DATE DUE			
Mar 2 '82			
Oct 31 '82			
Dec 10 '82			
Feb 20 '83			
8-9-83			

F

Transnational Terrorism

Transnational Terrorism

A CHRONOLOGY OF EVENTS, 1968 - 1979

Edward F. Mickolus

GREENWOOD PRESS WESTPORT, CONNECTICUT

909.827
M58t
118028
may 1981

Library of Congress Cataloging in Publication Data

Mickolus, Edward F
    Transnational terrorism.

    Includes index.
    1. Terrorism—Chronology. 2. Terrorism—History—
20th century. I. Title.
HV6431.M5   909.82'7   79-6829
ISBN 0-313-22206-1 lib. bdg.

Library of Congress Catalog Card Number: 79-6829
ISBN: 0-313-22206-1

First published in 1980

Greenwood Press
A division of Congressional Information Service, Inc.
88 Post Road West, Westport, Connecticut 06881

Printed in the United States of America

10 9 8 7 6 5 4 3 2 1

for FNU LNU

Contents

List of Tables

Acknowledgments

During the course of the research for this book, I have had the opportunity to speak and correspond with hundreds of people from the academic, diplomatic, legal, journalistic, business, intelligence, and policy communities. Any listing of people who aided an author always unintentionally omits several individuals, and I apologize beforehand for whomever I forget. Many business executives have given their counsel confidentially, and I shall not subject them to potential terrorist intimidation by publication of their names. I have similarly omitted the names of my colleagues in the intelligence community. Although many of them do not operate under the constraints of official cover, the compilation of even a short list of Central Intelligence Agency employees could be damaging to the national security, as well as their own well-being. Despite my institutional affiliation, descriptions of incidents should not be interpreted as representing validation or official positions of the Central Intelligence Agency or any other branch of the U.S. government.

I would like to thank the National Science Foundation and the University Consortium for World Order Studies for financing my graduate education and dissertation research. My Yale University dissertation board, consisting of H. Bradford Westerfield, Bruce M. Russett, and Garry Brewer, provided invaluable guidance. Professor William V. O'Brien of Georgetown University was kind enough to sponsor my study in Washington, D.C.

Several members of the scholarly community have been especially helpful in providing suggestions, data, and concepts. Among those deserving mention are: Dr. Yonah Alexander, director, Institute for the Study of International Terrorism, SUNY-Oneonta; Dr. Thomas Harries, Society for General Systems Research; the late Dr. Marius Livingston, Department of History, Glassboro State College; Dr. Michael Stohl, Department of Political Science, Purdue University; Dr. Robert Friedlander, Ohio Northern University College of Law; Dr. Martha Crenshaw, Department of Government, Wesleyan University; Dr. H. H. A. Cooper, American University; Dr. J. Bowyer Bell, Institute of War and Peace Studies, Columbia University; Dr. Ernest Evans and Bruce Blair, the Brookings Institution; Jay Mallin, Gainesville, Florida ; Dr. Lawrence C. Hamilton, Department of Sociology, University of New Hampshire; Dr. Douglas Simon, Department of Political Science, Drew University; Dr. Joseph B. Margolin, Behavorial Studies Group, George Washington University;

Eugene Methvin, Reader's Digest; Russell Osmond, Department of Political Science, Syracuse University; Dr. Robert Beattie, Inter-University Consortium for Political and Social Research, University of Michigan; Dr. W. Scott Thompson, Fletcher School of Law and Diplomacy, Tufts University; Dr. Robert Mandel, Lewis and Clark University; Dr. John Gleason, University of Nebraska; Dr. Stephen Sloan, Department of Political Science, University of Oklahoma; and Edward Heyman, Department of Political Science, University of North Carolina.

Several people in the U.S. government have made helpful comments on how this project could better serve policy needs. Among them are: Ambassador Anthony C. E. Quainton, Robert P. Myers, James Johnson, John Boehm, and Douglas Stevens, Department of State; Linnea Raine, Department of Energy; Brooks McClure, Department of Commerce; Richard Bond, U.S. Information Agency; Monte Belger and Virgil Krohn, Federal Aviation Administration; Robert Taubert, Federal Bureau of Investigation; Major John D. Elliott, U.S. Army Concepts Analysis Agency; Captain Larry Brown and Lieutenant Colonel Gary DeBusch, U.S. Army Institute for Military Assistance, Fort Bragg, North Carolina; and Major James P. Needham, U.S. Army Military Police.

The private research community has done more work than anyone in the development of data bases as policy tools. Those whose advice I especially appreciated include: Brian Michael Jenkins and Janera Johnson, RAND Corporation; Russell William Mengel, BDM Corporation; Marvin Leibstone, Science Applications, Inc.; Eric Shaw, CACI, Inc.; Benjamin Weiner, president, Probe International; Orval E. Jones, Sandia Laboratories; and Ric Blacksten, Ketron, Incorporated.

Introduction

Transnational terrorist attacks have captured the world's headlines in recent times, bringing the horror of atrocity into millions of homes. Each day we read of desperate men and women bombing, assassinating, kidnapping, hijacking, taking over facilities, and poisoning for a litany of disparate political motivations. Although terrorism has been with us for centuries (examples include the first-century sicarii, the twelfth-century assassins, the French Revolution's Reign of Terror, and the Russian anarchist movement of the turn of this century), its adoption in the last decade by hundreds of groups as a means of political expression is new. Increasing global interdependence has led to terrorism's becoming an international concern, involving nearly every nation-state in the world (see table 1), whereas it had previously been confined to domestic disputes.[1] Complex communication and transportation systems have greatly increased the possibility of virtually anyone becoming a victim of a conflict in some far-off corner of the globe. And the advent of weapons of mass destruction has enhanced the potential for terrorists' becoming a catalyst for Armageddon.

This menace has generated a cottage industry of writers, self-appointed security experts, apologists, symposium organizers, and novelists, but the literature in the field has been unsystematic, noncumulative, and distressingly unhelpful to the policy makers, as well as to the general public. This book is designed to fill one obvious gap: the lack of comprehensive description of worldwide terrorist incidents.

Although I acknowledge that a complete understanding of any phenomenon requires a multidisciplinary effort, I have tried to explore the utility of quantitative comparative data on the contemporary experience in dealing with the problem. My assumption is that transnational terrorist behavior is patterned and that discovery of these patterns through even the simplest of statistical procedures can be helpful in combating terrorism. The material in this book's chronology forms the data that comprise my ITERATE (International Terrorism: Attributes of Terrorist Events) computer system.[2] The types of incidents included in the data set are defined in this way: the use, or threat of use, of anxiety-inducing extranormal violence for political purposes by any individual or group, whether acting for or in opposition to established governmental authority, when such action is intended to influence the attitudes and behavior of a target group wider than the immediate victims and when, through the

TABLE 1 **Number of Incidents of National Involvement in Transnational Terrorism, 1968-1977**

Country	Starting Location	Ending Location	Victim	Terrorist	Demand Target	Asylum Grantor	Asylum Denier	Ancillary
Stateless			1					
United States	345	342	1,471	81	10			7
Puerto Rico	27	27	12	77				
Canada	18	26	23	7	4			1
Bermuda								
Bahamas	2	3	6					
Cuba	6	22	80	174	1	10	1	9
Haiti	4	5	10	4	1			1
Dominican Republic	20	18	14	10	3			
West Indies								
Federation			2	1				
Jamaica	11	11	2					1
Trinidad and								
Tobago	5	5	3					
Barbados	5	5						
Grenada								
Netherlands Antilles			2					
Mexico	65	62	29	29	7	8	1	5
Guatemala	30	31	7	19	4			
Honduras	5	5	2					1
El Salvador	13	13	8	5	1			
Nicaragua	6	5	7	8	2			
Costa Rica	18	18	6	4		1		
Panama	8	6	6	4		1	1	1
Indeterminate Latin			3					
Colombia	56	54	25	31	4			1
Venezuela	33	31	20	21	2		1	3
Guyana				3				
Ecuador	23	20	5	13				1
Peru	36	38	5	11			2	2
Brazil	45	46	15	16	5			1
Bolivia	39	40	15	21	2			1
Paraguay	3	4	8	2				1
Chile	27	28	28	6		4	1	4
Argentina	327	325	74	169	4			1
Uruguay	41	40	31	32	4			1
United Kingdom	212	245	334	8	5	1		5
Northern Ireland	9	8	5	221				
Ireland	55	54	42	5	1			2
Scotland		1						
Netherlands	112	36	43	6	8		1	2
Belgium	26	30	10	1	1		2	2
Luxembourg								
Corsica	1	1						
France	176	188	105	58	11	2		14
Monaco								
Liechtenstein								

Country	Starting Location	Ending Location	Victim	Terrorist	Demand Target	Asylum Grantor	Asylum Denier	Ancillary
Switzerland	22	27	27	5	4			5
Spain	42	42	102	35	4	1		3
Gibraltar		1						
Andorra								
Portugal	19	19	18	4				
West Germany	99	100	145	37	14			1
East Germany			3					
Poland	1		7					1
Indeterminate European	13	1						
Austria	21	22	17	4	2			2
Hungary	1		1	2				
Czechoslovakia		1	3					1
Italy	178	176	108	56	2			3
Vatican City	1	1	2					3
San Marino								
Malta	1	1	1					1
Albania			3	2				
Yugoslavia	9	9	51	36	2			2
Greece	120	118	40	36	6			3
Cyprus	14	15	8	8	3		1	7
Bulgaria	1	3	1	1		2		1
Rumania			1					1
Soviet Union	17	17	72					1
Finland			2					
Sweden	17	16	13	2	2		1	1
Norway	6	6	2	1				
Denmark	12	12	5	2			2	1
Iceland								1
Cape Verde								
Guinea-Bissau								
Gambia								
Mali								
Senegal			2					1
Benin, Dahomey						2		
Mauritania	2	2	2					
Niger								
Ivory Coast	1	1	1					
Guinea			1					
Upper Volta								
Liberia			1					
Sierra Leone	1	1						
Ghana	2	2		2				
Togo								
Cameroun								
Nigeria			2	1				
Gabon			1					
Central African Empire								
Chad	1			2				1

Table 1 (continued)

Country	Starting Location	Ending Location	Victim	Terrorist	Demand Target	Asylum Grantor	Asylum Denier	Ancillary
Congo-Brazzaville		1						
Zaire	2	5	2	2	1			
Uganda	3	4	3		1			
Kenya	3	3			1			
Tanzania	4	4	2					
Zanzibar	1	1						
Burundi	1	1		1				
Rwanda								
Somalia	2	3	2	1				2
Djibouti	3	3	3	3				
Ethiopia	39	35	20	10	1			
Eritrea	3	3	1	32				
Cabinda				2				
Angola	8	7	1	5				
Mozambique	2	1	7	2				
Zambia	7	8	2					1
Rhodesia, Zimbabwe	10	8	8	7				
Malawi		1	1					
South Africa	6	7	19	2	1			
Lesotho	1	1						
Botswana	2	2						
Swaziland								
Malagasy Rep.								
Comoros								
Mauritius								
Seychelles								
Indeterminate African			1	1				
Morocco	7	8	7	3				1
Canary Islands	1	1		1				
Spanish Sahara	2	2		8				1
Algeria	4	8	23	16	2	8	3	14
Tunisia	1	2	1		1	1	3	3
Libya	2	9	2	3		10	3	10
Sudan	3	4	1				1	6
Iran	27	27	24	15	2		1	4
Turkey	97	94	45	43	6			1
Iraq	4	5	13	14	2	2	1	6
Kurdistan				1				
Egypt	8	19	39	3	4	3	3	17
Syria	14	15	28	10	1	3	3	15
Lebanon	124	114	52	32	5	1	3	18
Jordan	39	47	35	14	5		1	2
Israel	142	174	417	20	17			3
Palestine			62	448	1			4
Saudi Arabia	2	3	17	1	2		1	
Yemen	3	3	2					1
People's Democratic Republic of Yemen, (PDRY)		2	2	3	1	5	5	8
Kuwait	9	12	8			1	1	6
Bahrain	1		1			1	1	1

Table 1 (continued)

Country	Starting Location	Ending Location	Victim	Terrorist	Demand Target	Asylum Grantor	Asylum Denier	Ancillary
Qatar			1					
Dubai	1	1	2		1	1	1	2
Trucial Oman				1				
Abu Dhabi	2	2				1	1	
Muscat-Oman			1	1				
United Arab Emirates	1	1	3					1
Afghanistan	1	1	1					1
People's Republic of China	1	2	2	1				
Mongolia								
Taiwan	6	6	5	2				
Hong Kong	5	4	3					
North Korea		1	3	1		1	1	2
South Korea	1	1	3	1	1			
Japan	18	18	35	25	4			3
Bhutan								
Sikkim								
India	99	64	42	16	1			1
Bangladesh	7	7	4	3				1
Pakistan	24	25	4	5	1	1	1	4
Burma	2	2		2	1		1	
Sri Lanka	4	4	1	1				1
Maldives								
Nepal	3	2	1	1				
Thailand	8	6	4	2	1			2
Cambodia	7	9	2					1
Laos	2	2	1					
Vietnam			1				2	1
North Vietnam								
South Vietnam		1	2					
Malaysia	59	22	3	45				
Singapore	3	3	4		2			2
Philippines	41	39	15	27	6			
Indonesia	1	1	12	14	1			
Australia	18	23	6	2				
Papua-New Guinea								
New Zealand	4	4	4					
Fiji								
Tonga								
Nauru								

Notes: "Demand target" refers to nations against whom the terrorists made specific demands in exchange for the release of hostages. "Ancillary" refers to involvement that is not described by one of the other types and may entail some other form of aid to the terrorists besides the provision of asylum at the dénouement of an incident, mediation between the demand targets and the hostage takers, joining rescue squads sent in by target or victim governments to free hostages, or other types of behavior.

The order of countries in the table follows that of the Russett-Singer-Small standardized nation codings suggested by the Inter-University Consortium for Political and Social Research, as used by ITERATE. Nations are grouped into geographical regions, and specific national orderings follow geographical borders rather than alphabetization.

nationality or foreign ties of its perpetrators, its location, the nature of its institutional or human victims, or the mechanics of its resolution, its ramifications transcend national boundaries.

It is widely believed that international terrorism is on the increase, that terrorists are resorting to more spectacular incidents involving sophisticated technology, and that terrorists aim at causing the greatest amount of death and destruction by their deeds. Whether this conclusion is correct can be evaluated by examining trends, noting the types of tactics that have been engaged in, logistic and tactical shifts, the extent of damage and casualties inflicted, and how terrorist attacks tend to involve governments.

TEMPORAL PATTERNS

Although the number of transnational terrorist attacks rose substantially in the 1970s, the continued rise alleged in the press does not appear to have taken place. What we find instead is a cyclical pattern:

Year	Number of Incidents
1968	123
1969	179
1970	344
1971	301
1972	480
1973	340
1974	425
1975	342
1976	455
1977	340

What may account for the discrepancy between these figures and conventional wisdom is the increasing attention paid to terrorism by the media, educators, and policy makers. Publicity generated by one or two spectacular terrorist events can further lend to the impression that this type of activity is on the rise. Fluctuations in annual totals are probably due to the multicausal nature of transnational terrorism. We might expect the normal level of terrorism to be 340 incidents annually, but rises could be due to a flurry of activity in protest to dramatic political events (such as the Sadat peace initiative in 1977, which led to numerous bombings throughout Europe) to commemorations of terrorist martyrs (Europe was host to several incidents in 1976 after the suicide of Ulrike Meinhof, a phenomenon that was repeated in 1977 with the suicides of her three colleagues). The periodicity might be the result of changes in security precautions made by governments experiencing severe terrorist onslaughts, which may subsequently let their guard down the next year. Another explanation might be that adversaries need a period of time to prepare for attacks designed to counter the counter-measures, introducing logistic innovations that may take another year for the governments to defend against.

Another way of looking at these long-term trends is to inquire into the stability of the increases and decreases. Heyman and Mickolus studied the tendency for transitions in the number of incidents to occur between quarters (see table 2).[3] They found that the international system is able to absorb increasing numbers of terrorist incidents. Stated differently, the system is getting worse; the annual totals (or, at least, some quarterly totals) can be expected to increase rather than decrease. Moreover, Western Europe is prone to higher levels of activity over the long run than is the Middle East.

This tendency for attacks to occur in industrialized nations, particularly Western Europe, is borne out by the data in table 1, which shows the locations of terrorist attacks. The bulk of politically violent incidents may occur in third world nations, but that is not true for transnational terrorism. Nearly half of all attacks are recorded in westernized democracies. Transnational attacks are very infrequent in Asia and Africa. The same patterns are found regarding the victims of terrorist attacks, with symbols of Western, particularly U.S., affluence being the most popular targets. These patterns are probably the result of the greater availability of publicity channels (such as television, radio, and newspapers) in advanced nations, as well as greater freedoms of association and movement. These two factors combine to create a more favorable environment for terrorists of any political stripe. Added to this is the greater availability of high-speed means of transportation to major Western capitals.

TACTICS OF TERRORISTS

Violence-prone groups can engage in numerous types of nonviolent actions to try to popularize their political views; here, however, we are concerned with actions that threaten or cause harm to property or individuals. Table 3 examines the frequency of various actions in the terrorist repertoires, and table 4 notes the probability of a specific type of incident resulting in casualties or damage.

Although the better-known terrorist groups have demonstrated an aptitude for the careful planning and coordination required for spectacular operations, the cost of such endeavors is high. One must be a dedicated full-time terrorist to mount such attacks. The vast majority of those engaging in terrorist incidents could be viewed as delving into a part-time hobby rather than a full-time profession. Hence, low-level attacks constitute the vast majority of reported operations. Particularly noteworthy is the ranking, as well as the rise, in bombings, arson and murder, which are low risk, not time-consuming, and do not involve the perpetrators in immediate confrontation with authorities but nonetheless have symbolic effect.

TABLE 2 **Quarterly Frequencies of Terrorist Incidents, 1968-1977**

Quarter	Number of Incidents
1	40
2	17
3	35
4	31
5	22
6	41
7	44
8	72
9	57
10	86
11	114
12	86
13	88
14	88
15	76
16	49
17	57
18	77
19	138
20	207
21	78
22	75
23	103
24	84
25	92
26	116
27	99
28	117
29	67
30	62
31	91
32	116
33	111
34	123
35	151
36	68
37	90
38	63
39	75
40	112

Note: Quarters begin with January 1, 1968. The first quarter includes all incidents that began on January 1 through March 31, 1968.

Rank orders of the quarters for a given year closely parallel the results noted in comparing the quarterly totals for the decade. Incidents tend to cluster toward the end of the year.

TABLE 3 **Annual Frequencies of Terrorist Attacks, By Type of Event**

Type of Attack	1968	1969	1970	1971	1972	1973	1974	1975	1976	1977	Total
Kidnapping	1	3	38	25	13	38	28	40	31	25	242
Barricade-hostage	0	0	5	1	3	10	12	16	4	5	56
Occupation	0	0	3	0	1	1	0	0	0	3	8
Letter bombing	4	5	5	1	245	23	17	3	11	9	321
Incendiary bombing	12	22	54	46	15	31	37	20	98	60	395
Explosive bombing	67	97	108	119	107	137	249	191	182	145	1,402
Missile attack	0	1	0	0	1	1	1	1	1	0	6
Armed attack	11	12	8	8	8	12	24	12	20	16	131
Aerial hijacking	3	12	22	10	15	6	7	2	6	6	89
Nonaerial takeover	0	0	1	0	1	0	2	3	0	2	9
Assassination or murder	7	4	16	13	10	18	15	20	48	23	174
Sabotage	1	2	0	4	3	2	2	0	2	0	16
Exotic pollution	0	0	0	0	0	1	0	0	0	0	1
Nuclear weapons	0	0	0	0	0	0	1	0	0	0	1
Threat	9	9	45	51	48	44	13	12	26	29	286
Theft or break-in	3	7	22	10	1	0	8	8	5	0	64
Conspiracy	3	4	2	0	1	9	4	3	2	2	30
Hoax	0	0	2	1	0	0	0	0	2	0	5
Sniping	3	2	7	3	4	3	3	9	14	6	54
Shootout with police	0	0	1	0	0	1	0	1	3	6	12
Arms smuggling	0	0	1	4	4	3	1	1	0	2	16
Other actions	0	0	4	5	0	0	1	0	0	1	11
Total	123	179	344	301	480	340	425	342	455	340	3,329

Also noteworthy is the infrequent resort to weapons or tactics involving technological sophistication, despite repeated warnings in the press and popular fiction about the consequences of such potential actions. Rifles, pipe bombs, and Molotov cocktails, easily acquired and handled, can be expected to remain far more popular with terrorists than an SA-7 heat-seeking missile or a home-built atomic bomb.

Differing patterns of destructiveness and frequency emerge for each type of incident. Each type of incident requires different skills, access to equipment and logistic support, planning, personnel, intelligence, and timing.

Kidnapping, in which an individual, usually a diplomat or business executive, is taken hostage, entails physically moving the hostage from one (generally known) location to another (usually unknown). Such operations are

TABLE 4 Incidents Resulting in Damage or Casualties, By Type of Attack

Type of Attack	Damage	No Damage	Casualties	No Casualties
Kidnapping	12	229	51	190
Barricade-hostage	11	41	27	28
Occupation	3	5	3	5
Letter bombing	56	216	5	273
Incendiary bombing	346	39	24	371
Explosive bombing	1,191	181	302	1,098
Missile attack	2	4	1	5
Armed attack	71	33	70	56
Aerial hijacking	15	71	25	62
Nonaerial takeover	2	7	3	6
Assassination or				
murder	13	154	157	17
Sabotage	12	4	0	16
Exotic pollution	0	1	0	1
Nuclear weapons	0	1	0	1
Threat	1	285	0	286
Theft or break-in	8	56	2	64
Conspiracy	0	30	1	29
Hoax	0	5	0	5
Sniping	29	18	8	46
Shootout with				
police	0	12	11	1
Arms smuggling	0	16	0	16
Other actions	6	5	3	8
Total	1,778	1,413	736	2,582

Note: Casualty and damage columns do not sum to each other or to totals reported in table 3, due to several cases in which the outcome is unknown.

somewhat less risky than a barricade and hostage operation since the terrorists are less exposed to the authorities. However, such operations have generally required more individuals to aid in the capture. People are needed for the seizure, to act as lookouts, drive successive getaway vehicles, guard the prisoner, negotiate with authorities, and so on. The hostage is usually viewed as a pawn to be used in obtaining concessions from the target of demands, which have included the release of prisoners, payment of a monetary ransom, and publication of a political manifesto. Casualties are less frequent than popularly believed, with the hostage being released unharmed after the securing of concessions. Most of the casualties mentioned in the fifty-one cases were incurred at the beginning of the incident, in which gun battles broke out between the terrorists and the hostage's security force. Because of the nature of these operations, damage is quite rare. In 1976-1977, there was a decline from the 1975 high of forty attacks because of increased security precautions taken by potential victims. But because kidnappings are lucrative (the record recorded ransom payment is $61.2 million), they will continue to be attractive options.

In barricade and hostage operations, terrorists seize one or more hostages but make no attempt to leave the original scene of the crime. Negotiations are carried on with the perpetrators themselves effectively being held hostage, unable to leave the scene at a time of their choosing. The situation frequently occurs at the end of an incident in which the seizure of hostages was not the terrorists' primary aim—for example, a bank holdup in which the robbers were discovered by the authorities before they were able to escape from an attack on an airport lounge or residence. However, the terrorist operations that have generated the greatest publicity have had hostage seizure as their primary aim and have frequently resulted in casualties. The 1973-1975 period saw an increasing popularity of this type of incident. Improvements in security measures at likely targets, such as embassies and other official installations, have made this type of action far more difficult to engage in, resulting in a noteworthy decline in 1976 and 1977.

Occupation of facilities without the seizure of hostages has been a comparatively infrequent terrorist tactic, although it has been often resorted to by student demonstrators worldwide.

Letterbombs plagued several postal systems in 1972 but quickly faded in frequency to technological curiosities. Many of the devices were intercepted before they damaged or injured their intended target. The inability of terrorists to control the devices' detonation once mailed, public outcry at the indiscriminate nature of the method, and the possible deaths in letterbomb factories of their creators have lessened the attractiveness of this type of operation. Innovations in detection hardware have also lessened the probability of the device reaching its intended target.

Incendiary bombing, from the thrown Molotov cocktail to simply lighting a match, is one of the easiest attacks to mount, leading to its high frequency in comparison to other types of attacks. Generally it results in some property damage, but fire alarms usually alert any potential human victims. Hence, terrorists are able to engage in symbolic property destruction without risking public criticism for causing injuries. Because of ease of operation and low risk to the perpetrator, incendiary attacks have risen in number while more difficult operations have grown more uncommon.

Rummel offers a useful definition of bombing: "any use of explosives to damage or destroy private or public property or wound or kill individuals including those used against the property of persons of foreign governments or their subjects, excepting what occurs in the context of open warfare between two countries."[4] Save for the 1972 letterbomb flurry, the planted or thrown bomb has ranked as the most popular terrorist tactic in each year of the 1970's.

It generally causes damage but, with sufficient warning, can avoid unwanted casualties. The tactic involves limited risk to terrorists, avoids direct confrontation with authorities, and gives terrorists an excellent chance of escape from the scene. Since it is very difficult to defend possible targets against bombing, this method can be expected to continue its popularity.

The resort to the use of missiles in attacks so far has been infrequent, but the use of other weapons in direct attacks on facilities has risen in the last few years. Such dramatic tactics frequently result in damage and casualties and generate publicity.

The resort to aerial hijackings by terrorists has generally been a mobile form of the barricade and hostage scenario. We can distinguish among those situations in which the hijackers are merely seeking a means of transportation to a nation giving them asylum; situations in which the hijackers force the pilot to land the plane, release the passengers and crew, and blow up the plane without making any ransom demands (engaged in for the shock value of the action); and incidents in which the skyjackers make specific demands upon governments or corporations, threatening the safety of the passengers, crew, and plane. These last attacks have attracted perhaps the greatest attention by the press and have sparked numerous books by hostages, negotiators, and commentators. International cooperation in denying safe haven to hijackers, as well as improved airline security measures (from metal detector screening at the boarding gates to sky marshals flying with the passengers), have greatly lessened the probability of a successful hijacking. The recent development of paramilitary rescue squads has added to what many hope will be a permanent deterrent against hijackers. The statistics for the past decade seem to bear out this belief; terrorist and nonterrorist hijackings have plummeted in recent years, although attempts will continue to be made against lesser-protected airlines and airports. Takeovers of nonaerial means of transportation (buses, trains, and ships) have not risen to fill the operational void created by the decline in aerial attacks. Threatening to force the plane into a power dive credibly jeopardizes the lives of more individuals than does any comparable threat against other modes of transportation. Moreover, it is simpler to control the actions of a large number of people on board a plane in flight than it would be to prevent the escape by passengers from a ship.

Three types of operations that may require ingenuity or technical expertise —sabotage not involving the use of explosives, nuclear weapons, and exotic (including chemical and biological toxins) forms of pollution—have not been popular terrorist actions. Difficulties in controlling the effects of these actions, generally aimed at personal injury, have led to resort to simpler forms of assassination, usually by guns.[5] Such attacks have generally been successful in inflicting injury or death to the intended victim and have thus seen an erratic rise during the past decade, with 1976-1977 finding more reported terrorist murders than any other three years combined. Sniping at facilities, which logistically involves many of the actions needed in assassination attempts, has similarly increased.

Over the 1970s, terrorists have tended to choose the line of least resistance in selecting types of attack. When one method, such as hijacking or letter-bombing, is found to be counterproductive or too difficult to engage in because of increased protective measures, adaptation and alteration in tactics has been the rule.

NATIONAL INVOLVEMENT

Although many of the more dramatic international incidents are carried on worldwide wire services, the vast majority of terrorist incidents involve nationals of only one nation. In our present sample, 74 percent of all incidents involved only two nationalities, with the mean being 2.539 nationalities. Table 5 indicates the range of nationalities involved. Extremely rare are cases involving more than four nationalities, probably because of selectivity in terrorist targetting. In most cases terrorists have attempted to victimize only ''enemy'' nationals, hoping to avoid offending citizens of potentially supportive governments.

TABLE 5 **Total Number of Nationalities Involved in Terrorist Incidents**

Number of Nationalities	Number of Incidents
2	2,464
3	521
4	190
5	49
6	30
7	23
8	14
9	10
10	1
11	9
12	4
13	1
14	2
15	2
17	3
18	1
19	1
22	1
24	1
25	1
27	1

LOGISTIC CONSIDERATIONS

The characteristics of adversaries against whom a security force must defend vary depending upon the type of action engaged in by the terrorists. Nevertheless, data can be aggregated for all types of actions to provide some generalizations.

On the average, approximately 4.4 terrorists (of 769 cases for which I have data) can be expected to participate in the attack. This number will be somewhat less for a simple planted bomb, and additional forces may be called into play for sophisticated operations that require separate teams for casing, logistics, planning, operational engagement, escape, negotiation, and postincident activities.

Most attacking groups consist of only one nationality and one terrorist group rather than an international team. The mean number of groups engaged in an action is 1.072, and the maximum recorded is 4. Often the names given by individuals engaging in an attack are fictitious to hide the identity of the action's true sponsors. The mean number of nationalities of the individuals composing the attacking force is 1.069, although one group boasted 5 separate nationalities. These figures may be skewed because of forged documentation used to hide the true identity and nationality of the perpetrators.

This is not to deny that cooperation between like-minded terrorists, and even sympathetic governments, takes place. Various guerrilla and terrorist groups have been funded, trained, armed, and received other forms of assistance from the Soviet Union, Cuba, North Korea, and several radical Arab nations. Terrorists have also obtained aid from each other or from intermediaries, such as the Paris-based Curiel Apparatus, in the form of forged documents, money, training, safe haven, intelligence, and even attacks for hire. Despite the apparent growth of these contacts in recent years, however, there does not appear to be the development of a single entity directing, or even promoting, all transnational terrorist violence because of ideological, organizational, and even personality clashes. Therefore most terrorist attacks can be expected to continue to be the work of individual groups.

The most popular weapons involve explosives or incendiary devices. Following a rough ordering of weaponry, and counting only the deadliest weapon evidenced in any given incident, I found that in 297 cases no weapon at all was used. Nonprojectile, nonexplosive weapons (mainly sharp instruments) were used in 21 cases. Handguns accounted for 65 cases, followed by longer-barreled weapons, such as rifles or machine guns, in 82 cases. Explosives were used in 2,305 cases (69.2 percent of the total, including unknown cases, 81.9 percent of the known cases). Missiles or other heavy projectiles were employed in 44 cases. Other weapons, such as chemical, biological, or nuclear contaminants, were employed in only 2 cases. It was impossible to determine what types of weapons, if any, were used in 513 cases.

Terrorists have shown a similar willingness to vary their targets, although certain preferences are readily apparent. In 281 cases, the victim's home was the scene. Nonresidential, nonvocational sites were attacked in 323 cases. By far the most popular target, however, was the victim's office or place of employment (including military bases or facilities), the scene of the crime in 1,698 cases. This was followed by attacks on 333 motor vehicles, 148 aircraft, 47 ships, 8 trains, 74 embarkation areas, and 417 indeterminate sites.

Although most terrorists prefer to stage simple raids, sophisticated groups have used operations that required detailed planning and careful timing. This is especially true of several recent operations which entailed multiple coordinated attacks. Hanafis seized three buildings in Washington, D.C.; Moluccans have attacked two places simultaneously twice in the Netherlands; and when West German anarchists kidnapped a prominent businessman, Palestinian hijackers later coordinated their efforts with those of the kidnappers. Although such cooperation is not new (witness the multiple hijackings by the Popular Front for the Liberation of Palestine on September 6, 1970), the frequency of these operations may portend a new logistical complication for antiterrorist forces.

Terrorists have not been successful in every case. In at least forty-two incidents, a serious logistical error or accident was committed by the terrorists (ranging from an assassin who killed the wrong man to a hijacker who mistakenly pulled the pin on her grenade while she was holding it, leaving her colleagues leaderless).

DESTRUCTIVENESS

Many observers have noted that the total number of individuals killed or wounded in terrorist incidents is far surpassed by the number of traffic fatalities in one year in the United States; however, the malevolent intent behind these casualties is not comparable to the inadvertent nature of traffic fatalities.

We should not interpret table 6 as meaning that there were .5 deaths and 1.4 injuries in each international terrorist incident in the decade surveyed. In only 401 cases (12 percent) was anyone killed. Injuries were reported in 523 (15.7 percent) cases, while casualties of any sort were noted in 736 (22.1 percent) cases. Injuries included 81 terrorists wounded, 703 foreign nationals, and 3,469 domestic citizens. The 6,453 casualties were accounted for by 285 terrorists, 1,417 foreign nationals, and 4,150 domestic victims.

Using average figures in estimating expected losses due to property damage can result in similar errors. For the 1,566 cases for which there are data, losses due to damage or theft (and not including ransom or extortion payments, security precaution costs, loss of investor confidence, company goodwill, psychic costs, and opportunity costs among others) totaled $332,600,000, or on average of $212,390 per incident. The record is a loss of $100 million in

TABLE 6   **Total Deaths and Injuries from Terrorist Incidents, 1968-1977**

Year	Total Deaths	Total Injuries
1968	34	202
1969	26	186
1970	125	207
1971	36	219
1972	153	366
1973	117	533
1974	328	1,047
1975	240	685
1976	409	881
1977	277	447
Totals	1,695	4,773

certain oil installation fires. In only 1,778 incidents (53.4 percent) was any damage reported.

Thus, although some incidents have resulted in high property damage costs and deaths in the scores, the vast majority of terrorist incidents do not involve losses in any way incurring an unpayable cost to society. So far nations and corporations have been able to shoulder the burden of these periodic attacks.

IMPLICATIONS

What does the experience of this decade tell us about the future of international terrorism? While prediction of the activities of a specific individual or small band is a hopeless task, we can nonetheless suggest that a few trends will continue well into the 1980s.

—Terrorists will continue to engage most often in simple forms of attacks, involving little risk to themselves, and entailing few casualties.

—Terrorists will adapt to measures taken by governments, corporations, and other potential victims to keep their activities in check.

—Although some bilateral cooperation between terrorist groups will continue, the widely varying ideological, personality, geographic, and operational characteristics of terrorists will hinder the formation of a Terror, Incorporated cartel.

—Although new terrorist groups will form to pursue idiosyncratic limited goals, the majority of terrorist attacks will be conducted against symbols of Western wealth and power.

NOTES

1. Material from table 1 was used to create an ITERATE computer file using nations, rather than incidents, as the unit of analysis. Due to lack of data or significance to the

study, the following entries were deleted from the data set: stateless, West Indies Federation, Netherlands Antilles, indeterminate Latin American, Andorra, indeterminate European, San Marino, Monaco, Liechtenstein, Gibralter, indeterminate African, Canary Islands, Spanish Sahara, Kurdistan, Tonga, and Nauru. Northern Ireland and Scotland have been merged with United Kingdom data. Corsica's data were added to those of France. Zanzibar data were merged with Tanzania's. Eritrea is considered part of Ethiopia for purposes of the study. Despite separatist aspirations, Cabinda is considered part of Angola. Data for Vietnam have been merged with North Vietnam.

The order of countries in the table follows that of the Russett-Singer-Small standardized nation codings suggested by the Inter-University Consortium for Political and Social Research, as used by ITERATE. Nations are grouped into geographical regions, and specific national orderings follow, roughly, geographical borders.

2. An early version of the computerized data set has been made available to the academic community through the auspices of the Inter-University Consortium for Political and Social Research, University of Michigan, Ann Arbor, Michigan. The updated version of the ITERATE, based upon this book's chronology, forms the basis of my own doctoral research and will be made available upon its completion. A description of the history of the ITERATE project can be found in Edward F. Mickolus, "An Events Data Base for Analysis of Transnational Terrorism," in Richards J. Heuer, ed., *Quantitative Approaches to Political Intelligence: The CIA Experience* (Boulder: Westview, 1978), pp. 127-163.

ITERATE data sources follow. The time period for all tables in this introduction is 1968 through 1977.

3. Edward Heyman and Edward Mickolus, "Imitation by Terrorists: Quantitative Approaches to the Study of Diffusion Patterns in Transnational Terrorism" (Paper presented to the joint national meeting of the Operations Research Society of America and the Institute for Management Sciences, New York City, May 1-3, 1978). As illustrated in the paper's appendix, Markov chains can generate the probability that a change from time T to time $T+1$ will be seen in the next transition period. This can be interpreted as the probability that a terrorist campaign can be sustained through two or more quarters. Changes in the overall magnitude of terrorist campaigns, as well as the simple fluctuations between quarters, can similarly be monitored.

4. See, for example, Rudolph Rummel, "Dimensions of Conflict Behavior Within Nations, 1946-1959" *Journal of Conflict Resolution* 10 (March 1966): 65-73.

5. This study has attempted to avoid the definitional morass that has encumbered the study of assassination. Most definitions suggested that the political office of the victims be taken into account. For example, ibid. defines assassination as "the politically motivated murder or attempted murder of national or local governmental officials, politicians, or nongovernmental personnel who support the government and its policies." Ali A. Mazrui, "Thoughts on Assassination in Africa" *Political Science Quarterly* 83 (March 1968): 40-48, observes that "neither the speed of killing nor the role of the killer is crucial in defining assassination. What is crucial is that an assassination is the killing of someone politically important by an agent other than himself or the government—for reasons which are either political or unknown." Difficulties in determining the importance of the victim (place in governmental hierarchy? influence in political party? degree of public support?) to the political system hinder this view's

utility in selecting cases for discussion. My study does not attempt to distinguish between the simple murder for political ends and the political assassination. Rather, any attack intended solely to cause bodily injury or death for political purposes has been tallied as a terrorist assassination or murder attempt.

ITERATE Data Sources

Analysis of the Terrorist Threat to the Commercial Nuclear Industry. Report submitted to the Special Safeguards Study, Nuclear Regulatory Commission, Washington, D.C., in Response to Contract No. AT (49-24)-0131. Vienna, Virginia: BDM Corporation, September 30, 1975, BDM/75-176-TR.

"Appendix A: Hijackings of Planes to Cuba and Frustrated Attempts to Hijack." In *Air Piracy in the Caribbean Area*, Report of the Subcommittee on Inter-American Affairs, Committee on Foreign Affairs, US House of Representatives, 90th Cong., 2d sess. December 10, 1968, pp. 9-11.

"The Arab Communist Organisation." IV-42, 350 *Fiches du Monde Arabe*, August 6, 1975.

Arey, James A. *The Sky Pirates.* New York: Scribner's, 1972.

Baumann, Carol Edler. *The Diplomatic Kidnappings: A Revolutionary Tactic of Urban Terrorism.* The Hague: Nijhoff, 1973.

Bell, J. Bowyer. "Assassination in International Politics: Lord Moyne, Count Bernadotte, and the Lehi." *International Studies Quarterly* 16 (March 1972): 59-82.

—————. *The Myth of the Guerrilla: Revolutionary Theory and Malpractice.* New York: Alfred A. Knopf, 1971.

Ben-Dor, Gabriel. "The Strategy of Terrorism in the Arab-Israeli Conflict: The Case of the Palestinian Guerrillas—Appendix: Arab Cross-National Terrorism, 1968-1974." Mimeographed. Israel: University of Haifa, 1976.

Bininsky, Yaroslav. "The Background of Contemporary Politics in the Baltic Republics and the Ukraine: Comparisons and Contrasts." In Arvids Ziedonis, Jr., Rein Taagepera, and Mardi Valgemae, eds., *Problems of Mininations: Baltic Perspectives.* San Jose: Association for the Advancement of Baltic Studies, 1973.

"Bomb Summary: A Comprehensive Report of Incidents Involving Explosive and Incendiary Devices in the Nation." Washington, D.C.: U.S. Department of Justice, FBI Uniform Crime Reports, 1972, 1973, 1974, 1975.

"Bombing Incidents, Mob Action and Harassment Against U.S. Installations Overseas, July 1, 1969-June 30, 1970." Washington, D.C.: U.S. Information Agency, September 4, 1970.

Bowden, Tom. "The IRA and the Changing Tactics of Terrorism." *Political Quarterly* (October-December 1976): 425-438.

"Briefing Packet." Washington, D.C.: U.S. Information Agency Seminar on International Terrorism, August 11, 1975.

"Chronology of Attacks upon Non-Official American Citizens, 1971-1975." Washington, D.C.: U.S. Department of State, Cabinet Committee to Combat Terrorism Working Group, January 20, 1976.

"Chronology of Hijackings 1968 through 1975." Washington, D.C.: U.S. Department of State, Cabinet Committee to Combat Terrorism Working Group, 1976.

"Chronology of Hijackings of U.S. Registered Aircraft and Current Legal Status of Hijackers, as of January 1, 1976." Washington, D.C.: Federal Aviation Administration, Civil Aviation Security Service, 1976, 1977.

"Chronology of Major Events in Domestic and International Terrorism." *Counterforce* (issues since January 1977).

"Chronology of Sabotage and Terrorism Against Cuba: 1973-1976." Paper distributed by Venceremos at Latin American Studies Conference. Pittsburgh, Fall 1976.

"Chronology of Significant Terrorist Incidents Involving U.S. Diplomatic/ Official Personnel, 1963-1975. Washington, D.C.: U.S. Department of State, January 20, 1976.

"Chronology of Terrorist Attacks in Lima, Peru in 1974." *Caretas* (November 11, 1974).

"Chronology of Unlawful Interference with Civil Aviation." (Montreal: International Civil Aviation Organization, 1969, 1970, 1971, 1972, 1973, 1974, 1975, 1976.

Clutterbuck, Richard. *Living with Terrorism*. London: Faber and Faber, 1975.

Clyne, Peter. *An Anatomy of Skyjacking*. London: Abelard-Schumann, 1973.

Cooley, John K. *Green March, Black September: The Story of the Palestinian Arabs*. London: Frank Cass, 1973.

Crozier, Brian. *Annual of Power and Conflict, 1974-1975*. London: Institute for the Study of Conflict, 1975. Volumes are published also for 1975-1976 and for 1976-1977.

Cutter, Curtis. Interview. February 1976.

Dobson, Christopher. *Black September: Its Short, Violent History*. New York: Macmillan, 1974.

———, and Payne, Ronald. *The Carlos Complex*. New York: Putnam's 1977.

"Domestic and Foreign Aircraft Hijackings, as of July 1, 1976." Washington, D.C.: Federal Aviation Administration, Civil Aviation Security Service, 1976, 1977.

Dortzbach, Karl, and Dortzbach, Debbie. *Kidnapped*. New York: Harper and Row, 1975.

Elliot, John D., "Action and Reaction: West Germany and the Baader-Meinhof Guerrillas." *Strategic Review* 4 (Winter 1976): 60-67.

"Explosions Aboard Aircraft, as of January 1, 1976." Washington, D.C.: Federal Aviation Administration, Civil Aviation Security Service, 1976, 1977.

Fly, Claude. *No Hope But God.* New York: Hawthorne, 1973.

Hacker, Frederick. *Crusaders, Criminals and Crazies.* New York: Norton, 1976.

"Hijacking Statistics, U.S. Registered Aircraft, 1961—Present, Updated January 1, 1977." Washington, D.C.: Federal Aviation Administration, Civil Aviation Security Service, 1977.

Jenkins, Brian Michael. "Hostage Survival: Some Preliminary Observations." Santa Monica: RAND Corporation, April 1975.

———. "International Terrorism: A New Mode of Conflict." California Arms Control and Foreign Policy Seminar Research Paper 48. Los Angeles: Crescent Publications, January 1975.

———. "International Terrorism: A New Mode of Conflict." In David Carlton and Carlo Schaerf, eds., *International Terrorism and World Security*, pp. 13-49. London: Croom Helm, 1975.

Jenkins, Brian Michael, and Johnson, Janera. "International Terrorism: A Chronology, 1968-1974." Santa Monica: RAND Corporation, R-1597-DOS/ARPA, March 1975.

———. "International Terrorism: A Chronology, 1974 Supplement." Santa Monica: RAND Corporation, R-1909-1-ARPA, February 1976.

"Meir Kahane: A Candid Conversation with the Militant Leader of the Jewish Defense League." *Playboy* 19 (October 1972): 69ff.

Kohl, James, and Litt, John. *Urban Guerrilla Warfare in Latin America.* Cambridge, Mass.: MIT Press, 1974.

"Legal Status of Hijackers, Summarization, Updated January 1, 1976." Washington, D.C.: Federal Aviation Administration, Civil Aviation Security Service, 1976, 1977.

Mallin, Jay, ed. *Terror and Urban Guerrillas: A Study of Tactics and Documents.* Coral Gables. Florida: University of Miami Press, 1971.

Messick, Hank, and Goldblatt, Burt. *Kidnapping: The Illustrated History.* New York: Dial, 1974.

Moss, Robert. *The War for the Cities.* New York: Coward, Mann and Geoghegan, 1972.

Nanes, Allan S. "International Terrorism." Washington, D.C.: Library of Congress, Congressional Research Service, Major Issues System, Issue Brief IB74042, May 11, 1977.

Parry, Albert. *Terrorism from Robespierre to Arafat.* New York: Vanguard, 1976.

Phillips, David. *Skyjack: The Story of Air Piracy*, London: Harrap, 1973.

Report of the Task Force on Disorders and Terrorism. Washington, D.C.: National Advisory Committee on Criminal Justice Standards and Goals, 1976.

Rich, Elizabeth. *Flying Scared*. New York: Stein and Day, 1972.

Russell, Charles A.; Schenkel, James F.; and Miller, James A. "Urban Guerrillas in Argentina: A Select Bibliography." *Latin American Research Review* 9 (Fall 1974): 53-89.

"Significant Worldwide Criminal Acts Involving Civil Aviation 1976." Washington, D.C.: Federal Aviation Administration, Civil Aviation Security Service, 1977.

Smith, Colin. *Carlos: Portrait of a Terrorist*. London: Sphere, 1976.

Snow, Peter, and Phillips, David. *The Arab Hijack War*. New York: Ballantine, 1970.

Sobel, Lester A., ed. *Political Terrorism*. New York: Facts on File, 1975.

Steinhoff, Patricia. "Portrait of a Terrorist: An Interview with Kozo Okamoto." *Asia Survey* 16 (September 1976): 830-845.

Stevenson, William. *90 Minutes at Entebbe*. New York: Bantam Books, 1976.

"Subject: Japanese Red Army." Mimeographed. Washington, D.C.: Embassy of Japan, n.d.

"Summary and Analysis of Security Incidents Overseas: August 1, 1953—May 20, 1959." Washington, D.C.: U.S. Information Agency, Office of Security, declassified by Richard Bond, IOS/P, June 7, 1976.

The Terrorist and Sabotage Threat to U.S. Nuclear Programs: Phase One Final Report. Prepared for Sandia Laboratories under Contract 82-9139 by the Historical Evaluation and Research Organization, Dunn Loring, Virginia, August 1974.

"Threats of Violence and Acts of Violence to Licensed Nuclear Facilities, 1969-1975." Washington, D.C.: U.S. Nuclear Regulatory Commission, 1976, 1977. Reports are also available for 1976 and 1977.

Tinnin, David B. "The Wrath of God." *Playboy* 23 (August 1976): 70-180.

————, with Dag Christensen. *The Hit Team*. Boston: Little, Brown, 1976.

U.S. Department of State. Airgram A-066 from American Embassy, Guatemala, June 14, 1976. Enclosure: "Major Terrorist Acts Attributable to the Extreme Left in Guatemala, January 1970-May 1976."

U.S. House of Representatives. *Political Kidnappings 1963-73*. Staff Study Prepared by the Committee on Internal Security. 93d Cong., 1st sess., August, 1, 1973.

U.S. Information Agency. "Dissident and Terrorist Acts Against U.S. Installations and Personnel Overseas, July 1, 1965-June 30, 1967." Available through Office of Security, USIA, Washington, D.C. Reports are also available for "July through December 1971, with Analysis of Targetting Against USIS Installations and Personnel," "January 1 through March 31, 1972," "April 1 through September 30, 1972," and "October 1, 1972 through December 31, 1972."

——. "Incidents Against US Installations Abroad July 1, 1967-June 30, 1968." Memorandum to IOS, Mr. Paul J. McNichol from IOS/P Charles M. Dulin, July 22, 1968.

——. "Report of Bombing Incidents, Mob Action and Harassment Against U.S. Installations Overseas July 1, 1968-June 30, 1969." Washington, D.C.: USIA, IOS 11997, July 31, 1969.

——. "Reports of Significant Security Incidents, Worldwide, 1976." Washington, D.C.: USIA IOS/P, 1977.

——. "Significant Security Incidents of Overseas Installations for Calendar Years 1973, 1974 and 1975." Washington, D.C.: USIA Office of Security, 1976.

——. Committee on the Judiciary. Subcommittee to Investigate the Administration of the Internal Security Act and Other Internal Security Laws. "Terroristic Activity: International Terrorism, Part 4, Hearings". 94th Cong., 1st sess., May 14, 1975.

United Nations. Document A/c.1/L.872, November 20, 1972.

Watson, Frank. *Political Terrorism*. New York: McKay, 1976.

Whelton, Charles. *Skyjack*. New York: Tower, 1970.

Wilkinson, Paul. *Political Terrorism*. New York: Wiley, 1975.

——. "Terrorism Versus Liberal Democracy: The Problems of Response." *Conflict Studies* 67 (January 1976).

Williams, Marilyn. "Chronology of Attacks upon Non-Official American Citizens 1971-1976." Washington, D.C.: U.S. Department of State, Cabinet Committee to Combat Terrorism Working Group, 1976.

——. "Chronology of Significant Terrorist Incidents Involving U.S. Diplomatic/Official Personnel and Installations 1963-1976." Washington, D.C.: U.S. Department of State, Cabinet Committee to Combat Terrorism Working Group, July 1976.

"Worldwide Criminal Acts Involving Civil Aviation 1974." Washington, D.C.: Federal Aviation Administration, Civil Aviation Security Service, 1975. Reports are available also for 1975 and for January-June 1976.

The aforementioned data sources have been supplemented by accounts given by the Associated Press, United Press International, and Reuter tickers, Foreign Broadcast Information Service, ABC FM Radio News, ABC, NBC, and CBS Evening News, the *Detroit Free Press*, *New Haven Register*, *New York Times*, *Washington Post*, and *Washington Star*. Chronologies from journalistic sources which have proven helpful include:

ABC News Olympic Special, 8 p.m., January 5, 1976.
Chicago Tribune (June 18, 1974).

Chronologies provided the author by Dr. Carol Edler Baumann.

The Economist (August 9, 1975).

New York Times (December 20, 1973), and (May 16, 1974).

"One Act of Guerrilla Violence After Another: Major Arab Terrorist Attacks in the Last 3½ Years" *U.S. News and World Report* (May 27, 1974).

"Terrorists: Where are they now?" *The Economist* (March 9, 1974).

Washington Post-Parade (March 16, 1975), p. 7.

Chronology of Events

This chronology attempts to centralize all unclassified reporting on transnational terrorism that occurred from 1968 through 1979. It begins with hundreds of examples of terrorist activities throughout history. These descriptions do not provide a comprehensive treatment of terrorist attacks prior to 1968; rather they illustrate that acts of violence that have some or all of the characteristics of contemporary transnational terrorism have been with us for a long, long time. In fact, many of these historical events today motivate terrorists seeking to settle ancient scores.

Scattered throughout the chronology are descriptions of incidents that were or are suspected of having been the work of governments. These listings are by no means exhaustive of the examples of state terrorism; they are included to provide readers a sense of the environments in which nonstate terrorist organizations operate. Many may believe that acts that governments deem to be morally acceptable, or at least pragmatically necessary, for them are thus also justified for nongovernmental actors.

Also included is a complete listing of aerial hijackings throughout history, whatever the motivation of the attacker or location of the incident. They are listed to illustrate the environment of violence that terrorists may believe exists. They also serve as a research tool for those who wish to investigate the possible diffusion, or even feedback, of violence by criminals, psychopaths, and terrorists who use the same forms of violent expression. In some hijacking summaries, mention is made of the behavioral profile developed by the Federal Aviation Administration to detect potential aerial hijackers on the ground. Details of this profile, still classified, are based upon patterns in demeanor and action discovered by psychiatrists and other social scientists working for the U.S. Department of Transportation. The FAA profile has been successfully used to screen out many potential hijackers from U.S. airline passengers.

Four-digit numbers follow approximately four thousand summaries in this chronology. The ITERATE-Common data file, based upon this chronology, was used to generate the statistical tables presented in the introduction. As part of my dissertation research, it lists only those incidents defined as transnational terrorism between 1968 and 1977; these incidents are 0001 to 3329. The ITERATE-Skyjack data file includes all incidents of skyjacking, including domestic and transnational attacks, as well as nonterrorist episodes, the latter numbered from 5000. Entries with no four-digit incident number are not part of any ITERATE computer file. These include major acts of domestic terrorism, noteworthy for the type of action engaged in, the precedents set by the action, the first act of a new group, or its particularly violent or symbolic nature. Interwoven with the terrorist incidents is a partial listing of threats and acts of violence against nuclear facilities. This list came about as a result of my research on the likelihood of terrorist exploitation of nuclear weapons or facilities in the future.

The chronology does not include incidents related to delared wars or major military interventions by governments, or guerrilla attacks on military targets conducted as internationally recognized acts of belligerency. It also does not include the numerous attacks between members of differing ethnic groups if such attacks are confined to the area in dispute (for example, Palestinian attacks in Israeli territory and attacks by the Irish Republican Army on British citizens in Northern Ireland), except for illustrative purposes.

The reporting on terrorist incidents is uneven, varying with the quality of the reporting source (usually a major U.S. or foreign newspaper but sometimes including government accounts), the importance of the incident to the source, and the success of the terrorists in publicizing their cause while masking the counterproductive aspects of their acts. Criminals or psychotics may wish to cloak their actions in terrorist garb, throwing police off their trail. Hence it is unavoidable that there are gaps in the descriptions of specific incidents, and some in fact may have been conducted by individuals not seeking political goals. Complete citations to the sources of information for specific incidents can be found in the bibliography of ITERATE Data Sources.

Transnational
Terrorism

Entries

Biblical times—Genesis 32:2-36 mentions the first recorded political kidnapping. Joseph, the seventeen-year-old son of Israel, was inclined to dreams of power and glory, which he felt compelled to share with his envious brothers. They ultimately decided to kill him and make his death appear to be caused by wild animals. However, one of them, Judah, eventually recognized the financial gains to be derived from their actions, noting, "What profit is it that we slay our brother and conceal his blood? Come, let us sell him to the Ish'maelites." Joseph was taken from the pit into which he was being held and was sold into slavery for twenty shekels of silver. He was taken to Egypt by the Mid'ianite traders, who in turn sold him to Pot'iphar, an officer of pharaoh, the captain of the guard.

1192—Austria—King Richard I of England, known as Coeur de Lion, was kidnapped on his return from the Third Crusade by Duke Leopold. Despite illegality of the act under civil and religious laws, Emperor Henry VI demanded Richard from Leopold and held him in a castle on the Danube. Richard's brother, Prince John, was informed that the ransom payment was 150,000 marks, twice the annual revenue of the British crown. The merchant class feared John's ambitions to the throne and raised the whole amount, securing Richard's release in 1194.

1532—Inca Empire—After the Spanish massacre of his Inca warriors, Atahualpa was taken prisoner by Pizarro in the town of Cajamarca. The king proposed that his people be allowed to ransom him, filling a great hall twenty-two feet by seventeen feet with gold as high as a man could reach (seven feet). Pizarro also demanded that an adjoining hall be filled twice with silver, giving the Incas two months as a deadline. The deadline was extended to five months, but Pizarro's troops became restless, and so the 1,326,539 gold pesos (approximately $170 million) was divided among them. Realizing the importance of Atahualpa to the Inca Empire's stability, Pizarro arranged a mock trial for him, accusing him of plotting against the Spanish, and sentencing him to death. When Atahualpa converted to Christianity, Pizarro altered the method of execution, and Atahualpa was killed on July 16, 1533.

1890—United Kingdom—Sun Yat-sen was kidnapped by members of his own government and held in the Chinese consulate in London.

August 22, 1890—Puerto Rico—General Barrienda, a prominent Guatemalan refugee, was assassinated by Guatemalan officers on the American steamship *Acapulco* at San José.

November 19, 1890—France—General Seliverskoff, a Russian agent, was assassinated in his Paris hotel.

July 23, 1892—United States—A young Russian-born anarchist attempted to assassinate industrialist Henry C. Frick in his Pittsburgh office. The assassin had decided Frick was an ideal object for anarchist propaganda-by-the-deed and shot and stabbed Frick. He was sentenced to twenty-two years.

June 24, 1894—France—President Sadi Carnot was assassinated by S. Caserio, an Italian anarchist in Lyons, to avenge the execution of Vaillant, who had thrown a bomb with no intent to kill. Carnot was stabbed in his carriage after his speech at a banquet. The dagger had been concealed in a rolled-up newspaper by Caserio, who was executed on August 15. Vaillant's case had previously been commemorated by Emile Henry, who killed one and wounded twenty when he threw a bomb in the Café Termenies on Gare St. Lazare in Paris on February 8. Henry was executed on May 21.

August 24, 1896—Turkey—The barricade-and-hostage scenario was developed by twenty-six Dasharak revolutionaries, led by seventeen-year-old Babken Suni, who seized the imperial Ottoman bank in Constantinople, making twelve demands on the behalf of Armenians. A foreign ambassador negotiated with the group, which had threatened to blow up the bank unless their demands were met. The ambassador agreed to their terms, arranging for their safe passage to the director's yacht. Suni and three others were killed and five persons were wounded by bombs used to secure the bank. The government retaliated with the massacre of more than six thousand Armenians.

August 8, 1897—Spain—Prime Minister Canovas was assassinated in Santa Agueda in the Basque mountains by Italian anarchist Michel Angiollilo to "avenge anarchist comrades." For firing three shots while Canovas read on the terrace, the assassin was garrotted.

May 18, 1904—Tangier—On the outskirts of Tangier, the bandit Raisuli and his cohorts broke into the Place of Nightingales villa and kidnapped Ion Perdicaris, a Greek-American, and his stepson, a Britisher named Varley. Raisuli demanded of the sultan: (1) release of Moorish political prisoners; (2) dismissal of the governor of Tangiers; (3) the recalling to Fez of government troops that had been sent out to keep order; (4) £11,000, to be obtained by the sale of the properties of the governors of Tangiers and Fez (money obtained from any other source would be refused); (5) two small districts—Zeenat and

Briesh—to be ceded to Raisuli; (6) arrest and imprisonment of two sheikhs and the two sons of one of them; and (7) free ingress and egress to and from town markets for turbulent tribesmen. President Theodore Roosevelt established a hard-line policy regarding the negotiations, declaring "Perdicaris alive or Raisuli dead," which would serve as a model for future U.S. policy. He also allowed U.S. Consul Gummere to handle negotiations. Perdicaris fell ill on June 8, and the sultan agreed to demands 1, 2, 4, 5, and 6. On June 15, Raisuli demanded the release of additional prisoners, two more districts, the arrest of other sheikhs, and British-American guarantees. In a show of force, U.S. and British ships were called in. Sheikh Zellal balked at his territory's being used to secure the release of hostages but was persuaded to cooperate. The hostages were released shortly after midnight on June 24.

August 25, 1906—Russia—Fifty-four people were killed and wounded when a bomb exploded in the residence of Russian Premier Stolypin.

June 28, 1914—Bosnia-Herzegovia—Austria's Archduke Francis Ferdinand and his wife were killed by seven members of the Union or Death group who fired on their automobile in Sarajevo. Gavrilo Princip, who was arrested with the other conspirators, fired the fatal shots. World War I began soon after this catalytic event.

January 31, 1919—United States—T. Wong, head of the Chinese Educational Mission to the United States, and two Chinese students were assassinated in Washington, D.C.

April 1919—United States—Bombs were sent through the mail by unknown persons to government officials throughout the country. One person was seriously wounded. On April 28 and May 1, acid packages were found in mail addressed to former Senator Thomas Hardwick of Georgia, Senator Lee Averman of North Carolina (who was active in suppression of enemy and bolshevik propaganda), Senator William King of Utah, and Frank Nebuker of Utah. Hardwick's package arrived on April 28, injuring his wife and her maid.

September 16, 1920—United States—A bomb exploded outside the House of Morgan on Wall Street. The time bomb killed thirty-four and injured over two hundred, causing damage estimated at $2 million. The U.S. attorney general proclaimed it a communist plot.

November 4, 1921—Japan—Japanese Premier Hara Takashi was assassinated by Korean rightist Rijichi Nakaoka, who was sentenced to jail.

December 31, 1921—Bessarabia—One hundred people were killed in the bombing of Siguranzia palace.

Feburary 24, 1922—India—The Prince of Wales' party was attacked by snipers as their car toured from Delhi to Puttiala.

March 11, 1922—Bulgaria—A bomb was thrown into the garden of the U.S. legation in Sofia.

March 28, 1922—Germany—Berlin was the scene of an attempted assassination against Paul N. Miliukoff, former minister of foreign affairs for the provisional government of Russia. The attack was frustrated by Valdimir Naboukoff, who was killed by a bullet.

June 23, 1922—United Kingdom—Two Irishmen, Joseph O'Sullivan and Reginald Dunn, attempted to assassinate Sir Henry Wilson, former chief of the imperial general staff, who had assisted the government of Northern Ireland. The two were hanged.

June 24, 1922—Mexico—A. Bruce Bielaski, ex-chief of the Bureau of Investigation of the U.S. Justice Department, was kidnapped near Cuernavaca. A $10,000 ransom was demanded for Bielaski, who escaped on June 27.

June 25, 1922—Mexico—Bandits occupied the U.S.-owned Cortez Oil Company facilities, holding its American employees hostage for fifteen thousand pesos ransom.

November 9, 1922—United Kingdom—Poisoned candy was sent by mail in a London assassination attempt against Sir William Horwood, chief of Scotland Yard.

November 17, 1922—China—Bandits kidnapped George Holm, an American missionary in Honan province.

1924—Rumania—A Korean assassinated prefect Manciu.

January 6, 1924—Japan—A Korean bombed the royal palace in Tokyo.

January 21, 1924—Hong Kong—Pirates hijacked a British steamer near Hong Kong, murdering the captain and kidnapping its passengers.

March 12, 1924—Greece—The front of the British legation in Athens was wrecked by a bomb.

June 19, 1924—China—The acting French consul and others were killed by a bomb thrown at them in Canton.

August 22, 1924—Brazil—Six bombs were thrown at the Argentine and Italian consulates in Rio de Janeiro, resulting in the postponing of King Umberto's visit.

November 19, 1924—Egypt—Sir Lee Stack, commander-in-chief of the Egyptian army, was shot by assassins in Cairo.

April 1925—Bulgaria—Radicals bombed the cathedral in Sofia where government officials were attending the funeral of a murdered general.

May 25, 1926—France—Symon Petljuria, a Ukranian official who had sought separation of the Ukraine from the Soviet Union, was assassinated in Paris.

April 7, 1927—Nicaragua—Two American Marine Corps planes were hit by sniper fire. Admiral Latimer ordered machine guns mounted on planes in the future.

December 24, 1927—Argentina—Considerable damage was caused by a bomb thrown by sympathizers of Sacco and Vanzetti against a Buenos Aires office of the National City Bank of New York.

February 21, 1928—United States—Envelopes containing lethal amounts of silver nitrate were sent to nine New York City officials.

February 27, 1928—Nicaragua—Five U.S. Marines were killed and eight injured in an ambush by rebels.

May 23, 1928—Argentina—The Italian consultate in Buenos Aires was bombed, resulting in the death of six, with thirty-four injured.

July 7, 1928—Lebanon—An artist and his wife employed at the U.S. consulate in Beirut were assassinated.

August 25, 1928—Mexico—E. J. Bumstead, a U.S. silver mine manager, was kidnapped near Ixtlan. A ransom of twenty thousand pesos was paid for him on September 15, leading to his release.

August 26, 1930—India—Anti-British rebels attempted to assassinate Eric Hobson.

August 30, 1930—India—Francis Lowman, a minor British official, was assassinated.

February 21, 1931—Peru—The first recorded skyjacking occurred when the American pilot of a local F7 Ford trimotor, Byron D. Rickards, turned "around and just as I did so armed soldiers rushed out. The soldiers had been hiding behind the hangar. They had rifles and their officers had handguns. They surrounded the plane and told me to cut the engines." The rebels agreed to allow a Panagra plane from Arica, Chile, collect the evening's mail and return. Rickards gave the impression that he was amenable to flying to Lima the next day to drop propaganda leaflets over the city. Rickards refused, allowing Colonel Cerro to drop the first batch of leaflets. (See next incident.) The Arequipa rebels were spurred on by Cerro's success and again attempted to force Rickards and Hillman, his copilot, to fly for them, but were again refused by the pilot, who was celebrating his twenty-second birthday with guests also trapped with them. On April 3, 1931, the *Chicago Daily News* reported that Rickards was given $100 by Pan-American Airlines for his bravery. Thirty years later, on August 3, 1961, Rickards became the first pilot to be hijacked twice. 5000

February 23, 1931—Peru—Colonel Cerro ordered Elmer Faucett to fly over Arequipa and drop government newsletters. Faucett then flew north on one of his company's scheduled flights. At Piura, Captain Jaramillo and two corporals, who were rebel sympathizers, seized his plane and forced him to fly to Talara to refuel. At Talara, the skyjackers and Faucett were arrested by government troops. Faucett was freed after he sent a cable to Cerro requesting his intervention. 5001

June 12, 1932—Netherlands—A German carrying a dagger and pistol climbed over a wall in Doorn and attempted to assassinate ex-Kaiser Wilhelm.

February 15, 1933—United States—Guiseppe Zangara, an Italian, attempted to assassinate President-elect Franklin D. Roosevelt in Miami, Florida. Zangara, who claimed to hate all rulers and capitalists, stood on a chair as Roosevelt was leaving after a speech and fired at him, fatally wounding Mayor Anton Cermak of Chicago. Zangara was executed.

February 22, 1933—United States—An apparent assassination attempt against President Franklin D. Roosevelt was thwarted in a Washington, D.C., post office when a shotgun shell wired to explode was found in an envelope mailed at Watertown, New York.

June 6, 1933—Germany—An Afghan student assassinated Afghan Minister Assis Khan, brother of King Nadir, in Berlin.

June 25, 1933—Holy See—An Egyptian resident of Spain threw a black powder bomb against the gate of St. Peter's in Vatican City.

August 14, 1933—Greece—An Albanian fruit merchant assassinated former Albanian Premier Hassan Bey Pristina in Saloniki. The killer claimed the premier had tried to induce him to assassinate King Zog.

September 2, 1933—India—British magistrate E. J. Burge was killed in Midnapur district.

November 22, 1933—Cuba—A bomb damaged an American-owned electric plant and sugar mill in Camaguey province.

October 9, 1934—France—King Alexander of Yugoslavia and Foreign Minister Louis Marthou were shot by Vlada Gheorghieff, a member of the Iron Hand (IMRO) who was aided by Croatians trained in Hungary. The Marseille crowd caught the assassin, who was sabred, beaten, and stamped to death. Three Croatians were sentenced to life imprisonment. The French interior minister resigned, and the police were reorganized.

March 12, 1935—Greece—Seventy million drachmas were taken from several banks by rebels who eventually surrendered to Turkish authorities.

June 25, 1935—Mexico—A bomb was tossed over the wall of the U.S. embassy grounds in Mexico City, shattering windows in the private office of the ambassador and the sleeping quarters of a secretary.

July 29, 1935—China—Manchurian bandits held up an express train between Heinking and Tumen. Twelve passengers, mostly Japanese, one Russian, and four Manchurians, were killed.

September 21, 1935—United States—Lieutenant Felix Waitkus of the U.S. Air Force Reserve hijacked a plane from Floyd Bennett Field in Brooklyn, New York, with the intention of flying to his native country, Lithuania. The plane ran out of gas, and crashed near Ballinrode, County Mayo, Irish Free State. The pilot was unhurt, although the plane was demolished. 5002

October 31, 1935—China—Anti-Catholic bandits seized Father Biron, a Catholic missionary in Lolo County (Szechwan) in southwest China, and dragged him by a rope until he was dead.

1936—China—Chiang Kai-shek was kidnapped by Chinese warlord Marshal Chiang.

February 4, 1936—Switzerland—A Yugoslavian medical student assassinated Wilhelm Gustloff, a Swiss Nazi leader in Davos. The Jewish student, a rabbi's son, was sentenced to eighteen years in prison in December 1936.

February 23, 1936—Puerto Rico—Two young nationalists shot E. F. Riggs, a retired U.S. Army colonel, who headed the insular police in San Juan. The assassins, who claimed to be avenging the massacre of four young nationalists in October 1935, were killed by gunfire at police headquarters. The district police Chief at Utuado was shot a few hours later.

May 4, 1936—Ethiopia—Natives attacked the U.S. legation in Addis Ababa. The American and other legations successfully held off repeated attacks. The British claimed they were unable to spare troops for protective purposes. Italian troops relieved the legations on May 5.

June 21, 1936—Palestine—Arabs attacked a train near Jerusalem, killing two Britons and forty Arabs.

June 22, 1936—Palestine—Another Arab attack on a train near Jerusalem led to the deaths of five Arabs.

June 22, 1936—Panama—A Venezuelan youth shot Ildemaro Urdaneta, a Venezuelan envoy, in the stomach. The youth then wounded himself in the leg.

June 26, 1936—Ethiopia—General Magliocci, assistant chief of aviation, and nine other Italian officers and pilots were killed in an ambush in western Ethiopia. Mass reprisals were ordered.

July 17, 1936—United Kingdom—Jerome Bannigan, an Irish journalist, pointed a loaded revolver at King Edward VIII as he rode to Buckingham Palace. The pistol misfired.

January 25, 1937—France—Dimitri Navashine, a former Soviet representative abroad, was stabbed to death in Paris. Navashine had intended to speak out against Stalin. His attacker escaped.

September 26, 1937—Palestine—Lewis Y. Andrews, district commissioner of Galilee, and his bodyguard were gunned down in Nazareth as they were leaving an Anglican church. Andrews was known for his strict rule.

October 12, 1937—Lebanon—The U.S. consul general was gunned down outside his Beirut consulate by an Armenian who had been refused visas.

January 21, 1938—United States—A peace advocate attempted to bomb the Japanese steamer *Hige Maru* in Seattle, Washington. The time bomb did not detonate, and the perpetrator drowned.

April 1, 1938—Mexico—The mayor of Juarez was killed by a package bomb mailed express from Chihuahua City.

April 6, 1938—China—Herman Chen en Liu, president of the U.S.-supported Shanghai College, and a British guard were shot by two Chinese gunmen in Shanghai, who claimed that the victim was "a traitor to China." One attacker was captured, and the other escaped.

May 14, 1938—Palestine—British troops escorting the partition commissioner were ambushed by Arabs in northern Palestine, resulting in the deaths of twenty-three Arabs.

May 26, 1938—Mexico—Followers of Cedillo, rebelling against Cardenas, cut train tracks, derailing an express from Laredo, Texas. Sketchy reports indicated that twenty-six American passengers were captured.

June 12, 1938—Iraq—Two natives murdered the Reverend R. C. Cumberland, an American missionary, north of Mosul.

July 15, 1938—Palestine—A bomb planted in an Arab market in Jerusalem killed ten Arabs and wounded twenty-nine.

July 25, 1938—Palestine—A bomb planted at a market entrance in Haifa killed sixty-five Arabs and one Jew.

August 26, 1938—Palestine—A bomb planted in a vegetable market in the Arab quarter of Jaffa killed twenty-one and wounded thirty-seven.

August 28, 1938—Palestine—Two Greek monks were abducted and shot in Kul Tarin in Caesarea in northern Palestine. The government imposed fines on eleven villages and destroyed one hundred twenty houses in Safad and Acre.

September 10, 1938—Palestine—An armed band seized arms in an attack on Beersheba, southwest of Jerusalem. A British policeman was killed.

November 7, 1938—France—Herschel Grunspan, a seventeen-year-old Jew protesting German treatment of Jews, assassinated Ernst von Rath, a German diplomat, in Paris. Germany retaliated with pogroms on November 9 and 10, burning synagogues and breaking shop windows.

January 1, 1939—Palestine—G. D. Sanderson, a British official, was assassinated. Sir C. Tegart escaped a similar attempt.

January 16, 1939—United Kingdom—Seven bomb attacks were made against power stations and power transmission lines in Manchester, London, Alnwick, and Birmingham. The IRA was responsible.

February 4, 1939—United Kingdom—Two bombs exploded in the London underground at Leicester Square and Tottenham Court Road. The IRA was responsible.

February 6, 1939—United Kingdom—An IRA bomb went off at Walton Jail in Liverpool.

February 28, 1939—Poland—An unsuccessful assassination attempt was made against Nikita Krushchev of the Soviet Union.

March 9, 1939—United Kingdom—The IRA was responsible for two major explosions in London, one at Hammersmith Bridge.

March 30, 1939—United Kingdom—The IRA was responsible for bombings in Liverpool, Coventry, and Birmingham.

March 31, 1939—United Kingdom—Seven IRA bombs exploded in London.

May 3, 1939—United Kingdom—The IRA set off tear-gas bombs in several London cinemas.

May 4, 1939—United Kingdom—The IRA set off four bombs in Coventry and two in London.

May 19, 1939—United Kingdom—Fires were started in eight English hotels by IRA delayed-acton incendiaries.

May 29, 1939—United Kingdom—The IRA set off four magnesium bombs in London movie theaters.

June 9, 1939—United Kingdom—The IRA bombed several post offices in Great Britain.

June 24, 1939—United Kingdom—The IRA bombed the major banks in Piccadilly Circus, London.

June 25, 1939—United Kingdom—The IRA set off a balloon bomb in Madame Tussaud's wax museum.

June 26, 1939—United Kingdom—IRA bombs exploded at King's Cross and Victoria stations in London.

June 27, 1939—United Kingdom—Three massive IRA bombs went off in Liverpool.

August 25, 1939—United Kingdom—Two members of the IRA used a bicycle to deliver a bomb in Coventry's Broadgate. Their hanging on February 7, 1940, led to massive protest demonstrations.

February 22, 1940—United Kingdom—Two IRA bombs exploded in the West End of London, injuring twenty-eight.

March 13, 1940—United Kingdom—Indian nationalist Mahomed Singh Azad assassinated Sir Michael O'Dwyer in Caxton Hall, London, to avenge those killed by O'Dwyer when he was lieutenant governor of the Punjab during the British killings in Amritsar in 1919. Two others were wounded in the gunfire.

May 3, 1940—Mexico—An armed posse in police disguise broke into the home of Leon Trotsky in Mexico City. Trotsky, his wife, and grandson were injured. His guard was shot by the attackers.

August 2, 1940—China—Karl Mezler, the leader of the White Russian Emigrants Association, was assassinated in Shanghai.

August 20, 1940—Mexico—Jacques Mornard von den Dreschel, a Persian-born Belgian journalist, broke into the villa of Leon Trotsky on the outskirts on Mexico City and murdered him with a pickax. Mornard was sentenced to twenty years.

November 25, 1940—Palestine—An explosion sank a French refugee ship in Haifa harbor. The ship had been refused admission to Palestine. Most of the 1,771 Jewish refugees swam ashore.

November 29, 1940—China—Guerrillas dynamited the Shanghai-Nanking express train, causing over one hundred casualties. The train had been carrying Japanese and Chinese officials who were to sign a peace treaty between Japan and the Wang Ching-wei government.

December 16, 1940—China—Chinese terrorists assassinated the French consular judge and a Japanese officer in Shanghai. The judge had dealt with the Wang regime.

January 14, 1941—Ecuador—Anti-German masked men assaulted the German transocean wireless station in Quito, beating the watchman and wrecking the station.

February 1941—Italy—An Italian merchant ship was bombed and sunk by Yugoslav intelligence agent Miloj Knezevich, who was executed.

March 11, 1941—Turkey—Six were killed when a bomb intended for the British minister to Bulgaria exploded in luggage in an Istanbul hotel lobby.

April 8, 1941—Cuba—A small bomb exploded in the German consulate in Havana, causing slight damage.

May 17, 1941—Albania—A Greek, Vasil L. Mihailov, attempted to assassinate King Victor Emmanuel of Italy and the Albanian premier. His shots hit a rear tire of their car. Mihailov was executed on May 27.

November 23, 1941—Indochina—The U.S. consulate in Saigon was bombed. The French governor-general expressed his regrets.

February 24, 1942—Turkey—A naturalized Turk from Czechoslovakia attempted to assassinate German Ambassador Franz von Papen in Ankara. The attacker was killed by his own bomb. Fifty foreigners, including five Russians, were arrested.

April 5, 1942—Northern Ireland—Six members of the IRA bombed the empty Royal Hippodrome theater in Belfast, which was used by British and American troops, causing slight damage. Several members of the IRA were captured.

May 1942—Italy—Yugoslavs assassinated an aide to King Victor Emmanuel.

September 9, 1942—Ireland—A group of men possibly connected to the IRA assassinated the detective sergeant of the Dublin Castle police force with submachine guns and revolvers.

March 13, 1943—Germany—Lieutenant Fabian von Schlabrendorff attempted to assassinate Adolf Hitler with a bomb captured from the British. The bomb, placed aboard Hitler's aircraft, failed to explode.

March 21, 1943—Germany—Colonel Wolf von Goersdorff planned to assassinate Adolf Hitler by setting off a bomb while showing Hitler a weapons exhibit. Hitler did not stop at the exhibit.

March 23, 1944—Palestine—Members of the Irgun Zvai Leumi killed six British constables and injured twelve in a series of bombings and gun battles in Jerusalem, Tel Aviv, and Haifa.

March 27, 1944—Palestine—A Jewish terrorist shot a British constable on a Tel Aviv street.

August 8, 1944—Palestine—Unknown attackers fired on the automobile of High Commissioner Sir Harold McMichael in a Jerusalem suburb. A curfew was imposed in the area, and its residents were fined $2,000.

November 6, 1944—Egypt—Lord Moyne, British resident minister in the Middle East, and his chauffeur were assassinated by gunmen as they were leaving his car at his residence in Cairo. Eliahu Bet Zouri, twenty-two, and Eliahu Hakim, seventeen, both members of the Fighters for the Freedom of Israel, were captured and hanged on March 22, 1945.

October 17, 1945—Java—Indonesian nationalists kidnapped Red Cross workers in Semarang, Ambarawa, Banjubiru. British troops were sent to the area.

November 4, 1945—Palestine—A raid on a British navy depot at Athlit by six Jews was repulsed.

November 23, 1945—India—Thirty were injured when Indian nationalists threw a hand grenade into a U.S. officers' Thanksgiving dance in Calcutta.

November 27, 1945—Palestine—Members of the Irgun Zvai Leumi bombed the Civil Investigation Department building in Jerusalem, dropping antitank mines to cover their retreat. British constables and soldiers engaged in a running gun battle with the attackers, arresting two hundred. Four British police and four Basuto soldiers were killed.

December 27, 1945—Palestine—A British corporal was killed in a raid on a Tel Aviv arms depot by fifty men with Haganah affiliations.

January 7, 1946—U.S. Zone, Germany—Three U.S. officials were found dead in their burned lodgings in Passau. "German werewolves" claimed credit.

January 28, 1946—Palestine—Fifteen terrorists dressed in RAF uniforms conducted a noon raid on an RAF camp in Aquir, taking two hundred machine guns. The high commissioner decreed the death penalty for offenses against defense regulations. The guns were later recovered.

February 6, 1946—Palestine—Jewish terrorists attacked a British camp in the vicinity of Tel Aviv. East African troops pursued the group, resulting in the deaths of one British officer, one African soldier, and three attackers.

February 28, 1946—France—Republican Spaniards and leftist French conducted raids on Spanish consulates in Sète and Auch.

March 6, 1946—Palestine—British troops drove off Jewish terrorists attempting to raid British military camps in Sarafand and Rehoboth.

April 6, 1946—Brazil—Tchyzaburo Nomura, former Japanese diplomat, was shot in São Paulo by Japanese terrorists for admitting that Japan lost World War II.

April 19, 1946—Germany—Anti-Nazis used arsenic to poison bread from a local bakery, which was sent to SS prisoners in Camp Stalag 13 in the vicinity of Nuremberg. 2,283 became ill.

April 25, 1946—Palestine—Seven British soldiers were killed when Jewish terorists seized arms at a British camp in Tel Aviv. Twelve hundred suspects were arrested.

May 5, 1946—Egypt—A bomb was thrown into the doorway of the British Young Men's Christian Association in Cairo, injuring twelve.

May 5, 1946—U.S. Zone, Germany—Two U.S. soldiers were shot by unknown gunmen while riding in their jeep in Nuremberg.

June 18, 1946—Palestine—Two Britons were wounded in an unsuccessful attempt by the Irgun Zvai Leumi to kidnap them in Jerusalem.

June 18, 1946—Palestine—Five British officers were kidnapped in Tel Aviv and held hostage by the Irgun Zvai Leumi to protest the death sentences of two Irgun members. One hostage escaped; two were released on June 22 and two on July 4.

June 22, 1946—India—Major M.O.S. Donald was kidnapped by Pathan tribesmen in the Waziristan area. The British bombed villages when the tribesmen refused to pay indemnity.

July 17, 1946—Italy—Yugoslav terrorists ambushed a U.S. jeep, murdering one soldier and shooting another in the vicinity of Gorizia.

July 22, 1946—Palestine—Members of the Irgun Zvai Leumi entered the kitchen of the King David Hotel, headquarters of the British army and secretariat of the Palestine government, disguised as Arabs. They held employees at bay with revolvers, while placing land mines in the basement. After escaping in a truck, they telephoned a warning to the Jerusalem hotel. Ninety-one were killed and forty-five injured when the blast went off. The British declared martial law, engaging in a house-to-house search that resulted in the arrests of 133 men and 10 women.

August 5, 1946—Lebanon—Two Arabs protesting the Anglo-U.S. policy toward Palestine bombed the U.S. and British consulates in Beirut. A guard was placed around the U.S. embassy.

August 16, 1946—Brazil—Members of the Japanese terrorist society Shindo Remmei assassinated two Japanese in Tupã who had admitted the defeat of Japan in the war. Seventy members of the group were deported.

August 26, 1946—Germany—A German assassinated the U.S. director of German universities on the Munich-Nuremberg highway. The attacker was trapped and killed by U.S. troops on September 4.

September 9, 1946—Palestine—Two British officers were killed when a bomb went off in a public building in Tel Aviv. A curfew was announced, and 101 were arrested.

September 30, 1946—Philippines—A U.S. soldier was killed when an unidentified gang attacked Fort McKinley.

October 6, 1946—Palestine—An RAF man was gunned down in Jerusalem.

October 8, 1946—Palestine—A mine planted by Jewish terrorists in the vicinity of Jerusalem went off under a military truck, killing two British soldiers and wounding fifteen others.

October 20, 1946—U.S. Zone, Germany—Members of a Nazi underground bombed U.S. military buildings in the vicinity of Stuttgart, causing some damage. Fifty-five suspects were detained and twelve arrested.

October 28, 1946—U.S. Zone, Germany—Nazi sympathizers threw a bomb into the Esslingen de-Nazification office.

October 30-31, 1946—Palestine—Jewish terrorists twice bombed British army trucks and attacked the Ras El Air airfield in the vicinity of Jerusalem, killing six British, injuring eleven, and damaging the airfield.

October 31, 1946—Italy—A wing of the British embassy in Rome was wrecked when two bombs concealed in suitcases left on the building's steps by members of the Irgun Zvai Leumi exploded.

November 9-13, 1946—Palestine—A campaign of land mining, suitcase bombing, and bombing of railroad stations, trains, and streetcars by Jewish terrorists killed eleven British soldiers and policemen and eight Arab constables.

November 17, 1946—Palestine—A land mine planted by Jewish terrorists exploded in Tel Aviv, killing three policemen and an RAF sergeant. The police rioted, beating Jews and firing into their houses.

December 2, 1946—Palestine—Land mines planted by members of the Irgun Zvai Leumi destroyed British jeeps, killing five soldiers.

December 5, 1946—Palestine—Jewish terrorists attacked the home of Sir Evelyn Barker, a British military commander, in Jerusalem.

December 29, 1946—Palestine—Members of the Irgun Zvai Leumi kidnapped and flogged a British major and three sergeants in retaliation for the flogging of bank robber Benjamin Kimkhin. All coastal communities were declared out of bounds to British troops.

January 5, 1947—Egypt—Jewish terrorists were suspected of engineering a hand grenade attack against a Cairo-Haifa train carrying troops to Palestine. The attack, in the vicinity of Benha, injured eleven Britons.

January 12, 1947—Palestine—Members of the Stern gang declared their truce with the government to be over by sending an explosive-laden truck into the central police station compound in Haifa, killing two British police and three Arab constables and wounding 140.

January 26, 1947—Palestine—Members of the Irgun Zvai Leumi kidnapped former Major H. A. I. Collins, a British banker, from his Jerusalem home and held him hostage for an Irgun member sentenced to death by the British. The high commissioner threatened martial law, but the execution was postponed. Collins, badly beaten, was released on January 29.

January 27, 1947—Palestine—In a related incident, Judge Ralph Windham was taken from his Tel Aviv court. He was released on January 28 when the British agreed to postpone the execution of an Irgun member.

January 27, 1947—Italy—A Yugoslav consul was beaten and murdered by Chetnik bodyguards of the British in the vicinity of Naples in a Chetnik camp. Yugoslavia blamed the British for the murder.

February 1, 1946—U.S. Zone, Germany—Nazis protesting von Papen's trial bombed the office of the president of the de-Nazification court in Nuremberg.

February 20, 1947—Palestine—Members of the Irgun Zvai Leumi used mortars and machine guns in attacks on an RAF base and Iraqi facilities in Hadera, which resulted in the destruction of the Iraq Petroleum Company's pipelines.

February 28, 1947—Palestine—Jewish terrorists bombed Barclay's Bank in Haifa in retaliation for the shipping of Jewish refugees to Cyprus. Two were killed and five injured.

March 1, 1947—Palestine—Members of the Irgun and Stern gang bombed the Goldsmith British Officers' Club in Jerusalem and fifteen other targets throughout Palestine, killing twenty-two and injuring twenty-seven. Martial law was declared.

March 3, 1947—Palestine—Members of the Irgun threw five hand grenades into the British military office in Haifa.

March 5, 1947—Palestine—Jewish underground members bombed the Haifa tax office to protest the deportation of illegal refugees.

March 8, 1947—Palestine—Jewish underground members attacked the British operational headquarters in Tel Aviv, resulting in the death of four attackers and one guard.

March 8, 1947—Palestine—The Jewish underground conducted an armed attack against the British army camp in Sarona.

March 9, 1947—Palestine—The Jewish underground attacked the Hadera British army camp.

March 12, 1947—Palestine—Jewish terrorists dynamited the British army pay corps offices in Jerusalem, killing one soldier.

March 28, 1947—Palestine—The Iraq Petroleum Company's pipeline in Haifa was bombed.

March 29, 1947—Palestine—Jewish terrorists ambushed and murdered a British officer in the vicinity of Ramle camp.

March 31, 1947—Palestine—Jewish terrorists dynamited the British-owned Shell-Mex oil tanks in Haifa, starting a waterfront fire that caused $1 million in damages.

April 2, 1947—Cyprus—Members of the Haganah damaged the *Ocean Vigour* with bombs in Famagusta Harbor.

April 6, 1947—France—The Czech consulate's economic expert was found dead on the steps of Chaillot Palace in Paris.

April 8, 1947—Palestine—Jewish terrorists assassinated a British constable in Jerusalem in reprisal for the slaying of Moshe Cohen, a Palestine freedom fighter, by a British patrol.

April 16, 1947—United Kingdom—Jewish terrorists attempted to bomb the Colonial Office in London in reprisal for the hanging of four terrorists in Jerusalem. The bomb failed to explode. Scotland Yard was ordered to investigate.

April 18, 1947—Palestine—Members of the Jewish underground gunned down two British soldiers and wounded two policemen in retaliation for the hanging of four terrorists.

April 18, 1947—Palestine—The Irgun attacked a field dressing station in the vicinity of Natanya in reprisal for the execution of Dov Bela Gruner, a Palestine freedom fighter.

April 18, 1947—Palestine—One bystander in Tel Aviv was killed in an attack by the Irgun on a British armored car in retaliation for the Gruner execution.

April 20, 1947—Palestine—Twelve British soldiers were injured in a series of Jewish bombings in Tel Aviv in retaliation for the Gruner execution.

April 22, 1947—Palestine—Jewish terrorists in Rehoboth bombed a troop train from Cairo, killing five British soldiers and three civilians and injuring thirty-nine.

April 25, 1947—Palestine—Members of the Stern gang drove a stolen post office truck loaded with explosives into a British police compound in Sarona, killing five policemen.

April 26, 1947—Palestine—Jewish terrorists gunned down Deputy Police Superintendent A. E. Conquest in Haifa, who was in charge of investigating underground activities.

May 4, 1947—Palestine—The Irgun bombed the Acre prison walls, freeing 251 Jews and Arabs during a gun battle. Fifteen Jews and 1 Arab were killed; 6 British guards and 26 others were injured. Twenty-three of the prisoners were recaptured, 3 were sentenced to death.

June 4-6, 1947—United Kingdom—Scotland Yard intercepted twenty letter bombs containing powdered gelignite that were mailed from Italy and intended by the Stern gang for Foreign Secretary Ernest Bevin, Anthony Eden, and eighteen others in London.

June 9, 1947—Palestine—Members of the Irgun kidnapped two British policemen from a swimming pool in Ramat Gen. They were released on June 10.

June 28, 1947—British Zone, Germany—A time bomb was discovered in an attempt to blow up a trainload of Allied personnel on the Hannover-Hamburg rail line.

June 28, 1947—Palestine—The Stern gang opened fire on a line of British soldiers outside a Tel Aviv theater, killing three and wounding two, in retaliation for the alleged slaying of a sixteen-year-old Jew being held in army barracks.

June 29, 1947—Palestine—The Stern gang attacked British soldiers on a Herzliyya beach, injuring four. The U.N. Inquiry Commission condemned such acts of terrorism as a "flagrant disregard" of the U.N. appeal for an interim truce.

July 12, 1947—Palestine—The Irgun kidnapped two British army sergeants in Natanya, holding them hostage for three Irgun members sentenced to be hanged. The two were sentenced by the Irgun to death and hung on July 30. The town was placed under martial law on July 14, and sixty-eight were arrested.

July 16, 1947—Palestine—The Irgun set road mines against military traffic in Natanya, killing one Briton and injuring sixteen. Two days later, another Briton was killed and seven injured by land mines.

July 22, 1947—Palestine—Jewish terrorists bombed the Iraqi Petroleum Company's pipeline in Haifa.

July 23, 1947—Palestine—The Haganah sunk the British transport *Empire Lifeguard* in Haifa.

July 25, 1947—Rumania—Three Rumanian army officers hijacked a Rumanian civilian plane carrying ten people to Canakkale province in Turkey and requested political asylum. One of the crew members was shot dead for refusing to pilot the plane to Turkey. The officers were taken into custody, but the seven civilians were freed. 5003

July 26, 1947—Palestine—A booby trap planted by Jewish terrorists killed two British soldiers and wounded eight others in Jerusalem.

August 5, 1947—Palestine—The Irgun bombed the Jerusalem Labor Department building in reprisal for the arrest of thirty-five leading Zionists, killing three British constables.

August 6, 1947—Canada—Three Doukhobors, members of the radical Sons of Freedom faction, committed arson against a provincial government building in Krestova to express their opposition to orthodox Doukhobors. They were sentenced on August 6 to seven years.

August 9, 1947—Palestine—The Irgun claimed credit for the mining of a troop train in the vicinity of Lydda, in an attempt to disrupt all railways. The train derailed, killing the engineer. On November 24, the British sentenced two Sternists to life imprisonment.

August 21, 1947—Palestine—Arab bandits stole $40,000 from the Ottoman Bank messenger in Haifa.

September 9, 1947—Germany—A bomb was found on board the *Empire Rival* in Hamburg harbor. The attempt was to protest the forcible return of Jews to the area.

September 26, 1947—Palestine—Jewish terrorists killed four British constables in an armed robbery of a police armored car outside a Tel Aviv bank, seizing $180,000 while dropping $300,000 in the street.

September 27, 1947—Palestine—The Swedish consulate in Jerusalem was damaged by a bomb placed by the Commandos for the Arab Holy War.

September 29, 1947—Palestine—The Irgun set off a barrel of explosives outside the Haifa police headquarters building in retaliation for the deportation of immigrants. Four British, four Arab policemen, and two Arab civilians were killed; forty-six were injured.

October, 1947—Chile—Unknown individuals machine-gunned the Soviet embassy in Santiago. The Chilean ambassador to Moscow apologized.

October 12, 1947—Palestine—The Polish consulate in Jerusalem was damaged by a bomb. Arabs were suspected of placing the device.

October 13, 1947—Palestine—Arabs were suspected in the bombing of the U.S. consulate general in Jerusalem, which resulted in damage and two people being injured.

November 14, 1947—Palestine—Two British policemen were murdered in Jerusalem.

November 30, 1947—Syria—Arab students claimed credit for the stoning of the U.S. legation and arson of communist headquarters in Damascus to protest the U.N. decision on the partition of Palestine.

December 2, 1947—Egypt—Arabs committed arson against the British Institute in Zagazig in protest of the U.N. partition decision.

December 3, 1947—France—Communists were suspected in the derailment of the Paris-Lille mail express in the vicinity of Arras, which killed twenty and injured forty.

December 4, 1947—Iraq—Iraqi students protesting the partition decision wrecked the USIS office in Baghdad.

December 5, 1947—Cuba—Members of the International Communist Brigade did considerable damage to the Dominican Republic's consulate in a ransacking operation.

December 12, 1947—Palestine—The Haganah attacked Arab quarters in Ramleh and Haifa, leading to the deaths of twenty Arabs, five Jews, and two British soldiers.

December 25, 1947—Palestine—Sternists machine-gunned a Tel Aviv café, killing two British soldiers.

December 29, 1947—Palestine—The Irgun tossed a bomb from a passing taxi near the Damascus Gate in Jerusalem, killing eleven Arabs and two British policemen.

January 4, 1948—Palestine—Sternists bombed the Arab National Committee Headquarters in Jaffa, killing fourteen and injuring one hundred.

January 5, 1948—Palestine—The Haganah bombed the Semiramis Hotel in Jerusalem, killing fifteen.

January 5, 1948—Palestine—Jewish terrorists threw bombs in Safad in northern Palestine, killing fourteen.

January 7, 1948—Palestine—Two bombs were thrown at the Jaffa Gate in Jerusalem by Irgun members disguised as Palestine police in a stolen armored car. Eighteen Arabs in the crowded area were killed, along with three attackers.

January 17, 1948—Palestine—Arabs machine-gunned Jewish men en route from Kfar Etzion, killing thirty-five.

February 3, 1948—Palestine—Sternists murdered two British policemen in Jerusalem because the bombers of the *Palestine Post* building on February 1 were Arabs wearing police uniforms.

February 22, 1948—Palestine—Arab terrorists bombed two truckloads of explosives being escorted by armored trucks with police insignia on Ben Yahuda Street in Jerusalem in retaliation for the Jewish bombing in Ramleh, which killed seven Arabs. Fifty-four were killed, and three city blocks were destroyed.

February 29, 1948—Palestine—Sternists set land mines in Rehoboth's Jewish area for the Cairo-Haifa train in retaliation for the Ben Yehuda Street bombing, which had been falsely blamed on the British. Twenty-eight British soldiers were killed and thirty-five injured.

March 1, 1948—Palestine—Unknown attackers shot at and set land mines for the car and escorting jeeps of British commander Lieutenant General G. H. A. McMillan, who was not in his vehicle at the time of the Jerusalem attack.

March 7, 1948—Indochina—Members of the Viet Minh Assassination Commission killed the director of the USIS and secretary of the U.S. consulate in Saigon, mistaking them for French women. The two killers were sentenced to death on December 14, 1949.

March 11, 1948—Palestine—Arabs stole a U.S. car and drove through the barricades of the Jewish Agency's building in Jerusalem with a load of explosives, killing thirteen and injuring eighty-four.

March 31, 1948—Palestine—Sternists set land mines near Haifa for the Cairo-Haifa train, killing forty Arabs and injuring sixty.

April 6, 1948—Czechoslovakia—Seventeen people, including the pilot and two crew members, hijacked the Prague-to-Bratislava domestic flight to the U.S. Zone of Germany, requesting political asylum. 5004

April 7, 1948—Palestine—Jews seeking firearms raided a British army camp in the vicinity of Pardes Hannah, south of Haifa, killing seven Britons.

April 9, 1948—Colombia—A bomb went off near the U.S. embassy in Bogotá following the assassination of Jorge Eliecer Gaitain, Liberal party leader, during the OAS conference. The assassin was beaten to death in the rioting that followed.

April 26, 1948—Japan—Fifteen hundred Koreans raided the prefecture in Kobe, kidnapping three officials in protest of Japanese control of Korean émigré schools. The group demanded the rescinding of the order that closed the schools and the release of seventy-three jailed Koreans. The demands were met.

May 3, 1948—United Kingdom—A Sternist letter bomb killed Rex Farran in Colverhampton. The bomb was intended for his brother Roy, who was acquitted for the murder of an Irgun member in 1947.

May 5, 1948—Palestine—Sternists ambushed and murdered seven British soldiers near Natanya to protest the British reinforcement of forces in Palestine.

May 5, 1948—Czechoslovakia—Three men and two women, all anti-communists, hijacked a domestic commercial flight from Brno, Moravia, to Ceske, Budegovice to the U.S. Zone of Germany, landing in Munich, where they requested political asylum. 5005

May 8, 1948—Greece—CBS correspondent George Polk was murdered by three communists who shot him and dumped his body in a bay after meeting on a boat in Salonika. They had hoped that the United States would blame nationalists and withhold future aid. One killer was sentenced to life and the two others to death in absentia.

June 3, 1948—Austria—Between six and twenty armed Russian soldiers invaded a British-run international police station in Vienna, freeing two MVD officials who were arrested after an attempt to kidnap an Austrian woman who had quit as a Soviet agent to work for the U.S. Army and for the kidnapping of a U.S. officer. The British denounced the attack.

June 4, 1948—Yugoslavia—Two men hijacked the Belgrade-to-Sarajevo local flight to Bari, Italy, and requested political asylum. 5006

June 17, 1948—Rumania—A Soviet-Rumanian Airways C47 on a domestic flight was hijacked to Salzburg, Austria, where all but one of the twenty-three people aboard asked for political asylum. 5007

June 30, 1948—Bulgaria—Strahil Mihalakev, a retired colonel in the Bulgarian Air Force, and several others skyjacked the Bulgarian Junkers 52 local flight from Varna to Sofia. Of the crew of four, the radio operator was shot dead, a pilot and the flight engineer were badly wounded, and the other pilot was overpowered. Mihalekev landed the transport plane in Istanbul, Turkey, claiming that the group was fleeing communist rule. 5008

July 7, 1948—Palestine—The Irgun kidnapped four Britishers in Jerusalem who were employed by the Jerusalem Electric and Public Service Corporation, accusing them of espionage.

July 16, 1948—Macau—The *Miss Macau*, a Cathay Pacific Catalina flying boat, crashed during its Macau-to-Hong-Kong flight during a skyjacking attempt by a band of criminals. The lone survivor of the crash, which occured twelve miles northeast of Macau, was a Chinese citizen, Wong Io, who suffered a broken arm and leg. Wong had planned to land the craft in the Pearl River estuary and hold the passengers for a ransom. He had recruited two other gunmen from his village to aid him: Chio Cheong and Chio Kei Mun, the latter dropping from the team a week before the attack and being replaced by Chio Choi. Chio Tok, the other member of the band, switched landing sites to a point northwest of Tao Munisland, planning to navigate the plane himself without telling the team leader. During the attack, Chio Choi stood over the pilot, Captain Dale W. Cramer, an American, and his co-pilot, flight officer K. S. McDuff, an Australian, and ordered them to relinquish the controls. The two refused, and a passenger tried to grab Chio Cheong's gun. Cramer swung the plane hard left as McDuff tried to club the two nearest gunmen. The three gunmen shot the pilots (police calculated that eighteen shots had been fired from three different types of revolvers). Chio Tok was unable to regain control of the plane and died in the air crash, the first resulting from a skyjacking. Wong Io was later freed by authorities who argued that although he had committed a crime, it had been outside Portuguese airspace and on board a British aircraft, carried out by foreigners against other foreigners. The case was sent to the Hong Kong colonial secretariat, whose attorney general declared that extradition would not be requested because Wong Io's confession did not constitute sufficient evidence. 5009

July 22, 1948—United States—Stephen J. Supina exploded a homemade dynamite bomb from an Aeronca plane over the United Nations headquarters building in Lake Success, New York, claiming that he wanted to "wake them up here and abroad to look to the U.N. for peace." No damage was caused. He surrendered to the *New Haven Register* on July 23.

September 12, 1948—Greece—Eight armed Greeks hijacked a Greek Dakota plane on the Athens-to-Salonika run, diverting it to Tetova, Yugoslavia, where they requested political asylum. 5010

September 17, 1948—Palestine—Four Sternists in a jeep halted the car of U.N. mediator Count Folke Bernadotte. One of the attackers fired point-blank through the car's window, hitting Bernadotte six times. Colonel Andrew Pierre Serot, chief of the French contingent of the U.N. truce-observer teams, was shot seventeen times. He had been unwillingly passing information to the LEHI, who now wished him silenced. The Hazit ha-Moledeth (Fatherland Front) of Bulgaria was used as a cover name for the LEHI operation.

January 4, 1949—Hungary—Janos Majoros, Milos Kuhn, and twenty others seeking political asylum hijacked a local Peos-to-Budapest Hungarian flight to Munich in the U.S. Zone of Germany. Majoros took over the plane's controls from the pilot, Kuhn, shortly after takeoff, by prearrangement. 5011

January 30, 1949—Republic of China—Six people hijacked the Shanghai-to-Tsingtao flight of China National Aviation Corporation to Tsinan, China, which was under the control of the Chinese communists. The hijackers took over the controls and made two unsuccessful attempts to land the plane in fog before turning over the controls to the regular crew members. The passengers (ten) and crew (three) were held for one month and then sent on to Tsingtao. The plane was not returned. 5012

March 17, 1949—South Korea—In Seoul, several men conducted an armed attack against a tea party attended by several members of a leftist student organization, with the intention of killing a Korean writer who had criticized Soviet policies, but they mistakenly killed the wife of a U.S. missionary instead. Four men were sentenced to death on October 20, 1949.

April 29, 1949—Rumania—Stoyan Korm, an anticommunist student, hijacked a Soviet-Rumanian Airlines Dakota flying from Timisoara to Bucharest and forced it to fly to Salonika, Greece. The hijacker, a female passenger, and a security guard requested and were granted political asylum. 5013

May 7, 1949—Philippines—A Philippine Air Lines DC3 crashed into the sea between Daet and Manila, with no survivors among the thirteen people on board. A time bomb had been delivered to the plane by two ex-convicts who were hired for the job by a man and woman who were attempting to kill the woman's husband, who was a passenger.

September 9, 1949—Canada—A Quebec Airways (subsidiary of Canadian Pacific Airlines) DC3 exploded forty miles from Quebec near Sault au Cochon on its flight from Quebec City to Comeau Bay, leaving no survivors from its twenty-three people on board. The explosion was caused by a bomb that had been put in the number 1 forward baggage compartment by J. Albert Guay, who was attempting to murder his wife. Three individuals were executed for the crime.

September 16, 1949—Poland—Five men seeking political asylum hijacked the Lot flight from Gdansk to Lódz, forcing it to land in Nykoeping military airfield, sixty-five miles south of Stockholm, Sweden. 5014

December 3, 1949—North Borneo—Two anti-British Malayans attacked Duncan George Stewart, the British governor, in Sibu, Sarawak, stabbing him to death. The two were charged with murder and sixteen others with conspiracy.

December 9, 1949—Rumania—Four people skyjacked a Soviet-Rumania DC3 flying from Sibiv to Bucharest and forced it to fly to Belgrade, Yugoslavia. A security guard was shot dead during the flight. 5015

December 16, 1949—Poland—Sixteen Poles skyjacked a Polish flight from Lódz to Gdansk and diverted it to Roenne, Bornholm Island, Denmark, where they were granted political asylum. The pilot, A. Vandofsky, appears to have been part of the plot. 5016

1950—Mexico—A Spanish diplomat was gunned down on a Mexican street.

March 6, 1950—Germany—German workers, hoping to halt the razing of the Goering Steel Works, sacked the offices of the British Dismantling Commission in Watenstedt-Salzgitter. Armored cars were sent in to disperse the workers. The U.N. high commissioner's determination to proceed strengthened.

March 24, 1950—Czechoslovakia—Three skyjackings took place, involving seventy-three passengers and twelve crew; sixteen passengers and eight crew were involved in the plot. One of the unsuspecting passengers was Katherine Komak, the assistant attaché of the U.S. embassy in Prague. Upon landing in the U.S. Zone of Germany, the U.S. Air Force treated the eighty-five people as their guests; fifty-eight of them wished to go home, but three passengers joined the plotters in requesting asylum. The plotters feared persecution because of their previous service in the RAF and their Roman Catholic religious beliefs. The U.S. Government rejected the Czech demand for extradition and dismissed allegations of ill treatment of the passengers. In the first skyjacking, a DC3 from Bratislava to Prague had to make only a slight deviation from its course and headed for Erding in the U.S. Zone of Germany near Munich. The four crewman—Oldrich Dolezal, Borijov Smid, Stanislav Sacha, and Jan Kralovansky—were in on the plot to divert the plane from its course. 5017

The second skyjacking found the pilot pulling the gun, heading his plane from Ostrava away from its course toward Prague, diverting the DC3 to the U.S. Zone of Germany, in Erding. Vladimir Svetlik and Viktor Popelka were among the crewmen responsible for the skyjacking. 5018

The pilot of the Brno-to-Prague DC3 was not part of the plot. He reported that "about fifteen minutes after the takeoff the copilot and the radio operator suddenly pointed revolvers at my head," after which he, too, flew on to Erding in the U.S. Zone of Germany. The responsible airmen were Vit Angetter and Kamil Mraz. 5019

April 1950—Canada—Thirty-six of the Sons of Freedom, a radical faction of the Doukhobors, engaged in an arson campaign against houses in Brilliant, British Columbia, to protest the tense world situation. They were arrested on April 14.

April 13, 1950—United Kingdom—An explosive device placed in the used towel receptacle in the lavatory of a British European Airways Viking 1B blew up as the plane was flying over the English Channel near Hastings, England, causing severe damage to the rear of the aircraft and wounding a stewardess. The aircraft aborted its London-to-Paris flight and landed at Northolt at night.

April 27, 1950—Indonesia—Terrorists kidnapped and murdered two Americans, Robert Doyle and Raymond Kennedy, in Sumedang, Java. The killings were condemned by President Mohammed Hatta.

May 28, 1950—United States—John O'Reilly, a mentally unbalanced passenger on a Los Angeles-to-Oakland flight, threatened passengers with a pistol and broke two windows. The pilot landed after a half-hour flight, and Fresno police arrested the twenty-six year old.

August 1950—United States—S. L. Simons, a research scientist, stole a vial of plutonium from the Los Alamos atomic laboratory, burying the bottle as a souvenir under his Denver, Colorado, home. He was arrested on August 22.

August 11, 1950—Czechoslovakia—Two people hijacked a Czechoslovakian transport plane on a local flight to Pottmes in the U.S Zone of Germany. 5020

November 1, 1950—United States—Two Puerto-Rican nationalists attempted to assassinate President Harry S Truman by rushing Blair House in Washington, D.C. The presidents' bodyguards opened fire. In the gun battle, one guard and one attacker died; two guards and the other attacker were injured.

1951—Spain—The Spanish government warned the U.S. ambassador of an assassination plot against him.

March 19, 1951—Iraq—Two men bombed the USIS reading room in Baghdad. They were sentenced to death.

March 20, 1951—Philippines—Huks murdered John Hardie, a U.S. citizen, and his wife on their farm fifteen miles east of Manila.

April 21, 1951—Philippines—Huks ambushed a group at Clark Field, killing five U.S. airmen and an airman's wife.

May 30, 1951—Northern Ireland—The IRA conducted bombing attacks on British property and made threats on the king's life. The king cancelled a planned trip to Northern Ireland.

July 16, 1951—Jordan—Lebanese ex-Premier Riad es-Solh, an opponent of the greater Syria plan for Jordan, Syria, and Lebanon to merge under Jordan's king, was assassinated by three members of the semifascist Syrian National Socialist Party, who attacked his car en route to the airport. Jordanian police killed one attacker; another committed suicide, and a third escaped. Supporters of es-Solh rioted in Beirut.

July 20, 1951—Israel—King Abdullah Ibn Hussein of Jordan was shot in Jerusalem while entering the mosque of Omar to pray. His assassin, Mustafa Ashu, a member of the Jihad Mukadess, gave as his reasons opposition to Jordan's annexation of Arab Palestine and support of the exiled mufti of Jerusalem. The assassin was killed; four other were hanged for complicity in the attack. Five hundred others were arrested during a period of martial law.

July 31, 1951—Indochina—A communist suicide volunteer in Sadec in southern Vietnam assassinated French Brigadier General Charles Marie Chanson and French-supported Governor Thai Lap Thanh when he exploded a grenade in his pocket, killing himself along with his victims.

August 2, 1951—Baltic Sea—Sixteen Polish sailors mutinied, directing its pilot at pistol point to bring the minesweeper to Ystad, Sweden.

September 11, 1951—Czechoslovakia—Frazek Jarda, the engineer of a Czech four-car passenger train, and accomplices hijacked his train to Selb-Ploeszberg in the U.S. Zone of Germany when a confederate switched a track at Asch station and crossed the border. The stationmaster held a gun on the communist fireman. The United States granted asylum for Jarda and thirty other anticommunists, while returning seventy-seven passengers on September 13.

September 16, 1951—Pakistan—Prime Minister Lisquat Ali Khan was shot dead while addressing a meeting in Rawalpindi by an Afghan fanatic who wished to protest opposition to the creation of the State of Pushtunistan on the Afghan-Pakistani frontier. The assassin was mobbed and killed.

October 6, 1951—Malaya—Malayan guerrillas in Kuala Lumpur ambushed the three-car convoy of British high commissioner Sir Henry L. G. Gurney, who had been campaigning for extermination of communist guerrillas and self-government for Malaya. Gurney was killed, and thirteen of his soldiers were wounded in the clash. British and Gurkha troops, aided by RAF planes, sought the killers, slaying four of them. A village was destroyed, with all inhabitants being arrested for harboring the assassins.

October 17, 1951—Yugoslavia—A Yugoslavian National Airlines DC3 on a domestic flight was hijacked to Zurich, Switzerland, by the pilot and copilot, who requested asylum for themselves, their wives, and two male children, claiming that they were ''no longer able to endure the regime of communist terror.'' Asylum was granted, and the three other crew members, along with twenty-two other passengers, were returned with the plane. 5021

October 25, 1951—Philippines—Huks ambushed a group near Olongapo, killing U.S. citizens John Grant and Harold Alden.

October 29, 1951—Cambodia—French commissioner Jean Léon François Maria de Raymond was stabbed while asleep in Phnom Penh by one of his servants, allegedly a member of a communist terrorist cell. The assassin escaped, but another servant was arrested as an accomplice.

December 14, 1951—Egypt—Two Egyptians protesting the presence of British soldiers in the canal zone were killed while attempting to raid a British army installation near Port Said.

December 20, 1951—Egypt—Unknown individuals attempted to sabotage a waterworks near Suez City, managing to blow up British railroad tracks and water mains. Five Egyptians were killed in the attack.

January 1, 1952—Egypt—No damage was reported when Egyptian students, protesting the British presence in the canal zone fired on a British army post in Ismailia.

March 13, 1952—Tunisia—Tunisian nationalists ambushed and killed two French gendarmes near Gafsa.

June 26, 1952—Yugoslavia—Vilim Inkret, Josip Tevek, and Bogdan Zigic hijacked the Belgrade to Puola flight of Yugoslavian National Airlines, diverting it to Foligno, Italy, where they requested political asylum. Inkret broke into the cockpit with an ax, took over the controls, and flew to Foligno while the other two pointed guns at the passengers. The nineteen passengers and five crew, as well as the plane, were returned to Yugoslavia. 5022

July 8, 1952—Argentina—The USIS library in Buenos Aires was bombed. A diplomatic protest was filed.

July 8, 1952—West Berlin—Three communists kidnapped Dr. Walter Linse, an economist for the anti-communist League of Free Jurists, carrying him by car into East Germany. Police arrested an East Berlin woman on November 14 and a man on March 9, 1953. A rally to protest the kidnapping turned into a riot.

September 24, 1952—Mexico—A bomb exploded in a suitcase in the forward baggage compartment fifteen minutes after a Mexicana DC3 took off from

Mexico City, flying for Oaxaca. The aircraft landed successfully, despite injuries to two, along with a seven-foot hole in the fuselage. Two men were convicted of the crime and sentenced to thirty years.

November 14, 1952—Western Pacific Ocean—Asiatic seamen mutinied, hijacking the Norwegian freighter *Rostro* to the People's Republic of China.

December 30, 1952—Philippines—After shooting a sixteen-year-old girl in front of her teacher and classmates because she did not return his love, armed Chinaman Ang Tiu-cho, age twenty-three, attempted to fly to his home of Amoy, a Chinese port five hundred miles to the northwest, by skyjacking the Laoag to Aparri DC3 flight of Philippine Air Lines, after escaping police. Mary Ireton of the local USIS was one of the other seven passengers on board and reported that Tiu-cho, who had boarded under the assumed name of Hung Chu-chun, shot the pilot and purser and wounded the copilot. Captain Ku Chung-yu of the Nationalist Chinese Air Force intercepted the plane as it flew fifty feet above the waves amid communist tracers and antiaircraft bursts, fired two warning shots, and forced the copilot to land in Quemoy, four miles from Amoy. Tiu-cho mistook the location for Amoy and threw down his guns and grenades, whereupon he was arrested. 5023

February 9, 1953—Israel—A missile was thrown into the garden of the Soviet legation in Tel Aviv in retaliation for anti-Semitism in the Soviet Union. Three people were injured. Fifty were arrested, many of them members of the Young Hebrews Association. The Soviet Union broke diplomatic relations with Israel on February 12.

March 2, 1953—Argentina—A bomb in the baggage room of a train carrying Juan Peron from Chile exploded as the train arrived in Buenos Aires.

March 23, 1953—Czechoslovakia—The pilot of the Prague-to-Brno C47 flight of Czechoslovakian National Airlines, Miroslav Slovak, and three other men with whom he had been plotting for two years, including Helmut Cermiak and Hana Cermiakova, diverted the plane to Frankfurt-am-Main, Germany. Political asylum was granted, and the other twenty-three passengers were returned to Czechoslovakia. 5024

April 15, 1953—Iran—The U.S. Point Four offices in Shiraz were attacked by communist and nationalist mobs.

April 16, 1953—Iran—Communist and nationalist mobs attacked the homes of U.S. embassy staff members in Tehran.

March 1, 1954—United States—Five U.S. congressmen were wounded when four Puerto Rican nationalists shouted ''Freedom for Puerto Rico'' and fired in the House of Representatives floor, expending twenty-five rounds from two German Lugers and two German P38 pistols. The three men and one woman were immediately arrested and subsequently convicted. Tighter security was instituted, and the FBI investigated. Seventeen leaders of the Puerto Rican nationalist party were arrested on March 6, with forty others being rounded up by the Puerto Rican police on March 8.

March 17, 1954—Israel—Jordanian terrorists halted a bus in the Negev desert with machine-gun fire, killing the driver and most of the passengers. The Mixed Armistice Commission investigated.

May 25, 1954—Morocco—One French soldier was killed and forty-one civilians injured when a bomb in a roadway in Marrakesh exploded after the car of General Augustin Guillaume, the retiring French resident governor, passed.

July 14, 1954—Egypt—The USIA reported that during the night, fires broke out in the USIS libraries in Cairo and Alexandria. Investigations the following morning revealed that incendiary devices had been planted. Three devices that failed to ignite were found in Cairo. The local police arrested three persons who admitted to the crimes and who said four incendiaries were placed in the Cairo library and one in the Alexandria facility. A number of other arrests were made. The Ministry of Information later announced that the library fires and other acts were the work of a ''Zionist leftist spy ring working for the Israeli Intelligence Service.''

July 15, 1954—Chile—At 1:15 A.M., a bomb containing explosive gelatin (mainly nitroglycerin) exploded in an areaway leading to the basement of the Binational Center in Santiago, causing minor damage to the basement and first floor and breaking a large number of windows in a building across the street.

December 23, 1954—Ecuador—An unknown individual fired a bullet through the bedroom window of a local employee of the USIS press section in Quito.

December 26, 1954—Ecuador—At 10:30 P.M., a large rock was thrown through the glass window of the living room of the U.S. public affairs officer's home in Quito, leading to a diplomatic protest by the United States.

December 27, 1954—Ecuador—The wall outside the front yard of the home of the U.S. information officer in Quito was damaged slightly by a fused bomb that went off at 10:30 P.M. The U.S. ambassador sent a protest to the foreign minister regarding all three incidents. The foreign minister expressed concern and blamed the attacks on communists.

Between 1955 and 1963—Egypt—Two Egyptian intelligence officers, Salah Mustafa and Mustafa Hafez, were killed by parcel bombs apparently sent by Shin Beth.

February 15, 1955—Switzerland—Six anticommunist Rumanian exiles seized the Rumanian legation in Bern, vowing to hold it until the release of jailed resistance leaders. Swiss police threatened to fire tank rounds after surrounding the building. In the fray, a chauffeur was killed. Three of the men finally surrendered. On February 16, three escaped, but one was later captured.

March 13, 1955—Soviet Union—A mentally deranged young Russian, V. A. Matveyev, attacked the British embassy in Moscow, shooting a Russian policeman in his attempt to gain entry. The Soviet government apologized to the British.

March 24, 1955—Israel—Egyptian terrorists threw grenades at a wedding party in Patish, killing one and injuring twenty-two.

April 11, 1955—Hong Kong—An Air India Constellation flying from Hong Kong to Djakarta, Indonesia, exploded en route to the Bandung conference with eleven Chinese delegates on board. A time bomb placed in the starboard wing root's wheel damaged the number 3 engine nacelle about five hours after takeoff. The plane soon caught fire and crashed near Great Natuna Island in the South China Sea. Chow Tse-ming, an employee of the Hong Kong Aircraft Engineering Corporation and reportedly an agent for the Kuomintang intelligence organization, was accused of planting the bomb, which killed eighteen and left three survivors.

June 28, 1955—Tunisia—A powerful bomb placed inside a grill at the ground-floor entrance of the USIS building in Tunis exploded at 1:30 A.M., severely damaging the first floor and shattering glass throughout the building and in neighboring stores and houses. The consulate general reported in March 1956 that three young perpetrators of the bombing had been expelled to France, although the instigators of the attack remained unknown.

July 25, 1955—South Vietnam—A USIS officer in Hue reported finding a small object with wires attached in an official USIS jeep. It was removed and examined by U.S. Army officers, who reported that the device was old and had become damp. If it had been in good condition, it could have done considerable damage.

August 13, 1955—United Kingdom—Ten armed members of the IRA made an arms raid on a British military depot in Arborfield, stealing sixty-eight weapons and 80,600 rounds of ammunition. Scotland Yard found most of the material and arrested three of the attackers.

August 15, 1955—United Kingdom—Five armed members of the IRA broke into a British artillery training camp near Rhyl, Wales, in an apparent attempt to secure arms but were frightened off by security guards.

October 1, 1955—Morocco—Berber tribesmen killed some Frenchmen in attacks on five French army posts in the Fez area. Tanks and planes were sent in to quell the disturbance.

October 17, 1955—Algeria—Algerian nationalists killed five French soldiers and eight French civilians in a shooting campaign.

November 1, 1955—United States—A United Air Lines DC6B flight from Denver to Portland disintegrated near Longmont, Colorado, eleven minutes after takeoff when a dynamite bomb detonated in the number four baggage compartment. John Gilbert Graham, twenty-three, was arrested by the FBI and convicted of planting the bomb in his mother's suitcase after buying $37,500 worth of insurance on her. He was executed for killing the thirty-nine passengers and five crew aboard the plane.

November 24, 1955—Cuba—During a showing of USIS films in a high school in Manzanillo, Oriente Province, a powerful bomb exploded outside the window, causing no material damage or injuries but panicking the audience of 350 students. Calm was restored and the film continued. It was believed that the bomb was set off by a group of youths who had been refused admission and had pounded on the door and torn off paper window covers used to darken the hall until the youth were scattered by the police.

January 7, 1956—Jordan—Anti-Americans in Amman, Jerusalem, Hebron, and Nablus protested U.S. support of the Baghdad Pact by stoning the U.S. consulate and burning offices and automobiles, causing $420,000 worth of damage. A one-week curfew was instituted.

March 4, 1956—Cyprus—A bomb exploded in the forward freight compartment of a Cyprus Airways (a British firm) Hermes while on the ground at Nicosia airfield. No casualties were reported.

March 9-10, 1956—Cyprus—Anti-British Cypriot nationalists bombed police patrols in Famagusta and Kathikas and a British home in Limassol.

March 10, 1956—Cyprus—A British patrol successfully drove off a group of attacking Cypriot nationalists in Paphos.

March 10, 1956—Crete—Anti-British demonstrators oposing the deportation from Cyprus of Archbishop Makarios attacked the British consulate in Heraklion, Candia. The consul and his staff fled as the attackers ransacked the building.

March 14, 1956—Cyprus—Unknown gunmen killed a British police sergeant and wounded a Turkish Cypriot policeman on their patrol in Nicosia. The center of the city was sealed off; ten families were expelled from their homes and eighteen shops were closed.

March 15, 1956—Cyprus—A bomb was thrown into the Nicosia home of a British soldier, wounding his wife and child.

March 15, 1956—Cyprus—An unknown gunman wounded a British soldier in Nicosia.

March 15, 1956—Cyprus—Two gunmen on cycles shot at but missed two British security policeman in Nicosia. One was later captured.

March 17, 1956—Cyprus—Members of EOKA ambushed a British motorized patrol in Khandria, resulting in the death of one terrorist. Khandria and six other mountain towns were placed under curfew.

March 17, 1956—Cyprus—One soldier was killed and two injured in the bombing of British army trucks in Lapithos. The village was fined $19,600 and was placed under a ten-day military curfew.

March 20, 1956—Cyprus—A time bomb was placed between the mattresses of Sir John Harding, the British governor in Cyprus, by his manservant, who disappeared. The bomb was removed to the garden, where it exploded. All Cypriots were removed from the staff on May 22.

March 21, 1956—Cyprus—A bomb was thrown into a British army truck by Cypriot nationalists in Famagusta, killing one and injuring two.

March 22, 1956—Cyprus—A bomb was thrown at a British patrol in Paphos, injuring a woman.

March 22, 1956—Cyprus—A U.S.-owned car was burned in Kyrenia.

March 27, 1956—Cyprus—Two were killed when a British security patrol was machine-gunned in Phrenaros. Sixteen villagers were arrested and a curfew was established. Twenty-one suspected EOKA members were arrested at Limassol. A £1,500 fine was revoked on March 29 upon the receipt of information by the authorities.

March 30, 1956—Algeria—Three French soldiers were kidnapped by Texenna.

April 10, 1956—Algeria—Members of the FLN ambushed French conscripts in western Algeria. The French returned the fire, resulting in the deaths of 120 rebels and 20 French troops.

April 27, 1956—Cyprus—A bomb destroyed a British-owned Cyprus Airways plane at Nicosia Airport.

May 4, 1956—Algeria—Twelve French soldiers were killed in an armed attack by Algeria nationalists on a French convoy near Tiemcen.

May 6, 1956—France—North African workers set fire to the Metz forest and shot at firemen.

May 9, 1956—Morocco—Moroccans kidnapped fourteen French Senegalese soldiers in Fez. A military search was threatened.

May 9, 1956—Cyprus—Three British soldiers and four Greek Cypriots were killed in Ktima in protest of the execution of two terrorists scheduled for May 10.

May 10, 1956—Cyprus—Leaflets distributed by EOKA in Nicosia claimed responsibility for the hanging of two British corporals who had been missing since November 1955 and April 17, 1956. The leaflets claimed this was in reprisal for the execution of two terrorists that day.

May 18, 1956—Algeria—Algerian rebels killed twenty French reservists in an ambush twenty-five miles from Algiers. The French retaliated with the razing of the village of Ouled Djerrah.

May 26, 1956—Algeria—Thirteen Europeans were killed when Algerian rebels conducted an armed attack on a French road crew in eastern Algeria.

May 30, 1956—Cyprus—Two British soldiers were killed and nineteen wounded when an EOKA bomb went off in the Famagusta area. Seventeen EOKA men were arrested.

June 6, 1956—Cyprus—Cypriot nationalists assassinated a British school teacher, Thomas A. Mylrea, in Limassol.

June 12, 1956—Cyprus—A bomb planted by Cypriot nationalists in the Limassol area killed three British soldiers and wounded seven.

June 18, 1956—Cyprus—A bomb intended for a Briton went off in a restaurant in the Greek EOKA section of Nicosia, killing U.S. Vice-Consul William P. Boteler and wounding three other U.S. consular employees. The U.S. State Department denounced the bombing, for which the EOKA expressed regret.

July 13, 1956—Hungary—A Hungarian twin-engined Malev flying from Gyor to Szombathely, Hungary, was hijacked by 7 anticommunist students—Georg Polyak, Joseph Jakaby, Gabor Kiss, Karl Tinter, Joseph Balla, and Mr. and Mrs. Fraz Isar—after a fight with the crew and other passengers in which twelve were injured. One of the hijackers took over the controls and landed the plane at Ingolstadt, West Germany, where the hijackers and two of the passengers requested political asylum. The other passengers, the crew, and the plane were returned to Hungary. 5025

August 1, 1956—Cyprus—EOKA kidnapped British civil servant John A. Cremer in Kyrenia, threatening to kill him in retaliation for the execution of three Cypriots. He was released on August 5.

August 13, 1956—Cyprus—EOKA frogmen planted bombs that sank the yacht of British Guard Captain C. W. B. Worthington.

August 13, 1956—Cyprus—Two Cypriot terrorists beat U.S. consular official Paul Sprenger in Nicosia.

August 30, 1956—Cyprus—Cypriot nationalists attached limpet mines to the bottom of a British tank landing ship in Famagusta Harbor, damaging it.

September 1, 1956—Cyprus—The British Middle East Command Headquarters in Episkopi was damaged by a bomb planted by Cypriot nationalists.

September 2, 1956—Cyprus—Time bombs planted by Cypriot nationalists wrecked the printing office of the British colonial government in Nicosia.

September 4, 1956—Cyprus—EOKA snipers killed a Turkish Cypriot and wounded a British captain in Larnaca.

September 27, 1956—Bolivia—An airliner flying from Santa Cruz to La Paz was hijacked by the forty-seven political prisoners it was carrying. The plane

landed in Salto, Argentina, where the group was granted political asylum.
5026

November 20, 1956—Lebanon—Arab terrorists protesting the Anglo-French attack on Suez bombed the French-owned bank of Syria and Lebanon in Beirut. Riots followed.

December 9, 1956—Northern Ireland—The IRA dynamited a British customs post in Killea, causing damage.

December 12, 1956—Northern Ireland—The IRA used hand grenades in an armed attack on a British army barracks in the Armagh area, which was repulsed by British soldiers.

May 26, 1957—France—Ali Chekkal, ex-vice-president of the Algerian Assembly, was assassinated in Paris. Mohammed ben Sadok was sentenced to life imprisonment at hard labor on December 11.

May 29, 1957—France—In Marseille, an unknown gunman assassinated Mohammed Mahiddine, who was believed to be the FLN chief for southeastern France.

June 4, 1957—Algeria—Three were killed and eleven wounded in an armed attack on a French Senegalese military post in Tlemcen.

July 25, 1957—United States—A Western Airlines CV240 flying from Las Vegas to Los Angeles was rocked over Daggett, California, by a bomb that exploded forty-seven minutes after takeoff, with the plane flying at seventy-five hundred feet and the cabin pressurized at four thousand feet. A hole was blown through the side of the plane, and a passenger who had detonated the dynamite in the lavatory was blown out of the aircraft. The plane landed successfully seventeen minutes after the explosion, with all thirteen passengers and three crew members reported safe.

July 30, 1957—Lebanon—At 11 P.M., four small stick bombs exploded at two USIS libraries and the Voice of America studio in Beirut, causing slight damage, mostly broken glass. The perpetrators were not apprehended, and no motive could be established.

August 2, 1957—France—Six Muslims were shot dead and four wounded by Algerian terrorists in Paris.

September 2, 1957—Jordan—During the night a bomb exploded on or near utility meter boxes outside the USIS building in Amman. The resulting damage to the water and electrical systems required three days to repair. The motive was not established, but the attack occurred during a period of extreme political tension.

October 22, 1957—Vietnam—At 1 P.M., a bomb exploded in the USIS library in Saigon, causing major structural damage and destroying thousands of books through fire and water. Because the library had been closed for approximately one hour, it appeared that the bomb was preset with a timed device and placed behind books on a shelf. Three other bombings were reported in front of an officers' quarters and under a bus loaded with enlisted men. Thirteen U.S. servicemen and fifteen Vietnamese were reported injured by the plastic bombs that were planted by individuals protesting the Colombo conference being held in Saigon.

October 28, 1957—France—Algerian rebels in Paris shot and killed Hocine Cherchalli, the ex-deputy mayor of Algiers, and Ahmed Bekhat, the secretary of the French Federation of the Union of Algerian Workers.

November 27, 1957—France—Algerian gunmen in Paris attempted to assassinate Abdelkader Barakrok, the state secretary for Algeria.

December 13, 1957—Greece—A series of three explosions between 1 and 2 A.M. almost completely destroyed the Athens USIS library. One of the charges was estimated at a minimum of ten pounds and contained an incendiary agent. In the opinion of Athens police, the incident was communist inspired and against NATO rather than being connected with the debate on Cyprus then taking place in the United Nations.

December 19, 1957—France—An Air France Armagnac flying from Oran, Algeria, to Paris was rocked over central France by a bomb that exploded in the lavatory. The damaged aircraft landed successfully at Lyons. No casualties were reported among the eighty-nine passengers and crew.

January 27, 1958—Turkey—A bomb thrown from a passing automobile destroyed about five feet of a stone wall in front of an Ankara bookstore at approximately 3 A.M. The bookstore was one block from the USIS library, and as the Turkish name of the commercial store was very similar to that of the library, it was believed that the store was mistaken for the library.

February 17, 1958—South Korea—A Korean National Airlines DC3 flying from Pusan to Seoul was hijacked by five communist sympathizers who drugged the two women and baby traveling with them so that they would sleep through their shooting off the cockpit door's lock. The United Nations demanded the return of the plane and passengers at the meeting of the Korean

Military Armistice Commission on February 19. North Korea refused the request, and the twenty-six crew and passengers, including the American pilot, Captain Willis Hobbs, were not freed from Pyongyang until March 6. 5027

February 19, 1958—Cuba—Cuban rebels dynamited the Santiago warehouse of the U.S.-owned Cuban Air Products Corporation, a manufacturer of bottled gas.

February 24, 1958—Cuba—Argentina's Juan Manuel Fangio, a world auto-racing champion, was kidnapped at gunpoint by three members of the Twenty-sixth of July Movement in the lobby of the Havana Lincoln Hotel. He was held from the evening before the race until the Gran Premio had been run, with the intention of embarrassing the government. The rebels then released him in the presence of reliable witnesses to the Argentine ambassador, so that Fangio could not be killed by Batista's police, who would then blame the murder on the movement.

April 9, 1958—Cuba—A Cubana plane flying from Havana to Santa Clara, Cuba, was hijacked to Mérida, Mexico. The plane and passengers were returned to Cuba on April 13. 5028

April 10, 1958—South Korea—A radioman was killed and the pilot and copilot of the South Korean Airlines C46 flying from Taegu to Seoul were wounded when a hijacker attempted to divert the plane to North Korea. The plane landed at Pyongtaek, South Korea, where the male hijacker was captured. 5029

April 13, 1958—Cuba—A Cubana DC3 flying from Havana to Santa Clara, Cuba, was hijacked by its three-man crew, including Carlos Villamar, and flown to Miami, Florida. The twelve passengers and the plane were returned to Cuba. 5030

May 28, 1958—Haiti—Rifle fire was directed at the Port-au-Prince home of the U.S. ambassador, Gerald A. Drew. The Haitian government apologized.

June 2, 1958—Czechoslovakia—Mr. and Mrs. Joseph Hornik and Jaroslav Vydra branished a broken pistol and forced the pilot of a domestic Czechoslovakian general aviation charter plane to fly to Vienna. The three were arrested for extortion under threats, but the charges were dropped on June 6, 1958. 5031

June 26, 1958—Cuba—Raul Castro and the Second Front of Frank Pais attacked the Moa Bay Mining Company, a subsidiary of the Freeport Sulphur

Company of New Orleans, located on the northern coast of Oriente Province. His two hundred rebels kidnapped ten Americans and two Canadians. During the attack, two Cuban civilians and six Cuban rebels were killed, and three Cuban army soldiers were wounded. The group also seized nineteen vehicles and a quantity of beds, surgical equipment, medical supplies, and food. One of the Canadians, Mr. Kristjansen, had previously been held for six hours in March by the rebels while they loaded stolen supplies from his plant. The rebels demanded that (1) the U.S. government announce that it would cease to furnish arms to the Cuban government under the Mutual Assistance Pact; (2) no Cuban military planes would be allowed to take on arms at the Guantanamo Naval Base; (3) negotiations would be held at the ambassadorial level; and (4) the United States would recognize the rebels' free territory of Cuba. The United States persuaded the Cuban government to stop bombing rebel positions from June 29 through July 18 while the hostages were being held. It also established direct contact with the rebels although Secretary of State Dulles on July 1 announced that the United States would never yield to blackmail to obtain the release of hostages. Some of the captives—Howard Roach, Edward Cannon, Henry Salmonson, and William Koster—were allowed to send a letter to a Moa subcontractor, giving their impression of the rebels, which was highly favorable. Castro claimed to have spent $1,400 on entertaining his captives. He decided to release them in small groups in order to gain more publicity. The first civilians were released on July 2, and by July 11 all of the civilians had been delivered to Guantanamo, along with a navy airman, T. R. Mosness, who had been kidnapped alone and was held with some of the civilians.

June 26, 1958—Cuba—Another group of Castro's rebels seized two sugar mill employees, one of whom was returning to his base by bus in Oriente Province. One was the U.S. field superintendent of the Ermita sugar mill, west of Guantánamo. The other, taken from his home, was the Canadian manager (a native of Toronto) of the Central Isabel mill, northeast of Guantánamo.

June 27, 1958—Cuba—In a night raid, Raul Castro captured a busload of Marine Corps personnel en route from Guantánamo to the port of Caimanera's naval base. First reports indicated twenty-four were taken, then twenty-eight, then twenty-nine, until another single abduction increased the tally to thirty. The driver and conductor of the bus, both Cubans, were also held. Negotiations for the United States were conducted by Robert Wiecha, U.S. vice-consul in Santiago, along with U.S. Consul Park Fields Wollam, who initially dealt directly with the Cuban government as had the Canadians. Newsman Jules Dubois claims to have convinced Castro to release the marines because of the Lebanese situation. Castro promised to release a group of four but then delayed. On July 15, he released seven men; on the sixteenth, another four; another four on July 17; and the remaining fifteen on July 18.

June 30, 1958—Cuba—Eight Cuban rebels kidnapped two officers of the Nicaro nickel plant in Oriente Province. The administrator-general and his assistant were captured when they were returning to their base by bus.

June 30, 1958—Cuba—Cuban rebels kidnapped four Americans working at a United Front sugar plantation near the village of Guaro. The four were the agricultural superintendent, his assistant, and two district superintendents.

August 16, 1958—Switzerland—Two Hungarian refugees conducted an armed raid on the Hungarian legation in Bern in an attempt to steal documents. Diplomats exchanged shots with the duo, who surrendered to arresting Swiss police. The Hungarians protested to the Swiss government.

August 17, 1958—Algeria—Algerians rebels kidnapped U.S. Methodist missionary Lester E. Griffith, Jr., from his car near Les Ouadhias, holding him until September 27. His auto was found burned in the mountains of eastern Algeria.

August 25, 1958—France—An Algerian was burned to death while attempting to set off a plastic bomb in an Esso refinery in Notre Dame-de-Gravenchon.

August 25, 1958—France—Algerian rebels conducted armed attacks in Paris against a police garage and a munitions factory in the suburbs, leading to the deaths of four policemen and two terrorists.

August 25, 1958—France—Algerian terrorists attacked oil refinery tanks near Marseille, injuring seventeen firemen.

August 26, 1958—France—Algerian gunmen wounded eight Paris policemen.

August 28, 1958—France—Algerian gunmen shot a French soldier in Paris.

August 28, 1958—France—Algerians were responsible for the explosion of four gasoline storage tanks in Rouen.

August 30, 1958—France—Algerians shot a French soldier in a Paris subway station.

September 15, 1958—France—Three Algerian terrorists shot at the car of Information Minister Jacques Soustelle near the Arc de Triomphe. In the ensuing gunfight, one bystander was killed and two were wounded. Two of the gunmen were immediately captured, with the third seized later. The three were sentenced to life imprisonment.

September 28, 1958—France—A time bomb was found unexploded at the Eiffel Tower. The arrests of Algerian terrorists was announced on September 30.

October 14, 1958—West Germany—The West German freighter *Atlas* was sabotaged in Hamburg harbor. The ship had been carrying arms from Hamburg free port to Algerian rebels.

October 20, 1958—Cuba—Raul Castro's rebels kidnapped two Americans and seven Cubans employed at the Texaco refinery in Santiago de Cuba. Ambassador Smith instructed Consul Wollam to inform the rebels that unless the hostages were freed at once, he would recommend that the United States renew shipments of arms to Batista. The group was released on October 23.

October 22, 1958—Cuba—Raul Castro's Column 6 seized a Cubana Airlines DC3 flying from Cayo Mambi to Moa Bay, Cuba, two weeks before Cuba's presidential elections. Three armed rebels posing as passengers forced the plot, Captain Francis Valliciergo, to land at their camouflaged airstrip. Eight other passengers and three crew members were on board. 5032

November 1, 1958—United States—A Cubana Airlines Viscount flying from Miami to Varadero airport, a resort area near Havana, was hijacked by five men, members of the Twenty-sixth of July Movement. According to Osiris Martinez, one of the three survivors of the attack, "Suddenly a man jumped up from his seat and pointed a gun at us. Four other men did the same thing. Nobody knew what was happening until the five men opened a small luggage compartment on the floor and pulled out fatigue-type uniforms and machine guns. . . . Some of the hijackers went into the cockpit. Later were were told that the pilot had refused to change the course of the aircraft and had been hit over the head." Martinez heard the group talking about getting off in Cuba with "a bundle of money" and letting the plane and the passengers go on to their destination. A hijacker attempted to find a landing area in Oriente Province but was unable to land in the darkness in Punta Tabaio. The plane crashed, with seventeen of the twenty on board killed. Martinez survived with cracked ribs and gashes, having lost his family. Castro disclaimed knowledge of the group's actions. 5033

November 3, 1958—West Germany—Unknown gunmen attempted to assassinate Ameziane Ait Ahcene, an anti-French rebel leader, in Bonn.

November 6, 1958—Cuba—A member of Castro's rebels hijacked a Cubana Airlines DC3 flying from Manzanillo to Holguin, Cuba, and diverted it to a rebel airstrip in Oriente Province. The aircraft was held, but the twenty-five passengers and three crew members were released. 5034

November 8, 1958—Cyprus—Two RAF men were killed when a Nicosia canteen was bombed by Cypriot nationalists. A curfew was imposed, and all Cypriot workers were banned from the British army and RAF bases.

January 1, 1959—Cuba—A group of ex-President Batista's supporters hijacked a Cubana airliner to New York. One of the passengers was Mario Cabas, Batista's minister of transportation. Other sources list the date as January 1, 1961. 5035

January 18, 1959—Argentina—A powerful bomb exploded at 2:30 A.M. in the doorway of the USIS office in La Plata, shattering glass in the front of the building, tearing open the iron window shutter, and blowing out the doors. The police chief believed the attack was connected with Peronist disapproval of President Frondizi's visit to the United States.

February 28, 1959—Algeria—Algerian rebels came down from the mountains in the vicinity of Aumale, sixty miles southeast of Algiers, posed as French soldiers, and kidnapped ten members of an Italian farm family: two couples, the Paul and Joseph Cesaros, one brother-in-law, and five children. The group traveled through the mountains at night and hid during the day. Five thousand French army troops were unable to corner the rebels, who promised to release the three men, and released the two women and three children on March 12. The rebels also machine-gunned and shelled the town (population thirty thousand) of Blidas.

March 4, 1959—Algeria—Between four and eight Algerian nationalist rebels ambushed an auto on the Morocco-Oran highway in the vicinity of Col du Juif, four miles west of Tlemcen, riddling the car with machine-gun fire at close range. An American photographer, sixty-five-year-old Homer Flint Kellens of Arkansas, and his German interpreter, nineteen-year-old Raymond Aircle, were killed, and twenty-seven-year-old William Hoggs, a second photographer who was filming in the desert, was seriously wounded. Authorities trapped and killed the suspected murderers.

March 11, 1959—Sea off Belgium—The Egyptian freighter *Alkahira*, carrying arms from Hamburg free port to Algerian rebels, was sabotaged.

April 10, 1959—Haiti—A Haitian DC3 flying from Aux Cayes to Port-au-Prince was hijacked by six men who killed the pilot and forced the copilot to fly to Cuba. 5036

April 16, 1959—Cuba—A Cuban Aerovias DC3 flying from Havana to the Isle of Pines, Cuba, was diverted by four Cuban gunmen, including Leonard and Jesus Serrate and Alfredo Mason y Sanchez, to Miami, where four U.S. border patrolmen arrested them. The group claimed that they had been imprisoned in La Cabana Fortress and were attempting to escape execution. They had requested the pilot to fly to the Dominican Republic, but the pilot indicated that he did not have enough gas to make the trip. Other reports indicate that the plane was a Cubana C46. 5037

April 23, 1959—Algeria—Mines set by the FLN in Azazga destroyed two jeeps in review of the Thirteenth Cavalry Regiment, killing one French officer and wounding five.

April 24, 1959—United States—John Gregory Feller, twenty-three, tried to climb Central Park's police barricade with a homemade bomb and kill Fidel Castro "for kicks." He was arrested and committed.

April 25, 1959—Cuba—A Cubana Vickers Viscount flying from Varadero Beach to Havana was hijacked by two men and two women, including Maria, Antonio, and A. S. Rodrigues Diaz, forcing the pilot to fly to Key West, Florida. Shortly after takeoff, the two women reached under their skirts, brought out pistols, and gave them to the two men. They then ordered the pilot to fly to Miami but agreed to Key West when the pilot claimed a lack of fuel. Antonio Rodrigues Diaz was a general under the deposed Cuban president, Batista. 5038

May 3, 1959—Haiti—An unsuccessful assassination attempt was made against Cuban Ambassador Antonio Rodriguez Echazabal.

June 7, 1959—Haiti—Another unsuccessful assassination attempt was made against Cuban Ambassador Antonio Rodriguez Echazabal.

July 8, 1959—Yugoslavia—A Yugoslavian airiner flying from Cattaro to Belgrade was hijacked by Cuckovic Obrad, who fired a warning shot, entered the cockpit, and ordered the pilot to land at the nearest Italian airport, which was in Bari. 5039

September 8, 1959—Mexico—A Mexicana DC3 flying over central Mexico from Mexico City to Veracruz was damaged by an in-flight explosion that tore a hole in the side of the fuselage. One of the passengers appears to have detonated the bomb and fell eleven thousand feet to his death. The aircraft with its thirteen passengers and three crew landed successfully. Eight occupants were injured, and a small fire caused by the explosion was extinguished during the flight.

September 13, 1959—Sea off the Netherlands—Saboteurs in the pay of French military intelligence successfully placed a bomb that exploded aboard the West German freighter *Brussard*, which was shipping arms to Algerian rebels. The ship was abandoned.

September 17, 1959—France—Five men armed with submachine guns attempted to assassinate Hadj Messali, leader of the Algerian National Movement and under detention in Chantilly. Two of the attackers were killed by bodyguards and police.

September 24-25, 1959—Algeria—A series of bombings and armed rebel attacks led to the deaths of nine French cilivians, with injuries to another twelve.

October 2, 1959—Cuba—A Cubana Viscount en route from Havana to Santiago was hijacked by Estaban A. and Gloria L. Betancourt and Osvaldo Hernandez, who threatened the pilot with hand grenades and a pistol, directing the pilot to fly to Miami, where they requested political asylum. 5040

December 2, 1959—Brazil—Eight men hijacked a Panair Do Brazil Constellation flying from Rio de Janeiro to Belém and forced the pilot to fly it to Aragarcas, Brazil. The hijackers were Brazilian military officers engaged in a revolt against the government. The revolt failed, and the hijackers flew on to Buenos Aires, Argentina. 5041

1960—Jamaica—Members of the Rastafarian religious cult ambushed and killed two British soldiers who were spying on them. Premier Norman Manley vowed to ''pursue ruthlessly and stamp out completely'' the Rasta sect.

January 6, 1960—United States—Three hours and four minutes after a National Airlines DC6B took off from New York on its flight to Miami, a bomb exploded at eighteen thousand feet, above Bolivia, North Carolina, scattering wreckage for thirteen miles. The explosion was caused by the detonation of dynamite by means of dry cell batteries located in the passenger compartment right of seat row number seven under the seat. The plane flew for sixteen miles before the pilot lost control of the plane. It appears that a passenger committed suicide after having bought a large insurance policy. All thirty-four on board the plane died.

March 6, 1960—Cuba—A series of explosions blew apart a French freighter loaded with explosives in Havana harbor. The perpetrators may have been an anti-Castro group. One hundred people were killed, and another two hundred injured.

April 9, 1960—South Africa—An anti-apartheid white farmer shot Prime Minister Henrik Verwoerd in the face with a pistol at a Johannesburg fair commemorating the country's fiftieth anniversary. The police seized the man, who was declared mentally unfit on September 26.

April 12, 1960—Cuba—A domestic flight of a Cubana Viscount was hijacked by the three-man crew and another individual to Miami. The four men—Gonzalo Herrera, Francisco Monnar, Angel E. Lopez, and Pedro Enrique—requested and were granted political asylum and were welcomed by Americans. The plane was not returned. Several American corporations sought court orders to declare the plane to be a partial payment on the Cuban debt to expropriated U.S. capital. 5042

April 28, 1960—Venezuela—A DC3 of Linea Aeropostal Venezolana flying from Caracas to Puerto Ayacucho was fourteen kilometers from Calabozo airport when an explosive device detonated in the cockpit, totally destroying the cockpit and killing all thirteen people aboard.

May 4, 1960—France—A terrorist fired five times and wounded Robert Abdesselam, an Algerian Muslim member of the National Assembly.

July 5, 1960—Spain—The two copilots (Miguel Acosta and Leslie Norbregas) of a Cubana plane flying from Madrid to Havana diverted their plane to Miami, where they requested political asylum. 5043

July 17, 1960—Cuba—A Cubana Viscount flying from Havana to Miami was diverted by its pilot, José P. Menendez, to Jamaica, where he requested political asylum. 5044

July 18, 1960—Cuba—A single-engine general aviation Cuban plane was hijacked from its flight from Havana to Veradero and forced to land in Fort Lauderdale by José F. Cardenas Adeas. 5045

July 19, 1960—Australia—A hijacker, Alex Hildebrant, attempted to divert a Trans-Australia Electra L188 flying from Sydney to Brisbane to Singapore. He was overpowered by a copilot and a deadheading pilot, and received a seven-year prison sentence. 5046

July 23, 1960—United Kingdom—An assassination attempt was made against Sir Edward D. Asafu-Adjaye.

July 28, 1960—Cuba—A Cubana flight from Oriente province to Havana was diverted to Miami by three men. The pilot, Eduardo Ferrer, locked himself in the cockpit while two armed passengers covered the sky marshal. Two woman and two children joined the hijackers in requesting political asylum. 5047

July 31, 1960—Algeria—Algerian rebels machine-gunned European bathers at Carobier Beach, killing thirteen and wounding six.

August 21, 1960—Soviet Union—A man and a woman attempted to hijack a domestic Soviet flight but were wounded and overpowered by the crew. 5048

August 29, 1960—Jordan—A time bomb planted in the premier's desk drawer went off in the foreign ministry in Amman, killing the premier and eleven others and wounding eighty-five. A second bomb went off twenty-four hours later, damaging the first-floor press office. Two Jordanians who appear to have been part of a United Arab Republic plot fled to Syria. King Hussein accused Syria of having advance knowledge of the attack and of being against the government and monarchy, and demanded the return of the two escapees. Eleven others were sentenced to death for complicity in the bombing.

September 21, 1960—Algeria—A mine planted by Algerian rebels exploded in Biskra, killing three French officers.

October 8, 1960—Algeria—A terrorist threw a grenade into a sidewalk café in Bône, killing a British seaman from the freighter *Chichester* and wounding four British sailors, five French soldiers, and seven civilians, including two women.

October 16, 1960—Switzerland—Unknown political assassins poisoned Dr. Felix Moumie, a leader of anti-French Cameroons Populations. Moumie died on November 3.

October 29, 1960—Cuba—A Cubana DC3 flying from Havana to the Isle of Pines was hijacked by nine men who diverted it to Key West. A Cuban guard on board resisted, and a gunfight broke out in which he was killed and the pilot, copilot, and two passengers were wounded. The copilot who landed the plane was one of the hijackers, who were greeted as heroes by anti-Castro Cuban exiles and hailed by the American press as people who escaped to freedom. The hijackers were granted political asylum, and the plane was held against Cuban debts to expropriated U.S. capital. 5049

December 8, 1960—Cuba—Five individuals attempted to hijack a domestic Cubana flight but were foiled by sky marshals and a pilot who, after being injured in a gun battle, crash landed at Cienfuego airport. One person died and four were injured during the attempt. Diosdado Martinez Hernandez, Enildo and Eloy Moreno Bacallado, Cesar Villarreal Garcia, and Raul Quian were seized and swiftly executed. 5050

December 25, 1960—Bolivia—The home of U.S. Ambassador Carl W. Strom was bombed.

January 5, 1961—Bolivia—Dynamite was thrown from a passing truck at the car of the U.S. ambassador, which was parked outside the university in La Paz, causing no injuries.

January 20, 1961—Algeria—A crude plastic charge with a burning fuse was placed at the door of a building housing the U.S consulate in Algiers. The fuse burned before reaching the charge. An anonymous phone caller told a local newspaper that the attack was "in honor of President Kennedy," who was in favor of autonomy.

January 22, 1961—Caribbean Sea—A Portuguese cruise ship was seized by twenty-four Portuguese rebels and two crewmen and diverted from its path from Lisbon to the Florida Everglades. Members of the Portuguese National Independence Movement, a group attempting to overthrow the regime, boarded the ship in Venezuela and the Antilles and took it over after a brief skirmish in which the third officer was killed and another person wounded. The Portuguese requested assistance of the U.S. and British navies. A U.S. naval patrol bomber sighted the ship and ordered it to put into San Juan. The rebels refused. After negotiations, the passengers were let off the ship in Recife, thirty rebels were given asylum in Brazil, and the ship was returned to its owner.

May 1, 1961—United States—National Airlines flight 337, which took off from Marathon in the Florida Keys at 3:30 P.M. bound for Miami and Key West, was hijacked to Havana by Antulio Ramirez Ortiz, who was born in Santurce, Puerto Rico, on November 20, 1926. The Latin hijacker, who met the FAA profile, had given his name as Elpir Cofrisi and then asked the ticket agent to add the letters "ata" to his Christian name, spelling out the name of an eighteenth-century Spanish pirate. As the Corvair 440 left with its seven passengers, Ramirez went onto the flight deck and shut the door behind him. Armed with a gun and knife, he pointed the revolver at the copilot, first officer J. T. Richardson, and ordered him to leave the cabin. He then directed Captain Francis X. Riley to head toward Cuba. The other crew member was a stewardess, Inez Barlow. Riley learned from the hijacker that he was an American citizen who had served in the Korean War and his reason for flying to Cuba was to warn Fidel Castro that he had been offered $100,000 by General Rafael Trujillo Molina of the Dominican Republic to assassinate him. Ramirez was taken away by Cuban soldiers, and the plane and occupants were briefly detained and then released. Ramirez was indicted by a federal grand jury in Miami, in the southern district of Florida, on July 28, 1961. He was arrested in Miami on November 11, 1975, by the FBI and sentenced to twenty years for the first hijacking of a U.S. plane. 5051

May 13, 1961—France—The OAS or another rightist group opposed to the end of the war in Algeria set off four bombs in Paris, wounding 10.

June 16, 1961—France—The OAS or another rightist group opposed to the end of the war in Algeria bombed the outside of the Paris home of the French ambassador to the United States, wounding five.

June 19, 1961—Tunisia—The OAS or another rightist group opposed to the end of the Algerian war bombed the office of the Tunis weekly *Afrique Action*.

July 3, 1961—Cuba—A Cubana DC3 bound for Veradero from Havana was hijacked by eleven men and three women and forced to land in Miami, where they requested political asylum after having shot and wounded a security guard. 5052

July 24, 1961—United States—Eastern Airlines flight 202, an Electra L188 flying from Miami to Tampa, was hijacked to Cuba by Wilfred Roman Oquendo, born in Havana on February 28, 1925. The hijacker had walked down the aisle, opened the cockpit door, pulled out a pistol, and informed the pilot that he wished him to "turn the plane around. We're going to Cuba." A U.S. Air Force F102 interceptor flew alongside the Electra until it reached Cuba. The FBI identified the hijacker as a thirty-six-year-old waiter in resort hotels who had boarded the plane under the name of J. Marin. He had lived in the United States for fifteen years and had become a naturalized citizen, although he visited Cuba frequently. The FBI claimed that he had been a secret policeman during the administration of President Soccares and had joined the Twenty-sixth of July Movement. The Latin probably met the FAA profile. The pilot, Captain W. E. Buchanan, the other four crew members, and the thirty-three passengers were well treated, fed, entertained, and sent back to Miami on July 25. Included among the passengers was a challenger for the world welterweight title, Luis Rodriguez, accompanied by his trainer and manager. The wife of an Eastern pilot, Mrs. Don Anderson, was on the plane with her five children, as was a Puerto Rican evangelist, the Reverend R. Quinones. Castro refused to return the $3.3 million plane because the United States was holding a hijacked Cuban naval vessel, a number of small boats, and six Cuban planes. During a speech to welcome Major Yuri Gargarin, the first Soviet cosmonaut, Castro told the crowd he would not return the Electra until the United States released the Cuban planes. He also suggested that the two countries sign a treaty agreeing to return each other's skyjacked planes, as well as arrest and extradite all hijackers. His plea was ignored, and several U.S. senators suggested sending in the marines. American corporations would not release their liens on the Cuban aircraft. After prolonged negotiations, Castro suggested that he would return the Electra for the patrol boat, the *40 SV8*, which had been hijacked a week before by three refugees who diverted it to Key West, where it was being held by the Coast Guard. The Electra was released on August 15. Oquendo was indicted on August 23 by a federal grand jury in the southern district of Florida. He remains a fugitive. 5053

July 31, 1961—United States—Bruce McRae Britt, born in Prescott, Arizona, on September 15, 1920, attempted to hijack the DC3 of Pacific Airlines Company flight 327 flying from Chico, California, to San Francisco. Britt boarded the plane without a ticket and claimed to wish to go to Arkansas to see his estranged wife. When he was told to get off the plane, he shot the passenger agent and told the pilot to take off. The pilot refused and was shot. The copilot and passengers charged Britt and disarmed him. The pilot was blinded and the ticket agent critically wounded. The passengers, some of whom had been shot at, had the impression that Britt really wished to go to Cuba. On September 5 he was sentenced in Orville, California, to three one to fourteen-year sentences to run consecutively for assault with intent to commit murder, the only American skyjacker to be convicted solely of this charge. Other reports listed Britt as being sentenced to twenty years. The profile was not applicable in this case of a white skyjacker. 5054

August 3, 1961—United States—Continental Airlines flight 54, a B707 flying from Phoenix to El Paso was taken over by an armed convict and his son, who directed the pilot to fly to Havana. The pilot landed in El Paso to refuel, where the plane was surrounded by two hundred FBI and police officers, who shot out the tires and arrested the duo. The plane was midway in its flight from Los Angeles to Houston, piloted by Captain B. D. Rickards, who had been the first pilot in history to be hijacked, (February 21, 1931). The nine-hour drama began when Leon Bearden, born on January 6, 1923, in Hayti, Missouri (a white who met the FAA profile), walked onto the plane with his son, Cody, who was born in Douglas, Arizona, on November 13, 1944. The elder Bearden had a history of criminal activity, first being sentenced to in 1941 for grand larceny in Graham County, Arizona. In 1942 he was sentenced to three to five years for forgery in Maricopa County, Arizona. After being released, he held jobs as a roofer and car salesman. In 1957 he was sentenced to from five years to life for armed robbery in Los Angeles County. He was paroled from Folsom Penitentiary in less than three years. He renounced his U.S. citizenship, claiming that he wished to live abroad. Bearden sat in the coach section, armed with a .38, while his son, a ninth-grade dropout, carried a .45. The plane left at

2 A.M., and minutes before the plane was to land in El Paso, Bearden stuck his .38 in the ribs of stewardess Lois Carnagey. Stewardess Antoinette Besset informed the hijackers that the passengers were becoming hysterical, that a pregnant woman had almost passed out, and that perhaps the passengers should be released. Bearden granted this wish for sixty-three of the passengers but demanded that the crew stay behind, along with four volunteer hostages. About half of the passengers volunteered, but only four remained behind. Outside the plane, members of Congress believed that the plane was hijacked by Cubans and were unsure whether there were two, three, or four hijackers. The plane was surrounded by members of the Secret Service, El Paso police, U.S. Border Patrolmen, deputies from the county shieriff's office, and agents from the U.S. Immigration and Naturalization Service, who became even more concerned when they discovered that Bearden had recently visited the Cuban embassy in Mexico City. The negotiating team pointed out that the plane was too big to land in Cuba and that they would give Bearden a smaller plane, an offer he refused. The FBI was told by President Kennedy to make their own decisions at the scene but to take "every precaution to bring about the safe rescue of the passengers and members of the crew." The FBI also noted that the Boeing 707 was structurally similar to a B52 bomber, the mainstay of the Strategic Air Command, and did not want such a plane falling into the hands of the Cubans or their Soviet mentors. After stalling for a few hours, the FBI allowed the plane to be refueled. During the refueling, a shot was fired on board. Cody had gone to the lavatory, and while passing the .45 to his father, Leon's finger accidentally jerked the trigger, causing a bullet to fire between the feet of the second officer, Norman Simmoms. At 6:50 A.M., clearance was granted for the plane to leave. As the plane taxied, four Border Patrol cars chased it and shot at its ten tires and engines with rifles and machine guns, the first time a skyjacked U.S. airliner was fired upon by law enforcement officials. A piece of glass cut the cheek of one of the crew, Louis Finch, Continental's director of passenger services. Bearden now was willing to swap planes, but President Kennedy vetoed the offer. Within an hour, Bearden had decided to allow the agent in charge, Crosby, to talk with him on board the plane. Meanwhile Louis Finch, the two stewardesses, and three of the passengers jumped down from the rear exit. An FBI agent and a Border Patrolman entered the cockpit through the electronics compartment grate through which the pilot and copilot, first officer Ralph Wagner, escaped, using a rope to slide from the window. When Crosby told Bearden that there would be no deals, Bearden vowed to kill himself. A tapping noise on the outside of the plane diverted Bearden's attention, and Gilman, the Border Patrolman and the last of the hostages punched Bearden just below the ear, breaking his hand. Gilman put an armlock on Bearden and took away his guns, while Crosby grabbed the thunderstruck Cody. It was learned that Bearden did not have anything against the United States politically but did not like being a former convict. He was

asked why he did not take a commercial plane from Mexico and replied that he did not have the necessary money. He was not considering stealing the plane for the benefit of another country but was intending to sell the $5 million plane to Castro so that he could retire to a life of luxury. Leon Bearden was indicted and convicted for obstruction of commerce by extortion and interstate transportation of stolen aircraft and sentenced to life imprisonment, which was later reduced to two terms of five and twenty years to run concurrently, on October 31, 1961. Cody Bearden was given a juvenile indeterminate sentence for obstruction of commerce by extortion and interstate transportation of a stolen aircraft and committed to a correctional facility. He was released in 1965. 5055

August 8, 1961—Atlantic Ocean—A Cuban freighter was hijacked by ten defecting crewmen and their captain. Armed with pistols, the group locked up twenty-three pro-Castro seamen and diverted the ship to Norfolk, Virginia, where they requested political asylum.

August 9, 1961—Cuba—Five anti-Castro Cubans attempted to hijack an Aerovias C46 flying from Havana to the Isle of Pines, Cuba, and divert it to Miami. When they attempted to force their way into the cockpit, two sky marshals fired on them. In the battle, three people died, including the pilot and a sky marshal, while six other people were wounded. The copilot managed to crash-land the spinning plane in a sugar cane field. The forty passengers were held for questioning. Some reports listed the plane as being a Cubana DC3. 5056

August 9, 1961—Mexico—Pan American Airlines flight 501, a DC8 enroute from Houston to Guatemala City, was hijacked after it left Mexico City by Albert Charles Cadon, a white who probably met the FAA profile and who was born in Paris on November 28, 1933. Cadon had come to New York City in 1957, the year he married his German-born wife, Charlotte, who told authorities that he had suffered a nervous breakdown recently, for which he had been treated at Bellevue Hospital. One of the crew recalled, "I thought that someone was sick, then I saw him point a gun [a .38] at the steward [some reports claim it was a stewardess] at the cockpit door. The steward shook his head and the man pushed him aside, kicked open the door, ran in, and closed it behind him." The captain, Carl V. Ballard, and his seven-person crew reported that Cadon claimed he was not a communist and was taking the plane to protest the U.S. position regarding France's Algerian policy. When the plane landed, Cuban soldiers took Cadon away for questioning. The rest of the passengers were well treated and given flowers. Two of the seventy-two passengers were greeted by Castro, who came to Havana to greet them as his personal guests; they were Colombia's foreign minister, Julio Cesar Turbay Ayala, and his wife. Colombia had recently followed the American lead and broke "diplomatic relations with Cuba. The plane and all eighty aboard were sent back to Miami within nine hours of being hijacked. Cadon was found by the Cubans to be mentally incompetent and was deported to Mexico, where he was convicted on charges of robbery and illegal possession of firearms, for which he served eight years and nine months. He is currently a fugitive from U.S. charges (although some reports claim that he was sent on to the United States from Mexico). The incident involved the greatest number of victims to date, and after it President Kennedy requested special antihijacking legislation. Some airlines, with the aid of FAA chief Najeeb E. Halaby, who would later become the head of Pan Am, put sky marshals aboard many of their flights. The FAA admitted that it had been assigning U.S. Border Patrolmen in plainclothes to many flights near Miami following the El Paso drama but that this protection did not include the DC8 flight. The FAA then issued a regulation requiring crews to keep the cockpit doors locked except during takeoffs and landings. The Congress made it a federal crime for unauthorized persons to carry concealed deadly weapons aboard planes, and also made it a federal crime to attempt to assault, intimidate, or threaten crew members in any way that would interfere with their duties or compromise the safety of the flight. Such sky piracy carried a prison sentence of up to twenty years or death. 5057

September 9, 1961—France—A member of the OAS who was attempting to overthrow the government planted a napalm and plastic explosive in the road in Aube département, which was being traveled by President de Gaulle. The bomb did not fire properly, and several persons were arrested for the plot.

September 10, 1961—Soviet Union—A YAK12 chartered passenger plane of the Russian domestic air service was flying from Erwan to Yekhegnadzor, Armenia, when three Armenians attempted to divert it to Turkey. As the plane banked toward Batumi airport, the three hijackers—Serge Tumanyan, Henri Sekoyan, and Haregin Movseyan—put a knife to the pilot's throat and ordered him to keep going. The pilot swerved the plane toward the ground, hoping to throw the attackers off balance. Instead they stabbed him several times. The pilot was able to bring the plane down in a crash landing in a field, an action that killed one skyjacker and wounded another individual, while the pilot collapsed from his severe wounds. The hijackers ran off but were soon captured and sentenced to death. 5058

November 10, 1961—Morocco—A Transportes Aeros (a Portuguese firm) L1049 flying from Casablanca to Lisbon was taken over by six heavily armed members of the Portuguese exile group Frente Antitotalitario, who forced it to circle Lisbon, where they dropped thousands of leaflets urging rebellion. The five men and one woman flew back to Tangier for what was to be a refueling stop, but they and the plane were held by the authorities. They were later expelled to Senegal and were finally granted asylum by Brazil, along with a rebel leader who had been expelled by Morocco. The plane was later returned. 5059

November 27, 1961—Venezuela—An Avensa DC6B flying from Caracas to Maracaibo was hijacked by five men to Curaçao. The Netherlands Antilles agreed to extradition, and the five were imprisoned for four years and seven months. 5060

January 1962—West Germany—The Yugoslavian news service reported that three members of a Ustasha group assassinated the caretaker, Popovic, of the Yugoslavian interests section of the Swedish embassy.

January 8, 1962—Indonesia—In an assassination attempt against President Sukarno, a bomb exploded a few hundred yards behind the presidential motorcade, killing three and wounding twenty-eight, in Makassar. Sukarno accused Dutch agents of the attack.

January 22, 1962—France—A plastic bomb planted by the OAS exploded in the courtyard of the Foreign Ministry's Quai d'Orsay headquarters in Paris, killing one and wounding thirteen.

January 25, 1962—France— The OAS bombed the Paris homes of fourteen prominent Frenchmen.

January 25, 1962—Algeria—The OAS bombed the French government's administration center in the Rocher Noir vicinity of Algiers.

March 6, 1962—Canada—The Doukhobor Sons of Freedom sect bombed an electrical power tower in the vicinity of Kootenai, British Columbia. Six members of the group were arrested.

March 17, 1962—France—A French plane flying from Paris to St. Martin de l'Ardoise, France, was the scene of a hijacking attempt by a suspected member of the Secret Army Organization who was being flown under guard. The hijacker, one of thirty-two prisoners on board the plane, was shot and wounded by a guard. 5061

April 13, 1962—United States—A Cessna 172 on a chartered sightseeing flight of the Miami area was hijacked to Havana. The FAA profile was probably not applicable in the case of the two white male hijackers—David Thomas Healy, born on June 4, 1939, in Coral Gables, Florida, and Leonard Malcolm Oeth, born on August 2, 1933, in Grandtoule, Illinois—who used a gun to force the pilot of the American Aviation plane to alter his route. Fidel Castro believed the hijackers to be CIA agents and deported them to Miami on April 20, 1962, on board a foreign commercial flight. They were tried and convicted on November 12, 1964, on charges of aircraft piracy and kidnapping, for which they were sentenced to terms of twenty years and one year to run concurrently. Oeth was paroled on December 16, 1968, and Healy followed him on December 15, 1969. Castro allowed the pilot and plane to return immediately to Miami. 5062

April 16, 1962—Netherlands—Edgar Da Silva, a Portuguese laborer, attempted to hijack a Royal Dutch Airlines (KLM) flight from Amsterdam to Lisbon and divert it to East Berlin. He claimed he was attempting to strike back at the Dutch government for not granting him a permanent visa and entered the cockpit with a pistol. The pilot gave the impression of following orders but banked the plane back to Amsterdam. Da Silva, believing himself to be in East Berlin, was quickly arrested by Dutch police, who discovered that he was carrying a harmless starter's pistol. 5063

May 2, 1962—Algeria—The OAS drove an explosives-laden car into an Algiers port area, killing 62 Moslem longshoremen and wounding 110.

May 15, 1962—Algeria—OAS gunmen went on a shooting spree in Algiers, killing fifty-one Moslems and injuring twenty-five, in reprisal for the previous day's Moslem machine gunnings from moving cars, in which seventeen Europeans and two Moslems were killed and thirty-five Europeans, five Moslems and four French officers were wounded in the first outbreak of anti-OAS counterterrorism since the March 18 cease-fire.

May 16, 1962—Algeria—Unknown gunmen in Algiers killed forty Moslems and two Europeans.

May 22, 1962—United States—Continental Airlines flight 11, the same B707 that had been hijacked by the Beardens on August 3, 1961, was en route from Chicago to Los Angeles via Kansas City when an explosion at thirty-nine thousand feet tore off the tail assembly and disintegrated the aft portion of the fuselage, hurling eight passengers to their deaths. The bomb was placed in the right rear lavatory's towel container and scattered pieces of the plane for 120 miles. The pilot was unable to regain control of the plane, and it crashed near Unionville, Missouri, killing thirty-six people on impact. The lone survivor lived long enough to tell fragments of the story. The FBI was unable to determine whether the motive was hijacking, sabotage, or insurance bombing.

August 17-18, 1962—France—Six members of the OAS dressed as French paratroopers and heavily armed looted the Pomponne arms depot.

August 22, 1962—France—A group of OAS members machine-gunned President de Gaulle's car as it was driving through the Paris suburb of Petit-Clamart. De Gaulle escaped unhurt from the attack, and security precautions were intensified. The leader of the ambush, Colonel Jean-Marie Bastein-Thiry, was sentenced to death by firing squad. The machine-gunner was a Hungarian deserter from the French Foreign Legion, Vaslo Varga, who was sentenced to life imprisonment but released in 1967 under an amnesty. He was killed on August 14, 1976, during an abortive holdup on a suburban Paris post office at age thirty-three.

September 10, 1962—Cuba—The Cuban exile group Alpha 66 used a forty-foot launch to attack a British freighter and two Cuban ships in Caibarién port on the northern coast of Cuba. A Cuban helicopter was called in for support, but the group escaped capture.

October 8, 1962—Cuba—Fifteen to twenty-five members of Alpha 66 raided Isabela de Sagna port, killing twenty people, including Russians, and capturing weapons and flags.

October 12-13, 1962—Cuba—Six members of an unidentified Cuban exile group on board a seagoing vessel sunk a Cuban patrol boat at sea near the northern coast of Catanzas province.

October 27, 1962—Venezuela—Four U.S.-owned electric power stations were dynamited, with damage reducing oil production. The bombings in the vicinity of Lake Maracaibo appear to have been in protest of the military mobilization decree of President Betancourt. Cuban radio credited the attack to elements of the Army of Venezeulan Liberation, while the Venezuelan government charged the act to a ''communist sabotage ring carried out by three men.''

November 2, 1962—Venezuela—Dynamite explosions damaged four pipes of U.S.-operated oil line installations in Puerto La Cruz. Damage was considerable, with one fire damaging a power station. Those responsible may have been members of the Army of Venezuelan Liberation.

January 1963—Venezuela—Members of the FALN armed with submachine guns carried off Cézanne's ''The Bathers,'' Braque's ''Still Life with Pears,'' and Van Gogh's ''Lilies in a Copper Vase,'' and still lifes by Picasso and Gauguin, all on loan in Caracas's Museum of Fine Arts. The four attackers declared themselves at war with the government to nine hundred touring grammar-school children who watched the seizure, claiming that they wanted to free Venezuela's oil from the United States. They said they would hold the paintings in ransom until their wishes were met, at which they would return the paintings to France. A protesting student was shot by the group. Police later found the paintings carefully wrapped and undamaged, hidden in furniture crates.

January 13, 1962—Togo—A junta of ex-soldiers assassinated by gunfire President Sylvanus Olympio outside the U.S. embassy during a coup.

January 29, 1962—France—Five people were arrested in a plot to assassinate President de Gaulle.

February 15, 1963—Venezuela—The Venezuelan freighter *Anzoategui*, en route from La Guaira to Houston, was hijacked by a leftist group with FALN connections, who held the freighter's crew hostage for political prisoners being held in Venezuela. The rebels radioed from the ship that the aim of the FALN was "to denounce to world opinion the crimes of the Betancourt dictatorship." The group asked Brazil for political asylum, and the ship was allowed to stop at Maraca Island. The rebels were taken to Rio de Janiero to face extradition for piracy.

March 1, 1963—France—An unsuccessful assassination attempt was made against President de Gaulle.

March 6, 1963—France—The OAS fired into a car in Neuilly, killing bank president Henri Lafond, a member of the AEC and director of firms with northern African interests.

March 12, 1963—Mozambique—Jaciento Cilozo, a first lieutenant in the Portuguese army, protested against the Salazar government by forcing a Portuguese military plane to fly from Mozambique to Dar-es-Salaam, Tanzania. The plane was returned. 5064

March 15, 1963—France—A plot to assassinate President de Gaulle was discovered. A group of officers and civilians, probably OAS members, planned to shoot him with a telescopic-sighted rifle during his visit to the Ecole Militaire.

March 19, 1963—Egypt—An Israeli and an Austrian attempting to bomb West German scientists killed six Egyptians and wounded one. The two were arrested.

April 25, 1963—Cuba—Members of an anti-Castro Cuban exile group, the Cuban Freedom Fighters, attempted to bomb oil refineries in the vicinity of Havana by dropping a one-hundred pound bomb and several smaller ones from a two-engine plane flying from an unidentified Caribbean island. Cuban sources claimed that the bomb did not explode.

June 11, 1963—Cuba—Ten anti-Castro commandos used a PT boat, machine guns, and a 30-mm cannon to attack a Matanzas Province sugar refinery. The group exchanged shots with a pursuing Cuban patrol boat, killing some soldiers. In the fray, their boat sank along with the Cuban vessel. The raiders fled to a small key and continued to fight their pursuers until they finally fled to Florida in a fishing boat.

July 18, 1963—United States—A Cuban-born naturalized U.S. citizen, Airman First Class Robert A. Ramos Michelena, stole a Beech T34 Mentor, which he flew to Cuba. He has not returned.

July 31, 1963—Uruguay—Members of the Movement for National Liberation, also known as the Tupamaros, stole firearms from the Swiss Rifle Club in Nueva Helvecia, Colonia. This is the first recorded armed action by this group. On September 6 a police raid found the arms in a cache on the bank of the Río Negro. Four suspects were arrested. On September 9 police reported that Tupamaros leader Raul Sendic was in Brazil, planning to seize and distribute land and a sugar mill to the UTAA, and accused him of directing the assault on the Swiss Rifle Club without PS sanction.

August 1963—Venezuela—The FALN kidnapped Argentine football star Alfredo di Stefano, who was touring with the Spanish team Real Madrid.

August 5, 1963—United States—Roy Siller was unsuccessful in his attempt to hijack a local private plane to Cuba and was fined $150. 5065

November 22, 1963—United States—President John F. Kennedy was assassinated while in a motorcade in Dallas, Texas.

November 27, 1963—Venezuela—The U.S. Army attaché and deputy chief of the U.S. military mission in Caracas, Colonel Chenault, was kidnapped by four members of the FALN as he stepped out of his home. The group demanded and received from the government the release of seventy political prisoners and released Chenault six days later.

November 28, 1963—Venezuela—Six young members of the FALN, including a woman, hijacked an Avensa Convair Twin Engine CV440 en route from Ciudad Bolívar to Caracas. They held machine guns on the pilot and fourteen passengers and forced the pilot to circle Ciudad Bolívar while they dropped leaflets telling its citizens not to vote in the national elections. They then diverted the plane to Port-of-Spain, Trinidad, where they were arrested. Commander and Olga Dilma, José Marin, Alberto Rojas, Patrick Toledo, and Armando Rojas were extradited. The president of Venezuela, Dr. Marcos Falcon-Briceno, charged the Cubans with being behind the action, pointing to the cache of Cuban weapons that had been discovered on the Venezuelan coast. He argued that taking the plane to Havana would have been unmistakable proof of Cuban complicity. 5066

December 6, 1963—Bolivia—Bolivian miners kidnapped seventeen people, including three U.S. officials and one Peace Corps volunteer, demanding the release of three labor leaders. Bolivian troops surrounded the Siglo Veinte area and negotiated, obtaining the release of the hostages.

January 18, 1964—France—An unsuccessful assassination attempt was made against President de Gaulle.

February 13, 1964—France—An unsuccessful assassination attempt was made against President de Gaulle.

February 18, 1964—United States—Two Spanish-speaking individuals chartered a private Piper Apache PA23 from Miami to Key West, but pulled a gun on the American pilot, Richard Wright of Miami, and forced him to fly to Havana. The U.S. Naval Air Station at Boca Chica scrambled two jet interceptors, which arrived too late to head the plane off. The skyjackers were two Cuban exiles, Enrique Castillo Hernandez, born June 30, 1930, in Havana, and Reinaldo Juan Lopez Rodriguez, alias Reinaldo Lopez Lima, born on March 22, 1939, in Havana, who were wanted for embezzlement and passing bad checks. The pilot was well treated by Cuban authorities and was allowed to spend the night in the Swiss embassy, leaving with his plane the next day. The hijackers were allowed to remain in Cuba. They were indicted on February 17, 1969, by a federal grand jury in the southern district of Florida and remain fugitives from the charges. The FAA profile does not appear to have applied in this case. 5067

March 19, 1964—France—An unsuccessful assassination attempt was made against President de Gaulle.

March 20, 1964—Cuba—Guillermo Santos and Andres Izaguire, both twenty-year-old Cuban soldiers assigned to the crew of a military helicopter, seized the aircraft during a routine patrol by firing seven shots into the pilot, who subsequently died. The hijackers flew six feet above the Caribbean, successfully evading North American Air Defense Commander radar, and landing in Key West. No charges were brought against the hijackers. The helicopter and body of the pilot were returned to Cuba. The penetration of U.S. radar caused concern among the military, who recalled the landing of a stolen Cuban plane in Miami during the Cuban missile crisis. 5068

March 24, 1964—Japan—An emotionally disturbed Japanese youth attempted to assassinate U.S. ambassador Edwin Reischauer by stabbing him when he was leaving the embassy. The youth was arrested, and the premier apologized for the incident.

March 25, 1964—France—An unsuccessful assassination attempt was made against President de Gaulle.

April 1, 1964—France—An unsuccessful assassination attempt was made against President de Gaulle.

May 1964—United States—A Pacific Air Lines F27 crashed, killing forty-four people on board, including several children, when the pilot was shot with a .38 revolver of Frank Gonzalez, twenty-seven, who had lost heavily at Reno, Nevada, gambling tables and carried $105,000 in flight insurance.

June 6, 1964—Cuba—Forty-two people were removed from a Cubana airliner in Havana on suspicion of conspiracy to hijack the plane to Florida. 5069

September 9, 1964—Uruguay—On the day that the Uruguayan government broke diplomatic relations with Cuba, members of the Tupamaros bombed the Montevideo offices of the First National City Bank, Moore-McCormack lines, and two cars with diplomatic plates parked in front of the U.S. embassy, the last with incendiaries.

September 10, 1964—Uruguay—A Tupamaro bomb exploded in the garden of the Brazilian ambassador. The homes of four government advisers were firebombed.

September 13, 1964—Caribbean Sea—Anti-Castro Cubans directed machine-gun fire from two small boats against a Spanish freighter, the *Sierra Aranzasu*, while it was in Caribbean waters, sixty miles off the eastern shore of Cuba, en route from Spain to Havana. The ship was set on fire, and the captain and two crewmen were killed; six others were injured.

October 3, 1964—Venezuela—Lieutenant Colonel Michael Smolen, deputy U.S. Air Force attaché in Caracas, was kidnapped by two armed men, members of the FALN, as he was about to enter his car in front of his home. He was forced into another car, which sped away from the Caracas suburb. The group claimed that the act was a political protest against the ''blatant interference of the U.S. in Venezuelan affairs.'' A widespread police search led to the capture of eleven terrorists on October 12 and three others on October 13. Smolen was freed on October 12.

October 19, 1964—Soviet Union—As a Soviet AN2 passenger plane flying from Shadur-Lungu to Izmail neared the Rumanian border, two skyjackers, identified by the Soviet press as "Fatso" and "Crewcut," pulled a gun and a knife on the crew and directed the pilot to fly over the Black Sea. The pilot pretended to comply but turned off the electric compass and put the plane into a slow turn, bring the craft to Kinishev airport. When the skyjackers realized the ruse, they shot the pilot and copilot seven times and stabbed them four times. The pilot rocked the plane to keep the hijackers off balance and managed to land safely, where he and the copilot were regarded as heroes. The hijackers were arrested. 5070

November 3, 1964—Venezuela—The FALN dynamited seven U.S. subsidiary-owned pumping stations and a pipeline for crude oil in El Tigre.

December 8, 1964—Bolivia—A Bolivian Alas Airlines C47 flying from Tipuani to La Paz crashed after an in-flight explosion, killing all fifteen on board. Authorities believed the dynamite was planted by a heavily insured passenger.

December 11, 1964—United States—Anti-Castro Cubans used an automatic timing device to fire a bazooka-type rocket shell across the East River during an anti-Castro demonstration in New York City. The shell exploded harmlessly in the river about two hundred yards from the United Nations headquarters building where Argentine-born Cuban revolutionary Ernesto "Che" Guevara, minister of industry, was addressing the General Assembly. Three anti-Castro Cubans were arrested on December 22, and said that they had deliberately missed the building and were trying to divert public attention from Guevara.

December 31, 1964—Israel—Four young men, members of El Fatah, blew up a water pump at El Koton. The first communiqué of El Fatah appeared the next day, claiming credit for the Ain Bone explosion, where Jordanian water was pumped through the main Israeli water pipe. The attack was condemned at Arab summit meetings and by government spokesmen, the Arab League, and Arab Unified Command, who viewed the action as a provocation that could bring war before the Arabs were prepared for such an engagement.

January 8, 1965—Ireland—The IRA set off a bomb that rocked several Ballacola houses, including the vacation house of Princess Margaret, causing a short circuit and touching off an explosion in a transformer station. Ten men were arrested.

January 15, 1965—Burundi—Prime Minister Pierre Ngendandumwe was assassinated in Bujumbura by a twenty-four-year-old Rwandan refugee who was employed as a U.S. embassy clerk. In what some believed to be a plot by Watusi extremists, the prime minister was shot in the back as he left a hospital after visiting his wife. Twenty-four were taken in for questioning, including a former prime minister, an ex-cabinet chief, and an ex-justice minister, five of whom were linked to a plot.

February 9, 1965—Guatemala—Members of the Revolutionary Movement of the Thirteenth (MR-13) were unsuccessful in their attempt to assassinate the chief of the U.S. military mission to Guatemala, Colonel Harold Hauser.

February 16, 1965—United States—A plot to blow up the Liberty Bell, Statue of Liberty, and Washington Monument was foiled by New York patrolmen who, with FBI aid, managed to infiltrate the group. Three New York men, one a member of the Black Liberation Front, were convicted for conspiracy in New York federal court on June 14. A Canadian woman, a member of the Montreal Separatist Party, pleaded guilty and testified for the prosecution. She had driven a dynamite-laden car from Canada.

March 28, 1965—France—An unsuccessful assassination attempt was made against President de Gaulle.

May 1965—Soviet Union—A Russian AN2 flying from Moscow to Leningrad was the scene of an unsuccessful skyjacking by a man and a woman who shot and killed a flight engineer. On June 15 Tass reported that a memorial had been dedicated to the crew member, whose bravery had given the rest of the crew a chance to overpower the hijackers. 5071

May 6, 1965—Uruguay—Tupamaros bombed offices of All-American Cable and Western Telegraph.

May 15-20, 1965—France—Two plots to assassinate President de Gaulle were thwarted by police. The OAS planned a May 20 bombing, when de Gaulle would be laying a wreath near the statue of Clemenceau in Saint-Hermine. Six right-wing extremists were arrested and accused of a similar bomb plot in Toulon.

May 18, 1965—Brazil—A bomb was found in the U.S. embassy.

June 1965—Argentina—U.S. Consul Temple Wanamaker was shot and seriously wounded by an unknown assailant.

June 1, 1965—Israel—Al Fatah was suspected of an armed attack on an Israeli settlement at Beit Jibrin in which two holes were blasted in a water reservoir. Israel filed a complaint to the Israel-Jordan Mixed Armistice Commission.

June 2, 1965—Israel—Al Fatah was suspected of sending infiltrators from Lebanon who dynamited a Yiftah house, north of the Sea of Galilee. Israel filed a complaint to the Israel-Jordan Mixed Armistice Commission.

July 8, 1965—Canada—A Canadian Pacific Airlines DC6B, flying from Vancouver, British Columbia, to Whitehorse, Yukon, crashed when an explosive device detonated within the fuselage, separating the tail section over British Columbia. None of the fifty-two on board survived.

July 10, 1965—Uruguay—The Brazilian embassy in Montevideo was bombed by the Tupamaros.

July 17, 1965—France—An unsuccessful assassination attempt was made against President de Gaulle.

July 27, 1965—Cuba—An unsuccessful assassination attempt was made against Premier Fidel Castro.

July 30, 1965—Brazil—A small bomb exploded in front of the Belo Horizonte Binational Center. The early morning explosion caused little damage.

July 31, 1965—Malaysia—A time bomb consisting of four and a half pounds of explosive was found at 7:10 P.M., 20 minutes before it was set to go off in front of the consulate general-USIS building in Singapore.

August 9, 1965—Uruguay—A West German chemical company, Warehouse of Bayer, was bombed by Tupamaros for the corporation's involvement with the U.S. Vietnam war effort. This was the first time the MLN commandos identified themselves as such.

August 27, 1965—Ecuador—A dynamite charge failed to go off during the night and was found in front of the Guayaquil Binational Center early the next morning.

August 27, 1965—Israel—Lebanese saboteurs, who were suspected of being Palestinians, bombed an irrigation pipeline in Ramin, formerly named Menara. Footprints were discovered leading from the pipeline to the Lebanese border.

August 29, 1965—Aden—Seven members of the Aden National Liberation Front fired seven shots at the British police superintendent as he was driving to his Aden City office. Five of the anticolonialists were arrested.

August 31, 1965—United States—Hawaiian Airlines Flight 358, a DC3 flying from Honolulu to Kauai, Hawaii, was diverted by Harry F. Fergerstrom, a white who met the FAA profile, who was born on January 1, 1949, in Kohala, Hawaii. He forced back the plane back to Honolulu. The hijacker was given an indeterminate sentence for interference with a flight crew member and committed to a juvenile correctional facility, from which he was paroled on November 3, 1967. 5072

September 1, 1965—Aden—Members of the Aden National Liberation Front assassinated the British speaker of the Aden state legislative council by shooting him two times as he was entering his car outside the Aden City tennis club. Five terrorists were arrested for this killing, as well as the assassination of a British police superintendent on August 29.

September 17, 1965—Aden—An Aden terrorist threw a hand grenade in the Aden civil airport as seventy-three schoolchildren were boarding a London-bound plane. Seven were injured.

September 20, 1965—Brazil—Shortly after the close of business, a small bomb exploded in the corridor outside the offices of the USIS and the American consulate on the twelfth floor of a downtown Belo Horizonte office building, causing minor damage. Another device, placed directly in front of a USIS bulletin board, failed to explode.

October 11, 1965—United States—Aloha Airlines flight TS755, an F27 on the ground at Molokai, Hawaii, scheduled to take off for Honolulu was attacked by two white males, Lawrence D. Hesiler, born on April 6, 1947, in White Earth, Minnesota, and Richard K. Boyd, born November 10, 1946, in Watonga, Oklahoma. The FAA profile was not applicable in their case. The captain used a flare pistol to disarm one attacker, while a ramp agent used a shotgun to apprehend the second hijacker, who did not have the opportunity to make their destination known. The two were subjected to a U.S. Navy court-martial and were sentenced to four years at hard labor and given a dishonorable discharge. Boyd was released on September 8, 1966, with Heisler following him four days later. 5073

October 26, 1965—United States—National Airlines flight 209, an Electra 188 bound for Key West from Miami, was the scene of an attempted hijacking by Luis Medina Perez, a Cuban exile and Bay of Pigs veteran who met the FAA profile and was born in Havana on August 19, 1945. He pulled a Lugar-shaped toy pellet pistol (which was unloaded) on the stewardess and directed her to escort him to the cockpit. She managed to send a warning message over the intercom to Captain K. I. Carlile, his copilot, and flight engineer Wiedemann. Carlile met Perez in the cabin and tried to reason with him in English and Spanish. Perez claimed that he wanted to go to Havana to free his relatives and would confront Castro with his open-door policy. Carlile reported that ''he said unless we took him to Havana, he would kill the crew and blow up the airplane.'' He had tried to hire a boat to Cuba but had been unsuccessful and saw this as his last alternative. Perez then accompanied Carlile to the cockpit and sat down in the jump seat behind the pilot. Wiedemann was waiting with a fire ax, which he used to pin Perez to the seat. Perez surrendered the gun. In a trial in which his mental competence was an issue, Perez was acquitted on June 24, 1966, of aircraft piracy and assault and became a front-page hero. 5074

November 11, 1965—Peru—A homemade bomb exploded during the evening in front of the Miraflores Binational Center, causing minor damage. Streets nearby were littered with handbills that proclaimed ''Down with Kennedy,'' a reference to the visit to Peru of Senator Robert Kennedy.

November 17, 1965—United States—National Airlines flight 30, a DC8 flying in the afternoon from Houston to Melbourne, Florida (twenty miles south of Cape Kennedy), with a stopover in New Orleans, was the scene of an attempted hijacking to Cuba by sixteen-year-old Thomas Harvey Robinson, a white male meeting the FAA profile who was born in Marion, Kentucky, on March 1, 1949. Described by the press as a ''brilliant youth,'' ''teen-aged honor student,'' ''straight-A student, just the kind of boy you'd want your son to be,'' ''never missed a day of Sunday school nor school until the day he boarded the plane,'' the Brownsville, Texas, high school junior boarded the plane in New Orleans and took his seat in the tourist section. Twenty minutes into the flight, he wandered into the first-class area and found a seat near the cockpit, across the aisle from Project Gemini Mission director Christopher Kraft, who was with twelve other NASA officials, including public affairs officer Paul Haney. Kraft noticed the youth fiddling with a newspaper and believed him to be hiding something. When Kraft asked him what he had, the youth jumped up and shoved his .22 caliber Colt automatic target pistol into Kraft's face. The youth fanned the hammer several times but did not pull it back far enough to discharge the bullets. He turned away from Kraft and attempted to open the cockpit door. Stewardess Nancy Taylor informed him that the door was locked and he could not enter. He then launched into a long speech before the ninety passengers about the dangers of Castro and how the U.S. government should be more militant in its anticommunism. He then drew a .38 caliber Smith and Wesson revolver and punctuated his address by firing nine shots into the floor, the first shots ever fired by a skyjacker aboard an American airliner while in flight. Taylor kept the pilot informed over the intercom as Captain Dean Cooper radioed New Orleans airport of his return. When Robinson lowered his guns to reload, Houston businessman Edward T. Haake tackled and disarmed him. Held under $50,000 bond, Robinson was indicted by a federal grand jury on counts of piracy, assaulting, intimidating, and threatening a stewardess, and intimidating and interfering with the pilot.

The judge granted the government's request for a sanity test, and the prosecution announced that it wished to try the juvenile as an adult because of the gravity of the charges. He was declared a juvenile delinquent and sentenced to an indeterminate term in a correctional facility on the assault charge. He was paroled on June 8, 1967, and the conviction was set aside on September 24, 1969. Airline manufacturers noted that the DC8 did not depressurize due to the nine bullet holes, despite its cruising altitude of twenty thousand feet. 5075

November 29, 1965—Israel—Palestinian terrorists fired five mortar shells into the Pitam Tigua town hall.

December 27, 1965—West Germany—An anonymous phone call advised that a bomb had been placed at the Munich Voice of America medium-wave transmitter. A search uncovered no evidence of intrusion and no bomb. Authorities believed it was a crank call.

February 5, 1966—Brazil—The Pôrto Alegre home of the U.S. consul was bombed.

February 25, 1966—West Germany—An anonymous telephone call to the Amerika Haus in West Berlin advised that a bomb was set to explode in the building soon after noon. Local police were unable to find a bomb.

March 8, 1966—Ireland—An explosion severely damaged the Nelson Column in Dublin. Irish police attributed the attack to the IRA.

March 20, 1966—Aden—An anticolonial terrorist killed a British official.

March 26, 1966—Argentina—Persons in a passing vehicle lobbed Molotov cocktails at the Mendoza Binational Center. The resulting fires were quickly extinguished and caused little damage. Leaflets found in the street attacked the U.S. position on Vietnam.

March 27, 1966—Cuba—A Cubana Ilyushin 18 was flying the sunset run from Santiago to Havana when the flight engineer, Angel Betancourt Cueto, locked the cockpit door as the craft was seventy miles west of Havana. He slugged the sky marshal behind the pilot and shot him dead. After being ordered to fly to Miami, the pilot contacted Cuban flight control, who agreed to the same ruse that had previously worked in Russia and Holland. The pilot flew on and began communicating in English to give the impression that he was nearing Miami. American radar screens picked up the plane as it was nearing Key West, and four U.S. Navy F102s were sent up. By the time they were aloft, the Cubana was in a slow curve, heading back to José Marti Airport.

Upon touchdown, Betancourt realized the trick and ordered the pilot to take off again. The refusing pilot was killed with one shot, and the copilot was wounded. Betancourt attempted to lift off himself, but the plane ran into the field at the end of the runway and skidded to a stop. Betancourt jumped off and fled into the darkness, becoming the subject of a massive manhunt. While Castro denounced the attempt as an American plot, anyone suspected of harboring the skyjacker was arrested. The hijacker was captured on April 11 in a Havana Franciscan monastery, along with three Franciscans who were hiding him. One of the passengers on the plane was a close aide and friend of Castro, Major Raul Curbelo. 5076

April 20, 1966—India—Anti-Indian Naga rebels bombed a train in Assam state, killing fifty-five and injuring eighty-four.

May 16, 1966—Peru—A Molotov cocktail was thrown against the front entrance of the Miraflores Binational Center but failed to explode. Leaflets found at the scene indicated that members of a Leninist youth group were responsible.

May 21, 1966—Turkey—Unknown individuals detonated two small fire-bombs and a moderately heavy explosive charge in USIS offices in Istanbul, destroying two hundred books, several pieces of furniture, and some shelves.

June 8, 1966—Brazil—A gasoline explosive device, along with two shotgun shells, were found in a charred package close to an outer wall of the São Paulo Binational Center. An igniting charge had failed to set off the device, resulting in little damage.

June 12, 1966—Brazil—During the late evening, an attempt was made to set fire to the Belo Horizonte Binational Center. The flammable substance, probably gasoline, that was poured under a rear door and around a window frame burned itself out quickly after being ignited, resulting in little damage.

June 28, 1966—Turkey—A local employee of USIS-Istanbul received an anonymous telephone call advising that a bomb was going to explode in the USIS Information Center. The building was cleared, and U.S. Marines found no explosive charge.

June 29, 1966—Brazil—At approximately 3 A.M., unknown individuals detonated a small explosive device in front of the Brasilia USIS Information Center, shattering the building's front window panes and causing light damage to the entranceway.

July 4, 1966—Northern Ireland—A seventeen-year-old boy dropped a thirty-pound concrete block on a car carrying Queen Elizabeth II and Prince Philip through Belfast. The couple escaped injury, and the boy was charged with the crime.

July 7, 1966—Cuba—A Cubana Ilyushin 18 flying from Santiago to Havana was hijacked by nine men, including the pilot, to Kingston, Jamaica. The copilot was shot and severely wounded during the incident. The plane and wounded man were quickly returned to Cuba. 5077

July 25, 1966—Brazil—An explosion damaged the USIS motion picture section located in the U.S. AID building in Recife. Two other bombs went off simultaneously in other parts of the city but did not involve U.S. property.

August 1966—West Germany—The Yugoslav press charged that Ustasha terrorists murdered the Yugoslav vice consul, Sava Milavanovic, in Stuttgart.

August 4, 1966—Colombia—A powerful bomb exploded in a ground floor ladies' room of the Bogotá Binational Center, killing an American citizen employed as a restaurant concessionaire and two Colombian citizens and causing six others to be hospitalized. The act was considered to be part of the predicted terrorist campaign connected with the Colombian president's inauguration.

August 9, 1966—Soviet Union—An attempt by three men to hijack a domestic Soviet flight to Turkey was foiled in a gunfight with the pilot in which one passenger was wounded. The plane landed in Batumi, and the hijackers were captured. 5078

September 20, 1966—Italy—A fairly heavy explosive charge consisting of black powder destroyed a show window and door, a large radiator, and several pieces of furniture, and shattered all windows in the USIS Cultural Center in the Marranello section of Rome. The center had been the target of several anti-Vietnam demonstrations during the previous eighteen months.

September 22, 1966—Canada—Members of the Miami-based Cuban National Association bombed the front of the Cuban embassy in Ottawa, causing little damage.

September 25, 1966—Israel—Arab terrorists from Jordan crossed six miles into Israel and sabotaged an electric transformer linked to a water pumping station near the Dead Sea. Israel filed a protest with the Israel-Jordan Mixed Armistice Commission.

September 28, 1966—Argentina—An Argentine Airlines DC4 bound from Buenos Aires to Río Gallegos was hijacked by twenty members of the Argentine nationalist group El Condor, led by the beautiful blonde star Maria Christina Varrier, who forced the pilot to fly to the Falkland Islands, a British colony in the south Atlantic, 350 miles east of the continent. The pilot landed in a level area that the inhabitants used as a race track near the capital, Port Stanley, whose population of 1,250 was half that of the island. The group announced to the crowd that gathered that the Falklands should be returned by Britain to their rightful owners, the Argentines. The islanders enjoyed the speeches and flag planting, although they did not speak Spanish. The El Condor group was successful in capturing the headlines for days. It was accused of shooting at the British embassy in Buenos Aires two days before Prince Philip's official visit to direct public attention to the Falklands issue. The DC4 was unable to fly off and was out of fuel, so the crew and twenty-five other passengers stayed in the homes of islanders. The hijackers were armed with rifles and stayed in the plane, surrounded by police, for two days, until they crept away and stayed in a church. They eventually surrendered and waited for someone to pick them up, which was a problem since no planes could land, as the plane blocked the makeshift runway, and the monthly mail ship was not due for another week. Some reports indicate that the group was extradited on October 1, with the three leaders being sentenced to five years and the others to three years. The Falklands remained under British sovereignty. 5079

October 27, 1966—Israel—A freight train struck and set off an explosive charge set by Arab terrorists southwest of Jerusalem. The train derailed while the group fired at it, injuring one Israeli. Train service between Tel Aviv, Haifa, and Jerusalem was canceled for three days.

October 30, 1966—Israel—Three Arab terrorists were responsible for the bombing of a water pipeline in the vicinity of Arad and Masada in the northern Negev. The Israelis found footprints of the three and traced them to the nearby Jordanian border.

November 22, 1966—Aden—An Aden (now southern Yemen) Airways DC3 flying from Wahidi's Paddy's Field in south Arabia (now southern Yemen) to Aden was disintegrated by an explosion that destroyed the aircraft. The explosive detonated in a hand baggage area on the port side of the passenger cabin shortly after the aircraft reached six thousand feet and about twenty minutes after it took off from Meifah (Maysaah), killing all twenty-eight people on board.

1967—Dominican Republic—An American teacher was killed by a Dominican terrorist. Subsequent events led to the deployment of the U.S. Marines.

1967—Canada—The Cuban Nationalist Association threatened to bomb the Cuban pavilion at Montreal's Expo 67. Felipe Rivero, the head of the group, was arrested by U.S. immigration authorities in Miami on May 12 and ordered deported on July 11. He had claimed credit for the September 22, 1966, bombing of the Cuban embassy in Ottawa, which shattered windows and splintered its door.

January 18, 1967—Israel—Members of the Heroes of Repatriation conducted an armed attack on the town of Beit Jibrim, in the vicinity of Jerusalem, and detonated thirty-three pounds of explosives at a nearby ammunition depot. According to the Israelis, the group then fled back into Jordan.

January 23, 1967—Uruguay—Tupamaros bombed the U.S. consulate in Montevideo.

January 26, 1967—South Vietnam—The American Director of the USIS Cultural Center in Can Tho discovered two sticks of dynamite and a timer concealed in a dictionary on a bookshelf. After ordering the building evacuated, he called in U.S. Air Force ordnance disposal technicians who defused the device minutes before it was set to explode.

January 29, 1967—United States and Canada—Six time bombs went off between 3:45 and 4:40 A.M. in Yugoslav diplomatic and consular missions in Washington, D.C., Chicago, San Francisco, New York, Ottawa, and Toronto, damaging walls, windows, and doors but causing no casualties. Antigovernment Yugoslav exiles were brought to trial but acquitted due to lack of evidence.

February 1, 1967—West Berlin—A few minutes before 6 P.M., an anonymous caller telephoned the Amerika Haus in West Berlin and warned that a bomb was set to explode there at 6 P.M. The building was evacuated, and a police search found no bomb.

February 7, 1967—Egypt—A Russian-built AN24 on a domestic Egyptian flight was hijacked by Riyad Kamal Hajjaj, who diverted the plane and its forty-one passengers to Jordan. Egyptian police described him as a common criminal with a long record. Hajjaj escaped to Sweden, where he was arrested and is serving a long sentence for other crimes. A while later, the FAA reissued its warning that all cockpit doors be kept locked. 5080

February 19, 1967—Israel—An explosion by a water pipeline near Arad caused no damage. The footprints of two Arab infiltrators led from the pipeline seven miles to the Jordanian border.

February 27, 1967—Ethiopia—Eritrean Liberation Front members were suspected of sabotage when more than a million tons of gasoline and oil was destroyed in an explosion at the Mobil terminal at Aseb, Eritrea.

February 28, 1967—Aden—Unknown individuals bombed an apartment of a British official, killing two and injuring eleven.

March 10, 1967—Chile—Leftist youths occupied and sacked the headquarters of the U.S. Peace Corps in Santiago. The group carried away much of the correspondence in the corps' files. Months later, charges were made that the Peace Corps had been paying informants for intelligence gathering. Paul C. Bell, the Peace Corps director in Chile, argued that the documents upon which the charges were based were forgeries and not those that had been stolen. He said that one of the letters offered as evidence may have been an authentic photocopy of a stolen document but that all of the damaging material had been inserted after the theft.

March 16, 1967—Israel—Five Arab infiltrators attempted to destroy a water reservoir and pipeline in the vicinity of Arad. The explosion killed two of the group instead.

March 22, 1967—Senegal—Mustafa Lo, a government employee, tried to shoot at the car of President Leopold S. Senghor. He was overpowered by police. The government charged that he was part of a plot by supporters of ex-Premier Mamadou Dia.

March 23, 1967—Bolivia—A rebel group organized by Major Ernesto Ché Guevara ambushed a government patrol, killing six soldiers and an Indian guard. Government troops counterattacked and supposedly surrounded the rebels.

April 3, 1967—United States—The acting chief of Cuba's United Nations mission, thirty-year-old Nicolas Rodriguez Astiazarain, was burned when a package exploded as he was opening it.

April 4, 1967—Turkey—At approximately 7 P.M. a marine guard at the U.S. consulate general in Istanbul received an anonymous phone call warning that a bomb had been placed in the USIS Information Center. A search proved negative.

April 12, 1967—Uruguay—A Burroughs building was bombed the day after anti-United States demonstrators clashed with police in Montevideo as President Lyndon Johnson arrived for a meeting at Punta del Este.

April 23, 1967—Nigeria—Five men hijacked a Nigerian Airlines F27 flying from Benin City to Lagos and forced it to land in Enugu in eastern Nigeria. 5081

April 24, 1967—Togo—President Etienne Eyadema was wounded when a military guard under orders from a former chief of staff shot him. The guard was sentenced to death.

May 27, 1967—Lebanon—A bomb exploded near the American embassy in Beirut, shattering several windows on lower floors and causing minor structural damage.

May 29, 1967—Iraq—An unknown individual threw a Molotov cocktail against the wall of the American Institute of Languages, a USIS facility in Baghdad, causing minor damage.

May 29, 1967—Colombia—A time bomb tore a three-foot hole in the rear fuselage of an Aerocondor DC6 flying between Barranquilla and Bogotá. The plane landed safely at Bogotá, and no casualties were reported among the four crew members and eighteen passengers.

June 4, 1967—Iraq—An explosive charge, possibly a hand grenade, was detonated on a side porch of the American Institute of Languages in Baghdad. No injuries were reported because classes had ended an hour earlier, but several windows were shattered and chunks of masonry were torn from the walls.

June 7, 1967—West Germany—A small firebomb was thrown through a display window into the library of the Hamburg Amerika Haus at 2 A.M. The fire was quickly extinguished by local police and caused only slight damage.

June 9, 1967—Dominican Republic—An explosive device, later described by police as a type used by communists in Venezuela, was found on a bookshelf of the USIS library in Santo Domingo. From the appearance of the fuse, it was judged that the device had been on the shelf for several days and had failed to detonate because of a malfunction.

June 9, 1967—France—An unsuccessful assassination attempt was made against U.S. Ambassador Charles E. Bohlen.

June 10, 1967—Sudan—Two bombs thrown over a rear gate landed on the second-floor balcony of the USIS in Khartoum. The explosion shattered a window and damaged part of the wall.

June 22, 1967—Haiti—An unsuccessful assassination attempt was made againt President François Duvalier.

June 30, 1967—South Yemen—An empty Aden Airways Viscount was bombed while parked on the tarmac at Aden airport. The aircraft caught fire and was destroyed; no casualties were reported. A piece of the time detonator pencil was found, and authorities believed that plastic explosive had been used in the forward compartment.

June 30, 1967—Spain—A British-owned and operated HS.125 air taxi, charted to fly from Palma de Mallorca to Ibiza, Spain, was hijacked to Algiers by François-Joseph Bodenan. The pilot, Captain Trevor Copleston, reported that Bodenan had chartered the flight, and he did not perceive him as a skyjacker and kidnapper of one of the passengers, former prime minister of the secessionist state of Katanga and former prime minister of Zaire, Moise Tshombe. Copleston claimed that "Bodenan came rushing up to the cockpit, holding a gun and looking all hot and sweaty and shouted in French 'To Algiers! To Algiers.' I thought, 'Well, it's his charter—better do what the man says!' Bodenan then explained that he was a member of the FLN." One of the shots fired by Bodenan ricocheted and wounded Michael Hambursin, one of the passengers, in the foot. The other passengers included two Belgians, Mr. and Mrs. Sigal, and Tshombe's two bodyguards. (In September 1966 Bodenan had formed SEDEFI, a Geneva- and Brussels-based company, which he used to lure Tshombe on board the plane in anticipation of closing a major business deal.) The passengers were released, but Copleston and his copilot, Taylor, were held for eighty-five days, during which they were questioned by Algerian authorities, who learned that Copleston was born in April 1928 on the Isle of Wight, had joined th RAF in 1945 as an apprentice, received his commission and later flew Hunter fighters, had married, and had four children. Taylor was born in 1940 in Oban, Scotland, was an RAF V-bomber pilot, and was single. After a ten-week detention, the International Federation of Air Line Pilots Associations began to threaten to boycott Algerian airports. After a second trip on September 15 to Boufarik to service the HS125, the pilots were released within the week. Tshombe had been accused of the assassination of Patrice Lumumba and was sentenced to death in absentia by a Congolese court on March 13, 1967, for murder and theft. It was argued in the Algerian supreme court that Bodenan had made a citizen's arrest of Tshombe, which does not appear to be true under Algerian and French law. The court nonetheless ruled that Tshombe should be extradited, but he was kept under house arrest in Algiers until he died of a heart attack, certified by a team of medical experts called in by his Algerian hosts on June 29, 1969, two years after the hijacking. Bodenan was released in September or October of 1969 and was found in Switzerland in December, where he was arrested. Spain demanded his extradition and the case was heard before the Swiss Federal Tribunal in Lausanne. On August 13, 1973, the tribunal decided to grant extradition, citing its contribution against hijacking. However, Bodenan, out on bail, disappeared during the trial. It has been argued that if Bodenan was acting solely for financial reward, he would have brought the plane to the Congo. Because he landed in Algiers, perhaps he had accomplices. 5082

August 1967—People's Republic of China—During the Cultural Revolution, a mob broke into the compound of the Soviet embassy, smashed the furniture, and burned files in a consular building and broke windows in the main building. No injuries were reported.

August 1, 1967—Brazil—The Peace Corps office in Rio was bombed.

August 4, 1967—Aden—Arab terrorists fired mortar rounds at the British military headquarters in the Crater District.

August 6, 1967—Colombia—A Colombian Aerocondor DC4 flying from Barranquilla to San Andres Islands in Colombia was hijacked to Cuba by five armed men, described as pro-Castro guerrillas. Castro granted political asylum to Pedro Buendia, Fermina Rojas, Roberto Lopez, Julian Alvarez, and José Angel Gomez Leon. The seventy-eight passengers, including three Americans, were allowed to leave with the plane the next day, with presents such as records, books, liquor, cigars, and flowers. Cuba sent Colombian Airlines a bill for everything, which the Colombians paid. Castro tied the hijacking in with the opening of the Latin American Solidarity Conference, where he held a major news conference to display six prisoners who, he claimed, were sent by the Central Intelligence Agency. On January 31, 1968, the Colombian army reported that its troops had killed 6 ELN guerrillas in the Santander mountains. One of the dead was Leon. Conflicting reports indicate that one of the hijackers was an Ecuadorean, while other reports list the passengers as totaling sixty-six, sixty-five, and seventy-eight individuals. 5083

August 11, 1967—Chile—An anonymous telephone caller warned members of the Santiago Binational Center that a bomb would explode. A search proved negative.

August 27, 1967—Saudi Arabia—Members of the National Liberation Front kidnapped Sheikh Ali Atil al-Kaladi, chairman of the Aden Supreme Council, in Jaar, in lower Yafa.

September 9, 1967—Colombia—A Colombian Avianca DC3 flying from Barranquilla to Maganqué, Colombia, was hijacked by three armed men,—

Ramiro, Fernando, and Joaquin Garcia—and forced to land in Santiago, Cuba. The plane and passengers were permitted to return to Colombia the next day. The Cubans sent the Colombians another bill. 5084

September 13, 1967—Hong Kong—A combination gasoline bomb and hand grenade was found on the outside window ledge of the USIS library. The following day, two bombs designed for their noise effect were found in the street gutter several yards away from the library. Police bomb squads handled all the devices without injury, but in their detonation of the devices found on the window ledge, the window itself was broken and a nearby showcase suffered minor damage.

September 19, 1967—Israel—Palestinian terrorists bombed several apartments and a printing shop in Jerusalem.

September 20, 1967—Israel—Palestinian terrorists dynamited a factory in Hadera.

September 25, 1967—Israel—Members of Al Fatah bombed a factory in Omez and Givat Habiba.

September 27, 1967—Brazil—The U.S. air attaché's Rio home was bombed.

September 28, 1967—Israel—Three men threw hand grenades outside the home of Premier Levi Eshkol in Jerusalem. They were seen running away.

September 29, 1967—Israel—A time bomb consisting of eight pounds of explosives was found in an abandoned briefcase in the American Cultural Center in Tel Aviv. The device failed to detonate because of faulty wiring.

October 1, 1967—Israel—Four Palestinian terrorists who had crossed the Jordan River bombed the village of Hamadia in the Baisan Valley. Three of their explosive charges failed to detonate. An Israeli soldier on leave was killed.

October 6, 1967—Israel—Palestinian terrorists attacked the United Nations Truce Supervisory Organization's headquarters in Jerusalem, dynamiting an antenna, but causing only slight damage. The PFLP claimed credit.

October 8, 1967—Bolivia—On October 10, the Bolivian army high command confirmed that Major Ernesto Ché Guevara de la Serña, age thirty-nine, was fatally wounded near Higueras in a clash with the army and had died on October 9. An army patrol had killed a nine-member guerrilla group on August 31 near Masiguri Bajo in the southeast. The dead included two or three

Cubans, including the group's leader, Joaquin, and a Bolivian woman, Laura Gutierrez, alias Tania. A prisoner, José Carillo, disclosed that Guevara had been instructing the rebels. Guevara's diaries indicated that thirteen members of his band were Cuban army officers and that four of them were members of the Cuban Communist party's Central Committee: Major Juan Vitalio Acuna, alias Joaquin; Major Antonio Sanchez Dias, alias Marcos; Major Alberto Fernandez Montes de Oca, alias Pachungo; and Captain Eliseo Reyes Rodriguez, alias Rolando. The Cubans had entered Bolivia in November and December of the previous year and had killed thirty-five Bolivian army members and wounded thirteen, while nineteen rebel bodies had been recovered, including thirteen Bolivians, five Cubans, and an Argentine, with twenty other rebels reported killed. Three other rebels, including Roberto Peredo, alias Coco, were killed on September 26. On October 14, four rebels—two Bolivians, one Cuban, and one Peruvian—were killed in a battle with the army, leaving only three Cubans and three Bolivians, led by Guido Peredo, alias Inti, at large.

October 12, 1967—Mediterranean Sea off the Island of Rhodes—A British European Airways Comet 4B flying from Athens to Nicosia at twenty-nine thousand feet crashed after an explosive device detonated in the tourist passenger cabin. A few floating pieces of debris were recovered along with some bodies. All sixty-six aboard died.

October 12, 1967—Dominican Republic—A plastic explosive device was found on a bookshelf of the USIS library in Santo Domingo at 2:30 P.M. Its detonator had fired but had failed to ignite the main charge.

October 15, 1967—Israel—Six members of El Fatah conducted an armed attack on the communal settlement of Maoz Haim. After blowing up a dining hall, a transformer house, and a trailer house, the group retreated two miles to the Jordanian border.

October 16, 1967—United States—A bomb exploded across the street from the Cuban, Yugoslav and Finnish U.N. missions in New York City.

October 23, 1967—Ecuador—Two Molotov cocktails were thrown through the second-story window of the Binational Center during a demonstration of sixty secondary school students who were protesting the death of Ché Guevara. Five Ecuadorians who were attending class received minor injuries, and the student lounge was slightly damaged.

October 24, 1967—Israel—A large fire damaged the Lod airport terminal building. George Habash of the PFLP claimed credit for his organization, but Israel said the blaze was an accident.

November 12, 1967—United States—A small explosion occurred in the rear baggage compartment of an American Airlines B727 one hour and forty-two minutes after taking off from Chicago, en route to San Diego. Three bags were destroyed by the blast over Alamosa, Colorado. The plane landed successfully three hours after takeoff with its seventy-two passengers and six crew members. A homemade crude explosive device was found on board, leading the FBI to arrest one man.

November 13, 1967—Israel—Palestinian terrorists shelled an army camp in the vicinity of Hebron. The camp was hit by a bazooka shell and several rounds of light weapon fire.

November 14, 1967—Israel—Palestinian terrorists were responsible for an explosion that damaged part of a building and some equipment of a Nazareth automobile assembly plant.

November 20, 1967—United States—A Crescent Airlines Piper Apache PA10, chartered by Louis Gabor Babler to fly from Hollywood, Florida, to Bimini in the Bahamas, was hijacked by Babler to Havana. Two U.S. jets tracked the plane, but the skyjacker warned them to move or he would shoot the two crewmen. The pilot, J. V. Raymond, described Babler as "a Russian." The pilots and plane were permitted to return to the United States. Babler was indicted on May 7, 1969, by a federal grand jury in the southern district of Florida, where it was noted that he was an American with a criminal record. Babler was born on March 10, 1934, in Budapest, Hungary. The FAA claims that the profile did not apply in the case of this white hijacker. 5085

December 13, 1967—Peru—A Molotov cocktail was thrown through a window of the Trujillo Binational Center during a demonstration by university students protesting suspension of classes. The fire was quickly extinguished, resulting in no damage.

December 26, 1967—Peru—At 2:20 A.M., the night watchman found a Molotov cocktail inside the entrance to the Lima Binational Center. He threw it into the street where it exploded, causing no damage or injuries.

January 2, 1968—United States—The U.S. government, citing lack of evidence, dismissed all charges against six anti-Castro Cubans who had been accused of plotting to bomb ships bound for Havana. 0001

January 7, 1968—Spain—Mohammed Khidder, a friend of Fatah's Yasir Arafat, was killed in Madrid, probably by an Algerian military intelligence agent. Khidder was a self-educated former streetcar conductor who became one of the Algerian revolution's top organizers and treasurer of the National

Liberation Front before falling out with Ahmed Ben Bella and President Houari Boumédienne. 0002

January 9, 1968—Cuba—A package mailed from New York City by the anti-Castro group El Poder Cubano exploded in a Havana post office, injuring five workers. 0003

January 13, 1968—Israel—Palestinian terrorists who had infiltrated from Jordan fired bazooka shells into an oil installation near Elath. While the resulting blaze was being extinguished, five mortar shells were fired into the town. 0004

January 16, 1968—Guatemala—Colonel John D. Webber, age forty-seven, commander of the thirty-four man U.S. Military Advisory Group (MAAG) in Guatemala, and Lieutenant Commander Ernest A. Munro, forty, head of the MAAG's naval section, as they were returning from lunch at the Guatemalan Air Force headquarters were killed by gunfire from an automobile that had pulled up alongside their own. Wounded in the attack were Sergeant Major John F. Forester, forty-two, of Salem, Oregon, and Chief Petty Officer Harry L. Greene, forty-one, of Omaha. The next day the Rebel Armed Forces distributed leaflets claiming credit for the attack and accusing the United States of having created Guatemalan army killer teams that were responsible for the deaths of thousands of leftists. They also claimed the attack was in revenge for the January 12 killing of Rogelia Cruz Martinez, Miss Guatemala of 1950, who was slain by La Mano Blanco, a right-wing terrorist group, because of her leftist sympathies. The Guatemalan government proclaimed a state of alarm, a form of martial law, and placed the U.S. embassy under special guard. U.S. officials stated that they would not lodge a formal protest to the Guatemalan government regarding the killings in Guatemala City. 0005

January 25, 1968—United States—Two parcels bombs placed by El Poder Cubano in package shipments being sent to Cuba exploded in Miami, injuring one person. The two businesses struck by the group had specialized in shipping packages that members of the refugee communiity in Miami were sending to relatives in Cuba. As the U.S. Post Office would mail only letters and medicines sent to Cuba, the firms arranged for other types of mail to be routed via Spain, Canada, and Mexico. A communiqué from El Poder Cubano warned that other bombs would follow, directed against people doing business with Cuba. 0006, 0007

February 8, 1968—United States—The British consulate in Miami was damaged by a bomb. El Poder Cubano or other anti-Castro Cubans were the major suspects. 0008

February 9, 1968—Argentina—At 1:40 A.M., the second floor of the U.S. embassy residence was struck by fifteen 9-mm machine-gun slugs fired from a passing automobile. The perpetrators and reasons for the attack were unknown. The next day, one hundred demonstrators marched on the U.S. embassy carrying Vietcong flags and anti-Vietnam war posters and distributed leaflets opposing U.S. actions in Vietnam. No violence or damage was reported. 0009

February 9, 1968—South Vietnam—A Pan Am DC6B, chartered by the U.S. military to fly soldiers from Da Nang to Hong Kong for rest and relaxation, was preparing for takeoff during the Tet offensive. A young marine private boarded the plane by force and announced that he wished to go to Hong Kong. After being informed that he was not on the passenger list, he pulled out his .45 automatic and entered the cockpit. The crew was checking the idling engines and was ordered to take off under threats of death. The plane was surrounded by armed troops while its engines were switched off. Colonel Paul Watson, the air force officer in charge of Da Nang military base, worried that Clark would take the plane to North Vietnam; others believed the skyjacking to be part of the Tet offensive. Clark again ordered the crew to start the engines, and they complied. While the plane was taxiing, four-star General William Westmoreland, the U.S. commander in Vietnam, ordered tear-gas canisters to be lobbed into the empty passenger compartment. The Pan Am flight engineer grabbed Clark while his attention was thus diverted. William L. Clark, born on November 15, 1948, in Cleveland, Ohio, was sentenced by a U.S. Marine court-martial to one and a half years hard labor and a bad conduct discharge. He was given an additional sentence for crimes committed while in prison. His convictions were set aside on December 3, 1969, and he received a medical discharge for schizophrenia on September 2, 1970. The FAA profile was not relevant in the case of this white hijacker. 5086

February 12, 1968—Dominican Republic—A homemade bomb was found behind books on the bookshelf in the USIS Lincoln Library in Santo Domingo. The bomb was a timed incendiary type that appeared to have ignited but did not have sufficient power to get outside its cardboard container and therefore caused no damage. 0010

February 13, 1968—Uruguay—A Molotov cocktail was thrown outside the U.S. labor exhibit in Montevideo at approximately 10:30 P.M., causing very minor damage. 0011

February 15, 1968—Dominican Republic—The remains of a Molotov cocktail were found at the entrance of the Santiago de Los Caballeros Binational Center. It did not explode because the bottle contained only a mixture of gasoline, oil, and an external wick. The bottle appeared to have been broken on impact after being tossed, but the wick did not light. 0012

February 16, 1968—West Germany—At 7:45, the USIS facility at Cologne received an anonymous call threatening a bomb explosion. A search proved negative. 0013

February 16, 1968—Colombia—A time bomb of extreme power exploded on U.S. embassy grounds at 1:32 P.M. No personal injuries were reported, but property damage resulted. Pro-Vietcong leaflets were dropped near the scene. 0014

February 17, 1968—United States—A Piper Apache PA24, chartered to fly from Marathon in the Florida Keys to Miami, was hijacked by its charterer to Havana. Thomas J. Boynton, born in Kalamazoo, Michigan on February 2, 1937, had lost his job as a researcher at the Fort Custer Job Corps Center in January. In December, his wife had filed for divorce. The FAA profile was irrelevant in the case of this thirty-two-year-old white male who held a gun to the pilot's head once the plane was aloft. Boynton hoped to find a way to put his talents as a sociologist to work in Cuba, but he was used there as a common laborer and complained about the food, the climate, the work, and his sporadic imprisonment. The Cubans suspected that he could be a Central Intelligence Agency employee. The pilot and plane had been allowed to return to the United States after a few days. On November 1, 1969, Boynton was one of six American hijackers who sailed into Montreal on board the Cuban freighter *Luis Arces Bergnes*. At Montreal the group asked Canadian authorities to escort them to the border at Champlain. On November 2 they were rearraigned at Plattsburgh, New York, and turned over to U.S. marshals, who jailed them in lieu of bail. On May 12, 1970, Boynton was sentenced to twenty years for kidnapping. 5087

February 18, 1968—France—One person was killed and fourteen injured when a bomb exploded in the basement of the Paris home of the Yugoslavian ambassador. 0015

February 19, 1968—Italy—An anonymous call warned that a bomb would go off in the USIS library in Milan at 7 P.M. A police search was negative. 0016

February 20, 1968—Chile—At 7:30 P.M., an explosion went off on the patio of the Santiago Binational Center, causing $21,000 damage to the building. Police surmised that a single stick of dynamite had been thrown from an adjoining building. 0017

February 20, 1968—Israel—Palestinians used a bazooka to shell a paramilitary settlement at Nahal Colan in the vicinity of Jebine. 0018

February 21, 1968—United States—The Soviet embassy was bombed at 5:45 A.M. The bomb was placed by unknown individuals on the window sill of a ground-floor office, which suffered considerable damage. No one was reported injured by the blast. Several persons were in the embassy at the time, including Ambassador Anatoly F. Dobrynin. Charges were made from Moscow and Washington by the Soviets that police protection was inadequate, and Tass claimed that the bombing "could have been committed only with the connivance of the American authorities." White House press secretary George Christian termed the charges "utterly ridiculous." A police and FBI investigation was ordered. 0019

February 21, 1968—United States—Delta Airlines flight 843, a DC8 en route from Chicago to Miami, had just left Tampa bound for West Palm Beach when a man in a white cowboy hat, jeans, and tennis shoes got up from his seat and put an automatic pistol to the head of Joy Bell, a stewardess. After forcing her to open the cockpit door, he instructed the pilot to fly the 102 passengers and crew to Cuba aboard the $8.5 million jet. The hijacker put on the pilot's earphones to listen for possible ploys and never removed the gun from Bell's temple. It was learned that the hijacker was Lawrence M. Rhodes, born November 12, 1939, in Welch, West Virginia. The FAA profile was not relevant in this case of a white hijacker who was wanted in West Virginia for a 1967 payroll robbery. Upon landing in Havana, Rhodes was led away by Cuban authorities, who granted him asylum. The passengers reported being well treated and were given souvenir posters of Ché Guevara. An air force enlisted man who tried to persuade the passengers not to buy anything was separated from them for a time but was not harmed by the authorities. The plane and passengers were allowed to return after three hours. On February 10, 1970, Rhodes appeared in Spain, where he surrendered. He was committed to a mental institution, and the hijacking charges against him were dropped on April 1, 1971. He was returned to jail on July 8, 1971. On July 17, 1972, he was sentenced to twenty-five years for robbery, with the effective sentencing date being declared to be January 12, 1971. This was the first successful hijacking of an American commercial airliner since 1961. 5088

February 21, 1968—Israel—Palestinian terrorists damaged a water pipe and fuel in the vicinity of Nedt Hakikir, south of the Dead Sea. 0020

February 22, 1968—Ecuador—A bomb exploded at 1:35 P.M. in the Quito Binational Center, causing extensive damage to three basement rooms. Authorities believed the charge was a volume of black powder that had been shoved into the building through a grating. 0021

February 24, 1968—Israel—Palestinian terrorists fired five mortar shells into the collective settlement at Masada, causing slight damage but no injuries. 0022

March 1-2, 1968—Soviet Union—Following the bombing of the Soviet embassy in the United States, the U.S. embassy in Moscow received three anonymous telephone calls threatening retaliation in kind and one threatening demonstrations against the United States. 0023-0025

March 5, 1968—Colombia—An Avianca DC4 flying from Riohacha to Barranquilla was hijacked by three members of the National Liberation Army (ELN, a pro-Castro Colombian guerrilla group), and forced to fly to Santiago de Cuba. The plane and its thirty-six passengers and crew members, including an aide to the Colombian president, were hijacked shortly after takeoff by Jairo Ortiz Acosta, Aristides Villalobos Rico, and Salim Hussein Sami Awadalla, alias Sani Analaye, all of them armed. 0026

March 8, 1968—Argentina—The USIS office in Rosario was machine-gunned between 1 and 3 A.M., presumably from a cruising taxi that had been seen in the area. Nine bullet holes were found in the protective curtain and several holes in the walls of a partition in the public affairs officer's office. A note left by the attackers identified them as the Frente de Liberacion Nacionel del Vietnam del Sur. 0027

March 12, 1968—Chile—A homemade bomb exploded in the women's restroom on the second floor of the U.S. consulate outside the USIS offices in Santiago, causing extensive property damage but no injuries. 0028

March 12, 1968—United States—National Airlines flight 28, a DC8 traveling between Tampa and Miami, was hijacked to Havana by two Spanish-speaking gunmen. One of the passengers appeared to know the hijackers and began to moan, ''I am killed, I am killed.'' After drinking all the whisky in sight and passing out his personal papers to the fifty-nine people on board, including comedian Flip Wilson, he left with the hijackers. It appeared that he was being kidnapped, but it was later learned that he was a hijacker who had lost his courage. The trio were identified as Cuban exiles, all having been born in Camajuani, Cuba, and fit the FAA profile: Gilberto Carrazana y Gonzales, born November 19, 1934; Jésus Armenteros, born July 1, 1929; and Ramon Donato-Martin, born August 4, 1922. The passengers and plane were allowed to leave within two hours. Castro viewed such skyjackings as a way to keep Cuba in the news, remarking, ''There now almost exists an air route of those who take over planes for sport.'' Havana television called such hijackings an extra added attraction for American tourists, pointing out that when they arrived in Cuba, they were ''not only caressed by our tropical sun, but they take with them an indelible memory of the new Cuba.'' The trio were indicted on October 14, 1969, by a federal grand jury in the middle district of Florida. They remain fugitives. 5089

March 12, 1968—Guatemala—A bomb was thrown over the wall surrounding the U.S. marine guards house in Guatemala City, breaking numerous windows but injuring no one. It evidently came from a moving car. 0029

March 15, 1968—Austria—A time bomb, probably planted by Croatian exiles, was found and disarmed at the Yugoslavian consulate in Klagenfurt. 0030

March 16, 1968—Chile—The U.S. Cultural Center in Santiago was bombed at 8:50 P.M. by a device believed to be composed of three dynamite sticks. Floors, walls, and ceiling were badly damaged; and many windows were broken; total damage was estimated at $7,500. No personal injuries were reported. 0031

March 16, 1968—Mexico—A Mexican twin-engined charter plane, hired to fly from Cozumel to Isla de las Mujeres, Mexico, was hijacked by its charterer, an American black named Hemingway, another man, the hijacker's wife, and two children. The pilot and plane were allowed to return to Mexico, while the hijacker stayed in Cuba. 5090

March 17, 1968—Guatemala—Roman Catholic Archbishop Mario Casariego was kidnapped in his car while driving to his home. The Rebel Armed Forces were initially blamed for the action but issued a speedy denial of responsibility. The government immediately declared a state of siege, granting security forces the right of search and seizure without judicial warrants. After the archbishop was released a few days later, the chief of the Guatemalan police claimed that the kidnappers were a group of ultrarightists who had hoped to split the church and army from the government. However, when the church's leaders publicly supported the president and the army remained loyal, the group gave up on their scheme.

March 18, 1968—France—Five French students bombed the Paris offices of Trans-World Airlines, Chase Manhattan Bank, and the Bank of America a couple of hours before dawn, breaking windows. The five were arrested by the end of the week and claimed to be protesting the U.S. involvement in the Vietnam war. 0032-0034

March 18, 1968—Israel—A bus carrying schoolchildren from Tel Aviv on a trip to the Negev Desert was blown up when it hit a mine planted by Al Fatah twelve miles north of Elath. Two Israeli adults were killed and twenty-eight children injured in the blast. The Israelis retaliated by attacking the village of Karameh, which was believed to be a major Fatah base in Jordan. 150 guerrillas were killed and another 150 captured by the Israelis, who lost 29 dead and 70 wounded. The Jordanians intervened with tanks, and the Israelis retreated. The Palestinians have since viewed this engagement as a major victory. 0035

March 19, 1968—United States—Anti-Castro Cubans attempted to bomb the Miami branch of the Spanish National Tourist Office. 0036

March 19, 1968—Brazil—A sizable bomb exploded in the USIS library in São Paulo at 1:30 A.M., damaging one-quarter of the premises and injuring three young Brazilians who were standing in front of the building. The bomb apparently was placed just inside the building. 0037

March 21, 1968—Venezuela—An Avensa CV440 flying from Caracas to Maracaibo was hijacked to Cuba by four armed men. The plane and fifty people aboard were permitted to return to Cuba. The four were given asylum. 5091

March 24, 1968—Austria—A time bomb, probably planted by Croatian exiles, exploded in the Yugoslav consulate in Graz. 0038

March 25, 1968—Spain—A bomb exploded in the Madrid Casa Americana at 6:35 P.M. in a second-floor restroom. Extensive damage was reported, including buckled walls and damaged plumbing and wiring, with estimates of damage as high as several thousand dollars. A librarian was hospitalized with three broken ribs. 0039

March 25, 1968—Spain—Five minutes after the Casa bomb, a second one exploded in the U.S. embassy, breaking windows in the building and those of a car belonging to a defense attaché. 0040

April 4, 1968—United States—Civil rights leader Martin Luther King, Jr., was assassinated in Memphis, Tennessee, by an individual with a long-range rifle in a local motel. James Earl Ray, a white with a history of criminal acts, was arrested in the United Kingdom on June 8 and charged with the killing. Racial violence erupted in over one hundred American cities.

April 5, 1968—Ecuador—A small anti-Poncista group threw an incendiary bomb at the Binational Center, causing little damage. 0041

April 13, 1968—Canada—Two time bombs believed planted by Croatian exiles exploded in the Yugoslavian embassy in Ottawa. 0042

April 15, 1968—Brazil—An armored car of the French and Italian Bank was attacked. One hundred thousand new cruzeiros were stolen. (At 1970 exchange rates, $1US=4.15 cruzeiros.) 0043

April 18, 1968—Israel—Tel Aviv police informed the U.S. embassy that they had received a bomb threat against the facility. An armed police guard was posted at the front entrance to reinforce regular patrols and examine all packages brought in by visitors. At police request, additional contract guards were added at the rear entrances of the embassy. The marine security guard increased irregular inspections and patrols of interior and exterior areas. 0044

April 22, 1968—United States—The Mexican consulate in New York City was bombed by El Poder Cubano, an anti-Castro Cuban group. Nine individuals were arrested for the attack. (See next incident.) 0045

April 22, 1968—United States—El Poder Cubano bombed the Spanish National Tourist Office in New York City. On August 13, police seized a supply of arms in Johnsonburg, New Jersey, after seventeen bombings and bombing attempts in major American cities of offices of nations that traded with Cuba. Leaflets found at some of the sites referred to "Cuban Power" and "United Cuban Power." On October 23, nine Cuban exiles were arrested in New York City and charged with six of the bombings, including those in New York of the Mexican Consulate and the Spanish National Tourist Office, as well as with plotting to assassinate Cuban officials and embassy personnel and to invade Cuba, and with arson, reckless endangerment, criminal mischief, and illegal possession of weapons and explosives. The nine members of El Poder Cubano were identified as Carlos Fernandez, 24; Oscar I. Acevedo, 38; Gabriel Abay, 49; Guillermo Miguel, 38; Arturo Rodriguez Vives, 25; José Rodone, 55; Ivan Acost, 24; Ramiro Cortez, 18; and Edgar Rivas, 21. 0046

April 25, 1968—Algeria—An unsuccessful assassination attempt was made against President Boumédienne at 2 P.M. as the president's car was leaving the Palais du Gouvernement, by a pistol-wielding individual, who was immediately apprehended by the police. The president was rushed to the Central Military Hospital.

April 29, 1968—Brazil—At 5 A.M., a Molotov cocktail was thrown onto the property of the U.S. consulate general in Recife. The bomb fell short of the building and burned a small garden area. 0047

April 29, 1968—Dominican Republic—Police removed and disarmed a time bomb placed in the bathroom of the Binational Center in Santiago de los Caballeros. The device was in clear view, taped to a water pipe, and was composed of a pocket watch and black powder, which was to be ignited electrically. The watch appeared to have stopped running immediately after being set. 0048

May 2, 1968—Uruguay—An unexploded Molotov cocktail was found on the steps of the main Binational Center building in Montevideo. No other attempts to damage USIS or USIS–affiliated buildings were reported. 0049

May 24, 1968—Canada—At 1:55 A.M., an explosion, probably caused by dynamite, damaged the entrance door of the U.S. embassy in Quebec, as well as breaking a number of windows. No injuries were reported. 0050

May 24, 1968—Belgium—A Molotov cocktail exploded in the basement window well of the USIS library in Brussels, causing no injuries. Minor physical damage was sustained in the living room of the concierge. A strong odor of gasoline was noted, but no fire broke out. In front of the building, police found political leaflets that criticized U.S. policy in Vietnam. 0051

May 26, 1968—United States—A bomb placed by El Poder Cubano damaged the Miami residence of the Mexican consul general. 0052

May 30, 1968—United States—El Poder Cubano bombed the Spanish National Tourist Office in New York City. 0053

June 5, 1968—United States—At a celebration of his winning the Democratic primary in California, presidential candidate Senator Robert F. Kennedy was killed by a Jordanian nationalist, Sirhan Bishara Sirhan, twenty-four, an eleven-year resident of California. Sirhan fired a pistol at Kennedy while the latter was passing through the hotel's serving kitchen. Five others were wounded in Los Angeles's Ambassador Hotel. Sirhan was immediately seized by members of Kennedy's staff and is currently in prison. His release was demanded in a subsequent terrorist incident (March 1, 1973). 0054

June 7, 1968—Bahamas—Haitian Consul Joseph Antoine Dorce was assassinated. Four Haitian exiles, members of the Haitian Coalition, a New York-based anti-Duvalier organization, were convicted of the murder, but their death sentences were voided on April 8, 1969, by the Bahamas Appeals Court. On February 8 the organization denied responsibility for the assassination, while admitting that the four were members of the group. 0055

June 19, 1968—Dominican Republic—A Venezuelan Airlines (VIASA) DC9, flying from Santo Domingo, Dominican Republic, to Curaçao, Netherlands Antilles, was hijacked to Cuba by three Dominican leftists identified only as Vargas, Radhames, and Mendez. The trio remained in Cuba, while the plane and passengers were permitted to depart the following day. A Dominican court sentenced them to twenty years on August 13, 1970. 0056

June 21, 1968—United States—The New York City branch of the Spanish National Tourist Office was again bombed by El Poder Cubano. 0057

June 29, 1968—United States—Southeast Airlines flight 101, a DC3 flying from Marathon, Florida, to Key West, was hijacked by a black fugitive gunman and diverted to Havana. The hijacker used the alias of E. H. Carter and probably met the FAA profile. No further identification was made of him, and he remains a fugitive. The fifteen passengers were allowed to leave the next day and the twin-engined plane the day after that; however, the pilot, thirty-six-year-old George Prellezo del Barrio, a former Cuban, was imprisoned by the Cubans. On the day of the hijacking, Prellezo was about to celebrate the eighth anniversary of his flying a Cuban Aeropostal on its regularly scheduled run to Miami. At that time, he informed immigration authorities that he feared arrest in Cuba and requested asylum. Another Cuban crew flew the plane back home, and Prellezo became a naturalized US citizen, married a Puerto Rican, and began a family. He flew the plane on its Miami-Marathon-Key West route when a coworker became ill. Havana radio announced that the pilot would be tried for desertion. His chances appeared bleak because the U.S. government had been unable to free the eight-two surviving crewmen of the *Pueblo*, who were still being held in Wonsan harbor in North Korea. But on the same day, a U.S. Army DC8 charter overflew Soviet airspace and was forced to land, loaded with 214 soldiers destined for duty in Vietnam. The Soviets released the plane and crew, providing an example for the Cubans. On July 12, the U.S. State Department permitted Prellezo's wife to go to Cuba, and Castro allowed her entry. With the help of the Swiss embassy in Havana, Olga and George Prellezo were allowed to fly to Mexico City on July 22 on their way back to the United States. 5092

July 1, 1968—United States—Northwest Airlines flight 714, a B727 en route from Chicago to Miami, was hijacked to Cuba by Mario Velasquez Fonseca, a Cuban born in Guantánamo on June 30, 1934, who had come to the United States earlier in the year. The nine-man crew was allowed to fly the plane out of Havana immediately. The eighty-five passengers were brought back on the plane normally used for the Cuban refugee airlift. The hijacker, who probably met the FAA profile, was allowed to remain in Cuba. 5093

July 4, 1968—United States—John Hamilton Morrow, born in Martin, Minnesota, on September 8, 1920, was flying on TWA flight 329 in the custody of U.S. marshals when he whispered to the stewardess that he had dynamite and would blow up the B727 if it did not fly to Mexico. The pilot of the Kansas City, Kansas, to Las Vegas, Nevada, flight pretended to comply but landed at Las Vegas. The white male who did not meet the FAA profile pleaded guilty to charges of escape and was sentenced to an additional five years, to run consecutively with his current sentence, on June 16, 1969. 5094

July 4, 1968—United States—El Poder Cubano bombed the Canadian consulate and tourist office in New York City. 0058

July 4, 1968—United States—El Poder Cubano bombed the Australian National Tourist Office in New York City. 0059

July 7, 1968—United States—El Poder Cubano bombed the Japanese National Tourist Office in New York City, slightly injuring two passersby with flying glass. 0060

July 9, 1968—United States—El Poder Cubano bombed the U.N. mission of Yugoslavia. 0061

July 9, 1968—United States—El Poder Cubano bombed the Cuban mission to the United Nations. 0062

July 11, 1968—United States—The U.S. Department of State announced that free space would be made available on planes for all Cubans who wished to return to Cuba. No questions would be asked by the U.S. government. No one applied.

July 12, 1968—United States—An Island City Flying Service Cessna 210, a small plane chartered to fly from Key West to Miami, was hijacked by Leonard S. Bendicks, born in Renovo, Pennsylvania, on June 16, 1935. He diverted the plane to Cuba. The FAA profile did not apply in the case of the white teacher from Williamsport, Pennsylvania, who was deported to the United States in September 1968. Bendicks was apprehended by U.S. authorities on September 24, 1968, at Champlain, New York. He was found competent to stand trial and was sentenced to ten years on a charge of kidnapping on March 4, 1971. He was granted a three-year parole on June 27, 1972. The pilot and plane had been permitted to return to the United States. 5095

July 12, 1968—United States—Delta Airlines flight 977, a Convair 880 flying from Philadelphia to Houston with a stopover in Baltimore, was the scene of an attempted hijacking to Cuba by Oran Daniel Richards, born in Columbus, Georgia, on May 26, 1935. Richards was described by passengers as a lanky six-footer with close-cropped hair and receding hairline, wearing clear-rimmed glasses, who met the FAA profile. One of the forty-eight passengers was Senator James O. Eastland (D-Miss.), at whom Richards pointed a silver-plated automatic, threatening to kill him. Eastland resumed his seat, and Richards told stewardess Elaine Hawes to let him into the cockpit. Once there, he talked to flight engineer Glenn Smith, pilot Captain Forrest Dines, and the copilot, informing them that he was a forklift operator in Springfield, Ohio, and complained that he was dying of cancer. Smith appealed to his moral sense, as well as pointing out that the plane had only enough fuel to reach Houston. After breaking down in tears, the hijacker handed his pistol to the captain, and allowed the plane, scheduled to arrive at Houston at 8:04 P.M., to make an emergency landing in Miami at 9:44 P.M. The FBI led Richards away. He was committed to a hospital in Springfield, Missouri, on September 3, 1969, after all charges against him had been dropped. He was released from a state mental institution in Dayton, Ohio, on January 10, 1970. It was learned that he had gone to police previously, admitting a compulsion to shoot someone but was discharged from Columbus State Mental Hospital on August 31, 1959. 5096

July 14, 1968—United States—The Chicago branch of the Mexican National Tourist Office was bombed by El Poder Cubano. 0064

July 15, 1968—United States—A hand grenade was thrown at the residence of the Cuban ambassador to the United Nations in New York City. 0065

July 15, 1968—United States—New York City police found and dismantled a bomb in front of the French National Tourist Office two minutes before it was set to explode. The bomb had been placed by El Poder Cubano. 0066

July 16, 1968—United States—Newark, New Jersey, police found and dismantled an El Poder Cubano bomb placed outside of the offices of the Mexican consulate and the Mexican national airline, Aeronaves de Mexico. 0067

July 17, 1968—United States—National Airlines flight 1064, a DC8 flying from Los Angeles to Miami, was hijacked between Houston and New Orleans by Rogelio M. Hernandez Leyva, who was born in Guantanamo, Cuba, on June 8, 1944. He waved a pistol and what he claimed was a hand grenade wrapped in cloth and told the pilot to fly to Havana. He allowed the plane to refuel the plane in New Orleans but would not allow the sixty-four passengers to disembark. He also would not allow the pilot to switch off the engines during the refueling. When asked by the pilot if he was aware of the State Department's shuttle service to Cuba, he vowed to use it the next time, stating, "Fidel ordered me back to Havana, dead or alive." The Cubans disarmed the hijacker in Havana, discovering the hand grenade to be a bottle of Old Spice shaving lotion. The hijacker had entered the United States illegally a year earlier and was allowed to remain in Cuba. The plane and crew were permitted to return home immediately but argued that the runways at José Martí Airport were too short to allow a safe takeoff with passengers. The passengers were well treated. They were bused eighty-five miles to Varadero and flown back on the refugee airlift plane. The hijacker was indicted on August 28, 1969, by a federal grand jury in the eastern district of Louisiana and remains a fugitive. 5097

July 18, 1968—Denmark—A time bomb was discovered and disarmed at the Yugoslav embassy in Copenhagen. Prime suspects were a Croatian exile group operating from Sweden. 0068

July 18, 1968—Norway—A time bomb was discovered and disarmed at the Yugoslav embassy in Oslo. Prime suspects were a Croatian exile group operating from Sweden. 0069

July 19, 1968—United States—El Poder Cubano bombed offices of the Mexican National Tourist Council, Mexican Travel Agency, Air France, Japan Air Lines, and the Shell Oil Building in Los Angeles. 0070—0074

July 20, 1968—Ecuador—A small bomb exploded at the Quito home of the U.S. public affairs officer. Minimum damage was caused by the early-morning explosion. 0075

July 22, 1968—India—Twenty Indian students broke into the U.S. consulate in Madras and threatened to burn the watchman. They instead set fire to a jeep and broke all the windows in the mobile unit. 0076

July 22, 1968—Italy—An El Al Boeing 707 on its way from Rome to Tel Aviv's Lod Airport was hijacked by three members of the Popular Front for the Liberation of Palestine. The two Palestinians and one Syrian attacked twenty minutes after takeoff, threatening to blow up the plane with grenades. They pistol-whipped the navigator, and then fired a shot in the cockpit. Captain Oded Abarbanel, the pilot, did not offer further resistance, and one of the skyjackers aided in bringing the plane with its ten crew members and thirty-eight passengers to Algiers' Dar al-Bayda Airport. (Two of the hijackers would engage in future actions. Yousef Khatib led a group of skyjackers in a February 22, 1972, Indian incident, and Ali Shafik Ahmed Taha, "Captain Rafat," joined Black September for a hijacking on May 8, 1972.) The Algerians had not been informed of the PFLP's plans, and one of PFLP leader George Habash's aides, who had arrived in Algiers the night before, asked a high Algerian security official to demand full diplomatic and material support for the group's demands, which was the release of an unspecified number of Arabs from Israeli jails. The trio initially was lauded, but they were refused exit visas on their fake passports the next day and held at a military camp in Algiers for the balance of the negotiations. The Algerians immediately released the twenty-three non-Israeli passengers, flying them to Paris aboard an Air Algerie plane. However, the ten Israeli crew members and twelve other passengers, including four women and three children, were held in a barracks near the airport. Within five days, the women, children, and three stewardesses were allowed to fly to Geneva and on to Israel. The PLO and Fatah sent a six-man delegation to Algiers to request that the other hostages be held until the release of twelve hundred Arab prisoners from Israeli jails, arguing that because Israel had claimed that one Israeli life was worth one hundred Arabs, the trade was fair. President Boumédienne was caught in the middle; the Arab nations began making their own demands. Iraq demanded the return of an MIG21 stolen by an Iraqi pilot who flew it to Israel in 1965. Egypt wanted Israel to withdraw from the occupied Sinai. Jordan wanted the old city of Jerusalem. Syria demanded the Golan Heights. International pressure against the continued detention of the hostages grew as well. The International Federation of Air Line Pilots' Associations (IFALPA) announced on August 13 that it would begin a boycott of Algeria on August 19. Swissair, Alitalia, and Air France made similar plans. African states threatened to boycott an upcoming African summit conference. On August 17, the IFALPA boycott was called off when it was learned that negotiations were taking place via the Italian consulate in Algiers. On September 1, the hostages were flown to Rome on an Italian jet and the French provided pilots to fly the $7.5 million B707 out of Algiers. On September 2, Israel Galilee, Israel's minister of information, informed the International Red Cross that, as a humanitarian gesture suggested by the Italian government, sixteen Arabs captured prior to the June 1967 war would be released. The PFLP criticized Algeria for releasing the hostages without consulting them. It was learned after the incident that the skyjackers had been studying passenger manifests and El Al logistics in Rome since mid-July (Israel charged that Egyptian intelligence agents aided in this operation), hoping to seize General Ariel Sharon, commander of the armored forces in Sinai in the recent war. The group believed Sharon to be on the plane they hijacked because one of them had seen a stewardess give what appeared to be a diplomatic pouch to the pilot. But Sharon had taken a direct flight from Paris after arriving from the United States. Algerian sources accused the Egyptian intelligence services of setting up the incident to embarrass Boumédienne. Other sources indicated that the PFLP skyjacking operations were planned by Dr. Wadieh Haddad shortly after the 1967 war. The PFLP charged that El Al had flown military spare parts during the war and was thus a legitimate target of war. Algeria wound up aiding a group of skyjackers in their demands, setting a precedent for future incidents, including the famed Entebbe affair of July 1976. 0077

July 30, 1968—United States—The British consulate in Los Angeles was bombed by anti-Castro Cubans, possibly El Poder Cubano. 0078

July 31, 1968—Philippines—Bandits entered the Villa Angela home of a Voice of America employee. The group tied up the individual and his wife while they ransacked the house. He was then abducted in his own car. When the car slowed down at the gate, the employee opened the door and rolled out. One of the bandits went after him and inflicted a slight stab wound in his abdomen.

August 3, 1968—United States—El Poder Cubano bombed the Bank of Tokyo Trust Company in New York City. 0079

August 4, 1968—United States—A Naples Airlines Cessna 182, chartered to fly near Naples, Florida, by a man who identified himself as Stewart Orth, was hijacked to Cuba. It was learned that the hijacker, accompanied by his three-year-old daughter who had been in the custody of his divorced wife, was Willis Jessie, a U.S. Army deserter from Fort Benning, Georgia, who was born on May 22, 1941, in Ethel, West Virginia. Havana authorities allowed the white hijacker, for whom the FAA profile was irrelevant, to remain in Cuba; the plane and pilot were immediately released. Jessie voluntarily returned to the United States via Mexico on January 10, 1969. He told a district court judge that he did not want his daughter to grow up in a ''slave country'' such as Cuba. His attorney asked for a delay in the trial due to the public mood regarding hijackers, but the judge doubted that the hostility would change and sentenced Jessie to ten years on June 61, 1969, for kidnapping, a charge to which Jessie had pleaded guilty. He was paroled on July 28, 1971. 5098

August 6, 1968—Israel—Palestinian terrorists fired three bazooka shells into the town of Ein Yahav, shattering an empty infirmary but injuring no one. The fleeing band was intercepted by an Israeli patrol, who killed five and wounded two attackers. 0080

August 8, 1968—Australia—Melbourne police advised the U.S. consulate general that it had received a bomb threat. The consulate was evacuated, but no device was found. 0081

August 8, 1968—United States—An underwater mine exploded, seriously damaging the British cargo ship *Caribbean Venture*, which was in Miami's Biscayne Bay. El Poder Cubano claimed responsibility. 0082

August 10, 1968—Turkey—Two firebombs were thrown at the USIS office in Izmir, but only one ignited, causing minor damage. Turkish police arrested a communist suspect. 0083

August 13, 1968—United States—Police raided a Johnsonburg, New Jersey, farm, thirteen miles east of the Delaware Water Gap, seizing a half ton of dynamite, automatic weapons, and crates of ammunition, as well as a uniform of the 2506th Cuban Assault Brigade of the Bay of Pigs, an anti-Castro organization. Michael A. DeCarolis, thirty-two, was arrested.

August 17, 1968—United States—En El Poder Cubano bomb damaged a Mexican airline office in Miami. 0084

August 18, 1968—Israel—Al Fatah exploded three grenades in Jerusalem's Jewish section, injuring eight Israelis and two Americans. One Arab was arrested for questioning. In retaliation, Israeli youths attacked east Jerusalem's Arab section, hurling stones at ships, buses, and taxis. 0085

August 19, 1968—Israel—An Al Fatah bomb went off a half mile away from the Parliament building in Jerusalem, causing no damage or injuries. 0086

August 21, 1968—Israel—A bomb planted by Palestinian terrorists exploded in the garden of the U.S. consulate in east Jerusalem, shattering windows but causing no injuries. 0087

August 22, 1968—Bahamas—An Island Flying Service Cessna Skymaster 336, chartered to fly from Nassau to Exuma, was hijacked by a person identifying himself as Bill McBridge, who diverted the plane to Cuba. The FAA profile did not apply. 5099

August 28, 1968—Guatemala—John Gordon Mein, fifty-four, U.S. ambassador to Guatemala since September 1965, became the first American ambassador assassinated by terrorists. As his limousine was driving to the embassy after a luncheon, a car forced his vehicle to the side of a downtown Guatemala City street, and a small truck blocked it from behind. Several youths armed with automatic weapons approached and ordered Mein out of the car. He opened the door on the other side and attempted to run but was struck from behind by a burst of submachine gun fire, which killed him instantly. The chauffeur was unharmed. The Rebel Armed Forces issued a statement the next day claiming that they had planned to kidnap Mein and demand the release of Camilo Sanchez, an FAR leader who had been arrested by the government on August 24. The U.S. State Department requested "a full investigation of all the circumstances" from the Guatemalan government, who proclaimed a state of martial law for thirty days. President Julio Cesar Mendez Montenegro later claimed that the assasins had been identified and offered a $10,000 reward for information leading to their arrest. Guatemalan police traced the automobile, which had been rented for the FAR on August 22, and went to the apartment of

Michele Firk, a young member of the French Communist party and a graduate of the Institute of Higher Cinematographic Studies, who had arrived in Guatemala in July. When the police entered her home, she shot and killed herself to avoid interrogation. Little was known of her activities, and French colleagues would only say that she worked with "an important man named Julien or Raymond." Four FAR members who later confessed to complicity in the assassination were among those whose release was demanded in the March 31, 1970, Von Spreti case. 0088

September 3, 1968—United States—Croatian terrorists planted a bomb aboard the *Kupres*, a Yugoslav ship, in Charleston harbor. An FBI tip arrived in time for the bomb to be disarmed. 0089

September 4, 1968—Israel—Three bombs went off in and near the central bus station in Tel Aviv, killing one Israeli and wounding seventy-one. Four hundred Arabs were arrested for questioning. On September 6, nineteen Arabs believed responsible for this attack and other bombings in Jerusalem were arrested. 0090

September 10, 1968—Uruguay—Five million pesos were stolen from a branch of the Bank of London and South America by Tupamaros. Prevailing exchange rates were $1U.S.=250 pesos. 0090

September 11, 1968—Canada—An Air Canada Viscount four-engine turbo-prop flying from St. John, New Brunswick, to Toronto was hijacked by gunman Charles Lavern Beasley, a U.S. citizen who wished to go to Cuba. He allowed the plane to land in Montreal for refueling and was talked out of his attempt by an RCMP officer who offered him guarantees of nonprosecution and possible asylum. Beasley claimed to be a member of a U.S. Black Power group and was fleeing the CIA. Dallas police claimed that he was wanted in his home town on a bank robbery charge. He was sentenced to a Montreal prison for six years on December 10, 1968, and was deported to the United States on March 25, 1971. He had been sentenced to ten-year and five-year concurrent terms for bank robbery and a related offense on August 19, 1968. 5100

September 13, 1968—Israel—Al Saiqa attacked a military police headquarters in Baniyas, an Israeli-occupied area of the Golan Heights. The facility was destroyed and all occupants were killed.

September 16, 1968—United States—El Poder Cubano terrorists shot at the Polish freighter *Polanika* with a rifle in the port of Miami. On November 15, Dr. Orlando Bosch, forty-one, Barbaro Balans and José Diaz Morejon were convicted of the charge. Bosch was also convicted of sending threatening telegrams to the heads of state of Spain, Mexico, and the United Kingdom. 0092

September 19, 1968—Israel—Five members of Al Fatah infiltrated eleven miles past the Jordan River cease-fire line and ambushed an Israeli army patrol in the vicinity of Jenin. All of the terrorists died. One member of the patrol died, and four were injured.

September 20, 1968—Puerto Rico—Eastern Airlines flight 950, a B720 flying from San Juan to Miami, was hijacked over the Bahamas by José Antonio Suarez Garcia and forced to fly to Havana. The hijacker, a Latin who fit the FAA profile, was born in Yateras, Cuba, on February 13, 1943, and claimed that he returned to Cuba to be reunited with his family. The forty-six passengers were given a bus ride to Varadero and a special Eastern Airlines Electra flight home from Cuba. After twelve hours on the ground, the crew departed with the plane at 10 P.M. after an overnight stay in the Hotel International. It was later learned that the hijacker had entered the United States illegally on July 26, 1968, and had been examined for psychiatric disturbance. A complaint was filed in district court in San Juan on June 16, 1969, but Garcia remains a fugitive. 5101

September 22, 1968—Colombia—An Avianca Airlines Boeing 727, flying from Barranquilla to Cartagena with seventy-one passengers and a crew of six, was hijacked by Ramon Garcia, who diverted the plane to Camaguey in central Cuba. The plane was immediately released and returned to Barranquilla without the hijacker. The airport security search had failed to turn up the knife and gun Garcia was carrying. 5102

September 22, 1968—Colombia—An Avianca Airlines DC4 flying from Barranquilla to Santa Marta with fifty-six passengers and a crew of four was hijacked by Carlos Londono, who diverted it to Santiago de Cuba. The plane returned the next day. There was no information on the hijacker's fate. The airport security search had failed to turn up the knife and gun Londono was carrying. 5103

October 1, 1968—Argentina—Two Molotov cocktails exploded on the sidewalk outside the U.S. embassy in Buenos Aires shortly after midnight, causing no damage. Pamphlets were found nearby signed ''Movemento Peronista.'' 0093

October 3, 1968—Ecuador—Student demonstrators in Guayaquil threw ten Molotov cocktails over the wall into the consulate general's garage, causing no damage. 0094

October 3, 1968—Argentina—In the early morning, a bomb exploded next to the Binational Center building but caused no injuries or damage in Córdoba. 0095

October 3, 1968—Argentina—A local guard at the U.S. Atoms-in-Action exhibit in Buenos Aires surprised two men placing an object in the USIA exhibit structure. The two fled, and as the guard picked up the object, it exploded and burned his hands, also tearing a large hole in the roof of the structure housing the exhibits. 0096

October 6, 1968—Mexico—An Aeromaya Airlines twin-engine Hawker Siddeley 748 turboprop, flying from Cozumel to Mérida, was hijacked over the Isla de Mujeres by thirty-five-year-old Judith Vazquez, an Argentine citizen residing in Mexico. Shortly after the plane took off, she ordered the pilot, Captain Ricardo Erosa, to fly to Cuba. The crew of four and fourteen passengers were allowed to return to Mexico. The hijacker, her twelve-year-old daughter Sylvia, and two-month-old son Ernesto stayed in Cuba. 5104

October 7, 1968—Uruguay—Tupamaros stole 11 million pesos from a branch of the Bank of London and South America. 0097

October 7, 1968—Dominican Republic—Two explosive devices believed to contain C-4 plastics were discovered and disarmed in Santo Domingo, one on the lawn of the marine security guard's residence and the other in front of the USIS. 0099-0100

October 8, 1968—Dominican Republic—A group of youths threw three Molotov cocktails at the entrance of the Santiago de los Caballeros Binational Center entrance. The director and a messenger extinguished the fire, which caused slight damage to the floor and porch but no injuries. 0098

October 9, 1968—Argentina—A bomb exploded in the early morning hours in Córdoba, shattering the ground-floor windows of the Binational Center library, as well as the windows in the director's office above the library. Several bookshelves were also destroyed by the bomb, which was planted at the side of the building. 0101

October 9, 1968—Bolivia—A bomb went off on the ground floor of the entrance to the USIS building in La Paz, which also houses a local insurance company. The bomb appeared intended for the USIS, but it seemed that the bomber did not know precisely which offices were used by the USIS. 0102

October 12, 1968—Brazil—Two members of the Popular Revolutionary Vanguard machine-gunned U.S. Army Captain Charles R. Chandler, thirty, in front of his home in São Paulo. The two sped away in a car after leaving pamphlets claiming that Chandler was a "Vietnam war criminal" (Chandler had served a year in Vietnam) who had been sent to Brazil "to train war criminals and show them the most advanced techniques of torture and cruelty." The VPR said that the killing was "a warning to all his followers who one day or another will answer for their actions to the revolutionary tribunal." Chandler was studying Brazilian and Portuguese history at the University of São Paulo before teaching at West Point. On October 14, Brazilian police arrested a São Paulo dentist, José Luis Andrade Maciel, who they believed planned the attack. Onofre Pinto, a former air force sergeant, and Ivens Marchetti, an architect, were charged in this case and were among the fifteen freed in the September 4, 1969, Elbrick kidnapping. 0103

October 14, 1968—Brazil—An unidentified object was discovered inside the gates of the Fortaleza Binational Center. Local newspapers described it as a valise containing eleven dynamite bombs with enough explosive power to demolish the building. 0104

October 16, 1968—Argentina—A bomb exploded inside the USIS library in Buenos Aires, blowing out plate-glass windows and damaging the interior. The resulting fire caused no injuries. 0105

October 18, 1968—Brazil—An anonymous bomb threat was received at the USIS office in Santos. A search was negative. 0106

October 23, 1968—United States—El Poder Cubano terrorists were arrested after an unsuccessful assassination attempt against the Cuban U.N. ambassador in New York. The ambassador was not injured. 0107

October 23, 1968—United States—A Key West Airlines Cessna 177 chartered to fly from Key West to Dry Tortugas Island was hijacked by Alben William Barkley Truitt, the grandson of a former U.S. vice-president, born on December 16, 1933 in St. Louis. The white hijacker, for whom the FAA profile was not applicable, forced the pilot, Charles Oliveros, employed by Key West Aviation Center, to fly to Cuba. The plane and pilot returned the following day. The hijacker was under arrest in Cuba until January 1969, when he was put aboard a ship going to France. He got off at St. John, New Brunswick, and was arrested at Champlain, New York, on February 8, 1969. On August 13, 1969, he was convicted of air piracy and kidnapping and received two twenty-year terms to run consecutively. He was paroled on September 11, 1972. Truitt claimed that hijackers were no longer treated by Cuba as heroes and reported, "Some, I was told by people of the Department of State Security, were imprisoned immediately. Others, I was told, were sent to work camps." 5105

October 26, 1968—West Germany—Three prominent Croatian émigrés known for their anticommunist leadership were found murdered in a Munich apartment. 0108

October 27, 1968—Brazil—A Sears Roebuck store was bombed. 0109

October 30, 1968—Mexico—Juan Francisco Garcia Zurita was unsuccessful in his attempt to hijack a Mexican SEASA C46 flying from Tampico to Reynosa. The plane landed in Brownsville, Texas. Zurita was extradited to Mexico. 5106

October 31, 1968—Ecuador—The U.S. chargé, visiting the Quito Binational Center, examined a thick volume on the library shelf. He discovered that it contained two sticks of dynamite, which had failed to detonate because of a fuse malfunction. 0110

November 2, 1968—United States—Roger Allen Pastorcich, born on February 27, 1951, in Bay Minette, Alabama, attempted to hijack Eastern Airlines flight 224, a DC9 flying from Mobile to Chicago, while it was parked in Birmingham, Alabama. The copilot diverted his attention, and the pilot grabbed the shotgun away from the white youth, for whom the FAA profile was not applicable. Pastorcich, who wanted to go to Saigon, was charged with carrying a weapon aboard an aircraft. Because he was a juvenile, he was placed on probation on July 18, 1969, after being in juvenile detention. He was placed under psychiatric care and was finally released on December 23, 1970. 5107

November 4, 1968—United States—National Airlines flight 186, a B727 en route from Houston to Miami via New Orleans, was hijacked to Havana by Raymond Johnson, Jr., a black who met the FAA profile, who was born on January 8, 1947, in Cheneyville, Louisiana. He renamed the plane the *Republic of New Africa* and pointed his .38 revolver at stewardess Sandra O'Brien, forcing her to collect $405 from the fifty-seven passengers. He did not attempt to rob the eight crew members, being content to call the passengers "economic devils," hitting the pilot over the head with his gun, and grinding the copilot's glasses underfoot. The Cubans immediately returned the money of the self-identified Black Panther. The hijacker was indicted on June 13, 1969, by federal grand jury in the eastern district of Louisiana and remains a fugitive. Twelve days later, he gave an interview to reporters in Havana, complaining that American black militants were not treated as revolutionaries but rather were isolated and imprisoned, subject to arrest for criticizing the Cubans. He asked Panthers in the United States to protest at the Cuban U.N. mission on behalf of Panthers in Cuba. Observers suggested that Eldridge Cleaver had overseen Johnson's speech and noted that there have been no hijackings to Cuba by black militants since Cleaver moved to Algeria. 5108

November 6, 1968—Philippines—A Philippine Airlines Fokker twin-engined plane flying from Aub to Manila was hijacked by four men who killed one passenger and wounded another, while robbing everyone. Upon landing in Manila, the hijackers escaped. One of the group, M. Rabuya, received a death sentence, and was electrocuted. 5109

November 8, 1968—France—An Olympic Airlines B707 flying from Paris to Athens was hijacked thirty minutes out of Orly Airport by two Italians, Umberto Giovine and Maurizio Panichi, who forced the plane back to Paris. Armed with a pistol and hand grenade, they passed out leaflets to the 130 passengers, telling them that they were being punished for flying to Greece, whose junta they opposed. The Paris press was sympathetic, but Olympic promised to prosecute "ruthlessly." Giovine received eight months, his partner, six months. 5110

November 10, 1968—Belgium—A bomb was found at the Yugoslav embassy in Brussels. Croatian exiles were suspected. 0111

November 15, 1968—United States—Nine anti-Castro Cuban exiles were convicted in federal court in Miami of conspiracy to damage ships of countries trading with Cuba. Among the defendants were Orlando Bosch, Aimee Miranda, Andrew Gonzalez, Marco Rodriguez Ramos, Jorge Luiz Gutierrez Ulla, Paulina Gutierrez, and Jésus Dominguez Benitez, who were each given sentences ranging from one to ten years. 0112

November 18, 1968—Mexico—A CMA DC6 four-engine propeller plane, en route from Mérida to Mexico City, was hijacked by two men who diverted it to Havana. The captain, José Ruiz Hernandez, reported that Hugo Torres pulled a homemade bomb consisting of seven sticks of dynamite ten minutes after the plane was airborne. Military police at Havana led the duo from the plane, which was allowed to return to Mérida. 5111

November 19, 1968—United States—A bomb went off in the lavatory of a Continental Airlines B707 flying from Los Angeles to Denver while it was flying over Gunnison, Colorado. None of the sixty-three pasengers and eight crew was injured by the resulting fire, which was quickly extinguished by the crew. The aircraft landed safely, and one of the passengers was arrested.

November 22, 1968—Israel—A bomb planted in the Jewish section of Jerusalem killed ten Israeli Jews and two Arabs and wounded fifty-five others, while destroying fruit and vegetable stalls and several nearby shops, apartments, and automobiles. Police reported that the explosives were hidden in a car parked in the crowded Mahane Yehuda market place two hours before the blast. Five hundred Arabs were rounded up for questioning; all but thirty were free three days later. The PFLP claimed credit for the blast, stating that it was "in retaliation for Israeli terrorist actions against our people" in the occupied territories. 0113

November 23, 1968—United States—Eastern Airlines flight 73, a B727 en route from Chicago to Miami with eighty-three passengers, was diverted to Havana by five armed Cuban males who met the FAA profile. They were accompanied by a woman and three small children, who were believed related to one of the hijackers. During the hijacking, one of the children was brought into the cockpit to see the bright array of dials and lights. The passengers were returned via an airlift flight. The plane was returned after twenty hours in Havana. The group was indicted on March 10, 1971, by a federal grand jury in the western district of Kentucky. They were identified as native Cubans: Aramis Suarez Garcia, born August 1, 1946, in Yateras; Miguel Mayor Valasques, born September 24, 1934, in Guantánamo; Alberto Arroyo Quintero, born September 12, 1949, in Cuba; Irardo Mendoze Viera, born August 3, 1938 in Havana; Teresa Nunez de Mendoza, born September 4, 1930 in Orte. They are still fugitives. 5112

November 24, 1968—United States—Pan American flight 281, a B707 flying from New York to San Juan, was hijacked to Havana by three Puerto Rican males who met the FAA profile. They were accompanied by a woman and small child. Although they were armed with knives and a gun, they attempted to calm the passengers by ordering them drinks and paying the stewardess. All ninety-six passengers were returned via an airlift plane, and the B707 was allowed to leave Havana after six hours. The hijackers, who were arrested by Cuban authorities, were identified as José Rafael Rios Cruz, born January 1941 in Barceloneta, Puerto Rico; Luis Armando Pena Soltren, born January 15, 1943 in Mayaguez, Puerto Rico; and Miguel I. Castro Cruz. The Air Line Pilots Association called upon President Johnson to "take immediate action" against hijackers. The trio was indicted by a federal grand jury in December 23, 1968, in the southern district of New York. David Gonzalez and Alejandro Figuera were arrested in New York and charged with conspiracy but were acquitted of aiding and abetting air piracy. Rios Cruz was apprehended in San Juan on August 2, 1975, and was sentenced to fifteen years. Castro Cruz was arrested in February 3, 1976, in San Juan, and received a twelve-year sentence on May 4, 1976. 5113

November 30, 1968—United States—Eastern Airlines flight 532, a B720 flying from Miami to Dallas with eighty-six passengers, was hijacked to Havana shortly after takeoff by a Cuban exile who "just couldn't stand life in the U.S." The plane and crew were allowed to depart after a four and a half hour wait. The passengers were given a bus ride to Varadero where they stayed overnight and put on board a special Eastern flight. Reports listed the hijacker as J. Sanchez or J. Lopez or Miguel Montesino Sanchez, born September 14, 1924, in Pinar del Río, Cuba, a Latin who met the FAA profile. He was indicted on April 9, 1969, by a federal grand jury in the southern district of Florida and remains a fugitive. Republican congressmen called for a nation-wide attack on hijacking and all other crimes. President-elect Nixon suggested bulletproofing the cockpits, an idea that was quietly dropped later. 5114

December 2, 1968—Cuba—The Cuban government announced on December 16 that it had captured five anti-Castro Cuban exiles two days after their landing at the northwestern port of Cabañas, thirty-eight miles southwest of Havana. The report noted that Ernesto Diaz Rodriguez and Emilio Nazario Perez Sargent were members of Alpha 66 and the Second Front of Escambray, which had merged their operations. 0114

December 3, 1968—United States—National Airlines flight 1439, a B727 flying from New York to Miami, was hijacked out of Tampa by Eduardo Canteras, a Cuban refugee, who permitted the plane to refuel in Key West. While on the ground, volunteers planned to deflate the tires and disconnect the engines' power units, but National vetoed the idea, not wanting to damage the plane and harm its winter season's prospects. The thirty-three-year-old hijacker, looking shabby and undernourished, complained about being unable to get a job in America and waved his .45 and hand grenade. The plane flew on the Havana where it and its crew left after eight and a half hours. Twenty-eight passengers stayed overnight at Varadero and returned on the next afternoon's Airlift International flight. Canteras did not meet the FAA profile. 5115

December 11, 1968—United States—TWA flight 496, a B727 flying from St. Louis to Miami, was hijacked by a black couple who met the FAA profile. They diverted the plane to Cuba. Included among the passengers were golfer Mason Rudolph and country singer Tex Ritter. The hijackers, who boarded the plane in Nashville, were identified as James Joseph Patterson, born November 15, 1947, in Jamaica, New York, and Gwendolin Joyce Patterson née Manual, born March 21, 1949 in Memphis, Tennessee. They were indicted on October 13, 1969, by a federal grand jury in the northern district of Georgia. Editorials noted that the average cost of a hijacking was $2,500 including food and lodging for the passengers. 5116

December 11, 1968—Ecuador—A student discovered a dynamite bomb in a hollowed-out book in the Quito Binational Center, approximately one hour before it was set to explode. 0115

December 13, 1968—United States—Orlando Bosch, an anti-Castro Cuban exile, was convicted of sending bomb threats to the heads of state of the United

Kingdom, Spain, and Mexico. He was sentenced to ten years. He was also convicted with eight colleagues on November 15 of conspiracy to damage ships of nations trading with Cuba. 0116

December 19, 1968—United States—Eastern Airlines flight 47, a DC8 flying from Philadelphia to Miami, was hijacked by Thomas George Washington, a black who probably met the FAA profile, who was born on February 1, 1941 in Philadelphia. That morning the unemployed chemist appeared at his former wife's apartment and asked to take his three-year-old daughter, Jennifer for a walk. Washington got up from his seat in the last row on the plane and handed a note to twenty-three-year-old German-born stewardess Uta Risse, after asking when they would reach Miami. The captain, Orris Firth, found that the note said: "Dear captain, this flight is going to Havana. I have a gun and nitroglycerin. I've studied chemistry." Washington was described as a tall and slender black man, who cried and said he was hijacking the plane to avoid having his daughter brought up in a land of hatred and bigotry. It does not appear that he was armed; he told the stewardess that he had only a cap pistol in the paper bag he kept his hand in. He was led away at José Martí Airport by six Cuban soldiers. The crew of seven and the plane returned to Miami immediately. The 142 passengers were bused to Varadero and flown to Miami aboard two Eastern Electra prop-jets. Eight months later Washington told reporters that he would like to return home. He returned via Canada with a group of hijackers in November 1969 and was sentenced on March 24, 1970, to two years for interfering with the flight crew. He was released on June 4, 1971. 5117

December 26, 1968—Greece—Two members of the PFLP threw incendiary grenades and fired a machine gun at an El Al plane waiting to take off for New York on its way from Tel Aviv. The stewardess suffered a fractured leg and spinal injuries when she jumped out of the plane with the forty-one passengers. One of the Israeli passengers, fifty-year-old Leon Shirdan, an Israeli maritime officer, was killed in the attack. Firemen managed to save the plane, but an engine was lost, and the plane was heavily damaged. The duo were immediately arrested by Greek police, who identified them as Mahab H. Suleiman, nineteen, of Tripoli and Mahoud M. Mohammad, twenty-five, a Palestinian refugee. The two had arrived earlier in the day on an Air France flight from Beirut. The PFLP claimed credit for the attack, charging that El Al was not "an airline undertaking innocent civilian transport," since it had "in secret flights under the supervision of the Israeli Defense Ministry" transferred "air force pilots trained in flying Phantom jets in preparation for a surprise attack and new aggression against the Arab states." During the trial of the terrorists, key Greek witnesses failed to appear in court, and the duo flashed the "V for victory" sign. They were convicted and sentenced on March 26, 1970.

Mohammad received seventeen years and five months, and Suleiman received fourteen years and three months. Both were convicted on charges of interference with air traffic, arson and illegal use and possession of explosives. A charge of premeditated murder against Mohammad for using the maching gun was lessened to a count of manslaughter by negligence. The two were freed on July 22, 1970, when six Palestinians hijacked an Olympic Airways plane to Beirut. 0117

December 28, 1968—Lebanon—The Israelis retaliated against Lebanon for the attack on an El Al airliner in Greece by PFLP members who had flown there from Beirut. A squad of commandos was flown into Beirut International Airpot. Five helicopters landed at the hangar, one on the runway, and two others hovered. The commandos placed explosives under the nose-wheel well and undercarriage-wheel well of thirteen civilian airplanes owned by Trans-Mediterranean Airways, Lebanese International Airways, and Middle East Airlines, destroying all of them. Damage was estimated at $43 million. No passengers were on board any of the aircraft, and no casualties were reported. Aircraft of non-Arab corporatons were not attacked. The U.N. Security Council unanimously condemned the attack on December 31, calling for compensation to the airlines.

December 29, 1968—Israel—Al Fatah claimed credit for shelling the town of Beisan, while Israeli army spokesmen claimed that five towns had been shelled in apparent reprisal for the Beirut raid. 0118—0122

December 31, 1968—Israel—Al Fatah shelled the settlement of Kiryat Shmona in upper Galilee. Lebanese authorities denied that the rockets had been fired from their soil. El Fatah claimed that they had operated within Israel. 0123

January 2, 1969—United States—Eastern Airlines flight 401, a DC8 flying from New York to Miami, was hijacked by two blacks who fit the FAA profile; they diverted the plane to José Martí Airport. The couple was identified as Tyrone Ellington Austin, born October 3, 1949, in Jersey City and his wife, Linda J. Austin, born October 15, 1948, in Brooklyn, who joined the evening flight with their baby strapped to her back. Austin went to the restroom and changed from his business suit into a Nehru shirt, heavy boots, and a white beanie. Ms. Austin took this as a signal to run screaming up the aisle. Austin took out his automatic pistol and grabbed two-year-old Alan Levy from his mother's lap, jamming the gun against the child's head. Screaming "Havana, Black Power!" he pointed his .45 at the stewardess to obtain entry to the cockpit. The pilot, Captain Dennis Vanhuss, informed the passengers that the child was calm. One of the 146 passengers was socialite Christina Paolozzi Bellin, who reported "When we landed in Havana the hijacker was treated like a hero. He paraded up and down, strutting, with a sort of honor guard of Cuban militia of about thirty. He marched so much he even bumped into them. I didn't see anybody leading him away, either.'' The passengers were bused to Varadero, from which they flew home. Austin was on wanted lists for shooting a policeman in April 1968. His wife was indicted by a federal grand jury on March 25, 1969, in the eastern district of New York. Austin managed to get back into the United States and was killed by a New York City patrolman after robbing $6,000 from the Manhattan branch of the Manufacturers Hanover Trust Company. His wife is still at large. 5118

January 2, 1969—Greece—After successfully avoiding arrest in a police trap on December 28 in which his companion was apprehended, twenty-five-year-old Giorgios Flamourides, a young construction worker who had previously been arrested for anti-junta activities and who had joined the clandestine communist resistance organization Patriotic Front, hijacked an Olympic DC6B flying from Crete to Athens, diverting it to Cairo, where he requested political asylum. While the pilot was attempting to contact authorities, the hijacker fired a shot through the windshield, narrowly missing the pilot's head. Flamourides may have preferred to go to the Soviet Union. The 102 passengers on board, including Elizabeth Peterson of Seattle, were not harmed. He was imprisoned for eight months in Egypt until the Swedish diplomatic service took him to Sweden, on the initiative of the U.N. refugee commission; however, he was tried for hijacking in Sweden. In his defense, he claimed that ''if he was apprehended for a minor offence of a political nature which he had previously committed, he risked being exposed to torture intended to force him to name other members of the opposition to the regime in power in Greece.'' Using the defense of necessity, he invoked chapter 24, section 4, of the Swedish Penal Code: ''A person who . . . acts out of necessity in order to avert danger to life or health . . . shall also be free from punishment if the act must be considered as justifiable in view of the nature of the danger, the harm caused another and the circumstances in general.'' In the event that a person used greater force than permissible, he should ''nevertheless not be punished so long as the circumstances were such that he could hardly have stopped to thing . . . lesser punishment than that fixed for the crime may be imposed.'' A resolution of the Committee of European Ministers of April 15, 1970, which had found that Greece had violated the European Convention on Human Rights, was not brought before the court. The court overruled many of his arguments but noted mitigating circumstances and sentenced him to twenty-two months in June 1970. A Greek request for extradition was formally denied in September 1970. 5119

January 7, 1969—Colombia—A lone gunman armed with a revolver entered the cockpit of an Avianca DC4 flying from Riohacha to Maicao, Colombia, and diverted it to Santiago, Chile. Sixty people were on board. The U.S. State Department denied a rumor which circulated after the incident that Castro received $30,000 ransom for each hijacked plane. 5120

January 8, 1969—West Germany—Arsonists set a fire in the Amerika Haus Library in Frankfurt. Total damage was estimated at $5,000, mostly to furniture and books. 0124

January 9, 1969—United States—Eastern Airlines flight 831, a B727 flying from Miami to Nassau, was hijacked by Ronald Thomas Bohle, a white student at Purdue University who did not meet the FAA profile and who was born on February 27, 1947, at Michigan City, Indiana. He diverted the plane to Cuba. He pulled a knife on stewardess Joyce Jernigan, informing her that he hated the United States and Eastern Airlines and was a communist who loved his state, Russia, and Cuba. He was initially well received in Cuba for taking seventy-nine people out of their flight plan but was later held in a political prison for several months. He returned to the United States via Canada on November 1, 1969, with several other hijackers. On July 6, 1972, he was sentenced to twenty years for aircraft piracy. On July 30, 1975, the sentence was changed to twelve years. 5121

January 9, 1969—Thailand—Two shots were fired at a U.S. Bangkok relay station vehicle during the night, causing no damage or injuries. 0125

January 11, 1969—United States—United Airlines flight 459, a B727 flying from Jacksonville to Miami, was hijacked by Robert McRae Helmey, a white hijacker for whom the FAA profile was not applicable, who was born on October 28, 1932, in Savannah, Georgia. Armed with a broken, unloaded shotgun, he diverted the plane to Havana, where the tall Green Beret reserve noncommissioned officer was placed in solitary confinement for 109 days. He was then put on a ship to Canada, which returned him on May 5, 1969. He was the first successful hijacker of an airliner to be arraigned in the United States. Helmey believed that he was part of an FBI-CIA plot to assassinate Fidel Castro. Two prominent psychologists, Dr. David Hubbard and Dr. Corbet Thigpen, testified that repeated head injuries during parachute training induced a mental breakdown and temporary insanity. After thirty minutes of deliberation, the jury agreed and acquitted him of charges of air piracy and kidnapping on November 20, 1969, making Helmey the first skyjacker of a commercial aircraft to be acquitted. Helmey sent an interesting letter to the Levi Strauss Company: "Gentlemen: On the morning of January 11, 1969, I put on a pair of 'Mr. Levi' Sta Press slacks and went to work. At 11 P.M. I arrived in Havana, Cuba, 'in a situation beyond my control.' I was taken to jail and put in solitary confinement for 109 days. The only clothing I had was what I had on. I lived in these slacks the duration of my confinement. I crawled on my hands and knees until there was no skin on them. After your inspection I would appreciate them being returned to me. These slacks are as good as new except where my wife cut them in search of a diary I had sewn inside the lining of my pocket. I highly recommend 'Mr. Levi's' to anyone who is confined or travels alot. As for everyday wear, I think the above is proof enough of the durability. The price is most remarkable for such comfortable and well-styled slacks. Thanks for making them.'' 5122

January 11, 1969—Bolivia—A bomb thrown from a moving automobile exploded in front of the U.S. consulate in Cochabamba, breaking windows in the consulate and the adjacent hotel but causing no injuries. 0126

January 12, 1969—Panama—A Peruvian ASPA CV990 flying from Buenos Aires to Miami was hijacked by twenty-five-year-old Jesus R. Anaya Roseque, an Ecuadorian using a Mexican passport, who used his pistol to enter the cockpit and force the pilot to fly to Havana. 118 people were aboard the plane. The hijacker was returned to Mexico, where he was sentenced to twenty-five years. On May 6, 1973, he was released and flow to Cuba with twenty-nine other prisoners Mexico released to secure the release of kidnapped U.S. Consul General Terrence Leonhardy. 0127

January 13, 1969—United States—An attempt was made to hijack Delta Airlines flight 297, a CV880 flying from Detroit to Miami, when the plane was on its final approach. Kenneth Carl McPeek, a white who probably met the FAA profile and was born on January 29, 1937, in Berkeley, Michigan, thrust a shotgun into the stomach of the stewardess and demanded to be taken to Cuba. The stewardess ran into the cockpit and locked McPeek out. While the plane was changing course, he went back to his seat to comfort his three-year-old son, who was ill. The course was changed from Havana back to Miami, and the former mental patient was arrested while sitting quietly at his seat with the unloaded shotgun at his feet. None of the seventy-five persons on board was injured. 5123

January 19, 1969—United States—Eastern Airlines flight 9, a DC8 flying from New York to Miami with 171 people on board, was hijacked by Aristofarez Antonio Navarro Payano, a Latin who met the FAA profile; he was born on July 12, 1949, in the Dominican Republic. Using a pistol and grenade, he entered the cockpit and forced the pilot to fly to Havana. It was reported that he was living in the Dominican Republic on May 9, 1970, where he was to stand trial. He was indicted by a federal grand jury in the southern district of New York on June 16, 1970. 5124

January 19, 1969—Ecuador—An Ecuatoriana International Lockheed Electra 188 on the Guayaquil-Quito-Miami run was hijacked to José Martí Airport by fifteen hijackers armed with machine guns, pistols, knives, a homemade bomb, and other weapons. The group allowed the pilot, Captain Dean Ricker, to refuel in Colombia, whose government held the plane until the group threatened to kill the pilot. One of the teenaged hijackers told stewardess Maria Flores that there were other groups in Ecuador hoping to hijack a plane to what he saw as a paradise of freedom and equality. None of the eighty-four passengers or four crew members was reported harmed. The hijackers, who ranged in age from fifteen to twenty-five, were identified as J. Quevedo Mora, Angel Quevedo Mora, Antonion Quevedo Mora, C. Quevedo Mora, J. A. Centurion Onofre, C. Pino, L. Pino, A. Viejo Romero, V. Moreno Merino, and C. Moreno Merino. The last two were reported in custody, and all were convicted in Ecuadorian court. 0128

January 22, 1969—Soviet Union—A lone gunman attempted to assassinate four cosmonauts and Leonid Brezhnev in Moscow by firing shots into their motorcade en route to a Kremlin celebration.

January 24, 1969—United States—National Airlines flight 424, a B727 flying the Key West-Miami-New York route with forty-seven passengers, was hijacked by Johnny Coulter, alias Ayre, a nineteen-year-old U.S. Navy deserter who did not want to go to Vietnam. He grabbed a stewardess and put a knife to her throat. Then he entered the cockpit and forced the pilot to fly to Havana. The white hijacker, who met the FAA profile, remains a fugitive. 5125

January 28, 1969—United States—Eastern Airlines flight 121, a DC8 flying from Atlanta to Miami with 113 people on board, was hijacked to Havana by three pistol-wielding American blacks who met the FAA profile. The trio were identified as Larry F. Brooks, born January 14, 1947, in Cleveland; Noble B. Mason, born February 26, 1943, in Cadiz Ohio; and Everett L. White, born May 9, 1945 in Wheeling, West Virginia. The last was apprehended in Cleveland on April 30, 1975. On September 24, 1975, he was given a ten-year suspended sentenced for interference with a flight crew member. A complaint had been filed on March 29, 1974, in the middle district of Florida. 5126

January 28, 1969—United States—National Airlines flight 64, a DC8 flying from Los Angeles to Miami, had just pulled out of New Orleans with its twenty-five passengers and seven crew when an alarm sounded on the cockpit call bell five seconds before two armed hijackers burst through the door, one of them carrying a stewardess with a .38 jammed into her ribs. The duo announced themselves as escapees from a California prison, where they were serving terms for robbery. They were identified as Byron Vaughn Booth, born September 1, 1944, in Chicago, and Clinton Robert Smith, born April 14, 1944, in Los Angeles, two blacks who met the FAA profile. One of the hijackers' coat pockets was full of bullets. The other held a cigarette carton with four sticks of dynamite with fuses wired to each stick. He attempted to light the fuse with a match. The pilot, in his testimony to the House Interstate and Foreign Commerce Committee, reported, "We had some fifteen minutes of negotiations take place before we could even so much as get a chart or map out of our flight kits. . . . All during this time, for one hour and fifteen minutes, from the point we were hijacked, until we got on the ground at José Martí Airport in Havana, the gun was behind my head. . . . There is a good ten-minute period at the initial outset of these hijackings when things are very much in the balance. The slightest move from anyone, or the slightest offending word by anyone, could really bring on an absolute holocaust." One of the passengers heard what was going on and pulled out a pistol from his jacket, saying that he would kill the duo in order to "save the crew." The crew and passengers dissuaded him. The airlines' associations announced that they would not pay reward money to anyone who attempted forcibly to subdue a hijacker in flight. One of the passengers, Luis Sierra Valdes, had planned to meet with his parents, two brothers, and their wives and seven children in Miami; all of them had been allowed to leave Cuba as refugees. While he was in Cuba he pretended to be a Peruvian and was allowed to return with the rest of the passengers to Miami, eight hours behind schedule. The hijackers remain fugitives from an indictment handed down on January 28, 1970, by a federal grand jury in the central district of California. 5127

January 31, 1969—United States—National Airlines flight 44, a DC8 on the San Francisco-Houston-New Orleans-Tampa-Miami run with eight crew and fifty-five passengers, was hijacked to Havana by Berkeley, California resident Allan Creighton Sheffield, a white who probably met the FAA profile; he was born on August 1, 1932. He jammed a gun into the ribs of stewardess Donna Golhinher (her second hijacking) and told her, "I am tired of TV dinners and seeing people starve in the world." The plane and crew left Havana immediately; the passengers were flown to Miami by another plane later that day. National mailed Castro a check for $2,500. The hijacker was indicted by a federal grand jury in the northern district of California on June 27, 1973. He was held in Yugoslavia for some time. On October 8, 1976, Sweden returned him to the United States aboard a flight to Kennedy Airport as the result an extradition proceeding. The FBI reported that he would be charged with air piracy. 5128

February 3, 1969—United States—Eastern Airlines flight 7, a B727 flying from Newark to Miami, was hijacked to Havana by a group of Cubans who used a revolver as well as held a knife to stewardess's throat. The hijackers were identified as Cubans: Wilfredo Hernandez Garcia, born November 13, 1926, in Placetas, Cuba; his wife, Marina L. Hernandez, born January 31,

1926; their daughter; and Joaquin Babin Estrada, born September 17, 1927, in Cuba. All met the FAA profile. The pilot, Captain Jack Moore, had been hijacked previously. Among the ninety-three passengers was Alan Funt of "Candid Camera." A complaint was filed on February 27, 1969, in the district of New Jersey. 5129

February 3, 1969—United States—A New York community college student with shoulder-length hair and his girl friend attempted to hijack National Airlines flight 11, a B727 flying from New York to Miami with seventy-thiree people on board. Holding a knife and a can of mosquito spray he claimed was a bomb, they held a stewardess hostage and demanded that the pilot fly to Havana. The hijackers identified themselves as Michael Anthony Peparo, born November 3, 1947, in Cold Spring, New York, and Tasmin Rebecca Fitzgerald, born July 4, 1950, in Poughkeepsie, New York. The white couple, who met the FAA profile, expressed doubts about what they really wanted to do. Peparo talked about problems at school, with his family, and with his draft board, while the pilot listened sympathetically. The crew talked them into allowing the plane to land to refuel. The ground crew at Miami became suspicious and alerted police. The FBI and pilot talked the hijackers out of their plan. At their trial, the captain, Harry Davis, pleaded for leniency for the two; he recalled how he had put his hands on Peparo's during the incident and prayed with him. The prosecution was willing to reduce the air piracy charge to unlawful interference with a plane in flight, and on May 7, 1969, the duo were sentenced to indeterminate terms in juvenile detention. They were paroled on December 7, 1970. 5130

February 3, 1969—Tanzania—A book bomb that arrived in a package in the mail killed FRELIMO president Dr. Eduardo Chivambo Mondlane, forty-eight, as he was opening it in a Dar es Salaam beach house where he was working. No proof was ever produced as to who was responsible. Suspects include PIDE (the Portuguese security service), Frente de Libertacao de Mocambique leaders Dos Santos and Reverend Uria Simango, defector Lazaro Kavandame, the Chinese, the CIA, and the Cubans. Dos Santos and Simango later received bombs in their mail. The executive committee of FRELIMO elected Vice-President Simango, a Methodist minister, on February 12 to succeed Mondlane. 0129-0131

February 5, 1969—Colombia—A Colombian SAM DC4, flying from Barranquilla to Medellín, with forty-nine persons on board was hijacked by Leonardo Fuentes, who used his revolver to force the pilot to fly to Havana. 5131

February 6, 1969—Venezuela—Seven men hijacked a Venezuelan airliner to Havana. 5132

February 8, 1969—Mexico—Victor Romo was overpowered by passengers when he atteempted to hijack a Mexican DC6 flying from Mexico City to Hermosa to Cuba. 5133

February 10, 1969—Puerto Rico—Eastern Airlines flight 950, a DC8 flying from San Juan to Miami with 110 passengers and 9 crew members, was hijacked to Havana by Pedro Pablo Alvarez-DeQuesada, who was born on September 29, 1937, in Havana and who met the FAA profile. The hijacker used a pistol and held a stewardess hostage. Castro ushered in a new policy by allowing the plane and passengers to leave immediately. The hijacker was indicted on September 24, 1970, by federal grand jury in the district of Puerto Rico. Eastern Airlines at the time was being sued by a former passenger who had been taken to Cuba during a hijacking for $5,880 for damages suffered to baggage, clothing, health, and lost time. 5134

February 11, 1969—Venezuela—A Venezuelan Aeropostal DC9 flying from Maracaibo to Caracas with seventy-three people on board was hijacked to Havana by five pistol-wielding men. A Cuban fishing boat had been seized by Venezuela a few days before, and Castro held the plane, claiming to wish to investigate whether the hijacking was ''legitimate or a provocation.'' After bargaining, the airliner and boat were released a few days later, with Venezuela paying $31,000 for expenses incurred in this and previous hijackings. 5135

February 17, 1969—Spain—The North American Study Center in Valencia, a USIS-supported facility, was bombed. The blast destroyed the auditorium window and all other windows up to the fourth floor but caused no personal injuries. No motive was determined. 0132

February 18, 1969—Switzerland—El Al flight 432, a Boeing 720B scheduled to fly from Zurich to Tel Aviv, was taxiing down the runway when a car driven by four PFLP terrorists came alongside it allowing the terrorists to fire 200 bullets from their machine guns (128 of which hit the fuselage) and lob 3 incendiary grenades at it. The pilot, Yorum Perez, was killed, and three other crewmen and three passengers were wounded. An Israeli security guard aboard, Mordecai Rachamin, returned the fire, killing Abdel Mohsen Hassan, thirty-eight, and chased the others away. Damage to the plane came to 250,000 Swiss francs (the plane had cost twenty million francs). Among the seventeen passengers and ten crew members was a high Israeli government official, who was unharmed in the attack. Apparently the group engaged in a practice of the attack five days previously. Authorities at the scene confiscated two Russian 7.62-mm machine guns, three more thermite bombs, several grenades, three large bombs, tear-gas grenades, and pamphlets explaining the group's actions. Defense counsel argued that Rachamin killed the attacker after he had surrendered to Swiss police, but Rachamin was acquitted. The three terrorists refused to speak during the trial, questioning only one witness. They did testify that they had chosen Switzerland for the attack because Basel was the site of the first Zionist congress in 1897. They were sentenced to twelve years' hard labor on charges of murder. The group were identified as Mohammed Abu el Haja, twenty-four; Ibrahim Tawfik Yusuf, thirty-four, a Catholic who later trained the Japanese Red Army group who attacked the Lod Airport on May 30, 1972; and Amina Dabbour, a twenty-one-year-old schoolteacher living in Lebanon. All were Palestinians. The PFLP immediately claimed credit for the attack, pointing out that El Al airliners were perceived by them to be military targets. Although the group was sentenced by a Winterthur court on December 22, they were released after the September 6, 1970, hijacking of a Swissair plane by the PFLP. The group told Swiss investigators that they were "trained in Jordan and some of them left Syria to carry out their attack in Zurich." Switzerland protested to Jordan, Syria, and Lebanon on February 28 for this support. On February 20, the Cairo newspaper *Al Ahram* revealed that the Egyptian government would provide health insurance for the commandos and their families and that sick or wounded commandos would be flown without charge to Egyptian hospitals "if they are unable to obtain treatment in Jordanian medical institutions." The Israeli Knesset held a four-hour crisis session on the day of the attack, and a statement was ready by Communications Minister Moshe Carmel, who warned the Arabs that Israel "retains the moral right and the operational ability to take any necessary means of protection, whenever required to break the strength of those scheming against us and our planes and to secure the free aerial traffic of Israel's air routes. . . . Compliance [by Arab governments] with hijacking and with scheming against and assault upon our air routes will cause serious damage to all, including the Arab states." Despite this statement, the Israelis did not engage in reprisals. The February 27 issue of *Pravda* attacked the Israeli policy of retaliation and praised the attackers as patriots. 0133

February 21, 1969—Israel—A bomb planted by the PFLP was found in front of the British consulate in east Jerusalem and disarmed in a nearby field. 0134

February 21, 1969—Israel—A bomb planted by the PFLP went off in a crowded Jerusalem supermarket during its busiest period when hundreds of shoppers were buying in preparation for the Jewish sabbath, killing two people and wounding twenty, including Australian Roy Skinner, a U.N. truce observer. A second bomb was found fifteen minutes after the blast and defused. On March 4, PFLP chieftain George Habash told the press that attacks on Israeli civilians would continue "if the Israelis continue to practice atrocities against us." In an interview two weeks later with John K. Cooley, the supermarket attack was seen as the PFLP response to "the murder at Zurich airport of Abdel Mohsen after he laid down his arms. We took care not to kill civilians at both Athens and Zurich. The killing at Athens was an accident; at Zurich an Israeli security guard fired at us from outside the plane. These attacks are answers to acts of savagery by the Israelis against Arabs in the occupied territories, especially the unknown acts in villages.'' A Ramallah woman was sentenced to life imprisonment. One hundred fifty Arabs had been questioned, and fifteen of them, mostly West Bank Palestinians, were sentenced for this and a bomb explosion in the cafeteria of the Hebrew Unversity. 0135

February 23, 1969—United States—Four men were removed from a plane in Chicago. A search discovered a .22 pistol. Two of the men were wearing Black Panther party badges, and one of them had mentioned Cuba to a stewardess. Three of the men were held for questioning on suspicion of hijacking. 5136

February 25, 1969—United States—Eastern Airlines flight 955, a DC8 flying the St. Louis-Atlanta-Miami-San Juan route, was hijacked out of Atlanta by Lorenzo Edward Ervin, Jr., a black who met the FAA profile. He was born on March 30, 1947, in Chattanooga, Tennessee. Using a small-caliber revolver, he forced the stewardess to allow him to enter the cockpit. He held the gun on the copilot, forcing the pilot to fly to Havana with seven crew and sixty-one passengers on board. An indictment for air piracy was handed down in March by a federal grand jury in Atlanta. Ervin, who had given his name as C. Green, surrendered to U.S. authorities in Prague, Czechoslovakia, in September 1969. He was arrested by the FBI as he stepped off a plane from Berlin at New York's JFK International Airport. On July 7, 1970, he was sentenced to life imprisonment for aircraft piracy and kidnapping. 5137

February 25, 1969—Israel—An Arab carrying a bomb on a tricycle in Lydda was wounded when the explosive detonated accidentally. Two other Arabs were arrested for questioning. 0136

February 25, 1969—Israel—A PFLP bomb went off in the British consulate in East Jerusalem, slightly injuring a secretary. The PFLP declared responsiblity for the attack, citing an alleged British decision to sell tanks to Israel, which the British called ''highly exaggerated.'' On March 5 the Jerusalem chief of police, Daniel Bareli, announced that eighty Arabs had been arrested on charges of conducting extensive guerrilla operations (twenty of them had been arrested the previous day). Most of the group were suspected PFLP members, and Bareli said that they would be charged with the recent supermarket bombing, as well as the attack on the consulate. It was alleged that the group operated in Jerusalem, the West Bank, and Gaza and received instructions from the Egyptian embassy in Jordan. The leaders were reported to be a female who directed the operations; Wodet Komeri, a prominent Ramallah lawyer; Bashir el-Hirri, who was accused of organizing the network; and a Ramallah Arab Anglican priest, Illya el-Khouri, who crossed the Jordan River frequently to maintain communications with the group's Amman leaders. 0137

March 2, 1969—Australia—The offices of the Australian-American Association in Melbourne were entered through a rear window and ransacked, after which fires were started in piles of paper in two rooms. One fire went out, but the other one caused $2,500 damage to supplies and equipment, with damage to the building much higher. Ten dollars was stolen from the cash box. 0138

March 2, 1969—Australia—A Molotov cocktail was thrown from a passing car, marring the paint but not breaking the windows of the U.S. consulate general building in Melbourne. The next day three hundred to four hundred young demonstrators marched in front of the building for twenty minutes. 0139

March 3, 1969—Ecuador—Five men attacked the U.S. consulate in Guayaquil, throwing Molotov cocktails that started a small fire in the consulate general's office. Three small fires were also started on the pavement in front of the buildings and red ink was thrown against the door. Property damage was slight. 0140

March 5, 1969—United States—A shipment of highly enriched uranium hexafluoride (UF^6) was reported missing on its Portsmouth, Ohio, to Hematite, Missouri, route. After an intensive search by the FBI and AEC, the shipment was found on March 19 in Boston's Logan Airport freight terminal.

March 5, 1969—United States—National Airlines flight 97, a B727 flying from New York to Miami with eighteen passengers, was hijacked to Havana by Anthony Garnet Bryant, a black who met the FAA profile. He was born on February 23, 1938, in San Bernardino, California. San Francisco police records show that he was convicted in 1961 of first-degree robbery and in 1964 for possession and sale of marijuana, for which he served eight years in San Quentin Prison. Bryant, who had identified himself as Jimmy Carver, told the seven crew that he had just been released three months previously on the narcotics sentence and that he had trafficked in narcotics to support his family. He was described as wearing a Fu Manchu mustache and beard, long hair, a dirty shirt, and carrying a .38. After informing the pilot, Captain Ed Buschser, that "I would rather be a prisoner in Cuba than here," he strolled down the aisle, putting a gun to the head of each passenger, asking them if they were poor or rich. James Tucker, a black soldier on leave from Fort Dix, replied, "Poor man!" and was left alone, as were other black passengers, a black stewardess, and anyone else Bryant believed looked "nice." He took $1,700 from a sleeping Cuban exile, Paul Rawman, and gave the money to two other passengers, claiming that he had stolen enough. Upon learning of the robbery, the Cubans in Havana returned the money and allowed the plane and passengers to take off. The next day, the Cuban daily newspaper, *Granma* announced that Bryant had been arrested, which was the first time the Cubans had disclosed the fate of any hijacker. However, he was not returned to the United States, where he remains a fugitive from an indictment handed down by the federal grand jury in the eastern district of New York on March 25, 1969. 5138

March 6, 1969—Israel—Two men and one woman, members of the PFLP and Popular Democratic Front for the Liberation of Palestine, were responsible for planting a bomb that exploded in the crowded cafeteria of the Hebrew University in Jerusalem, wounding twenty-nine Israeli students. The room was heavily damaged. 0141

March 6, 1969—Israel—A guerrilla hand grenade exploded in the Al Bireh West Bank branch of the Israeli National Bank, wounding one. Israeli security forces destroyed five Arab houses in east Jerusalem that contained terrorist arms, explosives, and other equipment. The families were permitted to leave first. 0142

March 9, 1969—West Germany—After the windows of the American Memorial Library in Berlin were broken, two Molotov cocktails were thrown inside, destroying a thousand books, and causing damage estimated at $2,000. 0143

March 11, 1969—United States—A shipment of highly enriched uranium, which was to be shipped from New York's JFK International Airport and arrive in Frankfurt, West Germany, on the afternoon of the next day, was reported missing. On March 17, the shipment was found in London, where it had been erroneously taken off the flight.

March 11, 1969—Colombia—Juan Cary Montoya, carrying a candle that he claimed was a stick of dynamite, attempted to hijack a Sociedad Aeronautica De Medellín EC4 on the Medellín-Bogotá-Barranquilla flight to Havana. He allowed the plane to land for refueling at Cartagena, where it and the thirty-eight people on board were surrounded by troops. When police entered the plane, a fight broke out in which the hijacker was wounded by gunfire and a flight mechanic was fatally shot by troops who mistook him for the hijacker. 5139

March 11, 1969—West Germany—A bomb planted by the Eritrean Liberation Front exploded aboard an Ethiopian Airlines B707 parked at Frankfurt airport, injuring several German cleaning women. The passengers, who had arrived from Athens, had deplaned before the two explosions rocked the tourist-class passenger compartment. The *Addis Zemen* said in its March 14 editorial that a

Syrian-Arab organization had claimed responsibility. "This band of gangsters which works under Syrian direction, has been given the name the Syrian-Arab Movement for the Liberation of Eritrea." The ELF claimed that the attack was designed to halt the use of Ethiopian Airlines to transport troops into Eritrea to attack local villages. 0144

March 12, 1969—West Germany—A Molotov cocktail was thrown through a ground-floor window of the Munich Amerika Haus, causing little damage. Police suspected that a skilled radical saboteur was responsible. 0145

March 16, 1969—Colombia—An Aerocondor Airlines DC6, flying from Barranquilla to San Andrés Island with forty people on board, was hijacked by a man carrying a revolver who was accompanied by his wife and child. The plane landed in Camaguey, Cuba. 5140

March 17, 1969—Peru—A Faucett Airlines B727, flying the Lima-Arequipa-Tacna route with eighty-one people aboard, was hijacked by six men carrying guns and a dynamite bomb. The group held the crew hostage while the plane refueled at Guayaquil. Seventeen people were allowed to deplane there, while the other sixty-four flew on to Havana, where the plane was parked next to a hijacked Delta DC8 at José Martí Airport. 5141.

March 17, 1969—United States—Delta Airlines flight 518, a DC9 flying the Dallas-Atlanta-Augusta-Charleston route, was hijacked to Havana by Robert Lee Sandlin of Vernon, Texas, a white who met the FAA profile; he was born on August 27, 1950, in Houston. He used a knife and pistol to hijack the plane and its sixty-four people aboard to José Martí Airport, where the plane parked next to a Peruvian airliner that had just been hijacked. Sandlin was reported drinking and laughing with the Peruvian group in the airport's dining room. He was confined for his first six months in a Cuban jail, held in a cell block with a number of other Americans. He returned to the United States via Canada with other hijackers on November 1, 1969. He was committed to a mental institution on February 1, 1972, but was released on a second eighteen-month furlough on December 5, 1973. 5142

March 19, 1969—United States—Delta Airlines flight 918, a CV880 flying the Dallas-New Orleans-New York route, was the scene of an unsuccessful attempt to hijack it to Havana. Douglas Alton Dickey, a white who met the FAA profile who was born on March 19, 1943, in Casa Grande, Arizona, produced a .22 pistol. He was persuaded by the pilot that refueling in New Orleans was necessary. While on the ground, he allowed the passengers among the ninety-five people on board to deplane. One of the passengers was an FBI special agent, who wrestled the gun from Dickey and placed him under arrest. One shot was fired during the scuffle, but no one was injured. Charges against him were dismissed due to insanity, and Dickey was transferred to Arizona State Institution on August 14, 1969, where local charges are outstanding. 5143

March 23, 1969—Israel—Portable rockets were fired on an Israeli command center and radar site in El Borg, Sinai, ten miles east of the Suez Canal, by commandos who claimed to be members of the Cairo-based Arab Organization of Sinai. The group claimed to have destroyed the facility, while the Israelis said the attack was ineffective. The same group claimed responsibility for an explosion at an Israeli artillery and supply depot in Ein Moussa, Sinai.

March 25, 1969—United States—Delta Airlines flight 821, a DC8 on the Newark-Dallas-San Diego-Los Angeles run, was hijacked out of Dallas by Luis Antonio Frese, a Latin who met the FAA profile, He was born on September 16, 1929, in San Juan, Puerto Rico. Frese used a revolver to force the pilot to divert the plane, its seven crew, and 107 passengers to Havana. He was indicted on June 26, 1969, by a federal grand jury in the northern district of Texas. He was reported to have died in Cuba on October 20, 1975. 5144

April 1969—Denmark—Croatian terrorists were believed responsible for planting a bomb that was disarmed at the Yugoslav embassy in Copenhagen. 0146

April 8, 1969—Peru—Five teenagers threw two Molotov cocktails at the front door of a USIS installation in Lima, several blocks from the U.S. embassy. The incendiaries were extinguished without causing extensive damage. The identity of the attackers was not established. 0147

April 11, 1969—Ecuador—An Ecuadorian Airlines DC6 flying the Guayaquil-Quito-Miami run was hijacked out of Guayaquil by three armed men who used a pistol and machine guns to force the pilot to fly to Havana. The hijackers were accompanied by six other men, three women, and four children. A total of sixty-eight people were on board. 5145

April 13, 1969—Puerto Rico—Pan American flight 460, a B727 flying from San Juan to Miami with ninety-one people aboard, was hijacked to Havana by four Latin males armed with various weapons who met the FAA profile. They were identified as José Diaz Claro, born October 2, 1943; Esmeraldo Ramirez Castaneda, born August 8, 1939; Manuel Vargas Agueros, born March 9, 1930; and Hiran Courouneau X. Sanchez, born February 10, 1944. All were born in Guantánamo. 5146

April 14, 1969—Colombia—A Colombian SAM DC4, on the Bogotá-Santa Maria-Medellín-Barranquilla run was hijacked out of Medellín by three men armed with knives and pistols. The plane was allowed to refuel at Cartagena and flew on the Havana. 5147

May 3, 1969—United States—John Kivlen, forty-two, informed a stewardess aboard a National Airlines DC8 bound for Miami from Los Angeles that he wanted to go to Havana. He meekly returned to his seat, and because he did not appear to be armed, the pilot landed in Tampa. Prosecution was declined. 5148

May 5, 1969—United States—National Airlines flight 91, a B727 flying from New York to Miami, was hijacked to Havana by two pistol-wielding white Canadians who met the FAA profile. Seventy-three people were on board. They were identified as Jean Pierre Charrette, born July 7, 1923, in Hull, Quebec, and Alain Allard, born January 21, 1947. They remain fugitives from an indictment handed down by a federal grand jury in the District of Columbia on January 23, 1975. 5149

May 11, 1969—United States—A fire at the Rocky Flats nuclear weapons fabrication facility in Colorado caused $45 million damage. It is believed that it was caused by spontaneous combustion of plutonium in a plant work room and that the fire, a common occurrence, was not extinguished because only one person was working in the plant that Sunday. Many suggested arson as a cause, but no evidence for such sabotage was ever presented. A group of independent Colorado scientists reported to Dr. Glenn Seaborg, AEC chairman, that plutonium deposits were found two to four miles from the plant as a result of the fire. Dow Chemical spokesmen attacked the credibility of the report, and the AEC concluded that "there was no danger involved and that the radiation was contained within the plant and the immediate vicinity."

May 15, 1969—Israel—Grenades and other explosive devices were thrown into market areas by Arab terrorists in the towns of Gaza, Jabaliya, Khan Yunis, Rafa, and Deir el Balah shortly before dawn, injuring thirty-five Arabs, many of them women, in a general protest of Israel's Independence Day, which coincided with the Hebrew lunar calendar's anniversary of Jordanian Jerusalem's 1967 capture by the Israelis. 0148-0152

May 20, 1969—Canada—Two anti-Castro Cuban refugees attempted to bomb the Cuban consulate in Montreal. They were arrested in New Jersey. 0153

May 20, 1969—Colombia—An Avianca B737 flying from Bogotá to Pereira was hijacked by Luis Eduardo Martinez Rusinke and three other gunmen who diverted the plane to Havana. Thirty-nine persons were on board the plane, which was allowed to refuel at Barranquilla. 5150

May 22, 1969—Denmark—An attempt by an Arab man and woman and a Swede to assassinate Israel's David Ben-Gurion in Copenhagen was thwarted by police. The trio was freed after three weeks on the grounds that intent to kill was insufficient reason to charge them. 0154

May 26, 1969—United States—Northeast Airlines flight 6, a B727 flying from Miami to New York City with fourteen passengers and four crew members, was hijacked to Havana by three Cuban exiles armed with pistols and a knife. The photographs of two of the hijackers were found in FBI files, although the FBI did not announce why their pictures were held. They were identified as Crecencio Parra Zamora, born July 15, 1946, in Cuba; Roberto Romero Gracial, born April 3, 1945, in Cuba; and Marino Bolivar Samon, born July 8, 1949 in Guantánamo, Cuba, the only one of the three who met the FAA profile. A complaint was filed on May 29, 1969, in the southern district of Florida, and an indictment was handed down on February 18, 1970. The three remain fugitives. 5151

May 30, 1969—United States—Texas International Airlines flight 669, a CV600 flying from Alexandria, Louisiana, to New Orleans, was the scene of an unsuccessful attempt to hijack the plane to Cuba. A prisoner who was being transported by law-enforcement officers handed a note to the stewardess indicating that he had a hand grenade and wanted to go to Cuba. The plane was already on its final approach to New Orleans and the pilot landed. The would-be hijacker was unarmed and was identified as a white male who did not meet the FAA profile; Terrance Jamison Niemeyer, who was born on November 2, 1937, in Chicago. On April 15, 1971, charges against him were dismissed due to insanity. He was committed to a state mental institution, from which he was released on probation on October 10, 1973. 5152

May 30, 1969—Bolivia—A small explosive device thrown from a moving car in La Paz exploded against a side wall of the Bolivian-American Center, causing no extensive damage and no personal injuries. 0155

May 30, 1969—Israel—Members of the PFLP placed an explosive charge in the Baniyas River, heavily damaging a section of the Trans-Arabian Pipeline, which is owned by Aramco, in the Golan Heights. The pipeline provides millions of dollars in royalties and transit fees to Saudi Arabia, Jordan, Syria, and Lebanon. The flow of oil through the one thousand mile pipeline, which connects Dharan, Saudi Arabia, to Sidon, Lebanon, was blocked due to the resultant fire. A PFLP spokesman claimed that his group had intended to pollute water supplied to Israeli settlements and fisheries in Hutch Valley. Oil was reported to be seeping into the northern part of the Sea of Galilee, and oil slicks were seen on the Jordan River. The Israelis managed to contain the blaze after fourteen hours. The PFLP was sharply criticized by Egypt, Saudi Arabia, and Lebanon for the attack. 0156

June 4, 1969—Haiti—Ten Americans and Haitians, probably members of Haitian exile group, used a four-engine plan to drop six homemade bombs on Port-au-Prince, Haiti's capital city, killing three people. The group made an emergency landing at a U.S. missile tracking base in the Bahamas and were charged with illegal entry. 0157

June 8, 1969—Angola—A Portuguese DIA Dakota twin-engined plane flying from Luanda to Cabinda was taken over by two Africans dressed in Portuguese army uniforms and armed with machine guns and grenades. They diverted the plane and all thirteen aboard to Point Noire, Congo Republic (Brazzaville). 0158

June 8, 1969—United States—Minor damage was caused to Loew's Orpheum Theater in New York City by a bomb. It was alleged that it was set by anti-Castro Cubans protesting the showing of the movie *Ché*. 0159

June 9, 1969—Australia—Croatian exiles were believed responsible for the bombing of the Yugoslav consulate in Sydney. No one was injured. 0160

June 11, 1969—Greece—A bomb wrecked the ticket booth of a theater outside the entrance to the Tameion building (which houses USIS facilities) in Athens. There was no damage to the USIS. 0161

June 11, 1969—Brazil—A USIS local employee discovered a tin containing eighteen sticks of dynamite with sufficient explosive power to destroy the two-story building housing USIS offices in Fortaleza. Police considered the bomb professionally constructed. 0162

June 14, 1969—Cuba—The Cuban Representation in Exile, an anti-Castro exile group, reorted that one of its military leaders, Angel Luis Castillo, a former captain in Castro's army, had been captured in Oriente province with a group of infiltrators. There were rumors that a ten-man group led by Amancio Mosqueda Fernandez, alias El Yarey, had been unsuccessful in a confrontation with Cuban troops in May; the group's members had all been killed, wounded, or captured. Radio Havana announced on December 7 that four of the group, including the leader, were executed by firing squad the previous night and that the others received twenty-year prison sentences. 0163

June 17, 1969—United States—TWA flight 154, a B707 flying from Oakland to New York with seventy-nine passengers and six crew, was hijacked to

Havana, making this the longest U.S. hijacking to date. The hijacker used a pistol to divert the plane as it was over Wilson Creek, Nevada, and the pilot suggested that he remain in the cockpit "for safety's sake." The tall, dapper black who met the FAA profile was identified by the FBI as a Black Panther captain who was accused of being involved in a shootout with police in San Francisco the previous November. William Lee Brent, born June 2, 1930, in Franklin, Louisiana, was taken into custody by the Cubans. He is a fugitive from an indictment handed down by a federal grand jury in the district of New York on June 24, 1969. 5153

June 18, 1969—Italy—An Eritrean student, Hagos Tesfai, died when a bomb he was preparing in his room in Rome exploded. Leaflets found in the room announced an impending attack by the Eritrean Liberation Front. 0164

June 18, 1969—Pakistan—Three Eritreans in their early twenties conducted an armed attack against an Ethiopian Airlines B707 parked at Karachi Airport. The ELF members hurled hand grenades and sprayed the jet with submachine guns, burning part of the plane but causing no casualties to the fifteen passengers who were waiting in the airport lounge area on their way to New Delhi from Addis Ababa. The trio, who had arrived from Beirut on June 16, claimed that they were dramatizing their opposition to Ethiopian rule in Eritrea. A. Abdulla, M. Idris, and S. Abrahim were convicted and sentenced to one year of hard labor. 0165

June 19, 1969—Argentina—Rosario students burned an American flag and threw explosives at the USIS building. Police did not interfere, and the demonstration broke up. 0166

June 19, 1969—Israel—Palestinian terrorists bombed a power line in Jerusalem, partially blacking out the city. 0167

June 20, 1969—Israel—The PFLP claimed responsibility for three bombs that exploded on a street leading to the Western Wailing Wall in Jerusalem, killing one Arab and wounding five others, including two U.S. tourists and one Israeli soldier. Twenty suspects were arrested. The PFLP the next day claimed that they were not trying to injure Jewish worshippers "but to remind the world and tourists of the Zionists' barbaric and Nazi-like acts and to warn the enemy to stop these actions." 0168

June 20, 1969—Uruguay—Following Nelson Rockefeller's visit, two Tupamaros dressed in police uniforms attacked a General Motors plant in Montevideo. MLN leaflets were left at the site of the $1 million fire. 0169

June 20, 1969—Colombia—Three men and one woman armed with machine guns hijacked a Colombian Urraca Airlines DC3 flying from Villavicencio to Monterrey, diverting it to Havana after a stopover in Santiago, Chile. 5154

June 22, 1969—United States—Eastern Airlines flight 7, a DC8 on the New York-Newark-Miami run, was hijacked by a family of Cuban exiles who diverted the plane to Havana. Agustin Esquivel-Medrano, who could speak only Spanish, bought tickets in Newark under the name of Perez. He was born on March 11, 1915, and probably met the FAA profile. His wife appeared very ill, and his fifteen-year-old daughter, a high school student, was the calmest of the group, which appeared conspicuous by having no luggage; each carried four or five shopping bags. The plane left Newark at 9:13 A.M., with eighty-one passengers and eight crew. The Perez family sat in the rear section. When it was a hundred miles north of Wilmington, North Carolina, the father jumped up and started addressing the stewardess, Rosemary Evans, in Spanish. The captain, Bernard L. Hautain, recalled, "We were just south of Norfolk, Virginia, when Rosemary let this Cuban in with a knife in his hand. He couldn't speak English, except to say, 'Havana, Havana,' so his daughter came in and translated." At 9:55 A.M. Hautain radioed that he was off to Havana. Second officer David Savage reported that the hijacker also had tied a bottle labeled "Danger: Explosives" to his wrist: "It looked like pink sugar, and inside this was a test tube of what looked like Merthiolate with wax on top of it. It probably was just a diversion, but you don't know what it was, of course." The hijacker recounted his difficulties with the language and cultural barriers in the United States and had reconsidered his decision to emigrate. His wife was also very ill and wanted to see her family in Cuba one last time. At 11:55 A.M., half an hour after the plane was due in Miami, it landed at José Martí Airport. When the mother's knees buckled, one of the militiamen on hand held her up. 5155

June 24, 1969—Israel—A fire caused by a PFLP bomb burned four hours at an oil pipeline in Haifa. One hundred seventy Arabs were arrested at roadblocks set up throughout Israel. 0170

June 25, 1969—United States—United Airlines flight 14, a DC8 flying from Los Angeles to New York, was hijacked to Havana, Cuba, by John Gerard Marques, a Latin who probably met the FAA profile; he was born on February 27, 1938, in Santa Monica, California. The stewardess, Patricia Redner, recalls that he said, "I'll give you three seconds to open the cockpit door," and was armed with a pistol. The plane carried fifty-nine passengers and three crew members. Marques remains a fugitive from an indictment handed down by a federal grand jury in the central district of California on January 14, 1970. The previous day, Ray Johnson, an earlier hijacker, had told of his mistreatment in Cuba, but this proved no deterrent to Marques. 5156

June 26, 1969—Argentina—Fourteen Rockefeller-owned Minimax super markets were bombed shortly before Governor Nelson Rockefeller arrived in Buenos Aires. Seven stores were totally destroyed; the other seven were damaged. Total damage was estimated at $3 million. 0171-0184

June 27, 1969—Uruguay—Tupamaros attacked a General Motors plant in Penarol, stealing 500 million pesos. 0185

June 28, 1969—United States—Eastern Airlines flight 173, a B727 on the Baltimore-Tampa-Miami run, was hijacked to Havana over Daytona Beach when a passenger pulled a pen knife and forced the stewardess to take him to the cockpit. The hijacker was described as Raymond L. Anthony, Sr., a white who did not meet the FAA profile, who was born in Midland, Maryland, on April 11, 1914. The unemployed Baltimore automobile salesman had a history of drinking, and he used a credit card he received unsolicited in the mail to have a few drinks before buying a ticket on the Eastern flight with the card. Anthony was dressed in shorts and sandals for the flight, which included ninety-six passengers and seven crew. He was indicted by a Baltimore grand jury on August 5 and wrote to his sister in Baltimore in October that he wished to return to the United States, describing Cuba as ''a terrible and horrible place.'' On November 1, 1969, he returned via Canada with several other U.S. hijackers. On October 6, 1970, he was sentenced to fifteen years for interference with a flight crew member. He was released on April 23, 1973. 5157

June 30, 1969—West Germany—A Croatian exile seriously wounded the head of the Yugoslav military mission in West Berlin, Anton Kolendic, and twenty others. 0186

July 1969—Kenya—Tom Mboya, the minister of economics, was killed by an assassin's bullet. Conditions in Kenya because of tribal enmity between Luo and Kikuyu were such that President Jomo Kenyatta and other members of the predominantly Kikuyu cabinet were unable to attend Mboya's funeral.

July 3, 1969—Ecuador—Thirteen armed individuals hijacked an Ecuadorian SEATA DC3 flying from Tulcán to Quito with twenty-three people on board. They forced it to refuel in Cali, Colombia, before flying on to Santiago, Cuba. 5158

July 10, 1969—Colombia—An Avianca DC4 flying from Barranquilla to Santa Marta was the scene of an unsuccessful hijacking attempt by Luis

Herrera, who wished to go to Cuba. Herrera was overpowered by the pilot, who returned to Barranquilla. 5159

July 10, 1969—Colombia—David Olarte was overpowered by a stewardess and other passengers when he attempted to hijack an Avianca DC4 flying from Cali to Bogotá to Cuba. The plane landed in Bogotá. 5160

July 17, 1969—India—Two time bombs exploded in the USIS reading room in the consulate section of the consulate general at Little Russel Street Annex in Calcutta. One library patron received a bruise on his ankle from a fragment, and one USIS local employee received minor burns on his hands. Only minor damage was done to the room. 0187

July 18, 1969—United Kingdom—A firebomb exploded in the Israeli ZIM shipping lines offices in London. The PFLP claimed credit. 0188

July 18, 1969—United Kingdom—A PFLP firebomb exploded in the Oxford Street branch of Marks and Spencer in London, a Jewish-owned chain store where most Arab visitors in London do their shopping. The PFLP warned that more bombings of Jewish facilities in the United Kingdom and United States would take place, with PFLP leader George Habash forecasting: "We shall expand our operations everywhere, in all parts of the world. The enemy camp includes not only Israel but also the Zionist movement, world imperialism led by the U.S. and reactionary powers bound to imperialism." 0189

July 19, 1969—Sudan—The USIS library in Khartoum was the target of a small bomb, which broke seven windows and caused minimal damage to window casements and sills but injured no one. 0190

July 22, 1969—Philippines—One of the two hand grenades thrown at the USIS library and consulate bulding exploded in Manila, killing one Filipino and damaging glass in front of the Library. 0191

July 22, 1969—Yugoslavia—A bypasser reported to the local fire department that a case of arson had occurred in the Belgrade office of the U.S. Binational Commission Cultural Exchanges during the night. The fire had not spread from the main reception room, where it was extinguished, and had caused no injuries. 0192

July 23, 1969—Greece—A cleaning woman discovered an explosive device in the Athens USIS Library. It was set to explode when the library was vacant and was disarmed by the policy without damage. 0193

July 26, 1969—United States—Continental Airlines flight 156, a DC9 flying the Los Angeles-El Paso-Midland, Texas-Lubbock, Texas route was hijacked to Havana by Joseph C. Crawford, a black who met the FAA profile; he was born on January 13, 1941 at St. Simons Island, Georgia. The plane was about to touch down in Midland that evening when it was taken over. Crawford allowed fifty-three passengers and three stewardesses to leave and flew on with the other four crewmen. Captain R. E. Green of Dallas reported, "He was polite, didn't talk much, and kept his knife out all the way to Havana." The hijacker returned to the United States via Canada with other U.S. hijackers on November 1, 1969, and on September 14, 1970, was sentenced to fifty years for aircraft piracy and kidnapping, the longest sentence meted out up to that time. 5161

July 26, 1969—Mexico—A Mexicana de Aviacion DC6 flying the Mexico City-Minatitlán, Veracruz-Villahermosa, Tabasco run was hijacked over Mexico's east coast just before noon by two pistol-wielding individuals who diverted the plane to Havana. The couple, identified as David Carrera Vasquez and Pilar Munos Ramos, held a stewardess hostage and entered the cockpit of the plane, which carried twenty-nine passengers and three crew. 5162

July 29, 1969—Nicaragua—A male hijacker dressed as a female was subdued after attempting to divert a Nicaraguan plane flying from Managua to the coast of Nicaragua to Cuba. 5163

July 30, 1969—Japan—A twenty-one-year-old Japanese youth attempted to assassinate the U.S. ambassador to Japan, Armin H. Meyer, as he was accompanying U.S. Secretary of State William Rogers at Tokyo International Airport. The youth, armed with a knife, was knocked to the ground, and no one was injured. 0194

July 31, 1969—United States—TWA flight 79, a B727 on the Philadelphia-Pittsburgh-Indianapolis-St. Louis-Los Angeles run, was hijacked to Havana's José Martí Airport. The hijacker had flown from Scranton to Pittsburgh aboard another plane and then transferred to the TWA flight, accompanied by a prison guard and a federal marshal who were escorting him to a federal prison. The bank robber was allowed to go to the washroom unaccompanied after the plane left St. Louis. He found a used razor blade in the receptacle and grabbed a stewardess, holding the blade at her throat. The captain, J. L. Wilmot, radioed, "There's a man in the cockpit who wants to go to Havana." One hundred thirty-one people were aboard the flight. The hijacker was identified as Lester Ellsworth Perry, Jr., a white male who did not meet the FAA profile, who was born on August 8, 1937, in Chicago. 5164

July 31, 1969—Ethiopia—The ELF issued a communiqué warning that they would resort to midair attacks on Ethiopian Airlines in retaliation for air force attacks on Eritrean villages. 0195

August 1, 1969—Mexico and Cuba—Cuba and Mexico signed a treaty providing for the mutual detention of hijackers. Extradition was not guaranteed.

August 4, 1969—Colombia—An Avianca DC4 flying the Barranquilla-Santa Marta-Riohacha run was hijacked to Cuba by three pistol-wielding males. Fifty-eight persons were aboard. 5165

August 5, 1969—United States—Eastern Airlines fight 379, a DC9 flying the Syracuse-Philadelphia-Tampa run, was the scene of a hijacking attempt by the oldest recorded hijacker. A man armed with a five-inch straight razor and a pocketknife identified as John Scott McCreery, a white who did not meet the FAA profile, who was born on August 14, 1895, in Philadelphia, wanted to go to Cuba. He allowed the pilot to refuel but commented that he would be apprehended if the plane touched down. He returned to his seat and was arrested in Tampa. Charges against him were dismissed on January 12, 1970, and he was committed to a mental institution, from which he was discharged on September 15, 1971. Eighty-six passengers were aboard the flight. 5166

August 5, 1969—Philippines—A passenger aboard a Philippine Airlines plane on a local flight committed suicide over Zamboanga by detonating gelignite in a lavatory, blowing himself out of the aircraft. Four other passengers were slightly injured. The plane carried twenty-seven passengers and four crew and was able to land successfully.

August 7, 1969—Israel—Palestinian terrorists attacked a potash works in Sodom. 0196

August 7, 1969—Israel—A PFLP terrorist set a bomb near El Hamma, which blew up an Israeli bus, killing the civilian driver and a soldier and wounding twelve other soldiers. The PFLP claimed it had killed fifty soldiers. The same day, Israeli jets crossed fifteen miles into Jordan, bombing camps, fortified positions, command posts, and transportation equipment. Israeli tanks shelled Jordanian positions.

August 8, 1969—India—Police theorized that an explosion at the Calcutta Post Office was directed at the USIS library. A book was hollowed out and an explosive device inserted, set to detonate by a time fuse or when it was opened. The book was being returned to the library by mail. 0197

August 9, 1969—Greece—A bomb exploded at an Olympic Airlines office in Athens, injuring two American tourists. 0198

August 11, 1969—India—During a demonstration of fifteen hundred college students, stones and two homemade bombs were thrown at the USIS office in Calcutta. One bomb did minor damage to the gate; the other failed to explode. 0199

August 12, 1969—Ethiopia—An Ethiopian Airlines DC3, flying from Bahr Dar to Addis Ababa, was hijacked by six students attending Haile Selassie University in Addis and an official of the Ministry of Community Development. Nineteen passengers were aboard the flight that the ELF males diverted to Khartoum, Sudan, using a revolver and knife to force a stewardess to allow them into the cockpit. The Sudanese jailed them for two weeks for passport violations. 0200

August 14, 1969—United States—Northeast Airlines flight 43, a B727 flying from Boston to Miami with fifty-two persons on board, was hijacked to Havana by two Latins who met the FAA profile and were armed with a revolver: Domingo Torres-Diaz, born February 17, 1943, in Niquero, Cuba, and Julio Lazaro Mena Perez, born October 1, 1939, in Cuba. They remain fugitives from a Massachusetts federal grand jury indictment handed down on November 14, 1969. 5167

August 15, 1969—Israel—Al Fatah bombed an oil pipeline and electric pylon in Haifa. 0201

August 16, 1969—Greece—An Olympic Airways DC3 on the Athens-Agrinion-Ioannina run was hijacked over the Bay of Corinth by Dr. Vassilios Tsironis, his wife, and two sons, who forced the plane to land at Valona, Albania. Tsironis was a minor Greek politician who had formed a political party that was highly critical of the Greek establishment and had served a number of terms in Greek prisons for his views. He and his wife carried pistols, while his children held knives aboard the plane, which was carrying twenty-eight passengers and three crew members. The forty-year-old former nurse in the Greek army, who had served in Greek prison camps after the civil war, apologized for any inconvenience. Passengers reported that the plane was intercepted by three MIGs and made a forced landing in a field near a deserted airstrip. After intervention by Turkey on behalf of Greece, the Albanians permitted the return of the plane. The family made their way to Sweden, which was highly critical of the Greek government and which rewarded the family with a generous allowance, quartering them in the Hotel Carlton in Stockholm. The U.N.

General Assembly took up the question of hijacking some months after the arrival of Tsironis, and criminal proceedings were suddenly begun against him. He was sentenced to three and a half years' imprisonment on July 7, 1971. 5168

August 17, 1969—United States—The PFLP firebombed a Marks and Spencers department store in London. 0202

August 18, 1969—Denmark—The Israel Tourist Office in Copenhagen was bombed. 0203

August 18, 1969—Egypt—An Egyptian Misrair Anatov-24 flying from Cairo to Aswan was hijacked to El Wagah, a small airstrip north of Jidda, Saudi Arabia. The plane was carrying a crew of six and thirty passengers, including several Americans, when it was hijacked by two brothers wielding a knife. They were identified as Mohamed Hashem El Moneiry and Soliman Hashem El Moneiry, an army physician who was accompanied by his wife and three children. They were arrested by Saudi Arabia and returned aboard the same plane under guard to Luxor, Egypt, under the orders of King Faisal. Soliman was sentenced to life imprisonment. 5169

August 21, 1969—Israel—The Al Aksa Mosque was gutted by fire in Jerusalem. Angry mobs throughout the Arab world denounced what they viewed as an Israeli desecration of one of their holy places. The Israelis later arrested the arsonist, a mentally disturbed Australian tourist who claimed to be a member of the Church of God, an evangelical denomination. He attacked the mosque because of a religious obsession.

August 23, 1969—Iran—A Jewish school in Tehran was bombed. 0204

August 23, 1969—Colombia—An Avianca AVRO-748 flying from Burcarmanga to Bogotá was hijacked by two men brandishing pistols. They allowed the pilot to refuel in Barranquilla before flying to Santiago de Cuba. The twenty-eight other people on board were lodged in Cuban hotels until the plane left. 5170

August 25, 1969—Turkey—Two Jordanians attempted to bomb the Israeli Commercial Fair in Izmir but were injured when the bomb exploded prematurely. One died from his injuries; the other was arrested. 0205

August 25, 1969—United Kingdom—The PFLP bombed the London office of the Israeli shipping line ZIM, wounding two people, including a female employee. Four days later in Amman, George Habash warned that similar attacks would be made against Israeli firms in London. 0206

August 26, 1969—Israel—Three rockets crashed into southern Jerusalem but caused no damage or casualties. A six-square-mile area southeast of Jerusalem was sealed off three days later when Israeli helicopters spotted thirteen other rockets on a barren hill two miles east of Bethlehem, between the Arab villages of Sur Bahir and Beir Sahhour. On August 26, Israeli jets bombed guerrilla bases in Jordan south of the Dead Sea in retaliation. 0207

August 26, 1969—Austria—Two people were killed and eleven injured when a naturalized Canadian citizen expressed his personal dissatisfaction by hurling a gasoline bomb into the library of the Canadian embassy in Vienna. The arsonist was arrested. 0208

August 29, 1969—United States—The files of the New York City office of the Palestine Liberation Organization were burglarized by the Jewish Defense League. 0209

August 29, 1969—United States—National Airlines flight 183, a B727 on the Miami-New Orleans-Houston run, was hijacked to Cuba by Jorge Carballe Delgado, a Latin who probably met the FAA profile, who was born on March 2, 1929 in Santo Domingo, Cuba. He was accompanied on the plane by his wife, a newborn baby, and two small sons. He used a pistol to force the stewardess to take him to the cockpit. When the plane and its fifty other people on board returned to Miami at 3:50 P.M., Barbara Aparicio Presley of Caracas, Venezuela, reported that she had sat next to the hijacker when she overheard him say to two of his children: ''Don't be ashamed of your father. We are doing it for our son in Cuba.'' Delgado is a fugitive from an indictment handed down by a federal grand jury in the middle district of Florida on November 6, 1969. 5171

August 29, 1969—Italy—TWA flight 840, a B707 flying the Los Angeles-Paris-Rome-Athens-Tel Aviv run had just picked up 85 of its 101 passengers and 12 crew members in Rome when it was hijacked over the Adriatic Sea by a man and a woman, members of the PFLP, who produced pistols. One carried a grenade and the other a time bomb in his pocket. The two, who stood up from their first-class seats, were identified as Leila Ali Khaled, born in 1944 in Haifa, Israel, and Salim K. Essawai, born in 1945 in Baghdad, Iraq, who identified himself as Captain Chadiyah Abu Ghazalah and called the plane ''PFLP Free Palestine.'' The passengers heard the following message from the cockpit: ''Ladies and gentlemen, please kindly fasten your seat belts. This is your new captain speaking. The Ché Guevara Commando Unit of PFLP, which has taken command of TWA flight 840, requests all passengers to adhere to the following instructions: Remain seated and be calm. For you own safety, place your hands behind your heads. Make no move that would endanger the life of other passengers. We will consider all your demands—within the safe limits of our plans. Among you is a passenger responsible for death and misery of a number of Palestinian children, women, and men, on behalf of whom we are carrying out this operation. This assassin will be brought before a Palestinian revolutionary court. The rest of you will be honorable guests in a hospitable and friendly country. Every one of you, regardless of religion or citizenship, is guaranteed freedom to go wherever he pleases as soon as the plane has safely landed. Thank you for your cooperation, and we wish you a happy journey.'' Khaled then ordered the captain, Dean Carter of Freeport, Bahamas, to fly over Lod Airport. The Israeli air controller heard over his radio: ''We have kidnapped this American plane because Israel is a colony of America and the Americans are giving the Israelis Phantom planes. Tel Aviv! We are from the Popular Front for the Liberation of Palestine. What can you do about it?'' Lebanese authorities offered permission to land at Beirut, but the plane flew on to Damascus, Syria. Two Israeli jets that had been scrambled to meet the plane turned back when it crossed the Lebanese-Syrian border. They were replaced by Syrian planes, which escorted the TWA plane down. Upon landing, Khaled informed the pilot that all passengers must immediately leave the plane because bombs were set to explode. All passengers successfully got off the plane just in time to watch hand grenades and an explosive canister device destroy the cockpit, causing $4 million damage. Khaled's orders had been to destroy the $8 million plane. Several passengers were injured during evacuation of the aircraft, including Caridad Roa Schaller of Leonardtown, Maryland, who broke her leg.

The Syrians released ninety-nine of the passengers, along with the twelve crew members, most of whom were Americans, French, Italians, and Greeks, but held six Israelis, saying that they would be held hostage for the release of Syrian prisoners in Israeli jails. Those released flew to Athens and Rome aboard an Alitalia plane. Four of the Israelis, three women and one teen-aged girl, were released after two days of questioning by the Syrians. Have Freud, who returned with her sixteen-year-old daughter Dalia, reported that they had been well treated and were served excellent meals and fruit. Victoria Shamash claimed that she had fainted because she had not been served kosher food. The Syrians continued to hold Hebrew University physiology professor Dr. Shlomo Samueloff and Saleh Muallem, a travel agent, whom the PFLP believed was responsible for torturing prisoners. They eventually changed their story, claiming that an Israeli of ''scientific and military importance'' was being held.

International pressure on the Syrians came from a number of sources, including the International Federation of Air Line Pilots Associations, which voted on September 1 to call a twenty-four-hour worldwide strike against Syria. U.N. Secretary-General U Thant cautioned IFALPA president Ola Forsberg of Finnair against such actions, as did the director general of the International Air Transport Association, Knut Hammarskjold.

Khaled and Essawai were held by the Syrians until October 13 inside the main Syrian Defense Ministry building in Damascus under heavy guard. It was learned that Khaled was a refugee who had left Haifa at age four and settled in Tyre, Lebanon, with her parents. She received PFLP training after the 1967 war and had forced the TWA pilot to overfly her city of birth. She was to become the most famous hijacker in the Arab hijacking campaign and in numerous interviews with the press observed that "hijacking is one of the operational aspects of our war against Zionism, and all those who support it, including the U.S. [The TWA plane was hijacked] because it brought visitors and tourists to our enemies who are occupying our land by force of arms. . . . It was a perfectly normal thing to do, the sort of thing all freedom fighters have to tackle." Despite poor relations between Habash and Syria due to differences between Habash's Arab Natonalist Movement and Syria's Baath Party, the duo were released. Khaled would later write her memoirs, as well as take part in another hijacking on September 6, 1970. It was also learned that Habash had told Khaled that the Israeli ambassador to the United States, Yitzhak Rabin, was aboard the plane. However, he had returned to Tel Aviv on an earlier flight. Rome police discovered that the two had come from Beirut on August 28.

On December 5, Samueloff and Muallem returned to Israel via Athens aboard the TWA plane, which had been repaired. Israel also received two pilots who had been shot down over Egypt. Israel released fifty-two civilians, five soldiers, and one air force pilot to Egypt and sent Syria thirteen of its citizens, including two air force pilots who had accidentally landed their MIG 17s in Israel sixteen months previously. The International Red Cross helped negotiate the deal, the last hostage arrangement Israel agreed to.

A complaint was failed on January 16, 1970, in the District of Columbia in the United States against the hijackers. 0210

August 30, 1969—West Germany—A postcard dated August 30, 1969, was received in Washington, D.C., postmarked Stuttgart and signed with the initials VFBP LBF. The card demanded that an unidentified Voice of America transmitter shift frequency during Radio Damascus's German-French broadcast from 5:30 to 6:30 P.M., warning, "If not, you are going to fly like the TWA plane," an apparent reference to the previous incident. 0211

September 1969—Cuba—José Antonio Quesada Fernandez, a leader of the Second Front of Escambray, led a small military group to Cuba to establish contact with the underground. Radio Havana announced on February 23, 1970, that he had been executed by firing squad. 0212

September 2, 1969—Israel—Palestinian terrorists shelled the town of Qiryat Shmona from positions in Lebanon, killing a nine-year-old boy and a twenty-six-year-old man and injuring five other civilians. Shells also hit the village of Kfar Giladi, causing no casualties. Army units counterattacked. In various border incidents, four Israeli soldiers were killed on September 2; six had died the previous day. 0213

September 3, 1969—Japan—After they were challenged by police, two young men dressed as students threw two Molotov cocktails at the U.S. embassy in Tokyo, causing no damage or injuries. One ignited next to the driveway; the other fell on the street. 0214

September 4, 1969—Brazil—Charles Burke Elbrick, sixty-one, U.S. ambassador to Brazil and former deputy assistant secretary of state for European affairs, was kidnapped from his car on his way to the embassy following lunch at home when four armed men, members of the Revolutionary Movement of October 8 and the National Liberation Action, blocked the path of his car with their cars on a Rio de Janeiro street. The group left a ransom note demanding the release of fifteen unidentified political prisoners who were to be flown to Chile, Mexico, or Algeria and the publication of a three-page manifesto. Elbrick's chauffeur, an embassy employee for four years, was left behind unharmed. Elbrick suffered a scalp-type wound on his right forehead where he was hit by the butt of a .38 caliber revolver. The group warned that if their demands were not carried out within forty-eight hours, they would "be forced to carry out revolutionary justice" by killing Elbrick. An hour after his capture, the group questioned him about the activities, membership, and contacts of the CIA in Brazil by two men whom the ambassador believed were outside communists, "unlike the kidnappers themselves who did not claim to be communists."

The Brazilian National Security Council, composed of three military ministers acting during the convalescence of President Arthur da Costa e Silva, met in emergency session on September 4 and the next day authorized the newspapers to print the manifesto, which claimed that the kidnapping was "not an isolated act. It is another one of the innumerable revolutionary acts already carried out: bank holdups, where funds for the revolution are collected, returning what the bankers take from the people and their employees; raids on barracks and police stations, where arms and ammunitions are obtained for the struggle to topple the dictatorship; invasions of jails when revolutionaries are freed to return them to the people's struggle; the explosion of buildings that signify oppression; the execution of hangmen and torturers. With the kidnap of the ambassador we want to demonstrate that it is possible to defeat the dictatorship and the exploitation if we arm and organize ourselves. We show up where the enemy least expects us, and we disappear immediately, tearing out the dictatorship, bringing terror and fear to the exploiters, the hope and certainty of victory to the midst of the exploited. Mr. Elbrick represents in our country the interests of imperialism, which, allied to the great bosses, the big ranches and the big national bankers, maintain the regime of oppression and exploitation.''

Foreign Minister José de Migalhaes Pinto announced the same day that fifteen political prisoners would also be released. Mexico and Chile immediately offered political asylum, and two hours later, the names of the prisoners that the terrorists wanted released were placed in a suggestion box at a suburban supermarket. They were identified as Gregorio Bezzerra, seventy, a leading member of the clandestine communist party, who had been in prison since 1964; Wladimir Palmeira, twenty-four, former president of the Metropolitan Student Union in Rio, arrested in 1968 and sentenced in August to three years imprisonment for leading student demonstrations against the government; Flavio Tavares, a newspapermen charged in 1966 with organizing guerrilla activities and recently arrested on charges of membership in a terrorist group called the Revolutionary Movement of July 26; Ricardo Zarattini, former National Student Union officer, jailed for subversive activities among peasants; Luiz Travassos, former National Student Union president who was also active in the radical movement of the Roman Catholic church; José Dirccu de Oliveira e Silva, also a former president of the National Student Union; Ricardo Villas Boas de Sarega and Maria Augusta Carneiro, both student leaders arrested May 1 for allegedly firing at a policeman who was attempting to prevent them from distributing antigovernment literature; Onofre Pinto, a former air force sergeant, arrested and charged with killing U.S. Army Captain Charles R. Chandler (see incident 0103); Ivens Marchetti, a São Paulo architect, also charged with Chandler's murder; José Ibrahim and Rolando Prattes, labor leaders in the São Paulo area; Argonauto Pacheco da Silva, labor leader and former São Paulo legislator; Joao Leonardo da Silva Rocha, a São Paulo lawyer; and Mario Galgardo Zanconato, twenty-two, former medical student, who said in Mexico City September 8 that he had organized eight bank robberies in Minas Gerais to raise funds for the revolutionary movement.

On September 6, members of the armed forces who disagreed with the government's capitulation attempted to prevent the prisoners' release. Two hundred navy men surrounded the airport but dispersed when they were ordered back to their barracks. The plane took off late for Mexico city with the fifteen, where they were granted political asylum. Thirteen of the group turned up later in Cuba.

Arrests soon followed. Police quickly surrounded the house where Elbrick was being kept (it had been rented in the true name of one of the kidnappers) but allowed the group safe passage in return for his release. One member returned to his parents' home for a change of clothes and was arrested. From him it was learned that the Revolutionary Movement of the 8th (MR-8) approached guerrilla theorist Carlos Marighella and the ALN with their plan for the kidnapping.

The Brazilian government had believed that it had previously crippled the terrorist movements. On July 27, it had arrested twenty-nine MR-8 members, seven more on August 7, and several dozen on August 10. This time a nationwide roundup was initiated, resulting in the arrests of over four thousand suspects. Institutional Act 14 was passed, which decreed the death penalty for subversion, the first time capital punishment was allowed in Brazil since 1891. Police powers of the military were also greatly expanded.

The groups still managed to send another manifesto after Elbrick's release, in which they argued that they had no personal hostility toward the ambassador but had taken him as a symbol of "big North American capitalists."

In November, the police announced the death of Carlos Marighella. In December, student Claudio Torres de Silva received a ten-year sentence for his part in the kidnapping, while three others were being held on related charges. In February, the army announced the eighteen persons had been in on the planning and execution of the kidnapping and that four had been apprehended; the others had fled to Cuba.

Members of the attack squad were interviewed in places of safety months after the incident. An MR-8 member in Algiers, Fernando Gabeira, claimed that he had been in on the two-month planning period, during which the group had infiltrated a female into the military intelligence agency, DOPS, where she collected information about the ambassador's travel habits. Twelve terrorists who had previously engaged in bank robberies used a rented villa on Marques Street, near Elbrick's home, as their headquarters. In late June, twenty-one-year-old Silvia de Araujo Magalhaes gave a similar interview in Algiers. She recounted that Elbrick was held in an apartment on the Barau de Petropolis in the Santa Teresa district. Elbrick had a bathroom with a shower, but the windows were sealed. His cook was Fernando Gabeira, a former editor of the *Journal do Brasil*. Elbrick was allowed to write three letters to his wife. The group felt compassion for him, giving him a book by Ho Chi Minh inscribed, "To our first political prisoner, with the expression of our respect for his calm behavior in action." 0215

September 6, 1969—Brazil—The public affairs officer of the USIS in São Paulo received a telephone call informing him, by name, "Your hour has come, wait for the blast." 0216

September 6, 1969—Ecuador—Two Tame Commercial Airlines C47 transport planes, operated by the Ecuadorian Air Force on domestic flights from Quito to Guayaquil, were hijacked and directed to fly to Cuba. Both landed in Tumaco, Colombia, to refuel. The first plane was taken over by six male hijackers armed with submachine guns. During the refueling, a fight broke out; the copilot was killed and the radioman wounded. The other crew member and fourteen passengers were left aboard the plane, and the six joined their colleagues, six men and a woman, all armed with submachine guns, aboard the other plane, which carried thirty-four passengers. Refueling stops were made at Panama and Jamaica before the plane landed in Santiago de Cuba. The passengers reported that the hijackers had referred to the attack as Operation Ho Chi Minh and that it was in retaliation for the May deaths of several students during antigovernment riots at the University of Guayaquil. 0217-0218

September 7, 1969—United States—Eastern Airlines flight 925, a DC8 that had left New York's Kennedy International Airport at 1:57 P.M., due to arrive in San Juan, Puerto Rico, at 5:19 P.M. with eighty-six passengers and ten crew, was hijacked east of the Bahamas one hour and forty-eight minutes into its flight. Captain John A. Themm landed the plane at José Martí Airport at 5:45 P.M. The plane was immediately released and allowed to fly for refueling to Miami, landing at 10:46 P.M., before continuing on to San Juan. The pistol-wielding hijacker was identified as Felix Roland Peterson-Coplin, a Latin who probably met the FAA hijacker profile; he was born on November 20, 1934, in La Romana, Dominican Republic. He remains a fugitive. 5172

September 8, 1969—Belgium—Three Arabs recruited by Al Fatah, two of them teenage boys, threw hand grenades at the El Al office in Brussels a few minutes past noon. Three El Al employees and a passerby were injured by flying glass and steel splinters. One of the teenagers fled to a nearby Arab embassy (reports differ as to whether it was the Tunisian or Iraqi mission). The adult returned to Syria via Budapest and East Berlin. The last member of the team, a sixteen-year-old boy, was arrested by a policeman while attempting to escape but was never brought to trial and eventually was handed over to the Libyan embassy. 0219

September 8, 1969—Netherlands—A Russian-made grenade was thrown by a PFLP terrorist at the Israeli embassy in the Hague, missing an open window and exploding harmlessly on a nearby balcony. One teenage boy was arrested but handed over to the Libyan embassy. Another sought refugee in the Algerian embassy. 0220

September 8, 1969—West Germany—While the other two attacks were occurring in Belgium and the Netherlands, a third PFLP group lobbed hand grenades at the Israeli embassy in Bonn. One grenade went off in the embassy courtyard, causing minor damage. Another exploded under the window of Ambassador Asher ben Nathan. One Arab youth was arrested; the other sought refuge in the Saudi Arabian embassy. The next day the PFLP claimed credit for the coordinated attacks, warning travelers not to use Israeli ships or planes and explaining that the embassies ''are the centers of espionage and collection points for mercenaries and immigrants to our occupied Palestine.'' The PFLP believed that the Netherlands and West Germany were places used by the United States to train Israeli pilots to fly their newly acquired Phantom jets. 0221

September 9, 1969—Argentina—Several hundred students conducted a street demonstration in memory of persons killed in previous disturbances. Tar bombs and Molotov cocktails damaged the USIS building's structure in Rosario. 0222

September 9, 1969—Ethiopia—Murray E. Jackson, U.S. consul general in Asmara, was kidnapped while driving in his official car with his chauffeur between Agordat and Keren. He and a British businessman were held by the ELF for two hours, who made no ransom demands and merely had him sign a statement saying that he had listened to the groups's differences with the government and that he had not been mistreated. 0223

September 10, 1969—Uruguay—Tupamaros robbed the Bank of London and South America of 5 million pesos. 0224

September 10, 1969—United States—Eastern Airlines flight 929, a DC8 flying from New York to San Juan, was the scene of an unsuccessful attempt to hijack it to Havana by José Luis Gonzalez Medina, a Latin who met the FAA profile, who was born on January 4, 1949 in Lares, Puerto Rico. He grabbed a stewardess and said, ''I want to go to Cuba.'' Unable to open the cockpit door with the keys she provided him, he returned to his seat, where he was subdued by the crew and members of the 192 passengers. He was committed to a mental institution on January 30, 1970, from which he was released in December 1971. 5173

September 12, 1969—Jordan—A bomb went off on the porch of the Amman home of the U.S. assistant army attaché, causing no injuries and slight damage. 0225

September 13, 1969—Italy—Two small Molotov cocktails were thrown at the entrance of the Palermo apartment building housing the American consul general, causing little property damage and no injuries. 0226

September 13, 1969—Ethiopia—An Ethiopian Airlines DC6, flying from Addis Ababa to Djibouti, French Somaliland, was hijacked by three members of the ELF to Aden, South Yemen. A gunfight broke out between the pistol-wielding hijackers and an Ethiopian secret police agent who was a passenger on board, who claimed that the group were attempting to escape. He fired six bullets into the stomach and arms of eighteen-year-old Mohammed Sayed, while the other two were captured. A Damascus spokesman for the group claimed credit for the attack, claiming that the operation was to gain publicity for their cause, as well as to retaliate ''for the mass and brutal annihilation campaign waged by the cowardly occupation forces in Eritrea.'' More attacks were promised. None of the sixty-six passengers or four crew members was reported injured. 0227

September 14, 1969—Honduras—A Honduran SAHSA DC3, flying from La Cieba to Tegucigalpa, was hijacked by Carlos Huete, armed with a .38 caliber revolver, who diverted the plane to San Salvador's Ilopango International Airport. He was immediately arrested. The plane and its thirty-four passengers and two crewmen continued on to their original destination. 5174

September 16, 1969—Turkey—A Turkish Airways Viscount flying from Istanbul to Ankara was hijacked by revolver-wielding Sadi Toker, a twenty-seven-year-old Turkish law student, who forced the pilot, Nazmi Kirsever, to fly to Sofia, Bulgaria, where the plane landed two hours after it took off. The Turks identified the hijacker as a former mental patient who had been hospitalized several times and who had been released ten days before the hijacking. He was involved in the stabbing of an American soldier in 1967 during a visit of the U.S. Sixth Fleet but was declared mentally ill and escaped punishment. He had served several prison terms in Turkey and other countries. The Bulgarians immediately allowed the plane, its six crew and the fifty-six passengers to leave and announced that it would return Toker by land to Turkish authorities at the frontier. He was later committed to a mental institution. 5175

September 19, 1969—Cuba—The Cuban government announced that it had established a law providing for the extradition of the hijackers of planes or boats, provided that reciprocity was followed. Cuba would retain the right to determine who was a common criminal or political refugee and noted that it would grant asylum to ''those persons, who, for political reasons, arrive in our country having found themselves in the necessity of using this extreme means to elude a real danger of death or grave repression." It also noted that it would not abide by relevant international agreements adopted in international organizations.

September 20, 1969—Brazil—Terrorists in two sedans pulled up in front of the U.S. consulate in São Paulo, dismounted, and forced the guard to kneel and forfeit his revolver. Two policemen arrived but were gunned down as they were leaving their Volkswagen. One of the six attackers appeared to be Japanese, but the others were masked. 0228

September 24, 1969—United States—National Airlines flight 411, a B727 flying the Newark-Charleston-Miami route, was hijacked to Havana by Alfred A. Hernandez, a Latin who met the FAA profile, who was born on March 20, 1943, in Placetas, Cuba. Seventy-two passengers and seven crew were on board. Hernandez remains a fugitive from an indictment handed down on November 19, 1969, by a federal grand jury in the middle district of Florida. 5176

September 27, 1969—Bolivia—A man threw a bomb in front of the U.S. consul's home in La Paz. He was frightened by pedestrians while he was running toward the house and threw the bomb early. It exploded in front of a car and caused no damage. 0029

September 29, 1969—Brazil—At 6:28 P.M., three terrorists robbed the cashier's safe of an American store. Then one of the group doused the merchandise around the front of the store with the contents of two five-gallon gasoline drums. The explosion caused a sheet of flame, which set off two sprinkler heads. Damage to fixtures, wiring, and walls were estimated at $2,000, and damage to merchandise came to $20,000. 0230

October 1, 1969—Ecuador—A large noise bomb was thrown from a small gray European car at the base of the wall adjoining the main entrance to the chancery of the U.S. embassy in Quito, causing no damage or injuries. 0231

October 1, 1969—Canada—A firebomb was thrown against the door of the U.S. consulate general in Vancouver by two "hippie"-looking women. 0232

October 6, 1969—Guatemala—A USIS officer in Guatemala City received three non-specific threatening telephone calls. 0233-0235

October 6, 1969—Argentina—The Córdoba offices of the First National City Bank, Pepsi-Cola, Squibb, and Dunlop Tires were damaged by bombs. 0236-0239

October 6, 1969—Argentina—The San Miguel de Tucumán offices of IBM and General Electric were damaged by bombs. 0240-0241

October 6, 1969—Colombia—A group identifying itself as the Invisible Ones attacked the car of the Swiss consul in Cali and wounded the consul, Enrique Straessle, while kidnapping his fifteen-year-old son, José, and the first secretary of the Swiss embassy. The two were held for seventeen days by the group, who demanded a $300,000 ransom. A state of siege was imposed in the state of Valle de Cauco to stop a spate of kidnappings in the area (eight persons had been kidnapped and $600,000 ransom had been paid between August and October). Police arrested four left-wing men but admitted that they had no immediate clues as to the location of the hostages and made no specific charges. Newspapers reported that the kidnappers were paid $110,000 of the ransom, although the family denied it. There was speculation that the kidnappers may have been a rightist group protesting Switzerland's representation of Latin American countries in Cuba. 0242

October 7, 1969—Colombia—Two sticks of dynamite exploded on the front porch of the Bucaramanga Binational Center, breaking windows but injuring no one. 0243

October 7, 1969—Argentina—The USIS library in Buenos Aires was damaged by a firebomb equipped with a timing device. No injuries were reported. 0244

October 8, 1969—Argentina—Bombs damaged a branch of the Bank of Boston in Buenos Aires and the Santa Fe office of Remington Rand. 0245-0246

October 8, 1969—Brazil—A Brazilian Cruzeiro do Sul Caravelle flying from Belém to Manaus was hijacked to Havana by six armed men. The group reported carried revolvers, submachine guns, nitroglycerin, and possibly dynamite. The plane carried seven crewmen and forty-two passengers, and was allowed to refuel at Georgetown, Guyana, and San Juan. 5177

October 8, 1969—Argentina—An Aerolineas Argentinas B707 flying from Buenos Aires to Miami with sixty-seven persons on board was hijacked to Havana via Santiago, Chile, by an Argentine student, E. Ugartteche, who was armed with a pistol. Americans numbered four among the twelve crew and fifty-four passengers. 5178

October 8, 1969—Uruguay—Members of the Tupamaros attacked the town of Pando, twenty miles east of Montevideo, robbing three banks and seizing the main police station. Fifteen were killed during a running gun battle in the streets.

October 9, 1969—United States—National Airlines flight 42, a DC8 flying from Los Angeles to Miami, was hijacked to Havana by Francisco Rivera-Perez, a Latin who probably met the FAA profile, who was born on August 24, 1920, in Vinales, Cuba. Seventy people were aboard the plane. A complaint was filed on October 10, 1969, in the western district of Texas. The hijacker remains a fugitive. 5179

October 10, 1969—Chile—The Binational Center director received a call warning that a bomb had been placed in the Santiago facility. A search found nothing. 0247

October 10, 1969—Peru—A bomb exploded in the Arequipa Binational Center, causing extensive damage but no injuries. 0248

October 13, 1969—Brazil—The wife of the U.S. consul general in São Paulo received an anonymous call stating, "We're going to get you," whereupon the caller hung up. 0249

October 14, 1969—Colombia—No one was reported injured when gunmen fired on the Swiss embassy in Bogotá. 0250

October 15, 1969—Lebanon—The headquarters of the Palestine Liberation Organization was shelled by four rockets in Beirut. The group blamed Israeli intelligence agents. 0251

October 19, 1969—Poland—A Polish Lot Ilyushin 18 flying the Warsaw-East Berlin-Brussels run with sixty-one passengers and nine crew members was diverted to West Berlin's Tegel Airport in the French sector by two East German automobile mechanics. They brandished pistols, only one of which was loaded, and entered the cockpit, demanding to be flown to the western half of Berlin so that they would be able to obtain political asylum. When the pilot and copilot refused, the hijackers hit them on the head with the pistols, inflicting slight injuries. Three hours later, the pilots complied, and the plane landed. The two were taken away by French authorities. None of the other twenty East Germans followed their lead. Among the passengers was fifty-eight year-old George Kucharski, an American residing in New York, who slept through the initial takeover. The two told police that they were in trouble with East German authorities for opposing the invasion of Czechoslovakia and identified themselves as Ulrich Juengen Von Hof, nineteen and Peter Klemt, twenty-four. The plane had landed at 1:55 P.M. and took off again just before 5

P.M. after the cordon surrounding it dispersed. On November 20, 1969, the two were sentenced to two years each, having been found guilty by a three-man French military court of having endangered air safety and of having hindered air traffic. The prosecutor had demanded three years, arguing for "exemplary punishment," and noting that West Berlin should not become a popular destination of hijackers. The hijackers emptied the bullets from their gun before leaving the plane. 5180

October 20, 1969—Japan—Several students were arrested after breaking into the South Korean embassy in Tokyo, breaking several windows. 0252

October 21, 1969—United States—Pan American flight 551, a B720 flying the Mexico City-Mérida-Miami run, was hijacked while descending at Mérida and forced to fly to Havana. The gunman was identified as Henry L. Shorr, a white who met the profile, who was born on November 3, 1951, in Detroit, Michigan. He told the thirty-six people on board that he had had an oppressed childhood. Among the passengers was state senator Tom Slade of Florida, as well as two Peruvian officials who had just submitted a hijacking resolution to the Interpol General Assembly. Shorr committed suicide in a Cuban hotel on September 28, 1970. 5181

October 22-23, 1969—Israel—Four apartments were bombed on October 22 and a fifth the next day in Haifa. Two were killed, twenty wounded, and two apartment buildings destroyed in the attacks. Premier Meir vowed to punish the perpetrators, whom police claimed were PFLP members. 0253-257

October 23, 1969—Peru—Five Molotov cocktails were thrown at the front doors of the U.S. embassy chancery in Lima. Only one bomb ignited, but did not cause damage or injuries. One of five youths involved was captured. 0258

October 25, 1969—Bolivia—A bomb exploded in front of the La Paz head-quarters of the U.S. Peace Corps, shattering fifteen windows but harming no one. 0259

October 26, 1969—Lebanon—A small explosive charge detonated in Beirut under the car of the U.S. embassy regional communications officer, which was parked in front of his home. 0260

October 28, 1969—Colombia—A Colombian Aerotaxi Airlines Beachcraft charted to fly from Buenaventura to Bogotá was hijacked by two armed men who diverted the plane and its eight passengers to Havana via Kingston, Jamaica. 5182

November 1, 1969—Japan—A time bomb was placed near the reception desk of the American Cultural Center in Tokyo. A Japanese worker who found the bomb managed to disarm it before it was scheduled to explode. 0261

November 1, 1969—United States—TWA flight 85, a B707 on the Baltimore-St. Louis-Kansas City-Los Angeles-San Francisco run, was hijacked twenty minutes out of San Francisco at 2:25 A.M. The hijacker had been sitting with a large bag, which he had told the stewardess contained a fishing rod. Later, he stood up and pointed his semiautomatic rifle at stewardess Tracey Coleman and told her that he was taking over the plane with forty-five on board. He diverted the plane to Denver, where he permitted thirty-nine passengers and three stewardesses to deplane. The pilot, Captain Donald J. Cook, thirty-one, flew on to New York. While the plane was refueling, the FBI attempted to board. FBI special agents recounted that Gerald W. Van Leeuwen talked to the hijacker through the window as a diversion while John F. Malone and Joseph Sullivan attempted to enter the plane but were unable to do so because the crew would not cooperate. The crew claimed that the FBI had not talked to the hijacker and had endangered the safety of the crew. During refueling, the hijacker fired one shot at the ceiling, which did not pierce the fuselage but hit an oxygen bottle. The plane was allowed to take off with two new pilots, Captain Billy N. Williams and Captain R. H. Hastings, who were qualified to fly transoceanic flights. They flew to Bangor, Maine, with a vacationing TWA pilot, Captain James F. Findlay, and then to Shannon airport in Ireland. The hijacker told the pilots to say that they were proceeding to Cairo but admitted that this was a ruse and that he would be deplaning in Rome.

During the flight, the hijacker identified himself as Lance Corporal Raphael Minichiello, a high-school dropout who had served in twenty-eight combat missions in Vietnam with the Second Battalion, Ninth Marines of the Third Division, where he was awarded the Vietnamese Cross of Gallantry. He was born in Italy on November 1, 1949, was white, and probably met the FAA profile. He also mentioned that he wanted to be an airline pilot. He was away without leave from Camp Pendleton. He claimed that he was being bilked out of $200 of his $800 he had saved while in the marines and had broken into the post exchange where he stole exactly $200 worth of radios and watches. His trial was to be on October 31, but he left the base. During the flight he showed suicidal tendencies, talking of how he expected to die in a gun battle with Italian police and showed how he would have killed himself by firing a bullet into his head if the FBI had attempted to storm the airplane. He took apart and cleaned his M-1 several times during the flight and left it on a seat near the pilot a few times. However, the pilot noted that he had spotted a knife and pistol in Minichiello's belt and did not know what type of combat training he had received so did not attempt to confront the hijacker. Minichiello spoke of problems he had experienced growing up in the United States, especially language and cultural problems, and said that he was going back to Naples to see his father, Luigi, who was living in the area.

On the approach to Rome's Leonardo da Vinci Airport, the hijacker radioed that he wanted a policeman to serve as a hostage and to have a car available. Dr. Pietro Guli, vice-chief of police at the airport, met him on the plane and escorted him to a waiting gray-green Alfa Romeo. Four police cars followed close behind, but Minichiello outdistanced them and had Guli leave the car (as well as his wallet and police credentials) with Minichiello. The hijacker later abandoned the car and took off on foot in an attempt to evade eight hundred searchers. Police claimed that they discovered he had been carrying 250 rounds of ammunition and ten dynamite caps in addition to his other arms. An early press release stated that the hijacker had been captured, but they had mistakenly gotten a quail hunter in the area. Finally, at 10 A.M., five hours after taking Dr. Guli hostage, Minichiello was arrested in a chapel ten miles south of Rome. The priests at the Sanctuary of Divine Love, saying All Saints Mass, suspected him when he walked in wearing only underpants and a shirt. Minichiello claimed that he was unable to remember the hijacking and asked police why he was being taken into custody.

He was indicted by a federal grand jury in the eastern district of New York on November 7, 1969, on charges that could result in life imprisonment. The Italian press and public opinion were against his extradition, and Italian lawyers representing him pointed to loopholes in the U.S.-Italy extradition treaty that allowed Minichiello to remain in their country, where he faced charges that could result in only thirty years of imprisonment. Deputy prosecutor Massimo Carli suggested that Minichiello should be charged with two counts of kidnapping the crew of the airplane and of an Italian policeman, two counts of using coercion by threatening armed violence against a public official, and three counts involving the illegal importation of a military weapon, its possession and carrying it without a license. He was also liable to counts of extortion for taking the policeman's wallet and credentials. The case received heavy press coverage in the United States and Italy, and the hijacker was sentenced to seven-and-a-half years, later reduced to three-and-a-half, with two years commuted. He was released on May 1, 1971, and remains a fugitive from U.S. charges.

TWA estimated that crew salaries and fuel for the trip cost $50,000. The hijacker could have flown from Los Angeles to New York for $149.10 and on to Rome for $286.50. 5183

November 2, 1969—United States—Six hijackers returned to the United States from Cuba via Canada. The six crossed into the United States at 2:15 A.M. after arriving in Montreal on board a Cuban freighter. One was carrying his four-year-old daughter. The six were identified as Thomas J. Boynton of Kalamazoo, Michigan; Thomas George Washington of Philadelphia; Ronald

T. Bohle of Michigan City, Indiana; Robert Lee Sandlin of Vernon, Texas; Raymond L. Anthony of Baltimore; and Joseph C. Crawford of Jacksonville, Florida. The group came back of their own volition, after complaining that they had been imprisoned during their stay in Cuba. No official pressure had been put on Cuba to return the individuals. Four of the men were held on bail of $100,000 each, one for $150,000, and one for $200,000, the differences due to stipulations in the relevant state laws applicable to where they were indicted.

November 4, 1969—Brazil—Brazilian police shot ALN leader Carlos Marighella to death after setting a trap for him based upon information on his whereabouts provided by arrested Dominican monks in São Paulo.

November 4, 1969—Nicaragua—A Nicaraguan Lanica BAC-111 flying the Miami-Managua-San Salvador-Mexico City route was hijacked by two armed Nicaraguan males out of Managua and forced to fly to Havana. The duo allowed the plane to fly to Grand Cayman Island, which they had been tricked into believing was Cuba. The twenty-five passengers disembarked at the island, along with one of the hijackers, who was disarmed and seized by the police. According to Jim Frazier, an FAA official, "The other man on the plane had a gun at the head of a stewardess and said he would start shooting if they didn't allow the other man to get back aboard." The pair flew on from the island with some of the crew and were later identified as Juan José Quezada Maldonado and Rena Lugo Valencia. 5184

November 4, 1969—Argentina—A Brazilian VARIG B-707 flying from Bueno Aires to Santiago with sixty passengers was hijacked while landing by five Argentine males and one woman, all of whom were armed. While the plane was refueled, they allowed a man and his pregnant wife to deplane and flew on to Havana. 5185

November 5, 1969—Brazil—P. Dolan, the son of a U.S. businessman, was kidnapped in São Paulo. A father and son attempted to extort $12,500 from the father. They were arrested. Dolan was found dead.

November 9, 1969—Australia—Two convicts attempted to hijack an East-West Airlines domestic flight with fifteen persons on board but were unsuccessful in overcoming their guards. 5186

November 8, 1969—Argentina—An Austral Airlines BAC111 was hijacked while flying from Córdoba to Buenos Aires with seventy-seven persons on board when a man seized a child from its mother's arms and threatened to shoot it unless the pilot flew across the Andes to Chile and then on to Cuba. The hijacker allowed the pilot, Gonzalo Gil, to return to Pajas Blancas airport for refueling, where seven passengers and a stewardess were allowed to deplane. The plane then flew to Montevideo, where the director of the airport, Victor Garin, talked the hijacker into letting the passengers and then the crew off, and left the plane with the hijacker one hour and twenty minutes later. According to Garin, ''He told me he had political problems in Argentina, and that's why he wanted to go to Cuba.'' Police arrested the hijacker, who was identified as twenty-year-old Luis Posadas Melgarejo, a Córdoban metal worker. He claimed that his brother hijacked another Argentine airliner on October 8 to Havana. He was sentenced to one to two years. 5187

November 9, 1969—Bolivia—A dynamite stick thrown at the La Paz Binational Center early in the morning bounced off the wall and exploded in the street, causing no damage to the structure. 0262

November 9, 1969—West Germany—A time bomb was discovered at the Berlin Jewish Community Center. 0263

November 10, 1969—United States—David Lawrence Booth, a fourteen-year-old freshman at Cincinnati's suburban Norwood High School, attempted to hijack Delta Airlines flight 670, a DC9 scheduled to fly from Cincinnati to Chicago with sixty-eight passengers and five crewman aboard, by holding a butcher knife to the back of eighteen-year-old ballet dancer Gloria Jean House, who had come to the airport to see her grandmother off. Booth, a white hijacker for whom the FAA profile was not applicable, was born in Cincinnati on June 24, 1955, and claimed that he wanted to go to Sweden, changing that to Mexico when informed that the plane could not fly that far. As the plane taxied, Booth was talked out of his attempt by Byron Kinman, chief of the airport police, and George East, Delta resident manager, one hour and fifteen minutes after he had grabbed the young woman. Booth's mother claimed that he had taken great interest in the Minichiello case of a few days ago and may have been influenced by his exploits. The federal authorities declined prosecution, and Booth was remanded to the custody of local juvenile authorities, who charged him as a juvenile incorrigible. He was found to be mentally incompetent and committed to a mental hospital, from which he was released on April 6, 1971. 5188

November 12, 1969—Brazil—An anonymous telephone call received at the U.S. embassy in Rio de Janeiro warned that a bomb had been placed in the structure. A search found nothing. 0264

November 12, 1969—Brazil—A Cruzeiro do Sol YS11, a Japanese-built twin turboprop flying from Manaus to Belém with twelve persons on board, was hijacked over the Amazon River by a lone male. The plane landed at Cayenne, the capital of French Guyana, as well as Trinidad for refueling, before flying on to Havana. 5189

November 12, 1969—Chile—A LAN Caravelle twin-jet plane flying from Santiago to Puerto Montt with sixty-two persons on board was hijacked fifteen minutes after takeoff by two teenagers who wished to go to Cuba. Beatriz de Gastoldi, thirty-four, a passenger, recalled, "They acted so quickly none of us realized what had happened until the crew announced that for reasons beyond their control they were rerouting to Antofagasta," a town 650 miles up the coast of Chile. While the plane refueled, a dozen of the fifty-six passengers who showed signs of hysteria were allowed to leave. As the plane was taxiing, the pilot reported a malfunction of the left jet. The hijackers allowed the other passengers to leave and took over another Caravelle parked nearby. When the plane was refueled, it took off for Havana. Fifteen minutes into the flight, the pilot and copilot disarmed the teenagers, bound them hand and foot, and flew back to Santiago, where they were taken away in a patrol car. The duo, who carried an automatic pistol and a revolver, were identified as students: fifteen-year-old Patricio Fernando Degach Vergue and sixteen-year-old Pedro Varas Flores. 5190

November 12, 1969—Chile—Five armed males hijacked a Chilean Airlines Caravelle with sixty passengers on board and diverted it from its Santiago-Punta Arenas flight to Cuba via Antofagasta. 5191

November 13, 1969—Colombia—An Avianca DC4 flying from Cúcuta to Bogotá was hijacked by six armed male students and diverted to Cuba. A pregnant woman and one other person were allowed to deplane during a refueling stop at Barranquilla. 5192

November 14, 1969—United States—The FBI arrested a forty-four-year-old passenger aboard a Delta plane in Dayton, Ohio, who approached the pilot during refueling, showed him a gun, and informed him that "other passengers on this plane are armed and planning a hijack, but don't worry. I am armed and will prevent it." Two FBI agents were summoned by the control tower. They arrested him without a struggle and found another pistol in his briefcase; none of the other sixty-five passengers was armed. He was identified as John Wilmot Kimball, who claimed to be a minister en route to Atlanta from Detroit.

November 17, 1969—Japan—An explosive device was placed near the guard box of the U.S. consulate in Yokohama. The guard who found it was able to dismantle it before it exploded. The perpetrators escaped. 0265

November 18, 1969—Mexico—A Mexican general aviation plane was hijacked on its flight from Mérida to Cozumel by a lone man who diverted it to Cuba. 5193

November 19, 1969—Israel—An Arab terrorist lobbed a grenade at the Khan Yunis branch of an Israeli bank, killing an Arab boy and wounding five other Arabs. 0266

November 19, 1969—Ecuador—A mob of two hundred to three hundred students attacked the Binational Center in Quito with rocks and Molotov cocktails, which were extinguished by police, causing no damage. 0267

November 20, 1969—Argentina—The Buenos Aires offices of fifteen foreign companies, including nine American firms, were damaged by bombs planted by the Péronist Armed Forces. 0268-0282

November 20, 1969—Poland—A Lot Antonov 24 flying the Wroclaw-Warsaw-Bratislava run was hijacking by two youths who forced the pilot to cirle Schwechat Airport three times before landing in Vienna, Austria. The two carried a fake time bomb, which consisted of some batteries connected to wires and switches on a wood panel visible in a blue bag, which also contained rags. They had also fashioned fake pistols, which had pipe barrels and Bakelite handles, but could not fire. They carried hunting knives, a pair of brass knuckles and a rubber hose. They were identified as Wieslaw Szymankiewicz, a twenty-year-old radio mechanic, and Ceslaw Romuald Zolotucho, an eighteen-year-old automobile mechanic. A Roman Catholic priest also asked asylum. The other fifteen passengers and five crewmen were not injured and were allowed to fly on to their destinations. Most of the passengers were surprised at the hijacking, and one, Peter Mieszalski, sixty-nine, speculated that LOT was filming a reenactment of the October 19 hijacking. In that case, two East Germans were sentenced in West Berlin on the day of the current hijacking. Austria ignored Poland's extradition demands and sentenced Szymankiewicz to twenty-seven months in jail, while his partner received two years. They were ordered expelled from Austria after serving their terms. 5194

November 24, 1969—Costa Rica—The U.S. embassy in San José received two phone calls warning that bombs had been placed in the chancery. A search found nothing. 0283-0284

November 27, 1969—Greece—Two Jordanians threw two hand grenades into the Athens office of El Al, killing a two-and-a-half-year-old Greek child, George Nastion, and wounding fifteen others, including three Americans, a

Briton employed by El Al, ten Greeks, and a three-year-old Greek child who lost an eye. No Israelis were injured in the attack, the moment that the trial of three terrorists in the February 18, 1969, Zurich attack began. The duo were identified as Elie Karabetian, twenty-three, and Mansur Seifeddin Mourad, twenty-one, who were formally charged on November 28 in Athens criminal court with "attempted premeditated murder." It was learned that they were members of the Popular Struggle Front, (PSF), a small group headed by Bahjat Abu Gharbiya, a Palestinian with links to Egyptian intelligence. The PSF sent apologies to the families of the victims and Greece and paid some reparations. The two received jail terms of eight years and eleven years respectively, but were released on July 22, 1970, after the hijacking of an Olympic Airways jet to Cairo. 0285

November 29, 1969—Australia—The Yugoslav embassy in Canberra was bombed by Croatian exiles. 0286

November 30, 1969—France—A Brazilian Varig B707 on the London-Paris-Rio de Janeiro route was hijacked while parked in Paris by an Algerian armed with a revolver and knife. As the plane was flying over Lisbon, he forced the pilot to divert the aircraft, carrying fourteen crew members and eighty-one passengers, including a nun and three children, to Puerto Rico for a refueling stop before proceeding to Havana. The plane, which had been hijacked to Cuba earlier in November on a Buenos Aires-Santiago flight, landed in Havana at 6:45 A.M. and left the next day. 5195

December 2, 1969—United States—TWA flight 54, a B707 flying from San Francisco to Philadelphia, was hijacked over Nebraska and forced to fly to Havana, where it landed at 9:20 P.M. The pilot, Captain C. Clyde Nixon of Los Altos Hills, California, reported that the plane carried twenty-one passengers and seven crew members and was hijacked by a black man who did not meet the FAA profile: Benny Ray Hamilton, who was born in Houston on May 11, 1946. A complaint was filed on December 8, 1969, in the district of Nebraska. The hijacker remains a fugitive. 5196

December 4, 1969—United States—The United States ratified the 1963 Tokyo Convention on Offenses and Certain Other Acts Committed on Board Aircraft, which then came into force.

December 5, 1969—United Kingdom—Four terrorists were arrested while planning an attack on a plane at the London airport. The group appears to have been Arabic. 0287

December 5, 1969—Argentina—A powerful bomb exploded in the restroom of the U.S. Binational Center in Rosario in the early morning, causing extensive damage but no injuries. 0288

December 5, 1969—West Germany—In the early morning a window was broken by two rocks, and two incendiary devices were thrown into the Frankfurt Amerika Haus, causing no fire damage. 0289

December 11, 1969—South Korea—A Korean Air Lines YS11 flying the Kangnung-Kimpo-Seoul route was hijacked by two North Korean sympathizers posing as South Korean officers and diverted to Sanduk, Wonsan, North Korea. Thirty-nine of the forty-seven passengers were returned sixty-five days later, but the other passengers, as well as the four crew, remained in detention. 5197

December 12, 1969—Spain—Two members of the ELF attempted to hijack an Ethiopian Airlines flight on the Madrid-Rome-Athens-Addis Ababa run but were foiled by security guards. One of the men, armed with a pistol, knife, and explosives, got up from his seat in the first-class section and walked toward the cockpit door when a guard grabbed his pistol and twisted it around, firing it twice. He then fired his own pistol six times, according to an American passenger, Harry Jacobi of Long Island. The other hijacker, armed with a pistol, jumped from his economy-class seat but was grabbed by three other men. Two shots were fired by the pistol-wielding trio, and a fourth man, according to Ray Culcutt, a passenger from London, "finished him off with another two shots." The two carried Senegalese and Yemeni passports and were identified as a nineteen-year-old student and a twenty-four-year-old businessman. The crew claimed that the two had intended to hijack the plane to Aden, South Yemen, but the ELF in Damascus said that they had merely wanted to distribute leaflets to the B707 passengers.

On December 14, Madrid police announced that Ahmed Mohammed Ibrahim, twenty-four, an Ethiopian student and suspected ELF member, was arrested four days earlier in the airport while carrying a suitcase containing explosives. Ibrahim claimed the group was to take the plane over Paris and London to distribute leaflets and then destroy the plane with explosives upon landing in Copenhagen.

None of the fourteen passengers and nine crewmen was injured, and the plane landed in Athens. Haile Selassie decorated the security guards. 0290

December 12, 1969—West Germany—A bomb was discovered in the West Berlin office of El Al. 0291

December 12, 1969—West Germany—A suspicious ticking package was found in the West Berlin Amerika Haus. On examination it proved to be an incendiary device and was removed and dismantled by police prior to detonation. 0292

December 13, 1969—West Germany—A bomb exploded outside a U.S. officers' club, causing slight damage. 0293

December 17, 1969—United Kingdom—Two Britons were arrested in London in an aborted conspiracy to bomb an El Al plane at Heathrow Airport. One was sentenced to twelve years, while his colleague went free after turning state's evidence. 0294

December 19, 1969—Chile—A LAN B727 flying from Santiago to Asuncion, Paraguay was hijacked by twenty-three-year-old student Patricio Alarcon Rojas, a member of the Maoist Leftist Revolutionary Movement. The hijacker allowed the plane to refuel at Arica and released fifteen women and children among the eighty-eight passengers and eleven crew membes. The plane proceeded to Cuba. Initial reports claimed that four hijackers were involved. The plane was returned to Santiago on December 20 after Chile paid the Cubans $20,000 for provisions, fuel, and landing rights. 0295

December 20, 1969—Turkey—A small bomb exploded at the edge of property behind the USIS office in Ankara at approximately 2:30 A.M., breaking six windows. 0296

December 21, 1969—Greece—Three members of the PFLP carrying forged Lebanese passports were arrested while attemptig to board the Tel Aviv-Athens-Rome-New York TWA B707 flight in Athens when a clerk became suspicious of three passengers with identical hand luggage. The luggage contained two guns, three hand grenades, and mimeographed announcements that the plane was being hijacked to Tunis by the PFLP. The group was headed by a twenty-one-year-old teacher, Maha Abu-Khalil, who denied any connection with the two men, the luggage, and a gun and explosives found in a ladies' room near where the trio and twenty-nine other passengers were waiting to board the aircraft. The flight was delayed for three hours, taking off at 2:30 P.M. One of the hijackers, Issam Doumidi, eighteen, made a full confession, claiming that he, the teacher, and twenty-year-old Sami Aboud planned to evacuate the passengers after landing in Tunis and blow the plane up "to warn the Americans to stop providing air communications with Israel." The group was released after the July 22, 1970, hijacking of an Olympic Airways jet to Cairo. 0297

December 22, 1969—South Vietnam—While on a domestic flight over Nha Trang, an Air Vietnam DC6B was rocked by an explosion in a lavatory. The pilot was injured, and the braking systems were damaged. Upon landing, the aircraft ran off the end of the runway and crashed into a school, killing thirty-two and wounding many others. Seventy people were on board the aircraft.

December 23, 1969—United States—An Air Icelandic plane flying from New York to Glasgow, Scotland, was the scene of an attempted hijacking by a man who claimed to be the U.S. secretary of defense. He was overpowered by the crew and arrested by police in Glasgow. 5198

December 23, 1969—Costa Rica—A LACSA C46 flying from Puerto Limón to San José was hijacked by a man who allowed thirty of the forty-four passengers to deplane at San Andrés Island before flying to Cuba. 5199

December 26, 1969—Uruguay—Tupamaros stole 380,000 pesos from the Montevideo branch of the Banco France e Italiano. 0298

December 26, 1969—United States—United Airlines flight 929, a B727 flying from New York to Chicago, was hijacked by a man identifying himself as M. Martinez, a Latin for whom the FAA profile was not applicable. The plane landed in Cuba. Martinez remains a fugitive from a complaint filed in the southern district of New York on December 29, 1969. 5200

December 29, 1969—New Zealand—The butler at the Wellington home of the U.S. ambassador found two Molotov cocktails on the driveway outside the house. One had exploded with no damage to property or injuries, while the second, a Coca-Cola bottle filled with gasoline, was found unignited leaning against the garage adjoining the residence. 0299

December 29, 1969—Philippines—Philippine nationalists attempted to assassinate U.S. Vice-President Spiro T. Agnew by throwing a bomb at his car but caused no damage. 0300

December 29, 1969—United States—Four men, probably members of the Jewish Defense League, broke windows and furniture and sprayed paint in the New York City offices of Aeroflot and Tass. 0301-0302

1970—Netherlands—A group of South Moluccans stormed the Indonesian embassy in the Hague, killing a Dutch policeman before being captured. 0303

1970—United States—An officer working at the U.S. Army's biological weapons warfare center was the subject of a blackmail attempt by a group of radicals who demanded his assistance in the theft of such material. The plot was discovered when the officer requested the issue of items unrelated to his job.

January 1, 1970—Israel—A grenade was thrown into a crowded Jerusalem marketplace, killing one Arab and injuring five other people. 0304

January 1, 1970—Israel—A grenade was thrown at an Israeli army vehicle in Hebron, but it missed and killed two Arab bystanders, identified as Moho Hilbi el Moukhtasseb, twenty-eight, son of the mufti of Jerusalem, and the mufti's uncle. 0305

January 1, 1970—Turkey—An explosion of undetermined origin occurred at 2:15 A.M. at the entrance of the U.S. consulate general in Istanbul. Damage was limited to broken windows on the ground floor of the building and a broken windshield of an official car parked adjacent to the building. No casualties were reported. 0306

January 1, 1970—Uruguay—A Brazilian Cruzeiro do Sul Caravelle flying from Montevideo to Rio de Janeiro was hijacked shortly after takeoff by five armed hijackers, including one woman described as pretty. The group, armed with grenades, knives, and revolvers, forced the pilot to fly to Buenos Aires to refuel and pick up maps to Havana. Its next refueling stops were Antofagasta, Chile, and Lima, Peru. When the pilot attempted to take off, the battery of one of the engines failed. Numerous mechanical difficulties extended the stopover to twenty-seven hours. Despite the heat, none of the seven crew and twenty-one passengers was allowed to leave the plane, necessitating the bringing in of meals. When the air conditioning broke down because of lack of electrical power, authorities suggested transferring to another plane. The group responded that their quarrel was with the Brazilian government and that they would accept only a Brazilian plane, a request that was turned down. The woman threw a letter out of the plane identifying the group as the Armed Revolutionary Guard-Joao Domingues Palmares Command (better known as VAR-Palmares) and telling that their mission was to pay homage to the dead guerrilla leader, Ché Guevara, as well as to escort the wife and two small daughters of a revolutionary who was being tortured in Brazilian jails. The mother vowed to return to fight in Brazil after the flight. The Caravelle finally took off and made only one more intermediate landing, in Panama, for a refueling and maintenance check, which took only a few hours. The plane landed in Havana forty-eight hours after the initial attack, where it was kept for a few days before flying out of Cuba. The hijackers were identified as Isolde

Sommers, Ados Magnos, Yanes Allen Luz, Claudio Galeno Megalhaes, and Luis Alberto Silva. 0307

January 4, 1970—Italy—A bomb caused slight damage to the Turin branch of the Bank of America and Italy. 0308

January 5, 1970—Greece—An unexploded bomb was discovered in the men's room of the U.S. consular section of the embassy in Athens. The device was taped to the underside of the toilet and ws discovered by a cleaning woman. The explosive was connected to an ordinary alarm clock set to detonate at 10 P.M. The bomb was removed at 4 P.M. and disarmed by Greek police an hour later. The bomb appeared to be of sufficient size to cause considerable damage but did not appear intended to cause injuries because it was set to explode after the close of business. 0309

January 6, 1970—United States—Anton Funjek, a white male who met the FAA profile and who was born on January 17, 1928, attempted to hijack Delta Airlines flight 274, a DC9 flying the Orlando-Jacksonville-Atlanta route, using a knife to hold the stewardess hostage in an attempt to go to Switzerland. During the scheduled landing, the pilot made a bumpy landing, allowing three of the sixty-three passengers and crew to overpower the hijacker. He pleaded guilty on July 7, 1970, and was sentenced on July 30, 1970, to twenty-five years for attempted aircraft piracy. 5201

January 7, 1970—Spain—Mariano Ventura Rodriguez, eighteen, attempted to use a toy gun to hijack an Iberian CV880 flying from Madrid to Zaragoza, Spain, and divert it to Athens and Albania. He was persuaded by the pilot to surrender to Zaragosa authorities, where he was sentenced to six years and one day. Forty-five persons were abroad. 5202

January 9, 1970—France—TWA flight 802, a B707 flying from Paris to Rome, was hijacked by Christian Reni Belon, a pistol-wielding white male who probably met the FAA profile and was born in France on December 22, 1943. He diverted the plane and the twenty people on board to Beirut, Lebanon. He fired several shots into the cockpit panel to speed up the refueling in Rome and several more in Beirut. He explained, ''I did what I did to spite America and Israel because America helps and encourages the Israelis and her aggression.'' He was arrested but released from jail on $8 bail on the orders of the minister of the interior, Kamal Jumblatt (who visited him while in prison) on January 15. Upon his release, he was surrounded by pretty women, television interviewers, and other well-wishers, and he then called on former Premier Abdullah Yaffi and Public Works Minister Pierre Gemayel. His French attorney, Christian Bourguet, noted that Belon was a member of a "very good family. ... his father was a dentist and his grandfather an industrialist." Bourguet first met Belon when he was sentenced to two years at Saint-Nazaire on a morals charge. When he was released from prison, he studied electronics in Germany, returned to France, and fell in love again. A fight with the woman's father resulted in Belon's being pushed down the stairs, where "he fell on his head and was in the hospital for several months." After that he suffered from occasional mental lapses. The French hijacker was later rearrested and sentenced to three years, which was quickly reduced to nine months; however, he was released on November 18, 1970, because he had already been in prison for nine months while awaiting trial. He returned to France, where he was sentenced to eight months for illegal possession of weapons. He was released from French jail on September 18, 1971. He remains a fugitive from a U.S. indictment handed down on July 15, 1971, by a federal grand jury in the District of Columbia. 0310

January 9, 1970—Panama—A RAPSA C47 flying from David City to Bocas del Toro was taken over by Jorge Julio Medrano Cabellero, twenty, who wished to go to Cuba. When the plane returned to David City to refuel, National Guard militiamen shot and killed him. 5203

January 11, 1970—Ethiopia—A U.S. soldier stationed in Ethiopia was shot and killed in a tavern outside Asmara by gunmen suspected to be ELF members. 0311

January 15, 1970—United States—After an anonymous call, an Eastern Airlines plane bound for Puerto Rico returned to New York, where a gun and ammunition were found in a waiting room; 178 persons were aboard. 5204

January 20, 1970—Guatemala—Unknown gunmen entered the British consulate in Guatemala City where they shot and killed the consul's bodyguard. 0312

January 21, 1970—Philippines—An unidentified Filipino male parked a sedan behind the Joint U.S. Military Assistance Group in the Philippines (JUSMAGPHIL) Headquarters in Manila. Six minutes later the sedan exploded, totally destroying it as well as damaging two other cars. The explosion was believed to be contained in the trunk of the car, caused damage to the JUSMAG Message Center, breaking most of the windows in the army section. Minor superficial injuries were suffered by an American officer and two Philippine armed forces sergeants. 0313

January 23-24, 1970—Brazil—The U.S. consulate general's commercial officer in São Paulo received two telephone threats by a caller who said, "As representative of economic imperialism you should not expect to see your family again.'' (The officer's wife and two of his children were in the United States.) When asked on the second call the purpose of the threats, the caller replied, ''To get rid of you.'' 0314-0315

January 24, 1970—Israel—Nineteen were killed and thirty-six injured when an ammunition truck exploded while unloading at the Elath dock. Al Fatah and the PFLP claimed responsibility, although the Israelis discounted sabotage. 0316

January 25, 1970—Dominican Republic—A Netherlands Antilles Airlines Fokker F27 flying from Santo Domingo, Dominican Republic, to Curaçao, Netherlands Antilles, with thirty-seven passengers was hijacked over Haiti by two men and two women who diverted it to Cuba. 5025

January 29, 1970—Japan—A firebomb was thrown through the first-floor window of the U.S. consular officer's office in Fukuoka in the early morning. Fireproof curtains halted the missile, which resulted in damage to a window and a scorched curtain. Police believed the attack was carried out by a student extremist group. 0317

February 2, 1970—Sweden—Approximately thirty Ethiopian student occupied the Ethiopian embassy in Stockholm to protest what they termed a ''fascist regime.'' The students destroyed books and documents before they were removed by local police on embassy request. 0318

February 6, 1970—Chile—A LAN Caravelle flying the Puerto Monta-Punta Arenas-Santiago route was the scene of an unsuccessful hijacking attempt by two armed Chilean male students, Oscar M. Vasquez and Pedro I. Venezuela Bravo, who wished to go to Cuba with the plane's seventy passengers. While refueling at Santiago, two policemen disguised as mechanics entered the plane, where a shootout ensued, resulting in the death of one hijacker and the wounding of the other hijacker, a stewardess, two detectives, and a uniformed policemen. 5206

February 10, 1970—West Germany—A team of three Arab terrorists with orders to hijack an El Al B707 were thwarted in their attempt and threw hand grenades at a shuttle bus and transit lounge, killing one Israeli and wounding eleven others, including actress Hanna Meron, whose leg was amputated as a result. The plane's pilot discovered the plot in the Munich lounge and grappled with one of the terrorists while the other two had boarded the bus carrying nineteen passengers. They had ordered the driver at gunpoint to open the door, but he drove off, so the third terrorist threw a grenade into the bus and another into the transit lounge. The trio also fired pistols in a gun battle with police before they were arrested and charged with murder. The group was identified as Mohammed el-Hanafi, an Egyptian who lost a hand when a grenade exploded prematurely (his arm was later amputated); Saleh Abder Rahman, a Jordanian who was wounded when he crashed through a skylight attempting to flee; and Mohammed Habibi, another Jordanian. Police later discovered that the group had orders to hijack the Tel-Aviv-Munich-London flight and to divert it to either Libya or Damascus. The group had arrived earlier in the day from Paris and carried a number of intructions. One of them, addressed to the passengers in the transit lounge, ordered them, "Go to the bus. We are leaving immediately. Tell the security guards on the plane to give themselves up or we well destroy the aircraft." Another text discovered at the lounge said that the group's leader would identify himself as El Hamid of the PLA and identify the hijackers as members of the Action Group for the Liberation of Palestine, threatening the passengers with the bombing of the aircraft if they did not cooperate. One of their hostages would have been Israeli Defense Minister Moshe Dayan's son Assaf, although the group apparently was not informed of his presence. On February 11 two groups in Amman, Jordan—the PFLP and the Action Organization for the Liberation of Palestine—claimed credit for the attack, stating, "We did not intend any harm to these Israelis, but intended [to capture them] in exchange for some Palestinian commando captives [held by Israel]." The AOLP was headed by Dr. Issam Sartwi, who had split from El Fatah before the incident but joined afterward. The trio received their freedom in the September 6, 1970, PFLP multiple hijacking. 0319

February 13, 1970—West Germany—Arsonists set fire to the Jewish Old People's Home in Munich, killing seven people and wounding nine. 0320

February 16, 1970—United States—Eastern Airlines flight 1, a B727 flying from Newark to Miami, was hijacked eighty miles south of Wilmington, North Carolina, by a shabbily dressed man traveling with his wife and two children. The stewardess, Eugenie Foxworth of New York City, reported that the man had two bottles he claimed contained gasoline with fuses extending from their mouths, as well as a revolver with a bayonet attached. He used a cigarette lighter to light one of the fuses and force the pilot, Captain Wayne A. Danielson, to fly the plane and all 104 on board to Havana, where it was on the ground for five hours. The plane then flew to Miami, landing at 6:55 P.M. The hijacker was identified as Daniel Lopez del Abad, a Latin who met the FAA profile, who was born on June 4, 1930 in Camaguey, Cuba. He remains a fugitive from an indictment handed down by a federal grand jury on July 1, 1970, in the district of New Jersey. The next day, Eastern Airlines reported that their detection equipment had not been in use at Newark Airport. On October 15 1969, Eastern had become the first airliner to adopt screening procedures that involved using weapons detectors on all boarding passengers as well as the scrutiny of passengers by airline personnel trained to note skyjacker behavioral characteristics. TWA and Pan Am had also adopted the system, with TWA experiencing only one hijacking, that by Christan Belon in Paris (see incident 0310), during its inception until this hijacking. 5207

February 17, 1970—West Germany—Acting on a pilot's suspicions, two Iraqis and one Jordanian were arrested by police in Munich's airport, who discovered several pistols in their luggage, as well as two statements indicating their intent to hijack an El Al plane. The group had arrived on a Yugoslav airliner that had flown from Paris en route to Belgrade and were identified as members of an Arab commando group. They were released in the September 6, 1970, PFLP multiple hijacking. 0321

February 19, 1970—Singapore—An apparent arson attempt against the chancery of the U.S. embassy in Singapore occurred when objects were thrown at the glass entrance door, cracking the shatterproof glass. A cardboard box filled with trash and probably doused with gasoline was set on fire directly in front of the entrance door. A marine security guard on duty reached the lobby security grill in time to see a young Chinese or Chinese-Malay male light the fire and flee. Police and fire officials arrived on the scene within five minutes, by which time the fire had burned itself out. 0322

February 21, 1970—Switzerland—Fifteen minutes out of Zurich's Kloten Airport, the pilot of Swissair flight 330 radioed, "We are on fire!" A bomb had exploded in the plane's rear luggage compartment. The resultant fire filled the crew's compartment with smoke, obscuring their vision, and resulting in the crashing of the Coronado in a forest near Wurenlingen, Switzerland, killing all thirty-eight passengers and nine crew, including fourteen Israelis, six Americans, Germans and Swiss. Investigators later discovered that the explosive was set off by an altimeter control, which detonated at fourteen thousand feet. In Beirut, Abu Meriam, the spokesman for Ahmed Jabril's PFLP-General Command, took credit for the operation, claiming that fourteen Israeli officials were aboard the plane (no Israeli officials were on board). Popular revulsion at the attack led him to withdraw the claim. A consortium of ten fedayeen groups, represented by Al Fatah, claimed that fedayeen had nothing to do with the attack, a statement echoed by the Soviets. Arafat's group claimed that the bombing was an Israeli provocation. The denial was reaffirmed two days later, and the group claimed that fedayeen were re-evaluating the use of attacks on airlines. Three Palestinians were arrested in West Germany and Austria but were released for lack of evidence. Two of them carried Israeli passports issued to Arabs living in pre-1967 Israel. After its day-long emergency cabinet meeting, the Swiss announced that entry visas would be placed on Arab passports only if their holders were known to consular officers and if their entry was justifiable on humanitarian grounds or because of 'important Swiss national interest.'' Due to a similar bombing, Austria also adopted the new controls. Six European airlines suspended all cargo flights to Israel, and SAS canceled its weekly passenger flight to Tel Aviv. The Israeli domestic airine, Arkia, demanded extra government protection, temporarily suspending operations. 0323

February 21, 1970—West Germany—An Austrian Airlines Caravelle flying from Frankfurt to Vienna with thirty-three passengers and five crew was rocked twenty minutes after takeoff by a bomb detonated by an altimeter reading of fourteen thousand feet. The bomb, placed in a mail bag intended to be carried on a flight to Israel later in the day, exploded in the cargo hold, creating a jagged three foot by two foot hole through the bottom of the fuselage. The mailbag had been packed between layers of tightly wadded newspaper, which absorbed most of the shock, allowing the plane to land safely in Frankfurt. No one was injured. The attack is generally attributed to the PFLP. A Palestinian from Israel with an Israeli passport was arrested by Austrian police for this and the previous incident but was released for lack of evidence. The Austrian foreign minister asked Arab ambassadors to ask their governments to take action to prevent attacks on international flights. 0324

February 23, 1970—Israel—Arab terrorists attacked a tourist bus near the occupied town of Hebron, killing an American woman. 0325

February 27, 1970—Guatemala—During preparations for a national election, four armed gunmen kidnapped Foreign Minister Alberto Fuentes Mohr from his car in Guatemala City. The Rebel Armed Forces gave the government twenty-four hours to release José Vincente Giron Calvillo, a university student who was identified as an FAR member and to publish an FAR policy statement, or Mohr would be executed. With the Mexican ambassador acting as intermediary, the student was delivered to the residence of Ambassador Delifin Sanchez Juarez. He was then flown to Mexico City, where on March 1 he said that he hoped that the FAR's twenty thousand active members (whom he described as nationalists rather than communists) would provoke U.S. intervention ''to unite the people of Guatemala behind us and start a full-scale revolution.'' Mohr was released on February 28, after the FAR arranged with a local newspaper to deliver him safely to their offices. 0326

March 1970—Ethiopia—Five members of a National Geographic film team, including its American producer, were kidnapped by the ELF, which made no ransom demands and released the hostages unharmed seventeen days later. 0327

March 1, 1970—Italy—A bomb was found in the luggage aboard an Ethiopian Airlines B707 in Rome. The plane was to fly its thirty-nine passengers to Athens, Beirut, Asmara, and Addis Ababa. An agent used an emergency chute and threw the bomb onto a field, causing no injuries. The ELF was responsible. 0328

March 3, 1970—Argentina—A noise bomb exploded in front of the office building housing the USIS Rosario branch, causing no casualties or damage. It was placed in a travel agency on the ground floor of a building in which USIS occupies the seventh floor. 0329

March 4, 1970—Philippines—Police and troops fired shots into the air and used tear gas to keep about a thousand rampaging anti-American demonstrators from the U.S. embassy in Manila. Two hours after the demonstration, an explosion rocked the embassy area and slightly damaged a passing tanker truck carrying gasoline. Police said the tanker had apparently run over a bomb. Another bomb was also found in the embassy area. A jeep loaded with Molotov cocktails was intercepted en route to the embassy. 0330-0331

March 6, 1970—Turkey—The USIS building in Ankara was invaded at 6:15 P.M. by 50 students with 150 more observing outside. Damage was limited to three windows and seveal door locks broken, as well as two American flags destroyed. No Americans were injured, but two police guards outside were beaten. Riot control police arrived within minutes and removed the attackers. 0332

March 6, 1970—Guatemala—Five armed male FAR members kidnapped Sean M. Holly, the U.S. labor attaché, and threatened to execute him within forty-eight hours if the government did not release four political prisoners. The government agreed and turned over José Antonio Aguirre Monzon and Vidalina Antonieta Monzon into the custody of the Costa Rican embassy the next day. Aguirre Monzon, arrested on March 4, was the intermediary between the FAR and government in the Mohr kidnapping (February 27, 1970). The government claimed it was unable to locate the other two prisoners. José Antonio Sierra, a bakery workers' union organizer, had been freed earlier in the week and contacted the FAR from Tapachula, Mexico, where he had been staying. The fourth prisoner, Mario Leonel del Cid Garcia, appeared at the Costa Rican embassy on March 8 and flew with the other two prisoners to Mexico City. Del Cid told Mexican newsmen that police kept moving him to different prisons while denying knowledge of his whereabouts. Holly was released on March 8. 0333

March 7, 1970—Argentina—A heavy bomb exploded at 4 A.M. in the front entrance of the Córdoba Binational Center, severely damaging steel shutters and the building's facade, and breaking glass, including at the rear of the building and on the second floor. No injuries were reported. Metal particles embedded in the wall indicated a fragmentation device. 0334

March 10, 1970—East Germany—A young married couple, both about twenty, attempted to hijack an East German Interflug Antonov 24 flying from East Berlin to Leipzig by drawing guns and attempting to enter the cockpit. The doors were locked, and the duo could not force their way in. The pilot, realizing what was occurring, turned back to Schoenfeld Airfield. The couple then committed suicide with their pistols. None of the other passengers was injured. 5208

March 11, 1970—Brazil—The Japanese consul general in São Paulo, Nobuo Okuchi, was kidnapped by members of the VPR. On March 12, the group demanded the release of five prisoners, immunity from retaliation, a pledge of no retaliation against remaining political prisoners, and a suspension of a massive nationwide search for the kidnappers. The government reiterated its pledge on March 13, when it received a list from the VPR stating the names of the prisoners it wanted released: Sister Maurina Borges da Silveira, mother superior of a convent in Ribeirão Préto; Damaris Oliveira Lucena, wife of a guerrilla leader who was reportedly killed February 20 by São Paulo police; Shizuo Ozawa, a member of the Popular Revolutionary Vanguard who had been arrested February 26 for bank robbery; Otavio Angelo, a mechanic arrested December 20 in what the government called a raid on a terrorist arms factory; and Diogenes José Carvalho de Oliveira, about whom the government gave no details, although a man of the same name had been arrested in 1969 on charges of murdering U.S. Army Captain Charles R. Chandler. Four of the freed prisoners flew to Cuba on March 27. Sister da Silveira decided to remain in Mexico City. There had been a slight delay in getting clearance for the plane with the prisoners from São Paulo, as the guerrillas had demanded the reduction of heavy security measures. Ten hours after the plane landed in Mexico, Okuchi was released on March 15.

In an interview with reporters months later, a man identified as Dobor recalled his involvement in the kidnapping: "The kidnapping of the Japanese consul was really rather funny. On one side of the place where we seized him is the federal police headqarters; on the other side, less than one hundred yards away, is the headquarters of the civil police; on the third side is the district police station; and only fifty yards away is the state security agency! Militarily this type of action is usually very simple. He was in his car with a chauffeur. One person in a Volkswagen began to swerve about the road as if his car were out of control, and he motioned to the ambassador's chauffeur to stop, which of course he did because he didn't want to ram into the VW. Six of our people stepped in at this point. I was on the corner and explained to the ambassador's chauffeur that he should remain calm. Two people then took the consul and put him into a car and drove away. There was also a second car. We always have one main car and one security car. Both cars have firing teams and if one there is any police intervention we try to get the police car in the middle between the two. That's what happened in this case. A few kilometers away, the police managed to find us, seemingly by coincidence. They took a look at our car. The car behind blocked them; we turned to the left and the police just went straight. They didn't want any trouble.''

Japanese are prominent in São Paulo industry and two VPR leaders were of Japanese origin, which may explain the selection of the victim. 0335

March 11, 1970—Colombia—An Avianca B727 flying from Bogotá to Barranquilla was hijacked by four men carrying explosives, who directed the pilot, Captain Sinforoso Gutierrez, to fly to Cuba. The hijackers allowed the plane with its seventy-eight persons on board to refuel at Cartagena for five minutes and at Barranquilla, where it landed a second time to repair a faulty landing gear. The hijackers demanded that the government collaborate in the repairs or they would blow up the plane. 5209

March 11, 1970—United States—United Airlines flight 361, a B727 flying the Cleveland-Atlanta-Tampa-West Palm Beach route with a crew of seven and ninety-nine passengers aboard was hijacked after leaving Cleveland by a black male who met the FAA profile, Clemmie Stubbs, a Cleveland resident who was born October 3, 1934, in Pittsburgh. Stubbs allowed the plane to refuel in Atlanta at 10:04 A.M. Thirty-two minutes later it took off for Cuba, where it landed at 12:13 P.M. None of the passengers was allowed to leave the plane while it was on the ground in Atlanta. A United spokesman, Jim Ramsey, said that federal agents and detectives in the terminal had ''strict orders to stay away from the plane'' while Stubbs was in the cockpit. Stubbs, his wife, and four children remained in Cuba, and the plane was allowed to return to Miami. He was imprisoned in Cuba for attempting to escape the country and was shot and killed while trying to escape from prison on March 26, 1973. His wife and children returned to the United States on May 30, 1974. 5210

March 12, 1970—Hong Kong—Three calls were made by unknown individuals, two to the Hong Kong poice and one to the U.S. consulate general switchboard, warning that a bomb was set to explode ''within an hour.'' The search found no bomb. The Hong Kong police reported that this was the first bomb threat to a consulate in sixteen years. 0336-0338

March 12, 1970—Chile—A Brazilian Varig B707 flying from Santiago, Chile, to London, United Kingdom, via Buenos Aires was hijacked by one armed man, D. Romulo de Souza, who diverted the plane to Cuba. 5211

March 14, 1970—Greece—A United Arab Airlines Antonov 24 flying from Athens to Cairo via Alexandria was four minutes out of its stopover when a bomb exploded in the landing gear well of the rear of the left engine, causing extensive damage to the undercarriage and injuring two of the ten passengers. The plane landed safely. 0339

March 14, 1970—Gulf of Siam—The U.S. freighter *Colombian Eagle* en route to Sattaship with U.S. Air Force ammunition was hijacked to Cambodia by two armed crewmen who were protesting the U.S. war effort in Vietnam. Twenty-four crewmen were released in lifeboats, and a U.S. Coast Guard cutter followed the ship into Cambodia, where the duo requested political asylum. The ship was released on April 8.

March 14, 1970—Jamaica—The butler at the home of the U.S. ambassador in Kingston received a call from an American or Canadian female who asked to speak to the ambassador. She refused to give her name when informed that the ambassador was not in and warned that the chancery and residence would be bombed within fourteen days. Security measures were tightened. 0341

March 17, 1970—Ecuador—USIA reported that intelligence reaching them noted terrorist plans for the kidnapping of the American consul in Quito and that students planned to place several bombs in either the embassy, the consulate, or the Quito Binational Center. 0342-0343

March 17, 1970—United States—Eastern Airlines flight 1320, a DC9 7:30 P.M. shuttle from Washington, D.C., to Newark, New York, and Boston, was the scene of an attempted hijacking by John J. DiVivo, a white male who met the FAA profile and who was born on June 24, 1942, in Englewood, New Jersey. The stewardesses were collecting the shuttle fares from the passengers when they came to DiVivo, who was sitting by himself in a back row. He gave the stewardess, Sandra Saltzer, less than the exact fare, and when she told him that more was required, he pulled a .38 revolver from a small black case on the floor. She persuaded the mumbling DiVivo to hold the gun inside his shirt so that the passengers would not become alarmed, and quietly told the pilot, Robert M. Wilbur, Jr., and copilot, James Hartley, that a man with a gun wished to come into the cockpit. The two did not understand her, as passengers were not allowed in the cockpit during landing approaches. The plane was five thousand feet over Franklin, Massachusetts, on their five-minute approach to Logan Airport. After she tried a second time to warn the pilots. Hartley opened the cockpit door to find out what was wrong and was faced with the .38. DiVivo told the captain, "Fly east. I don't have any place to go. Just fly east until the plane runs out of gas." (Other accounts claim that DiVivo wished to be informed when the plane had five and two minutes left of gas.) Wilbur and Hartley began talking to the man, explaining to him that sixty-eight passengers and five crew members, including stewardesses Christine Peterson and Arlene Albino, who were calming the passengers, would be killed because the plane had little gas left. They thought that DiVivo would allow them to land at Logan Airport in Boston, but when the pilot banked the plane, DiVivo became enraged and began shooting. A bullet went through the copilot's chest, and a slug passed through Wilbur's right arm and lodged in his left. Hartley grappled wth DiVivo for control and the pistol and shot him twice with it. The plane landed safely at Logan Airport. Hartley was dead on arrival at Massachusetts General Hospital, while Wilbur and DiVivo, on the danger list, underwent surgery. Wilbur was grounded for four months while recuperating but recovered sufficiently to continue flying. He and Hartley were given ALPA's Gold Medal Award for Heroism. After DiVivo was released from the hospital, he was arraigned for murder in Suffolk Superior Court and committed to Bridgewater State Mental Hospital for observation. At 3:20 A.M. on October 31, 1970, his body was found suspended by a neckerchief tied to the bars of his cell. It was learned that DiVivo was a ninth grade dropout, a "lone wolf type" to those who knew him, who lived with his widowed mother, two brothers, and a sister in West New York, New Jersey. The five-story brick building was known to local police as the "house of horrors," being the scene since 1967 of two suicides, a murder, and a double murder and suicide. DiVivo himself suffered from a bullet in his head, which changed the youth from gregarious to reticent. His family explained that he had sustained the injury during an abortive robbery attempt at Palisades Amusement Park where DiVivo was working. Local police said that when DiVivo was sixteen, he put a .22 caliber revolver to his head in a suicide attempt. 5212

March 18, 1970—Colombia—The son of the Belgian consul to Medellin, Luis Fernando Uribe Bernal, and his fiancé, Gloria Piedrita Diaz, were found shot to death. 0344

March 19, 1970—Turkey—Turkish students threw three Molotov cocktails at three foreign-owned buildings, causing slight damage. 0345-0347

March 24, 1970—Argentina—An Aerolineas Argentinas Comet IV flying from Córdoba to Tucumán and Buenos Aires with fifty-nine persons on board was taken over after takeoff from Córdoba by an armed couple, Atilio Ortiz and Maria A. Herrera. The couple allowed eight passengers off the plane during a nine-hour repair stop in Lima, Peru. The plane landed in Cuba the next day. 5213

March 24, 1970—Dominican Republic—A powerful bomb exploded in a restaurant on the third floor of the Santo Domingo building housing the USIS offices. The bomb caused no great damage, and apparently had been placed there to call attention to a sign that read "Freedom for the 21." 0348

March 24, 1970—Dominican Republic—Lieutenant Colonel Donald J. Crowley, U.S. air attaché, was kidnapped by six members of a group calling itself the United Anti-Reeletion Command, a leftist group opposing President Balaguer's reelection. He was taken shortly after 6 A.M. from a polo field on the grounds of the Embajador Hotel. The group demanded the release of twenty-one prisoners by March 25 at 10 A.M., threatening to kill Crowley if the deadline was not met. They later increased their demands to twenty-four prisoners. The chief of police initiated an active search for the attaché, but the government agreed to release twenty prisoners, although not in the center of Santo Domingo's main square, as the group had demanded. Archbishop Monsignor Hugo Polanco Brito acted as an intermediary and was able to achieve a compromise solution in which the twenty prisoners were placed on board a plane headed for Mexico. Crowley was freed before the plane took off rather than ten hours afterward, as the group had suggested, on March 26. Police dispersed crowds gathered in the main square with tear gas. Most of the prisoners were common criminals but included several members of radical antigovernment organizations, including Maximiliano Gomez, secretary general of the leftist Dominican Popular Movement (MPD), which some accounts credit with the kidnapping). On July 16, police shot and killed Otto Morales, an MPD leader who was a suspect in the kidnapping. 0349

March 24, 1970—Argentina—Police seized a substantial ERP arms cache in the Jujan section of Buenos Aires. The cache included jeeps painted in military colors, uniforms, molds for military insignia, weapons, ammunition, and surgical equipment.

March 24, 1970—Argentina—Joaquin Waldemar Sanchez, Paraguay's consul in Buenos Aires, was kidnapped by a group of armed men claiming to belong to the Armed Forces of Liberation (FAL) in the border town of Ituzaingo in Corrientes province. The group claimed that he was an agent of the CIA and a representative of the Stroessner dictatorship and demanded the release of two political prisoners by March 25 at 10 P.M., or they would execute him and begin killing managers of American business firms. The government announced that Alejandro Baldu was a "fugitive from justice" who had yet to be captured and that Carlos Della Nave was being "processed for common crimes" and would not be released because he was in the hands of the federal court of San Martín, Buenos Aires, and it would be contrary to the constitution for the executive branch to interfere. President Stroessner of Paraguay, vacationing in Argentina, concurred in the position of Argentine President Juan Carlos Ongania in rejecting the FAL demands. The kidnappers extended their deadine several times, and the government displayed Della Nava on television to show that he had not been tortured or killed, but they remained steadfast in their refusal to release him. Sanchez was released unharmed early March 28 in a Buenos suburb on what the FAL termed "humanitarian grounds," claiming that they did not want to shed blood needlessly. Argentina thus became the first Latin country to refuse successfully demands made in a political kidnapping. 0350

March 25, 1970—British Honduras—A British Honduran chartered Cessna 180 on a local flight was hijacked by a couple, Tyrone Won and Edna Lee, who allowed the plane to refuel in Mexico before flying on to Cuba. Won later committed suicide. 5214

March 27, 1970—Argentina—As a reprisal for the March 24 kidnapping of the Paraguayan consul, the MANO, a right-wing terrorist group, threatened to kill the Soviet ambassador and his family. 0351

March 28, 1970—Turkey—Police apprehended four students carrying dynamite and gasoline in the U.S. consulate and Turkish-American Association area in Adana. Two of the students admitted intending to bomb the Turkish-American Association and implicated the other two, who were later arrested. 0352

March 28, 1970—Lebanon—The American Insurance Company in Beirut was bombed by the PFLP, causing little damage and no injuries. 0353

March 28, 1970—Lebanon—The U.S. embassy in Beirut was bombed by the PFLP, causing little damage and no injuries. Another bomb exploded in the sea three hundred feet from the chancery in the direction of the Saint George Hotel. On March 29, the PFLP said that this and other raids were in retaliation for "plans of the U.S. embassy in Beirut to foment religious strife and create civil massacres in Lebanon aimed at paralyzing the Palestine resistance movement." 0354

March 29, 1970—Lebanon—The U.S.-owned Medreco oil refinery near Sidon was bombed by the PFLP, causing little damage and no injuries. 0355

March 29, 1970—Lebanon—The Bank of America in Beirut was bombed by the PFLP, causing little damage and no injuries. 0356

March 29, 1970—Lebanon—Two sticks of dynamite planted by the PFLP exploded at the rear entrance of the USIS Kennedy Center in Beirut. The first-floor office at the rear entrance was heavily damaged, and glass was broken in all windows on the first and second floors on that side of the building. No injuries were reported; the center was unoccupied at the time of the explosion. 0357

March 29, 1970—Netherlands—The U.S. consulate general received a bomb threat in the form of a letter signed by Al Fatah. Amsterdam police were informed, who replied that the Israeli consulate general and seven others in the city had received similar threatening letters, which were probably the work of a psychopath.

March 29, 1970—Argentina—Four armed members of the Argentine National Organization Movement, a right-wing terrorist group, ambushed two Soviet embassy officials in a commercial garage as they were returning from a family drive. One of the diplomats fell from the getaway car into which he had been forced at gunpoint. The other victim was identified as Yuri Pivovarov, the Soviet assistant commercial attaché, whose wife's screams alerted a local guard, who fired at the car. A passing squad car chased the terrorists' vehicle through the street of Buenos Aires, firing many rounds into the car and injuring three of the abductors. The car finally smashed into another car and a tree, resulting in the escape of one of the kidnappers and the capture of three attackers. Pivovarov was apparently not seriously injured. The Soviet Union issued a formal protest to the government of President Ongania, who apologized and claimed that gangsters and armed delinquents were responsible. On March 30 the government claimed that a deputy federal police inspector, Carlos Benigno Balbuena, was one of the kidnappers who had been captured. The other two were identified as Guillermo John Jansen and Albert Germinal Borrell, who had no governmental affiliation. 0358

March 31, 1970—Japan—A Japan Air Lines B727 left Tokyo at 7:30 A.M. on a flight to Fukuoka but was hijacked shortly after takeoff by nine members, aged sixteen to twenty-seven, of the Japanese United Red Army (also known as Sekigun-ha, Red Army Faction), who wielded samurai swords, daggers, pistols, and pipe bombs and demanded to be flown to Pyongyang, North Korea. The plane carried three crew, four stewardesses, and 122 passengers, mostly Japanese, including tourists, businessmen, students, a group of doctors on their way to a three-day medical conference in Fukuoka, a Maryknoll priest, and two Americans, including Herbert Brill. The group of terrorists tied up the male passengers, while others passed out candy to the children on board. The copilot, Teiichi Ezaki, was tied to his seat. The pilot, Captain Shinji Ishida, claimed that the plane could not make the flight to North Korea without refueling and was allowed to land at Itazuke air base outside Fukuoka at 8:59. Negotiations continued for five hours, and the group finally agreed to allow twelve children, ten women, and one ailing elderly man to leave the plane in exchange for refueling. As had been the case with the plane's landing, two escort planes were scrambled to accompany the plane as it left the air base and ended their surveillance when the plane approached Korea.

In an elaborate ruse, the South Koreans attempted to give the impression to the students (as well, as it turned out, to the crew) that the plane had entered

North Korean airspace. They fired rounds of antiaircraft shells at the plane, scrambled fighter planes, and escorted it to an airfield that identified itself as Pyongyang (at 131.4 megacycles, a frequency suggested by an unidentified radio station) but was really South Korea's Kimpo Airport in Seoul. The airport had been disguised to look like what Pyongyang might be, with all soldiers and policeman in communist uniforms, girls singing greetings, and a bullhorn calling for them to enter North Korea. The terrorists, however, saw through the ruse, noting an American car parked nearby, as well as a U.S. Northwest Airlines plane and a U.S. Air Force DC3 parked on the runways. The officials were unable to produce a photograph of Kim Il Sung at Pyongyang airfield and were tripped up on several points of communist dogma. The group threatened to blow up the plane if any more attempts to end the hijacking were made but agreed to the pilot's suggestion to delay takeoff until morning, when flight would be safer. The plane was moved to a corner of the airfield so that other flight traffic could continue. The hijackers flicked the passenger cabin lights continually during the night in an attempt to demoralize the occupants. They also denied attempts to send food aboard, accepting only a few sandwiches. When mechanics wheeled a battery cart near one of the engines, the group interpreted this as meaning that they would try to dismantle one of the engines and again threatened to set off the pipe bombs that two of them were carrying. Japanese officials had identified two of the group as being wanted on explosives charges—Takamaro Tamiya, twenty-seven, the group's leader, and Tsuneo Umeuchi, a medical student—which tended to give credibility to the threat. The following day the temperature in the cabin rose to 107 degrees, and the hijackers finally allowed food, water, cigarettes, and blankets to be brought on board. They had also let an 8 A.M. deadline for clearance to fly out of Seoul pass by. As stewardess Juniko Kubata reported later, they were often extremely agitated and gave the impression that they were serious about harming the passengers despite their general politeness. Japanese Ambassador Masahide Kanayama urged caution on the part of the South Koreans, who took full responsibility for the failed ruse. The Japanese vice-minister of transportation, Shinjiro Yamamura, flew to Seoul from Tokyo and began negotiating with the hijackers, along with the ambassador, who had established radio contact with the hijackers, the captain, and two of the passengers. Yamamura, thirty-six, offered to serve as a substitute hostage and called for the group to release the passengers and allow a fresh crew to fly the plane. The group refused and demanded to have Yamamura identified by an individual they respected, a socialist member of the Japanese Diet, Sukeya Abe. Abe flew to the airport and also offered to become a substitute hostage, but the South Korean Government refused this suggestion. When they learned of Yamamura's plan, the South Koreans objected. The Japanese minister of transport, Hashimoto, who had joined Yamamura, decided to tell the Koreans that the plan had been dropped. However, the Koreans were listening to the radioed negotiations and translated enough Japanese to discover that the plan was still on. South Korean Defense Minister Chung Nea Hiuk issued a protest to the Japanese government against their "unilateral action." The students finally agreed to allow the plane to be moved to a takeoff position, to allow passenger baggage to be removed, and to release fifty passengers, then allow Yamamura to board, then release the other fifty, at which time the plane would fly on to North Korea. The agreement was consummated eighty hours after the hijacking began.

During the flight to North Korea, the communist government made ominous warnings about the possible incarceration and torture of the hostages. The plane never reached Pyongyang airport but did land in North Korean territory. A journalist who was a member of the Japanese Communist party reported that the hijackers bounded from the plane and struck karate poses, acting as heroes. The pilot reported that the North Koreans forced them to relinquish their weapons and separated them from their hostages, who were questioned in a local hotel by officials from the Social Security Department. The communists announced that the hijackers would be given political asylum and that appropriate steps would be taken in their case but refused to elaborate. On Saturday they informed Yamamura and the crew that they were illegal immigrants. Yamamura had heard reports from former hijack victims that they had been beaten while held in North Korea and also recalled that the crew of the *Pueblo* was still being held. However, his group was allowed to leave, apparently because of the world publicity about Yamamura's bravery in offering to serve as a hostage. Pressure may also have been placed on North Korea by the International Committee of the Red Cross, which had served as a mediator between Japan and North Korea during the negotiations in South Korea. The jet was returned to Tokyo on April 5, and Yamamura was given a porcelain vase by the Diet. On April 6 North Korean broadcasts called the hijackers "strangers who came uninvited."

Sources differ as to the identity of the hijackers. During the attack, the sixteen-year-old youth identified himself as "Boya," who had played hookey from Kobe High School that day. The FAA identifies the group as O. Takeshi, W. Mariaki, A. Shiro, S. Yasumiro, K. Takahiro, A. Kimihiro, Takamaro Tamiya, twenty-seven, Yoshizo Tanaka, twenty-five, and Kintaro Yoshida, twenty-four. Various sources claim that a brother of the hijackers was involved in the Lod Airport massacre.

On April 4, a Red Army leader gave a clandestine press conference from his Tokyo hideout, in which he observed, "I think we succeeded. Our objective was to reach North Korea. We had no advance contacts with the North Koreans, yet now it is clear they are going to let our people stay there. World revolution is our ultimate goal, while our immediate objective is to set up revolutionary bases overseas. . . . We are no longer just a student organization, but a revolutionary organization in the real sense. We have to show that violent revolution is not only possible but necessary in an advanced industrialized country like Japan.'' Two years later, eight of the hijackers met in North Korea with visiting Japanese journalists and informed them that they felt that the hijacking had been ''a mistake.'' 0359

March 31, 1970—Guatemala—The West German ambassador, Count Karl von Spreti, was kidnapped by armed members of the Rebel Armed Forces (FAR) from his car outside his home after having left the embassy shortly after noon. On April 1, a note from the ambassador was dropped in the mailbox of the West German chargé d'affaires, saying, ''I am in the hands of the FAR. I am feeling well and expect to be returned soon.'' The group demanded the release of seventeen political prisoners. To the surprise of all, given the government's previous capitulation in political kidnap cases, the demands were refused. The government claimed that it was unconstitutional for the executive to release prisoners who had already been convicted by the judicial branch. In a letter to the papal nuncio, Gerolamo Prigione, who served as intermediary, the kidnappers threatened to kill the ambassador and increased their demands to twenty-five prisoners (other accounts claim twenty-two) and $700,000 ransom. International pressure was mounted. A group of foreign diplomats met with Alberto Fuentes Mohr, the foreign minister, on April 3 to protest the government's stance and to demand better protection for themselves, the latter of which was granted. West Germany sent a special envoy, William Hoppe, to confer with President Julio Cesar Mendez Montenegro on April 4, and Chancellor Willy Brandt made a similar request. The president declared a state of martial law and a national emergency but refused to give in. Security precautions were increased in a number of other countries, such as Venezuela, which provided guards to ambassadors and other diplomats, as well as increasing protection of embassies. A last-minute attempt to resume negotiations failed, and a terrorist-imposed deadline of one hour passed on April 5. Von Spreti was shot to death during the evening of that day. His body was found after an anonymous phone call. The next day the government announced that four of the prisoners whose release was demanded had confessed to involvement with the August 1968 killing of John Gordon Mein, the U.S. ambassador (see incident 0088), and ''We could not let those go.'' Walter Scheel, the West German foreign minister, recalled the acting chief of the West German mission, as well as most of the aides, and let it be known to the Guatemalan ambassador in Bonn that he should leave the country. The initiation of a house-to-house search in Guatemala City that day did not help to ease strained relations between the two countries. 0360

April 1970—United States—A drum of nuclear waste containing a small amount of 70 percent enriched uranium was reported lost while in transit from two firms in a California city. It had been mistakenly sent to Tijuana, Mexico.

April 2, 1970—Colombia—The U.S. embassy telephone operator in Bogotá received two short phone calls stating that the consular officer would be murdered by a local protest organization. 0361-0362

April 5, 1970—Brazil—The U.S. consul general in Pôrto Alegre, Curtis S. Cutter, forty-one, successfully escaped a kidnapping attempt. As he was driving his wife and a friend home from a party, a Volkswagen blocked his path. Four or five armed men jumped out and approached his car. According to Cutter, the attackers, members of the VPR, had been watching his movements for weeks. Cutter remembered the recent successful escape by the Soviet ambassador in the MANO attack in Argentina, so he instructed his passengers to get down while he stepped on the accelerator. One of the terrorists was hit by the car and thrown onto the Volkswagen. He aimed his machine gun at Cutter as though to fire but was waved off by the group's leader. The others responded with covering fire, and Cutter was wounded in the back. He successfully continued on to a local hospital, where a bullet was removed from his shoulder. Four attackers were later captured, although the driver of a second vehicle remains at large. Cutter later visited the ''people's prison'' he was to have been held in while being used as a pawn in obtaining the release of political prisoners. 0363

April 6, 1970—United States—A TWA B707 flying from San Francisco to Pittsburgh was the scene of a hijacking attempt by twenty-two-year-old Lynn L. Little who used a pistol to get to the cockpit, where he demanded to be taken to Cuba. He appeared confused and surrendered his weapon to the pilot. Sixty-six persons were on board. 5215

April 10, 1970—Dominican Republic—A medium-intensity bomb exploded in the Santo Domingo headquarters of the Peace Corps, causing minimal damage. Two Peace Corps volunteers and an embassy watchman who were in the building at the time were not injured. 0364

April 13, 1970—Lesotho—The foreign minister advised the U.S. ambassador in Maseru that the government of Lesotho had received information indicating a strong possibility of the abduction of some member or members of the local diplomatic community, including the strong possibility that the victim would be a child. Police were requesting permission to interrogate all diplomatic servants because their information indicated that a servant was in collusion with kidnappers. The tentative decision of the United States was to allow police to interrogate staff. 0365

April 13, 1970—Argentina—Rosario newspapers alleged that threats of kidnapping had been directed at the USIS branch public affairs officer, which had resulted in increased protection by the police for USIS. The officer had been subjected to such threats in the past and had received threats subsequent to April 13. As a result, it was decided to evacuate him from his post and replace him. 0366

April 15, 1970—Jordan—The USIS Cultural Center in Amman was attacked by a large mob, broken into, and subsequently completely destroyed by fire. All U.S. government personnel were evacuated safely from the center. 0367

April 15, 1970—Jordan—Palestinian terrorists attacked the U.S. embassy compound in Amman, tore down the flag, broke windows, burned cars, and attempted to enter the chancery. The mob was successfully kept from the inside of the chancery. They stayed in the compound and chanted slogans. One hundred thousand dollars of damage was reported, although no injuries were sustained. 0368

April 16, 1970—Czechoslovakia—A group of young men, all around age twenty-three, attempted to hijack a local flight from Prague to Karlovy and divert it to West Germany. They were overpowered by the crew and were tried in Ostrava on charges of trying to leave the republic. 5216

April 18, 1970—Costa Rica—Marvin Right Lindon, twenty-four, and his twenty-year-old brother attempted to hijack a Costa Rican National Airways C46 to Cuba on its way to San José from Puerto Limón. They used a revolver and grenades and locked the crew inside the plane. Police fired tear gas into the plane, and the brother surrendered. 5217

April 20, 1970—Ecuador—Telephone calls were received at the U.S. ambassador's residence in Quito (on an unlisted gate guardhouse phone), the U.S. embassy chancery, and the Deputy Chief of Mission's residence, threatening kidnapping of the ambassador, DCM, or other American personnel. 0369-0371

April 21, 1970—Brazil—According to a leftist source, ALN leader Juarez Guimarez de Brito was killed in an attempted kidnapping of West German Ambassador von Holleben. 0372

April 21, 1970—Philippines—A Philippine Air Lines HS748 on a local flight near Pant Bangan, seventy-five miles north of Manila, exploded at ten thousand five hundred feet. The tail secton ripped off, and the plane crashed, killing all thirty-six on board. Investigators found bomb fragments at the site of the crash and claimed that the explosion occurred in a rear lavatory.

April 21, 1970—Ethiopia—Jack Fry, a U.S. Peace Corps volunteer, and his wife were kidnapped from a train by members of the ELF. No ransom demands were made, and they were released unharmed five days later. 0373

April 22, 1970—United States—Ira David Meeks, a black ex-convict born in York, South Carolina, on February 23, 1944, and Dianne Vivian McKinney, a black born on June 25, 1952, in Baltimore commandeered a taxi to the Gastonia, North Carolina, airport, where they hired a Caldwell Aviaton Corporaton Cessna 172 to fly over the city. After they were airborne, they forced the pilot to fly to Havana, alowing refueling stops in Rock Hill, South Carolina, Jacksonville, Florida, and Fort Lauderdale, Florida. McKinney was arrested in New York on July 10, 1975, as she returned from Cuba. The FBI arrested Meeks in New York after he flew there from Barbados. They were held on an indictment handed down by a federal grand jury in the western district of North Carolina on September 21, 1970, on charges of air piracy and kidnapping. They were declared mentally incompetent to stand trial, and charges were dismissed on December 6, 1976. The FAA profile was inapplicable in this case. 5218

April 22, 1970—Bolivia—USIS intelligence sources in La Paz reported that a dissident group within Bolivia was preparing a list of prominent diplomats as targets for kidnapping. They were to be held hostage for the release of Regis Debray, who was being held prisoner by the Bolivian government. Among members of the U.S. embassy supposedly included were the ambassador, the Deputy Chief of Mission, and the public affairs officer. 0374

April 22, 1970—West Germany—A group of six hundred Germans, composed of members of SDS, Young Democrats, Young Socialists, and a smattering of other students, marched through the streets of Heidelberg and shouted for Lenin and against Vietnam and capitalism as they passed the Amerika Haus. Twenty minutes before the marchers arrived, a smoke bomb exploded in the library. The bomb had been placed under a bookshelf, apparently timed to go off when it did. Protection was requested, and thirty policemen were provided. 0375

April 22, 1970—Jamaica—The U.S. embassy switchboard operator in Kingston received an anonymous call that there was a bomb in the chancery. An evacuation and subsequent search revealed nothing. 0376

April 23, 1970—United States—Joseph A. Wagstaff, born June 24, 1928, a white for whom the FAA profile was inapplicable, hijacked a bus from Petosky, Michigan, to the Pellston airport, where, wielding a knife and toy gun, he used the driver as a hostage in order to enter North Central flight 945, a DC9 picking up passengers on its way from Detroit to Sault Sainte Marie. The crew stalled, allowing the passengers to disembark. Some of them phoned Michigan state police, who overpowered Wagstaff after he threatened the crew. Wagstaff, who was later committed, had wanted to go to Detroit. 5219

April 24, 1970—United States—Nationalist Chinese Premier Chiang Ching-kuo was shot while entering the Plaza Hotel in New York City in an unsuccessful assassination attempt by a Taiwanese, Peter Huang, a member of the World United Formosans for Independence, who wanted Taiwanese freedom. He was arrested along with the organization's executive secretary. 0377

April 25, 1970—West Germany—During the early morning hours, the U.S. consulate general building in Bremen was attacked with five Molotov cocktails, one of which landed after being thrown through the second-floor window, causing $300 damage to the room used by USIS. Three bombs failed to ignite, and the fifth burned harmlessly in the motor pool open area. 0378

April 25, 1970—Turkey—Dynamite placed by several members of the Popular Struggle Front exploded in the Istanbul ticket office of El Al, breaking windows and causing minor damage inside but causing no injuries. 0379

April 26, 1970—Brazil—A Brazilian Viacao Aerea de São Paulo B737 flying from Brasilia to Manaus was hijacked by a lone gunman later identified as Joaqium Terreira, who was considered to be the ALN successor to Carlos Marighella. The hijacker allowed the pilot to refuel at Georgetown, Guyana, where thirty-six passengers deplaned. One male hippie remained voluntarily and accompanied the crew and hijacker to Havana. 0380

April 28, 1970—Turkey—A small group of young men attacked a U.S. AID warehouse on the outskirts of Ankara by cutting the barbed wire to allow their entry to the grounds. They shot four times at the night watchman, who retreated into the building. Molotov cocktails were then thrown at vehicles and equipment in the parking lot but not at the warehouse itself. The main damage reported was a gutted truck and separate truck trailer. 0381

May 1-3, 1970—West Germany—The director of the German-American Institute in Heidelberg received anonymous phone calls by two different German voices speaking in English. The comments made were, "You will die very soon, you killer," and "You burn children, you will burn tomorrow." The director notified police, who increased patrols in the vicinity of his home. 0382-0383

May 1, 1970—Jamaica—Two American males, A. Jacobs and R. R. Wiggins, armed with a pistol and a knife threatened a stewardess on board a British West Indian Airways (a Trinidad and Tobago corporation) B727 flying from Kingston to Miami. They claimed they had an appointment with Eldridge Cleaver in Algiers and demanded to be flown there. The pilot persuaded them that a faulty oil pressure gauge necessitated the plane's landing in Havana for repairs and refueling. The two demanded to be flown to Senegal, but were talked out of this idea by British and Cuban negotiators. Sixty-six persons were aboard the plane. 0384

May 3, 1970—Uganda—Brian Lea, a first secretary at the British High Commission in Kampala, was allegedly kidnapped. A telephone informant announced the abduction but gave no reason for the kidnapping and made no ransom demands. Lea appeared the next day after police had launched a search. The High Commission instructed Lea and his wife to make no statements to the press. The press believed that Lea may have been taken because of his involvement as first secretary for administration and consular affairs, which entailed his refusing British entry vouchers to East African Asians holding British passports (a protest against such British immigration restrictions had taken place at the British passport office in Kampala on March 10). Uganda's president, Milton Obote, claimed that the incident was a hoax and called for an official inquiry. The United Kingdom meanwhile recalled Lea. The press suggested that Lea had voluntarily gone into hiding on a small island in Lake Victoria and had been involved in an illicit affair. A subsequent investigation claimed that Lea had engineered the incident to point out the plight of Asians in Uganda. 0385

May 3, 1970—Italy—At 5 A.M., a Genoan carabiniere found six sticks of dynamite weighing three-and-a-half pounds with an ignited fuse in the alleyway around the corner from the U.S. consulate general entrance. He stifled the fuse and prevented an explosion, which police estimated would have broken most of the windows in the consulate general and adjoining buildings. The police posted a two-man, twenty-four-hour guard around the building. 0386

May 4, 1970—Paraguay—Two Palestinian gunmen, claiming to be members of Fatah, ran into the Israeli embassy in Asunción, intending to assassinate the ambassador. They instead killed the wife of the first secretary and seriously wounded an embassy employee. They were captured and sentenced to jail terms. Sketchy evidence indicates that they were still incarcerated as of February 1975. Reports differ as to whether they were Paraguayans hired by Fatah, were Fatah members, were PFLP members, or whether the incident was even fedayeen inspired. 0387

May 5, 1970—Pakistan—A bomb exploded directly in front of the door to the USIS library in Dacca, causing no damage but injuring a library patron, who suffered scratches on the leg. The library was near closing time, and all protection grills had been lowered except those over the library door. The USIS Cultural Center was also the scene of two student demonstrations protesting U.S. action in Cambodia. 0388

May 5, 1970—Czechoslovakia—Pavel Verner, thirty-two, a junior executive for a Czech uranium plant, hijacked a twin-engined private executive plane flying from Pribram to Košice. He intended to seek political asylum and a job by diverting it to West Germany but flew to Linz, Austria, instead. Upon landing, he stabbed the pilot with a penknife and knocked the other passenger, his boss, unconscious. Austrian authorities arrested Verner, who was sentenced to one year in jail on September 2, 1970. 5220

May 5, 1970—West Germany—An anonymous German phone caller told the USIS duty watchman in the Frankfurt housing area, "I am tipping off; the consul will be kidnapped." 0389

May 6, 1970—West Germany—The Amerika Haus in Berlin was attacked with rocks and Molotov cocktails by twelve to fifteen people. Two cars pulled in the parking lot on one side and started the rock-, and bomb-throwing assault. Three additional cars pulled up in front of the building, and its occupants attacked library and foyer windows. Two interior showcases were burned out, and floors at the main entrance and corridor to the auditorium were slightly damaged by fire. Two men and one woman were taken into custody by police. 0390

May 6, 1970—United Kingdom—Two Molotov cocktails were thrown at the U.S. embassy in London, breaking a glass window and causing minor fire damage in the visa waiting room but injuring no one. 0391

May 6, 1970—Venezuela—A bomb broke windows in an American firm's store in Caracas. 0392

May 8, 1970—West Germany—A Molotov cocktail was thrown at the offices of Pan American Airlines in Munich. This attack came in the context of general disturbances in the city, marked by two groups of demonstrators who attempted to rush barricades erected in front of the Amerika Haus. A small group of twenty to thirty apparently benign protesters congregated on the consular general lawn but were dispersed without difficulty by police. Additionally, the Bank of America lost a window and a glass door, American Express Bank lost two windows, and several bags of paint were lobbed at the office of the Armed Forces Network. 0393

May 8, 1970—South Africa—The assistant U.S. naval attaché in Capetown reported that he was kidnapped during the early evening. The officer was held overnight and released. He was forced to telephone the demands of the kidnappers for the release of twenty-two people being held under the Suppression of Communism Act. 0394

May 9, 1970—United Kingdom—Five hundred antiwar demonstrators marched on the U.S. consulate general in Edinburgh, denouncing U.S. actions in Laos, Cambodia, and Vietnam and protesting the presence of American submarines in Holy Loch. Marbles, stones, and a gasoline bomb were thrown at the building, cracking two window panes but injuring no one. Police pulled three agitators from the crowd and hustled them away in a van. 0395

May 10, 1970—Lebanon—Two hand grenades were thrown at the gendarme post adjacent to the residence yard of the U.S. ambassador in Beirut, causing no damage but slightly wounding one of the guards. 0396

May 10, 1970—Jordan—The U.S. military attaché in Amman was assassinated by automatic weapons fired at close range at his home. 0397

May 10, 1970—Switzerland—Fifty passengers and six crew members were removed from an Iberia Air Lines DC9 in Geneva before an incendiary device exploded in the plane's baggage compartment. Officials discovered one suitcase too many aboard the plane and began a luggage search. They evacuated the plane after an anonymous call. 0398

May 10, 1970—Netherlands—A firebomb that was to have been planted on board an Iberia Air Lines plane bound for Spain exploded in Amsterdam airport. 0399

May 10, 1970—West Germany—A firebomb that was to have been planted on board an Iberia Airlines plane bound for Spain exploded in Frankfurt airport. 0400

May 10, 1970—United Kingdom—Security agents in London received a telephone warning that a firebomb had been placed in a suitcase on board a loaded Iberia Air Lines plane bound for Spain from Heathrow Airport. The bomb was found before exploding. It was speculated that all four bombs on board the Spain-bound planes had been planted by opponents of the Franco regime, possibly members of the ETA. However, the Paris offices of the

Basque and Spanish Republican governments denied responsibility on May 12. On May 11, anonymous telephone callers in New York claimed that a group of anti-Castro Cubans had placed the bombs to protest Spain's trade with Cuba. 0401

May 11, 1970—Switzerland—A telephoned bomb threat was received in Basel, delaying the takeoff of an Iberian Air Lines plane. 0402

May 11, 1970—Switzerland—A Barcelona-bound plane was delayed when an anonymous caller warned of a firebomb on board. 0403

May 11, 1970—New Zealand—An anonymous telephone call was received by the owners of the Auckland building housing the U.S. consulate, warning that a bomb was on the consulate floor and would explode in ten minutes. An evacuation and search found nothing. 0404

May 12, 1970—India—Early in the afternoon, police stationed outside the entrance to the American University Center in Calcutta were subjected to a bomb attack by unidentified terrorists believed to be Naxalites. Two policemen and one passerby were injured. The AUC is on the third floor of the building and was closed at the time of the incident, escaping damage. 0405

May 13, 1970—Dominican Republic—Eight heavily armed members of a Dutch revolutionary group hijacked a Netherlands Antilles Airlines Fokker F27 on its way from Santo Domingo to Curaçao and diverted it and the twenty-nine people on board to Cuba. Six of the group were later identified as V. de Los Santos, Enrique Frias, Miguel A. Nina, Arsenio Veloz, F. Taveras, and Ventura. 0406

May 14, 1970—Australia—Theodore N. Perrotis, armed with a toy gun, threatened the pilot of an Ansett Airlines DC9, attempting to hijack it from its Sydney to Brisbane route. A six-year-old girl accidentally opened an emergency exit door while the plane was on the ground at Sydney, allowing the passengers to escape. The hijacker was overpowered by the ground crew and surrendered to police who had come on board. He was sentenced to five years on October 30, 1970. 5221

May 14, 1970—Brazil—A young Brazilian male armed with two guns and two tubes of nitroglycerin around his neck hijacked a Viacao Aerea de São Paulo B737 on its was from Brasilia to Manaus. He allowed the passengers to leave while refueling in Georgetown, Guyana, and refueled again in Curaçao, Netherlands Antilles, before proceeding to Cuba. Forty-seven people had begun the flight. 5222

May 14, 1970—Austria—The U.S. embassy in Vienna received a telephoned threat, advising that a bomb was being planted in the chancery. A search was negative. Elsewhere in the city, a protest demonstration of two thousand university students was protesting the U.S. move into Cambodia. It was generally peaceful, save for tear gas being thrown by a far rightist group against the leftist majority. 0407

May 15, 1970—West Germany—A window of the library facing the parking lot of the Amerika Haus in Frankfurt was broken. Two bottles containing a flammable liquid, which had been ignited, were thrown inside. The fire damaged the floor at the end of the library and darkened two columns. Soot damage to books and magazines was slight. 0408

May 16, 1970—Mexico—On May 19 the Mexican government announced that the leader of the Guatemalan Revolutionary Movement of November 13, Marco Antonio Yon Sosa, and two of his followers were shot to death near the Guatemalan border. According to the report, ''A routine army patrol, which was investigating reports of the presence of armed persons in the area, Saturday encountered a cabin which, at first view, appeared unoccupied. But when the soldiers approached it, they were received with small-arms fire. They responded to the fire.'' Several guerrillas apparently escaped. Sosa was a lieutenant in the Guatemalan army until 1960, when he joined a rebellion against President Miguel Ydigoras Fuentes. 0409

May 17, 1970—Ecuador—Terrorists in Guayaquil dynamited the U.S. branch public affairs officer's Mustang automobile in his residence driveway as he was giving a small dinner party with the U.S. cultural affairs officer and his family. There were no injuries, but the blast blew out the front windows of his home, and the rear of the car was badly damaged. A telephone call was later received from a person identifying himself as a member of a dissident group who claimed that the blast was in retaliation for U.S. entry into Cambodia. 0410

May 21, 1970—Colombia—An Avianca DC3 flying from Yopal to Sogamoso en Boyaca was hijacked by four men, identified as D., A. and M. Silva Mahecha and J. Patino Hormaza, and forced to fly to Cuba. The plane stopped unexpectedly in Barrancabermeja and later refueled in Barranquilla. 5223

May 22, 1970—Israel—Members of the PFLP-General Command crossed five hundred yards from the Lebanese border near Avivim, Israel, and fired four bazooka shells at a school bus, killing twelve children and wounding twenty-two. In reprisal, the Israeli military shelled four Lebanese villages, killing twenty and wounding forty. 0411

May 24, 1970—Mexico—A Mexicana de Aviacion B727 on the Cozumel-Mérida-Mexico City run was hijacked by three Brazilians and one Mexican (three men and one woman), who diverted the plane to Cuba. The hijackers were identified as V. L. P. Preskovski, Selva A. Mendez, F. Navarrete, and L. E. P. Pineda. 5224

May 25, 1970—United States—Delta Airlines flight 199, a CV880 on the Chicago-Atlanta-Miami run, was hijacked out of Atlanta by a Latin woman who did not meet the FAA profile, Graciella C. Quesada, who was born on April 29, 1942, in Havana and who was accompanied by her son. She used a .38 caliber revolver to force the pilot to fly to Cuba, where she remains a fugitive from an indictment handed down by a federal grand jury in the middle district of Georgia on July 27, 1970. 5225

May 25, 1970—United States—American Airlines flight 206, a B727 flying from Chicago to New York, was hijacked by a Latin male who did not meet the FAA profile, Nelson Molina, born on May 20, 1946, in Havana. He allowed the passengers to leave in New York while the plane refueled. He remains a fugitive in Cuba from an indictment handed down by a federal grand jury in the eastern district of New York on August 13, 1970. 5226

May 30, 1970—Ireland—Fifteen members of the Sinn Fein, an above-ground IRA political group, took over a British Airways Trident at Shannon Airport. Police evacuated the plane in half an hour, with no violence reported. The plane was empty at the time of the takeover. 0412

May 30, 1970—Italy—An Alitalia DC9 flying from Genoa to Rome was hijacked by Gianlucca Stellini (also known as Gianlocca Stellipi and Gianluca Stellino), a young Italian student armed with a toy pistol, who diverted the plane and its thirty-five persons on board to Cairo in protest of the Middle East conflict. He refused to let passengers leave the aircraft while it was refueling in Naples but did allow the stewardess to leave the plane to check its doors. He forced the pilot to change course twice during the incident. 0413

May 31, 1970—Colombia—An Avianca twin-engined Avro 748 flying from Bogotá to Bucaramanga was hijacked by a couple, José Armando Sanchez and Berta Bueno, with their five children, and diverted to Cuba. The two were armed with a gun and a knife and allowed the pilot to refuel in Barrancabermeja. 5227

June 2, 1970—Philippines—A hand grenade exploded at thirteen thousand feet under the seat of passenger Francisco Santos, who was on aboard a Philippine Air Lines Fokker 27 flying from Manila to Bacolod in the Negros

Islands. A nine-square-foot hole was torn in the fuselage by the explosion. Santos later died of his wounds. Twelve other passengers were severely injured. The plane, carrying forty passengers and four crewmen, landed safely at Roxas.

June 4, 1970—Colombia—A group of students attacked the USIS Cultural Center in Baranquilla at 11:15 A.M. A second attack came at 5:10 P.M. when rocks and three Molotov cocktails were used to damage the building and a USIS vehicle. No one was injured. 0414

June 4, 1970—United States—Arthur Barkley, a white male whom the FAA claimed met the profile exactly, and who was born on May 23, 1921, in Logan, Texas, hijacked TWA flight 486, a B727 flying from Phoenix to St. Louis, demanding $100 million when the plane landed in Washington, D.C. The hijacker had been fired from the Continental Baking Company and began a series of unsuccessful suits against the company and the International Brotherhood of Teamsters for lost sick leave. In 1964 he dropped the suits against them and decided to take out the nineteen days' unpaid sick leave, amounting to $471.78, from his federal income tax. The Internal Revenue Service (IRS) disagreed and sued him for the back taxes plus a penalty tax. Barkley began a series of suits against the IRS, asking damages of $100 million in federal court, where his case was thrown out. The U.S. Supreme Court refused to hear the case.
    Barkley appears to have decided to change tactics on June 4 when he boarded the plane in Phoenix, which took off at 10:30 A.M. with seven crew and fifty-one passengers. At 11 A.M. he confronted stewardess Robin Urrea with a gun, straight-edge razor, and what the crew believed to be a can of gasoline. He entered the cockpit and ordered Captain Dale C. Hupe to fly directly to Washington's Dulles Airport. He radioed that Barkley was demanding that the Supreme Court provide $100 million in small bills to the plane upon its landing. An internationally qualified pilot, Captain Billy Williams, offered to take over the controls when it landed at Dulles. (Williams had flown in the November 1, 1969, Minichiello episode.) At 3:40 P.M. the plane landed at Dulles, where Barkley was greeted with $100,750 in small bills which was all two nearby banks could provide. During its fifty-four-minute stopover, the plane also took on forty-seven thousand gallons of kerosene jet fuel. After attempting to count the money and soon discovering that he was shortchanged, the infuriated Barkley allowed the pilot to take off, demanding to be flown south. He radioed: "To the president and the State Department: You don't know the rules of law. You don't even know how to count money." Six minutes later he ordered the captain to change course and fly northeast. At 4:45 Barkley radioed, "Send a message to the president. Tell him his orders failed. They were not carried out."

Between constant demands to change course, Barkley began to utter ominous observations to the crew, including copilot Donald Salmonson: "It's a shame to go by yourself. When you go, you shouldn't go alone. You ought to take a lot of money and people with you. You ought to take as much money and as many people as possible. You should never go alone." He also began referring to the passengers as his hostages, who included a six-day-old baby, an elderly woman suffering from a bad heart, several college students, and several married couples and their children. Barkley demanded more money from the president at 5 P.M. and considered pouring gasoline over the cash and setting fire to it. At 5:35 the pilot informed Dulles that "the money is to be in hundred-dollar bills and nothing less" and that he was returning to Dulles. At 6 P.M., Barkley demanded that the bills be placed in one hundred sacks. At 6:40, he demanded more fuel for the plane. The FAA offered to provide two people to refuel the plane and two to provide the money. Barkley would allow only one for each task. At 7:02, the plane landed on a runway two miles from the main terminal. Barkley demanded that several emergency vehicles leave the adjoining runway but did not notice a small truck pull up behind the airliner. Two FAA police fired .30-caliber rifles at the plane's tires, missing with initial shots but flattening the four tires on the main landing gear and immobilizing the plane.

Sacks had been placed on the runway to get Barkley to allow the landing. The sacks were filled with shredded newspaper rather than money, a fact that Barkley was not intended to learn. Upon diverting his attention with the sacks, authorities sent trucks, police cars, and other vehicles to barricade the plane. Barkley demanded that the pilot end this siege at 7:18. However, authorities had decided that Barkley was murderous and had no intention of letting him take off again, possibly to commit suicide with all on board. Richard Gillen, a passenger, managed to open an exit door and aid the passengers in leaving. According to his account, "When we finally came back after that ridiculous ride, I looked out and saw the gasoline truck lined up for another refueling, and I said to myself, 'the heck with that.' I asked the senior captain if it would endanger the crew to pop the door, and he said, yes, it would. I told him it might endanger us all the more to stay. So I turned the big handle on the door, flopped open the chute, and told my wife, 'Honey, out you go!'" FBI agents were waiting to greet the escaping passengers. Barkley stared dumbfounded, pointed his pistol at one of the passengers, and ordered him to stop but did not fire when his orders were ignored.

While Barkley's attention was diverted by the escape, Dulles Airport manager Dan Mahaney tossed a .38 through a door to Captain Williams, who had boarded the plane on its previous stopover. At 7:30, an FBI agent wearing a bulletproof vest was hoisted into the doorway nearest the cockpit, causing Barkley to fire four shots. Captain Hupe, fearing that he was shooting two of the remaining passengers, leaped at Barkley while copilot Salmonson jumped at Barkley's shoulders. In the ensuing fight, Hupe was shot in the abdomen by the hijacker who himself was wounded in the left thumb. He was quickly subdued and brought before a federal magistrate in Alexandria, Virginia, later that night. He declared his innocence and told newsmen, "It's all pending in the Supreme Court of the United States Tax Court." He was arraigned and jailed without bond on charges of air piracy. On June 15, a federal judge ordered him sent to a mental institution to determine his sanity during the attack. On November 16, 1971, he was acquitted due to temporary insanity.

Captain Hupe successfully underwent surgery and returned to work on September 22. He and three other crew members received the FAA's award for extraordinary service on that date.

Eight days after the attack, an anonymous donor paid Barkley's $471.78 tax bill. The IRS refused to reveal the individual's identity. 5228

June 5, 1970—Poland—A LOT AN 24 flying from Sczeczin to Gdansk was hijacked by Zbigniew Ivanicki, who, armed with two grenades, forced the pilot to land in Copenhagen, Denmark. He was tried by a Danish court and sentenced to six years on January 4, 1971. The sentence was later reduced to three-and-a-half years. 5229

June 6, 1970—Philippines—A bomb was found in the morning in the USIS Thomas Jefferson Cultural Center in Manila. It had been placed between the first and second floors above a doorway on a window outside the building. It was removed by the Philippine police's bomb disposal forces. At 6:05 P.M., a bomb exploded in the music library of the center, injuring no one but damaging the card catalog file and the plywood wall behind it. 0415-0416

June 7, 1970—Jordan—Morris Draper, forty-two, chief of the political section of the U.S. embassy, was taken from his car in Amman as he was driving to an evening dinner party. The PFLP demanded the release of forty prisoners who had been captured in fighting with Jordanian troops. While being held, Draper was questioned by the group. His release was apparently negotiated by the Jordanian government, which had a cabinet-level meeting, as well as a meeting chaired by King Hussein of his chief officials. The government refused to give in to the demands, but Draper was released unharmed twenty-two hours after being kidnapped. 0417

June 7, 1970—Jordan—U.S. Army Captain Robert Potts, assigned to the U.S. defense attaché's office in Amman, and his wife were wounded after their car was stopped and fired upon at a commando roadblock. 0418

June 8, 1970—United States—Members of the Students for a Democratic Society were reported in the area shortly before a bomb damaged the Chicago headquarters of the National Socialist White People's party.

June 8, 1970—Czechoslovakia—A Czechoslovakian National Airlines IL14 carrying twenty-eight persons from Karlovy Vary to Prague was hijacked by four men and four women, accompanied by a child, two minutes after takeoff. The group, five of whom were armed with revolvers and knives, forced the pilot to fly to Nuremburg, where they surrendered their arms and asked for asylum. They were taken into police custody and because they were carrying arms were sentenced to eight to thirty months. A stiffer antihijacking law was subsequently passed. The hijackers of the twin-engined plane were identified as Stanislava and S. Cihakova, Rudol Cihak, Jini Calasek, Jaroslav Porer, Vera Klementova, Eva Galaskova, and Marie Prochazkova. 5230

June 9, 1970—Jordan—In Suweilih, a small town west of Amman, the motorcade of King Hussein was the subject of an assassination attempt against the head of state, who had a summer villa in the area. The king was returning to his palace in Amman to deal with the current crisis when his bodyguard was killed and five others were wounded in the attack. Reuters reported that Hussein was also wounded.

June 9, 1970—Iran—The Tehran offices of El Al were bombed. 0419

June 9, 1970—Jordan—Members of the PFLP took over two hotels, the Philadelphia and the Intercontinental, in Amman, holding over sixty foreigners hostage, including seven Americans, one U.S. foreign service officer, thirty-five newsmen (including reporter John K. Cooley), Cooley's Greek wife, and citizens of the United Kingdom, West Germany, Canada, and Australia. The group threatened to bomb the hotels if PFLP camps in Amman and Zarqa were smashed in renewed fighting with the Jordanian army. A small group of royal guards tried to surveil the Philadelphia Hotel, perhaps planning to storm the facility, but were forced back when the terrorists fired Kalashnikovs and machine guns. It was later learned that King Hussein gave orders not to attack the hotel, although two Fatah 340-mm heavy rocket units were sent to bolster the guerrillas holding the Intercontinental Hotel.

Hussein agreed to dismiss his uncle, Major General Sharif Naffer ibn Jamil, as army commander-in-chief, and to replace him with chief of staff Brigadier General Mashrour Haditha, whom the Palestinian leadership trusted. After a three-day siege, the hostages were released on June 12. George Habash, head of the PFLP, talked to a group of hostages in the basement of the Intercontinental, musing about how the human spirit is changed by the refugee experience, but warning, "Believe me and I am not joking—we are determined to blow up the hotels with the hostages in them if we had been smashed in our camps." The brother of hijacker Leila Khaled, Walid, suggested holding Cooley's wife as a hostage for the release of seven terrorists held in Greece. Vania Cooley successfully argued that Greece would not be willing to concede to spare her life. 0420-0421

June 9, 1970—Poland—Two armed male Poles, Roman Jasinski and Andrzej Rybak, attempted to force their way into the flight deck of a LOT AN24 flying from Katowice to Warsaw. Their hijacking attempt was foiled by the crew, and they did not make it to Warsaw. 5231

June 10, 1970—Jordan—U.S. assistant army attaché Major Robert Perry, thirty-four, was shot to death in his Amman home when the PFLP fired automatic weapons through a locked door when they attempted to enter. 0422

June 10, 1970—Jordan—Two fedayeen terrorists broke into the homes of American personnel in Amman, where they searched and looted the residences and raped the wives of two U.S. Officials. PLO leader Yasir Arafat announced that the two Palestinians responsible for the attack were not members of the PFLP or Fatah. They were hanged on June 13. 0423

June 11, 1970—Brazil—Eight armed members of the Juarez Guimarez de Brito command of the ALN and VPR kidnapped West German ambassador Ehrenfried von Holleben in Rio de Janeiro. The sixty-one-year-old envoy was taken from car a few hundred yards from his home. Bystanders reported that the group had been waiting in the area for two hours. Von Holleben's Brazilian bodyguard was killed and two others, following in a station wagon, were injured. Brazilian police had discovered the plot forty-five days prior to the attack but believed that with fifty arrests they had successfully prevented it.

Leaflets left at the scene warned that the group would not attack any members of the Rio diplomatic community, and not merely diplomats from major capitalist nations. They also pointed out that increasing security guards would merely increase the risk to the target, noting "We are determined to use as many combatants as are necessary to achieve our ends. . . .We regret we have once more to resort to methods which we have always tried to avoid. However, as long as patriots are being tortured and killed in the prisons we will not have any other choice, even knowing that the physical integrity and the lives of people not directly involved in the revolutionary struggle are at risk. . . .All search for and attempted imprisonment of revolutionary combatants should cease immediately." In a letter the next day, the group demanded the release of forty political prisoners. The Brazilian government agreed to the demand on June 13 and published a revolutionary manifesto in the daily newspapers calling for "revolutionary war, guerrilla actions and rural guerrilla warfare [which] will lead the Brazilian people to free themselves." The group called for expropriation of all foreign holdings and large plantations, an independent and anti-imperialist foreign policy, and guarantees of civil liberties and human rights.

The kidnappers agreed to release the ambassador after foreign news agencies confirmed the safe landing of the plane carrying the forty political prisoners to Algeria. The prisoners numbered thirty-four men and six women and were accompanied by four children. Among them were four accused in the kidnapping of Ambassador Elbrick (see incident 0215): Fernando Paulo Nagle Gabeira, a former newsman who had pleaded guilty; Cid de Queiroz Benjamin, a student; Daniel de Arao Reis Fillio, a student leader; and Vera Silvia de Araujo Magalhaes, a student. A spokesman for the prisoners, former army officer Apolonia de Carvalho, warned that kidnappings would continue. The Algerians granted the group asylum for "humanitarian reasons" and allowed them to give a news conference in which they claimed that they had been tortured and made to believe that their execution was imminent. A group of four of those freed were allowed to grant another interview, and were identified as Ladislaw Dobor (VPR), Carlos Eduardo Fleury (ALN), Fernando Nagle Bageira (MR-8), and Angelo Pezzuti.

Von Holleben was released the evening of June 16. The kidnappers claimed that police surveillance in Rio was too strict and delayed the release for twenty-four hours while street patrols were reduced. The West Germans congratulated President Emilio Garrastazu Medici for his handling of the incident.

On February 9, 1971, military sources reported that at least half of those freed had secretly returned. On February 6, Aderval Alves Coqueiro, one of those released, was killed by police while resisting arrest. Fleury was killed by Rio police on December 10. Joao Carlos dos Santos, leader of the kidnappers, was captured on July 24, 1971. It was learned that Chile and Mexico would also have been acceptable places of asylum. 0424

June 12, 1970—Uruguay—Tupamaros raided the Swiss embassy in Montevideo, stealing documents, typewriters, and a photocopying machine. 0425

June 15, 1970—Bolivia—The USIS Binational Center in Cochabamba was damaged by students who tore down a sign, ripped off metal screening, and broke five windows. They were unsuccessful in an attempt to dynamite a door. 0426

June 15, 1970—Soviet Union—A group of twelve Soviets were prevented at 8:30 A.M. on Monday from boarding a twelve-seat Aeroflot AN2 at Leningrad's Smolny Airport. The plane was bound for Petrozavodsk, Karelia, near the Finnish border. It was claimed that the eleven men and one woman had intended to hijack the plane to Finland and then to Sweden, from which they would work their way to Israel. The attempt to flee the country was treason under Soviet law. It appears that several of the group attempted to escape, but they were captured and were found carrying several knives and two pistols. Tass expanded this into "revolvers, ammunition, and knuckle dusters." It was learned that several of the group had been in labor camps in the 1960s for "anti-Soviet propaganda" and had attemped to emigrate to Israel but were repeatedly refused by Russian authorities. Six of them had signed a letter to U.N. Secretary-General U Thant appealing for his aid. One was an activist in her home town of Riga in support of this cause. The government initiated an immediate crackdown on the group's associates, arresting eight Jewish residents of Leningrad at their homes, places of work, and in a vacation spot. Another fifty Jewish homes were searched within the next few hours, with scores of Jews held for questioning in Kharkov, Riga, Leningrad, and Moscow. Twenty-six more Jews were arrested at the end of the month in Riga, Tifils, and Kishinev.

On December 15, the trial of the Leningrad eleven opened (nine of them Jews) for Eduard Kuznetsov; his wife, Silva, the Riga dissident; her brother Izrael Zalmanson; Mark Dymshits, a former air force pilot; Alexei Murzhenko; Iosif Mendelevich; Yuri Fyodorov; Mendel Bodnya; Arye Khnokh; Anatoli Altman; and Boris Penson. A three-judge court sentenced the group on December 24. Dymshits and Eduard Kuznetsov, the alleged leaders of the group, were sentenced to death before a military firing squad. The rest were given sentences ranging from three to fifteen years. International protest, especially from the United States, Israel, and the Vatican, was especially strong. The Soviets responded that they had been lenient, pointing out their kindness to Mary Mendelevitch, the pregnant wife of Iosif, who had received a fifteen-year sentence. The pressure seemed to have worked; the death sentences were commuted to fifteen years in labor camps on December 31. The terms of three others were also reduced. On Janury 7, 1971, a Leningrad military court sentenced Lieutenant Vulf Zalmanson, brother of two of the group, to ten years in prison for attempted hijacking (which differed from the primary charges against the other eleven of attempting to emigrate to Israel without permission). Thirty-four other people accused of the plot (thirty-two of them Jews) were eventually sentenced. 5232

June 16, 1970—Brazil—A group of students in Sucre attacked the USIS Binational Center with Molotov cocktails and broke into the facility. They carried out the furniture and burned it, alone with books, in the streets, before police were able to respond. Three typewriters, two tape recorders, and one record player were also lost. 0427

June 17, 1970—Brazil—A group of rioting students in La Paz threw Molotov cocktails at the USIS Binational Center, setting fire to property. The fire was extinguished with little damage. 0428

June 17, 1970—Brazil—A U.S. embassy vehicle on the way to the La Paz USIS Binational center to find out about the situation was attacked by 100 to 150 students, who stoned it and threw Molotov cocktails at it. The three

Americans and duty driver escaped without injury, but the vehicle was completely destroyed by the fire. 0429

June 18, 1970—Argentina—The Parke Davis pharmaceutical plant on the outskirts of Buenos Aires was severely damaged by a bomb. Three employees were reported missing and feared dead. 0430

June 19, 1970—Thailand—Three USIS foreign service local employees were killed in an ambush by communist terrorists while traveling in a USIS vehicle on the main highway in Chieng Mai. 0431

June 21, 1970—Iran—Three Iranian males, aged twelve, nineteen, and twenty, armed with pistols and gasoline bottles, hijacked an Iranian Airlines B727 flying ninety-eight people from Tehran to Abadan. Ali Mollahzadeh and his brother Hassan, along with Maswd Hamidi Asl, threatened to light the gas, forcing the pilot to land in Baghdad, Iraq, where they were given asylum. The plane returned to Tehran. 5233

June 21, 1970—Canada—A plot by 3 FLQ members to kidnap U.S. Consul-General Harrison W. Burgess was foiled by police in a raid on their cottage in the Laurentians. Police discovered twenty-four detonators, a wired alarm clock, three hundred pounds of dynamite, a liquid anesthetic, a large syringe, adhesive tape, handcuffs, hoods, a sawed-off shotgun, four revolvers, matching ammunition, 150 mimeographed copies of what the authorities were to do to obtain Burgess's release, and a number of press clippings, among them a picture of company directors.

   The group was arraigned on July 3 and identified as Claude Morency, nineteen, a Place Fleury laborer who faced twenty charges (including one of having conspired with the two others and "persons unknown" to commit acts intended to explode bombs and kidnap the consul-general, as well as steal $58,775 in an armed holdup at the University of Montreal on May 28—$28,000 of this money was found hidden in the cottage); André Roy, twenty-three, an unemployed taxi driver of Morgan Boulevard; and François Lanctot, twenty-one, of the same address, the latter duo facing twelve charges each. A fourth man, Pierre Carrier, thirty, an unemployed plumber, was arrested the same day and sentenced to forty-five days in jail for contempt for failing to answer questions at a fire commissioner's hearing. He was not charged with the kidnapping due to lack of evidence.

   The name of the American consul-general was found underlined in three diplomatic directories on the premises. The mimeographed sheets identified the group as Front de Liberation Quebeçois, operation Marcil-Lanctot, and demanded the release of thirteen political prisoners, including Pierre-Paul Geoffroy, who was servng a life term for bombings, Pierre Valieres, and

Charles Gagnon, the last two out on bail. According to press reports, the group was to be "freed at once and taken to Montreal International Airport where they will be permitted to communicate with their lawyers and others. They must be allowed a one-hour broadcast on CBS television and 'the population' must be invited to meet the 'patriot prisoners' and to be present at their departure for Cuba in a plane placed at their disposal. Legal counsel and two newspapermen must go along on the flight." The group also demanded the reemployment of "revolutionary workers of Lapalme by the federal government on the sole terms of the revolutionary workers of Lapalme," and payment of "voluntary tax of $500,000 in gold bars." They also warned police not to institute searches or arrests or to take other steps that might threaten the life of the consul general. The group would agree to release the hostage once their demands had been met and the Cubans had checked the $500,000. The manifesto ended by saying, "By the kidnapping of Consul Burgess, the FLQ wishes to emphasize its revolutionary solidarity with all the countries which struggle against the economic, social, and cultural domination of the Americans in the world." 0432

June 22, 1970—Lebanon—Pan American flight 119, a B707 flying from Beirut to New York with a stopover in Rome, was hijacked by Haxi Hassan Xhaferi, an armed male who was born in Albania on January 10, 1938, and probably met the FAA profile. Using a pistol, he forced the pilot to fly to Cairo, claiming that he was against American imperialism in Vietnam and was seeking asylum (he was a U.S. resident). He also claimed to be a supporter of the Palestinian cause. He fired a shot into the cockpit as the plane landed. Cairo police briefly detained him, while the plane and 144 others on board were allowed to continue their flight. On February 15, 1973, he was arrested in Los Angeles, California. He was tried and sentenced to fifteen years for interference with a flight crew member on June 8, 1973. Reports differ as to whether his citizenship was Albanian or American. 0433

June 23, 1970—United States—The offices of Amtorg Trading Corporation in New York City were damaged in an attack by members of the JDL who were protesting Soviet treatment of Jews. 0434

June 23, 1970—Uruguay—Tupamaros robbed the Banco Palestino del Uruguay, fleeing with 18 million pesos ($72,000). Some reports claimed that its manager was kidnapped. The Banco de Pan de Azucar was also robbed by the Tupamaros, who stole 8 million pesos ($28,000). A branch of the Union of Uruguay Banks had been robbed of $28,000 on June 17. 0435

June 26, 1970—India—A group of twenty-five to thirty young male Naxalites threw several homemade bombs at police who were guarding the entrance to the American University Center in Calcutta. One bomb hit the side of the building at the third-floor level in an apparent attempt to throw it through the window of the Center. No damage to U.S. property and no U.S. casualties were reported. Press reports claimed that police opened fire, killing one man and wounding four others. 0436

June 26, 1970—Colombia—An Avianco B727 flying from Cúcuta to Bogotá was hijacked by two armed men, Jairo Cardenas and Mauricio E. Carrillo del Castro, who allowed the plane to refuel in Barranquilla before flying on to Cuba. 5234

June 27, 1970—Argentina—Nine bombs exploded in Buenos Aires, Rosario, and Córdoba. Among the targets were several U.S.-owned firms. 0437-0445

June 30, 1970—Uruguay—Members of the Tupamaros occupied the Sayago branch of the Bank of London and South America, stealing 12 million pesos ($63,000). 0446

July 1970—Guatemala—Owen Smith, a British-Guatemalan coffee, tea, and cattle rancher, was kidnapped. He was released seventeen days later after his family paid $75,000 to ''young revolutionaries.'' 0447

July 1, 1970—United States—Members of the Revolutionary Force Seven firebombed the Washington headquarters of the Bank of London and South America, stealing 12 million pesos ($63,000). 0448

July 1, 1970—United States—National Airlines flight 28, a DC8 flying the San Francisco-Las Vegas-New Orleans-Tampa-Miami run, was hijacked out of New Orleans by a man who had boarded in Las Vegas. George E. Lopez, a Latin who met the FAA profile, was born in New Orleans on December 5, 1949. The weapons he used to divert the plane and its thirty-nine persons on board to Havana were not identified. Four servicemen who were passengers were roughed up at José Martí Airport. The hijacker is a fugitive from an indictment handed down by a federal grand jury in the eastern district of Louisiana on December 18, 1970. Other reports list his identity as Bob Serra. 5235

July 1, 1970—Brazil—Three men and one woman, members of the ALN, attempted to hijack a Cruzeiro do Sul Caravelle flying the Rio de Janeiro-São Paulo-Buenos Aires run, and use a machine gun to divert it, its thirty-four passengers, and three crewmen to Cuba. One of them used a revolver to shoot the pilot in the legs, but he managed to fly back to Rio, unknown to the hijackers, who were identified as Eiraldo and Fernando Palha Freire, Colombo

Veria de Souza, and Jessie Jane. When the attackers discovered where they were, they demanded to be allowed to take off again, threatening to kill the passengers one by one. The president of Brazil gave orders that the plane was not to leave. Ten minutes after the plane landed, air force policemen shot out two of the four tires under the right wing, immobilizing the plane. After three hours of stalemate, with vehicles and loading ramps slowly being moved into place, airport fire engines blasted firefighting foam at the plane, while military police used smoke generators to add to the confusion. Thirty officers armed with machine guns and other weapons made their way to the plane. Four of them managed to get on top of the fuselage and on a wing to attempt to open the front cabin door. One of the passengers opened the door and another opened an emergency exit, allowing the passengers to scramble to safety while the authorities poured in. The hijackers, all in their twenties, claimed that they were going to use the passengers as hostages for the release of political prisoners but were arrested before their demands could be made. One of the ALN members shot himself in the neck during the scuffle. 0449

July 1, 1970—Bolivia—A U.S. embassy officer in La Paz, responding to a telephone call regarding the sale of his car, was confronted by a gun and an unsuccessful kidnap attempt. 0450

July 2, 1970—Austria—The U.S. embassy telephone operator in Vienna received a threat that the embassy would soon be blown up. A search proved negative. 0451

July 2, 1970—United States—Members of Revolutionary Force Seven claimed credit for the early morning firebombings of the Washington embassies of Argentina, Haiti, Uruguay, and the Dominican Republic, which caused minor damage and no injuries. 0452-0455

July 4, 1970—Brazil—A Cruzeiro do Sol YS11 flying from Belém to Macapá was hijacked by a lone armed man, Carlos A. Afraytes, who diverted the plane to Cuba. During a refueling stop at Cayenne, French Guyana, he allowed forty of the fifty-six passengers to deplane. At the second refueling stop at Georgetown, Guyana, the remaining sixteen were allowed to leave. 5236

July 4, 1970—United States—The New York City office of BOAC was bombed protest of British actions in Northern Ireland, causing little damage. 0456

July 6, 1970—Colombia—Three powerful incendiary devices were found unexploded in the Cali facility of a U.S. firm. 0457

July 7, 1970—Uganda—During the night, the U.S. ambassador in Kampala received two anonymous telephone calls. The first threatened that the ambassador would be kidnapped. The second warned that he and his children would be killed within a day unless certain political prisoners were released. Security precautions were tightened, and local police guards were posted. 0458-0459

July 7, 1970—United States—A pipe bomb exploded at the Haitian consulate in New York City, injuring three people but causing little damage. 0460

July 7, 1970—United States—Two hours after the Haitian consulate bombing, a pipe bomb was found at the Portuguese Travel and Information Agency office in New York City, while police removed an explosive device from the South African Consulate. Both devices were defused by police. 0461-0462

July 11, 1970—Lebanon—An attempt was made to kill Dr. Wadi Elias Hadad, the forty-year-old second in command of the PFLP and founder of the Arab Nationalist Movement, and schoolteacher Leila Khaled, famed PFLP hijacker, in Hadad's Beirut home on the third floor of the Katarji Building in Almala district on Muhi Aldin Alhayat Street. Khaled and Hadad, automatic pistol and Kalashnikov assault rifle always at the ready, were finishing off a bottle of whisky, coffee, and cigarettes when at 2:14 A.M. six Katyusha rockets blasted through his home.

The rockets were fired from the fifth floor of a building facing the Katarji building, one hundred meters away. Three rockets went through the salon and bedroom of Hadad's apartment. Two rockets malfunctioned. A fire broke out in the apartment, and doors and windows in the apartment and of cars in the street were damaged. Hadad suffered a cut hand, while his wife, Samia, and son Hagi, eight, were treated for burns at the American University Hospital. According to Sami Hadad, an American refused to treat the child without payment until Dr. Hadad, whom the American recognized as another physician, intervened. Adla Khaled el Zayn, fifteen, Hadad's maid, was also injured. Leila Khaled was unharmed.

Inside the launch apartment were a wardrobe, bed, and some cheap furniture. Surgical gloves had apparently been used to avoid leaving fingerprints in the assembling of the missiles. A man claiming to be Ahmad Batzrat and carrying an Iranian passport had rented the apartment after arriving in Beirut three months previously. He had purchased the furniture and drove a beige Volkswagen. He had written on the launching assembly, "Made by Fatah, 1970." He was described as a dark-skinned man in his thirties, thin, mustached, wearing black glasses, with a poor command of Arabic. He avoided meeting people.

The PFLP claimed the Israeli and U.S. intelligence were responsible.

Hadad had returned to Beirut from France only two days before.

Investigations indicated that the terrorist had come from Europe via Lufthansa and Air France, according to labels on two valises left in the apartment. The valises had false bottoms and sides and apparently were used to smuggle the rockets through Beirut airport. Palestinians alleged that he would have needed local support to handle surveillance, planning, renting of the apartment, and setting up the rockets. They suggested that Ahmad Rauf, who came from and returned to West Germany, was involved and that the weapons had been purchased in Lebanon. 0463

July 12, 1970—Brazil—Eduardo Leites of the VPR was arrested in an attempt to release political prisoners by hijacking an airliner. 5237

July 12, 1970—Saudi Arabia—A Saudi Arabian B707 was hijacked on its Riyadh-Beirut run by a lone Arab, Fahad Bakheet Salem Al Harbi, who diverted it to Damascus, Syria, where he requested political asylum. 5238

July 15, 1970—Bolivia—A bomb was thrown into the USIS Binational Center in La Paz late Wednesday night, breaking library windows and frames. 0464

July 16, 1970—Brazil—The USIS reported that a kidnapping threat was received, targeted against a consular officer in Recife. 0465

July 21, 1970—Bolivia—Members of the ELN occupied the town of Teoponte, ninety-three miles north of La Paz, for several hours. They burned the offices of the U.S.-owned gold mining firm, South American Placers, Inc., stole $5,000 and kidnapped two West German technicians, with whom they fled into the jungle. A radio station received a letter in which the group threatened to shoot the duo, Gunter Lerch and Eugene Schulhauser, unless ten prisoners were released by the government within forty-eight hours. The government agreed on July 22, flying the ten to Arica, Chile. The technicians were released in Teoponte the next day. The group included several individuals held for being guerrilla followers of Ché Guevara. They were identified as Loyola Guzman, the group's only woman, Enrique Ortega, Gerado Bermudez, Felix Melgar Antel, Oscar Busch, Victor Cordoba, Roberto Moreira, Rodolfo Saldana, Juan Sanchez, and Benigno Coronado. They reached Cuba via Mexico on August 30. 0466

July 22, 1970—South Vietnam—A twenty-year-old U.S. serviceman, Private George M. Hardin, tried to hijack an Air Vietnam DC4 from its Pleiku to Saigon route and divert it to Hong Kong. He held the pilot at knifepoint for two hours after the air had been let out of the plane's tires. The pilot persuaded him to surrender at Tan Son Nhut Airport. The navigator was reported injured.

Thirty-nine others were on board the plane. Hardin escaped from military custody on August 10, 1970, and was recaptured while trying to hijack a C141 from Bien-hoa Air Base. 5239

July 22, 1970—Lebanon—An Olympic Airways 727 carrying forty-seven passengers and eight crewmen from Beirut to Athens was hijacked over Rhodes by five men and a woman, members of the Palestine Popular Struggle Front (some reports claim it was the PFLP), who allowed the plane to land in Athens, where they negotiated for eight hours for the release of their comrades in Greek jails. According to an American passenger, "We had just had breakfast and I was looking at a young Arab and a pretty girl who looked like newlyweds. They suddenly got up and the man, holding a gun, struck it in the ribs of the stewardess. The girl held a grenade. The man said, 'Don't get excited and you won't get hurt.' Then four more heavily armed Arabs got up. One of them, holding a submachine gun, confided to the passengers: 'We have a plan. We will land in Athens and no one will get hurt.'''

The group members were identified as Farid Abdel Meguid, the group's leader, his sister Mona, Yusef Fakhi, Khaled Abul Abd, Khaled Abul Walid, and Mansur Seif Ed Din. They demanded the release of seven Arab terrorists who were being held for the December 21, 1969 attack on an El Al airliner (incident 0117), the December 21, 1969 attempted hijacking of a TWA plane (incident 0297), and the November 27, 1968, attack on the El Al office in Athens (incident 0285). Three people negotiated for the Greek authorities: Deputy Prime Minister General Patakos, Aristotle Onassis, the owner of Olympic Airways, and M. André Rochat, the International Red Cross delegate for the Middle East, who was in Athens (and knew the correct code words for talking with the Arab hijackers). Onassis twice offered to serve as a substitute hostage, but the hijackers radioed back their rejection of his proposal. Rochat acted as an intermediary and got the parties to agree to allow the trial of Elias Dergarabetian and Mansur Mourad to go ahead as scheduled on July 24 for their November attack on the El Al offices. After the trial, the prisoners would be freed. The hijackers allowed the passengers to deplane, with the crew remaining and Rochat joining them as a guarantor of the agreement. It was suggested that the plane fly back to Beirut, but the hijackers preferred Cairo, where officials welcomed them and praised their revolutionary determination to free their comrades. Rochat returned to Athens the next day.

Heavy diplomatic pressure, especially by the. Israeli government, was placed upon Prime Mininster George Papadopoulous to reneg on the agreement arrived at under duress. However, Dergarabetian received an eighteen-year sentence, and Mourad received eleven years. Together with the other five who had already been sentenced, they were released in the custody of the ICRC and flown to Cairo. The prosecutor who had tried them on charges of murder and had succeeded in convictng them of premeditated manslaughter told them that he hoped to see them again in his country as tourists. Reports differ on whether the seven landed in Cairo on August 12 or 13. 0467

July 23, 1970—United Kingdom—Two canisters of tear gas were thrown onto the floor of the House of Commons by an Ulster Catholic in the visitors' gallery. The hall was evacuated, but sessions were resumed later in the day. James Anthony Roach, twenty-six, was arrested by police and accused of violating the Firearms Act. An adviser to Bernadette Devlin, a member of Parliament, was arrested on July 28. Bowes Egan was charged with conspiring with Roach. Minor damage was reported in the London attack. 0468

July 24, 1970—Brazil—By arresting three terrorists, police foiled an attempted kidnapping of U.S. consul Donner Lyon in Recife. 0469

July 25, 1970—Mozambique—L. De Campos and A. Da Silva attempted to hijack to Tanzania a Portuguese general aviation Etapa Air Taxi flying from Porto Amerlia, Moazambique, to the island of Ibo. The plane landed in Ibo. The hijackers were captured on March 2, 1972, and sentenced to fourteen years. 5240

July 25, 1970—Israel—Israeli security forces arrested Christopher Moreau, a young Italian Swiss, as he stepped off a Greek liner, the *Enotria*, in Tel Aviv. He was carrying five pounds of Soviet-made explosives, detonators, and six copper labels inscribed ''PFLP.'' He claimed that he had contacted the PFLP in Beirut and had been given several weeks of training. He had always been interested in left-wing politics but could not go to Vietnam and thus joined a geographically closer cause. He was paid $900 in advance and was to receive another $5,000 when his bombs exploded. He was sentenced to fifteen years. 0470

July 25, 1970—Mexico—An Aeronaves de Mexico DC9 flying from Acapulco to Mexico City was hijacked by four armed males, one Mexican, and three Dominican Republic nationals, who diverted the plane to Cuba. They allowed a thirty-minute refueling stop in Mexico City but did not allow anyone to deplane. 5241

July 28, 1970—West Germany—The Frankfurt Amerika Haus library was broken into, fuel poured over the floor, and books (primarily those dealing with U.S. foreign policy) and three firebombs ignited. The building and books were damaged before the fire was extinguished. 0471

July 28, 1970—Argentina—An Aerolineas Argentinas B737 flying from Salta to Buenos Aires was hijacked by a man armed with two pistols, who wished to divert it to Cuba. The man was identified as Jurado Albornoz, although other reports list his name as Germin Albornoz, Fermin Jorado Albornoz, and Lorenzo Hermin Jurado Albornoz. He allowed twenty-three of the forty-eight passengers to deplane in Córdoba during a refueling operation. The plane refueled again at Mendoza. An Andes snowstorm forced the plane back to Córdoba. After a fourteen-hour wait in which it was determined that the plane could not take off again due to refueling difficulties, the hijacker surrendered. Six crewmen were on board. 5242

July 28, 1970—Mozambique—A Mozambiquan commercial traveler attempted to hijack a plane by threatening the pilot with a gun, but the pilot refused to divert the aircraft. 5243

July 30, 1970—Chile—The U.S. Embassy in Santiago received a kidnap threat against three employees, including a USIS officer. 0472

July 30, 1970—United States—The Purple Sunshine Clan, probably a faction of the Weather Underground, claimed credit for a bombing of the Alameda County Courthouse in Oakland, California. The letter claiming credit was dated several months after the blast.

July 31, 1970—Uruguay—In the first of a series of raids in Montevideo, hooded Tupamaros attempted to kidnap members of the U.S. embassy in an underground garage of their apartment in the early morning. Michael Gordon Jones, twenty-seven, the second secretary of the embassy, and Nathan Rosenfeld, forty-eight, the cultural attaché officer, both received head wounds by being beaten with revolvers. Rosenfeld broke loose and ran, while Jones was tied and blindfolded, wrapped in a blanket, and thrown into the back of a pickup truck. Upon regaining consciousness while being driven through the streets of the city, he rolled out of the truck onto the street during a stop for a red light. 0473

July 31, 1970—Uruguay—At 8:40 A.M., four men dressed as public utilities servicemen entered the Casa Avda, Calle Potosi home of the Brazilian consul in Montevideo, Aloysio Mares Diaz Gomide. The group seized his wife and two children and demanded that he accompany them. He was blindfolded and bound and thrown into their car. On August 2 the kidnappers revealed in a statement to the newspaper *El Dairio* that the Tupamaros chose Gomide because he was a representative of a dictatorship that had tortured and killed hundreds of Brazilian patriots, and demanded the release of 150 imprisoned Tupamaros in exchange for the release of Gomide and Dan Mitrione, a U.S. adviser who had also been kidnapped (see incident 0475), as well as Judge Daniel Pereyra Manelli, a criminal court judge who had been taken from his

Montevideo home on July 28. On August 3, in its first official communication on the kidnappings, the government announced that it was not prepared to negotiate but it did not rule out the possibility. Gomide was held for a time with Dr. Claude Fly and was given a Portuguese Catholic Bible to read. President Jorge Pacheco Areco obtained passage of legislation that suspended all individual civil rights for twenty days, allowing a nationwide search which included the August 7 arrest of several suspected Tupamaros leaders, including the group's founder, Raul Sendic, as well as Raul Bidegain Greis-sing who was wanted for kidnappings and bombings. On August 6, Pacheco had reiterated an Interior Ministry ruling that the prisoners were common criminals and could not be released as political prisoners. On August 9, three messages were sent by a ''justice squad'' that threatened to kill fifty ''antisocial'' individuals for every foreigner killed by the terrorists and five for every soldier or policeman murdered. On August 10 Brazilian Foreign Minister Mario Gibson Barbosa requested the Uruguayan government to assure Gomide's safe release. The same day the Tupamaros threatened to kill Gomide if the prisoners were not released. (Mitrione's body was found on the tenth.) The group later changed their demands to $250,000 as a ransom. Reports differ as to whether Gomide's wife paid the ransom, but he was released outside Montevideo on February 21, 1971. 0474

July 31, 1970—Uruguay—Tupamaros kidnapped forty-nine-year-old Daniel A. Mitrione, a U.S. AID public safety adviser to the Uruguayan police, on his way to work. A wild shot hit him as he was being dragged to the same car used in the Gomide kidnapping. The group announced that they had performed surgery on him and demanded the release of all political prisoners, who were to be flown to Mexico, Peru, or Algeria. The government again refused the demands of the Tupamaros. After an anonymous telephone tip, the police found letters from Gomide and Mitrione to their wives, claiming to be in good condition. Mitrione noted that he was being questioned extensively, especially about his work with the police and asked his wife to have the U.S. ambassador ''do all he can to free me as soon as possible.'' The State Department asked the kidnappers to release him to allow him to receive hospital care. On August 8, several radio stations received a communiqué setting a deadline of noon the next day. The U.S. ambassador, Charles W. Adair, Jr., broadcast an appeal for mercy twenty minutes before the deadline. The radio station Carve received a call soon after noon claiming Mitrione had been shot: ''In the face of the president of the republic's failure to fulfill the demands of the movement, Mr. Dan Mitrione was executed.'' The caller threatened to execute Gomide and Fly if the demands were not met. Three Uruguayan leaders had offered themselves as substitute hostages but were refused. Mitrione's body was found in the trunk of a car on a Montevideo residential street the next day. He had been shot in the head twice, apparently early that morning. The United States had pressured the government to obtain Mitrione's release but agreed with the decision not to pay ransom or give in to political blackmail. Over one hundred individuals were arrested during a street search by five thousand Montevideo police before the killing. Their numbers swelled to over ten thousand after Mitrione's death in a house-to-house search for the two remaining hostages.

Leopoldo Madruga of Havanna's *Tricontinental Bulletin* printed interviews with "Urbano," a Tupamaro spokesman, in his publication's December and January issues. Urbano claimed that the government was split over how to respond to the terrorists and was further divided when a deadline was established: "Minister Fleitas . . . was negotiating with our imprisoned leaders, proposing the release of the student prisoners and making the others subject to trial by ordinary courts in exchange for the release of the diplomats. There was another try at negotiations through Judge Diaz Romeu, who requested a seventy-two-hour extension of the deadline for the execution of Mitrione from Sendic. This effort failed because of the refusal of Colonel Rivero, the Police Chief."

Urbano also showed a conception of the actions as a propagandistic chess game: "There are a series of factors involved, relating to the Movement, to Mitrione, and to those with whom negotiation was attempted. In the first place, Mitrione represented the presence of the CIA and the Agency for International Development, which sends advisers to the countries of Latin America to aid the repressive forces. He had educated the Uruguayan police in the art of mass repression and torture. His record in Brazil was not a very good one. He is mentioned in the book Who's Who in the CIA. Mitrione was clearly an agent of the repressive forces of the United States. He was tried by a revolutionary tribunal, and his crimes were serious enough to warrant his receiving the sentence he did. But this was not all that was involved—it was not even the most important of the factors involved, because otherwise we wouldn't have proposed his exchange. We were willing to negotiate for the release of our comrades. The U.S. Embassy, acting through Pacheco, decided to sacrifice Mitrione. We gave them a deadline, sentenced him, and warned that if our comrades were not released or a reply was not made to our negotiation proposals within that period, Mitrione would be executed. In such a case, the decision made by the revolutionary movement should be carried out, especially in view of the existing factors. These are the reasons for his execution. The carrying out of this sentence implies a responsibility of the Movement not only to its people but to other revolutionary movements of Latin America as well. This is what you mentioned a moment ago. The kidnapping-exchange method must be carried to its logical consequences in order to save it as a tool. This was also taken into consideration. In taking a step of this kind we were thinking not only of our situation here but of the situation faced by all the other revolutionary movements in Latin America and what kidnappings mean to them. Imperialism is fully aware of this, and this was one of the reasons for its 'no' in the case of the Mitrione exchange.''

On March 29, 1973, security officials announced the capture of Antonio Mas Mas, a Spanish student who joined the Tupamaros at Montevideo University, who reportedly killed Mitrione; Henry Engler, who orchestrated the kidnapping and ordered the murder; and Esteban Pereira and Rodolfo Wolf. Police killed Armando Blanco during the arrest. On February 16, 1977, Mas Mas, twenty-eight, was sentenced to thirty years' imprisonment and 12 years of additional unspecified security measures, the maximum punishment provided by the penal code. It was revealed to the Uruguayan supreme military court that Mitrione had been shot in the back with his hands tied. The court also charged Mas Mas with having murdered Pereira Garay, a police agent, and Ruben Zambrano, a guard, in collaboration with other terrorists, and with the shooting of police officer Hector Moran Charquero. It was claimed that Mas Mas had also participated as an accessory in the kidnapping of Uruguayan politician Ulysses Pereira Reverbel and British ambassador Sir Geoffrey Jackson. 0475

August 1, 1970—Belgium—A bomb planted by Croatian terrorists was found in the Yugoslavian embassy in Brussels before it was able to explode. 0476

August 1, 1970—United States—The Revolutionary Affinity Group Six claimed credit for an explosion outside the New York City branch of the Bank of Brazil. The word *Weatherman* was found painted on the bank, and a Vietcong flag was near the scene of the pipe bomb explosion. 0477

August 2, 1970—United States—Pan American flight 299, a B747 flying with 19 crew members and 360 passengers, 2 short of capacity, on its New York to San Juan run, was hijacked by a Latin who met the FAA profile, Rodolfo Rivera Rios, two hundred miles and twenty-six minutes out of San Juan. The hijacker got out of his first-class seat and confronted the stewardess with a switchblade knife, a bottle containing what he claimed to be nitroglycerin, and what he claimed to be a pistol. He appears to have been born in Aibonito, Puerto Rico, but reports differ as to whether the date was May 23, 1942, May 2, 1943, or May 15, 1943. Captain Augustus Watkins reported that the hijacker was wearing a black beret with a Cuban flag, fatigue jacket, khaki pants, and a goatee, resembling that of Ché Guevara. He disappeared upon the plane's landing in Havana's José Martí Airport. Prime Minister Fidel Castro greeted the pilot and peppered him with questions about the plane's capacity and capabilities. He declined to enter the plane for a tour, saying ''I would probably scare the passengers.'' The plane departed for San Juan within an hour. The hijacker remains a fugitive in the eastern district of New York. 5244

August 3, 1970—West Germany—Pan American flight 742, a B727 carrying 118 passengers from Munich to West Berlin, was the scene of an attempted hijacking by Johann Huber, who appeared to meet the FAA profile, and was born on July 1, 1942, in Germany. He threatened a stewardess with a starting pistol and said that he wanted to go to Budapest. The pilot claimed that the plane did not have enough fuel for the trip, and Huber was taken into custody by police in Berlin. The pilot believed that the white male hijacker appeared to be deranged. No charges were brought against him, and he was committed to a mental institution, from which he was released on November 13, 1970. 5245

August 4, 1970—Chile—A box containing what appeared to be a time bomb with four sticks of dynamite was discovered in the Santiago USIS Binational Center. The device was removed by a center employee who removed one of the sticks from the container and found it to be a candle wrapped in red paper. Further investigation revealed that all of the sticks were candles. 0478

August 7, 1970—Poland—Waldemar Frey, armed with a hand grenade, attempted to hijack a LOT AN24 flying from Szcregin to Katowice and divert it to Hamburg. The hijacker was denied entry into the cockpit, and the pilot landed the plane in East Berlin. He was extradited to Poland and sentenced on September 19, 1970, to eight years for aircraft hijacking and five years for rape and blackmail. 5246

August 7, 1970—Uruguay—Dr. Claude Fly, sixty-five, an FAO agronomist working as a contractor for the International Development Services, a private corporation headquartered in Washington, D.C., was kidnapped from his office by five male members of the Tupamaros who flashed police credentials. Two more with rifles were stationed at the pickup truck, into which he was placed. He was transferred to the trunk of a second vehicle after a half-hour ride through Montevideo. On the third day of his imprisonment, he was driven to another location and placed in a cage. He was held for 208 days. Harassment of Fly included the charge of working for the CIA but ended during his third week. The Tupamaros appeared to be using him for training others as guards of kidnapped prisoners. They gave him a copy of the New Testament, works of Lincoln and Wilson, and a book on Uruguay by Gerassi. The guards often played cards and other games with him and permitted him to write a six hundred-page diary of his experience, which turned out to be profoundly religious, and a guide to the Bible. He also wrote an essay on freedom and security, which was well received by his captors. An Argentine reporter was allowed to interview him at one point. His son offered himself as a substitute hostage, but this offer was refused. The leader of the guards mentioned to Fly that they wanted a proclamation published for his release.

In late October, it appeared that Fly would be released, and he was driven to another location. However, he was merely being transferred to another Tupamaro safe house. Police searched this apartment four times, but the hiding place had been cleverly camouflaged. During this stay, a European communist reporter, probably of Belgian extraction, was allowed a press interview with Fly. Around the turn of the year, another cell took charge of him, bringing him back to his original cell, this time with Brazilian consul Gomide (see incident 0474) being held in the wire cage. In mid-January, Fly was told that he would be released when the state of martial law was lifted. A few days after Gomide's release, Fly suffered a heart attack. The Tupamaros kidnapped a prominent heart specialist, who verified Fly's condition. The doctor ministered to him with an ECG and two oxygen tanks, but claimed to be unable to do anything more for him, so the duo were released in front of the Hospital Britannica in Montevideo on March 2, 1971.

In the wake of the simultaneous kidnappings of other foreigners, great concern had been expressed over Dr. Fly's fate. On August 10, U.S. State Department spokesman Robert J. McCloskey stated that the United States had maintained close contact with the Uruguayan government but had not pressed for release of the 150 prisoners whose freedom it had originally demanded, as it would mean "great risks for all Americans overseas." He also claimed that security measures for American diplomats had been improved.

Uruguay's President Pacheco had refused to negotiate with the Tupamaros and threatened to seize any news media that published the Tupamaro manifesto. He also had refused anyone the right to contact the group and negotiate with them or act as a mediator for negotiations. On September 20, he turned down the group's demand for the publication of a twelve-hundred-word manifesto by three radio stations, three television stations, and six daily newspapers. The manifesto claimed that the government was conducting secret negotiations with the group for the release of the two hostages, whom it did not name. On October 7, Deputy Ariel Collazo and Senator Zelmar Michelini read, in their respective chambers, the text of the MLN manifesto.

The day after Fly's release, Miriam Fly, his wife, and his son John charged in Fort Collins, Colorado, that the Uruguayan and U.S. governments had refused to negotiate for Fly's release. John Fly claimed that "there were no negotiations about his release. It was just the fact that he had a heart attack and the Tupamaros were compassionate enough to release him. I believe the refusal to negotiate is responsible for the death of Dan Mitrione and nearly for the death of my father." 0479

August 8, 1970—Costa Rica—A fire completely destroyed a half-block of buildings in Limón, including the USIS Binational Center. Its library was completely destroyed. 0480

August 8, 1970—Czechoslovakia—A Czechoslovakian IL14 flying from Prague to Bratislava was hijacked by Vladimir Rehak and his two sons, Vladimir, Jr., and Jaromir, who diverted the plane to Vienna, Austria, where they requested political asylum. Czechoslovakia requested extradition. 5247

August 9, 1970—Argentina—The FAP conducted an armed attack on the Italian Hospital in Sante Fe. 0481

August 10, 1970—South Vietnam—George Hardin, a U.S. serviceman being held for a July 22, 1970 hijacking attempt, escaped custody and attempted to hijack a C141 from Bien-hoa air base, but was recaptured. 5248

August 12, 1970—West Germany—Two bombs exploded in West Berlin, damaging private cars belonging to three U.S. military personnel and a Department of the Army civilian. 0482

August 13, 1970—Israel—The telephone operator of the U.S. embassy in Tel Aviv received a call warning that a bomb would explode in the embassy within five minutes. A search was negative. 0483

August 13, 1970—United States—An unidentified male phoned to warn that a bomb would go off when a Western Airlines 720 flying from Anchorage to Seattle descended to 10,000 feet. A search of the plane found no bomb.

August 18, 1970—United States—Leon Zelwanski, seeking additional restitution for the deaths of 250 relatives in World War II, fired four shots at two attachés in the West German consulate in New York City and was subsequently arrested. 0484

August 18, 1970—Northern Ireland—A bomb placed by the IRA caused heavy damage to the British Naval Recruiting Stations in Belfast.

August 18, 1970—Bolivia—A time bomb was found outside the La Paz Peace Corps headquarters around midnight and was successfully disarmed. 0485

August 19, 1970—Bolivia—A bomb exploded in a La Paz sidewalk policeman's box in front of the U.S. AID building, causing minor damage to the building. 0486

August 19, 1970—Poland—A LOT IL14 flying twenty-two people between Gdansk and Warsaw was hijacked by Krbystov Krynski and two couples. One man used a hand grenade to force the pilot to land on the Danish island of

Bornholm, where they surrendered to police and asked for political asylum. The rest of the passengers and crew returned to Poland. 5249

August 19, 1970—United States—Trans-Caribbean Airlines flight 401, a DC8 flying 147 people from Newark to San Juan, was hijacked by three men armed with a gun and hand grenades, who diverted the plane to Havana, where it remained for six hours before flying on to Miami. The three Latins met the FAA profile and were identified as José Arrue-Martinez, born April 20, 1948, in Guantánamo, Cuba; Jesus Ramos-Cobas, born April 3, 1947, in Colona, Spain; and Brilan Torres-Llurdan, born November 27, 1945, in Cuba. They remain fugitives from an indictment handed down on March 25, 1971 by a federal grand jury in the district of New Jersey. 5250

August 19, 1970—Japan—An All Nippon Airways B727 flying from Nagoya to Sapporo with six crew members and seventy-four passengers was hijacked by twenty-four-year-old Sachio Inagaki, who demanded that the plane land at Hamamatsu Air Defense Base. Upon landing, he demanded a rifle, ammunition, and two drums of gasoline in exchange for the passengers. Reports indicated that he had broken up with a girl friend and was going to commit suicide. After two hours of negotiations, a passenger feigned labor pains. The hijacker and pilot agreed that she should be let out of the plane. When an ambulance arrived, a plainclothesman ran up the rear ramp of the plane, jumped the hijacker, disarmed him, and clapped handcuffs on his wrists. His gun turned out to be a toy. 5251

August 19, 1970—Uruguay—U.S. AID public safety officer Spann was kidnapped by Tupamaros and held while his car was used in two bank robberies in Montevideo. He was subsequently released unharmed. Another report indicates that a Stephan Spann was the son of a local southern Baptist missionary and was kidnapped. 0487

August 20, 1970—United States—Delta Airlines flight 435, a DC9 flying from Atlanta to Savannah, Georgia, with eighty-one persons on board was hijacked by a marine absent without leave who claimed he had a bomb inside a briefcase. Although no one saw the bomb, the plane was diverted to Havana, where he surrendered to Cuban officials. He was identified as Gregory A. Graves, a black who did not meet the FAA profile, who was born on April 17, 1949, in Kansas City, Missouri. An indictment was handed down on February 2, 1971, by a federal grand jury in the middle district of Georgia. Graves was arrested in San Juan on June 1, 1975, and flown to Georgia to stand trial. He was convicted of air piracy and sentenced to twenty years on October 25, 1975. 5252

August 22, 1970—Jordan—Unknown individuals, possibly Palestinian commandos, kidnapped Salim al Sharif in Amman. Sharif was a Palestinian newspaper editor thought to back the government view on a settlement with the commandos. It appeared that he was taken so that his captors could learn about the financing of his newspaper. 0488

August 22, 1970—Brazil—A guard sitting in the entrance of the USIS offices in Fortaleza was shot and slightly wounded by an unknown attacker. The guard was not part of the regular·police guard but was a night watchman hired to protect a nearby commercial building. 0489

August 24, 1970—United States—The New Year's Gang phoned a University of Wisconsin underground newspaper to claim credit for the bombing of the Army Mathematics Research Center, which killed a postdoctoral researcher and destroyed the contents of the building, including its $1.5 million computer. Four other people were injured. Police received a warning call two minutes before the explosion.

August 24, 1970—United States—TWA flight 134, a B727 flying from Las Vegas to Philadelphia with ninety-two persons on board, was hijacked by Robert J. LaBadie, who had joined the flight in Chicago. LaBadie entered the cockpit and informed the crew that a companion had access to a bomb. He allowed the plane to land in Pittsburgh to refuel but did not allow anyone to deplane. The plane flew on to Cuba. LaBadie was identified as a white hijacker who met the FAA profile; he was born on February 27, 1943, in Detroit, Michigan. The Cuban government found him undesirable and flew him back on September 24, 1970, making him the first hijacker they had returned. He was found incompetent to stand trial on December 28, 1970, and was committed to a mental institution, from which he was released on October 30, 1973. 5253

August 25, 1970—United States—An anonymous caller warned of a bomb aboard a Pan American B707 taking off from San Francisco on a flight to Hawaii, and demanded $100,000. A search revealed no bomb, and the airline decided not to pay the money. The aircraft took off an hour later with 148 persons on board.

August 25, 1970—Poland—Five youths hijacked a Polish trawler at sea near Darlowo, Poland, and diverted it to Bornholm, Denmark, where they requested political asylum.

August 26, 1970—Poland—Twenty-seven-year-old Rudolf Olma, accompanied by his wife and child, attempted to hijack a LOT AN24 flying from

Katowice to Warsaw and divert it to Vienna, Austria. The bomb he was carrying accidentally exploded, injuring him and ten other passengers, tearing off the door of the flight deck, damaging electrical equipment, and setting the plane on fire. The pilot managed to land the plane with its thirty-one persons on board safely at Katowice. Olma was sentenced to twenty-five years in prison on April 8, 1971. 5254

August 28, 1970—Bolivia—Bombs exploded at the La Paz residence of a U.S. embassy officer and at the U.S. consulate building. There was no damage to the consulate, but most windows on one side of the house were shattered and a three-foot diameter hole was blown in the wall. 0490-0491

August 29, 1970—United States—The Revolutionary Action Party claimed credit for the Washington, D.C., bombings of the Portuguese embassy and the Rhodesian Information Office, which caused minor damage. 0492-0493

August 30, 1970—Chile—Shots were fired from a passing car at a guard stationed in front of the U.S. ambassador's Santiago residence. 0494

August 30, 1970—United States—A suitcase full of dynamite was found behind the Portuguese embassy in Washington, D.C. An army demolition team disarmed the device. 0495

August 31, 1970—Netherlands—Thirty-two armed Amboinese youths seized the Hague residence of the Indonesian ambassador, killing a guard in the attack. The embassy was taken in the early morning, with the group using pistols and Sten guns to hold the family and servants hostage. They demanded the independence of the South Moluccan Islands but were talked into surrendering. President Suharto's visit to the Netherlands was delayed for one day. 0496

August 31, 1970—Poland—A Polish trawler was seized by ten Poles at sea off Poland and diverted to Bornholm, Denmark, where they requested political asylum.

August 31, 1970—Algeria—An Air Algerie Convair 640 flying from Annaba to Algiers with forty-four persons on board was hijacked by three Algerian males who wished to obtain political asylum in Albania. The trio, identified as Rabah Boultif, Allova Layachi, and Muhamed Tovanti, were armed with pistols, knives, and grenades. They allowed the plane to refuel in Sardinia, Italy. The Albanian government refused to allow the plane to land, so the group flew on to Dubrovnik, Yugoslavia, where they surrendered to police. 5255

August 31, 1970—Turkey—During the early morning hours, an explosion in a U.S. Air Force Tuslog Detachment 30 building in Ankara broke several windows but injured no one. Later two unexploded devices were found in the vicinity of the same building. The hospital annex was evacuated following what proved to be a false bomb threat. 0497-0498

September 1970—Guatemala—The Uruguayan embassy was machine-gunned by the FAR. 0499

September 1970—United States—Dynamite was found at the Wisconsin-Michigan Power Company Point Beach licensed nuclear facility.

September 1970—Guatemala—A U.S. embassy car was intercepted in Guatemala City by men who identified themselves as FAR members. After they seized weapons in the vehicle, the driver and the car were released. 0500

September 1, 1970—Jordan—Palestinian commandos in Amman attempted to assassinate King Hussein by firing on his motorcade. Army troops and commandos exchanged gunfire in and around Amman following the attack. A government communiqué read, "The Jordanian government assures the Jordanian people and the Arab nation that the situation in the capital and the kingdom is under full control. Any rumors by the army of a crackdown on the commandos are completely untrue, and the aim of these rumors is to create confusion." 0501

September 2, 1970—Bolivia—A nearby bomb blast broke thirty windows in the La Paz residence of a U.S. embassy officer. 0502

September 2, 1970—Greece—A bomb exploded in a parked car in the area adjoining the U.S. embassy in Athens, killing a Cypriot man and an Italian woman. Two other cars were burned, and glass was shattered throughout that side of the embassy. A few local employees suffered minor cuts. The embassy was cordoned off, and local employees were sent home. Investigations suggested that the dead were terrorists from the Patriotic Front who intended to bring the bomb into the embassy. 0503

September 2, 1970—Jordan—Two U.S. Embassy vehicles were taken at gunpoint in Amman. One was stopped on the street and the other by forcing an embassy officer at his residence to hand over the keys. 0504-0505

September 3, 1970—Jordan—Another U.S. embassy vehicle was taken at gunpoint on an Amman street. A personal vehicle was taken from a U.S. mission employee at his residence. 0506-0507

September 4, 1970—Uruguay—Tupamaros machine-gunned the headquarters of the U.S. embassy marine guard. Six businesses and private homes were also bombed in Montevideo. 0508

September 6, 1970—West Germany—Two members of the PFLP, identifying themselves as M. Vasques and A. Lapez, Arabs who probably met the FAA profile, took over TWA flight 741, a B707 flying from Frankfurt to New York with 145 passengers and 10 crew members. The attack occurred over Belgium at 12:20 P.M. The plane was diverted to Dawson's Field, Zerka, Jordan, a former RAF landing strip in the desert. This was the first of a well-coordinated series of hijackings carried out by the PFLP this day. The group demanded the release of three PFLP members being held in West Germany for the attack on the airline bus in Munich (see incident 0319), three held in Switzerland for the Zurich attack on the El Al plane that had resulted in the killing of the copilot (see incident 0133), and an unspecified number of fedayeen held in Israeli prisons. The demands later expanded to include Leila Khaled, who was being held in a British jail after an unsuccessful hijacking attempt. The group threatened to blow up the planes with the passengers inside by 3 A.M. on Thursday, September 10.

On September 5, *Le Soir*, a Brussels newspaper, had reported that ham radio operators had intercepted an Interpol message warning that Palestinians were on their way from Beirut to Europe. On September 6, a Beirut spokesman for the PFLP explained that the U.S. planes were seized ''to give the Americans a lesson after they supported Israel all these years'' and to retaliate for U.S. peace initiatives in the Middle East.

Upon landing, the guerillas allowed 127 passengers from the planes at Dawson Field, mostly women and children, to go to two Amman hotels and were told that they were free to leave. The remaining hostages were men from West Germany, England, Israel, and the United States. The planes were surrounded by commandos, who in turn were surrounded by troops from Jordan's army, including fifty tanks and armored cars. Negotiations thus began, with the Swiss and Germans initially being willing to deal unilaterally with terrorists to free their own nationals, but British Prime Minister Edward Heath called upon all five governments to take a common position. Hence on Tuesday, the Berne Five was formed. Its first act was to instruct Red Cross representative M. Rochat, who had acted as intermediary in the Athens Seven case (see incident 0467), to inform the PFLP in Amman of their stand, which was to release the seven prisoners upon the release of all passengers. In addition, the Germans sent Mr. Wischnewski, a German Social Democrat party member, to Amman to negotiate on September 7. On September 10, the ICRC incorrectly reported that an American woman had given birth at Dawson's Field. On the eleventh, two more Americans were released from the TWA jet. Eighteen other hostages were secretly taken to Zerka and hidden in homes, because the attack squad began to distrust their PFLP leaders in Amman and wanted extra insurance against a doublecross. The PLO sent Munif Razzaz to calm the militants. He had been secretary general of the Syrian Ba'athist party before his faction lost in a party split.

The Israelis preferred to be observers in the Berne Five, and thus the Red Cross was named by only four of the members as their intermediaries. A three-member liaison group of ICRC officials was sent to Amman to confer with PFLP member. The hijacking of the BOAC VC10 led to an extension of the deadline to early Sunday morning. It appeared that the PFLP altered the deadline in hopes that the United States would have more time to pressure Israel to capitulate. The negotiation group was joined by journalists and author Michael Adams, a leader of the Council for the Advancement of Arab-British Understanding. None of these negotiators was immediately successful. On September 12 the PFLP gave a five-minute warning that women and children would be released in Amman. This appeared to be in response to a Baghdad commando radio broadcast picked up on September 11 by the BBC Monitoring Service. In it, the PFLP's Central Committee announced, ''The committee has decided the following: 1. To transfer all the passengers to Amman. . . .2. To release all passengers of various nationalities with the exception of Israelies of military capacity. These passengers will be released when an official statement is issued by the foreign countries concerned that they are ready to free the Palestinian girl and other fedayeen held . . .in Western Germany, Switzerland and Britain. 3. To release the three aircraft and their crews as soon as the fedayeen in question arrive in Jordan or in any other Arab country. . . .4. To hold the Zionist passengers of military capacity in Amman until an agreement is reached in the current negotiations with the Red Cross on the release by the Zionist authorities occupying Palestine of a number of Palestinian men and women fedayeen imprisoned in enemy jails.'' On the twelfth, the planes held at Dawson's Field were evacuated and destroyed by PFLP explosives experts. On the thirteenth, the release time of the last West German hostages was put back twice. An appeal by the pope to free the hostages was delivered to the PFLP by Monsignor Jean Rodhain. With the release of the West Germans, fifty-eight hostages remained, including the eighteen being secretly held in Zerka.

The activities of the PFLP on Jordanian territory proved too much for King Hussein to tolerate, and Jordanian troops engaged the fedayeen in a series of bloody battles, in which approximately seven thousand died. Negotiations became of secondary importance to the embattled PFLP, and hostages were rescued sequentially by Jordanian army troops. On September 25, sixteen Swiss, German, and U.K. hostages were found in the Wahdat refugee camp near Amman, apparently abandoned by the PFLP guards. The next day thirty-two Americans were released to the ICRC after being held in Amman. The final six Americans—three members of the U.S. government, two rabbis, and one teacher—were released to the ICRC on September 29. Also on the twenty-ninth, the Swiss government announced that seven Arab guerillas would be released by Switzerland, West Germany, and the United Kingdom when the Americans had safely left Jordan, and called upon Israel to release ten Lebanese soldiers and two Algerians taken from an airliner on August 14 as a humanitarian gesture. The seven were released the next day (see incidents 0319, 0321, 0512).

It was later reported that one hundred hijacking pupils were led through the planes for a quick course on jet operations. 0509.

September 6, 1970—Switzerland—At 1:14 P.M., a Swissair DC8 carrying 143 passengers and 12 crew members were seized over France thirty minutes out of Zurich on its New York-bound flight by two men and a woman belonging to the PFLP. Among the passengers was Jack Detwiler, head of Alcan Cable in Jersey Shore, Pennsylvania, who reported that the plane was forced to land in Zerka, Jordan, almost on the tail of the TWA plane (see incident 0509). Guy Winteler, ICRC delegate in Amman, was chosen to relay the PFLP demands, which called for the release of Leila Khaled for the British passengers (this was a bluff because no British passengers were being held at the time), three terrorists in West Germany for the German passengers, three terrorists in Switzerland for the Swiss passengers, and an unspecified number of guerrillas in Israeli jails for the Israeli and American passengers (on August 15, 1970, it was reported that there were thirty-four Arabs in Israeli jails). The guerrillas set a seventy-two hour deadline, and the Swiss initially were willing to capitulate, until intervention by British Prime Minister Heath. The next day, General Mashour Haditha got the guerrillas to release 127 women and children in return for the Jordanian army's retreating two miles from the planes. However, the guerrillas kept the passengers' passports, allowing them to go only to the Intercontinental Hotel in Amman. On September 10, Yasir Arafat called a meeting of the PLO Central Committee. The 2 PFLP representatives abstained on a vote taken to release all passengers save Israelis of military age. The next day, the passports of sixty-eight of the hostages in the hotel were returned, allowing them to fly to Cyprus. Thanks to the intervention of Adams, Abu Maher granted the release of three Dutch passengers. On September 12, Dr. Wadieh Haddad, who was PFLP operations chief and who was acting for George Habash, in North Korea and China during the bargaining, gave the order to destroy the planes in Zerka. A $30 million plane was reduced to rubble in the blast. Arafat's proposal to suspend the PFLP from representation on the central committee of the PLO was subsequently approved. The next day, M. Rochat of the ICRC negotiations group left.

During negotiations, the commandos became suspicious of the intentions of their leaders and moved some of the hostages to Amman. They also turned away Red Cross supplies, as well as PLO buses that had been sent to collect the hostages. However, they did let another twenty-three hostages into Amman, most of them Indians. Of those hostages remaining, all but thirty-eight, including five Israeli girls, were allowed to go to the hotel. The thirty-eight were split up, being sent to various locations in Amman. These included nationals of Israel, Switzerland, West Germany, the United States, and the United Kingdom. During the fighting that followed, major leaders of the fedayeen, including Salah Khalef (also known as Abu Ayad) and three other Fatah leaders, were captured in a house. The Egyptian embassy received several shellings, possibly due to their attempts to get the PFLP to release the hostages being held in the Wahdat camp. (See previous incident for subsequent events.) 0510

September 6, 1970—Netherlands—According to the log of Pan Am flight 93, code 9052 (denoting a skyjacking) had been reported at 7:17 A.M. for a TWA plane flying over Zagreb, Yugoslavia. At 7:30 A.M., it received the same message for an El Al plane. At 8:14 A.M., the same message was received for a Swissair over Luxeuil, France. At 10 A.M., the Pan Am, which was late in getting out of Amsterdam, was hijacked by two Arabs who probably met the FAA profile. They forced the plane to refuel in Beirut before picking up another PFLP member, who flew with the group to Cairo, where the plane was destroyed. The trio were identified as Sa'id Ali Ali, Samir Abdel Majid Ibrahim, and Mazin abu Mehanid Khalil. The hijackers of the 747 appear to have been Palestinians whose forebears came from Chad. Scattered reports claim that they were born in Jerusalem. One hundred fifty-two passengers and twenty-three crew members were on board, including four members of a deadheading crew captained by Paul La Chapelle and Valerie Priddy, the wife of the pilot, John Priddy, who had received a garbled warning message that was too vague to be of use. Two of the passengers, supposedly students registered in the names of Diop and Gueye, and carrying Senegalese passports, had been denied entry on an El Al plane (which had claimed to have oversold its first-class section). They had booked a flight to New York's JFK Airport, from which they would fly to Chile. They were supposed to have been part of a PFLP group that was to hijack the El Al flight but instead seized the 747. Each carried a revolver and hand grenade and had the plane circle Beirut for two hours because the Lebanese government did not wish to be involved in the incident.

A PFLP member, who identified himself as Walid Kaddoura, alias Abu Khaled, talked to the hijackers from the control tower and gave them instructions. He told Gueye, alias Samir Abdel Maguid, who claimed that this was his third hijacking, that he was with Abu Ahmad Yones Njeim. The latter told the terrorists that Ashraf and Abu Hani, Amman party leaders, had not planned for them to land in Beirut. At times, the Israelis contacted the plane and suggested flying to Tel Aviv. A message from Jordan instructed the hijackers to fly to Cairo (apparently to embarrass President Nasser), where the plane was to be destroyed. PFLP Captain Ali allowed five men to refuel the plane. He was then instructed to separate the Jews from the other passengers, collect their passports, and keep them as hostages after leaving the plane. Ali found that he was holding a French diplomat, plus two Englishmen he suspected. (The pilot later reported that a Belgian or Dutch Jew in his seventies was not spotted.)

Nine members of the PFLP, including a woman, then boarded the plane, armed with .45 caliber pistols and eighty pounds of dynamite. The group's bomb expert stayed on board the plane with a pregnant woman and her husband; the others left. The demolitions expert, in his early twenties, set the fuses before the plane landed. The stewardesses activated the emergency chutes and the passengers ran for cover before the $24 million plane was destroyed. In the rush, seven passengers were injured and later hospitalized. The rest went safely to an airport hotel. Egyptian authorities detained the trio of hijackers and began looking for a fourth hijacker they believed had escaped. 0511

September 7, 1970—Netherlands—The last attempted hijacking of the day was against El Al flight 291, en route from Tel Aviv to New York, thirty minutes out of its stopover in Amsterdam. It was the only airliner of the four that included armed guards among its 145 passengers and 13 crew members. However, the sky marshal of the first-class cabin of the B707 had been mistakenly locked in the pilot's cabin with pilot Bar-Lev when the attack began. The original plan had called for a four-member PFLP team to hijack the plane. However, two members of the group had been denied boarding and instead hijacked a 747 to Cairo (they did not have navigational plans for Zerka). The duo had orders to meet Leila Khaled of the PFLP (who had participated in a hijacking on August 28, 1969) and Patrick Joseph Arguello, a member of the FSLN, in the airport lounge after checking in. However, they made no attempt to warn their compatriots of their failure and boarded the 747, leaving Khaled and Arguello to fend for themselves. Khaled was posing as a Latin American, Maria Sanchez, while Arguello claimed to be Enrico René Diaz, a professor.

The hijacking began twenty-five minutes after takeoff. Arguello, armed with a grenade and pistol, held his gun to the head of a stewardess and demanded the crew open a security door leading to the cockpit. A steward seized his gun arm but was shot in the chest. Arguello's automatic jammed when he tried to shoot him again. What happened next is unclear. Arguello pulled the pin from his grenade and rolled it down the aisle. An Israeli security man stood up with a drawn revolver in the path of the grenade but was not harmed because the fuse was improperly set. Khaled claims that two or three Israeli security men plus three passengers jumped Arguello, beat him, tied him up, and shot him in the back four times. The Israelis claim that the tall security man shot him once. Khaled tried to use two grenades she had hidden in her bra, but was overpowered by two male passengers. An elderly American disarmed her. Some accounts indicate she pulled the pin on one of her grenades, but it was rusty and failed to explode. One crew member, Shlomo Vider, was injured by five shots. Israel radioed the pilot and pleaded that he return to Tel Aviv with the injured Khaled. However, he proceeded to London to allow prompt medical attention for Vider. Bar-Lev was criticized by his government for this decision. Arguello died under an oxygen mask in an ambulance, but Vider was saved. Later a note was found with Khaled that was to identify her as "Shadia, of the Abdel Jader command unit of the PFLP," ordering the plane to fly to Amman.

Reports on Arguello's biography conflict. Some say he was born in San Francisco on March 30, 1943, and lived in Nicaragua as a child. Others find his father to have been a Nicaraguan physician who married an Irish-American woman and settled in Los Angeles. In 1966, Arugello graduated from the University of California at Los Angeles. Two years later, he travelled through Mexico to the Nicaraguan University to begin a postgraduate program. In 1969, he went to Geneva to study for a master's degree in sociology, where he may have been recruited by the PFLP. Other reports find him studying in Chile on a Fulbright scholarship.

Khaled had previously captured headlines with a hijacking on August 28, 1969. When the plane landed in Heathrow Airport, the El Al security guards refused to let her go, and a tug-of-war ensued, with the Israelis pulling at her legs while the British police grabbed her shoulders. She was held in Ealing police station. Three days later the Israelis formally informed the British government that they intended to request extradition of Khaled. The same day a BOAC jet was hijacked, and Khaled's name was added to the list of those whom the PFLP wanted released. She was flown on board an RAF Comet on September 29, when it was announced that the British hostages had been flown to the RAF base in Akrotiri, Cyprus. The Comet made stops in Zurich and Munich to pick up the other freed terrorists. On October 1, the seven Palestinians arrived in Cairo in time for Egyptian President Nasser's funeral but were not allowed to attend, being kept in a government guest house. Eleven days later they flew to Damascus and Beirut. 0512

September 7, 1970—United Kingdom—The U.S. embassy duty secretary in London received a call threatening "Unless girl [Khaled] is released, no U.S. aircraft will be safe." 0513

September 7, 1970—Bolivia—The USIS Binational Center in Sucre was attacked with Molotov cocktails. 0514

September 7, 1970—Argentina—A small bomb exploded at the USIS Binational Center in Mendoza, causing insignificant property damage and no injuries. 0515

September 8, 1970—Greece—Two Arabs planning attacks against Israeli targets in Greece were arrested. A report claims that they were freed in the context of the Zerka hijackings (see incidents 0509, 0510, 0511, and 0512). 0516

September 8, 1970—Greece—An attempt to hijack an Ethiopian airliner in Athens by two members of the ELF was foiled by security guards. 0517

September 8, 1970—Philippines—A contract mechanic at the U.S. Voice of America transmitter in Tinang, Tarlac, was shot through the head and killed while repairing a bulldozer in the antenna field. 0518

September 9, 1970—Argentina—Three armed men entered the fifth floor offices of the USIS in Córdoba, and, after binding and gagging the BPAO and an Argentine employee, set off incendiary devices and a bomb in the store-room. The two men were able to escape, and no injuries were reported. The blaze was confined to the USIS area of the building. 0519

September 9, 1970—Greece—A TWA B707 flying from Athens to New York with 143 passengers was delayed two hours after two anonymous phone calls warned of a bomb on the plane. A search found no bomb. 0520-0521

September 9, 1970—Jordan—U.S. Staff Sergeant Ervin Graham, assigned to the U.S. defense attaché's office, was kidnapped by members of the Palestine Liberation Army as he tried to proceed around a military roadblock in Amman. He was held for eight days, interrogated, and released unharmed. No ransom was demanded. He reported that he was well treated. 0522

September 9, 1970—West Germany—A bomb threat was received by tele-phone at the U.S. consulate in Frankfurt, warning that three bombs had been placed there. A search was negative. 0523

September 9, 1970—Bahrein—BOAC flight 775, a VC10 piloted by Captain Cyril Goulborn and carrying 105 passengers and a crew of ten from Bombay to London, was hijacked by three members of the PFLP who were identified as M. J. Haddad, A. M. S. Ahmed, and H. M. Hassan. The trio forced the pilot to divert the plane to Beirut, where it took on eighteen thousand kilograms of fuel, before it flew on to join the other two planes at Zerka's Dawson's field near Amman. Among the passengers were fifty-two British, including thirty children, twenty-one of whom were returning to boarding school. The PFLP now put their deadline back to the early hours of Sunday morning, having gained new leverage against the British in their attempts to achieve the release of Leila Khaled. The three hijackers, who had named the plane *Leila*, had been joined in Beirut by three more PFLP members, including a woman named Mona Saudi. Twenty-three of the passengers on board the BOAC plane were quickly released; twenty-one of them were Arabs. The other two were a Persian mistaken for an Arab and his English fiancée, Lesley Pressley. The evening of the eleventh, other hostages were released, including nineteen Indians, one Saudi Arabian, and one Indonesian from the BOAC plane. Abu Fadi, a PFLP airstrip leader, forced everyone back into the planes after noting a military buildup near the area. The next day, all three planes were destroyed by PFLP demolitions experts after being evacuated, causing a loss of $20 million in the case of the VC10. A disagreement within the PFLP seems to have occurred regarding this action, with the PFLP headquarters leaders wanting to spare the planes. Captain Goulborn and Major Potts were kept as hostages by the airstrip PFLP members until the end of the incident. They were among twenty-eight hostages, including British, Americans, and five Israelis, who were taken to Wahdat refugee camp during the negotiations. On the twelfth, PFLP leader Ibrahim, with PFLP translator Bassam on hand, held a news conference, in which he claimed that forty hostages were being held, which proved to be an underestimate. Some reports indicate that twenty-two of the hostages were being held in the home of George Habash in Wahdat. On September 17, the British asked for the intervention of Egyptian President Nasser in the negotiations. On September 25, Potts and the other hostages were found inside the house by members of the Jordanian army. The hostages included eight British, six Swiss, and two West Germans. (See incidents 0509 through 0512.) 0524

September 10, 1970—Bolivia—At 2 A.M., the USIS office in La Paz was hit by a bullet, which broke the window of the book office. 0525

September 10, 1970—Guatemala—A bomb exploded in the home of Atilio Arrillaga, the Uruguayan ambassador, who was not at home at the time. 0526

September 10, 1970—Lebanon—Three Arabs attempting to hijack an Egyptian plane flying from Beirut to Cairo were overpowered by security officers shortly after their attack. 0527

September 10, 1970—Jordan—The U.S. cultural affairs officer, John Stewart, was kidnapped by members of the Palestine Liberation Army in Amman. No ransom demands were made. Stewart reports that he was questioned and released unharmed twenty-eight hours later. 0528

September 10, 1970—Canada—An anonymous telephone call threatening to hijack a BOAC jet flying between Toronto and London resulted in a brief delay of its takeoff. 0529

September 11, 1970—Canada—A threat to hijack a Canadian Wardair jet flying between Toronto and London resulted in a search of all 183 passengers on board. 0530

September 11, 1970—Uruguay—Tupamaros robbed the Esso Standard Oil Company's Montevideo offices of $1,800. 0531

September 11, 1970—United States—A bomb threat was made against the licensed nuclear facility at Kansas State University.

September 12, 1970—Libya—A male from Chad attempted to hijack an Egyptian plane flying from Tripoli, Libya to Cairo. He was apprehended by security officers aboard the aircraft shortly after the hijacking attempt was initiated. 0532

September 12, 1970—United Kingdom—Members of the Jewish Defense League in London announced that they had kidnapped three employees of the Egyptian embassy, claiming that they were Iraqi, Jordanian, and Syrian members of Al Fatah, and demanded that those being held hostage by the PFLP in Zerka airstrip be released. 0533

September 13, 1970—United States—Members of the Weather Underground aided Dr. Timothy Leary, a former Harvard professor and advocate of the use of LSD, in an escape from minimum security in San Luis Obispo Men's Colony.

September 14, 1970—Romania—A Romanian TAROM BAC111 flying from Bucharest, Romania to Prague, Czechoslovakia, with eighty-nine persons on board was hijacked by a Hungarian group using pistols and a fake bomb. The group managed to divert the plane to Munich, where they were disarmed by West German police, and asked for political asylum. Piroschka Biro, a hijacker who was accompanied by her two children, was found innocent. The other three hijackers were sentenced to two-and-a-half years by a West German court on January 20, 1971. They were identified as Miklos Biro, twenty-nine; Geza Karaczony, twenty-three; and Janos Mamuzsits, twenty-five. 5256

September 15, 1970—Argentina—The USIS Binational Center in Sucre received a warning to evacuate, which was followed by a dynamite charge against the front door that broke its locks. Police were able to disperse assembled demonstrators before they could enter the center. 0534

September 15, 1970—United States—TWA flight 15, a B707 flying from Los Angeles to San Francisco with fifty-nine persons on board, was the scene of an attempted hijacking to North Korea by Donald Bruce Irwin, a white who probably met the FAA profile, who was born in Detroit on November 19, 1942. Armed with a pistol, he remained in his seat after handing the chief stewardess a note stating that he wished to go to North Korea. He allowed thirty-five women, children, and military officers to leave the plane while it refueled in San Francisco. A stewardess informed a Brinks guard, who was a passenger on board the flight, of the attempt, and he shot and wounded Irwin. No further injuries were reported. Irwin was convicted in state court and sentenced on November 23, 1971, to twelve-and-a-half years for attempted kidnapping. 5257

September 15, 1970—Canada—A message threatening sabotage was dropped off at a ticket office of Air Canada in Montreal. Flights leaving Montreal were delayed while a search of all buildings was conducted, revealing no bomb. A ransom was demanded in the note. Seven men and a woman were held in police custody in connection with the threat.

September 16, 1970—Egypt—Sayed Seif el-Nasr, armed with a revolver and dagger, attempted to hijack an Egyptian Airlines Antonov 24 flying between Cairo and Luxor with fifty-one persons on board and divert it to Saudi Arabia. A security officer on board disarmed el-Nasr, who was subsequently sentenced to ten years in prison. 5258

September 17, 1970—Canada—A sabotage threat against an Air Canada plane was received in Toronto. The 127 passengers disembarked on a runway away from the main building. No bomb was found.

September 17, 1970—Jordan—Partially as a result of the multiple hijacking conducted on his soil, King Hussein began a series of attacks against the fedayeen. During street fighting in Amman, mortar explosions damaged the U.S. Embassy, with several local employees receiving slight shrapnel wounds. Elsewhere a fedayeen attempt to capture the unoccupied residence of the U.S. ambassador was beaten off by guards. 0535-0536

September 18, 1970—Jordan—The U.S. AID parking lot in Amann was burned, and the U.S. embassy received more sniper fire. 0537-0538

September 18, 1970—Thailand—Pretending to be a movie scout, thirty-six-year-old U.S. citizen Robert Joseph Keesee hijacked a Bira Air Transport general aviation Cessna 182 flying in northern Thailand and diverted it to Dong Hoi, North Vietnam. The plane was fired upon while landing on the beach. Keesee was the only passenger on board the ten-seat plane, which also carried a pilot and copilot. Keesee was released to U.S. authorities with a group of

American prisoners of war on March 14, 1973. He next showed up in the kidnapping and murder of an American official in Mexico (see incident 1855). 5259

September 19, 1970—United States—Allegheny Airlines flight 730, a B727 flying ninety-nine people from Pittsburgh to Boston, was hijacked by Richard Duwayne Witt, a black male who met the FAA profile, who was born in Pittsburgh on December 22, 1952. Holding a gun at the throat of the stewardess, he initially demanded to be flown to Cairo. This threat to the woman's safety discouraged a professional wrestler among the passengers from trying to overpower the hijacker. The plane landed in Philadelphia for refueling, where the passengers, but not the crew, were permitted to leave. Witt eventually settled for a flight to Havana. He remains a fugitive from an indictment handed down on July 27, 1972 by a federal grand jury in the eastern district of Pennsylvania. 5260

September 22, 1970—United States—Eastern Airlines flight 945, a DC8 flying between Boston and San Juan, was the scene of an unsuccessful hijacking attempt by David W. Donovan, a white male who did not meet the FAA profile, who was born in Boston on June 25, 1934. Donovan, a federal prisoner being transported to San Juan, locked himself in a lavatory and threatened to burn the plane if it was not flown to a destination of his choice (which he never specified). His two escorting U.S. marshals overpowered him, and the plane flew on to San Juan. Federal charges against him were dropped in favor of unrelated state robbery and murder charges. He was sentenced to six years for robbery and life imprisonment for murder. 5261

September 22, 1970—Bolivia—On September 19, a USIS vehicle had been slightly damaged when it was caught in a student demonstration. Damage was not severe due to the quick action of the driver. At 12:30 on the twenty-first a mob of several hundred people attacked the U.S. embassy, forcing the marine guard to use tear gas to clear the alley by the embassy. A number of windows were broken by rocks and a dynamite stick placed near the entrance blew out the glass in the door. Molotov cocktails were also hurled at the building. One was thrown through a second-floor window but was thrown back before it could explode. Three embassy employees were stoned as they sought to reach the embassy. On September 22, two bullets penetrated USIS premises in La Paz. 0539-0540

September 22, 1970—Cuba—Bolivia—The USIS reading room in Oruro was the target of a group who attempted to burn the front door. 0541

September 22, 1970—Bolivia—The one-room USIS office in Trinidad was sacked and burned. 0542

September 23, 1970—Cuba—The Cuban government announced that it had killed or captured all members of a nine-man commando squad. The anti-Castro Cuban exile group Alpha 66 claimed on September 28 that two separate groups of invaders had landed on the island. It further claimed on November 7 that one of the groups had reached its destination in Oriente Province. 0543

September 24, 1970—United States—A ten-inch pipe bomb exploded in a woman's restroom near the offices of the Japanese and Kuwaiti governments in New York City. The restroom sustained slight damage. 0544

September 25, 1970—Italy—Eleven vehicles bearing U.S. armed forces license plates were firebombed in Rome. Two of the cars were completely destroyed. 0545-0555

September 25, 1970—Italy—A fire damaged the home of the U.S. ambassador in Rome during the early morning. 0556

September 26, 1970—United States—A pipe bomb exploded outside the Ivory Coast U.N. mission in New York City, causing minor damage. 0557

September 27, 1970—France—A woman deposited a suitcase with a bomb at the Iberia counter at Paris's Orly Airport. When she did not show up for the flight, the suitcase was set aside in an adjoining room, where it exploded, injuring a stewardess. 0558

September 27, 1970—United Kingdom—A bomb exploded in a suitcase that was to be loaded on an Aer Lingus flight. No injuries were reported at London airport's international baggage section. 0559

September 27, 1970—United States—A BOAC VC10, loading sixty-eight persons for a flight from New York to London and Tel Aviv, was the scene of an unsuccessful hijacking attempt. Security guards discovered weapons carried by a couple and arrested them before boarding. The two were identified as twenty-five-year-old Gordon Rider (also known as Avraham Hershovitz) and twenty-year-old Nancy McGovern (also known as Nancy Hershovitz). 5262

September 30, 1970—Brazil—A small bomb exploded in the USIS Thomas Jefferson Library in Rio de Janeiro, partially shattering a large plate glass window and knocking down some bookshelves. 0560

October 1970—Guatemala—FAR members shot a policeman outside the Costa Rican embassy. 0561

October 2, 1970—Argentina—The door to the USIS Binational Center in Sucre was dynamited. 0562

October 2, 1970—Turkey—A bomb exploded outside the U.S. Air Force Tuslog commissary in Izmir, destroying approximately thirty feet of rear wall valued at between $500 and $1,000. No injuries were reported. A second bomb, consisting of seven sticks of dynamite, was found outside the commissary and defused. 0563

October 3, 1970—Turkey—A bomb exploded against a U.S. CENTO element building in Ankara, resulting in forty-four broken windows on two sides of the building and a damaged vehicle. No injuries were reported. 0564

October 3, 1970—Turkey—At 6:27 P.M., an explosive device was thrown at the USIS offices in Ankara. Seven window panes and one glass door were broken on the third floor, and one window and a balcony door were broken on the ground floor. 0565

October 5, 1970—Lebanon—Forty-three commandos who wanted to remain in Beirut held an airport officer hostage. They were persuaded to release him. Forty-two of the group left, with the last individual following later. The group was armed with six guns and five grenades. 0566

October 5, 1970—Argentina—A time bomb was left on the window ledge of the USIS Binational Center in Tucumán. Police were alerted and the bomb was defused. 0567

October 5, 1970—Canada—James Richard Jasper Cross, the British trade commissioner in Quebec, was kidnapped from his Montreal home and thrown into a taxi by five members of the Quebec Liberation Front who were carrying M1s. The kidnappers were later identified as Marc Carbonneau, Jacques Lanctot, Jacques and Louise Cosette-Trudel, and Yves Langlois. In a series of notes sent to the Canadian government, the group demanded publication of a political manifesto in all Quebec newspapers; release of certain political prisoners; a chartered aircraft to fly the prisoners to Cuba or Algeria; $500,000 in gold bullion to be placed in the plane as a voluntary tax; federal jobs for 450 truck drivers belonging to Lepalme Service, a private postal firm, who had lost their jobs in a recent dispute with the federal post office; the publication of the name and photograph of an FLQ informer who led police to the discovery of an FLQ cell; and the stopping of a police manhunt for Cross. The terrorists imposed a forty-eight-hour deadline. On October 10, another cell of the FLQ kidnapped Pierre Laporte, the Quebec minister of labor, to increase pressure on the government. The government again rejected the demands but offered safe conduct out of the country for the kidnappers. On October 16, the government invoked emergency powers, authorizing police and troops to conduct searches and arrest without warrants. On the eighteenth, the minister's body was found in a car trunk. This led to a massive hunt for the kidnappers, with five hundred individuals being arrested. Cross's kidnappers released him unharmed on December 3. Seven individuals were flown to Cuba under the safe conduct agreement. On August 6, 1974, it was reported that France had granted temporary asylum to an FLQ member and his wife who had been flown to Cuba. During the Montreal trial of Paul Rose, who had been charged with the murder of Pierre Laporte, the government introduced evidence claiming that the USIS branch PAO had been marked for kidnapping along with Cross. 0568

October 6, 1970—Italy—One of two Molotov cocktails placed against the front door of the USIS offices in Milan exploded at 1:45 A.M. The resulting fire, which was quickly extinguished, went under the front door and burned the inside footmat. 0569

October 6, 1970—United Kingdom—Two parcels with grenades inside and addressed to the embassy of Israel and the El Al office in London were found in the BOAC London office. 0570-0571

October 6, 1970—Turkey—An undetonated bomb was found under the vehicle of a USAR member near his Ankara apartment. 0572

October 6, 1970—United States—A pipe bomb exploded in the New York City office of the Palestine Liberation Organization, causing some damage. 0573

October 7, 1970—Bolivia—The USIS office in Oruro was sacked after the door to the building was dynamited and entrance gained by a crowd estimated at one hundred. All equipment and materials were carried out of the offices and classrooms. Later an American flag was taken and burned in a nearby square. 0574

October 7, 1970—Bolivia—The USIS Binational center in La Paz was dynamited and taken over by demonstrators. A U.S. embassy residence building was entered and sacked by demonstrators. Eighteen armed students entered the Peace Corps office and stole a short wave radio. The USIS warehouse was broken into and a few items were stolen. 0575-0578

October 8, 1970—Uruguay—A man rang the front door bell at the marine guard residence in Montevideo. When the maid answered the door he pulled out a pistol and ordered her to call the "chief marine." The maid screamed and fainted, and the man fled. An intensive search by the marines and police failed to turn up a suspect. 0579

October 8, 1970—United States—American terrorist groups celebrated the anniversary of Ché Guevara's death in Bolivia with a series of bombings along the West Coast. The Purple Sunshine group claimed credit for planting an undetonated bomb at the University Study Center in Berkeley, California. The Perfect Park Home Garden Society planted a bomb at the Santa Barbara National Guard facility, causing $400 damage. The Quarter Moon Society bombed a Navy Reserve Officers Training Corps facility in Seattle, Washington, causing $150,000 damage. The group claimed that the bomb was planted in commemoration of Diana Oughton, a Weather Underground member who died in a New York City Weather bomb factory. The Weather Underground planted a bomb in a women's restroom in the Marin County Courthouse in California, causing $100,000 in damages. Their publication, *Prairie Fire*, claimed that the bombing was to protest the death of three prisoners.

October 8, 1970—Chile—The Santiago offices of the Ford Motor Company were bombed. 0580

October 8, 1970—West Germany—Two young men entered the USIS Amerika Haus in Munich at 4 P.M., setting off homemade firebombs in the second-floor exhibit room. The main damage was to the exhibit room, posters, and equipment. Police arrested the pair. 0581

October 9, 1970—Peru—Small incendiary devices went off in the Lima store of an American firm, causing slight damage. 0582

October 9, 1970—Iran—An Iran National Airlines B727 flying between Tehran, Abadan, and Kuwait with forty-nine persons on board was hijacked to Baghdad, Iraq, by three armed Iranian youths who threatened to blow up the plane with all passengers and crew aboard if Iran did not release twenty-one political prisoners. A stewardess was wounded by the gun-wielding trio, identified as Hassan Tahrani, Ali Reza, and Mohammed Mahmoudi. The group was held by Iraqi authorities for questioning. 0583

October 10, 1970—Canada—To bolster the position of the kidnappers of forty-nine-year-old British Trade Commissioner James Cross, members of the FLQ kidnapped forty-nine-year-old Pierre LaPorte, Quebec minister of labor and immigration. Two masked men armed with submachine guns took him from his home at 6 P.M., the time of the deadline set by Cross's kidnappers, and identified themselves as the Chenier cell of the FLQ. Upon his release, Cross, for whose release the government had broadcast a fourteen-hundred-word manifesto, claimed that his kidnappers had been surprised by the actions of the Chenier cell.

The kidnappers threatened to kill LaPorte if the Cross group's demands were not met by 10 P.M. The group sent a note in LaPorte's handwriting pleading for compliance. Five minutes before the deadline, Premier Robert Bourassa appeared on television to reject the demands and asked the terrorists to free Cross and LaPorte. On October 11, police arrested Robert Lemieux, a radical lawyer who had served as spokesman for the cells, and charged him with obstructing their investigations. The next day, the Quebec cabinet appointed Robert Demers, a Montreal lawyer, to represent the cabinet in the hostage negotiations. However, the terrorists wanted Lemeiux to represent them, and the talks opened that day in his jail cell. He was released on October 13 and the next day claimed that the government had not told him whether it would agree to release twenty-three political prisoners. The next day, an FLQ note refused to guarantee the hostages' safety other than a "solemn pledge to the people of Quebec," and would not surrender one cell member each, a government suggestion. On October 15, Lemieux claimed that the police had found where Laporte was being held. Bourassa asked Ottawa to send troops to guard public buildings and major officials' homes, a request that was granted. He refused to release all twenty-three prisoners but suggested a compromise: the release of five prisoners and safe passage for the kidnappers. Among the twenty-three were FLQ members accused or convicted of conspiring to kidnap, armed robbery, and involuntary homicide. Four of them had received life terms, and others had received twenty-five-year sentences.

On October 16, Prime Minister Trudeau invoked the War Measures Act, which outlawed the FLQ and gave the government power to do anything deemed "necessary for the security, defense, peace, order and welfare of Canada." Civil liberties were suspended for members of the separatist group and possible witnesses, the first such measure by Canada in peacetime. Between the invocation and November 24, 3,068 raids were conducted by police, resulting in the arrests of 453 persons and the seizure of 159 firearms, 677 sticks of dynamite, 912 detonators, and 4,962 rounds of ammunition.

On October 18, around midnight, Laporte's body was found in the trunk of the kidnap vehicle. The previous day, the government had offered safe conduct if the kidnappers brought him to the Concordia Bridge on the Expo 67 site in Montreal. Cuban consular officials would take custody of the hostages, and the kidnappers would be allowed to travel to Cuba. On October 18, an arrest warrant was issued for Paul Rose, twenty-seven, and Marc Carbonneau, thirty-seven. The next day, police found the FLQ's safe house on an unpaved street in the Montreal suburbs. A neighbor had recognized a suspect from televised police photographs of Rose. Rosa Rose, mother of Jacques and Paul, said on November 7 that she and her two sons, along with Francis Simard, had been motoring through the United States when they heard of the Cross kidnapping. The youths decided to return immediately to Canada.

On November 6, Montreal and Quebec police arrested Bernard Lortie, nineteen, who confessed at a coroner's hearing the next day to participating in the Laporte kidnapping, but denied that he had been involved in his murder or Cross's kidnapping. On December 2, police surrounded the kidnappers' hideout at 10949 Des Recollets Street in a Montreal working-class suburb. The next day, the kidnappers expressed willingness to negotiate. A police bomb squad arrived and later determined that the house was booby-trapped. Quebec justice minister Jerome Choquette joined the negotiations between Robert Demers, the government's representative, and Bernard Mergler, a radical lawyer and FLQ representative. The kidnappers were then allowed to drive to St. Helen's Island in Montreal. Cross was handed over to Ricardo Escartin, Cuban acting consul in Montreal, at the Canadian Pavilion. A helicopter flew the terrorists and their relatives to Montreal's Dorval Airport, where an RCMP plane flew them to Cuba. The passengers were Marc Carbonneau, a thirty-seven-year-old Montreal taxi driver; Jacques Lanctot, twenty-five, his wife, Suzanne, and their child; Pierre Seguin; and Jacques and Louise Cossette-Trudel. The Cubans noted that they agreed to the exchange for "humanitarian reasons."

Three Laporte suspects were captured on December 28. Paul Rose, his brother Jacques, and Francis Simard surrendered at a St. Luc farmhouse, thirty miles south of the U.S. border. Michel Viger, thirty, who had rented the house to the trio, was also apprehended. Police had searched the house three times previously, and this time had found a twenty-five-foot-by-four-foot chamber under the house the previous day. Jacques Ducros, a Montreal lawyer, served as the suspect's negotiator. The trio had arms and food supplies and demanded that bail be set for fifty persons held under the War Measures Act. The government agreed, and the three surrendered.

Simard claimed that Laporte had cut himself on a broken window while trying to escape, and "we decided to strangle him with the [religious] chain he had been wearing since his kidnapping."

On March 13, 1971, Paul Rose was sentenced to life imprisonment for capital murder. On November 20, he received a second life term for kidnapping Laporte. On May 20, 1971, Simard was convicted of noncapital murder and received a mandatory life sentence. On November 2, 1971, Lortie was given twenty years for kidnapping. On December 9, 1972, Jacques Rose was acquitted of kidnapping and on February 22, 1973, was acquitted of murdering Laporte.

The War Measures Act expired and was not renewed, because the authorities had effectively ended the FLQ's threat to public order. 0584

October 11, 1970—United States—A passerby found fifteen sticks of dynamite wired to a clock in an attaché case twenty minutes before it was set to explode outside the Greek consulate in Chicago. 0585

October 11, 1970—Norway—The U.S. embassy in Oslo received an extortion letter, threatening the destructon of local buildings, including the embassy, unless a sum of money was paid. Although a church was burned by an arsonist, as threatened in the letter, to authenticate the writer's intent, nothing further developed. 0586

October 12, 1970—Taiwan—A bomb exploded early in the evening in the lobby of USIS Tainan. One USIS contract employee was injured, though not seriously, but three students in the building were seriously wounded. Extensive damage was done to the building. 0587

October 13, 1970—Argentina—A small time bomb disguised as a book on a shelf of the USIS Binational Center in Rosario exploded, causing minimal damage and no injuries. 0588

October 14, 1970—Peru—A small incendiary device exploded in the Lima store of an American firm, causing slight damage. 0589

October 14, 1970—United States—The Proud Eagle Tribe, a Weather Underground women's group, sent a letter claiming credit for the bombing of the library of the Center for International Studies of Harvard University.

October 15, 1970—Argentina—The October 8 unit of the FAL hijacked an airplane in Rosario and used it to drop leaflets on the city. 5263

October 15, 1970—Soviet Union—An Aeroflot AN24, flying between Batumi and Sukhermi with fifty-one persons on board, was hijacked by forty-six-year-old Pranas Fransizkas Koreyevo, a Lithuanian truck driver, and his son Algedas (reports differ as to his age, citing him as somewhere between fifteen and eighteen years old). The man claimed that he had planned the hijacking for three years but was unable to persuade his wife and daughters to come with him. The two broke into the cockpit and thrust a note at the pilot, Captain Valery Adeyev, demanding to be taken to Turkey. The pilot took evasive action, making a steep, banking turn. However, the hijackers were not thrown off balance and began shooting instead. One shot killed stewardess Nadezhda Kurchenko, and another hit the pilot, seriously wounding him. Other shots hit the radio operator and a passenger. The copilot, Surikov, took over and flew one hundred miles out of the Soviet Union to Trebizond, Turkey.

The hijackers surrendered to Turkish authorities and requested political asylum. The police discovered that the two had been armed with two shotguns, five pistols, and three hand grenades and had been carrying $6,300 in cash. The Soviet government immediately demanded extradition of the pair, but the Turkish government refused, pointing out that the two countries had no extradition agreement for crime and that Turkey considered this a political crime, for which extradition does not apply. *Pravda* claimed that the elder hijacker was a thief and embezzler, had been dismissed from several jobs, and had served five years for theft and "economic crimes." A later report claimed that he had acquired $6,500 through illegal activities and had been convicted of abuse of state funds and black marketeering. It denied that he had ever participated in political activities. Rumors appeared, later proven false, that the two were Soviet Jews. Shortly after the Soviet government announced the institution of a new security policy, in which two thousand armed guards would be assigned to travel on Soviet planes flying near Soviet borders or from airports from which a plane might be hijacked. Another five hundred detectives would be posted at airports to check passengers and luggage before boarding.

The two were tried on hijacking charges, convicted, and jailed. Their sentences were reduced due to a Turkish general amnesty decree, and they were released from prison on May 21, 1974. Fearing the possibility of Soviet retaliation, such as kidnapping, the two fled to a Turkish camp for displaced persons in Yozgat, Anatolia. In June 1976, they left camp, complaining that they were sick and suffering from depression. On June 28, they appeared at the U.S. embassy in Turkey to request political asylum in the United States. The two Lithuanians said they feared that the Turks would turn them over to the Soviets. At one point, the older Brazinskas stabbed himself with a small knife. Ambassador William B. Macomber, Jr. received assurances that the Turks would not return them to the Soviets, and they were placed in Turkish custody after a three-day stay in the U.S. embassy. On July 11, the two flew from Istanbul to Rome. Turkey had given them international identification papers in lieu of passports. They next appeared in Venezuela on thirty-day tourist visas. When these ran out, they flew to Canada. While changing planes in New York on August 24, they were given permission for transit within eight hours but disappeared from Kennedy Airport. Nine days later, the son, Algedas, now no longer a minor, was married to an American citizen of Lithuanian descent in Worcester, Massachusetts. Immigration and Naturalization (INS) officials arrested him there on September 14. On September 15, his father turned himself in to INS officials in New York. Both requested asylum, which INS officials promised to consider. They were released on bonds of $5,000 each, provided by Dr. J. K. Valiunas of New Rochelle, New York, a leader of the Lithuanian-American community. As of November 1977, asylum had been denied and they faced deportation to Venezuela. 5246

October 16, 1970—Argentina—Firebombs destroyed the home of the U.S. Defense attaché in Buenos Aires. The house and furnishings were completely destroyed, but no injuries were reported. 0590

October 18, 1970—Norway—The Norwegian State Broadcasting Company received an anonymous telephone call warning that a bomb would explode in the USIS library in Oslo before midnight. No bomb was found. 0591

October 20, 1970—Argentina—Bombs exploded in the homes of two U.S. officials in Buenos Aires, causing no injuries. 0592-0593

October 21, 1970—Australia—Croatian terrorists were believed responsible for planting a bomb found at the Yugoslav consulate in Melbourne. 0594

October 21, 1970—Argentina—In Buenos Aires, members of the FAL robbed Chilean industrialist Jorge Yarur Rey and hs family, taking jewels and personal documentation. 0595

October 21, 1970—Costa Rica—A LACSA BAC111, flying between Limón and San José, Costa Rica, was hijacked by five men and two women, all members of the FSLN, who demanded to be taken to Cuba. On their way to San Andrés Island, Colombia, where they refueled, they learned that four Americans were on board the plane. Upon landing, they handed a note to airport officials, demanding the release of four FSLN members who were being held in a Costa Rican jail. The group said that they would proceed to Cuba whatever the response of the government but that the four Americans would be killed and the plane blown up if their colleagues were not freed and sent to Mexico. During the negotiations, thirty-two people were allowed to leave the plane, but the four Americans, as well as the crew, remained on board. One of the guerrillas whose release was demanded was Carlos Fonesca Amador, who had fled from Nicaragua to Costa Rica in 1969 to avoid being captured by Nicaraguan National Guardsmen. However, he had been arrested for unlawful possession of a firearm and was imprisoned. A group of FSLN members attacked the prison in an attempt to help him escape, killing two guards, but the rescue failed, and several of the attackers were captured. Costa Rica agreed to release the four, and they arrived in Mexico, where they said, ''We want to get to Cuba as soon as possible so we may continue the fight against the government of General Anastasio Somoza.'' The FAA reported that the seven hijackers transferred to a second plane, which flew them to Havana. 0596

October 23, 1970—Burundi—The U.S. embassy in Bujumbura was warned of a plan to kidnap the U.S. ambassador or another ranking officer. Although the reliability of the informant was unknown, his story was backed up by a letter from a rebel group. Precautionary measures were taken. 0597

October 23, 1970—Portugal—The U.S. embassy in Lisbon received a letter indirectly threatening the life of the U.S. ambassador. Security measures were increased. 0598

October 24, 1970—Italy—The U.S. Education '70 exhibit in Rome was the subject of a commando-type raid executed by twenty to twenty-five young people. A tear-gas grenade was thrown, and a computer and some teaching machines were damaged. The lights were cut off, and several panels were knocked over. A photograph of Angela Davis with a message saying, "To American School of Assassins, we reply with revolutionary violence," was left. The exhibit was open to the public on schedule after the weekend. 0599

October 26, 1970—Sierra Leone—The U.S. embassy in Freetown discovered a threat to kidnap the chargé d'affaires. On October 15, two hundred demonstrators pulled down the American flag at the embassy and ripped it up in spite of the presence of riot police and troops. Several windows in the embassy were broken. 0600

October 27, 1970—Soviet Union—An Aeroflot twin-engined IL14 (other reports claim it was an AN2 or a Morave IL14 Aeroflot Air Taxi) flying the Kerchi-Krasmodar-Sevastopol domestic route was hijacked by two students, Nikolai Gilev (also known as F. Ginlov), twenty, and his cousin, twenty-five-year-old Vitaly M. Pozdeyev. They had planned their hijacking for two years and designed a bag to put over the pilot's head so that he could not see his instruments. The plane landed in Turkey, at Akliman, Sinop, the site of a U.S. radar monitoring station. One other person was on board. The two asked asylum but were extradited to the Soviet Union. In September 1972, one was sentenced to ten years, the other thirteen years. 5265

October 27, 1970—United States—A bomb threat was made against the Commonwealth Edison Company (Dresden), a licensed nuclear facility.

October 27, 1970—United States—The Orlando, Florida, city hall received a note threatening to blow up the town with an atomic device unless $1 million was paid, safe passage out of the country was granted, and a television station acknowledged receipt of the letter. A diagram of the device was later sent to substantiate the threat. The money was collected and prepared for delivery before it was discovered that a fourteen-year-old honors science student had fabricated the hoax.

October 28, 1970—Argentina—The Emilio Juaregui group of the FAL claimed to have assaulted three police guards at the U.S. embassy in Buenos Aires, stealing their weapons and uniforms. 0601

October 29, 1970—Argentina—At 3 P.M., the telephone operator of the U.S. embassy received an anonymous call warning that a bomb would explode within the embassy in twenty minutes. No bomb was found. 0602

October 30, 1970—United States—National Airlines flight 43, a DC8 flying fifty persons from Miami to Tampa and San Francisco, was hijacked by a Cuban male accompanied by his wife and five children, forcing the plane to fly to Havana. He gave his name as L. Rosas, which appeared to be an alias. No positive identification of him was made, and he remains a fugitive. The plane and passengers were allowed to return to Miami. Rosas probably met the FAA profile. 5266

October 30, 1970—Italy—Two letters were received in Rome threatening the lives of U.S. officers assigned to NATO. 0603-0604

November 1, 1970—United States—United Airlines flight 598, a B727 flying with seventy-one persons from San Diego to Los Angeles and Portland, was hijacked by Felipe F. Larrazolo, who was born in Mexico on November 13, 1935. He was accompanied by his two children and probably met the FAA profile. Using a pistol to threaten a stewardess, he forced the pilot to refuel at Tijuana, Mexico, and fly on to Havana. The plane was returned to the United States after several hours in Havana. Larrazolo remains a fugitive from an indictment handed down by a federal grand jury in the central district of California on December 9, 1970. 5267

November 1, 1970—Pakistan—Feroze Abdullah drove a catering van into a reception line at Karachi Airport that had been set up to greet the Polish president and his entourage. Four persons were killed and ten wounded in the attack on the group, which had arrived from Islamabad. Those killed were identified as Zygfryd Wojniak, deputy foreign minister of Poland; Chowdhury Nazir Ahmed, deputy director of the Pakistani intelligence bureau; and Ashrah Ali Beg and Mohammed Yasin, both photographers. Those injured were Abrar Hassan Khan, chairman of the KMC; Mohammed Khan Bajwa, a sub-inspector of the B.B.; Alay Ali, controller of the branches of the Habib Bank; Anwar Kamal Quzi, a television cameraman; S. H. Ran, a press and commercial photographer; Jamil Ahmad Ansart, an editor of *Dawn*; P. Konecki, a Pole; W. Duda, Polish consul; Captain Khalid Ahmad, director of the excise du taxation; and Mohammad Ansar of the Pakistani navy. The attack was initiated at 11 A.M. as the Polish president was moving along the reception line after deplaning. The assassin had come back to the airport four hours after having gotten off work, found the van with the keys in it, and drove into the reception line. Feroze surrendered without any resistance to authorities, saying that he had completed his mission. He sent a plea for clemency to the chief martial law administrator, which was reprinted in Pakistani newspapers, which claimed that he bore no ill will against the Poles and that "I had expressed my ill feeling against America in my statement before the court and not against any Communist country." He also claimed to have been under the influence of drugs at the time of the attack. The Pakistan special military court found him guilty of murder and sentenced him to death by hanging on March 24, 1971. It found that no conspiracy was involved. 0605

November 6, 1970—Israel—A bomb exploded in the central bus station in Tel Aviv, followed by another explosion there twenty minutes later. Two people were killed and thirty-four injured in the attack which was credited to Al Fatah. Two hundred Arabs were questioned and nine held in the bombings. On November 8, Abu Iyad of Fatah issued a statement in Amman saying that these were "the start of more and bigger operations within our occupied homeland." 0606

November 7, 1970—Colombia—the personal vehicle of a U.S. embassy officer in Bogotá was slightly damaged when a bomb was placed or thrown under it while it was parked. 0607

November 9, 1970—South Africa—A parcel bomb mailed to Joel Carlson, a lawyer involved in a major political trial, failed to explode when it arrived in his office. The parcel carried a Lusaka postmark and Zambian stamps. 0608

November 9, 1970—South Africa—An officer of the U.S. consulate general in Johannesburg received two threatening telephone calls warning that he would be dead by evening. 0609–0610

November 9, 1970—Soviet Union—Vitautas Simokaitis, thirty-four, and his wife, Grazhina Mitskute, twenty-one, attempted to hijack an Aeroflot AN2 from its flight between Vilnius and Palanga on the Baltic Sea and divert it to Sweden. The pilot had allowed the two on board without tickets. The man had a gun, but the two were overpowered and tried in Vilnius. He was sentenced to death, but the sentence was commuted to fifteen years in a labor camp. Unlike the Dymshits case, there had been no worldwide protest over his initial harsh sentence. 5268.

November 9, 1970—Dubai—A DC3 owned by the Air Taxi Company of Iran and chartered to Iran Airlines was hijacked by a group of criminals and forced to fly to Baghdad, Iraq. Reports differ as to the details of the hijacking. It appears that the plane was carrying three crewmen, ten passengers, and nine hijackers. Six of the hijackers were petty criminals wanted in Iran, who had fled the country and settled in Dubai without passports, exit visas, or work permits. When they were discovered, they were expelled from Dubai in the custody of three armed guards who were to bring them to Iran. The group, armed with knives and pistols, rushed the cockpit and ordered the pilot, Sidney Strody Jordan, an Australian, to "fly to Baghdad or Basra." Jordan attempted to fool the hijackers by unobtrusively altering his course and flying to Bandar Abbas, Iran, as was originally planned in his flight, but the hijackers threatened to pour gasoline over the seats and destroy the plane if he did not comply with their demands. Reports differ as to whether Jordan was able to refuel, with some claiming that he refueled in Doha, Qatar. While he was flying over Kuwait, the authorities got the impression that he intended to make an unauthorized landing. He was initially unable to inform the government of its mistake because the hijackers had pulled out his communications transmitter. When a plane of the group sent up by the military forces came dangerously close to the DC3, the hijackers allowed him to explain the situation. When the plane got to Iraq, the government initially refused to allow Jordan to land. It is possible that language barriers gave the Iraqis the impression that the pilot was from Jordan rather than named Jordan. He was finally allowed to land after pleading that he had very little gasoline left. The hijackers, who asked for political asylum, were taken away by the local police. The passengers and crew members were questioned for four hours and released with the plane. Iran requested extradition. 5269

November 10, 1970—United States—The Idaho State University licensed nuclear facility received a bomb threat.

November 10, 1970—Jordan—A Saudi Arabian Airlines DC3 flying from Amman, Jordan, to Riyadh, Saudi Arabia, with twelve persons on board was hijacked by a gunman and his wife, Grazina, and diverted to Damascus, where the hijacker was arrested by Syrian police. 5270

November 12, 1970—Argentina—A mob of demonstrators forced entry to the Córdoba USIS Binational Center through steel door shutters and burned out a large portion of the ground floor. 0611

November 13, 1970—United States—Eastern Airlines flight 257, a DC9 flying between Richmond, Virginia, and Atlanta, Georgia, was hijacked after leaving Raleigh, North Carolina, by a black gunman who met the FAA profile, who used the alias of G. Jones. He allowed the plane to refuel at Jacksonville before flying on to Cuba. He remains a fugitive. 5271

November 14, 1970—Puerto Rico—The Armed Commandos of Liberation claimed credit for five bombings in the San Juan hotel district.

November 19, 1970—Argentina—The U.S. embassy switchboard operator in Buenos Aires received an anonymous telephone call warning that a bomb on the second floor (occupied by the USIS) would explode. No bomb was found. 0612

November 20, 1970—Argentina—A small explosive device was detonated outside the Buenos Aires home of the U.S. agricultural attaché by members of the FAP. 0613

November 20, 1970—Argentina—Four hours after the U.S. agricultural attaché house bombing, another device was discovered at the front door of the Buenos Aires home of another U.S. embassy officer. 0614

November 20, 1970—Argentina—Members of the FAP entered the homes of members of the U.S. air mission in Argentina. 0615

November 20, 1970—Portugal—Three bombs exploded in Lisbon, damaging a training school for Portuguese political police, a dock area, and the USIS library. The library was extensively damaged by the explosion of a fragmentation bomb introduced through a window that was forced open. All of the windows were blown out, and damage to rear shelves, the ceilings, and the rear wall was heavy. Major equipment, fixtures, and furniture suffered only slight damage. Three policemen in the area were injured by flying glass, and another was injured in one of the other explosions. A man who had set the bomb in the training school died while trying to set a second charge. He could not be identified. The dock bomb, which caused extensive damage, was hidden in a metal suitcase that was to have been loaded on board the ship *Niassa*, which was scheduled to bring soldiers to Africa on November 21. A letter was later sent to the press by the ARA, claiming responsibility for the bombings. 0616

November 21, 1970—Turkey—At 7:30 P.M., a homemade bomb was thrown from a passing automobile in the general direction of the garden area behind the U.S. embassy parking lot in Ankara. The device exploded outside the fence, causing no injuries or damage. 0617

November 22, 1970—Philippines—At 7:50 P.M., an explosive device went off at the base of the front wall of the USIS Thomas Jefferson Cultural Center in

Quezon City. The device, evidently located on the concrete terrace against the wall, created a hole about five inches deep and eighteen inches in diameter. Books and furnishings of the center were not damaged, although many windows were blown out. 0618

November 23, 1970—Puerto Rico—An anonymous telephone caller to United Press International claimed that the Armed Commandos of Liberation were responsible for a bomb that caused some damage to the Dominican Republic consulate in San Juan. No one was in the consulate at the time the bomb went off, hours after Dominican President Joaquin Balaguer had ended his visit to Puerto Rico. 0619

November 25, 1970—United States—A ten-inch pipe bomb placed in an attaché case hidden in a doorway exploded, causing extensive damage to the New York City offices of Aeroflot and Intourist. The JDL was believed responsible, although Rabbi Meir Kahane, the group's leader, said that no one in his organization was involved, although he "heartily applauded" the attack. On December 11, the Soviet Union cancelled a 1971 tour of the Bolshoi Theater's opera and ballet companies. Vasily V. Kuznetsov, Soviet first deputy foreign minister, read a note in Moscow to U.S. Ambassador Jacob D. Beam, in which he claimed that the United States had "not taken necessary measures to stop these criminal actions, thereby encouraging them. . . .The provocations not only create obstacles to the implementation by Soviet institutions in the U.S. of their official functions, and threaten to disrupt measures within the sphere of cultural exchange, but also endanger the personal safety of Soviet citizens." 0620

November 25, 1970—West Germany—The Frankfurt Amerika Haus was broken into and a fire was set that resulted in $5,000 to $7,000 in book damages. 0621

November 26, 1970—Greece—A statue of President Truman was slightly damaged in Athens when a bomb exploded. Thirty people were arrested in connection with the incident. 0622

November 26, 1970—Canada—An anonymous telephone call was received by the Montreal police warning that a bomb had been placed at the main offices of the U.S. consulate general. A search of the building revealed no bomb. 0623

November 27, 1970—Argentina—The homes of three U.S. military attachés in Martínez, a suburb of Buenos Aires, were raided by armed men who left leaflets identifying them as members of the Péronist Armed Forces. They stole official documents, weapons, uniforms, and U.S. currency. 0624-0626

November 27, 1970—Turkey—Three bombs exploded in the U.S. officer's open mess in a military installation in Ankara. Three other bombs detonated at the U.S. military annex, also in Ankara. There was minor damage, but no injuries were sustained in either incident. 0627-0628

November 27, 1970—Philippines—Benjamin Mendoza Amor, a mentally unstable Bolivian artist, attempted to assassinate Pope Paul VI with a knife at Manila airport. He was dragged to the ground by Bishop Anthony Galvin of Miri, Sarawak, and was subsequently arrested.

November 28, 1970—Ivory Coast—The U.S. ambassador in Abidjan received a telephone threat warning him to leave the country within forty-eight hours. 0629

November 30, 1970—Iran—Iranian terrorists attempted to kidnap U.S. ambassador Douglas MacArthur II and his wife as they were returning home. MacArthur suspected a kidnapping attempt when two cars tried to stop his limousine. He directed his chauffeur to drive through the ambush, and they successfully escaped without injury, although at least one shot was fired at the ambassador, and a hand axe was hurled through the rear window of the car. On February 9, 1972, an Iranian military tribunal sentenced four guerrillas to life imprisonment and another sixteen to jail terms ranging from three to ten years for a series of antigovernment activities, including the kidnapping attempt. 0630

November 30, 1970—Argentina—The Maria Pacheco group of the FAL stole 8 million pesos (approximately $23,000) in a raid on the French Hospital. 0631

December 1, 1970—Cambodia—A bomb exploded in the north chancery of the U.S. embassy in Phnom Penh, extensively damaging the building's first and ground floors where major renovation construction was in progress. 0632

December 1, 1970—Uruguay—Members of the Tupamaros bombed the Montevideo offices of International Telephone and Telegraph, causing much damage. 0633

December 1, 1970—Spain—Eugen Beihl, fifty-nine, the honorary West German consul in San Sebastián and representative of several German industrial concerns, was kidnapped from his San Sebastián home in Guipuzocoa Basque Province by members of the ETA (Basque Nation and Liberty), who demanded that a group of fifteen ETA members not be given death sentences in a Burgos court-martial trying them for the 1968 murder of the provincial head of the political police. Consul Beihl was allowed to send notes to the outside during his incarceration and indicated to the German embassy that he was being held by the ETA and that Germany should do what they asked. After being freed, he indicated that he had been held by masked, armed men. The Spanish government instituted a three-month state of emergency, conducting a house-to-house search for Beihl in San Sebastián. Executives of the Second West German Television Network (ZDF) helped arrange for his release. Reports are unclear as to the extent of government participation in any agreements worked out with the kidnappers. On December 22, Basque spokesmen claimed that an arrangement was being made in exchange for lenient treatment of the prisoners. This was confirmed by the official Spanish government news agency, which said that ''parties interested'' had met with the ETA. In an act involving symbolic timing, the ETA released Beihl on Christmas Day. He was driven to Wiesbaden, West Germany, by ZDF executives. Two ZDF technicians who were held hostage were freed in France on December 26, after Beihl had arrived safely in West Germany. On December 28, six of the Basques in the trial were sentenced to death, with nine others receiving long jail terms. Great international and domestic pressure was placed upon the government, and on December 30, President Franco commuted all of the death sentences to thirty-year prison terms. The ETA pointed out that it had released Beihl first so that Franco's move could appear to be an act of clemency rather than giving in to political blackmail. 0634

December 2, 1970—Bulgaria—The U.S. embassy in Sofia received a telephoned bomb threat. A search was negative. 0635

December 3, 1970—Japan—At 11:45 P.M., two bottles containing flammable liquid were discovered and removed from the front grounds of the U.S. consulate in Yokohama. 0636

December 6, 1970—Malaysia—Three shots were fired at the home of a U.S. Army officer in Kuala Lumpur. 0637

December 7, 1970—Bolivia—Around midnight, the door of the USIS office in Santa Cruz was dynamited, resulting in the breaking in of the door, a wall, and broken windows, including those of neighboring buildings. 0638

December 7, 1970—Brazil—Giovanni Enrico Bucher, the Swiss ambassador to Brazil, was kidnapped by members of the VPR and the Juarez Guimarez de Brito Command of the ALN. Six or seven men armed with submachine guns used four cars in the attack, which involved blocking Bucher's vehicle and seizing him. During the attack, Bucher's chauffeur-bodyguard was killed. A roadblock set up in Rio de Janeiro located one of the cars, but Bucher was not found. Switzerland was at the time of the kidnapping the third most important foreign investor in Brazil, tied with Japan behind the United States and West Germany. Its government had also recently expelled two Brazilian terrorists who were freed among the forty prisoners whose release had been demanded in the von Holleben incident (see incident 0424).

The kidnappers made an extensive series of demands, including the release of seventy political prisoners, to be flown to Chile, Algeria, or Mexico, in that order of preference. Of the thirty-seven whose occupations were listed, four were civil servants, one was a priest, three were technicians, three were army defectors, and eighteen were students. The group also demanded the broadcast of an antigovernment manifesto on all radio and television stations for two consecutive days, which promised that "the armed struggle in the cities and countryside" would be stepped up with spontaneous uprisings by workers. It claimed that Brazil was "the country that has the highest index of infant mortality and of prostitution in the world, and the most glaring social injustices. Slavery still exists in certain states, the people are exploited, and Brazil has become the favorite hunting-ground of foreign enterprise." The group further demanded that all future communiqués be published, that the press carry photos of the released political prisoners, that workers be given a 100 percent wage increase, that free public transportation be provided for city workers, and that Swiss bank deposits be confiscated.

Twenty-five hundred government soldiers began an intensive search for Bucher, but without success. During their search, eight thousand suspects were arrested, but most were released after two or three days on the personal instructions of Brazilian President Emilio Garrastazu Medici.

After conferring with the chiefs of the three armed services, as well as the ministers of justice and foreign affairs, the president issued a statement saying that the government would be willing to negotiate upon receipt of a handwritten, dated note from Bucher listing the prisoners to be freed. On December 19, such a message was received, and the government agreed to release fifty-one of those specified. The government claimed that the others were guilty of kidnapping and murder and considered these nonpolitical crimes. Three different lists of prisoners eventually made their way to the government authorities. On January 13, 1971, President Medici decreed that sixty-eight prisoners would be stripped of Brazilian citizenship and two foreign prisoners would be deported. The group was freed and flown to exile in Chile the next day. However, three of the prisoners refused to leave Brazil, including Irgeu Mengon, a former VPR member, who said, "I joined the VPR thinking that I could do something for Brazil. But I have been completely deceived. The VPR only uses terror and violence, which horrify me." Other released prisoners claimed that the Brazilian government had used physical and psychological torture against them during their incarceration. Chile's chief of police told the prisoners, "During your stay in Chile, you will not make political statements nor any other statements which could damage the good relations between Chile and other countries." On January 16, 1971, Bucher was released unharmed in downtown Rio. He claimed that he had been blindfolded during his period of captivity and was unable to identify where he had been held. Brazil had ignored the groups' demands for publicity. 0639

December 10, 1970—Czechoslovakia—A lone man attempted to hijack a Czechoslovakian Morave Aero Taxi flying between Bratislava and Brno. The plane landed safely in Brno after passengers overpowered the hijacker while the plane was in the air. One passenger was wounded. 5272

December 11, 1970—Uruguay—Unidentified individuals broke into the Montevideo offices of the Inter-American Development Bank, destroying furniture and stealing documents. 0640

December 14, 1970—United States—The New York City corporate headquarters of General Electric was bombed by MIRA, a Puerto Rican militant group. 0641

December 15, 1970—Canada—An Eastern Airlines plane flying seventy-four passengers between Montreal and New York City was recalled twenty minutes into its flight. It was delayed one hour during a search, which revealed no bomb.

December 16, 1970—United States—The United States signed the Hague Convention for the Suppression of Unlawful Seizure of Aircraft. The U.S. Senate approved the convention on September 8, 1971, and it entered into force on September 14, 1971.

December 18, 1970—Argentina—The FAL raided the Spanish consulate in Rosario, setting the building on fire and escaping with 300,000 pesos. 0642

December 19, 1970—United States—Continental Airlines flight 144, a DC9 flying from Albuquerque to Tulsa, was the scene of an attempted hijacking by a black male who met the FAA profile; Carlos Denis was born in New York City on November 25, 1935. He handed the stewardess a note claiming that he had a gun and demanded to be flown to Cuba. He allowed the plane to land at Tulsa to permit the passengers to deplane; however, the crew members also deplaned, stranding the hijacker. Police entered the aircraft and arrested Denis, who was unarmed and hiding in a lavatory. After being subjected to a medical and mental examination, he was found guilty of conveying false information concerning an attempt to commit air piracy and sentenced to five years on February 9, 1971. 5273

December 21, 1970—Puerto Rico—A Puerto Rican International Airlines (Prinair) Heron 157 flying from San Juan to Ponce, Puerto Rico, was the scene of an unsuccessful hijacking by a male for whom the FAA profile was inapplicable; Victor Lopez Morales was born in Salinas, Puerto Rico, on July 10, 1948. He claimed that he had a bomb and demanded to be flown to Mexico. The crew persuaded him to allow them to refuel in San Juan, where they overpowered him on board the general aviation craft. The criminal complaint against him was dismissed due to his mental incompetence. He was committed to a mental institution, from which he was released on November 29, 1973. 5274

December 24, 1970—Turkey—Two students from Ankara University were arrested while attempting to set explosive charges consisting of dynamite at the U.S. Air Force Tuslog Detachment 30 in Ankara. 0643

December 24, 1970—United States—An attempt to hijack a plane by three criminals in New York was forestalled by police using eighty squad cars and three helicopters. Early in the morning, three bandits entered a Locust Valley (Nassau County) bank, forced an employee to open the vault, and bound the three employees, along with three female employees who entered the bank later. After filling sacks with money, the robbers found that their getaway car driver had panicked when he saw police responding to an alarm tripped by one of the employees. The police and robbers engaged in a short gun battle, which ended when the trio took three hostages and piled into a young woman's nearby car. During a prolonged chase, the robbers decided to drive to the airport and hijack a plane. However, they gave up this plan after finding three police helicopters hovering over them after they entered the airport. The robbers drove to Brooklyn, where they were surrounded by forty squad cars. They pushed the car's owner out, and then police dragged the suspects out of the car. One of the robbers banged his head on the car door, becoming the adventure's only injury. Their stolen $19,200 was returned. The trio were arraigned in Mineola, New York, on charges of armed robbery, kidnapping, and assault. 5275

December 27, 1970—United States—The Soviet Union complained to the U.S government on January 4 that a protest demonstration by members of the JDL had included the throwing of a bottle through a window, which injured a staff member and wakened a child. The United States replied that two U.S. diplomats in Moscow had received threatening calls to their unlisted home phone numbers and suggested that official complicity was involved.

December 28, 1970—Spain—The Burgos trial of ETA members accused of assassinating Meliton Manzanas, chief of the political police in Guipuzcoa Province in 1968, was concluded by a five-man military tribunal. The death sentences were commuted, possibly due to an agreement between President

Franco and the kidnappers of Eugen Beihl (see incident 0634). Originally sentenced to death were Francisco Izco, twenty-nine (who was charged with actually shooting Manzanas); Eduardo Uriarte, twenty-five; Joaquim Gorostidi, twenty-six; Francisco Larena, twenty-five; José Dorronsoro, twenty-nine; and Mario Onaindia, twenty-two. Izco, Uriarte, and Gorostidi had also received death sentences for banditry. Each was ordered to pay a $14,285 indemnity to Manzanas's widow. Franco's order changed each death sentence to a thirty-year term. Those receiving the double sentences also were to serve twenty to thirty years for other charges. However, Spanish law prevented any prisoner from serving more than thirty years. The Burgos trial handed down the other sentences for the following: Victor Arana, seventy years imprisonment; Jesus Abnisqueta, sixty-two years; Reverend Juan Echave, Enrique Guesalaga, and Juana Dorronsoro, Izco's wife, each fifty years; Lopez Irasuegui, thirty years; Iciar Airpurua, Gorostidi's wife, fifteen years; Antonio Carrera, twelve years; and Maria Aranzazu Arruti, wife of Lopez Irasuegui, acquittal.

December 29, 1970—Switzerland and West Germany—Attacks being planned against Israeli targets in West Germany and Switzerland were forestalled when two Arab terrorists were arrested. 0644

December 29, 1970—Turkey—Two policemen outside the U.S. embassy in Ankara were wounded when fired upon by terrorists in a fast-moving car. 0645

December 30. 1970—Turkey—The USIS office in Istanbul received a telephoned bomb threat. 0646

January 1971—Mozambique—On March 5, Portugal charged that Zambia had allowed members of COREMO, the Mozambique Revolutionary Council, to bring eleven kidnapped farm workers of Portuguese nationality across its borders. It claimed that five of the black men had escaped but that one Portuguese had been killed. Zambia denied the charge, saying that it had refused COREMO's request to bring the kidnapped men into the country and on March 8 accused Portugal of kidnapping five Zambians from villages near the Mozambique border. 0647

January 1, 1971—Greece—Bombs exploded on New Year's Eve outside a hotel used by the U.S. Air Force and at a U.S. servicemen's club in Athens, causing minimal damage. The bombs appeared to be timed devices. 0648-0649

January 2, 1971—Soviet Union—Two U.S. embassy officers in Moscow received threatening phone calls at their unlisted home phone numbers. One caller warned that he planned to bomb the embassy. A call was also received at the marine desk in which a barely understandable message included some reference to bombs. This harassment appeared to be in response to JDL demonstrations in the United States against the Soviets. Several incidents occurred in the following weeks. On January 6 at 7 P.M., a small-scale demonstration took place next to the U.S. embassy. The demonstrators briefly rocked a staff member's automobile parked in front of the embassy but did no damage. An embassy officer was accosted on the street by three men who expressed outrage over U.S. actions. On January 8, several small, well-behaved groups of protestors presented petitions at the embassy, expressing veiled threats. Two embassy officers were accosted on the street by a group of four men. One officer was grabbed by the lapels, shaken, and shoved. The next day, an embassy officer's car was briefly rocked by three men in front of the embassy. Both headlights and one tail light were smashed and two tires deflated on the personal car of an embassy officer while it was parked in front of a hotel. The windshield of the car of an embassy officer was smashed in front of another hotel. Also, an embassy officer was shoved and then grabbed briefly on the arm by a man who emerged from a car that had tailed him. 0650-0652

January 3, 1971—United States—National Airlines flight 36, a DC8 flying the Los Angeles-Tampa-Miami route, was hijacked out of Los Angeles and flown to Cuba by a group of two men, their wives, and four children. One of the group threatened a stewardess with a gun and then kept his gun trained on the engineer. The plane returned to Miami without the hijackers. Ninety-six people were aboard the plane hijacked to Havana. The hijackers were identified as blacks, two of whom met the FAA profile: James Arthur Wilson, born in New York City on November 1, 1946, and Lolita K. Graves, born in San Diego on May 5, 1947. Two other blacks probably met the FAA profile: Carl White, born in Detroit on August 29, 1946, and Norma Jean White, born in Haynesville, Louisiana, on August 5, 1947. They were indicted by a federal grand jury in the southern district of California on January 27, 1971. White, his wife, and four children were apprehended in San Juan, Purto Rico, on May 24, 1975. They were flown to San Diego to stand trial. All charges were dropped against his wife, but Carl White received twenty years for air piracy on November 24, 1975. Wilson and Graves were arrested on November 18, 1975, in Chicago. He was sentenced to twenty years for air piracy on March 22, 1976, and she received five years for smuggling. 5276

January 7, 1971—Pakistan—Several reports were received in Lahore of American cars being stopped, including an attempt by students to commandeer the car of an embassy officer's wife. 0653

January 7, 1971—United States—An explosion at the Pomona, California, headquarters of the Campfire Girls caused $50,000 damage.

January 8, 1971—Uruguay—Sir Geoffrey M. S. Jackson, fifty-five, British ambassador to Uruguay, was kidnapped in Montevideo by twenty Tupamaros, who surrounded his car with five vehicles four blocks away from his office in the British embassy. His driver and bodyguards were dragged from the limousine and beaten. The kidnappers had trapped the car in a narrow one-way street. On January 20, a note discovered in the lavatory of a downtown bar claimed that the attack was against "British neocolonialism" and called upon the government to begin negotiations. This appeared to be an attempt to increase the pressure on the government, which was concerned about the kidnappings of Claude Fly and Dias Gomide (see incidents 0479 and 0474). As before, when kidnapping Gomide, the group again demanded the release of 150 political prisoners. On January 11, President Pacheco Areco asked Congress for a ninety-day special police power to conduct a search. The eleven-member Legislative Commission granted him a forty-day suspension of individual rights, which allowed twelve thousand police and troops to begin Operation Fan, a search of private homes without warrants and the power to hold suspects without court hearings. On March 10, the Tupamaros kidnapped Uruguay's attorney general, Guide Berro Oribe, in Montevideo and held him in the same "people's jail" as Jackson. According to Tupamaro communiqué 18, the group questioned him "on the matter of serious irregularities that have occurred during his term as court prosecutor." On March 22 he was set free, having admitted handing over political prisoners to military tribunals and detaining prisoners after their sentences expired. At the end of March, the head of the UTE, Ulises Pereyra Reverbel, a personal friend of the president, was kidnapped a second time by the Tupamaros, who claimed to have sentenced him to life imprisonment in one of their people's jails. The government remained firm in its refusal to negotiate for Jackson's release and on May 22 offered a $50,000 reward for information regarding his location. On September 6, 106 Tupamaros, including their leader Raul Sendic, as well as Maneras Lluveras, Marenales Saenz, Martinez Platero, and Amodio Perez, escaped from Punta Carretas prison by digging a tunnel. On September 8 the MLN announced that they no longer had a need to detain Jackson, who was found the next day on the steps of a parish church in a Montevideo residential district after an unidentified woman had phoned the U.K. embassy. Embassy officials drove him to a hospital for a physical examination. The next day he left for Britain. He stated that he found his captors intelligent "with certain reservations," and that although they would have killed him if their hideout was found, he agreed with the no-ransom policy. His relations with the kidnappers had been correct, stressing his dignity as the representative of a sovereign government. He managed to stay healthy by exercising each day. 0654

January 8, 1971—United States—A bomb exploded outside the Soviet cultural offices in Washington, D.C., causing slight damage. The JDL took credit for the blast. The same day U.S. ambassador Jacob D. Beam received a "stern protest" from Soviet Foreign Minister Andrei A. Gromyko. A campaign of harassment against U.S. embassy officials in Moscow followed. On January 17, President Nixon sent sixty federal guards to protect the Soviet U.N. mission in New York. On January 19, JDL leader Meir Kahane called an "indefinite moratorium" on his organization's campaign, begun January 10, to "follow, question and harass" Soviet diplomats in New York City. Kahane was being brought before a New York criminal court on charges of resisting arrest in 1969. He was convicted on February 23. He was rearrested on February 15 on charges of harassment and verbal abuse outside the Soviet U.N. mission. On February 22 he had declared an end to the harassment moratorium. 0655

January 10, 1971—United States—Patrick E. Miranda, twenty-five, attempted to hijack a TWA B707 flying from New York to Denver and divert it to Las Vegas, although reports are unclear regarding his preferred destination. A stewardess talked him out of his attempt, and the plane landed in Denver, where he was arrested. He was sentenced to life in prison pending a mental examination. 5277

January 11, 1971—Argentina—The USIS offices and Binational Center in Santa Cruz were taken over by students and systematically looted. 0656

January 12, 1971—Ethiopia—The U.S. Embassy in Addis Ababa was informed of a rumored plan to kidnap a high-ranking western diplomat. Additional security precautions were initiated regarding the U.S. Ambassador's movements. 0657

January 12, 1971—Ethiopia—A U.S. Army enlisted man assigned to Kagnew station in Asmara was fatally shot on the road to Massawa. A pouch containing documents was missing from the truck he was driving. Limited evidence indicates that the attack was the result of opportunity rather than calculation on the part of a roving rebel band. 0658

January 13, 1971—Japan—A group of thirty radical students assaulted Kadena Air Force Base in Okinawa to protest the storage of mustard gas at the Chibana ammunition dump. The group was ejected by U.S. riot policemen, but the gas was later moved to Johnston Island. 0659

January 15, 1971—United States—Members of the JDL smashed windows of the New York office of Aeroflot. 0660

January 16, 1971—West Germany—A surreptitiously planted explosive device went off in the main entrance hall of the Munich Amerika Haus, causing extensive damage. 0661

January 17, 1971—United States—A Molotov cocktail was thrown into the United Arab Republic's U.N. mission in New York. 0662

January 17, 1971—Northern Ireland—The IRA was suspected of having placed a bomb that caused damage to a customs post in Lifford, Northern Ireland, on the Irish border.

January 17, 1971—Australia—Two Bulgarians were arrested after throwing three gelignite bombs at the Soviet embassy in Canberra, breaking some windows but causing no injuries. 0663

January 20, 1971—Guatemala—Four terrorists entered the British consulate in Guatemala City, killed a PMA guard, and then sprayed the consulate with machine-gun fire. 0664

January 22, 1971—Philippines—Bombs went off at the Manila headquarters of the U.S. oil companies Esso and Caltex, killing a Filipino employee and damaging the offices. A note signed by the People's Revolutionary Front was left at the Caltex office and said, ''This is the anger of the Filipino people against American imperialism.'' 0665-0666

January 22, 1971—Ethiopia—An Ethiopian Airlines DC3 flying from Bahr Dar to Gondar, Ethiopia, with twenty-three persons on board was hijacked by four armed male Eritrean students, members of the ELF, identified only as Sebhatu, Selassie, Michael, and Yohanneso. The hijackers refused to allow anyone to deplane in Khartoum while the plane refueled. The plane landed in Benghazi, Libya. The ELF denied responsibility for the hijacking. 0667

January 22, 1971—United States—Northwest Airlines flight 433, a B727 flying the Minneapolis-Milwaukee-Detroit-Washington run, was hijacked out of Milwaukee by a black male who met the FAA profile. He was Garland J. Grant (also known as Gerald Grant), who was born in Milwaukee on October 20, 1950. He claimed he had a bomb in his briefcase and also carried a hatchet. He originally demanded to be flown to Algeria, but after allowing the plane to refuel in Detroit, he settled on flying to Havana with the sixty persons on board the flight. He remains a fugitive from an indictment handed down by a federal grand jury in the eastern district of Wisconsin on March 9, 1971. 5278

January 23, 1971—Philippines—Approximately twenty-five demonstrators appeared in front of the USIS offices in Cebu. Speeches in opposition to U.S. imperialism and foreign oil companies drew a crowd of about one hundred passersby. The demonstrators shouted that the USIS should leave the country and that they would return. The same afternoon a bomb threat led to the evacuation of the library. A search by local police was negative. 0668

January 23, 1971—United States—The mayor of Tucson, Arizona set a curfew and declared martial law after the third night of violence near the University of Arizona campus in which six police were injured and four people were arrested during a fire-bomb outbreak. The disorders were attributed to hippies or street people who demanded a people's campground and the abolition of the city's antiloitering and antihijacking ordinances.

January 23, 1971—South Korea—Twenty-two-year-old Kim Sang-tae, a South Korean, attempted to hijack a Korean Airlines F27 flying sixty-five persons from Kangnung to Seoul and divert it to North Korea. He was armed with four hand grenades and a razor-sharp kitchen knife. He used two of the grenades to blast his way into the cockpit, where he made his demands known to the pilot, who sent out a radio message and flew false patterns. South Korean fighters were scrambled in an attempt to halt the flight, while antiaircraft fire was directed at the plane. The pilot managed to land the plane on a beach near the border, shaking up the passengers. A sky marshal fired twice at the hijacker with his pistol, causing the skyjacker to drop his grenades. Both of them exploded, killing the skyjacker and the copilot and injuring sixteen others, four of them seriously. 5279

January 23, 1971—Turkey—Unexploded bombs were found on the grounds of the U.S. embassy and USIS building in Ankara. 0669-0770

January 25, 1971—Turkey—Two Molotov cocktails were thrown onto the balcony of the apartment of a U.S. foreign service officer in Ankara. The family was at home, but there were no injuries, and the fire was extinguished immediately. 0671

January 25, 1971—Turkey—Following an explosion heard elsewhere in Istanbul, police received a bomb threat against a U.S. armed forces Tuslog building. 0672

January 25, 1971—Turkey—A bomb, apparently directed at the Police Assistance Fund building, broke three windows in the American noncommissioned officers' club next door in Ankara. 0673

January 26, 1971—Dominican Republic—Enrique Jimenez Cano, a male U.S. resident, attempted to hijack an Aerovia Quisqueyana (a Dominican airline) L1049 Super Constellation flying from Santo Domingo to San Juan with fifty-eight passengers, and divert it to Cuba. He used a vial of colored water, which he claimed was nitroglycerine, to threaten the crew. He refused to allow the plane to land in Haiti, but did allow it to land in Cabo Rojo to refuel. The crew overpowered him, and a passenger was injured in the struggle. 5280

January 28, 1971—United States—The Siberian Dancers and Singers of Omsk's dance performance in New York's Carnegie Hall was disrupted so that police could search for a bomb in response to a threat made over the telephone by a man claiming to be a member of the Student Struggle for Soviet Jewry. 0674

January 29, 1971—United States—The Chicano Liberation Front bombed a federal building in Los Angeles, killing a Chicano employee. The group was severely criticized by the local community for this action, which may have led to a curtailment of its activities.

January 30, 1971—India—An Indian Airlines Fokker Friendship F27 flying thirty persons from Srinagar to Jammu was hijacked to Lahore, Pakistan, by two armed males, members of the Kashmiri Liberation Front, who were armed with pistols and hand grenades. The duo, Hashim Quershi and Mohammed Ashraf, allowed the passengers and crew to leave the plane on February 1 but remained on it, demanding that they be given asylum and freedom from prosecution by the Pakistani government. They also demanded that the Indian government release thirty-six prisoners being held in jails in Kashmir. Pakistani citizens rushed to the airport, treating the hijackers as heroes and hoping to drape garlands around their necks. They also called for holding the Indian passengers and crew members as hostages "for Moslems kept in Indian jails." However, the Pakistani police managed to head off both pursuits. The Indian government refused to negotiate with the terrorists, accusing the Pakistanis of stalling in returning the plane, crew, and passengers by refusing to allow a relief plane to pick up the people. The Pakistanis argued that the crowd was hostile and would not allow an Indian plane to land. Two days later, the passengers and crew returned overland to India. Hundreds of Indians demonstrated in front of the Pakistan High Commission in New Delhi, demanding the return of the plane and hijackers. However, the Pakistanis had granted them political asylum and allowed them to confer with a Liberation Front leader at the airport. The Indians again refused their demand to "release . . . all political prisoners rotting in Indian jails for refusing to succumb to India's repression to accept its sovereignty over Kashmir." With that, the hijackers blew up the plane with their hand grenades, remaining on board to ensure that a fire consumed the plane and preventing Pakistani firefighters from halting the blaze. Upon jumping from the plane, one of the hijackers was seriously wounded; the other suffered minor wounds. They were both brought to a hospital under guard. The Indians loudly protested the Pakistani handling of the case and denied them overflight privileges for military and eventually commercial planes.

The hijackers were charged with conspiracy and subversive activities. On May 17, 1973, a special tribunal found Hashim guilty of being an Indian agent who had received his orders from Delhi intelligence officers. The court found that he acted as an intelligence agent rather than as a member of the Liberation Front and sentenced him to stiff jail terms under the Pakistani Penal Code and the Official Secrets Act. The court held that Ashraf was unaware of Hashim's conspiracy and thus was charged, along with the other officers of the Liberation Front, with sending arms and ammunition to Indian-occupied Kashmir. They received only minor sentences. 0675

February 1971—Nicaragua—Between February and May, threats were received in Managua against the U.S. ambassador, his wife, and a USIS officer. 0676-0678

February 2, 1971—United States—The OAS Convention to Prevent and Punish Acts of Terrorism was signed by the United States in Washington. The U.S. Senate approved the convention on June 12, 1972.

February 4, 1971—United States—Delta Airlines flight 379, a DC9 flying twenty-eight persons from Chicago to Nashville, was hijacked by a black male who met the FAA profile: Walter Chico Hines, born in Itta Bena, Mississippi, on November 12, 1937. He claimed he was carrying explosives and forced the pilot to fly to Havana. The plane was allowed to return to Miami. He was apprehended on September 24, 1975, in Barbados. A complaint had been filed against him on November 11, 1974, in the northern district of Illinois. He was brought to Chicago to stand trial and convicted on April 23, 1976, of air piracy. 5281

February 4, 1971—United States—The Armed Forces Induction Center in Oakland, California, was bombed. The Bay Bombers said in a note that the attack was in retaliation for the U.S. invasion of Laos, Cambodia, and Vietnam.

February 5, 1971—Brazil—At 2:30 A.M., three armed men attempted to break into the home of a U.S. Consular officer in Recife. The men, discovered by civilian guards at the home, fled following an exchange of ten shots. 0679

February 7, 1971—Greece—Small homemade bombs damaged three cars in Athens, two owned by U.S. military personnel. 0680-0681

February 8, 1971—Turkey—A bomb wrapped as a package was left outside an American enlisted man's Ankara apartment. A son took the package into the kitchen where his mother noticed smoke and hurried her family from the apartment. The device exploded with enough force to have killed the family had they been inside, and it caused heavy damage. The night before, the family's car had been vandalized. 0682

February 9, 1971—Denmark—A telephone call warned of a bomb placed outside the chancery of the U.S. embassy in Copenhagen. A police search found nothing. The day before, between two hundred and four hundred demonstrators had peacefully protested in front of the embassy against U.S. action in Laos. 0683

February 10, 1971—Turkey—A bomb was found in an Ankara building occupied by seven Turkish and three American military families. Although the device was left on the ground floor, which housed three Turkish families, the rest of the building would have been damaged had it detonated. 0684

February 10, 1971—Sweden—The Yugoslav consulate in Goteborg was taken over by two Croatian émigrés, who threatened for twenty-four hours to kill their hostages unless a Croatian militant who had been sentenced to death in Belgrade was released. Rolovic, the consul, informed the terrorists that the Yugoslavian government rejected their demands. The pair released the hostages and were imprisoned. 0685

February 11, 1971—Turkey—A bomb exploded in a second-floor bathroom of the Turkish-American Association in Ankara, cracking a water pipe and causing considerable damage to the USIS library downstairs. Many windows were broken, a hole was blasted in the exterior wall, and two people in the library received minor cuts. 0686

February 12, 1971—West Germany—A bomb threat was received by telephone at the America Haus in Cologne at 4:30 P.M. Thirty minutes later a protest march of three or four hundred demonstrators was kept away by police barricades. 0687

February 12, 1971—Philippines—At 5:10, a sizable explosion went off near the wing of the U.S. chancery building in Manila, breaking several windows and damaging a metal awning but injuring no one. The explosion apparently was the result of a bomb planted on a motor scooter parked in the area. 0688

February 14, 1971—Pakistan—Two persons hurled Molotov cocktails at the front door of the American Center in Islamabad. The door was badly damaged but not penetrated, and an embassy vehicle parked nearby was slightly damaged. 0689

February 15, 1971—Turkey—Three armed members of the Turkish People's Liberation Army kidnapped an unarmed USAR security policeman, James Finlay, as he was patroling the Ankara Air Station on the outskirts of that city. The U.S. government requested the Turkish Foreign Ministry to do everything possible to obtain his safe release. The kidnappers made no demands for ransom or the release of prisoners and released Finlay unharmed seventeen hours after his capture. 0690

February 16, 1971—Philippines—Following the fatal shooting of a University of Mindanao student, students roved through the city, burning shops and attacking police. The USIS Davao office was attacked, and its windows were smashed. Two hundred books were burned with Molotov cocktails, and two thousand more books received water damage. 0691

February 16, 1971—United States—A bomb threat was received at the Yankee-Rowe Atomic Electric Company licensed nuclear facility.

February 17, 1971—Turkey—A bomb exploded outside the perimeter fence of the U.S.A.R. Tuslog Detachment 29's Fargo Building motor pool, breaking a few windows but causing no injuries. 0692

February 17, 1971—Turkey—A bomb was thrown into the lower parking lot of the U.S. consulate-general in Istanbul at 1 A.M. It was defused by police. 0693

February 19, 1971—Soviet Union—The U.S. embassy received a telephone threat against Americans on the streets in Moscow. 0694

February 19, 1971—Turkey—A bomb damaged a U.S. Army J-Boat belonging to Detachment 33-1 in Istanbul, causing no injuries. Another bomb found in a second boat was defused. 0695-0696

February 20, 1971—Turkey—Two explosive devices, consisting of plastique, were discovered on the grounds of the main USIS building in Ankara. The fuse had been lit, but the bombs failed to explode. 0697

February 20, 1971—Yugoslavia—A bullet was fired through the opaque glass of the locked U.S. consulate general main entrance in Zagreb. There was no injury to personnel. A woman was seen hiding a pistol outside on the sidewalk. 0698

February 23, 1971—Burma—Two hundred members of the Kachin Independence Army ambushed a passenger train in North Kachin State by using a mine to derail the engine and five coaches. The group shot at the train from all sides, but government troops exchanged the gunfire. The rebels looted the train and fled.

February 25, 1971—Israel—Muhmad Sa'id, twenty-eight, attempted to hijack a Swiss airliner by running toward the cockpit brandishing a pocket knife. Security agents overpowered him and handed him over to Israeli police. 0699

February 25, 1971—United States—Western Airlines flight 328, a B737 flying ninety-seven persons from San Francisco to Seattle, Washington, was hijacked out of Ontario, California, by Chappin Scott Patterson, a white male who did not meet the FAA profile, who was born on August 23, 1951, in Long Beach, California. The hijacker, who wished to avoid military service, threatened to blow up the plane if he was not flown to Cuba. He settled on flying to Vancouver, Canada, where he surrendered to the RCMP. He was ordered deported to the United States on March 2 and returned on March 8, 1971. He was sentenced on June 11, 1971, to ten years for interference with a flight crew member. 5282

February 25, 1971—Soviet Union—The rear window and both tail lights of a U.S. embassy officer's car were smashed while he and his wife were in the car in Moscow. The damage was done with a crowbar and a club. Both occupants of the vehicle were showered with broken glass but were not injured. 0700

February 27, 1971—Cambodia—A plastic bomb was discovered next to a U.S. mission vehicle after it had stopped briefly at a Phnom Penh hotel. Serious injuries were averted when the fuse burned out before detonating the bomb. 0701

February 28, 1971—Ireland—D. Reynolds, an IRA political organizer, was kidnapped and found beside a road. Two individuals were arrested, one of them from Ulster. 0702

March 1971—United States—JDL members crashed a diplomatic reception in Washington and poured blood on the head of a Soviet official.

March 1, 1971—West Germany—Unconfirmed reports were received in Bonn that the kidnappers of a seven-year-old German boy who was held between February 22 and 27 had intended to seize the son of a U.S. embassy official. 0703

March 1, 1971—United States—At 1:32 A.M., a powerful bomb exploded in an unmarked men's lavatory in the Senate wing of the U.S. Capitol, damaging seven rooms, some of them 250 feet away, but injuring no one. Damage was estimated at $300,000. Thirty-three minutes before, the Capitol telephone operator had received a warning saying, "This building will blow up in thirty minutes. You will get many calls like this, but this one is real. Evacuate the building. This is in protest of the Nixon involvement in Laos." A few days later, the *New York Times*, *New York Post*, and Associated Press received letters postmarked March 1 in Elizabeth, New Jersey, in which members of the Weather Underground said, "We have attacked the Capitol because it is, along with the White House and the Pentagon, the worldwide symbol of the government which is now attacking Indochina." In Senate Public Works Committee hearings on March 2, U.S. Army Captain Edwin Joyner, a bomb expert, testified that the bomb could have entailed fifteen to twenty pounds of dynamite hidden in "an ordinary briefcase." Capitol police chief James M. Powell claimed that two hundred to three hundred threats against the Capitol had been received in the past few years. On April 27, Leslie Bacon, nineteen, was arrested in Washington as a material witness to the bombing. She was flown to Seattle on April 29 to be questioned by a federal grand jury.

March 1, 1971—United States—The New School for Social Research in New York City was bombed by the Puerto Rican Resistance Movement. 0704

March 2, 1971—United States—Two unidentified people threw a firebomb from a passing car at the Iraqi mission to the United Nations in New York City, causing minor damage. 0705

March 2, 1971—Israel—After receiving a bomb threat, the U.S. embassy was partially evacuated and searched. Nothing was found in the Tel Aviv building. 0706

March 4, 1971—Israel—A man walked into the USIS Library in Tel Aviv and said that a bomb would explode shortly in the building. A marine security guard apprehended the man when he ran into the embassy. A search was negative. 0707

March 4, 1971—Taiwan—The USIS office in Kao-hsiung received a telephone call threatening a bomb explosion in the library. Nothing was found. 0708

March 4, 1971—Turkey—Four U.S. airmen stationed near Ankara—Sergeant James J. Sexton and Privates Larry J. Heavner, Richard Caraszi, and James M. Gholson—were kidnapped by five armed members of the TPLA as they drove from a radar base outside Ankara to their billets. The car in which they were traveling was also taken. The kidnappers set a March 6 deadline, demanding 400,000 Turkish lire (approximately $44,444 at the time) and the publication of a manifesto, threatening to shoot the airmen. The same day, the Turkish government arrested a suspect, Mete Ertekin, a twenty-four-year-old student at Middle East Technical University in Ankara. The kidnappers immediately demanded his release as well. Under interrogation, Ertekin yielded the names of his accomplices, and forty-five thousand police and soldiers began searching for them. The Turkish news agency and a radio station received a manifesto from the TPLA that claimed credit for the kidnapping, as well as that of James Finlay (see incident 0690), and for two bank robberies and recent bombings. The group called for armed struggle against the conservative Turkish government and U.S. imperialism and other foreign enemies. The U.S. ambassador in Turkey announced that he had established contact with the Turkish foreign ministry but claimed that no pressure was being placed upon Turkey to negotiate. President Nixon stated that the United States "would not suggest that the Turkish government negotiate." The United States appealed to the kidnappers to release the four men. During the search, riots broke out at Ertekin's university when troops attempted to enter a dormitory, resulting in the deaths of a student and a soldier in a gunfight, as well as injuries to twelve soldiers and students; 356 persons were held for questioning, with twenty-six arrested. Many of these were suspected of receiving training from Palestinian guerrillas. The Turkish government announced that it refused to accede to the terrorists' demands. On March 8, the airmen were freed unharmed when the kidnappers left them alone late that evening in the apartment where they had been held, seven hundred yards away from the U.S. embassy. According to Turkish officials, the kidnappers had phoned friends several times attempting to get rid of their hostages. The kidnappers were eventually arrested, tried, and convicted. On May 6, 1972, three were hanged, one was imprisoned, and one was killed in a gunfight with Turkish authorities. 0709

March 6, 1971—Ceylon—The U.S. embassy in Colombo was attacked with rocks and firebombs. Two vehicles were burned, and a number of car windows and windows in the chancery were broken. Up to forty men out of a group of one hundred overpowered the police guard and scaled the embassy wall. Three policemen were stabbed, one fatally. 0710

March 7, 1971—West Germany—A number of U.S. military vehicles were firebombed in Frankfurt, causing $6,000 worth of damage. 0711

March 8, 1971—United States—National Airlines flight 745, a B727 flying the Mobile-Pensacola-New Orleans route with forty-five persons on board, was the scene of a hijacking attempt by Thomas Kelly Marston, a white for whom the FAA profile was inapplicable; he was born in Augusta, Georgia, on September 4, 1954. He had boarded the plane in Mobile and initiated his attempt while the aircraft was on the ground, loading for departure from New Orleans. He pulled a .38 caliber pistol and asked the stewardess to take him to the cockpit. He allowed the other passengers to deplane and demanded to be flown to Montreal. While flying over Knoxville, Tennessee, the crew persuaded the hijacker to surrender, and he turned his gun over to the pilot. The plane flew back to Miami, and Marston was taken into custody by the FBI. He was released to his father's custody and was sentenced on November 8, 1971, to an indeterminate term under the youth corrections act for interference with a flight crew member. 5283

March 10, 1971—Ceylon—The U.S. embassy in Colombo received a postcard, believed to have originated with the same group that attacked the embassy on March 6 (see incident 0710), warning that the lives of all Americans in Ceylon were in danger and threatening death to "U.S. imperialists." 0712

March 12, 1971—Pakistan—Two small bombs were thrown into the ground floor of the building housing the U.S. consulate in Dacca. A watchman was ordered away at gunpoint while the bombs were thrown. 0713

March 13, 1971—Greece—Members of the Greek Militant Resistance bombed the Athens offices of the Esso-Pappas Oil Company. 0714

March 14, 1971—Turkey—A small bomb was thrown over the back wall of the U.S. consulate general in Istanbul, causing a small hole in the ground. 0715

March 15, 1971—Argentina—In Córdoba, a city-wide labor-student strike resulted in fifty vehicles burned and a number of foreign businesses destroyed, with damages estimated at $4 million. A group broke into the USIS Binational Center library and burned books, wrecked furniture, broke windows, and burned the card catalog. On March 18, the strike resumed, with clashes with the army continuing. A state of emergency was decreed, with Córdoba being declared a military zone. Thirty-five hundred troops were called in to occupy the city. 0716-0717

March 15, 1971—Netherlands—Europeans operating on a contract from Rasd, the Fatah intelligence organization, sabotaged the Gulf Oil refinery in Rotterdam. Among them was Evelyne, twenty-five, an English teacher in the

Paris suburbs who also worked as a cashier at the Theatre de l'Ouest, which was sponsored by the French government and managed by Mohammed Boudia, a Palestinian terrorist leader in Europe. Evelyne spent a week in Rotterdam planning her operation with an Algerian. She next drove to Holland with a Frenchman and Palestinian. The group cut through the protective fence surrounding the oil tanks, set delayed-action bombs, and escaped across the French border. At midnight their 150 kilograms of plastic explosive went off in three blasts.

Evelyne's gang was ultimately arrested because of an error by two members of her Paris group, Nadia and Marlene Bardali, daughters of a rich Casablanca merchant. The three women, along with an elderly French couple who had been given 850 pounds sterling and airline tickets, were the "Easter commando," which was to smuggle detonators and timing devices into Israel. From there the group would bomb nine tourist hotels during the 1971 Easter ceremonies. The Israelis immediately arrested the girls, whose confessions led them to Evelyne and the French couple. The authorities discovered that the girls had hidden explosives in their brassieres, girdles, lipsticks, Tampax, and shoe heels. The Moroccan girls' long coats hid an explosive liquid, while Evelyne carried a second chemical that was part of a binary napalm bomb.

During their trial, the sisters said that they had acted out of love for their Arab boyfriends, which quickly brought Lebanese press characterizations of them as "nymphomaniac terrorists." Evelyne was sentenced to fourteen years. She later gave the Israelis a list of French addresses and names. When the explosives laboratories were raided, authorities found that the Algerian bomb makers had escaped. 0718

March 15, 1971—Turkey—Members of the TPLA bombed the U.S. consulate in Ankara, as well as a branch of the American-Turkish Trading Bank and the offices of the right-wing Ankara newspaper *Dunya*. No injuries were reported in the consulate bombing. 0719-0720

March 16, 1971—Pakistan—Several shots were fired at the home of the U.S. consul general in Dacca, penetrating the master bedroom suite. 0721

March 20, 1971—Pakistan—A U.S. embassy officer in Lahore received a threat against his life. 0722

March 20, 1971—Pakistan—Three Molotov cocktails were thrown into the services compound of the U.S. consulate in Dacca. 0723

March 20, 1971—Netherlands—Two males jumped from a car near a KLM Royal Dutch Airlines plane and threatened passengers and crew with a submachine gun. Authorities took both men into custody. 5284

March 21, 1971—Pakistan—A homemade bomb was thrown at the American center in Chittagong by two men on a motorcycle. Three small window panes were broken, and seven others were cracked. 0724

March 22, 1971—Israel—The U.S. embassy in Tel Aviv was partially evacuated and searched after receiving a bomb threat. Nothing was found. 0725

March 22, 1971—France—The U.S. ambassador in Paris received a letter threatening the kidnap for ransom of a member of his family. 0726

March 25, 1971—Turkey—A pipe bomb exploded at the rear of the U.S. consulate in Izmir, causing no damage or injuries. 0727

March 25, 1971—France—Forty members of the Movement of Youthward Brothers in War of the Palestinian People threw stones and three Molotov cocktails at the offices of the Bull Computer Company, a subsidiary of General Electric. 0728

March 26, 1971—Pakistan—A bomb threat was received at the American School in Lahore. 0729

March 28, 1971—Turkey—At 6:55 P.M., a bomb exploded in the garden of the consulate general residence in Izmir, causing no injuries or property damage. 0730

March 29, 1971—Zambia—A bomb exploded in the Lusaka office of FRELIMO, seriously injuring Matteus Childende, an official of the group, and damaging the building. 0731

March 30, 1971—United States—The Secret Cuban Government claimed responsibility for the bombing of the New York City office of the Cuban Health Exchange. 0732

March 30, 1971—Kuwait—The former Iraqi vice-president and air marshal was assassinated. He had worked against the Baathist regime since his 1970 dismissal. Authorities speculated that Baathists were involved in the murder. 0733

March 30, 1971—Philippines—A Philippine Air Lines BAC111 flying from Manila to Davao City was hijacked by six long-haired Filipino youths who were members of Kabataang Makabayan, a Philippine leftist student organization. The group members, identified as Daniel Lotibana, Fructuoso Chua,

Edgardo Mausisa, Domingo Baskinas, Glen Rosauro, and Edgardo Tigulo, demanded to be flown to Peking. Armed with pistols, a carbine, and scissors, they allowed twenty passengers and an infant not on the passenger list to deplane while refueling in Hong Kong. The other twenty-four passengers and crew of five remained on board the plane, which took off for the People's Republic without requesting landing permission there. Four Americans were among their hostages. Maps and charts to Peking were not available, so the hijackers allowed Captain Antonio Misa to land in Canton's White Cloud Airport, where all were courteously received. The passengers spent the night in a dormitory of an airport compound and were given communist publications in a number of translations during their twenty-four-hour holdover. They were released the next day, with the hijackers being forced to apologize to their hostages for the inconvenience. According to the pilot, the Chinese "impressed it on us that they don't approve of air piracy, and that they don't want this kind of incident of going to China on a hijacked aircraft." However, Russell Ebersole, an American missionary on board the plane, was told by one of the hijackers that they were to receive training in China and would eventually return to the Philippines, possibly to hijack again. Two of the hijackers returned to Manila in June 1977 and were taken into military custody. They were charged in August 1977 before a military court. 0734

March 31, 1971—United States—The Government Center in Boston was letter-bombed.

March 31, 1971—United States—Eastern Airlines flight 939, a DC8 flying from New York to San Juan, Puerto Rico, with eighty-two persons on board was hijacked by America's oldest hijacker, a Latin who met the FAA profile; Diego Ramirez was born on August 30, 1906, in Caracas, Venezuela. Armed with a child's toy, which he used to threaten the crew, he demanded to be flown to Havana. A complaint was filed against him on April 8, 1971, in the southern district of New York. He was returned to the United States via Bermuda on October 8, 1974. His case is pending. He has also been identified as Diego Ramirel Landeatta. 5285

March 31, 1971—United States—The United States' youngest hijacker attempted to commandeer Delta Airlines flight 400, a DC9 scheduled to fly from Birmingham, Alabama, to Chicago with seventy passengers. John M. Mathews, Jr., a white male for whom the FAA profile was inapplicable, was born on March 1, 1957, in Birmingham, Alabama. He enplaned without a ticket at the airport and held a gun on stewardess Mrs. Foster Jordan for forty-five minutes while he allowed the passengers and other hostesses to deplane. He demanded to go to Cuba but was talked out of it by the hostess. In court the stewardess testified that Mathews felt rejected because of his parents' divorce. She offered to give him a home during the summer, and Mathews accepted the offer. He was given a suspended three-year probation on June 7, 1971, for carrying a weapon aboard an aircraft. Other reports claim that he had surrendered to the FBI after a ramp agent convinced him he should surrender. 5286

April 1, 1971—West Germany—Roberto Quintanilla, the former Bolivian consul general in Hamburg, was killed by a member of the ELN who entered the consulate and shot him. The next day the ELN issued a communiqué in which it claimed responsibility and said the consul was responsible for the death of Inti Peredo, one of their leaders, in 1969. Quintanilla had retired but had remained in Hamburg, waiting for his replacement to arrive. On May 13, 1973, two ELN members, Oswaldo Ucasqui, an Argentine citizen, and Monica Ertl, were killed in a shootout with police. Ucasqui was believed to be the consul's killer. 0735

April 2, 1971—Jordan—Members of a fedayeen group damaged a pipeline carrying 440,000 barrels a day of crude Saudi Arabian oil to the Zarka refinery, resulting in the loss of transit fees to Jordan, Syria, and Lebanon (with no losses to Israel). The pipeline, crossing the occupied Golan Heights, is an extension of the Tapline, also known as the Trans-Arabian Pipeline, owned by Aramco. 0736

April 5, 1971—Jordan—A fragmentation grenade was tossed over the back wall of the U.S. embassy in Amman. The grenade landed in a parking lot, causing no injuries and slight damage. 0737

April 5, 1971—United States—American Air Taxi flight 208, a Cessna 402 nine-passenger aircraft (general aviation) flying from Key West to Miami, was hijacked by a Latin male for whom the FAA profile was inapplicable: Carlos L. Hernandez-Tranhs, who was born in Cuba on October 18, 1948. He remains a fugitive from an indictment handed down on June 8, 1971, by a federal grand jury in the southern district of Florida. The plane landed safely in Havana. 5287

April 6, 1971—Uruguay—Automatic weapons fire and a bazooka-like projectile were directed at a U.S. embassy residence in Montevideo. 0738

April 6, 1971—Venezuela—An explosive charge went off near a Caracas restaurant in which a U.S. National War College group was scheduled to have lunch. The explosion occurred twenty-five minutes before the group was to arrive, and the luncheon was held on schedule. Leaflets found near the scene indicated that the bomb was in protest of the "Yankee operation in Laos." 0739

April 6, 1971—Venezuela—A U.S. embassy officer was forced to the side of the road by another vehicle near his Caracas home. As he sped off, a shot was fired at him. 0740

April 6, 1971—Turkey—Five bombs with fuses still smoking were discovered outside the CENTO Ankara secretariat building. A bomb exploded outside the U.S. element CENTO facility in Ankara. The U.S. officer open mess in Ankara was hit with two black powder bombs thrown by four young Turks, causing some damage but no injuries. 0741-0743

April 7, 1971—Sweden—Two Croatian terrorists entered the Yugoslavian embassy on the pretext of obtaining passports and shot Vladimir Rolovic, the Yugoslavian ambassador to Sweden, a number of times and wounded a secretary, Mira Stemphihar, who tried to protect the ambassador. Rolovic died of his bullet wounds on April 15. The attackers were identified as Andjelko Brajkowic and Miro Barzico, and were charged with murder on April 16 in a Stockholm court, along with a third man suspected of aiding them. On April 12, Barzico's lawyer, Lars Bergmark, told reporters that the two had planned to kidnap the ambassador and hold him for the release of Croatians being held in Yugoslavia, but that they had opened fire when Rolovic had thrown his gun. They were sentenced by the Stockholm city court to life imprisonment on July 14. Marinko Lemo and Stanislav Milicevic were given two-year terms for complicity, while Ante Stojanom, the group's leader, received a four-year term. On July 14, the *London Times* reported that the group had planned to form a terrorist group that would attack people in Sweden suspected of working for Yugoslavia against the Croatians.

On September 15, 1972, three Croatian émigrés hijacked an SAS airliner and obtained the release of six Croatian terrorists being held in Swedish jails. The aircraft was flown to Spain, where Spanish authorities apprehended the nine Croatians. The six who had been released in Sweden were permitted to leave Spain for Paraguay on June 23, 1974. Sweden has requested that three of the group be extradited for involvement in the 1971 murder of Rolovic. Paraguayan authorities have issued warrants for their arrest, but they have not been found. Press reports speculate that the men may have fled to Uruguay. 0744

April 7, 1971—Uruguay—Fifteen rifles were seized from an artist; the home of Police Inspector Washington Carrerras was firebombed; and the U.S. Marine billet in Montevideo was damaged by a bomb. The Tupamaros were responsible for all of the incidents. 0745

April 7, 1971—Trinidad and Tobago—The U.S. embassy in Port-of-Spain was partially evacuated following a bomb threat. A search was negative. Later cars of guests attending a social function at the U.S. ambassador's residence were damaged. 0746-0747

April 7, 1971—Haiti—The U.S. embassy in Port-au-Prince was partially evacuated after receiving a bomb threat. A search was negative. 0748

April 11, 1971—Israel—Authorities arrested two sisters, Evelyn and Nadia Bardeli, as they were entering Israel at Lod Airport. The two were carrying detonators in their bras, lipstick, hollow heels, and transistor radios and claimed that they belonged to the French section of the PFLP. They had had affairs with Arab terrorists who had asked them to engage in the smuggling. The two had been born to a French Christian mother and Arab Moslem father and felt an affinity for the Palestinian cause. Under interrogation, they told of the entry two days earlier of an elderly French couple posing as tourists, Edith and Pierre Burghalter, who had also smuggled in explosives. This information of the Casablanca-born sisters led to the arrest of the couple at a Tel Aviv seafront hotel. The following day, twenty-three-year-old Evelyne Barges, a French student, was arrested after flying into Lod Airport. Upon this arrest, the Israelis announced the capture of the terrorist cell. They claimed that Barges was involved in the destruction of the Rotterdam oil refinery (see incident 0718), as well as the September 1970 airline hijackings (see incidents 0509 to 0512). All of the group received prison sentences. In March 1972, Pierre Burghalter was given amnesty and flown to Frnace. Due to ill health, Edith Burghalter and one of the sisters were given amnesty in December 1974. German-born Barges remained incarcerated. 0749

April 12, 1971—United States—Members of the Black Revolutionary Assault Team claimed credit for a bomb that exploded at 11 A.M. at the New York City consular office of the Republic of South Africa, destroying an outer wall. The group was protesting apartheid. 0750

April 12, 1971—United States—An unidentified male threatened the pilot of a private aircraft on an excursion flight with a toy pistol. When the plane's fuel ran out, the pilot landed in a field and then overcame the passenger. Police treated the attempted hijacking as a minor offense. 5288

April 13, 1971—Canada—Three juveniles used sharpened toothbrushes to hijack a Midwest Airlines Piper Navajo flying between Dauphin and Winnipeg with eight persons on board. The youths, identified as Jeffrey M. Howdle, Leslie Lamirande, and Gary G. Rusk, wanted the Transair-Midwest plane to fly to Yorkton, Saskatchewan, but the plane used cloud cover to foil the youths and landed in Winnipeg, where the trio were taken into custody. 5289

April 14, 1971—Argentina—Members of the Angel Bengochea unit of the ERP, in conjunction with the Tupamaros, stole documents from the home of the Uruguayan naval attaché in Buenos Aires. 0751

April 15, 1971—Netherlands—A bomb caused heavy damage to the Amsterdam office building housing the Soviet trade delegation. Four of the twenty occupants and a passerby were injured and the windows of nearby buildings, including the U.S. consulate general, were broken. A board was found on the gate of the building, with JDL slogans "Never again! Let my people go!" written in English. Dutch police arrested an American Jew living in the Netherlands as a suspect. 0752

April 18, 1971—France—The Paris connection to the Easter Commando group of the PFLP, which had been arrested in Israel, was found by French counter-intelligence agents. Sidi Mohammed ben Mansour, an Algerian student at the Vincennes Faculty of the University of Paris, and René Caudan, a French mechanic, were arrested and accused of furnishing detonators to the group which had arrived in Israel intending to bomb Israeli buildings for the PFLP. Israeli police claimed that the girls had fallen in love with PFLP agents in France, and that all were well paid. All were sentenced to prison. 0753

April 19, 1971—United States—A pipe bomb containing smokeless powder and steel bearings injured one person and caused considerable damage to the New York City offices of the South African Tourist Corporation. A notice to news media claimed that the attack was in opposition to apartheid. 0754

April 21, 1971—Kenya—The U.S. embassy in Nairobi received an anonymous phone call warning that a bomb was planted in the university hall where the U.S. ambassador was speaking. Local police and security officials were alerted, and the ambassador concluded his speech as planned. 0755

April 21, 1971—United States—Eastern Airlines flight 403, a DC8 flying forty-four passengers from Newark to Miami, was the scene of a hijacking attempt by an individual who had been searched prior to boarding and had been found to have no weapons on his person. Francesco F. Anile, a white male who met the FAA profile, was born on August 9, 1940, in Italy. He told the pilot that he had a gun and grenade and would allow the pilot to land in Miami but wished to go to Italy. The pilot called his bluff, determined the hijacker was unarmed, and flew on to Miami where federal agents took Anile into custody in Miami. The hijacker had no weapons. He was charged with conspiracy to commit air piracy and on February 15, 1972, was given a three-year (some sources claim five years) suspended sentence for interference with a flight crew member. The flight had begun in New York. 5290

April 21, 1971—Denmark—About five thousand demonstrators peacefully staged an anti-Vietnam march in Copenhagen. By the time the group reached the U.S. embassy, it was reduced to about 2,000. Earlier in the day, three telephone bomb threats were received against the homes of U.S. military personel. Elsewhere in Copenhagen, a bomb destroyed the Greek embassy. 0756-0759

April 22, 1971—Taiwan—A bomb threat led to the evacuation of the American School in Taipei. A search was negative. 0760

April 22, 1971—Argentina—The Angel Bengochea command of the ERP stole equipment from the offices of the Parke-Davis Laboratory in La Plata. 0761

April 22, 1971—United States—The New York City offices of AMTORG, the Soviet Trading Corporation, were damaged by a bomb. No injuries were reported. Twenty minutes earlier, an individual using JDL slogans had phoned United Press International and Associated Press to warn of the bombing. The JDL denied responsibility. The Soviets sent an official protest to the United States on the twenty-fourth, and summoned U.S. ambassador Jacob D. Beam to see First Deputy Foreign Minister Vasily V. Kuznetsov. Seven members of the JDL were charged with conspiracy to violate the National Gun Control Act of 1968, the Federal Explosive Act of 1970, and with possessing 2 dynamite bombs. Sheldon Siegel, twenty-six, was convicted of conspiracy in the case. 0762

April 23, 1971—Malta—The U.S. embassy in Valletta received a telephoned bomb threat at 4:45 P.M. While previously noted signs of attempted jimmying of the embassy front door gave some credence to the call, nothing was found. 0763

April 23, 1971—Turkey—A device exploded in an empty lot beside the Turkish-American Association Theatre in Ankara. No damages or injuries resulted. Three unexploded dynamite sticks were found on the sidewalk adjacent to the theater. Ten minutes later, an explosion occurred in front of the Maltese-American facility, breaking windows and slightly injuring the Turkish guard. 0764-0765

April 25, 1971—Colombia—A man identified only as Rivadeneira attempted to hijack an Avianca plane flying from Barranquilla to Medellín but was overpowered by passengers and crew members. 5291

April 26, 1971—Greece—A small bomb exploded in a trash barrel outside the headquarters of the USAF Group to protest the U.S. presence in Athens. A Greek employee was seriously wounded, and there was glass breakage and damage to a U.S. government vehicle. Elsewhere in Athens, a bomb exploded outside the headquarters of the General Confederation of Labor. 0766

April 26, 1971—Ceylon—The U.S. embassy in Colombo received a threat to Americans through the mail. 0767

April 27, 1971—Argentina—The Luis Blanco and Adolfo Bello units of the ERP placed eleven bombs in U.S. business offices in Rosario. 0768-0778

April 27, 1971—Argentina—A bomb found in the auditorium of the USIS Binational Center in Rosario was safely removed by police. 0779

April 29, 1971—United States—A lone man identified only as Vega attempted to hijack an Avianca plane flying from Los Angeles to Bogotá and divert it to Cuba. The plane landed in Panama, where the hijacker was arrested. 5292

April 30, 1971—France—At midnight, a plastic bomb was thrown over the rear gate of the Paris residence of the U.S. ambassador, causing no injuries but breaking a number of windows. 0780

May 3, 1971—Argentina—The ERP claimed credit for the bombing of three foreign businesses in Buenos Aires. 0781-0783

May 3, 1971—Argentina—A homemade bomb exploded in the La Banda affiliate of the USIS Binational Center in Santiago del Estero, destroying windows and part of the front wall. Leaflets were distributed claiming the bombing for the Revolutionary People's Army. 0784

May 4, 1971—Turkey—A bomb exploded at the USAF Tuslog Detachment 30 billet in Ankara, shattering all of the windows in the building but causing no injuries. The residence was unoccupied at the time. 0785

May 5, 1971—Iran—In an apparently well-planned daylight attack, building and exhibit windows at the Binational Student Center, a USIS facility in Tehran, were broken by three young men. Elsewhere one window of the Binational Center's English Teaching Academic Center was broken. A bomb exploded in a restroom at the Binational Center IAS Cultural Center. Damage was confined to the one room. 0786

May 6, 1971—Taiwan—The U.S. embassy in Taipei received an anonymous letter threatening the life of the U.S. ambassador. 0787

May 7, 1971—United States—Two well-dressed women threw two stink bombs into the South Vietnamese consulate in San Francisco, causing no damage. "VC Will Win" was painted on the consulate wall. 0788

May 7, 1971—New Zealand—A local newspaper in Auckland reported a bomb threat at the U.S. consulate. A search revealed nothing. 0789

May 8, 1971—Colombia—An Avianca DC4 flying twenty passengers from Montería to Cartagena was hijacked by twenty-one-year-old José Rafael Moreno, who was armed with a pistol and grenade. He allowed the passengers to leave in Cartagena. The plane landed in Maracaibo, Venezuela, where the hijacker was apprehended by Venezuelan authorities. The plane was released. 5293

May 12, 1971—Bolivia—Bolivian peasants kidnapped the manager of a U.S.-owned gold mine. He was released in exchange for a tractor to be used in road construction. 0790

May 13, 1971—United States—An indictment was handed down against the leader of the JDL, Meir Kahane, and six other JDL members for conspiring to violate federal gun laws. On July 23, Kahane received a five-year suspended sentence, was fined $5,000, and was placed on probation in New York. U.S. district court judge Jack B. Weinstein gave Chaim Bieber a three-year suspended sentence and a $2,500 fine and placed him on a three-year probation. Stewart Cohen received the same sentence but was only fined $500.

May 13, 1971—Japan—An All Nippon Airways YS11 flying from Tokyo to Sendai was the scene of an attempted hijacking by a male, Eiki Kurosawa, also known as Yong Ki Chung, who threatened to blow up the airplane if he was not flown to North Korea. The pilot returned to Tokyo where the hijacker offered no resistance and was arrested by police. 5294

May 14, 1971—Greece—A Greek policeman was killed while trying to defuse a bomb that exploded in Athens near the statue of President Harry S Truman. The same day, foreign correspondents received a pamphlet from a rightist underground organization, Free Greeks, who claimed that "the official American policy (is) an enemy of the Greek people," and threatened to increase their anti-American attacks unless the United States ceased its support of the regime. One other person was injured in the explosion. 0791

May 15, 1971—Argentina—Approximately ten terrorists detained one of the U.S. embassy's security patrol automobiles in a Buenos Aires suburb. An attempt to burn the embassy's vehicle was thwarted by the guards. 0792

May 16, 1971—Dominican Republic—A U.S. embassy contract watchman was killed by an unknown assailant, who fired on him through the wire fence surrounding the embassy warehouse in Santo Domingo. 0793

May 17, 1971—Turkey—Four armed members of the TPLA or TPLF kidnapped Ephraim Elrom, fifty-nine, Israel's consul general in Istanbul. The attackers bound twelve persons in his residence and then dragged him away to a waiting car. The terrorists demanded the release of ''all revolutionary guerrillas was under detention'' by 5 P.M. on May 20, threatening Elrom's life. The government rejected the demands and initiated a massive search for the kidnappers, whom they believed were from the Turkish Revolutionary Youth Federation (Dev-Genc), which had been banned on May 12 by court order. Among the members of the group that had been arrested were Omer Ayna, who was apprehended after robbing an Istanbul bank on May 3, and three individuals who were arrested on May 8 while attempting to cross into Syria, where they planned to receive Arab guerrilla training.

On May 18, Deputy Premier Sadi Kocas told the Senate that the government had ''no intention of bargaining with a handful of adventurers,'' and announced the arrest of Ayhan Yalin in the case. In a two-hour cabinet meeting, the Israeli government expressed its support of the Turkish handling of the case. On May 23, police found Elrom's body in an apartment five hundred yards from the Israeli consulate. Elrom had been shot three times in the head the previous evening. The government asked Parliament for a two-month extension of the April state of martial law. Police rounded up nearly one thousand people for questioning, including university professors, writers, and other intellectuals, but most of them were quickly released. The next day, martial law authorities said they were looking for one female and eight male university students. The police also announced that, on May 23, three persons who had been taken into custody had confessed to planning the kidnapping and surveilling the Elrom apartment and Israeli consulate.

On June 1, 1971, Sibel Erkan, fourteen, the daughter of an army major, was rescued from two armed kidnappers who had held her since May 30. Huseyin Cevahir was killed in a police shootout, and Mahir Cayan was seriously wounded. The TPLA duo were wanted for the Elrom murder. They had taken Erkan hostage in her own home after allowing her mother and brother to leave and threatened to kill her unless they were given passports and safe passage out of Turkey. After a fifty-one-hour siege, police stormed the apartment. Cevahir was hit by twenty-three bullets. The wounded Cayan attempted to flee but surrendered to police when surrounded by an angry mob. One policeman was wounded in the battle. Cayan later became a martyr for future Turkish leftist terrorists.

On November 30, 1971, five TPLA members escaped from Istanbul's maximum security military prison. Among them was Ulas Bardakci, a participant in the Elrom murder. He was shot and killed in a police shootout on the shores of the Bosporus on February 19, 1972. Police captured Ziya Yilmaz, another escapee, who on March 17 was given a death sentence by an Istanbul military court for Elrom's killing. 0794

May 17, 1971—Argentina—The son of one of the U.S. embassy patrol security guards was severely beaten by three armed men in Buenos Aires and told, "We know your father works for the U.S. embassy." 0795

May 17, 1971—Sweden—An SAS DC9 scheduled to fly from Malmo to Stockholm was the scene of an aborted hijacking attempt by a male identified only as Pennington, who threatened to kill his girl friend unless he was taken to an unspecified destination. He was talked into surrendering before the plane took off. 5295

May 21, 1971—Northern Ireland—Thirty were injured when an IRA bomb exploded in a British ex-servicemen's hall in Suffolk.

May 23, 1971—Argentina—Stanley M. F. Sylvester, the honorary British consul in Rosario and executive of the Industrial Britanico de Carne Envasada and of the Swift and Company de la Plata packing plant, was kidnapped by three members of the Luis N. Blanco command of the ERP. The group left a note claiming that the attack was carried out in Blanco's memory. Blanco was a left-wing university student killed in the May 1969 riots in Rosario. The group also vowed to try Sylvester before "a people's court of justice." Later the group demanded that Swift rehire the four thousand workers who had been laid off Swift's fifteen thousand-member work force, grant better working conditions, and distribute $62,500 worth of food, clothing, and school supplies to the poor in Rosario slums. No contact was made between the governments of the United Kingdom and Argentina and the terrorists. Despite Argentine government protests, the company indicated that food would be distributed to the poor, but they ignored the other demands. A major search by police failed to locate Sylvester and his captors, and the company went ahead with the distribution on May 29. The next day, Sylvester, Argentine-born, was released unharmed. (Sources disagree as to whether the ransom was $50,000, $60,000, or the total $62,500 demanded. No mention is made of the workers laid off in 1970.) 0796

May 23, 1971—Belgium—Maximiliano Gomez, the twenty-eight-year-old exiled secretary-general of the Dominican Republic's MPD, was found dead in Brussels. The May 27 and June 4 issues of *Le Monde* carried statements by Gomez's friends in Paris that he may have been murdered by killers contracted by political allies of Dominican President Balaguer. 0797

May 25, 1971—United States—Steven M. Street hijacked an Air West F27 flying from Redmond, Oregon, to Klamath Falls, Oregon, and demanded to be flown to Denver, Colorado. He was arrested by police on a trespass charge. 5296

May 26, 1971—Australia—A Mr. Brown telephoned asking for $500,000 in exchange for directions to dismantle a bomb that he claimed was on board a Qantas 707 flying from Sydney to Hong Kong with 128 persons on board. Upon receiving the money, he phoned to say that there was no bomb. Two men were later arrested. On the twenty-seventh, an unidentified male claiming to be Mr. Brown threatened to sabotage a Qantas 707 flying from Perth to Adelaide with seventy-seven passengers on board. The plane landed safely in Adelaide, and a search revealed no bomb.

May 27, 1971—Rumania—A Rumanian Tarom IL14 flying from Oradea to Bucharest with nineteen persons on board was hijacked by five armed men and one woman who demanded to be flown to Munich, where they would seek political asylum. They allowed the pilot to land at Vienna's Schwechat Airport to refuel, but the nose wheel was damaged. Police persuaded the hijackers to surrender, and they were sentenced to terms ranging from twenty-four to thirty months in December 1971. The hijackers were identified as Sandor Miheller, Adalbert Moka, Janos and Joszef Papp, Robert Vamos, and Janos Veizer. 5297

May 28, 1971—United States—Eastern Airlines flight 30, a B727 flying from Miami to New York with 143 persons on board, was hijacked by a former New York policeman, James E. Bennet, a white male who met the FAA profile, who was born on May 22, 1931, in New York City. He threatened the stewardess with what he claimed was acid (but later proved harmless) and threatened to blow up the aircraft (with fake explosives) if he were not flown to LaGuardia Airport (the original destination of the flight). He also demanded that his wife and son be at the airport. Upon landing, he allowed the passengers and stewardesses to deplane. Still claiming that he was wrapped in explosives, he waited for one-and-a-half hours for his family to arrive. When they did not appear, he ordered the plane to take off and demanded to be flown to Nassau in the Bahamas. He also demanded that $500,000 be placed on the runway and that the New York representative of the IRA be waiting for him. He claimed that he wished to donate this money to that organization. Upon deplaning in Nassau, Bennet was overpowered and arrested before he could fly to Ireland. A complaint was filed against him on May 29, 1971, in the eastern district of New York. The Bahamas deported him to the United States on that date. He was acquitted of air piracy due to lack of criminal responsibility on December 29, 1971. He was committed to a mental institution the following day. 5298

May 29, 1971—Venezuela—Pan American flight 442, a B707 flying from Buenos Aires to Miami with sixty-eight persons on board, was hijacked out of Caracas by Ivan Gustavo Garcia Landaetta, a Latin male for whom the FAA profile was not applicable, who was born in Venezuela on January 8, 1949. The hijacker held a knife at the throat of a thirteen-year-old girl and demanded to be flown to Havana. The aircraft, passengers, and crew were detained in Havana for four days, but were eventually allowed to fly on to Miami. This may have been due to the recent seizure of eight Cuban fishermen by the U.S. Coast Guard. The hijacker remains a fugitive from an indictment handed down on April 12, 1973, by a federal grand jury in the southern district of Florida. Some reports claim that the hijacker was politically motivated. 5299

May 29, 1971—Spain—Members of the ETA attempted to kidnap the French consul in San Sebastián, Henri Wolimer, who resisted and escaped. 0798

June 1971—Uruguay—Six local employees of the USIS in Montevideo received identical threatening letters, personally addressed. 0799-0804

June 1, 1971—Cambodia—Two Phnom Penh houses occupied by U.S. embassy personnel were heavily damaged by explosions in the early morning. Although there were no serious injuries, two of the occupants suffered cuts from flying glass. 0805

June 4, 1971—United States—United Airlines flight 796, a B737 flying from Charleston, West Virginia, to Newark, New Jersey, with seventy-one persons on board, was hijacked ten minutes after takeoff by a white male who did not meet the FAA profile and was armed with two pistols: Glen Elmo Riggs, who was born on December 1, 1912, in Powellton, West Virginia. The crew told him that they did not have enough fuel to fly to Israel, Biggs' demanded destination, so he allowed them to land at Washington, D.C.'s Dulles Airport to refuel. While there, he allowed two stewardesses and the passengers to deplane and requested a larger airplane. After three hours on the ground, the hijacker went to get a drink of water, leaving his pistol on his seat. The crew disarmed him, and he was taken into custody. He was convicted on November

29, 1971, and sentenced to two concurrent twenty-year terms for aircraft piracy and interference with a flight crew member on January 7, 1972. 5300

June 4, 1971—Israel—PFLP terrorists on a speed boat fired ten bazooka shells at the Liberian-registered oil tanker *Coral Sea*, causing several fires but no injuries. The tanker was taking oil to Israel and was navigating the Strait of Bab el Mandeb at the entrance to the Red Sea at the time of the attack. The PFLP claimed that they were dramatizing their opposition to the trade in oil between the Persian Gulf and Israel and wished to deter tankers from using the Israeli port of Eilat on the Red Sea. 0806

June 7, 1971—Bolivia—The head of the Volcan metallurgy firm, Swiss industrialist Alfred Kuser, was kidnapped. His company paid between $35,000 and $45,000 in ransom, and he was released unharmed on June 9. 0807

June 10, 1971—Philippines—Police acting on a tip arrested a young man at the Cebu City airport before he boarded a Philippine Airlines BAC111 scheduled to fly to Manila, on suspicion of intending to hijack the plane. 5301

June 11, 1971—Israel—Grenades were thrown at Arab laborers waiting for Israeli buses to take them to work near the Muwazzi refugee camp in south Gaza. Two Arabs were killed and eighty-one injured. 0808

June 12, 1971—United States—TWA flight 358, a B727 flying from Chicago to Albuquerque and New York City, was hijacked at the boarding gate by a black male for whom the FAA profile was inapplicable: Gregory L. White, who was born in Chicago on September 25, 1947. Armed with a pistol, he forced his way on board the plane and held a stewardess hostage. Howard L. Franks, age sixty-five, was killed by the hijacker when he attempted to come to the aid of the stewardess. He was the first passenger to be fatally shot on board a U.S. aircraft by a hijacker. White allowed the passengers, bodyguard, and stewardesses, except for his hostage, to deplane, and took off for New York. During the deplaning, a deputy U.S. marshall sneaked on board the plane. After the hijacker had demanded $75,000, a machine gun, and a flight to North Vietnam, the crew, Marshall, and hijacker exchanged several shots. The plane landed at New York's JFK Airport, where the crew and Marshall escaped. During a gun battle between White and FBI agents in which he and an FBI agent were wounded, White surrendered. He was charged with air piracy and murder but was found incompetent to stand trial and was committed to a mental institution on October 7, 1971. It appears that he flew to New York to attempt to acquire a plane large enough to make the trip to Vietnam. 5302

June 12, 1971—United States—A faulty timing device prevented a JDL bomb from exploding at the Soviet Union's estate in Glen Cove, New York. On September 26, 1972, three individuals pleaded guilty in a New York federal court to being involved in two anti-Soviet bombings. Sheldon Siegel, twenty-six, had conspired to bomb and make two bombs planted at Amtorg in April 1971. Eileen Garfinkle, twenty-one, and Jacob Weisel, twenty-five, admitted to illegal possession of dynamite, some of which was used in the Glen Cove case. 0809

June 12, 1971—Zaire—Two deserters from the Portuguese army, R. Rodrigues de Sousa and J. Rodrigues Reis, hijacked an Angolan Air Taxi (general aviation) scheduled to fly from Luanda, Angola, to Cabinda, and diverted it to Pointe Noire in the Republic of the Congo. 5303

June 12, 1971—Philippines—Three thousand pro-Maoist demonstrators staged a protest against U.S. imperialism in front of the U.S. embassy in Manila. Six pillbox grenades were thrown against the main gate, resulting in minor injuries to one local security guard at the embassy. Later nine unexploded devices were found on the embassy grounds. 0810

June 12, 1971—Philippines—Three Molotov cocktails were thrown at the JUSMAAG motor pool in Manila, causing minor damages. 0811

June 12, 1971—Philippines—A Molotov cocktail exploded at the U.S. AID parking lot storage house in Manila, causing slight damage. 0812

June 13, 1971—United States—A bomb exploded outside the building housing the Mexican Government Tourism Department, causing minor damage. The explosion, which took place at 11:45 P.M., was the third bombing of Mexican-oriented agencies in two days in Los Angeles and was in protest of the deaths of six students in Mexico City riots. 0813

June 16, 1971—Cambodia—A small plastic bomb was thrown at a U.S. embassy vehicle in Phnom Penh, injuring two Cambodian pedestrians and damaging the vehicle. 0814

June 18, 1971—Peru—A threat was made against the life of the U.S. ambassador in Lima. 0815

June 18, 1971—United States—Piedmont Airlines flight 25, a B737 that had landed in New York after flying from Winston-Salem, North Carolina, was boarded by a white male for whom the FAA profile was irrelevant: Bobby R. White, who was born on July 23, 1944, in Kingsport, Tennessee. Only the pilot was on board when the hijacker, claiming to have acid and explosives, demanded to be flown to Cuba. The captain informed him that the aircraft needed fuel and additional crew. While a second pilot was entering the plane, White was overpowered by the pilot and two sky marshals. He was sentenced to five years for conveying false information concerning an attempt to commit air piracy on September 14, 1971. 5304

June 21, 1971—Colombia—J. Anaya attempted to hijack an Avianca DC4 flying from Montería to Medellín and divert it to Cuba, but he was overpowered and disarmed by the crew. 5305

June 22, 1971—United States—Members of the JDL attempted to bomb the Russian-owned estate at Glen Cove, New York. A young male phoned a warning, and fifteen sticks of dynamite wired to a clock were disarmed. 0816

June 23, 1971—Israel—A hand grenade was thrown into a marketplace at Khan Yunis, killing two Arabs and wounding forty-four others. 0817

June 23, 1971—Uruguay—Alfredo Cambon, a legal adviser to several large U.S.-backed Uruguayan companies, was kidnapped and held two days for questioning. Reports differ as to whether he was seized by the Tupamaros or the OPR-33, the Organization of the Popular Revolution 33, named for thirty-three heroes of the nineteenth-century independence movement. 0818

June 23, 1971—United States—The Purdue University licensed nuclear facility received a bomb threat.

June 28, 1971—Soviet Union—During the course of the preceding weekend, U.S. embassy personnel reported eight cases of harassment. Two tires on the automobile of an embassy officer were punctured on May 29. Additionally the embassy received three telephone calls warning of possible bombings. 0819-0821

June 29, 1971—Finland—A woman armed with a pistol attempted to hijack a Finnair DC9 flying from Helsinki, Finland, to Copenhagen, Denmark, and divert it to Cuba. A stewardess disarmed the woman, whom police claimed was mentally disturbed. 5306

June 30, 1971—Pakistan—A threatening letter was received, addressed to the USIS librarian in Dacca. 0822

July 1971—Jordan—Fedayeen sabotaged the Tapline. 0823

July 1971—United States—The Secret Cuban Government bombed a theater in New York City. 0824

July 1, 1971—Venezuela—Fire was set in front of the quarters of one U.S. military group official in Caracas, and a rock was thrown through the window of another, causing no personal injuries or extensive property damage. 0825

July 2, 1971—Mexico—Braniff flight 14, a B707 flying 102 passengers on the Acapulco-Mexico City-San Antonio, Texas, run, was hijacked by a couple who boarded at Mexico City and handed a note to the pilot as the plane approached San Antonio. The duo did not meet the FAA profile and were identified as a white male, Robert Lee Jackson, who was born on December 25, 1934, in Townsend, Tennessee, and his girlfriend, Ligia L. Sanchez Archila, also known as Lydia Lucrezia Sanchez, who was born in Guatemala on June 7, 1948. They forced the pilot fly to Monterey, Mexico, where they received $100,000 from a Braniff official in exchange for the release of the passengers. The plane with the crew and hijackers flew on to Lima, Peru, and Rio de Janeiro where police tried and failed to arrest the hijackers. Still waving their pistols, which they had used to threaten a hostage while the Braniff official obtained the money, they flew to Buenos Aires, looking for an Algerian representative who would arrange political asylum for them. The Argentine government refused to negotiate with the hijackers and surrounded the plane with three hundred policemen, who held them at bay for sixteen hours. After allowing the crew to disembark, the hijackers surrendered to Argentine authorities, ending a forty-four-hour, seventy-five-hundred-mile ordeal. The Argentine police took the money from them when they surrendered, although Jackson had tried to keep some of the cash, hiding $10,000 in his socks. Complaints were filed against the pair in the western district of Texas on July 2, 4, and 6, 1971. An Argentine court sentenced Jackson to five years and his girl friend to three years on December 15, 1971. The two were extradited to Mexico on July 25, 1974. They remain fugitives from U.S. charges. 5307

July 3, 1971—Greece—A bomb completely destroyed a U.S. vehicle belonging to EES and used to transport Greek employees to the U.S. air base in Heraklion, Crete. 0826

July 4, 1971—Thailand—The U.S. embassy in Bangkok received an anonymous telephoned bomb threat. 0827

July 4, 1971—Pakistan—A small bomb exploded in the consul general's residence garden, leaving a small crater but not damaging the U.S. Dacca residence. 0828

July 7, 1971—Israel—Seven Arab members of Al Fatah fired rockets at a suburb of Tel Aviv, killing four and wounding thirty. An Israeli patrol pursued the attackers, killing six; one escaped to Jordan. 0829

July 8, 1971—Greece—Bombs exploded in the night in Athens, damaging a railway track and a tank truck of Esso-Pappas. 0830

July 9, 1971—Northern Ireland—Rioters set fire to a U.S.-owned factory, Essez International Brakelining of Fort Wayne, Indiana, in disturbances in Londonderry. 0831

July 9, 1971—Argentina—Police arrested more than a dozen young men and women, all Uruguayan and Argentine members of the Revolutionary Peoples' Army, who were found with arms and explosives and planning to kill Argentine president Alejandro Lanusse and Uruguayan president Jorge Pacheco Areco at a military parade on Argentine Independence Day. A tank truck loaded with gasoline was to explode near the presidential reviewing stand. 0832

July 9, 1971—Argentina—The USIS Lincoln Library in Buenos Aires was extensively damaged by a firebomb. The librarian had received a telephoned bomb threat earlier. The bomb was in a one-liter soft-drink bottle hidden in the book stacks and timed to explode when the library was closed. 0833

July 11, 1971—Cuba—Two armed men, Angel Lopez Rabi and Nelson Alvarez Lopez, attempted to hijack a Cubana IL14 flying from Havana to Cienfuegos by threatening the pilot with guns and grenades. The pair was overpowered by crew members, but in the scuffle, a grenade exploded, killing one passenger and wounding three others. The plane landed safely in Havana, and both offenders, who did not specify where they wished to divert the plane, were handed over to authorities. 5308

July 11, 1971—Ireland—A TWA 707 with 143 on board and flying from Shannon to Washington, D.C., made an emergency landing upon discovery of a hijack note. No bomb was found. 5309

July 12, 1971—Uruguay—Argentine-born Jorge Berembau, an industrialist, was kidnapped. In a broadcast on July 28, the Tupamaros demanded that his family, owners of Uruguay's largest textile factories, would have to pay a ransom of 1 million pesos ($300,000) to three textile unions to compensate for recent factory closings. Berembau was released on November 26. 0834

July 14, 1971—Czechoslovakia—Karel Dolezel, twenty-four, and Antonin Lerch, twenty-eight, two miners, were convicted of hijacking the Prague-to-

Carlsbad flight to West Germany. They claimed that they had patterned their actions on those of the hijackers of a Czech plane on June 8, 1970 (see incident 5230). During their attack, the eight passengers and two crew members were threatened by revolvers and plastic explosives. Lerch shot the copilot twice. (Reports are conflicting as to whether the copilot survived.) Czechoslovakia demanded extradition but was refused. After pleading guilty, the pair was sentenced to seven years under Germany's new hijacking law. 5310

July 14, 1971—Greece—A bomb exploded at the USIS Hellenic American Union, a Binational Center in Athens, in the early morning hours, doing considerable surface damage. 0835

July 16, 1971—United Kingdom—An unidentified male called the National Airlines office in Miami and asked for $50,000 for information that would deactivate a bomb he claimed was on board a DC8 flying from London to Miami with 110 passengers. The plane landed in Stephenville, Newfoundland, and a search revealed no bomb.

July 16, 1971—United States—Warren Cooksey, forty-six, phoned an airline in San Francisco, demanding money in exchange for information on a bomb that he claimed was on board a San Francisco to Hawaii flight. He was apprehended when he was about to receive the money.

July 17, 1971—United States—John Berry telephoned Aer Lingus that a bomb was on board its 747 flying from New York to Europe. He was apprehended while attempting to take the money he had demanded. The plane landed in Boston, where a search revealed no bomb.

July 20, 1971—France—An unidentified individual telephoned the Montreal office of Air Canada and said that there was a bomb on board flight 871, a 747 flying from Paris to Montreal with 159 passengers on board. The plane landed at Shannon airport, where a search revealed no bomb. The plane landed in Montreal four hours late.

July 20, 1971—Canada—The pilot of an Air Canada 747 flying from Toronto to Vancouver with 252 persons on board learned of a bomb threat and landed in Milwaukee, where a search revealed no bomb.

July 22, 1971—Italy—A cyclist threw a bomb at the U.S. consul general's front door in Palermo, causing minor damage to the occupied building but no injuries. 0836

July 23, 1971—Australia—Five males threatened to blow up an Ansett Airlines plane in Sydney unless they were given $66,000. One man was arrested at the airport, and the other four were eventually apprehended.

July 23, 1971—United States—TWA flight 335, a B727 flying fifty-five passengers on the New York-Chicago-Los Angeles run, was hijacked by a white male who met the FAA profile: Richard A. Obergfell, who was born on September 26, 1944, in Brooklyn, New York. He commandeered the aircraft after takeoff from LaGuardia Airport and demanded to be flown to Milan, Italy. When the crew informed him that a larger plane was needed, he used a stewardess as hostage to force the crew to fly back to LaGuardia. He drove to JFK Airport in a maintenance van while still holding the hostage and was shot by FBI marksmen while waiting for a TWA 707 to be prepared. He was severely wounded in the shoulder and stomach and died twenty-five minutes later. He was the first U.S. hijacker to be killed on U.S. soil during a hijacking attempt. 5311

July 24, 1971—United States—National Airlines flight 183, a DC8 flying eighty-three persons from Miami to Jacksonville, Florida, was hijacked by a Latin who met the FAA profile who was armed with a small-caliber pistol and a stick of dynamite; he was Santiago M. Guerra-Valdez, who was born in Remedios, Cuba, on August 19, 1932. While on the way to Havana, he opened fire, wounding passenger Larry Evans of Redding Ridge, Connecticut as well as the stewardess, Sue Bond. Both received medical treatment in Havana, where the plane safely landed. The hijacker remains a fugitive from an indictment handed down by a federal grand jury on May 25, 1972, in the southern district of Florida. 5312

July 25, 1971—United States—A JDL firebomb destroyed a Soviet Union embassy official's car in New York City. 0837

July 28, 1971—Canada—An unidentified caller said an Air Canada DC9 flying from Montreal to Miami would have difficulties if a ransom was not paid. The plane landed in Raleigh, North Carolina, where a search revealed no bomb. The plane continued to Miami.

July 28, 1971—Switzerland—Two unidentified males phoned the TWA Geneva office and demanded $960,000, claiming that a bomb was on board a TWA 707 flying from Geneva to New York with 145 passengers. The plane landed in Shannon airport, where a search revealed no bomb. The two were arrested.

July 28, 1971—Italy—A male PFLP member gave a Western woman who believed she was his girl friend booby-trapped luggage to take on board an El Al plane flying from Rome to Lod Airport. Israeli security men prevented the plot from succeeding. 0838

July 30, 1971—United States—Time, Inc., in New York City received a written note threatening the kidnapping of the U.S. ambassador in Lima by the MTR. 0839

July 30, 1971—United States—The JDL bombed a Beverly Hills building housing a travel agency, causing $3,000 damage.

July 31, 1971—Guatemala—National police dismantled an explosive device in a sewer near the U.S. consular section in Guatemala City. Had the bomb exploded, the blast would have killed anyone in the immediate vicinity but would not have seriously damaged the consulate. 0840

August 1971—Dominican Republic—The PCV was temporarily held captive by unknown persons in Santo Domingo, a report was received that the MPD might be planning the kidnapping of a U.S. diplomat, suspicious persons approached the residences of two U.S. mission employees, and there were two instances of break-ins of U.S. mission residencies. 0841-0844

August 1971—United States—An intruder entered the Vernon, Vermont, Yankee nuclear power plant, walking past guard towers and fences and shooting a night watchman before escaping.

August 1971—Denmark—A riding instructor and his wife, claiming to be working for Al Fatah, kidnapped the managing director of Tuborg Breweries in Copenhagen and demanded a $240,000 ransom. The ransom was paid, the victim was released, and the two were arrested. 0845

August 2, 1971—Canada—An unidentified caller said that a barometric bomb was on board a BOAC 747 flying from Montreal to London with 378 persons. The flight was diverted to Denver, where a search revealed no bomb. The plane returned to Montreal.

August 3, 1971—United States—An unidentified caller said that either a Pan Am 747 flying from New York to Dakar with eighty-seven persons on board or a Nigerian Airways flight could be diverted. 5313

August 9, 1971—Uruguay—A Molotov cocktail was left near a vehicle assigned to a U.S. public safety officer, causing no damages. 0846

August 11, 1971—United States—The JDL phoned to claim credit for the bombing of a trucking firm in New York City.

August 17, 1971—United States—An unidentified male ordered a stewardess to tell the captain fo fly a United Airlines 747 on the Honolulu to New York run to Cuba. Security officers took the man into custody. 5314

August 17, 1971—United States—The Duke Power Company Oconee licensed nuclear facility received a bomb threat.

August 19, 1971—Honduras—A USIS building was bombed, but damage was not serious because the office was closed. 0847

August 21, 1971—Honduras—Both Peace Corps and U.S. military group headquarters were bombed during the night and early morning, causing no injuries and minor damage. 0848-0849

August 21, 1971—Lebanon—Fedayeen detained an adult dependent of a U.S. Department of Defense officer in Beirut for questioning. The victim was unharmed and treated courteously. 0850

August 21, 1971—Bolivia—During civil strife in La Paz, a vehicle was taken from a U.S. embassy official at gunpoint, and another U.S. embassy official ran his vehicle through a roadblock of armed students. Both were unhurt, although one car sustained bullet impacts. 0851-0852

August 21, 1971—Bolivia—The U.S. embassy marine house in La Paz was attacked by armed civilians using small automatic weapons, tear gas, and dynamite. Over 180 rounds were fired into the house, but the occupants were able to deter the attackers by using tear gas. Damage was considerable. 0853

August 22, 1971—Egypt—K. Farag, a Jordanian, attempted to hijack an Egyptian Airlines IL18 flying from Cairo to Amman and divert it to Israel. He was overpowered by sky marshals. 5315

August 22, 1971—United States—The MIRA, a Puerto Rican independence group, was credited with nine firebombings of groceries and supermarkets in Greenwich Village and Harlem. In Hoboken, New Jersey, the group claimed credit for the firebombings of seven stores. 0854-0869

August 24, 1971—Spain—A bomb exploded in a B707 of the Royal Jordanian Airline, Alia (named after King Hussein's eldest daughter), which was parked at Madrid's Barajas Airport. The explosive device was placed in the aft lavatory complex and blew a hole in the top of the fuselage, tearing a gash three feet long in the metal but causing no injuries because the plane was out of service at the time. It appears that the target was Hussein's mother, Queen Mother Zien, who had boarded the jet at Amman but deplaned in Istanbul. No group claimed responsibility, although Al Fatah members have been reported as the prime suspects. One report claims Black September was responsible, although the group did not publicly surface until November 1971. 0870

August 24, 1971—Ecuador—A bomb exploded at 9:35 P.M. in front of the U.S. consulate section in Guayaquil, causing no injuries. Damages were limited to a bad dent in the steel door and a shattered inner glass door. 0871

August 25, 1971—Brazil—Information was received that terrorists were planning to kidnap the U.S. Base Public Affairs Officer in Salvador. On September 2, the ALN proposed the assassination of a U.S. embassy official to commemorate Patriotic Week in Rio de Janeiro. 0872

August 30, 1971—Philippines—Information was received at the U.S. embassy that the KM (Nationalist Youth) planned to abduct the U.S. ambassador or a U.S. embassy official to obtain money for the purchase of arms and ammunition. On October 5, it was learned that a leftist organization planned to kidnap a foreign diplomat of ambassadorial rank in order to raise funds but excluded the U.S. ambassador because of security afforded him. 0873

August 31, 1971—Greece—An explosive device was found on the roof of a common building housing U.S. and several other pavilions in Thessaloniki. The device was defused by authorities. 0874

September 3, 1971—United States—Eastern Airlines flight 993, a DC9 flying from Chicago to Miami with eighty persons on board, was the scene of an attempted hijacking by a Latin male who met the FAA profile: Juan Miguel Borges Guerra, who was born on June 24, 1951, in Oriente, Cuba. The hijacker held an ice pick at the throat of a stewardess and demanded to be flown to Cuba. A deadheading three-man crew, sensing something amiss, over-powered the hijacker with the assistance of passengers. The hostess and the trio were stabbed in the scuffle. The hijacker was sentenced on March 16, 1972, to twenty years for interference with a flight crew member. Some reports claim that the plane was a B727 flying to the Virgin Islands. 5316

September 4, 1971—Ireland—The U.S. embassy in Dublin received a threat from a man claiming he was an IRA member and vowed that if Joe Cahill, a noted Irish revolutionary, was not allowed to leave the United States, the IRA would "declare war" on the U.S. government, its buildings, and its properties. 0875

September 5, 1971—United States—Two attempts to smuggle explosives on board El Al planes flying from New York to Israel. Woman tourists—one from the Netherlands, the other from Peru—had been given explosive charges to take into Israel but were arrested on arrival at Lod Airport. They had been duped by two Arab terrorists and were later released. 0876-0877

September 7, 1971—Uruguay—It was reported that the PCU was attempting to locate the residences of U.S. diplomatic personnel in order to take reprisals for bombing attacks against the Frente Amplio. Molotov cocktails were thrown at the entrance to the American Women's Club, causing little damage. 0878-0879

September 7, 1971—Cambodia—Two men attempted to assassinate U.S. ambassador Emory C. Swank in Phnom Penh by rolling a bicycle carrying a bomb made of C3 explosive in front of his car. The assailants apparently had failed to activate the fuse mechanism, and the bomb did not detonate. 0880

September 8, 1971—Canada—An unidentified male in Vancouver said that a bomb was on a C P Air flight and demanded $20,000 to specify which one. He was arrested later in a suburb at the designated place for him to pick up the money. A search revealed no bomb.

September 8, 1971—Lebanon—An Alia Caravelle flying forty-six persons from Beirut to Amman was hijacked by a member of Al Fatah, Lieutenant Mohammed Jaber, who ordered the plane to fly to Benghazi, Libya (although some reports claim Syria), after fighting off a security officer and threatening the captain with a grenade. He was arrested by local police but given political asylum. The plane and passengers were allowed to return immediately. Fatah claimed that Jaber had been sentenced to death by a Jordanian military court for his part in battles with Jordanian troops that summer and that he had acted on his own "to get rid of the bloodbaths and intimidation to which Palestinian commandos are being subjected in Jordanian prisons and detention camps." 0881

September 9, 1971—Jordan—Fedayeen damaged the Trans-Arabian Pipeline (Tapline) near the Syrian border. Jordan accused the Syrians of involvement. 0882

September 11, 1971—Honduras—A bomb was placed on the back wall of the U.S. embassy at the rear of the parking lot. The explosion knocked down several U.S. Marines who were playing basketball in the vicinity and caused minor damage to the wall. 0883

September 12, 1971—Pakistan—The U.S. consular general received two telephoned bomb threats from anonymous callers. A search was negative. 0884-0885

September 15, 1971—Israel—An El Al 707 made an emergency landing at Rome when a young passenger said he thought a woman had planted a bomb. A search of a suitcase revealed no bomb.

September 15, 1971—El Salvador—Seventeen incendiary devices resembling cigarette packs were planted in the San Salvador store of a U.S. corporation between 6 and 6:30 P.M. Four of the devices ignited, causing $40 loss. 0886

September 15, 1971—Jordan—Fedayeen terrorists, possibly from Syria, bombed a section of the Trans-Arabian Pipeline (the Aramco-owned Tapline). 0887

September 16, 1971—Israel—Fedayeen terrorists in Jerusalem threw a hand grenade into a crowd of U.S. tourists, killing a child and wounding six others, as well as hitting five American tourists with shrapnel. 0888

September 16, 1971—Lebanon—Sky marshals prevented a hijacking of an Alia Cravelle to Baghdad. The hijacker, armed with a hand grenade, was identified as a seventeen-year-old Palestinian, Hilal Abdel Kader Hassan (also known as Ali), who claimed he had been given a specially made pair of shoes to carry the grenade in at Beirut airport by Fatah agents. The plane was to fly from Beirut to Amman. The hijacker was sentenced to death on October 7, 1971. 0889

September 18, 1971—Mexico—Two members of the People's Armed Command were arrested in Mexico City. They claimed that their group had planned to kidnap the U.S. ambassador. 0890

September 18, 1971—United States—The VEPCO licensed nuclear facility in Surry received a bomb threat.

September 20, 1971—United Kingdom—A male PFLP member attempted to bomb a London-to-Tel Aviv El Al flight by giving a booby-trapped suitcase to a woman passenger. The suitcase was discovered. 0891

September 20, 1971—United States—A caller to United Press International claimed credit for the bombing of the entrance of Zaire's U.N. mission in New

York City for the Black Revolutionary Assault Team. He claimed, "We bombed it because they refused to allow our freedom fighters to cross their country to get to Angola." No one was injured inside the building, although sixteen persons were in the second-story suite of offices when the blast went off at 11:33 A.M. Jodie Della Femina, a three-year-old girl who was walking on the sidewalk with her mother and brother, was severely cut by flying glass, suffering six facial lacerations including cuts of the eyelid, cheek, lip, and chin, requiring seventy-five to one hundred stitches, as well as losing an upper front tooth. Her mother and brother were also hit by the glass. Minutes later, police arrested a black youth attempting to flee in a taxi. He was found with fifty rounds of ammunition and an incriminating note and was charged in criminal court with arson, possession of a bomb and a loaded weapon, and criminal mischief and was held in $50,000 bail. He was identified as eighteen-year-old Larry Pearson, a student at Louis Brandeis High School. Police described him as a black militant without any affiliation with a revolutionary group. He had placed the bomb at the top of a stairway and immediately outside the door to the Zaire offices. The main force of the blast was down the stairwell, cracking the wall open and jolting the glass panel street door off its hinges, as well as shattering glass. 0892

September 20, 1971—United States—Minutes after the bombing of the Zaire U.N. mission (see incident 0892), a low-grade pipe bomb approximately fifteen inches long was found at the Malawi U.N. mission. It was disarmed by police while the mission was evacuated. The caller claiming credit for the Zaire bombing also said that the Black Revolutionary Assault Team was responsible for this attempt. 0893

September 22, 1971—Northern Ireland—The U.S. consulate general in Belfast was damaged by a bomb directed at the police station opposite the consulate. 0894

September 23, 1971—Canada— The United States signed the Convention on Aircraft Sabotage at Montreal. It was approved by the U.S. Senate on October 3, 1972, and entered into force on October 26, 1973.

September 24, 1971—United States—American Airlines flight 124, a B727 flying from Detroit to New York City, was the scene of an attempted hijacking by a White Panther, a white female who did not meet the FAA profile: Barbara H. Pliskow, who was born in Detroit on September 14, 1933. She had carried a diaper bag filled with dynamite onto the plane. Because of a tip from a police informant, the passengers, including the hijacker, were deplaned prior to takeoff on the pretext of mechanical difficulties. Pliskow was apprehended in the airport terminal after threatening to shoot the arresting officer with her pistol and to blow up the explosives. She had intended to threaten to blow up the aircraft to secure the release of two Black Panthers from prison and then accompany them on board the aircraft to Algeria. She was released on bond on October 18, 1973, and was given two years' probation for assaulting a federal officer on July 23, 1974. Some reports claim that she was accompanied by a male White Panther. 0895

September 24, 1971—Bolivia—An anonymous phone call in La Paz alleged that an attempt would be made on the life of the U.S. ambassador. The U.S. embassy had been receiving reports that a series of terrorist acts aimed at Americans would be mounted the week of October 3, the day that Ché Guevara was killed by the Bolivian army. 0896

September 26, 1971—Yemen—Three bombs exploded at a U.S. consular officer's home in San'a, causing limited structural damage but no injuries. The bombing was believed to be part of a civil disturbance campaign aimed at the Yemen Arab Revolutionary Government and not specifically at Americans. 0897

September 26, 1971—Cambodia—Terrorists threw hand grenades onto a softball field three blocks from the U.S. embassy chancery in Phnom Penh, killing two U.S. Marine security guards and injuring ten other Americans playing softball. 0898

September 29, 1971—Egypt—An explosive device was found near the office of the minister of information, Abdel Kader. Bombs were found in other areas, including a district inhabited by Russians. A bomb alert was called in Cairo, according to a report released in Beirut. Anti-Soviet pamphlets were circulated in the city by the Egyptian National Front, which attacked Soviet imperialism. Egyptian officials claimed that Israeli intelligence had mailed the pamphlets to cause friction between the United Arab Republic and the Soviet Union.

October 1971—Guatemala—The PGT/FAR was responsible for the theft of $12,000 from a Coca-Cola plant. 0899

October 1971—United States—The unauthorized sale of a nuclear radiation device took place at Brigham Young University. According to a BDM Corporation report, "Unauthorized personnel at Brigham Young University inadvertently sold a radiation device (irradiator) as scrap to a junk salvage yard in Provo, Utah. The reports did not indicate who had sold the device, but stated that the radiation source was still in the device when sold. The device is one which was typically used for classroom or laboratory work under an AEC license, by authorized personnel. The discovery that the device was missing was not made until September 1974—three years after it had been sold. University personnel located the device at the salvage yard in late September

1974. The radiation source was intact and no health or safety hazard was present. According to the salvage dealer, the device was not moved from the time it arrived in October 1971 until its recovery in October 1974. The AEC's Directorate of Regulatory Operations fined the University $1000 for 3 apparent violations of AEC Regulations. The violations were: failure to secure a radiation device against unauthorized removal; transfer of the device to an unauthorized person; and failure to report promptly to the AEC when the loss of the device was discovered.''

October 1971—Netherlands—Four tons of small arms from the Czech Omnipol arms factory were intercepted by Dutch police at Schipol Airport en route for Ireland. It was suspected that the arms would have worked their way to the Provisional IRA.

October 1, 1971—Colombia—Ten firebombs were found at the Chapinero store of a U.S. firm at midnight. One of the devices exploded, causing no damage. The firm's Barranquilla office reported unspecified problems with students, resulting in the closing of the store for a half-day. 0900

October 2, 1971—Mexico—Police reported that an anonymous phone call indicated that a bomb would go off at the U.S. embassy in Mexico City. The previous day information was received from a U.S. Army deserter that there was a plot to bomb the embassy. A search was negative. 0901

October 4, 1971—United States—A Big Brother, Inc., general aviation charter flight of an Aero Commander Hawk 681 from Nashville, Tennessee, to Atlanta, Georgia, was hijacked by two armed men for whom the FAA profile was irrelevant. They diverted the plane to Jacksonville for refueling and supplies before demanding that it proceed to the Bahamas. The two were identified as George Giffe, Jr., a white who was born on July 11, 1936, in Chattanooga, Tennessee, and Bobby Wayne Wallace, who was born on November 23, 1938, in Humphreys County, Tennessee. An FBI agent shot out the plane's tires at Jacksonville, whereupon Giffe killed his wife, the pilot, and himself. The copilot and Wallace were unharmed. Wallace was later charged with piracy and kidnapping but was acquitted on June 22, 1972. 5317

October 4, 1971—Lebanon—An Alia Caravelle flying from Beirut to Amman was the scene of an unsuccessful hijacking by two members of Fatah, a Palestinian man and woman, one of whom was reported killed when overpowered by security guards during the flight. The woman had attempted to pull the pin from a grenade she had carried on board inside a wig and wanted to divert the plane to Iraq. They were identified as Wafa Badel R. T. Awad and Tewfik Hussein Zaiden. 0902

October 6, 1971—Lebanon—A delay to take off from Beirut for technical reasons saved a Jordanian Airlines Caravelle. A time bomb that had been placed inside a suitcase exploded under the wing while being loaded. 0903

October 6, 1971—Greece—Two bombs exploded in U.S. vehicles, causing no injuries and slight damage to the vehicles. 0904-0905

October 6, 1971—Syria—An attempt was made to assassinate Yasir Arafat, chief of the PLO and Fatah, while he was visiting his commandos in Syria's Golan Heights. Fatah blamed "elements which have infiltrated guerrilla ranks." 0906

October 8, 1971—Uruguay—Two light aircraft were hijacked by Tupamaros to distribute leaflets commemorating the takeover of Pando village and Ché Guevara's death. One of the hijacking groups was captured. 5318-5319

October 8, 1971—Venezuela—Incendiary devices were found in the Bello Monte store of an American firm at 5:30 P.M. 0907

October 8, 1971—El Salvador—A bomb exploded in front of a U.S. Peace Corps Training Center near San Salvador. The bomb was discovered by a local guard who threw it into the street before it exploded, preventing serious damage. 0908

October 9, 1971—United States—Eastern Airlines flight 953, a B727 flying from Detroit to Miami and Puerto Rico with forty-four persons on board, was hijacked by a man who threatened a stewardess with a pistol and forced the pilot to fly to Cuba after he had pushed his way on board the plane. The hijacker, for whom the FAA profile was irrelevant, was identified as a white male, Richard Frederick Dixon, who was born on August 5, 1940, in Pontiac, Michigan. The plane, crew, and passengers were allowed to return to Miami from Havana immediately. Dixon was indicted by a federal grand jury in the eastern district of Michigan on January 19, 1972. He returned to the United States on January 8, 1976, and was apprehended in Michigan the next day for the murder of a South Haven, Michigan, police officer. The FBI later identified him as the hijacker. He was convicted of air piracy and kidnapping on December 16, 1976. 5320

October 12, 1971—Cuba—Members of the Cuban Liberation Front claimed credit for an armed attack on a small fishing village on the northern coast, holding the town for more than an hour. In the attack, a border patrol guard and an interior ministry policeman were killed, and four others were injured. The group machine-gunned the town, tore down telephone lines, and sabotaged the village electrical plant before escaping in two boats in the night. Guillermo

Martinez Marquez, the New York spokesman for the Miami-based group headed by José de la Torriente, claimed credit for his organization. 0909

October 12, 1971—Turkey—Turkish terrorists bombed a car belonging to a U.S. Consular Affairs Office in Istanbul, as well as a car owned by the consulate general. Another bomb exploded in the vicinity of a hotel used frequently by transient U.S. government employees. Two days before, a bomb exploded in a Tuslog building but caused no injuries or damage. On October 15, police reported that the Turkish Revolutionary Youth Federation was considering kidnapping diplomats, including the U.S. ambassador. 0910-0913

October 12, 1971—Venezuela—Two men hijacked an Avensa Convair 580 flying from Barcelona to Caracas and diverted it to Cuba. 5321

October 14, 1971—United States—Antimonarchist Iranian students dynamited the Iranian consulate in San Francisco, causing $1 million damage to the consulate and nearby houses and injuring four people. The group was protesting the shah's lavish celebration of the twenty-five hundredth anniversary of the Persian Empire. 0914

October 14, 1971—Colombia—Members of the United Front for Guerrilla Action bombed the Sinclair pipeline. 0915

October 16, 1971—Greece—Bombs detonated in vehicles belonging to JUSMAAG and USAF personnel but caused no personal injuries. 0916-0917

October 16, 1971—Greece—A man attempted to hijack an Olympic Airways YS11A flying from Kalamata to Athens and divert it to Beirut. Claiming to have a bomb, he allowed the plane to land at Athens to refuel. Police boarded the plane and arrested the hijacker, who was identified as Constantine Yannopolous. He was sentenced on October 11, 1972, to eight years and two months. 5322

October 18, 1971—United States—Wein Consolidated Salta flight 15, a B737 flying from Anchorage to Bethel, Alaska, with thirty-five persons on board, was hijacked by a man armed with a pistol who threatened the stewardess and wanted to be taken to Cuba. He was identified as a white male who met the FAA profile and who had served a prison sentence for manslaughter: Del Lavon Thomas, who was born on December 29, 1942, in Hawthorne, California. He allowed the plane to land in Anchorage to permit the passengers to leave. He flew on to Vancouver for refueling and then demanded to fly to Mexico City. However, an hour out of Vancouver, he ordered the plane to turn back, hoping to obtain a larger aircraft (although the stewardess claims that he decided to give up at this point). Upon landing, an RCMP police inspector boarded the plane. One hour later, the crew was allowed to leave, and Thomas surrendered to the RCMP. He was deported to the United States on October 19, 1971, and sentenced on May 12, 1972, to twenty years for air piracy. 5323

October 18, 1971—Canada—A member of the Canadian Hungarian Freedom Fighters Federation assaulted Soviet Premier Aleksei N. Kosygin in Ottawa. 0918

October 18, 1971—United States—The JDL bombed a travel agency in Los Angeles.

October 20, 1971—United States—Members of the JDL fired four rifle shots through the bedroom window of an apartment occupied by members of the Soviet Union's U.N. mission in New York City. 0919

October 20, 1971—Ecuador—A Saeta Viscount flying from Quito to Cuenca with twenty-six passengers was hijacked to Cuba by four men and two women. The plane was allowed to return to Quito. 5324

October 22, 1971—Nicaragua—A plot to kidnap the U.S. ambassador in Managua was revealed. 0920

October 24, 1971—Jordan—Aramco's Tapline was damaged by an explosion. 0921

October 25, 1971—United States—American Airlines flight 98, a B747 flying from New York to San Juan with 221 passengers, was hijacked by a Latin male who did not meet the FAA profile: Angel Lugo Casado, who was born in Ponce, Puerto Rico, on March 1, 1949. Using a dummy gun, he diverted the plane to Cuba. Among those aboard were three sky marshals and a vacationing FBI agent. 5325

October 26, 1971—Greece—A man identified as Thalassinos attempted to hijack an Olympic airliner flying from Athens to Crete and divert it to Rome, but he was overpowered. 5326

October 27, 1971—Portugal—A powerful bomb exploded outside the new NATO headquarters in Lisbon, causing considerable damage to the building but no injuries. 0922

October 30, 1971—Brazil—At 5:30 P.M., a Molotov cocktail was tossed at the back of the car of the president of a Brazilian facility of an American firm, at his home. The back of the car was badly burned. 0923

November 1971—Dominican Republic—A band of leftist guerrillas robbed the Royal Bank of Canada of $50,000. On January 12, 1972, a day-long battle with a group of suspects resulted in police using bazookas and mortars, with eight policemen and four guerrillas dying in the firefight. Plinio Matos Moquete, a communist lawyer accused of being the group's leader, and Harry Jiminez Castillo, who managed to escape, were promised an impartial trial by President Joaquin Balaguer if they surrendered. The fight began at a guerrilla hideout fourteen miles east of the capital and led to riots by students in Santo Domingo. 0924

November 3, 1971—Bolivia—A group of eleven political prisoners and five mutinous guards hijacked an army plane delivering supplies to a prison camp in the jungle and used it to escape to Peru. Upon landing, the Peruvians transferred the hijackers to Chile, where they were granted political asylum. 5327

November 3, 1971—Brazil—A car belonging to the U.S. consul general in São Paulo was damaged by Molotov cocktails, as were the homes of officials of Chicago Bridge Company and Swift and Company. 0925-0927

November 4, 1971—Peru—An anonymous phone call was received at the USIS, threatening to blow up the "cinema section." 0928

November 4, 1971—United States—Five million dollars in damages was caused by a fire set by a seven-year maintenance employee of Consolidated Edisons' nearly completed Indian Point Number 2 plant near Buchanan, New York. According to the BDM Corporation report, "An operating mechanic at the plant was arrested for the crime and later pleaded guilty to arson in the third degree. The fire apparently was set on the first floor of an auxiliary building which housed the control panels, cables, and pumps for the facility. The reactor building and generator building at the site were reportedly not endangered by the fire and there was no release of radioactive material in this case. During the course of the investigation of this case, a group calling itself 'Project: Achilles Heel,' sent a letter to the *New York Times* saying 'Indian Point Guerrillas' were responsible for the fire. Due to the evidence in the case and the tight security precautions employed at the plant, however, the perpetrator of the attack was suspected to be an employee at the plant. . . . The man who admitted the crime was on duty at the plant at the time and was reported to be one of the first persons on the scene of the fire. No reported motive for the attack was found in the press reports, although the arsonist was obviously venting some grievance held against his employers. Some support for his mental incompetence is evidenced by the fact that the employee was arrested at a Veterans Administration psychiatric hospital, where he was a patient. The extent of his psychiatric problems were not disclosed in the report."

November 8, 1971—Portugal—A bomb exploded at a NATO military base at Caparica. 0929

November 9, 1971—Brazil—At 10:05 P.M., the Agua Branca store of an American firm was found to contain an explosive device that had been placed in the folds of a wool blanket. The device, which did not explode, was composed of a pack of cigarettes containing permanganate of potash crystals added to glycerin inside a glass blister with a small cotton fuse. 0930

November 10, 1971—Jordan—Four explosions went off in Amman's Intercontinental Hotel, which is managed by U.S. personnel and which used to have a small amount of U.S. backing. 0931

November 11, 1971—Spain—A sabotage threat was made against an Iberian Airlines 747 flying from Madrid to New York with 259 persons on board. The plane landed at Yarmouth, Nova Scotia, and the passengers were evacuated while the RCMP searched for a bomb. The search was negative.

November 13, 1971—Canada—An Air Canada DC8 flying from Calgary to Toronto with 115 passengers was hijacked by a twenty-six-year-old Canadian, Paul Joseph Cini, a self-styled member of the IRA. Extremely disturbed and upset, he used a shotgun to take over the plane and shot a hole in a partition. However, he allowed the passengers to deplane in Great Falls, where he was given $50,000 of the $1.5 million he had demanded, threatening to blow up the aircraft. He then demanded to be flown to Ireland, where it was assumed he would attempt to contact the IRA. Instead he attempted to jump from the craft with his money, thereby avoiding capture. However, he confused a safety belt with a parachute strap and was knocked out by the pilot as the plane was flying over Calgary. He was later charged with kidnapping and extortion and was sentenced to life imprisonment on April 12, 1972. 5328

November 15, 1971—United States—The Sons of Liberty attempted to bomb a bank in Cambridge, Massachusetts.

November 17, 1971—Trinidad and Tobago—A man attempted to hijack an Arawak Convair on a domestic flight and divert it to Cuba, but he was persuaded by police to surrender at Trinidad. 5329

November 19, 1971—Mexico—Dr. Jaime Castrejon Diez, the rector of the State University of Guerrero and millionaire owner of the Coca-Cola bottling concession in that town, was kidnapped by a group of leftist rural guerrillas believed to be operating in the mountains near Acapulco and led by Genaro Vazquez Rojas, a former schoolteacher. The group demanded the release of nine political prisoners, $200,000 ransom, and trials for fifteen other political prisoners. On November 28, the Mexican government agreed to release the prisoners, who were flown to Cuba. Radio Havana said that the eight men and one woman were accepted for humanitarian reasons. They included five individuals who were said to be close associates of the guerrilla leader, as well as a woman who may have been his sister-in-law. The rector's family paid the ransom on November 30. The government made no reply regarding the fate of the other fifteen prisoners, but the captive was released on December 1. 0932

November 20, 1971—Taiwan—A China Airlines Caravelle flying from Taipei to Hong Kong exploded, probably due to a bomb, over the South China Sea, killing all twenty-five on board.

November 22, 1971—United States—Two members of the Puerto Rican Liberation Front were arrested after firebombing an office building and a bank in Camden, New Jersey. 0933-0934

November 23, 1971—Australia—Croatian terrorists were believed responsible for throwing a bomb at the Yugoslav travel agency in Sydney. 0935

November 24, 1971—United States—Northwest Airlines flight 305, a B727 flying from Washington, D.C., to four other stops, including Portland and Seattle, with thirty-six passengers and a crew of six, was hijacked by an individual who identified himself as D. B. Cooper. He had boarded the flight at Portland and met the FAA profile. Cooper showed a stewardess a briefcase containing several red cylinders conected with wires and gave her a note for the pilot, which demanded $200,000 in $20 bills to be placed in a knapsack, two back parachutes, and two chest parachutes. He allowed the passengers and two of the stewardesses to deplane in Seattle and then demanded to be flown to Reno and Mexico. While the plane was cruising at 197 miles per hour at ten thousand feet (at seven degrees below zero, with a wind-chill of sixty-nine below zero), Cooper used two of the parachutes and bailed out with the twenty-one pounds of money strapped to his body. One was a training chute used by stunt flyers, and the other was a training chute used for demonstrations, the panels of which had been sewn shut so that it could not open. Cooper, wearing a business suit and street shoes, was never seen again. In April 1972, two hundred army troops from Fort Lewis, Washington, spent eighteen days in the area (somewhere in the lowlands of western Washington and Oregon). The FBI reported that it has checked out more than one thousand suspects but had yet to find a substantial lead. Two men were arrested for trying to bilk *Newsweek* magazine of $30,000 for an interview with Cooper, whose spectacular leap spawned imitators. On September 9, 1975, the *Washington Post* reported that the FBI was investigating Fairfax City's Jerry A. Cooper, who fit the hijacker's description. It appears that he has been cleared of all suspicion. On November 23, 1976, a federal grand jury in Portland, Oregon, handed down an indictment against "John Doe, also known as Dan Cooper," who was described as "a male Caucasian, age mid-forties, height 5' 10" to 6 feet, weight 170-180 pounds, physical build average to well built, complexion olive, medium smooth, hair dark black or brown, parted on left, combed back . . .of greasy appearance, sideburns at low ear level, eyes brown or dark, voice without particular accent, using an intelligent vocabulary, and a heavy smoker of cigarettes." The government claimed that this was a capital crime with no statute of limitations, making sure that a possibly relevant five-year statute would not be invoked. One count of the indictment charged Cooper with aircraft piracy, while a second alleged obstruction of interstate commerce by extortion. Cooper's escapades by then had become folk history. A song written about the hijacking became popular in Washington and Oregon. T-shirts and bumper stickers were marketed within seventy-two hours of his jump. On November 28, 1976, a few days after the indictment, the four hundred citizens of Ariel, Washington, and several visitors celebrated Cooper Caper Sunday, with sky-diving, buffalo stew, and souvenir sweatshirts. A public invitation was extended to Cooper, but his presence was not reported. 5330

November 26, 1971—Colombia—Fourteen incendiary bombs were placed in the San Martín store of a U.S. firm. Four of them worked but caused a merchandise damage of only $184.36. 0936

November 27, 1971—Northern Ireland—Individuals suspected of belonging to the IRA conducted armed attacks against five British customs posts.

November 27, 1971—United States—Three armed blacks, for whom the FAA profile was inapplicable, hijacked a TWA B727 and diverted it to Cuba. Forty-six persons were on board the plane, which was taken over on the ground at Albuquerque, refueling from its flight from Phoenix and being prepared to fly on to Chicago and Washington, D.C. The trio used a knife and automatic weapons and demanded to be flown to Africa. They were identified as Michael R. Finney, born in San Francisco on December 9, 1950; Charles R. Hill, born December 15, 1949 in Olney, Illinois; and Ralph L. Goodwin, born on April 29, 1947, in Berkeley, California. The trio were wanted in the slaying of a New Mexico policeman and claimed to be members of the Republic of New Africa. They allowed flight 106 to refuel at Tampa, where the passengers deplaned. Upon arrival in Cuba, the plane was allowed to return to Miami. Goodwin drowned while swimming in Cuba on March 4, 1973. The other two remain fugitives from an indictment handed down by a federal grand jury in the district of New Mexico on December 14, 1971. 0937

November 28, 1971—Egypt—Black September claimed credit for the assassination of Jordanian Prime Minister Wasfi Tell, fifty-two, in Cairo's Sheraton Hotel. Tell was returning from a meeting of the Arab League's Joint Defense Council and was hit point-blank by five pistol bullets as he entered the door, trying to draw his own gun. Jordanian foreign minister Abdullah Sallah was slightly injured, and an Egyptian policeman was seriously wounded. The group of four assassins were immediately captured. They were identified as Monzer Suleiman Khalifa, twenty-seven; Gawad Khali Boghdadi, twenty-three; Ezzat Ahmad Rabah, twenty-three; and Ziad Helou. There appear to have been two others in the squad who managed to escape detection: a female student in Cairo, who was to throw a grenade if the shots missed, and an organizer who provided the money and arms for the attack. According to Khalifa, who stooped to drink Tell's blood after he was hit, "I am proud. Finally I have done it. We have been after him for six months. We have taken our revenge on a traitor." Rabah, the man who fired the shots, said, "We wanted to have him for breakfast, but we had him for lunch instead." The group claimed that the killing was in revenge for the slaying of Palestinian guerrillas in the Jordanian civil war of September 1970, which Palestinians refer to as Black September. They alleged that Tell tortured to death Abu Ali Iyad, Al Fatah's field commander, during the summer of 1971.

Egypt came under heavy Arab pressure, led by Libya, to free the assassins, although Fatah's Khaled al-Hassan said the attack was "one of the acts of terrorist, fascist thinking which conflicts with the thinking of the revolution." Large amounts were allocated to their defense funds, and Egypt finally relased them on bail of 1,000 Egyptian pounds ($2,300) each. They were never brought to trial. Reportedly they lived in Cairo for a year with Libyan financing. They were then told that they were free to leave Cairo and were given transit documents for Beirut. However, the judiciary balked and prevented their travel. In April 1973, a Datsun in Beirut was bombed. A similar Datsun, parked nearby, was owned by Ziad Helou, one of Tell's released assassins.

More information on the planning of the assassination was revealed upon the arrest in Amman in 1973 of Abu Daoud, a Black September leader whom many credited with the planning of the Olympics massacre (see incident 1116). Under interrogation, Daoud claimed that the Tell assassination planner was Mohammed Youssef el Najjar (also known as Abu Youssef), who "personally assigned the men through Yahya Ashur, he transported them to Cairo and subsequently he himself carried their weapons to Cairo. At that time Abu Youssef was a member of the PLO's political department and chairman of the Higher Committee for Palestinian Affairs in Lebanon, a body that serves as a liaison between the three hundred thousand Palestinians in Lebanon and the Lebanese authorities." Youssef appears to have died on April 10, 1973, in an Israeli raid on Black September facilities in Beirut.

Other reports claimed that the PLO provided the assassins' bail on February 29, 1972, and that the PFLP claimed responsibility for the assassination. 0938

November 29, 1971—Uruguay—Michele Ray, a French journalist, claimed that she was kidnapped and held for thirty-eight hours by members of the OPR-33. Some officials in Uruguay speculated that the thirty-four-year-old Ray had arranged her kidnapping in order to interview the terrorists. 0939

November 20, 1971—United States—Richard Golden Adams told the stewardess of an Eastern Airlines flight that he ''might want to go to Cuba.'' He was arrested by security guards when a gun was found in his hand luggage. 5331

December 3, 1971—France—A Pakistan International Airlines 720B flying from Paris to Karachi, Pakistan, was hijacked by Jean Mena Kay, who threatened to blow up the plane if he was not given twenty tons of medicine and flown to Bangladesh. He was overpowered by a policeman. During the scuffle, another policeman was slightly wounded. Twenty-two persons were on board the flight, which had not yet taken off. Kay was given a five-year suspended sentence in October 1972. 5332

December 5, 1971—United States—The Jewish Armed Resistance claimed credit for bombing two Russian gift shops, one in New York City and the other in Shakopee, Minnesota. Bombs placed in the doorways shattered glass. A call to the Associated Press identified the perpetrators. 0940-0941

December 7, 1971—United States—Two bomb explosions that went off at 4 A.M. rocked the Stanford Linear Accelerator, causing around $100,000 damage. According to the BDM report, ''2 bombs caused heavy damage to the electronics equipment in the control room. . . .According to Dr. Wolfgang Panofsky, Director . . .' the bombs destroyed a master oscillator and a device that controls the burst of the beam. Damage was well under $100,000 and should have little impact on the operation of the accelerator.' The blasts occurred while the accelerator was closed for routine maintenance. The entire center is regarded as a minimum security operation and does not use any licensed nuclear materials. The fact that this facility had minimum security status undoubtedly aided the perpetrators of this incident. In terms of access, the accelerator was a relatively easy target. The building, made of corrugated metal, has many windows, most of them open at the time of the incident. In addition, the doors to the facility were not locked. A three-foot chain-link fence was the only obstacle between the building and a nearby road. Although guards were on duty at the time of the explosions, they did not detect any intruders. The damage was discovered by workmen who were arriving at the plant the morning after the bombing. No information was available concerning the perpetrators of the bombing. The only clue uncovered, according to the sources, was the fact that people were seen in the general vicinity of the accelerator several days prior to the blast. A radiation technician reported that he had seen people on a ridge 3,000 yards from the accelerator several days prior to the incident. There were no clues, suspects, or motives for the bombing.''

December 11, 1971—Pakistan—An armed man entered the USIS library and ordered the local employees out. Minutes later a deafening explosion was heard. Destruction of the library was almost total. On December 18, a Bengali mob went to the wrecked office and demanded that the U.S. flag be hauled down and the Bangladesh flag be raised. The Americans complied. In Lahore, the first anti-U.S. demonstration in West Pakistan occurred when fifteen persons, mostly students, entered the USIS library. Some were armed with clubs and were shouting anti-U.S. slogans. After causing minor damage, the group was forced out. 0942

December 12, 1971—Nicaragua—A Lancia BAC111 flying from San Salvador to Managua and Miami with fifty-four persons on board was hijacked out of Managua by three armed members of the FSLN, who demanded to be taken to Cuba. They were identified as Gustavo J. Villanueva Valdes, Raoul Arana Irias, and Leonel M. Valladares. Upon landing at San José, Costa Rica, for refueling, over two hundred civil guards, on the orders of President José Figueres, stormed the plane. One of the hijackers was fatally shot during the battle, and a passenger and another hijacker were wounded. Several passengers were injured when they jumped from the plane as it burst into flames. The two captured hijackers were returned to Nicaragua but escaped custody during the Nicaraguan earthquake of December 23, 1972. They are still at large. 0943

December 13, 1971—Ireland—Two explosive devices were attached to a U.S. Marine security guard vehicle. One device failed to go off. Damage was minor, and no personal injuries were reported. 0944

December 15, 1971—United Kingdom—A member of Black September attempted to assassinate Jordanian Ambassador Zaid Rifai on a London street. His chauffeur-driven Daimler was winding through the streets of Kensington on its way to the embassy in Campden Hill when it reached the Duchess of Bedford's Walk junction. William Parsons, an Electricity Board worker who was repairing cables, noticed a man standing in a traffic island pull a Sten gun from under his raincoat and fire thirty rounds into the car. One of the bullets pierced Rifai's right hand, shattering almost every bone in it. He ordered the driver to speed on, and after the engine stalled, Rifai was taken to safety. The attacker ran down Holland Street and drove off in a red Hillman Hunter, which had its engine running. He was later identified as Frazeh Khelfa, an Algerian who used the alias Khelfa Same, and was arrested in Lyons the next month.

The Lyons court recommended that France grant the United Kingdom's extradition request, but the French Ministry of Foreign Affairs decided to send him to Algeria, which, according to many reporters, invented a charge against him so that he could return there.

An Al Fatah Cairo broadcast the next day approved of the attack, claiming that Rifai was Hussein's liaison with American intelligence. The Jordanian government on December 17 claimed that Black September was "only a mask used by Fatah to hide its treacherous schemes. . . . We know very well those in Fatah who are in charge of these schemes. . . . They shall not escape punishment." Reports claim that a former senior official of Razd, the Fatah intelligence service, Ali Hassan Salameh, organized the attack. Reporter David Tinnin learned that the ammunition had been stored in Libya's Bonn embassy. The U.K.-made Sterling 9-mm submachine gun used in the Rafai attack, as well as those used in an attack on five Jordanians in West Germany, were traced to a consignment sold to Libya. 0945

December 16, 1971—Bolivia—A Lloyd Air Boliviano F862 flying from Sucre to La Paz was hijacked by Wilfred Urdininea, who killed the pilot and injured the copilot and a passenger. The hijacker, who never specified where he wanted to land, was killed by police. Some reports claim that he may have wanted to fly to Cuba. 5333

December 16, 1971—Switzerland—Black September sent a parcel bomb to Jordan's U.N. mission in Geneva, addressed to Ambassador Ibrahim Zreikat. Police and firemen were called in to examine the parcel, which exploded as they were opening it, injuring three people, including two Swiss policemen, and destroying the mission's reception room. Zreikat was in another room and escaped unharmed. 0946

December 18, 1971—United States—Five members of the East Coast Conspiracy to Save Lives, an antiwar group, were arrested after attempting to pour concrete on the Penn Central Railroad tracks near an American Machine and Foundry Corporation bomb-casing factory. According to the FBI's J. Edgar Hoover, the group was led by the Berrigans, two radical priests active in left-wing causes.

December 19, 1971—Japan—Masaaki Arai set fire to the toilet of an All Nippon Airways Fokker F27 flying from Fukui to Tokyo with fifteen persons on board. He then attacked the captain in the cockpit with a knife and was subdued by a copilot and passenger after injuring three people. He later died of a self-inflicted wound.

December 20, 1971—Sudan—An unidentified person called the principal officers of the U.S. Interests Section and stated that a bomb had been placed in the Interests Section. A search of the premises, including the USIS facility, by U.S. Marines and the Sudanese police and bomb disposal squad was negative. 0947

December 22, 1971—Dominican Republic—An Alas Del Caribe Air (a Dominican Republic airline) Islander BN2A flying from Santiago to Santo Domingo was hijacked by Urbano M. Porcilio. The plane landed in Dajabón, Dominican Republic, where the hijacker was overpowered by the pilot and passengers. 5334

December 24, 1971—United States—Northwest flight 734, a B707 flying from Minneapolis to Chicago with twenty-nine passengers, was hijacked by a white male who met the FAA profile: Everett Leary Holt, who was born on December 19, 1946 in Indianapolis, Indiana. Shortly after the plane took off, he fired a revolver into the bulkhead and ordered a stewardess to inform the captain that he had just killed a man. He demanded $300,000 and two parachutes. The flight landed at Chicago, where the money was delivered, and the hijacker allowed all but two of the passengers to deplane. While Holt was counting the money the cockpit crew escaped. Holt next went to the lavatory, and one of the three stewardesses escaped. The plane was then spotlighted, and the other two stewardesses and one of the passengers jumped to the ground. Holt threw out the money and surrendered. He was indicted by a federal grand jury in the northern district of Illinois on December 29, 1971. Charges were dismissed on May 2, 1975 due to mental incompetence. He was remanded to the custody of the state. He was committed to a mental institution on June 21, 1972. 5335

December 26, 1971—United States—American Airlines flight 47, a B707 flying from Toronto to San Francisco, was hijacked out of Chicago and diverted to Salt Lake City by a white male who did not meet the FAA profile: Donald L. Coleman, who was born in Chicago on September 17, 1947. Holding a plastic replica of a pistol, he claimed he had a pressure-type bomb on his person that was set to explode if the aircraft descended to twenty-five hundred feet. He demanded $200,000. He was subdued by two passengers and two stewardesses, with no injuries to any of the ninety passengers. Personal effects and statements made following his arrest indicated that he wanted to prove that any person could hijack an airliner. He was convicted on June 5, 1972, and sentenced to two ten-year concurrent terms on July 28, 1973, for air piracy and interference with flight crew members. He was released on five years' probation on September 16, 1974. 5336

December 26, 1971—Canada—An Air Canada DC9 flying from Thunder Bay to Toronto with eighty-nine persons on board was hijacked by a U.S. citizen, Patrick D. Critton, who was armed with a revolver and hand grenade, and wished to escape prosecution. He allowed the passengers to deplane in Toronto but kept the crew for a flight to Cuba. The plane was returned the next day, without the bank robber. 5337

December 29, 1971—United States—An explosive device placed on a seat in the cabin of a general aviation Turbo Commander plane that was not in service exploded, destroying the plane and making a large hole in the roof of the hanger at Elkhart, Illinois. The door of the hangar and the door of the aircraft had been forced open prior to the explosion. A suspect was identified. No casualties were reported.

1972—United States—In early 1972, it was discovered that two college students had planned to place typhoid fever bacteria in the Chicago water supply. The bacteria culture, developed in the school's laboratory, would have been destroyed by the cholorination systems used in the Mid-west.

1972—Philippines—On February 10, 1976, President Ferdinand Marcos disclosed that he had discovered a plot to kidnap Philippine Foreign Secretary Carlos P. Romulo and U.S. Ambassador Henry Byroade before he proclaimed martial law in 1972. Marcos claimed that he had to send the ambassador out of the country because "I laughingly told him, 'You better go out, I'll never pay any ransom for you.' " 0949

January 1972—Guatemala—An American businessman's home was bombed. 0948

January 1972—Kuwait—Facilities of the Kuwait Oil Company, which is partially U.S.-owned, were damaged twice. One of the incidents was confirmed as sabotage. 0963-0964

January 2-9, 1972—Worldwide—At least thirteen letter bombs were mailed by the PFLP-GC from various locations in Europe to individuals in Israel. Most of the letters were posted in Vienna. One bomb disposal expert was injured while dismantling one of the bombs in a Tel Aviv police station on January 3. Many prominent Israelis, including General Ezer Weizman, former air force commander, received the bombs. 0950-0962

January 3, 1972—Northern Ireland—A bomb exploded on the back of a beer truck on Callender street in Belfast, injuring sixty-two people but killing no one. The IRA was believed responsible.

January 5, 1972—Israel—Palestinian terrorists set bombs in Kfar Saba and Nethanya, injuring seven people. 0965-0966

January 7, 1972—United States—In San Francisco, Chicago, and New York City, police defused bombs with nine-month timing devices. Between January 13 and 19, Ronald Kaufman, a thirty-three-year-old psychologist and an army private absent without leave, was indicted for placing eight bombs in safe deposit boxes in eight bank branches in those cities. Letters he sent to newspapers demanded the release of imprisoned radicals.

January 7, 1972—United States—Pacific Southwest flight 902, a B727 flying from San Francisco to Los Angeles with 145 persons on board, was hijacked by a black couple who met the FAA profile and were accompanied by their child. They wanted to go to Africa and were identified as Allen G. Sims, who was born on September 8, 1948, in New York City, and Ida P. Robinson, who was born on February 11, 1951, in San Francisco. Sims used a pistol and shotgun to threaten the stewardess and passengers. They allowed the passengers to deplane at Los Angeles and demanded a plane large enough to fly to Africa. They were told that none was available, so they settled on flying to Cuba. They refueled at Tampa airport, which closed down for two hours. The plane and crew were returned safely. The hijackers remain fugitives from an indictment handed down on August 2, 1972, by a federal grand jury in the central district of California. 5338

January 9, 1972—Jordan—The U.S. embassy in Amman received an anonymous phone call warning that a bomb had been placed in embassy grounds. A search was negative. 0967

January 11, 1972—Brazil—A uniformed state military guard stationed at the Pôrto Alegre residence of the U.S. consul was shot in the leg by two unidentified assailants at 3:30 A.M. The attackers fled on foot. 0968

January 12, 1972—United States—Braniff flight 38, a B727 flying from Houston to Dallas, was hijacked by a white male who met the FAA profile: Billy Eugene Hurst, Jr., who was born on September 29, 1949, in Walters, Oklahoma. Claiming his briefcase was stuffed with dynamite, he demanded $1 million and ten parachutes. He also demanded to be flown to South America. While he held seven crew members hostages while waiting for the money to be delivered in Dallas, the pilot was informed that the starter plugs of the number two engine were being pulled, and the gun that Hurst had asked to be sent to the plane had been fixed so that its firing pin would not strike. Unfortunately the radio broadcast this information to the Dallas public during the incident, nearly foiling the police's plans and endangering the hostages. The crew and passengers managed to deplane, and Hurst surrendered to the police. He was sentenced to twenty years for aircraft piracy on February 2, 1973. 5339

January 14, 1972—Canada—Rejean Turpin, thirty-three, threatened to sabotage an Air Canada flight from Montreal to Barbados if one of the passengers did not repay him some money. His phone call was traced, and Turpin was later arrested. He was sentenced to three years in the penitentiary.

January 16, 1972—Israel—An American nurse was killed and a minister and other individuals were wounded when Palestinian guerillas ambushed a car in the Israeli-occupied Gaza strip. 0969

January 17, 1972—Iran—The U.S. mission premises in Tehran were subjected to four bombings. Two local guards suffered minor injuries at the USEA commissary, and twenty-four windows were broken at the Iran American Cultural Center. 0970

January 19, 1972—Spain—The ETA kidnapped Lorenzo Zabala, an industrialist, near Bilbao. He was freed on January 22 after his instruments company rehired 120 of 183 dismissed workers, increased wages by $4 weekly, and granted workers a voice in management decisions. Police released two priests and ten workers arrested during a search for the kidnappers.

January 20, 1972—United States—The VEPCO Surry licensed nuclear facility was subjected to a bomb threat.

January 20, 1972—United States—Hughes Airwest flight 800, a DC9 flying from Las Vegas to Reno with seventy-one on board, was hijacked by a white male who met the FAA profile: Richard Charles LaPoint, who was born in Boston on September 10, 1948. LaPoint, a Denver salesman who had been a helicopter gunner in Vietnam, claimed he had a bomb (which turned out to be fake) and demanded $50,000 and two parachutes. He allowed the passengers and two stewardesses off the plane and parachuted in daylight outside Denver, spraining an ankle upon landing. He was spotted by the pilot of a BAC111 plane, which had joined the search for him. The pilot led Colorado highway patrolmen to the field with a set of locator beacons of the type used to find downed Vietnam pilots. He was sentenced to forty years for aircraft piracy on May 25, 1972. 5340

January 22, 1972—United States—A pipe bomb exploded in the New York City office of Portuguese Airlines. The bombing was in protest of Portuguese rule in Guinea-Bissau. 0971

January 25, 1972—Northern Ireland—A telephoned bomb threat caused evacuation of the U.S. consulate in Belfast. A search was negative. 0972

January 26, 1972—United States—An SFO Helicopter Company general aviation helicopter that was to fly from Berkeley, California, to San Francisco was seized on the ground be a white male for whom the FAA profile was irrelevant: Patrick H. McAlroy, who was born in Santa Monica, California, on January 31, 1945. He demanded a cash payment and the use of a commercial helicopter to take him to San Francisco airport where a jet was to ready to take him to Cuba. He surrendered prior to being provided an aircraft and was committed to a mental institution by the state on January 15, 1972. 5341

January 26, 1972—Sweden—A Jugoslovenski Aerotransport DC9, flying from Stockholm to Belgrade with stops in Copenhagen and Zagreb, crashed after a bomb exploded in the forward luggage compartment. The plane fell near České Kamenice, Czechoslovakia, killing twenty-nine persons. The sole survivor, a stewardess who was injured, fell approximately fifteen thousand feet in the tail section. A Croatian nationalist organization claimed credit for the bombing, which it said was an attempted assassination of the Yugoslav premier. 0973

January 26, 1972—United States—A woman died of smoke inhalation as a result of a bomb that exploded in the New York City offices of Columbia Artists, a talent-booking organization located a few blocks away from Sol Hurok's offices, which was also firebombed (see next entry). Witnesses claimed that the bomb was set by two "clean-cut and white" young men. Anonymous phone calls to the Associated Press and NBC claimed that the bombs were to protest "deaths and imprisonment of Soviet Jews . . .Soviet culture is responsible . . .Never again! (the JDL slogan)." JDL Leader Meir Kahane said that the acts were "insane. It isn't the first time our slogan has been used. I know our group wouldn't do this."

January 26, 1972—United States—A few minutes later, a firebomb exploded in the New York offices of Sol Hurok Enterprises, which booked Soviet performers. A Jewish receptionist, Iris Kones, was killed, and thirteen people, including Hurok, were injured. Considerable damage to the offices was reported. Four JDL members were arrested for the bombings at Hurok's and Columbia's offices.

January 26, 1972—United States—Mohawk flight 452, an FH227 flying from Albany, New York, to New York City with forty-five persons on board, was hijacked by a white male who met the FAA profile: Merlyn L. St. George, also known as Heinrick von George and W. St. George, who was born in St. Paul, Minnesota, on July 13, 1926. Using a fake bomb and a track starter's pistol, he demanded $200,000, four parachutes, and a flight to Poughkeepsie, New York. He allowed the passengers to get off in Purchase, New York, where the money was paid. He held a stewardess hostage for seven hours and was killed by an FBI agent as he and the stewardess entered a car. 5342

January 27, 1972—Austria—A time bomb believed to have been placed by Croatian terrorists exploded on a train en route from Vienna to Zagreb, injuring six persons. 0974

January 28, 1972—United Kingdom—An individual threatened to blow up a BOAC 747 in flight unless he was given $260,000. When he arrived at the airport office to collect the money, he was arrested.

January 29, 1972—United Kingdom—A mentally disturbed Polish émigré spilled paint thinner in the lobby of the U.S. embassy in London and ignited it. The fire was quickly brought under control and damage was negligible.

January 29, 1972—United States—TWA flight 2, a B707 flying from Los Angeles to New York with 101 persons on board, was hijacked by a white male who met the FAA profile: Garrett Brock Trapnell, a former mental patient who was born in Boston on January 31, 1938. He hid an automatic pistol in a false plastic cast on his arm and threatened the crew and passengers. He changed his demands several times, which included a flight to Dallas, a flight to Europe, $306,800, and the release of Angela Davis and a friend from jail. An FBI agent posing as a crewman shot and captured the hijacker in New York City. Trapnell was ordered to undergo mental tests before arraignment on air piracy charges. During his trial, he claimed that his evil alter ego Gregg Ross was responsible. During the first trial, a juror believed him to be insane, necessitating a retrial. On July 20, 1973, he was ultimately sentenced to concurrent terms of twenty years, ten years, and life imprisonment for unlawful interference with the crew, possession of a gun, and aerial piracy. 5343

February 1, 1972—Austria—A bomb threat was telephoned to the U.S. embassy in Vienna. It received another bomb threat by telephone against the Amerika Haus, and a nonspecific telephone threat was made against the U.S. ambassador. 0975-0977

February 2, 1972—Ireland—The British embassy in Dublin was firebombed by the IRA. 0978

February 2, 1972—West Germany—The Second of June Movement placed a bomb in a boathouse used by British army officers, killing a German employee who was checking the explosive device. The group claimed to be commemorating the anniverary of a bloody event in Northern Ireland. 0979

February 4, 1972—Canada—Konstantinos Issoghos, twenty-nine, phoned the Vancouver office of CP Air and threatened to blow up planes in flight if he was not given $200,000. One bomb was found and dismantled in the airport. Three flights were delayed. The money was not paid, and Issoghos was later arrested.

February 5, 1972—Brazil—A British sailor on shore leave in Rio de Janeiro was killed by a blast of machine-gun fire from a passing car. A leaflet claimed the action was in solidarity with the "combatants of Ireland and of all the world" and was signed by four Brazilian extremists. 0980.

February 6, 1972—Netherlands—Oil tanks belonging to Gulf Oil's gas-pumping station in Ravenstein were set on fire by explosions. Black September accused the company of helping the Israelis. Reports claimed that two Palestinians, a Jordanian, a Belgian, an Algerian, and a Frenchman were responsible for the sabotage. French authorities arrested the Algerian. In March 1974, the Belgian was caught and sentenced in April 1972 to three years' imprisonment, with thirty months of the sentence suspended. 0981

February 6, 1972—West Germany—Five Jordanian workers who were allegedly spying for Israel were murdered in Bruehl, near Cologne. Black September took responsibility. Reporter David Tinnin learned that the ammunition had been stored in the basement of Libya's Bonn embassy. The U.K.-made Sterling-9mm submachine gun used in the attack on Rifai (see incident 0945) as well as those used in this attack were traced to a consignment sold to Libya. 0982

February 8, 1972—West Germany—Black September claimed responsibility for bombing the Streuber Motor factory in Hamburg. The company's plant made electrical generators for Israeli aircraft engines. 0983

February 10, 1972—Northern Ireland—Two British soldiers were killed when their car hit an IRA mine placed in the road in Cullyhanna.

February 16, 1972—United States—Two bombs exploded in the Manchester, New Hampshire, police department. Three were discovered in the fire department in the same building, and a fourth was recovered from the police chief's office before detonating. Damage was estimated at $5,000. A white couple was apprehended while fleeing the building. Letters found on the woman were addressed to New Hampshire newspapers and signed by the People's Liberation Army, claiming that the attacks were to protest the Vietnam war and the recent arrest of demonstrators.

February 17, 1972—Greece—In Athens, the private automobile of the JUSMAAG commander received minor damage from a bomb that went off around midnight while the vehicle was parked in front of his residence. Two other cars belonging to U.S. diplomats in Athens were bombed. The attacks were credited to the Resistance, Liberation, and Independence Organization (AAA). 0984-0986

February 18, 1972—Japan—Five members of the United Red Army held the wife of a mountain lodge caretaker hostage in the lodge, ninety miles northwest of Tokyo. The incident caused a national sensation, and during a televised attack by the police, two policemen and one bystander were killed.

February 19, 1972—Egypt—An Alia Caravelle flying from Cairo to Amman with thirty-seven persons on board was the scene of an abortive hijacking. Salah Mahdi Mustafi, also known as Jamil Abdel Hassan Ayoub, used a hand grenade in an attempt to divert the plane to Tripoli, Libya, as it left Cairo. He was overpowered by Jordanian security guards. The Jordanian National Liberation Movement claimed responsibility. 0987

February 22, 1972—West Germany—The Esso Oil pipeline near Hamburg was sabotaged by Black September, which accused the company of aiding the Israelis. 0988

February 22, 1972—United Kingdom—A bomb planted inside a car in front of the kitchen of the Aldershot Army Base, thirty-five miles from London, exploded, ripping through the officers' mess of the parachute brigade, which had been involved in what the IRA described as the "Londonderry massacre," which had entailed the shooting of several Northern Ireland residents. Seven people were killed immediately, including five waitresses, a gardener, and an army chaplain. Nineteen others, including fourteen soldiers, were injured. Two people later died of their wounds. The dining room was empty at the time of the blast, which was the first attack by the IRA in Britain since World War II. Three people were later arrested, and two were charged with conspiracy. Noel Jenkinson, a forty-two-year-old IRA explosives expert, was sentenced on November 14 to life imprisonment in England. 0989

February 22, 1972—India—Lufthansa flight 649, a B747 flying from New Delhi to Athens with 173 passengers and a crew of sixteen was hijacked thirty minutes after takeoff by five Palestinian guerrillas who burst into the cockpit armed with hand grenades, dynamite, and pistols. According to the pilot, Captain Erwin Zoller, the group gave him a set of compass readings, which would place the plane in the desert along the Red Sea on the Arabian peninsula's coast. He persuaded the hijackers to land at Aden, Southern Yemen, instead. Among the passengers was Joseph P. Kennedy, the nineteen-year-old son of the late Senator Robert Kennedy, who had been touring India. Many speculate that the hijackers would use Kennedy as a bargaining chip to obtain the release of Sirhan Sirhan, but they apparently were unaware of his presence. Reports of the demands of the group vary. The Rand Corporation lists them as requesting the release of three Arabs held for the slaying of five Jordanians (see incident 0982), as well as the release of four Palestinians who murdered Wasfi Tal (see incident 0938). There is a similar question regarding their organizational affiliation. Various reports claim that they called themselves the Organization for Victims of Zionist Occupation, the Organization for Resistance to Zionist Conquest of Palestine, and the Organization for Resistance to Zionist Occupation. The individual members were identified as Yusaf Al Khatib, the group's leader who was one of the three PFLP men involved in the 1968 hijacking of an El Al airliner (see incident 0077); Kasim Ben S. Mohamad; Abdel R. Almaki; Sudan M. Aljram; and one unidentified male. Baghdad radio broadcast what it claimed was a message read to the passengers attacking ''the flagging and defeatist attitude certain Arab regimes are adopting'' regarding Israel and German aid to Israel. ''We will pursue the enemy everywhere and strike him and uproot him throughout the world.'' The Tuesday morning of the hijacking, an individual in Cologne sent a letter that arrived that afternoon at the office of the chief of Lufthansa, which is partially government-owned. Although the passengers had already been released and only the crew members, seven of them stewardesses, remained on board the plane, it threatened to blow up the plane along with the passengers and crew if $5 million was not paid by 9 A.M. Wednesday. Meanwhile the hijackers wired the plane with explosives. The letter demanded that the money be carried to a secret location outside Beirut. Georg Leber, West German minister of transport, ensured that the instructions were carried out and sent two officials from the Foreign Ministry to inform the hijackers of the government's decision. Lufthansa sent one of its security agents as a courier via Athens on a charter flight. Ninety minutes before the deadline, Aden's civil aviation chief, Mahmoud Asari, talked the hijackers into freeing the passengers. After being informed that the money had been delivered, the group surrendered to South Yemeni authorities, who released them on February 27. The West Germans had announced the payment of the ransom on February 25. Israeli security sources claimed that

$1 million of the ransom was paid by the PFLP to the South Yemeni government as landing fees. On March 14, PFLP chief George Habash announced in a Beirut news conference that his organization was not responsible for the hijacking.

Reporter John Cooley learned that a rightist faction of the PFLP was responsible and was denounced by the left at a PFLP conference in Beirut. Habash accused them of hiding the ransom in secret bank accounts. The leftists said they would form the Popular Revolutionary Front for the Liberation of Palestine. Reconstruction of the case discovered that the first skyjacker had boarded the plane at Hong Kong. He was joined by two others at Bangkok, and the last two boarded at Delhi. 0990

March 1972—United States—The Secret Cuban Government claimed credit for bombing a theater in New York City. 0991

March 1972—Puerto Rico—The Secret Cuban Government claimed credit for bombing two drugstores in San Juan. 0992-0993

March 1, 1972—Northern Ireland—Forty-three people were injured in a bomb explosion in Londonderry. Two teenagers were found dead in the back of a van outside a Belfast hospital.

March 2, 1972—Greece—A bomb went off in the private automobile of the USIS press officer in front of his home. The explosion damaged the car but caused no injuries. 0994

March 4, 1972—Northern Ireland—Two young girls were killed and 130 people were injured when a bomb exploded in the busy Abercorn Restaurant in the center of Belfast. Many of the injured were badly mutilated.

March 6, 1972—Northern Ireland—A bomb exploded in a Belfast theater, injuring fifty-two.

March 7, 1972—United States—A Chalk's Flying Service Grumman Goose 73, a general aviation craft, was entered on the ground in Miami by two fugitives from justice who forced the copilot to fly to Havana. They were identified as two black males for whom the FAA profile was not applicable: Joseph T. Bennett, who was born in Chicago on August 25, 1948, and James W. Brewton, who was born on March 30, 1950, in Chicago. The two shot and wounded the pilot, James Cothron, and a mechanic, Douglas McKenzie, as well as a bystander. Cothron had refused to start the plane's engines. Five passengers were on board the flight, a sixth jumped off and sounded an alarm that the Bahamas-bound plane had been diverted. Brewton was killed during an attempted robbery in Jamaica on December 15, 1975. Bennett remains a fugitive from an indictment handed down in March 25, 1972, by a federal grand jury in the southern district of Florida. 5344

March 7, 1972—United States—National Airlines flight 67, a B727 flying from Tampa to Miami and Melbourne, Florida, with forty-seven passengers, was hijacked by a white youth for whom the FAA profile was not applicable: Edmond M. Mckee, Jr., who was born in the Panama Canal Zone on March 30, 1957. Waving a gun, he forced his way aboard the aircraft and demanded to be taken to Sweden. The captain talked him out of this idea, and he was overpowered by a federal marshal. Charges against him were dismissed on July 25, 1973. He was placed under state supervision. No charges were brought against him by the state. 5345

March 7, 1972—United States—An anonymous caller warned that four TWA planes would be blown up at six-hour intervals unless he was paid $2 million. A bomb exploded in a TWA B707 in Las Vegas. The plane had been searched in New York, and the device exploded ten hours after the crew and passengers had deplaned, causing no injuries to those seventeen persons. The bomb had been placed in the right rear portion of the cockpit. President Nixon ordered tighter security measures. Dynamite was found in unclaimed luggage at Seattle Airport from a United flight from San Francisco. The device was found to be inoperable. A TWA B707 flying fifty-two persons from New York to Los Angeles was turned back. Dogs found plastic explosives less than one hour before they had been timed to detonate. All flights were delayed from half an hour to an hour. An attempt to pay the money failed.

March 8, 1972—United States—A man carrying a pistol was arrested in New York City. A phone call later warned that a Lufthansa plane flying from New York to Munich would be hijacked. The plane was searched in Cologne and then continued on to Munich. 5346

March 10, 1972—Columbia—At 10:30 P.M., a timed explosive device placed in a grated vent of the Medellín USIS Binational Center outside the director's office exploded, causing no injuries and minor damage. The bomb was judged to be of sufficient force to have caused casualties. 0995

March 10, 1972—Yugoslavia—The USIS library in Belgrade received a letter stating that a bomb was to be placed in the library at "exactly 18:15" by the "Trotskyist Organization." The library was closed and searched, but no bomb was found. 0996

March 11, 1972—Italy—An Alitalia Caravelle twin engine flying thirty-seven persons from Rome to Milan was hijacked by Mrs. Attillia Lazzeri, fifty-five, who was armed with a pistol and what she claimed were grenades in her handbag. She was protesting her sister's commitment to a mental institution and forced the plane to fly to Munich, where she allowed the passengers and crew to deplane. The pilot talked her into surrendering to police. The Germans issued a warrant for her arrest on suspicion of air piracy. Italian authorities charged her with abduction and illegal possession of arms. 5347

March 11-12, 1972—United States—Billy Owen Williams, forty-six, threatened to blow up the New York facilities of Pan Am, demanding $160,000. He had been threatening to blow up the aircraft and installations for some time. When he came to collect the money, he was overpowered by authorities.

March 13, 1972—United States—Ronald D. Rearick threatened to sabotage airline facilities in Salt Lake City. He was arrested immediately after taking possession of a parcel containing a ransom payment.

March 13, 1972—United States—The General Electric Company's licensed nuclear facility in San José, California, received a bomb threat.

March 19, 1972—France—French riot police were sent to guard Soviet Aeroflot planes after threats were made against them if 2 million Swiss francs were not paid.

March 19, 1972—United States—A Tortugas Airways Cessna 206, a general aviation plane chartered to fly five persons from Key West to Dry Tortugas Islands, was hijacked by a white couple for whom the FAA profile was not applicable; they diverted the plane to Havana harbor. No injuries were reported, and it is not known if they used weapons. They were variously identified as Mr. and Mrs. Bob Sands, and as John H. Jennings, who was born in Butte, Montana, on January 14, 1943, and Janyce Reed, who was born in El Paso, Texas, on June 28, 1948. They remain fugitives from an indictment handed down by a federal grand jury in the southern district of Florida on June 5, 1972. 5348

March 20, 1972—Northern Ireland—Six people were killed and another died later when a bomb exploded on Belfast's Donegall Street. Two of the dead were policemen, 146 others were injured.

March 20, 1972—Ireland—Two of three letter bombs mailed to three IRA offices in Dublin exploded when their packages were opened. The only injury reported was to Sean MacStiofain, the Provisional IRA's chief of staff, who was slightly wounded. 0997-0999

March 21, 1972—Jamaica—A Jamaica Air Taxi Ltd. Cessna 182 that had been chartered to take an excursion flight from Kingston around Jamaica was hijacked by the two people who had rented the plane for sightseeing. One man pulled a knife and ordered the pilot to fly to Cuba. The pair identified themselves as Mr. Hughes and Mr. Garth and were later identified as Charles Schwandner and Steven Pera. 5349

March 21. 1972—France—At 9:15 A.M., a shot was fired through the open French doors of the U.S. vice-consul's home in Strasbourg, causing no injuries. The quarters are located in the consulate. 1000

March 21, 1972—Uruguay—The Armed Popular Front (FAP) claimed credit for the robbery of $5,000 from the Israeli Bank of Uruguay. In its April 3 communiqué, it claimed it would fight "Zionist capitalism" and would kill "the two strongest figures of Zionism" in Uruguay if the bank did not meet its monetary demands. 1001-1002

March 21, 1972—Argentina—Eight members of the ERP's Luis Pujales and Segundo Telesforo Gomez units kidnapped Oberdan Sallustro, the president and managing director of the Italian-owned company, Fiat of Argentina, while he was en route to work. The group demanded the release of fifty of the more than five hundred political prisoners being held by the government, giving $1 million worth of school supplies and shoes to schoolchildren in poor areas of the country, the reinstatement of 250 workers who had been fired in a 1971 labor strike, the release of SITRAC/SITRAM workers who had been jailed, and publication of ERP communiqués. The group claimed that the fifty-six-year-old manager was responsible for the repression of workers. Fiat agreed to the ransom demand, but President Lanusse on March 24 said, "I will not negotiate with common delinquents," and warned Fiat that its executives would be prosecuted for "illicit association" if they continued contact with the kidnappers. A police car on April 10 was fired on by several guerrillas when their people's prison was discovered. During the attack, Sallustro was executed by his captors, all but one of whom escaped. The same day, General Juan Carlos Sanchez, who had claimed that his counterinsurgency program had eliminated 85 percent of the country's guerillas, was assassinated by a combined ERP-FAR tactical unit that left a flyer: "Sanchez, the 15% lives!"

The government continued to take a hard line against the terrorists and engaged in a nationwide search for the killers. Among those captured was José Joe Baxter, who had begun his guerrilla career in the 1960s with the ultra-rightist Tacuara movement.

On April 11, President Lanusse rejected Italian President Giovanni Leone's request for negotiations with the ERP, saying that this was an internal matter. The ERP replied that it would kill Sallustro "at the appropriate moment." On

April 18, the army announced its capture of an eight-member ERP team in the case. On April 19, police in San Javier, Tucumán Province, captured Eduardo Coppo and Manuel Negrin, ERP members who were also involved. Fifteen women and three men, alleged ERP members, were also arrested. Six accomplices were at large. Two of those held, Andres Ernesto Alsina Bea and Ignacio Ikonicoff, charged in the May 12 press that they had been tortured in Buenos Aires jails. Bea, a *La Opinion* journalist, claimed he was kicked severely and electric shock was applied to his genitals and mouth. Ikonicoff, an Inter Press journalist, said he was beaten and that other prisoners were burned with acid. On March 16, 1973, three individuals were given life sentences, and seven others received terms of one to twelve years. A three-judge court held that two of the suspects had been tortured. Buenos Aires business man José Marinasky, who had been kidnapped on May 14, 1973, but was freed four days later, was an uncle of Mario Raul Klacho, who was sought for the Sallustro kidnapping. Klacho's wife, Giomar Schmidt, was acquitted of all charges regarding the Sallustro case.

On May 26, at least 375 prisoners (some reports claim 500) were released, including several held for the killings of Sallustro, ex-President Pedro Aramburu, and Army General Juan Carlos Sanchez. 1003

March 22, 1972—Northern Ireland—Over seventy were injured when a bomb planted by the IRA exploded in a car parked in front of Belfast's Europa Hotel. Two boys were injured by a one hundred-pound bomb that exploded in Enoiskillen.

March 24, 1972—United Kingdom—The British government suspended the Northern Ireland Parliament and imposed direct rule as of March 30.

March 27, 1972—Turkey—Five members of the TPLA stormed an apartment in Kizeldere and kidnapped three NATO radar technicians. They held them in a hut, demanding the release of three terrorists who had been sentenced to death for the kidnapping of four Americans (see incident 0709). The NATO technicians had been employed at a Turkish air force radar base at Unye. They were identified as Gordon Banner and Charles Turner of the United Kingdom and John Stewart Law of Canada.

The government refused to negotiate or to grant the terrorists' subsequent demand for safe passage out of Turkey. On March 30, police raided the terrorists' shack in Kizildere, a village sixty miles south of Unye on the Black Sea. The terrorists shot the hostages, who were bound, in the head. Police rockets and small arms fire killed the ten terrorists, who included Mahir Cayan, wanted for the killing of Israeli consul Ephraim Elrom, Cihan Alptekin, and Omer Ayna (see incident 0794). The trio had escaped from prison in November 1971.

The next day, Interior Minister Ferit Kubat, who had led the assault, announced to the National Assembly that Ertugrul Kurkcu had been captured alive near the shack. A letter found in the shack written by the terrorists claimed they killed the technicians because they were "English agents of the NATO forces which occupy our country, and . . .we consider it our basic right and a debt of honor to execute them." 1004

March 29, 1972—Sweden—A bomb planted by Croatian terrorists exploded in the Stockholm office of Yugotours, a Yugoslav travel agency. 1005

March 29, 1972—United States—A Soviet research ship in Biscayne, Florida, was bombed by the JCN, an anti-Castro Cuban group. The JCN may be a cover name. 1006

March 31, 1972—South Africa—Nuts and bolts were removed from the rails for trains eight miles north of Potgietersrust in the Transvaal. This caused the derailment of a train carrying black workers, killing 38 and wounding 174 of them.

April 1972—United States—The Crystal River licensed nuclear facility of the Florida Power Company received a bomb threat, as did the Beaver Valley licensed nuclear facility of the Duquesne Light Company.

April 4, 1972—Canada—Two plastic bombs exploded in the Montreal offices of the Cuban Trade Commission, killing a Cuban guard and damaging the building. Seven Cubans were arrested. The next day an anonymous caller informed the Miami United Press International that the Young Cubans claimed credit for the attack "in the name of Alejandro Del Valle, who died in the Bay of Pigs invasion." Fidel Castro complained of the police handling of the incident and blamed the Central Intelligence Agency for the attack, in which seven others were injured. 1007

April 5, 1972—Indonesia—A Merpati Nusantara Airlines Vickers Viscount flying from Surabaya to Jakarta with forty-three persons on board was hijacked by a twenty-one-year-old male, Hermawan Harjanto, who used a grenade to divert the plane to Jogakarta, Java. The hijacker demanded 20 million rupiahs and a parachute and was shot and killed by the pilot while negotiating. 5350

April 7, 1972—Tanzania—Three Africans and an Arab assassinated two leaders of the Revolutionary Council of Zanzibar. 1008

April 7, 1972—United States—United Airlines flight 885, a B727 flying from New York to Los Angeles with ninety-five persons on board was hijacked out of Denver by a white male who met the FAA profile: Richard Floyd McCoy, Jr., a student major in law enforcement at Brigham Young University, who was born in Kingston, North Carolina, on December 7, 1942. Using two guns, a hand grenade, and plastic explosives, he demanded $500,000 and six parachutes. He diverted the plane to San Francisco, where he allowed the passengers to deplane. He then flew to Salt Lake City, where he was given the money. He jumped in the vicinity of Provo, Utah, but was arrested at his home by the FBI on April 10. During his trial, he feigned illness and escaped from the restroom into the street. He was captured three blocks away. On July 10, 1972, he was sentenced to forty-five years for air piracy. He escaped on August 10, 1974, and was killed resisting capture in a shootout on November 10, 1974. According to McCoy, he and a friend had talked about parajacking after Richard Charles LaPoint had received $50,000 in January (see hijacking 5340), which led to his night jump. Other reports claim he was paid off in San Francisco. 5351

April 7, 1972—Puerto Rico—José Luis Lugo used a gun to kidnap banker José Luis Carrion and hijack a four-engine commuter plane in San Juan. He demanded $290,000 and flew to Camaguey, Cuba. The U.S. Department of State demanded the return of the plane, money, hijacker, and banker. 5352

April 8, 1972—Peru—A Faucett B727 flying from Piura to Chiclayo with 119 persons on board was hijacked by two armed men identified as J. Bustamente and Juan A. Vallejos, who were armed with a gun and a bottle of gasoline and attempted to divert the plane to Cuba. When the gas failed to ignite, the crew overpowered them. 5353

April 9, 1972—United States—Pacific Southwest flight 942, a B727 flying ninety-two persons from Oakland, California, to San Diego, was hijacked by a white male for whom the FAA profile was not applicable: Stanley H. Speck, who was born on November 11, 1940, in Glendale, California. Claiming he had a pistol and a hand grenade, he demanded $500,000, four parachutes, and a flight to Miami. He left the plane in San Diego to obtain charts and was overcome by FBI agents. He was charged with hijacking but was committed to a state mental institution for an indefinite period on December 19, 1972. He was discharged on June 14, 1973. 5354

April 11, 1972—United States—A Continental Airlines B707 flying from Portland to Seattle with fifty-six passengers was hijacked by Major Burton Davenport, fifty-six, who claimed he had a bottle of nitroglycerin and demanded $500,000, but did not specify a place for the plane to land. He was talked out of his attempt. 5355

April 13, 1972—United States—Frontier Airlines flight 91, a B737 flying from Albuquerque to Tucson and Phoenix with thirty-three persons on board, was hijacked to Los Angeles by Ricardo Chavez-Ortiz, a Latin who met the FAA profile and who was born in Mexico on September 19, 1935. The father of eight, who had been married for seventeen years, lived in the Los Angeles barrio and worked as a short-order cook. On two occasions welfare social workers had sent him to psychiatrists, who diagnosed him as having paranoid schizoid tendencies. He was treated with drugs and psychotherapy for several months but still believed that his coworkers and his children were plotting against him. He informed his wife that he had decided to go to Mexico to become a police officer and then used the last of his savings to purchase a ticket in Albuquerque under an assumed name. He also bought a gun and some ammunition, which he hid in the closet of his hotel room. The next morning he boarded the plane. When a stewardess asked him if he would like a drink, he requested access to the cockpit, where he had the pilot surrender his cap and fly to Los Angeles. Although his pistol was not loaded, he successfully demanded television and radio time to deliver a two and a half hour speech in Spanish in which he asked for world peace and better educational opportunities for poor Mexican and other children. During his speech he kept his pistol trained on the crewmen but immediately surrendered to the FBI after completing his talk. He wrote a letter to President Nixon requesting either the death penalty or acquittal. Frederick Hacker, a famed psychologist who has been consulted in other cases, was called in as an expert witness. Chavez-Ortiz was found sane and sentenced to life imprisonment for air piracy on July 24, 1972. The sentence was later reduced to thirty years and was further reduced to twenty years on November 29, 1972. 5356

April 15, 1972—Uruguay—A bomb went off in the Soviet embassy in Montevideo. 1009

April 16, 1972—Sweden—The USIS office in Gothenburg was damaged by firebombs during the night. No injuries were reported. On April 12, there had been a bomb threat against the U.S. ambassador's plane in Jokkmokk. 1010-1011

April 16, 1972—Puerto Rico—Prinair flight 179, a DH114 general aviation flight from Ponce to San Juan, was the scene of an unsuccessful hijacking attempt at the boarding ramp by a Latin for whom the FAA profile was inapplicable: Uriel A. Ojeda Perez, who was born on March 27, 1949, in Mayaguez, Puerto Rico. He was overpowered by a boarding passenger and a mechanic at the ramp and charged with air piracy. On August 18, 1972, he was sentenced to two years for conveying false information concerning an attempt to commit air piracy and was released on January 10, 1974. 5357

April 17, 1972—United States—An Alaskan flight AS-1861, a B727 flying from Seattle, Washington to Annette Island, Alaska, was hijacked by a black male who forced his way on board the plane and for whom the FAA profile was not applicable. Kenneth L. Smith, who was born in Portland, Oregon, on February 17, 1946, demanded to be flown to Cairo, Egypt. He was captured and committed to a mental hospital on May 4, 1972, from which he was released on July 10, 1973. 5358

April 17, 1972—Switzerland—A Swissair DC9 flying from Geneva to Rome with twenty persons on board was hijacked by a man who claimed to have a bomb and demanded to go to Argentina. He was identified as Mario Victor Maimone, who held U.S. and Italian citizenship. He was talked out of the idea at Rome airport, where he was arrested. He was sentenced to two years and three months on March 8, 1973, and was released on provisional liberty on March 14, 1973 after posting a 3 million lire bail. 5359

April 17, 1972—United States—Delta Airlines flight 952, a Convair 880 flying from Miami and West Palm Beach to Chicago with ninety-one persons on board, was hijacked by a white male who did not meet the FAA profile: William Herbert Greene III who was born in Berea, Ohio, on August 15, 1941. He demanded to be flown to the Bahamas and to be given $500,000, according to a note he sent to the captain. He was persuaded to fly to Chicago and let the passengers deplane and was captured less than an hour later. He was later charged by a grand jury with air piracy and was sentenced to twenty years on September 25, 1972.

Although he was ultimately declared sane, there was some question about Greene's mental state. After the breakup of his marriage, he came to believe that he was in a battle against the devil. He wore women's clothes after a divine order in a song, committed several thefts, visited Cape Canaveral, and finally interpreted a "Delta is ready when you are" road sign as his final divine order. He never left his seat during the hijacking, did not possess a gun, and had no idea what he was to do in the Bahamas. 5360

April 18, 1972—Czechoslovakia—A Slovair L410 flying from Prague to Marianske and Marienbad with twelve persons on board was hijacked by two Czech miners identified as Karel Dolezal, twenty-eight, and Antonin Larch, twenty-four, who diverted the plane to Nuremburg, West Germany. The two were armed with two pistols and shot and slightly wounded the copilot. They were arrested and sentenced to seven years imprisonment on July 31, 1972. Their request for political asylum was denied in April 1973. Czechoslovakia requested extradition. Asylum was granted by West Germany on December 9, 1976. 5361

April 19, 1972—Pakistan—Eleven Pakistani males attempted to hijack a Pakistan International Airlines 707. The group was armed with five guns and ammunition hidden in books. No details are available regarding their arrest. 5362

April 19, 1972—Spain—Eight or nine young men with their faces covered and iron bars in hand broke most of the glass in the entrance to the USIS Binational Center library and auditorium in Barcelona. They fled, throwing two Molotov cocktails that burned on the sidewalk, causing no damage. 1012

April 20, 1972—Greece—In Athens, a small timed explosive device detonated in the rear wheel well of the personal auto of the U.S. consul general, causing slight damage. The consul, his wife, and a guest had just entered the car, and the consul's wife sustained a slight cut on the ankle from flying metal. Elsewhere in Athens, a USAR sergeant noticed a man tampering with his private auto. The man fled, but the sergeant found a green plastic package on top of the right rear tire. The sergeant called OSE and the Greek police, but the device exploded prior to their arrival, doing damage to the wheel, tire, and wheel well. In Piraeus, a U.S.-owned car was damaged by an explosion. The AAA took credit for two of the bombings. 1013-1015

April 21, 1972—Italy—Three pipe bombs exploded almost simultaneously in the inner court of the chancery of the U.S. embassy in Rome, causing no damage or injuries. 1016

April 21, 1972—United States—Two unidentified males called a Pan Am official in St. Louis, threatening to destroy nine aircraft unless he left $1 million at a store near Collinsville. The men were later arrested.

April 22, 1972—Jordan—The U.S. embassy in Amman received a telephoned bomb threat. A search was negative. 1017

April 24, 1972—Netherlands—A timed gasoline incendiary device was discovered by a local employee in the waiting room of the U.S. consulate general in Amsterdam. He took it outside where police deactivated it. 1018

April 27, 1972—Kenya—Hours after the official opening of the U.S. Cultural Center in Nairobi, a call was received that a bomb would explode there in five minutes. A search was negative. 1019

April 28, 1972—United States—The North Anna, Virginia, licensed nuclear facility of VEPCO received a bomb threat. Similar threats were received on May 5, 11, and 12.

May 1972—Japan—Japanese authorities discovered the bodies of fourteen members of the United Red Army, who had been slain by their colleagues in a factional dispute. Among those killed was a woman who had worn earrings, which others claimed was bourgeois revisionism.

May 1972—United States—The Crystal River licensed nuclear facility of the Florida Power Company received a bomb threat.

May 1972—United States—Twelve members of the JDL staged a sit-in at the Austrian embassy in Washington, D.C., protesting the acquittal in Austria of a former concentration camp guard. The group hung a Nazi flag outside a window and traded blows with embassy officials.

May 1, 1972—Israel—The U.S. consular office in Jerusalem received a telephoned bomb threat. 1020

May 3, 1972—Sweden—The Turkish tourist office was bombed in response to Ankara's parliament ratifying the death sentences of three TPLA members convicted of kidnapping three U.S. servicemen in 1971 (see incident 0709). The trio—Deniz Gezmis, twenty-five, Yusef Aslan, twenty-five, and Huseyin Inan, twenty-two, were hanged on May 6. Bombs went off in Ankara and Istanbul the next day, injuring three passersby and one terrorist. 1021

May 3, 1972—Turkey—Four armed individuals placed bombs on the parking lot of the Ankara U.S. base civil engineering facility. The bombs did not explode. 1022

May 3, 1972—Turkey—A Turkish Airlines DC9 flying from Ankara to Istanbul with sixty-eight passengers and crew members was hijacked by four armed members of the TPLA, who diverted the plane to Sofia, Bulgaria. The hijackers were identified as three students and an electrician: Iashar M. Aidan, Ainoulla A. Akcha, Seffer A. Shemshek, and Mehmed H. Youlmaz. They demanded the release of the three TPLA members who had been sentenced to death (see incident 1021) for kidnapping three U.S. servicemen and threatened to blow up the plane and everyone aboard. The Turkish government refused to negotiate with the pistol-wielding crew but agreed to allow the Bulgarians to grant them amnesty if they would put down their hand grenades and pistols and not harm the people or plane. The group extended their deadline several times and finally agreed to the governments' suggestion on May 4. One passenger had suffered a heart attack during the siege. Although the Bulgarians gave the hijackers asylum, they were sentenced to three years on November 3, 1972. 1023

May 5, 1972—United States—Western Airlines flight 407, a B737 flying from Salt Lake City to Los Angeles with seventy-five passengers, was hijacked by a white army draftee who met the FAA profile: Michael L. Hansen, who was born on October 18, 1950, in Fargo, North Dakota. He wanted to divert the plane to Hanoi to protest the U.S. bombing of North Vietnam but was persuaded by the captain, Gary Harding, that the plane lacked the range, and he settled for Cuba. He allowed eleven passengers to deplane in Los Angeles while refueling. The plane refuelled again in Dallas and Tampa before flying for Cuba. Hansen was returned to New York from Cuba via Barbados on June 14, 1975. After being tried in Los Angeles as a result of an indictment handed down against him by a federal grand jury in the central district of California on September 2, 1972, he was sentenced to ten years on December 23, 1975, for his act of aerial piracy in which he had used a pistol. 5363

May 6, 1972—United States—Eastern Airlines flight 175, a B727 flying from Allentown, Pennsylvania, to Washington, D.C., and Miami with forty-five passengers and a crew of seven, was hijacked by Frederick William Hahneman, a white male who met the FAA profile, who was born in Puerto Castilla, Honduras (although he was an American citizen), on July 5, 1922. Hahneman, armed with a gun, forced the plane to land at Washington's Dulles Airport, where he allowed the passengers and a stewardess to leave but demanded $303,000, six parachutes, two bush knives, two jumpsuits, two crash helmets, and two cartons of his favorite brand of cigarettes. He flew to New Orleans, where he used his six hostages as a shield to walk the fifty feet to a reserve airliner. According to the flight's pilot, Captain Hendershot, "He talked like there was another country and he wanted the money for a cause." Hahneman bailed out over the village of Yoro in the jungle of northern Honduras. According to Eastern's senior vice-president, William R. Howard, the company received a tip in late May in response to their reward of $25,000 that the hijacker was living in Honduras. The FBI named him in a warrant on June 1. On June 3, he appeared at the U.S. embassy in Tegucigalpa with a childhood friend, José Gomez Rovelo. The hijacker, who had been in the air force and had worked as a technician for American firms abroad, was indicted on counts of air piracy, kidnapping, and extortion. He informed authorities that "a contact who came to Honduras from Panama took the money and deposited it in the Chinese Communist bank in Hong Kong." Judge Oren R. Lewis, observing that "money is replaceable," sentenced him to life imprisonment on September 29, 1972. The money was recovered in May 1973. 5364

May 8, 1972—Austria—Sabena Airlines flight 517, a B707 flying the Vienna-Athens-Tel Aviv route with eighty-seven passengers and ten crew members, was hijacked over Zagreb by four members of Black September (two males and

two females), who forced the British pilot, Reginald Bernard Levy, to fly to
Lod Airport. The group was armed with pistols and grenades, and threatened
the passengers, including the 'Jewish pilot's wife, who was a passenger. The
plane landed at Lod at 7:15 P.M. The group demanded the release of 317
fedayeen prisoners, most of them held at Ramleh prison, including early
members of Al Fatah, William Nassar and Fatma Bernawi; they threatened to
blow up the plane and all aboard. The twenty-one-hour negotiations were
supervised by Defense Minister Moshe Dayan, who used Captain Levy as a
go-between. The Belgian government established contact with Black September through their embassy in Beirut.

The group's leader was identified as Ali Shafik Ahmed Taha, also known as
Captain Rafat, who was a member of the PFLP team that had hijacked an El Al
airliner to Algeria in 1968 (see incident 0077). In 1969, he had supervised the
two Young Tigers of the PFLP's Ho Chi Minh section, who bombed the Brussels
offices of El Al (see incident 0219). He also was a member of the Revolution
Airstrip commando squad in 1970 (see incident 0509-0512). In 1971, he joined
Black September.

Dayan set up an operations center in the airport control tower, one mile away
from the plane. With him was chief of staff David Elazar, central command
chief Aluf Rehav'am Ze'evi, and air force chief Mordechai Hod. One of their
first actions was to have two airport workers let the air out of the plane's tires
and drain its hydraulic fluid during the night. Their next concern was getting
the 5:30 deadline extended. To do this, they offered the terrorists another
plane. This stalling would allow them to plan for a daylight attack upon the
disabled 707. Levy radioed, "I understand they are prepared to wait until 8
o'clock in the morning. . . .The hijackers have asked to speak with the International Red Cross and we have agreed to this request."

The identities of the two female hijackers were learned: Rima Tannous,
twenty-one, and Therese Halaseh, nineteen. Five days before the attack, Rima
met Rafat, who was introduced as Youssef, and flew with him to Frankfurt,
where they met Therese and Zacharia, also known as Abdel Aziz al Atrash, a
Syrian Druse. They had trained in pistol shooting and explosives handling in
Fatah's camp at Sidon, Lebanon, and flew on to Brussels, where they purchased the wigs they wore on the flight. They also obtained false passports,
along with special girdles whose fabric contained a TNT-like explosive. The
women hid hand grenades in their cosmetic boxes and detonators in their
brassieres. Because the search procedures at the airport boarding gates were
superficial, the men carried aboard a revolver each, ammunition, and the
battery for the explosives. The group's leader had a great deal of experience in
such stressful situations, but the women did not and were very nervous, which
worried the pilot. Levy recalled, "The Arabs were getting very agitated
because the Israelis would not hand over the fedayeen. The two girls had
already mined the plane with plastic charges. They were all carrying grenades

and they decided to blow us all to Kingdom Come, themselves included. When I saw the girls crying and kissing the two men goodbye before they let off the charges I knew something had to be done. I grabbed one man's gun. I squeezed the trigger. It didn't go off. The safety catch was on. Don't ask me why, but they didn't shoot us. And we managed to talk them into delaying the blowing-up operation.'' Levy's success in stalling them gave Dayan's men time to train in methods to open the doors, climb inside, and begin shooting within ninety seconds, General Elazar's goal. The Israelis in the control tower led Rafat to believe that his plane was being readied and the prisoners would be released. The terrorists would be flown to Cairo, where they would release the passengers. The Arab prisoners would then be flown to Cairo in another plane. Another Boeing was towed out near the Sabena plane, and an airport bus drove up, containing men wearing prison uniforms whose heads were shaven; however, they were Israeli soldiers in disguise.

At 3:45 P.M., eighteen men in white overalls arrived at the plane, appearing to be members of the Red Cross and airport mechanics. The Red Cross negotiator suspected a trick, and the guerillas sent three of the crew out of the plane, two of whom searched the group, finding nothing. The eighteen left the airline service vehicle, climbed ladders onto the wings, opened the two emergency doors, and engaged in a ten-second gun battle with the terrorists. In the fighting, the two male hijackers, identified by Black September as Major Ahmed Mousa Awad and Lieutenant Abdel Aziz el Atrash, were killed. Therese Halasah was wounded, as were three paratroopers. Five passengers were injured, including one who stood up in panic during the shooting. Twenty-two-year-old Miriam Anderson later died in a hospital, hit in the head by a bullet. Also wounded were Wilfred Kordovski, fifty-five, a German tourist, who sustained bullets in the jaw and body, and Paula Rubin, fifty, who was shot in the ear. The other passengers, fifty of them Israelis, were unharmed.

The two female hijackers were tried in a military court in the theater of the old British army camp at Sarafand. Halaseh was born near Nazareth to a middle-class Arab family. She completed high school and became a nursing student. She was recruited into Fatah by a fellow student and in 1971 went across the border to a Fatah camp. Her colleague, Tannous, was an orphan who was reared by nuns. She entered nursing in Amman. She claimed that she was raped by a young man and then became a mistress to a Fatah doctor who gave her drugs. She said that she was forced to sleep with Fatah members and was beaten or refused morphine if she refused. She claimed that she was totally dependent upon Fatah for food and money. ''I had to comply with their orders. I had as much free will as a robot.'' She was selected for a special course in sabotage and subjected to an intense loyalty test. The two women were then sent on their mission with the two men, known to them as Yosef and Zechariah. They also knew that their linen body belts contained plastic explosives and that their handbags and talcum powder cans hid grenades and pistols, but they were not informed of their target, which they learned only when the plane took off from Vienna for Tel Aviv. They had boarded the plane with forged Israeli passports and spoke pidgin Hebrew.

The court tried them for terrorist crimes in violation of point 58d of the 1945 British Mandatory Government's Defence (Emergency) Regulations and for being members of the unlawful El Fatah association, contrary to point 85.1.a. The women, claiming constraint according to section 17 of the Criminal Code Ordinance of 1936, said that they were forced to carry the arms and were not willing members of Fatah. Tannous's addiction was apparently used to force her compliance with Fatah's orders. Halasah claimed that she had been kidnapped by Fatah. The tribunal rejected these defenses, noting that the law allowed that defense only if there was an immediate threat of death or grievous harm, which did not appear to be the case. One of the judges demanded the death sentence for the women after they were found guilty of the three charges, saying, "They were both nurses, angels who should have saved people's lives. Instead they brought death to innocent people. Life imprisonment should be sufficient for them and the death sentence would serve as a deterrent. "His colleagues disagreed, and on August 14, 1972, the two were sentenced to life imprisonment.

Black September accused the ICRC of aiding the Israelis, whose commandos had followed a vehicle with a Red Cross flag that was to carry refreshments to the passengers. The group warned that, in future hijackings, such humanitarian considerations as food and drink for the hostages might not be important. It also suggested possible reprisals against the Belgian government. 1024.

May 9, 1972—United Kingdom—A small petrol bomb was thrown against the entrance to the U.S. embassy in London, causing no damage except for smoked glass. 1025

May 10, 1972—France—Four young men entered the U.S. Trade Center in Paris and set off two firebombs, causing an estimated $100,000 damage but injuring no one. 1026

May 11, 1972—West Germany—A series of bombs exploded in the Frankfurt headquarters of the Fifth U.S. Army Corps, killing Colonel Paul Bloomquist and wounding thirteen others. Responsibility was claimed by members of the Petra Schelm command of the Red Army Faction, also known as the Baader-Meinhof Group, in retaliation for U.S. action against North Vietnam. In 1977, three members of the group were sentenced to life imprisonment for the killing. The group had demanded an end to the mining of North Vietnam's harbors and immediate withdrawal of all U.S. troops from Indochina. The group took credit for a number of other bombings in West Germany in May. 1027

May 11, 1972—Guatemala—A national police lieutenant who was the chief of the U.S. embassy national police security detail was assassinated near his Guatemala City home. 1028

May 11, 1972—Philippines—In Manila, a group of five hundred radical students demonstrated at the U.S. Embassy, throwing ''pillboxes'' and Molotov cocktails, injuring nine persons and causing minor damage to the embassy. 1029

May 12, 1972—Argentina—The Buenos Aires offices of one Dutch and four U.S. firms were bombed by the Comite Argentino de Lucha Anti-Imperialisto to protest U.S. escalation of the Vietnam war. One report speculated that the group was composed of ERP members. 1030-1034

May 12, 1972—United States—The Beaver Valley licensed nuclear facility of the Duquesne Light Company, as well as VEPCO's North Anna nuclear facility, received bomb threats.

May 12, 1972—West Germany—An incendiary device planted in a book on a shelf of the Hamburg Amerika Haus Library went off. Damage was limited to the book, which did not belong to the library. 1035

May 15, 1972—United States—Arthur Bremer attempted to assassinate presidential candidate Governor George Wallace in a Laurel, Maryland shopping center. Bremer fired a gun at Wallace from close range as the candidate was moving through a crowd after a political rally. The assailant was apprehended by police.

May 16, 1972—Iran—A bomb exploded in the washroom of the Tehran international fairgrounds about seventy-five yards from the U.S. industrial and medical exhibit. No information was available to indicate that the bomb was directed at the U.S. exhibit.

May 17, 1972—West Germany—The Berlin Amerika Haus was closed for forty-five minutes after a phoned bomb threat. The search was negative. 1036

May 17, 1972—United States—Vinicio Estrella Ruiz, twenty, was arrested in New York while trying to sneak a sawed-off shotgun aboard a National Airlines plane bound for Miami. 5365

May 17, 1972—Venezuela—Four incendiary devices ignited in the USIS Binational Center library in Caracas in the early evening. Seven more were removed by Venezuelan police prior to detonation and were found to consist of potassium chlorate contained in cigarette and match boxes. 1037

May 18, 1972—Venezuela—In Caracas, a pipe bomb that had been discovered and removed from the USIS Binational Center exploded while being deactivated, severing the arm of a Venezuelan police officer. 1038.

May 19, 1972—United States—A bomb detonated in the Pentagon, causing $75,000 damage. A few minutes before the blast, a Weathermen member called the *Washington Post* to claim credit. The *New York Post* also received a call, saying that the bomb was to celebrate the birthday of the late Ho Chi Minh, the North Vietnamese leader. The caller directed the *Post* to a phone booth, in which was placed a six-page statement attacking President Nixon's Vietnam war policies. The *Washington Post* received a similar statement, signed by Weather Underground No. 12.

May 20, 1972—Puerto Rico—The Dorado Beach Hotel where Tanya Wilson was being crowned Miss USA was hit by a series of bombs planted by a Puerto Rican independence group.

May 20, 1972—Philippines—Leftists and student activists staged a demonstration but were prevented from reaching the U.S. embassy in Manila by police. The confrontation with police resulted in the throwing of "pill boxes" and Molotov cocktails, injuring twelve to fifteen persons. On May 22, a small demonstration with some bombing was directed at the U.S. embassy in protest of the Vietnam war and the previous vigorous police measures of two days ago. On May 25, fears that an anti-Vietnam demonstration might become uncontrollable were proved unfounded. Security was excellent, and two thousand demonstrators were kept away from the embassy.

May 21, 1972—Venezuela—A small-caliber bullet was fired into the parked auto of a U.S. embassy officer in Caracas. The unoccupied car was parked in front of his residence.

May 23, 1972—Venezuela—A bomb went off in ITT headquarters in Caracas, causing heavy damage. Reports indicated that the blast was to protest ITT opposition to President Allende of Chile. 1040

May 23, 1972—Ecuador—An Empress Ecuatoriana de Aviacion DC6B Electra Turbo-Prop flying from Quito to Guayaquil with forty-five persons on board was hijacked by J. V. Baguero Cornejo, who threatened to blow up the aircraft unless provided with $39,000 and two parachutes. He allowed the passengers to deplane and was then killed by two air force men. 5366

May 24, 1972—United States—The Long Island residence of the Soviet U.N. mission was bombed by the JDL. 1041

May 24, 1972—Rhodesia—A South African Airways B727 flying from Salisbury to Johannesburg, South Africa, with sixty-six persons on board was hijacked by two Lebanese, Fyad H. Abdul Kamil and A. J. Yaghi, who threatened to blow up the aircraft. At a refueling stop in Salisbury, they allowed some of the passengers off. They diverted the plane to Balantyre, Malawi, and demanded money from the Anglo-American Mining Company. On May 25, all passengers and crew escaped. Troops fired on the jet after the last of the hostages were safe. No injuries were reported, and the hijackers were captured. On September 18 they were sentenced to eleven years. They were released in Malawi in 1974. Some reports claim that they then went to Cairo, while others record them being deported to Zambia on May 21, 1974. 1042.

May 24, 1972—West Germany—Two bombs planted in parked cars at U.S. Army-Europe headquarters in Heidelberg exploded within seconds of each other, wounding five and killing three Americans: Captain Clyde R. Bonner, twenty-nine, of El Paso, Texas; Specialist 5 Ronald A. Woodward, twenty-six, of Otter Lake, Michigan; and Specialist 5 Charles L. Peck, twenty-three, of Hawthorne, California. The bombs also ripped a hole in the wall of the base's computer center. The Baader-Meinhof Group claimed responsibility for the attacks, charging that the data-processing facility was used to plan U.S. bombing in Vietnam. The major members of the group were arrested in June and held in pretrial detention for over three years. A twenty-three-month trial ensued, with three leaders of the group being sentenced on April 28, 1977 to life imprisonment by a five-man tribunal in Stuttgart. The trio were identified as Andreas Baader, thirty-three; Gudrun Ensslin, thirty-six; and Jan-Carl Raspe, who were also convicted of thirty-four counts of attempted murder and of joining in a criminal conspiracy, and were sentenced to life plus fifteen years. The counts included bomb attacks on two police stations, a publishing house, and a judge's car and the attempted murder of policemen during a shootout when they were arrested. Their chief lawyer, Otto Schilly, argued that their actions had been legitimate protests against the Vietnam war and that they should be treated as prisoners of war.

The trial and events occurring during the group's incarceration were a topic of national discussion. West German authorities cracked down successfully on the terrorist gangs but resorted to bugging the conversations of the group's lawyers, which resulted in the defendants' and their advocates' boycotting the last six weeks of the trial, engaging in a hunger strike. In November 1974, one of the original accused, Holger Meins, died in jail during a hunger strike. The next day Judge von Drenkmann was killed in West Berlin in retaliation. The group's intellectual founder, Ulrike Meinhof, forty-one, was found hanging in her jail cell in May 1976, an apparent suicide. Leftists protested what they viewed as murder and bombed several German locations in Europe in protest. Three weeks before the end of the trial, a motorcycling member of the Ulrike Meinhof Action Group shot and killed the chief public prosecutor, Siegfried Buback, who had been involved in the trial. 1043

May 25, 1972—Venezuela—For two successive nights. the U.S. Marine security guard received threatening phone calls at the U.S. embassy in Caracas. The second call was a bomb threat, but a search of the chancery was negative. 1044-1045

May 25, 1972—Iran—A small bomb exploded in a classroom of the Iran American Society Academic Center in Tehran, causing no injuries and $50 damage. 1046

May 25, 1972—United States—Virgil Lee Fugua kidnapped Mrs. J. Roberts in Waco, Texas and drove to Dallas Airport, where he demanded an airplane in order to leave the country. Braniff refused, and after discussions, Fugua surrendered to police. 5367

May 25, 1972—Panama—An LAN 727 flying from Santiago to New York with stops in Panama City and Miami was jolted after it left Panama City when a pipe bomb planted in the ice water fountain service compartment exploded while the plane was over the Caribbean Sea near Cuba. The bomb caused extensive damage to the rear end of the aircraft. The pilot managed to land safely at Montego Bay, Jamaica, and reported no injuries to the fifty people on board. 1047

May 25, 1972—France—Bombs caused some damage to the U.S. consulate and offices of the American Legion, Pan Am, and TWA in Paris. The Committee of Coordination took responsibility, claiming that it was protesting U.S. bombing in North Vietnam. 1048-1051

May 26, 1972—Belgium—In Brussels, the U.S. Marine security guard at the embassy received a call stating that a bomb was in the building. A search was negative. 1052

May 26, 1972—Norway—The U.S. embassy in Oslo received a telephone call warning that a bomb would explode at 2 P.M. A search was negative. 1053

May 28, 1972—Italy—A Lebanese woman in possession of arms was apprehended in Rome. Her destination was unknown. She was freed and expelled to Beirut. 1054

May 28, 1972—Crete—An Olympic Airlines 707 flying from Iraklion to Athens with 130 persons on board was hijacked by Evangelos Savvakis, twenty-five, who used a toy pistol and demanded that he be given money and a ticket to London, where he wished to receive medical treatment. The captain asked him to allow the plane to refuel at Athens, where he was persuaded to leave the plane. Police rushed him, and he was arrested. On February 10, 1973, Savvakis was sentenced to two years. 5368

May 30, 1972—France—The U.S. consul in Lyons received a bomb threat against the consulate. A search was negative. 1055

May 30, 1972—Brazil—A Varig Airlines Lockheed Electra 188 flying from São Paulo to Pôrto Alegre with ninety-six persons was hijacked out of Curitiba by Nelson Mesquita, twenty-five, also known as G. D. J. Silva, who was armed with a gun and demanded $260,000 and three parachutes. The crew on the ground sabotaged the engines, and when troops rushed the plane, the hijacker committed suicide with his pistol. 5369

May 30, 1972—Israel—Three members of the Japanese Red Army, on contract from the PFLP, fired machine guns and threw hand grenades at passengers arriving from an Air France flight, killing twenty-eight and wounding seventy-six. Two of the attackers died in the massacre. The plane, Air France flight 132, had arrived from Paris and Rome, when the trio picked up their weapons at the luggage area, opened their suitcases, and pulled out their Czech VZ-58 automatic rifles, whose butts had been removed, and six shrapnel grenades. One hundred sixteen passengers had just deplaned, and about three hundred people were crowding into the waiting lounge. One hundred thirty-three shots were fired from the 7.63 caliber M43 weapons. Among those killed were sixteen Puerto Rican Catholic pilgrims on a visit to the Holy Land. Twenty-seven others of the sixty-eight-member tour group were injured. Others killed included Israeli Professor Aharon Katchalsky, one of the world's foremost biophysicists. One of the terrorists, identified as Yasuyuki Yasuda, was killed accidentally by bullets from the rifle of Takeshi Okudeira, who was blown up by a grenade. The surviving member of the squad, Kozo Okamoto, ran onto the tarmac outside the terminal in an attempt to blow up an SAS plane parked outside. He was tackled with two grenades in his hands by El Al traffic officer Hannan Claude Zeiton.

In reconstructing the movements of the group, police discovered that they had carried tiny paper dolls as good luck charms. The group had also used symbolism in their selection of passports. Okamoto claimed to be Daisuke Namba, who had been executed for the attempted assassination of Crown Prince Hirohito in 1923. His birthdate was given as December 7, Pearl Harbor day. Jiro Sugisaki, whose real name was Takeshi Okidoro, gave his birthday as Feburary 26, 1937, when Japanese army officers had mutinied. The other dead man, who claimed to be Ken Torio, was Yasuiki Yasuda, who claimed to be born on March 30, the date of the Red Army's hijacking of a Japanese airliner. Included among those hijackers was Okamoto's brother (see incident 0359). Their passports identified Namba as being twenty-two, Torio as twenty-three and Sugizaki as twenty-three, although other reports claim Okamoto was twenty-four.

A PFLP spokesman, Bassam Towfik Sherif (also known as Bassam Zayad), claimed credit for the attack, saying that the group were members of the squad of the martyr Patrick Arguello (see incident 0512) in which Leila Khaled and an FSLN member were unsuccessful in hijacking an El Al plane. Bassam gave their PFLP names as Bassem, Salah, and Ahmed and said that the attack was in reprisal for the deaths of two Black September terrorists in the Sabena hijacking (see incident 1024) three weeks earlier. After his gang had killed eight Israelis, Okamoto told Israeli officers that his group was named the Army of the Red Star.

Okamoto was initially unwilling to talk to the authorities, asking for death. His interrogator, General Zeevi (who had questioned Tannous and Hallasah in the Sabena hijacking), threw his pistol on the table in front of him and told Okamoto that he could turn it on himself if he would sign the confession. Okamoto then began talking (it appears that Zeevi never intended to fulfill his part of the bargain). Okamoto studied agriculture at Kagoshima University. In early 1970, an Iraqi revolutionary, Bassim (who later married Leila Khaled), visited Tokyo and contacted the Red Army. There the two organizations made a movie, *PFLP-Red Army Declare World War*. In November 1971, Okamoto was asked to show the film at Kagoshima and was invited to go to Beirut, where his brother was undergoing PFLP training. He said: "I received a letter requesting me to leave for Tokyo at the end of February or the beginning of March, and to go from there to Montreal, New York and Paris. From New York I was supposed to fly by El Al 747 first-class, to observe everything closely and remember every detail and when I reached Beirut to make contact with a certain Japanese who would make all the arrangements for me....After arriving in Beirut, I went by taxi to Baalbek. In the house where I arrived, we stayed all three of us, Okidoro, Yasuda and I. We did gymnastics to get fit and afterward we trained in Port Said, in explosives, shooting with pistols and Kalashnikovs, and hand grenades. On May 16, I was told by Okidoro that four Japanese would take part in a military operation, and from May 17 we went through training for this military operation." On May 22, they left Beirut for Paris and arrived in Rome on May 30. They booked a night in the Anglo-

American Hotel and then moved to the Scaligera Pension on the Via Nazionale, where Arabs often stay. On May 30 they arrived at Leonardo da Vinci Airport for a flight to Tel Aviv. They passed through a body search, but their baggage was not searched. It appears that their trainer was Abu Hija, who had participated in the Zurich attack under the name of Youssef (see incident 0133). Maruoka Osamu was the fourth JRA member to be trained with the group and is wanted as an accomplice in the incident.

The Lod Airport assassin was charged with the military offense of political terrorism, which carried a death penalty under the 1945 British Emergency Regulations, which had initially been applied to Irgun members. Max Kritzman, a Chicago-born attorney, was appointed to be Okamoto's lawyer. Okamoto at first refused any counsel but accepted when told that the trial could not proceed without one. He sabotaged all attempts by Kritzman to provide a defense and tried to convince the court to sentence him to death. His address to the court is of particular interest: "This was our duty, to the people I slaughtered and to my two comrades, who lost their lives. It is my response with the other soldiers, to the people I killed. I take on myself full responsibility for it. . . . The revolutionary struggle is a political struggle between the classes. It is a just struggle. We strive to build a world where wars will be banished. But it will be a long struggle and we are preparing World War III through our own war, through slaughtering and destruction. We cannot limit warfare to destruction of buildings. We believe slaughtering of human bodies is inevitable. We know it will become more severe than battles between nations. . . . This incident had been reported worldwide, but it seems to me nobody has grasped the motivation for it. But when a similar operation takes place the next time, what will the world think? When I was captured, a certain Japanese asked me: 'Was there no other way?' Can that man propose an alternative method? I believe that, as a means toward world revolution, I must prepare the creation of the world Red Army . . . a means of propelling ourselves onto the world stage. . . . The Arab world lacks spiritual fervor, so we felt that through this attempt we could stir up the Arab world. The present world order has given Israel power which has been denied the Arab refugees. This is the link between the Japanese Red Army and the Popular Front for the Liberation of Palestine, with whom we collaborate. . . . I want you to know that the next target may be New York or San Francisco. I would like to warn the entire world that we will slay anyone who stands on the side of the bourgeoisie. This I do not say as a joke. We three soldiers, after we die, want to become three stars of Orion. When we were young, we were told that if we died we may become stars in the sky. I may not have fully believed it, but I was ready to. I believe some of those we slaughtered have become stars in the sky. The revolution will go on, and there will be many more stars. But if we recognize that we go to the same heaven, we can have peace.'' Lieutenant Colonel Abraham Frisch, the presiding judge, sentenced Okamoto to life imprisonment. His release has since been demanded in a number of subsequent incidents, including the September 5, 1972 Olympics massacre (see incident 1116), a July 20, 1973 JAL hijacking (see incident 1595), and the Entebbe affair of July 1976 (see incident 2762).

In interviews since his incarceration, it was learned that Okamoto and his colleagues tore their passports in a lavatory of Lod Airport so that they could not escape, a further expression of their determination to go through with the act. They had also planned to explode their last grenades in their faces to make the job of identifying them much harder. At the last moment, Okamoto apparently decided to attack the SAS plane as well but missed with his last grenades and was captured. 1056

May 31, 1972—Iran—At 5:45 P.M., a bomb placed in an alley against the outer side wall of the USIS building in Tehran exploded, breaking many windows, blowing in two steel doors, and killing one person and wounding two others. The bomb was placed by Iranian terrorists. It was reported that one American, three local employees, and a guard were in the building at the time of the explosion. 1057

May 31, 1972—Iran—A bomb was thrown at the car of USAF Brigadier General Harold L. Price, resulting in damage to the car and serious injury to the general, including two broken legs and multiple minor lacerations. The attack by anti-Shah guerrillas occurred near his Tehran home and resulted in all windows in the house being broken. 1058

May 31, 1972—Iran—A bomb virtually destroyed the private vehicle of a U.S. civilian attached to the FAA working with the Iranian air force. No injuries were reported. 1059

May 31, 1972—Iran—At 7:45 A.M., a car belonging to a civilian employee parked in the USAF parking area in Tehran was destroyed by a magnetic bomb attached to the gas tank. No injuries were reported. 1060

May 31, 1972—Iran—An anonymous call warned that a bomb would go off at the U.S. IAS Cultural Center in Tehran. All classes were cancelled, but no bomb was found. 1061

May 31, 1972—United States—Rodney Williams, eighteen, threatened to blow up the Pan Am passenger terminal in New York City unless he was given $350,000. He was arrested when he arrived at the payoff location.

June 1972—United States—The West Valley station of the Los Angeles County Police Department received a live bomb through the mail, with a note signed, "Chris, the pig killer."

June 1, 1972—West Germany—Andreas Baader, head of the Baader-Meinhof Group, was captured after a gunfight with Frankfurt police. Baader was wounded in the hip when police surrounded his garage hideout. Also captured were Holger Meins, thirty, and Jan-Carl Raspe, twenty-seven. On June 7, Gudrun Ensslin, thirty-one, was arrested in a Hamburg shopping center. Ulrike Meinhof, thirty-seven, was arrested, along with Gerhard Mueller, twenty-three, in a Hanover suburb on June 15. Siegfried Hausner, twenty-one, was picked up on June 19.

June 2, 1972—United States—The licensed nuclear facility at Iowa State University received a bomb threat.

June 2, 1972—United States—United Airlines flight 239, a B727 scheduled to fly from Reno to San Francisco with twenty-nine persons on board, was taken over on the ground by a pistol-wielding youth who forced his way on board but allowed the passengers to leave the plane. He was identified as Robb D. Heady, a Reno car park attendant who had learned parachuting while in Vietnam. The FAA profile was not applicable in this case. Heady had been born in Laramie, Wyoming, on March 8, 1950. The white hijacker demanded $200,000 and jumped from the plane near Reno during the night, but he was unable to carry all the money and had to leave $40,000 on the plane. He was arrested six hours later when he approached a car he had left in the desert approximately twenty miles from Reno. FBI and police officials had kept the car under surveillance. On August 25, 1972, he was sentenced to thirty years for aircraft piracy. 5370

June 3, 1972—United States—Western Airlines flight 701, a B727 flying from Los Angeles to Seattle with ninety-six persons, was hijacked by two people who did not meet the FAA profile. They were identified as William Roger Holder, a black Vietnam veteran who claimed to be a Black Panther Party member, who was born in Middlesex, North Carolina, on June 14, 1949, and Katherine Mary Kerkow, a white female who was born in North Bend, Oregon, on October 6, 1951. The two threatened to blow up the plane unless they were given $500,000. The plane landed in San Francisco, where they were given the money and allowed to transfer to a B720H, taking thirty-six hostages with them to New York City. They flew on to Algiers, Algeria, where they asked for asylum. The Algerians placed them under house arrest and returned the money on June 28, 1972. On September 29, 1972, the international section of the Black Panther Party in Algiers announced that Holder had succeeded Pete O'Neal, who had in turn succeeded founder Eldridge Cleaver, as chief of the Panthers' international section in Algiers. The Algerian government had formally accorded the Panthers the status of a liberation movement. On March 28, 1973, the Algiers office was abandoned, and the party members apparently left Algiers. The government had restricted the group's activities because of internal party disputes. It was announced that the duo had been arrested in Paris on January 24, 1975. A French court refused an extradition request for Holder and Kerkow on April 14, 1975, saying that the French would try them for hijacking and would set a date later. On May 6, 1977, Holder said in Paris that he would set a date to return to the United States to stand trial under an indictment handed down on June 6, 1972, in the eastern district of New York. 1062

June 3, 1972—Italy—The offices of U.S. firms in Milan were damaged by four bombs. The firms were identified as IBM, Honeywell, and the Bank of America and Italy. Honeywell's factory in a Milan suburb was also bombed. Leaflets at the sites hailed "the struggle of the Vietnamese people against American imperialism" and victories "of the revolutionary and Communist army in Vietnam. 1063-1066

June 3, 1972—Northern Ireland—Seventy were injured by a bomb in an East Belfast pub.

June 5, 1972—Philippines—An anonymous phone call warned of a bomb in the USIS library in Manila. The building was cleared, but no bomb was found. 1067

June 7, 1972—Belgium—The American Library in Brussels was evacuated after a bomb threat. A police search was negative. 1068

June 8, 1972—Ireland—Two members of the Eire security forces were injured when a bomb exploded near the Ulster border. 1069

June 8, 1972—Venezuela—The USIS Binational Center director in Caracas received a telephone call warning that a bomb was planted in the third-floor area of the center. The building was cleared and programming cancelled, but no bomb was found. 1070

June 8, 1972—Czechoslovakia—A Slov-Air L410 flying seventeen persons from Marianske Lazne (Marienbad) to Prague was hijacked by seven men and three women, accompanied by one child. The group killed the pilot when he refused to change course. The copilot was shot in the chest but survived, as did a wounded passenger. The group landed in a small airfield inside West Germany after having demanded to be flown to Nuremburg. All offenders were charged with air piracy. Czechoslovakia sought their extradition. In January 1973, one of the group committed suicide in prison. On December 14, 1973, nine of the group were convicted by the Nuremburg state court and sentenced to terms ranging from three to seven years. On December 9, 1976, the court in Ansbach, West Germany, granted political asylum to two of the hijackers, Karel Doleal, thrity-two, and Antonin Lerch, twenty-eight. Other reports claimed that the hijackers landed in Weiden, West Germany. On August 8, 1977, the other nine were denied asylum. 5372

June 9, 1972—Argentina—Bombs planted by Argentine terrorists damaged the offices of four U.S.-owned firms. A total of sixteen bombs went off in Buenos Aires, Córdoba, Rosario, and Sante Fe, damaging the offices of the newspaper *La Opinion* and a steel plant, among the other facilities. The terrorists were celebrating the sixteenth anniversary of an abortive Peronist military coup. 1071-1074

June 10, 1972—Ireland—A bomb placed by supporters of the Baader-Meinhof Gang damaged the West German embassy in Dublin. 1075

June 14, 1972—India—A JAL DC8 flying from Tokyo to London crashed out of New Delhi, killing eighty-seven of the eighty-nine persons on board. Airline officials have not ruled out the possibility of sabotage.

June 14, 1972—Puerto Rico—A San Juan liquor store was bombed by the Anti-Communist Commandos. Authorities suggested that this might be an alias of the Cuban National Liberation Front. 1076

June 15, 1972—West Germany—Croatian terrorists were suspected of placing a bomb in the Yugoslav consulate in Munich. 1077

June 15, 1972—Thailand—A Cathay Pacific Airlines Convair 880 flying the Singapore-Bangkok-Hong Kong run exploded over the central highlands of South Vietnam, killing all eighty-one aboard. The bomb had been placed in a suitcase under a passenger seat on the right side over the wing. A police officer whose fiancée and daughter were aboard and who had been heavily insured before boarding was arrested and charged with the crime. The next day a Cathay Pacific Convair 880 flying from Paya Lebar to Bangkok was delayed for three hours while the plane was searched after a bomb threat. No bomb was found.

June 16, 1972—United States—Joseph Anthony Landisi, forty-nine, wrote several letters demanding $300,000, threatening to blow up the terminals and aircraft of American Airlines in New York, as well as damage the liner *Queen Elizabeth II*. He was later arrested in his store.

June 18, 1972—United States—The pilot of a private aircraft in Gonzales, Texas, was shot in the back by Lydia Morales in what appeared to be a murder-suicide. Five people were killed in the incident. A note was found in the Morales home indicating a suicide motive.

June 18, 1972—Netherlands—The Revolutionary Peoples Resistance of the Netherlands claimed responsibility for an early morning fire in Amsterdam that did extensive damage to the library of the Netherlands-American Institute. 1078

June 20, 1972—Israel—Members of the PFLP General Command fired rockets at an Israeli bus in the Golan Heights, killing two civilians and injuring several others. The Israelis retaliated by shelling Lebanese frontier villages, killing about fifty Lebanese civilians and guerillas. The U.N. Security Council condemned Israel. 1079

June 20, 1972—Yugoslavia—Nineteen Croatians infiltrated into western Bosnia and Herzegovina. Near the town of Bugojnok, they conducted an armed attack against a security force, killing thirteen officers before they were captured. 1080

June 22, 1972—Belgium—The U.S. embassy in Brussels received a telephoned bomb threat indicating that a bomb would explode in the chancery in thirty minutes. A search was negative. 1081

June 23, 1972—United States—American Airlines flight 119, a B727 flying the New York-St. Louis-Tulsa run with ninety-four passengers and a crew of seven was hijacked by a white male who did not meet the FAA profile: Martin Joseph McNally, who had been born in Trenton, Michigan, on March 16, 1944. His last job had been as an attendant in a gas station. He carried a machine gun (which one report described as a pistol with a barrel fifteen inches long), what appeared to be a smoke grenade, and what he told a stewardess was dynamite in an attaché case. He forced the captain to fly back to St. Louis, where he allowed all of the women and children plus some of the men on the plane to disembark. While the plane was circling St. Louis, he demanded $502,200, plus parachutes and a shovel. While the plane was on the ground, a man in a late-model Cadillac drove through police lines and crashed his car into the plane, disabling it from taking off. The driver was taken to the hospital in critical condition. The hijacker transferred planes and demanded that the captain fly him to Toronto. While en route, he had the pilot show him how to strap on the parachute. He bailed out over Peru, Indiana, but lost the money in the slipstream. The pilot had told McNally that the plane was going much slower than its true speed. A farmer later found the money in a field, and the hijacker's gun was found three miles away. The FBI arrested the hijacker in Detroit on June 28. An accomplice was arrested two days later and identified as Walter J. Petlikowsky, who was born on January 21, 1941 in Poland. The white accomplice's case was not relevant to the FAA profiling system. McNally was sentenced to two concurrent life terms for aircraft piracy on December 14, 1972. Petlikowsky was sentenced to ten years on May 18, 1973, for aiding and assisting one sought for air piracy. 5373

June 26, 1972—Italy—Dagmar Jensen, twenty-one, was arrested while trying to sneak a gun aboard a Scanair plane due to fly from Rome to Copenhagen. Mengesha Befekadu, twenty-three, was accused of being an accomplice. 5374

June 26, 1972—United States—William John Macicak, Jr., phoned Ozark Airlines in Chicago and threatened to blow up an aircraft if he was not paid $50,000. He was arrested when he went to pick up the money left by the airline.

June 30, 1972—United States—Airwest flight RW 775, a DC9 flying from Seattle to Portland, was hijacked by a white male who met the FAA profile: Daniel B. Carre, who was born in Hood River, Oregon, on April 26, 1947. He demanded $50,000 and a parachute but was apprehended at Portland. He was committed to a mental institution on July 5, 1972. 5375

June 30, 1972—United States—The licensed nuclear facility of Babcock and Wilcox, a Virginia firm, received a bomb threat.

June 30, 1972—Argentina—Ernanno Barca, the president of the Buenos Aires branch of the Banco di Napoli, a leading Italian bank, was kidnapped by four armed men and released unharmed after the payment of a $200,000 ransom. 1082

July 1972—Lebanon—The assistant manager of Beirut's Rifbank was injured by a letter bomb. The firm did some business with Palestinians. 1095

July 1972—Lebanon—Shafiq al-Hout, PLO director in Beirut, was sent a letter bomb, but it was detected before it could explode. 1096

July 1972—Lebanon—Marwan Dajani, an Al Fatah leader, and Abu al-Hassan, a PLO intelligence officer, were sent letter bombs, which were discovered before they exploded. 1097-1098

July 1972—Lebanon—Dr. Azmi Awad, a Palestinian physician working for the Red Crescent relief organization, found a bomb in his car engine. 1099

July 2, 1972—South Vietnam—Pan Am flight 841, a B747 flying from San Francisco to Honolulu and Saigon, was hijacked out of Saigon by an Oriental who did not meet the FAA profile: Nguyen Thai Binh, who was born in Vietnam on January 14, 1948. Using a switchblade and a bag of explosives, he demanded to fly to Hanoi in protest of U.S. bombing of North Vietnam. The pilot, Gene Vaughn, had given his gun to a retired policeman. The pilot grabbed the hijacker and instructed the policeman to "shoot the s.o.b." He fired five shots at the hijacker, killing him. Seventeen crew members and 164 passengers were reported on the flight, and several of them were injured while leaving the plane. 5376

July 4, 1972—Philippines—A group of leftist demonstrators throwing explosive pillboxes attacked the police guarding the U.S. embassy in Manila. They were repulsed, but thirty people were injured by fragments. 1083

July 4, 1972—United States—The licensed nuclear facility of the Colorado Public Service Company at Fort St. Vrain received a bomb threat.

July 4, 1972—Guam—A Pan American 707 received a sabotage threat and landed with its fifty-four passengers at Osaka International Airport. No bomb was found.

July 5, 1972—United States—A Pacific Southwest B737, flight 710 flying from Sacramento to Hollywood and San Francisco with eighty-four persons on board, was hijacked by two Bulgarian white males who probably met the FAA profile: Dimitri K. Alexiev, who was born on January 30, 1944, and Michael D. Azmanoff, who was born on January 24, 1944. They were armed with pistols and threatened the passengers and stewardesses. They forced the pilot to fly to San Francisco, where they kept everyone on board the plane for four hours while they demanded $800,000, two parachutes, and a flight to Siberia. FBI agents carrying the money entered the plane but fired on the hijackers, killing them and a passenger in the crossfire, as well as wounding two others. An accomplice, a white male for whom the FAA profile was not applicable, was identified as Lubomir Peichev, who was born on March 19, 1943, in Sofia, Bulgaria. He was sentenced to concurrent terms of life imprisonment and twenty years on December 21, 1972, for aiding and abetting air piracy and conspiring to interfere with commerce by extortion. 5377

July 5, 1972—United States—Charles E. Smith, a black for whom the FAA profile was not applicable, and who had been born on December 16, 1948, in Canton, Mississippi, entered a parked empty American Airlines B707 at Buffalo's airport and demanded to be flown out of the United States. He had just stabbed his wife and a friend before arriving at the airport and held his daughter at knifepoint for three hours before surrendering. He was convicted of custodial interference, a state kidnapping statute, on June 6, 1973, and was sentenced to five years' probation on July 18, 1973. 5378

July 6, 1972—United States—Pacific Southwest flight 389, a B727 flying from Oakland to Sacramento, was hijacked by a white male who met the FAA profile: Francis M. Goodell, who was born on March 31, 1951, in Omaha, Nebraska. He used two pistols to force the pilot to land in San Diego, where he freed the passengers and was given $455,000 and a parachute. He claimed the money was for "two organizations involved in the Mideast crisis" and flew to Oakland, where he demanded a helicopter. He surrendered to the FBI. On January 17, 1973, he was convicted of aircraft piracy and using a firearm to commit a felony, and sentenced on February 12, 1973, to twenty-five years and five years, to run consecutively. Fifty-seven persons were on board the flight. 5379

July 9, 1972—Lebanon—Gassan Kanafani, painter, poet, editor of the PFLP's weekly journal *Al Hadef*, PFLP spokesman, and number four in the group's hierarchy, died when a bomb exploded in his car, in front of his home in Hazmiyeh, outside Beirut. His niece, Lamis Najem, seventeen, was also killed while walking to his car. His wife, the former Annie Hover of Copenhagen, and his small son and daughter were in the area but unharmed by the blast. The PFLP vowed vengeance and charged that Israeli or Jordanian agents, or a conspiracy of the two, were responsible for the killing. His widow said it was not possible for Palestinians to have committed the attack. In mid-June, the Israeli newspaper *Haaretz* had blamed Kanafani for organizing the Lod Airport attack. According to reporter David Tinnin, Israeli frogmen had slipped ashore in Beirut and planted a radio-triggered bomb in the car but had not intended to kill his niece. Kanafani liked to keep up on Israeli information programs abroad and while in the car was reading a packet of Israeli materials sent him through Arab diplomatic channels in Denmark. After the explosion, a card reading, "With the compliments of the embassy of Israel in Copenhagen," was found. The Israelis put a less benign interpretation upon Kanafani's possession of the card. On July 9, a spokesman for Israel's National Police Headquarters in Jerusalem said that the bomb had gone off accidentally and was apparently intended as part of an Arab terrorist plot to kill Israelis overseas. Spokesman Mordechai Tavor noted that Kanafani's brother lived in Denmark and may have been involved in a plot to send parcels that would be mistaken as having been sent from the Israeli Copehagen embassy. The Lebanese security service reported that the same assassination technique had been used in 1955 in Gaza against Egyptian intelligence officers and against German missile and rocket specialists working for Egypt in 1962.

July 10, 1972—West Germany—A Lufthansa B737 flying from Cologne to Munich was hijacked by an Algerian, N. Bachalt, who demanded $100,000. He was apprehended aboard the plane by German police. 5380

July 11, 1972—Israel—In reprisal for Kanafani's death on July 9, the PFLP threw a grenade in a Tel Aviv bus terminal, wounding nine. 1084

July 12, 1972—Ivory Coast—A man planned to hijack a French UTA plane flying from Abidjan to Paris, but the plane was diverted prior to landing at Abidjan, depriving him of the opportunity to attack it. He was shot and apprehended after he shot his wife. 5381

July 12, 1972—United States—American Airlines flight 633, a B727 flying from Oklahoma City to Dallas with fifty-seven persons on board, was hijacked by a white male who met the FAA profile: Melvin Martin Fisher, who was born in Norman, Oklahoma, on November 26, 1922. Using an empty revolver, he demanded $550,000 and a parachute. He released the passengers in Norman and surrendered to a stewardess after he received $200,000. He was sentenced to life imprisonment for air piracy on September 28, 1972. 5382

July 12, 1972—United States—National Airlines flight 496, a B727 flying from Philadelphia to New York City was hijacked by two black males who met the FAA profile: Michael S. Green, who was born in Washington, D.C., on March 2, 1938, and Lulseged Tesfa, who was born on March 10, 1950, in Addis Ababa, Ethiopia. Armed with a pistol and a sawed-off shotgun, they forced the plane to return to Philadelphia, where they demanded $600,000 and three parachutes and released the passengers. National paid $501,600. The plane flew on to Lake Jackson, Texas, where the pilots swerved the plane, blowing the tires. The pair surrendered and were indicted on two counts of air piracy. Green was convicted of air piracy on June 19, 1973, and sentenced on March 18, 1974 to fifty years. Tesfa was sentenced on December 2, 1974 to sixty years for air piracy. 5383

July 13, 1972—France—Thirty members of the Jura separatist group Les Beliers occupied the Swiss embassy in Paris, demanding autonomy for the Jura canton. 1085

July 16, 1972—Japan—Two fourteen-year-old boys phoned All Nippon Airways and said that a bomb was on board a 727, which made an emergency landing.

July 17, 1972—Colombia—The first secretary of the Swedish embassy in Bogotá, Kjell R. Haeggloef, was shot to death by unidentified gunmen. 1086

July 17, 1972—Mexico—A panel truck containing plastic cans filled with gasoline to which were attached dynamite caps exploded in front of the U.S. consulate general in Monterey, destroying the truck but causing no damage to the consulate general or any injuries. 1087

July 18, 1972—Colombia—An Aero Opita Tao flying from San Andrés Island to Bogotá was hijacked by Benjamin Suarez, who killed the pilot and severely wounded the copilot, who was nonetheless able to land the plane with its fifty-two persons on board. Suarez was overpowered by other passengers. 5384

July 18, 1972—Philippines—An attaché case containing fifteen pounds of explosives was discovered in the USIS Cultural Center in Manila. The case had been checked at the desk by an unknown patron on Friday evening, and the device was timed to explode at 1 A.M. Saturday. The guard did not check the case until Monday morning, and the building was saved only by the failure of the timing device. 1088

July 19, 1972—Lebanon—The director of the PLO research center in Beirut, Anis Sayegh, who is also the brother of Fayez Sayegh, director of the Arab League's information service in the United States, was partially blinded when a package bomb exploded. 1089

July 20, 1972—South Africa—The U.S. consul general in Pretoria received a phone call from an unidentified male threatening to firebomb the "American embassy" if the consul general attended a ceremony in Natal unveiling the tombstone of Chief Albert Luthuli, a Nobel Prize-winning South African black leader. 1090

July 21, 1972—Switzerland—A telephone call at 2:55 P.M. from a Swiss-German speaker advised that the U.S. consulate general in Zurich would be reduced to rubble at 4:15 that afternoon. After evacuation and a negative search of the premises, business was resumed. 1091

July 22, 1972—Northern Ireland—On Bloody Friday, twenty-two bombs exploded in Belfast in the space of eighty minutes, killing eleven people and wounding 130. The IRA claimed credit. Military action against the IRA was intensified.

July 22, 1972—Lebanon—The successor as PFLP spokesman to the assassinated Ghassan Kanafani, twenty-five-year-old Bassam Abu Sharif, was blinded in his right eye and severely wounded elsewhere in the face and body, losing several fingers, when a book bomb exploded in his hands in the Al Hadaf office. The book was entitled Days of Terror. 1092

July 28, 1972—Uruguay—Hector Menoni, United Press International manager in Uruguay, was kidnapped by OPR-33 but released unharmed the next day. 1093

July 31, 1972—United States—Delta Airlines flight 841, a DC8 flying ninety-four persons from Detroit to Miami, was hijacked over Florida by five Black Panther Party sympathizers and their three children, who met the FAA profile. They used guns to demand that they be given $1 million and be flown to Algeria. The passengers were freed in Miami, and the ransom was paid. The plane refuelled in Boston before landing in Algiers the next day. The group was taken into custody but freed on August 4. The money was returned to Delta on August 23, 1972. The three children who accompanied the hijackers returned to the United States in December 1972. The hijackers were identified as Melvin McNair, born in Greensboro, North Carolina, on October 31, 1948; Jean McNair, born in Winston-Salem, North Carolina, on October 11, 1946; George E. Wright (also known as Burgess), born in Halifax, Virginia, on March 29, 1943; George Brown (also known as Singleton), born on March 28, 1944, in Elizabeth, New Jersey; and Joyce Burgess (also known as Tillerson), born in Spartanburg, South Carolina, on June 6, 1941. The group minus Wright were arrested in Paris on May 28, 1976. They faced possible extradition to the United States and appealed to the French people on October 11, 1976, that they not be sent home, arguing that because of racial discrimination, ''we would not be judged impartially and we would be condemned to spend the rest of our days in infernal prisons. . . .We are ready to face the consequences of our act. But at the same time we ask not to be delivered to the American authorities.'' They had been arrested for carrying false U.S. passports. The U.S. extradition request was turned down by France in November 1976. They were ordered to stand trial in France on hijacking charges. 1094

August 1972—Guatemala—An American businessman was kidnapped but freed after paying a sizable ransom. Leftist guerrillas were suspected. 1100

August 1972—United States—The Southern California Edison Company's licensed nuclear facility at San Onofre received a bomb threat.

August 1972—United States—The VEPCO licensed nuclear facility at North Anna, Virginia, received bomb threats on August 1, 10 (two), 11, 14, and 15.

August 1, 1972—United States—The Gulf-United Nuclear Fuels Corporation's licensed nuclear facility in Elmsford, New York, received a bomb threat.

August 3, 1972—United Kingdom—Two telephone calls threatening sabotage against various airlines on transatlantic routes disrupted Heathrow Airport for two hours while searches were made for bombs. Nothing was found.

August 5, 1972—Italy—A joint PFLP-Black September squad led by Mohammed Boudia set off four explosives, including at least one time bomb, at the
trans-Alpine oil terminal at Trieste, destroying six of twenty-five oil tanks in a
fire that burned for two days. Damage was estimated at $7 million. The group
claimed that the attack was against Zionist and imperialist interests, which
they called the enemies of Palestinians, pointing out that the port facility
supplied oil to West Germany and Austria, both of which supported Israel.
Warrants were issued for the arrests of Boudia, another Algerian, two French
women, and Ludovico Codella, an Italian who was ultimately arrested. The rest
escaped to France. Italy was never able to produce enough evidence to back an
extradition request. 1101

August 8, 1972—Iran—A small bomb exploded in the washroom of the Iran
American Society in Shiraz around 10 A.M., causing extensive damage but no
injuries. 1102

August 15, 1972—According to the ICAO, Armando Disdiel, fifty-four, an
unarmed individual, attempted to force his way into the cockpit of a domestic
flight but was overpowered and charged with interfering with the crew while in
flight. 5385

August 15, 1972—Argentina—An Austral BAC111 flying from Trelew to
Buenos Aires was hijacked by nine men and one woman, including prison
escapees, who forced the pilot to refuel at Puerto Montt, Chile, before landing
in Santiago, Chile, where they were granted political asylum by President
Allende, who allowed them to fly to Cuba on August 25. The Argentine
government, which had demanded extradition, recalled its Ambassador the
next day. The group was among twenty-six political prisoners who had
escaped during a mutiny at an army maximum security prison at Rawson,
fifteen miles from Trelew. The group went to the airport, where ten of them
entered the Austral plane, which had ninety-six people already on board. The
others waited for the next flight, but they were captured by Argentine police.
On August 22, thirteen of the guerillas were killed in an alleged breakout
attempt from the prison at the naval air base near Trelew, in the southern
province of Chubut. The three other prisoners were wounded. Casualties
included twelve members of the ERP, one member of the FAR, and two
Montoneros. The wife of ERP leader Roberto Mario Santucho was among
those killed. (Other reports claim that all sixteen died in what appeared to be
official retaliation for the hijacking.) The response of the government caused
demonstrations throughout Argentina and has become a major anniversary for
leftist revolutionaries in that country. Those who flew to Havana were ERP
members Mario Robert Santucho, a public accountant; medical student
Domingo Menna, twenty-five, Enrique Gorriaran, Alejandro Ferreyra, and
Victor Fernandez Palmeiro; Fernando Vaca Narvaja, twenty-four, of the

Montoneros; and FAR members Marcos Osatinsky, lawyer Robert Jorge Quieto, thirty-four, Ana Dora Wiesen, and Carlos Goldenberg. Santucho's (secretary-general of the Revolutionary Workers' Party (PRT)) wife died at Trelew, as did Susana Lesgart, twenty-three, Narvaja's wife. 1103-1104

August 16, 1972—Italy—A bomb placed in a portable record player stored in the aft baggage compartment of an El Al B707 flying from Rome to Tel Aviv with 148 persons on board exploded shortly after takeoff. The bomb contained two hundred grams of explosive and used a barometric firing device. The blast caused a crack in the rear door and a hole in the baggage compartment, which had been armored by the Israelis. Reports differ on whether there were any casualties, with some claiming that four people were slightly injured. The plane returned safely to Rome. The Nationalist Youth Group for the Liberation of Palestine claimed credit for the blast, although reports also give responsibility for the bombing to Black September and the PFLP-GC. Two British women who had been on vacation informed authorities that they had been given the phonograph (which had also been reported as a radio, tape-recorder, and gramaphone) by two men they had been dating in Rome. The men, Adnam Ali Hasham and Ahmed Zaid, a student leader, told the women they were Persians and said that they had to fly to Tehran to collect money rather than fly on with them to Israel. However, they bought the women's tickets, gave them the device, and promised to meet them in Jerusalem. Given their descriptions, Rome police arrested the men, who were identified as an Iraqi and a Jordanian. In February 1973, they disappeared from Italy after being given provisional liberty on the grounds that the bomb ''was not adequate to destroy the airliner.'' 1105

August 17, 1972—Northern Ireland—Fifty-five people were injured by one of three bombs exploded in Belfast.

August 18, 1972—United States—United Airlines flight 877, a B727 flying from Reno to San Francisco with twenty-two passengers, was hijacked to Seattle by a white male for whom the FAA profile was not applicable: Frank M. Sibley, Jr., who was born in Baltimore on June 4, 1929. Armed with a rifle, he forced his way aboard the aircraft and demanded $2 million, fifteen pounds of gold, and a flight to Vancouver. The money and gold were paid, but he was shot and captured by the FBI in Seattle. He was convicted of aircraft piracy on October 18, 1972, and on February 28, 1973, sentenced to thirty years. 5386

August 22, 1972—Lebanon—A Southern Yemeni Al Yemda Airlines DC6 flying sixty-one persons on the Beirut-Cairo-Aden run was hijacked by two males and a woman who were armed with guns and claimed to be members of the Eagles of National Unity. The plane refueled in Cyprus and then flew on to Benghazi, Libya, where they requested political asylum. The plane was allowed to fly to Cairo without the hijackers, who were freed by the Libyans on August 27. The Southern Yemeni government claimed that the hijackers were a reactionary group supported by Saudi Arabia. 1106

August 25, 1972—Colombia—An Opita Air Taxi (TAO) four-engined turbo-prop flying from Neiva to Bogotá with thirty-one persons was hijacked in flight by four men, who allowed the plane to refuel in Barrancabermeja before proceeding to Cuba. 5387

August 25, 1972—Philippines—A grenade exploded fifty feet from the guard barracks at the Tinang transmitter site of the Voice of America's Philippine relay station. The grenade, apparently directed by a launcher, landed near a group of contract guards during a change of shift guard mount just before midnight. 1107

August 26, 1972—Philippines—A bomb exploded near the wall of the sea-front embassy staff housing apartments of the U.S. embassy in Manila at 4:45 A.M. Two hundred panes of jalousie glass were broken in several apartments, but no one was injured. 1108

August 29, 1972—Greece—A small bomb exploded in the basement women's restroom of the U.S. embassy in Athens at 2:30 P.M., causing no injuries. A warning had been telephoned to the Associated Press office, and police and bomb experts were arriving at the embassy as the bomb exploded. On September 4, the Popular Revolutionary Resistance claimed responsibility for it, as well as for two 1971 bombings related to the visit of U.S. Vice-President Spiro T. Agnew. 1109

August 30, 1972—Greece—In Athens, telephoned bomb threats were received at the U.S. embassy commercial library and the USIS offices and library. 1110-1112

August 30, 1972—France—The son of the Jordanian ambassador to France was kidnapped but released the following day after his father paid a $40,000 ransom. It was initially believed that Arab guerrillas were responsible, but the ambassador later stated that he believed this was not the case. 1113

August 30, 1972—United States—An unidentified individual phoned Milwaukee airport, warning that a bomb would go off if he was not paid $100,000. A fake bomb was found in a locker, and the money was not delivered.

September 4, 1972—Iran—The USIS Binational Center in Tehran at 8 P.M. received a telephoned bomb threat, prompting classes at the academic center to be dismissed ten minutes early. Nothing was found. 1114

September 5, 1972—Argentina—Six Montoneros kidnapped Dutch citizen Jan J. Van de Panne, who headed the Philips Argentina electronics firm in Buenos Aires. The group demanded a $500,000 ransom, which the company paid. The executive was released unharmed two days later. 1115

September 5, 1972—West Germany—Eight members of Black September broke into the Israeli quarters at the Olympic Games in Munich, killing two Israeli athletes and taking nine others hostage. They demanded the release of 236 guerillas in Israeli jails, including Kozo Okamoto, the release of Andreas Baader and Ulrike Meinhof, and safe passage to a foreign country. After a shootout with police, the hostages were killed, as were five of the terrorists and a West German policeman. The three surviving terrorists, two of whom were wounded, were released after the hijacking of a Lufthansa jet the next month (see incident 1257).

Two German workmen first saw six terrorists at the village fence at 4:15 A.M., as did a Uruguayan shotputter, but thought they were pranksters or members of a track team coming home late. The group cut through the fence and made their way to dormitory building 31, which housed the Hong Kong, Uruguayan, and Israeli teams. At 5:30 A.M., the group burst into the Israelis' quarters. Only one Israeli, weight-lifting coach Tuvia Sokolsky, escaped in the first attack, although Gad Tsobari, a wrestler, escaped during a fight with the attackers. In all, six of the team managed to reach safety. One of the team members, wrestling coach Moshe Weinberg, thirty-three, held the door against the attackers while shouting for his friends to flee. He was cut down by bursts from the AK-47s. Joseph Romano, a thirty-three-year-old weight lifter, was killed while fighting the terrorists. The nine Israelis who were trapped were reported to have fought their attackers with knives but were soon overcome and tied with cords precut to the correct length. Their hands were tied behind their backs, and they were forced to hobble to a central location. Soon afterward, the terrorists threw a note out of a window with their demands—the release of the 236 prisoners within four hours and safe passage out of Germany. They threatened to kill two of their hostages every half hour after the 9 A.M. deadline. During their negotiations, deadlines were moved back to noon, 1 P.M., 3 P.M., and 5 P.M. The Germans offered an amount of money to be specified by the terrorists, and the German interior minister, Hans Dietrich Genscher, offered himself and his colleagues as substitute hostages. These suggestions were turned down. The initial negotiations were established between a police officer, Amalise Graes, and the terrorists' leader, Esa, who trained a machine gun on Graes and kept a hand grenade ready. He told her that his father was Jewish, his mother Jordanian, and that his brothers, eighteen and twenty-eight years old, were prisoners in Israeli jails.

The police were unsuccessful in plans to trick the terrorists, which included a suggestion to poison food sent to them. Schreiber and the head of the Egyptian Olympics team, Ahmed Touni, repeated their monetary offers to the terrorists, who replied "Money means nothing to us; our lives mean nothing to us." The terrorists again extended their deadline but threatened to shoot two hostages in front of the building. At 12:30, a third deadline postponement was granted when Genscher and Merk told the terrorists that they were still talking to the Israeli government. The deadline was then extended to 2:30 P.M., and the Tunisian ambassador later got an extension to 5 P.M. At 4:30, while the police squad assembled to storm the building, the terrorists demanded to be flown to Cairo with their hostages. They also called for a swap of hostages for the prisoners in Israel when the plane touched down.

The West Germans traced calls made by the terrorists to Beirut and Tunisia. The Beirut number belonged to a Palestinian refugee organization. Tunisia's ambassador said that the Tunis number belonged to an unnamed "honorable personage." In any case, the calls were unanswered. After these calls, at around 3:30 P.M., Tunisian Ambassador Mahmoud Mestiri managed to get the deadline extended.

Chancellor Willy Brandt had phoned the Israeli government, who urged that the demands of the terrorists not be granted, although the Israelis were willing to give the group safe passage if their athletes were released. Brandt also attempted to reach Egyptian President Sadat, but could only get Prime Minister Sidki, to whom he suggested that the terrorists be allowed to fly to Cairo. Sidki claimed that this was not Egypt's affair and that he could do nothing about it. Egypt would later claim that Brandt misunderstood Sidki, who meant Egypt was powerless to influence the terrorists, as were the West Germans. One last delay of the deadline was achieved between 6:30 and 9 P.M. During this time, the Libyan ambassador in Munich offered to mediate but was turned down. He had suggested that he attempt to reduce the demands from 236 to 13 imprisoned guerrillas' release. At 9 P.M., the terrorists agreed to leave the building with their hostages. At 10:10 P.M., using underground corridors, the terrorists boarded a bus with their hostages and were taken to their helicopters, which flew them to Fürstenfeldbruck Military Airport, instead of Riem, Munich's main civil airport. A Lufthansa B707 was waiting when the helicopters landed at 10:35. Although Mohammed (also known as Esa) had agreed not to hold the four pilots hostage, the Black Septemberists now kept their guns trained on them. Two of the terrorists traversed the 165 yards from their helicopter to the plane. Police had initially been on board the plane disguised as the plane's crew, but this plan had been vetoed at the last minute. The two terrorists walked back to the helicoper, suspecting a trick by the authorities, and were fired upon by the five police snipers. Two terrorists standing beside the helicopters and one of the men walking across the tarmac were immediately killed. However, the leader, Mohammed Masalhah, dove for cover. The other terrorists fired on the hostages and control tower, killing a policeman and damaging the tower's radio. At 10:50, the police called upon the terrorists in English, German, and Arabic to surrender, but were fired on. The terrorists were armed with automatic machine guns; the Germans had only single-shot rifles. At 12:04, a terrorist jumped from a helicopter and threw a grenade into its cabin. Another terrorist emerged from where he had been hiding. Both were immediately shot by the police snipers, but the grenade had already gone off, killing the nine hostages. Arriving firemen were kept at bay by the surviving three terrorists. Armored cars moved in and captured the trio near the un-damaged helicopter. One of the volunteer helicopter pilots was badly wounded in the lung. One of the Israelis apparently died of smoke inhalation. During the attack, Bonn's official government spokesman erroneously informed reporters that all of the hostages had been successfuly rescued.

Among the German authorities with major roles in the negotiations were Dr. Georg Schmidt, the police director of the Munich state police, who would later escort the surviving trio to freedom in Yugoslavia; Dr. Manfred Schreiber, the president of the Munich State Police and a member of the crisis staff, who was the primary negotiator with the terrorists and who was in charge of all police action; Lieutenant Colonel Peter Schulze, a member of the German Luftwaffe, who was in charge of communications at Fürstenfeldbruck; and Dr. Georg Wolf, vice-president of the Munich State Police, who was in charge of the police operations at Fürstenfeldbruck. Some reports claim that the chief of Israeli intelligence was at the airport, advising the Germans.

Three senior officials of the Shin Beth, Israel's Department of Internal Security, were fired as a result of the poor security arrangements for the Olympics. Germany later toughened immigration and registration restrictions on Palestinian students and workers.

The games had been allowed to continue during the negotiations, but were postponed for one day while a remembrance service was held for Israeli athletes. The service was marred when Arab athletes refused to participate and Soviet and Eastern European teams kicked soccer balls on practice fields near the service.

The dead Israelis were identified as David Berger, Zeev Friedman, Yosef Gutterfreund, Eliezer Halfin, Yosef Romano, Amitzur Shapiro, Kehat Shorr, Mark Slavin, Andrei Spitz, Yaacov Springer, and Moshe Weinberg. Romano was born in Libya, Berger was an American (his body was flown back to Cleveland), and Slavin, eighteen, had emigrated from the Soviet Union four months previously, after having demonstrated in front of the Minsk KGB headquarters in support of Jewish emigration. A nationwide funeral was held for the slain athletes in Israel.

Four days later, the dead terrorists were flown to Libya, where they were mourned at Tripoli's main mosque. Official radio called them martyrs and heroes. The Voice of Palestine broadcast the terrorists' will, which was sent to the station a few hours before their attack. With it they sent $500 and 37 marks, to be given to the Palestinian revolution. In their will, they said, "We are neither killers nor bandits. We are persecuted people who have no land and no homeland." They also said that they "give up our lives from the very first moment. . . .This time we shall force them to know we are serious. . . .We will the youth of the Arab nation to search for death so that life is given to them, their countries and their people. Each drop of blood spilled from you and from us will be oil to kindle this nation with flames of victory and liberation.'' They apologized for interrupting the games. ''We are asking them to know that there is a people with a twenty-four-year-old case. . . .It would do no harm to the youth of the world to learn of our plight only in a few hours. We are not against any people, but why should our place here be taken by the flag of the occupiers . . .why should the whole world be having fun and entertainment while we suffer with all ears deaf to us?'' It was also rumored that Libya's Colonel Qaddafi paid Black September $5 million for the operation.

On September 14, the PLO Executive Committee in Damascus stated that it was not responsible for the attack and that its objective ''was only aimed at pressuring Israel to release detained guerillas from Israeli jails.''

In February 1973, a Palestinian, Abu Daoud, who would later figure prominently in a 1977 extradition squabble between Israel, West Germany, and France, was arrested by Jordanian police and questioned. Daoud told his Jordanian interrogators that in August 1972 he had traveled to Sofia to buy arms for Fatah, carrying a forged Iraqi passport for Saad ad-Din Wali. Abu Iyad and Fakhri al Umari arrived from Geneva and informed him of the Olympics plan. Daoud was ordered to give Umari his passport because it contained a valid German visa. Daoud claims that he did so after returning from Libya and that he took no other part in the attack. Many observers disagree with this claim and believe that Daoud was a major organizer of the attack. German police found that Umari and Wali (whom they believed was Daoud) were in Munich at the same time. Wali was registered at a small Munich hotel from late June until September 5. Daoud's account was broadcast over Amman radio. He claimed that ''three days after my return to Libya, Abu Iyad contacted Fakhri al Umari and asked him to go to Munich with Yusaf Nazzal, who was traveling on an Algerian passport. In Munich, Fakhri al Umari tried to enter and reconnoiter the Olympics Village, but he was turned away. He was obliged to get another person to help him. He got Mohammed Masalhah from Libya because he knows several languages, including German, and had worked as an architect in the Olympic Village while it was being built. . . .It was Masalhah who reconnoitered the village, using his cleverness, his good German and his knowledge of the entrances. He was able to learn where the Israelis were staying, which was opposite the Saudi team. The Saudis did not know anything about this operation, but Masalhah got into their quarters in his capacity as an architect and he was able to find out that the Israeli building was similar to the Saudi building and so plan the attack. . . .Maslahah had taken with him the instructions for the operation from Abu Iyad. He had a statement written in English and a list of the fedayeen detainees whose release was to be demanded. Two groups totaling six were to take part in the operation, making eight with Masalhah and Yusuf Nazzal. They were to detain the Israeli team and negotiate for the release of the fedayeen. The code name for the operation was Ikrit and Birim (the names of two Arab villages which the Israelis occupied in 1948 and have refused to give back). If the Israelis released their prisoners and took them to any Arab country except Lebanon or Jordan, the members of the Israeli team were to be taken with the eight men by plane to Tunisia, and there they would have been released. In the event of a refusal, they were to go in a plane to Tunis, provided they were able to safeguard their travel to the airport in a closed van. The instructions did not include opening fire on the Israeli team. . . .The youths had come from Libya. Some of them came via Rome to Munich and the others came via Belgrade. Each group was composed of three people. The first group arrived on September 2 and the second the following day. Fakhri al Umari supplied the arms in two installments, the first on September 1 and the second on the morning of September 4. The arms consisted of eight Kalashnikovs and ten grenades. Mohammed Masalhah took the arms from a box at the railway station, where they had been left by Fakhri al Umari. Mohammed Masalhah and Yusuf Nazzal booked the youths into hotels in Munich. . . .Fakhri al Umari left on September 4 for Rome before the operation started and from there he went to Tripoli in Libya. After one day he flew to Beirut and then went to Damascus, where he remained. . . .The man responsible for the Munich operation was the acting political officer Mohammed Masalhah. No German nationals or Arabs resident in Germany took part in the operation. . . .The plan was that the young men would jump over the wall at 0400 on September 5.''

Daoud's testimony should be compared to the account given by reporter David Tinnin of the activities of Ali Hassan Salameh. According to Tinnin, Salameh assigned Umari, chief of Black September assassins, to the case. Umari collected the weapons, possibly from an Arab diplomatic facility in West Germany, hid them in airline flight bags, and checked them in the luggage room of Munich's train station. When he tried to case the Olympics Village, he was sent away by guards. Mohammed Masalhah, a Libyan architect, was then given the assignment and was later chosen to lead the terrorists. Two other BSO members were told to get village jobs. The Syrian embassy vouched for them on their employment questionnaires. The other five terrorists underwent training in a refugee camp near Deraa, Syria, and then left on a circuitous route to Munich. The terrorists were ultimately to take the hostages to Tunis, which accounted for the phone calls. But according to Tinnin, the Tunisian contact apparently panicked and backed out.

On October 29, 1972, Black September hijacked Lufthansa flight 615 flying from Damascus to Frankfurt and successully obtained the release of the three remaining terrorists, identified as Abdullah Samir, Abdel Kadir el Dnawy, and Ibrahim Badran, picked them up at Zagreb airport, and flew on to Libya, where they disappeared.

The Israelis retaliated for the attack by raiding refugee camps in Lebanon on February 21, 1973, killing thirty-one. They later shot down a Libyan airliner that had overflown Israeli air space, killing all 107 aboard. Israeli officials had blamed Egypt, Syria, and Lebanon for being behind the Olympic attack, saying, "The Egyptians are the prime party in this incident. They have the power and influence to stop these groups, and instead they encourage them." Some reporters also claim that the Olympics attack led the Israelis to establish assassination squads, which killed more than a dozen members of Black September in the coming year. Salameh died on Janaury 22, 1979, when a bomb exploded in a car his entourage was passing in Beirut. 1116

September 6-8, 1972—Jamaica—The U.S. embassy chancery and residence in Kingston received numerous bomb threats. Three searches were all negative. 1117-1119

September 9, 1972—Greece—The Greek government announced that a Greek underground organization had planned to kidnap foreign diplomats, including U.S. Ambassador Henry Tasca. The threat was uncovered while questioning arrested members of the organization, which also led to the discovery of weapons planned for use in the kidnappings. 1120

September 9, 1972—France—A bomb was found in the washroom of an Air France B747 flying from Paris to Montreal with 354 persons on board. The plane landed in Gander, where the bomb was dismantled. There were no injuries.

September 10, 1972—Iran—At 11:30 A.M., a bomb blew up in a room near the washroom of the toilet building in the rear of the USIS Binational Center in Meshed. A dozen windows of the nearby center building were also broken. No injuries were reported, although one class was in session at the time of the explosion. 1121

September 11, 1972—Belgium—Ophir Zadok, an Israeli security officer at the Israeli embassy in Brussels, was lured to Prince's Café in De Brouckere Square by a caller who claimed to have information about a terrorist plot against the embassy, and who gave his name as Mohammed Ahmed Rabbah. Two fedayeen terrorists fired weapons at him, critically wounding him with two bullets. Some accounts credit the attack to Fatah or Black September; others believe Zadok was an undercover Mossad officer, the caller was one of his Palestinian contacts, or the caller was a Moroccan who had once been an agent for Israeli intelligence. According to the café's owner, Jean Redding, "I noticed a man looking like an Arab pacing the pavement as if waiting for someone. He was soon joined by another man of the same type and they both came into the café. Another man had come in and was sitting in a dark corner without ordering. The two Arab-looking men stood there for a moment, one of them nodding toward the seated man as if pointing him out. Then he walked out in a hurry. I then heard five shots and saw the man sitting alone stand up, covered in blood. He staggered toward the front door and collapsed on a seat. The gunman, holding a light machine gun, rushed past him into the street and disappeared.'' 1122

September 12, 1972—The crews of two El Al planes were threatened with assassination. Both planes took off without incident. 1123-1124

September 14, 1972—Tanzania—An East African Airways DC9 that was due to fly from Dar es Salaam to Nairobi was parked overnight in Dar. When the crew reported for duty, the plane had disappeared. It was found later in Kilamanjaro, with burst tires and other damage. No injuries were reported, and no one was on board.

September 14, 1972—United States—In retaliation for the Olympic massacre, a bomb was thrown at a Hollywood apartment house where a Palestinian Arab was a tenant. 1125

September 14, 1972—Northern Ireland—Two people were killed and forty-nine injured by a bomb explosion in a Belfast hotel.

September 15, 1972—Sweden—SAS flight 130, a DC9 flying from Goteborg to Stockholm with seventy-nine passengers and four crew members, was hijacked by three Croatian males, Tomislav Rebrina (their leader), Nikila Lisac, and Rudolf Preskalo, who forced the plane to Malmo. They demanded the release of seven Croatians in Swedish jails, including two who had been convicted of the 1971 murder of the Yugoslav ambassador, Rolovic (see incident 0744). Marinco Lemo and Stanco Milicevic were scheduled to be free at the end of their short sentences on November 1, 1972. Milicevic thus refused to be released, but Lemo, after being pressed into negotiating with the hijackers by the minister of justice, agreed to board the plane in exchange for the passenger. The hijackers had threatened to blow up the plane if the prisoners, including Milo Bareshic, twenty-one, and Adnjelko Brajkovic, were not released. After releasing thirty passengers, the group demanded $200,000 but settled for $105,000 and the six prisoners. They flew to Madrid, Spain, where another three hours of negotiating followed, much of which entailed squabbling between the hijackers. They apparently were not certain that many countries would be willing to accept them and surrendered to Spanish authorities. The six who had been released in Sweden were permitted to leave for Asunción, Paraguay, on June 23, 1974. Sweden requested that three of them be extradited for involvement in the 1971 murder of Rolovic. Paraguay issued warrants for their arrest, but they have not been found. Press reports speculated that the group fled to Uruguay. On December 5, 1974, a Spanish military court sentenced the three hijackers to twelve years in prison, but on February 13, 1975, General Franco granted them a full pardon. Sweden's extradition request initiated Spanish legal proceedings. Complicity in the hijacking was alleged against the five Croats, who had all touched a revolver that was passed around during the negotiations. It is not clear under what law extradition was demanded of Lemo, who slept during the hijacking. On June 12, 1974, the Audiencia Provincial dismissed the extradition request, saying that Sweden had not guaranteed that the Croats would not be jailed for crimes committed before the hijacking. According to Spain's 1958 Act of Extradition, "The concession of extradition by the Spainsh government shall always be understood as conditioned by . . .the formal promise on the part of the government making the request that the subject of the extradition shall not be prosecuted for offenses committed prior to and unrelated to that for which the request for extradition is formulated without his express consent to that effect." 1126

September 15, 1972—Spain—At 9:10 P.M., five well-dressed youths entered the doorway of the USIS cultural center in Madrid and hurled four Molotov cocktails into the entrance area before a guard, seated at a desk in the area, could stand up. Two of the devices ignited, causing some fire damage. 1127

September 16, 1972—Mexico—Twelve bombs exploded in four cities, injuring one person and causing considerable property damage. Seven of the blasts damaged the offices of U.S.-owned businesses on Mexico's Independence Day. 1128-1134

September 16, 1972—Philippines—A bomb exploded in an Air Manila Fokker F27P flying from Manila to Iligan City with thirty-eight passengers and four crew members. The explosion occurred at about eleven thousand feet, blew a large hole in the cargo compartment and damaged a propeller. It appeared to have been caused by a hand grenade. Two other hand grenades were found in the plane, which landed at Roxas City. There were no injuries.

September 16, 1972—Netherlands—Black Septemberists mailed sixty-four letter bombs from Amsterdam to various locations across Europe and the United States. Most of the bombs were intercepted by authorities before exploding. Eight of the items have not been accounted for.
    Each bore the correct postage and had been neatly addressed in ordinary manila or airmail envelopes, which made them difficult to detect. Some of the envelopes contained a powder, probably TNT. Others used two thin strips of plastic explosives five inches long. The plastique, developed in World War II,

is a mixture of Hexogen, TNT, and rubber compound, allowing easy molding. When the letter is opened, a spring hits a detonator the size of an aspirin, exploding the plastique. The entire device weighs an ounce and is an eighth of an inch thick; it has an effective range of three feet. Other types of letter bombs ignite a fuse or scratch a percussion cap.

The Israelis retaliated with attacks against fedayeen positions in Lebanon, killing sixty and taking seventeen prisoners. They also blew up or bulldozed 112 houses and damaged 200 others. The Lebanese government charged that the Israelis killed fifteen Lebanese soldiers and two hundred civilians. 1135-1142

September 16, 1972—Israel—Two men, one a former leader of the Irgun Zvai Leumi, were arrested for attempting to smuggle guns abroad to the JDL. Ammunition and grenades were also seized. 1143

September 17, 1972—Lebanon—A Venezuelan Airlines DC8 flying from Beirut to Caracas with ninety-seven persons on board landed at Cyprus after a caller said that there was a bomb on board. A powerful time bomb was found in the rear toilet. Dr. Atef Harkous, Hussein Harkous, and Adnan Harkous were arrested. 1144

September 17, 1972—Australia—Two offices of the Yugoslav Travel Agency in Sydney were bombed by Croatian terrorists, injuring fifteen. Yugoslavia threatened to break off diplomatic relations, claiming that Australia had allowed the growth of terrorist training camps and that some Australian politicians backed the terrorists because they were anticommunist. 1145-1146

September 19, 1972—An unnamed terrorist group threatened to hijack a Swissair plane to Damascus and demand the release of the Olympics terrorists. Ten days later, a hijacking obtained their release. 1147

September 19, 1972—United Kingdom—Dr. Ami Schechori, Israel's agricultural attaché in London, was killed when he opened one of the Black September letter bombs personally addressed to him in ink and mailed from Amsterdam. Schechori, who had just returned to his office from a long weekend after the Day of Atonement, did not expect such an attack, because all parcels were first checked by embassy security guards. He told a colleague, "Now this is really important," assuming that the package contained Dutch flower seeds he had planned to plant back home, where he was scheduled to go soon. Because the blast caused by the three ounces of plastique funneled downward toward his desk, the attaché missed the initial effects of the explosion, but was killed by a large splinter from the desk, which drove through his heart. The thick, buff-colored envelope measured six inches by three inches. 1148

September 19, 1972—United Kingdom—The Israeli security guards searched the embassy mail and discovered four more of the letter bombs, all working on the same principle, with the same handwriting and mailed from Holland, with the same postmark. They were addressed to individual staff members of the embassy. One of them contained a leaflet from Black September, threatening to attack Israelis around the world. 1149-1152

September 19, 1972—United Kingdom—Four more letter bombs were found in the Israeli embassy, addressed to Ambassador Michael Comay. 1153-1156

September 19, 1972—United Kingdom—Four more letter bombs addressed to members of the Israeli embassy were found in a London post office later that day. 1157-1160

September 19, 1972—France—The Israeli embassy in Paris discovered two large envelopes containing explosives. The devices were defused. 1161-1162

September 20, 1972—West Germany—The International Anti-Terror Organization announced that it would bomb Arab airlines, embassies, and organizations in retaliation for Arab attacks on Israelis. 1163

September 20, 1972—United Kingdom—Eight letter bombs addressed to Israeli officials were intercepted in London. 1164-1171

September 20, 1972—Canada—Six letter bombs addressed to Israeli officials were intercepted in Ottawa. A seventh was found in Montreal. 1172-1178

September 20, 1972—United States—Three letter bombs addressed to Israeli officials were intercepted in New York City. One was addressed to Josef Tekoah, Israel's U.N. ambassador. 1179-1181

September 20, 1972—Austria—Five letter bombs addressed to Israeli officials were intercepted in Geneva. 1187-1189

September 20, 1972—Belgium—A letter bomb addressed to an Israeli official was intercepted in Brussels. 1190

September 20, 1972—Israel—Two letter bombs addressed to Israeli officials were found in Tel Aviv and Jerusalem. One of them was addressed to Shimon Peres, minister of transport. One exploded in the Jerusalem Post Office, injuring a postal worker. 1191-1192

September 20, 1972—Australia—A few days later, five letter bombs addressed to Israeli diplomats were intercepted. 1193-1197

September 20, 1972—West Germany—Lufthansa Airlines received letters threatening the bombing of one of its aircraft unless $700,000 was paid.

September 21, 1972—Italy—A phone caller warned that a bomb was on board an Alitalia 747 flying from Rome to New York with 162 persons on board. The plane made an emergency landing in London, but no bomb was found.

September 21, 1972—Colombia—According to a security officer of a service station of an American firm, in the morning "we received an unknown call threatening us with an attack to our Barranquilla store by the Group of the Black September. Later on at 1:35 A.M., a man was noticed by the side of the gasoline island. Our watchman ordered him to stop, but this man ran away. Immediately reinforcements arrived at our store. So far everything indicates that it was a false alarm and everything is in perfect order." 1198

September 21, 1972—Canada—A phone caller said an Air Canada 747 flying from Montreal to Paris with 244 passengers on board was carrying a bomb. No bomb was found, but four passengers were injured using emergency chutes.

September 21, 1972—Israel—Ten more of the Amsterdam-postmarked letter bombs were intercepted in a Jerusalem post office. 1199-1208

September 21, 1972—Zaire—A letter bomb was found in the Israeli embassy in Kinshasa, but security guards prevented it from doing damage. 1209

September 21, 1972—Belgium—Israeli security guards found a letter bomb in the Israeli embassy in Brussels. 1210

September 21, 1972—Argentina—Israeli security guards found a letter bomb in their embassy in Buenos Aires. Amsterdam police believe that the BSO members had entered their country the previous week and slipped out after sending the letter bombs. On September 22, the British police volunteered to coordinate global efforts to investigate the letter bombs. Information was to be sent to Scotland Yard. 1211

September 21, 1972—Cambodia—Israeli security guards found a letter bomb in their embassy at Phnom Penh. 1212

September 23, 1972—Philippines—The *Washington Post* reported on February 11, 1977, that "an American and 3 Filipino opponents of President Ferdinand Marcos were sentenced to 6 years imprisonment and fined $1,333 each today [Feb. 10] after they admitted plotting to kill Marcos and take over the government. The American, August McCormick Lehman, twenty-six, of

Nashville, Tenn. . . . There had been reports during his 4½ years in prison indicating that he had been tortured. . . . Lehman's treatment since his arrest the day after Marcos declared martial law on Sept. 22, 1972, had been unusual for a person accused of so serious a crime. . . . The defendants tried today are among 10 persons, including 2 other Americans and prominent Filipino political cal figures, who have been charged with at least 7 attempts to Marcos' life and with trying to raise an army of 4300 men to stage a coup. The other 2 Americans and a Briton are being tried in absentia, although the Briton is believed to be dead. Larry Tractman, described as a California businessman who was to supply the rebels with equipment, and Robert Pincus of Jericho, N.Y., are believed to be living in the U.S. There is no extradition treaty between the Philippines and the U.S. The Briton involved in the case, Brian Borthwick, is believed to have died recently in a Singapore prison. The others sentenced today along with Lehman were Eduardo Figueras, son of a former mayor of Manila, and businessmen Manuel Crisologo and Antonio Arevalo. . . . Not before the court were former newspaper publisher Eugenio Lopez, Jr., former senator, and presidential candidate Sergio Osmena Jr., the alleged mastermind of the plot, and Osmena's son Sergio Osmena III. Former senator Osmena is in exile in the U.S. and is being tried in absentia. . . . The defendants were taken into custody in 1972 but formal charges were not filed until last year. Fugueras submitted an affidavit to the court claiming that the group also planned to set fire to government buildings throughout Manila but the martial law decree upset their timetable. He said the elder Osmena offered $333 for every building burned but the would-be arsonists were arrested before they could carry out their orders." 1213

September 23, 1972—Jordan—The Amman post office discovered and defused four more of the Amsterdam letter bombs addressed to Jordanian officials, according to a government spokesman. 1214-1217

September 25, 1972—United Nations—U.S. Secretary of State William P. Rogers urged the General Assembly to adopt a convention on terrorism and to convene a meeting in 1973 to define and establish a legal basis for fighting terrorism. The United States circulated a draft convention defining terrorism and legal jurisdiction and providing for the prosecution or extradition of persons who killed, seriously injured, or kidnapped innocent civilians in a foreign state for the purpose of harming or obtaining concessions from another state or from an international organization. President Nixon also established the Cabinet Committee to Combat Terrorism.

September 25, 1972—United States—The Metropolitan Edison Company's licensed nuclear facility on Three Mile Island near Harrisburg, Pennsylvania, received a bomb threat.

September 25, 1972—Northern Ireland—A five-hundred-pound bomb wrecked a luxury hotel, the Russell Court, in Belfast. Damage was estimated at £1 million. The next day, twenty-seven were injured by a bomb in Belfast.

September 27, 1972—Cambodia—A motorcycle loaded with plastique explosives was electrically detonated as the vehicle carrying the U.S. deputy chief of mission and chargé passed on its way to the embassy. While extensive damage was done to the outside of the vehicle, no one riding in the car was injured. However, a Phnom Penh military policeman motorcycle outrider was killed, as was a passing civilian bicyclist. Another Cambodian military policeman in a follow car was wounded. 1218

September 28, 1972—France—An El Al 747 scheduled to fly from Paris to Tel Aviv was held in Paris for one hour when a woman passenger alerted authorities regarding a parcel she was asked to take to Israel. No bomb was found.

September 28, 1972—United States—Robert W. Gupton, Jr., demanded that Delta Airlines pay him $1 million or he would blow up the company's planes. He was arrested by federal agents.

September 29, 1972—Israel—Three were wounded when Palestinian guerrillas bombed a supermarket in Jerusalem. Police questioned 134 people. 1219

September 30, 1972—Iran—A young female warned by telephone that a bomb was set to go off in twenty minutes in the Tehran Binational Center's academic center. The center was evacuated, but no device was found. 1220

October 1972—Cuba—Forty-four Cubans hijacked a boat to Mexico, seeking political asylum.

October 1972—Malaysia—Black September sent a series of eight letter bombs to Israelis all over the world. The disposition of four of the devices is unknown. 1221-1224

October 1, 1972—United States—A police car awaiting repair at a Los Angeles shop was bombed, causing extensive damage to the car and surrounding buildings. On October 7, United Press International received a call from the Afro-American Liberation Army, claiming credit. Many believed it to be the same as the Black Liberation Army, composed of Eldridge Cleaver's supporters.

October 3, 1972—Northern Ireland—A car bomb injured thirty-three in Belfast.

October 4, 1972—Italy—One of the Malaysian-postmarked letter bombs arrived at the Rome office of United Hias Service, a Jewish immmigration office. Italian explosives experts defused the device. The letter bore Black September inscriptions. 1225

October 4, 1972—France—An Arab bookstore serving as the Paris headquarters of the PLO was slightly damaged by a bomb blast. A Paris newspaper received a message signed by the Massada Action and Defense Movement, claiming that this was the group's first action, in response to terrorism against Israelis and Jews. It vowed to continue to strike back against future Arab terrorism. Israeli officials denied any knowledge of the group. 1226

October 5, 1972—Ireland—The Ulster Defense Association claimed credit for a raid on an IRA arms dump. 1227

October 6, 1972—France—An anonymous male caller stated that two bombs in the U.S. embassy in Paris were set to go off in ten minutes. A search was negative. 1228

October 6, 1972—United States—The Cooper Station licensed nuclear facility of the Nebraska Public Power District received a bomb threat.

October 6, 1972—Algeria—Palestinian students held hostages in the West German consulate in Algiers, demanding the release of the three Black September terrorists held for the Olympics massacre in Munich (see reference 1116). The hostages were released after one hour. 1229

October 7, 1972—Mexico—At 10:20 P.M., a fire broke out on the upper floor of an American firm's store, destroying merchandise, tandem equipment, and display tables. The water from the sprinkler system also damaged much merchandise; damage was placed at $23,673.64. After getting the fire under control, a small bottle (approximately fifteen cubic centimeters) was found, leading investigators to believe the fire was intentional. 1230

October 7, 1972—Italy—An Aero Transporti Italiani Fokker F27 flying from Ronchi Del Legionari to Bari, Trieste, and Venice was hijacked by an armed teenager, Ivano Baccaccio, who threw a bomb in the runway and demanded $344,000 and a flight to Cairo. He allowed the six passengers to deplane at Ronchi, and the crew escaped, whereupon the police opened fire on the plane.

During the battle, one policeman was wounded. The hijacker was later found dead inside the empty plane. 5388

October 8, 1972—United States—A phone caller warned that a bomb was on board a chartered 707 due to carry a baseball team from Oakland to Detroit. The flight was delayed for an hour during a search that was negative.

October 10, 1972—Venezuela—A four-tube mortar was set up across a major Caracas thoroughfare and was fired at the U.S. embassy. Only one of the tubes fired. The round hit a tree in the embassy grounds and exploded before hitting the building, causing no damage. 1231

October 10, 1972—Chile—The USIS Binational Center in Chillán was attacked by leftists who broke windows and hurled a Molotov cocktail.

October 10, 1972—United States—Two of the Malaysian-postmarked letter bombs were delivered to two New York women active in American Zionist circles. They opened the envelopes, but the bombs did not explode. 1233-1234

October 10, 1972—Rhodesia—Letter bombs were mailed to Jewish families in Bulawayo. 1235

October 11, 1972—Ceylon—A U.S. embassy officer in Colombo received a telephone call from someone claiming to be from Black September and threatening to shoot him. 1236

October 11, 1972—Portugal—A Lufthansa B727 flying from Lisbon to Frankfurt with fifty-eight passengers was hijacked by Friedrich Schutz, also known as Friedhelm Schuetz, who claimed to have a bomb and threatened to blow up the plane unless he was given $650 in marks. He was shot by police while trying to move to a car. 5389

October 13, 1972—Chile—The USIS Binational Center in Concepcíon received a bomb threat. No bomb was found. 1237

October 14, 1972—United States—A clerk in a New York City post office was seriously injured when a letter bomb exploded. The letter, another of the Malaysian-postmarked series, was addressed to a former national officer of Hadassah, the women's Zionist organization. 1238

October 15, 1972—United States—Eight members of De Mau Mau, a gang consisting primarily of black Vietnam veterans, were charged with the murder of nine whites in Illinois from May to September. Chicago police claimed that not all eight participated. The group was apparently roaming the countryside looking for someone to kill.

October 16, 1972—Argentina—Radical supporters of Juan Perón bombed the new U.S.-owned twenty-four-story Sheraton Hotel in Buenos Aires. Initial reports claimed that an American tourist was killed and two other Americans injured. Later reports claimed that a Canadian woman was killed in the blast. According to the *Washington Post*, ''An anonymous telephone call to the newspaper *La Prensa* said the blast was the work of the Marxist Liberation Armed Forces, but hotel employees said pamphlets signed by the 'Maximo Mena Command' had been found in the hotel. The command is an extremist group of Perón followers. A dozen bombs exploded earlier in Buenos Aires and other Argentine cities, mostly at the homes of military officers.'' October 17, 1945, was the day Perón was released from prison under the pressure of public demonstrations. 1239

October 16, 1972—Italy—A Jordanian resident of Rome for sixteen years, who was employed as a translator for the Libyan embassy, Abdel Wael Zuaiter, was assassinated as he approached an elevator in his apartment house by two gunmen who fired twelve shots from their .22 caliber pistols and then escaped into a waiting Fiat 125. The Fiat was found a few hundred yards away. A spent cartridge matched those found in the Jordanian's body. The thirty-eight-year-old victim, described by Fatah as their representative in Italy, was born in Nàblus, Jordan. A Jordanian embassy official said Zuaiter was a nephew of Akram Zuaiter, Jordan's ambassador in Beirut, but declined to confirm reports that he was also a second cousin of Yasir Arafat. The car was traced to a rental agency, whose records showed that the Fiat had been leased the previous Sunday to a man with a Canadian driver's license, claiming to be Anthony Hutton, forty-seven, of Toronto. Many suggested that Hutton was actually a member of the Israelis' Wrath of God assassination squad attached to Mossad and that members of the team included ''Mike,'' ''Tamar,'' and General Zwi Zamir.

Zuaiter had a history of political involvement with the Palestinian cause. Two of his brothers were killed in 1968 during an Israeli incursion into Lebanon. He had contributed to *Palestina*, a pro-Palestinian periodical, and led meetings of Italian leftist pro-Arab and rightist anti-Jewish movements. He also collected money to build a hospital in a Palestinian guerrilla camp. He was questioned in connection with the attempt by two Jordanians to blow up an Israeli airliner on August 17 (see incident 1105). The Israelis claimed that he worked for Black September. Reporter David Tinnin learned that Rome police had seen him with Razd, Fatah's intelligence service, and suspected that he had knowledge of BSO operations. He was questioned after the BSO bombing of a Trieste pipeline in August 1972. His brother was expelled from West

Germany after the Olympics attack. The Israelis believed that he was BSO's chief in Italy, and held him responsible for the hijacking of a Rome-Tel Aviv flight to Algeria (see incident 0074), as well as the explosion of a bomb on an El Al B707 in August (see incident 1105). Publicly, Zuaiter had been an apologist for the Munich attack, claiming that the Israelis had plotted to have the hostages killed so that they could gain world sympathy.

The assassination had taken place around 10:30 P.M. One of the bullets lodged in a copy of *1001 Nights* (a book Zuaiter had translated into Italian), which he had kept in his pocket. 1240

October 18, 1972—Netherlands—The U.S. consulate general in Rotterdam received an anonymous telephoned bomb threat. A search was negative. 1241

October 20, 1972—United States—The licensed nuclear facility of the Southern California Edison Company in San Onofre received a bomb theat.

October 22, 1972—Turkey—A Turkish Airlines B707 flying from Istanbul to Ankara with sixty-nine passengers and a crew of eight was hijacked by four male members of the TPLA who used guns to force the pilot to fly to Sofia, Bulgaria, where they threatened to blow up the plane if the Turkish government did not release thirteen political prisoners, abolish the strike ban in martial law areas, reorganize the universities by giving them greater freedom, engage in land reform, and abolish antidemocratic articles of the constitution. The Turks refused to talk to the hijackers, who surrendered to the Bulgarians the next day. The pilot and one passenger were reported wounded in the hijacking. Bulgaria granted the hijackers political asylum but sentenced them to two to two and a half years' imprisonment on February 2, 1973. The group were apparently university students and were identified as Haji Yuzdenir, Ahmed Maden, Yudzel Zoskurt, and Dervis Elmadjoglu. 1242

October 25, 1972—Netherlands—Dutch authorities arrested a Jordanian carrying an Algerian diplomatic passort whose luggage at Amsterdam's airport contained hand grenades, explosives, and forty unaddressed letter bombs. Officials described him only as ''R.H., a thirty-three-year-old Palestinian traveling on an Algerian diplomatic passport from Damascus and attached to an Algerian embassy in South America.'' The courier told a magistrate that he was unaware of the contents of his suitcases, which he had received in Damascus. Police claimed that they could not prove that he was aware of the contents of his two suitcases and released him after twenty-four hours to continue on his journey. An Israeli inquiry brought the same response from the Dutch justice ministry. 1243

October 25, 1972—Israel—Black September mailed three letter bombs to President Nixon, Secretary of State William Rogers, and Defense Secretary

Melvin R. Laird from the northern town of Kiryat Shmona. Suspicious Israeli postal workers intercepted the bombs. Authorities believe that the explosive devices were either smuggled across the Lebanese border or were posted by a local Arab. 1244-1246

October 25, 1972—Lebanon—A letter bomb addressed to a Palestinian businessman in Beirut exploded in his office, injuring his secretary. The firm was a trading company that arranged arms deals with Arab countries. The Palestinian partner was traveling outside the country at the time. 1247

October 25, 1972—Lebanon—Another letter bomb exploded in the Beirut post office, blinding a postal worker sorting letters. The letter was addressed to a Palestinian businessman. 1248

October 25, 1972—Algeria—Abu Khalil, PLO and Fatah representative in Algiers, was injured when a parcel bomb exploded in his face. 1249

October 25, 1972—Libya—Mustafa Awad Abu Zeid, PLO secretary in Tripoli, was blinded by a parcel bomb, which caused less serious injuries to two other people. Zeid was flown to London for treatment. 1250

October 25, 1972—Egypt—At Cairo airport, Egyptian officials intercepted a parcel bomb addressed to a PLO official. 1251

October 26, 1972—Egypt—Three letter bombs were intercepted at Cairo airport. Reports differ as to whether one or all three exploded. An Egyptian security officer who was examining the envelopes was injured by the explosion. The letters were addressed to three members of the Cairo PLO office. 1252-1254

October 27, 1972—Lebanon—A letter bomb addressed to the PFLP's newspaper offices in Beirut was intercepted in the post office, where it was rendered harmless. 1255

October 28, 1972—Pakistan—An anonymous telephone caller claimed that he would come by the USIS office in Lahore in fifteen minutes and "throw dynamite." The threat was not carried through. 1256

October 29, 1972—Lebanon—Lufthansa flight 615, a B727 flying thirteen passengers and seven crew on the Damascus-Beirut-Ankara-Munich run, was hijacked after it flew out of Beirut at 7 A.M. on Sunday by two Arabs who had booked first class. They informed the pilot, Capter Walter Claussen, at 10:45 that they would blow up the plane if the surviving members of the Munich massacre (see incident 1116) were not released. Eight of the passengers were

Arabs (only one was a West German), and it was believed that some of them would have aided the Black September hijackers if they were needed. The pair, identified as Samir Arif El Shahed and Mahmoud Saleh, were armed with two revolvers and two grenades and had used Yemeni and Lebanese passports. They flew on to Nicosia, Cyprus, to refuel, and then to Munich, where they had demanded that Mahmud el Safadi (also known as Abdel Kadir el Dnawy), twenty-one, Samer Mohammed Abdullah, twenty-two, and Ibrahim Badran, twenty, be brought. However, there was no Arab airliner available in West Germany to transport the prisoners to their destination, so the plane circled for one hour while the terrorists decided how to receive their colleagues, who were accompanied by five hundred security officers. The hijackers flew to Zagreb, Yugoslavia, and were soon met by the trio, who were flown there in a smaller plane. The group boarded the 727 at 5:30 P.M. The Yugoslavs had refused to refuel the plane unless the passengers were released when the prisoners boarded the plane, but allowed the plane to take off at 9:10 P.M., landing soon afterward in Tripoli, Libya, where the terrorists were given a heroes' welcome. The passengers and crew were allowed to return to Frankfurt aboard a special flight the next day. Some reports claimed that Abu Ali was the leader of the hijacking. This is the same name of the individual who met members of the Japanese United Red Army in North Korea and who may have also been involved in the June 1976 Air France-Entebbe hijacking (see incident 2762). Rumors abounded that the West Germans had prearranged the hijacking with the PFLP, hoping to get the Munich killers out of the country so that its citizens would not be subject to a bloody incident. 1257

October 30, 1972—United States—Eastern Airlines flight 496, a B727 flying from Houston to Atlanta with thirty-five passengers and seven crew members was hijacked on the ground by four armed men who forced the pilot to fly to Havana, with a refueling stop in New Orleans. The group members were identified as four white males for whom the FAA profile was inapplicable: Charles A. Tuller, born in Detroit on November 5, 1923; his two sons, Bryce M. Tuller, who was born in Bronx, New York, on January 16, 1953, and Jonathan R. Tuller, who was born in Bronx, New York on September 4, 1954; and their friend, William W. Graham, who was born in Evanston, Illinois, on August 9, 1954. The group was standing in the boarding line at 1:45 A.M. when they darted for the plane. When Stanley Hubbard, the ticket agent, tried to stop them, they shot him dead. Wyatt Wilkinson, a maintenance man, continued the chase but was wounded in the arm. An indictment was handed down against the hijackers by a federal grand jury in the southern district of Texas on November 6, 1972. It was learned that they were also charged with the murder of Arlington policeman Israel P. Gonzalez and bank manager Harry J. Candee during an attempted robbery of the Arlington Trust Company's Crystal Mall branch on October 25, 1972. They were also charged with attempted bank robbery and attempted murder of Gladys Willier, a bank clerk who was wounded in the attempt. The senior Tuller was a former $26,000-a-year Commerce Department worker, who became a self-styled white-collar revolutionary and harangued the passengers about the freedoms he would find in Cuba. The three Tullers found Cuba not to their liking, describing periods of solitary confinement, starvation, and boredom and secretly returned to the United States via Jamaica in June 1975. Bryce Tuller was captured July 3 during an attempted robbery of a K-Mart store in Fayetteville, North Carolina. His father and brother turned themselves in to the FBI soon afterward in Washington, D.C. After a trial that received heavy press coverage, the three were found guilty of air piracy on June 24, 1976, and sentenced to fifty years on July 16, 1976. Graham remained in Cuba, saying that he was going to college. 5390

October 31, 1972—United States—An unidentified male appeared at the boarding gate of a National Airlines DC10 scheduled to fly from New York to Miami. He claimed that he had a bag of nitroglycerin and would blow everyone up. He was overpowered by security guards and was ordered to undergo mental tests. None of the eighty-one persons on board were injured. 5391

October 31, 1972—United States—The General Atomic Company's licensed nuclear facility at San Diego, California, received a bomb threat.

October 31, 1972—Malaysia—The Malaysian Home Affairs Ministry confirmed that fifteen letter bombs meant for Jewish groups in London, Rome, and the United States had been discovered in the Kuala Lumpur post office and defused by the army. A local Malay-Arab group was responsible. 1258-1272

October 31, 1972—Malaysia—Malaysian officials announced on November 2 that the same Malay-Arab group was responsible for another twenty letter bombs. 1273-1292

October 1972—Malaysia—The same group was responsible for mailing nine other explosive devices from Penang. 1293-1300

October 31, 1972—United Kingdom—A letter bomb received at Egypt's London embassy was rendered harmless. 1301

November 2, 1972—United Kingdom—One of the Penang letter bombs was destined for the British Technion Society, which was connected with the University of Haifa, Israel. It was defused by London police. 1302

November 2, 1972—Spain—Three youths, members of the left-wing Hammer and Sickle Cooperative, entered the French consulate in Saragossa, tied up the consul, Roger Tur, and two employees, and set fire to the building. Tur died on November 7 of injuries, and the other two were also injured. On February 1, 1973, five members of the group were sentenced to thirty years for the arson; a sixth was acquitted. The students said that they were protesting the October 8, 1972, ban by the French government on ETA activities in France. 1303

November 3, 1972—Northern Ireland—A stewardess on board a British European Airways Viscount flying from Belfast to Glasgow found a suspicious parcel in the pantry. The pilot descended to five thousand feet and dropped the parcel out a window.

November 3, 1972—Israel—A woman telephoned to warn that there was a bomb in the U.S. Mission building in Tel Aviv. The U.S. embassy and cultural center were searched, with negative results. 1304

November 3, 1972—Jordan—A French female member of the PFLP was killed in Amman while handling a bomb, which police reported she had intended to plant in the U.S. embassy. 1305

November 5, 1972—El Salvador—A bomb exploded in the main ticket office of Pan Am in San Salvador, causing considerable damage but no injuries. 1306

November 6, 1972—India—A letter bomb exploded in Bombay's post office, wounding an employee. 1307

November 6, 1972—Japan—A JAL B727 flying from Tokyo to Fukuoka with 126 persons on board was hijacked by Tatsuji Nakaoka, a male armed with a gun and explosives, who demanded $2 million and a flight to Cuba, threatening to blow up the plane if his demands were not met. He returned to Tokyo to get the ransom and held the crew and plane hostage while a DC8 was prepared. He allowed the passengers to deplane and was overpowered while entering the second plane by police who had hidden inside it. He was sentenced to twenty years on March 13, 1974. 5392

November 7, 1972—Argentina—Italian industrialist Enrico Barrella was kidnapped in Buenos Aires and released unharmed on November 10 after the payment of $500,000 ransom. 1308

November 8, 1972—Mexico—A Mexicana de Aviacion B727 flying from Monterrey to Mexico City with 104 passengers and a crew of six was hijacked by four armed members of the Armed Communist League (two of whom were identified as German Segovia and Ricardo Rodriguez Moya). They allowed the plane to return to Monterrey, where 29 passengers deplaned. The group demanded the release of five of their comrades who had been arrested on November 7 during a police search, a government promise to drop charges against two guerrillas who joined them, a doctor for a wounded prisoner, two machine guns and ammunition, 4 million pesos ($330,000), and a flight to Havana. The Mexican government complied. The plane and passengers returned to Mexico the next day. Mexico requested extradition of seven of the group on November 16 but was refused on November 30 because the terrorists' action was deemed political. The ransom and weapons were returned to Mexico on January 2, 1973, but the eleven guerrillas were given political asylum by the Cubans. 1309

November 9, 1972—Argentina—The San Miguel de Tucumán offices of IBM were damaged by a powerful bomb explosion. 1310

November 10, 1972—Morocco—Two senior U.S. mission officers in Rabat received letters threatening death to them or other Americans. 1311-1312

November 10, 1972—United States—Southern Airways flight 49, a DC9 flying from Birmingham to Montgomery, Alabama, with twenty-six passengers and five crew members, was hijacked by three wanted criminals who demanded $10 million and forced the pilot to fly to nine different locations before finally landing in Cuba, where they were arrested. The group, all black males who claimed to be Black Panther sympathizers and who met the FAA profile, were identified as Henry D. Jackson, Jr., who was born in Detroit on September 28, 1946; Louis D. Cale, who was born on August 30, 1945, in Bibb County, Alabama; and Melvin C. Cale, who was born in Anderson County, Tennessee, on October 30, 1950. After leaving Havana and landing in Orlando, Florida, the FBI shot out the tires of the plane. In retaliation, the hijackers shot the copilot in the hand and forced to pilot to return to Cuba. The three were found guilty by Cuba on September 27, 1973; Jackson and Louis Cale were sentenced to twenty years, and Melvin Cale received fifteen years. On August 12, 1975, the *Washington Post* reported that Cuba had returned the ransom money, which had been paid to the hijackers. A Royal Bank of Canada branch honored the check. The Cuban government had previously attempted to repay the money with a check drawn on a New York bank account holding Cuban funds from dictator Fulgencio Batista's regime. The account had been frozen, however, and the check was not honored. Southern Airways had borrowed the $2 million ransom. The trio remain fugitives fron an indictment handed down by a federal grand jury in the northern district of Alabama on November 27, 1972.

Jackson and Moore were free on bail in Detroit, where they were accused of rape. Cale, Moore's half-brother, was an escaped convict. He had taken part in an armed robbery on two stores near his former Oak Ridge, Tennessee, home.

Jackson and Moore had sued Detroit, its mayor, and the police commissioner for $4 million, alleging that in March 1971 police had brutalized them while arresting them for concealing weapons. Although the charge against them was dropped, their suit continued.

During the twenty-nine-hour siege, the hijackers forced the pilot to circle the towns against which they had grudges. They ordered the men to strip to their underwear and forced the women to throw their purses in the aisle to ensure that no passengers were armed.

The DC9 refueled in Jackson, Mississippi before flying on to Detroit, where the hijackers demanded money, ten parachutes, and stimulants to keep the four crewmen alert. It was learned that the hijackers were armed with grenades as well as guns. While the Detroit City Council met to consider the demands and determine where the money could be obtained, the plane headed for Cleveland to refuel because weather conditions in Detroit precluded landing there. Seven sharpshooters (three FBI, two Secret Service, and two Cleveland police) drove toward the tail of the plane in a van. However, the plane took off when the group was within five hundred feet. The plane headed for Toronto, and Jackson informed ground control that if he did not receive the $10 million there, he would crash the plane into the Oak Ridge atomic facility. Another Southern Airways DC9 flew from Atlanta with $500,000 from the company and arrived in Toronto around 4:30 A.M. The company offered this money for the release of the passengers, one of whom, Alvin Fortson, eighty-two, a Trumann, Arkansas, farmer, had an emphysema attack. But Jackson demanded the entire sum. In Detroit, the council raised $500,000 from the National Bank.

The DC9 then circled the Knoxville area for five hours. At one point, it refueled (for the fourth time) at Lexington's Blue Grass Field at 9:34 A.M. The federal government donated $1 million to the ransom fund, which was flown with the Detroit money in a Lear jet chartered by the city. The hijackers set a 1 P.M. deadline for the $10 million, their logistic demands, and an official U.S. document stating that the ransom was a federal grant. The money was passed to them at Lovell Field Airport in Chattanooga, Tennessee.

During the flight to Cuba, the hijackers had two southern stewardesses, Donna Holman and Karen Chambers, and a Delta stewardess, Rita Tidwell, count the money. The hijackers at one point offered the passengers some of the ransom.

Upon landing, Cale stayed in the plane to guard the crew. Captain Hass considered knocking out Cale with an emergency ax but decided that his grenade might explode in a struggle. On the ground, the Cubans refused to allow the hijackers to keep the ransom. Jackson returned to the plane and announced, "These people here treat you worse than George Wallace." The plane left Cuba at 6:49 P.M., becoming the first plane to take off from Cuba with its hijackers still aboard. Jackson decided to go on to Switzerland and was persuaded by the pilot to land at Orlando to collect navigation charts and fuel. In Orlando, agents fired at the tires after the refueling. Jackson then shot the copilot in the shoulder and threatened to shoot everyone else. He directed the copilot to stand so that he could shoot him in the head. One hijacker pulled the pin on his grenade, held it to the pilot's head, and threatened to shoot people if the plane was not allowed to take off. They then ordered the pilot to circle over Key Biscayne, where President Nixon was relaxing after his reelection victory. They demanded to speak with him over the radio. After an hour, the DC9 headed for Havana.

The disabled plane landed bumpily at Havana, injuring two passengers.

Atomic Energy Commission officials said that the plane would not have caused a nuclear explosion if it had crashed into the Oak Ridge facility. 5393

November 10, 1972—India—Forty-two letter bombs addressed to Jewish firms in Europe were intercepted in Bombay. They were in colored envelopes, mostly pink, and many carried more than the required postage. 1313-1354

November 10, 1972—India—Ten letter bombs addressed to Jewish firms in Europe were intercepted in New Delhi. 1355-1364

November 10, 1972—Switzerland—Five letter bombs postmarked in New Delhi on November 10 were intercepted at Geneva's airport postal center. The letters were addressed to the Israeli mission to U.N. agencies in Geneva and Jewish organizations. 1365-1369

November 10, 1972—United Kingdom—Twenty letter bombs sent to Jews were intercepted by British officials. All had Indian postmarks. 1370-1389

November 10, 1972—United Kingdom—One of the letter bombs exploded while it was being opened by the managing director of a diamond brokers' firm in London, severely wounding Vivian Prins, a diamond merchant. 1390

November 10, 1972—United States—One of the Indian letter bombs was sent to a woman heading the Hadassah organization in New York City. 1391

November 10, 1972—United States—A New York City post office worker was wounded when one of the Indian letter bombs exploded. 1392

November 10, 1972—Netherlands—A Dutch Jew received one of the Indian letter bombs, which contained forty grams of cyanide powder, resembling fine grains of salt. Upon contact with oxygen, it would have produced a poison gas, but the device was detected in time. 1393

November 13, 1972—France—Three Arab gunmen, apparently members of Black September, forced their way into the Paris apartment of Khodr Kannou, a Syrian journalist, and fatally shot him. The group escaped in a Peugeot 304. Reports differ as to who the killers were. Most reports claim that Kannou was writing a story on the BSO but that his assassins believed he was a Mossad agent. Other reports claim that he was a contact of Mohammed Boudia, a BSO chieftain in Europe, and that he was assassinated by the Shin Beth's Wrath of God squad. 1394

November 14, 1972—United States—Two unidentified individuals took five hostages after a bank robbery in Greensboro, North Carolina, and tried to board an aircraft. The group was finally stopped at a police roadblock. 5394

November 15, 1972—Australia—An Ansett Airlines Fokker Friendship F27 flying from Adelaide to Alice Springs and Darwin with thirty-eight persons on board was hijacked by a lone man armed with a rifle, who held a stewardess hostage. When the plane landed at Alice Springs Airport, he demanded a light plane and a parachute. He was shot by police while trying to escape in the second plane. He finally shot and killed himself. A policeman was reported wounded during the incident. The hijacker was identified as M. Nelson or Miloslav Hrabinec. Some reports claim that he had demanded a ransom and a flight to the interior of Australia. 5395

November 15, 1972—El Salvador—A small bomb exploded in a ladies' restroom of the Argentine/Brazilian pavilion of the Fifth International Trade Fair in San Salvador. 1395

November 23, 1972—Jordan—A bomb was thrown into the house of an Arab National Union official in Amman. Three members of Al Fatah were arrested by Jordanian authorities and confessed to their part in the attack. 1396

November 24, 1972—West Germany—An Air Canada DC8 scheduled to fly from Frankfurt to Montreal and Toronto with twenty-nine persons on board was hijacked on the ground by Viktor Widera, an armed gunman, who forced everyone off the plane except a stewardess whom he held hostage for twenty-four hours. Widera demanded the release of a Czech being held by West Germany for hijacking a plane from Prague to Nuremburg, as well as the release of several other Czechs. When a radio was passed to him and he was attempting to close the cockpit door, police marksmen shot and killed him aboard the aircraft. 5396

November 27, 1972—Morocco—The USIS public affairs officer in Rabat received a letter in English threatening ''to finish with you.'' 1397

November 27, 1972—United Kingdom—Several phone calls threatening to seize an airliner in order to secure the release of a prisoner led to the institution of strict security measures at British airports.

November 28, 1972—United States—Robert Dickens pulled a knife when a stewardess insisted he fasten his seat belt. The plane, a Frontier Airlines flight from Denver to Oklahoma City with twenty-eight persons on board, returned to Denver. 5397

December 1972—Cyprus—Police frustrated a Black September plan to hijack an Italian passenger ship voyaging between Cyprus and Israel. 1398

December 1972—United States—The FIN, an anti-Castro group, bombed a travel agency in Queens, New York. 1399

December 1972—United States—An Atomics International licensed nuclear facility received a bomb threat.

December 1, 1972—Ireland—One man was killed and twenty were injured when a bomb exploded outside Liberty Hall, the headquarters of the Irish Congress of Trade Unions, in Dublin. The IRA and UDA denied involvement in this and the following bombing. Heavy damage was reported. 1400

December 1, 1972—Ireland—A bomb went off behind a Dublin department store, killing one man in a nearby office and injuring eighty. The next day, the Dail approved a bill giving the government extensive powers to combat terrorism. 1401

December 1, 1972—Northern Ireland—An explosion in the center of Belfast injured twenty-two people.

December 1, 1972—Egypt—Fifteen shots were fired from a machine gun at a departing Egyptian aircraft. The crew was unaware of the attack until landing at Cairo.

December 5, 1972—Venezuela—Unidentified persons sprayed the Caracas residence of the Honduran ambassador with machine gun fire, injuring no one. 1402

December 6, 1972—Argentina—Felix Azpiazu, a Spanish industrialist, was kidnapped by unknown persons. He was released unharmed on December 8 after his firm paid $100,000 of the $180,000 originally demanded by the kidnappers. 1403

December 7, 1972—Greece—Time bombs exploded under the cars of two U.S. servicemen in Athens, causing only slight damage and no injuries. The cars were parked in front of the officers' homes in the vicinity of the USAF base. The Independence, Liberation, Resistance group claimed responsibility, indicating that the bombings were a token protest against U.S. support of the Greek regime. 1404-1405

December 8, 1972—Ethiopia—An Ethiopian Airlines B720 flying from Addis Ababa to Asmara and Paris was hijacked shortly after takeoff by seven students, all members of the ELF, who demanded the release of fellow members of the front. Security guards immediately opened fire, exchanging shots with the five men and two women hijackers. One of the hijackers exploded a hand grenade, which tore a twelve- to fifteen-inch-diameter hole in the floor in the first-class cabin section, damaged electrical wires and some control cables, stopped one of the engines, and damaged the rudder. Of the one hundred persons on board, eleven were wounded, including seven passengers and two stewardesses. Six of the hijackers died, and one of the women was seriously injured and was arrested. The plane landed safely in Addis Ababa. Other reports indicate that all of the hijackers were killed. 1406

December 8, 1972—Australia—A vacationing American businessman was killed when a bomb exploded in an automobile parked outside a Serbian Orthodox church in Brisbane. 1407

December 8, 1972—France—Mahmoud Hamshari, PLO and Al Fatah representative in Paris, was killed in his apartment at 175 rue d'Alesia when a high-pitched whine over his telephone line activated a detonating mechanism for a bomb that had been planted in his phone. The Israeli intelligence service's Wrath of God team was suspected. Hamshari had been contacted by an individual claiming to be an Italian journalist who wished to interview him. While he was gone, an impression was taken of his apartment's door lock. A second meeting was arranged at a café, when the device was implanted. Surveillance of the habits of Hamshari, as well as his wife, Marie-Claude, and his daughter, Amina, had led the assassins to believe that his relatives would be away at that moment. When Hamshari answered the ringing telephone and was asked if it was he on the other end, he replied "Oui, lui-même." The signal was then sent through his receiver. Hamshari lived long enough to inform French police of the Italian journalist's interest in him. According to the Israelis, Hamshari had been responsible for an attempted assassination of David Ben Gurion in Copenhagen in 1969, as well as for the bombing of the Swissair plane that killed forty-seven persons (see incidents 0154 and 0323). It was claimed that he was a Black September operative, with connections to Mohammed Boudia's group. 1408

December 10, 1972—Argentina—Ronald Grove, the managing director of the British Vesty Industrial Group, a meat-packing concern in South America, was kidnaped in Buenos Aires by members of the ERP. His firm paid a ransom on December 14. Reports differ as to the precise figure, with estimates ranging from $500,000 to $1 million. He was released unharmed on December 19. On February 21, 1973, La Plata police captured a seven-person FAR cell, implicated in the kidnappings of Grove and Enrico Barella (see incident 1308). The group was headed by Francisco Urondo, a journalist and poet. 1409

December 11, 1972—United States—The FIN bombed the VA-Cuba Forwarding Company in New York City. 1410

December 12, 1972—United States and Canada—The Cuban Secret Government claimed credit for bombing a travel agency and three offices handling packages bound for Cuba. Reports claimed that the offices, located in Miami, New York, and Montreal, were destroyed. No one was injured. The group warned of further attacks aimed at individuals and firms doing business with Cuba. 1411-1415

December 14, 1972—Canada—A Quebecair BAC111 flying from Wabush to Montreal with fifty-seven passengers on board was hijacked by Larry Maxwell Stanford, who pointed a rifle at a stewardess and held two stewardesses hostage. He forced the pilot to fly to Montreal and then shuttle between Montreal and Ottawa. He allowed the passengers to deplane in Ottawa. He surrendered after ten hours when his father, a psychiatrist, arrived and persuaded him to give his gun to a stewardess. He was ordered to undergo mental tests but was convicted on April 26, 1973. 5398

December 19, 1972—Switzerland—A telephone caller warned that a bomb was in the U.S. mission building in Geneva as a protest against the U.S. Vietnam policy. The building was evacuated and a search was negative. 1416

December 20, 1972—United States—Robert Dobbelaer used a gun to wound two security officials while trying to use a food truck to get to a BWI plane about to depart from the Pan American terminal at New York. He was overpowered by other guards. 5399

December 20, 1972—Lebanon—The U.S. embassy in Beirut was hit by two rockets, which caused extensive damage. The 7.5-inch U.S. antitank-type rockets were fired by remote control from a car parked across the street. A note in the car claimed that the attack was in protest of the Vietnam war, but many officials attributed the attack to the Black September Organization. 1417

December 23, 1972—France—A university-aged group of about fifty attacked the USIS building in Paris, beating up a policeman guarding the building and hurling several Molotov cocktails. The policeman was hospitalized, and damage was estimated at $3,000. 1418

December 24, 1972—West Germany—At 10 P.M., a small bomb that had been placed against the door of the U.S. Berlin brigade non-commissioned officers' club opposite the U.S. headquarters exploded, causing little damage and no injuries. 1419

December 24, 1972—Belgium—Shortly before midnight, a Molotov cocktail was thrown from a passing automobile over the fence of the U.S. chancery in Brussels, causing no damage or injuries. 1420

December 24, 1972—United Kingdom—British police arrested Mohammed Abdul Karin Fuheid, twenty-four, a Palestinian Fatah lieutenant who was attempting to smuggle weapons through London airport for an attack on Israel's Stockholm embassy. Because he was in transit, his baggage would not normally be searched. He was charged with illegal possession of a Browning automatic pistol and fifty-one rounds of ammunition. He was sentenced to eighteen months' imprisonment at the Old Bailey. Authorities later received threats of sabotage to airports and airliners unless the Black September courier was freed. He earned full remission of his sentence and was released after one year. His flight had originated in Beirut. 1421

December 26, 1972—Turkey—Two Black September members driving out of the country were arrested when their car was searched and found to be carrying explosives, detonators, firing devices, and a plastic bomb. The group claimed to be en route to Paris. 1422

December 26, 1972—Bangladesh—One hundred fifty demonstrators from the university in Rajshahi arrived at the USIS shouting anti-United States and pro-North Vietnamese slogans. Ten minutes after their arrival, seven of them, equipped with gasoline cans and an unidentifiable white powder, crashed into the building, forcing the door with a crowbar. The interior was sprayed with the gasoline-powder combination and set on fire. Police and a fire truck arrived after the inside of the structure was destroyed. No injuries were reported. 1423

December 27, 1972—Argentina—Vicente Russo, director general of operations for Standard Electric of Argentina, a subsidiary of the International Telephone and Telegraph Corporation, was kidnapped in Buenos Aires by members of Descamisados Peronistas Montoneros. He was released unharmed on December 30. Company officials refused to comment on local newspaper accounts of a ransom payment of between $100,000 and $1 million. 1424

December 28, 1972—West Germany—A firebomb was thrown over the fence near a rear gate of the U.S. military air base portion of Tempelhof Airport in West Berlin. The only damage caused was a small grass fire, which was quickly extinguished. 1425

December 28, 1972—Thailand—Four members of Black September took over the Israeli embassy in Bangkok. During a party at the embassy, two men in white tie and tails opened the gate and walked into the compound. The Thai guard, Private Sunchait Pienkana, thought they were guests. Then two others, armed with machine guns, climbed over the wall and aided the other two in seizing the embassy. They allowed all of the Thais to leave but held Rehavam Amir, the Israeli ambassador, and his wife, visiting Israeli ambassador to Cambodia Simon Avimor, Nitzan Hadas, first secretary of the embassy, and his wife, Ruth, and another embassy staff member, as hostages. They were forced at gunpoint to the second floor of the tri-story embassy. The terrorists demanded the release of thirty-six terrorists held in Israeli jails, including Kozo Okamoto, the survivor of the Lod massacre (see incident 1056), and the two survivors of the Sabena hijacking (see incident 1024). They threatened to blow up the embassy if their demands were not met and the Thais attempted to storm the grounds. An 8 A.M. December 29 deadline was set. Negotiations were conducted by two Thai officials, Marshal Dawee Chullaspaya, the armed forces chief of staff, and the deputy foreign minister, Chartichai Choonhavan, along with the Egyptian ambassador, Mortafa el-Essaway, acting on the personal orders of President Sadat. After nineteen hours of negotiations in which the group attempted to wear the terrorists down, the terrorists agreed to what has been termed the Bangkok solution; they would release their hostages and drop all other demands in return for safe passage out of the country. The negotiators had also pointed out that December 27 and 28 were holidays for the Thais, who were celebrating the investiture of Crown Prince Vijiralongkorn, the heir to the throne, and said that these days of national joy should not be marred by bloodshed in a dispute that did not involve the Thais. A blue and white bus carried the terrorists and their hostages to the airport. During that time, the hostages were bound with rope and were not untied until the terrorists boarded the Thai Airways DC8. The three negotiators accompanied the terrorists to Cairo as a guarantee of safe conduct. On January 5, 1973, Thailand announced that Israel had agreed to release to their families the bodies of two slain Palestinian hijackers. Black September strongly criticized their operatives for backing down and losing face for the organization. 1426

December 29, 1972—Bangladesh—The Public Affairs Office of the USIS in Dacca received an anonymous telephone call threatening a repetition of the December 1971 bombing of the USIS and advised that all Americans in Bangladesh were marked for death (see incident 0942). 1427

December 29, 1972—United States—The Consumers Power Company licensed nuclear facility at Palisades received a bomb threat.

1973—United Kingdom—Libyan president Muammar Qaddafi ordered an Egyptian submarine commander to torpedo the British liner *Queen Elizabeth II* as it voyaged toward Israel filled with Jews celebrating the twenty-fifth anniversary of the founding of Israel. President Sadat, whose nation was theoretically federated with Libya, ordered his vessel back to port after the commander had requested verification of his orders.

January 1973—Guatemala—A letter bomb mailed in November 1972 in India arrived at the Israeli embassy. 1428

January 1973—Ireland—A steel erector, a member of a local defense regiment, was shot to death in his home by the IRA. 1429

January 1973—United States—Black September made threats against the families of members of the Israeli consulate in Brookline, Massachusetts. 1430

January 1, 1973—Jordan—A Syrian and a Palestinian who had been sent into Jordan from Syria by Al Fatah to cut the Trans-Arabian Pipeline were captured by a Jordanian army patrol. 1431

January 1, 1973—Ireland—A young couple was murdered in Donegal County, on the border with Northern Ireland. The IRA denied responsibility. 1432

January 2, 1973—United States—Piedmont Airlines flight 928, a YS11A propjet flying from Atlanta to Washington, D.C., and Baltimore was hijacked by Charles A. Wenige, a white male who fit the FAA profile and who was born on June 14, 1935, in Baltimore. The hijacker used a gun to take over the plane on the ground in Baltimore and held two stewardesses hostage for three hours. The passengers had disembarked previously. Wenige claimed to want a flight to Toronto. He was persuaded by a church cardinal and his own psychiatrist to surrender to federal agents. He pleaded guilty to charges of assaulting a federal officer and interstate transportation of a stolen weapon and was sentenced to twenty years on February 16, 1973. 5400

January 4, 1973—Canada—A Pacific Western Airlines Convair turboprop scheduled to fly from Vancouver International Airport to Penticton and Castlegar with nineteen persons on board was taken over on the ground by C. K. Neilson, who used a toy gun and threatened to blow up the plane if he was not paid $2 million and flown to North Vietnam. He released the passengers.

Police boarded the plane and overpowered the hijacker, who was ordered to undergo a mental examination. 5401

January 4, 1973—Spain—An unidentified male phoned TWA's Madrid office to warn that a bomb would explode when a 747 flying from Madrid to New York with 236 persons on board flew below thirty-two hundred feet. He demanded $237,000 for information on how to disarm the bomb. No money was paid, and no bomb was found when the plane landed in South Dakota.

January 5, 1973—United States—On December 5, 1972, Congress had passed legislation that strengthened airport security. It went into effect a month later. Airports were required to station armed law-enforcement officers at passenger checkpoints, search all carry-on items, and use electronic screening devices on all boarding passengers.

January 7, 1973—Greece—Incendiary devices damaged two privately owned cars of two U.S. government employees in Athens. No injuries were reported. 1433-1434

January 7, 1973—Canada—A sabotage threat was made against an Air Canada DC8 flying from Vancouver to Toronto. The plane was searched in Calgary, but no bomb was found.

January 8, 1973—France—Black September claimed credit for placing a bomb that destroyed the Paris offices of the Jewish Agency, which arranges for the emigration of Jews to Israel. 1435

January 9, 1973—Cyprus—Authorities arrested four Arabs who planned to attack targets in Haifa, where the group intended to arrive by ship. They were later freed. 1436

January 10, 1973—West Germany—The USIS Amerika Haus in Frankfurt was broken into and a fire started in the library, causing over $25,000 worth of damage. 1437

January 11, 1973—West Germany—A group of six to eight Arab terrorists attacked a Kaiserslautern restaurant and fired on foreign tourists. During the battle, a tourist whose parents lived in Tel Aviv was killed. Several other persons were reported injured. 1438

January 17, 1973—Lebanon—A small dynamite charge wrecked a basement restroom in the American University of Beirut. 1439

January 17, 1973—Italy—Four cars in Terrenia belonging to U.S. military personnel were vandalized, with their windows broken, gasoline thrown inside, and ignited. 1440-1443

January 17, 1973—Spain—Four ETA members kidnapped Felipe Huarte from his Pamplona home. From France, the group demanded the rehiring of 114 workers who had been dismissed for striking at Torfinasa, a Huarte subsidiary, a $47-per-month wage increase at the plant, fully paid sick leave, and a one-month annual vacation. The company agreed to the terms, and his family paid a 50 million peseta ($800,000) ransom. He was released on January 25 after the payment of the ransom in France. On January 31, the government revoked the labor concessions as having been granted under duress.

The government sent thousands of civil guards to the mountains north of Pamplona to search for the kidnappers, but Huarte was released on the French border near Irun. On April 19, 1973, Eustaquio Mendizabal, leader of the ETA's military wing, was killed in a police shootout in a village near Bilbao. Police said that he was killed while attempting to escape. He was wanted for three major kidnappings since 1970. The semiofficial news agency implied that his location was disclosed by ETA rivals after a dispute over the disposal of the Huarte ransom. 1444

January 18, 1973—United States—Seven Hanafi Muslims were murdered in their Washington, D.C., home. Five black Muslims from Philadelpha were convicted for the crime. A group of Hanafis took over three buildings in Washington in 1977, attempting to obtain custody of the murderers for retribution (see incidents 3037-3039).

January 19, 1973—United States—A seventeen-year-old male soldier who was absent without leave used a shotgun to force a mechanic on board an Ozark Airlines DC9 in Louisville. A guard estimated that two hundred persons were in the area at the time, but no injuries were reported. The soldier demanded a flight to an African country that would give him asylum. Early the next day, a policewoman grabbed him in a ruse and overpowered him. 5402

January 20 and 27, 1973—Austria—Three Black Septembrists were arrested in Vienna, followed by the arrest of three colleagues a week later who were trying to escape to Italy. Italian border guards handed them over to Austria after they crossed the border. The police found sketches of Schonau camp (used to help Soviet émigrés proceed to Israel), and one Arab admitted that he had twice cased the camp to determine when there would be many immigrants. He was then to telephone "the East" (presumably Prague or Budapest) and give a code word indicating that the operation was set. Arms and more terrorists would then go to Vienna. He claimed that an airline ticket from London had nothing to do with his political activities. All six were given suspended sentences and deported. A special gendarmerie unit was established to handle camp security. Reconstruction of the movements of the terrorists revealed that they had begun in Beirut and flew on to Geneva, where they traded their Syrian passports for forged Israeli ones, which they were to use to pose as Israelis while entering Schonau, which they were to seize and blow up. 1445-1446

January 23, 1973—Eritrea—Two Italian businessmen residing in Eritrea were kidnapped by the ELF while attempting to negotiate with a guerrilla group demanding protection payments. The victims were released on February 4, probably after a ransom payment. 1447

January 23, 1973—Haiti—The U.S. ambassador to Haiti, Clinton E. Knox, was seized by two men and a woman while driving to his home in Port-au-Prince and forced at gunpoint into another car. He was then forced to call the U.S. consul general, Ward L. Christensen, who joined him as a hostage in Knox's residence. The group demanded the release of thirty prisoners and $1 million ransom. The French ambassador acted as an intermediary and reduced the demands to twelve prisoners and $70,000. The United States government had refused a ransom demand of $500,000. It was unclear as to who paid the ransom, but the hostages were released the next day after eighteen hours in custody. The trio flew with the released prisoners to Mexico, which granted the group asylum but confiscated the money. The group was allowed to continue on to Chile, which granted them transit visas. In New York, the Coalition of National Liberation Brigades, a Haitian anti-Duvalier exile group, claimed credit. The group then claimed to be members of the National Anti-Duvalierist Movement, and were identified as four men and a woman, most of them teachers. The leader of the kidnappers was identified as Raymond Napoleon. 1448

January 24, 1973—Chile—One of the letter bombs that had been mailed from India in November 1972 arrived at a Santiago post office, injuring a police technician who was handling it (see incidents 1313-1364). 1449

January 24, 1973—Iran—A small bomb caused slight damage to the Tehran office of Pan Am. 1450

January 25, 1973—Cyprus—Three days after arriving in Nicosia from Beirut, the chief of the forty-man Fatah contingent was killed when a short-range radio signal detonated a bomb placed under his bed. The victim ws identified as Bashir Abu Khair (also known as Hussian Al-Bathis, Hussein Bashir, and Hussein Abad Al Chir). Reporter David Tinnin claims that he was

Black September's contact with the KGB in Cyprus, and had just returned with a meeting with a Cypriot agent who had given him a check for $5,000. After the Black Septembrist clicked off the light in his room at the Olympic Hotel on President Makarios Avenue, a Mossad Wrath of God member pressed a button, which transmitted the signal to the detonation device. It was later claimed that Khair carried a Syrian passport and a Lebanese laissez-passer, although he was a Palestinian. 1451

January 26, 1973—Spain—Black September claimed that it had begun to retaliate for the Mossad campaign of attacking its operatives in Europe by assassinating a Shin Beth officer in a Paris café. The officer, posing as a tourist named Uri Molou (who also carried a false passport claiming he was Moshe Hannan Yishai), was lured to a meeting at a café on the Grand Via in Madrid with one of his Palestinian student contacts, who had promised to provide him with the names of the most politically active Arab students on his campus. The officer, later identified by the Israeli prime minister's office as Baruch Cohen, suspected a trap. He put his hand in his coat to grab his gun but was fatally shot by his contact, who successfully fled to the airport and left the country. Some reports claim that Mohammed Boudia was involved in the killing and may have been the agent responsible for Cohen's death. Others claim that the assassination was engineered by Wadi Haddad, who may have had aid from Iraqi and Syrian intelligence. Black September said that Cohen had been subjected to execution by a firing squad for killing Palestinian representatives in Italy and France. At the time of his death, it was reported that he had uncovered a plot to kidnap prominent Spanish Jews. 1452

January 26, 1973—Corsica—A man armed with guns and grenades held five people hostage at Calvi airport in an aborted attempt to hijack an Air Inter Airlines plane. In the struggle that ensued, the man, reported to be a French Foreign Legionnaire, was killed by police gunfire. No other injuries were reported. 5403

January 27, 1973—Lebanon—A bomb exploded in a Beirut apartment building, killing the man carrying it and wounding another person.

January 27, 1973—United States—The Turkish consul general in Los Angeles, Mehmet Baydar, and the deputy consul general, Bahadir Demir, were assassinated by Gourgen M. Yanikian, who shot them in the head at a luncheon in the Santa Barbara Biltmore Hotel. The consul general died almost instantly, and Demir died shortly after arrival at a local hospital. Yanikian, who surrendered to authorities, claimed that members of his Armenian family had been killed in attacks by Turkey in 1915. 1453

January 28, 1973—France—A powerful bomb exploded in the Paris branch of the Spanish Banco Popular, causing considerable damage but no injuries. 1454

January 28, 1973—Cuba—The Cuban fishing boat *Plataforma* was attacked in international waters.

January 30, 1973—Guatemala—A U.S. AID employee and his vehicle were seized by the PGT, who released him several hours later. The vehicle was found several days later in a south coast town. 1455

February 3, 1973—Argentina—The FAL kidnapped Norman Lee, an Argentine executive of a Coca-Cola bottling company in Buenos Aires. He was released on February 21 after the payment of a $1 million ransom. (Lee would be kidnapped a second time.)
    In the face of the continued threat of kidnappings and assassinations, several companies moved their American executives and their families out of Argentina. They included Coca-Cola, John Deere, IBM, ITT, and Otis Elevator. 1456

February 5, 1973—United States—The licensed nuclear facility of the Gulf-United Nuclear Fuels Corporation at Elmsford, New York, received a bomb threat.

February 5, 1973—Argentina—An incendiary bomb found in the car of the Paraguayan ambassador was deactivated. 1457

February 7, 1973—Brazil—David Cuthberg, a British naval officer, was assassinated in Rio de Janeiro. Rubens Berado, a deputy and former vice-governor of Guanabara, was also assassinated. 1458

February 15, 1973—Jordan—Jordanian authorities arrested Abu Daoud and sixteen other terrorists planning to assassinate King Hussein in Amman and overthrow his government. Daoud was reconnoitering government buildings for terrorists who were to cross the border in cars containing explosives and arms hidden in special compartments. Police discovered him dressed as a Saudi sheik, accompanied by a fifteen-year-old who claimed to be his wife. Because his passport indicated he had six children, the police became suspicious and asked him to come to the police station. The girl panicked and dropped the gun and ammunition she was carrying under her robe.
    Daoud provided the Jordanians with extensive information about Black September operations, possibly believing that Abu Iyad had sent him on a suicide mission. He claimed that he had been a member of Fatah's Revolutionary Council since 1970 and was a major BSO leader. His assignment was to

''occupy the prime minister's office, arrest the ministers and to bargain for the release of detainees in Jordan.'' He claimed that Saleh Khalef (Abu Iyad) had planned the Olympics massacre as well as the murder of an Israeli agent in Madrid in January (see incidents 1116 and 1452). He claimed Fatah leader Abu Youssuf arranged the 1971 murder of Wasfi Tell, the 1972 hijacking of a Belgian jet to Tel Aviv, and the takeover of Israel's Bangkok embassy (see incidents 0938, 1024, and 1426). He said the Munich attack had been planned in Sofia and that the participants had left Libya for Munich.

Two fedayeen incidents were engaged in (the March 1, 1973, takeover of the Saudi Arabian embassy in Khartoum and the seizure of the Saudi embassy in Paris) to effect his release, but he was finally freed in September 1973 with 753 others in a general amnesty called by King Hussein as a result of his rapprochement with Egypt and Syria. Hussein had given him a reprieve of his death sentence.

According to reconstructions of Daoud's movements, his group had entered Jordan from Kuwait and Syria. Daoud claimed that Black September was merely an operating arm of Fatah. He denied having extensive involvement in the major attacks, claiming that he was asked to give his Iraqi passport to Fahri Umari when he met with him and Abu Iyad in Sofia in August 1972 in preparation for the Olympics attack. The press reported that Daoud took a two-month intelligence course in Cairo in 1968 and made a March 1972 visit to North Korea and China in his capacity as a Fatah representative. Daoud was later arrested in France in January 1977, causing an international debate over Western handling of terrorist suspects. The amnesty under which Daoud was released was called by Hussein in September 1973. 1459

February 15, 1973—United States and Cuba—The United States and Cuba signed a memorandum of agreement regarding the return of hijackers of boats and planes, which was to be in force for five years. Upon Cuban Premier Castro's denunciation of the agreement on October 15, 1976, the treaty became nullified on April 15, 1977. Similar accords were signed by Cuba with Canada on February 15, with Mexico on June 7, with Venezuela on July 6, and with Colombia on July 22, 1974.

February 20, 1973—United Kingdom—Three Pakistani youths, members of Black December, attacked the Indian High Commission in London, injuring some of the staff members. They held the group hostage, but two of them were shot by British police and a third was captured. He claimed that the group wished to obtain an audience with Indian Prime Minister Indira Gandhi so that they could demand the release of Pakistani prisoners of war. 1460

February 21, 1973—Israel—A Libyan Boeing 727's French pilot was blinded by a sandstorm and overflew Israeli territory. The Israelis, claiming that numerous threats had been made by Black September to hijack an airliner and crash it into Tel Aviv, scrambled Phantom fighters, which shot it down over the desert, killing all 106 aboard.

February 21, 1973—Greece—A U.S. serviceman's car in Athens was destroyed by a bomb, and another American military officer's car was damaged. It was assumed that the bombs were planted by opponents of the Greek regime. No injuries were reported. 1461-1462

February 21, 1973—Brazil—Manuel Henrique de Olivera, a Portuguese national and alleged to be a police informer, was assassinated by the Aurora Maria Nacimiento Furtado Command. 1463

February 27, 1973—United States—Two hundred supporters of the American Indian Movement seized a strategic hamlet in Wounded Knee, South Dakota, and demanded a Senate investigation of Indian problems. Eleven local hostages were released on March 1. Several gun battles took place against federal agents, with both sides suffering casualties. The occupation did not end until May 9.

March 1973—United States—The Cuban Secret Government bombed the Center for Cuban Studies in New York City. 1464

March 1, 1973—Sudan—Eight Black Septembrists, driven in a Land Rover with PLO diplomatic plates, seized the Saudi Arabian embassy in Khartoum. After unsuccessfully bargaining for the release of imprisoned terrorists, they murdered two American and one Belgian members of the diplomatic corps: U.S. Ambassador Cleo A. Noel, Jr., George C. Moore, the departing U.S. chargé (for whom the diplomatic reception was being held), and Guy Eid, the Egyptian-born chargé at the Belgian embassy. The attack began at 7 P.M. when a Land Rover, driven by Abu Salem, deputy chief of Fatah's Khartoum office, crashed through the embassy's unguarded gate. The terrorists fired machine guns and revolvers, while some guests escaped by jumping over the embassy wall. Others hid and fled. Noel sustained an ankle wound from a ricochet, and Eid was shot in the leg. Noel and Moore were bound with ropes, punched, and kicked, according to Shigeru Nomoto, the Japanese chargé d'affaires. The terrorists also held Sheik Abdullah el-Malhouk, the Saudi ambassador and party host, his wife, and four children, and Adli el-Nazir, the Jordanian chargé d'affaires. Later the children were allowed to leave. Some diplomats identified themselves as representatives of Arab or Eastern-bloc states and were also immediately released. The terrorists had hoped to seize the West German ambassador, but he had left earlier in the evening. Also on the group's assassination list was Raymond Etherington-Smith, the British ambassador, who left the party earlier to greet at the airport the British under secretary of state, Anthony Kershaw, who was arriving for an official visit.

The group set a twenty-four-hour deadline for their demands for the release of prisoners to be met. They demanded that the United States release the killer of Senator Robert Kennedy, Sirhan Sirhan (see incident 0054); that Israel release all women detained in Israeli jails, including the two surviving hijackers of the Sabena plane (see incident 1024); that West Germany release imprisoned members of the Baader-Meinhof Gang (see incident 1027); and that Jordan release Abu Daoud and the sixteen Black Septembrists accompanying him (see incident 1459), as well as Major Rafreh Hindawi, a Jordanian officer who had been sentenced to life imprisonment for plotting against the Amman government. To underline the group's determination, one of the terrorists appeared on a balcony, tossing a grenade from one hand to another. The group's leader allowed a doctor to enter the embassy to treat Moore's wounds.

On March 2, Mohammed el Baghir, Sudan's interior minister, told the terrorists by telephone that Jordan had refused their demands for Daoud, Hindawi, and others. The terrorists then dropped their demand for release of prisoners in Israel "since Sudan cannot contact the Zionist enemy," as well as for those held in West Germany, since they were unable to capture the West German ambassador, but "we insist and reconfirm that we will not leave the embassy or release the hostages or even guarantee their lives except if the Palestinian prisoners held in the prisons of the reactionary regime of Jordan are freed." The group also held firm on their demand for Sirhan's release.

President Nixon sent Deputy Under Secretary of State William Macomber, Jr., to Khartoum to advise the Sudanese on their negotiations. Macomber and his group initially landed at Cairo. The attendant publicity of his visit appeared to please the terrorists, and officials got the impression that the group was willing to fly to Cairo to continue the negotiations. Unfortunately Macomber's flight to Khartoum was detained by the continuing sandstorm. In addition, President Nixon refused the demand for the release of Sirhan, claiming that the United States could not give in to political blackmail: "We cannot do so and we will not do so. Now, as to what can be done to get these people released, Mr. Macomber is on his way there for discussions; the Sudanese Government is working on the problem...but we will not pay blackmail." Many foreign service officers later criticized Nixon's statements, claiming that these had deleterious effects upon the negotiations.

Egyptian President Sadat had attempted to defuse the situation by sending an Egyptian plane to Khartoum to pick up the terrorists and their hostages and fly them back to Cairo. At the time of the murder of the trio, senior members of Fatah were waiting at Cairo airport. Sadat hoped that the Fatah members would be able to persuade the group to surrender.

Members of Israeli intelligence managed to monitor the ultrahigh-frequency shortwave that the terrorists were using to keep in touch with their leaders at headquarters. At one point, Beirut said, "Remember the blood, Nahr el Badawi," a Palestinian refugee camp in Lebanon that had been attacked a few days previously by the Israelis. Many took this to mean that the group had been instructed to execute their hostages. (Other reports claim that the message was "Cold River" or "The organization orders, repeat orders, you to carry out Operation Cold Water on numbers one, two, and three.") At around 9:30 P.M. on March 2, the group took the trio to the basement and emptied forty rounds, beginning by firing at their legs after the ambassador and chargés had been allowed to make out their wills and had thanked the Saudi ambassador for the party, saying, "I'm very sorry it has turned out this way, but I want you to know it is not your fault." The terrorists phoned the U.S. embassy, announcing, "We have executed the two Americans and the Belgian." The terrorists were informed that they would not be allowed a flight out of the country, and a few hours later they ended the sixty-hour siege by releasing their remaining hostages and surrendering to Sudanese authorities.

Black September soon released a statement in Beirut vowing to continue attacks against "Zionist and American imperialism and their agents in the Arab world." The Khartoum operation was characterized as "not at all aimed at bloodshed but had sought the release of our imprisoned heroes . . . as a result of the arrogance and the obstinacy of American imperialism, represented by Nixon's statements and by the attitude of hireling tools in Jordan, our revolutionaries carried out the death sentences on three hostages . . . The United States shared in plotting to slaughter our people, conspiring against our Arab nation and our national struggle . . . [Moore was seen as] the plotting brain of the American Central Intelligence Agency and one of those directly responsible for the September massacres. . . . We wish to affirm to the world that the Black September militants have never known fear and will not know it. . . . Its members would not be intimidated by the hypocritical cries of condemnation or the tears of those whom we have never seen shed a tear throughout a quarter of a century during which this people has been subjected to all kinds of torture and persecution. Those who ostensibly weep today over the execution of three enemies of the Arab nation, for which the United States has been directly responsible, realize that thousands of the sons of this people have been atrociously slaughtered and that thousands of others are suffering all kinds of torture in Jordanian and Israeli jails. . . . War against Zionist and American imperialism and their agents in the Arab world will continue. Our rifles will remain brandished against both the substance and the shadow." Many observers believed that Black September had intended to kill the diplomats before initiating the attack to recoup the prestige the organization had lost in the Bangkok operation (see incident 1426).

The Sudanese conducted raids on the Khartoum office of the PLO and discovered many documents that linked Fatah and the PLO to the operation. Reporter Christopher Dobson learned that the PLO Khartoum office's chief, Fawaz Yassin, organized the attack, his deputy, Rizig Abu Gassan, led the team, and the number three man, Karam from Fatah, drove the Land Rover. Documents seized included instructions for the raiders and a map of the embassy. Karam later confessed to Fatah complicity, and Gassan, who had made Fatah broadcasts over Sudanese radio, said at a magistrate's court preliminary hearing, "We are proud of what we have done." Yassin was in Libya a few days prior to the attack. He met the seven BSO members at the airport when they arrived from Beirut and saw their luggage through customs. They had smuggled in five pistols, eight grenades, and Kalashnikovs. Yassin then flew to Libya a few hours before the raid and left instructions for the attack and the assassination of Emperor Selassie and the F.R.G. and U.K. ambassadors. Colonel Qaddafi refused a request for the return of Yassin and helped him to a PDRY sanctuary. It was also learned that the Black Septembrists had hoped to fly their American hostages to the United States, where they would assassinate them.

A Sudanese court of inquiry indicted the eight on five counts, including murder, but released two of them for lack of evidence in October 1973. A Khartoum court convicted them of murder on June 24, 1974, and sentenced them to life, but Sudanese President Gaafar el-Nimeiry immediately commuted each sentence to seven years. He also announced that the group would be handed over to the PLO. They were flown to Cairo the next day. It appears that Egypt placed the group at the disposal of the PLO in November 1974. 1465

March 3, 1973—Morocco—A watchman discovered a shoe box containing a bomb underneath the U.S. consul's station wagon in Casablanca. 1466

March 4, 1973—Lebanon—The Greek-Cypriot charter ship *Sounion-Sanya*, carrying 250 U.S. Christian tourists to Haifa, Israel, sank in Beirut harbor when a Black September bomb exploded. The device had been placed against the side of the ship below the water line. No injuries were reported, but the ship was badly damaged. 1467

March 5, 1973—Morocco—A bomb was found in a package placed inside a paper towel dispenser in a public washroom at the USIS Cultural Center in Casablanca. 1468

March 7, 1973—United States—An elaborate network of explosives was found in the trunks of cars parked in front of the El Al warehouse at Kennedy Airport, the First Israel Bank and Trust Company, and the Israel Discount Bank, Ltd. Police, having been tipped off by Israelis, were able to dismantle the bombs. A search of the vehicles also revealed a quantity of paper with Black September's letterhead. The FBI reported that the bombs were set to go off on March 4 during Israeli Premier Golda Meir's New York visit, but an error in their circuits caused them not to explode. On March 15, a U.S. federal warrant was sworn out for the Black Septembrist believed to have escaped the country after planting the bombs: Khalid Danham Al-Jawari, an Iraqi. 1469-1471

March 7, 1973—Dominican Republic—During a riot in Santo Domingo, the residence of the U.S. air attaché was attacked by a rock-throwing mob, which attempted to enter the home.

March 7, 1973—United States—A man armed with a rifle took two hostages and attempted to seize a plane at Spokane airport. He was injured by a guard after refusing to surrender. Three people were injured in the attack. 5404

March 8, 1973—United Kingdom—Two bombs exploded in London, killing one man and injuring 243. The *London Times* received an anonymous call forty-five minutes before the first explosion, giving the locations of three bomb-laden cars. The first bomb went off in an auto parked in front of the British army's central London recruiting office, off Trafalgar Square, shattering windows of a nearby pub, the Agriculture Ministry, and other Whitehall government offices. Ten minutes later, a bomb went off in front of Old Bailey, the criminal court. A third bomb was defused near the headquarters of the British Forces Broadcasting System. Several other bomb scares were reported at Windsor Castle, the *London Times* offices, the stock exchange, and twenty other buildings. A bomb was defused outside Scotland Yard, and tough security precautions were put into effect at airports and near the prime minister's home. Police believed that the IRA was protesting a referendum on Northern Ireland's staying within the United Kingdom or joining Ireland. On November 15, eight of ten Provisional IRA members accused of these bombings were sentenced to life imprisonment. The ninth defendant received a fifteen-year term, and the tenth was acquitted. 1472-1495

March 10, 1973—United Kingdom—An IRA bomb exploded in a Glasgow hall where Protestant supporters of British rule in Northern Ireland had scheduled a dance. 1496

March 10, 1973—Canada—A lone male boarded an Eastern Provincial Airways Dart-Herald plane flying from Halifax to Montreal with forty-six persons on board at its stop in Charlo, New Brunswick. A stewardess informed the captain that the man was carrying a gun in his belt. Upon arrival in Montreal, the man was arrested and a mental examination was ordered.

March 12, 1973—Cyprus—Simha Gilzer, fifty-nine, described by police as an Israeli businessman, was shot to death on the steps of the Nicosia Palace Hotel by a Jordanian. Cairo's fedayeen radio claimed Gilzer was a ''Zionist intelligence officer.'' On March 13, the Iraqi news agency reported that Black September had claimed responsibility for the murder, charging that Gilzer was a senior Israeli security officer who was responsible for the death of a BSO operative in January (see incident 1451). Christopher Dobson reported that Gilzer had also been a member of the Irgun Zvai Leumi in the 1940s. 1497

March 15, 1973—United States—A break-in was discovered at the fuel storage building in Oconee of the Duke Power Company's licensed nuclear facility. No material was reported stolen.

March 15, 1973—France—French police arrested two Arabs who were attempting to smuggle explosives across the Italian-French border for use in attacks against the Israeli and Jordanian embassies as part of a Black September campaign. Mohammed Tabab, a Jordanian, and Sakar Mahmoud al Khalil, a Palestinian, drove from a Lebanese Fatah base in a Mercedes carrying thirty-five pounds of plastique. The Israelis learned of the car and tracked it to La Grave in France's Haute Alpes. They passed the information to the French, who found that the car had a spare license plate, CDK 59, which belonged to the Israelis' Paris embassy. The French later arrested Jamil Abdel Hakim, a Palestinian, and Diane Campbell-Lefevre, thirty-one, a British doctor who had worked in Palestinian refugee camps. She was deported to London on March 22, and the Palestinian was deported to Damascus on March 23. The two Fatah members were imprisoned for six months and then expelled from France. 1498-1499

March 19, 1973—South Vietnam—A bomb exploded in the cargo area near the main wing spar of an Air Vietnam DC4 on its landing approach at Ban Me Thuot, after flying from Saigon with fifty-nine on board. There were no survivors.

March 21, 1973—West Germany—A man and a woman entered the grounds of the U.S. consulate general in Frankfurt. One fired a pistol, and the other hurled a bottle against a window. No injuries were reported. Police found a quantity of Molotov cocktails on the roof of a garage near the consulate general. The attack may have been part of a general protest by local radicals; during the night a number of windows were broken at the Greek Central Bank and at several travel agencies in the downtown area. 1500

March 22, 1973—Greece—An explosive incendiary device caused minor damage in Athens to the private vehicle of a U.S. government employee. The initials *EAN* were painted on the door, denoting the Greek Anti-Dictatorial Youth. 1501

March 23, 1973—Belgium—On the day the Greek embassy was celebrating its Independence Day, a Molotov cocktail was thrown through the basement window of the Greek ambassador's residence in Brussels, causing minor damage. 1502

March 23, 1973—United States—The licensed nuclear facility of the Metropolitan Edison company at Three Mile Island near Harrisburg, Pennsylvania, received a bomb threat.

March 26, 1973—Argentina—Fifteen members of the ERP seized the nearly completed Atucha nuclear station. The plant was not seriously damaged, although the ERP left political slogans on the building. Weapons were stolen from the guards, which may have been the primary motive for the attack.

March 28, 1973—Argentina—Gerardo Scalmazzi, the manager of the Rosario branch of the First National Bank of Boston, was kidnapped by Argentine guerrillas, who released him on April 4 after the bank paid a ransom of between $500,000 and $1 million. 1503

March 28, 1973—Argentina—Bombs placed by unidentified terrorists damaged a Jewish nursery school in Rosario but caused no injuries. 1504

March 28, 1973—Colombia—Three persons phoned Avianca Airlines, demanding $250,000 for information on the location of a bomb they claimed was on board a Bogotá to Barranquilla flight with seventy persons on board. The trio was later arrested.

March 28, 1973—South Vietnam—Using guns and dynamite, nine males and one female forced a bus driver to take them to Don Muang airport. The group demanded a plane to take them out of the country. One of them was injured, and all of them were arrested. Thirty persons were on board the bus. 5405

March 29, 1973—United States—The Cuban National Front was suspected of an attempted bombing of a bookstore in Union, New Jersey. 1505

April 1973—Singapore—An Arab parcel bomb was discovered. 1506

April 1, 1973—Lebanon—A bomb placed in a Datsun sedan parked in a Beirut residential area exploded, damaging several surrounding cars but causing no injuries. The owner was not involved in politics or crime. However, it was later discovered that a similar Datsun parked in the area was owned by Ziyad Al Hilu, a Black Septembrist who had assassinated Wasfi Tell in Cairo (see incident 0938). The BSO claimed that Jordanian intelligence operatives had attemped to retaliate, and Hilu demanded Lebanese protection from "acts of sabotage by the Jordanian, American, and Israeli intelligence departments." 1507

April 2, 1973—Argentina—Anthony R. DaCruz, a naturalized U.S. citizen and technical operations manager of Kodak Argentina S.A., a subsidiary of Eastman Kodak Company, was kidnapped by six members of the FAL while on his way to work in Buenos Aires. The group freed him unharmed on April 7 after the company paid $1.5 million. Many reports list him as the first U.S. businessman kidnapped in Argentina, but the *New York Times* wrote that before the DaCruz kidnapping, approximately fifty businessmen had been kidnapped in Argentina in the previous two years, with $5 million being paid in ransoms. On the same day, Francisco Agustin Aleman, a retired Argentine admiral, was kidnapped by the ERP, who demanded justice for the death of sixteen prisoners. He was released unharmed on April 7. 1508

April 4, 1973—Italy—Two Arab members of the PFLP were arrested while attempting to attack passengers of an El Al plane in Rome airport. Carrying forged Iranian passports, they carried two pistols each and had special belts around their waists that held six hand grenades. Although they were sentenced to four years, they served only four months, being released in August and expelled to Lebanon. According to reports by Christopher Dobson, four suitcases full of explosives and weapons were discovered in passenger lounges at Rome airport, and an attractive young Lebanese woman attempting to board an airliner was found to have two pistols strapped to her inner thighs. 1509-1511

April 4, 1973—France—Several persons believed to be of Armenian origin threw tear-gas grenades into the Turkish consulate general and the Turkish airlines office in Paris. 1512-1513

April 4, 1973—France—Dr. Bassel Rauf Kubeisy (also known as Basil Raoud Al Kubaisi) was shot to death on a Paris street as he was returning to his hotel in the shadow of the Madeleine Church soon after midnight. According to an eyewitness, the Iraqi law professor at the American University in Beirut was walking fast, apparently trying to outdistance two young men following him. When they caught up to him, he yelled, "Non, non, ne faites pas cela," but they shot him ten times with .22 pistols. The next day the PFLP issued a statement in Beirut claiming that Kubeisy was carrying out a PFLP mission. Other reports indicated that he was planning with Mohammed Boudia an attack in Austria against Soviet Jewish emigrants headed for Israel. The Mossad Wrath of God teams were suspected in the death of the forty-year-old professor, who was, they claimed, in charge of the arsenals of firearms and explosives kept in Arab diplomatic missions in Europe. 1514

April 5, 1973—Italy—A bomb exploded in the garden of the U.S. embassy marine guard quarters in Rome, breaking windows and causing moderate structural damage to the building. No injuries were reported. 1515

April 5, 1973—Italy—A fire at the USIS library in Rome, originally attributed to a short circuit, was discovered to have been caused by an incendiary device. It caused extensive damage but no injuries. 1516

April 8, 1973—Argentina—Francisco Victor Brimicombe, president of Nobleza Tabacos, Argentina's largest cigarette company and a subsidiary of British-American Tobacco Company, was kidnapped outside his Buenos Aires home by the ERP. He was freed unharmed after his company paid a ransom of $1.8 million on April 13. 1517

April 9, 1973—Cyprus—The replacement for the Black September contact man with the KGB who had been murdered three months earlier was killed when he switched on a light on his Nicosia hotel room after returning from a meeting with the KGB. The switch triggered a detonating device. Zaiad Muchasi had arrived in Cyprus only two days earlier. 1518

April 9, 1973—Italy—Two young men firebombed the USO facility in Rome, causing some damage. They also attacked and disarmed a policeman on duty outside the building. 1519

April 9, 1973—Cyprus—Four members of Black September dynamited the apartment house in Nicosia where the Israeli ambassador, Rahamin Timor, lived. They had timed their attack to coincide with his normal after-lunch walk, but he left a few minutes early. His family was in the apartment house, but no one was reported injured.

After driving up to the house, the terrorists shot a Cypriot police guard in the back. They then placed forty pounds of dynamite by the front door but did not put it close enough to the house. It knocked a hole in the home but did more damage to the terrorists' car. A local explosives expert said the terrorists "had absolutely no idea about explosives." The terrorists hijacked a passing car at gunpoint. Police gave chase, fired on the car, and wounded one of the terrorists. They arrested the other two. Some reports indicate that a fourth terrorist escaped. The group was sentenced to seven years' imprisonment, but on December 6, President Archbishop Makarios said that he did not want Cyprus to become a battleground for the Middle East conflict and released them to Cairo, where they flew on to an unidentified Middle Eastern nation. 1520

April 9, 1973—Cyprus—Thirty minutes after the attack on the apartment building, a Land Rover and another car crashed through the gates at Nicosia airport, driving toward an El Al Viscount whose passengers from Tel Aviv had just deplaned. The terrorists fired machine guns at the plane. A police guard and Israeli guard fired back. The latter killed one of the terrorists with a pistol shot and then fell to the floor. The terrorists moved in, but the guard's ruse had worked; he fired a Uzi submachine gun at the remaining terrorists, killing another one. The Land Rover crashed into a mobile generator. The rest of the terrorists were arrested. Three of the terrorists were wounded, as were two Cypriot policemen. Seven terrorists were arrested. Six carried passports: two each from Oman, Saudi Arabia, and Ras al-Khaima, a Persian Gulf emirate. An Israeli security official said, "Let's say we knew the Arabs would strike, so we brought in help from Israel and warned the Cypriots. We were at the airport early this morning waiting for something to happen."

Inside the Land Rover of the foiled hijackers, police found a terrorist message reading, "We are the new pilots and commanders of this plane. Please don't force us to use violence. Remain in your seats. We are representatives of the Arab Nationalist Youth Organization for the Liberation of Palestine. [Other reports claim that they were members of Black September.] To the friendly people of Cyprus: We are very sorry for the fight on your beautiful island. We did not start this fight. We are only struggling to regain our land and our homes."

Two months later, the seven terrorists were brought before a magistrate's court, where they shouted at the prosecutor and threatened a police witness. One of them yelled, "We did what we did for the ideal of the Palestine Revolution. By detaining us you are preventing us from fighting against Israel. How can Cyprus say that it was a friend of the Arabs?" This logic escaped the court, and on July 27, the group received seven-year sentences. However, on December 6, they received an amnesty from President Makarios and were flown to Cairo. From there they flew to an unidentified Middle Eastern destination. 1521

April 10, 1973—Lebanon—In a spectacular series of raids that took only ninety minutes, approximately thirty Israeli commandos attacked headquarters of Black September and the PDFLP, killing seventeen terrorists and wounding several others, as well as bombing the Black September letter-bomb factory. Preparations for the attack were conducted by six Israeli agents holding forged Latin American passports, who checked into two hotels near the seafront on April 6 and hired three white Buicks, a Plymouth sedan, a Plymouth station wagon, and a Renault from a local automobile rental firm. One of them claimed to be British; he stayed at the Coral Beach Hotel, where he developed a pattern of going fishing at night. On the tenth, he delivered the cars to Israeli units who had landed at the beach. Three of the cars took fifteen commandos, armed with submachine guns and grenades to two apartment blocks off Rue Hamra. The raiders attacked three apartments belonging to prominent Fatah leaders: Abu Youssef (also known as Mohammed Yussef Najjar), one of two Fatah representatives on the PLO Executive Committee, Kamal Adwan, a Black September leader, and Kamal Nasser, a former member of Jordan's parliament and official PLO spokesman. Only three guards were stationed at their posts, and they were quickly killed. Among the dead was Youssef's wife, who threw herself in front of her husband to shield him from the bullets, and a seventy-year-old Italian woman who looked out her adjoining apartment door to see what was causing the noise. Ziad Helou, who was responsible for the Wasfi Tell killing, was injured in the battle. His two colleagues, Essat Rabah and Monzer Khalifa, led the procession in Omar Makram mosque in Cairo's Liberation Square, carrying pictures of the dead Palestinians a few days later. Lebanon claimed that twelve persons were killed in the attack: four Palestinians, two Lebanese policemen, two Lebanese civilians, three Syrians, and an Italian woman. The Israelis later announced that two of their group had been killed and two others were wounded.

Meanwhile, nine Israeli commandos arrived at the headquarters of the Democratic Popular Front near a refugee camp near southern Beirut. The commandos killed two guards sitting in a car. Guerrillas inside the building fired from the top floors at the Israelis. Several Arabs were cut down when their elevator doors opened to greet Israeli submachine gunfire. Arab reinforcements arrived, and cases of mistaken identity occurred on both sides. In the confusion, an Arab tried to carry to safety a wounded Israeli, who freed himself. After thirty minutes, the Israelis placed a large bomb in the building. Firing bazookas, they set the charges and then escaped in autos with their two dead and two wounded.

Elsewhere Israeli paratroopers moved north to a group of warehouses used by Black September to manufacture letter bombs and car bombs. Encountering little resistance, they blew up the facility.

During these attacks in Beirut, Israeli air force helicopters picked up a wounded army officer and carried off some files from the apartments of the three dead Arabs. Aiding the automotive escape, the helicopters dropped spikes on the streets behind the cars to burst the tires of pursuit vehicles.

There were rumors that the Israelis had planned to kill Yasir Arafat and Abu Iyad, who were supposed to have attended a meeting at Nasser's apartment but were called away to Damascus before the attack began.

April 12, 1973—Greece—Ahmed Aboussan, an Arab carrying a Jordanian passport, was killed when a bomb exploded in his Athens hotel room. Initial investigations indicated that he had been carrying the bomb in his luggage. Other reports claimed that he was an agent of Razd and died when the bomb was tossed into his room. 1522

April 12, 1973—Italy—A bomb in La Spezia demolished a car belonging to a British official assigned to NATO. No injuries were reported. 1523

April 14, 1973—Lebanon—Twenty members of the Lebanese Revolutionary Guard overpowered a guard and set explosive charges on twenty oil storage tanks belonging to the U.S.-owned Caltex-Mobil Company in the Sidon area. One of the tanks was destroyed, two were badly damaged, and a fourth was slightly damaged. An army demolitions team removed charges from sixteen other tanks. The group was protesting American support of Israel and appear to have all been males wearing masks. 1524

April 14, 1973—Saudi Arabia—The Saudi Arabian National Guard discovered and detached an explosive device wired to the Tapline near Rafha. 1525

April 16, 1973—Lebanon—Saboteurs attempted to blow up the Tapline in Zahrani but succeeded only in denting it. The oil flow was not affected. On February 27, 1974, a military court sentenced two Palestinians who were working for the PFLP and the PFLP–GC to seven years for the attack, which they claimed was in retaliation for the April 10 Israeli attack against Black September quarters. 1526

April 16, 1973—United States—A single shot was fired through the bedroom window of the home of the New Zealand chargé d'affaires in Washington, D.C. A slogan was painted in red, reading: "There will be a homeland for all or a homeland for none. Death to the Zionists and their functionaries." It was signed by Black September and included a star. The chargé speculated that this was a case of mistaken identity; the Jordanian ambassador, who was probably the group's real target, had lived in the house at one time. 1527

April 21, 1973—West Germany—Bonn authorities received a telephone call threatening to hijack a plane to Moscow. The lone male was later arrested. 5406

April 21, 1973—Israel—Israeli troops captured three Fatah members two miles south of the Lebanese border. The group had planned to attack civilians at a bus station in Safad, fourteen miles southeast. Shehada Ahmed Mustafa confessed at a Tel Aviv news conference on April 22 that they were on a "suicide mission to sabotage the bus station, a restaurant, and other public places and had been ordered to "kill as many as we could and not permit ourselves to be captured." 1528

April 21, 1973—Greece—A bomb placed under the car of the Italian vice-consul in Athens caused severe injuries to a Greek citizen passing by. A car owned by a U.S. employee of the European Exchange Service was slightly damaged by a small bomb. Leaflets attributed the bombings to the National Youth Resistance Organization. 1529-1530

April 23, 1973—West Germany—Rocks and firebombs were thrown at the U.S. consulate in Frankfurt, causing no injuries. 1531

April 23, 1973—Soviet Union—A lone male attempted to hijack to Switzerland an Aeroflot TU104 flying from Leningrad to Moscow. The hijacker killed himself and the copilot when he exploded a bomb. The man was standing in an area between the passenger compartment and the cockpit, and the blast blew a hole in the right side of the fuselage. The plane landed safely at Leningrad. 5407

April 24, 1973—Puerto Rico—A bomb exploded at the Dominican Republic consulate in San Juan, causing slight damage and no injuries. An anonymous Spanish-speaking male phoned to explain that the bombing was the work of Dominican exiles and was timed to coincide with the celebration of the eighth anniversary of the Dominican revolt. 1532

April 25, 1973—Japan—A firebomb was thrown at the main entrance of the U.S. Ikego ammunition storage area, about fifteen miles from Yokosuka Naval Base, causing no injuries or damage to U.S. government facilities. 1533

April 27, 1973—Lebanon—Airport officials arrested two Lebanese and a Palestinian who were about to board an Air France flight to Nice and Paris. The luggage contained explosives and timing devices. 1534

April 27, 1973—Italy—Vittorio Olivares, an Italian employee of El Al, was shot twice in the stomach by an Arab armed with a long-barreled pistol fitted with a silencer. As he ran from the scene of the crime, outside a Rome department store, the gunman fired several shots to keep the crowd away but was arrested by Italian police. He said that he was Zaharia Abu Saleh and had been sent by Black September to kill Olivares, whom he claimed was an Israeli agent responsible for the death of BSO operative Abdel Zuaiter in Rome in October 1972 (see incident 1240). The Lebanese citizen was committed to an Italian psychiatric institution and not brought to trial on the grounds that he was mentally unfit. On July 17, 1975, he was released on a 30-million-lire bond. It was believed that he left Italy. 1535

April 28, 1973—Lebanon—Black September placed a bomb in a lavatory in Beirut International Airport. The device was found and dismantled by authorities one hour before it was set to go off. Security around the airport was tightened. Callers claimed that the attack was designed to secure the release of the three Arabs who had been arrested the previous day (see incident 1534). The callers said another bomb was near an oil storage area, but none was found. 1536-1537

April 29, 1973—Lebanon—A stick of dynamite thrown at the Beirut residence of the Jordanian ambassador exploded in a vacant lot, doing negligible damage and causing no injuries. 1538

April 29, 1973—El Salvador—A bomb caused extensive damage to the San Salvador offices of IBM. 1539

April 30, 1973—Lebanon—Four members of Black September were arrested by Lebanese troops as they approached the U.S. embassy in Beirut in a car that contained weapons, explosives, and a radio transmitter. Police later reported that five other armed Palestinians were taken into custody in connection with the incident. 1540

April 30, 1973—Argentina—A bomb exploded in a Córdoba building owned by Goodyear, causing serious damage but no injuries. The ERP later claimed credit for the attack. 1541

May 1, 1973—Lebanon—Palestinian guerrillas kidnapped two Lebanese officers in Beirut and demanded the release of the three Arabs arrested on April 27 for carrying explosives into Beirut International Airport (see incident 1534). The hostages were released when fighting erupted between Lebanese troops and Palestinian guerrillas in Beirut and other parts of Lebanon on May 2 and 3. A cease-fire was called on May 2 but fighting resumed on May 3 after a Palestinian ambush of a Beirut police barracks in which three policemen died and seven others were injured. 1542

May 1, 1973—Spain—The Barcelona office of British European Airways was damaged by firebombs. 1543

May 1, 1973—Argentina—Santiago Soldati, son of the Swiss chairman of the Italo-Argentine Electric Company and of a new Italian bank in Buenos Aires, was kidnapped by armed men in that city. His family paid a $1.5 million ransom, and he was released unharmed on May 4. 1544

May 1,1973—Afghanistan—A member of Black December shot at an assistant manager of the Indian Airlines office in Kabul. The attacker was overpowered by the assistant manager, who held him for police. 1545

May 1, 1973—Argentina—An ERP bomb exploded in front of the Goodyear office in Córdoba. 1456

May 2, 1973—Spain—Two firebombs were thrown at the Barcelona offices of Pan Am, breaking all of the windows and causing considerable smoke damage. 1547

May 2, 1973—Lebanon—Rockets were fired from an unknown location at the Beirut residence of the U.S. ambassador, causing no damage or injuries. 1548

May 3, 1973—United States—A bomb threat was received at the Lynchburg, Virginia, licensed nuclear facility of the Babcock and Wilcox Company, which received a similar threat on May 8.

May 4, 1973—Burma—Rebel Shan tribesmen kidnapped two Soviet doctors and demanded the release of Chang Chipu, their imprisoned leader. On May 30, the government's forces attacked a rebel hideout where the hostages were being held, but the rebels escaped. Some reports claimed that Soviet and U.S. intelligence services engaged in the negotiations for the hostages, but the results of those talks were not made public. One of the doctors was released on February 2, 1974; the other was released on June 19, 1974. 1549

May 4, 1973—Mexico—The U.S. consul general in Guadalajara, Terence G. Leonhardy, was kidnapped by members of the People's Revolutionary Armed Forces, who demanded the release of thirty prisoners in Mexican jails who were to be flown to Cuba, publication of an antigovernment communiqué, suspension of the search for Leonhardy and his kidnappers, and a television appearance by the Cuban ambassador to confirm that the prisoners had arrived safely in Havana. The Mexican government's president, Luis Echeverria Alvarez, quickly agreed to the demands, and the twenty-six men and four women arrived in Havana on a Mexican airliner on May 6. Among those released was José Bracho Campos, an associate of the late guerrilla leader Genaro Vasquez Rojas.

The guerrillas' communiqué, which was published in the press and broadcast over television and radio on May 6, denounced Mexico's health standards, illiteracy, and exorbitant credit rates. It pointed to concentration of wealth, capital flight, and repression of student, worker, and peasant dissent as the causes of this impoverishment. The group said the government tried to ''convince the people that we are common delinquents, hired killers, cattle rustlers, enemies of the country. Today, for the first time and was not voluntarily, the mass media are serving the proletarian cause.'' Leonhardy's wife borrowed $80,000 from a local bank and paid the money to the FRAP as ransom for her husband, who was released unharmed on May 6. On December 24, 1973, Pedro Orozco Guzman was wounded by police in a shootout. Before he died of his wounds, he confessed to participation in the kidnappings of Williams, Mexican industrialist Fernando Aranguren, and Leonhardy. On August 28, 1974, three of those who were released to Cuba participated in the kidnapping in Guadalajara of General José Zuno Hernandez, who was required to restate his belief in revolution. The release of a man imprisoned for the Leonhardy incident was unsuccessfully sought by two FRAP bus hijackers in Mexico City in August 1977. 1550

May 7, 1973—Greece—Pipe bombs caused extensive damage to cars belonging to two U.S. servicemen and a Greek-American movie producer in Athens. No injuries were reported. 1553-1555

May 13, 1973—Bolivia—Two ELN members were killed in a shootout with police in La Paz. They were identified as Oswaldo Ucasqui, an Argentine citizen, and Monica Ertl, who was alleged to be the killer of the Bolivian consul in West Germany in 1971 (see incident 0735). 1556

May 14, 1973—United States—A man holding two persons hostage threatened to blow up a fuel tank at the Lockheed Air Terminal at Portland airport if his wife and children were not brought to him. He fired shots at several airliners and was eventually killed by authorities.

May 18, 1973—Brazil—A fire caused by an incendiary device thrown at the home damaged the São Paulo residence of a U.S. diplomat but caused no injuries. 1557

May 18, 1973—Venezuela—An Avensa Convair 580 flying from Valera to Barquisimeto with thirty-seven passengers and five crew members was hijacked by Federico Bottini Marin, the leader of the People's Revolutionary Army Zero Point (also known as Punto Cero), who was accompanied by two other men and a woman who were armed with guns. They threatened to blow up the plane if seventy-nine prisoners were not released from Venezuelan jails. On May 19, the Venezuelan government announced that it refused to discuss the demands of the terrorists. The plane refueled in Curaçao and flew on to Panama City, where five passengers were allowed to deplane. The plane next flew to Merida and Mexico City, where a Mexican official, Miguel Nazar, persuaded the hijackers either to accept political asylum in Mexico or allow the Mexican government to aid them in reaching Cuba. The group accepted the latter offer, and Nazar flew with them to Havana, from which the plane returned with its passengers and crew on May 20. The hijackers were taken into custody. 1558

May 20, 1973—United Kingdom—British police arrested two Arabs who were believed to be planning terrorist actions. After interrogation, they were expelled from the country two days later. 1559

May 21, 1973—Argentina—Several armed men kidnapped the manager of the Córdoba Coca-Cola bottling plant, Oscar Castells, and released him on June 2 after a payment of a $100,000 ransom. 1560

May 21, 1973—Argentina—In an unsuccessful kidnapping attempt, gunmen from the ERP shot two Ford Motor Company executives as they left the Ford factory in the General Pachecho area of Buenos Aires. One of the victims, Luis Giovanelli, died on June 25 from his wounds. The ERP issued a communiqué claiming that the duo had been shot attempting to resist a kidnapping attempt and warned that the kidnapping of Ford executives would continue if the company did not pay it a $1 million charitable contribution. 1561

May 23, 1973—Argentina—An ERP bomb was defused at the Ford Motor Company offices in Buenos Aires. As a result of this attack and the earlier machine-gunning of Luis Giovanelli and a female employee in a second car when plant security guards attempted to intervene, Ford gave in to ERP demands for a $1 million contribution. According to press reports, Ford's vice-president for Asian, Pacific, and Latin American operations, Edgar R. Molina, said at the company's Dearborn, Michigan, headquarters that Ford would pay $200,000 in medicine for the Buenos Aires children's hospital and $200,000 in instruments for the Catamarca children's hospital; provide twenty-two ambulances equipped for emergencies, one for each province (154 ambulances had initially been demanded, but Ford said it did not produce ambulances and would have difficulty obtaining them from other companies immediately); $180,000 for food for poor areas of Buenos Aires; and $300,000 in school supplies for needy schools in the Buenos Aires area. The money was donated directly to the specified hospitals in Buenos Aires and Catamarca. The Argentine military government, due to leave office in two days because of upcoming elections, loosened its restrictions on foreign companies' negotiating with domestic terrorist groups. This appeared to be the first case of a U.S. firm's paying protection money to an Argentine terrorist group, and other foreign firms criticized the decision. 1562

May 24, 1973—France—A bomb caused heavy damage to the Senegalese embassy in Paris. Damage to other buildings was slight, and no injuries were reported. 1563

May 25, 1973—Soviet Union—An Aeroflot TU104 flying from Moscow to Chita with one hundred persons on board was hijacked by a lone man. Authori-

392   May 26, 1973

ties believe a gunfight between the hijacker and a guard caused the plane to crash in southern Siberia, leaving no survivors. 5408

May 26, 1973—Crete—Fire, possibly caused by an incendiary device, caused minor damage to a car of a U.S. military officer in Iraklion. 1564

May 30, 1973—Colombia—An SAM Lockheed Electra flying the Cali-Pereira-Medellín route with eighty-six persons on board was hijacked out of Pereira by two young men who claimed they were members of the ELN and were identified as Francisco Solano Lopez Dominguez and Oscar Eusebio Borjas Gonzales. They used guns and threatened to blow up the plane if 140 Colombian prisoners were not released and a ransom of $200,000 was not paid. They ordered the plane to fly to Aruba and then to Ecuador, Peru, Argentina, Aruba, Argentina, and finally to Paraguay. The Colombian government refused both demands. All of the passengers escaped or were permitted by the hijackers to leave at different stops along the way. At one of the stops, the hijackers agreed to settle for a $50,000 ransom provided by SAM. The duo escaped from the plane in Resistencia, Argentina. 1565

May 31, 1973—Argentina—The ERP demanded a $500,000 ransom for the release of John Thompson, the British manager of the Golov Lopez y Carva textile company. 1566

May 31, 1973—Argentina—The ERP threatened to attack and kidnap Otis Elevator Company executives and their families if the company did not pay $500,000 in charitable contributions similar to those made by Ford (see incident 1562) and double the wages of thirteen hundred Otis employees in Argentina. The company refused and ordered the families of thirteen executives flown to São Paulo, Brazil. On June 3, the ERP released business executive Aaron Belinson, an Argentine citizen, after 10 days' captivity, after a $1 million ransom was paid. At a press conference, Belinson read an ERP statement that pledged to use the money to "help finance the revolutionary struggle." 1567

June 2, 1973—Iran—Lieutenant Colonel Lewis L. Hawkins, an American military adviser serving as the financial comptroller of the U.S. Military Aid and Assistance Group in Tehran, was shot and killed by gunmen belonging to an Iranian leftist group. The gunmen jumped on a motorcycle driven by a confederate and escaped. On June 15, security forces killed the leader of the group, Reza Rezai, when they surrounded his home. A pistol used by Rezai was found to have been a weapon taken from the body of Iranian General Taheri by his assassins. According to the *Washington Post* of January 1, 1975,

''An Iranian army tribunal has sentenced 10 Marxist guerrillas to death by a firing squad for the killing of 3 American colonels, an Iranian employee of the US Consulate and 4 other Iranians. An 11th defendant, one of 2 women in the group, was sentenced to solitary confinement for 15 years. . . .They . . .admitted the slaying.'' 1568

June 6, 1973—Argentina—Members of the ERP-August 22, an ERP splinter group, sent six of their group to kidnap Charles Agnew Lockwood, British director of the firm of Roberts, Meynell y Compania, an Argentine affiliate of Britain's Acrow Steel, which represents U.S. and U.K. interests in Argentina. In a June 9 press interview, members of the ERP denied responsibility for Lockwood's kidnapping, as well as threats against the Otis Elevator Company. The abductors initially asked for $7.5 million ransom. After fifty-three days of negotiations, Lockwood was released on July 30 after the company agreed to pay $2 million. 1569

June 9, 1973—West Germany—Black September bombs partially destroyed the Fritz Werner GMBH Arms Plant in West Berlin. Agence France-Press reported that a BSO communiqué released in Cairo claimed that the firm dealt with Israel. 1570

June 9, 1973—Peru—A homemade bomb was placed outside a building owned by a U.S. firm in San Isidro. The device exploded on Friday at 10:55 P.M. close to the iron curtain that protects the entrance door and adjacent windows. The device, a three-inch galvanized pipe 20 cm long filled with black explosive power and a cotton hydraulic fuse, caused glass breakage of a window and doors and dented two of the iron curtains. Officials claimed losses came to $866. 1571

June 10, 1973—Nepal—A Royal Nepalese Airlines Twin Otter on a domestic flight from Biratnagar to Katmandu with eighteen persons on board was hijacked to Forbesganj, India, by three hijackers armed with guns. The trio, identified as Basanta Bhattari, Prasad Subedi, and Nagendra P. Dhungel, was led by a leader of a Nepalese student organization connected with the Nepalese Communist party. The plane was carrying a Nepal State Bank shipment of 3 million India rupees, worth approximately $400,000, which the group seized. The trio escaped into the jungle on a waiting jeep. None of the passengers was reported injured. 1572

June 10, 1973—Italy—Members of the Mafia kidnapped Gene Paul Getty II in Rome. On October 21, they cut off his right ear and mailed it to a Rome newspaper to establish that they were holding him. A postal strike delayed delivery. Billionaire J. Paul Getty paid a ransom of $2.9 million (3 billion lire, which weighed a ton) for his grandson's release, which came on December 15.

June 13, 1973—United States—The brother of Sirhan Sirhan, the killer of Senator Robert Kennedy, Sharif Bishara Sirhan, thirty-two, was convicted of sending a threatening letter to U.S. Secretary of State William Rogers warning that Golda Meir would be shot. 1573

June 17, 1973—Italy—Two members of Black September were seriously injured when their car, laden with explosives, blew up on a Rome street. They were identified as Abdel Hamid Shibli, a Jordanian, and Abdel Hadi Nakaa, a Syrian, and were believed to be driving their booby-trapped car toward their next mission, which may have been against the transit camp in Austria for Soviet Jewish émigrés. Some reports claim that the Mossad Wrath of God teams arranged for the bombs' premature detonation. A quantity of automatic weapons and plastic explosives was found in the car. In August 1973, Italy freed all imprisoned terrorists, including the duo, who had yet to stand trial for transporting weapons in their Mercedes. 1574

June 18, 1973—Guatemala—The FAR kidnapped Roberto Galvez, the general manager of the U.S. company Corn Products, in Guatemala City. He was released after the payment of a $50,000 ransom. 1575

June 18, 1973—Argentina—U.S. citizen John R. Thompson, president and general manager of Firestone Tire and Rubber Company's subsidiary in Buenos Aires, was kidnapped by several armed male ERP members. Thompson's chauffeur said he was driving from the plant when five ERP autos intercepted his car. They smashed the window, grabbed Thompson, threw the chauffeur into a ditch, fired a few rounds, and then fled. Thompson, an amateur actor, was to have appeared in a suburban community theater play, *The Desperate Hours*, the tale of two criminals who hold a family hostage in their home. On July 6, Thompson was released unharmed after his company paid a $3 million "revolutionary tax." Firestone officials bargained with an ERP negotiator at the Presidents Hotel in Buenos Aires. The ransom was in bundles of five-hundred-peso notes, and filled an armored car provided by the ERP. 1576

June 19, 1973—Argentina—Guerrillas in Buenos Aires kidnapped Jan Hans Kurt Gebhardt, sixty-one, a West German who was technical manager for Silvania, S.A., a women's hosiery plant. His attackers pulled him from his car as he was about to leave his home in the morning. A ransom of $100,000 was paid, and he was released on July 1. 1577

June 19, 1973—Soviet Union—A lone male hijacked a Russian domestic plane scheduled to fly between Rostov and Batum. The copilot succeeded in taking off before the passengers embarked. The man was taken into custody by authorities upon landing in Trebizond, Turkey. 5409

June 19, 1973—United States—The Southern California Edison Company's licensed nuclear facility at San Onofre received a bomb threat.

June 20, 1973—Argentina—In a gun battle between police and members of the ERP, FAR, and Montoneros at Buenos Aires's Ezeiza Airport, twenty were killed and three hundred injured. A crowd was awaiting the arrival of General Perón from Spain.

June 20, 1973—United States—A car owned by Anatoly V. Grodski, a member of the Soviet U.N. mission in New York, was destroyed by fire. An anonymous telephone caller, apparently a JDL member, claimed that the firebombing was in protest of the visit of Leonid Brezhnev to the United States and the treatment of Jews in the Soviet Union. 1578

June 23, 1973—Argentina—Mario Baratella, vice-president of the Bank of Italy and Rio de la Plata, was kidnapped by ERP gunmen in Buenos Aires, who demanded a $2 million ransom. He was released unharmed on July 5 after an undisclosed amount was paid. 1579

June 28, 1973—France—Mohammed Boudia, an Algerian boss of the Black September network in Europe, was killed in Paris when a bomb exploded in his Renault 16 on the Rue des Fosses-St.-Bernard. According to documents the Israelis acquired in the April 10 raids on Black September headquarters in Beirut, it was Boudia's job to coordinate the activities of the numerous left-wing terrorist groups operating in Europe.
Boudia was wanted by Italian police for the bombing of the Trieste oil terminal. He had been named by Evelyne Barges, a French woman picked up by the Israelis, as the orchestrator of her sabotage operations. Boudia, an Algerian, was a member of a secret Marxist group opposed to Colonel Houari Boumédienne's regime. He managed the Theatre de l'Ouest, an avant-garde Paris establishment. He and Mahmoud Hamshari recruited Left Bank intelligentsia for BSO operations. He was particularly adept at seducing French women and then sending them on BSO missions. He had spent the night with a girl friend at her apartment in Rue Boinod in the eighteenth arrondissement. In the morning he drove to another girl friend's house in the fifth arrondisement, in front of the Faculty of Science. A mechanic across the road reported seeing a forty-year-old man open the front door of the car and place something between

the front and back seats. It turned out to be a bomb attached to a string tied to the car door. When the door was opened, it pulled the pin on a ten-second time-delay fuse, allowing Boudia enough time to get inside the car before it exploded. Reporter David Tinnin claimed that the assassination was the work of the Mossad Wrath of God team, and that seated less than one hundred yards away, peering through slits in black masking tape on the window, were agent "Mike" and General Zvi Zamir. 1580

June 20, 1973—Northern Ireland—A bomb went off near the freight terminal of Belfast's Aldergrove Airport, injuring several people.

July 1973—Guatemala—The son of a resident U.S. businessman was slain by unknown assailants. 1581

July 1, 1973—United States—Colonel Yosef Alon, forty-three, one of Israel's most famous pilots and air and naval attaché of the Israeli embassy in Washington, D.C., was shot five times and killed in his front garden in Chevy Chase, Maryland, as he was parking his car after he and his wife returned from an embassy party. Some reports claim that Mossad has information showing that Alon was shot by Black Power gunmen on a $20,000 contract from a Black September representative. In Beirut, the Arab general commando of Ahmed Jebreel claimed responsibility. In Beirut, the newspaper *Al Moharrer* announced, "The fact that the arm of the Palestinians has reached the American stronghold in Washington is another piece of evidence that there is nothing—absolutely nothing—which will stop the Palestinian people from expanding the scope of the war against its enemies." The Voice of Palestine claimed that the assassination was in retaliation for the death of Mohammed Boudia (see incident 1580). 1582

July 1, 1973—India—The U.S. consul in Calcutta received three telephoned bomb threats. Although assumed to be crank calls, precautions were taken. 1583-1585

July 2, 1973—Argentina—Raul Bornancini, assistant manager and head of banking operations for the Córdoba branch of the First National City Bank of New York, was kidnapped en route from his home to his office. Several hours later a ransom demand of $1 million was made by an individual who said that the abductors were not politically motivated. Bornancini was released unharmed on July 13 after the ransom was paid. The Argentine government increased security measures to prevent the numerous kidnappings that were occurring, including the creation of a special antikidnapping unit in the federal police. 1586

July 4, 1973—United States—The shop window of a Cleveland store selling Yugoslav newspapers, books, and other goods was shattered. Police arrested Joza Misetic, Milan Butina, and Petar Perun, Yugoslav émigrées.

July 4, 1973—Argentina—Norman Lee, an executive of the Coca-Cola Bottling Company in Buenos Aires, was kidnapped for a second time by a group of armed men. They released him unharmed after he successfully argued that no more ransoms would be paid for him, but they took his car and approximately $100 from his wallet. 1587

July 4, 1973—Argentina—An Aerolineas Argentinas B737 flying from Buenos Aires to Tucumán with eighty persons on board was hijacked by a gun-wielding man, Basilio J. Mazor, who claimed to be a member of the ERP. The hijacker demanded that Argentina pay $200,000 to charitable organizations. The government turned down his demand. He forced the pilot to fly to Mendoza, Argentina, Santiago, Chile, Lima, Peru, Panama City, Panama, and finally Havana, Cuba, having released all but twenty-eight of those on board at those stops. The hijacker was offered asylum in Cuba, although the Argentine government demanded his return. The ERP denied that he had ever been affiliated with the organization. 1588

July 4, 1973—Peru—A small bomb destroyed the iron gate of the French embassy in Lima. The attack was thought to be a protest of the planned French nuclear tests in the South Pacific. 1589

July 6, 1973—Argentina—The ERP hurled incendiary bombs and opened fire on the Buenos Aires residence of the Uruguayan ambassador, causing some damage but no injuries. 1590

July 8, 1973—Argentina—Two men and one woman, all ERP members, seized the Uruguayan consulate for fifteen minutes, painting signs on the walls proclaiming "solidarity with the Uruguayan revolutionaries and workers." No one was reported injured in the brief takeover in La Plata. 1591

July 10, 1973—Barbados—A bomb exploded in the British West Indies Airways office. The firm represents the interests of Cubana in Barbados. 1592

July 11, 1973—United States—A JDJ Flying Service Bell 47GS helicopter chartered to allow its passenger to take photos between Gainesville, Texas, and Marietta, Oklahoma, was hijacked over Marietta by a white male for whom the FAA profile was not applicable: Daniel Clark, who was born in Riverside, California, on May 26, 1953. The hijacker forced the pilot at pistol point to fly to Wichita Falls, Texas. He was captured in Dallas, Texas, on July 13, 1973. He was indicted on September 18, 1973, by a federal grand jury in the northern district of Texas. On February 11, 1974, he was convicted of air piracy and sentenced to twenty years or until discharged by the Federal Youth Correction Division's board of parole according to the Federal Youth Corrections Act. 5410

July 19, 1973—Israel—The U.S. embassy in Tel Aviv received a telephoned bomb threat. A search was negative. 1593

July 19, 1973—Greece—A lone Palestinian armed with a submachine gun and grenades attempted to attack the El Al offices in Athens but was prevented from entering when an alert guard pressed a security lock that closed inner doors made of bulletproof glass. The attacker fled to a nearby hotel, where he took seventeen hostages (some reports claim he took forty hostages, while others claim two hostages), holding off two policemen who gave chase. He threatened to kill the hostages unless Greek Deputy Premier Stylianos Patakos escorted him to Athens airport for safe passage out of the country. Patakos refused. The ambassadors of Libya, Egypt, and Iraq negotiated with the terrorist in the lobby of the hotel for two and a half hours, and persuaded him to end the five-hour siege and fly to Kuwait, where he vanished, leaving the hostages unharmed. He claimed to be a member of the Organization of Victims of Occupied Territories. Arab officials denied knowledge of the organization. 1594

July 20, 1973—Netherlands—JAL flight 404, a B747 flying from Paris to Tokyo and Anchorage, was seized thirty minutes after leaving Amsterdam at 3:42 P.M. by four hijackers armed with grenades and pistols. The hijacking was precipitated when one of the hijackers, identified on her forged Ecuadorian passport as Mrs. Peralta but later identified as an Iraqi Christian member of Habash's group, Katie George Thomas, sipped a glass of champagne and asked a purser how to place her seat back. Upon following the purser's instructions and swiveling her chair in the upper deck of the first-class section, she noticed that she was leaving behind her handbag, which contained a grenade. Reaching back to retrieve it, she accidently pulled the firing pin. After placing the handbag in her lap, the grenade exploded, killing her and injuring the purser. This led the other four hijackers (three Palestinians and one Japanese member of the Japanese Red Army, identified as Osamu Maruoka) to take over the plane, informing Cyprus ground control that this was Operation Mount Carmel. Unfortunately for the hijackers, the planner of the operation, believed to be Ali Hassan Salameh, instructed only Katie regarding what they were to seek in the operation. It appears that they were to act in response to Japan's paying $6 million in compensation for the Lod Airport massacre (see incident 1056). The group demanded the release of the last surviving member of that attack, Kozo Okamoto, as well as a ransom of $5 million. Israeli Transport Minister Shimon Peres turned down the demand the next day. Moreover, due to Mossad intelligence reports that Black September was planning to crash a plane into Haifa, Israeli Phantom jets were ordered to shoot down the 747 if it reached Israeli air space. However, the plane flew on to Beirut, where it was refused landing privileges. They next attempted Basra, Iraq, but the landing strip was deemed too short. Bahrain also denied permission to land. Captain Kenzi Konuma was finally successful in landing in Dubai for refueling.

The group variously identified themselves as the Organization of Sons of Occupied Territories, the Mount Carmel Martyrs, and the Japanese Red Army acting for the People of Palestine. It is possible that they were a splinter group of the PFLP. Maruoka, a student said by the Japanese to have married the leader of the JRA, Fusako Shigenobu, and the other terrorists allowed the wounded purser, as well as the body of the dead hijacker, to leave the plane. However, they demanded that the body be returned in a coffin, which was placed in the first-class section of the plane before it flew off again. The rest of the 123 passengers and 22 crew members were forced to remain on board. According to one of the passengers, a West German businessman, Holger Gauger, "We were forced to put our hands on our heads for a total of twelve hours. Anytime there was any action or anyone approached the plane, it was hands up, sometimes for half an hour at a stretch."

The terrorists turned down negotiation offers by JAL and Sheik Mohammed bin Rashid, the UAE defense minister, who had boarded the plane on July 21. On July 23, the Dubai control tower relayed a message allegedly sent by a West German group to the hijackers: "If you intend to kill the passengers on board . . .do it at once, otherwise be human enough to release them. . . .Please give up your intentions. There are other means of unbloody possibilities to reach your political aims." Shortly afterward, the hijackers forced Dubai authorities to refuel the plane, which took off on July 24.

They were refused landing privileges at Bahrain, Saudi Arabia, and Abu Dhabi, and Beirut turned off the lights on its landing strip, barring them a second time. Damascus allowed them to refuel but sent them on their way after three hours. The plane flew on to Benghazi, Libya, where Colonel Qaddafi allowed it to land for "humanitarian reasons." Before the plane landed, the terrorists informed the pilot that the passengers had two minutes to deplane before it would be blown up. All disembarked safely, and the £10 million plane was destroyed when the fire started by the hijackers' bombs hit the plane's fuel tanks. According to the captain, the hijackers received instructions from terrorists in Amsterdam to destroy the plane upon landing. This guidance was relayed via control towers in Bahrain and Kuwait. The group was initially accorded a heroes' welcome, with the Libyan government attempting to explain their motivations, but they came to be condemned by Qaddafi a few days later. On July 29, Libyan Minister of Information Abu Zaid Durda described the attack as "a crime for which the perpetrators have not been able to give any justification. . . .Some hijackers seek to become rich by demanding a ransom for the release of their victims. Others seek fame and some want to travel free of charge. Some hijackers, however, try to justify their crime as being in the defense of a national cause. . . .Just as it condemned robbery, megalomania and parasitism, Libya also condemned the reducing of methods of defending national causes to such a low level. The Libyan Arab Republic has therefore decided to bring the hijackers to trial. They will be tried according to Armed Robbery Law No. 148 of 1972 which was enacted in line with Islamic law." It does not appear that the hijackers were tried, although Osamu reportedly was kept in prison for a year. Upon his release, he wrote in the left-wing weekly *Shinsayoku* that he had been treated as a special political prisoner with his cell equipped with color television. The Japanese police were unable to locate him in order to question him about his suspected involvement in the planning of the Lod massacre. Reuters reported that the hijackers had been released and were at liberty in Damascus, where they arrived on August 13, 1974. The PLO, PFLP, and all other major Palestinian organizations denied responsibility for the attack. 1595

July 21, 1973—Norway—Ahmed Bouchiki, thirty, a Moroccan waiter mistaken by Israeli intelligence for Ali Hassan Salameh, a Black September leader, was gunned down on a Lillehammer street by two Wrath of God members firing .22 caliber pistols. Two Israelis were arrested in the Oslo apartment of diplomat Yigal Eyal on July 25. The group believed that BSO had planned to hijack an El Al plane in Denmark and was to assemble the attack squad in Norway. On February 1, 1974, an Oslo court convicted five Jews, including the two Israelis, for accessory to murder and spying for Israel. A sixth Israeli defendant was acquitted. Sylvia Rafael, a South African, and Abraham Gehmer, an Israeli, received five-year sentences. Ethel Marianne Gladnikoff of Sweden received two-and-a-half years, and Swi Steinberg of Israel received one year. In October 1974, two Israelis were expelled to Israel. In May 1975 the last two of the convicted group were pardoned. Salameh died on January 22, 1979, when a bomb exploded in a car his entourage was passing in Beirut. 1596

July 22, 1973—Peru—Bombs thrown from a passing car damaged a Lima annex of the Colombia embassy, as well as the Miraflores USIS Binational Center (Peruvian-North American Cultural Center) and the Society of Industries. 1597-1598

July 23, 1973—Lebanon—In Beirut, the marine guard from the U.S. embassy in Kuwait was kidnapped by Palestinians but released unharmed after several hours of questioning. 1599

July 23, 1973—Israel—The U.S. embassy in Tel Aviv received two telephoned bomb threats, including one from an English-speaking young man. A search was negative. 1600-1601

July 24, 1973—United States—The Secret Cuban Government claimed credit for the bombing of New York City's Martin Luther King, Jr., Labor Center. A pro-Castro Cuban cultural and political exposition was scheduled to be held there. A maintenance worker was injured, and the top floor of the Times Square building was damaged. Due to the late-night bombing, as well as egg and brick throwing and repeated bomb threats by anti-Castro exiles, the show closed on July 28, a day ahead of schedule. 1602

July 25, 1973—Chile—A bomb planted on the fourteenth floor damaged the offices of the Czechoslovakian embassy in Santiago. 1603

July 26, 1973—Honduras—A tear-gas bomb was fired into the offices of the OAS in Tegucigalpa by several unidentified persons. 1604

July 26, 1973—West Germany—The U.S. embassy in Bonn received a note warning that it would be blown up on July 30. Additional police protection was requested. 1605

July 27, 1973—Chile—A bomb was thrown at the Santiago residence of the second secretary of the Democratic People's Republic of Korea. No injuries were reported, but a car parked in front of the home was destroyed. 1606

August 1973 —United States—Twenty-one capsules of radioactive iodine-131 were stolen from the Arcadia, California, hospital.

August 2, 1973—France—Juan Felipe de la Cruz Serafin, a member of the Cuban Revolutionary Directorate, an anti-Castro Cuban group, was killed when a bomb exploded in his Avrainville hotel room. Serafin was a U.S. citizen. The Cubans claimed that the bomb exploded in his hands and that he had intended to use it against the Cuban embassy. 1607

August 4, 1973—Yugoslavia—The Belgrade railway station was bombed, killing one and injuring seven.

August 5, 1973—Greece—Two Black Septembrists opened their suitcases at an Athens airport inspection, pulled out machine guns and grenades, and killed three and wounded fifty-five passengers, most of them waiting to board a TWA flight to New York. It was later learned that they had been ordered to attack the TWA flight to Tel Aviv, but the passengers had already boarded. The dead included two Americans and an Indian. Two of the wounded, one a sixteen-year-old U.S. girl, Laura Haack, later died of their injuries in a local hospital. The terrorists claimed that their mission was to exact revenge for the Mossad execution of Abu Youssef in Beirut on April 10, 1973. The duo then seized thirty-five hostages but soon surrendered to Athens police.

On August 7, Shafik el Arida, twenty-two, a Palestinian, and Tallal Khaled Kaddourah, twenty-one, of Lebanon, told a court that they had "orders to hit at emigrants to Israel because they kill our wives and children." Arida had flown from Benghazi, Libya, on August 3 to surveil the Athens transit lounge. They took off for Beirut and returned on August 5 to carry out their attack. In their court testimony, they claimed, "Our orders were to strike against the passengers of the third TWA aircraft leaving Athens that afternoon, because our leaders had established it was carrying Jewish immigrants to Israel disguised as tourists to settle in the land from which we were uprooted." A group calling itself the Seventh Suicide Squad took responsibility for the attack, claiming that it was named "Bahr al-Bakr" after a Cairo suburb where Israeli planes bombed a school in 1970. However, the two were later identified as belonging to Ahmad Abd-al Ghaffur's group of Fatah dissidents. After a one-day trial, a Greek court sentenced the two to death on January 23, 1974. The sentences were commuted to life imprisonment on April 23, 1974. Their release was demanded in two subsequent incidents: the armed attack/hijack on December 17 in Italy and the February 2, 1974 thirty-three-hour takeover of a Greek ship in Karachi, Pakistan (see incidents 1731 and 1809). The two were released and expelled to Libya on May 5, 1974. It appears that they were granted their freedom in Libya; one of them was with Abd-al Ghaffur when he was killed in Beirut on September 13, 1974. 1608

August 9, 1973—Northern Ireland—Fifty houses were damaged and sixteen people injured when a four-hundred-pound bomb planted by the IRA went off in an army housing compound in Armagh.

August 10, 1973—Lebanon—Iraqi Airways flight 006A, a Caravelle flying from Beirut to Baghdad, was intercepted by two Israeli fighters and forced to land in Haifa. After two hours, the aircraft and the eighty-two persons on board were allowed to return to Beirut.

August 11, 1973—Argentina—After the ERP threatened to attack its executives if $1 million was not paid to specified charities, the Coca-Cola Export

Corporation, a U.S.-based firm, ordered its executives and their families moved to Brazil and Uruguay. 1609

August 12, 1973—Ecuador—A bomb exploded outside the U.S. consulate general in Guayaquil, hurting no one but breaking thirty-five windows. 1610

August 12, 1973—Chile—A bomb in Santiago destroyed a car parked near a USIA employee's residence. 1611

August 15, 1973—New Zealand—A bomb thrown from a speeding car gutted the U.S. consular agency in Christchurch but caused no injuries. 1612

August 15, 1973—Chile—Pipe bombs were found in the driveways of the Santiago homes of three U.S. embassy officers, including that of the air attaché. Police disarmed the bombs before they could explode. 1613-1615

August 16, 1973—Northern Ireland—Six IRA gunmen hijacked a booby-trapped freight train on the border of Ireland and Northern Ireland. British police detonated the bomb with rifle fire, causing damage to the train.

August 16, 1973—Libya—Middle East Airways B707 flight from Benghazi to Beirut was hijacked by Mohammed Ahmed Al-Toumi, a Libyan who had gotten drunk and used two pistols to threaten the crew and passengers. All 125 on board were flown to Tel Aviv's Lod Airport, accompanied by Israeli Phantoms. When the hijacker's attention was diverted, Israeli antiterrorist forces boarded the plane and overpowered him. The plane and its passengers, including the Libyan ambassador to Iraq, were allowed to fly on to Beirut. Al-Toumi claimed that he wished to ''show Israelis not all Arabs are enemies of Israel.'' Golda Meir said that the hijacker ''will be our guest for a while.'' He was committed to a mental institution on December 11, 1973. One person was injured during the hijacking while jumping from the aircraft upon landing. 5411

August 18, 1973—Zambia—A letter bomb exploded at the Lusaka embassy of the People's Republic of China, killing Sun Yen, the wife of the chargé d'affaires ad interim, and seriously injuring Hua Chin-liang, another embassy staff member. 1616

August 18, 1973—United Kingdom—Members or sympathizers of the IRA launched a letter-bomb and firebomb campaign in England and against its foreign embassies. By September 28, more than forty bombs had exploded, and many others had been discovered and defused. At least twenty-nine people were reported injured. Many bomb hoaxes also plagued the United Kingdom, especially in the London area. The locations of ten of the bombings are unknown (the other thirty are chronicled below). 1617-1626

August 18, 1973—United Kingdom—Two IRA bombs were discovered in London's Harrods department store. Other devices were discovered later in the month in several other stores. Most of them were hidden in cigarette packages. Tourists were stopped and searched in London's central shopping district. 1627-1628

August 20, 1973—West Germany—The U.S. Embassy in Frankfurt received two phone calls warning that bombs would explode. A search was negative. 1629-1630

August 20, 1973—Yugoslavia—The Yugoslav press carried stories about an aborted plan by three Slavs to hijack an American Trans-International Airways charter DC10 flying from Cleveland to Ljubljana and divert it to South Africa or Rhodesia, where they would demand $1 million for the safe release of 340 Slovenian and northwest Croatian emigrants and ten crew members on board the plane. The plan went awry at Brnik airport two hours before the plane was due to land at 11 A.M. when a local citizen noticed the machine-gun-carrying trio acting suspiciously and warned local officials. They were identified as Dusan Cirin, twenty-four, a cadet at the Secondary Vocational School at the Secretariat for Internal Affairs of Slovenia in Ljubljana; Milan Gasparini, nineteen, a machinist at the ROG bicycle factory; and Goran Mise, twenty-one. A fourth hijacker was supposed to join, but the group was unable to locate him. On the night before their attempt, the group broke into an arms depot and stole four machine guns, a revolver, and ammunition. After being spotted, two of the conspirators escaped into the woods but were captured two hours later. 5412

August 20, 1973—Argentina—Six members of the ERP took over the La Plata airfield, hoisting a flag and painting slogans. Two of them forced a pilot to fly over the town, showering the city with ERP propaganda leaflets. 5413

August 21, 1973—United Kindgom—An IRA letter bomb was intercepted at the prime minister's official residence at 10 Downing Street. It was opened by a mechanical letter opener and "dealt with under normal security arrangements." 1631

August 22, 1973—United Kingdom—A parcel bomb hidden in a booby-trapped book sent to Conservative party headquarters was defused. 1632

August 22, 1973—United Kingdom—A mail bomb sent to the Ministry of Defense was defused. 1633

August 23, 1973—United Kingdom—A bomb was found and defused at the Baker Street subway station minutes before it was set to explode during the evening rush hour. 1634

August 24, 1973—United Kingdom—A chief administrative officer and his secretary were wounded when a letter bomb exploded in an office of the London Stock Exchange. 1635

August 24, 1973—United Kingdom—A secretary was injured when a letter bomb exploded in the House of Commons. 1636

August 25, 1973—United Kingdom—A letter bomb exploded at the Bank of England, injuring two persons, one of them critically. 1637

August 25, 1973—Czechoslovakia—A man, accompanied by his wife and son, flew a Zlin cropduster to Blankense, West Germany, after seizing it. He had to be guided in for landing and severely damaged the aircraft. 5414

August 25, 1973—Yemen—A Yemen Airways DC6 flying fifteen persons from Taiz to Asmara, Ethiopia was hijacked by a Yemeni armed with a gun, Nasser Ahmed Abu Bakr, who forced the pilot to refuel at Djibouti before he surrendered in Kuwait after being guaranteed his safety. 5415

August 27, 1973—United States—A letter bomb, apparently flown in a Royal Air Force plane from the United Kingdom after the letter had been mailed in London, exploded in the hands of Nora Murray, a secretary to the military attaché in Washington, D.C. Her hand was severed in the blast, which also knocked out windows and damaged furniture in the sixth-floor office. An embassy official denied that the bomb had traveled in the diplomatic pouch. Most authorities attributed the attack to the IRA, although the IRA's spokesman denied responsibility. 1638

August 27, 1973—Paraguay—Ian Martin, a U.K. citizen and manager of Liegib's Meat Company, was kidnapped in Asunción. A ransom note found in his car was signed by the Argentine ERP. However, Paraguayan authorities blamed the attack on the MoPoCo, a dissident faction of the ruling Colorado party. On September 6, Paraguayan police rescued Martin. Two of his kidnappers were killed and an undisclosed number arrested. 1639

August 27, 1973—Chile—Six sticks of dynamite were found in the entrance to the USIS Binational Center Temuco in Santiago before they could explode. 1640

August 27, 1973—Chile—Bombs exploded at the Santiago homes of two Cuban diplomats and in the car of a third. There was considerable property damage, but no injuries were reported. 1641-1643

August 28, 1973—France—A letter bomb was intercepted in the U.K. embassy in Paris. 1644

August 29, 1973—United Kingdom—Two bombs exploded in a bank doorway and outside another Solihull building near Birmingham, slightly injuring three persons. 1645-1646

August 29, 1973—Japan—The U.S. embassy annex in Tokyo, which houses the Defense Attaché Office and other embassy facilities, was slightly damaged by a Molotov cocktail. No injuries were reported. A twenty-four-hour guard was subsequently placed at the door. 1647

August 30, 1973—United Kingdom—An IRA firebomb burned a Birmingham shoe shop. 1648

September 1, 1973—United States—The Convicts Retaliatory Action Movement claimed responsibility for the bombing of an auditorium at the Washington State Penitentiary in Walla Walla.

September 1, 1973—Soviet Union—A homemade bomb exploded in the Lenin Mausoleum on Red Square in Moscow, causing no damage to the facility but killing two women waiting in line as well as the man carrying the device, whom Soviet sources described as an insane individual who had recently been released from a hospital.

September 4, 1973—Chile—A small bomb exploded against the door of the USIS Binational Center in Santiago, injuring no one but breaking forty window panes. 1649

September 5, 1973—France—Five Palestinian commandos seized as hostages the Saudi Arabian embassy in Paris, taking thirteen people, including Françoise Goussault, the French-born mother of the earl of Shaftesbury, who was serving as the secretary to the Saudi ambassador, and three other women. The group demanded the release of Abu Daoud (see incident 1459) and safe passage out of the country. At one point, the leader of the group, describing himself as a doctor, radioed for an ambulance, claiming that he had shot one of the hostages in the leg. He was bluffing. The Kuwaiti ambassador aided in the negotiations, as did a number of other Arab diplomats. At the end of twenty-eight hours of negotiations, the French agreed to grant the group safe passage out of the country if they would release the four women. On September 6, Syrian President Hafez al-Assad sent a Syrian Arab Airlines Caravelle at the disposal of the terrorists, who claimed to be members of Al Icab Punishment Organization, which had been unknown before this incident. The Iraqi ambassador offered to take the place of the women but they were released at Le Bourget Airport along with all but four Saudi diplomats, who were bound and forced into the plane. It appeared that the group had dropped their demands for the release of Daoud, but on landing in Kuwait after a refueling stop in Cairo, the group transferred to a Kuwait Airways B707, and flew over Riyadh, Saudi Arabia, threatening to throw the hostages out of the plane unless pressure was put on the Jordanians to release Daoud. The governments refused, and the plane returned. The terrorists, who had threatened to blow up the embassy with their hand grenades, asked for yet another plane to fly them to Damascus but were refused. During the negotiations, Ali Yassin, the PLO representative in Kuwait, was taken hostage by the group while he was serving as a mediator. On September 8, the Kuwaitis offered to give the terrorists safe passage to Iraq in a car if they would release all of their hostages. The terrorists demanded that they be allowed to bring along Yassin or a Kuwaiti security official as a guarantee of their safe passage, but this demand was refused. Yassin was released two hours later, and the terrorists gave up later that day. According to press reports, the five were handed over to the PLO by Kuwait on October 11, apparently to continue the fight against Israel. All of the principal Palestinian organizations denounced the attack, with Yasir Arafat saying that he would seek out those responsible and punish them. It appears that the operation was a freelance attack carried out by Iraqi-based Fatah dissident Sabri al-Banna. It is also possible that the group wished to punish Daoud for giving the Jordanians useful information about Black September during his incarceration. On September 18, King Hussein announced a general amnesty for Arab guerrillas and two days later supervised the release of 754 fedayeen, including Daoud. The Yom Kippur war took place later that month. 1650

September 5, 1973—Thailand—A bomb exploded in the galley of an Air Vietnam B727 flying from Bangkok to Saigon, injuring three persons. The plane and its forty-eight passengers returned safely to Bangkok. 1651

September 5, 1973—Italy—Italian military police raided an apartment in Ostia, four miles from Fiumicino Airport in Rome, and arrested an Arab who

408   September 7, 1973

was hiding two SAM-7 Strela missiles in his wardrobe. The thirty-pound, four-and-a-half-foot missiles are able to hit low-flying aircraft up to three miles away and had been supplied by the Soviet Union to Egypt. The terrorist claimed that he and his colleagues had planned to attack an El Al plane. The other four were arrested later in the day. The terrorists may have acquired the missiles from Libya, which had planned to unite with Egypt and had pressed for coordinated military training. Two of the group were released on bail and flew to Libya. The five (with the other two in absentia) were tried and sentenced by an Italian court to five years and two months on February 27, 1974, as well as fined $2,500 each. They were freed on bail on March 1 pending an appeal. It is assumed that they left Italy. 1652

September 7, 1973—West Germany—A West German news agency received a letter in which Black September claimed responsibility for the bomb explosion that destroyed the Israeli exhibit at the West Berlin International Radio and Television Fair. Damage was extensive, but no injuries were reported. 1653

September 8, 1973—United Kingdom—Two IRA bombs exploded in the King's Cross and Euston railway stations, seriously injuring two men and a woman and causing lesser injuries to ten others. There was a three-minute warning in one of the bombings and no warning in the other. 1654-1655

September 8, 1973—United Kingdom—Four persons were injured by an IRA firebomb at London's Victoria rail station. 1656

September 8, 1973—United Kingdom—Three IRA firebombs exploded in Manchester store doorways. 1657-1659

September 10, 1973—Italy—A small bomb exploded in the mailbox at the Bologna home of a U.S. citizen, causing no injuries. Italian police ruled out the possibility of a letter bomb. 1660

September 11, 1973—Zambia—A parcel bomb exploded and killed a U.K. employee of the Zambian Ministry of Information and his wife and injured their son. The explosion occurred outside the main post office after the victim had picked up the parcel and placed it in his car. Extensive damage was also done to nearby vehicles. Two anonymous telephone calls were received at the *Times* of Zambia following the explosion. The first caller said, "Ian Smith did it," and the second warned, "Tomorrow we will bomb the airport and the British High Commission." Both callers reportedly sounded like expatriate men. 1661-1662

September 11, 1973—Australia—An Arab member of Al Fatah was arrested by Australian authorities on suspicion of planning terrorist activities. He was released after interrogation. 1663

September 12, 1973—United Kingdom—A bomb exploded in a shopping bag in a crowded London shopping area, injuring eight. Another bomb exploded in London's Chelsea district. 1664-1665

September 14, 1973—Switzerland—Eight hundred demonstrators gathered outside the United States consulate general in Zurich to protest the Chilean coup. Molotov cocktails were thrown, but no damage was reported. In Zagreb, fifty demonstrators protested the Chilean coup in front of the USIS library. In Amsterdam, red paint was splashed on the sidewalk in front of the U.S. consulate general, apparently to protest the Chilean coup. 1666

September 17, 1973—Gibraltar—A letter bomb sent to a senior British official was defused. 1667

September 17, 1973—Zaire—A letter bomb sent to the U.K. embassy in Kinshasa exploded, injuring a U.K. security officer. 1668

September 17, 1973—Portugal—A letter bomb sent to the British ambassador in Lisbon was defused in the embassy. 1669

September 17, 1973—West Germany—Two explosive charges were detonated in Munchen Gladbach, adjoining the British Army of the Rhine premises, causing no damage. It was presumed to be part of the IRA worldwide letter-bomb campaign. 1670

September 17, 1973—United Kingdom—An army officer who was a bomb disposal expert was critically wounded in Birmingham while attempting to defuse a bomb. He died of his wounds on September 23. 1671

September 18, 1973—Argentina—Two bombs exploded in the garden of the home of the U.S. ambassador in Buenos Aires, causing extensive damage to windows but no injuries. The bombs appeared to have been launched from motor-type weapons. 1672

September 18, 1973—Belgium—Two letter bombs, one addressed to Sir Christopher Soames, the U.K. representative to the European Economic Community, and the other to a member of the U.K. permanent EEC delegation, were defused by Brussels police. 1673-1674

September 19, 1973—Argentina—Members of the Montoneros and FAR claimed to have attacked the U.S. embassy in Buenos Aires. 1675

September 21, 1973—United States—A bomb went off in a Tusco Navion plane on the ground at Crestwood, Illinois. The device was placed in the engine manifold and ignited by an exterior fuse.

September 21, 1973—Ghana—The U.S. embassy in Accra received a telephoned bomb threat. A search was negative. 1676

September 21, 1973—Argentina—David George Heywood, an accountant with Nobleza Tobacco, a subsidiary of the British-American Tobacco Company, was kidnapped in Buenos Aires by six gunmen. His family paid a $300,000 ransom. On October 20, police announced they had rescued Heywood, recovered $280,000 of the ransom, and arrested four of the kidnappers. 1677

September 23, 1973—Greece—The U.S. pavilion at the Thessaloniki Fair was the target of a bomb scare. A search was negative. 1678

September 23, 1973—Norway—The U.S. embassy in Oslo received a telephone call indicating that a bomb was in the building. A search was negative. 1679

September 24, 1973—Lebanon—Unknown individuals attempted to blow up the Tapline in the An-Nabitiyah district. The explosion made a hole in the ground without damage to the pipeline. Security in the company's installations was increased. 1680

September 28, 1973—United States—A time bomb planted by the Weather Underground demolished four rooms in the Latin American section of ITT headquarters in New York. No one was injured, although damage was estimated at $80,000. The attack was reported to be a protest of ITT activities in Chile.

September 28, 1973—Italy—A blast occurred outside the office of ITT Standard S.A. in Rome. Police reported that unknown individuals poured gasoline on the main doors of the office and ignited it, but the fire was quickly extinguished and caused only slight damage. 1681

September 28, 1973—Austria—Two armed Palestinians claiming to be members of the Eagles of the Palestinian Revolution (but later determined to be using that as a cover name to avoid embarrassment to their Syrian sponsors, who backed their organization, Saiqa) took five hostages on board diesel passenger train number 2590, which left Bratislava, Czechoslovakia, and entered Marchegg, Austria, at 10:43 A.M. A customs official, Franz Bobits, boarded the train and was greeted by one of the Palestinians who pointed a Bulgarian submachine gun at him, as well as another terrorist holding an FN automatic pistol and a grenade. During the confusion of transferring to a Volkswagen Kombi, two of the hostages escaped. The terrorists unsuccessfully demanded their return. They later took off for Vienna's Schwechat Airport, where they demanded that Austria close down the Schonau Castle facility for Soviet Jewish émigrés and not allow further émigré transit through Austria. The hostages were identified as newly arrived Soviet Jews on their way to Israel. The terrorists allowed a number of deadlines to pass while the fifteen-hour negotiations went on with diplomats from Egypt, Iraq, Lebanon, and Libya serving as mediators. Two psychologists, Dr. Willibald Sluga and Professor Frederick Hacker of the University of Southern California, also talked to the terrorists and determined that they had taken drugs that could distort their behavior as the effects wore off. At one point, Karl Soherr, a drunken middle-aged doctor armed with a Walther automatic, managed to get through the police cordon by claiming to be an army marksman. He was conversing with the terrorists in English and having coffee with them when Dr. Schuller led him away and disarmed him.

The Austrian turned down the terrorists' demands that the hostages accompany them out of the country but agreed to grant them safe passage early the next day. Two Austrian pilots and two substitute hostages were on board an Austrian plane given to the terrorists. After refueling stops in Yugoslavia and Italy, the plane was denied landing by Tunisia and Algeria. After the terrorists threatened to blow up the plane, it was allowed to land in Libya.

In December 1973, Libya announced that the two had been released to fight in the war against Israel. Some reports claimed that the two terrorists had been trained in a PFLP camp in Lebanon. It was also claimed that one of them participated in the December 1975 OPEC raid (see incident 2527). The two were identified as Mahmoud Youssef Sheik Khaldi and Mustafa Soudeidan. Only one of them did the negotiating during the incident, which some reports claim had been planned by Mohammed Boudia before he died, with the notorious Venezuelan-born PFLP operator, Ilich Ramirez Sanchez, alias Carlos, taking on that task after his death. Although Austrian Prime Minister Bruno Kreisky was internationally criticized for closing the camp, he held to his decision, while continuing to allow Soviet Jews to pass through other Austrian facilities and customs checkpoints.

A note delivered by the terrorists read: "By the name of the Palestinian Martyrs who had been martyred in struggling to return back, and by the name of the Palestinian Revolution. We, the Eagles of the Palestinian Revolution, declare our responsibility about this operation. We have done this mission, because of feeling that the immigration of the Soviet Union Jews form a great danger on our cause. We haven't done this mission because we are murderers by nature, but because of the crimes of Zionists who bombed our camps, killing our infants and children, women and olds, and when they murder our leaders by meagre methods and because they had declared that they will fight and destroy our people any where will be found. We have done it because we have rights, have the will of determination and decision to fight the Zionists wherever can be found, as ever as they are recruits to the enemy. It is not our first strike, it will not be the last, and nothing we will accept, but liberating our land by force. And to those who are acting to let us think and imagine the peaceful projects as a way to give us our rights, let them know that we refuse any project except liberating our whole land from the Zionists. The Eagles of the Palestinian Revolution.'' 1682

September 28, 1973—Dominican Republic—Claiming to be a left-wing revolutionary, Manfredo Casado, who took political asylum in the Mexican embassy in Santo Domingo in 1972, was given safe conduct to fly to France after he held the twelve-year-old son of Francisco Garcia, the Mexican ambassador, and threatened to kill himself and the boy by using a gasoline cache and a grenade to blow up the room they were in. Casado released the boy unharmed at Santo Domingo's airport and was flown to France. 1683

September 28, 1973—United Kingdom—A bomb exploded in a fire exit in the West London air terminal, injuring six persons. Fear of a second bomb delayed some flights.

October 1973—United States—The first of fourteen ''Zebra'' murders took place in San Francisco, California. The murders, always of whites, were linked to a fanatic religious cult calling themselves the Death Angels, which appeared to be a splinter group of the Nation of Islam, who believed that ''white devils'' should be killed. Four black men were convicted of the murders in 1976.

October 1, 1973—Argentina—Pan Am and Braniff received notes from an ERP splinter group demanding the payment of $1 million. The companies did not report what the group threatened to do. 1684-1685

October 1, 1973—Brazil—A Brazilian man walked into the LAN-Chilean Airlines office in Rio de Janeiro and handed the clerk a package, saying, ''I have a message for the government of Chile.'' Upon giving the clerk the parcel, the man ran out of the office. The clerk discovered a note saying that the bomb would explode and went for help. While police were opening the parcel, it exploded, injuring fifteen people and destroying most of the office. 1686

October 2, 1973—Yugoslavia—It was believed that an intruder in the U.S. consular section of the embassy in Zagreb was attempting to plant a lethal device. 1687

October 2, 1973—West Germany—A KLM DC9 flying twenty-six passengers from Düsseldorf to Amsterdam was hijacked by Franz-Josef Stremmer, who used a gun to hold a stewardess hostage. Stremmer was disarmed by the crew while talking to the pilot and was arrested when the plane landed in Amsterdam. 5416

October 4, 1973—Colombia—Fifty ELN guerrillas attacked a facility of Frontino Goldmines and kidnapped two U.S. citizens, Willis Leon Dotsun and Rene Francis Kast, who were employed there. In a letter received the next day by International Mining Company, the gold mine's owner, the group demanded a ransom of 4 million pesos ($168,990). The company attempted to pay the ransom, but Colombian authorities seized the money when its representative tried to pay off the kidnappers. The Colombian army rescued the two men on March 7, 1974, after surrounding the terrorist hideout. 1688

October 5, 1973—Italy—Two gasoline bombs placed at the front door of the building housing the U.S. consulate general in Genoa exploded in the early morning, injuring no one and causing no reported damage. Spanish-language leaflets found at the scene were signed by the Proletarian Action Group. Local police believed the attack was related to Chilean politics. 1689

October 5, 1973—Mozambique—FRELIMO guerrillas attacked a village in the Tete district, killing twenty-four civilians, including some women and children, and kidnapping a couple. A woman reported that her husband had been executed by FRELIMO while trying to escape from their captors' hideout in Tanzania. 1690

October 7, 1973—Cyprus—In what appeared to be an attempt to assassinate Archbishop Makarios, four bombs exploded on a rural road near Famagusta minutes before he was scheduled to drive by. Police arrested a Greek Cypriot, claiming that he was working for a pro-Enosis group.

October 8, 1973—Argentina—The anniversary of Ché Guevara's death was commemorated in Buenos Aires with an ineffectual rocket attack on the Sheraton Hotel. Twelve rockets were fired, but only two hit the building, causing little damage and no injuries. 1691

October 8, 1973—Argentina—The Bank of America in Buenos Aires was firebombed by a group of young demonstrators who threw Molotov cocktails that did considerable damage. 1692

October 9, 1973—Argentina—ERP bombs exploded in front of the Córdoba offices of two U.S. firms, Coca-Cola and Firestone Tire and Rubber, as well as a German company, Mercedes Benz, causing some damage but no injuries. 1693-1695

October 10, 1973—Mexico—A Mexicana Airlines B727 scheduled to fly seventy-two persons from Mexico City to Monterrey was taken over on the ground by Roberto Garcia Perez, who was armed with a gun and threatened to kill the passengers. He was overpowered by a security officer dressed as a crewman who boarded the aircraft before takeoff. 5417

October 10, 1973—Mexico—Members of the Twenty-third of September Communist League claimed credit for the kidnapping of the U.K. honorary consul, Anthony Duncan Williams, in Guadalajara. The group demanded the release of fifty-one political prisoners and $200,000 ransom. The government refused to release any prisoners. It is not known whether a ransom was paid. Williams was released unharmed on October 14, 1973. On January 10, 1974, Jalisco State authorities announced the arrest of José de Jesus Ramirez Meza, who, they claimed, had participated in the kidnapping. Pedro Orozco Guzman, who was killed in a police shootout on December 24, 1973, confessed before dying that he also had participated in the kidnapping of Williams, as well as the abduction of U.S. Consul Leonhardy (see incident 1550) and the kidnap-murder of Mexican industrialist Fernando Aranguren. 1696

October 11, 1973—Philippines—A PAL BAC111 flying from Davao to Manila and Bacolod with fifty-four passengers was hijacked by three young Filipino males armed with a hand grenade and homemade .22 caliber pistols. The president of the airlines, Benigno Toda, offered to serve as a substitute hostage for the release of the passengers. The hijackers, Roger Riga, Armando Naval, and Basilio Montojo, agreed and landed in Hong Kong. President Marcos granted them amnesty in the Philippines. The hijackers agreed, and surrendered their weapons. 5418

October 11, 1973—A woman stabbed the pilot of a private aircraft several times. The pilot managed to land the plane safely, and the woman was detained.

October 16, 1973—Cuba—A lone anti-Castro Cuban kidnapped the Belgian ambassador, Jean Somerhausen, and took him to the French embassy, where he demanded to leave Cuba. French Ambassador Pierre Anthonioz offered himself as a voluntary hostage. The Cuban government rejected the gunman's demands and killed him in a shootout after security guards had secretly entered the embassy. 1697

October 18, 1973—France—An Air France B727 flying from Paris to Nice with one hundred passengers was hijacked by Danielle Françoise Cravenne, née Batisse, who used a rifle to force the pilot to land at Marseille, where all passengers and all but two of the crew were released. She attempted to force the pilot to fly to Cairo, but police disguised as stewards boarded the plane and shot, wounded, and captured her. She died on the way to the hospital. 5419

October 18, 1973—West Germany—West Berlin police arrested four Arab members of Black September in their apartment in the U.S. sector of Berlin and confiscated over twenty pounds of plastic explosives with which they had planned to attack El Al offices and other targets. Two of them were acquitted. One was sentenced to four years' imprisonment, and the other, a seventeen-year-old, to three years' confinement as a juvenile offender. The two in detention were released and deported to Cairo on June 10, 1974. 1698

October 18, 1973—Lebanon—Five members of the Lebanese Socialist Revolutionary Organization seized thirty-nine hostages in the Beirut Bank of America. During a twenty-five-hour negotiation session, they demanded that the bank pay them $10 million to help finance the Arab war effort against Israel, that Lebanon release all fedayeen guerrillas, and that Algeria or Southern Yemen grant them safe haven. All of their demands were refused, and an American citizen, John Crawford Maxwell, was killed by the terrorists. Police and army commandos stormed the bank amid a hail of bullets and grenades. In the battle, two guerrillas and one policeman were killed, and six policemen, five bank employees, five passersby, and one terrorist were wounded. A fourth terrorist surrendered unharmed, and a fifth was captured later. On March 9, 1974, a Lebanese military tribunal in Beirut sentenced the surviving terrorists to life imprisonment. Adel Najin Abu-Asi was sentenced to death for murdering Maxwell. 1699

October 19, 1973—Malaysia—Nine passersby were injured when a bomb exploded at the USIS Lincoln Cultural Center in Kuala Lumpur. No injuries to U.S. or local employees were reported. The center reported some damage. Three days previously, fifteen hundred students had thrown stones at the windows of the center during a demonstration, and a thousand more had protested the Middle Eastern war at the U.S. embassy. 1700

October 20, 1973—Argentina—An Aerolineas Argentinas B737 flying from Buenos Aires to Salta with forty-three passengers and six crew was hijacked by four armed terrorists (two men and two women) who claimed to be Tupamaros but may have been ERP members. The group forced the plane to fly to Tucumán and then to Yacuiba, Bolivia, where they released all but five hostages and demanded a smaller plane so that they could take off from the border town and fly to Cuba. The Bolivian government refused their demands, and after two days of negotiations, the group surrendered after Bolivia promised them safe passage to Cuba. The hijackers were identified as Mario Pagola Nicolini, Luis Arturo Sienrra Mata, Mirtha Susana Pedroso Silva, and Lidia Elena Biere Diaz. 1701

October 21, 1973—Soviet Union—Two Palestinians claiming to be members of Black September threatened Soviet physicist Andrei Sakharov, a dissident, and his wife in their Moscow apartment and warned him against making any further statements in support of Israel. 1702

October 22, 1973—Argentina—The ERP kidnapped Kurt Schmidt, the Swissair manager for Latin America, as he was being driven by his chauffeur in a Buenos Aires suburb. The group demanded a ransom of $10 million. He was released on November 29 after the payment of an undisclosed sum and immediately left the country. Swissair refused to say if it had paid a ransom. 1703

October 23, 1973—Argentina—David B. Wilkie, Jr., a U.S. citizen and president of Amoco Argentina, a subsidiary of Standard Oil of Indiana, was kidnapped in suburban Buenos Aires by individuals believed by Amoco to be common criminals. A ransom of between $1 million and $3.5 million was demanded. Wilkie was released unharmed on November 11 and immediately returned to the United States after the payment of what the company claimed was ''well below'' the amount demanded. 1704

October 26, 1973—United States—A parcel containing a smoke bomb and a letter addressed to the Turkish consulate by the Yanikian Commandos was received by the Turkish Information Office in New York. The bomb did not detonate. 1705

October 31, 1973—Ireland—Two men forced the pilot of an Irish Helicopters Alouette, which had been hired for filming at Stradbally, to fly from Dublin to a prison where three men were picked up. The helicopter then flew to Baldoyle, where the three men were picked up by a car. 5420

October 31, 1973—Venezuela—An Avensa DC9 flying from Maracaibo to Caracas was hijacked out of Barquisimeto by José Gabriel Lorenzo who threatened a stewardess with a pistol and demanded to be flown to Cuba. When the pilot told the hijacker he was about to land at Caracas and had very little fuel, the hijacker shot and seriously wounded himself (some reports claim that he died from his wounds). 5421

November 2, 1973—Soviet Union—An Aeroflot YAK40 flying from Bryansk to Moscow with twenty-seven persons on board was hijacked by four males armed with a shotgun who demanded $1 million. The plane landed at Moscow's Vnokovo Airport, where the hijackers demanded a flight to Stockholm, Sweden. After five hours of negotiations, police stormed the aircraft. They killed two of the hijackers, wounded a passenger, and captured the other two hijackers. 5422

November 5, 1973—United States—The Three Mile Island licensed nuclear facility of the Metropolitan Edison Company near Harrisburg, Pennsylvania, received a bomb threat.

November 6, 1973—United States—The Symbionese Liberation Army claimed credit for the ambush and murder of Marcus Foster, a black superintendent of Oakland, California schools, who was shot with cyanide bullets. A deputy was wounded in the attack.

November 7, 1973—Argentina—The ERP kidnapped Colonel Florencio Crespo of the Argentine infantry and accused him of collaborating with the United States by receiving instruction in U.S. military schools in how "to repress the Argentine people and its revolutionary vanguards."

November 16, 1973—United States—The Turkey Point licensed nuclear facility of the Florida Power and Light Company received a bomb threat.

November 17, 1973—Argentina—Enrique (Henry) Nyborg Andersen, the Danish regional manager of the Bank of London and South America, an Argentine affiliate of Lloyds International Exchange Bank of London, was kidnapped in Buenos Aires by the ERP, which demanded a ransom of $1.2 million. Andersen was released on February 19, 1974, after payment of $1,145,000. 1706

November 17, 1973—West Germany—Two subsidiaries of ITT, one in Nuremburg and one in West Berlin, were damaged by bomb blasts. No injuries were reported, although parked cars in the area were also damaged. 1707-1708

November 20, 1973—Venezuela—Kurt Georg Nagel, thirty-seven, honorary West German consul in Maracaibo and a university professor, was kidnapped during the night by members of the Bandera Roja. It was reported that the kidnappers had drafted a ransom note demanding 100,000 Bolivars ($22,000), but before they were able to deliver it, four local farmers found their hideout in Concepción, twenty-five miles south of Maracaibo. The kidnappers had threatened the farm's owner and several employees. National Guardsmen and the kidnappers engaged in a gun battle in which Nagel was rescued two days later. Two of the kidnappers were wounded and two others were captured. Three others fled during the exchange of gunfire. One farmer was reported wounded. 1709

November 22, 1973—Canada—A lone male entered an aircraft while it was being serviced to fly from Montreal to Toronto. When questioned, he demanded to be flown to London in the Air Canada DC8. While the attendant went for help, the man tried to start the engines. He was later arrested and sent for a mental examination. 5423

November 22, 1973—West Germany—According to United Press International in Bonn, "West German government officials refused to comment today on reports that Arab partisans are blackmailing the government with threats of germ warfare. Nearly all of West Germany's national-circulation newspapers carried versions of a report that unidentified blackmailers had demanded about $8,200,000 from the government and threatened, failing payment, to mail bacteria-laden letters to officials and dump potent germs into various city water systems." 1710

November 22, 1973—Argentina—John Albert Swint, fifty-six, a U.S. citizen and general manager of Transax, a transmission and axle plant owned by the Ford Motor Company, was assassinated by fifteen FAP youths who trapped his chauffeur-driven car and the follow car of guards, firing automatic weapons and shotguns. Swint was on his way to work in Córdoba when two trucks blocked him in front and two small cars boxed his cars in the rear. Two of his bodyguards were killed, and a third was critically injured. Police claimed that a tall, blond gunman finished the attack with a machine gun burst before the group fled. Swint had been receiving threats in the previous months and had increased the number of bodyguards he employed. Ford moved twenty-five U.S. executives and their families out of Argentina during the next few days. 1711

November 23, 1973—Argentina—Jacob Marinott, an Austrian industrialist, was reported kidnapped by three armed guerrillas in Buenos Aires. 1712

November 25, 1973—Lebanon—A KLM B747 flying from Beirut to New Delhi and Tokyo with 247 passengers and 17 crew members was hijacked by three members of the Arab Nationalist Youth for the Liberation of Palestine, who used pistols to force the pilot to fly to Damascus, Syria, where it was denied refueling privileges. It flew on to Nicosia, Cyprus, where the group demanded the release of seven of their colleagues who were jailed in April (see incidents 1520 and 1521). Their demands were rejected, but the seven were quietly amnestied by President Makarios and flown to Cairo on December 6. The plane next flew to Tripoli, Libya, where they were rebuffed, and then landed at Valletta, Malta, where the gunmen freed all of the 247 passengers, most of them Japanese, and 8 stewardesses. They flew on to Dubai the next day, November 28, with 10 crew and a substitute hostage, KLM vice-president A. W. Withholt. His airline had agreed to halt transporting arms to Israel, and his government had given a solemn pledge on November 26 not to "allow the opening of offices or camps for Soviet Jews going to Israel" and banning "transportation of weapons or volunteers for Israel." The hijackers next flew on to Aden, South Yemen, but were denied landing permission. They returned to Dubai, where they surrendered after promises of safe passage to an undisclosed country. On December 8, 1973, the hijackers were taken to Abu Dhabi, where they presumably were turned over to the PLO. The trio, identified as Fawzi Darwish, Husayn Ahmad Al-Sanuri, and Isnu Zhbgeen, had threatened to blow up the plane at one point. Other reports listed four hijackers. 1713.

November 26, 1973—Mexico—Homemade bombs caused considerable damage to the Bank of London branch in Guadalajara, as well as to the Commercial Bank and to a monument. No personal injuries were reported. A fourth bomb was found by firemen before it exploded. 1714

November 27, 1973—United States—The Bay Area Americans for Justice claimed credit for a bombing in San Francisco.

November 28, 1973—Argentina—After the ERP threatened Ford executives with death if they remained in the country, twenty-two executives and their families departed. 1715

December 1973—France—Four hundred forty thousand gallons of oil were lost in a fire set at a storage depot in Besançon. In Belfort, valves at an oil installation were deliberately opened. 1716-1717

December 1973—United States—The Cuban Secret Government bombed a New York City business office. 1718

December 1973—United States—The FLNC, using the Cuban Anti-Communist League as a cover name, bombed a Bahamian cargo ship in Miami. 1719

December 1, 1973—Switzerland—A Swissair DC8 flying from Zurich to Geneva with 160 persons on board was hijacked by Daniel Buholzer, who was armed with a gun and demanded $50,000 for starvation-threatened Africa and a ticket to New York and safe conduct. When the plane landed in Geneva, he asked to speak to reporters. Police boarded the plane posing as news people and quickly overpowered him. He had previously released all but four crew members. 5424

December 3, 1973—United States—A bomb exploded in the hallway leading to the offices of the U.S.-Latin America Justice Committee, a group "dedicated to seek justice for political prisoners in Latin America," according to the group's spokesman. Three persons were injured, and some damage was reported. The building in New York City also houses offices of the Angela Davis Defense Fund, the Hashommer Hatzair Zionist youth organization, and the American Friends of Israel. 1720

December 3, 1973—Greece—A bomb exploded outside the Piraeus building housing a branch of the Bank of America, causing no injuries but damaging the bank building and adjacent area. The Greek People claimed credit for this explosion, as well as for a bomb that exploded in the basement of a branch of the Commercial Bank of Greece in Athens, which caused some damage but no injuries. 1721

December 3, 1973—Mexico—A time bomb exploded in the early morning in front of the Cuban embassy's chancery in Mexico City, causing some damage but no injuries. 1722

December 4, 1973—Israel—An Arab terrorist member of the Palestinian Revolutionary Forces tossed a hand grenade into a shopping area in the Old City of Jerusalem, injuring twenty. 1723

December 5, 1973—Israel—Palestinian terrorists bombed a bus in the Natanya area. 1724

December 6, 1973—Argentina—Victor E. Samuelson, thirty-seven, manager of the Esso Argentina oil refinery at Campana, was kidnapped at gunpoint by ERP members while he was having lunch at the company club restaurant. Slogans painted on the wall attributed the attack to the ERP. The group demanded a ransom of $10 million to be paid in the form of food, clothing, and construction materials to poor neighborhoods across Argentina "as a partial reimbursement to the Argentine people for the copious riches extracted from our country by Esso in long years of imperialist exploitation." The group later demanded an additional $4.2 million in supplies for victims of floods for "the superprofits that Esso has obtained in the country, thanks to the exploitation of its workers." The group demanded that an ERP communiqué be printed by twelve Buenos Aires newspapers and in thirty others throughout Argentina. However, all but three papers in the capital refused, fearing government reprisal. Neither the group's name nor initials appeared in the ads because of a government decree, which also outlawed the organization. Unspecified problems made the payment of the goods unfeasible, and the company made a direct cash payment to the group of $14.2 million on March 11, 1974, setting a record for political ransom payments as of that date. According to the *Washington Post*, "Industry sources said the ransom money was brought into Argentina packed in wooden boxes and duly declared in customs. It was not known when the payoff was made. . . . One military expert said the ransom money was enough to equip and maintain nearly 1500 guerrilla fighters for more than a year." Samuelson was allowed to send a letter to his wife and three children on March 16, indicating that the ransom had arrived. He was released on April 29, 1974, and left for the United States. On June 12, 1974, the ERP announced that it had donated $5 million of the ransom money to the Revolutionary Coordinating Junta, a group whose existence had been announced in Buenos Aires on February 14 by Enrique Gorriaran and Domingo Mena. The group was composed of the ERP of Argentina, the Revolutionary Movement of the left of Chile, the National Liberation Army of Bolivia, and the Tupamaros of Uruguay. 1725

December 7, 1973—France—The Chilean embassy in Paris was occupied by thirty members of the French Communist Youth Movement. Members of the embassy staff were not mistreated, and embassy property and records were not damaged. Riot police entered the building in force, and the occupiers surrendered peacefully.

December 8, 1973—Chile—A fire broke out in the commercial section of the former Soviet embassy in Santiago, causing little damage. Almost simultaneously an incendiary bomb was thrown from a speeding car at the front door of the former residence of the Soviet ambassador. A security policeman suggested that the attacks were in retaliation for the occupation of the Chilean embassy in Paris the previous day. 1726-1727

December 10,1973—Jordan—A clandestine radio broadcast by Black September threatened the life of U.S. Secretary of State Henry A. Kissinger during his trip to that area. 1728

December 11, 1973—United States—Two bricks were thrown through the first-floor windows of a building housing the French Press and Information Office, the office of the Counselor for Cultural Affairs of the French Embassy, and the French National Center for Scientific Research in New York City. An anonymous caller to United Press International claimed credit for the JDL to protest "cowardly French submission to Arab oil blackmail." 1729

December 14, 1973—France—An eyewitness saw a man throw a plastic explosive bomb into the Algerian consulate in Marseilles, killing four Algerians and wounding twenty others, ten of them seriously. The Charles Martel group claimed responsibility for the attack, which came during a period of racial tension in the city, following an incident in August in which an Algerian stabbed a French bus driver to death. 1730

December 17, 1973—Italy—After a customs official discovered a gun in the luggage of an Arab who had reached Rome's Leonardo da Vinci (Fiumicino) Airport from Tripoli, Libya, and Madrid, Spain, four other Arabs, claiming to be members of the Arab Nationalist Youth Organization for the Liberation of Palestine, took out their machine guns and began firing into the crowded transit lounge. Police returned their fire. Taking six hostages, they moved on to a Pan Am B707 waiting to take off for Beirut and Tehran and threw in two phosphorus grenades. The aircraft immediately caught fire, killing many of the passengers, including four Moroccan officials en route to Tehran for a state visit and fourteen American employees of the Arabian-American Oil Company who were among the fifty-nine people on board the plane. Having killed twenty-nine people and injured eighteen up to this point, the terrorists dragged their hostages to a Lufthansa B737 being prepared for a flight to Munich. During the gun battle in which they herded five of their Italian hostages on board the plane, an Italian customs policeman was killed, and a second man shot outside the plane died on the way to the hospital. They forced Captain Joe Kroese to fly to Beirut but Lebanese authorities would not allow the plane to land, so they flew instead to Athens, where they landed and demanded the release of Arida and Kaddourah, who were being held for an August attack on that airport (see incident 1608). The duo, awaiting trial, refused to join the hijackers, claiming that they belonged to a different organization. During these negotiations, the hijackers called Domenico Ippolito, a ground staff worker, to accompany them. According to Helen Hanel, an Austrian ground staff employee of Lufthansa who had taken cover in the plane, "They called Mr. Ippolito up from the rear of the plane, where he was sitting alone. He walked up calmly. Nobody had any idea of what was about to happen. They asked him politely to go into the galley. He walked in and they closed the curtain. Then we heard 2 shots and it was finished. They threw his body out of the plane." While the bargaining continued, the terrorists kept firing their guns and told the pilot that they had killed copilot Rolf Kiess and three others, but they were bluffing. Being unable to secure the release of the two Athens terrorists, the hijackers flew on to Damascus, where they were allowed to refuel and take on food. The plane then landed in Kuwait on December 18, where the terrorists surrendered to Kuwaiti authorities and released their twelve hostages after receiving a safe-conduct guarantee. On March 2, 1974, the terrorists were flown to Cairo where they were to be tried by the PLO, which had denounced the attack, but Egyptian authorities did not release them. On the demand of the four hijackers who seized a BOAC VC10 on November 22, 1974, the five Rome terrorists were flown to Tunis, and on December 7, 1974, went to Libya with the hijackers and two other terrorists released by the

Netherlands. Libya reportedly imprisoned all eleven, but later they appeared to be at liberty in Libya. It was suggested that the group was a breakaway faction of the PFLP or Black September and had scheduled their attack to wreck the Geneva peace conference on the Middle East. Under questioning in Kuwait, they claimed that they were originally charged with assassinating Henry Kissinger. They were to fire the Kalashnikovs and throw the phosphorus bombs at his plane when it landed in Beirut. His flight was diverted to the Rayak military airfield, forty-five miles east of Beirut, when the Lebanese found out about the plot. The terrorists claimed that they were then directed by their Libyan patrons to attack Rome airport and sabotage the Geneva conference by seizing hostages. They said they were sent by a Libyan diplomat and that their weapons traveled in the Libyan diplomatic pouch. They also said that the Libyans offered to insure them for £250,000, payable to their families if they were killed. 1731

December 17, 1973—United Kingdom—Between December 17 and 26, over twenty IRA bombings were reported in London, injuring eighty-one people. The location of eleven of those bombings, injuring eighteen, is unknown. The other bombings are reported below. 1732-1742

December 17, 1973—United Kingdom—Two letter bombs were received in London. One of them blew off the right thumb of an aide to Queen Elizabeth. The device was placed in a hollowed-out paperback book delivered to the aide's home. The IRA was suspected. These and other attacks were believed to be in reprisal for the jailing of IRA terrorists who bombed the Old Bailey in March 1973 (see incidents 1472 to 1495). 1743-1744

December 18, 1973—United Kingdom—A car bomb exploded outside a government office building in London, injuring thirty-four persons. Another car bomb injured twenty-five people in London. The IRA was suspected. 1745-1746

December 18, 1973—Belgium —The Charles Martel group, reportedly a French organization, phoned the Belga Agency, a news service, to warn that it would kill a Palestinian family at 2 A.M if the Palestinian commandos who seized the Lufthansa plane refused to release their hostages (see incident 1731). 1747

December 18, 1973—Bangladesh—Three Molotov cocktails were thrown into the motor pool of the U.S. embassy in Dacca, causing no damage. 1748

December 18, 1973—Portugal—The main office of Mobil Portuguesa in Lisbon was stoned by fifteen to twenty youths. There were no injuries, but damages were estimated at $8,000 to $10,000. Leaflets at the scene identified the perpetrators as members of the reorganized Movement of the Portuguese Proletariat, a small Maoist far left faction. One leaflet was headlined, ''Kissinger out of Portugal.'' The downtown Lisbon offices of Reader's Digest and Ford were also stoned, possibly by the same group.

December 20, 1973—France—Paris police arrested ten Turks, one Algerian, and two Palestinians in a villa in Villiers-sur-Marne, southwest of Paris, and other locations, seizing U.S. M-26 grenades that had been stolen by the Baader-Meinhof Gang and transferred to the Venezuelan-born PFLP operative Carlos, explosives, equipment to make bombs, false identity cards, passports, and documents detailing terrorist plans. The terrorists, who did not put up a fight, were identified as members of the TPLF and PFLP. The same M-26 grenades would turn up in five incidents in four countries within the next eighteen months; they had apparently been brought into France by car. Four of the terrorists were freed on March 14, 1974. Nine others were sentenced on May 11, 1974, to prison terms varying between five and thirteen months. Other reports claim that they were also quickly expelled.

The cell had been organized by the Turkish killer of Ephraim Elrom, Israel's consul general in Istanbul, in 1971, an action taken as a favor to the PFLP. The villa, a large nineteenth-century building with a fake Gothic tower, was used by Carlos as an arms drop and communications center.

Acting on an Israeli tip, French police stopped a red Dodge with black mudguards at Modane on the Franco-Italian frontier. The occupants, including a German woman, had delivered explosives and equipment from Bulgaria via Belgium to the Villiers-sur-Marne villa.

Sophisticated radio transmitters and receivers found in the villa matched those left by Carlos at one of his Paris safe houses. 1749-1750

December 20, 1973—Spain—Premier Luis Carrero Blanco, seventy, was assassinated in Madrid by six ETA members who planted a bomb in the street in which his car was riding. Blanco, his chauffeur, and a police guard were killed in the explosion, which lifted their car five stories off the street and into the courtyard of a church where the premier had just attended mass. In a statement released in Bordeaux, France, the ETA claimed that the attack was in revenge for the killing of nine Basque militants by the government, as well as to fight Spanish repression. According to interviews given to Julen Agirre by four ETA members who claimed to have been responsible for the assassination and who were identified only as Txabi, Iker, Jon, and Mikel, the terrorists had initially planned to kidnap Blanco but were forced to change their plans after a lengthy surveillance. The preparation for the attack took approximately one year and involved digging a twenty-five-foot-long tunnel leading from a rented basement room out under the middle of the street, where the explosives went off at 9:30 A.M.

On July 9, 1975, two Basque nationalists were arrested in Bilbao and charged with transporting the dynamite used in the killing. In a shootout with police on July 30 in Barcelona, Ignacio Perez Beotequi, a suspect, was captured by police. Four others were captured with him, and a fifth was killed.

On September 20, 1975, Madrid police announced that a three-city dragnet led to the capture of José Mugica Arregui, thirty, believed to be the ETA's military chief and a key suspect in the assassination. Thirteen suspects were arrested in Madrid, and one more committed suicide when cornered by police. In Barcelona, five persons—one of them critically wounded by police bullets—were arrested. One was shot dead in a gun battle. Several others were arrested in Bilbao. The arrests came after the discovery of a plot to free forty political prisoners. 1751

December 20, 1973—Greece—A watchman discovered a bomb in an elevator of a Piraeus building where the local branch of the Chase Manhattan Bank is located. The device was turned over to police, who disarmed it. 1752

December 21, 1973—United Kingdom—Two bombs exploded outside the London Hilton Hotel bar. Both devices were small and caused minimal damage and no injuries. 1753

December 21, 1973—Argentina—Charles Robert Hayes, construction superintendent for McKee-Tesca, a joint venture between an Argentine firm and Arthur G. McKee and Company, a Cleveland engineering and construction company, was kidnapped at gunpoint while driving to work in La Plata. A ransom of $1 million was demanded for his release. The amount paid was not revealed, although some reports list the full million as having been delivered by the time Hayes, in "delicate health," was freed and secretly flown to the United States on January 31, 1974. 1754

December 22, 1973—United Kingdom—British General Ward received a letter bomb at his London home. A police constable was injured when the IRA parcel exploded while being inspected. 1755

December 26, 1973—United Kingdom—Two more IRA bombs exploded, one shattering a bar adjacent to a crowded theater. There were no injuries, although two persons were treated for shock. 1756-1757

December 28, 1973—Argentina—Seven armed men, reportedly members of the FAR, kidnapped Yves Boisset, plant production manager and director of Safrar-Peugeot, a subsidiary of the Peugeot Motor Company of France, in Buenos Aires. In early January 1974, the Associated Press reported that the Peugeot Motor Company had received two letters from Boisset, who said he was in good health. French sources claimed the ransom demand was $4 million. Boisset was released unharmed on March 18, 1974, apparently in good health. Peugeot officials did not announce how much ransom was paid. The FAR denied responsibility for the attack. 1758

December 28, 1973—United States—The United States signed the Convention for the Prevention and Punishment of Crimes against Internationally Protected Persons, including Diplomatic Agents.

December 28, 1973—Northern Ireland—Thomas Niedermayer, honorary West German consul and manager of the Grundig Electronics Company in Belfast, was kidnapped from his home, apparently by an IRA faction. Possible motives for the abduction included the release or transfer to Northern Ireland of two sisters, Dolours and Marion Price, who were jailed in the United Kingdom for a car-bomb attack in London in March, a ransom payment, or frightening off foreign investment. According to various reports, it was believed that the ransom was paid and that Niedermayer was released, although other reports claimed that he had been killed by IRA or Protestant extremists. He was presumed dead by a court of law in August 1976. On March 11, 1980, Northern Ireland police identified a body discovered at a garbage dump as Niedermeyer's. 1759

December 29, 1973—United Kingdom—Heathrow police arrested Allison Thompson, eighteen, of Santa Barbara, California, Abdelkhir el-Hakkaoui, twenty-five, of Morocco, and Athar Nassem, twenty-one, of Pakistan, for carrying five automatic pistols and more than 150 rounds of ammunition. On January 6, Robin Oban, twenty-five, another U.S. citizen, was deported to the United States after three days of police questioning, which did not result in formal charges. On January 5, FBI agents at Travis Air Force Base in California arrested Theodore Brown, thirty-one, on charges of helping Thompson smuggle guns and ammunition to the United Kingdom. On July 16 a U.S. federal prosecutor in Los Angeles dropped charges against Thompson of violating the Neutrality and the Firearms and Control Assistance Acts.

The three were charged on January 4 in England with arms conspiracy in a plot to kidnap a high French official and hold him for the release of thirty Moroccan political prisoners. Thompson was cleared of all charges by a British jury; el-Hakkaoui received a three-year jail sentence and Nassem one year. 1760

December 30, 1973—United States—Two bombs damaged the 573-ton *Mereghan II* as it awaited cargo in a Miami river dock. In a call to news media, a man identifying himself as a member of the Cuban Liberation Front said the attack was directed against the government of the Bahamas for the murder of Cuban nationals. Reports also credited the attack to the Cuban Action and the

FIN-National Integration Front. Other reports suggested that these were cover names for the Frente de Liberación Nacional Cubana. 1761

December 31, 1973—Italy—Explosions in downtown Rome heavily damaged three buildings housing ITT subsidiaries. Leaflets found on the scene charged that "ITT organized the coup in Chile and it is made up of Fascist and reactionary elements." 1762-1764

December 31, 1973—Italy—A bomb was thrown in Turin at a building housing the Spanish consulate and Spanish Chamber of Commerce, neither of which was damaged. No injuries were reported in what appeared to be an attack by Spanish extremists protesting the death sentence of a Barcelona student radical. 1765

December 31, 1973—Switzerland—A bomb exploded in a Zurich post office located beneath the Spanish consulate general, causing no injuries. The attack appeared to be related to the protest of the death sentence of a Barcelona student radical. 1766

December 31, 1973—United Kingdom—A member of the PFLP attempted to assassinate Joseph E. Sieff, president of the Marks and Spencer store chain, honorary vice-president of the Zionist Federation of Britain, and president of the Joint Palestinian Appeal, which collects funds for welfare in Israel. The shot broke two of Sieff's teeth and lodged in his head. Many accounts credit Venezuelan terrorist Carlos with the attack, which the PFLP said was in response to Sieff's hospitality for Menachem Begin, the leader of the Likud faction, which won the Israeli elections in 1977 and who had called for Jewish settlement of the occupied territories.

Shortly after 7 P.M., a man knocked on the Queens Grove, St. John's Wood door of Sieff. Manuel Teloria, the butler, opened the door and found a young man wearing a parka with its hood over his head and dark woolen material covering his face. Wielding a 9-mm automatic, he forced the butler to lead him into the empty lounge and then to the second-floor bathroom. The gunman fired at Sieff's head from less than three feet away. Meanwhile Mrs. Sieff was calling the police, who arrived ninety seconds later. The bullet had gone into Sieff's upper jaw, immediately under his nose, missing his jugular vein. Sieff praised his strong teeth for deflecting the bullet's power and saving his life. The gunman escaped before the police and an ambulance arrived.

When police later discovered Carlos's list of targets, Sieff's name was near the top. Carlos was suspected of the shooting when the gun was found among his weapons nearly two years later.

The PFLP claimed responsibility because "the British Zionist billionaire Joseph Sieff . . .gives every year millions of pounds to the Zionist usurper and his war machine." 1767

1974—Italy—Neofascist extremists plotted to introduce radioactive material into the water supply of Italian cities. Police discovered the plot before any material was acquired.

1974—Netherlands—Dutch Development Minister Jan Pronk and Economics Minister Ruud Lubbers were given special police protection after kidnap threats believed to originate from South Moluccans. 1768

1974—United States—Unknown individuals threatened to use an atomic bomb against the U.S. Capitol in an attempt to extort $10 million worth of food for hungry Americans.

January 2, 1974—Argentina—José Judvig, sixty-one, a Yugoslav-born Italian general manager of the Schconik paper manufacturing firm, was kidnapped during the night in Hurlingham, a Buenos Aires suburb. 1769

January 3, 1974—Argentina—Four ERP gunmen kidnapped Douglas Gordon Roberts, forty-six, an Argentine administrative director of Pepsi-Cola S.A., a local affiliate of the U.S. firm of PepsiCo, outside his home in the Buenos Aires suburb of Martínez. Two ERP cars blocked Roberts's car as he was leaving for work. He was then forced into a getaway vehicle. Both ERP cars were found not far from Roberts's home. He was freed on February 2, 1974, after the company paid a ransom of undisclosed size. Some of the kidnappers were arrested by Argentine police, who had followed them after they picked up the ransom. 1770

January 3, 1974—Jamaica—Rodoballo S. Sanchez, a young man alleging that he had a hand grenade wrapped in a handkerchief, walked through a shop area, avoiding the Kingston airline terminal, and boarded an Air Jamaican CD9 scheduled to fly to Detroit. When asked for his ticket, the hijacker threatened to blow up the plane and demanded to be flown to Miami. Two security guards boarded the plane and overpowered him. 5425

January 5, 1974—United Kingdom—Two hundred twenty soldiers and two hundred police sealed off five square miles around Heathrow International Airport after receiving reports that terrorists had smuggled in SAM-7 anti-aircraft missiles by using the diplomatic pouches of Arab embassies, and planned to shoot down an El Al airliner. 1771

January 6, 1974—United Kingdom—A suitcase filled with thirty pounds of explosives was discovered in the basement of the London home of the adjutant general of the British army, Sir Cecil Blacler. The bomb was defused. The IRA was suspected. 1772

January 6, 1974—United States—The Crystal River licensed nuclear facility of the Florida Power Corporation received a bomb threat.

January 6, 1974—United Kingdom—The London home of Major General Philip Ward, the general officer commanding the London district, was seriously damaged by a ten-pound IRA bomb. 1773

January 6, 1974—France—A fire set by arsonists burned five storage tanks in Macon containing 660,000 gallons of fuel oil. 1774

January 7, 1974—West Germany—Four Arab members of Black September were arrested in West Berlin and charged with attempting to smuggle explosives that were to be used in attacks on Israeli property. 1775

January 8, 1974—Peru—The ambassador of Haiti, Guillaume Tambronne, denounced threats he had received and requested police protection. 1776

January 9, 1974—Greece—A homemade, clock-activated bomb was discovered and deactivated under a U.S. government car outside an American residence in Kiffisia, an Athens suburb. 1777

January 10, 1974—Switzerland—The offices of Air Iberia were sprayed by red paint by several youths who wrote the letters MIL (Movimiento Iberico de Liberacion) on the windows.

January 11, 1974—Switzerland—A bomb placed in a telephone booth adjacent to the Zurich building housing the Spanish consulate went off. The consulate itself was not severely damaged, but the lobby was destroyed and the ground-floor post office was extensively damaged. There were no injuries. 1778

January 11, 1974—Italy—A bomb damaged the door of a Turin building housing the Spanish consulate and chamber of commerce, but caused no injuries. The attack may have been related to the death sentence of Salvador Puig Antich, an anarchist convicted of murdering a policeman in Spain. Elsewhere three bombs exploded in Rome, heavily damaging offices of firms linked to ITT. A fourth bomb went off in a Rome suburb, slightly damaging a truck owned by a telephone line maintenance firm. Leaflets found in the area claimed ITT was responsible for the 1973 Chilean coup and charged that the firm was involved in a "reactionary and fascist plot" in Italy. 1779-1783

January 12, 1974—Iran—An Iranian terrorist organization threatened over the telephone in Tehran to kill four Americans for each prisoner ordered executed by the shah. 1784

January 16, 1974—United Kingdom—A bomb found on the perimeter of Heathrow Airport in London was destroyed by bomb disposal experts.

January 17, 1974—United States—The Ginna licensed nuclear facility of the Rochester Gas and Electric Corporation received a bomb threat.

January 18, 1974—Greece—Homemade pipe bombs caused minor damage to three cars owned by U.S. military personnel, as well as to four other U.S. official cars in Athens. The cars all carried distinctive yellow foreign mission license plates. Calls to the press identified the perpetrators as dissident students belonging to LAOS People Number One and LAOS Number 13. The groups said the bombings were "in memory of the students killed last November by CIA agents." 1785–1791

January 18, 1974—Greece—A bomb damaged a car belonging to a Rumanian embassy employee. Calls to the press identified the perpetrators as dissident students in Athens. 1792

January 19, 1974—Argentina—The ERP released Giulio Baraldo, director of the local subisidiary of the Italian Beretta arms firm, in exchange for an undetermined quantity of arms. 1793

January 20, 1974—United Kingdom—A Libyan possessing explosives and planning attacks on Israeli targets was arrested in London and sentenced to two years imprisonment. He was expelled in July 1974. 1794

January 20, 1974—Mexico—A homemade bomb was thrown from a truck at the Cuban embassy in Mexico City. The bomb exploded in the embassy garden, causing no injuries and little damage. Police later discovered and removed four unexploded bombs from the embassy compound. The Cuban National Liberation Front claimed credit. 1795

January 21, 1974—Canada—The Cuban embassy reported receiving a package containing high-power explosives through the mail from Cuban Action. 1796

January 21, 1974—Peru—A Cuban Action package containing high explosives detonated in the Cuban embassy in Lima. 1797

January 21, 1974—Spain—A Cuban Action package containing high explosives blew up in the Cuban embassy in Madrid. 1798

January 21, 1974—Argentina—The Cuban embassy reported receiving a package containing high explosives through the mail from Cuban Action. 1799

January 21, 1974—United Kingdom—The IRA was suspected of sending a bomb contained in a Bible to the London home of the Right Reverend Gerard William Trickle, Roman Catholic bishop to the British forces, after he had spoken in defense of British troops in the Irish conflict. 1800

January 21, 1974—Colombia—An Aeropesca Vicker Viscount with fifty persons on board flying between Pasto and Popayán was hijacked by a young man, J. Tapia Carrion, who had hidden a carbine rifle in a towel when he boarded the aircraft. He forced the pilot to refuel at Cali, where twenty-three passengers were released. The aircraft was slightly damaged upon landing in Barranquilla. Two tires were changed, the plane was refueled, and four more passengers were released. The plane then took off for Havana. The plane and its remaining passengers were allowed to return to Colombia. Some U.S. citizens were reported to be on board the flight. 5426

January 21, 1974—Italy—Two telephone bomb threats were received by the U.S. embassy in an extortion attempt. A suspect was apprehended while picking up a satchel of fake money that had been delivered to the pickup point. 1801–1802

January 22, 1974—United States—The Crystal River licensed nuclear facility of the Florida Power Corporation received a bomb threat.

January 23, 1974—Cyprus—Followers of underground leader General George Grivas were believed responsible for four bombs that caused heavy damage at the Limassol post office, wrecking two parked cars and damaging a power line.

January 24, 1974—Ireland—Four IRA men armed with guns took over an Irish Helicopter Ltd. chartered Bolkow Bo 105 on the ground and forced the pilot to fly to Strabane, Northern Ireland, where they dropped two milk churns filled with explosives on a police station. The bombs missed their target and did not explode. The helicopter was flown back to Eire, and the hijackers escaped. 1803

January 24, 1974—United Kingdom—An individual described as a young man in his mid-twenties opened the door of the Bank of Hapoalim, Israel's third largest bank, on Lawrence Lane, off Cheapside in London's financial district, and threw in a bomb packed in a shoe box. The bomb bounced off a door, exploding in front of the counter. A typist was slightly injured by flying glass. Extensive damage was reported. A woman employee gave a description, which vaguely matched that of Carlos, the Venezuelan terrorist working for the PFLP, which claimed credit for the explosion. 1804

January 31, 1974—United Kingdom—A British judge in Edinbridge was slightly injured by an IRA letter bomb. 1805

January 31, 1974—Singapore—Two members of the Japanese Red Army, Haruo Wako and Yoshiaki Yamada, and two members of the PFLP attempted to set on fire three storage tanks belonging to a Royal Dutch Shell Oil Company refinery on Pulau Bukum Island off Singapore. Only one tank was set on fire, and the blaze was quickly extinguished. The terrorists claimed that they had acted in support of the ''Vietnam revolutionary people and for making a revolutionary situation after considering the situation of today's oil crisis.'' They then took hostages to a ferryboat in an attempt to escape but were intercepted by Singapore police. Five of their eight hostages jumped overboard, but the terrorists threatened to kill themselves and their remaining hostages if Singapore did not grant them free passage to an Arab country. The Singapore government refused but offered them sanctuary on February 4 in any of the forty-two embassies in Singapore. The situation remained at an impasse until February 6 when five PFLP members seized the Japanese embassy in Kuwait, holding twelve hostages, including Ambassador Ryoko Ishikawa, and demanded that their colleagues on the ferryboat be flown by the Japanese government to Kuwait. A JAL picked up the four terrorists, flew to Kuwait and picked up the five PFLP members, who released their hostages, and arrived in Aden on February 8. The nine were released by the PDRY government two days later. 1806

February 1, 1974—Botswana—Abraham Onkgopotse Tiro, the permanent organizer of the black South African Students' Organization who had been dismissed from a South African teaching post after classes with school officials over apartheid, was killed by a parcel bomb explosion in Gabarone. The airmail parcel was stamped by the International University Exchange Fund in Geneva, Switzerland. 1807

February 1, 1974—France—Henry Haim, president of the Association of Honest Allies of Israel and the Mediterranean, was attacked in his Paris clothing store by two unidentified men who cut a Star of David into his chest and stole $2,000. 1808

February 2, 1974—Pakistan—Three gunmen who initially identified themselves as members of Black September but later claimed to be affiliated with Moslem International Guerrillas, ''a group like Black September,'' hijacked the Greek freighter *Vori* in the west wharf of Karachi port, threatening to blow up the ship and kill their two hostages if the Greek government did not free two Arab terrorists who had been sentenced to death for the August 5, 1973, attack on Athens airport (see incident 1608). After negotiations with Pakistani authorities, as well as members of the PLO and the ambassadors of Syria, Libya, and Egypt, the attackers accepted a Greek government agreement to commute the sentences of the Athens terrorists. Accompanied by Pakistani officials, as well as the Egyptian and Libyan ambassadors, a PIA plane flew them out of Karachi to Cairo on February 3, thirty-two hours after the attack began. The hijackers flew on to Libya the next day.

The ship, owned by the Companina Carica S.A. Athens, was bringing sugar from Brazil to Afghanistan and was seized around 4 P.M. after the three had boarded the boat carrying suitcases. According to the captain, Constantinos N. Bliziotis, sixty-five, the terrorists ran into his cabin with pistols and forced him to call his chief officer and chief engineer on the intercom. The captain was allowed to leave after a few hours, suffering from what appeared to be a heart attack but which may have been hysteria. The group did not allow any of the crew to leave the ship and used them to serve food to themselves and their hostages. At one point, the trio claimed, "We are Muslims. We are not against the Islamic summit which is equally dear to us. We are working for the cause of humanity. We support all liberation movements including the liberation of Kashmir, Palestine, Cyprus, and Eritrea." They demanded the immediate release of the two terrorists in Greece and that the two be flown "to Uganda or to some other friendly country." Press reports listed the commandos as being armed with Italian Bereta automatic pistols and a few hand grenades. The chief negotiator for the Pakistani government, Karachi Port trust chairman Rear Admiral Zahid Hasnain, said the guerrillas also had " 'apple size' plastic bombs. One of the bombs was kept on the table all the time and one was being held by one of the commandos during the negotiations . . .the arms could not damage the cabin and were not sufficient to blow up the ship as was threatened by the commandos." At one point, the terrorists held a press conference, with reporters being allowed within one hundred yards of the ship. They also allowed the chief officer, Nicolas Lambropoulos, and the chief engineer, George Permimenis, to inform the reporters that they were being well treated. The terrorists permitted their hostages to send messages to their families, which were carried over telegraph to Athens. Although they began the attack with masks, one of the terrorists posed for photographers, flashing a victory sign.

The terrorists had established a twenty-four-hour deadline, due to expire at 4 P.M. that Sunday, for the release of the Athens pair. They extended the deadline for twenty-four hours after meeting with Khalid Abdul Ghann, the PLO representative in Pakistan, and his colleague, Nasir. A few hours later, the ambassadors of the three Arabic nations flew from Islamabad to meet with the terrorists and inform them that their heads of state had personally requested that they not harm their hostages. The terrorists said that they would rather kill themselves than harm them. After meeting three times with Aly Abou el Fadi

Khaahaba of Egypt, Ibrahim el Jerby of Libya, and Abdul Aziz Allouni of Syria, the terrorists accepted the Greek offer to commute the death sentences and traveled with the ambassadors by car to the airport, where they took a Pakistan International Airlines B707 to Cairo. Omar Ali Deeb, a Syrian seaman of the *Vori* who had facilitated the interaction between the terrorists and the crew, accompanied them to the airport. Before leaving the ship, one of the terrorists wrote on his cap, "To my friend, Nicolas," signing his name as Dilon, MIG. The hat was traced to a hatter in Karachi.

The terrorists initially requested that they be flown to Libya but were told that due to communications problems between Karachi and Tripoli, they would first have to fly to Cairo. The three surrendered their arms to the Egyptian ambassador, who kept them in his briefcase during the flight. According to the Pakistani English-language press, "The plane, also carrying the Egyptian and Libyan Ambassadors to Pakistan, landed at Cairo's international airport at 3:20 A.M., 1020 GMT. . . .The commandos, who surrendered to Cairo airport security authorities, will continue their flight to Libya. They will be accompanied by Ibrahim Jerbi, the Libyan Ambassador to Pakistan." Some reports indicated that the terrorists threatened to commit suicide if they were not flown to Libya.

On April 30, the terrorists' death sentences were commuted to life imprisonment. President Phaidon Gizikis later pardoned them. On May 5, they were deported to Libya at the request of Tripoli. Greek Justice Minister Stylianos Triandafyllou said Libya promised they would be "held answerable for their actions." Israel and the United States criticized Athens for the decision.

Questions remained as to the identity and nationality of the terrorists. Some reports indicated that the MIG was active in the Philippines and Indonesia and received funds and arms from Arab states. During the negotiations, one of the terrorists mentioned to the captain that he was an Indonesian. According to the local press, the chief officer "was convinced that at least one of them was either a Filipino or an Indonesian . . .the guerrillas were extraordinarily sharp and intelligent . . .using English for their conversation with negotiators, they relied on some unidentified foreign languages for whispering in the presence of visitors." They also read Urdu dailies that were given them, as well as physics and chemistry texts, giving the impression that they were students in their twenties, although one of the hostages claimed one of them was in his forties. One of them said, "Not all of us are Arabs." 1809

February 3, 1974—United Kingdom—A fifty-pound IRA bomb, apparently concealed in a suitcase in the rear luggage compartment of a British military bus, exploded, killing eleven people and wounding fourteen. The dead included the entire family of a British soldier (his wife and two children). The bus was taking soldiers and their families back from leave to their County Durham camp when it was hit by the bomb near Batley, Yorkshire. 1810

February 3, 1974—United Kingdom—Four IRA gunmen stole $80,000 from a bank at Stansted Airport near London. 1811

February 4, 1974—United Kingdom—An IRA letter bomb slightly wounded Reginald Maulding, a prominent Conservative politician and a former home secretary, in London. 1812

February 4, 1974—United Kingdom—A London newspaper security guard handling mail was injured by the explosion of a book-sized parcel addressed to the chairman of the *Daily Express*. 1813

February 4, 1974—Peru—A package mailed from Mexico exploded in the afternoon at the Cuban embassy in Lima, injuring a secretary, Pilar Ramirez Vega, who was hospitalized. A few days later, the Secret Hand Organization claimed credit. 1814

February 5, 1974—United States—Two male and two female members of the Symbionese Liberation Army kidnapped Patricia Hearst, nineteen, from her Berkeley, California, apartment. The group demanded that her father, Randolph A. Hearst, president and publisher of the *San Francisco Examiner*, distribute $70 worth of food to each person in California ''with welfare cards, Social Security pension cards, food stamp cards, disabled veteran cards, medical cards, parole or probation papers and jail or bail release slips,'' which would have run to $400 million. On February 19, Hearst announced details of a $2 million food giveaway program. The hostage was not released, and in a series of tapes left for a local radio station, it was learned that Patricia Hearst had grown to sympathize with, and ultimately join, the members of the SLA, adopting the name of Tania, a colleague of Ché Guevara. Six of her kidnappers died in a gun battle with police in Los Angeles on May 17, 1974, but Hearst and two of her captors escaped from the police, who were searching for her in connection with an SLA bank robbery of April 15. Hearst and her two companions were captured in 1976.

February 5, 1974—Peru—A letter bomb carrying stamps and postmarks from Mexico exploded in the Cuban embassy in Lima, injuring an attaché and damaging the building. The Movimiento Armado Nacionalista Organizado (MANO), a Peruvian terrorist group, issued a communiqué, saying, ''This is a first warning to those who, like the agents of Fidel Castro's international communism, seek to disrupt law and order in the republic and poison our people with Marxism-Leninism.'' 1815

February 6, 1974—Kuwait—Five fedayeen terrorists claiming to represent the PFLP, JRA, and the Sons of the Occupied Land seized the Japanese embassy and Ambassador Ryoko Ishikawa and fifteen of his staff at gunpoint, threatening to kill them unless the PFLP-JRA team stranded in the Singapore stalemate (see incident 1806) was freed and flown to Kuwait. Four non-Japanese staff members were permitted to leave the building, which the terrorists held for two days while negotiations continued. Kuwait would not allow a Japanese Airlines plane to land, refusing to grant asylum to the Singapore group. After a plea by the Japanese government, Kuwait agreed to allow the plane to land if the terrorists released their hostages. The JAL plane flew to Kuwait airport later that day, where it picked up the five terrorists and flew on to Aden, where they surrendered to the Southern Yemeni authorities. After being greeted by senior PDRY officials, the terrorists appear to have been released. 1816

February 8, 1974—Spain—A Molotov cocktail was thrown at an Air France office in Barcelona. 1817

February 11, 1974—Israel—Three Christian establishments in Jerusalem, two of them U.S.-owned, were firebombed: the Baptist House, operated by the U.S. Southern Baptist Convention, the Zion House Bible Shop, and the chapel of the Swedish Theological Institute. Those responsible were unknown, but the JDL and extremist Yeshiva students had conducted similar attacks in February 1973. 1818–1820

February 12, 1974—Argentina—The Montoneros and the ERP joined representatives of Brazilian, Bolivian, Chilean, and Uruguayan terrorist organizations to coordinate urban operations across South America.

February 12, 1974—Argentina—Federal police in Buenos Aires arrested thirty Uruguayans upon discovery of a plot to assassinate President Juan Péron, his wife Isabel, and Uruguayan President Juan M. Bordaberry. The Montoneros and the FAR were also implicated in the plot. FAR founder Carlos Alberto Caride was arrested near an intersection where the presidential motorcade was to pass. Reports indicate that he had been carrying a gun and grenades. 1821

February 12, 1974—United Kingdom—A fifty-pound IRA bomb exploded in the records section of the Latimer National Defense College in Little Chalfont, Buckinghamshire, about thirty miles west of London. Ten people were injured, none critically. Three hours after this explosion, bomb disposal experts detonated another bomb found nearby. 1822

February 12, 1974—Zambia—John Dube, deputy representative of the African National Congress of South Africa and a member of Spear of the

Nation, was killed when a letter bomb exploded in the ANC office in Lusaka. Two other people were wounded in the blast, which destroyed the office and damaged nearby offices. Dube was believed to have planned joint ANC-ZAPU attacks in Rhodesia in 1967 and 1968. 1823

February 13, 1974—Spain—A package addressed to the Cuban embassy exploded in a Madrid post office, wounding a postal worker. 1824.

February 16, 1974—Belgium—Bombs exploded at a Spanish tourist office and a Spanish bank in Brussels. 1825–1826

February 16, 1974—West Germany—Arsonists set a fire that damaged a Spanish travel agency in Frankfurt. 1827

February 16, 1974—Colombia—The M-19 occupied the University of Cali, painting slogans calling for the dismissal of the government on the walls and issuing a demand for the release of twenty jailed members of a leftist group.

February 17, 1974—United States—A young army private stole a military helicopter and flew it to Washington,D.C., where he hovered over the Washington Monument. He landed one hundred yards from the White House on the White House lawn after security guards hit the craft with shotgun blasts. He was arrested.

February 19, 1974—Brazil—Several officers of the U.S. consulate general in São Paulo received telephoned threats of bombing or assault on their residences. 1828

February 20, 1974—United States—J. Reginald Murphy, editor of the *Atlanta Constitution*, was kidnapped after accompanying a man who appeared at his home claiming to be Lamont Woods, who needed help in distributing $300,000 worth of fuel oil to the needy. Murphy was blindfolded and thrown into the trunk of a car, from which he was released after forty-nine hours. A group claiming to be the American Revolutionary Army, which wanted to "stop these lying, leftist, liberal news media," said that it was the rightist counterpart of the Symbionese Liberation Army, whose exploits had dominated the news that month. The group called for the resignation of all federal officials so that free elections could be held. It also demanded a ransom of $700,000, which was paid by managing editor Jim Minter at a prearranged location. A few hours later the FBI arrested William A. H. Williams, thirty-three, a Lilburn, Georgia, building contractor, and his wife, Betty, at their home, where the money was found. Williams admitted that he dreamed up the

ARA after reading about the SLA. He was convicted on federal extortion charges and sentenced to forty years. The conviction was reportedly overturned in 1976 by a three-judge federal court on the grounds that pretrial publicity and inflammatory prosecution arguments deprived Williams of a fair trail. U.S. attorney John Stokes said in January 1976 that he had petitioned the U.S. Fifth Circuit Court of Appeals for a rehearing.

February 20, 1974—South Vietnam—An Air Vietnam DC4 flying from Da Lat and Qui Nhon to Da Nang with fifty-two persons on board was hijacked by a South Vietnamese youth, Nguyen Cuu Viet, who demanded that the flight, which had originated in Saigon, be diverted to Hanoi or Dong Hoi, North Vietnam. The pilot and American copilot persuaded the hijacker that fuel was low, engines were malfunctioning, and a landing at Dong Ha, a North Vietnamese–controlled area, was necessary. The pilot actually landed the plane at Phu Bai Airport in Hue, South Vietnam. While on the ground, two passengers attempted to apprehend the hijacker, who, realizing that he had been tricked, detonated the hand grenade he had concealed in a bag, killing all three. A hole about two by three meters was made in the port side of the fuselage, and three starboard windows were broken. The aircraft was not considered economically repairable. Five passengers and a stewardess were reported injured. Passengers for the flight had had their hand baggage searched, but there was no body search. 5427

February 22, 1974—United States—According to the BDM Corporation, "A 500-foot-high meteorological tower, erected as a preliminary step for a planned nuclear reactor in Massachusetts, was toppled. . . .Sam Lovejoy, a 27 year old college graduate and organic farmer, deliberately sabotaged the tower as a protest against the ' . . .symbol of a future nuclear power plant.' The man entered the site at night by cutting the barbed wire on top of the cyclone fence that surrounded the area. By loosening one of 3 sets of high-tension cables that served as guy wires for the tower, he was able to bring down the top 360 feet of the 500 foot tower. Damage to the tower was estimated by the Northwest Utilities Company as in 'the neighborhood of $100,000.' Following the sabotage, Mr. Lovejoy turned himself in to the local police headquarters where he presented a 4-page typewritten statement taking full responsibility for the deed. The man had many objections to the proposed nuclear power plant, including what he called 'the safety rap, the background radiation and ecosystem rap,' and the 'whole Madison Avenue dance.' It was these considerations that led him to conclude 'it was tower tippin' time.' In addition to citing ecological reasons for not building the plant, he also mentioned a series of accidents and shutdowns that occurred at the nearby Vermont Yankee power plant."

February 22, 1974—United States—Delta Airlines flight 523, a DC9 scheduled to fly from Baltimore-Washington InternationalAirport to Atlanta, had emplaned eight passengers when it was the scene of an attempted hijacking. Samuel J. Byck, a white male for whom the FAA profile was not applicable and who was born in Philadelphia on January 30, 1930, shot and killed a policeman, George N. Ramsburg, in the airport terminal, forced his way aboard the aircraft, killed the copilot, Fred Jones, and wounded the pilot, Reese Lofton, thirty-nine, with three shots in the chest and abdomen from his pistol. While the plane was still on the ground, an airport policeman from outside the aircraft fired a rifle through the door's glass porthole and hit Byck twice in the chest. Byck then shot himself in the head and died. A booby-trapped incendiary bomb he had carried with him was dismantled on the runway. 5428

February 23, 1974—Argentina—The ERP kidnapped Antonio Vallocchia, an executive of Swift and Company in Rosario, accusing him of "unjustified dismissal of forty-two workers demanding decent salaries." Three days later Swift agreed to the ERP demands for reinstatement and payment for the days the employees were out of work. 1829

February 23, 1974—Greece—The People's Resistance Organized Army placed five bombs in the Dow chemical plant at Lávrion, about forty miles from Athens. Four of the bombs exploded, causing material damage. Two Greek demolition experts were killed attempting to defuse the fifth bomb. 1830

February 24, 1974—Mexico—Seven bombs went off in the night at the offices of U.S. and other companies. In Guadalajara, Pepsi-Cola and Union Carbide plants were damaged, while Coca-Cola offices, a bakery, and federal offices were targeted in Oaxaca. Damage was estimated at more than $400,000. No injuries or arrests were reported. 1831–1833

March 1974—United States—A case of possible intrusion at a Nike-Hercules missile site near Woodstock, Maryland, was reported when several men drove to a guarded gate. One of the men attempted to talk his way in, telling the guard that he had worked there years ago. When challenged, the group fled. It appeared that the group was testing security precautions rather than planning to steal a missile.

March 1974—United States—The Cuban exile magazine *Areito* reported being the target of bomb attacks. 1834

March 1, 1974—France—The Sonolar factory in Paris, owned by a French subsidiary of ITT, was destroyed by fire. Agence France Press was phoned by a group calling itself We Must Do Something, which said that this was their welcome to the Chilean ambassador to France. 1835

March 2, 1974—Spain—The death sentence of Salvador Puig Antich, twenty-six, a Catalan anarchist convicted of killing a policeman in 1973, was carried out when he was garroted in the Barcelona city jail. A number of bombings and demonstrations were reported in protest of the death sentence of the Iberian Liberation Movement member. Numerous groups around the world had requested clemency for Antich.

March 3, 1974—Lebanon—A British Airways flight from Bombay to London with ninety-two passengers and ten crew members was hijacked shortly out of its Beirut stopover by Adnan Ahmad Nuri and Sami Hussin Taiman, who demanded that the pilot fly to Athens, where they intended to demand the release of the terrorists in the Athens airport incident (see incident 1608). The Greek authorities refused to grant permission to land, so the plane flew on to Amsterdam's Schipol Airport, where all passengers and crew were allowed to flee before the terrorists threw inflammable liquids, including the plane's liquor supply, around the cabin and set the plane on fire. The terrorists were captured by police while running from the plane. They had identified themselves as members of the Palestine Liberation Army, but after the PLO in Beirut disavowed connection with the attack, the Organization of Arab Nationalist Youth for the Liberation of Palestine claimed credit, warning the Dutch government against prosecuting the two prisoners. The hijackers claimed that the arms and explosives for their operation had been hidden on board the plane by accomplices before they boarded in Beirut. On June 6 a Dutch court convicted them on charges of air piracy and arms violations and sentenced them to five years. They were released on November 24, 1974, and flown to Tunis as part of an agreement reached with four hijackers of a British Airways plane at Dubai on November 22 (see incident 2145). On December 7, 1974, the two terrorists went to Libya with the four hijackers who had demanded their release and five other terrorists released from Egypt. The two hijackers of the VC10 apparently were given their freedom in Libya. 1836

March 3, 1974—Italy—A Molotov cocktail was ignited at an entrance adjacent to the USIS building in Milan. There were no personal injuries or extensive property damage, and it was not determined whether the USIS building was the actual target. 1837

March 7, 1974—Netherlands—An early morning fire partially destroyed the building housing the Spanish tourist agency in The Hague. A local daily newspaper received an anonymous phone call from a woman speaking with a Spanish accent who said the fire was a protest against the Madrid execution of a Spanish anarchist on March 2. 1838

March 7, 1974—Iran—A bomb was thrown into the U.K. embassy compound in Tehran during the evening, causing no injuries but breaking some windows. A bomb exploded in front of a Tehran theater as well. 1839

March 8, 1974—Northern Ireland—A powerful IRA bomb exploded at the front of the British army's headquarters in central Belfast, causing no injuries.

March 10, 1974—Peru—At 10 P.M. in Lima, an unknown individual threw an explosive at the principal residence of the Swiss ambassador at Avenida Salaverry 3290, breaking the door's windows. 1840

March 11, 1974—United States—The licensed nuclear facility of the Maine Yankee Atomic Power Company received a bomb threat.

March 12, 1974—Ireland—William Fox, a Protestant senator, was shot dead near a Clones farmhouse where he was visiting his fiancée. The twelve masked men responsible for the killing near the Northern Ireland border also ransacked and burned the farmhouse. 1841

March 12, 1974—Argentina—A bomb exploded at the front door of the Córdoba USIS Binational Center at 2:10 A.M., causing $350 damage. 1842

March 12, 1974—Japan—A JAL B747 flying 426 persons between Tokyo and Naha, Okinawa, was hijacked by Katsuhito Owaki, a Japanese youth who claimed to have a bomb in a briefcase. Upon landing in Naha, he demanded $55 million, 200 million yen, fifteen parachutes, and mountain-climbing gear. Having allowed the passengers to deplane, he requested food and was over-powered by police who boarded the plane dressed as food handlers. No bomb was found on board the plane, whose passengers had been screened prior to boarding. 5429

March 13, 1974—United States—The Diablo Canyon licensed nuclear facility of the Pacific Gas and Electric Company received a bomb threat.

March 14, 1974—Mexico—The Mexico City offices of Cubana de Aviacion were damaged by a dynamite explosion, claimed by the FLNC. 1843

March 14, 1974—Venezuela—Three incendiary bombs were discovered and disarmed at Sears stores in El Marques and Bello Monte. Incendiaries went off in the main Sears store in Caracas, but the fires were extinguished with little damage. During the presidential inauguration period, other pipe bombs and Molotov cocktails exploded in Caracas and Maracaibo. A fire was also set at a new supermarket partially owned by the Rockefeller family. The FALN and the Red Flag, along with several other groups, claimed responsibility for these attacks. 1844–1847

March 15, 1974—Lebanon—Security police arrested six Arabs after they attempted to smuggle arms and explosives in food containers and luggage aboard a KLM Royal Dutch Airlines B747 en route from Amsterdam to Tokyo via Beirut. One of the suspects was a Lebanese employee of KLM. His accomplices carried Jordanian, Egyptian, and Yemeni passports. Reports claimed that the individuals were members of the PFLP, as well as the Arab National Youth Organization for the Liberation of Palestine, and that they included two Palestinians, two Lebanese, and one Libyan. It appeared that two of the group, which included Fawzi Darwish, a fedayeen, Muhamud Subhi Albal'us, a Palestinian refugee from southern Lebanon, and Husayn Nasvi Al'Kebir, a.k.a. Abu Mu'tarzz, a Palestinian refugee from Syria, participated in the November 26, 1973, hijacking of a KLM plane (see incident 1713). Police at Beirut International Airport had earlier received intelligence information concerning a possible hijacking attempt. 1848

March 16, 1974—Lebanon—The Lebanese Revolutionary Socialist Movement claimed responsibility for throwing a bomb at the car of the Iranian Ambassador, blowing a tire and causing minor damage to the body of the car. 1849

March 16, 1974—Argentina—A bomb exploded at the front door of the USIS Binational Center in Cordoba, causing no personal injuries but $1000 damage. 1850

March 16, 1974—Jamaica—The Cuban embassy in Kingston was bombed by the FLNC. 1851

March 17, 1974—Northern Ireland—Four armed and hooded IRA members entered the U.S. Naval Communications Station, a center for the U.S. Polaris Submarine fleet, in Londonderry, where they forced the gate sentry and three other U.S. sailors, whom they bound, into a stolen van and drove to the base armory in an attempt to steal arms and ammunition. The servicemen managed to escape during the arms foray, and the terrorists fled on foot when the alarm sounded, jumping over a boundary wall and fleeing into a nearby public housing area. They fired four shots at the guards and may have deliberately misaimed, injuring no one. The had used wirecutters to break through a chained rear gate upon entry. 1852

March 20, 1974—United Kingdom—A white Ford driven by Ian Ball, twenty-six, halted the car of Princess Anne and her husband, Captain Mark Phillips, as they were driving down London's Mall toward Buckingham Palace. Ball's shots hit the royal bodyguard in the chest, arm, and shoulder and the chauffeur in the stomach. He was unable to open the car door and ran to the rear of the car. A reporter who jumped out of a taxi to stop him was wounded, and a policeman was shot in the stomach. Ball continued to fire and one bullet missed the princess by inches. He then fled into St. James' Park, where he was overpowered by policeman Peter Edmonds.

Inside the Ford was a ransom note demanding $4.6 million in "reparation" for blacks, workers, and victims of inflation and the Irish Troubles. Ball was carrying three pairs of handcuffs, tranquilizers, and $700 cash.

March 20, 1974—Kenya—An East African Airways Fokker F27 flying thirty-five persons from Nairobi to Malindi and Mombasa was hijacked by an Ethiopian married couple, Kasete Al'Azhar and Niget Kiflu, who demanded to be flown to Libya via Khartoum, threatening to blow up the plane. (Other reports claim that the male hijacker appeared to be an Arab armed with a gun and that he demanded to be flown to Moscow.) It appears that the couple smuggled the pistol on board the plane in the woman's hair. The hijackers agreed to stop at Entebbe, Uganda, to refuel, where they let the passengers deplane. After negotiating (some reports claim that President Idi Amin joined in the bargaining) for several hours, the couple surrendered to authorities. It is unclear whether they were arrested or freed. 5430

March 20, 1974—United States—A man armed with a knife entered a real estate office at the Indianapolis airport and seized a woman, holding the knife to her throat. He demanded $1 million and an aircraft and was shot by an airport policeman after asking for a gun. 5431

March 21, 1974—Mexico—Five members of the Twenty-third of September Communist League were arrested while planning the kidnapping of a U.S. Nobel Peace Prize winner. 1853

March 22, 1974—Corsica—A French Air Inter Caravelle III scheduled to fly from Bastia, Corsica, to Marseille was destroyed on the ground at Bastia by an explosive device placed in the forward landing gear compartments in the movable flap of the wheel housing. The bomb exploded at 4 A.M., damaging the forward landing gear, everything under the forward galley floor, the flight deck, parts of the fuselage, the underflooring, and the cabin area. 1854

March 22, 1974—Mexico—U.S. Vice-Consul John S. Patterson was reported kidnapped after leaving the consulate in Hermosillo (Sonora State) with an unidentified man. A ransom note demanding $500,000 for his release was received at the consulate, signed by the People's Liberation Army of Mexico. Although Patterson's wife, Ann, attempted to deliver the ransom, she was unable to make contact with the abductors. Patterson's mutilated body was found in a creek bed near the town on July 7, 107 days after his abduction. On May 28, Bobbie Joe Keesee, forty, a U.S. citizen, was arrested in San Diego on U.S. federal charges of planning and participating in the kidnapping (he had also participated in a hijacking, incident 5259). Greg Curtis Fielden was named as an unindicted co-conspirator. On April 29, 1975, Keesee was sentenced to twenty years for conspiracy to kidnap a diplomat. The PLAM turned out to be a hoax. 1855

March 23, 1974—Eritrea—The Debawa site of an Ethiopian-Japanese mining operation near Asmara was attacked by members of the ELF-General Command armed with grenades and automatic weapons. The Eritrean flag was raised at the site, and leaflets were scattered. Damage to the mine generator and other equipment was placed at $3 million. There were no casualties at the mine, but two guards at the village school were killed by fleeing terrorists. 1856

March 23, 1974—Peru—At 5 A.M., cyprus trees were set on fire by arsonists who attacked the residence of the Colombian ambassador, Dr. Jaime Barra Ramirez, on Avenida Arequipa 3220, Lima. 1857

March 25, 1974—Argentina—Jorge Oscar Wahelich, a Brazilian industrialist, was killed in Buenos Aires while resisting a kidnapping attempt. 1858

March 26, 1974—United Kingdom—The headquarters of an army bomb disposal regiment in northern England was bombed, slightly injuring a woman who managed an army canteen. 1859

March 26, 1974—Ethiopia—Four Tenneco Oil Company employees, including three Americans and one Canadian, along with their Canadian pilot were kidnapped by the ELF after their helicopter made a forced landing due to bad weather near Massawa, Eritrea, forty-five miles west of that city. The ELF set fire to the helicopter, which had been used by the group on their geological survey mission for a new concession granted Tenneco by the Ethiopian government. The ELF said that it would try three of the five hostages for exploitation of the national resources of Eritrea and demanded that Tenneco aid the ELF in obtaining the release of seventy-five prisoners, employ a journalist to publish the ELF story, suspend further explorations until the fighting between the government and ELF had ended, and specify that the hostages not return to Ethiopia. Tenneco agreed to discuss the demands. At one point, the ELF announced that it would release two of the hostages. A helicopter pilot who was sent to retrieve them was kidnapped on May 27, 1974. An American nurse who was taken prisoner the same day and the second pilot were freed on June 23, with a ransom demand of $1 million accompanying the first pilot, who was released three days later. After prolonged negotiations, the remaining four hostages were released unharmed on September 10. 1860

March 30, 1974—United States—A young man identified as Ernest E. Smith, who was born in Waterloo, Iowa, on April 15, 1953, armed with a shotgun and holding two hostages, forced his way on board a parked National Airlines B727 at Sarasota, Florida. An airline maintenance man, the only person on board the aircraft, managed to wrestle the shotgun away from the white hijacker, for whom the FAA profile did not apply. The hijacker fled but was arrested by police four hours later. On September 16, 1974, he was sentenced on state charges of kidnapping to fifteen years and convicted of two counts of aggravated assault and sentenced to two concurrent terms of five years. 5432

April 1974—India—According to BDM Corporation, ''an apparent uranium smuggling operation was uncovered. . . .It is believed that a smuggling ring had been supplying uranium (of unspecified grade) from the Juduguda plant in Bihar, to Nepal. From Nepal, the uranium was smuggled to Hong Kong where Chinese or Pakistani agents took delivery. The sources described the thieves as being mostly Indians with possible contacts in Delhi, Bombay, and Calcutta. Some reports indicate that as much as $2,500,000 worth of uranium may have been involved. A restaurant run by a foreigner near the mountain mine's store camp is suspected of being the starting point for the gang's operations. Despite various theories concerning the incident, some facts are available to study the events. On April 21, according to the Deputy Superintendent of Police in Jamshedpur, a raid on a house in Jamshedpur resulted in the arrest of five persons and the recovery of about 3.5 Kg of uranium. The material consisted of 750 grams of 'yellow-colored powder' and the rest 'ash-colored powder,' packed in plastic bags. Two of the men arrested were workers at the Jaduguda plant. An atomic mineral scientist attached to the plant, Dr. Swapan Sarkar, disappeared in October, 1973. His wife thought his disappearance had something to do with the uranium smuggling. In addition, a man believed to be important in the smuggling was killed near Katmandu. Following the arrest of the 5 persons, a government report was issued stating that the stores of uranium concentrate were intact. Mr. K. C. Pant, Minister for Irrigation and Power, stated that the source of the recovered material was not known and the material had not yet been fully analyzed. He also stated that there was no obvious connection between the missing scientist and the material. 'Informed sources' believe that smuggling had gone on for 2 years and that the police only caught on following the arrests at Jamshedpur. Whether or not the thefts are as widespread as some believe, theft of some material has been accomplished using inside assistance at the plant.''

April 1974—Netherlands—The Amsterdam office of the Indonesian Airline Garuda was sabotaged by fire. 1861

April 4, 1974—Argentina—The FAP murdered Roberto Francisco Klecher, an Argentine who was personnel manager of the mechanical section of Fiat-Concorde, the Argentine branch of Fiat, on a downtown Córdoba street shortly after he left the plant. 1862

April 4–10, 1974—Puerto Rico—Abdala, an anti-Castro group, was responsible for eight bombings in San Juan. 1863–1870

April 6, 1974—United Kingdom—IRA bombs damaged an office building and railway station in Birmingham and store in suburban London and injured two policemen in Manchester. 1871–1874

April 8, 1974—Eritrea—A rocket struck a control van about twenty-five feet below a parabolic antenna at the U.S. Kagnew tracking station near Asmara, causing slight damage but no injuries. The ELF was suspected. 1875

April 8, 1974—United States—A bomb placed in the breezeway of a Washington, D. C., diplomatic residence failed to detonate. 1876

April 9, 1974—Colombia—Prior to takeoff from Medellín for its flight to Turbo, a Cessnica general aviation Beechcraft C45 was the scene of an attempted skyjacking by Elkin Tobon, seventeen, who pointed a knife at the pilot and demanded to be flown to Lima, Peru. A cargo handler grabbed the hijacker from behind and overpowered him. 5433

April 9, 1974—Spain—The FLNC called a Spanish-language Miami radio station to claim credit for the bombing of the entrance of the Cuban consulate in Madrid. Heavy damage was done to the apartment building housing the consulate, but no serious injuries were reported. 1877

April 11, 1974—Israel—Three members of the PFLP-GC identified as one Palestinian, one Syrian, and one Iraqi entered Israel via the Lebanese border and attacked an apartment complex in the border town of Kiryat Shmona, opening doors of apartments and firing indiscriminately. They killed eighteen people, including five women and eight children, and wounded sixteen. According to communiqués released by the PFLP-GC during the attack, the group demanded the release of one hundred prisoners held in Israeli jails, including Lod Airport survivor Kozo Okamoto (see incident 1056). Israel denied that the terrorists were holding hostages and refused the demands. Israeli troops engaged in a gun battle with the terrorists, who had attacked a second building, losing two troops but killing all three terrorists when explosives they were carrying blew up. According to PFLP-GC Politburo member Abdul Abbas, who spoke in Beirut the next day, "This operation was just the beginning of a campaign of revolutionary violence within Israel that is aimed at blocking an Arab-Israeli peace settlement." Another PFLP-GC communiqué said, "Our men carried out their instructions. They set off explosive belts they wore for the operation when the enemy stormed the building they were holding. They died along with their hostages." Israel retaliated the next day in southern Lebanon, raiding the villages of Dahira, Yaroun, Muhebab, Blida, Ett Taibe, and Aitarun, blowing up houses belonging to Arab guerrilla sympathizers after the inhabitants had been evacuated. 1878

April 12, 1974—Argentina—Alfred A. Laun III, chief of the USIS in Córdoba, was kidnapped in the morning from his home by the ERP, who shot and beat him when he resisted abduction, wounding him in the head, abdomen, and shoulder. Shortly aferward, the ERP sent a message to a Córdoba radio station, saying that he would be "interrogated on counterrevolutionary activities in Vietnam, Santo Domingo, Brazil and Bolivia, and for his active participation as a liaison in the fascist military coup against our brother people in Chile. He will also be interrogated on his ties with the Central Intelligence Agency." Laun was released in the evening, fifteen hours after his abduction, when his kidnappers realized the seriousness of his wounds and worried that he would die in their hands. Laun was treated in Córdoba and Panama and survived. On April 28, police shot Claudio Alberto Luduena, one of Laun's abductors, as he was attempting to kidnap a business executive in Córdoba, Antonio Minetti. 1879

April 13, 1974—United States—José Elias de la Torriente, sixty-nine, an exile leader who planned to lead an armed attack against the Castro regime in 1969 and 1970 and who was accused by Cuba of being a CIA agent, was shot to death by a sniper's bullet in his Coral Gables home while watching television with his wife. Four days later, the "Secret Organization Zero" claimed credit. 1880

April 13, 1974—Philippines—Three U.S. Naval officers were shot and killed while inspecting road construction at the perimeter of the Subic Bay Naval Base, fifty miles northwest of Manila. 1881

April 14, 1974—United States—A bomb at the Lebanese consulate in Los Angeles caused $1,500 damage but no injuries. The bombing appeared to be in retaliation for the Kiryat Shmona attack (see incident 1878); two news services received anonymous phone tips that the bombs would go off, followed by the JDL slogan "Never Again!" 1882

April 17, 1974—United States—The Westinghouse Electric Corporation's licensed nuclear facility at Columbia, South Carolina, received a bomb threat.

April 17, 1974—Austria—A man claiming to be a "justice guerrilla" daubed radioactive iodine 131 on seats in passenger compartments of a Vienna-to-Rome express train. Some reports claimed that this was a vendetta against the government over prison conditions. A phone call warned that the passengers' lives were endangered, but when scientists examined the seats, they reported that the amount of radioactivity was not harmful to human life and that the substance was similar to that used in medical diagnoses. The same type of material found in the first-class compartment was believed stolen on April 12 on its way from a Vienna drug company to its destination in Linz, Austria. 1883

April 18, 1974—Italy—Genoa's deputy prosecutor, Mario Sossi, was kidnapped from his home by the Red Brigade, which claimed that he was being held in a "people's jail" awaiting trial by a "people's tribunal." On May 6, the kidnappers threatened to kill Sossi unless eight members of the Maoist October 22 group, whom Sossi had prosecuted, were released and flown to Cuba, North Korea, or Algeria. Sossi was released on May 23 after the Genoa court agreed to release the prisoners on the condition that Sossi be freed first. On June 18, the supreme court overturned the Genoa court's decision to release the prisoners. 1884

April 18, 1974—United States—The Burlingame, California, headquarters of an international trade union and an adjacent building were extensively damaged by a bomb. 1885

April 18, 1974—Egypt—Members of the Islamic Liberation Organization attacked the Military Technical Academy in Cairo, killing eleven and injuring twenty-seven in a gun battle with police. The group was led by Saleh Abdalla Sariya, an individual carrying Iraqi and Libyan passports who had worked in Cairo with the Arab League. According to reports in the *London Guardian*, he had been a political assassin since 1960 when, as a refugee in Iraq, he was sponsored by Haj Amin Hasaini, the grand mufti of Jerusalem. He had also been a member of the Jordanian Communist party, the Muslim Brotherhood, the Islamic Liberation party, and numerous Palestinian organizations. Sariya had visited Libya in June 1973 and apparently discussed the attack, which was to lead to a coup attempt against President Sadat, with Libyan President Muammar Qaddafi. Muhammad Abdel Qader, a medical student, was arrested and confirmed this report. Approximately eighty were arrested in connection with the attack. 1886

April 19, 1974—Austria—An anonymous phone call led police to a Vienna-to-Linz train, where they discovered that twelve passengers had been contaminated by a radioactive substance sprayed on the train's seats. The liquid was identified as material used in medical diagnoses. On April 22, a phone call alleging a third use of the substance turned out to be a hoax. The Austrian police offered a reward for the capture of the person who applied the substance and called himself a "justice guerrilla."

April 19, 1974—Greece—A USAF sergeant found a suspicious package under his auto in Athens. It was discovered to contain an anti-personnel bomb. 1887

April 20, 1974—India—A Kuwait Airways flight from Bombay to Baghdad with Dr. Syedna Mohammed Burhanuddin, the spiritual head of the Dawoodi Bohras, aboard, was held up at Santa Cruz Airport for two and a half hours while authorities searched for a bomb after an anonymous telephone tip. 1888

April 21, 1974—Italy—A section of the railway line near Bologna was sabotaged, but the driver of the Paris express was able to stop the train before crashing. 1889

April 21, 1974—Yemen—A dynamite charge exploded in the garden of the Soviet embassy in Sana, causing no damage or injuries. 1890

April 21, 1974—Chad—Members of a Toubou rebel group in the Tibesti region of Chad, calling themselves the Armed Forces of the Chadian Revolution and believed to be associated with the National Liberation Front of Chad (FROLINAT), kidnapped five Europeans in a raid on a medical research center at Bardai in northern Chad. The hostages included Christian Staewen, a physician and nephew of West German President Gustav Heinemann, Françoise Claustre, a French archeologist, and a Frenchman, Marc Combes. Staewen's wife was killed in the attack, and Combes escaped to Libya shortly after being captured. The rebels kept altering their demands, which revolved around the provision of money and arms. The German government agreed to pay a $1.2 million ransom and broadcast a FROLINAT manifesto for the release of Staewen, who was freed on June 11, 1974. In April 1975, a French military officer sent to contact the Toubous was shot by the insurgents, who demanded $2.7 million for her release. Claustre's husband was taken hostage in July 1975 when he flew to the Toubou camp in a private plane in an attempt to begin negotiations. The terrorists threatened to execute Mrs. Claustre on September 23 if the French government did not pay $880,000 and provide eighty-eight tons of military supplies. The group granted her a stay of execution when the French government agreed to the cash ransom, which the Chadian government criticized as interference in a domestic issue. The French were ordered to close their military bases in the country. On September 24, 1975, Chad's foreign minister, Kamougue Wadal Abdelkader, announced at a New York City news conference that his government would take charge of the negotiations through a former spiritual leader of the Toubous, le Derdei. The group still demanded military equipment, including jeeps, binoculars, and uniforms, but France refused to supply them with weapons. In March 1976, French Prime Minister Jacques Chirac went to Tripoli to request the intervention of President Muammar Qaddafi, who attempted to negotiate with the group's leader, Hissein Habre. Negotiations were unsuccessful, and Qaddafi backed a rival faction of the group, which ousted the main Toubou group. The new faction appeared to be led by Habre's younger second in command, Goukouni Guddei, who agreed to release the Claustres. He appeared with them at a press conference in Tripoli on January 31, 1977, the date of their release, and praised Qaddafi's efforts. 1891

April 22, 1974—West Germany—Two Palestinian terrorists in West Berlin were convicted of plotting to bomb the office of El Al, the police registration office for foreigners, a hotel, and a Jewish-owned nightclub. They were released on June 9, 1974, after West Berlin authorities received threats that other terrorists would attack the World Cup soccer matches in West Berlin, as well as at other locations within West Germany, if the two were not released. The two were flown to Egypt. 1892

April 22, 1974—Puerto Rico—A bomb exploded outside the Argentine consulate in Guaynabo during the evening, causing no injuries. Damage was estimated at $5,000. 1893

April 23, 1974—Italy—A bomb went off at the Lecco Socialist party headquarters, destroying two adjacent shops and shattering windows for three hundred yards. Another bomb damaged the main support pillar in a three-story building housing a Milan tax office. In Lecco, leaflets were found signed "Group for the Black Order, Mishima Section." After a telephone call, leaflets signed by the same group were found in a Milan telephone booth. Yukio Mishima, a Japanese writer, led a paramilitary nationalist group until his suicide.

April 23, 1974—Puerto Rico—The Venezuelan consul reported to Guaynabo police that he had received a telephone call during the morning from a Spanish-speaking person who warned that the consulate would be bombed next. The Argentine consul suggested to Puerto Rican police that "anti-Castro elements" were responsible for the recent bombing and threats because Argentina and Venezuela had recently signed a Cuban trade agreement. 1894

April 23, 1974—Thailand—Two missionary nurses, one Dutch and one from New Zealand, who had been treating lepers in a Moslem village about five hundred miles south of Bangkok were kidnapped by four armed Moslem members of the Pattani Liberation Front, which demanded a ransom of 10 million baht ($500,000), a halt to Israeli aggression against Palestinians and Arab countries, a halt to U.S. and U.K. military and economic aid to Thailand, and an end to Thai government "persecution" of the people of Pattani and legalization of their quest for independence. Two bodies found on March 20, 1975, in southern Thailand were believed to be the remains of the nurses. 1895

April 24, 1974—Yemen—A large explosive device exploded under an unoccupied taxi that had been driven into the midst of several cars belonging to chiefs of diplomatic missions who were attending an evening film showing at the North Korean embassy in Sana. There was some property damage, and one Yemeni official was slightly injured. 1896

April 24, 1974—Peru—An unexploded bomb was found in the bathroom of the Arequipa USIS Binational Center in Lima. 1897

April 26, 1974—Ireland—Bridget Rose Dugdale and four other armed men stole nineteen paintings valued at $19.2 million from the home of Sir Alfred Beit, a British millionaire. A week after the attack, a letter was received demanding the transfer of four convicted IRA members, Dolours and Marion Price, Hugh Tenny, and Gerald Kelly, from England to Ulster jails. It also demanded a $1.2 million cash ransom by May 14, threatening the destruction of the paintings. The paintings were recovered unharmed on May 3. Dugdale, after her arrest, was sentenced to nine years. On October 3, 1975, two IRA terrorists kidnapped a Dutch businessman, demanding the release of Dugdale and two others. The Irish police refused to negotiate. 1898

April 30, 1974—El Salvador—Four gunmen claiming to be members of the People's Revolutionary Army allowed a watchman to take his child out of the building before planting a bomb that destroyed the offices of the Chilean embassy in San Salvador. No injuries were reported, and the terrorists escaped after the attack. 1899

May 1, 1974—United States—Without prior warning, a bomb exploded in a public locker in the international arrivals terminal for Alitalia and SAS Airlines at JFK International Airport in New York, injuring 2 airline employees among the 115 people in the terminal. The Alitalia flight to Rome was rescheduled. 1900

May 1, 1974—Lebanon—The Organization of Arab Nationalist Youth for the Liberation of Palestine claimed credit for a dynamite blast that damaged the Tapline telemetering station in Maysat, two kilometers west of the Hasbani River in the vicinity of the Israeli border. The Lebanese army extinguished the resulting fire, which had no effect on pipeline operations. 1901

May 3, 1974—France—Balthazar Angel Suarez, manager of the Paris branch of the Bank of Bilbao, was kidnapped by three individuals as he was about to get into his car in the suburb of Neuilly. The Iberian Liberation Movement claimed responsibility, demanding the release of two colleagues in Spanish prisons. The International Revolutionary Action Group (GARI), which appeared to be affiliated with the MIL, also claimed credit, demanding the release of political prisoners in Spain, including Santiago Soler Amigo, an MIL member said to be in poor health, and publication of an anarchist communiqué in Spanish newspapers. Suarez was freed on May 21 after the payment of 3 million francs ($621,000). Police in Barcelona announced the arrest of eight suspects on July 7. The ransom was later recovered. 1902

May 3, 1974—United States—The Indian Point licensed nuclear facility of the Consolidated Edison Company received a bomb threat.

May 3, 1974—Argentina—Eleven bombs caused substantial damage to sales outlets for foreign cars in greater Buenos Aires during the early morning hours, following a strident speech by Juan Perón on May 1. No injuries were reported in the bombings, whose targets may have been chosen as symbols of foreign influence. 1903–1913

May 4, 1974—United Kingdom—A bomb placed on the window sill of a London house adjacent to the Cuban embassy was detonated by means of a safety fuse giving a three-minute delay. The blast caused only minor damage and no injuries. An anonymous telephone call to a Miami newspaper credited the FLNC with the attack. 1914

May 7, 1974—Haiti—A bomb that had been shipped in a fertilizer package addressed to the brother of the Haitian minister of interior and shipped by air cargo from Miami exploded at Port-au-Prince airport, causing extensive damage to the Pan Am cargo facility but no injuries. A second parcel bomb addressed to an officer of the presidential guard was discovered at the same facility and placed in safekeeping. On June 6, 1974, a Cuban exile residing in Florida was arrested in connection with the letter bombs. 1915–1916

May 8, 1974—Lebanon—An explosive device placed by the Lebanese Socialist Revolutionary Movement (Shibbu Gang) against the outside of the reinforced concrete wall of the USIS Regional Service Center in Beirut blew an eighteen- by twenty-four-inch hole in the wall. The shaped plastic charge did not cause any major damage to the printing presses, and no injuries were reported. 1917

May 11, 1974—Colombia—An Avianca B727 flying from Pereira to Bogotá with ninety-four persons on board was hijacked by Carlos A. Tabares, Jorge E. Avila Campos, and Pedro J. Rodriguez Hernandez, who used pistols and grenades, along with what they claimed to be a bomb, to force the pilot to fly to Bogotá, where they released twenty-six passengers. The plane flew to Cali, Pereira, and back to Bogotá after several airports refused to allow the plane to land during its seventeen-hour flight. The hijackers demanded a flight to Cuba and 8 million pesos (approximately $317,300), but officials refused to pay the ransom. Police disguised as mechanics at El Dorado airport stormed the plane, killing one hijacker and capturing the other two, one of whom was wounded in the leg. Six others were reported injured. 5434

May 14, 1974—Mexico—Two FLNC bombs almost completely destroyed the Mérida offices of the Cuban consulate and caused serious damage to the residence of the Cuban consul. A third bomb was found at the building. Police believed the bombs were thrown. 1918

May 14, 1974—United States—A possible intrusion took place at the Nike-Hercules missile site near Woodstock, Maryland. A guard inside the perimeter gate and a sentry dog handler claimed to have noted an intruder near the warhead building. The *Washington Post* reported, "Exclusion lights were turned on at the same time that the site's alert force was called into action. The primary alarm system was not tripped, however, and the alert force found no evidence of intrusion or forcible entry into the warhead building." A Pentagon spokesman said that no indication of sabotage or missing items was found.

May 15, 1974—Israel—Three members of the PDFLP crossed the Lebanese border into Israel where they attacked a van bringing Arab women home from work, killing two and injuring one. They then entered the town of Maalot, bursting into the apartment of Yosef Cohen, killing three of the family members. A deaf-mute child escaped because he had hidden and was unable to make a sound. The neighbors sounded an alarm, but there were no troops or effective police forces in the small border town. An officer in a neighboring city attributed the cry for help as hysteria and ignored it. The terrorists moved on to a nearby school, where they shot a janitor and then herded over ninety schoolchildren from their dormitories, kicking and clubbing them. Three adults and seventeen children escaped through windows. Later that morning, the commandos sent out a female hostage with the demands for the release of twenty-three Arab prisoners by 6 P.M. They demanded that the prisoners go to Damascus or Cyprus with Francis Hure, French ambassador to Israel, and Red Cross representatives, or they would blow up the school. Israeli officials said they agreed to the demands. Defense Minister Moshe Dayan and Army Chief of Staff Lieutenant General Mordechai Gur arrived to direct rescue operations. The terrorists demanded that Hure and Ion Covaci, Rumania's ambassador, act as mediators. They were to give the terrorists a code word indicating that the prisoners had arrived, at which time half the hostages would be released. The terrorists planned to fly to an Arab capital, preferably Damascus, with Covaci and the rest of the hostages. After the terrorists refused to extend their deadline, the Israelis stormed the building.

Apparently the prisoners, including Kozo Okamoto (see incident 1056), had been taken out of their cells in anticipation of their being traded for the hostages when the negotiations broke down. The Israelis decided to attack within half an hour of the deadline. One terrorist was shot as he ran to detonate an explosive, and the two others fired on the children before they died, machine guns in hand. Sixteen of the children were killed immediately, and five of the seventy injured children died later. One of the Israeli commandos also was killed in the raid. Premier Golda Meir promised revenge for the attack, and on May 16 Israeli jets attacked guerrilla camps at Ein el Halweh and Nabatieh in southern Lebanon. Some reports said that twenty-one were killed and 134 wounded. Later PDFLP leader Naif Hawatmeh claimed that the raid was designed to prevent peace negotiations, which would return the West Bank of the Jordan to the kingdom of Jordan. 1919

May 15, 1974—Israel—Police defused three Soviet-made rockets minutes before they were set to go off. One had been aimed at the Wailing Wall. 1920

May 17, 1974—United States—The Indian Point 1 licensed nuclear facility of Consolidated Edison Company received a bomb threat.

May 17, 1974—Ireland—Three car bombs exploded simultaneously and without warning in downtown Dublin at 5:30 P.M. during the rush hour, killing twenty-three persons immediately, with two more dying later from injuries. One hundred eighty were reported injured. The cars had been stolen or hijacked in Northern Ireland and driven across the border. The IRA and UDA denied responsibility. At 6 P.M., a bomb exploded in front of a bar in Monaghan, eighty miles north of Dublin, killing five and injuring more than twenty. On June 25, a new Protestant group, the Young Militants Association, claimed credit, warning that it would retaliate in Eire for any IRA bombings in Northern Ireland. 1921-1924

May 19, 1974—United Kingdom—A one-hundred-pound IRA bomb exploded in a public parking garage at Heathrow Airport near the British

European Airways terminal, damaging fifty cars and injuring three people, including an American tourist. Fifteen minutes earlier, a man using an IRA code word had telephoned British authorities to warn of the blast. Several flights were cancelled. 1925

May 22, 1974—Belgium and Netherlands—A stolen automobile loaded with jerrycans of gasoline and bottles of butane gas exploded outside the Iberian Airlines office in downtown Brussels, injuring two people and heavily damaging the building, which also houses the First National Bank and the U.S.-owned Westbury Hotel. Cars containing similar explosive devices were discovered and disarmed by Belgian police in front of Iberian Airlines offices in Liège and Antwerp, and a similar device was found in the Netherlands. Based upon pamphlets found at similar subsequent incidents, as well as the bombings' timing, which coincided with the arrival in Brussels of a Spanish parliamentary group, Belgian authorities believed GARI to be responsible. 1926-1929.

May 22, 1974—Italy—A bomb that exploded in the courtyard of the Albanian embassy in Rome caused serious damage. Three more bombs were found and dismantled. 1930

May 22, 1974—Israel—Israeli forces killed an infiltrator near the Lebanese border and killed six more the next day who had crossed the Syrian lines into the Golan Heights. Questioning of two PDFLP guerrillas who had been captured earlier led to the interceptions. The duo said they were to take civilian hostages at the Ein Gev and Haon kibbutzim near the Sea of Galilee and demand the release of thirty terrorists held in Israeli jails and the return of the bodies of the trio killed at Maalot on May 15. 1931

May 22, 1974—United States—An explosive device mailed and delivered to the Peruvian embassy in a package was discovered and neutralized by the Washington, D.C., metropolitan police bomb squad. A nineteen-year-old Maryland resident responsible for the attempt surrendered to authorities on June 21, 1974, and was placed in confinement at a local hospital for mental observation. 1932

May 23, 1974—United States—A Wall Street general aviation Bell 206A Jet Ranger Helicopter with three persons on board at the Thirty-fourth Street heliport in New York City was hijacked when David F. Kamaiko took the aircraft refueler hostage, forced his way on board the helicopter, and forced the pilot to fly to a number of locations before landing on the Pan Am building. Upon landing, the white hijacker, who was born in New York City on July 11, 1952, shot the pilot, who was attempting to escape. The hostage then struggled with the hijacker, who had demanded that $2 million be delivered to him by a bikini-clad woman so that he could buy guns for the JDL. Police rushed the helicopter and captured the hijacker. He was indicted on May 28, 1974, by a federal grand jury in the southern district of New York, where he was charged with aircraft piracy and kidnapping. The prosecution said that a decision to prosecute would be made pending a one-year psychiatric treatment beginning on December 30, 1974. Kamaiko was examined at Bellevue Hospital where, according to the U.S. attorney's office in Manhattan, he was found competent to stand trial. He was released in $50,000 bail into the care of his parents. He next underwent an examination at St. Vincent's Hospital in Harrison, New York, where doctors were to determine his sanity during the hijacking attempt. Some reports indicated that Kamaiko had been armed with two guns during his attack. 5435

May 23, 1974—United States—Acting Attorney General Richard G. Kleindienst announced the arrest of Mark I. Binsky, David Levine, Robert E. Fine, and Ezra S. Gindi at the Lido Beach Jewish Center on Long Island after Nassau County police received a telephone tip. The group was assembling bombs to be placed at the residence of the Soviet U.N. mission in Glen Cove, New York. The four JDL members were held without bail on state and federal charges of conspiracy and bomb possession. Directions to Glen Cove were found in their possession. 1933

May 27, 1974—Argentina—A U.S. citizen was robbed of $52,000 in currency and valuables by the ERP in Buenos Aires. 1934

May 27, 1974—Eritrea—Four members of the ELF carrying rifles and machine guns attacked the American Evangelical Mission Hospital at Ghinda, near Asmara, kidnapping two nurses, one a pregnant American citizen, Debbie Dortzbach, and the other a fifty-two-year-old Dutch nurse, Anna Strikwerda. The Dutch nurse was killed by her abductors shortly after they left the scene of the noon attack. Her body, with a gunshot wound in the forehead, was found in a nearby valley. The ELF later claimed that they had intended to kidnap the head of the mission to obtain medicines and demanded the provision of medicines as well as supplies for Dortzbach, who was held for a time with Tenneco employees who had been kidnapped by the ELF. Through a series of notes to members of the mission, including Dortzbach's husband (who also received letters from his wife), the ELF demanded $5,000 worth of cholera medicines (a cholera epidemic had broken out in the area), $5,000 worth of malaria medicines, five Tigrinya typewriters, two English typewriters, two duplicators, seven battery microphones, $75,000, and the publication and broadcast of an ELF message noting the ELF's sorrow over the death of Strikwerda. The mission personnel, negotiating through a local intermediary, rejected the group's demands. The ELF lowered their demands to $12,500 cash and medicines but finally decided to release Dortzbach to a Muslim sheikh's custody on June 22. One of her captors was reported shot in battle in September 1974. 1935

May 28, 1974—Lebanon—A small explosive went off at the USIS John F. Kennedy Center's Library and Cultural Center in Beirut, causing minor injuries to three local employees and some damage to the installation. The Revolutionary Arab Youth Organization claimed credit. Several terrorists were sentenced to prison for the bombing in May 1975. 1936

May 28, 1974—Italy—A bomb timed to explode at an antifascist meeting in Brescia killed eight and injured ninety-five.

May 29, 1974—Italy—Gasoline bombs were thrown at the Milan offices of Iberia Airlines. 1937

May 29, 1974—United States—The Calvert Cliffs 1 licensed nuclear facility of the Baltimore Gas and Electric Company received a bomb threat.

May 29, 1974—West Germany—A homemade bomb consisting of a potassium chlorate mixture packed in a Nescafé tin exploded in the entrance of the Japan Airlines office in West Berlin, damaging a glass door and some of the office furniture. Two pieces of paper found at the scene credited SOLO as the attacker. It is believed that this referred to the Sons of the Occupied Land Organization, the name used by the group that hijacked a JAL plane in July 1973 and has PFLP connections (see incident 1595). 1938

May 30, 1974—United States—The licensed nuclear facility of the Connecticut Yankee Atomic Power Company at Haddam Neck received a bomb threat.

June 1974—Guatemala—The Nicaraguan consulate was bombed. 1939

June 1974—United States—According to reports by the BDM Corporation, "A nuclear device (Strontium 90) used to measure the density of roadbeds was stolen near Deerfield Beach, Florida. . . .The device was later recovered on a freeway overpass where an examination indicated that it had been tampered with. According to Avery Sedell of the Department of Transportation, 'there is a strong possibility that whoever took it may have received enough exposure to prove fatal. It looks as if they worked on it for quite a while.' Radiation from the device had the potential of causing bone cancer to the thieves." BDM also reported "possible sabotage . . .at the Zion nuclear power plant in Illinois during the summer. . . .There had been repeated failures of a single valve, and other valves and switches had been found in incorrect positions, which a

Consolidated Edison spokesman called 'suspicious.' Jerry Standbrough, nuclear news coordinator for the company, said in an interview, 'it's the kind of thing you would expect a disgruntled employee to do for nuisance value.' He claimed that none of the incidents endangered the safety of the plant. Several bomb threats have also been received by the plant. . . .According to Jon Strasma, an AEC official, the valve failures, if intentional, could only have been caused by a company employee.''

June 1974—Ethiopia—The ELF shot a German motorist on a local road. 1940

June 1, 1974—Haiti—A bomb in a trunk that had been shipped on an Air France flight from Miami exploded in a baggage room at the Port-au-Prince airport, injuring a policeman. The trunk was shipped by a man who had a ticket for the flight but did not board the aircraft. 1941

June 2, 1974—Greece—Athens police removed two unexploded bombs that had been placed next to a wheel of vehicles owned by two U.S. servicemen and parked overnight near their residences. According to Paris and London wire services, an anonymous caller said that the Popular Liberation Organized Army was responsible, while another caller claimed credit for the LAOS-11. It appeared that these initials stood for Popular Resistance Sabotage Groups, followed by a number. It was reported that these groups were established by the Panhellenic Antidictatorial Movement. 1942-1943

June 3, 1974—Argentina—José Chohelo, Peugeot's representative in Buenos Aires, was kidnapped and released on June 11 after a ransom of $200,000 was paid. 1944

June 4, 1974—Ethiopia—Eritrean rebels kidnapped an Italian farmer from his Eritrean plantation. 1945

June 4, 1974—Israel—Two Arab terrorists were captured by Israeli police, apparently on a mission to kill persons at random in Haifa. The duo, Israeli citizens from Galilee, had crossed the Lebanese border the previous day but were arrested after a suspicious taxi driver tipped off police. 1946

June 5, 1974—United States—Two unidentified individuals suspected of being anti-Duvalier Haitian exiles threw a bomb on board a Haitian navy patrol boat drydocked at Ryder Yacht Basin in Miami. 1947

June 9, 1974—West Germany—After West Berlin authorities received threats that terrorists would attack the World Cup soccer matches, as well as other locations in West Germany, two Palestinians who were convicted of plotting to blow up the West Berlin office of El Al and other locations (see incident 1892) were released. 1948

June 11, 1974—United States—Two incendiary bombs exploded within five minutes of each other shortly after 2 A.M., causing slight damage and work delay at the construction site for a Soviet residential complex in Riverdale, New York. Reuters and United Press International received anonymous calls claiming that this was a warning to the Soviet Union to allow Soviet Jews to emigrate. 1949

June 12, 1974—Greece—In Athens, Greek army explosives experts disarmed and safely removed an unexploded time bomb that had been placed by LAOS-11 underneath a car belonging to a senior U.S. Navy officer. 1950

June 12, 1974—West Germany—A bomb exploded on the second floor of the Chilean consulate in West Berlin, causing considerable damage to the consulate's offices and two other floors in the building. Four German nationals living in the buildings, including the honorary consul, were slightly injured. In a letter to the German news service DPA in Düsseldorf, the Revolutionary Cell claimed credit for the blast, which it said was to publicize "terrorism under which the people of Chile live." 1951

June 13, 1974—United States—The Gulf Oil offices in Pittsburgh were bombed, causing $450,000 damage. The Weather Underground claimed that the bombing was in protest of Gulf's fomenting a Portuguese war in Angola.

June 13, 1974—West Germany—Five Palestinians planning to attack the World Cup soccer matches, which were opening that day, were arrested by West German police. It was reported that one of the terrorists was a student in Saarbrücken who intended to attack the Israeli embassy in Bonn, El Al aircraft, and an El Al office. It appeared that two of the Arabs had intended to leave for Scandinavia when they were arrested in Hamburg. 1952

June 13, 1974—Israel—Four PFLP-GC members slipped across the Lebanese border and attacked the village of Shamir, six miles away. They killed a New Zealand woman volunteer worker and wounded a man leaving a dining hall. Six armed male settlers killed one attacker. The surviving trio ran into a factory building and fired on the Israelis. They blew themselves up with grenades and explosives after shooting two more women to death inside the building. Two other men were reported wounded in the battle. The group carried leaflets demanding the release of one hundred prisoners, including Kozo Okamoto (see incident 1056), within six hours. Israel carried out retaliatory air strikes against Palestinian camps in Lebanon, killing one hundred and wounding two hundred. Libya's Colonel Muammar Qaddafi informed the PLO's Yasir Arafat in a June 24 cable that Libya "places all its capabilities at your disposal." In Beirut, the terrorist group announced that the attack was timed to coincide with the beginning of the Middle Eastern tour of President Nixon. 1953

June 14, 1974—United States—Two FALN bombs exploded in Chicago. 1954-1955

June 15, 1974—United States—A man displayed a gun and a knife and spoke incoherently on a flight from Columbus, Georgia, to Fort Campbell, Kentucky. The man, who had chartered the small aircraft, was apprehended when the plane landed. 5436

June 15, 1974—United Kingdom—Rubens's "The Adoration of the Magi," one of the world's most valuable paintings, was vandalized by an unknown individual who scratched the letters "IRA" across its face. The seventeenth-century painting, hanging in the King's College chapel of Cambridge University, was bought at auction in 1959 for $660,000 and has since been appraised by some experts at $4 million. 1956

June 17, 1974—Argentina—German-born Herbert Pilz, an executive of Mercedes Benz, was kidnapped on his way to the company's plant in the southern suburbs of Buenos Aires, presumably by left-wing guerrillas. He was released unharmed on July 10 and immediately left the country for West Germany. Mercedes spokesmen claimed a large ransom had been paid. 1957

June 17, 1974—United Kingdom—A twenty-pound IRA bomb injured eleven and caused damage to Westminster Hall, the oldest and most historic part of the House of Commons in London. Firemen spent eight hours dousing the flames from a gas main that had burst as a result of the bomb blast. The British Press Association received a warning six minutes before by an individual using the IRA code word. According to press accounts, the Belfast and Dublin leaders of the IRA denied prior knowledge of the details of the attack and claim they had no part in its planning. They indicated that the London IRA unit was responsible. 1958

June 18, 1974—Switzerland—A powerful bomb damaged the Zurich branch of the U.S.-owned Manufacturers Hanover Trust but caused no injuries. Swiss police arrested members of the Krause Group in connection with the blast. 1959

June 19, 24, 1974—Argentina—A series of bombs that exploded between 6 P.M. and midnight on the evenings of June 19 and 24 damaged the offices of business establishments, most of them foreign owned. Among those attacked were two branches of the First National City Bank, two branches of the Bank of Boston, a branch of the Bank of America, a Coca-Cola warehouse, Eveready offices, a Ford showroom, and offices of Parke-Davis and Xerox. Three branch offices of the Bank of London were also bombed. The blasts caused material damage but no injuries. 1960-1972

June 24, 1974—Yugoslavia—A bomb composed of antitank shells exploded in the Skopje office of the French Cultural Center's director in the evening, after the center had been closed. The explosion caused serious damage but no injuries. 1973

June 25, 1974—Israel—After landing on the coast of Israel, three Fatah members killed four and wounded eight before being killed in a gun battle with Israeli troops in a raid on a Nahariya apartment house four miles south of Lebanon.
A small boat was found beached south of Nahariya, indicating that the terrorists had come from Lebanon. An armed volunteer guard fired at the night raiders. Police and troops surrounded an apartment house held by the guerrillas and quickly stormed it, killing the three Palestinians, who were armed with guns and grenades. Some reports claim that in response to a demand to surrender, the terrorists killed a woman and her two children. In the battle, one Israeli soldier was killed and six others were wounded. Fatah claimed credit in Baghdad the same day, while the Israelis retaliated by shelling Palestinian targets in southern Lebanon. On July 8, Israeli naval commandos raided the southern Lebanese ports of Ras a-Shak, Saida, and Tyre, destroying thirty fishing boats believed to be used to smuggle terrorists into Israel. 1974

June 25, 1974—Argentina—At 2:30 A.M., a small truck passed in front of the U.S. embassy chancery in Buenos Aires. Individuals inside the vehicle fired machine guns on an Argentinian police patrol car protecting the chancery and then fled. The police car sustained bullet hits, but no police were injured. 1975

June 26, 1974—United States—A prisoner identified as Edwin Claude Rowell, a white male for whom the FAA profile was inapplicable and who was born in Le Compte, Louisiana, on November 1, 1950, was being transported in an Air Charter Piper Commanche from Alexandria, Louisiana, to Angola, Louisiana, in the custody of a deputy sheriff when he produced a pistol and diverted the plane to Hammond, Louisiana. Rowell fled to a wooded area after handcuffing the deputy and the pilot to a tree. He was captured an hour later about one and a half miles from the plane. He allegedly received his weapon from his girl friend at his trial. He was sentenced by the state on April 14, 1975,

462   June 27, 1974

to ten years' imprisonment for aggravated kidnapping. The sentence was to be served in addition to thirty-four years for previous crimes. 5437

June 27, 1974—Israel—Rabbi Meir Kahane was convicted by a Jerusalem district court of trying to harm Israeli-U.S. relations by conspiring to bomb foreign embassies in Washington, D.C. He was given a two-year suspended sentence the next day but was acquitted of charges of conspiracy to murder and kidnap Soviet and Arab diplomats in the United States Kahane confessed he had urged American JDL members to bomb the Soviet and Iraqi embassies in Washington and New York financial institutions with Soviet ties. 1976

June 27, 1974—United States—Three men robbed an Ashland, Montana, bank and used a Big Horn Airways Cessna 172 they had chartered as a getaway vehicle. The hijackers were identified as having been born in Hardin, Montana, with the FAA profile being inapplicable in this case. Douglas Arthur Kirkaldie was an Oriental born on July 11, 1950; William Henry Conrad Beck was a white born on April 13, 1954; and Stanley Dean Naylor, also white, was born on March 18, 1953. While in the air, the pilot agreed to change the plane's course from its Ashland, Montana, route to Sheridan, Wyoming, but when he started to report the change of his flight plan, the microphone was taken from him and guns were pointed at him. Upon landing at Yellowtail Dam in Montana, the pilot was bound and left in the plane. Two of the hijackers were captured an hour later forty-five miles from the landing area. Kirkaldie was captured on July 6, 1974, in Janesville, Wyoming. Naylor and Beck were sentenced to twenty years for bank robbery on July 16, 1974, and July 23, 1974, respectively. Their sentences were reduced to eight years under the Youth Correction Act on October 21, 1974, and October 22, 1974, respectively. Kirkaldie was sentenced on November 11, 1974, to twenty years for bank robbery and interference with a crew member. 5438

July 3, 1974—Lebanon—A columnist and coeditor of *An-Nahar* was kidnapped in Beirut. The leader of the PLO, Yasir Arafat, cooperated in the search. The abductee was released five days later. Three men—a Lebanese, a Syrian, and a Palestinian—were arrested in connection with the incident. 1977

July 3, 1974—France—A plastic bomb exploded in front of the Cuban embassy in Paris, demolishing the door frame and furnishings in the foyer and knocking out windows in neighboring buildings. No injuries were reported. The FLNC phoned a Miami newspaper to claim credit. 1978

July 4, 1974—United Kingdom—Large lumps of metal were discovered behind the turbofan engine of a Nigerian Airways B707 in London Airport. 1979

July 6, 1974—United States—A police sergeant in Compton, California, reported the theft of ninety-six M-16 rifles with 3,360 rounds of ammunition, machine guns, grenades, launchers, smoke and riot grenades, and gas masks from the National Guard Armory.

July 15, 1974—United States—The Farley licensed nuclear facility of the Alabama Power Company received a bomb threat.

July 15, 1974—Japan—A JAL DC8 flying from Osaka to Tokyo with eighty-four passengers and five crew members was hijacked by Akira Iwakoshi, a young Japanese male who belonged to the Japanese Red Army, who was armed with a knife and what he claimed to be a bomb. He held the passengers hostage for more than five hours, demanding the release of imprisoned JRA leader Takaya Shiomi and a plane to take them both to North Korea. After landing in Tokyo and Osaka, the plane flew on for refueling to Nagoya, where the passengers escaped while the hijacker was in the cockpit. Police ran into the plane, where Kwakoshi attempted suicide by cutting his throat. He was arrested before he succeeded. A female purser was slightly injured during the incident. 1980

July 16, 1974—United Kingdom—Two persons were injured when an IRA bomb exploded in a downtown Manchester building. In Birmingham, a bomb blasted a twenty-story office building but injured no one. Prior to the bombings, a telephone caller used the special code word used in the past by the IRA to identify genuine bomb warnings. 1981-1982

July 16, 1974—France—A series of bombs planted by the GARI destroyed thirteen buses in a parking lot and along the route of the Tour de France bicycle race near Lourdes and Saint-Lary in which Spanish riders competed. 1983

July 17, 1974—Argentina—Machine-gun fire from a passing car was directed at the Buenos Aires home of Juan Courard, an Argentine national and head of the Ford Motor Company in Argentina. One guard was injured in the attack. 1984

July 17, 1974—United Kingdom—A ten-pound bomb exploded at the ground-floor level of the White Tower, the oldest of the thirteen structures comprising the Tower of London. Little damage was done to the building, but part of the cellar armory collection was damaged. The armory was packed with tourists at the time, and one British tourist was killed and forty-one others, including four young U.S. tourists, were injured. Two minutes before the explosion, the *Daily Mirror* received a telephoned warning identifying the IRA-Provisional Wing as responsible. 1985

July 18, 1974—Argentina—David Kraiselburd, a newspaper executive, was kidnapped and later shot to death by persons reputed to have associations with one of the organized guerrilla groups operating in the country.

July 21, 1974—United States—The window of a New York City tourist agency doing business with Yugoslav travel agencies was shattered, and gasoline was poured in the premises and set on fire. The damage was estimated at between $15,000 and $20,000. 1986

July 21, 1974—Lebanon—Four members of the Lebanese Revolutionary Socialist Organization (Shibbu Gang) fired shots at Chilean Ambassador Alfredo Canales Marquis and his wife as they were entering their Beirut apartment in the evening. General Canales was hit by five bullets and was critically injured, but surgeons at the American hospital successfully operated on him. In a communiqué to several Beirut newspapers, the attackers said that they wished to ''underline the unity of the struggle of the peoples of Latin America, Asia and Africa against American imperialism.'' Investigators found a case of anaesthetic in the porter's lodge at the apartment building, indicating that the group had intended to kidnap the general but changed their plans when his wife screamed. 1987

July 22, 1974—United States—A man armed with a starter's pistol held a cab driver hostage in his taxi at Pittsburgh's airport and demanded that an aircraft take him to Florida. Police surrounded the vehicle and subsequently subdued and arrested the man. 5439

July 22, 1974—United States—The pleasure boat *Spook* was hijacked by Clifford Thomas and his wife Patrice Ann McRary with their two children. The captain of the boat, Earl Werner Widner, and a crew member, Molly Christine de Witt, were forced to take the seajackers to Havana after leaving Key West. The captain and one of the crew members were allowed to return, and the four seajackers were turned over to competent courts to be tried in accordance with Cuban law for the most severely penalized offense in accordance with the acts they had committed.

July 23, 1974—United States—A pipe bomb inside the basement stairwell of the French military materiel mission in Washington, D.C., exploded, causing minor damage. The two persons inside the building at the time of the blast were not injured. Local newspapers speculated that the bomb may have been intended for the Israeli or Cypriot embassies, both of which are located within two blocks of the French mission. It was also suggested that the building housing the offices of the Chilean military and naval attachés, located five doors away, was the intended target. 1988

July 23, 1974—Northern Ireland—A telephone call was received warning that a bomb was aboard a British Airways Trident en route between Belfast and London. The aircraft made an emergency landing at Manchester with its eighty-five passengers. The bomb, found under a seat in the cabin, had failed to detonate. 1989

July 23, 1974—Argentina—Erich Breuss, an Austrian national and executive of Argentina's largest steel manufacturing firm, Acindar, was kidnapped on his way to work in Rosario by four men posing as provincial policemen. The ERP claimed credit. 1990

July 24, 1974—United States—The San Onofre licensed nuclear facility of the Southern California Edison Company received a bomb threat.

July 24, 1974—Colombia—An Avianca B727 flying between Pereira and Medellín was hijacked by a couple, with their infant, who forced the pilot to land at Cali, where the emergency doors were opened and 128 passengers escaped. The hijackers, identified as Luis Eduardo Martinez Rusinke (who participated in the hijacking of a plane on May 20, 1969; see incident 5150) and Mercedes Forero de Suarez, demanded the release of several political prisoners and $2 million. A policeman disguised as a mechanic boarded the aircraft and shot Martinez three times when he attempted to resist capture. The hijacker's wife, who was sentenced to prison in Colombia, allegedly brought the pistol on board in her brassiere. Martinez died in a hospital an hour later. Two days before, Cuba and Colombia had signed an agreement to curb air and maritime piracy and similar crimes. 5440

July 25, 1974—France—No one was injured when a homemade bomb exploded in front of a Spanish bank in Nîmes. Spanish anarchists were suspected. 1991

July 26, 1974—Puerto Rico—A bomb at the Peruvian consulate in San Juan destroyed two cars and damaged the consulate building. The Associated Press in Miami received a call claiming credit for the Cuban exile group M-7. 1992

July 26, 1974—United Kingdom—A bomb exploded in a multilevel parking lot at London's Heathrow Airport, damaging several cars but causing no injuries.

July 26, 1974—France—A French customs inspector arrested Furuya Yutaka (also known as Yoshiaki Yamada and Suzuki Furuya) who had arrived at Orly from Beirut. It appeared that he was a courier from Fusako Shigenobu and her PFLP colleagues and that he was to deliver $10,000 in counterfeit bills and messages to the JRA network in Europe. In the courier's briefcase were a few rolls of 35-mm film, along with three forged passports: Taiwanese, American, and Japanese. The false bottom of his briefcase contained several coded letters, one of which was translated by the Japanese, to whom it had been turned over, as "Little Miss Full Moon, I am ill with desire for you. Let me embrace your beautiful body again. Your love slave. Suzuki!" The note, written in Japanese on perfumed rice paper, appeared to be intended for Mariko Yamamoto, who ran a Japanese shop in Avenue de l'Opera and who was the JRA contact point in Paris. Furuya's arrest was not announced for several days, and Yamamoto's flat was put under surveillance. Among her visitors was Takahashi Taketomo, the head of the JRA in Paris. Within a week, the flats of Yamamoto and two others were raided, and eleven Japanese were arrested. Eight of them were expelled from France, with six of them returning to Japan. The other two were freed because they had allowed their homes to be used as meeting places, although they had not necessarily known what the meetings were about. The eight were expelled because intention alone under French law is not an indictable offense. Furuya was charged with issuing false passports. Taketomo said that his eventual destination was Poland, but he asked to be flown to Amsterdam, where a JRA cell would take over the French embassy in a few months and obtain the release of Furuya. Over one hundred people had been interrogated in the investigation, including a JRA film critic, a sociology professor, and individuals with ties to the Curiel apparatus, a Paris-based leftist group that has aided scores of revolutionary organizations.

It was later learned that Furuya was one of the JRA members who attacked the Singapore refinery (see incident 1806) and that his messages, tied in with one that Taketomo attempted to swallow upon his arrest, were parts of a plot to kidnap representatives of Mitsubishi and Marubeni in Düsseldorf, as well as other wealthy Japanese. Their ransoms would be used to finance a general uprising of JRA members in Europe. Yamamoto was found to possess a coded notebook with the addresses of fifty safe houses throughout Europe which could be used in the operations. She was also part of the ten-member VZ58 group, which was named after the type of assault rifle used in the Lod Airport attack (see incident 1056). Taketomo was found to have ties with individuals called Acheme, who furnished him with weapons, and Jean Baptiste, who provided papers and money. Acheme was identified as a Brazilian, Perera Carvalho, who had never been arrested and was eventually discovered to have ties to Carlos, the famed Venezuelan terrorist. Jean Baptiste was a Frenchman, André Haverman, a photographic microfilmer. He was arrested and charged with forgery and the use of forged documents but was then released. The attack was code named "Operation Translation." 1993

July 28, 1974—France—Three policemen in Toulouse were injured when a bomb exploded on the roof of a covered playground near the Spanish consulate. Spanish anarchists were suspected. 1994

July 30, 1974—Lebanon—Four Palestinian guerrillas and a civilian were killed in Dekwaneh, a Beirut suburb, in a battle between PLO members and the right-wing Falange party.

August 1974—Angola—A lone male hijacked a light charter aircraft on a domestic flight within Angola and forced the pilot to fly to South-West Africa (Namibia), where he turned himself over to South African authorities. 5441

August 1974—United States—According to the BDM Corporation, "9 radio-active radium needles were stolen from Scenic General Hospital in California. . . . The theft was not discovered until November, when hospital employees planned to turn them over to federal authorities for disposal. The theft was apparently perpetrated by a night porter at the hospital, who was found in possession of 7 of the needles. Another needle was found in the possession of an uncle of the porter, and a 9th needle was still missing. . . . The police had not learned the motive for the theft, but stated it was elaborately planned. It included the removal of lead blocks which surrounded the needles in storage, one at a time, over a period of several days to reduce the container's weight so it could be easily carried from the hospital.''

August 1974—France—The Soldier of the Algerian Opposition movement claimed credit for a bombing that damaged the offices of the Algerian National Tourist Bureau in Paris. 1995

August 2, 1974—Lebanon—A man was observed leaving a briefcase at the Pan Am office in Beirut and then departing quickly. The briefcase contained a dynamite bomb, which experts defused. The man was subsequently arrested. 1996

August 3, 1974—France—Bombs in two small cars and a minibus parked outside the offices of two anti-Arab newspapers, *L'Aurore* and *Minute*, and a welfare organization, the United Jewish Social Fund, exploded within minutes of each other, injuring two people. Police defused a fourth bomb outside the office of the national television network. Police arrested the man who rented the three vehicles from the same touring agency. On August 5, the PFLP claimed responsibility in the name of Commando Muhammad Boudia, saying that the papers "have consciously made themselves into instruments of criminal actions by Israeli secret agents.'' It was rumored that Carlos, the famed Venezuelan terrorist, was linked to the explosions because detailed diagrams of all three offices, carefully annotated, were found among his papers when his apartment was raided in 1975. 1997-2000

August 4, 1974—Peru—At around 10 P.M., a bomb caused damage in the area of the French embassy in Lima on Jiron Lopez 234. 2001

August 4, 1974—Italy—The Ordine Nero (Black Order) claimed credit for the bombing of a Rome to Munich express train. The bomb exploded as the train emerged from a tunnel between Florence and Bologna, and killed twelve and injured forty-eight. Three men were arrested two days later, and two more were being sought in connection with the attack. The Black Order claimed responsibility in a note on August 5, saying that the bomb was "to demonstrate that we are capable of placing bombs where we want, at any time, in any place." It said that because the government was banning such fascist groups (as was the case of what appeared to be the Black Order's predecessor, the New Order, which was banned in November 1973), it was "bringing Italy under Marxism." It asserted that "the Nazi flag did not die in Berlin in 1945. It still lives for a powerful Fascist and Nazi Italy. Nazism will return for the salvation of a renaissance Italy." 2002

August 5, 1974—Belgium—Bombs exploded during the night in front of three branch offices of the Spanish Bank in Brussels, and one bomb caused slight damage to a Spanish bank in Saint-Gilles. During the morning rush hour in Brussels, a bomb exploded in front of the downtown office of Iberia Airlines, wounding five people. Pamphlets found at one of the banks were signed by GARI. 2003-2007

August 5, 1974—Netherlands—When a suspected bomb at the chancery of the U.S. embassy in The Hague was discovered, a wing of the building was evacuated. Police and a military demolition team detonated the device by use of a secondary charge. 2008

August 5, 1974—Australia—Sydney Airport was evacuated twice after phone calls warned that a bomb was in the airport. Several flights were delayed, but no bomb was found.

August 5, 1974—United States—The New World Liberation Front attempted to bomb an insurance agency in Burlingame, California.

August 6, 1974—France—A bomb was placed in the forward landing gear compartment of an Air Inter Caravelle III (some reports list the plane as a Fokker F27) parked on the ground for the evening at Quimper airport. The bomb exploded, causing damage to the plane but no injuries.

August 6, 1974—Jamaica—A small bomb exploded on the lawns of the Cuban embassy in Kingston in the early morning, causing slight damage but no injuries. Embassy officials claimed that the explosion took place soon after a car slowly passed the gate. 2009

August 6, 1974—Puerto Rico—An explosive device containing nuts and bolts was detonated in the early morning at the front door of the Venezuelan consulate in San Juan, causing extensive damage but no injuries. The Associated Press in Miami received a call that evening from a woman who claimed that the Cuban M-7 organization set the bomb to protest "deals of the Venezuelan government with Cuban Premier Fidel Castro." 2010

August 6, 1974—Argentina—Maurice Kember, an Argentine citizen and president of Inti, a Coca-Cola subsidiary, was kidnapped in front of his Córdoba house as he was leaving for work. He was freed in a gun battle on October 8 in which one of his abductors was killed, two were wounded, and three were captured. A $1.5 million ransom had been demanded. 2011

August 6, 1974—United States—At 8:07 A.M., a bomb exploded inside a coin-operated locker at Satellite II, a building that houses numerous foreign airlines at Los Angeles International Airport. The bomb went off in the Pan Am lobby of the International Carrier Building, killing three persons and injuring thirty-five others. Damage was estimated at $200,000. Three days later, a telephone call received by a news broadcasting company led to the discovery of a cassette recording that claimed that this was the first in a series of planned bombings. The first letter of each location would spell out the name of the Aliens of America. On August 16, another call directed a local newspaper to a second tape, which claimed that a bomb was located in a locker at a bus station. The bomb was recovered by the Los Angeles bomb squad. On August 20, Muharem Kurbegovic, a Yugoslavian immigrant and hydraulic engineer, was arrested and charged in connection with both attacks. On January 20, 1975, he was committed for ninety days to a mental hospital for observation. It was learned that he called himself Isaac Rasim during the bombings. Coworkers reported that he was known as "Mu" and had emigrated from British Columbia in 1967; he had not spoken a word to them since arrival. A psychiatrist had previously diagnosed him as brain damaged and mentally ill after he had sought medical treatment for self-inflicted head injuries. Police claimed that he had set fires at three locations in November 1973. The previous June he had attempted to bomb the car of one of the three commissioners who had denied him a dancing hall license. After setting three more fires on July 4, 1974, he phoned a local radio station, claiming to be a member of the Symbionese Liberation Army and announcing that he would set three more fires. The next day, the individual who came to be known as the Alphabet Bomber said that the Aliens of America would take over the government of the world if the U.S. immigration and naturalization laws were not abolished and if the United States did not deal with the Soviet Union in a more forthright manner. He also threatened in five more taped messages that he would put dangerous nerve gas on postage stamps. His only successful bombing was of the locker at the airport.

August 7, 1974—Israel—The PFLP kidnapped four Druses employed by Israel to build a security fence between Lebanon and Israeli-occupied Golan Heights areas. Israel retaliated by kidnapping six Lebanese civilians who had crossed the border and by conducting air attacks on two villages. 2012

August 7, 1974—United States—A dynamite bomb planted at the U.N. General Assembly building was dismantled by bomb specialists. 2013

August 9, 1974—Japan—A small incendiary device was thrown against the U.S. consulate in Sapporo. The resulting fire was quickly extinguished by a caretaker, and property damage was minimal. 2014

August 10, 1974—Israel—An Israeli naval vessel patroling the coast of Lebanon spotted a rubber dinghy heading south in the Mediterranean and blew it out of the water after Arabs had opened fire. The Israeli military command claimed that the three to five Arabs were bound for a raid on the northern coast of Israel and mentioned that the group that had attacked Nahariya (see incident 1974) had come to Israel in a boat. The dinghy was carrying explosives. 2015

August 11, 1974—United States—The Zion licensed nuclear facility of the Commonwealth Edison Company received a bomb threat.

August 14, 1974—Syria—A bomb exploded near the entrance of the U.S. pavilion at the Damascus International Fair, causing moderate damage to the building and more serious damage to the Skylab exhibit. The building facade was damaged, with all glass windows shattered. Part of the terrazzo tile ramp and cinder block wall built for crowd control was ripped out by the force of the blast, which injured one pavilion guard and a Syrian policeman. The next day, the Arab Communist Organization claimed credit for its first operation. 2016

August 15, 1974—South Korea—President Park Chung Hee's wife was fatally wounded by an assassin's bullet intended for her husband. A seventeen-year-old girl was also killed by a stray bullet during the National Day rally in Seoul. The assassin, Mun Se Kwang, twenty-two, a Korean who had resided in Osaka, Japan, was arrested after being wounded by security guards. South Korean investigators charged that the attempted assassination of President Park had been plotted by the North Korean government. Kwang had been a member of the Osaka branch of the Korean Youth League, an anti-Park organization of Korean residents in Japan. He was reported to have been recruited by North Korean agents in 1972 and assigned to kill Park in November 1973. During his trial, he claimed that he had been ordered to assassinate

Park by Kim Ho Ryon, the leader of the Chosen Soren in Japan. He had received funds from Kim and worked out the assassination plan with him. Another unidentified agent whom Mun had met on board a North Korean cargo ship in Osaka harbor had told him that President Kim Il Sung of North Korea had personally ordered the killing. 2017

August 16, 1974—Peru—Four pieces of shrapnel hit the Cuban embassy in Lima after two bombs exploded at 3:10 A.M. The Soviet embassy in the same district was bombed. 2018-2019

August 16, 1974—United States—The Indian Point licensed nuclear facility of the Consolidated Edison Company received a bomb threat.

August 17, 1974—Italy—The official station wagon of the station manager of the U.S. Rhodes Relay Station was destroyed by fire under circumstances pointing to deliberate sabotage. 2020

August 19, 1974—Canada—The U.S. consul general in Montreal received a telephone threat from an English-speaking male claiming to be of Greek origin saying that he intended to kill someone in the consulate within the week. 2021

August 19, 1974—Cyprus—The U.S. ambassador to Cyprus, Rodger P. Davies, and a Greek Cypriot embassy secretary were shot to death by EOKA-B members during a riot in Nicosia by a group protesting what they claimed to be a pro-Turkish policy of the United States in the Greek-Turkish clash over Cyprus. In the attack against the U.S. embassy and official residence, fire-bombs were thrown at official vehicles, destroying several cars, including that of the defense attaché. Nearly one hundred bullets ripped into Davies's L-shaped office from two angles, leading police to conclude that a conspiracy was evident. His secretary died as she came to his assistance. The office windows were later plated with steel panels. Some reports claimed that American intelligence services knew the identities of the killers one hour after the attack, because a local film crew had taken movies of the demonstration. Three defendants were identified firing automatic weapons, including a machine gun, into the office, while three others were firing in other directions. After years of American pressure, the six suspects were arrested on February 4, 1977. Three of them, Ioannis Ktimatis, a former policeman serving a prison term for illegal possession of firearms, Loizos Savva, a former policeman, and Neoptolemos Leftis, were charged with homicide. Three others, including a lieutenant in the Greek Cypriot National Guard, were accused of crimes, which included the illegal use of firearms, threats of violence, and rioting. All six were identified as belonging to the EOKA-B organization. The first three were arraigned on charges of manslaughter on February 11, 1977. On June 3, a Cypriot court threw out the homicide charges against Greek Cypriots Ktimatis, thirty-nine, and Leftis, fifty, citing lack of evidence. The decision insured that the two would not be asked to testify in court about any links between the gunmen and EOKA-B leaders who might have planned and ordered the assault, as well as held government posts. Two of the other defendants were acquitted, one on a technicality, while the other two were sentenced to a few months in jail after pleading guilty. On June 20, 1977, Ktimatis was convicted of illegal use and possession of firearms, riot, and property damage, while Leftis was convicted of illegal possession of firearms and riot. Ktimatis was liable to a sentence of fifteen years, while Leftis faced a possible eight-year sentence. On June 21, 1977, the court sentenced them to seven and five years, respectively. The press reported that these were considered unexpectedly stiff sentences. 2022

August 23, 1974—France—A plot was discovered to kidnap Don Juan, the exiled father of Prince Juan Carlos, on the sea as his yacht approached Monte Carlo. 2023

August 23, 1974—Netherlands—A Pan Am 707 flying from Amsterdam to New York with 143 passengers made an emergency landing in Scotland after a phone call warned that a bomb was on board. No bomb was found. 2024

August 25, 1974—West Germany—The Commando Muhammad Boudia claimed credit for bombing a Mannheim crane construction factory, causing $2,400 damage but no injuries. The *Beirut Daily Star* reported that the group, which was believed affiliated with the Venezuelan terrorist Carlos, bombed the Korf-owned factory because the owner had invested in an Israeli steelworks two years previously. 2025

August 26, 1974—United States—An explosion was reported in a men's room at Chicago's O'Hare Airport, causing damage but no injuries. An investigation by the bomb squad revealed that one or more U.S. Army firecrackers had been placed on the restroom floor.

August 26, 1974—United States—An incendiary device was detonated in a public area of the Pilgrim licensed nuclear facility of the Boston Edison Company, near Plymouth, Massachusetts.

August 26, 1974—Greece—After a TWA B707 landed at Rome from Athens, a fire was discovered in the aft baggage compartment. The fire was confined to an area near a suitcase containing an explosive device that malfunctioned and caused the fire. 2026

August 26, 1974—West Germany—A homemade bomb placed in front of a window of the Israeli State Travel Office in Frankfurt exploded, causing $20,000 damage to the office and slight damage to two cars parked in front of the office building but no injuries. 2027

August 27, 1974—Argentina—Ricardo Goya, the labor relations manager of the French-owned IKA-Renault Motor Company in Córdoba, was assassinated by a group of FAP men armed with machine guns who blocked his vehicle as he was driving to work. 2028

August 28, 1974—Mexico—The FRAP kidnapped José Guadalupe Zuno Hernandez, the father-in-law of President Luis Echeverria, in Guadalajara. They threatened in an August 30 communiqúe to a Mexico City newspaper to kill him unless the government paid a $1.6 million ransom, released ten political prisoners and flew them to Cuba, and authorized publication of a FRAP manifesto in leading newspapers. The government refused to negotiate. During his incarceration, an interview with Zuno was published in which he praised FRAP leader Lucio Cabanas, said that his treatment by his captors was ''magnificent,'' and criticized the government for being on the side of ''capitalist reaction.'' He was released on September 7 and announced at a press conference that his statements were not made under duress. The government arrested one of the kidnappers on September 3 and fourteen others on September 26. Zuno had been Jalisco State's governor. 2029

August 28, 1974—West Germany—Ninety M-72 A1 light antitank missiles, also known as LAWs, were reported stolen from a U.S. weapons facility in Miesau. One of the weapons was discovered in the hands of a Croatian terrorist group in Zagreb, Yugoslavia, in November 1974. Most of the weapons were recovered. 2030

August 29, 1974—Lebanon—The Arab Communist Organization attacked the headquarters of the American Life Insurance Company in Sidon. 2031

August 31, 1974—United States—An FALN bomb exploded at 12:55 A.M. without warning in Damrosch Park in New York City's Lincoln Center. Except for uprooting a row of hedges at Amsterdam Avenue and Sixty-second Street, the bomb caused no damage. 2032

September 1974—Northern Ireland—IRA gunmen killed a judge and a magistrate within five minutes of each other.

September 1974—United States—One hundred mildly radioactive copper plates were stolen from the Berkeley Lawrence Radiation Laboratory. The plates had been contaminated with cobalt-60 as a result of their recent removal from a cyclotron. The AEC claimed that the plates represented no health hazard to the general public or to the thieves.

September 1974—Lebanon—The Arab Communist Organization robbed a branch of the Banque Libano-Française in Tyre, escaping with 30,000 Lebanese pounds (approximately $68,400). 2033

September 1, 1974—Lebanon—An explosion damaged the Beirut office of Iran Airlines during the night, breaking windows of nearby shops but causing no injuries. It was reported that the time bomb had been planted inside the office the previous day. 2034

September 2, 1974—Greece—A large bomb exploded in the Athens parking lot of the U.S. embassy chancery, killing the two terrorists who were carrying it and causing extensive damage. 2035

September 4, 1974—United States—The U.S. Nuclear Corporation's licensed nuclear facility in Oak Ridge, Tennessee, reported an attempt to breach its fence.

September 2-4, 1974—Israel—Two Arab terrorists attempting to enter Hanita from the western end of the Lebanese border were killed by Israeli troops. A second squad met a similar fate. Israelis intercepted a Palestinian group near Fasuta, three miles south of the Lebanese border. The PDFLP group intended to seize hostages in exchange for eleven guerrillas and Greek Orthodox Archbishop Hilarion Capucci. Two terrorists and two Israeli soldiers were killed. The PDFLP claimed that its forces had captured an Israeli installation and were negotiating for the release of their hostages through foreign diplomats, presumably the French and Finnish ambassadors. The terrorists said that some hostages were killed by attacking Israeli troops. The Israelis denied this claim. A later Damascus PDFLP communiqué admitted the deaths of two terrorists. On September 5, Nayef Hawatmeh, PDFLP chieftain, said the raids would continue. 2036-2037

September 4, 1974—United States—Upon landing at Boston's Logan Airport from a flight from New York with ninety-nine persons on board, Eastern Airlines flight 1160, a DC9 was taken over by Marshall Collins III, a black who did not meet the FAA profile, who was born on June 27, 1954, in Providence, Rhode Island. He released everyone on board save the pilot and kept an arm around his neck, cutting him slightly with a razor blade. He also pressed a nail into the pilot's arm and hit him with an emergency ax about the head and shoulders. Collins demanded that $10,000 be paid to the people of Boston's Roxbury ghetto and that he be flown to New York City's La Guardia Airport. After three hours of negotiations, he surrendered to police and FBI agents. He was charged with air piracy. 5442

September 7, 1974—United States—The Brunswick licensed nuclear facility of the Carolina Power and Light Company received a bomb threat.

September 8, 1974—Argentina—A bomb thrown from a passing automobile in Rosario damaged the USIS center but caused no injuries. The three terrorists in the car, who may have been Montoneros, threw four more bombs at other locations in Rosario. During a chase by police, a bomb in the terrorists' car exploded, killing all three. 2038

September 8, 1974—Spain—The Chilean consulate in Barcelona was bombed in connection with the first anniversary of the overthrow of the Allende government. There was property damage. 2039

September 8, 1974—Greece—After landing for a scheduled stopover in Athens, the pilot of a Tel Aviv to New York TWA 707 radioed that he was having trouble with one engine. The plane subsequently entered a steep climb and then went into a steep nose-down spin and crashed into the Ionian Sea, killing all eighty-eight on board. The Organization of Arab Nationalist Youth for the Liberation of Palestine said in Beirut that one of their members exploded a charge he was carrying around his waist. This claim was at first doubted, but on January 11, 1975, investigators from the National Transportation Safety Board, as well as a British team of investigators, who examined a relatively small quantity of debris found after the plane sank in 10,800 feet of water, announced that laboratory tests showed conclusively that a high-explosive bomb had gone off in a rear cargo compartment. 2040

September 11, 1974—Argentina—A high explosive bomb detonated during the evening at the entrance of the Yugoslav emigrants' hall in Buenos Aires, causing no casualties. 2041

September 11, 1974—Argentina—A series of bombs exploded at U.S. and other foreign companies' offices in Buenos Aires, Mendoza, Córdoba, and Lomas de Zomar. Extremist groups were suspected of celebrating the anniversary of Allende's overthrow in Chile. 2042-2045

September 11, 1974—Argentina—A bomb exploded at the Salta residence of the Chilean consul, causing considerable damage but no injuries. 2046

September 11, 1974—Spain—A bomb caused property damage but no injuries at the LAN-Chile Airlines office in Barcelona. 2047

September 13, 1974—Spain—It was believed that the ETA and members of the Spanish Communist party collaborated in planting a bomb in the Rolando Cafeteria next to Madrid police headquarters. It exploded, killing twelve and injuring seventy.

September 13, 1974—France—A bomb placed at the entrance of the Air Algeria office in Marseilles shattered the front door and caused extensive damage inside the office, as well as to cars parked in front of the building. 2048

September 13, 1974—France—A bomb thrown at the Albanian embassy in Paris caused minor damage. 2049

September 13, 1974—Netherlands—Three members of the JRA identified as Haruo Wako, Junzo Okudaira, and Jun Nishikawa, armed with handguns and M-26 grenades, burst into the French embassy in The Hague at 4 P.M. with machine guns blazing and took eleven hostages, including the ambassador, Jacques Senard. In the gun battle, one of the Japanese terrorists was wounded in the arm; a Dutch policeman and a policewoman were also injured. During what would become a siege lasting 101 hours, the nearby U.S. embassy served as a command center for the government's negotiations team. The Dutch immediately deployed a counterterrorist squad, as well as a platoon, around the barricaded French embassy. The terrorists threatened to kill their hostages, setting a deadline, unless the French government released Furuya Yutaka (also known as Yoshiaki Yamada), a JRA member who had been arrested at Orly Airport on July 21 in the group's aborted Operation Translation (see incident 1993). The group vowed to kill their hostages one by one if their demand was not met. On the third day, they relented, releasing three ill Dutch women. They also demanded a $1 million ransom, which the French refused to pay. Eventually they agreed to a $300,000 ransom, which was paid by the Dutch (the French eventually repaid the Dutch, whose money was returned by Syria upon the terrorists' arrival in their country). Furuya proved difficult, initially refusing to join his fellow JRA members after being flown to Schipol Airport. Observers believed that he was concerned about possible reprisals by the JRA for erring in his mission. Professor DeVos, a Dutch expert on Japan, interviewed Furuya, who said the JRA had not carried out their attack vigorously enough. The French guards were ordered to kill Furuya if any hostages were murdered, according to a Dutch psychiatrist. In a poll taken by a French newspaper, a small plurality wanted the embassy stormed in any case, and an overwhelming majority said it would support killing Furuya if any French hostages were harmed.

Relations between the French and Dutch became strained during the negotiations. French Minister Poniatowski was unsuccessful in conducting the negotiations over long-distance telephone from Paris, and at one point, the

French apparently informed the Dutch that they were no longer responsible for what happened in the incident. Some reports claim that the French sent a team of eight sharpshooters to The Hague and advocated a shootout with the terrorists but were overruled by the Dutch. Other reports credit the Dutch with wishing to pursue this approach. The Dutch used unique negotiating methods, at one point resorting to writing messages in large Japanese characters on a paper roll spread out on the street below the embassy. The French eventually gave in on the demand for a French plane to take the terrorists to an unnamed Middle Eastern country but did not wish to endanger any more French lives by providing a French crew to pilot the plane. The Dutch government was willing to provide the crew but demanded that the hostages be released and that the terrorists surrender their weapons. According to some reports, two women hostages were freed on September 16, and the other nine on September 17 after Furuya was freed. Three of the hostages were left at the embassy, with the other six being freed at the airport.

Lebanon refused the plane permission to land, but it was allowed by the PDRY government to refuel in Aden. Some reports claim that the terrorists were even allowed to take along the code book that Furuya had been carrying when he was arrested. However, the terrorists were not granted safe haven by the PDRY government, which refused to allow anyone save the British flight engineer, Bernie Knight (who lived in the Netherlands), to leave the plane. The plane finally landed in Damascus, Syria, where the government agreed to grant the terrorists safe conduct in return for their surrendering their weapons and the ransom money (which was returned to the Dutch).

The Syrians initially did not want the terrorists to leave the plane and conducted negotiations for three hours over the disposition of the trio. The group finally gave their guns to the crew of the plane. Reports indicate that the terrorists were handed over to an official of the PLO. The PFLP denied involvement in the incident. According to the Japanese government, which was consulted by the Dutch during the incident, Jun Nishikawa was arrested in Stockholm and was indicted on May 2, 1975, on charges of attempted murder and unlawful arrest and confinement. Fusako Shigenobu, Kazuo Yoshimura, and his two Hague partners were placed on an international wanted list as accomplices.

There were some indications of involvement by Carlos, the Venezuelan PFLP terrorist. Shortly after the attack, French police arrested Taketomo Takahashi, a former assistant professor at Tokyo's Rikkyo University, who had become a Paris JRA leader. He had tried to swallow a piece of paper that had two code names: "Acheme" and "Jean Baptiste." The latter was Andrew Haberman, a microfilm specialist identified in DST files as the Curiel Apparat's document forger. He was charged with forgery and released. Acheme was identified as Antonio Perera Carvalho, a Brazilian who held messages for the Japanese and who may have given them arms for the Hague attack. The notebook of Michel Moukharbel, Carlos's assistant, listed him as Felipe Fereira.

Carlos traveled to Amsterdam the day before the embassy attack. Bank records show that he changed a substantial amount of money, which he gave to Acheme for safe keeping. The police believed that Carlos and the Japanese used these Curiel figures to set up the Hague attack. Other reports claim that the JRA left behind in the embassy some M-26 grenades that Carlos had given them. It is also claimed that the notebook of Michel Moukharbel, the terrorist who was killed by Carlos in Paris when French police raided his apartment in July 1975, had written on one of his checkbook stubs, "Affaire Japonais. 2000 francs." 2050

September 14, 1974—Syria—A medium-sized bomb planted by the Arab Communist Organization exploded on the ground floor of an empty building under renovation and publicly designated for future use by the USIS in Damascus. The blast caused damages to three stories of the structure and to many other buildings in the area and injuries to six Syrian pedestrians. 2051

September 14, 1974—Argentina—Three FAL men driving past the Chilean embassy in Buenos Aires fired a machine gun at the building, injuring the driver of a car parked in front of the embassy. Simultaneously several antitank grenades were fired at the embassy from an adjacent public park. 2052

September 14, 1974—South Vietnam—An Air Vietnam B727 flying from Da Nang to Saigon was hijacked by Le Duc Tan, thirty-four, a major in the South Vietnamese army, who demanded to be flown to North Vietnam. The pilot attempted to land at Phan Rang to refuel, but the hijacker, who was in the cockpit, pulled the pins on his two hand grenades. The plane veered off course and crashed, killing all seventy-one on board. One or two Americans were believed to have been on board. Reports indicate that the hijacker was allowed to bypass security screening by an army acquaintance. 5443

September 15, 1974—France—At 5:30 P.M., a young man stood on the balustrade in the Drugstore Saint-Germaine, a popular Paris complex comprised of a café, pharmacy, and other shops, and pulled the pin on an American M-26 grenade, killing two Frenchmen and wounding thirty-four others. The attacker escaped in the confusion. The Group for the Defense of Europe, an extreme right-wing organization, claimed credit. The complex is owned by a Jew, Marcel Bleustein-Blanchet. Many accounts have credited the attack to the Muhammad Boudia Commando, suggesting that the Venezuelan terrorist Carlos was responsible. A man speaking heavily accented French phoned Reuters and Agence France-Presse to explain that the attack was a warning to the Dutch and Japanese governments to agree to the JRA's demands at The

Hague (see incident 2050): "If the government does not do what it should we shall attack a cinema next." A follow-up note read, "Enough of lying Jewish propaganda." 2053

September 16, 1974—United States—A fire was caused by an incendiary device in a suitcase destined for a TWA flight to Israel from Boston's Logan Airport. Some damage resulted to the TWA baggage security cage, but there were no injuries. 2054

September 16, 1974—Argentina—Forty bombs exploded throughout the country, most of them directed against ceremonies dedicating the military revolt that ended Juan Perón's first administration. Montoneros slogans and banners were found at many of the bomb sites. Among the offices targeted were three Ford showrooms, Peugeot and IKA-Renault showrooms, Goodyear and Firestone tire distributors, Riker and Eli Lilly pharmaceutical laboratories, Union Carbide Battery Company, Bank of Boston and Chase Manhattan Bank branches, Xerox Corporation, and Coca-Cola and Pepsi-Cola bottling companies. 2055-2069

September 19, 1974—Peru—The Condor organization left a document at the scene of a bombing in Arequipa of the Bolivian consulate in the Hotel Presidente building . The explosion damaged the consulate and eight other offices and injured two people. It was believed that the Condors had ties to the National Liberation Army. 2070

September 19, 1974—Argentina—In an attack that involved dozens of Montoneros, including some disguised as telephone repairmen, two sons of Juan Born, Sr., the co-proprietor of Bunge y Born, the world's sixth largest grain exporter and Argentina's largest private company, were kidnapped in Buenos Aires shortly after they had left for work. The group noted that the hostages would be "tried for the acts committed against the workers, the people and the national interest by the monopolies to which they belong." They were found guilty and sentenced to one year in a people's prison. Juan Born, thirty-nine, was freed in April 1975, suffering from psychological problems caused by undergoing intensive interrogations. Although the group claimed to give him psychiatric help, he was released after partial payment of a ransom. Born was secretly flown out of the country and is believed to have recuperated in Paris. The Montoneros demanded that the company pay a cash ransom of $60 million, a record for a political kidnapping, as well as distribute $1.2 million worth of food and clothing in various parts of the country. They also demanded improved wages and working conditions in the company's plants and the publication of advertisements in local newspapers itemizing goods delivered to shanty towns. Political statements by the Montoneros were placed in various European newspapers, as well as the *Washington Post*, which reported that the full-page ad cost $6,971.04. The communiqúe accused the company of being behind the 1955 ouster of Perón and of exploitation of the workers. Because Argentine law prohibits negotiating with political kidnappers, it was reported that most of the bargaining took place in other countries, including Spain, Switzerland, and the Soviet Union. The company gave in to all of the demands, and in a clandestine June 20 press conference run by the Montoneros chief, Mario Firmenich, twenty-seven, Jorge Born, forty, was freed in a house in a Buenos Aires suburb. It was only then that Jorge was informed of the deaths of his chauffeur and a close friend, Juan Bosch, another company executive, who were killed in the initial attack. It was pointed out that given the black market exchange rate, $60 million was worth one-third of the Argentine defense budget. Firmenich said that the equivalent of 480 million cruzeiros would be used in "establishing the popular authority, in developing the total war against imperialism and in the efforts to obtain definitive national liberation." Two company executives were later arrested by Argentine police. 2071

September 22, 1974—Peru—At 9:30 P.M., three grenades exploded on a Lima crosswalk near a Sears store, causing cracks in the cement. 2072

September 27, 1974—Dominican Republic—A group of seven armed men from the Twelfth of January Liberation Movement kidnapped Barbara Hutchison, USIS director in Santo Domingo, as she left her office and then seized the Venezuelan consulate, holding seven more hostages, including the Venezuelan consul and vice-consul, a Spanish priest, and four Dominican consulate employees.

Radhames Mendez Vargas told reporters by telephone that he demanded $1 million from the United States and the release of thirty-eight political prisoners by the Dominican government. He threatened to kill his hostages one by one and said that the consulate would be blown up if police rushed it. Security forces surrounded the consulate but allowed two daily food deliveries, which were cut to once daily on October 1. President Joaquin Balaguer, supported by the U.S., Venezuelan, and Spanish governments, rejected the demands. On September 27, Mendez, a convicted hijacker who had been released from prison in 1974, said that the attack was to protest the government's rejection of "demands for democratization" and was aimed at freeing "patriots who are rotting in jail under the Balaguer dictatorship." Mendez demanded the release of his movement's leader, Plinio Matos. The guerrillas later named thirty-two other prisoners, ten of whom, along with the Dominican left, including the Dominican Popular Movement (of which the terrorists were supposedly members), condemned the attack.

Robert Hurwitch, the U.S. ambassador, and government officials negotiated with the terrorists. On October 3, they dropped their ransom demand and asked for safe conduct to Mexico or Peru for themselves and the prisoners. This was rejected by Balaguer, Mexico, and Peru. On October 7, Balaguer gave an "absolutely final" offer of safe conduct, which was accepted the next day. Panama agreed to grant asylum to "end this unfortunate case," according to Panamanian Ambassador Alejandro Cuellar Arosemena on October 9. After freeing the seven hostages, the terrorists flew to Panama City. 2073

September 28, 1974—United States—No one was reported injured when two bombs exploded in an alley separating Newark, New Jersey, police headquarters and city hall. It was believed that the bombing was in retaliation for the deaths of two Puerto Ricans during Labor Day weekend disorders in Newark.

September 29, 1974—Ireland—Four IRA members armed with pistols and homemade bombs took over the Dundalk Aero Club. While two of them held persons in the club at gunpoint, the other two forced a pilot of a Rallye Club plane to fly them to Jonesborough, across the Northern Ireland border, to a British army base in County Armagh. They intended to drop four explosive canisters onto the base, but the first bomb they threw struck a wing of the plane, five miles away from the target. The three other bombs could not be pushed through the hatchway, and the hijackers gave up the attack. Twenty other IRA terrorists fired mortars and machine guns at the base but caused no casualties. The hijackers flew to Revensdale, Ireland, where they escaped. 2074

September 30, 1974—Argentina—Retired General Carlos Prats Gonzalez, who had commanded the Chilean army under President Salvador Allende, and his wife were killed when a bomb exploded in or under their car as they were driving to their home in Buenos Aires. A close friend of Prats claimed that the deceased had told him of information he had received of a plan to kill him and that the murder would appear to be the work of the Argentine Anti-Communist Alliance, but it would actually be the responsibility of Chilean or American rightists. Prats had been living in voluntary exile since the coup. 2075

September 30, 1974—Argentina—The ERP kidnapped a senior executive of Bunge y Born, Alfonso Marguerite, in Buenos Aires.

October 1974—Italy—According to a report by the BDM Corporation, "A plot to poison Italy's water supply with uranium was uncovered....Italian Defense Minister Giulio Andreotti reportedly informed his Parliament that right-wing terrorists had planned to poison water supplies with radioactive uranium stolen from a nuclear center, and placed in various aqueducts. According to press reports, the scheme also involved a plan to assassinate the Prime Minister, the Communist Party leader, and other top officials. The alleged purpose of the plot was to create a large scale panic that would force the army to intervene and open the way for a rightist government takeover. Reports indicate that as of October 1974, 8 people had been arrested in the case, 12 others were being sought and 55 others may be facing some form of legal action.''

October 2, 1974—Peru—In the afternoon, a bomb exploded on the roof of the Soviet embassy in Lima, causing no major damage to the interior garden. A similar explosion took place at the Instituto Nacional de Planificacion. 2076

October 2, 1974—United States—After a warning call, a hotel associated with ITT was bombed by the New World Liberation Front in San Francisco. A similar attack was made in Los Angeles three days later.

October 5, 1974—United Kingdom—Two Guildford pubs frequented by British soldiers were bombed by the IRA. The first blast, at the Horse and Groom, killed three men and two women; two of the men were military personnel. Fifty-four were injured in the two explosions, including thirteen members of the Women's Royal Army Corps and thirty other persons affiliated with the military. Thirteen IRA members were arrested on November 30. 2077-2078

October 6, 1974—Peru—After a bomb threat, a stick of dynamite was thrown at the Yugoslavian embassy in Lima but did not explode. 2079

October 6, 1974—Italy—The Avis office in Milan was bombed, with damage totaling $15,000. That same evening, four terrorists invaded Face-Standard, a local ITT communications subsidiary, and set fire to a warehouse, causing $9 million damage. An unsigned note delivered to the Milan office of the Italian news agency said the attack was in retaliation for ITT's role in Chile. 2080-2081

October 7, 1974—Taiwan—A Far Eastern Air Transportation Corporation Viscount 810 flying from Tainan to Taipei was hijacked by a man armed with a knife and four bottles filled with gasoline, who demanded to be flown to the People's Republic of China. He was overpowered by a security guard and cabin attendant and was arrested when the plane landed in Taipei. 5444

October 8, 1974—Peru—Terrorists conducted armed attacks in Lima against a Coca-Cola factory, the residence of the U.S. ambassador, and the Bolivian embassy. 2082-2084

October 8, 1974—Puerto Rico—The FLNC and the M-7 claimed credit for the bombings of two theaters. On October 13, an individual called the San Juan office of United Press International to claim credit for the Latin American Anti-Communist Army. 2085-2086

October 9, 1974—Puerto Rico—The FLNC and the M-7 claimed credit for the bombing of the San Juan office of Mexicana de Aviacion. On October 13, an individual phoned United Press International in San Juan to claim that the Latin American Anti-Communist Army was responsible. 2087

October 10, 1974—Syria—The Arab Communist Organization bombed the Damascus two-story office building that houses National Cash Register, killing a Syrian office boy and injuring a cleaning woman. The building was severely damaged, and most of its contents were destroyed. The group said the company was one ''which represents a form of imperialist exploitation of the area.'' The bombing took place on the eve of the visit of U.S. Secretary of State Henry Kissinger. The ACO bombed NCR offices in Aleppo the next day. 2088-2089

October 10, 1974—United Kingdom—Three IRA bombs exploded in two London military clubs, injuring one person. Two of the bombs caused slight damage in western London's Victory Ex-Servicemen's Club, and the third destroyed a room in Pall Mall's Army-Navy Club. 2090-2091

October 11, 1974—Lebanon—An Arab Communist Organization bomb caused considerable damage to the Beirut offices of the First National Bank of Chicago but caused no injuries. A statement found in the entrance to the bank demanded the release of Adel Abn Asi, a Lebanese sentenced to death for his participation in the attack on the Bank of America on October 18, 1973 (see incident 1699). 2092

October 11, 1974—Spain and Morocco—Fifteen terrorists planning to assassinate the chiefs of state of various Arab countries attending the Rabat Summit Conference were arrested in Morocco. Two others were arrested in Spain. 2093-2094

October 21, 1974—Argentina—The USIS Binational Center in Rio Cuarto was bombed at 4 A.M., causing considerable damage but no injuries. An Argentine official of the Ford affiliate Transax was seriously injured by a bomb that exploded as he left his San Carlos home. A Ford showroom and a Pepsi-Cola bottling plant were bombed in Rio Cuarto, causing minor damage but no injuries. 2095-2098

October 22, 1974—United States—A firebomb was thrown during the night into a Cleveland store selling Yugoslav newspapers and records.

October 22, 1974—United Kingdom—The IRA bombed London's Brooks Club, injuring three. 2099

October 25, 1974—France—A Mexican male held a French ground hostess hostage for thirteen hours at Nice Airport before surrendering. He had demanded his wife's release from prison and a pledge to be allowed to live in Mexico. 2100

October 25, 1974—Venezuela—At 10 P.M., a bomb exploded in a maintenance closet in the El Marques store of a U.S. firm. 2101

October 26, 1974—Netherlands—Two Arab terrorists and two Dutch criminals took twenty-two hostages at Scheveningen's prison chapel, near The Hague, using guns that had been smuggled to them. The hostages included a priest, members of a visiting choir, and relatives of the singers including children, women, and old men. During the 105-hour siege, the terrorists demanded a plane to take them out of the country, presumably to asylum in an Arab nation, and the release of the other member of the Arab National Youth Organization for the Liberation of Palestine, Sami Houssin Tamimah, who had participated with one of the hostage takers in the March 3, 1974, hijacking incident (see incident 1836) for which they had been placed in separate Dutch prisons. The terrorists, led by Palestinian Adnan Ahmed Nuri, and the Algerian Mohammed Koudache, were backed by two criminals, one extremely violent and the other described as mentally defective. Authorities promised Tamimah a reduced sentence if he would not go along with the terrorists' demands. He subsequently aided in the negotiations, talking with his former compatriot four times. Although the terrorists threatened to kill the hostages one by one, pointing out to each hostage the spot on his body where he would be shot, seven of the hostages were released during the negotiations. On the fifth day, police engaged in a three-pronged assault on the chapel during the morning, causing confusion by howling wildly, shooting wildly, and accompanied by a huge whining siren and swirling searchlights. No one was wounded or killed in the attack. The Dutch attorney general said the four would be charged with unlawful deprivation of liberty. Nuri and Tamimah were released a month later as a result of demands made by hijackers (see incident 2145). 2102

October 26, 1974—United States—The FALN caused $970,000 damage by setting off five bombs at around 3 A.M. in New York City. No one was injured. One bomb exploded in a car, blasting a two foot by two foot hole in the street between Marine Midland and Chase Manhattan banks, scattering debris for a block and a half. In one of the blasts at Rockefeller Center, windows thirty-one stories up were broken by shock waves. All of the blasts tore out building fronts and smashed windows and glass walls. The Exxon and Banco de Ponce buildings in Rockefeller Center and the Union Carbide and Lever Brothers building on Park Avenue were damaged, as were the Marine Midland Bank and Federal Reserve Bank of New York. A man and woman with Puerto Rican accents phoned to direct reporters to a phone booth at Broadway and Seventy-third Street, where they left an FALN statement: "We have just bombed imperialist banks. Free all Puerto Rican political prisoners."

The statement called for the immediate independence of Puerto Rico and the release of five Puerto Rican prisoners held by the U.S. government. Among them was Oscar Collazo, who, along with Griselio Torresola, had attempted to shoot into Washington's Blair House on November 1, 1950, to assassinate President Truman. Torresola and a guard died from wounds suffered in the gun battle. Collazo recovered and was convicted of murder and sentenced to death. President Truman commuted the sentence to life imprisonment. Also named were Lolita Lebron and three men who fired pistols in the House of Representatives in 1950, wounding five congressmen. The terrorists ultimately were released in September 1979.

The group claimed credit for bombings and attempted bombings in the spring and on September 28 in Newark, saying that they were celebrating the October 30, 1950 "uprising against yanki colonial domination" in Puerto Rico.

Police later reported that the explosions went off during a forty-minute period, beginning at 2:55 A.M. with the explosion of the auto bomb. Sophisticated timing devices were employed. The car bomb, the most powerful, had the explosive force of forty sticks of dynamite or twenty pounds of plastic explosives. 2103-2107

October 28, 1974—Puerto Rico—The Latin American Anti-Communist Army claimed credit for the bombing of the San Juan office of Iberia Airlines in the Caribbean Towers building, causing moderate damage but no injuries. 2108

October 29, 1974—United States—Three JDL males broke into the New York PLO office, fired two shots, and beat the assistant director, Kasan Rhaman, with lead pipes before fleeing. 2109

October 29, 1974—Iran—Three bombs exploded during the night in Tehran on the eve of the arrival of U.S. Secretary of State Henry Kissinger. The offices of ITT were completely gutted; a company dealing in agricultural machinery and bus transport was slightly damaged; and offices of a film export-import company were badly damaged. All of the firms had American trade connections. According to an Arabic-language broadcast, Iranian terrorists were responsible. 2110

October 29, 1974—United States—In a communiqué to station KPFK, the New World Liberation Front claimed credit for setting off a bomb on the lawn of Robert D. Hallock, a former ITT executive, at 3 A.M. in Los Angeles. The group called upon ITT to "admit to the American people their complicity" in Allende's overthrow. It also demanded the release of all Chilean political prisoners and that "ITT put an end to the murder and torture by the military junta in Chile."

October 30, 1974—Turkey—The Ankara apartment of a U.S. sergeant attached to the defense attaché's office was fired on from the street with an automatic weapon. Thirteen bullets hit the front of the apartment, with two entering the home. No one was injured. 2111

October 30, 1974—Venezuela—The Cuban-Venezuelan Friendship Institute in Caracas was attacked. 2112

October 31, 1974—Argentina—The Montoneros bombed the motor launch of Argentina's police chief, Alberto Villar, killing him and his wife soon after they left the river port of Tigre, eighteen miles northeast of Buenos Aires. The Montoneros claimed that he sanctioned torture and murder of political activists and that they regretted the death of his wife. Villar was commander of the police blue squad, which rode tandem motorcycles into street demonstrations with the rear men hitting demonstrators with long truncheons.

November 1974—United Kingdom—Two persons were killed and twenty wounded when an IRA bomb exploded in a bar in Woolwich, East London, near a military base. 2113

November 1, 1974—United States—The Haddam Neck licensed nuclear facility of the Connecticut Yankee Atomic Power Company received a bomb threat.

November 1, 1974—Lebanon—The Arab Communist Organization attacked the headquarters of Sohat, a Lebanese mineral water firm, in the Beirut suburbs. 2114

November 2, 1974—United States—Demonstrations were held in front of the permanent mission of Yugoslavia to the United Nations against sentences of a group in Zadar, Yugoslavia. A mission window was broken.

November 3, 1974—Italy—Gasoline bombs were thrown into the Rome offices of IBM and Minnesota Mining and Manufacturing Company, causing light damage, and into three branches of the Italian affiliate of the Bank of

America. One of the branches was damaged extensively, but no one was reported injured. U.S. Secretary of State Henry Kissinger was due to address the World Food Conference in Rome the next day. 2115-2119

November 4, 1974—United States—The Pilgrim licensed nuclear facility of the Boston Edison Company near Plymouth, Massachusetts, received a bomb threat.

November 5, 1974—Italy—A group of youths tossed firebombs into the Rome offices of Honeywell. 2120

November 5, 1974—Italy—Three Molotov cocktails were thrown into the Milan Trade Center, which is under the jurisdiction of the U.S. Commerce Department, causing minor fire damage to an office but no injuries. 2121

November 6, 1974—Jordan—A Royal Jordanian Airlines Caravelle 50 flying between Amman and Aqaba was hijacked by three off-duty security guards who used a gun borrowed from one of the flight's security guards to divert the plane to Benghazi's Benina Airport, where the trio released the passengers and crew after being granted political asylum. Reports differed as to the number of passengers on the plane, ranging from eight to twenty-one people. The trio, identified as Salem Hiyari, Yassin Al Zaiban, and Muhammad S. Al Auran, attempted to land in Beirut, but officials closed the airport. The plane returned to Amman later that day. The hijackers claimed membership in the Jordanian Free Officers Movement. 2122

November 6, 1974—United Kingdom—The IRA killed four British soldiers in reprisal for the death of a Maze prisoner. 2123

November 7, 1974—United Kingdom—A London newspaper received a call from a man claiming membership in the left-wing Red Flag 74 group, saying that his organization was responsible for the bombing of London's King's Arms Tavern in which one man died and nineteen others, including several soldiers, were injured. 2124

November 7, 1974—Ecuador—Two bombs exploded near the conference site in Quito of the OAS. The meeting was intended to discuss the lifting of economic sanctions against Cuba. One bomb damaged the Bolivian embassy, injuring two persons. The second damaged the Brazilian Cultural Institute. A third was disarmed at the Paraguayan embassy. 2125-2127

November 8, 1974—Mexico—A bomb exploded in the car of the Cuban ambassador to Mexico, Fernando Lopez Muino. 2128

November 9, 1974—United States—At 8:30 P.M., a high order explosive detonated on the second floor of the Pan American Union building in Washington, D.C., which serves as the headquarters of the Organization of American States. Damage was estimated at $100,000. Two persons were in the building, but police reported no injuries. At 2:05 A.M. the next day, offices of United Press International and Associated Press were phoned, with the caller requesting that a tape recording of his message be made. He said, "We are responsible for the bomb placed at the headquarters of the OAS. This is our answer to the re-establishment of relations with Cuba. This is our answer to the recognition to the Castro Communist Government of Cuba...Cuban C-4 Movement." This may have been a cover name used by the FLNC. 2129

November 10, 1974—United States—A bomb exploded early in the morning in the Los Angeles offices of the U.N. Information Center bookstore, injuring no one but causing $5,000 damage to the building and destroying $10,000 to $15,000 worth of UNICEF Christmas cards and U.N. calendars. The *Los Angeles Times* and a radio station received anonymous calls from a male who said the bomb was "a thank you note from the PLO to the U.N. for letting them address the U.N." He closed with the JDL slogan, "Never again!" A judge dropped charges against a JDL member due to insufficient evidence. 2130

November 12, 1974—Puerto Rico—Anti-Castro Cubans were believed responsible for a bomb that caused $200 damage to the door of the San Juan office of Avianca Airlines. 2131

November 12, 1974—United States—Members of the JDL publicly vowed to assassinate Yasir Arafat, leader of the PLO delegation to the United Nations. 2132

November 13, 1974—United States—Yasir Arafat, leader of the PLO, gave a ninety-minute speech to the U.N. General Assembly, saying, "I have come bearing an olive branch and a freedom fighter's gun. Do not let the olive branch fall from my hand." Arafat had been accorded the reception of a head of state from the General Assembly chairman, Algerian Foreign Minister Abdelaziz Bouteflika. Arafat denied claims that two of his bodyguards had participated in the Khartoum attack in which two U.S. diplomats were killed (see incident 1465). During that evening, a reception was given for Arafat in the U.N. delegates' dining room by the head of the Egyptian delegation, Ambassador Ahmed Esmat Abdel Mequid. It was reported that standing behind Arafat in the reception line was Ali Hassan Salameh, believed by many to be a leader of Black September.

November 14, 1974—Japan—Several Japanese extremists, wearing red helmets and insignia of the Maruseido (Marxist Youth League) threw Molotov cocktails at the U.S. chancery in Tokyo, causing little damage. They then charged the embassy main gate, injuring seven guards. All were apprehended by police. President Ford was scheduled to visit Japan shortly. 2133

November 14, 1974—Japan—Almost simultaneously, Maruseido members threw firebombs at the Soviet embassy in Tokyo. Some managed to enter the embassy lobby and do some damage, as well as slightly injure five Soviet embassy personnel and two guards. The attackers were arrested. 2134

November 14, 1974—Mexico—Sara M. Davis, the wife of a U.S. real estate dealer, was kidnapped in the Mexican resort of Cuernavaca. Her captors demanded a ransom of $1 million in food and land for the poor. The United Popular Liberation Army of America left two communiqués in a Mexico City subway station. 2135

November 16, 1974—Italy—The Holger Meins Kommando claimed credit for a bomb planted at the West German consulate in Florence. 2136

November 18, 1974—United Kingdom—Alan Quartermaine, a London insurance broker, was shot twice in the neck and killed when his chauffeur-driven Rolls Royce stopped at a King's Road traffic light. He usually used neither the car nor the route.

Speculation centered on Venezuelan terrorist Carlos, who may have mistaken him for a Jewish member of Parliament who drove a Rolls and lived nearby. Carlos spent three or four weeks in London, then two in Paris, and then went back to London on a routine basis. He and his friend Bouvier may have been involved.

Other theories suggest IRA involvement. Quartermaine's firm had recently acquired extensive holdings in the Irish Republic. However, Quartermaine was not personally involved in the transaction. Several IRA men operating in London were captured and charged with various offenses but not this particular murder. 2137

November 18, 1974—Mexico—Literature traceable to the Twenty-third of September Communist League was found at the sites of numerous bombings of Mexico City commercial establishments, including Sears and a U.S.-owned restaurant and drugstore. 2138-2139

November 18, 1974—United States—Napoleon Bagaya Lechoco, forty-four, a former Philippine law clerk and president of his community's civic association, entered the Philippine embassy in Washington, D.C., for his 3:30 appointment with the ambassador, Eduardo Z. Romualdez. He pulled a pistol on the ambassador and demanded that his son, Napoleon, Jr., fifteen, whose exit visa from the Philippines had been delayed, be permitted to join the rest of his nine-member family in Washington, D.C. The economic attaché, Mario S. Lagdameo, attempted to subdue Lechoco, but as police entered the building, Lechoco fired several shots, wounding the attaché superficially in the arm. For the balance of the ten-hour siege, he lay on the floor of the ambassador's office pretending to be dead. Lechoco tied and gagged the ambassador. At 2 A.M. the next day, having received assurances that his son would be permitted to leave for the United States, Lechoco surrendered. His son arrived two days later. In 1975, Lechoco was found guilty by a U.S. district court jury of armed kidnapping and other charges. In a separate phase of the trial, he was also found sane and sentenced to ten years in the federal prison at Danbury, Connecticut. He served fifteen months of his sentence. On September 23, 1976, a U.S. court of appeals ruled that the judge had improperly excluded certain defense witnesses who would have supported Lechoco's credibility as to his insanity plea. On May 3, 1977, a U.S. court jury decided that Lechoco, a lawyer, was insane at the time of the incident. In a hearing before U.S. District Judge Howard F. Corcoran on May 11, 1977, Dr. Thomas Polley of St. Elizabeth's Hospital testified that he and other staff members at the institution found that Lechoco was not currently suffering from a mental illness and presented no further danger to himself or to others. Corcoran then ordered Lechoco's unconditional release. 2140

November 19, 1974—Israel—Three PDFLP members entered a Beit Shean apartment house and killed four unarmed civilians before they were themselves killed by an Israeli commando squad. Five others were wounded in the battle, and nineteen others were injured, including several children whose parents tried to save them by dropping them out of the apartment's windows. The group carried communiqués in which they demanded the release of twenty terrorists held in Israeli jails, as well as Archbishop Hilarion Capucci, who had been accused of arms smuggling. The group would have had the French and Austrian ambassadors summoned as negotiations to ensure their safe flight to Damascus. The residents were enraged by the attack and battered the corpses, throwing them out of the windows and setting a bonfire of their bodies. They did not realize that they had also burned a victim of the guerrillas. 2141

November 21, 1974—Peru—A bomb exploded in a Sears Roebuck store in Lima, causing $30,000 damage and injuring eleven. Police received an anonymous call warning of the bomb thirty minutes before the blast. In June 1975 the Lima press reported that the Revolutionary Vanguard, an extreme leftist group, was responsible. 2142

November 21, 1974—United Kingdom—Bombs exploded in two bars in Birmingham, killing nineteen and injuring 202. The blasts had the characteristics of an IRA attack, but the Red Flag 74 claimed credit. 2143-2144

November 21, 1974—Dubai—After climbing over an airport fence, four members of the Arab Nationalist Youth Organization for the Liberation of Palestine (ANYOLP) rushed to a British Airways VC10 while the aircraft was refueling en route from London to Singapore, Calcutta, and Brunei. The group, armed with automatic weapons, pistols, and hand grenades, fired their weapons as the attack began, wounding an Indian stewardess in the back during a shootout on the plane and injuring an airport employee. The plane carried twenty-two passengers, thirteen crew members, and twelve ground service employees who had been on board when it was taken over. The hijackers demanded the release by Egypt of thirteen Palestinians and that the Netherlands release two other Palestinians (see incidents 1465, 1731, 1836, and 2102), threatening to blow up the plane. Five of the guerrillas were awaiting trial by the PLO for their attack on Rome airport in December 1973. The demands were initially rejected by Egypt and the PLO. The hijackers released four passengers on November 22 in Tunis after a refueling stop in Tripoli, Libya. Thirteen more were released after the five terrorists held by the PLO were flown to Tunis. The Netherlands released their two Palestinians. The seven released prisoners then boarded the plane. Werner Gustav Kehl, a West German hostage, was shot and killed by the hijackers during the negotiations on November 23. The remaining hostages were released on November 25, and the hijackers demanded asylum in Tunisia. The government agreed, and those on the plane surrendered that day. On November 27, the PLO claimed it had arrested twenty-six persons in Lebanon and other Arab countries for their involvement in the incident and that the suspects would be tried in public. On December 7, 1974, the Tunisians handed over the eleven terrorists to the PLO. The group left Tunis in PLO custody for an undisclosed destination. The PLO claimed on January 24, 1975, that the four hijackers, who claimed to belong to the Martyr Abou Mammoud Squad of the ANYOLP, had been tried and sentenced to long prison terms. 2145

November 22, 1974—Japan—Three members of Maruseido attacked the U.S. consulate in Fukuoka, causing minor damage and slightly injuring the consul. They broke ground-floor windows and set off an incendiary device. Japanese police arrested the trio. On February 25, 1976, the Fukuoka district court sentenced Hikaru Koishi, twenty-seven, to six years and Toshiaki Higashitani, twenty-five, to three years. Both were former university students. Yasuo Morioka, twenty-six, was sentenced to four years the next day. They were protesting President Ford's visit to Japan and South Korea. 2146

November 23, 1974—Japan—An All Nippon Airways B727 flying from Chitose to Tokyo and Sapporo was hijacked by a sixteen-year-old Japanese youth, armed with sticks resembling dynamite and a gas lighter, who demanded to be flown to North Korea. He was overpowered by the copilot and the flight engineer. One of the crew members was injured slightly. 5445

November 25, 1974—Argentina—Leftist guerrillas in Buenos Aires were believed responsible for the bombings of a branch of First National City Bank of New York and two General Motors showrooms, which caused damage but no injuries. 2147-2149

November 25, 1974—United Kingdom—At least twenty persons were injured by IRA bombs planted in London sidewalk mailboxes. 2150

November 25, 1974—Mexico—Three incendiary devices went off in the Guadalajara store of an American firm, causing $80,000 worth of damage to inventory and fixtures. The same night an explosive device went off at the Xerox office in Guadalajara, causing considerable damage. 2151-2152

November 25, 1974—United Kingdom—Two IRA bombs exploded in London's Chelsea district, injuring six. One bomb went off in a curbside mailbox, and the other exploded outside the Chelsea army barracks. 2153-2154

November 29, 1974—Canada—A Canadian Pacific Airlines B737 flying 88 persons on the Montreal-Winnipeg-Edmonton-Vancouver run was hijacked out of Winnipeg by a Canadian citizen, Naim Djemal, who held a knife to the throat of a stewardess and demanded to go to Cyprus. Upon landing at Saskatoon, Saskatchewan, for refueling, the pilot persuaded the hijacker to surrender. The stewardess was treated for minor facial cuts. On February 5, 1975, Djemal was sentenced to seven years for attempted hijacking. 5446

November 30, 1974—Israel—Two members of Fatah entered the town of Rihaniya where they entered a house and shot an Israeli Moslem to death and wounded his wife. They then spoke to the nine-year-old daughter in Hebrew. She answered in Arabic, explaining that this was a Moslem Circassian (descendants of migrants from czarist Russia) area. The dismayed Arabs (one of whom accidentally wounded his partner) apologized to the girl for the attack and surrendered to Israeli authorities. It appears that they believed they had entered a Jewish village and were searching for hostages to exchange for five imprisoned terrorists in Israel. Some reports claim they were members of the PDFLP. 2155

November 30, 1974—Ethiopia—Explosive charges were set off in an attempt to blow up jet fuel tanks at Bole Airport.

December 1974—Lebanon—The Arab Communist Organization robbed a branch of the Société Nouvelle de la Banque de Syrie et du Liban in Beirut of 29,000 Lebanese pounds ($66,000). 2156

December 1974—United States—Luis Reque, a Bolivian and executive secretary of the Inter-American Commission for Human Rights, informed Montgomery County, Maryland, police that he had received a note in his Bethesda home saying, "Your daughter Leslie will be kidnapped." The family also reported receiving a call at home, and Reque said he received several at the commission's offices. The FBI was called into the case, but no arrests were made, and no harm came to the girl. At the time, Reque was writing a report attempting to show that the death of Chile's Salvador Allende was not a suicide. 2157

December 1, 1974—India—A Swissair DC8 flying from Bombay to Karachi was hijacked by Mohammad Aslam, twenty-four, who pointed a gun at the crew and demanded to be flown to Libya or Lebanon. Shortly after the aircraft landed at Karachi to refuel, Aslam was overpowered by the crew and taken into custody. He was sentenced on March 10, 1975, to three years and fined $200 for attempted hijacking. 5447

December 5, 1974—Mexico—A member of the Twenty-third of September Communist League held two French diplomats at gunpoint in their embassy for five hours. He was tricked by police into believing that his demand for political asylum in France had been met. Upon releasing the diplomats unharmed, he was captured on his way to the airport. 2158

December 6, 1974—Israel—PLO terrorists raided the Rosh Hanikra kibbutz, wounding two Israelis. One terrorist was killed. 2159

December 7, 1974—Peru—A group of unidentified persons fired submachine guns at Lima's Sheraton Hotel, wounding two guards. Several Latin American foreign ministers were housed in the hotel, which was the center for celebrations of the one hundred fiftieth anniversary of a battle for independence in Latin America. The terrorists escaped during a gun battle with police. 2160

December 9, 1974—Pakistan—Two employees were slightly wounded when a bomb exploded at the USIS center in Peshawar. An initial inspection revealed that the library and offices were nearly a total loss from fire and water damage. 2161

December 10, 1974—Lebanon—Scores of rockets were launched at dawn by sophisticated timing devices from wooden cases on the roofs of empty rental cars. Several damaged three Beirut PLO offices and wounded five persons. Ten rockets slammed into the second-story offices of the PLO on the Corniche Mazraa and a furniture store downstairs, slightly injuring two Lebanese and one Palestinian. According to PLO spokesman Shafiq al-Hout, PLO employees returned to the building. But guards spotted another car twenty-five yards from the first. "They shouted a warning and we barely managed to scramble out to safety when the wooden case on top began to lift automatically. Then five or six small rockets whistled overhead, crashing into my offices with an ear-splitting explosion."

Two pedestrians sustained minor cuts when four rockets hit the PLO's Western Sector Bureau in residential Mazraa. This office was in charge of guerrilla operations in Israel.

A third rocket attack was aimed at the library of the PLO's Palestine Research Center on Hamra Street. No one was in the library at the time.

Police discovered that the four cars had been rented from four different Beirut agencies five days previously by individuals using British, West German, Irish, and Mexican passports. The four men who rented the cars left the country before the attacks.

Some observers suggested that the Israeli Wrath of God teams were responsible. The Israeli military command in Tel Aviv denied responsibility, and the government refused to comment. Others suggested that Palestinian dissidents or an underground Lebanese extremist group were responsible. 2162-2164

December 11, 1974—Israel—In reprisal for the rocket attacks against the PLO offices the previous day, a PFLP member threw hand grenades into a Tel Aviv movie theater audience, killing himself and three others and wounding fifty-four. He was described as a Ghana-born holder of a British passport (which appeared to be forged) who had lived in Turkey. His explosives and detonators had been smuggled inside his suitcase lining. He made the grenades in his hotel room out of soft-drink cans packed with locally bought key rings and dismantled toy cars, which were used as shrapnel. The Israelis retaliated the next day with air strikes against Palestinian refugee camps in Beirut. 2165

December 11, 1974—United States—During the evening, two New York City patrolmen responded to an anonymous telephone call that reported that a body was located inside an abandoned, condemned building in East Harlem, a Puerto Rican district. One of the officers, Angelo Poggi, a twenty-two-year-old rookie, opened an outside door, and a pipe bomb, apparently booby-trapped, exploded. Poggi suffered a broken arm, facial wounds, and the loss of sight in his right eye. Damage to the building was estimated at $25,000. The FALN claimed responsibility, saying it was avenging the death of a young Puerto Rican while in police custody. The police listed the death as a suicide by hanging in a police cell, but some Puerto Rican groups charged that the youth had been abused and murdered by the police. 2166

December 12, 1974—United States—Two cesium-137 gauges slated for disposal were stolen from a locked room at the E. I. Du Pont de Nemours and Company plant near Gibbstown, New Jersey. They were found in damaged condition after an anonymous phone tip made several days after they were missed. The theft led to considerable media coverage and a widespread search of the area.

December 12, 1974—Lebanon—The agency that had rented a car to a man with a West German passport that had been used in a rocket attack against the PLO (see incidents 2162-2164) was destroyed in a bomb explosion. 2167

December 12, 1974—United States—After meeting the pilot of a Tampa Flying Service twin-engine Piper Seneca he had chartered to fly from Tampa to Naples, Florida, a man using the alias of Robin Harrison pulled a gun and demanded to be flown to Havana. He was taken into custody by Cuban officials. The hijacker, a white male for whom the FAA profile was inapplicable, had phoned to charter the flight, and pointed the handgun at the pilot in the company's operations facility. A complaint was filed against him on December 18, 1974, in the middle district of Florida. 5448

December 15, 1974—Lebanon—Three members of a tour group, all teachers at the Dependent's School of the U.S. air base in Italy, were detained, beaten, and interrogated by Palestinian guerrillas in Beirut. The three were accused of being Israeli agents and were questioned extensively about biographic matters. At the conclusion of their interrogation, the teachers were given an anti-NATO lecture and released. 2168.

December 15, 1974—United States—The Latin American Anti-Communist Army bombed the Miami offices of the Bahama Cruise Line, causing moderate damage but no injuries. 2169

December 15, 1974—France—Bombs exploded outside the TWA and Coca-Cola offices in Paris. A bomb exploded the next day at the Minnesota Mining and Manufacturing Company, shattering windows. No injuries were reported in any of the attacks. The Youth Action Group, an extreme right-wing organization, claimed credit, saying that they were protesting the meeting in Martinique of the presidents of France and the United States. 2170-2172

December 16, 1974—Argentina—A *Times* of London correspondent was kidnapped by Buenos Aires rightists who threatened to kill him if he did not immediately leave the country. He complied. 2979

December 16, 1974—United Kingdom—The IRA bombed three central London telephone exchanges, killing one man and injuring four others. Three policemen clearing the area outside a Chelsea exchange were injured. The second bomb went off under a parked car near a telephone exchange off Shaftesbury Avenue in the theater district of the West End, injuring no one. The third bomb exploded on the Chenies Street telephone exchange near Tottenham Court Road, badly injuring an employee. The bomb apparently was left in a parcel outside the exchange. 2173-2175

December 16, 1974—United States—A bomb exploded in the Eastern Steamship Lines office in Miami, causing a small fire and minor damage. The company, which owns two cruise ships operating between Miami and the Bahamas, is U.S. owned and has no legal connection to the Bahamian government. The FBI reported that the bomb was different from those used in recent Cuban exile bombings. However, the FLNC had recently claimed that it would conduct attacks against the Bahamas government. 2176

December 18, 1974—United Kingdom—An IRA bomb exploded in a car parked across the street from Selfridge's department store on London's Oxford Street, slightly injuring five persons. 2177

December 18, 1974—United Kingdom—Two IRA bombs went off in garbage cans in downtown Bristol, injuring twenty. 2178-2179

December 19, 1974—France—A French news agency received an anonymous telephone call in which the Raul Sendic International Brigade claimed credit for the Paris assassination of the Uruguayan military attaché to France and the United Kingdom, Colonel Ramon Trabal. The gunmen may have been connected with the Tupamaros, whose leader, Raul Sendic, had been detained by Uruguay. The group said the attaché had tortured Tupamaros in Uruguay. The following day the bodies of three women and two men, all Tupamaros, were found riddled with bullets thirty miles outside Montevideo, Uruguay. Some reports claimed that Trabal had been an intelligence officer. 2180

December 20, 1974—Israel—Terrorists threw a hand grenade at a busload of Christmas pilgrims from the United States who were touring Jerusalem, wounding Dejean Replogle, sixteen, of Jacksonville, Florida, who had to have her right leg amputated, and injuring an Arab bystander. The bus belonged to a local company. The PLO issued a statement warning visitors ''not to go to occupied Palestine during the escalation of commando activities against the Israeli enemy.'' On September 10, 1975, Replogle announced that she would lead another group of pilgrims to Israel in November 1975. 2181

December 20, 1974—Israel—A PDFLP bomb exploded on central Jerusalem's Ben Yehuda Street, an avenue of cafés, shops, and offices, just after lunchtime when it was crowded with shoppers, injuring thirteen. 2182

December 21, 1974—Lebanon—The Arab Communist Organization set off two bombs in the U.K.-owned Spinney's department store in Beirut, causing extensive damage but no injuries. The group threatened further "reprisals" as a lesson to all "monopolist companies" and set a New Year's Eve deadline for the free distribution of one ton of sugar, one ton of rice, and one thousand cans of powdered milk to poor Beirut families. The demands were not met and another Spinney's store was bombed on January 28, 1975. 2183

December 21, 1974—United Kingdom—The IRA bombed Harrod's, one of London's most exclusive department stores, causing no injuries. 2184

December 22, 1974—United Kingdom—An IRA bomb exploded at the home of former Prime Minister Edward Heath in London, causing no injuries. 2185

December 24, 1974—Australia—Two firebombs were thrown into a downtown ticket office of Pan Am in Sydney, causing $3,900 damage but no injuries. Two men were arrested for the explosion. A socialist youth group may have been responsible. 2186

December 25, 1974—Lebanon—An Air India B747 flying 155 passengers on the Bombay-Beirut-Rome-New York run was hijacked out of Beirut by Josef Homolov, a Czechoslovak-born Canadian who entered the cockpit and flashed a pocketknife. While holding a flashlight over the pilot's head, he demanded a gun and passage to a place of his choice. During the two-hour seige, he attempted to force the pilot to put the plane into a sharp dive over the center of Rome. At this point, the hijacker was overpowered by members of the crew. Homolov received a minor head injury and was arrested by Italian authorities upon landing safely in Rome. 5449

December 27, 1974—Netherlands—Five hundred South Moluccans demanding secession from Indonesia firebombed the Hague Peace Palace, headquarters of the International Court of Justice, causing $180,000 damage. Several people were injured, including police officers. Other demonstrators went to the Dutch prime minister's residence, where they read a petition protesting alleged torture of South Moluccans in Indonesia. Police surrounded the demonstrators, seized their firearms, and took them to police headquarters. On May 5, 1976, six South Moluccans were given jail terms ranging from two weeks to two months for the demonstrations. It was reported that Dutch police had foiled an attempt by South Moluccans to firebomb the Indonesian embassy in December as well. 2187-2188

December 27, 1974—Nicaragua—Nine FSLN members invaded the Managua suburban home of the former agricultural minister, Dr. José Maria Castillo, who was hosting a party in honor of U.S. Ambassador Turner B. Shelton. Shelton had already left the party before the initial assault, in which three guards and Castillo were killed and two others were injured. Twenty-five hostages were taken, including Alejandro Montiel Arguello, Nicaragua's foreign minister, Guillermo Sevilla-Sacasa, Nicaragua's ambassador to the United States and dean of the Washington diplomatic corps, the Nicaraguan ambassador to the United Nations, the mayor of Managua, the local Esso manager, and Chile's ambassador to Nicaragua. The terrorists, wielding submachine guns, threatened to shoot one of their hostages every twelve hours if they were not paid $5 million. They also demanded that the government release fourteen political prisoners and fly them with the prisoners to Havana and that it broadcast a revolutionary communiqué, which took over an hour to read. After sixty-one hours of negotiations, which included the archbishop of Managua and the papal nuncio acting as intermediaries, the government agreed to pay $1 million and release the prisoners, as well as broadcast the statement. The hostages were released at the airport as crowds cheered the terrorists, who flew with the intermediaries and the ambassadors of Spain and Mexico to Havana to ensure their safety. Mauricio Duarte Alvarez, who was suspected of planning the attack, was killed in Jinotepe on January 10, 1975. The government had suspended all constitutional guarantees after the attack and created a special antiterrorist unit recruited from members of the U.S.-trained National Guard. The government claimed that the FSLN, which had been established in 1958 by Carlos Fonseca Amador, had received guerrilla training in Cuba and the Soviet Union. The FSLN is named after General Augusto Sandino, who had opposed the U.S. occupation of Nicaragua from 1927 to 1933 and who was shot on orders given by the father of the current Nicaraguan president, Anastasio Somoza. 2189

December 28, 1974—United States—A man drove his car through an unlocked airport gate at Grand Forks, North Dakota, and parked it under a Northwest Airlines B727, which was boarding passengers. He entered the plane and informed a stewardess that he was going to steal a ride on the plane and that his car contained explosives. He deplaned after being told to move his car and was arrested. 5450

December 28, 1974—Puerto Rico—An individual threw a hand grenade onto the berthed Soviet cruise vessel *Maxim Gorki*, injuring two Soviet crew members, one of them seriously. One injured crewman followed the assailant a short distance and described him as a Latin male, forty years old. An anti-Castro group claimed credit. The ship is of Soviet registry and carried Soviet crewmen and Canadian passengers from New York to San Juan and St. Thomas. 2190

December 31, 1974—South Africa—A bomb concealed in a book exploded in the Johannesburg post office, injuring a local employee. The bomb was addressed to a Jewish family. Police did not disclose where the parcel was posted from. 2191

1975—Peru—The Vanguardia Revolucionaria was believed responsible for robbing a Sears store and attacking a policeman on duty outside the Panamanian embassy. 2192-2193

1975—France—The Baader Solidarity Group, Holger Meins Brigade, and Ulrike Meinhof Commando claimed credit for attacking the Mercedes branch in Paris, near the Etoile, the German television offices in Paris, and a German coach in the south. French police believed that Germans and native Frenchmen were responsible. The Puig Antich Ulrike Meinhof Commando sent a message to the French newspaper *Le Figaro* in which they threatened the life of French Minister of Justice M. Lacanuet, saying, ''In France our international collectives have avenged the death of Holger Meins by attacks on Mercedes.'' 2194-2197

January 1975—Syria—The PLO announced in Damascus that hijackers would be executed if their crimes caused loss of life. Sentences of fifteen years' hard labor would be given to those engaging in attacks not involving injuries. Western journalists were shown a farm fifteen miles southeast of Damascus, which the PLO had converted into a prison.

January 1975—United States—A man who became an Israeli citizen after fleeing the United States set fire to a car belonging to John Artukovich, whose brother, Andrea, was a Croatian Nazi leader sentenced to death in absentia in Yugoslavia for the murder of 800,000 people. The arsonist said that he burned the car because he was unable to get to the brother, who was protected at all times by bodyguards. Todd Michael Schwartz, twenty-two, jumped a $10,000 bail in Los Angeles and arrived in Israel as a tourist in February 1976. He became an Israeli citizen in April 1976 and joined the Israeli armed forces after Hebraizing his name to Tuvia. On June 16, 1976, members of the Israeli Knesset attempted to prevent the United States from extraditing him, pointing out that seventy-three Nazis were still living in the United States and that the government had refused to extradite them to Europe on the grounds that their offenses were political and not criminal. 2198

January 1975—United Kingdom—Seven people, including six women, were injured when the Portman and Carlton Tower hotels were machine gunned from a passing car. Later in January, five bombs exploded in London shopping centers, injuring seven. A bomb in a Lewis's store in Manchester injured nineteen. 2199-2206

January 3, 1975—Syria—The Arab Communist Organization bombed the Jordanian and Egyptian embassies in Damascus. The Jordanian embassy was severely damaged. The bomb at the Egyptian embassy was apparently placed outside a door and caused damage primarily to windows and doors. The date coincided with the opening of the Quadripartite Conference in Cairo. 2207-2208

January 3, 1975—United States—Carrying a .22 caliber rifle, a man climbed over a four-foot fence at Pensacola Municipal Airport in Florida, boarded an out-of-service National Airlines B727 and announced to the three men cleaning the aircraft that he was hijacking the plane. Two of the cleaners grabbed the gun from the hijacker and held him until airport police arrived. The hijacker was identified as a white male for whom the FAA profile did not apply, who was born in Long Beach, California, on September 19, 1947. On January 14, 1975, a federal grand jury in the northern district of Florida handed down an indictment against Paul T. Landers, who apparently hoped to attract attention to himself. He was convicted of air piracy on January 20, 1975, and committed suicide by hanging himself in prison three days later. 5451

January 6, 1975—Taiwan—The USIS Center in Taipei received a telephone call at 3:15 P.M. through its switchboard in which a male told the operator that his friend was "going to place a time bomb at USIS." He hung up before the operator could question him. The building was searched, but no bomb was found. 2209

January 7, 1975—United Kingdom—A British Airways BAC111 flying from Manchester was hijacked before landing in London by an Iranian citizen in an Arab headdress identified as Saed Madjid, who pointed a pistol at a stewardess and threatened to use a hand grenade to blow up the plane. He allowed the forty-six passengers to deplane but threatened to kill the five crew members still on board if he was not given £100,000 ($235,000), a parachute, and a flight to Paris. After hours of negotiations, the money and parachute were delivered, and the plane took off. The pilot pretended to go to Paris, but an hour later landed at Stansted Airport, Essex, forty miles from London. The hijacker got off the aircraft and tried to escape, holding a steward as a hostage. He was subsequently captured. It was revealed that the gun and explosives were fake. The hijacker was eventually brought to trial in London. 5452

January 8, 1975—Ethiopia—Three bombs were thrown through the main entrance of the Asmara USIS Library, causing minor damage but no injuries. One of the hand grenades shattered the display window, and a few books were damaged. The attack appeared to be timed to minimize the loss of lives. The bombing may have been carried out by the Popular Liberation Forces, although the group's leadership had called for a lessening of terrorist activity. 2210

January 12, 1975—United States—An employee of the Zephyrhills, Florida, airport was approached in a hangar by an individual who appeared to be either drunk or under the influence of drugs, who demanded to be taken to Mexico. The employee told the man that he was a janitor and could not fly a plane. The man pulled out a knife but dropped it on the floor without threatening the employee. The individual finally ran from the facility and was not apprehended. 5453

January 13, 1975—United States—A young man activated a metal detector at the screening area of Minneapolis-St. Paul International Airport. A physical search revealed a paring knife. The suspect admitted his intent to hijack an aircraft. 5454

January 13, 1975—United States—Laughlin Wright, a black male for whom the FAA profile did not apply, and who was born on June 4, 1928, in Atlanta, attempted to hijack Eastern Airlines flight 140, a B727 flying from Atlanta to Philadelphia with sixty passengers. He had boarded without a ticket. He started pounding on the cockpit door, demanding to be flown to San Juan, Puerto Rico. He agreed to allow the pilot to land at Washington's Dulles Airport for refueling and locked himself in the plane's lavatory while the other passengers deplaned. Police boarded the plane and arrested the hijacker, who was not armed. He was committed to a mental institution on March 28, 1975. 5455

January 13, 1975—France—Two men, one described as being about thirty, fired two RPG-7 rockets at an El Al 707 scheduled to fly 136 passengers and 9 crew, mostly Americans, to Montreal and New York. The first round missed the El Al and hit the fuselage of a Yugoslav DC9 scheduled to fly from Orly Airport to Zagreb. The rocket failed to explode but slightly injured a Yugoslav steward, a French security guard, and a workman. The second round hit an administration building, causing some damage. The duo, whose rocket launcher had smashed through their Peugot 504 saloon's windshield, escaped.

The white car, with two rockets in the back seat, was found in a cemetery in the suburb of Thiais, a few miles from the airport. A 9-mm Tokarev automatic pistol was found on the ground. It was later learned that on January 10 a German calling himself Klaus Muller had rented the car from the Hertz car rental desk at Les Invalides air terminal. His real name was Johannes Weinrich, a lawyer and friend of Ernst Bose. He was also codirector of the Roter Stern publishing house. Police were initially unsure of whether the attack was caused by Palestinian or Croatian terrorists. A phone call was received at Reuters in which an individual claimed credit for the Muhammad Boudia Commando, saying, "Next time we will hit our target." The police guard at Orly Airport was increased to 750. The planning for the attack was traced to Carlos, the PFLP Venezuelan terrorist, and Moukharbel, who led the PFLP squad in Europe. Police knew that the Arab had made a reconnaissance of Orly, because they had discovered a two-franc ticket to the public viewing terraces at the airport in his apartment. It appeared that he wished to discontinue the operation, but Carlos ordered one more attempt, which took place six days later. 2211

January 15, 1975—United States—Four international air carriers received handwritten notes threatening hijacking of aircraft or kidnapping of airline officials unless each air carrier paid $250,000. The extortionists were not apprehended.

January 19, 1975—United States—Rifle shots hit the Soviet U.N. mission building in New York City. 2212

January 19, 1975—France—An Orly Airport policeman fired a submachine burst at an Arab who was setting up an RPG-7 rocket launcher to fire at an El Al scheduled to fly to Tel Aviv. He was joined by two other Arab terrorists, who fired machine guns and threw hand grenades at the police. During the battle, one of the terrorists was injured, along with twenty-one bystanders, including a security guard. The terrorists, identified as a Palestinian, an Algerian, and a Lebanese, all members of the Muhammad Boudia Commando, seized ten hostages and herded them into a second-floor washroom. Most of the hostages initially believed that the trio were policemen trying to get them to safety. One of the terrorists fired a gun through the shoe of a woman who was not crawling to the lavatory fast enough. She escaped by locking herself into the first lavatory available as the terrorists moved past her. The hostages were asked if they were Americans or Israelis, but they admitted only to being French or Portuguese. The CRS attempted to storm the washroom but retreated when the terrorists threatened to kill all the hostages. One of the terrorists, who had been wounded in the arm, held a grenade, forcing the hostages to stand during the eighteen-hour negotiation session. French Interior Minister Poniatowski took personal charge of the police negotiations team, who had been slipping notes under the washroom door. The Egyptian ambassador eventually arrived to act as an intermediary. At one point, the terrorists fired several shots during the ninth hour of the negotiations to prove their commitment. The CRS suggested boring a hole through the door with a laser and pumping in a nerve gas but decided that no gas would act quickly enough. They managed to place various listening devices in the area during the night, as well as jerryrig a periscope composed of mirrors, which allowed them to determine the number of people kept hostage in the screened-off room. Photographs were also taken of the barricaded area. The duo demanded to be flown out of the country and released a pregnant woman and her four-year-old child after Poniatowski refused to bargain until they were freed. The other hostages were freed after a plane was given to them on January 20. The Air France jet flew over Europe and the Middle East for fourteen hours, searching for a country that would accept the three guerrillas. Iraq finally allowed the plane to land at Baghdad on ''humanitarian grounds'' after sending them away after a refueling stop.

A grenade found in an abandoned Simca 1100 matched those later found in Carlos's flat. Several other grenades and a Russian automatic were also found in the car. An abandoned Citroen contained Hertz contracts for the two cars as well as for one used in the raid six days before. The French DST believed Carlos used the Citroen to get away when he discovered that the operation had gone awry. A Klaus Muller had rented both cars. The West German Interpol branch determined that his license was among those stolen by the Baader-Meinhof Gang in West Berlin in November 1970. German police determined that Muller was really Johannes Weinrich, twenty-eight, who was arrested in March 1975. 2213

January 24, 1975—United States—The FALN claimed credit for bombing the Fraunces Tavern annex in New York City at noon, killing four, wounding fifty-three, and causing $300,000 damage. Three communiqués found taped to telephone booths demanded the release of four men and one woman imprisoned since 1950 for attempting to assassinate President Truman and attacking the House of Representatives. The group said the bombing was in retaliation for the ''CIA-ordered'' bombing of an independence meeting in Puerto Rico in which two were killed. The note said, ''You have unleashed a storm from which you comfortable Yankees cannot escape.'' A passerby informed police that he may have seen one of the individuals taping the messages to the booths. Police said that two suspects had been described. One was forty to forty-five years old, 190 pounds, and about six feet tall. The second was of medium build, with a short neck, large head, and thick mustache. 2214

January 26, 1975—Poland—A sabotage threat was made against a Polish airliner flying 133 passengers from Warsaw to New York. The plane was searched for three hours at Ireland's Shannon Airport, but no bomb was found. 2215

January 27, 1975—Mexico—A large bomb exploded either in front of a store of an American firm in San Luis Potosí or a nearby building. Shop windows were broken and window frames were damaged in the 3 A.M. bombing. Another bomb exploded several blocks from the store at 8 A.M, killing eight people and wounding several others, including one of the firm's employees, whose leg was broken. 2216-2217

January 28, 1975—Mexico—A union official who attempted to stop members of the Twenty-third of September Communist League from passing out leaflets at the General Electric factory gateway in Ecatepec, Mexico City, was shot by the group, who fled in three cars. The same fate was suffered by another union official on May 3, 2218

January 28, 1975—Lebanon—The Arab Communist Organization, Lebanon Region claimed credit for bombing the British-owned Spinney's Center department store, which caused moderate damage but no injuries. Pamphlets said that the bombing was engaged in because Spinney's had failed to respond to its previous demands (see incident 2183) to distribute food in the ACO's name. 2219

January 29, 1975—United States—A bomb exploded at 1:17A.M. in a washroom of the main building of the U.S. State Department, causing $367,000 damage but no injuries. The bomb may have been aimed at the AID offices, which have been accused of serving as cover for intelligence operations. Thirty minutes earlier, a member of the Weather Underground had phoned a wire service, warning that State, as well as a Department of Defense building in Oakland, California, would be bombed. The bomb in Oakland was recovered and detonated in an open area while a navy explosive ordnance detachment was trying to dismantle it. No injuries were reported. The caller also led the reporters to a telephone booth that contained messages signed by the group.

January 31, 1975—Colombia—Canadian-born Eric Leupin, fifty, the honorary Dutch consul in Cali and a businessman, was kidnapped by thirty members of the FARC at his lumber farm near his southwestern Colombia villa. The group demanded a ransom of $1 million and the release of the FARC member imprisoned in 1971. Leupin's wife was arrested on May 3, 1976, attempting to deliver a $50,000 ransom. On October 3, 1976, he was released unharmed in Cali. The Dutch government denied that the embassy or any governmental officials had negotiated for Leupin's release and did not pay the ransom, denying all knowledge of the amount paid. 2220

February 1975—United States—Luciano Nieves, forty-three, an outspoken advocate of peaceful coexistence with the Castro regime and an associate of weekly newspaper publisher Rolando Masferrer, chief of Cuba's secret police in the Batista regime, was fatally shot with a .45 caliber pistol in the parking lot of a children's hospital in Miami after visiting his son. The Movement for Cuban Justice claimed credit. Some reports alleged that one suspect's gun jammed during what began as a kidnapping attempt, and the second gunman shot off the first's left index finger by mistake. Several of the nine alleged co-conspirators, believed to be members of the Pragmatistas, apparently fled to Mexico after jumping bond. Three of the others were reported to be at large. Two of those accused were identified as Enrique Velasco and Hector Carbonnell. County Judge Richard Fuller revoked their $10,000 bonds on November 23, 1976, when they failed to appear in his courtroom as ordered. 2221

February 1975—Lebanon—The Arab Communist Organization robbed the Banque Libanaise pour le Commerce in Beirut of 192,000 Lebanese pounds ($438,000). 2222

February 1, 1975—United States—Just before midnight, a homemade bomb packed in a plastic container exploded outside the Venezuelan consulate general in New York City, causing moderate damage. Shortly after the explosion, a Spanish-speaking male phoned CBS television, claiming that Omega-7, an anti-Castro Cuban group, was responsible. Abdala, another anti-Castro group, also claimed credit. 2223

February 3, 1975—United States—The sixth floor men's restroom of the Denver regional office of the Securities and Exchange Commission was bombed, injuring four. The next evening a note attached to a rock was thrown on the porch of a local television station. The Continental Revolutionary Army took credit, saying that it was protesting U.S. involvement in Cuba, Chile, Puerto Rico, and Vietnam.

February 3, 1975—Thailand—On board a Pan Am 747 flying from Bangkok to New Delhi, a passenger poured gasoline from a whiskey bottle into a restroom toilet bowl and around the lavatory as the plane was approximately sixty miles west of Rangoon, Burma. He then broke the needle of a butane refiller cartridge, which sprayed over the lavatory. The man struck a match, and an explosion and fire ensued. It was quickly extinguished by the crew. There was no structural damage to the aircraft, and damage to the restroom was minor. The passenger who set the fire received minor burns. None of the other seventy-seven on board was reported injured.

February 4, 1975—United States—The National Socialist Liberation Front, a Nazi group, was suspected of planting a fragmentation bomb that exploded in the Los Angeles headquarters of the Socialist Workers party. Its members inside were almost killed.

February 6, 1975—United States—The Cuban Action Commandos were suspected of bombing Unidos, a Los Angeles socialist bookstore run by the October League. 2224

February 8, 1975—France—The Mercedes agency in Paris was bombed. 2225

February 9, 1975—Switzerland—An anarchist group was suspected to have been responsible for two explosions at the German mission to the United Nations in Geneva, which caused considerable damage but no casualties. 2226

February 11, 1975—United States—The JCN and Abdala were suspected in one attempted and one successful bombing in Elizabeth, New Jersey. 2227-2228

February 11, 1975—Lebanon—An Arab Communist Organization bomb exploded at the Tyre branch office of the American Life Insurance Company, causing extensive damage but no casualties. A leaflet claimed the attack was a protest against Secretary of State Henry Kissinger's Middle Eastern tour. During the Lebanese civil war, Palestinian guerrillas were freed in a massive jailbreak on March 24, 1976. Among those who fled were ACO members charged with bombing U.S. businesses. The group's freed leader, a Lebanese Christian, said that she turned communist after learning how much money Americans spend on pet food in a starving world. Another who escaped was a Bulgarian woman linked with the Palestinian guerrillas. 2229

February 17, 1975—Lebanon—The eleven-year-old son of Robert Walker, chaplain and professor of culture at the American University of Beirut, was slightly injured when a hand grenade attached to his father's car exploded. 2230

February 18, 1975—Ethiopia—During periods of heavy firing in Asmara, the USIS and U.S. consulate general compound received rounds. 2231

February 20, 1975—Lebanon—A bomb caused serious damage to the Turkish Airlines office in Beirut, but no injuries were reported. A note found in the offices said, "The Slave Kortin Yanikyan groups will continue the just struggle of the Armenians against the imperialists." 2232

February 20, 1975—United States—The Diablo Canyon licensed nuclear facility of California's Pacific Gas and Electric Company received a bomb threat.

February 21, 1975—Argentina—Ten bombs in Rosario damaged the First National Bank of New York, the Boston Bank, the Bank of London and South America, Massey-Ferguson tractor firm, the New Italian Bank, the German Roemer Laboratories, and several automobile showrooms, causing two injuries. 2233-2242

February 22, 1975—Brazil—A VASP B737 flying from São Paulo to Brasilia with eighty persons on board was hijacked out of Goiânia by Joel Siqueira, Jr., who had passed through preboard screening with a pistol. Shortly after takeoff, he carried an infant to the cockpit. At the door, he put the infant down and grabbed a stewardess around the neck, putting a gun to her head. He then took the copilot's seat and pointed the gun at the pilot. During the eight-hour negotiations, he threatened to blow up the plane if he was not given 10 million cruzeiros ($1.3 million), pistols, parachutes, the release of two political prisoners, and radio time for a broadcast. After the plane landed, Siqueira agreed to release twenty-eight women and children in exchange for fuel for the aircraft. Four policemen were able to slip aboard the plane during the refueling. They shot and critically wounded the hijacker before he made known his final destination. 5456

February 23, 1975—United States—The fence of the Nuclear Fuel Services licensed nuclear facility at Erwin, Tennessee, was breached, but nothing was reported stolen.

February 23, 1975—Yemen—A Yemen Airways DC3 flying from Hodeida to Sana was hijacked by a Yemeni passenger, Ali Ben Ali Al Awadi, who pointed a gun at the pilot and forced him to fly north, demanding to be taken to Abu Dhabi. The pilot landed at Qizan, Saudi Arabia, to refuel. Saudi security officials boarded the plane and arrested the hijacker. They accompanied the hijacker and crew in the plane to Sana International Airport and turned him over to Yemeni authorities. He was tried and sentenced to death, but the president commuted his sentence to life imprisonment on March 2, 1975. 5457

February 24, 1975—Puerto Rico—A bomb was discovered in the Santurce office of Avianca Airlines. The device had been ignited but failed to detonate. 2243

February 25, 1975—United States—A bomb threat was made against the Farley licensed nuclear facility of the Alabama Power Company.

February 25, 1975—Philippines—Two men disarmed a Philippine sky marshal with hand grenades, taking his rifle to hijack a PAL DC3 flying the Pagadian-Mindanao-Zamboanga route. They forced the pilot to return to Cebu

City, where twelve passengers were released. Eighteen others were still on board and flew with the hijackers to Manila, where ten hours of negotiations began. The hijackers demanded liquor, cigarettes, food, and a full pardon by the president for one of the hijackers for a previous jail sentence. They released the remaining passengers and crew after the president agreed to the demands, and they surrendered to authorities. On December 7, 1976, a Philippines military court sentenced the two Filipino men to death by firing squad. 5458

February 26, 1975—Argentina—John Patrick Egan, the U.S. consular agent in Córdoba, was kidnapped from his home by the Montoneros, who demanded that the Argentine government prove that four missing guerrillas were alive and well. The government refused to negotiate, and forty-eight hours later Egan was shot and killed by the guerrillas. His body was found soon after. 2244

February 26, 1975—United States—A man attempted to board an American Airlines flight without a ticket or boarding pass. When questioned by a stewardess, the man stated that he had a gun and ordered her to have the ramp truck removed from the plane. The stewardess escorted the man to the aircraft door, and he was taken to an airport operations area where he was turned over to law officers. 5459

February 26, 1975—United States—The Cuban Action Commandos were suspected in the bombing of KCET, a Los Angeles radio station that had announced the showing of a Cuban film, *Lucia*. 2245

February 27, 1975—West Germany—Three days before the West Berlin mayoral election, the Second of June Movement kidnapped Peter Lorenz, chairman of the Berlin Christian Democratic Union (CDU) and his party's mayoral candidate. The two armed men and a woman stopped his car, knocked out his chauffeur, and drugged Lorenz. The group issued a communiqué the next day, demanding the release of individuals arrested during a Berlin demonstration protesting the November 1974 death in prison of Holger Meins, as well as six others imprisoned for terrorist activities. They demanded that the six be flown out of the country, each with £3,600. The CDU was to publish these demands in thirteen newspapers, and police were to stop a nationwide search for the kidnappers. They also warned that Lorenz would be killed if the demands were not met, although they also planned to try him for his connection with "fascist governments." Chancellor Helmut Schmidt offered a reward of £18,000 for information leading to Lorenz, but such searches were fruitless.

The group had links with the Baader-Meinhof Gang, some of whose members had appeared in their demands. The group received its name in commemoration of the death of student Benno Ohnejorg, who died in a demonstration against a visit of the shah of Iran to Berlin in 1967.

The government agreed to the demands within seventy-two hours. Verena Becker, twenty-two, a telephone operator serving six years for bank robbery and bombings, and Ingrid Siepmann, thirty, a technical pharmaceutical assistant serving twelve years for similar crimes, were flown from their West Berlin prison on a French military plane to Frankfurt. The release was televised to give the terrorists maximum publicity and to show that their orders had been carried out. Pastor Heinrich Albertz, a former Berlin mayor, flew in the plane as an additional hostage. Upon landing, the two were joined by Rolf Pohl, thirty-three, a lawyer who was sentenced to six years for belonging to the Baader-Meinhof Gang, and Rolf Heissler, twenty-six, a student serving eight years for armed robbery. Pohl and Heissler had arrived from their Bavarian prison and were joined by Gabriele Krocher-Tiedemann. The last terrorist whose release was demanded, Horst Mahler, one of the original Baader-Meinhof four, chose to stay imprisoned so that he would not desert the class struggle. Some observers believed that his toying with Maoism had led to his comrades' being irritated with him, and perhaps hoping to change his thinking forcibly.

Krocher-Tiedemann, whom some suspected of being involved in the Entebbe hijacking of June 1976, initially refused to accompany the terrorists because her eight-year prison sentence could soon be shortened by parole hearings. Pohl and her mother debated with her the merits of remaining in prison, and she finally compromised, saying that she would leave with the group but end her connections with them: "I am going to take up my studies again abroad." The takeoff of the Lufthansa plane carrying the terrorists to Tripoli was televised on March 3, but the plane was denied landing privileges in Tripoli, Beirut, Damascus, and Amman. The PDRY finally granted the terrorists political asylum in Aden. Albertz was allowed to fly back the next day and broadcast a communiqué from the terrorists, which apparently included a code to their colleagues. Six hours later, Lorenz was released in a West Berlin park. The reward for the terrorists' arrest was increased to £55,000. One of the terrorists was reported killed in a shootout with police. On September 14, 1975, West Berlin police arrested Fritz Teufel, thirty-two, for the kidnapping after he was detained in a police sweep following a bombing in Hamburg that injured eleven.

Those who were released continued to appear in the headlines. Rolf Pohl arrived in Athens on May 27, 1976, using a false passport from Peru. After his arrival from Corfu, he was identified from photographs brought to Athens by West German policemen after his arrest on July 22, 1976. A long legal battle in Greek courts ensued regarding the status of West Germany's extradition request. A lower court ruled that he was not covered by the 1907 Greek-German extradition agreements because his acts were those of a genuine revolutionary, not a criminal. He had been convicted in 1974 in West Germany of conspiracy, forgery, and fraud. Pohl's lawyers also argued that he had in effect been given amnesty by the Bonn government when he was exchanged for

Lorenz. However, the supreme court reversed the decision in a six to one vote, agreeing with public prosecutor Vassilios Papanastasiou that the lower court decision would ''make Greece a haven for international terrorists, for any fugitive on the lam.'' It was also believed that Greece was afraid that Carlos, the famed Venezuelan terrorist and an apparent friend of Pohl, might attempt to engage in an attack to free Pohl. Under strict security procedures, he was brought on board a West German aircraft on October 3, 1976, and extradited to Munich.

On July 7, 1976, four women held in West Berlin's prison for terrorist activities, including the Lorenz kidnapping, escaped. They included Inge Viett, thirty-two; Gabriele Rollnik, twenty-five; Juliane Plambeck, twenty-three; and Monika Berberich, thirty-three. The first three were being held to determine the extent of their participation in the kidnapping. Viett, a former kindergarten teacher, was a leader of the Second of June Movement. Berberich, a Baader-Meinhof Group member, was serving a twelve-year sentence for bank robbery. Plambeck was also suspected of participating in the kidnap-murder of West Berlin's chief judge, Gunther von Drenkmann, in November 1974. The escape had been carried out at 1:15 A.M. from the Tiergarten area. Viett pointed what appeared to be a gun at two female guards, who opened her cell. She obtained the warden's keys and freed the others. They climbed knotted sheets down the prison wall to a waiting getaway car. Police found several steel spikes on the road, apparently designed to foil pursuers.

Viett and Plambeck had been arrested in September with Ralf Reinders, twenty-seven, the suspected leader of the Second of June Movement. Terrorists who had hijacked an Air France jet to Entebbe in June 1976 had demanded the release of Reinders and Viett. On July 21, 1976, West Berlin police arrested Berberich as she was walking. 2246

February 28, 1975—Japan—The East Asia Anti-Japanese Action Front exploded two bombs at the Tokyo headquarters of a large industrial organization, giving themselves the code words Wolf and Scorpion.

March 1975—United States—In Chicago, John Badovinac, chairman of the Croatian Brotherhood Community, an emigrant organization, was attacked in an assassination attempt. 2247

March 1975—Netherlands—Security services uncovered a South Moluccan plot to kidnap the Indonesian ambassador. 2248

March 1, 1975—Iraq—An Iraqi Airways B737 flying from Mosul to Baghdad with ninety-three on board was hijacked by three Kurdish sympathizers, who demanded a ransom of $5 million and freedom for eighty-five political prisoners, threatening to blow up the plane and all aboard. The men were identified as Taha Naimi, Faud Al-Qeitan, and Ahmad Hasan. During the flight, an Iraqi security officer engaged in a shootout with the hijackers, leaving two passengers dead and ten others, including Hasan, wounded. The plane landed in Tehran, Iran, and the passengers were allowed to disembark without interference. The terrorists surrendered to Persian authorities. Naimi and Al-Qeitan were executed by an Iranian firing squad on April 7. Hasan died from wounds received during the flight. 2249

March 2, 1975—United States—Alexander P. Grosser, a white male for whom the FAA profile was not applicable and who was born in Breslau, Germany, on July 5, 1940, approached Air New England's flight XQ911, a Twin Otter scheduled to fly from Hyannis, Massachusetts, to Nantucket, and demanded that the pilot, the only person on board, fly him to New Haven, Connecticut. The pilot refused and radioed for help. Grosser boarded the plane and repeated his demand, claiming to have a knife. Trucks blocked the aircraft, and the pilot jumped out. Police struggled briefly with the hijacker and arrested him. A complaint was filed the next day in the district of Massachusetts. Grosser was convicted on April 9, 1976, for carrying a weapon aboard an aircraft. 5460

March 2, 1975—France—The Charles Martel Club bombed the Toulouse office of Air Algérie. The firm's Lyons office was also bombed. 2250-2251

March 4, 1975—Burma—Gert Windhein, a West German geologist, was kidnapped at a tin mine in northern Shan state by the Kachin Independence Army, which demanded a ransom of 1 million marks ($390,000). The West German government agreed to pay, but the Burmese government refused the demand. It is not known if the demands were met, but Windhein was freed unharmed on May 7. 2252

March 5, 1975—Sweden—Two members of the Japanese Red Army, Jun Nishikawa and Kazuo Tohira, were arrested by the Stockholm police while they were taking photographs and making sketches of a building housing the embassies of Lebanon, Austria, and four other countries. It was believed that the three hundred photographs, diagrams, and background notes that were found later were part of their preparation for a break-in of the Lebanese embassy. They were charged with using forged passports. A third member of the group, Toshikiko Hidaka, escaped. One of the two had been involved in the Hague incident the previous September (see incident 2050). One of them carried an emergency retreat address, which was found to be that of a high North Korean diplomat in East Berlin. On March 13, 1975, the two were deported from Sweden and were arrested by the Japanese police at Tokyo International Airport on charges of forging and using official documents. They were indicted on April 3, 1975. Their accomplices, Osamu Maruoka and Toshihiko Hidaka, were placed on an international wanted list.

Nishikawa confessed to Japanese police of involvement in a plot to kidnap Japanese businessmen in Europe, and detailed the JRA's September 1975 reorganization. Fusako Shigenobu's political committee handled relations with Venezuelan terrorist Carlos and the PFLP. Three subcommittees included the military committee (comprised of commando fighters), an organization committee, and a logistics committee. Nishikawa was charged with attempted murder for having fired a shot over the heads of the Hague hostages (and hitting a picture of President Pompidou).

Tohira said his group was to surveil Lebanese embassies in Copenhagen, Oslo, and Stockholm in preparation for a seizure of hostages and ransom demands. The group members were given instructions and forged passports at a Beirut PFLP camp by Haruo Wako and Osamu Maruoka.

Shigenobu said that she planned to stage operations to secure the release of the arrested JRA members. In June 1975, the group published "Form Ranks, a Declaration by the JRA," which said that it would be reunited with Nishikawa and Tohira, who would be welcomed.

Nishikawa and Tohira, along with other terrorists in Japanese jails, were freed as a result of demands made in the JRA takeover of the U.S. consulate in Kuala Lumpur, Malaysia, on August 4, 1975. They were flown with their colleagues to Libya. 2253

March 5, 1975—Israel—Eight members of Fatah used two rubber dinghies to land in Tel Aviv. The terrorists had hoped to attack the Municipality Youth Center but were spotted by a policeman, who called in reinforcements. Firing wildly, the terrorists attacked the Hotel Savoy in the city's prostitution district, taking ten people hostage (thirty others managed to escape). A one and a half hour gun battle ensued, ending at 1 A.M. with the terrorists forcing one of their hostages, Mrs. Kochava Levy, thirty-one, to yell out the window the demands of the terrorists. The group demanded the release of ten Palestinian guerrillas and Greek Archbishop Hilarion Capucci, who was imprisoned for smuggling guns to Palestinian terrorists. The group also wanted a plane to fly them to Damascus and asked for the ambassadors from the Vatican, France, and Greece to serve as intermediaries. The Israelis stalled for time but did not intend to give in to the group's demands. Levy was allowed to escort one wounded hostage from the hotel. She decided to return to the hostages to aid in the negotiations (she was the only hostage who spoke Arabic). The group was armed with explosives, grenades, and Kalashnikov submachine guns. Prime Minister Yitzhak Rabin ordered Israeli troops to storm the building at 2:15 A.M. The attack began at 5:30 A.M. and lasted for fifteen minutes. The terrorists set off one of their explosives, destroying the fourth floor of the hotel and seriously damaging most of the rest of the building. In all, seven of the eight terrorists were killed, three Israeli soldiers died, and eight hostages, including a Dutch boy of fifteen, a German national, a Swiss citizen, and a Somali, were killed. Twelve others were reported injured, as was the surviving terrorist, Moosa Jummaa, twenty-three, who was discovered around noon during a cleanup operation, hiding behind a wooden wall. The Israelis also seized the terrorists' ship, which had begun its journey from the Lebanese port of Sidon and was found between Beirut and Cyprus. Hammid Nadim, twenty, a Palestinian, was discovered on board. He claimed that he had been ordered to join the attack squad but refused, staying on board the craft to supervise the operation. Two other crewmen, described by Israeli authorities as Egyptian sailors and not members of Fatah, were also arrested on the ship. The Israelis allowed Nadim and Jummaa to appear before a press conference. Jummaa claimed to have been born in Beersheba; Nadim came from Nablus on the occupied West Bank. They claimed that the operation was organized by Abu Jehad, whom they decribed as the second in command of Fatah. "We were asked to say in case we were taken prisoner that we came from Port Said, Egypt." The group was aiming at sabotaging talks between Israel and Egypt that were to get underway with the arrival in the Middle East of U.S. Secretary of State Henry Kissinger. Painted on one of the boats was an Arabic inscription, which translated as, "Kissinger's efforts will fail." According to the terrorists, their seven-month training period began near Damascus. They went to Latakia, a port city, for naval training and moved to Lebanon in February for their final training. Before the Israeli commando attack, the group had lessened their demands to safe passage to Damascus for themselves. 2254

March 6, 1975—Chile—A Cuban exile journal in Miami reported that Chile's General Pinochet promised "unconditional help" to Cuban exile groups.

March 6, 1975—France—A bomb caused slight damage to a Paris office of a West German publishing group. Leaflets from the Sixth of March Group demanded freedom and amnesty for Baader-Meinhof members in German jails. 2255

March 6, 1975—United States—Ralph Gonzalez, a Latin who was born in Las Vegas, Nevada, on August 4, 1954, and Edward E. Rodriguez, a Latin born in Los Angeles on January 2, 1953, chartered a Sawyer Aviation Cessna 310 to fly them from Phoenix to Tucson. During the flight, they pointed a gun at the pilot and forced him to fly to Nogales, Mexico. The hijackers turned the plane and pilot over to a group that met the plane. The pilot escaped the next day and notified the authorities of the hijacking. Rodriguez was captured in Las Vegas on March 21, 1975, and Gonzales surrendered to federal agents on April 11, 1975. They were sentenced to six years in prison for kidnapping on July 17, 1975. The FAA profile was not applicable in their cases. 5461

March 7, 1975—Mexico—Police discovered and disarmed a powerful nitro-glycerin bomb at 9:10 A.M. in the Mexico City offices of Cubana de Aviacion, fifty minutes before it was set to explode. Two Molotov cocktails were defused in a subway station. 2256

March 8, 1975—United States–The Zion licensed nuclear facility of the Commonwealth Edison Company received a bomb threat.

March 8, 1975—United States—On New York City's Lower East Side, police discovered a Hell's Angels cache of seventy-five pounds of explosives. The group claimed to have taken the explosives from the FALN to aid them in getting a prisoner released.

March 9, 1975—Argentina—The Montoneros bombed new cars on a San Justo production lot at the Chrysler-Fevre plant, fifteen miles west of Buenos Aires, causing no casualties. The group warned of future attacks against "octopus" U.S. interests and said that they were protesting the forthcoming visit by a U.S. assistant secretary of state. 2257

March 10, 1975—Turkey—A packet of explosives thrown into the garden of the U.S. consulate in Istanbul only partially exploded and caused no damage. An anonymous phone call to the Anatolian News Agency claimed credit for the Mahir Cayan Suicide Group. Cayan had been involved in the 1971 assassination of the Israeli consul general and had himself been killed in a shootout with police. The bombing was to protest U.S. Secretary of State Henry Kissinger's visit to Turkey. 2258

March 12, 1975—Syria—The chief of the PLO military division, Zouheir Mohsen, threatened to launch terrorist attacks on Israeli targets in the United States. 2259

March 14, 1975—United States—The licensed nuclear facility of Mallinckrodt Chemical Works in St. Louis, Missouri, received a bomb threat.

March 15, 1975—United States—A small explosive device believed to be an M-80 firecracker exploded near a ticket counter at San Francisco international airport, blowing out one and a half inches of stucco wall but causing no injuries.

March 17, 1975—United States—A young man walked into a general aviation airport in Ohio and pointed a shotgun at a hangar secretary, saying that he wanted an aircraft. An employee in an adjacent office who had overheard the conversation talked to the man and led him out of the office to an aircraft tie-down area. As they approached a plane, the gunman lit and tossed a flare underneath its wing. A policeman arrived at the scene and disarmed the individual, who later claimed that he intended to crash an aircraft into a terminal tower as a protest against abortion. 5462

March 22, 1975—United States—A crude homemade device resembling a pipe bomb was found at a lost-and-found baggage area at the Hawaiian Airlines terminal in Honolulu international airport. It was later determined that the device could have caused substantial damage had it detonated during a flight.

March 23, 1975—Somalia—Jean Gueury, the French ambassador, was kidnapped by members of the Somali Coast Liberation Front as he was leaving a church. The group took him to a suburban villa, which was quickly surrounded by security police. The Italian ambassador, Giorgio Jacomelli, served as an intermediary in the negotiations. The group demanded $100,000 in gold and the release of two political prisoners being held in France. The duo, Omar Osman Rabeh and Omar Elmi Khareh, had been imprisoned in 1968 for life for attempting to assassinate the FTAI political leader, Ali Aref. The group set a thirty-six-hour deadline, due to expire at noon on March 25, 1975. In Algiers, Mohamed Fara, an FLCS spokesman, said Gueury would be killed if the demands were not met or if the Somalis attempted to use force. France agreed to the demands, and Gueury was freed in Aden on March 28. 2260

March 24, 1975—United States—During the evening, two fires were set at the Colombian consulate in New York City. One fire caused extensive damage to the second floor, and the second caused minor damage to the third floor. The consulate had received threats from a Cuban exile group. 2261

March 27, 1975—United States—A powerful bomb planted by the Red Guerrilla Family exploded in the FBI office in Berkeley, California.

March 27, 1975—United States—The Cuban Action Commandos claimed credit for bombing two Los Angeles buildings, one of which housed the Costa Rican consulate. The other caused minor damage to the offices of Apex International Exporting Company. A man claiming to be a member of a pro-Castro Cuban group phoned radio station KFWB saying that he supported Fidel Castro's attempts to get Cuba into the OAS. He claimed that the bomb was aimed at the offices of the Panamanian Tourist Bureau. An employee, Nick Nell, said, "If any pro-Castro group did that, it sounds very weird. Panama has opened relations with Cuba." No injuries were reported. 2262-2263

March 30, 1975—France—Croatian exiles were believed responsible for an assassination attempt in which the Yugoslav vice-consul in Lyons was shot and seriously wounded as he got out of his car in a garage near his home. 2264

April 1975—Colombia—Although he had identified himself, rioting students in Bogotá set fire to the car of the apostolic nuncio. 2265

April 1, 1975—United States—The Peace Bottom licensed nuclear facility of the Philadelphia Electric Company received a bomb threat.

April 2, 1975—Mexico—Fire was reported in the U.S. consulate in Guadalajara, causing no major damage to USIS premises. 2266

April 3, 1975—United States—Four FALN bombs exploded in downtown New York City after a warning was given. Damage was estimated at $155,750, including 120 shattered windows.

The first bomb exploded at 11:44 P.M. at the New York Life Insurance Company annex at 51 Madison Avenue. The second went off at 12:03 A.M. at the Bankers Trust Company plaza at 45 East Forty-ninth Street. A third bomb exploded at 12:08 A.M. at the Metropolitan Life Insurance Company headquarters at 340 Park Avenue South. Four firemen injured their hands clearing glass from the site. At 12:19 A.M., the last bomb exploded outside the Blimpie Base restaurant at 5 West Forty-sixth Street. A pedestrian was cut in the head by flying glass. Fire Department Chief Schryver suggested that the bombers had intended to go elsewhere, but when spotted when somebody came out of the building, threw their last bomb away before it was about to explode. The bomb went off in the middle of a dozen plastic garbage bags.

At 12:53 A.M., a man phoned Associated Press and speaking with a hispanic accent, said, "This is the FALN. We just threw bombs. You will find a communiqué in a telephone booth at 88th Street and Lexington Avenue." The news service gave the unopened envelope to the police, who released the statement. The terrorists said that their victims were "important decision makers in planning of domestic and foreign policy and benefit from the exploitation and oppression of Puerto Rico and other Third World nations as well as the North American working class." The group demanded independence for Puerto Rico and the release of five terrorists serving prison sentences for attempting to assassinate President Truman and shooting at members of the House of Representatives. The Bureau of Prisons denied that one prisoner, Andres Figueroa Cordero, was dying of cancer. 2267-2270

April 3, 1975—United States—The Cuban Action Commandos were suspected of planting a bomb that misfired in the Los Angeles office of the Communist party. 2271

April 4, 1975—United States—Rifle or pistol shots cut a telephone line of the Point Beach licensed nuclear facility of the Wisconsin-Michigan Power Company.

April 5, 1975—United States—An unexploded dynamite bomb was found in a window air-conditioner unit at the Heron Travel and Tourist office in Los Angeles. Philip John Goodman, a suspected JDL member, was convicted of two felony charges related to the attempted bombing.

April 5, 1975—United States—An explosive device caused considerable damage to the Los Angeles office of Iraqi Airways but caused no injuries. A young man was arrested. An anti-Arab message was telephoned to a local news agency after the evening explosion. 2272

April 8, 1975—Angola—A South African Airways jet flying 287 passengers from Johannesburg to London was hit by small arms fire as it came in for a landing at Luanda. Six shots hit the jet, causing slight damage and no injuries. 2273

April 9, 1975—Japan—As a JAL B747 flying 212 passengers from Sapporo began its approach to Tokyo, Kazuo Oshima, a young man, pointed a pistol at a steward and demanded two parachutes and 30 million yen ($100,000). The plane taxied to a parking area at Haneda Airport, where the passengers were allowed to deplane. While the pilot engaged Oshima in conversation, three policemen entered the plane through a rear door. During the ensuing struggle, a shot was fired. No injuries were reported, and the hijacker was arrested. 5463

April 10, 1975—United States—The JDL was supected of firebombing the Iraqi U.N. Mission in New York City, causing minor damage. 2274

April 10, 1975—United States—The Millstone licensed nuclear facility of the Northeast Nuclear Energy Company received a bomb threat.

April 10, 1975—France—In a letter to Reuters, the Charles Martel Club claimed credit for planting a bomb that exploded in a car outside the Algerian consulate in Paris. The group was protesting the French president's visit to Algeria. 2275

April 11, 1975—Kuwait—The American Life Insurance Company office in Kuwait sustained considerable damage by a bomb. Kuwaiti press credited the blast to the Communist Labor Organization-Lebanon, which may be the Arab Communist Organization. Three of the terrorists responsible were arrested in July 1975 and sentenced in late December to prison terms of from three to fifteen years, to be followed by deportation. Several other group members were arrested in July 1975 in Syria and Lebanon. Those in Syria were sentenced shortly after their arrest, and some were executed. The fate of those arrested in Lebanon was not reported. 2276

April 13, 1975—United States—An anonymous caller claimed credit for the Cuban Action Commandos after a bomb was dropped through the roof of the Unidos book store in Los Angeles. The store is reputedly leftist in orientation. 2277

April 14, 1975—United States—The Calvert Cliffs licensed nuclear facility of the Baltimore Gas and Electric Company received a bomb threat.

April 16, 1975—Lebanon—John McKay, a U.S. Drug Enforcement Agency official, was kidnapped and held for two days by Palestinians in Beirut's Sabra refugee camp. He was interrogated and released unharmed. 2278

April 16, 1975—United States—A Consolidated Edison Company licensed nuclear facility received a bomb threat.

April 18, 1975—Argentina—A bomb exploded at the door of the Chilean consulate in Mar del Plata, causing serious damage to part of the building. The Chilean president had recently visited Argentina. 2279

April 19, 1975—Japan—A bomb exploded in the early morning in the Tokyo building housing the South Korean Industrial and Economic Research Institute. Another bomb exploded in a building housing a company engaged in a joint venture with the institute. Threatening letters were found in both companies' mail boxes. Eight young extremists were arrested on May 19 for these and other bombings. Police found ties between these members of the Anti-Japan Armed Front of East Asia and the South Korea Youth League, an organization opposed to President Park of South Korea. 2280

April 21, 1975—Greece—The U.S. embassy in Athens was attacked by part of a crowd of leftist demonstrators protesting U.S. support of the military junta that had ruled Greece until July 1974. Considerable damage was reported to the consular section, and fifteen Greek police were injured. 2281

April 24, 1975—Sweden—Six members of the Socialist Patients' Collective took over the West German embassy in Stockholm. They were part of a group of mental patients led by Heidelberg psychiatrist Dr. Huber and his wife who believed that the cause of mental illness is society, which must be changed through violent action. The group, five men and a woman, identified as Hanna Elisa Krabbe, a former companion of Hans Joachim Klein (an associate of Venezuelan terrorist Carlos), entered the embassy at noon, searched for an individual with keys to the upstairs floors, and took eleven staff members, along with Ambassador Dieter Stoecker, hostage on the third floor. In the initial attack, a Swedish woman was injured. The group, whose ages ranged from twenty-three to thirty-one, was led by a male named Hausener and carried

American-made M-26 grenades (suspected of being part of Carlos's cache), automatic weapons (two Suomis, believed supplied by Baader-Meinhof lawyer Siegfried Haag), and thirty-three pounds of explosives, which they wired to the upstairs floors. They demanded that West Germany release twenty-six prisoners held in jail for the deaths of eight people and injuries to one hundred others, including Baader-Meinhof members Andreas Baader, thirty-two, Ulrike Meinhof, forty, Gudrun Ensslin, thirty-four, and Jan-Carl Raspe, thirty. The prisoners were to be given $20,000 each and placed on board a B707, which would fly to an unannounced location. They were to be accompanied by the Swedish ambassador to Bonn, Sven Baechlund. During the initial assault, Swedish police refused to move away from the building, and the terrorists fired four bullets into the military attaché, Lieutenant Colonel Andreas Baron von Mirach. Police were allowed to take his body from the embassy grounds; he died soon afterward. The German government refused to accept the terrorists' demands despite threats to kill one hostage each hour. Upon receiving this refusal, the terrorists killed the economic counselor, Heinz Hillegaart. The group allowed three of the female hostages to leave the embassy with the message that they had dropped their demands, which included the televising to Germans and Swedes of the transfer of the prisoners onto the plane. At approximately midnight, two loud explosions, believed to have gone off accidentally, were heard. Most of the top floor of the embassy was destroyed in the blast, which also killed one of the terrorists. Some reports claim that he took his own life rather than allow himself to be arrested. Thirteen others were injured, including Ambassador Stoecker, who reported an ear injury and minor burns on his hands, and one of the terrorists, who suffered burns on 40 percent of his body. The terrorists were found wandering about the embassy grounds and had thrown down their submachine guns. Police noted that only one of them had a criminal record. It was later discovered that Krabbe had also been wounded in the blast. The four terrorists who did not need extensive hospitalization were immediately extradited to Germany, to be joined later by their wounded colleague. Some reports listed seven terrorists as taking part in the attack and noted that Swiss terrorists were believed to have aided in providing arms to the attackers, who initially identified themselves as members of the Holger Meins Commando. On July 20, 1977, a Düsseldorf court sentenced Hanna-Elise Krabbe, Lutz Manfred Taufer, Karl-Heinz Dellwo, and Bernard Maria Roessner to life imprisonment. 2282

April 25, 1975—United States—United Airlines flight 344, a B727 flying sixty-seven persons from Raleigh, North Carolina, to Newark, was the scene of an attempted hijacking by Francis P. Covey, a white male who did not meet the FAA profile and who was born in Richmond, Virginia, on March 6, 1931. He called to a stewardess and informed her that the plane was going to Havana, claiming to have a bomb and gun and threatening to blow up the plane if his demand was refused. The pilot talked him into allowing him to land in Atlanta to refuel. Covey agreed to allow all passengers and all but one crew member to deplane. In the confusion, all managed to escape. External doors were locked until FBI agents were able to board the aircraft and arrest Covey, who was unarmed. On October 17, 1975, he was sentenced to five years (after having been indicted on May 20) for conveying malicious false information regarding destruction of aircraft. 5464

April 25, 1975—Argentina—A bomb placed in a car parked in front of the British embassy residence in Buenos Aires exploded, killing a police guard and injuring two others. The ambassador and his family were not injured. 2283

April 28, 1975—United States—A self-professed revolutionary group claimed credit for the Denver bombings of the American National Bank and the home of a CIA employee.

April 28, 1975—South Africa—The Israeli consulate in Johannesburg was taken over by a mentally unstable security guard, David Protter, twenty-four, who killed two consulate employees and wounded thirty-three others during a sixteen-hour siege, which included many gun battles with police. Initial reports claimed that six terrorists had taken over the building and had seized twenty-one hostages. Protter was armed with three revolvers, two submachine guns, and hand grenades. He had hidden in the consulate before dawn and informed each employee who entered the consulate that he was conducting a security exercise. He then locked each one up. When one of the consulate's security officers, Giora Raviv, Protter's superior, objected, Protter shot and killed him. Also reported dead was Edwin Malpo, a South African employee. Protter negotiated with police by using a walkie-talkie, employing various voices and accents to give the impression that he had several accomplices. He ran from window to window firing into the streets, injuring several passersby. On November 13, 1975, he was sentenced to twenty-five years for murdering Raviv. Protter had been born in Austria to a Jewish family, which emigrated to South Africa when he was a small child. When he was seventeen, he went to Israel to continue his studies, which were cut short when he suffered a nervous breakdown. Upon being told that he was to return to South Africa, he climbed to the roof of a building, threatening to jump. He also attempted to slash his wrists. While being driven to the airport, he stabbed himself in the stomach. Later he was discharged from the Israeli army for psychiatric reasons. He had been arrested several times in Israel for impersonating a paratroop officer. Israeli officials were at a loss to explain how he had passed their background investigations to join the consulate staff. 2284

April 29, 1975—Spanish Sahara—It was speculated that Sidemech Muhammad al-'Arusi, twenty-two, a member of the Polisario (Popular Front for the

Liberation of Saguia el Hamra and Rio do Oro), was kidnapped by individuals seeking political vengeance. Others suggested that he had decided to rejoin the group.

May 1975—Spanish Sahara—Fourteen Spaniards who were kidnapped in May by the Polisario were reported released on September 9, 1975, at the behest of Algeria. 2285

May 1975—France—The Warriors of Christ the King, a rightist group allegedly composed of Spanish police, were suspected of attacking ETA targets in the south. A Hendaye bookshop selling Basque and ETA literature was bombed. In Biarritz, three men attempted to place a bomb in the car of José Antonio Urruticoechea, a suspected ETA member named as one of fifteen persons wanted by the Spanish government for the Carrero Blanco murder (see incident 1751). One of the trio died when the bomb exploded prematurely. Another was wounded. He was carrying a fake Australian passport. The *New York Times* claimed he was a member of the Spanish secret police. The third man escaped. 2286-2287

May 1, 1975—United States—The Nat Turner-John Brown unit of the New World Liberation Front claimed credit for bombing the Sacramento office of the California Department of Corrections.

May 2, 1975—United States—The Cuban Action Commandos bombed a Socialist Workers party bookstore in Santa Monica, California. 2288

May 3, 1975—United States—Ivan Lukic, Bozo Delava, Zvonko Luburic, and others were reported to have assaulted the Yugoslav consul general, M. Bulajic, and his wife at a New York City party.

May 3, 1975—France—Seventy minutes before two explosions took place at the construction site of a French nuclear power station in Fessenheim, an anonymous call was made to *L'Alsace*, a local newspaper, claiming credit for the Puig Antich-Ulrike Meinhof Commando, which was believed to be composed of German and Spanish anarchists. No fissionable material was on hand at the time of the explosions, which caused considerable damage to the building and equipment but no injuries. According to reports by the BDM Corporation on the attack, ''Electricity workers on duty at the time of the explosion stated that the explosion had occurred inside the concrete building housing the reactor. They report damage to a steam generator pump and the system for lowering uranium rods into the reactor. Despite the various reports of damage in this incident, the damage did not appear to be severe enough to significantly delay the completion of the reactor. Because the reactor was still under construction, no fissionable materials were involved. There is some agreement on other facts of this case. Reports indicate that a man telephoned 2 Alsatian newspapers . . .claimed 3 bombs would go off in the toilets of an administrative building 900 feet from the reactor. The caller said he wanted everyone to get out in time. The bombs were located either in a building much closer to the reactor or in the reactor building itself." 2289

May 6, 1975—United States—The Forked River licensed nuclear facility of the Jersey Central Power and Light Company received a bomb threat.

May 7, 1975—France—GARI bombed the Paris IBM office, injuring no one. 2290

May 7, 1975—United States—The Cuban Action Commandos were suspected of bombing the leftist-oriented Midnight Special Bookstore in Los Angeles. 2291

May 10, 1975—United States—A small bomb placed inside a stack of newspapers in front of an Aeroflot office door in Washington, D.C., exploded in the early morning, causing minimal property damage and no injuries. A mile away, the Mexican chancery was bombed, with minor damage and no injuries. The next day the Associated Press received a note from El Alacran (the Scorpion), apparently an anti-Castro group, claiming credit. 2292-2293

May 13, 1975—United States—TWA officials received a phone call warning that there was a bomb aboard one of its flights. The caller described the bomb and demanded $500,000. The flight arrived safely at its destination. The extortionist was not apprehended.

May 13, 1975—United States—The Millstone 3 licensed nuclear facility of the Northeast Nuclear Energy Company received a bomb threat.

May 13, 1975—Lebanon—U.S. foreign service officer Michael Konner was kidnapped from a Beirut marketplace by three Palestinians. He was interrogated and beaten but not seriously injured. He was released fourteen hours later. 2294

May 14, 1975—United States—Mission staff prevented two unidentified armed individuals from breaking into the New York building housing the Yugoslav U.N. mission. 2295

May 15, 1975—United States—A young woman aboard United Airlines flight 509, a B737 flying from Eugene, Oregon, to San Francisco with eighty persons on board, advised a stewardess that she did not want to land in San Francisco. She claimed to have a knife and threatened to harm the other passengers if she was not allowed inside the cockpit. The captain talked to her over the intercom phone, trying to calm her. She was grabbed by one of the crew as the plane landed and held for police. The FAA profile did not apply in the case of this white hijacker, identified as Deborah Lynn Crawford, who was born on March 30, 1959. She was returned to a state hospital in California. 5465

May 16, 1975—Spain—Five or six Catalan separatist youths broke windows in a Pan Am ticket office in Barcelona and threw a Molotov cocktail, which caused smoke and fire damage estimated at $3,500. No injuries were reported in this protest of the U.S. use of force in the *Mayaguez* incident, according to leaflets found at the scene. 2296

May 17, 1975—Mexico—Five sticks of dynamite with an acid fuse were found in a store of a U.S.-owned firm in the morning. 2297

May 19, 1975—Tanzania—Forty armed members of the People's Revolutionary Party, a radical Zairian group, attacked an animal research center run by British anthropologist Dr. Jane Goodall for Stanford University, kidnapping four Stanford students. On May 25, one, Barbara Smuts, twenty-four, of Ann Arbor, Michigan, was released with the guerrillas' demands for $500,000, American arms, and the release of two PRP members from Zaire jails. She reported that the other hostages had been taken by boat across Lake Tanganyika to Zaire. While Stanford let it be known that it would be willing to provide some form of humanitarian aid, the U.S. government refused to grant monetary or military aid in a terrorist situation. The Zaire government refused to allow safe conduct to intermediaries who wished to contact the guerrillas. Contact was made through a group of fishermen. An attempt was made to rescue the students, but the rescue boat was shelled by a Zairian gunboat as it neared the lake shore. On June 28 Carrie Jane Hunter, twenty-one, of Atherton, California, and Emilie Bergman, twenty-five, of the Netherlands, were released. On July 26 the last hostage, Kenneth Stephen Smith, twenty-two, of Garden Grove, California, was released. Stanford announced that part of the agreement with the terrorists was that neither side would disclose ransom terms. The press speculated that $40,000 had been paid. The U.S. government and the university president claimed that no such cash payment had been made by them. On August 15, 1975, Secretary of State Henry A. Kissinger was rumored to have fired W. Beverly Carter, the U.S. ambassador to Tanzania who played a central role in negotiations leading to the release of the students. Carter was to lose his appointment to be ambassador to Denmark and was to be transferred to the USIA at a reduction in status and pay. When he returned to the United States in December, he was given the job of special assistant in the State Department's Bureau of African Affairs, where he had served as deputy assistant secretary in 1969. On March 19, 1976, Carter was nominated to be ambassador to Liberia. 2298

May 21, 1975—Iran—Five members of the Iranian People's Strugglers (although some reports claimed they were the Crusaders of the Iranian Nation) shot and killed two U.S. Air Force officers in Tehran as they were being driven to work at the U.S. Military Assistance Advisory Group. They were identified as Colonel Paul R. Shaffer, Jr., forty-five, a native of Bryan, Ohio, and Lieutenant Colonel Jack J. Turner, forty-five, of Christopher, Illinois. On July 29, 1975, two Iranian terrorists were arrested and charged with the crime. They later confessed to killing Turner and Shaffer, as well as Lieutenant Colonel Lewis Hopkins in 1973 and an Iranian interpreter at the U.S. consulate on July 3, 1975. They were identified as Vahid Rahman Afrakteh and Mohsen Khamoushi. Seven others were reported arrested on August 10, 1975, at a hideout that held ten pistols and twenty-five hand grenades. Others held after the gun battle included a pregnant woman and another suspect. A third individual was reported killed by members of his own gang. On December 31, 1975, ten of the group were sentenced by an Iranian army tribunal to death by a firing squad. An eleventh defendant, one of two women in the group, was sentenced to solitary confinement for fifteen years. The sentences were carried out against nine of the terrorists on January 24, 1976. The sentence of the tenth was commuted to life imprisonment. 2299

May 22, 1975—France—The Puig Antich-Ulrike Meinhof Commando bombed the West German consulate in Nice and a Paris building containing the Swedish tourism office and several other Swedish facilities. 2300-2301

May 22, 1975—Turkey—A bomb heavily damaged a U.S. Army truck on an Istanbul street and broke windows in nearby buildings but caused no injuries. The joint U.S.-Turkish supply depot was also bombed, but no injuries or property damage was reported. An anonymous caller to the Associated Press said a Marxist group was responsible. 2302-2303

May 26, 1975—United States—A pipe bomb exploded in the doorway of the Manhattan building housing the Mexican consulate and U.N. mission, damaging the entrance but causing no injuries. 2304

May 27, 1975—United States—Two shots were apparently fired at a security guard at the Zion licensed nuclear facility of the Commonwealth Edison Company.

May 31, 1975—Lebanon—An Arab Communist Organization bomb blew out windows and damaged ITT offices in downtown Beirut. Most of the offices and shops in the building had closed, and no injuries were reported. 2305

May 31, 1975—United States—A bomb placed by the George Jackson Brigade caused $100,000 damage to a state adult corrections office in Olympia, Washington. Communiqués to the news media claimed support for inmate demands at Walla Walla prison.

June 1975—France—Harkis, a group of Algerian migrants who had fought for the French in Algeria and now hold French citizenship, held a French official hostage for twenty-eight hours to demand an inquiry into their conditions and indemnification for their losses in Algeria.

June 1975—United States—An FALN black-powder pipe bomb damaged the Mid-Continent Plaza building in Chicago. 2306

June 3, 1975—Italy—Firebombs were thrown at three American companies' offices only hours after President Ford ended his visit to Rome. Windows were broken at a branch of the Bank of America and Italy. A fire in a storage area caused minor damage at Goodyear Tire Company. Bombs exploded but did not break windows at an ITT subsidiary. 2307-2309

June 3, 1975—Philippines—A bomb placed inside a lavatory in the rear of a PAL BAC111 exploded, injuring forty-five and killing one person. The explosion occurred as the plane was flying from Legaspi to Manila, two hundred miles southwest of its destination. The bomb badly damaged the tail section and tore a hole four feet in diameter in the fuselage.

June 5, 1975—France—The Nationalist Intervention Group, believed to be right-wing Spaniards, bombed the Paris offices of the Committee for Solidarity with Spain on the Rue St. Jacques. 2310

June 6, 1975—United States—Morris Colosky, a white male for whom the FAA profile did not apply, who was born in Lansing, Michigan, on August 30, 1954, chartered a Hi-Lift Helicopters Bell 47J2 helicopter to fly him from Plymouth, Michigan, to Lansing. After takeoff, he flashed a knife at the pilot, forcing him to land at a marked rendezvous point inside the walls of Southern Michigan State Prison. One waiting prisoner boarded the helicopter and then directed it to a point six miles away from the prison. They sprayed mace in the pilot's face and escaped in waiting vehicles. The convict was apprehended the next day. Colosky was captured on June 17, 1975, and indicted ten days later by a federal grand jury in the eastern district of Michigan. He was sentenced to twenty years for aircraft piracy on November 20, 1975. 5466

June 8, 1975—Peru—In a telephone call to a French press service, the Movement of the Revolutionary Left (MIR) claimed credit for throwing a small bomb over a wall, exploding in the garden of the Lima residence of the

U.S. ambassador. The bomb caused no injuries or damage. The ambassador and his wife were away at the time of the attack. 2311

June 10, 1975—United States—The Hatch licensed nuclear facility of the Georgia Power Company received a bomb threat.

June 12, 1975—France—A bomb exploded in Saint-Jean-de-Luz, a summer resort, in a building housing a group giving aid to Basque refugees from Spain. A second bomb exploded during the night in a high school in nearby Hasparren. Spanish authorities suspected that the school had been the site of a recent assembly of the ETA. Damage was slight in both bombings. A third bomb was discovered in a Basque-owned bookshop in Bayonne. 2312-2314

June 14, 1975—Iran—A bomb placed on the wall of the Mashad USIS Binational Center in Tehran exploded, damaging the wall and several windows but injuring no one. Damage was placed at $300 to $500. 2315

June 14, 1975—United States—An FALN bomb exploded in Chicago's plaza at 12:45 A.M., having been thrown from a passing car. Seven minutes later, another bomb exploded at a bank. An FALN letter stated that the two banks and a federal building had been targetted. The attacks coincided with the annual Puerto Rico Day parade. 2316-2317

June 15, 1975—Israel—After crossing the Lebanese border, four members of the Arab Liberation Front, an Iraqi-backed organization led by Abdul Wahab Kayyali, attacked the cooperative farm village of Kfar Yuval, holding a family hostage. The group demanded the release of twelve prisoners, including the Greek Catholic archbishop of Jerusalem, Hilarion Capucci. The Israelis refused the group's demands and stormed the house, killing all four guerrillas. Also killed was the father of the family taken hostage, Yakov Mordechai, who joined the troops who rushed the house where his wife, baby son, and relatives were being held. His brother-in-law died in the original takeover in which six persons were wounded, including his wife and son. 2318

June 16, 1975—United States—At 4:40 A.M., a bomb went off at the Banco de Ponce in New York City. A search of the blast area disclosed that a high-order bomb had been used. A nine-volt battery, a piece of light wire, and metal fragments were recovered at the scene. The Weather Underground claimed credit through a telephone call and several letters in which they said that they were showing support for striking Puerto Rican cement workers and opposing the "superexploitation" of Puerto Rico. One person was injured, and the building sustained $250,000 damage. 2319

June 16, 1975—Guatemala—Nine pistol shots were fired from a moving car at the U.S. embassy chancery in Guatemala City at 8 P.M. No one was injured, and property damage was slight. One shot broke a downstairs window, while others struck trees, concrete, and metal window frames. 2320

June 19, 1975—Sweden—A McDonald's restaurant in Stockholm was bombed. 2321

June 23, 1975—Israel—A small bomb exploded in Tel Aviv, damaging a car belonging to a TWA employee but causing no injuries. The vehicle was parked fifty meters from the U.S. embassy. 2322

June 23, 1975—United States—A powerful bomb exploded shortly after midnight near the facade of the Yugoslav U.N. mission in New York City, causing extensive property damage but no injuries. 2323

June 27, 1975—France—After lengthy interrogation by members of the French DST, Michael Waheb Moukharbal, a member of the PFLP's Muhammad Boudia Commando, led three unarmed policemen to 9 Rue Toullier at 9:40 P.M. The Venezuelan terrorist known as Carlos, Illich Ramirez Sanchez, was slightly drunk at a party being held in the apartment of one of his girl friends, Nancy Sanchez. After half an hour of questioning, the DST men asked him to accompany them to Paris police headquarters. After being excused to go to the men's room, Carlos returned with a Czech automatic pistol in hand and killed Moukharbal along with officers Raymond Dous and Jean Donatini, and wounded commissaire principal Jean Herranz in the throat. Despite an extensive manhunt, he managed to escape. Some accounts claim that he made his way to Lebanon (where Moukharbal had been recently detained for questioning) and then on to East Germany. A few days later, the French expelled three members of Cuba's embassy whom they claimed were members of the Direccion General de Inteligencia and who had extensive contacts with Carlos. A bag of weapons and explosives left by Carlos was found in an apartment of friends with whom he had stayed. Three of them were taken in for questioning, among them being Angela Otaola, a Spanish Basque from Bilbao in whose London apartment the arms were discovered, her boy friend Barry Woodhams, and a woman described only as a Latin American about thirty-five. On July 26, 1975, Angela Armstrong, twenty-nine, who was another associate of Carlos and who had been charged with arms possession and collusion with agents of a foreign power, was given provisional liberty in Paris. 2324

June 28, 1975—France—FRAP sympathizers held up the Lyons-Barcelona express train. 2325

June 28, 1975—Bulgaria—A Balkan Airlines (Bulgarian) Antonov-24 flying forty-eight passengers and crew from Varna to Sofia was hijacked by Nodsio I. Gakof, a young Bulgarian man armed with an automatic pistol, who forced the pilot to fly to Thessaloniki, Greece (some reports claim it was Salonica, Greece), where the hijacker requested political asylum. The hijacker, who apparently had mental problems, was extradited to Bulgaria. It was later reported that Gakof committed suicide. 5467

June 29, 1975—Lebanon—Colonel Ernest R. Morgan of the U.S. Army was kidnapped in Beirut from a taxi by members of the PFLP-GC, who demanded that the U.S. government distribute food, clothing, and building materials to a slum area of the city. He was released thirteen days later after a distribution of food was made by unknown parties believed to be private Lebanese encouraged by the Lebanese government. Morgan was attached to the U.S. military aid mission in Turkey and was reported to be vacationing in the area after attending a CENTO meeting. Some sources claimed that the forty-three-year-old colonel had left his hotel to go to the airport to obtain some reading material. The Petersburg, Virginia, resident was dragged out of the taxi at a roadblock at a traffic circle near the airport. Some reports claimed that the PFLP was responsible for the attack, while others noted that the Revolutionary Socialist Action Organization (RSAO) claimed credit and was pressured by Syria, Lebanon, and the PLO to release Morgan. Other reports stated that he was taken by twenty armed men and turned over to the PFLP in the Palestinian refugee camp of Shantila. On July 6, two cassette tape recordings were left outside the office of Agence France-Presse, along with recent photographs and a letter to U.S. Ambassador McMurtrie C. Godley. The RSAO demanded that the food and other materials be distributed in the Abattoir district, setting a seventy-two-hour deadline. They also demanded that the search for Morgan be ended and that their message be publicized in U.S. media, including overseas Voice of America broadcasts. The Lebanese government announced the next day that it was in touch with the kidnappers, who were demanding the distribution of thirty tons of sugar, thirty tons of rice, ten tons of cooking fat, ten tons of powdered milk, twenty tons of flour, three thousand pairs of shoes, three thousand new shirts and trousers, four hundred tons of cement, and two hundred tons of iron construction rods. The PLO, which helped in the attempts to free Morgan, threatened retaliation against the PFLP-GC if Morgan was killed. The PLO said Morgan was abducted by three Lebanese belonging to a minor Palestinian cell, who turned him over to the PFLP-GC, which in turn consigned him to a Lebanese urban guerrilla organization. Although the group had claimed that Morgan was a spy, they released him on July 12, saying that he was black and blacks rarely attain such high rank in the U.S. Army. His release was intended to safeguard black American relations with the Arab cause. The kidnappers also claimed that the U.S. government had complied with their ransom demands. The United States denied this claim. Further reports suggested the possibility of Socialist Labor party links to the attack. 2326

July 1975—Netherlands—Several Moluccans were given prison sentences of up to five years for plotting to kidnap Queen Juliana and members of her royal family. 2327

July 2, 1975—United States—The Kerr-McGee Nuclear Corporation reported an attempted forced entry at its licensed nuclear facility in Oklahoma City.

July 3, 1975—Iran—Members of the Iranian People's Strugglers cut off a U.S. embassy car in downtown Tehran during the afternoon rush hour and fatally shot Hassan Hossnan, twenty-five, an Iranian employee who had been in the visa section for eighteen months. Reports claimed that the car was cut off about two blocks from the embassy. Two men jumped out, and one dressed in a police uniform fired, killing Hossnan but leaving the driver and another passenger uninjured. A young woman was seen in the terrorists' car, but she did not participate in the shooting. An anonymous telephone caller said the group was fighting for "freedom and democracy." Individuals identified as Afrakhteh and Khamoushi were accused in this case, as well as in the slayings of three other U.S. Air Force colonels. On December 31, 1975, an Iranian army tribunal sentenced ten of the group to death by a firing squad, while an eleventh defendant, one of two women in the group, was given fifteen years of solitary confinement. 2328

July 4, 1975—Israel—A bomb placed in an old refrigerator in Zion Square, a Jewish section of West Jerusalem, exploded in a crowd of shoppers in the early-morning rush hour, killing fifteen, including two children and a social worker, Mira Berger, thirty-four, and injuring seventy-five, including two Americans, Mark Katz and Deborah Levine, both from Richmond, Virginia, who were visiting Jerusalem as part of a United Synagogue Youth Group. The bomb was believed to have contained thirty pounds of explosives and had been left in front of a hardware store. Security forces rounded up more than three hundred Arabs for questioning within three hours of the blast. The PLO claimed credit for the attack, as did the Martyr Farid Al Boubaly Brigade, a Fatah unit named in memory of a fedayeen killed earlier in 1975 in an unsuccessful attack on an Israeli patrol. Three days later, Israeli forces attacked PLO bases in south Lebanon. On June 27, 1977, an Israeli military court in the occupied West Bank of Jordan sentenced Ahmed Haj Ibrahim Mousa Assad Jabara, from the village of Tourmus-Aya, to life imprisonment for the Zion Square bombing. 2329

July 4, 1975—United States—The Vallecitos licensed nuclear facility of the General Electric Company received a bomb threat.

July 5, 1975—Pakistan—A bomb placed under a seat in the passenger compartment of a Pakistan International Airlines B707 blew a hole three to four feet in diameter in the fuselage. The bomb went off half an hour after the 150 passengers had deplaned, injuring no one. The plane was on the ground at Rawalpindi-Islamabad airport, having flown from Karachi.

July 9, 1975—Israel—An Israeli oil pipeline running from the Red Sea to the Mediterranean was shut down by an explosion at a pumping station near Eilat. Palestinians claimed credit, and Israeli national radio attributed it to either sabotage or a malfunctioning pump. 2330

July 14, 1975—Japan—Molotov cocktails were thrown in the vicinity of a hangar at Tokyo international airport. The bottles exploded but did not cause any serious damage.

July 14, 1975—United States—The Brunswick licensed nuclear facility of the Carolina Power and Light Company received a bomb threat.

July 14, 1975—Ethiopia—Two American civilians and four Ethiopians were kidnapped from the U.S. Navy's Kagnew Station transmitter site near Asmara by members of the Eritrean Liberation Front-Revolutionary Council. The Americans were identified as Steve Campbell of San Leandro, California, and Jim Harrell of Milwaukee, Wisconsin, both civilian technicians employed by the Collins International Service Company of Richardson Texas, a Rockwell Corporation subsidiary. The ELF-RC said in Damascus that it was holding the six for security reasons but did not elaborate. The attack occurred about 10:45 A.M., when the six were driven off in a company truck that security forces later found abandoned seventeen miles west of Asmara. No messages were found in the truck. On August 14, 1975, Osman Sabbi, the leader of the ELF-Popular Liberation Forces, a second faction of the ELF, said in Beirut that the Americans would be set free without ransom within two weeks. Photographer Ahmed Abu Sada was allowed to release a photograph he had taken of the two with their captors ten days earlier. On May 3, 1976, the two were released in good condition in Sudan. V. H. Burwood-Taylor, the honorary British consul in Asmara who had been kidnapped in October 1975, was released with them. The U.S. State Department claimed that the United States had paid no ransom but that it was possible that a private transaction had been worked out for their release. 2331

July 15, 1975—United States—A bomb exploded inside the crowded offices of the Mexican consulate in Los Angeles, injuring four and causing $35,000 damage. A man informed the City News Service that the Peace and Freedom Fighters were responsible and demanded the release of Cuban political prisoners and that relations not be established with Cuba. Other reports noted suspicions of a joint attack by the Hungarian Peace and Freedom Fighters, the Cuban Action Commandos, and the Nazi Group. 2332

July 15, 1975—United States—A young man on board a National Airlines DC10 flying from New York to Miami entered a restroom, spread newspapers on the floor, and set himself on fire. The plane made an unscheduled landing at Jacksonville, Florida, where the man was found dead on arrival. There was little damage done to the restroom, although part of the interior showed heavy scorching. None of the other fifty-seven passengers was injured.

July 17, 1975—Japan—Two members of the Okinawa Liberation League attacked Crown Prince Akihito during his visit to the island.

July 18, 1975—Israel—Two terrorists were arrested by police at Tel Aviv airport for carrying dynamite in their car. 2333

July 18, 1975—United States—A small bomb exploded a few feet from the ambassador of Costa Rica as he left the embassy offices at 2112 S Street in northwest Washington, D.C. Ambassador Rodolfo Silva was uninjured, and part of an outer wall suffered minor damage. Ninety minutes after the 5 P.M. blast, a caller told United Press International and Associated Press that the Cuban Scorpion was claiming credit and that ''our goal is to punish anyone who recognizes Cuba.'' Costa Rica was the site of a meeting of the OAS that was discussing hemispheric relations with Cuba. According to one report, statements from an FLNC leader implicated Abdala and the Cuban Action Commandos. Police were also called to the Colombian embassy at 2118 Leroy Place to check on what was reported as a suspicious package. 2334-2335

July 19, 1975—El Salvador—The Workers Revolutionary Organizaton bombed the Salvadoran Tourist Institute in San Salvador, damaging doors and windows in nearby buildings but injuring no one in the early morning.

July 19, 1975—Mexico—Five armed terrorists claiming to be members of the Twenty-third of September League kidnapped an American Express executive outside his Mexico City house. He was released two days later after the payment of an $80,000 ransom in Mexican pesos. 2336

July 22, 1975—United States—An explosion occurred in Tampa airport when a baggage handler picked up a valise that contained numerous M-80 firecrackers and cherry bombs. The explosion was not sufficient to cause damage to the surrounding area, although the baggage handler suffered minor injuries.

July 23, 1975—United States—A case of possible arson to an equipment storage barn was reported by employees of the licensed nuclear facility in West Valley, New York, which is owned by Nuclear Fuel Services.

July 23, 1975—Japan—Two men in a motorboat threw eight firebombs at a Chilean naval training vessel, a Kobe University ship, and two other boats docked at the International Ocean Exposition in Naha, Okinawa. Two crewmen of the Chilean sailing trainer *Esmeralda* were injured in the dawn attack, one seriously. The attackers were believed to be members of the Okinawa Liberation League. A Japanese patrol boat arrived thirty minutes after the beginning of the attack and chased the suspects to nearby Toguchi port, where police arrested a man in wet clothes carrying a flashlight. The suspect refused to answer questions. Police recovered an abandoned boat carrying Molotov cocktails at a nearby pier. 2337

July 24, 1975—United Kingdom—A young man brandishing a fake pistol took a girl hostage and used her to get through the screening area at Manchester airport. After reaching the international pier area of the apron, he ran up to and entered a parked aircraft. The man was confronted by a cleaning crew, which he ordered off the plane. Shortly thereafter police overpowered the individual. 5468

July 25, 1975—Philippines—A Danish plantation manager in Malangas, southern Philippines, was kidnapped by Moslem rebels who demanded a $13,300 ransom. The Philippine subsidiary of the Goodyear Tire and Rubber Company paid over $10,000 to Moslem rebels for the release of a hijacked motorboat with fifteen people on board. 2338-2339

July 26, 1975—France—The Algerian Cultural Center in Lyons was bombed, as were offices in Paris and Roubaix of the Amicale des Algériens en Europe. Considerable damage was reported. On August 6 the government closed the last Harkis camps so that it could spend £15 million on rehousing and training. 2340-2342

July 28, 1975—Argentina—A suspicious package was found in the corridor of a Rosario building that housed Samon Federal, an office of two local lawyers, as well as the USIS field representative. 2343

July 28, 1975—Japan—An All Nippon Airways Lockheed Tristar L1011 flying 275 passengers and 11 crew members from Tokyo to Hokkaido and Sapporo was hijacked by H. Oshima, seventeen, a Japanese high school student, who entered the cockpit feigning that he had a knife in his pocket. He demanded to be flown to either Hawaii or Okinawa. The pilot persuaded him to allow him to land in Tokyo, where the passengers and crew deplaned. Police disguised as engineers subdued the hijacker, who claimed that he had acted on an impulse and had wanted to get as far as possible from home. Oshima was unarmed. 5469

July 31, 1975—Argentina—Charles Agnew Lockwood, sixty-five, president of the British firm Roberts and Company, was kidnapped in suburban Caseros by twenty members of the ERP. This was the second time in two years that Lockwood was kidnapped. He had been released in 1973 after the payment of a $2 million ransom (see incident 1569). In this attack, he was taken at 8 A.M. shortly after he had left home for his downtown Buenos Aires office. He was accompanied by his two daughters and a chauffeur; bodyguards followed them in another car. The kidnappers, dressed as railway workers, stopped Lockwood's car at a railroad crossing not far from his suburban home. There was a gun battle, and two bodyguards and the chauffeur were wounded. Lockwood was uninjured and was driven away in a green station wagon. On August 31, 1975, Lockwood was rescued after a police shootout in which four of his ERP captors were killed. 2344

August 2, 1975—Lebanon—Constance Stransky, a U.S. citizen, was kidnapped by Palestinians who released her unharmed eleven days later. 2345

August 2, 1975—Syria—Four Palestinians and a Syrian, all Arab Communist Organization members, were executed in Damascus for attacks against Syrian and American installations. Among them was Ali Ahmed al Gahdban, twenty-five, who was believed to be the founder and leader of the group. Nine others were sentenced to prison terms ranging from four years to life.

August 4, 1975—United States—A small incendiary device exploded shortly after midnight at the Venezuelan consulate in New York City at 7 East Fifty-first Street. A plate glass window was shattered, but no injuries were reported. 2346

August 4, 1975—Malaysia—Five members of the Japanese Red Army armed with hand grenades and guns took over the U.S. consulate in Kuala Lumpur and held fifty-three hostages during a seventy-nine-hour siege. The group wounded a watchman and two policemen as they entered the consulate on the ninth floor of the twelve-story American International Assurance Building, which also houses the Japanese, Canadian, and Swedish embassies. One of the hostages, Bernard Joseph, thirty-four, a Malaysian Air Lines employee, was wounded the evening of the second day of the siege when a terrorist's pistol accidentally fired as the hostage was being searched. Observers pointed out that the attack came on the eve of a meeting between President Ford and Japanese Prime

Minister Takeo Miki in Washington, D.C. Among those taken hostage in the morning raid were U.S. Consul Robert C. Stebbins, forty-two, three other U.S. embassy employees, Swedish chargé d'affaires Fredrik Bergenstraahle, forty-eight, and his secretary, Ulla Odqvist. Senior Malaysian, Japanese, and American officials conducted negotiations by phone with the terrorists, who threatened to blow up the building and kill the hostages if their demands were not met, but they allowed three deadlines to pass without incident.

Several reports credited the planning of the incident to the JRA's female leader, Fusako Shigenobu, who wanted seven prisoners flown to Libya: Junich Matsuura, a bank robber; Jun Nishikawa and Kazuo Tohira, who had been captured in Stockholm (see incident 2253); Hisahi Matsuda, a bank robber; Hiroshi Sakaguchi; Norio Sasaki, chief of the Wolf bombers, which victimized businesses; and Kunio Bando, the rifleman of the Karuizawa siege. Matsuura refused to be released because he was in poor health and soon to be paroled. Sakaguchi also refused to go because he considered the JRA not revolutionary enough. Shigenobu initially believed this response to be a police trick, but Sakaguchi talked to the terrorists, who became convinced of his sincerity. Some observers suggested that he was worried about possible mistreatment by the rival JRA.

The group allowed Stebbins to talk to the negotiators on the telephone, telling them that the hostages were being well treated and were waiting patiently. The terrorists had a telephone conversation with the *Kuala Lumpur New Straits Times* newspaper, in which they said, "We want to announce our solidarity with the Laotian, Vietnamese and Cambodian revolutionary people. Long live the Palestinian people's struggle." The Paris office of the PLO denied any connection with the attack.

The Japanese government agreed to the terrorists' demands on August 4 during the evening and flew the five prisoners on a DC8 to Kuala Lumpur. Also on board were a crew of eleven and more than thirty Japanese officials, including a number of police officers. On August 6, the terrorists released nine of the hostages they were holding, including three Americans (two women and a young girl). All of those freed were women and children. The attackers were reported to be holding the diplomats, along with a Singaporean and thirty-four Malaysians. The three freed Americans were Mrs. Ng Wai-Han, forty-seven, her daughter Susan, twenty-seven, and her five-year-old granddaughter. An Australian woman and her three young sons were also released. She was identified as Joan Lancaster, wife of Gerald Lancaster, a Houston man who remained as a hostage. A Malaysian woman, Mrs. S. C. Choo, sixty-three, was carried out on a stretcher and taken to an ambulance. A doctor said she had previously suffered a heart attack. It was reported that the terrorists had ended their random sniper attacks, which had punctuated the immediate aftermath of their takeover of the building. Malaysian Prime Minister Tun Abdul Razak took part in the negotiations with the terrorists. It was agreed that the terrorists would release their last hostages (only fifteen remained after a second group was released) upon reaching the plane. Several Malaysian and Japanese officials offered to serve as substitute hostages along with the nine crewmen of the DC8. They were identified as Ramli Omar, parliamentary secretary to the Malaysian Communications Ministry; Osman Cassim of the Malaysian Home Ministry; Ryohei Murata of the Japanese Foreign Ministry; and Misao Matsumoto of the Japanese Transportation Ministry. Relations between the Japanese and Malaysian negotiations teams soured at one point, with the Malaysians accusing the Japanese of attempting to stall and threatening to "hijack" the plane with an all-Malaysian crew that would fly out the terrorists, who were becoming anxious during the delays. Problems also arose over where the terrorists would fly. The Japanese initially informed the Malaysian government that the Libyans had refused to accept the terrorists, although the Malaysians were told by the Libyans that landing privileges would be granted. Kuwait refused to accept the terrorists. Cuba, Syria, and Southern Yemen were also canvassed by the Malaysians. It was planned that the flight would take eleven hours, with a stopover in Karachi, Pakistan, for refueling. The pilot was Captain Tomio Mashiko, a JAL pilot who had flown the Singapore JRA-PFLP terrorists to South Yemen in 1974 (see incident 1806). JAL later said that the cost of the Boeing and crew of nine was $618,000. Another snag came over whether the terrorists would be allowed to retain their weapons during the flight. After the substitute hostages entered the plane and the original hostages were released, a car containing two members of the Malaysian police bomb squad drove up to the plane. Two of the terrorists carried a large sachel down the stairs of the plane's ramp. The package contained an undisclosed quantity of plastic explosives and was detonated at the southern fringe of the field. The plane was then allowed to fly off, but it stopped in Colombo, Sri Lanka, for refueling. Plans for the refueling in Pakistan were changed when India and Iran refused to allow the plane to cross their territory. Iran's air force was ordered to shoot down the DC8 if it entered Persian airspace. Israeli authorities declared a state of alert at Tel Aviv's Ben Gurion Airport. While the Sri Lankans allowed the plane to refuel, it informed the terrorists that no one would be allowed to leave the plane and that the JRA members were not to show their faces. The plane landed in Libya, where the terrorists surrendered to authorities.

In Tokyo, police checking files on the JRA said they believed one of the terrorists was a participant in the JRA hijacking of a 747 from Amsterdam to the Netherlands (see incident 1595) on July 20, 1973. They identified him as Osamu Maruoka, twenty-four. It was also noted that one of the hostages freed in Libya, Director General Keisuke Ochi of the Japanese Foreign Ministry's Immigration Bureau, said that earlier reports that one of the terrorists was a female were incorrect. On August 26, Japan decided to request extradition of the ten terrorists who were flown to Tripoli. However, in a visit to Vice-Foreign Minister Shoji Sato in Kyoto on October 29, 1975, Libyan Vice-

Interior Minister Younes Abulgasem Ali said that the terrorists were still in Libya and that he was not in a position to discuss their future with the Japanese officials because he did not have any authority over the matter. 2347

August 5, 1975—Colombia—Five men and a woman wearing masks and armed with pistols and submachine guns kidnapped U.S. business executive Donald E. Cooper from his Bogotá home during the evening. Cooper, fifty, of North Platte, Nebraska, had recently returned from a vacation in the United States, where his Peruvian wife and two children were staying. He was vice-president for merchandising for the Sears chain in Colombia and had twenty years of service with Sears in Latin America. His maid and chauffeur were reported wounded in the attack in which a shot was fired that barely missed the ear of the chauffeur. After months of negotiations by Sears, Cooper was released unharmed on November 2, 1975. 2348

August 5, 1975—Argentina—A bomb exploded in the basement of the Ecuadorean embassy in Buenos Aires, causing serious damage but no injuries. 2349

August 9, 1975—United States—The Miami office of the Dominican Republic's consul was bombed by a Cuban exile group protesting the extradition to the United States of a Cuban exile leader. 2350

August 13, 1975—Spain—Madrid police were placed on alert after receiving information through Interpol from French intelligence that two squads of Japanese terrorists, composed of nine men and four women, were planning to free fifty jailed Spanish terrorists. 2351

August 13, 1975—Argentina—Four members of Accion Cubana shot from an automobile at two Cuban embassy vehicles entering the embassy compound in Buenos Aires. The Cuban ambassador, Emilio Aragones, was in one car, and a visiting Cuban official and an attaché were in the other. No one was injured in the machine-gun attack. 2352

August 16, 1975—Italy—A group of individuals who had served in the French army released a hostage on August 18 whom they had seized as part of a campaign to get France and Algeria to permit Harkis to travel freely between the two countries. 2353

August 16, 1975—United States—Roper McNair, a black male for whom the FAA profile was not applicable and who was born on May 6, 1952, in Washington, D.C., entered a private Piper Cherokee 140 that was taxiing for departure from Woodbridge, Virginia. Pointing a gun at the pilot, he demanded to be flown to Jamaica, Puerto Rico, the Bahamas, and Madrid. The plane headed south but ran out of fuel and landed on a highway near Fayetteville, North Carolina. One of his two hostages escaped. McNair commandeered a car and drove his remaining hostage to Fayetteville airport, where he unsuccessfully attempted to board several parked aircraft. He was finally persuaded to surrender by local authorities. 5470

August 18, 1975—United Kingdom—A bomb was found and defused in the Algerian embassy in London. A telephone caller told news agencies that the bomb had been placed by the Soldiers of the Algerian Opposition, which seeks the overthrow of Algerian Colonel Houari Boumédienne. 2354

August 18, 1975—West Germany—A bomb placed by the Soldiers of the Algerian Opposition was found and defused in the Algerian embassy in Bonn. 2355

August 18, 1975—Italy—A bomb exploded in the Algerian embassy in Rome, damaging a parked car and the ground-floor office but injuring no one. A message left in a telephone booth near the embassy claimed credit for the Soldiers of the Algerian Opposition. 2356

August 19, 1975—West Germany—Police evacuated the Indonesian embassy in Bonn after an anonymous telephoned bomb threat. A search was negative. 2357

August 19, 1975—Sweden—A bomb exploded in a McDonald's restaurant in Stockholm in the early morning, smashing windows and much of the interior but causing no injuries. The restaurant had been bombed on June 19, 1975 (see incident 2321). McDonald's Stockholm manager, Paul Lederhausen, said, "Last time I thought it was just an isolated case. But now I see there must be somebody with a negative attitude toward the United States." 2358

August 20, 1975—West Germany—An explosive device mailed to the West Berlin Jewish Community Center went off inside a police bomb-disposal squad truck. The center received the parcel with its regular mail, but a staff member became suspicious on opening it. He phoned the alleged sender, who knew nothing about the parcel. 2359

August 21, 1975—Corsica—Forty farmers armed with hunting guns seized a vineyard farmhouse near Aleria, to protest the owner's complicity in the adulteration of wine. During the Bastia attack, two policemen died in a gun battle with the members of the Action for the Rebirth of Corsica. Four other policemen were injured, and a Corsican had his foot blown off by a tear-gas grenade. French Interior Minister Michel Poniatowski gave police the order to attack the farmhouse after the separatists refused to free their six hostages—four North African farm workers and two French tourists. The leader of the separatists, Dr. Edmond Simeoni, forty-one, raised a white flag, ending the thirty-three-hour siege. Simeoni and seven others were put on trial on May 17, 1976, accused of leading a revolt against the French government.

April 21, 1975—United States—A licensed nuclear facility of the Consolidated Edison Company received a bomb threat.

August 22, 1975—United States—The Millstone 1 licensed nuclear facility of the Northeast Nuclear Energy Company received a bomb threat.

August 22, 1975—Spain—A U.S. Marine, Donald Croswaye, twenty, on shore leave in Valencia, was shot and wounded by FRAP men who fired from a passing car. 2360

August 22, 1975—Argentina—A powerful bomb placed by the Montoneros exploded in the engine room of an Argentine naval destroyer under construction in Buenos Aires, damaging the engines and blowing a hole in the hull. The $70 million ship sank in shallow water. The navy claimed the damage was reparable but gave no estimate of the cost. The ship, the *Santisima Trinidad*, was being built under license to a British company, Vickers. Members of the ERP and Montoneros appeared to be coordinating a series of attacks throughout Argentina in commemoration of the anniversary of the 1972 Rawson jailbreak, in which sixteen guerrillas were killed after being captured and sent to the Trelew naval facility. 2361

August 22, 1975—Canada—A member of the JRA, Yoshima Gyoja, was arrested when he attempted to enter the United States from Canada using a forged voter registration card (purportedly issued by the New York City Board of Election) and another false document. He was deported to Japan on September 1 and was arrested at Tokyo International Airport by Japanese police on charges of forgery and using forged personal documents. Gyoja was alleged to have been a member of the JRA's Operation Translation plan to kidnap Japanese businessmen in West Germany. He had studied in Berlin between September 1972 and January 1973 and then returned to Japan. In April 1974 he went back to West Germany and was last seen a month later in Düsseldorf. It was believed that he was attempting to enter the United States to sabotage the visit of Emperor Hirohito scheduled for October 1975. 2362

August 23, 1975—Ethiopia—Two Americans were killed when an ELF land mine exploded while they were driving on a road near Asmara on the way to the U.S. transmitter facility. They were employed by Collins International Service Company, working under contract for the navy at the facility. They were identified as William D. Trower, twenty-five, of Vandalia, Missouri, and Aldworth R. Brown, Jr., twenty-seven, of Fort Worth, Texas. 2363

August 25, 1975—United Kingdom—An anonymous caller said a bomb was on board a British Airways VC10 scheduled to fly 112 passengers from London to Montreal. The plane was evacuated, but no bomb was found. 2364

August 26, 1975—Philippines—Moslem rebels kidnapped Yoko Seki, a Japanese stewardess for Lufthansa, at gunpoint while she was swimming off a southern Philippines beach. She was released at night, sixty-one hours later, after the Philippine government paid a ransom equivalent to $27,000. The guerrillas told her she had been kidnapped to show the outside world "the real situation" in the area. 2365

August 26, 1975—United Kingdom—British security officials in Great Yarmouth said that a threat to blow up the U.S.-owned Phillips Petroleum Company's gas drilling rigs in the North Sea was a hoax. Royal Navy divers checked the rigs mentioned in telephone warnings but found nothing. The deadlines mentioned in the calls passed without incident. 2366

August 27, 1975—United Kingdom—An IRA bomb exploded in the Caterham Arms bar in Surrey, injuring thirty-three people, eight of them seriously. The bar was crowded with about one hundred customers, including a score of British army troops who had been paid earlier in the day at the barracks fifty yards away. 2367

August 28, 1975—Peru—Approximately one hundred people attacked the Lima USIS Binational Center at 8:30 P.M. Three Molotov cocktails were thrown into the mezzanine offices, causing window damage and superficial burns on walls. Total damage was estimated at $100. No injuries were reported because the center had closed for the evening. One unexploded Molotov cocktail bore the initials of the National Federation of University Employees of Peru. 2368

August 28, 1975—United Kingdom—An IRA bomb exploded outside the Prudential Insurance Company offices on Oxford Street in a busy London shopping district, injuring seven persons. 2369

August 28, 1975—Spain—A Burgos military tribunal condemned two ETA members to death for killing Gregorio Posada, a member of the Civil Guard, in San Sebastián in 1974. They were identified as José Antonio Garmendia, twenty-three, a student, and Angel Otaegui, thirty-three, a mechanic. On September 18, a Madrid military court sentenced to death five FRAP guerrillas for the shotgun slaying of a policeman. A sixth defendant, José Fonfria, twenty-nine, was given a twenty-year prison sentence. The five included two pregnant women: Concepcion Tristan Lopez, twenty-one, a nurse, and Maria Jesus Dasca Penellas, twenty, a student. The three men were Ramon Garcia Sanz, twenty-seven, a welder, and students Manuel Canaveras and José Luis Sanchez Bravo, both twenty-one. They had killed Lieutenant Antonio Pose Rodriguez, a traffic policeman. All but Fonfria retracted their confessions, claiming they had been tortured.

August 28, 1975—France—In Bayonne, three gunmen ambushed a truckload of Spanish refugees leaving a demonstration against the Burgos trial. Two protestors were injured in the night raid. 2370

August 29, 1975—France—Two groups of masked men bombed the Spanish consulate and the Bank of Bilbao in Bayonne. 2371-2372

August 29, 1975—United Kingdom—An IRA bomb exploded in a shop in West London's Kensington district, killing one man. 2373

August 29, 1975—United Kingdom—A bomb disposal expert, Captain Good of Scotland Yard, was killed while trying to defuse an IRA bomb in London's Kensington High Street. The bombers were believed to be an IRA splinter group opposed to the IRA cease-fire. 2374

August 30, 1975—Philippines—Two U.S. employees of Boise-Cascade were kidnapped by Moslem dissidents at a timber concession near Zamboanga. They were released less than twenty-four hours later. 2375

September 1975—United Kingdom—Two IRA bombs exploded at the Hilton and the Portman hotels in London, injuring no one. 2376-2377

September 1975—Angola—Donald Lutes, a Canadian missionary, was kidnapped. 2378

September 1975—Lebanon—Fifteen Egyptians died in a Beirut hotel that was set on fire during the fighting in the civil war. 2379

September 1, 1975—United States—The Zion licensed nuclear facility of the Commonwealth Edison Company received a bomb threat.

September 2, 1975—Mexico—A bomb misfired at the Ejercito store of a U.S. firm. Later that night three carloads of terrorists were discovered by the police driving around the store. Police followed the cars and a gunfight broke out. Two of the terrorists were killed, one of whom was identified as the assistant to the leader of the Twenty-third of September League. 2380

September 3, 1975—Sweden—Akira Kitagawa, who had been expelled from France for his involvement in JRA's Operation Translation, and Kyoichi Shimada, a member of a group that had sent out Junzo Okudaira, were deported to Japan under Sweden's Anti-Terrorism Act. Japanese police arrested the two upon their arrival at Tokyo international airport. Kitagawa was held for violation of the passport law, while Shimada was charged with forging and using personal documents. 2381

September 3, 1975—Soviet Union—A crew member on board an Aeroflot flight to London apparently shot and killed himself. No other injuries were reported.

September 5, 1975—United States—The Weather Underground bombed the Kennecott Building in Salt Lake City, causing $50,000 damage. The group said, ''We attack Kennecott for all the years it has robbed the Chilean people of their copper and wealth, for its role in the overthrow of the Unidad Popular Government in Chile and the murder of Salvador Allende, and for its oppression and exploitation of working people here in the United States.''

September 5, 1975—United States—Lynnette ''Squeaky'' Fromme, a member of the Manson family, attempted to assassinate President Gerald Ford in Sacramento but was unsuccessful when her handgun jammed.

September 5, 1975—United Kingdom—A bomb exploded in the crowded lobby of the London Hilton Hotel in Park Lane at 12:20 P.M., shattering the front entrance, killing a man and a woman, and injuring sixty-three, seven of them seriously. Four Americans were reported injured by the blast. There were perhaps one hundred people in the lobby at the time of the blast, including a Canadian. A bomb warning was received at 11:59 A.M. at the Associated Newspaper Group, Ltd., owners of the *Daily Mail* and the *Evening News*. Police apparently did not have enough time to effect an evacuation. A second bomb was found in the hotel and detonated by army bomb experts. The IRA was believed responsible. 2382

September 5, 1975—Australia—The Australian government and the International Committee of the Red Cross suspended relief flights to Timor after a soldier, believed to be a member of the Timorese Democratic Union, forced the pilot of an Australian air force plane to fly him and forty-two other Timorese to Darwin. The group was detained by police. They included other soldiers and their families. 5471

September 5, 1975—Netherlands—Amsterdam police detectives arrested four armed Syrians who were planning to take over the daily 0836 D-train from Moscow at Amersfoort station the next day. They intended to kidnap immigrating Russian Jews in the sleeping car and demand a plane to fly them and their hostages out of the country. The group would have fired their automatic weapons to frighten people away from a station building easily defended. Three days later, they were sentenced to eighteen months' imprisonment. Amin Salamah, leader of the Al Saiqa terrorists, and Joseph Assad Azar claimed that they had been trained in 1972 in a village outside Moscow. Their preliminary six-month course covered the use of arms and explosives, as well as propaganda and interrogation survival techniques. Shortly after the terrorists' arrest, Soviet consular official Aleksandr Rylov told the Dutch Foreign Ministry that his government might be able to identify the Syrians from their passport numbers. 2383

September 8, 1975—United States—A group of Yugoslav exiles assaulted Ziggi Leone in a New York restaurant after he claimed to be from Yugoslavia. A Yugoslav emigrant, Hamo Salkovic, was seriously injured in the attack, which was reportedly organized by Ivan Jorgic, a Croatian exile. Two days later, Marijan Buconjic, Ilija Curic, and Ivan Jurid threw leaflets, chanted slogans, and tried to unfurl a Croatian flag during the U.N. General Assembly's general debate.

September 8, 1975—France—Fifty youths were evicted from a Spanish office in Paris that they had occupied to protest death sentences handed down against ETA members. Fifty-nine Spanish priests signed a letter asking for clemency.

September 9, 1975—Spain—A bomb was found in a railway tunnel through which the Madrid-Paris express passed. 2384

September 9, 1975—United States—A bomb exploded at an oil company facility in Carteret, New Jersey. Threatening letters demanding a total of $45.5 million were sent to Gulf, Texaco, Exxon, Union, Phillips, Standard, and Amoco oil companies.

September 9, 1975—Abu Dhabi—The U.S. embassy received a bomb threat over the telephone. The embassy was closed for the remainder of the day, and all local and nonessential U.S. employees were sent home as an added security measure. 2385

September 9, 1975—Haiti—A Haiti Air Inter Dehavilland Twin Otter flying from Port-au-Prince to Cap Haitien was hijacked by three young Haitians, P. Laurent, C. Laurent, and E. Charles, who used knives and Molotov cocktails to threaten the pilot and demand to be taken to Cuba. The pilot persuaded the hijackers to allow a refueling stop at Gonaives. One of the hijackers left to find fuel at the deserted airport. Shortly thereafter the other two hijackers were overpowered by the crew and two passengers. Local authorities arrived and took the hijackers into custody. 5472

September 11, 1975—Portugal—Bombs exploded during the early morning at the Lisbon building housing Royal Morocco Air, the Spanish embassy, and the Sheraton Hotel, causing slight damage. An anonymous caller claimed that the Revolutionary Internationalist Solidarity had bombed the Spanish embassy. 2386-2388

September 11, 1975—Sweden—A bomb was defused outside the Spanish tourist office in Stockholm. It was believed the action was part of an international protest against Spanish death sentences for ETA terrorists. 2389

September 12, 1975—United States—The People's Forces Unit IX of the New World Liberation Front set bombs that failed to explode in a federal building in Phoenix, Arizona, and a Veterans Administration building in Seattle, Washington.

September 13, 1975—Ethiopia—The ELF-Revolutionary Council kidnapped two Americans and six Ethiopians from the Kagnew communications facility near Asmara. Early reports claimed that nine were killed and that the facility was gutted by fire and practically destroyed, although the equipment was apparently salvageable. The Americans were identified as Navy Electronics Technician 3 Thomas C. Bowidowicz of Jersey City and Army Specialist 5 David Strickland of Orlando, Florida. The ELF-RC in Damascus claimed credit for the kidnapping. On October 3, an ELF-RC spokesman in Beirut, Muhammad Dad, said, "We will not be responsible for the safety of the hostages, but we are not saying we will execute them." The group demanded that the United States halt military assistance to the government and close all installations in Eritrea Province. They also demanded compensation for areas of Eritrea that suffered heavy damage in attacks by the U.S.-equipped Ethiopian air force plane during fighting in February; U.S. government pressure on Ethiopia's military government to free all Eritrean rebels it held in prisons; and dismantling of an Ethiopian naval base under construction at Massawa, Ethiopia's chief Red Sea port. Later reports claimed that the group had demanded a $5 million ransom and had tied this case to the kidnapping of Harrell and Campbell (see incident 2331). It appeared that the attack was timed to coincide with the first anniversary of the overthrow of former Emperor Haile Selassie. The two were released unharmed on January 9, 1976, in neighboring Sudan, whose government had participated in negotiations for their release. The U.S. State Department claimed that it had not complied with any of the kidnappers' demands. 2390

September 14, 1975—United States—Israeli security officials reported that a window was broken by a bullet in the sixth floor of the embassy annex. Several bullet marks were found on a window ledge three floors below. 2391

September 14, 1975—Greece—A grenade that failed to detonate was discovered lying on the floor of a restroom at Athens airport.

September 14, 1975—United Kingdom—The countess of Onslow, fifty-nine, a central figure in a spying operation against the IRA in 1973, was wounded in the hands and face by a letter bomb mailed in Dublin. Hospital officials said her condition was not serious. She had arranged clandestine meetings between government officials and Kenneth Littlejohn, a bank robber who later claimed he was ordered to spy on the IRA by British intelligence. 2392

September 14, 1975—United Kingdom—A letter bomb mailed in Dublin exploded in the London office of Canadian-based Alcan, slightly injuring a secretary. Two weeks previously, the company had announced plans to build a plant in the Republic of Ireland. 2393

September 15, 1975—Greece—A time bomb destroyed a car owned by a U.S. Air Force sergeant, causing damage to the surrounding area but no injuries. The car was parked in the seaside town of Glyfada, just south of Athens. The yellow license plates indicated that the auto belonged to a member of the U.S. military or the staff of a diplomatic mission. 2394

September 15, 1975—United States—Fred Saloman, a Latin who was born on October 28, 1950, and whose case was inapplicable to the FAA profile, commandeered a vehicle, took a hostage, and, armed with a knife and pistol, attempted to secure an airplane and a pilot. Unsuccessful in this attempt, he took another hostage and drove to the San José municipal airport. There Saloman and his hostages climbed over a fence and boarded a parked out-of-service Continental Airlines B727. Two engineers who were aboard the plane were taken as hostages. Saloman threatened the lives of his hostages if his demands for a pilot and ammunition were not met. Two of the hostages managed to escape, and another was shot and seriously wounded by the hijacker. After agreeing to surrender, Saloman, using his one remaining hostage as a shield, appeared at the top of the boarding stairway and pointed his pistol at a policeman on the ground. He was then fatally shot by a police marksman. 5473

September 15, 1975—Spain—Four Palestinian terrorists took over the Egyptian embassy in Madrid, threatening to blow it up and kill the ambassador and two aides unless Egypt abandoned its disengagement pact with Israel. The group set a midnight deadline. The group claimed membership in the Group of the Fallen Abd al Kadir al Husayni, although the press speculated that the attackers were members of the PFLP, whose spokesman, Bassam Abu Sherif, ascribed responsibility to ''some Arab students'' but did not issue a denial. The PLO denied responsibility, although Egyptian President Sadat claimed that Yasir Arafat would be held personally responsible. The group, which took over the embassy shortly before noon, was armed with pistols, a shotgun, and a bag containing explosives. They claimed to have dynamited all of the entrances to the twelve-room embassy apartment. Negotiations were conducted by the ambassadors of Iraq, Algeria (Mohammed Khaled), Kuwait, and Jordan. A bullhorn was used, and notes were also slipped under the door of the study of Egyptian Ambassador Mahmoud Abdel Ghaffar. The guerrillas demanded that Egypt refrain from signing implementing documents for the accord with Israel; that it issue a public declaration attacking the Geneva implementation conference, noting that the September 4 agreement is ''a betrayal of the Egyptian and Arab people''; and that Egypt leave the conference. One hour before the deadline, the Spanish government announced that the Palestinians had agreed to fly to Algiers with their hostages. Cairo agreed to allow the Algerian and Iraqi ambassadors to accompany them. The group received a welcome from the Algerian government and announced at a news conference that they had obtained a written denunciation of the Sinai pact signed by the Egyptian, Algerian, Iraqi, Kuwaiti, and Libyan ambassadors in Madrid, as well as a sixth unnamed envoy, believed to be the Syrian ambassador. The group sought asylum in Algeria. Sadat's government called the denunciation ''a worthless piece of paper.'' The Kuwaiti newspaper *Al Rai Al Am* said the terrorists included two Fatah members. 2395

September 16, 1975—France—During the evening, bombs exploded outside three Spanish banks in Paris, causing extensive damage. 2396-2398

September 16, 1975—United States—A bomb was disarmed two minutes before it was set to detonate in a stolen car placed next to a Denver building housing a convention of the International Association of Chiefs of Police.

September 18, 1975—United States—Bill and Emily Harris, Wendy Yoshimura, and Patricia Hearst were captured by the FBI in San Francisco. The apartment in which Yoshimura and Hearst were arrested was rented to Hearst by Stephen Soliah, who was captured later. The next day, a bomb exploded in a Seattle grocery store. A warning call from the George Jackson Brigade said the bomb was in retaliation for the arrests. Nine were injured.

September 22, 1975—United States—Sara Jane Moore fired a pistol shot at President Gerald Ford as he was entering his limousine in San Francisco.

September 22, 1975—United States—A man ran through an Allentown, Pennsylvania, airplane terminal building and out a fire exit door leading to the ramp area. He was apprehended as he ran toward a parked plane. The man was discovered to have six knives and a box of .22 caliber ammunition. A .22 caliber rifle was found in his car later. He told authorities that God had told him to board the aircraft and would be giving him further instructions. 5474

September 23, 1975—United States—The Brunswick licensed nuclear facility of the Carolina Power and Light Company received a bomb threat.

September 23, 1975—Panama—Eight hundred leftist Panamanian students demonstrated against U.S. military bases in the Canal Zone and threw rocks, red paint, and three Molotov cocktails at the U.S. embassy in Panama City. No one was injured, but eighty-five windows were broken and five embassy automobiles were damaged. The group demanded U.S. force withdrawal and denounced the governments of the United States and Panama for considering a joint defense treaty for the Canal Zone. The Panamanian government later apologized for the attack. 2399

September 24, 1975—Argentina—A bomb exploded in the Córdoba offices of Xerox Argentina, a subsidiary of the American Xerox Corporation, smashing windows but causing no injuries. 2400

September 24, 1975—United States—Evidence found in the apartments rented to Patricia Hearst and William and Emily Harris, members of the Symbionese Liberation Army, led to the arrest in Seattle of Larry Handelsman, a member of the Weather Underground.

September 25, 1975—United States—Officials at the Massachusetts Institute of Technology reported an attempted forced entry at their licensed nuclear facility.

September 26, 1975—United States—The Indian Point licensed nuclear facility of the Consolidated Edison Company received a bomb threat.

September 26, 1975—Philippines—Twenty members of the Moro National Liberation Front hijacked the *Suehiro Maru*, a Japanese ship in the southern Philippines, and demanded a $133,000 ransom within two days. The group threatened to kill a Philippine hostage and take reprisals against twenty-six Japanese crewmen unless the Philippine navy's ten ships left the area and allowed them safe passage to their island hideout. The owners of the vessel cabled Manila that they were willing to pay the ransom. A five-man mission of American Steamship took a PAL flight to Zamboanga City to conduct negotiations, carrying the ransom money with them. After ninety hours of negotiations, the hijackers surrendered on September 29. The ship and crew returned to Japan, while the hijackers were reported to be on board a Philippine naval vessel. 2401

September 26, 1975—Northern Ireland—The IRA denied responsibility for a booby-trapped bomb that injured two British army soldiers patroling a school in a Catholic district of Belfast.

September 26, 1975—Belgium—Demonstrators destroyed the windows of the Spanish embassy in Brussels and burned part of the facility. They also destroyed the local offices of the Spanish national airline. 2402-2403

September 26, 1975—France—Demonstrators protesting the execution of ETA terrorists in Spain attacked a Spanish bank in Paris and the Spanish cultural center in Toulouse. 2404-2405

September 26, 1975—Switzerland—Demonstrators attacked the Spanish consulate in Geneva. 2406

September 27, 1975—Denmark—The windows of the Spanish embassy in Copenhagen were smashed. 2407

September 27, 1975—Italy—Rome demonstrators set six Spanish tourist buses on fire after ten thousand persons attended rallies organized by the Italian Communist party and splinter Marxist groups. 2408

September 27, 1975—Portugal—Following the sacking of its Lisbon embassy by angry demonstrators, Spain recalled its ambassador. 2409

September 27, 1975—Colombia—A bomb exploded at the Soviet chancery in Bogotá in the early morning. Shortly afterward a bomb exploded at the site of a Cuban film festival sponsored by the Cuban embassy, causing no injuries and minor damage. Leaflets found at both sites credited the attacks to the Military Liberation Front of Colombia. 2410-2411

September 27, 1975—Greece—S. Marketos, a young man, entered the cockpit of an Olympic Airways SC7 flying from Athens to Mykonos. Holding a spray bottle, which he claimed contained nitric acid, he threatened to blind the pilot if he was not flown to Albania. He was overpowered by the crew and turned over to authorities at Mykonos. 5475

September 27, 1975—Burma—Unidentified individuals attacked a Union of Burma Airways flight as it was preparing to take off from Bhamo airport. The plane was hit with three rockets and considerable rifle fire, which left over one hundred bullet holes in the plane. Four persons were injured and one was killed.

September 28, 1975—Netherlands—Fires, which Dutch authorities refused to rule out as arson, damaged the Spanish embassy in The Hague and the home of the sister of the Dutch ambassador to Spain. 2412

September 28, 1975—Turkey—A stick of dynamite was thrown into the garden of the Ankara residence of the Spanish ambassador. 2413

September 28, 1975—Spain—A time bomb exploded under the locomotive of a Spanish train traveling from Madrid to Paris. 2414

September 28, 1975—United Kingdom—After bungling a morning robbery attempt, three gunmen seized eight hostages in the basement storeroom of the Spaghetti House restaurant in Knightsbridge, London. The group claimed to be members of the Black Liberation Front, although the organization denied any links with them. Two West Indians were led by Frank Davis, a Nigerian. They demanded to be flown to Jamaica, but the police refused to grant their demands and surrounded the restaurant. The police allowed the gunmen water, coffee, cigarettes, and playing cards but did little else to improve the conditions in the cramped basement. They continually pressured the gunmen, telling them there was no way out but surrender. The Italian consul general, Mario Manca, talked with the gunmen often and was able to pass secret messages to the hostages in Italian. The police gave the gunmen a transistor radio, permitting them to listen to broadcasts that had been calculated to wear down their resistance. Two ill hostages were released during the first 24 hours of the 122-hour siege. On October 1, the radio announced the arrest of two other men on charges of involvement in the robbery. Police surmised that this led to the gunmen's capitulation. On October 3 the group informed police that they were releasing the remaining six hostages. Two of the gunmen accompanied them; Davis shot himself in the stomach, seriously injuring himself. On June 30, 1976, the three were found guilty of attempted robbery. 2415

September 30, 1975—United States—In Boston, a man was slightly injured and the window of the Iberia Airlines office was shattered by a small bomb. 2416

September 30, 1975—Hungary—A Malev Hungarian Airlines TU154 flying from Budapest to Beirut crashed into the Mediterranean Sea, killing all sixty-four on board after an explosion occurred. 2417

October 1975—United States—The Dominican government sent two soldiers to serve as bodyguards to Consul General Quilino Ricardo, Jr., who had received a number of telephone threats. Cuban terrorists were believed responsible. 2418

October 1975—United States—Humbert Lopez, Jr., thirty-four, a Cuban exile, was arrested in Miami after a bomb he was apparently preparing exploded at his home. Lopez lost his left eye and three fingers in the explosion. A jailed friend, Luis Crespo, lost an arm in 1974 in a similar accident. He had fled the United States to avoid serving a possible fifteen-year jail term for violation of federal and state laws regulating the use of explosives and firearms. Lopez was held without bail pending arraignment. 2419

October 3, 1975—Ireland—A man posing as a policeman kidnapped Teide Herrema, the Dutch manager of the Ferenka metal plant in Dublin, a few hundred yards away from his home as he drove his Mercedes to work. The Limerick plant is a subsidiary of Enka Glantzstoff, a multinational corporation based in Arnheim, Netherlands. Police officers found his car less than one hundred yards from his house, with the door open and the key in the ignition. There was no sign of a struggle. One report claimed that four terrorists took part in the kidnapping, with four or five other renegade IRA members providing safe haven and cars. Herrema and his kidnappers, Eddie Gallagher, twenty-seven, and Marion Coyle, nineteen, first drove to Kinnity, where cars were switched at a farmhouse. They next drove to a Mountmellick house where Herrema was kept for eight days in a small room. For five days he was tied up, blindfolded, and had cotton stuffed in his ears to deprive him of sensory detection. He was then moved to 1410 Saint Evins Park in Monasterevin.

The kidnappers demanded that three IRA terrorists be released within forty-eight hours or Herrema would be executed; that Ferenka close for forty-eight hours as an act of good faith; and that police not search for the kidnappers or set up roadblocks. The corporation agreed and offered to pay a ransom. The Irish government refused all of the kidnappers' demands. The group later demanded safe passage out of the country. The kidnappers used the code word previously employed to identify IRA members. The prisoners whose release was demanded were Kevin Mallon, Bridget Rose Dugdale (see incident 1898), and Jim Hyland, who were being held for attempted murder, complicity in an art theft, and possession of explosives, respectively. Four thousand Irish police searched for the kidnappers, and the deadline passed without incident. A Capuchin priest, Reverend Donal O'Mahoney, was nominated by Bernard Cardinal Alfrink of the Netherlands to serve as an intermediary but was unsuccessful in obtaining the fifty-three-year-old hostage's release. It was later learned that Gallagher was the father of the baby born in jail to Dr. Dugdale, thirty-four, who had been jailed for nine years. On October 16, Herrema broadcast a statement in which he claimed to be alive and noted that his captors threatened to cut off his foot if police continued to demand proof that he was being held by them.

On October 20, police discovered the house where the kidnappers were hiding. They attempted a rescue by storming into the house, but the kidnappers fired five shots and retreated to an upstairs bedroom, holding a gun to Herrema's head. Gallagher then pushed Herrema to a window of the house, yelling, "He's a dead man if you try anything." Gallagher claimed to have explosives tied to himself and threatened to blow up the house if security forces attempted to enter again. On October 28, a friend of the kidnappers told television interviewers that the kidnappers had hung explosives around the neck of Herrema. Two days previously, Ruairi O'Bradaigh, the leader of the Provisional Sinn Fein, said at the annual conference of his group in Dublin that the kidnapping served no useful purpose and that his group condemned the attack. Police hooked up a listening device to a drainpipe in the house and were able to monitor conversations between Herrema and his captors. At one point, Gallagher offered to surrender if Coyle was given safe passage out of the country. It appeared that Coyle was against this suggestion. Gallagher also offered to surrender, but again Coyle refused. Union leader Philip Flynn, another mediator, said on November 4 that the kidnappers wanted safe passage out of the country in return for Herrema's release. At times, however, the two hardened their positions and threw milk bottles at the police. The bottles were found to contain urine and were accompanied by excreta wrapped in newspaper. The police continued to pressure the terrorists to release Herrema, making loud noises and shining spotlights in an attempt to prevent sleep. Once two police went to the back bedroom window to attempt a surprise attack, but one detective was wounded in the hand by a gunshot from the kidnappers. At 9:30 P.M. on November 7, Gallagher became ill and called out to police that he would release Herrema. On March 11, 1976, an Irish court sentenced Gallagher to twenty years; Coyle received fifteen years. On November 24, 1975, the Irish government announced that it would confer honorary citizenship on Herrema and his wife, Elizabeth. 2420

October 4, 1975—Lebanon—Four terrorists attacked Beirut international airport in an attempt to sabotage the Egyptian-Israeli Sinai accord. The terrorists shot their way past the terminal doors and sprayed the lobby with machine-gun fire. Three people, including one of the terrorists, were killed, and fourteen others were wounded. One of the terrorists was captured in the terminal; another was found on a Middle East Airlines B707. Those killed included a policeman and an Egyptian tourist who was hit during the forty-five-minute gun battle. One of the potential hijackers escaped but was captured by the PLO and handed over to Lebanese authorities. Interrogation was conducted in secrecy, but it was reported that the man killed was a Syrian and the wounded terrorist was a Palestinian. The other two were a Lebanese and an Egyptian. It was believed that the Al Fatah identification card carried by one of the group was a forgery. 2421

October 5, 1975—United States—A young man gained entry to the air operations area at Cincinnati airport by going to the observation deck, climbing a fence, and jumping onto the ramp. He approached a maintenance man and offered him money if he would help him hijack a plane. Rebuffed, he ran up to and entered an aircraft that was being boarded. He announced to the stewardess that he was taking over the plane and wanted to speak to the captain. An airline representative arrived and escorted the man off the plane and into the custody of security personnel. 5476

October 5, 1975—Argentina—Fifty Montoneros attacked the Twenty-ninth Infantry Regiment's barracks near Formosa in an attempt to steal guns and ammunition. In the ensuing battle, fifteen guerrillas and eleven security officers were killed. The terrorists fought their way to Formosa airport, where they were met by a second group, who held the provincial governor captive. Simultaneously fifteen to twenty of their group hijacked an Aerolineas Argentinas B737 flying from Buenos Aires to Corrientes. They forced the pilot to land at Formosa, where all of the passengers were permitted to leave. Fighting off authorities, the other terrorists boarded the plane, which was directed toward Brazil. The plane ran out of fuel and landed at Rafaela, where the hijackers were met by three waiting cars, allowing their escape. The jet's tires blew out and the landing gear sank into the ground, but none of the occupants was injured. The next day several people attacked El Pacu Airport in Formosa, killing a security guard. 5477

October 5, 1975—Israel—A suitcase packed with explosives was discovered at Tel Aviv's international airport after it had circled on a conveyor belt for more than an hour. The suitcase apparently had been abandoned by a terrorist who had entered the country. 2422

October 6, 1975—Philippines—A PAL BAC111 was hijacked by Camilo Morales, twenty-five, as it was approaching Manila on its flight from Davao. The hijacker, armed with a grenade and a .45 caliber pistol, demanded that the plane be readied for a flight to Benghazi, Libya. Several passengers were released in exchange for a PAL vice-president and eight stewardesses. Morales was persuaded to surrender eight hours later after Philippine authorities agreed to help him locate his four-year-old daughter, whom he claimed had been kidnapped several days previously in the Mindanao region where Moslem rebels were conducting an insurgency against the government. 5478

October 6, 1975—Italy—The former vice-president of Chile, Bernardo Leighton, sixty-six, and his wife, Anita, were shot by an unknown gunman during the evening. He was a spokesman for the Christian Democratic Party in Exile and had been a prominent critic of the military government in Santiago.

He had lived in Rome for three years. Friends claimed he had received anonymous death threats. 2423

October 6, 1975—United States—A bomb planted by the Youths of the Star, an anti-Castro Cuban exile group, exploded in the Dominican Republic's consulate in Miami, breaking all of the windows of the two-story building and causing extensive property damage but no injuries. The consul, Aquilino Ricardo, and his family escaped injury. It was believed that the attack was related to the Dominican Republic's recent extradition to the United States of a Cuban exile wanted as a federal fugitive (see incident 2419). 2424

October 7, 1975—United States—Three men chartered an Atlantic Aero Cessna 177 to fly from Greensboro, North Carolina, to Atlanta, Georgia. Shortly after takeoff, one of them pulled a .22 caliber revolver, pointed it at the pilot's head, and demanded to be flown to Florida. After a refueling stop, the plane landed in Florida. Two of the hijackers walked away from the plane, while the third went with his hostage to the airport. Authorities were alerted and the hijacker surrendered to police. The other two were subsequently apprehended. The FAA profile did not apply in this case. The trio were indicted by a federal grand jury in the middle district of Florida on October 16, and were identified as white males: Ronald F. Ralph, who was born on January 7, 1948, in Weymouth, Massachusetts; David P. Burke, who was born in Washington, D.C.; and Jeffrey Murphy. Prosecution against Murphy was declined on January 7, 1976. Ralph and Burke were sentenced to twenty years for air piracy on January 30, 1976. 5479

October 7, 1975—France—French officials were unable to confirm press reports that three Basque members of the ETA were shot to death during the night near Saint-Jean-de-Luz in French Basque country. 2425

October 8, 1975—West Germany—The Spanish consulate in Mainz was extensively damaged by a bomb, which caused no injuries. 2426

October 8, 1975—France—A gunman fired three revolver bullets into the stomach of Captain Bartolomé Besto Garcia Plata Valle, who was arriving at his Boulogne-sur-Seine apartment for lunch. Valle was hospitalized in grave condition. The Juan Paredes Manot International Brigade claimed credit in a statement to a leftist Paris newspaper. Paredes was a Spanish Basque militant executed in Barcelona the previous fall. On May 11, 1976, the Ché Guevara Brigade said in a communiqué that the 7.65-mm revolver it used to kill diplomat Zenteno was the same weapon used in this case (see incident 2696). On May 13, 1977, French police arrested three men for the attacks. They were in possession of the weapons used and admitted to membership in the Maoist Armed Nuclei for Popular Autonomy. 2427

October 8, 1975—Argentina—Eleven Chileans and a Brazilian took over the Buenos Aires offices of the U.N. High Commission for Refugees, holding fourteen employees hostage, including Robert Jean Muller of Switzerland, the chief commission representative, and his Austrian deputy, and Chilean and Argentine nationals. The group threatened to kill them unless they were allowed to leave for a democratic country. The Argentine government guaranteed safe passage the following day but had difficulties finding a country willing to accept the terrorists. The group claimed to be protesting the treatment of fifteen thousand Chilean refugees who had fled to Argentina after the 1973 military coup. They said, "We have grenades and guns, and we will blow ourselves up with the hostages unless the United Nations people arrange to transport us to Sweden or another European country that will accept us." The federal police chief, Omar Pinto, entered the building to negotiate with the Chileans, who also claimed to be in telephone contact with U.N. officials in New York. Sweden, Denmark, and the Netherlands turned down the Argentine request to accept the terrorists. Four other countries, including Belgium and an unidentified socialist nation, were contacted. John Kelley of Ireland, the legal representative for Prince Sadruddin Aga Khan, the U.N. commissioner for refugees at Geneva, flew to Buenos Aires to meet with the group, who had taken over the building at midday, but reported that he was unable to enter the building. The group released eight women and an Argentine man who had suffered an epileptic attack. On October 10, the group released the hostages and flew with their families to Algeria, which granted them asylum. 2428

October 9, 1975—Angola—John S. Robinson, an American missing in Luanda, was turned over to civilian police on October 28 by the Popular Movement for the Liberation of Angola. 2429

October 9, 1975—United Kingdom—An IRA bomb exploded in the Green Park subway station in London, a quarter mile from Buckingham Palace. One person was killed and eighteen others wounded by glass from shattered store windows. 2430

October 10, 1975—United States—The FLNC bombed the Broward County courthouse in Fort Lauderdale, Florida. 2431

October 11, 1975—Turkey—Shortly before midnight, a bomb was thrown from a passing car into the parking lot of an Ankara building occupied by the U.S. Base Civil Engineer Detachment. A second explosion occurred at the Ankara Officers' Club, which was occupied by U.S. servicemen. No injuries were reported, although there was property damage. 2432-2433

October 12, 1975—United Kingdom—A coach bolt bomb was defused at Lockets Restaurant in Westminster. 2434

October 13, 1975—United States—The Emiliano Zapata Unit threw a Molotov cocktail at a Pacific Gas and Electric Company tower in Belmont, California. The device fizzled out.

October 14, 1975—France—A bomb exploded in the early morning at an anti-Franco Spanish-language publishing house in Paris, causing considerable damage but no injuries. 2435

October 14, 1975—United States—The Westinghouse Electric Company's licensed nuclear facility in Columbia, South Carolina, received a bomb threat.

October 16, 1975—Argentina—Reinaldo Dalbosco, an Italian executive of an electrical supplies factory, and Corporal Raul Sanguinetti were killed by submachine gunfire in the morning by terrorists who intercepted their car in a Buenos Aires suburb. The policeman resisted the kidnapping attempt. It was reported that their bodies had nearly one hundred bullet wounds each. 2436

October 17, 1975—United States—The Pilgrim licensed nuclear facility of the Boston Edison Company received a bomb threat.

October 17, 1975—United States—A bomb exploded in a locker at the Miami international airport, blowing a section of lockers in the main terminal fifty-seven feet from the wall and destroying part of the ceiling. No injuries were reported. An anonymous caller had warned of the bomb. Police said that the bomb may have been directed at a nearby ticket counter for Dominicana Airlines, which had received several bomb threats. The thumbprint of Rolando Otero, thirty-three, a Cuban exile, was found on the locker. He was convicted of the bombing on January 27, 1977, by a Fort Walton Beach, Florida, jury, which deliberated only one hour in his case, although he was acquitted of eight other bombing charges. 2437

October 18, 1975—Spain—Two members of the Civil Guard patroling the western bank of the Bidassoa River near the frontier town of Behovia came under fire from the French side of the river. One of them was slightly wounded in the leg. 2438

October 20, 1975—United States—A time bomb that apparently malfunctioned was discovered by a janitor as he walked into the office of Dominicana Airlines in Miami. The bomb was disarmed by a police bomb squad. 2439

October 22, 1975—West Germany—Governor George Wallace received a telephoned death threat at his Berlin hotel. The male caller told an operator that the Red Army Faction had the power to kill Wallace. Police officials believed the call was harassment and not from the group. Wallace flew to Paris with tightened security arrangements for his five-nation European tour. 2440

October 22, 1975—Austria—Three gunmen fired submachine guns at the Turkish ambassador, Danis Tunaligil, sixty, after asking his secretary if they could see him in his office around noon. Police experts identified the weapons as an Israeli-designed Uzi and a U.S.-designed Thompson submachine gun. The Justice Commandos of the Armenian Genocide took credit for the assassination. The gunmen appear to have escaped. 2441

October 22, 1975—Lebanon—The director and assistant director of the USIS regional service center in Beirut's Christian quarter of Sin el-Fil were kidnapped on Corniche Mazra at 7 A.M. while on their way to work. They were taken from their car after stopping at a roadblock set up by a Nasserite street gang in a Moslem and Palestinian section of Beirut. Two Lebanese employees of the printing center were also in the station wagon, which carried diplomatic plates. They were released by the gunmen and reached the printing center where they reported the kidnapping. The two hostages were identified as Charles Gallagher, forty-four, and William Dykes, fifty-five. It was believed that they were handed over to an arm of the PFLP, although the group denied any links with the attack. There were also reports that the Socialist Labor party was connected with the incident. The demands by the kidnappers changed constantly; they ranged from monetary ransom to the release of captured guerrillas in Israel and Lebanon. On February 25, 1976, they were unexpectedly released during the evening at the home of Kamal Jumblatt, the titular leader of the Lebanese left. The State Department said that no ransom had been paid, although spokesmen refused to comment upon the possibility that the release of two Palestinians by the Israeli government was linked to Gallagher and Dykes's freedom. The two Americans flew to Athens to join their families. They had lost weight during imprisonment. They were not allowed to discuss their treatment as hostages with members of the press. 2442

October 23, 1975—Angola—Patricia Thornton, thirty, of New York City, who worked as a teacher in a Luso school, was reported to have been kidnapped and taken to Luanda by the MPLA. 2443

October 23, 1975—Ethiopia—Two armed members of the Popular Liberation Forces broke into the British consulate at 9:45 A.M., locked up an assistant, and kidnapped the honorary consul, Basil V. H. Burwood-Taylor, from his Asmara office. The fifty-eight-year-old consul also ran an import-export business in Asmara and looked after the interests of Britons in Asmara. It does not appear that any ransom demands were made. On November 1, 1975, Taylor's wife received the first message from his abductors that her husband was alive. He was released in Khartoum, Sudan, with Americans Steven Campbell and James Harrell (see incident 2331) on May 3, 1976. 2444

October 23, 1975—United Kingdom—An IRA bomb planted under the front wheel of a Jaguar owned by Conservative Member of Parliament Hugh Fraser exploded at 8:53 A.M., minutes after he delayed his drive to Sotheby's to answer a telephone call. He had been scheduled to drive Caroline Kennedy, seventeen, the daughter of the late U.S. president, to her art classes. Seven people were injured and a leukemia specialist, Dr. Gordon Hamilton Fairley, a professor in the department of medical oncology at St. Bartholomew's Hospital in London, was killed as he walked past the car with his dog. A number of houses had broken windows and chipped facades from the blast, which threw huge pieces of jagged metal over the square. Police assumed that Kennedy was not the target of the attack. Fraser had on occasion spoken out against terrorism. On October 29, Scotland Yard announced the arrest of eight suspects, four of them women, in the recent wave of bombings in London, including this car bombing. 2445

October 24, 1975—Argentina—Montoneros kidnapped Franz Heinrich Metz, the West German production manager of the Mercedes-Benz truck factory in Buenos Aires, after he left the factory. They demanded that Mercedes rehire 119 workers who were dismissed and recognize the strike leaders as the workers' representatives. A large ransom, reported by some to total $7.5 million, was paid for his release, although Mercedes refused to confirm the figures. On December 24, Mercedes ran an advertisement in newspapers in Europe, Latin America (including Mexico), and North America, including the *Washington Post*, outlining the group's arguments against Perón's government and denouncing the "economic imperialism" of multinational corporations in developing countries. The group had demanded the publication of the statement as one of the conditions of Metz's Christmas Eve 1975 release. The labor concessions were also granted. 2446

October 24, 1975—France—An anonymous phone call to a radio station in Paris warned that the Turkish embassy would be bombed in the evening. A police search was negative. 2447

October 24, 1975—France—The Turkish ambassador to France, Ismail Erez, fifty-three, and his chauffeur, Talip Yener, twenty-three, were machine-gunned to death as they were driving back to the embassy after a luncheon at the Austrian embassy on the Left Bank. As the car neared the end of Bir Hakeim Bridge, the driver slowed down. A gunman on the right side of the street fired his machine gun into the car, killing the ambassador instantly. A second gunman on the left killed the driver. The assassins escaped with a third gunman. Several calls claimed credit for the attack, including the Secret Armenian Army for the Liberation of Armenia, EOKA, and the Justice Commandos of the Armenian Genocide. French police detained fourteen persons for questioning and searched the homes of twenty Armenian families, finding no weapons or other evidence related to the killing. 2448

October 24, 1975—Israel—Authorities fought off a group of Arab infiltrators south of the Dead Sea. The group had attempted to enter Israel from Jordan and left behind a 60-mm mortar, shells, explosives, and small arms. It was believed that they intended to shell Neo Hakikar and to sabotage installations in the area. Israelis believed that the group had evaded Jordanian border patrols. 2449

October 25, 1975—Lebanon—Three diplomats from France, Denmark, and Sweden were kidnapped from a Beirut hotel by leftist gunmen. They were released unharmed after the intervention of Al Fatah and the PLO. 2450

October 25, 1975—Ethiopia—Eritrean secessionist gunmen kidnapped Egizio Fralaschi, an Italian teacher, in Asmara. 2451

October 25, 1975—Argentina—A major synthetic fiber plant in Buenos Aires with 40 percent Dutch ownership announced that it was going out of business because textile workers had threatened to kill its executives if wages were not raised.

October 25, 1975—Lebanon—Leftist gunmen broke into Beirut's Myrtom House, a small hotel and restaurant owned by an Austrian resident of the city, smashed furniture and windows, and set the place on fire. A fire truck called to the blaze was shot at and retreated. 2452

October 26, 1975—Lebanon—Philip Caputo, thirty-four, of Westchester, Illinois, a staff correspondent for the *Chicago Tribune* in Beirut, claimed that he was deliberately shot at by leftist gunmen after being directed to walk down a street. He was wounded in both feet and in the back. According to Caputo, he was stopped as he left his office: ''They checked my credentials and then told me to walk down to Hamra Street, a distance of about one hundred yards. I had gone about thirty yards when one of them fired a shot at me. I shouted at them to stop but then another joined in and fired a burst of bullets, one of which literally went through my hair. I ran zigzagging and rolling low and was grazed across the back and arms by flying bullets. Then one hit me in the right ankle and just as I reached the corner, another one got me in the left ankle. I crawled down Hamra Street toward the central bank and a householder took me in.'' 2453

October 26, 1975—Lebanon—Twelve men carrying AK-47 assault rifles burst into the sixth-floor office apartment of *Washington Post* reporter Jonathan C. Randal just before dawn and led him to a waiting car. Driving the Volkswagen through the Moslem neighborhoods of Beirut, the group, claiming to be communists, went to their headquarters. They were greeted by an individual claiming to be Abu Daoud. Randal suggested calling Algerian Ambassador Mohammed Yazid, who vouched for him after the 6:15 A.M. phone call. Randal was then delivered safely to the ambassador's home. 2454

October 27, 1975—Lebanon—Michael Ross, an American newsman with United Press International, was detained for more than an hour by gunmen from the Ain El Mreisse quarter of Beirut near the U.S. embassy. He said he had gone to rescue his brood of kittens in his house. 2455

October 27, 1975—Lebanon—Several mortar rounds landed on the Beirut residence of the Austrian ambassador in the Kantari neighborhood. No injuries were reported. 2456

October 27, 1975—United States—The FALN took credit for ten bombings throughout the country: one bank and two office buildings in Chicago; one at the State Department and one at the Bureau of Indian Affairs in Washington, D.C.; four at four New York City banks; and one at the United States Mission to the U.N. building. The group demanded immediate independence for Puerto Rico and the release of Puerto Rican political prisoners, and it mentioned exploitation of the working class. No one was injured in the explosions, which caused minor structural damage to the buildings. Fifteen thousand dollars of damage was done to the State Department building, including the shattering of thirty-seven windows at three levels. The Washington Bureau of the Associated Press received a call claiming credit for the State bombing, protesting "Kissinger's sellout of Israel to Sadat." The caller ended with the words, "Never again," the slogan of the JDL. State spokesmen ruled out any connection of the JDL to the bombings. Police found a bomb that failed to go off in Chicago and said that it was made of five sticks of dynamite and a detonator. It had been placed in a flower stand outside the Standard Oil building in Chicago's Loop section. Bombs in Chicago caused minor damage at the Sears Towers, the IBM Corporation, and the Continental Bank building. Chicago damage was estimated at $50,000; BIA sustained $200 damage; and the New York building damage was placed at $150,000. The first New York bomb went off at 1:43 A.M. outside a branch of the British-owned West Minster Bank at 100 Wall Street. At 2:01 A.M., a bomb went off in the doorway of the Chase Manhattan Bank at Madison Avenue and East Fifty-seventh Street. A third bomb went off at 2:04 A.M. at the First National City Bank at 111 Wall Street. At 2:11 A.M., a bomb went off at the U.S. U.N. mission, punching out fifty-five windows and damaging an entrance door. A minute later, a bomb went off at the First National City Bank at 40 West Fifty-seventh Street. 2457-2467

October 27, 1975—Israel—A thirty-three-pound bomb planted in a French car parked in front of Jerusalem's Eyal Hotel exploded, wrecking the ground-floor lobby of the hotel, shattering windows in stores and apartments as far as one hundred yards away, damaging ten shops, and injuring eight persons, including two young Swiss women, two Israelis, and an Arab. Arab terrorists were suspected, and fifteen to twenty Arabs were taken into custody for questioning. 2468

October 28, 1975—United States—The U.S. Senate approved U.S. ratification of the U.N. Convention on the Prevention and Punishment of Crimes Against Internationally Protected Persons, Including Diplomatic Agents.

October 28, 1975—Lebanon—Officials of the French embassy were pinned down in their spacious compound on Rue Clemenceau in Beirut by gunfire. 2469

October 28, 1975—Lebanon—Gunmen looking for a sniper broke into the vacated Indian embassy in the Kantari district of Beirut. The group's leader, Ibrahim Koleilat, later called the Indian ambassador and apologized for the incident. 2470

October 29, 1975—Lebanon—Herman Huddleston, forty-eight, a U.S. pilot for Trans-Mediterranean Airlines, was kidnapped from his beachfront home in Beirut by four Palestinians armed with machine guns. He had been watching television during the evening with his wife at the time of the attack. The group was suspicious of his amateur radio equipment and accused him of being a CIA employee. He was released unharmed three days later. Huddleston was unable to identify the group's affiliation. 2471

October 29, 1975—United Kingdom—An IRA bomb exploded without warning inside an Italian restaurant, the Trattoria Fiori at Mount and South Audley streets in the Mayfair district of London, injuring eighteen. The U.S. embassy, only two hundred yards from the restaurant, was not damaged. 2472

October 29, 1975—Argentina—Four Montoneros gunmen parked in a car outside the Córdoba home of Alberto Salas, forty-three, personnel manager of the products division of Fiat-Concord, Argentina's largest auto firm, shot him to death as he got behind the wheel of his car. The group had threatened to kill company executives if their demands were not met. The company had closed its plant on October 20 but was compelled by the government to reopen the installation. 2473

October 29, 1975—Turkey—Two Molotov cocktails exploded during the evening in Istanbul in the garden of the Iranian consulate and in the parking lot of the British consulate. A dynamite bomb exploded in front of the Turkish-Iranian Association Building (some reports list it as the Turkish-Iranian Friendship Society). No injuries were reported, although there was property damage. Police speculated that the attacks were to protest the visit of the shah of Iran. 2474-2476

November 1975—Lebanon—Unidentified gunmen made an unsuccessful kidnapping attempt against two U.S. officials—Drug Enforcement Agency special agent Michael Holm and security officer John Jarrell—who were driving in Beirut in separate cars two hundred yards apart. The assailants were using 9-mm automatic weapons and fired several rounds at the cars but missed. Using evasive driving techniques, the men escaped unharmed from their attackers. 2477

November 1, 1975—Puerto Rico—A bomb exploded on the Soviet cruise ship *Maksim Gorky*, docked in San Juan, causing minor damage but no injuries. 2478

November 1, 1975—United States—Rolando Masferrer, fifty-eight, a former pre-Castro Cuban official known as "el Tigre" and a leading Castro foe, died in Miami when a bomb placed under his car wheel exploded when he turned on his ignition. The Secret Organization Zero said he had been killed because of his "systematic work in the destruction of the anti-Communist struggle" as well as his relation to Cuba's internal intelligence organization. "His assassination, like that of José Elias de la Torriente [see incident 1880] should serve as an example for those who disdain the cause of Cuban liberation. It is necessary to cleanse the exile community in order to liberate Cuba." 2479

November 3, 1975—United Kingdom—An IRA bomb destroyed a London lawyer's car near Marble Arch and Hyde Park in the West End. Attorney Richard Charnley, thirty-three, and his wife received minor injuries. 2480

November 3, 1975—Venezuela—A U.S. firm in Caracas received a threat that its store would be bombed and its executives kidnapped. 2481

November 3-4, 1975—United States—The General Atomics, Inc., licensed nuclear facility in San Diego, California, received two bomb threats.

November 5, 1975—Bangladesh—The *Washington Post* reported on December 14, 1975, that a mission had been taken over. According to Lewis M. Simons, "Indian-backed Bengali guerrillas have captured a Catholic mission and hospital on the northern border of Bangladesh and are holding an elderly priest hostage there, 2 escaped nuns said today. The guerrillas, supporters of assassinated Bangladesh President Sheik Mujibur Rahman, are threatening to kill the priest if they are attacked by troops of the Bangladesh Rifles, the national border-defense force. The rebels—about 15 of them, well-armed with rifles, machine guns and mortars—have occupied the mission since Nov. 5, according to the nuns, Sister Pascale, who is French, and Sister Cecilia, a Bengali. Thirty-five patients, some of them critically ill, were forced to leave the hospital, the nuns said in an interview here [Dacca]. . . . The rebels are led by Kader 'Tiger' Sidiqui, a popular guerrilla leader and warlord in the central district of Tangail during the 1971 Bangladesh struggle for independence from Pakistan. Between 30,000 and 40,000 aborigines live on the Bangladesh side of the frontier. According to the 2 nuns, Sidiqui has promised them self-rule once they help him 'avenge Mujib.' 'Kader came to the mission with 3 of his brothers and I appealed to him to take his men away, telling him it was a neutral zone,' said Sister Pascale. 'But he refused. He said that in time of war nothing was neutral.' The 2 women said none of the mission personnel nor the patients was treated badly by the guerrillas. 'But after we escaped, we heard that they were very angry and that they looted the mission and the hospital,' said Sister Pascale. The 2 nuns escaped individually about 3 weeks ago by changing from their uniforms into saris and slipping away to a nearby village. They were interviewed in Dacca, a few hours after they arrived here with (Rev. Joseph Dutta, a physician at a mission hospital in the northern district town of Mymensingh).'' 2482

November 6, 1975—United States—Two explosive devices were discovered in two unclaimed suitcases in Buffalo airport. The cases had been taken off a flight originating in Columbus, Ohio. The timing devices on the explosives had malfunctioned.

November 7, 1975—Philippines—Ten armed MNLF members kidnapped six Japanese from their fishing vessel off Basilan Island. The group demanded a monetary ransom and the release of two jailed guerrillas. The government offered them a pardon, and the kidnappers surrendered on December 6 after freeing their hostages. 2483

November 8, 1975—United States—The Pilgrim licensed nuclear facility of the Boston Edison Company at Plymouth, Massachusetts, received a bomb threat.

November 8, 1975—United States—Jack R. Johnson, a white male for whom the FAA profile was not applicable and who was born on July 5, 1956, in Evansville, Indiana, chartered a Tri State Aero Cessna 150 for a flight around the town. Intent upon committing suicide, he pointed a gun at the pilot and told him to dive the aircraft into the ground. The pilot put the plane into a high-speed dive, grappled with Johnson, and managed to push him out of the plane to his death. The pilot then regained control of the aircraft and made a safe landing. 5480

November 9, 1975—Israel—Four ALF members were killed in a clash with Israeli forces in the north. The group was armed with grenades and sabotage equipment. 2484

November 9, 1975—Soviet Union—Twenty members of the 250 crewmen of the Kotlin-class antisubmarine patrol vessel *Storozhevoy* mutinied and attempted to take the destroyer, armed with guided missiles, to a Swedish port. The three-hundred-ton ship carried no identification save for the serial number on its bow. Sweden reported that approximately ten Soviet planes strafed and bombed the ship, killing around fifty of the crewmen. The chief mutineers were sentenced to death and others were imprisoned in Riga, where the ship was taken after the attack.

November 9, 1975—United Kingdom—Police defused a ten-pound IRA bomb outside the London home of Edward Heath minutes before it was set to explode in the Belgravia section in the morning. The former prime minister returned home after the bomb was defused. 2485

November 11, 1975—Angola—There were unconfirmed press reports that a gunman firing a pistol with a silencer attempted to assassinate Prime Minister Agustinho Neto from one of the main Luanda hotels as he passed in a car. MPLA troops wounded and captured the attacker.

November 11, 1975—Tunisia—Police overpowered and arrested a gunman in Tunis who had taken hostages in the Belgian embassy and had demanded that his estranged wife living in Belgium be brought to him. 2486

November 11, 1975—Chile—The Pinochet government announced the arrest of fourteen leftist guerrillas involved in a plot to infiltrate twelve hundred terrorists who would cross the Andes mountains from Argentina and engage in attacks against the government, including the assassination of Pinochet. The government claimed that some of the guerrillas had been trained in Cuba.

November 12, 1975—Bangladesh—A live grenade was found on the grounds of the residence of Samar Sen, the Indian ambassador. 2487

November 12, 1975—United Kingdom—An IRA bomb exploded in Scotts Restaurant in London's Mayfair district, killing one man and injuring fifteen. 2488

November 12, 1975—Lebanon—David Dodge, a longtime U.S. resident of Beirut, was picked up by gunmen during the evening and robbed of his car and $50 before being released unharmed. 2489

November 13, 1975—Lebanon—Two Saiqa members entered the Pan Am hangar at Beirut international airport and held five maintenance men at gunpoint, demanding jeeps or trucks. Finding none at the hangar, they left. Army troops intercepted them and killed them in a gun battle after they refused to surrender. 2490

November 13, 1975—Israel—A twenty-three-pound bomb exploded inside a porter's luggage cart left on the sidewalk in front of a coffeehouse twenty feet from Jerusalem's Zion Square, killing seven and injuring forty, ten of them seriously. An American woman tourist was among the injured. Glass was blown out of store fronts in the 7 P.M. rush hour attack. Al Fatah's Damascus offices claimed credit, saying that it was commemorating Yasir Arafat's U.N. address of the year before, as well as the passage of three pro-Palestinian resolutions in the United Nations including one that equated Zionism with racism. The Martyr George Haddad Unit of the PDFLP also claimed credit. 2491

November 18, 1975—United Kingdom—An IRA bomb loaded with ball bearings, nuts, and bolts was thrown from a passing car into Walton's restaurant in London's Chelsea district, injuring twenty people and killing a British woman celebrating her husband's birthday and a British businessman. Two Americans were injured: Barbara Matthews, thirty-nine, of New York City, and Elizabeth Petroy, seventy-one. Police and Scotland Yard initiated a search for three men and a "pretty girl with long blond hair." 2492

November 19, 1975—Australia—Federal police in Canberra found and defused a letter bomb addressed to Prime Minister Malcolm Fraser shortly after a letter bomb addressed to John Bjelke-Petersen, premier of Queensland State, went off in a Brisbane mail room, injuring two clerks. Two days later, the Canberra post office defused a letter bomb addressed to Governor-General Sir John Kerr.

November 20, 1975—Israel—Three members of the PDFLP broke into a school dormitory at Ramat Magshimim, lined students against the wall, and began shooting them in the back. A survivor fled to warn others on the farming settlement. The terrorists, armed with submachine guns and hatchets, killed three and wounded another before escaping into Syria. A spokesman for the PDFLP said that four Israeli soldiers were killed and that the purpose of the attack was to capture hostages in order to demand the return of the remains of terrorists killed in previous attacks. The students were also army sergeants. 2493

November 21, 1975—Angola—Members of the MPLA kidnapped Don Webster of CBS and Bill Mutschmann, a freelance photographer, and accused them of being CIA agents. Upon their release on December 11, 1975, they complained of poor treatment, inedible food, unsanitary conditions, and much harassment by their captors. They reported that at least one prisoner was horribly beaten every night but that the two of them were not beaten. 2494

November 22, 1975—Northern Ireland—British and Irish troops searched both sides of the border near South Armagh for men who killed three British soldiers in an attack on an observation post.

November 23, 1975—Australia—The British governor-general, who had recently fired Australian Prime Minister Whitlam, received his third letter bomb.

November 23, 1975—Israel—A time bomb killed one person in Jerusalem. 2495

November 24, 1975—Lebanon—A British businessman was fatally shot by Arab gunmen in Beirut who apparently mistook him for an American. 2496

November 24, 1975—United States—A man chartered a California Air Charter twin-engine Piper Navajo to fly musical instruments from Palomar, California, to Dallas, Texas. The individual pulled a gun on the pilot while the plane was over Phoenix, Arizona, and ordered him to fly to Mexico. The pilot landed the plane on a deserted beach near Mazatlán, where the plane became mired in mud. The hijacker was met by fifteen accomplices, who unloaded the cargo, which turned out to be guns. The hijacker then set fire to the plane and fled with his accomplices. The pilot returned to the United States unharmed. The hijacker was identified as Gary C. Bruton, a white male for whom the FAA profile was inapplicable, who was born on May 31, 1947, in Claremont, California. 5481

November 26, 1975—Bangladesh—Six men attacked Indian High Commissioner (the British Commonwealth equivalent of ambassador) Samar Sen, sixty-one, as he arrived for work, shooting him in the right shoulder. Police and guards killed four of the attackers and wounded the other two, whom Bangladesh said would receive "exemplary punishment." A government spokesman in Dacca said the assailants belonged to the defunct National Socialist party (Jatyo Sanajtrantrik Dal, JSD) and were followers of former Prime Minister Sheik Mujibur Rahman. Other reports claimed that the attack was not an assassination attempt but was planned as a kidnapping to secure the release of party leaders being held in Dacca's central jail. 2497

November 27, 1975—United States—A mechanic discovered a ticking bomb behind a wall panel behind the lavatory on a Bahamasair BAC111 at Miami international airport before forty-one passengers boarded. Police disarmed the device, which investigators said would have killed everyone on board had it gone off in flight. An anonymous telephone caller claimed credit for Cuban Power 76, saying that the group was protesting Bahamas' policy toward Cuba. Another bomb was found in front of the dormitory room of a Cuban exile student at the University of Miami. No injuries were reported to those on board the Nassau-bound flight or in the university. 2498-2499

November 27, 1975—United Kingdom—Ross McWhirter, coeditor with his identical twin brother Norris D. McWhirter of the *Guinness Book of World Records*, was killed by gunmen who fired on him at night on the doorstep of his northern London home. He had offered a $100,000 reward for the arrest of those conducting the recent bombing campaign in London. Two days later, an individual using the IRA code word claimed credit for that group. On February 10, 1977, four IRA gunmen were sentenced to forty-seven life terms and additional prison terms totaling 616 years for killing McWhirter, Professor Gordon Hamilton-Fairley, police bomb disposal expert Captain Roger Goad, and three others. The group was identified as Martin O'Connell, Edward Butler, Harry Duggan, and Hugh Doherty and were convicted of twenty-five counts of murder. The judge, Sir Joseph Cantley, recommended that they not be considered for parole for at least thirty years. 2500

November 28, 1975—Mexico—An anti-Castro exile organization was believed responsible for planting a bomb that destroyed the front end of the Cuban ambassador's car in Mexico City when the chauffeur started it. The chauffeur was not injured, and the ambassador, Fernando Lopez Muino, was not in the car. 2501

November 29, 1975—Mexico—Cuban Anti-Castro Cuban exiles were believed responsible for planting a bomb that caused property damage to the entrance of an office in the Soviet embassy in Mexico City. No injuries were reported. 2502

November 29, 1975—Ireland—Two bombs exploded at Shannon International Airport, killing one airport employee and wounding seven others. Speculation concerned whether the bombs were planted by the IRA or by a Protestant group striking back at the IRA. 2503

November 30, 1975—Pakistan—A bomb exploded in the baggage storage area in the domestic terminal of Karachi international airport. The resulting fire destroyed eight rooms and baggage and injured two people. Several flights were delayed for hours.

December 1975—Ethiopia—An Italian and several Taiwanese were kidnapped by Eritrean separatists. 2504

December 2, 1975—United States—The Palisades licensed nuclear facility of the Consumers Power Company received a bomb threat.

December 2, 1975—Netherlands—Seven members of the Free South Moluccan Youth Organisation, led by Freddy Aponno, seized a train in Beilen, killing the engineer and a passenger later in the takeover. The group, armed with automatic pistols and a hunting rifle, released their demands, written in Dutch, through two women and a child who were hostages. Immediately after, the bodies of the thirty-year-old train engineer and the passenger were removed from the train. The group demanded that the Dutch government recognize the nonexistent Republic of South Molucca, that it release twenty-five terrorists held in Dutch jails (see incident 2327), that it initiate U.N. mediation on Moluccan independence and a three-way meeting between Dutch, Indonesian, and Moluccan representatives, and that it provide a bus to take them to a plane that would fly to an undisclosed destination. They also demanded food for the hostages and themselves, which was granted, and another engineer for the train, which was refused. An approaching train was shot at by the gunmen. Approximately seventy hostages were initially seized, although five passengers escaped the first day and thirteen more during the evening. A Moluccan who attempted to mediate with the group was shot at by the terrorists. When the Dutch government refused to meet the group's demands, another passenger was killed on December 4, the same day that a second group of terrorists seized the Indonesian consulate (see below). When an accidental explosion occurred on December 5, one passenger and one of the terrorists were rushed to a local Red Cross facility. A doctor who was held hostage on the train reported that he was able to treat two other hostages who were not as seriously injured. A team of four local South Moluccan leaders, led by Johan Alvares Manusama, president of the self-styled Republic of the Moluccas, negotiated with the hijackers and obtained the release of two eighty-year-old hostages on December 7. The terrorists demanded a Dutch statement on television admitting injustices to the Moluccans, as well as television time for the Moluccans. These demands were also refused, although the police provided food, water, blankets, medicine, and other articles. The police pointed out that the hundreds of troops surrounding the train would be ordered to attack if any more of the hostages were killed by the terrorists. On December 11, two more hostages were released, and the next day a sixteen-year-old girl was released and rushed to a nearby hospital. The terrorists finally gave up fighting the freezing temperatures and the determination of the authorities and surrendered on December 14. The hostages claimed that they had been well treated. The Dutch government later met with other members of the Moluccan community to discuss their problems. On March 26, 1976, the seven terrorists were sentenced to fourteen years in prison. Their release was demanded in attacks on a train and a school by South Moluccans in 1977 (see incidents 3099 and 3100). 2505

December 4, 1975—United States—The New Black Revolutionary Front, the Cuban Youth Group, the JIN, an anti-Castro group, and El Condor claimed credit for seven bombings of government buildings, including the Miami police department and Metropolitan Justice Building, and a bank, causing minor damage and one injury. A note in Spanish demanded that $50 million be given to the poor. 2506-2512

December 4, 1975—Netherlands—A group of seven South Moluccans seized the Indonesian consulate in Amsterdam, holding twenty-one children attending school in the building, as well as fifteen other hostages, including three Dutchmen. During the takeover four employees escaped down a rope. Three of them were injured in the fall, and the fourth was wounded by gunfire and died from his injuries on December 9. Five of the children were immediately released. The group made the same political demands as those made by the group holding the train in Beilen (see incident 2505), but the Dutch government again refused to give in to their demands, saying that the Moluccan issue was beyond their power now that Indonesia was an independent nation. On December 8, the group released the last four children, two boys and two girls. The next day, two ill hostages were released. The Reverend Semeul Metiary, a fifty-eight-year-old Moluccan pastor, was requested by the group as an intermediary. The group also demanded that an Indonesian official participate in the discussions, but Surjadi Kromomihardje, the political counselor, said he would act only in his private capacity and not as an official emissary because that would be an indirect recognition of the group. It was reported that over six thousand telephone and letter threats against South Moluccans were received in the Netherlands during the two incidents. The group, armed with a carbine, pistol, and knives, had seized the consulate at midday. On December 19, they fired eight shots, claiming to be checking their weapons. They then released the last of their hostages shortly after 1 P.M. and joined Metiery and Johan Alvares Manusama, a local Moluccan leader, in leaving the building. None of the hostages had been hurt during the negotiations, although on the second day of the siege two blindfolded hostages, including one of the children, were pushed onto a balcony at gunpoint and were threatened by the terrorists. The

Dutch had not given in to the demands, although they did agree to discuss joint problems with Moluccan community representatives. On April 8, 1976, Dutch judges sentenced the seven to six years in jail. Their release was demanded in attacks on a school and a train by South Moluccans in 1977 (see incidents 3099 and 3100). 2513

December 6, 1975—Argentina—Argentine rightists dragged five Bolivian students from their Córdoba hostel, shooting them to death along with four Argentine students in apparent retaliation for the murder of former federal police chief General Jorge Steban Caceres Monie and his wife. 2514

December 6, 1975—Lebanon—Robert Mardiroussian, forty-five, a second secretary at the Soviet embassy, was paralyzed from the waist down after being hit by five bullets when gunmen challenged his car in Beirut. A second Soviet diplomat was released from the American University hospital after being treated for a minor gunshot wound. 2515

December 6, 1975—United Kingdom—Four IRA gunmen fired two shots at Scott's Restaurant (which had recently been bombed by the IRA) in London and then fled in a car. They were pursued by policemen and seized a Dorset Square apartment on Balcombe Street, taking hostage a British postal inspector, John Matthews, fifty-four, and his wife, Sheila, fifty-three, that evening. The four demanded a plane to fly them to Dublin, Ireland. Among them was Michael Wilson, who was wanted in connection with the murder of A. Ross McWhirter, coeditor of the *Guinness Book of World Records* (see incident 2500). The police refused to allow the group to leave but offered them food, a telephone hookup, and a chemical toilet. Negotiations were tense at times; the terrorists threw out the telephone and refused other items. Mrs. Matthews was released on December 12, and her husband was freed 2 hours later when the group ended the 130-hour siege. 2516

December 8, 1975—Lebanon—Two French journalists were wounded by Phalange mortar rounds fired behind the Beirut post office building. They were identified as Noel Alexandre, a cameraman for the British Visnews television company, and Bernard Estrade of Agence France-Presse. 2517

December 8, 1975—United States—The Nuclear One licensed nuclear facility of the Arkansas Power and Light Company received a bomb threat.

December 8, 1975—Argentina—The Mexican consulate in Buenos Aires was bombed. Property damage but no injuries were reported. A caller to the Associated Press said this was "repudiation against that traitor Luis Echeverria who embraced Fidel Castro." On April 2, 1977, CORU leader

Orlando Bosch said in his Venezuelan jail cell, "Is it that you have forgotten ...the blasting of the Mexican Embassy ...when the traitor Echeverria announced his visit to Havana?" 2518

December 10, 1975—France—Pamphlets at the scene credited the rightist Portuguese Liberation Army with the bombing of the main entrance of the Portuguese embassy in Paris. Extensive damage but no injuries were reported. 2519

December 11, 1975—United States—The Barnwell licensed nuclear facility of Allied-General Nuclear Services received a bomb threat.

December 12, 1975—United States—Two bombs exploded in Miami, one outside the offices of Almacen el Espanol in the Little Havana section and the other outside a beauty shop next to Almacen offices in Hialeah. The firm ships medicines to Cuba for relatives of Cuban exiles. The midnight bombs caused considerable damage but no injuries. 2520-2521

December 12, 1975—United States—The JDL announced a campaign of following and harassing diplomats from at least sixty of the seventy-two nations that voted in favor of a U.N. resolution that equated Zionism with racism.

December 15, 1975—United States—A pipe bomb exploded outside the U.N. building in New York City, causing minor property damage and no injuries. 2522

December 16, 1975—Colombia—A bomb consisting of two sticks of dynamite with a timing mechanism exploded at 11:25 P.M. in the Chapinero store of a U.S. firm, causing $2,000 damage. 2523

December 17, 1975—Lebanon—Farouk Mokkamdam, a Moslem leftist leader, seized a six hundred-ton Panama-registered ship belonging to Christian owners of a chemical fertilizer plant in Tripoli, a northern port. Mokkamdam threatened to blow up the ship unless the two businessmen agreed to pay workers four months' back wages, honor minimum wage regulations, and distribute one thousand tons of wheat to the needy. Kassem Imad, the governor of northern Lebanon, mediated in the negotiations. He was gunned down in Tripoli on December 20 by three masked gunmen as he and his wife left their home.

December 18, 1975—Lebanon—The Secret Armenian Army fired rockets during the evening at the Turkish embassy in Beirut. 2524

December 19, 1975—United States—A helicopter at Angels Camp, California, was damaged by six to eight blasting caps that had been placed between the landing gear and the fuel tank of the aircraft. The detonation produced a hole measuring two to three inches in the fuel tank. The ensuing fire caused $10,000 damage.

December 20, 1975—Ethiopia—Joan Emmerson, thirty-nine, a British nurse, and two Ethiopians were wounded in an ambush by thirty to fifty rebels wearing uniforms and armed with automatic weapons and rocket launchers. The attack took place near Goro, several hundred miles west of the Ogaden. The Galla nationalist movement was believed responsible, although others suspected Somali irregulars. 2525

December 21, 1975—United Kingdom—The Young Militants splinter of the IRA, as well as Protestant militants from Northern Ireland, claimed credit for a bomb that injured five people in Biddy Mulligan's public house in Kilburn, an Irish section of London. 2526

December 21, 1975—Austria—Six members of the Arm of the Arab Revolution, believed to be a cover term for the PFLP, attacked a ministerial meeting of the Organization of Petroleum Exporting Countries in Vienna, seizing seventy hostages, including eleven oil ministers. In the attack and subsequent shootout with police, three people were killed and eight injured, including one of the terrorists. The group was led by the famed Venezuelan terrorist, Illich Ramirez Sanchez (known as Carlos). According to various popular accounts, although the PFLP-Habash wing denied any connection to the attack, planning was initially engaged in by Carlos and Wadi Haddad of the PFLP. Participants included Hans-Joachim Klein, a Second of June Movement member (a friend of Hanna Elisa Krabbe, who had been involved in incident 2282, the takeover of the West German facility in Sweden), and a female, who had been identified as Gabriele Krocher-Tiedemann, who had been released in the Lorenz kidnapping (see incident 2246). Other sources claim that the woman was Klein's last known girl friend, Mechthild Rogali. The group was armed with Beretta model 12 machine pistols, Chinese grenades, plastic explosives, fuse wires, batteries, and detonators and also carried vitamin C tablets and amphetamines, to aid them in a siege operation. The identity of the three other members of the attack force is less clear, with most accounts making them out to be Palestinians. The warrant of arrest handed down by the Vienna criminal court on December 23 lists the participants as: "1. Salem, aged about 30, about 180cm tall, slender but sturdy figure, round face, bold shaped roman nose. 2. Khalid, aged about 30, about 175cm tall, slender figure, curly black hair combed back to the neck, moustache. 3. Joseph, aged about 30, about 175 cm tall, slender figure, curly black hair combed back to the neck, moustache. 4. A woman, aged about 25, delicate, small figure. 5. A man at least 180 cm tall, who was wounded during the incident in question. 6. Another man who, already detained in connection with the facts of the case in question and in custody in Algiers, has committed the undermentioned crimes in conjunction with the 5 persons listed above (in that armed with submachine guns and pistols they killed 3 men, broke into OPEC, etc.).''

In the initial attack, the group members ran up the stairs toward the meeting hall where the OPEC conference was in session. The only security measures were two guards looking forward to retirement, Inspectors Janda and Tichler. Anton Tichler, an Austrian, was killed in the gunfire, and Josef Janda was taken hostage by the group. He managed to get to a phone and relayed a message to his headquarters that OPEC was under attack. The second individual killed was Ali Hassan Khafali, a security officer with the Iraqi delegation, who attempted to surprise Carlos and seize his carbine. He was killed by the woman. The third killed was Yousef Ismirli, a Libyan economist, who wrestled with Carlos for control of his weapon and was shot dead by the terrorist. One of the rounds passed through Ismirli and wounded a member of the Kuwaiti delegation in the right arm. By this time the Austrian security police had sent in reinforcements, and in a gun duel with Inspector Kurt Leopolder, Klein was shot in the stomach. He was taken out of the building on a stretcher but later returned after demands made by the other terrorists. One of the RGD-5 grenades exploded during the attack, killing no one.

The terrorists rounded up their hostages and barricaded themselves in the conference room, where they discovered that they held eleven ministers: Delaid Abdesselam of Algeria, Jaime Duenas-Villavicencio of Ecuador, Edouard Alexis M'Bouy-Boutzit of Gabon, Lieutentant General Dr. Ibnu Sutowo of Indonesia, Dr. Jamshid Amouzegar of Iran, Tayeh Abdul-Karim of Iraq, Abdul Mutalib Al-Kazemi of Kuwait, Ezzedin Ali Mabruk of Libya, Dr. M. T. Akobo of Nigeria, Ahmed Zaki Yamani of Saudi Arabia, and Dr. Valentin Hernandez-Acosta of Venezuela. Some reports claim that the original plans were for the assassinations of Yamani and Amouzegar, two of the most important participants in the OPEC meeting, representing countries in disagreement with the Rejection Front of the Palestinian movement. During the beginning of the thirty-six-hour siege, the hostages were separated into four groups. The Libyans, Algerians, Iraqis, Kuwaitis, and Palestinian OPEC employees were considered friends. Neutrals included citizens of Gabon, Nigeria, Indonesia, Venezuela, and Ecuador. Austrians were placed by themselves, and the rest were considered to be enemies. The terrorists selected Griselda Carey, the British secretary of Chief Feyide, the Nigerian OPEC secretary-general, to carry their demands to the Austrians. The group's demands included the return of Klein, the publication of a political manifesto over Austrian radio and television, a bus to take them to the airport, where a DC9 with three crewmen was to be waiting, rope, scissors, and adhesive tape. The manifesto, translated from the French, read: "Reaffirmation of the 3 fundamentals of the 1976 Khartoum Arab summit: no treaty with, no negotiation with, and no recognition of the state of Zionist aggression. Denunciation of all compromise and all political plans aimed at destroying this anti-capitulation plan and aimed at giving tacit or explicit legality to aggression from any part of the Arab Palestinian land. In the light of this, condemnation of the treacherous agreements over the Sinai and the reopening of the Suez Canal to Zionist trading, with a claim that they be dropped, to allow the heroic Egyptian Arab Army to pursue its victories of the October war by leading a war of total liberation with the armies of the north-east front. Condemnation of attempts to lead Arab states and the Palestine resistance to the negotiating table, and condemnation of treaties and recognition in Geneva, or any other place, of other capitulation formulas. Formation of the north-east front with Syria, Iraq and the Palestine resistance on the basis of refusal to compromise, and reinforcement of the war of total liberation. The reawakening of the process of Arab unification, whose realization is a fundamental condition for national salvation, by moves towards unification among Arab states who partner each other geographically and politically. The declaration of the principle of full sovereignty over 'our' petroleum and financial wealth through nationalization of petroleum monopolies and the adoption of a national petroleum and financial policy which will enable the Arab people to use its resources for its development, its progress, the safeguard of its national interests and the strengthening of its sovereignty alongside the friendly people of the Third World so they can emerge from their economic stagnation, on condition that priority be given to financing the confrontation countries and the Palestinian resistance. Declaration of clear position over the dramatic conflict taking place in Lebanon by condemning and opposing the denominational isolationist plot which is only one among many faces of the great Zionist reactionary-American plot, and the effective equipment and moral support for the Lebanese national Arab forces and the Palestinian resistance who are defending Lebanon and its national Arab adherence." The Kreisky government agreed to broadcast the manifesto.

During the negotiations, the Iraqi chargé d'affaires, Riyadh Al-Azzawi, served as mediator. Carlos's first choice, the Libyan ambassador, was in Budapest at the time of the attack. The Iraqi was able to obtain the release of several hostages, including an Austrian secretary who had become hysterical, the Kuwaiti who had been injured, and an English interpreter employed by the Algerian oil minister. Later seven female hostages were allowed to leave to do their Christmas shopping.

A possible rescue attempt failed when the car of two armed Israelis crashed outside the building.

Despite surrounding the building with troops, the Austrian government soon gave in to the terrorists' demands for a flight out of the country. They also granted the demand that a doctor travel with Klein and recruited Dr. Wiriya Rawenduzy, a Kurd who had obtained Austrian citizenship. Forty-two of the hostages, none of them Austrians, were herded onto the DC9, which was piloted by Captain Manfred Pollack and Otto Herold. The plane flew first to Algiers Dar El Beida Airport, where Klein was taken to a hospital in a Red Crescent ambulance (later reports claimed that he was transferred to a Libyan hospital, and had been paid £100,000 by Libya's Colonel Muammar Qaddafi for his participation in the operation). The neutrals were also allowed off the plane. Kreisky stated that Carlos had agreed to allow all of the hostages off in Algeria, but the terrorists instructed the pilot to fly on to Tripoli and Baghdad. The plane flew to Tripoli, where the terrorists instructed air traffic control to have Libyan Prime Minister Major Abdul Salam Ahmed Jalloud ready to meet them. Carlos requested a larger plane but was not given one. Hostages from Saudi Arabia, Iran, the UAE, Qatar, Algeria, and Libya were released.

Some details of the terrorists' demands are unconfirmed. Colin Smith learned that they demanded a large ransom from Saudi Arabia and Iran for the release of their oil ministers. On midnight, December 22, the king phoned the shah from Amman about the case. An hour later, a Zurich banker was phoned by the Iranian embassy in Geneva and told to transfer an undisclosed sum of money to an Aden bank. A PFLP man in London months later said the sum was $5 million. In Beirut, Fatah sympathizers said it was ten times that and that Haddad, Habash, and Carlos received much of it (the last perhaps recouped $2 million). Three months later, Chancellor Kreisky was reported to have confirmed the ransom tale.

After being refused landing rights in Tunis, the plane flew back to Algiers. Apparently after receiving a code word from Algerian Foreign Minister Bouteflika that Haddad had received the money, the terrorists surrendered and released the hostages. Reporters claimed that the terrorists did not appear to have been arrested, and an Austrian government extradition request was refused on the grounds that no treaty existed between the two countries. Christopher Dobson and Ronald Payne reported that Carlos moved to the Albert I Hotel, where he was joined by his girl friend from Paris, Maria-Teresa Lara. Other reports claimed Carlos flew on to Libya, having apologized to the government for the unintentional death of their national.

Gabriele Krocher-Tiedemann was captured after a shootout with Swiss police on December 20, 1977 (see incident 3321). 2527

December 22, 1975—Ethiopia—Ronald Michalke, a U.S. citizen employed by the Collins International Service Company at the Kagnew communications base in Asmara, was kidnapped from his home, along with an Ethiopian servant, by five armed members of the ELF. On December 30, Osman Saleh

Sabbe, ELF secretary-general, said, "We still are negotiating with our military colleagues to insure the release of all the captives without any conditions." He claimed that he had persuaded the military group to drop a demand for a $5 million ransom for their hostages, which at the time included five Americans. Michalke was released on June 2, 1976. 2528

December 23, 1975—United States—The licensed nuclear facility of the Duke Power Company at Oconee received a bomb threat, as did the Shoreham licensed nuclear facility of the Long Island Lighting Company.

December 23, 1975—Colombia—A SAM Beechcraft D80 flying eight persons from Barrancabermeja to Medellín was hijacked by R. Rodelo, a man who entered the cockpit after takeoff. Upon landing, he demanded $65,000 and safe conduct to an unspecified country. Local authorities entered the plane, shot him twice in the head, and took him into custody. Rodelo died later in a hospital. 5482

December 23, 1975—Greece—Richard S. Welch, forty-six, the Athens station chief of the CIA, was killed in Palaion Psyhiko by three gunmen as he and his wife returned home after a Christmas party at the home of U.S. ambassador Jack B. Kubisch. His wife was not injured. The Union of Officers Struggling for the National Idea claimed credit for shooting him as he got out of his car. Welch's name, along with that of other U.S. embassy employees, had been published on November 25, 1975, in the *Athens Daily News*, which claimed that his position of special assistant to the ambassador and first secretary at the embassy was a cover for his CIA position. On December 28, 1975, an advertisement was placed in Athens by the Organization of November 17, claiming responsibility. The Army Officers Representing the Free Greek Spirit (which may be another translation of the name of the former group) also claimed credit. Welch's home on Vassilias Frederikas had been used by six other CIA station chiefs. On December 15, 1976, Evanghelos Mallios, forty-three, whom reports claim was one of the most brutal torturers in the former Greek regime, was assassinated outside his home. Ballistics tests found that the .45 caliber gun was the same one used to kill Welch. The identity of the killers of Mallios and Welch has yet to be discovered. The Fiat the killers drove away in has not been found. Most police theories credit the attack to either extreme left- or right-wing individuals attempting to drive a wedge between the United States and Greece. Other sources suggest Turkish responsibility, while still others suggest that Rejectionist Front Palestinians opposed to improved U.S.-PLO relations may have been involved. 2529

December 24, 1975—West Germany—The Yugoslav Aero Transport office in Stuttgart was bombed, with property damage but no injuries. 2530

December 25, 1975—Lebanon—A bodyguard of Soviet Ambassador Alexander Soldatov was slightly wounded by a stray bullet while escorting Soldatov on a drive through an eastern suburb of Beirut. 2531

December 29, 1975—United States—A bomb exploded in a baggage locker at 6:30 P.M., in a Delta, Eastern, and TWA claims area of New York City's La Guardia Airport, killing eleven and injuring seventy-five. Damage was estimated at $750,000. A caller said a commando attack squad of the PLO had carried the armed struggle into the United States and threatened more attacks. Another caller warned that two more bombs had been planted, but this turned out to be a hoax. A Puerto Rican group claimed responsibility for the blast. The next day, the PLO denounced the blast, which police said was equal to twenty to twenty-five sticks of dynamite. Numerous bomb threats were received at other airports around the country, and they continued into 1976. Later telephone calls credited the attack to the Symbionese Liberation Army, as well as the underworld. A twelfth person later died of a heart attack. The nation's airlines offered a $50,000 reward for information regarding the bombing, which has so far gone unsolved. 2532

December 29, 1975—United States—A bomb exploded in the home of Sava Temer, assistant to the Yugoslavian consul general in Chicago. No injuries were reported, but there was some property damage to the Morton Grove residence. 2533

December 29, 1975—United States—Four members of the JDL were arrested after spray-painting a Star of David and ''Viva Israel'' inside the Mexican consulate in Philadelphia.

December 31, 1975—United States—The Oyster Creek licensed nuclear installation of the Jersey Central Power and Light Company received a bomb threat.

1976—Argentina—Washington Perez Rosini, thirty-five, a Uruguayan unionist, claimed he was kidnapped by Uruguayan men who wanted him to aid in negotiations involving a group of ten Uruguayan members of the outlawed Worker Student Resistance who had been kidnapped. A ransom of $2 million had been demanded for their release. Rosini fled to Sweden after becoming convinced that the organization would not be able to raise the money. Fifty other Uruguayans had been reported missing in Argentina during a six-month period. 2534

1976—Venezuela—Caracas dailies reported that the Cuban embassy had received several unexploded letter bombs. The Aerotur tourist firm, which conducts tours to Cuba, also received a package containing unexploded bombs. 2535

1976—United States—Los Angeles County undersheriff Sherman Block reported that a terrorist group warned that they had planted a nuclear device in an industrial complex and demanded an undisclosed amount of money. A task force determined that the threat was a hoax, although Block refused to identify the target or the group's name. Block said, ''Federal people with monitoring equipment finally determined the threat was not real, but the threat provided an opportunity for us to test our plans and procedures during what appeared to be a real emergency.''

January 1976—Algeria—The Polisario Front kidnapped two French teachers, whom it accused of cooperating with the Moroccan army. The hostages were identified as Pierre Secguro, thirty-five, and Jean-Paul Dieff, twenty-four, who were released in Tindouf, Algeria, on October 28, 1976. 2536

January 1976—Lebanon—Radical Palestinian guerrillas robbed the British Bank of the Middle East. Some sources claimed that $50 million was taken. A minimum of $20 million was stolen. According to Gabriel Badaro, vice-president of Beirut's Chamber of Commerce, ''only the owners know what was in the [safe deposit] boxes. It could be $50 million or it could be $100 million or more.'' 2537

January 1, 1976—West Germany—Three homemade bombs were discovered in the Chilean consulate in Frankfurt and defused. A safe and cupboard in the consul-general's office had been burglarized. 3158

January 1, 1976—Lebanon—A sudden explosion aboard a Middle East Airlines 720 flying from Beirut to Dubai and Oman caused the plane to crash into the Saudi Arabian desert, killing all eighty-two on board. The explosion took place in the forward baggage compartment as the plane was flying above Saudi and Kuwait. 2538

January 1, 1976—United States—The Native Underground Red Cloud Group phoned a bomb threat to the Bureau of Indian Affairs building in Parker, Arizona. Six sticks of dynamite were discovered, leading to three arrests.

January 1, 1976—Spanish Sahara—Five French tourists were mistakenly killed in a Polisario Front ambush when their bus hit a land-mine. The group had set out in a minibus from Tafaya, Morocco. The son and daughter of the political counselor of the French embassy in Rabat, Jean Guyot, were driving to the provincial capital of El Aaiun. 2539

January 2, 1976—Israel—A fire believed set by arsonists caused millions of dollars worth of damage to a three-story building housing *Haaretz*, Tel Aviv's leading newspaper. 2540

January 3, 1976—Algeria—A bomb exploded in the Algiers office of the country's official newspaper. The Algerian press claimed that French intelligence was responsible, although others credited the attack to a domestic opposition group. In March, seven people, including three non-Algerians, were tried and found guilty of planting explosives. 2541

January 3, 1976—West Germany—A time bomb exploded in front of the garage of the Yugoslavian consulate general in Stuttgart, causing minor property damage but no injuries. The offices were empty at the time. 2542

January 5, 1976—Philippines—A JAL DC8 flying from Bangkok to Tokyo with 199 passengers and 23 crew members was hijacked in Manila by two Filipinos armed with handguns and explosives, who threatened to kill a stewardess if they were not given a free ride to Tokyo. The hijackers, Prudencio Dono and Renato Dono, have been identified as brothers, although some reports claim they were father and son. They released the passengers early in the twelve-hour negotiations, in which they also demanded a pardon, a ban on publishing their photos, and an improvement in living conditions. The Japanese government refused to allow them to land, and they surrendered to authorities shortly afterward. 5483

January 7, 1976—United Kingdom—British Airways flight 661, a B747 flying 212 passengers and 18 crew members from London to Miami, was diverted to Ireland's Shannon Airport when it received a bomb threat. It was on the ground for eight hours before flying on. 2543

January 8, 1976—Jamaica—One man was killed and a second injured when two gunmen opened fire outside the U.S. consulate in Kingston, the scene of an earlier demonstration in which hundreds of individuals, many of them throwing stones, protested the South African presence at an International Monetary Fund meeting. 2544

January 9, 1976—Israel—A time bomb exploded in a crowded Jerusalem supermarket, injuring eight pre-Sabbath shoppers. Police rounded up 130 Arab suspects for questioning. PFLP claimed credit. 2545

January 9, 1976—France—The Front de l'Auto-Defense Juive (Jewish Self-Defense Front) claimed credit for throwing firebombs at two UNESCO headquarters buildings in Paris during the night. The United States and other nations had cut off or cut back their contributions to the UNESCO budget since 1974, when Israel was excluded in an Arab-led move from any regional grouping of the organization. 2546-2547

January 10, 1976—United States—The New World Liberation Front sent bombs in candy boxes to the homes of two members of the San Francisco board of supervisors.

January 10, 1976—Lebanon—The U.S. embassy in Beirut came under heavy sniper fire, although no one was injured. At the American University of Beirut, two groups of armed men entered the campus and hospital, fired guns to scare off guards, and stole two station wagons. 2548

January 12, 1976—France—The Jewish Self Defense Front threw a gasoline bomb at an Arabic bookstore on the Rue Saint Victor in Paris, causing $30,000 damage. The victim was a Palestinian militant, Mahmoud Saleh, who had served as a temporary PLO representative in Paris. Other sources claimed that he was a member of the Rejection Front and had represented the PLO since 1972, when Mahmoud el Amchari was assassinated. Saleh himself was assassinated in Paris on January 3, 1977. 2549

January 12, 1976—United States—The terminal area of La Guardia Airport was evacuated after a telephoned threat. No bomb was found.

January 12, 1976—United States—Three pipe bombs were discovered by a New York City electrician inspecting a subway maintenance entrance near the U.N. Library. The devices were set to explode at 3 P.M. when the Security Council was scheduled to debate the Palestinian question. The bombs were disarmed half an hour before the debate began. The Jewish Armed Resistance Strike Movement and the Young Croatian Republican Army claimed credit. 2550

January 12, 1976—United States—Two time-delay bombs were discovered in a basement exit in front of the Iraqi U.N. mission after the Jewish Underground Army telephoned a warning. On August 19, 1976, four members of the JDL were indicted by a New York court on eleven charges, including attempting the bombing of the Iraqis. The individuals were identified as Russell Kelner, thirty-five, of New York City; Thomas MacIntosh, thirty-six, formerly of Woodbury, New Jersey; Jeffrey Weingarten, twenty-one, of New York City; and Steven Ehrlich, twenty-one, of San Francisco. Named as unindicted co-conspirators were Sheryl MacIntosh, wife of Thomas MacIntosh, and a John Doe. 2551

January 12, 1976—West Germany—A bomb was thrown onto the terrace of the Yugoslav consulate in Dortmund, causing minor damage. 2552

January 13, 1976—Israel—Israeli troops killed four members of the Palestinian Rejection Front armed with submachine guns and axes. Statements from the guerrilla coalition in Damascus and Beirut said that the group had intended to seize hostages to obtain the release of thirty prisoners, including Archbishop Hilarion Capucci, who was serving a twelve-year sentence for smuggling weapons. 2553

January 14, 1976—United States—A bomb planted by the Red Guerrilla Family exploded in the men's restroom adjacent to the Iranian consulate in San Francisco. Two persons were slightly injured by flying glass, and damage was estimated at $200,000. A warning had been phoned to news agencies before the evening explosion. The group said it was "in support of the Iranian people's struggle to rid themselves of the CIA-backed shah" and proclaimed solidarity with revolutionaries in Angola, Greece, Puerto Rico, Iran, and the United States. 2554

January 14, 1976—Colombia—Fred Archibald, a Colombia employee of Intercol, an Esso subsidiary, was kidnapped by communist guerrillas who released him on January 17 after his company paid a ransom. The press speculated that the group was the Colombian Revolutionary Armed Forces (FARC). 2555

January 15, 1976—Ethiopia—Plastic explosives were placed under two power units at the U.S. Navy's Kagnew communications station in Asmara. The explosion caused minor damages and no injuries. 2556

January 15, 1976—Argentina—The British Cultural Institute in Córdoba was bombed, causing property damage but no injuries. Reports credited the attack to nationalists protesting Britain's refusal to recognize Argentine sovereignty over the Falkland Islands. 2557

January 16, 1976—United States—A pipe bomb was thrown from a passing car in New York City, exploding outside the Polish consulate general. A caller claimed credit for the New Jewish Armed Resistance, using the JDL slogan, "Never Again." The caller warned that India would also be attacked for voting in favor of a UN resolution that equated Zionism with racism. 2558-2559

January 16, 1976—Switzerland—Swiss authorities dispatched security agents to Saint Moritz, a famed winter resort, following reports that the

Venezuelan terrorist Carlos might arrive at the same time as the shah of Iran, who was expected in four days.

January 16, 1976—Portugal—A Soviet freighter in the northern port of Oporto was bombed, causing no injuries or serious damage. 2560

January 17, 1976—United States—An anonymous call to the United Nations in New York City warning of a pipe bomb led to the discovery of a piece of pipe in bushes on U.N. grounds; however, the sealed pipe was empty. 2561

January 18, 1976—United States—The Emiliano Zapata Unit sent money orders to two San Francisco homes near the Berkeley branch of the Bank of America that had been bombed in December. Notes said, ''We apologize for the inconvenience this has caused, but we are certain you would willingly sacrifice a few windows to get these parasites out of our community.''

January 19, 1976—United States—The B&W Naval Fuel installation in Lynchburg, Virginia, received a bomb threat.

January 19, 1976—Mexico—A package containing TR-4 plastic explosive with a remote firing device was found at 2:50 P.M. in the parking lot of a U.S. firm. 2562

January 20, 1976—United States—Passengers on an Eastern Airlines B727 flying from New York left the plane in Charlotte, North Carolina on an emergency chute after a telephone threat was received shortly before the scheduled landing. No bomb was found, but three of the sixty-three persons on board were injured in deplaning.

January 21, 1976—Italy—Three Molotov cocktails were thrown at the Iranian embassy in Rome. 2563

January 22, 1976—United States—A four-month search for a weapons cache belonging to Neustra Familia, a prison-based gang, ended when police uncovered ten shotguns, rifles, one-hundred rounds of assorted shells, and bullets in the backyard of a San José, California, home.

January 22-23, 1976—United States—The licensed nuclear facility at the Massachusetts Institute of Technology received two bomb threats.

January 24, 1976—Kuwait—The U.S. embassy in Kuwait received a telephoned bomb threat. The premises were evacuated, but a police search found nothing. 2564

January 25, 1976—Kenya—Three Palestinian terrorists, apparently members of Wadi Haddad's splinter faction of the PFLP, were arrested by authorities at Nairobi's Embakasi International Airport before they could fire their SAM-7 heat-seeking missiles at an EL AL plane scheduled to stop over during its flight from Johannesburg, South Africa, to Tel Aviv. Some reports claimed that two of the three had been involved in an abortive operation with SAM-7s at Orly Airport in January 1975 (see incidents 2211 and 2213). The group had received visitors' visas issued by the British embassy in Beirut in December 1975. Some reports claim that the machine guns, grenades, pistols, and SAM-7s were provided by Idi Amin of neighboring Uganda. A few days later, West Germans connected with the Baader-Meinhof Gang were sent to find out what had happened to their colleagues but were also arrested, apparently as a result of a tip by Israeli intelligence to President Jomo Kenyatta's security service, the General Service Unit. They were identified by the Israelis on March 30, 1977, after they learned that the press was about to leak their identities, along with the fact that the five terrorists had been turned over to Israel by Kenya. The two were Brigitta Schultz, twenty-three, and Thomas Reuter, twenty-four. The woman had instructions written on her stomach in invisible ink ordering the terrorists to carry out their attack. The Israelis announced that they would try the group in secret. The release of the terrorists was demanded by a PFLP group that hijacked an Air France plane to Entebbe, Uganda, on June 27, 1976. 2565

January 26, 1976—Soviet Union—A Soviet Jew attempted to hijack an Aeroflot over Moscow but was overpowered in the air. A Swedish airport received a radio message from the hijacker and Tel Aviv's Ben Gurion Airport went on alert for ninety minutes, but nothing further was heard from the hijacker. The plane apparently landed in the Soviet Union. 5484

January 27, 1976—United States—An intrusion was reported at the Metropolitan Edison Company's licensed nuclear facility at Three Mile Island 1 and 2 in Goldsboro, Pennsylvania.

January 28, 1976—Turkey—A bomb placed under an unoccupied U.S. government-owned truck parked in front of a U.S. military transient building, Merhaba Palas, exploded in Ankara, damaging the building and truck and injuring the desk clerk. 2566

January 29, 1976—Argentina—Fifteen Montoneros, including two women, burst into the offices of the local Bendix subsidiary and shot and killed two Argentine executives. A small bomb destroyed the interior of the general manager's office. A policeman was killed when he tried to interfere with the terrorists, who painted a Montonero slogan on the outside wall of the offices. 2567

January 30, 1976—Colombia—A bomb éxploded at the Spanish embassy in Bogotá, destroying the front gate and fatally injuring the guard on duty. 2568

January 30, 1976—United States—The licenced nuclear facility at the Massachusetts Institute of Technology received a bomb threat.

January 31, 1976—France—The Iran Air office on the Avenue des Champs Elysees in Paris was attacked. 3154

January 31, 1976—Uganda—Authorities announced that a plane piloted by a PLO officer crashed into Lake Victoria. It was the third recent crash involving PLO pilot trainers in Uganda.

February 2, 1976—United Kingdom—A lone male demanded a multimillion dollar payment, threatening to blow up a Concorde. He was arrested as he picked up bags supposedly containing the money and was sent for a mental examination.

February 3, 1976—Thailand—A lone male used gas and butane to set fire to himself in a lavatory of a Pan Am plane flying seventy-five persons from Bangkok to New Delhi. The door was blown off, and he suffered burns. He was later sentenced to fifteen years in prison.

February 3, 1976—United States—The Westinghouse Nuclear Fuel Facility in Columbia, South Carolina, received a bomb threat.

February 3, 1976—Central African Republic—President Jean Bedel Bokassa escaped an assassination attempt at Bangui airport, in which two of his bodyguards were killed by grenades.

February 3, 1976—French Territory of the Afars and Issas—Four members of the Front for the Liberation of the Somali Coast hijacked a bus carrying thirty-one children of French military families to the Somali border post of Loyada. The Somalis later allowed the terrorists to be joined by two more of their colleagues and massed troops along the border. One African was also reported on the bus. The group demanded the immediate and unconditional independence of FTAI without the referendum planned by France, release of all political prisoners, and the departure of all French troops from Djibouti. The group threatened to slit the throats of their hostages. On February 4, French troops engaged in a shootout with the terrorists, killing five of them. One of the guerrillas opened fire on the children. killing one and wounding four, one of whom later died from his wounds. The bus driver and a social worker were also wounded. A sixth terrorist fired off a burst of shots before being killed by the troops. The attack touched off a firefight with Somali soldiers, resulting in the death of a Somali and the wounding of a French officer. The terrorists had taken one of the hostages, Frank Rutkovsky, seven, over the Somali border. He was released in Mogadishu to the French embassy on February 7. The French called upon the U.N. Security Council to consider the matter, pointing out that the Somalis allowed the group to establish their headquarters in the country's capital. Uganda's Idi Amin called for the Security Council to condemn the French for their attack on the Somalis. 2569

February 4, 1976—United States—The Susquehanna Units 1 & 2 licensed nuclear facility in Berwick, Pennsylvania, owned by the Pennsylvania Power and Light Company, received a bomb threat.

February 5, 1976—Italy—A police patrol was fired on by two gunmen carrying machine guns at the Egyptian embassy in Rome during the evening. 2570

February 6, 1976—France—Three bombs destroyed the offices of the Iranian Atomic Energy Organization in Paris's tallest building, the Montparnasse Tower. The International Solidarity sent a letter to a French newspaper in which it said it was protesting the recent execution of opposition elements in Iran. On February 2, Iran had executed two Marxist terrorists. 2571

February 7, 1976—West Germany—Yugoslavian Vice-Consul Edwin Zdovc was assassinated by two gunmen at 7:30 A.M. in the driveway outside his home in the Sachsenhausen quarter of Frankfurt. A caller told a New York radio station that the Young Croatian Army for Freedom was responsible. 2572

February 8, 1976—West Germany—A bomb consisting of one kilogram of commercial explosives caused extensive property damage but no injuries on the third story of a building housing the Office for Israeli Economic Affairs on West Berlin's Kurfuerstendamm at 7 P.M. A typewritten leaflet was signed by the Arm of the Arab Revolution, claiming that the office was an "official agency of the Israeli Finance Ministry."2573

February 9, 1976—United States—A man threw an unlighted Molotov cocktail through a glass door on the lower level of a terminal building at Chicago's O'Hare International Airport, shattering the glass but injuring no one. The man was arrested.

February 9-10, 1976—India—Poisonous snakes were sent through the mail to a university official and a government worker in New Delhi. A two-foot-long cobra tried to attack H.L. Batra, secretary to the vice-chancellor of Meerut University, but was captured and placed in a jug. A snake charmer said the cobra belonged to a deadly species. A worker at the central government's

Public Service Commission found a live, poisonous, small snake in a package he opened.

February 10, 1976—Malaysia—The U.S. embassy in Kuala Lumpur received a bomb threat, but no bomb was found. 2574

February 11, 1976—France—New Order firebombs damaged the Paris offices of Aeroflot and *Liberation*. 3155

February 12, 1976—United Kingdom—The IRA's Frank Stagg died in a British jail on the sixty-first day of his hunger strike. In the following four days, eleven people died and £1 million of damage was done in Belfast, with over one hundred acts of violence reported.

February 12, 1976—United Kingdom—A twenty-pound IRA bomb was defused by police during rush hour at London's busy Oxford Circus subway station. 2575

February 12, 1976—Ireland—Thirteen IRA incendiary bombs went off in Dublin stores. 2576-2588

February 12, 1976—Portugal—Bombs damaged a town hall in the north where a showing of Soviet photographs was being conducted. 2589

February 12, 1976—France—The Somali embassy in Paris was attacked, and its front door was smashed. 2590

February 12, 1976—Bahamas—The Soviet ship *Dzhordano Bruno*, anchored five miles from the U.K.-owned Anguilla Cays island of Cay Salbank, was fired on by a small boat. No one was injured. 2591

February 13, 1976—Venezuela—A bomb exploded in the Barquisimeto Shopping Center, across from a U.S. firm. No damage or injuries were reported. Reports claimed that the device was a noise bomb and that FALN pamphlets were attached to it. 2592

February 14, 1976—United Kingdom—A man aboard a National Airlines flight from London to Miami informed the captain that he wanted to go to Cuba and would blow up the plane if his demand was not met. The crew overpowered him, and the plane landed safely in Miami, where the man was taken into custody. No bomb was found. 5485

February 15, 1976—Colombia—The M-19 kidnaped José Raquel Mercado, sixty-one, the anticommunist president of the million-member Colombia

Workers Confederation. He was killed in Bogotá on April 19, marring the government's election victory.

February 16, 1976—Colombia—The director of the Renault plant in Envigado, a French citizen, and his bodyguard were wounded by machine-gun fire by National Liberation Army guerrillas. 2593

February 16, 1976—Lebanon—The first secretary of the Turkish embassy in Beirut was assassinated by an unknown assailant. 2594

February 16, 1976—Northern Ireland—IRA gunmen ambushed British troops on a mountain outside Belfast. No British were injured, but two of the attackers were believed hit.

February 17, 1976—Lebanon—A Palestinian student was arrested and charged with shooting two professors at the American University of Beirut. It is believed he was acting out of revenge, having been expelled in 1974 for radical activity.

February 17, 1976—Venezuela—At 4:25 A.M., three shots were fired at the U.S. embassy in Caracas from a passing automobile, causing no injuries and slight damage. On the morning of February 16, a Cuban news agency in Caracas reported an attack on the U.S. embassy closely paralleling the actual attack, leading investigators to suspect that the Cuban news agency source knew about the attack before it took place. 2595

February 18, 1976—United Kingdom—Assassination threats were made against Home Secretary Roy Jenkins, Northern Ireland Minister Merlyn Rees, and the labor government's chief whip, Bob Mellish, in the aftermath of the death in a British prison of IRA member Frank Stagg, a hunger striker. 2596-2598

February 18, 1976—Belgium—Rabbi Meir Kahane, the JDL leader, was dragged away from the World Conference on Soviet Jewry by Belgian police after he tried to enter the conference hall in Brussels. Kahane had been refused a request to join the U.S. delegation.

February 19, 1976—Venezuela—Two bombs were placed outside the El Marqué stores of a U.S. firm in the evening. Only one of them exploded, causing minor glass damage, as well as damage to the door frame. A third bomb was found inside the store. When disarmed by police, it was found to be without explosive material. All schools were closed because of student riots protesting the death of two students in San Felipe and one in the 23 de Enero District. 2599

February 20, 1976—Philippines—Moslem rebels ambushed a bus at New Calamba as it went up a hill, killing twenty-one persons and wounding several of the fifty people on board, eighty-seven miles north of Zamboanga.

February 20, 1976—France—Bombs exploded in the Algerian consulate general in Paris, the consulate in Strasbourg, and the Air Algérie office in Lyons. The airline office was heavily damaged by the blast, which caused no injuries but also damaged windows of nearby apartments and those of a French airline company, UTA. 2600-2602

February 21, 1976—United States—Police Special Weapons and Tactics (SWAT) teams and the FBI raided a home in Richmond, California, before dawn, arresting six members of the Emiliano Zapata Unit and confiscating 130 pounds of explosives. Among the items found was a plan for blowing up a larger city's water system.

February 22, 1976—France—The Unified Liberation Front of New Algeria bombed the Algerian government tourist office in central Paris in the early morning. Windows were smashed, and two passersby were treated for shock. There was also an attempted bombing of the Algerian consulate in Besançon. 2603-2604

February 23, 1976—Lebanon—Mohammed Haymour, a Lebanese gunman, and six armed relatives took over the Canadian embassy in Beirut, holding twenty-three hostages. They demanded that his four children be returned to Lebanon, that he be given $500,000 for his share of an island, which he claimed he had been bilked out of by his wife and a doctor, and that the government of Canada reverse a medical opinion that he was mentally unbalanced. The group initially allowed eight women to leave. They released their remaining hostages and surrendered after eight hours. No one was injured. 2605

February 26, 1976—United States—An intrusion was reported at the Pacific Gas and Electric Company's licensed nuclear facility in Diablo Canyon, California.

February 27, 1976—Greece—Homemade bombs damaged the Athens offices of American Express and Chase Manhattan. 2606-2607

February 27-March 4, 1976—Colombia—The night watchmen of a Barranquilla store of a U.S. firm reported continued harassment. At 9:50 P.M. on February 27, the inside night watchman received a call, saying, "Are you sleeping? Tonight we are going to attack the store to steal and to kill the night watchman.'' The call was repeated three times, not giving the watchman a chance to talk. It was believed the call was a recording. At 9:55 P.M. on February 29, the following call was repeated three times: ''It's going to be this night; we are going to steal inside the store, and who we are going to kill is the outside watchman.'' This time the voice was clearer, and no other noise was heard over the telephone. At 3:45 A.M. on March 4, the outside watchman noted a car without plates stationed outside the store with three people in it. One of them shouted through a window, ''You know we are going to burn you; open your eyes.'' The car kept on going but came back five minutes later and parked in the same place. This scene was repeated four times, perhaps with the perpetrators looking for the watchman, who had taken precautions and hid himself in the rear of the store. A special security service was hired from 7 P.M. to 7A.M. to aid the watchman. 2608

February 27, 1976—United States—Four rifle shots were fired at a Soviet residential complex in New York City at 2:45 A.M. An M-1 rifle was found in a schoolyard across the street. A woman claiming membership in the Jewish Armed Resistance phoned several news services, saying, ''Four .30 caliber bullets have been fired into the Soviet diplomatic residence located at Riverdale in the Bronx on behalf of Marina Tiemkin,'' a fifteen-year-old Soviet Jewish girl who wished to emigrate but who had been placed in a mental institution. The caller threatened to kidnap Soviet diplomats unless Tiemkin was allowed to emigrate to Israel. On August 19, 1976, an eleven-count indictment was handed down against Russell Kelner, thirty-five, of New York City; Thomas MacIntosh, thirty-six, formerly of Woodbury, New Jersey; Jeffrey Weingarten, twenty-one, of New York City; and Steven Ehrlich, twenty-one, of San Francisco. Named as unindicted co-conspirators were Sheryl MacIntosh, Thomas's wife, and a John Doe. All were JDL members. On December 16, four of the group were sentenced to prison terms of up to six years, while the fifth received a suspended sentence. 2609

February 27, 1976—Venezuela—William Niehous, forty-four, president of the Owens-Illinois glassmaking operations in Venezuela, was kidnapped from his home while watching television in the evening with his wife by seven armed uniformed men. The group tied up Mrs. Niehous and the couple's three teenage sons and injected a sedative into Mr. Niehous. The Group of Revolutionary Commandos-Operation Argimiro Gabaldon claimed credit for the attack. The Owens company agreed to pay a $116 bonus to each of its sixteen hundred employees in Venezuela and paid for the publication of a leftist political manifesto in the *New York Times*, *London Times*, and *Le Monde*. The Venezuelan government announced that it would expropriate Owens's holdings, which amounted to $25 million in its eighteen years of operations in Venezuela. On March 1, police found a car used to transport Niehous in

Maracay, a western city. Also in March, Henry Niehous, William's father, pleaded with terrorists to free his son. His letter to the kidnappers read, "I know I don't have long to live. I want to see my only son again." Niehous was not released, and his father died of leukemia at age seventy-seven in Toledo, Ohio, on October 20, 1976. The guerrillas added a $2 million ransom demand, which Owens said it was willing to contribute towards. Mrs. Niehous collected $500,000 from her family and friends and offered it as a reward for information leading to her husband's whereabouts. The group holding him said that he had been "arrested and imprisoned" and was to stand trial for "political and economic sabotage" because he was a representative of a multinational corporation. On August 12, 1976, a local newspaper reported that Marcos Gomez (also known as El Nego) was arrested in connection with the kidnapping, as well as his membership in the Revolutionary Organization. The government had announced on August 4 the arrest of two left-wing congressmen, Salom Mesa Espinoza and Fortunato Herrera, for questioning. A guerrilla communiqué issued on August 6 said that Jorge Antonio Rodriguez, whom the group claimed had died on July 25 from torture, had not been responsible for the kidnapping. It was alleged that the political police intercepted the delivery of a ransom to two of the group's mailboxes by friends of the Niehous family. The group ended a second communiqué by saying that "David Morales Bello [a high-ranking member of the ruling Democratic Action party], José Casals [development minister], Muchacho Bertoni [state governor], Carmèlo Lauria [state minister for basic production], and Pedro Tinoco [former finance minister] are all accomplices in the Niehous kidnapping." It was also reported that David Niehous, who had been arrested on July 20, was apparently involved in the kidnapping of Venezuelan Congress President Gonzalo Barrios in 1974. The negotiations with the kidnappers bogged down, and various reports claimed that the body of Niehous could be found in several locations. On March 4, 1977, a Venezuelan policeman was shot and killed while watching an apartment thought to be used by a suspect in the kidnapping. This followed a report that Niehous's wife had identified five of the guerrillas who had kidnapped her husband, including Carlos Rafael Rodriguez Lanz (also known as Commander Anibal), the leader of the PRV-FALN (Venezuelan Revolutionary Party—Armed Forces of National Liberation), which had claimed credit for the Gabaldon operation. It was later noted that Gabaldon was a guerrilla leader active in the west, who had been killed in 1967 when a colleague's weapon accidentally went off. On March 28, 1977, Orlando Bottini Marin was arrested in Mérida while carrying documents belonging to Niehous.

The group later demanded a $3.5 million ransom in addition to the bonus payment to each of the two thousand Owens employees.

Niehous was rescued after a June 20, 1979, gun battle between a police patrol and his guerrilla captors in a secluded ranch south of the Orinoco River, 350 miles southeast of Caracas. Niehous was found at a house by police searching for cattle rustlers, identified himself, and escaped with a policeman. The two later separated for safety, and Niehous's whereabouts were unknown for a few hours. Police said they found a large quantity of arms, including hand grenades and rifles near the hideout. Two men were killed in a gun battle at the location. Niehous returned to the U.S., to a promotion from his firm. 2610

February 28, 1976—Philippines—The MNLF kidnapped Eunice Diment, a British missionary, from a boat off Basilan Island in the Mindanao provinces. She was released unharmed on March 17. 2611

February 29, 1976—Colombia—An Aces Airlines general aviation Saunders ST27 flying from Medellín to Apartado was hijacked by José Cardona, an armed man who took over shortly after takeoff. Cardona demanded a $300,000 ransom. The plane first flew to Chigordo, where the hijacker allowed the passengers to disembark. The plane returned to Medellín, where he began shooting at police who were converging on the plane. He was shot in the throat during the gun battle and died in a hospital a few hours later. The fifteen passengers and five crew were unharmed. 5486

March 1976—Ethiopia—The Tigre People's Liberation Front kidnapped a British family: Lindsey Tyler, his wife, and their two small children. They were held for a time with Jon Swain, *London Sunday Times* foreign correspondent, who was kidnapped later in the year. The family was released in the Sudan on January 6, 1977. 2612

March 2, 1976—Japan—The East Asia Anti-Japanese Armed Front claimed credit for a bomb that exploded at 9:03 A.M. in a crowded Sapporo government office building on Hokkaido, killing two and injuring eighty-five. The group protested oppression of the Ainu.
'
March 3, 1976—Costa Rica—A Miami-based Cuban exile group bombed the Soviet embassy in San José. 3161

March 4, 1976—United Kingdom—A ten-pound IRA bomb placed under a seat exploded in a commuter train in the morning, minutes after hundreds of rush-hour passengers had disembarked at a London railway station. Eight people traveling in a second train alongside suffered shock in the explosion. They were treated and discharged from a local hospital. Two more bombs exploded later in central London, injuring one. 2613-2615

March 5, 1976—United States—The Carolina Power and Light Company's Brunswick 1 and 2 licensed nuclear facility in Southport, North Carolina, received a bomb threat. A similar threat was reported against the Susquehanna

Units 1 and 2 licensed nuclear facility of the Pennsylvania Power and Light Company in Berwick, which was threatened again three days later.

March 6, 1976—Northern Ireland—The Belfast Brigade of the Provisional IRA fired a battery of fourteen mortars mounted in sand and clay on a dump truck at Aldergrove airport. Damage was slight, and no injuries were reported. The shells were launched by a sophisticated electric, delayed-action mechanism. Nine of the shells exploded.

March 6, 1976—Italy—Three Libyans attempting to board a flight at Rome's Fiumicino Airport were discovered to be carrying a briefcase containing pistols and hand grenades. The three were involved in a kidnapping plan against a former Libyan Revolutionary Command Council member who had gone into exile. Some reports claimed the trio had planned to hijack the plane, which they believed Major Abdel Moneim Hony was aboard.

March 7, 1976—France—Shots from automatic weapons were fired at the windows of an Aeroflot office in Paris, causing considerable property damage but no injuries. 2616

March 8, 1976—Egypt—Seven Libyans were arrested in Cairo on charges of planning to kidnap Omar Mahayshi, the former planning minister of Libya, who was said to be a leader of an aborted coup attempt against Libyan leader Muammar Qaddafi. The Egyptians also claimed to have arrested former Tunisian Foreign Minister Mohammed Masmoudi, whom they claimed was a Libyan agent. Some Egyptian officials charged that Qaddafi hired the Venezuelan terrorist Carlos to kidnap an Egyptian diplomat and hold him hostage for the forced return of such exiles as Mahayshi and Hony.

March 8, 1976—Mexico—Mexico City police reported that four young left-wing terrorists kidnapped Juan de Dios de la Torre, chairman of the Mexican Soccer Federation, from his Guadalajara office.

March 8, 1976—United States—A young man phoned the *New York Post* to claim that the Jewish Armed Resistance Strike Force had been responsible for a bomb that exploded shortly before midnight at the doorway of a building in New York housing the offices of Aeroflot and the Czechoslovakian national airline. The bomb caused considerable damage but no injuries. 2617

March 8, 1976—France—A Zionist group was believed responsible for throwing numerous Molotov cocktails at the Syrian embassy in Paris, causing slight damage and no injuries. A similar group had harassed a Syrian delegation in Paris the previous evening. 2618

March 9, 1976—United States—The Turkey Point licensed nuclear facility in Florida City of the Florida Power and Light Company received a bomb threat.

March 9, 1976—West Germany—Rudi Manz, twenty-four, a gunman wearing a green ski mask, seized two hostages after being foiled in his attempt to free a courtroom defendant. He demanded a ransom of 1 million marks ($390,000) and a plane to Cuba. The German government gave him the money, but he refused to leave the Frankfurt courthouse, which was surrounded by 350 police armed with submachine guns. On March 10 his captives jumped him, and he was injured in the shootout. The hostages were not injured at the end of the twenty-nine-hour siege. 5487

March 11, 1976—United States—A lone man made several telephoned bomb threats against United Airlines in Brooklyn, New York, demanding $10,000. He was arrested when he went to pick up the money.

March 12, 1976—El Salvador—Seven unexploded incendiary bombs were discovered in the San Salvador store of a U.S. firm at approximately 6:40 P.M. The FMLLF took credit. 2619

March 12, 1976—Mexico—Two hooded, armed men, members of the American Escape Committee, raided a Mexican jail during the evening, overpowered the guards and freed eleven Americans and five Mexicans, who were guided to the Rio Grande, two blocks away. The escapees swam to the border town of Eagle Pass, Texas. It was claimed that the group was financed by parents of Americans jailed in Mexico, and was comprised of a coalition of left- and right-wing Americans operating in concert with Mexican guerrillas. On May 8, 1976, it was claimed that the group was funded by a Dallas psychologist, Dr. Sterling Blake Davis, and led by Don Fielden, thirty-one, an unemployed Dallas truck driver who was said to have been with the marines in Vietnam. Fielden and William Hill, thirty-two, an unemployed wrecker yard operator, were indicted on May 18, 1976, in San Antonio, Texas on charges of taking an illegal twelve-gauge shotgun into Mexico. The indictment charged that they had exported a shotgun with a barrel less than the legal length of eighteen inches without a license or government permission.

March 12, 1976—Laos—Two grenades exploded on the grounds of the Soviet embassy in Vientiane, injuring two men and two women, all Soviet citizens. 2620

March 14, 1976—United States—The JDL tried to disrupt a concert at Lincoln Center, New York, when three of its members attempted to throw eggs on the stage during a recital by a Soviet musician. The night before, windows were broken in several stores by Save Our Israel, which also picketed the Chase Manhattan Bank for its cooperation with Arabs. At 6:30 A.M., a caller to Reuters said that windows would be smashed at ten banks. The B'nai B'rith Antidefamation League had cited the banks for demanding proof of compliance with the Arab boycott from U.S. exporters.

March 14, 1976—Italy—The Spanish embassy was damaged when twenty youths threw ten firebombs at it. In the resulting skirmish, a passerby was killed and two others injured. It is not known if the individual was killed by Roman police bullets or by bullets fired by one of the youths. 2621

March 15-16, 1976—United States—The Sequoyah Nuclear Plant in Daisey, Tennessee, operated by the Tennessee Valley Authority, received bomb threats.

March 15, 1976—United Kingdom—Nine persons were injured and one was killed when an IRA bomb went off in a London subway train during rush hours. The perpetrator was injured in the explosion. While running from his pursuers, he shot and killed the train's engineer, who had given chase. 2622

March 15, 1976—United States—A plot to assassinate President Ford and Ronald Reagan, chief contenders for the Republican party's presidential nomination, was revealed by the FBI. The plotters planned to attack the National Republican Party Convention in Kansas City in August 1976. Gregg Daniel Adornetto, twenty-seven, an FBI informer of the terrorist Emiliano Zapata Unit (EZU) in the San Francisco Bay area, claimed that an agent of the Cuban intelligence services (DGI) had advised the group in their plans. He was identified as using the code name of Andres Gomez. The DGI agent had reportedly fled to Mexico shortly after a police shootout, in which Adornetto and six other EZU members were arrested.

March 18, 1976—Argentina—Argentine officials and police foiled an attempt to assassinate President Isabel Perón when they chased off two people placing a bomb as her helicopter was landing at the presidential palace in Buenos Aires.

March 19, 1976—Lebanon—Two rockets hit a YAK-40 jet of the Syrian air force scheduled to fly Lebanese Premier Rashid Karami and former Premier Saeb Salem from Beirut to Damascus for crisis talks about the Lebanese civil war. Saiqa claimed that a soldier had fired three rounds from his machine gun in an apparent assassination attempt. 2623

March 19, 1976—Thailand—At 11:30 A.M., the USIS office in Chiang Mai was informed by a local newspaper that it had received an anonymous telephone warning that a bomb was in the USIS center. The center was evacuated, but a police search was negative. 2624

March 19, 1976—Turkey—A Turkish terrorist group was believed responsible for setting fire to a building at the Ortakoy U.S. Army installation, which was destroyed. No injuries were reported. 2625

March 20, 1976—Israel—The PLO in Damascus claimed credit for setting a predawn fire that gutted the eight-story Park Hotel in Netanya, killing four tourists and injuring forty-six, including two Americans (one of whom was a Florida woman who jumped from a window). The Israelis doubted that guerrillas were responsible. 2626

March 21, 1976—France—Felicia Perez Revilla, the wife of Tomas Perez, a leading Basque nationalist refugee, was seriously wounded during the night when their car was machine-gunned near their home in Saint-Jean-de-Luz. A passing car fired on them. She was wounded in the lung, and one of her hands had to be amputated. Her husband was slightly wounded by a ricochet, and her fifteen-month-old son was injured by flying glass. 2627

March 22, 1976—Tunisia—Four Libyans were arrested on charges of trying to kidnap or assassinate President Habib Bourguiba or Premier Hedi Nouira, Bourguiba's designated successor, in Tunis. A planned Libyan-Tunisian merger had collapsed in 1974. On April 23, 1976, the Tunisian state security court sentenced Mohammed Ali Nail to death.

March 22, 1976—United Kingdom—Scotland Yard detectives announced the discovery of two IRA bomb factories in the Lavender Hill section of south London. They detained five men and a woman.

March 23, 1976—Japan—A young star of pornographic films crashed his Piper Cherokee into the home of Yoshio Kodama. a rightist leader accused of accepting $7 million in payoffs from the Lockheed Aircraft Corporation. A fire in the house was quickly extinguished. Kodama, sixty-five, was not injured, but the pilot was killed. He was identified as Mitsuyasu Maeno. twenty-nine, (also known as Shimoichiro Maeno) who had no known criminal or political affiliations and was described as an emotionally disturbed young man who had previously attempted suicide. Maeno wore the uniform and headband of Kamikaze pilots and gave their cry over his radio before the crash.

March 25, 1976—Soviet Union—After U.S. embassy employees in Moscow received over seventy harassing phone calls, a bomb threat was phoned to the embassy in which an anonymous caller, speaking in fluent English, warned a U.S. Marine guard that a four-pound plastic explosive would go off in twenty minutes on the ground floor. A search was negative. It appeared that the callers believed that the campaign had governmental approval, coming at a time of strained relations between the two nations. 2628

March 25, 1976—Puerto Rico—In San Juan, the son of the secretary-general of the Puerto Rican Socialist party, Juan Mari Bras, was found fatally shot in the head in a car along a mountain highway. The party called the murder of Santiago Mari Pesquera, twenty-four, a political assassination. On March 28, a former mental patient, Henry Walter Coira Stori, twenty-three, was charged with first-degree murder.

March 25, 1976—Thailand—A bomb exploded at a political rally in the north, killing seven and wounding ten.

March 25, 1976—United States—The licensed nuclear facility of Purdue University received a bomb threat, as did the Diablo Canyon Unit 1 nuclear facility of the Pacific Gas and Electric Company in California.

March 25, 1976—United States—An unexploded time bomb was found on the fire escape of a New York City office of Amtorg Trading Corporation, the Soviet trade agency. In a message to the Associated Press, a male member of the Jewish Armed Resistance claimed responsibility. The JDL denied any connection with the group or the bombing. 2629

March 26, 1976—Argentina—Two security guards of a Ford executive were killed by machine-gun fire from a speeding car. 2630

March 27, 1976—United Kingdom—An IRA bomb exploded without warning in a trash bin at Olympia, a London exposition center that was hosting a mobile home show. The blast injured eighty persons, including eight children. 2631

March 27, 1976—Turkey—Two small bombs exploded outside a U.S. military apartment building in Istanbul, causing minor damage but no injuries. Another bomb exploded at an Italian bank building. 2632-2633

March 29, 1976—West Germany—A bomb was thrown through the second-floor window of the office building housing the Swedish consulate in Düsseldorf.The bomb exploded in the offices of a German firm. Although the Swedish offices are on the first floor, its flag is flown from the second floor. It was believed that the attackers were protesting the trial of terrorists who seized the West German embassy in Stockholm in April 1975 (see incident 2282). 2634

March 30, 1976—Soviet Union—The Soviet Foreign Ministry warned the U.S. embassy in Moscow that it had received a telephoned bomb threat at 1 P.M. that a device would go off in one hour. No bomb was found. 2635

March 30, 1976—Northern Ireland—A British soldier was killed when a booby-trapped bomb exploded outside a Protestant hall near Lurgan. Three more British soldiers were killed the next day when their vehicle hit a land mine in Ulster.

March 30, 1976—Colombia—The Lebanese consul in Barranquilla was shot dead. 3162

March 31, 1976—Turkey—Bombs exploded outside the offices of Pan Am and Philips Electronics in Ankara, causing extensive damage but no injuries. 2636-2637

March 31, 1976—United States—The Bahamian-registered lobster boat *Sea Cat* was slightly damaged when it was bombed in the night in Miami. Police arrested four persons seen leaving the vicinity in another boat when the bomb went off. 2638

March 31, 1976—United States—A bomb threat was telephoned to the New York University Arab Student Club, cutting short the speech of Mouffak el-Allaf, the Syrian delegate to the United Nations. Six hundred people were in the audience. The event was also picketed by the JDL. 2639

March 31, 1976—Soviet Union—A bomb scare at the U.S. consulate in Leningrad forced evacuation of the mission. 2640

March 31, 1976—Ireland—Twelve gunmen dressed in rail workers' clothing stopped the Cork-Dublin train near the village of Sallins by littering the tracks with warning flares. The group took mailbags containing $1 million, which police believed would be used to finance terrorists in Northern Ireland. A few days, later, police arrested four men in Dublin and another seven in Dundalk, fifty-four miles to the north. They held the group under the antiterrorism act. 2641

March 31, 1976—United States—An unidentified individual broke a display window at the Yugoslav Airlines office in New York City and then attemped to spread paint around the area. No injuries were reported.

April 1976—Ireland—A Czech diplomat about to defect to marry his Irish girl friend died in Dublin after a visit by an unknown individual. The press suggested that the deceased had planned to detail Czech support of Provisional Irish Republican Army terrorists. 2642

April 1976—Lebanon—Radical Palestinian guerrillas were believed responsible for emptying the safe deposit vaults in major Beirut banks, the Banco di Roma and the Bank Misr-Liban. 2643-2644

April 1, 1976—Ghana—At 12:50, a marine security guard at the U.S. embassy in Accra received a call from a Ghanaian female asking for the second secretary. The call was placed to the economic counselor, who was told, "A bomb will be exploded in your embassy in 5 minutes. This is your April Fool." A search was negative. The embassy was unable to contact police due to telephone difficulties. 2645

April 1, 1976—Dubai—A passenger knifed a steward on a KLM 747 flying from Dubai to Zurich with 397 passengers on board. The plane made an unscheduled landing in Vienna, where the steward was hospitalized with a severe face cut. The male attacker was arrested by Austrian police and sent for a mental examination. 5488

April 2, 1976—United States—Three men stole 140 M-16 rifles, 4 M-14 rifles, 18 .45 caliber revolvers, 2 M-60 machine guns, 1,440 rounds of 5.56-mm tracer ammunition, and 1,140 rounds of 5.56 blanks from a marine-navy reserve armory in Knoxville, Tennessee. It was pointed out by the press that U.S. sympathizers had been supplying the IRA with weapons.

April 2, 1976—Laos—Two grenades were thrown in the evening into the grounds of the Cuban embassy in Vientiane, wounding a militia man and slightly damaging some windows. 2646

April 2, 1976—United States—A lone male attempted to extort $300,000 by threatening to bomb the Eastern Airlines terminal of the Atlanta airport. He was paid off with a bundle supposedly containing all of the money but was not apprehended.

April 2, 1976—United States—The Jewish Armed Resistance (JAR) took credit for firing two rifle shots through the ninth-floor window of the Soviet U.N. mission, vowing more attacks if a nineteen-year-old Jewish woman was not allowed to emigrate. U.S. Ambassador Scranton apologized for the incident, which occurred at 3:50 A.M. Police found a rifle a block away at a construction site. The JAR threatened to kidnap Russian children if harassment of Soviet Jews was not ended. One of the shots entered a ninth-floor apartment occupied by a couple and their child; the other shot hit the building. No one was injured. Five JDL members were arrested for this and other incidents. On December 16, four of them were sentenced to prison terms of up to six years, and the fifth received a suspended sentence. 2647

April 3, 1976—United States—A bomb exploded at the student union of the University of Miami shortly before black Marxist Angela Davis was scheduled to speak. No injuries were reported. On January 31, 1977, state officials charged a Cuban exile, Pablo Gustavo Castillo, thirty, an unemployed carpet layer from Hialeah, Florida, with the bombing. He had been arrested in Puerto Rico and brought to Miami two days later. He was called before a federal grand jury probing international terrorism. 2648

April 3, 1976—Colombia—After two bombs had exploded during the night of April 2 at the national headquarters of the Liberal and Conservative parties, a bomb exploded at 10 P.M. at the entrance of a branch of the First National City Bank in Bogotá, near the U.S. embassy chancery. No injuries resulted, but damage was extensive. 2649

April 3, 1976—Greece—An incendiary bomb exploded in the Athens offices of American Express, causing limited damage. The company later received several telephone calls warning of two additional bombs, but no devices were found. 2650

April 3, 1976—Argentina—Security forces killed Eduardo Castellano Soto, a Peruvian member of the ERP, in Córdoba. 2651

April 4, 1976—Spain—Five Molotov cocktails were thrown into the Madrid store of a U.S. firm, activating sprinkler systems. They contained the fires but caused damage estimated at 200,000 pesetas ($3,000). 2652

April 4, 1976—Soviet Union—Half a dozen men jostled and threatened Raymond Benson, the U.S. cultural counselor, as he was entering Moscow's Tchaikovsky Concert Hall. The group said, ''You live quietly here. Why don't you let our people live quietly in New York? If anything more happens there, it'll happen here, too. Tell your ambassador.''

April 5, 1976—Angola—A heavily armed Cuban soldier serving as a security guard at Luanda airport hijacked a Portuguese TAP B747 as it was taking off for Lisbon. He demanded that he be flown to Lisbon, where he was granted political asylum. He claimed that he opposed Cuban intervention in Angola. Three hundred eighty passengers were on board the plane. 5489

April 6, 1976—United States—The Millstone Units 1 and 2 licensed nuclear facility of the Northeast Nuclear Energy Company in Waterford, Connecticut, received a bomb threat.

April 6, 1976—Cuba—The FLNC and Brigade 2506 claimed credit for the machine-gun attack on two Cuban fishing vessels, *Ferro 123* and *Ferro 119*, in which one of five fishermen was killed. The attack took place in the Straits of Florida. Fidel Castro threatened to abrogate the U.S. 1973 antihijacking agreement over this incident. 2653

April 7, 1976—Angola—Two Roman Catholic missionaries, a Dutchman and a Portuguese, were killed by a uniformed man who fired on them with a machine gun. 2654

April 7, 1976—Argentina—Left-wing guerrillas attacked the home of Hugo Carlos Sardan, an Argentine executive of the U.S. Pfizer Drug firm, killing one guard and wounding another. 2655

April 7, 1976—Philippines—A PAL BAC111 flying seventy-two passengers from Cagayan de Oro to Mactan was hijacked by three MNLF members who threatened the passengers if they were not flown to a country of their choice, given $300,000, and granted the release of four political prisoners. The plane landed at Manila, where negotiations began. The hijackers exchanged the seventy-two passengers for twelve airline employees and flew on to Bangkok after refueling in Kota Kinabalu and Kuala Lumpur. Their progress was stalled when Burma refused overflight privileges, and the pilot noted that the plane could not make such a long flight. The group pulled the pins on two grenades and demanded another PAL plane. They were given a DC8 and agreed to release ten of their hostages and surrender all but one of their weapons. The BAC111 was also reported to have run into mechanical difficulties. The plane flew on to Karachi, Pakistan, where officials refused refueling privileges. The plane landed in Benghazi, Libya, but the hijackers were told that they would not be allowed off the plane and would have to fly off once the DC8 refueled. The group asked to speak to Colonel Muammer Qaddafi, and were granted political asylum after threatening to blow up the plane and kill the hostages. They surrendered to Libyan authorities shortly thereafter, freeing their hostages. The Libyans immediately turned the money over to PAL officials. Among the released hostages was an American, Frederick Schrader of California. The plane flew with the freed hostages to Rome. 2656

April 8, 1976—Soviet Union—Four Russians surrounded a U.S. diplomat and lectured her about violence against Soviets in New York. Soviet officials denied permission for a U.S. military jet to land in Moscow and fly out U.S. Ambassador Walter J. Stoessel, Jr., on a routine trip.

April 8, 1976—United States—JDL members picketed the Soviet U.S. mission in New York, carrying signs saying, "2 Russian Diplomats in Ransom for Marina Tiemkin" a sixteen-year-old Jewish girl imprisoned in Moscow for applying for a visa to Israel, and "Russian Blood on New York Streets." Mordechai Rosenberg, a local JDL leader, led the JDL protest.

April 8, 1976—Spain—The Spanish government announced that it had found the body of industrialist Angel Berazadi, who had been kidnapped three weeks earlier by the ETA in a Basque village. The group's demands for $3 million had not been granted. On April 13, the government announced that it had arrested ninety-seven Basque guerrillas, including three of the four terrorists who had kidnapped Berazadi.

April 12, 1976—Somalia—A small fire in the USIS offices in Mogadishu destroyed the main electrical distribution complex and caused some smoke and water damage to a corridor and stairwell. 2657

April 12, 1976—France—Two Molotov cocktails exploded at the U.S. consulate in Nice, destroying the steel front door but causing no injuries. A local extreme right-wing nationalist group said it was protesting refusals by several U.S. cities to permit landings of the Concorde jet. 2658

April 13, 1976—Argentina—Two men and two women firing from a moving car sprayed the Buenos Aires suburban home of Antonio Claudia Trigo, the Argentine administrative manager of the local subsidiary of the Goodyear tire manufacturing firm, with machine-gun bullets, killing a father and son bodyguard team. Neither Trigo, his wife, nor his two children were hurt. Jorge Alberto Carbone was an off-duty federal police agent moonlighting for a private security agency. His father, Alberto Carbone, was a retired noncommissioned air force officer. 2659

April 13, 1976—Chad—An attempt to assassinate President Felix Malloum with hand grenades failed at a military parade in N'Djamena marking the first anniversary of the coup that brought him to power. Seventy-two were wounded and four were killed, including one of Malloum's bodyguards.

April 14, 1976—Italy—The Armed Communist Formations claimed credit for the firebombing of the Texaco Oil Company offices in Florence. 2660

April 14, 1976—Northern Ireland—A gang of teenagers in Belfast, believed to be Protestants, doused two Roman Catholic children with gasoline and set them on fire. The eight-year-old boy was badly burned, and the twelve-year-old boy was treated in a hospital for hand and facial burns.

April 14, 1976—Libya—President Muammar Qaddafi escaped unharmed from an assassination attempt.

April 14, 1976—Argentina—Gunmen in Buenos Aires shot a navy captain, an Argentine executive of the U.S. Chrysler Corporation, and three policemen to death. 2661

April 15, 1976—United States—The FAA instituted a system of selective searching of cargo-hold luggage.

April 15, 1976—United States—A Pan Am B747 flying from New York to Germany with 329 passengers and nineteen crew members received a bomb threat. It dumped its fuel load before landing at Logan International Airport in Boston. Eight right-hand brakes were frozen. They were replaced and inspected, but no bomb was found. No injuries were reported. 2662

April 15, 1976—Soviet Union—Three Russian men surrounded U.S. embassy political officer Igor Belousovitch in his Moscow residential compound in the early morning and lectured him about anti-Soviet activity in New York.

April 17, 1976—Italy—A Molotov cocktail was thrown at the Spanish consulate in Florence. 2663

April 18, 1976—Rhodesia—Zimbabwe guerrillas killed three South Africans returning from a motorcycle visit sixty miles from the South African border. During the evening, they had held up three cars near Nuanetsi on the road from Fort Victoria to Beitbridge. As two motorcycles drew up, the terrorists opened fire, killing three men and wounding a woman passenger. 2664

April 18, 1976—United States—Roger Lentz, thirty-one, of Marquette, Nebraska, hijacked a Heinzmann Engineering Company general aviation Piper Navajo at Grand Island, Nebraska, by pointing his pistol at the pilot and forcing him to fly to Stapleton International Airport in Denver. Lentz demanded a larger aircraft for a flight to Mexico. At various times he threatend the lives of his hostages and several times shot out windows of the plane, which he took over at 6 P.M. He demanded a United Airlines plane but was refused. Governor Richard Lamm offered a DC8 trainer, but Lentz requested a Convair

990 of the Ports of Call Travel Club because of its longer range. His brother, Larry, was flown from Nebraska to talk to him, but Roger refused to listen to him. The brother claimed that the hijacker had threatened suicide and was despondent about marital problems. Authorities said he had a criminal record and may have been attempting to avoid prosecution. The hijacker and his hostages transferred planes, but as Lentz was walking down the aisle of the 990, he was shot and fatally wounded by FBI agents who were hidden in the plane. Neither hostage—pilot Robert Blair of Grand Island nor mechanic Harlin Hillers—was injured. 5490

April 20, 1976—Lebanon—Los Angeles correspondent Joe Alex Morris was kidnapped during the evening by two armed men while driving home after work in west Beirut. He was taken to a deserted area where his kidnappers forced him from the car, took his identity papers, and released him. 2665

April 20, 1976—Lebanon—Gerald Utting, a visiting journalist with the *Toronto Star*, was kidnapped after leaving for the Beirut airport by taxi. He was released on April 22 after the intervention of PLO leader Yasir Arafat. Utting was later reported missing in July 1977 after flying to Uganda to investigate reports of widespread massacres in the wake of an unsuccessful coup attempt against Idi Amin. 2666

April 21, 1976—Italy—The Armed Communist Formations claimed credit for severely wounding the Italian president of Chevron Oil Italiana in Rome. Chevron is a subsidiary of Standard Oil of California. 2667

April 22, 1976—Greece—A bomb exploded at the Athens branch of the First National City Bank. 2668

April 22, 1976—Lebanon—In an attack on Beirut international airport, a commercial transport plane was heavily damaged, twelve people were injured, and three other planes were hit but able to fly away.

April 22, 1976—Lebanon—The U.S. embassy was hit by a shell that crashed into an empty office. 2669

April 22, 1976—United States—An individual threatened to intrude into the grounds of the St. Lucie Unit 1 licensed nuclear facility of the Florida Power and Light Company on Hutchinson Island.

April 22, 1976—Portugal—A power bomb exploded at the Cuban embassy in Lisbon, killing two Cubans and seriously injuring five Portuguese. Extensive property damage was reported, and two floors of the building housing the embassy were completely wrecked. The dead were listed as Adriana Corcho, twenty-six, wife of the embassy's first secretary, and Efren Monteagudo, twenty-three, an embassy staff member. It was believed that Portuguese right-wing extremists or embittered returnees from Angola were responsible. The Portuguese Anti-Communist Movement, a right-wing group, claimed credit. On August 9, 1976, the Portuguese government arrested nine individuals it believed were connected with the bombing. Several of them were members of a terrorist organization, and others were identified as figures linked to the former right-wing dictatorship. 2670

April 23, 1976—France—A powerful bomb exploded at a Spanish bank in Paris, causing extensive property damage but no injuries. 2671

April 23, 1976—Venezuela—An incendiary device was found in the Maracaibo store of a U.S. firm. 2672

April 23, 1976—United States—The Turkey Point Units 3 and 4 licensed nuclear facility in Florida City of the Florida Power and Light Company received a bomb threat, as did the Grand Gulf installation of the Mississippi Power and Light Company in Port Gibson. The latter received a second bomb threat three days later.

April 24, 1976—Turkey—A bomb exploded at the entrance to the American Language and Trade Institute in Istanbul, causing negligible damage. The facility is a private girls' school funded by the American Board Mission and the YWCA. 2673

April 24, 1976—Turkey—A bomb exploded at the Iran Air ticket office in Istanbul, causing extensive damage and injuries to four passersby. The bombing was believed connected with the visit of the shah of Iran to Izmir. 2674

April 24, 1976—Colombia—Alfonso Hernandez produced a revolver shortly after takeoff and forced a stewardess to bring him to the cockpit of an Avianca B727 flying from Pereira to Bogotá. He instructed the pilot to continue to Bogotá, where he released all of the passengers. Saying that he was protesting "the government's neglect of the peasants," he turned his gun over to the pilot and surrendered to authorities. 5491

April 28, 1976—Burma—Rebels of the Karen National United Army ambushed a ferry boat traveling between Pann and Shwegun in Karen State, killing forty-five passengers and wounding seventy-five others.

April 29, 1976—Argentina—A Frenchwoman, the widow of an Argentine journalist, was kidnapped from her Buenos Aires home by five men wearing civilian clothes but claiming to be security forces. The press said the incident "bore the earmarks of right-wing terrorism." 2675

April 29, 1976—People's Republic of China—A powerful bomb exploded at the gates of the Soviet embassy on Peking's Anti-Revisionist Street. Reports conflicted on the extent of damage and casualties. The Soviets said two Chinese guards were killed, while other reports listed the bomber as also dying in the blast. The Tokyo newspaper *Asahi* reported that five or six Chinese youths struggled with three Chinese soldiers at the gates and that two of the soldiers and most of the attackers were killed. The Chinese termed the action "an act of sabotage by a counterrevolutionary." There were also unconfirmed reports of one arrest at the site of the explosion. 2676

April 30, 1976—United States—Emilio Milian, forty-four, a Cuban exile who was news director and commentator for WQBA, a radio station serving the Miami Spanish-language community, was injured when a bomb exploded in his car as he turned on his ignition. The car's hood was thrown over a cement wall, the left front fender was ripped, and the driver's door was torn open. Milian's legs were blown off at the knees. He had spoken out against terrorism and violence. 2677

April 30, 1976—France—A Turkish Airlines DC10 flying from Paris to Istanbul with 255 persons on board was hijacked by Zeki Ejder, thirty-six, a Turkish migrant worker who had entered France illegally in 1974. Armed with a knife, he threatened a stewardess and demanded to be flown to either Marseille or Lyons. Permission to land was refused by both airports, and the plane returned to Orly two and a half hours after takeoff. He surrendered without incident and was taken into custody. He informed a French policeman that he was attempting to avoid expulsion and "to rejoin a woman he loves and who is under arrest in France." On May 1, he flew on the same plane with fifty-five of the original passengers and two French plainclothesmen to Istanbul, where he was taken into custody. 5492

May 1976—Argentina—General Videla informed the West German embassy that his government had never taken into custody two Germans who disappeared soon after the military coup. The embassy believes the men were seized by armed groups.

May 1976—Egypt—General Hassan Abu Basha, Egypt's assistant interior Minister, anounced in Cairo the arrest of Libyan-trained agents who were to plant bombs in Alexandria movie theaters, at a wine factory in the Beheira

Governorate on the Nile delta, and at a civilian radar station west of Alexandria. The attacks were to coincide with President Sadat's Labor Day speech. At least one bomb went off in Alexandria, injuring six Egyptians.

Those arrested said they were trained with Soviet-made bombs and guns at 'Alsho'ba, 176 kilometers south of Tobruk, Libya, by the chief of Libyan intelligence, Mohammed Idriss el Sherif el Shoheibi. Abu Basha said that the attacks were to give the impression of unrest in Egypt. A letter attached to two time bombs in an Abu Matamir street threatened the Egyptian government with more bombings if anti-Qaddafi broadcasts in Cairo did not cease.

May 1976—Iran—The Iranian newspaper *Rastakhiz*, the organ of the only legal party, claimed that documents taken from terrorist hideouts established that Libya's Colonel Qaddafi had paid the anti-Shah terrorists $100,000 and had planned to pay an additional $100,000 every three months. The paper claimed that a large amount of U.S. currency was found in a terrorist hideout raided in Tehran and that the Libyans had provided the group with machine guns and hand grenades. The paper also wrote that the PFLP had provided the terrorists with training.

May 1976—Rhodesia—Gideon Becking, a South African-born Rhodesian farmer, was kidnapped in eastern Rhodesia and taken into Mozambique. 2678

May 1, 1976—Chile—Several pistol shots were fired at the Santiago residence of the U.S. ambassador from a car with three occupants in the early morning. There was no damage or injuries. 2679

May 1, 1976—Panama—The Panama National Guard discovered a plot by Miami-based Cuban exiles to attack the Cuban embassy. 2680

May 2, 1976—United States—Five pipe bombs exploded in New York City in the early morning at the Four Continents Bookstore, a Soviet publication outlet; two banks; the Communist party headquarters; and a site near the U.N. library. Police said the bombs were designed more to attract attention than to cause damage. The *Daily News* received an anonymous call claiming credit for the Jewish Armed Resistance Strike Unit, which planted the bombs to protest Soviet treatment of Jews. 2681-2682

May 3, 1976—United States—The display window of the JAT offices (a Yugoslav firm) in New York City was shattered.

May 3, 1976—Israel—A booby-trapped motor scooter exploded on Ben Jehuda Street, Jerusalem's main commercial thoroughfare, injuring thirty people, including the Greek consul-general. The explosion blew out store windows and set fire to another motor scooter and a Peugeot. Few people were on the streets because stores were closed in honor of Remembrance Day. Arab terrorists were blamed, and dozens of suspects were detained. 2683

May 4, 1976—Corsica and France—Sixteen bombs planted by the Corsican National Liberation Front exploded in Corsica and in southern France.

May 4, 1976—Argentina—Vedro Rota, an Italian executive of Fiat, was assassinated by leftist terrorists as he left his Buenos Aires home in the morning. 2684

May 4, 1976—United States—The North Anna Units 1, 2, 3, and 4 licensed nuclear facility of the Virginia Electric and Power Company in Mineral, Virginia, received a bomb threat. Another bomb threat was received three days later.

May 6, 1976—Turkey—A pipe bomb exploded in the garden of the U.S. consul general's residence in Izmir, causing minor damage and no injuries. A car belonging to a DOD instructor at an air force facility in Izmir was set on fire and destroyed. No injuries were reported. 2685-2686

May 6, 1976—United States—The Diablo Canyon Units 1 and 2 licensed nuclear facility of the Pacific Gas and Electric Company of California received a bomb threat.

May 9, 1976—West Germany—Ulrike Meinhof, forty-one, the cofounder of the Baader-Meinhof terrorist group known as the Red Army Faction, hanged herself in her prison cell in Stammheim. She was last seen alive by a prison guard and was heard typing in her cell until 10:30 P.M. She was found in the morning hanging at the window rails from a piece of prison toweling. Authorities said she had given no indication of suicidal tendencies. Along with other BMG members, whose trial had lasted for one and a half years at the time of Meinhof's death, she had been indicted on charges of leading a wave of terrorist attacks in which four U.S. servicemen were killed and approximately one hundred people were endangered. The group had also engaged in bank robberies netting $200,000. Protest bombings took place across Europe in the ensuing weeks.

May 9, 1976—France—Two West German steel company offices were bombed in Paris. Klocker and Thyssen reported damage. 2688-2689

May 10, 1976—France—The Daimler Benz office in Nîmes and the West German cultural center in Toulouse were bombed. 2690-2691

May 10, 1976—Italy—The West German tourist office and a German Academy building in Rome were bombed. 2692-2693

May 10, 1976—Bolivia—A bomb exploded at the entrance to the Uruguayan consulate in Santa Cruz nine hours before the arrival of the Uruguayan president. 2694

May 11, 1976—Israel—A small bomb exploded in a Tel Aviv movie theater, slightly injuring one person. 2695

May 11, 1976—France—The Ché Guevara Brigade claimed credit for the assassination of Bolivian Ambassador Joaquin Zenteno Anaya, who had commanded the troops who captured and executed Guevara in 1967. Witnesses disagreed on whether there were two gunmen. Two bullets were fired into the ambassador's back as he was unlocking his car in an exclusive Paris neighborhood on Avenue de President Kennedy during the lunch hour. His attacker was described as thirty-five, bearded, and wearing a black beret and glasses. The assassin escaped into a nearby subway station. The brigade said the 7.65-mm revolver used in the murder had also been used in the nearly fatal shooting of the assistant Spanish military attaché, Captain Bartolome Garcia Plata Valle, in October 1975 (see incident 2427). Zenteno died less than one hundred feet from the spot where the Turkish ambassador to Paris was killed by the Secret Armenian Army on October 24, 1975 (see incident 2448). On May 26, 1977, Paris police announced that they had arrested three leftists on suspicion of three armed attacks, including Zenteno's killing. The trio had in their possession the weapons used in the attacks on Valle and Zenteno and admitted membership in the Maoist Armed Nuclei for Popular Autonomy. 2696

May 12, 1976—Spain—A West German business was bombed in Barcelona. 2697

May 12, 1976—United States—The Zion Units 1 and 2 licensed nuclear facility of the Commonwealth Edison Company in Zion, Illinois, received an intrusion threat.

May 12, 1976—Italy—An attempted arson was reported at the German Table restaurant in Rome. 2698

May 12, 1976—United States—The Washington Monument was closed for twenty minutes at 8:40 P.M. when a dog trained to detect bombs found two canisters at a military display on the grounds. U.S. Park Police said the canisters were grenades found in a compartment underneath a helicopter.

May 13, 1976—United States—Franklin M. Solesby chartered a Royal American Flyers general aviation Cessna 210 to fly from Denver to Houston. After takeoff, one of the two pilots saw Solesby holding a .22 caliber pistol in both hands with his arms outstretched. The hijacker cocked the weapon twice, but it failed to fire. Solesby was overpowered by one of the pilots and was taken into custody by local authorities at Lamar, Colorado. Prosecution against him was declined on June 7, 1976. 5493

May 14, 1976—Portugal—A bomb destroyed a five-floor building housing a radar installation at Lisbon international airport.

May 14, 1976—France—Jean Bilksi, twenty-two, a suspected political extremist, killed himself with a single shot after assassinating Crédit Lyonnais chairman Jacques Chaine, sixty-one. Chaine was shot twice in the chest at point-blank range as he stepped from his car outside the bank's Paris headquarters at 9:45 A.M. His wife, who was beside him in their chauffeur-driven limousine, was wounded in the jaw by a bullet.

May 14, 1976—Italy—The West German consulate in Venice was firebombed. Bombs exploded at the offices of Volkswagen and the Bosch Company in Milan. 2699-2701

May 15, 1976—Italy—A bomb exploded at the German Archaeological Institute in Rome. 2702

May 15, 1976—Philippines—Seven Moslem gunmen kidnapped a Japanese pearl technician, Masato Oki, off the southern port city of Zamboanga. They were last seen heading for nearby Basilan Island. 2703

May 16, 1976—Lebanon—Edouard Saab, editor of the French language daily *L'Orient le Jour* and reporter for *Le Monde*, was killed by a sniper's bullet while driving across a line dividing Christian and Moslem sectors of Beirut. The forty-six-year-old writer was a passenger in a car driven by Henry Tanner of the *New York Times*, who was slightly injured. 2704

May 16, 1976—Lebanon—Twelve mortar rounds hit the French embassy compound during the evening, injuring no one. 2705

May 17, 1976—United States—A group calling itself a secret anti-Castro Cuban army claimed credit for bombing a Cuban social club at West Fourteenth Street near the Avenue of the Americas in New York City. 2706

May 17, 1976—United States—Firebombs exploded at 4:30 A.M. outside the New York City branches of First National City Bank and Bankers Trust, causing minor damages and no injuries. An anonymous male caller told the Associated Press that Save Our Israel (SOIL) attacked the banks because of their cooperation "with the Arab racist boycott of Israel and American Jewry."

May 17, 1976—France—French police reported that bomb attacks heavily damaged the offices of the right wing newspaper *L'Aurore*, a courthouse in Augoulême in the southwest, and the offices of a Spanish company in Paris. Two West German-registered cars in Paris were firebombed. 2707-2709

May 17, 1976—West Germany—Firebombs were thrown at the Turkish consulates in Cologne, Essen, and Frankfurt, damaging the last. 2710-2712

May 19, 1976—Italy—Molotov cocktails were thrown at a German automobile outlet in Rome. An arson attempt against Lufthansa Airlines at the Rome airport was reported in mid-May. 2713-2714

May 20, 1976—Belgium—Molotov cocktails were thrown at the West Germany embassy in Brussels. 2715

May 21, 1976—Argentina—Manuel Liberoff, an Argentine-born Uruguayan labor leader, was kidnapped. 2716

May 21, 1976—Philippines—A PAL BAC111 flying from Davao to Manila with ninety-three passengers and ten crew members was hijacked by six MNLF males armed with pistols and hand grenades who diverted the plane to Zamboanga, where they demanded $375,000 and a DC8 to fly them to Libya. After food and water were sent aboard the plane, the hijackers released five women and nine children. One of those freed was an American woman, Martha Talton of North Charleston, South Carolina, manager of the U.S. Ravenel Travel Agency. Two Americans remained on board and were identified as Andres Macs, general manager of Weyerhauser Philippines, and John Mallett, manager of a United Brands banana plantation near Davao. Military officials negotiated with the hijackers by radio and offered them amnesty if they released all of the hostages, but they were refused. The military officers arranged for the relatives of the leader of the hijackers, Pendatun Domiangca (also known as Commander Zapata) and Maranao political leaders to fly to Zamboanga to talk with him. Philippine sharpshooters deflated the nose wheels of the plane to keep it from taking off. After forty-eight hours of stalemate, a shootout began, and fifty-four passengers escaped. Ten of the passengers and three of the hijackers were killed. The other three hijackers and twenty-two Philippine passengers were wounded. Philippine authorities said they did not begin firing until one of the hijackers killed two passengers near him. The hijackers set off hand grenades, and a PAL spokesman said the $4 million BAC111 was a total loss. Passengers claimed the troops first fired a tear-gas grenade. A government spokesman said that a woman killed in the battle may have been responsible for smuggling the .45 caliber pistols and two grenades aboard the plane inside a large cake. However, the passengers said the gunmen had boasted of sneaking in the weapons past security guards by hiding them in their underwear. The released American woman said, "We all became sort of one unit, the passengers, the hijackers, the pilot, against the outside world. We found ourselves wanting to explain the cause of the hijackers." The three surviving hijackers were convicted of air piracy, multiple murder, and illegal possession of firearms and explosives. The Philippine military announced on November 4, 1976, that the group had been sentenced to death by firing squad. It was also reported that a special hijacking task force instituted by the Philippine government had been deployed for the first time in this incident. 2717

May 22, 1976—Argentina—The bodies of four Uruguayan exiles were found in an abandoned car in Buenos Aires during the evening. Two of the victims were identified as former Uruguayan Senator Zelmar Michelini and former Speaker of the Chamber of Deputies Hector Gutierrez Ruiz. They had been kidnapped from the center of Buenos Aires earlier in the week. Two other Uruguayan exiles killed by the gunfire were identified as William Whitelaw Blanco and his wife, Rosario Barbedo. Michelini was a cabinet minister in the government of Uruguayan President Oscar Gestido in the late 1960s and had been working for the leftist newpaper *La Opinion*. He was also a leader of the leftist faction of the ruling Colorado party. Gutierrez was a businessman. Police said papers signed by a leftist group and found in the car claimed credit for the killings. On May 24, 1976, the London-based Amnesty International said that security forces in Chile, Argentina, and Uruguay were cooperating in a campaign of terror against refugees and exiles and may have been responsible for this kidnap-murder.

May 23, 1976—United States—Two shots were fired at an apartment at 3450 Toledo Terrace, Hyattsville, Maryland, injuring no one. The apartments were rented to two second secretaries of the Soviet embassy, Kimgaudas K. K. Malishauskas and Ivan I. Zavrazhnov. On June 29, the FBI arrested Dr. William Perl, seventy, a psychologist and founder of the Washington, D.C., branch of the JDL, and charged him with conspiracy. It was brought out in his trial that he had made contact with Reuven Levtov, a naturalized U.S. citizen, who had worked at one time as a chauffeur with the Israeli embassy. Levtov turned out to be an FBI agent and claimed that Perl had instructed him to fire a .22 caliber rifle at the apartment. Instead Levtov fired two shots at it with an air pistol he had obtained from the FBI. He then phoned Perl and let the phone ring twice, giving the signal that the attack had been made at 11:20 P.M. On November 24, a federal jury in Baltimore deliberated for six hours before convicting Perl, who had negotiated with Adolf Eichmann in the late 1930s for the release of thousands of German Jews, of conspiracy to shoot out the windows and of obtaining a .22 caliber rifle without a license. He was found innocent of using a stolen rifle. 2718

May 23, 1976—Mexico—The Armed Vanguard of the Proletariat kidnapped Gayle Moony, eight, the daughter of an American businessman, and demanded $400,000 ransom. She was released on June 15, 1976. 2719

May 23, 1976—United States—Incendiary devices damaged two Pan Am vehicles in the cargo center of New York City's JFK Airport. No injuries were reported.

May 25, 1976—Mexico—Nadine Chaval, sixteen, the daughter of the Belgian ambassador, was kidnapped at 7:15 A.M. after leaving her home on Francisco Sosa No. 27 in Cohoacan to go to school. Her car was intercepted by two individuals riding another car. The ambassador, Andreé Chaval, who usually traveled in the same car but did not that day, was the intended victim. Various reports claimed that four men and a woman, all members of the Twenty-third of September Communist League, took part in the attack on the chauffeur-driven embassy car. The group threatened to kill the "bourgeoisie prisoner" if a ransom of $800,000 (10 million pesos) was not paid by midnight of May 27. A family friend, Dr. Fernando de Laye, said the family home in Mexico City had been put up for sale to help raise the ransom. Eighty Belgian families aided in contributing to the ransom, as did Mexican friends, including a nine-year-old boy who donated his clay piggy bank containing nine dollars. Chaval had a nervous breakdown after his daughter's abduction, while his wife, Mireille, was reported on the verge of collapse. With the aid of a Roman Catholic priest who acted as a courier, the negotiators got the kidnappers to lower their original demands to $408,000, which was paid. The blonde schoolgirl was freed, blindfolded, near the Turkish embassy during the night of May 29, twenty-four hours after the ransom payment. The girl described her kidnappers as "violent, aggressive, and rude." Federal police promised an $8,000 reward for the capture of each of the sixteen persons believed involved in the abduction. On June 4, the Twenty-third of September Communist League responded to this announcement by machine-gunning a group of policemen at a police station in the industrial suburb of Ecatepec, killing at least five and leaving five others seriously wounded. On May 6, four individuals had shot down a group of policemen eating breakfast in a Mexico City restaurant, killing nine. On June 11, twenty-one of the twenty-six policemen in the town of Tulpeclac walked off their jobs, raising to 110 the number of policemen in municipalities outside Mexico City who had resigned since the June 4 attack. 2720

May 25, 1976—Israel—A booby-trapped suitcase exploded when a passenger with a Dutch passport opened it in a security office off the luggage area of Tel Aviv's Ben Gurion International Airport. The passenger and a security officer were killed, and ten Israelis were injured. The PFLP claimed credit for the 2:45 P.M. bombing. A second suitcase was exploded by security officials, but contained no explosives. A third suitcase examined contained no bombs. Initial reports conflicted on the origin of the suitcases. Some said that the individual arrived on an Austrian jet from Vienna, but others said he had traveled on an El Al plane for Tehran or on a Lufthansa plane from Frankfurt. On June 14, two Dutch students in the Netherlands admitted to giving the dead Baader-Meinhof terrorist a passport. The dead terrorist was identified as a West German, Bernard Hausmann, twenty-five, who had been given the passport of Hugo Mueller, twenty-five, a Dutch political science student. He and a fellow student, identified only as Rudy M., twenty-six, were charged with embezzling a state document.

Hausmann, according to reporter David Tinnin, was given an altered Dutch passport by a member of Wadi Haddad's supporters in Amsterdam. He proceeded to Vienna, where he phoned another member of the network. His contact told him to fly round trip to Bangkok, with stopovers in Tel Aviv and Tehran. He was to deliver a suitcase in Israel along the way. At the Austrian Airlines counter in Schwechat Airport, Hausmann paid in cash for his ticket, as well as $800 for his overweight baggage, which contained twenty-six pounds of plastique inside hollowed-out compartments of the suitcase. His luggage passed an inspection in Vienna. At Tel Aviv's Lod Airport, a female security officer thought he looked suspicious—he wore jeans and small-lensed, wire-rimmed glasses—and asked him to go to a private inspection room. When he opened the case a second time, he and Marguerite Ben Yishy, the security officer, were killed, and a second officer was injured. A glass wall was shattered, cutting travelers with shards. 2721

May 26, 1976—India—A vanity case exploded in the customs area of New Delhi airport, causing slight property damage and no injuries. The case had been left in the passenger cabin of a Japanese Airlines plane arriving from Bangkok and was taken to the customs area, when no one claimed it. The Indonesian package was addressed to Aeroflot-New Delhi. 2722

May 26, 1976—Spain—Arson was reported at the West German consulate in Bilbao. 2723

May 26, 1976—Italy—Two bombs were thrown at the Milan Volkswagen Agency. 3157

May 27, 1976—France—A bomb exploded in the Armenian Cultural Center in Paris, killing one and injuring another. A second bomb in the building was defused. The injured man was found hiding in another building some blocks away. Police speculated that the two were setting some bombs when they exploded. 2724

May 27, 1976—United Kingdom—Several letters bombs were discovered in London. One was sent to a British judge, who opened a package wrapped in brown paper that arrived with his morning newspaper. The judge said the package contained a book on Irish shipping, which made him suspicious, so he called the police bomb squad. The package carried a Northern Ireland postmark and was addressed in "an illiterate scrawl." Authorities feared that this was the beginning of a new campaign of IRA violence. 2725

May 28, 1976—Switzerland—During the evening, two bombs exploded within twelve minutes of each other in a Turkish bank and at the Turkish consulate in Zurich, causing heavy damage but no injuries. 2726-2727

May 28, 1976—France—Police found the bullet-riddled body of José Bernardo Badiola-Achega, twenty-three, a member of the Spanish Basque independence movement, near the border town of Sare. He had been dead for two weeks. 2728

May 29, 1976—United States—The body of Jesus Gonzalez-Carta, fifty-three, a Cuban exile, was found in a field south of Miami. He had led an extreme right-wing group, Accion Guiteras, during Cuban political gang wars in the 1940s. In 1944, Eduaro Chibas, head of the Cuban Orthodox party, publicly accused him of killing the chief of the Cuban secret police, Gonzalez-Carta. Gonzalez had been killed within twenty-four hours of the time his bullet-riddled body was found on the fringe of the Everglades. 2729

May 31, 1976—Brazil—Forrest E. Fitzpatrick, fifty-one, of Detroit, the manager of a Ford tractor plant in São Paulo, was found dead in his apartment there. Reports gave no indication of the cause of death.

May 31, 1976—United States—The General Electric Fabrication Plant in Wilmington, North Carolina, a licensed nuclear facility, received a bomb threat.

June 1976—Costa Rica—Reports indicated that a group of anti-Castro Cuban exiles met to form CORU, a confederation of organizations that included the FLNC, Cuban Action, Cuban Nationalist Movement C-4, Bridge 2506, and F-14.

June 1976—Kuwait—A Syrian airlines office was bombed by Palestinians in reprisal for the movement of Syrian troops into Lebanon. 2730

June 1976—Ethiopia—The ELF kidnapped three Britons and a Pole who disappeared in the Danakil desert. The Britons were identified as Ian McChesney, a chemical engineer, Bruce Thompson, a forester, and Brian Hazelhurst, a schoolteacher. The Pole, believed to be an Ethiopian citizen, was serving as their guide. On September 17, the Beirut office of the ELF announced, "No ransom is demanded, and the British authorities have been duly informed of this. The three will be released if they are found innocent. Otherwise they will be court-martialed." The group decided that the trio were not spies, and were reported to have treated the hostages well. The group arrived in Rome from Sudan on October 5, 1976, after having been released unharmed. 2731

June 1, 1976—West Germany—The Revolutionary Cell Brigade Ulrike Meinhof claimed credit for setting two time bombs that exploded in a shopping area and at the army officers' club at the U.S. Army's V Corps headquarters in Frankfurt. The injured included six U.S. soldiers, three military dependents, including several wives, an American civilian employee, and a German civilian. The early afternoon blasts caused extensive property damage. The group said that this was a continuation of the struggle of their colleagues who were in prison or dead, including Ulrike Meinhof, who committed suicide on May 9. Four suspects, all wearing civilian clothing, were held for questioning. 2732

June 1, 1976—Argentina—Former President Juan José Torres Gonzalez of Bolivia, living in exile in Buenos Aires, disappeared from his home at 8:30 A.M. after telling his wife that he was going to take the car for a few errands. His body was found two days later on a rural roadside, blindfolded and shot twice in the neck and once behind the ear. A ranch hand sixty-five miles from Buenos Aires heard shots and saw four men in a car speeding off, leaving the body behind. Torres had helped plan and carry out the attack on Ché Guevara's forces in 1967 that resulted in Guevara's death. There was speculation that the Venezuelan terrorist Carlos had entered Uruguay and planned the operation with the Ché Guevara International Brigade, a group that had operated overseas. Torres's family said that they doubted a leftist group killed the leftist president. The Bolivian government cancelled plans for burial in La Paz, and President Luis Echeverria Alvarez of Mexico allowed the body to be buried in his country. 2733

June 2, 1976—Canary Islands—Members of a Spanish Canary Islands independence group were suspected of kidnapping tobacco industrialist Eufemiano Fuentes, sixty-five, from his bedroom before dawn. A ransom of $900,000 was demanded. His decomposed and mutilated body was recovered from a deep well in Las Palmas on October 6. Police accused Angel Cabrera Batista of the kidnap-murder.

June 2, 1976—United States—The Pilgrim Unit 1 licensed nuclear facility of the Boston Edison Company in Plymouth, Massachusetts, received a bomb threat.

June 2, 1976—West Germany—Two U.S. military trucks were firebombed at the Lindsey Air Base in Wiesbaden, causing property damage but no injuries. 2734

June 3, 1976—France—The International Revolutionary Front claimed responsibility for a firebombing in Brittany. Police investigated the possibility that the group was responsible for an explosion that had touched off a fire in Paris the previous week, killing four people in their sleep. No one claimed credit for the incident. 2735

June 3, 1976—United States—Bomb threats were received at nuclear power plants, including Susquehanna Units 1 and 2 of the Pennsylvania Power and Light Company in Berwick.

June 3, 1976—United States—A package bomb found in the mail of the Republic of China's embassy was defused by police, who said the bomb was contained in a white rectangular cardboard box mailed in the U.S. The box was designed to slide open. At 10 A.M., First Secretary Ching Yen Chang slid the box open two inches, saw wiring inside, and called the police. The box was found to contain batteries and wires and weighed five ounces. It had been addressed to Ambassador James C. H. Shen. It had arrived the day before, but the embassy staff did not report for work in observance of the Chinese holiday of the Fifth Moon, the Dragon Boat Festival. 2736

June 4, 1976—France—Molotov cocktails were thrown at the Mercedes Benz office in a Paris suburb. 2737

June 5, 1976—Mexico—A commando-style raid was carried out at Punta Banda against six groups of California residents and a busload of University of Illinois biology students. 2738

June 6, 1976—United States—A bomb exploded at the front door of the Cuban U.N. mission, causing significant property damage and breaking windows in other nearby buildings. The Associated Press and CBS News received anonymous calls from an individual who said this was part of a plan, code named Omega 7, "to hit communists everywhere." Anti-Castro Cubans were suspected. 2739

June 7, 1976—Paraguay—Carlos Abdala, the Uruguayan ambassador, died in a hospital after being shot in Asunción by a Croatian, Jozo Damjanovic, who thought he was shooting at the Yugoslav ambassador. 2687

June 7, 1976—United States—Bomb threats were received at nuclear power plants in Massachusetts.

June 8, 1976—United States—Four bombs exploded in Chicago, damaging the First National Bank Plaza, the John Hancock Center of North Michigan Avenue, the Bank Leumi Le Israel, and police headquarters. Five persons were injured at the 10:45 P.M. bombing at the First National Bank. Police claimed that the timing of the bombings, which took place within twenty minutes of each other, was near to the anniversary of bombings by the FALN in 1975 in Chicago and other cities and that the bombs were similar. No one claimed credit for the explosions. 2740-2743

June 9, 1976—West Germany—The U.S. Army reported that a crate containing fifteen antitank shoulder-fired weapons, two feet long with a range of up to four hundred yards, was missing from the arms depot of its training unit at Wildflecken, near Bad Kissingen.

June 9, 1976—United States—A bomb exploded on a concrete slab at the bottom of stairs in the basement of the Yugoslav embassy at 12:07 A.M., blowing open a heavy metal door and blasting a hole in the concrete about eighteen inches wide. Jovica Mijhailovic, twenty-four, and Nevenka Radic, thirty-seven, were cut by flying glass. Nearby homes reported broken windows. Four hours later, a caller to the Associated Press in Washington, D.C., said the Pan Epirotic Federation of America and Canada was responsible for placing the bombs, without the sanction of their leadership (which denied responsibility). He said he wished to "free our Greek brothers who are being enslaved and tyrannized as minorities in Albania, Yugoslavia, and Bulgaria."

Epirus was identified as an ancient district in northwest Greece and southern Albania. 2744

June 9, 1976—Jamaica—A bomb exploded in luggage that was to be loaded onto a Cuban plane. 2745

June 10, 1976—Canada—At the U.N. Habitat Conference in Vancouver, the Canadian Greenpeace Foundation said that it had been offered an ounce of stolen plutonium to present at the conference to publicize the dangers of nuclear materials but had declined out of fear that it could fall into the wrong hands.

June 10, 1976—Uganda—In an unsuccessful attempt to assassinate Idi Amin, three grenades were thrown during a graduation ceremony of police recruits at Nsambya Barracks, two miles from Kampala. Reports differed on the number of people killed, ranging from one to ten, and wounded, ranging from seven to seventy-six. Some reports claimed that Amin had staged the incident to prevent a coup and used the attack as an excuse to round up potential plotters. Reports claimed that more than two thousand people were killed in the ensuing purge. Amin announced on August 26 the release of seven Africans who had been accused of the attack, as well as the release of a Briton, farmer Robert C. Clegg, who had been accused of spying.

June 11, 1976—Ethiopia—Teresa Piccioni, an Italian vice-consul, and a companion were kidnapped in Massawa by the ELF, who released them on June 26 without making any demands. 2746

June 11, 1976—Argentina—A group of forty men armed with machine-guns entered the Hilton and Pinot hotels in Buenos Aires and abducted twenty-five political refugees—twenty-three Chileans, one Uruguayan, and the Paraguayan-born hotel administrator—in two raids at 2 A.M. The refugees included two boys aged sixteen and seventeen, a cripple, a man sick with mumps, and a Chilean ill with bronchitis. The day before, the offices of the Catholic International Migration Committee were raided by armed men who stole a master list with the names and addresses of thousands of political refugees living in Argentina. The property of the refugees was damaged, and the individuals were roughed up. Reports indicated that their attackers appeared unhurried, although a police station was a half-block from one of the hotels. The group drove off in a convoy of Ford Falcons, which had been used by right-wing death squads, as well as members of the police force. The government denied any link with the attackers. The hostages were released the next day at 4 A.M. on various Buenos Aires streets and forced to walk home. They all had been beaten, and some claimed that they were unable to walk because of the severity of the tortures they had endured. The kidnappers told them not to report their experiences to the press and if they had not left Argentina within forty-eight hours, they would be killed. The deadline passed without incident, although eighteen of the refugees left for Sweden and the Netherlands on June 23. 2747

June 13, 1976—Zambia—Two bombs exploded in Lusaka, blowing out windows in the main post office and demolishing a stone lion at the gates of the high court. No one was injured in the bombings, which President Kenneth Kaunda blamed on the Rhodesian government.

June 14, 1976—Philippines—A boy threw three grenades in Notre Dame of Dulawan, a school in Data Piang, Cotabato, a Moslem town in the central area of Mindanao Island, killing four and wounding twenty-six. The school is run by three Maryknoll Sisters of St. Dominic, a Roman Catholic order of nuns, including two Americans, who were not among those injured. The perpetrator escaped. 2748

June 14, 1976—United States—Sixteen letter bombs were sent to various American and foreign corporations throughout the United States. Only one of the devices was not intercepted in time; it injured four women employees of Merrill, Lynch, Pierce, Fenner and Smith. Other bombs, most of which were postmarked from Atlanta, Texas, or Texarkana, Texas, were mailed to Bunge (an Argentine firm, which received three bombs), the Bank of Israel, Continental Grain, Exxon Pipeline, Marathon Oil, Beatrice Foods, Cargill, The Combined Insurance Company, E. I. DuPont de Nemours and Company, Exxon Corporation, and McDonald's Systems. A letter containing what the writer claimed to be infected ticks was received at one corporation. The letter ended with the typed name of "J. Foxworth, Fort Walton Road," with a smudged city and zip code from somewhere in Connecticut. The FBI noted that over two hundred American corporations had received extortion letters from a "B.A. Fox" over the preceding months. National Life was instructed to give $175,000 to the account of a person in the Matamoros, Mexico, bank. Beatrice Foods was told to deposit a certified check for $16 million in the account of a person with a "German sounding name" in the same bank. 2749-2752

June 15, 1976—Ethiopia—Jon Swain, twenty-eight, foreign correspondent of the *London Sunday Times* and Britain's Journalist of the Year 1975, was kidnapped from a bus by the Tigre Popular Liberation Front while traveling east of Axum, 350 miles north of Addis Ababa. After that he was marched by the group, crossing into Eritrea around the end of July, when they were joined by guerrillas of the Eritrean Popular Liberation Front. At one point his group linked up with a band that had kidnapped Lindsey Tyler, a Briton, and his family. He was released at the British embassy in Khartoum the night of September 5. It is not known what negotiations, if any, led to his release. 2753

June 15, 1976—Jamaica—Peru's ambassador, Fernando Rodriguez Oliva, was stabbed to death in his living room after he returned from a walk and surprised some burglars. Authorities ruled out any political motives in the slaying.

June 16, 1976—Lebanon—U.S. Ambassador Francis E. Meloy, fifty-nine, economic counselor Robert O. Waring, and the ambassador's chauffeur, Zohair Moughrabi, were taken from their light green armor-plated Chevrolet Impala with diplomatic plates on Beirut's Corniche Mazraa. After a period in which it was assumed that they had been kidnapped, their bodies were found in a garbage dump near Beirut's beach, each with bullets in their heads.

The ambassador had left the U.S. embassy in the Moslem sector of Beirut at 10:40 A.M. to meet with President-elect Elias Sarkis, whose headquarters was in the Christian sector on the other side of Beirut's Green Line, which separates the two tribes. Prior to the departure, the three security officers in the follow car were briefed by the chauffeur as to his plan of action. (It was later learned that Moughrabi had overridden the orders of the embassy's security officer, leading many to believe that Moughrabi had been part of the assassination plan. The State Department discounted this theory, arguing that he had worked for the embassy since 1951.) At 10:55 A.M., the embassy received a radio transmission from the chauffeur that gave the impression that the car had crossed into the eastern sector inhabited by the Christians and had successfully passed their roadblocks. The security officers in the follow car returned to the embassy at a prearranged point. However, the party did not appear at Sarkis's office for their meeting, and shortly before 1 P.M., the embassy was informed that the wife of the chauffeur had received an anonymous phone call saying that her husband and two others had been kidnapped but were unharmed. The embassy initiated many contacts attempting to locate the group but failed. In the late afternoon, two Swiss representatives of the International Red Cross informed the embassy that they had recovered the bodies on a sidewalk in West Beirut. It was reported that the trio had not been tortured and that they were found between 4 and 4:30 P.M. next to the Ouzai Boulevard. The next day the PLO's news agency reported that it had arrested three individuals, later increased to five and later eight, who were connected with the killing and that they were willing to surrender them to an Arab League force being formed. The PLO also said that Yasir Arafat would transfer the transcripts of their interrogation to the Arab League delegation in Lebanon. There was some confusion as to the identity of the group to which the suspects were affiliated. Fatah's radio station WAFA reported them as being with the Arab Socialist Revolutionary Movement. Others alleged that two of them were members of the Arab Communist Organization. Still others reported their membership in the Socialist Workers' party, the Lebanese wing of a pan-Arab leftist movement led by George Habash, who also serves as the chief of the PFLP. This particular group was reported to be part of the Libyan-backed Alliance of Moslems and Palestinians.

Many other questions remained unanswered in the assassination of Meloy, who had arrived in Lebanon on May 12 and had not had the opportunity to meet with high-level Lebanese leaders because of the chaotic situation in Beirut. The transmission by Moughrabi that the car had arrived safely in the Christian sector conflicted with the fact that it had been intercepted somewhere between the Moslem and Christian sectors, controlled by the more radical and violence-prone groups. The degree of inside information available to the murderers had not been determined. In testimony to the congressional committee investigating the assassination, a security officer said, "I, myself, would stand on the balcony in front of the embassy looking down at the telephone box down on the street and see a little fellow with a khafia on his head and an AK-47 on his back with earphones on, sitting crosslegged listening on the wire. This would happen in broad daylight every other day. Other than that, in the various parts of the city, the telephones were compromised." The ambassador appears to have made the arrangements for his appointments with Sarkis over a telephone. The State Department claimed that the ambassador's car was never recovered and was believed to have fallen into the hands of Fatah. This conflicts with press accounts claiming that the PLO, to demonstrate that it had nothing to do with the attack, had turned the car over to the CIA to examine. The chauffeur had been given training in defensive driving techniques, including the running of roadblocks, but apparently had not used them. The Associated Press suggested one possible explanation, noting that Meloy's car was recovered by Palestinians undamaged. The doors had apparently been opened willingly by Meloy, who, according to a Western diplomat, believed that a direct, friendly approach was the best guarantee of safety. Hence the gunmen would not have had to break into the car, which was equipped with electric locks that could be opened only from the inside, as well as with bulletproof windows fixed in a closed position. Others suggested Zohair Moughrabi, the chauffeur, was bribed or that his family had been threatened. There were also rumors that a major leader of Fatah, Salah Khalaf, was involved in planning the operation and that the assassins were responsible for the previous murder of the sister of leftist leader Kamal Jumblatt. Those responsible for the murder have yet to be brought to justice.

Meloy had previously experienced international terrorism while ambassador to the Dominican Republic in March 1970 when he negotiated for three days for the release of Lieutenant Colonel Donald J. Crowley (see incident 0349). 2754

June 19, 1976—Italy—A Milan supermarket jointly owned by Dutch and West German citizens was firebombed. 2755

June 21, 1976—Argentina—Leftist terrorists killed Osvaldo Trinidad, industrial relations manager for the Swift meat packing firm, with bursts of machine-gun fire as he left his La Plata home for work. 2756

June 22, 1976—United States—A homemade incendiary bomb was discovered and disarmed aboard a small aircraft at the Lubbock,Texas, airport.

June 23, 1976—United States—Bomb threats were received at several licensed nuclear facilities, including the Susquehanna Units 1 and 2 of the Pennsylvania Power and Light Company in Berwick.

June 23, 1976—United States—Two Pan Am vehicles parked adjacent to the Pan Am cargo facility at Kennedy Airport were slightly damaged by incendiary devices. No injuries were reported. Several news services received anonymous calls claiming credit for the Dov Gruner Strike Unit of the Jewish Armed Resistance. The individual charged that Pan Am serves as the cargo agents for Aeroflot and warned Americans to stay away from Soviet buildings and to stop trading with them.

June 24, 1976—United States—Two Molotov cocktails were thrown from a car at the South African embassy at 12:55 A.M., causing no injuries and minor damage. The first bomb hit the second story of the building, and the second landed in a tree and caused a small brushfire. Serious race riots had recently caused several deaths in South Africa, whose prime minister had met with U.S. Secretary of State Henry Kissinger in West Germany the week before. 2757

June 25, 1976—Argentina—A bomb exploded at the Paraguayan consulate in Clorinda, causing extensive damage just across the border from Asunción. 2758

June 25, 1976—United States—A bomb exploded near an escalator on the first floor of the Pan Am Building in Manhattan, causing minimal damage and no injuries. Reuters received an anonymous call from a spokesman for Save Our Israel, who said that Pan Am flies to Syria and Iraq.

June 26, 1976—Argentina—Two U.S. missionaries were kidnapped in Corrientes by the Political Military Organization of Paraguay and taken over the border to Paraguay. They were released on June 30 after police raided the terrorists' hideout. 2759

June 27, 1976—Israel—A suitcase bomb was disarmed at Ben Gurion Airport in Tel Aviv. The luggage belonged to a passenger scheduled to leave on an Air France flight for the Far East. 2760

June 27, 1976—Lebanon—A Middle East Airlines B707 that had arrived from Amman was hit by four rockets, presumably fired by right-wing Christians, and burned to the frame. Five people were injured, including, according to some reports, an American engineer. The pilot, Zuheir Maqati, thirty-nine, a Lebanese, was killed. Beirut international airport was closed after the shelling. 2761

June 27, 1976—Greece—Air France flight 139, an A300 Aerospatiale Airbus carrying 257 people, including twelve crew members, from Tel Aviv to Paris, was hijacked out of Athens by seven members of the PFLP. The Athens authorities reported that the plane had left on schedule at 12:25 P.M. Fifty-six persons had boarded there, including fourteen French, ten Greeks, nine Americans, three Canadians, five New Zealanders, two Britons, a Jordanian, a Lebanese, a Cypriot, and a Japanese. The plane first landed in Benghazi, Libya, for refueling. While on the ground, the terrorists allowed Patricia Suzan, thirty, a British citizen, to deplane. She had been hemorrhaging. Upon leaving Libya, the plane attempted to land in Sudan, but the government refused. It flew on to Entebbe Airport in Uganda. During the initial seizure, the West German leader of the hijackers announced over the loudspeaker: "This is the Che Guevara Brigade of the Popular Front of the Liberation of Palestine. I am your new commandant. This plane is renamed *Haifa*. You are our prisoners." The passengers, including M. Cojot, who acted as liaison with the hijackers, reported that the terrorists attempted to keep their identities secret, referring to each other only by numbers. Upon landing at Entebbe, where the hijackers were provided with additional weapons by the Ugandans, who also guarded the hostages while the terrorists left to freshen up, three additional terrorists joined the original seven.

The demands of the terrorists were initially unclear, because they were written in Arabic and had to be translated. There was some question as to the identities of several of the fifty-three terrorists imprisoned in Israeli, Swiss, West German, French, and Kenyan jails whose release was demanded. Some reports claimed that the five terrorists mentioned in Kenyan jails had plotted to assassinate Idi Amin, who added their names to the end of the hijackers' list. Others believe that the group had attempted to fire heat-seeking missiles at an El Al plane in January but had been captured and either killed or turned over to the Israelis. The hijackers named Hashi Abdullan, the Somali ambassador to Uganda, as their representative and instructed France to name an envoy for the side of the governments. However, President Amin refused to allow French Ambassador Pierre Renard or a special French envoy to deal with the hijackers directly, claiming that he was negotiating with them. The hijackers set a deadline of noon on July 1 for the release of the prisoners, threatening to destroy the plane and all on board. They demanded that the French release Intos Silvia Masmela, a girlfriend of the Venezuelan terrorist Carlos, and the release from Switzerland of Petra Kraus, the leader of a Baader-Meinhof-type urban terrorist group. West Germany was to release Werner Hoppe, Jan-Carl Raspe, Ingrid Shubert, Raphael Rendat, Inge Viet, and Fried Tufail, most of them Baader-Meinhof members. They claimed Kenya was holding Abdul Hanafi, Sad, Ibrahim Qasim, Hasan, and Sals. The remaining prisoners were held in Israeli jails: Kozo Okamoto (see incident 1056), Dollo, Carlos Musallim Jaru, Abd ar-Rahman Habir, Archbishop Hilarion Capucci (who was held for smuggling guns to the PFLP), Shaykh Muhammad Abu Tahir, Ash-Shaykh Asud, Aha Said, Fatim Brinawi, Shukran Shukran, Abd al'Adhim, Ativa Bamor, Hasan Kamal Nicholas, William Nasir, Abd ar'Rahman Qasim, Mahmud Abd an'Nasir, Hafidh Abd al'Aziz, Ahmad Hammun Hamad, Mahmed Al'Afif, Abd al'Latif Qadi, Taha Abd a 'Jabbar, Yabu Qasiz, Mahmud Ja'Far Qawwash, Izzat Bin Rashid, Ahmad Hamid Jabir, Fatim Badir Jabir, Yusuf Sulayman Najah, Kamal Numayr, Azim Musa Ogiedo, Mamud Herman, Samir Darwish, Jabir Amah, Hafidh Qasim, Hasan Ilyan, Habib Ekwi, Tall al'Yasin, Umar Abduh, Abd ar'Rahman Qasim, Dawud Khalfan, and Jabir Shita. According to Kampala radio, the terrorists demanded that Air France "bring all these freedom fighters to Entebbe International Airport, to be exchanged with the hostages and the aircraft. Air France to transport the freedom fighters held in Israel to Entebbe International Airport and it should only carry the freedom fighters and the crew. They should inform the Uganda government of the date and time of the arrival and the flight number, well in advance. Those freedom fighters from countries other than Israel should be transported to Entebbe International Airport through those countries' own means. . . .The PFLP supports the struggles of the peoples of Zimbabwe, Azania, South-West Africa and Djibouti."

None of the governments gave in to the demands. The Israelis initially suggested that the plane of Idi Amin, who at one point flew to Mauritius for a meeting of the Organization for African Unity, be hijacked and Amin held prisoner. Others suggested that relatives of PFLP members in Israel be held and killed if any passengers were injured. Still others suggested that Moshe Dayan fly to Entebbe to negotiate personally with Amin, who had many of his troops trained by the Israelis before he had broken diplomatic relations with them. All of these suggestions were rejected. On June 30, the hijackers released forty-seven elderly women, sick persons, and children and allowed an Air France 707 to fly them to Nairobi, Kenya. Ugandan officials said that among those released were thirty-three French nationals, three Moroccans, two Greeks, two Americans, two Dutch nationals, a Canadian, a Cypriot, a Paraguayan, a Venezuelan, and a stateless person.

The next day, the Israeli cabinet announced that it was willing to negotiate for the release of some of the prisoners in return for the hostages. This decision followed a demonstration by fifty relatives of the Israeli hostages, who stormed the office of Prime Minister Yitzhak Rabin. A delegation of three of them were allowed to speak to him. The hijackers extended their ransom

deadline to July 4. On July 1, the terrorists released one hundred more
hostages. It was learned from this group that a selection had taken place; the
non-Jewish hostages were separated from the Israelis or persons of dual
nationality. The crew of the Air France plane decided to stay with the Israeli
hostages, who were threatened with death by 0700 EDT. After intervention by
France, Yasir Arafat sent a senior Fatah member to Kampala to attempt to
secure the release of the rest of the hostages. The terrorists refused to meet with
him, but allowed Amin to speak to the hostages once more. Israeli Lieutenant
Colonel Baruch Bar-Lev telephoned Amin several times, pleading with him to
take action to release the hostages but was unsuccessful. On July 2, the
terrorists increased their demands, adding $5 million in compensation for the
return of the Air France plane. The Israelis also learned from the tapped
telephone of Wadi Haddad (the PFLP's planner of terrorist operations) in
Mogadishu, Somalia, that he had ordered the deaths of the Jewish hostages
regardless of the response of the Israelis. At this point, planning for Operation
Thunderbolt, a daring rescue of the hostages, began in earnest.

The plan called for flying several C130 Hercules transport planes twenty-
five hundred miles to Entebbe from Tel Aviv, secure the release of the
hostages, and return. The Israelis claimed that no other nations were involved
in the rescue operation, although many reports held that the Kenyans allowed
the planes to refuel in Nairobi, and it was noted that the Israelis were allowed to
treat the wounded there with a thirty-three-doctor medical team. Other reports
suggested that fifty Israeli agents had arrived in Kenya a few days before the
midnight July 4 raid to arrange details. It was noted that the hijacking was
named "Remember the Kenyan Treachery," making many believe that Kenya
had cooperated with the Israelis in the arrest of the five PFLP members in
January. Western governments claimed that they had not been informed of the
Israeli plans, although reporters wrote that the former Israeli ambassador to
France, Asher Ben Nathan, was flown to Paris to discuss a suggested joint
mission with French Interior Minister Michel Poniatowsky. However, plans
for this suggestion were abandoned.

Because of superior intelligence, which many believed was derived from
questioning the released hostages, overhead photography, and Israeli agents
on the scene in Entebbe, the Israeli mission was a success. The operation was
commanded by Brigadier General Dan Shomron, thirty, head of the paratroopers and infantry: the attack force was led by Lieutenant Colonel Jonathan
Netanyahu, thirty, a U.S.-born officer shot in the back by Uganda gunfire
during the assault. Before the raid, two practice sessions were held: one for the
pilots of the four planes involved and another for the ground forces.

Flying low to avoid hostile radar, the planes landed at a deserted section of
the airfield. A black Mercedes led the first group of commandos, who raced to
the airport lounge where the hostages were being held. Some reports claimed
that a burly Israeli was made up to look like Amin and confuse the Ugandan
soldiers. A second group set off bombs in another section of the field, creating

a diversion. They later destroyed 11 MIGs of the Ugandan air force so that their planes would not be attacked while returning to Israel. A third group secured the airfield entrance gate, holding off a squad of Ugandan soldiers. In the gun battle, the terrorists were taken by surprise and did not have a chance to shoot any of the hostages before they all were killed. A few hostages were killed or wounded when they stood up in the cross-fire. The operation lasted fifty-three minutes, and all of the planes successfully returned to Israel, with a stopover in Nairobi.

Reports conflict regarding casualties. Israeli authorities believed seven of the terrorists were killed and three who were not present at the airfield escaped (although other reports alleged that the trio were captured by the Israelis and returned to Israel). Eleven other Israelis, civilian and military, were wounded. The Israelis believed that about twenty Ugandan soldiers were killed, saying that Amin's claim of one hundred deaths was an exaggeration. Amin later claimed that twenty soldiers died, thirteen were seriously wounded, and nineteen others were hospitalized. Among the dead hostages were Jean-Jacques Maimoni, nineteen, and Ida Borowicz, fifty-six. Later reports indicated that forty-two persons were injured and forty-five Ugandans were killed. Several governments condemned the Israeli action in press statements and during a U.N. debate, while others, including the U.S., congratulated the Israelis. Amin telephoned the Israelis later in July to add his own congratulations, to request weapons and military spare parts, and to announce that he had broken relations with the Palestinian terrorists. Amin was ignored by the Israelis, although it was reported that Libya delivered twenty French-built Mirage jet fighters to replace the destroyed MIGs.

Amin was reported to have engaged in a wide-scale purge of individuals connected with the guarding of Entebbe airport, with some claims of 245 killed by Amin's troops as punishment. Among those killed was Dora Bloch, seventy-five, an Israeli-British citizen who was left behind in a Ugandan hospital where she had been taken after choking on some meat at the airport lounge. Israeli officials attempted to obtain her release through the use of third parties, but it has been reported by a number of sources that two to four men dragged her from the hospital and strangled her. Some reports claimed that her burned body was found in a field in Uganda after being taken from Kampala's Mulago Hospital. Although a British official had visited Bloch the day after the raid, Ugandan Radio claimed that she had been returned to the airport and was among those freed in the Israeli attack.

The identity of the terrorists is still disputed. Most reports agreed that the initial leader of the group was Wilfred Boese, twenty-six, an associate of Venezuelan terrorist Carlos. One of the terrorists who joined the group at Entebbe was Antonio Degas Bouvier, an Ecuadorian associate of Carlos. The identity of the woman, whom the hostages claimed had acted "like a Nazi" and mistreated all of them, was subject to much speculation. Many claimed that she was Gabriella Teidman Kreiger, aka Gabrielle Kroecher-Tiedemann, who had taken part in the OPEC raid of December 1975 (see incident 2527). Others suggested that she was Turkish-born Barin Acturk, who was arrested in Paris in 1973 for gun smuggling, where she was released after six months and flown to Baghdad. Still others offered the name of Eleanore Honel-Hausman, the widow of "Hugo Muller," who died on May 25, 1976, when his suitcase exploded in Tel Aviv's airport (see incident 2721). The identity of the Palestinians was also difficult to ascertain. The PFLP claimed that one of them was a founder of their group, Al Haj Jayez Jaber, who had also founded the terrorist group Heroes of the Return, which had merged with other groups to form the PFLP. Uganda claimed that the dead were Haji Fayez Jaber, Abdel Razzark Sammarraie, Jayel Arjam, Aboh Khaled Khalayli, and Aboh Ali. The two Europeans were given Arabic pseudonyms, Mahmoud and Halima, saying that the woman was a member of the German Revolutionary party. French counterespionage said that Boese had used the alias Claudius Axel. Others were identified by them as Jail el-Arja, thirty-nine, in charge of South American activities for the PFLP; Faiz Jaber, forty-four, a member of the PFLP's military branch in charge of guerrilla operations; Abd al'Latif Abd al'Razaq, forty-three, an Iraqi friend of Haddad. Reports by investigative reporters Christopher Dobson and Ronald Payne listed Jayel Naji el Arja as second in command of the PFLP's Department of Foreign Relations. They also mentioned that an Abu Ali (Arabic slang for one who is boastful) had contacted the Japanese Red Army in Japan and suggested that the dead terrorist may have been this person. It was learned that the terrorists had flown on Singapore Airlines to Athens from Kuwait and had taken their weapons on board the plane because they stayed in the Athens transit lounge, where they were not subjected to searches. Several suits were filed by hostages against Air France and Air Singapore for these security breaches. The Air France plane was eventually returned by Amin, who had demanded several million dollars in compensation for the attack, which had greatly buoyed the spirits of Israelis and aided the domestic popularity of the government. 2762

June 28, 1976—West Germany—Marko Krpan, twenty-four, fired four shots at the Yugoslav vice-consul in Düsseldorf, Vladimir Topic, as he was entering his office building at 7:00 A.M. None of the revolver shots hit Topic, who escaped into the garage. The attacker jumped into a car driven by Pavle Perovic, twenty-three. Both were arrested later. 2763

June 30, 1976—Argentina—Enrique Rodriguez-Larreta, Sr., a Uruguayan, asked the government in an open letter the whereabouts of his son, who had been jailed in Uruguay on charges linking him to the Tupamaros.

July 1976—Barbados—An early morning bomb blast ripped apart the offices of British West Indian Airways. 2764

July 1976—Brazil—A German-born Roman Catholic missionary was killed in northern Mato Grosso when seventy squatters invaded an Indian reservation whose lands the priest was trying to protect. 2765

July 1, 1976—United States—A bomb threat was received at the licensed nuclear facility of the Joseph M. Farley Nuclear Power Plant installation of the Alabama Power Company in Dothan.

July 1, 1976—United States—The Lucio Cabanes Unit of the New World Liberation Front claimed credit for a bomb that exploded behind the residence of the South African consul in San Francisco, causing extensive damage but no injury to the consul or his family, who were in the house at the time. The group said they were in sympathy with the black man on death row in a Louisiana state prison and called for the release of a California prisoner. They also were protesting the recent deaths of over one thousand blacks in South Africa. 2766

July 1, 1976—United States—During the Entebbe hijacking negotiation period, the Ugandan embassy in Washington received two threatening phone calls, and the *Washington Post* received a call that said the embassy was to be firebombed. 2767-2769

July 2, 1976—Argentina—The Montoneros claimed credit for a bomb that went off at noon in the dining room of the federal police security department in Buenos Aires, killing eighteen and wounding sixty-six. In what appeared to be AAA retaliations the next day, the bodies of three murdered Roman Catholic nuns were found in quarters attached to the Pompeya Church south of Buenos Aires. The bullet-riddled bodies of three Irish-born priests and two Argentine seminarians were discovered at San Patricio Church in western Buenos Aires by an altar boy. A message on the church's walls accused them of being Montoneros. Grenades were found beside their bodies. 2770

July 2, 1976—United States—An Eastern Air Lines Electra II Lockheed prop jet valued at $500,000 was destroyed when an explosive that had been placed between the strut and landing gear detonated at 1 A.M. at Boston's Logan International Airport. One person was injured. A courthouse built in 1805 sustained $100,000 damage in another Boston blast. A National Guard truck was destroyed in a third Boston bombing. A man claiming to be Dennis Callahan of the South Boston Defense League, an antibusing group, claimed credit. On July 15, grand juries in Boston and Portland, Maine, indicted members of the Sam Melville-Jonathan Jackson Unit, which was responsible for this and other bombings. The individuals were identified as Joseph Aceto, twenty-three; Everett Carlson, thirty-eight; Richard J. Picariello, twenty-eight; and Edward P. Gullion. All were also members of the Fred Hampton Unit of the People's Forces. On October 8, Carlson was sentenced in U.S.

district court to ten years for transporting explosives. Gullion and Picariello were also wanted for an attempted kidnapping of Polaroid Corporation President William J. McCune on August 12, 1976, outside a company plant in Waltham, Massachusetts.

July 2, 1976—Kuwait—The Syrian Airline Offices was destroyed by firebombs, which caused no injuries. The bombing occurred the day after Palestinian organizations and resistance groups met in Kuwait to send a cable to Yasir Arafat urging him to retaliate for the Phalangist and Syrian "atrocities" at Lebanese refugee camps. Police arrested a Palestinian with a Syrian passport who confessed to the bombing and was sentenced on August 9 by the Kuwait Criminal Court to two years imprisonment with labor, followed by deportation from Kuwait. 2771

July 3, 1976—Brazil—A group of sixty squatters ambushed American Amazon ranchers John Weaver Davis, fifty-eight, and his two sons, John Mallory Davis, thirty-three, and Bruce Davis, twenty-nine, shooting them to death. Although the Davises held title to the property, there was some dispute as to the boundaries of their land. Some reports indicated that they had tried several methods to prevent the squatters from taking over the property, including blocking access roads to their shacks, fencing off a lake, hitting the peasants, and setting fire to their huts. Twenty-three suspects were taken into custody. 2772

July 3, 1976—Ireland—The Ulster Volunteer Force planted bombs that exploded in famous hotels frequented by tourists: the Gresham in Dublin, the Great Southern in Killarney and Rossiare, and the Royal George Hotel in Limerick, where one person was seriously injured. 2773-2776

July 3, 1976—United States—The Peace Bottom licensed nuclear facility of the Philadelphia Electric Company received a bomb threat.

July 4, 1976—France—Observers believed that the bombing of an electric power plant was related to protests over the suicide of Ulrike Meinhof in a West German jail (see incident, May 9, 1976).

July 5, 1976—United States—A bomb exploded under the tail section of a Bell helicopter parked at a temporary landing strip in Zortman, Montana, causing extensive damage to the cargo area but no injuries.

July 6, 1976—Libya—A Libyan Arab Airlines B727 flying eighty-six passengers and twelve crew members from Tripoli to Benghazi was hijacked by Mustafa Hasdlumagid, twenty, who demanded to be flown to Tunis. The airport refused him landing permission after he claimed to be a member of a

Libyan underground movement called Vigilant Youth opposed to Qaddafi's regime. The pilot next tried to land at Algiers airport, but he was unable because the runway was blocked. The plane landed twenty miles south at Boufarik air base but stayed only ten minutes. It is not known if the plane refueled there. It flew on to Palma de Majorca, where the hijacker surrendered, ending the early-morning episode. He was found to be carrying two toy pistols and two knives, which he turned over to the chief of the airport. He was sentenced in Majorca on July 1, 1977, to six years in prison. 5494

July 9, 1976—Jamaica—A Cuban flight on the ground at Norman Manley International Airport, loading for a flight to Havana, was delayed. During the delay a bomb exploded in a piece of luggage that was to be loaded onto the plane, destroying the cart and the luggage, but causing no injuries. The Cuban Revolutionary Organization in Miami claimed responsibility. It was learned on October 16, 1976, that an individual held for the bombing of a Cubana plane off Barbados in October 1976 was on the Cubana airliner damaged at Kingston (see incident 2913). He was identified as Hernan Ricardo and was detained in Trinidad. Barbados requested his extradition. 2777

July 9, 1976—Lebanon—Three French embassy guards were kidnapped and released unharmed the next day after the intervention of Raymond Edde, a Christian who ran unsuccessfully for president with Moslem-leftist backing in May 1976. He pledged that a relative of the Moslem kidnappers would be freed by the Christians. 2778

July 10, 1976—Barbados—The three-story office building in Bridgetown housing the British West Indian Airways offices was damaged extensively by a bomb explosion. The Coordination of United Revolutionary Organizations (CORU), a confederation of anti-Castro Cuban exiles, claimed credit, saying that BWIA is the Cubana Airlines agent in Barbados. 2779

July 10, 1976—Syria—Syrian radio charged that Iraqis were responsible for the morning bomb death in Damascus of Ahmed al-Azzawi, an Iraqi who defected to Syria eighteen months previously and who had been a leader of the Arab Baath Socialist Party. 2880

July 10, 1976—France—A bomb caused damage but no injuries at the Paris headquarters of an Israeli organization. 2781

July 12, 1976—United States—The first of six incendiary devices planted by the FALN in New York City went off at 12:40 P.M. at Macy's on Thirty-fourth Street. Other devices caused fires at Ohrbachs on Thirty-fourth Street, Altman's and Lord and Taylor's on Fifth Avenue, and Korvettes on Thirty-fourth Street. A device at Gimbels on Thirty-third Street did not go off. The devices were placed inside cigarette packs, using a chemical mixture with a flashlight bulb and a wristwatch battery. No injuries were reported, and there was little damage. The *New York Post* received a telephone call from a man who directed him to a communiqué in a telephone booth at Park Avenue and Seventy-third Street: "Today July 12, the armed commando unit Andres Figueroa Cordero detonated 12 incendiary bombs in the Herald Square area near Madison Square Garden in Manhattan. This is in protest of the presence of 22 colonial leeches attending the national convention of one of the ruling parties of the United States." The Puerto Rican delegation was attending the Democratic National Convention. Cordero was being held for shooting members of the U.S. House of Representatives in 1954. 2782-2787

July 13, 1976—Argentina—Seventeen Uruguayan and three Chilean refugees were kidnapped in the early morning in Buenos Aires by men identifying themselves as plainclothes Argentine police. Two days later, the Chileans were released after being beaten. Among the Uruguayans abducted was two-week-old Antonio Riquelo and Enrique Rodriquez Larreta, fifty-three, a relative by marriage of a former Uruguayan legislator who had been kidnapped on May 18. Others kidnapped included the surviving daughter and son-in-law of former Senator Zelmar Michelini, who was murdered: Margarita and Raul Altuna, both twenty-six. On July 16, fifteen Chilean refugees staged a sit-in at the Canadian embassy, demanding to be flown to safety in Canada. 2788

July 14, 1976—France—The Avengers, a group of World War II Resistance fighters, claimed credit for burning the home of ex-Waffen S.S. Colonel Joachim Peiper, sixty-one, who was killed in the blaze. Peiper had been condemned to death for ordering the execution of seventy-one U.S. prisoners of war during the Battle of the Bulge. The death sentence was commuted to life imprisonment, but he was released in 1957. Police found a revolver and his shotgun near Peiper's body. His home was littered with cartridges and the remains of firebombs. It was reported that the Avengers intended to kill other ex-S.S. men living in France. 2789

July 14, 1976—United States—A bomb threat was received at the Northern States Power Company's licensed nuclear facility in Minneapolis.

July 16, 1976—United States—The Beaver Valley licensed nuclear facility of the Duquesne Light Company in Shippingport, Pennsylvania, received a bomb threat.

July 16, 1976—Puerto Rico—An Eastern Airlines plane flying 149 persons from San Juan to Chicago was the scene of an attack by a lone male against a boy in the lavatory. He was brought under control, but while being removed from the plane he seized a gun and shot a policeman. The offender was sent for a mental examination.

July 16, 1976—Mexico—A Drug Enforcement Administration official was injured in Tijuana when a gunfight broke out in his hotel, where a heroin transaction was believed to be taking place. One Mexican man was reported to have died in the battle; five were wounded. Members of the Twenty-third of September Communist League reportedly had been trading marijuana for stolen U.S. M-16 rifles. 2790

July 17, 1976—Colombia—Anti-Castro exiles claimed credit for the bombing of an Air Panama office in Bogotá, which caused heavy damage but no injuries. The bomb was set off in a car that once belonged to the Chilean embassy and still carried a diplomatic license plate. The group said it was protesting the renewal of flights to Cuba. A demolition squad disarmed another bomb at the offices of the Colombian subsidiary of Burroughs, the computer company. 2791-2792

July 18, 1976—United States—The Zion Units 1 and 2 licensed nuclear facility of the Commonwealth Edison Company in Illinois reported an automobile intrusion.

July 18, 1976—Israel—Three Arabs were among the eleven injured when a bomb planted inside a can of food exploded on board a Tel Aviv bus, spewing nails and metal fragments when it went off in the luggage rack. It was believed that the Arabs had planned to plant the bomb in the bus station but that the device went off prematurely. 2793

July 18, 1976—Colombia—Two Americans were killed by Spanish-speaking men who boarded the *Feisty*, a fifty-four-foot sloop, anchored ten miles off the Colombian coast. Two survivors were picked up by the tanker *Esso Lincoln*, where they were questioned by the FBI and Coast Guard, who learned that the four were from Miami. A spokesman for the Coast Guard said, "It could be considered a case of piracy because it happened aboard the high seas."

July 18, 1976—Thailand—A bomb exploded in a crowd of students at a welcoming celebration for freshmen at a Khon Kaen school in the northeast, killing eight and wounding eighty-two.

July 19, 1976—Argentina—The leader of the ERP, Mario R. Santucho, thirty-nine, and his chief lieutenant, Enrique Goriarran Merlo, were killed in a gun battle with police at Villa Martelli, a suburb five miles from Buenos Aires. Eight others were reported killed in the clash, among them two policemen, including Captain Juan Carlos Leonetti, who led the attack on the apartment. A military official said the break in the case came on July 10 during a raid of a guerrilla hideout in which ERP kidnap victim Air Force Vice-Commander Roberto Echegoyen was killled. Two clandestine printing shops and a central office of the ERP were located soon after, where a list of names and addresses of the group's members was found.

July 20, 1976—Italy—A bomb exploded outside the Rome office of Syrian Airlines, causing considerable damage but no injuries. An anonymous phone call led to a leaflet denouncing Syria, the U.S.-Soviet accords, and the union of Palestinian and Lebanese revolutionary forces. 2794

July 20, 1976—Argentina—Two French Roman Catholic priests, Gabriel Lomvill and Carlos de Dios Muriat, affiliated with the parish church of El Chamical in La Rioja Province, were assassinated after being taken from their parish dining hall for ''questioning'' by men claiming to be policemen. Church authorities believed that they were killed by rightists and rejected allegations that they had any connection with subversive elements. 2795

July 20, 1976—Spain—A bomb wrecked the door of the Netherlands embassy in Madrid. 2796

July 21, 1976—Portugal—A bomb destroyed a large section of DETA, the Mozambican airlines, in Lisbon but caused no injuries in a morning attack. 2797

July 21, 1976—Northern Ireland—A bomb smuggled into a heavily guarded British army barracks in Londonderry exploded during the night, killing one soldier and demolishing part of the building.

July 21, 1976—Ireland—The IRA was suspected of detonating a remote-controlled land mine that exploded under the limousine of the new U.K. ambassador, Christopher Ewart-Biggs, fifty-four, and Judith Cook, twenty-seven, his secretary. The blast ripped the car apart, tore a huge crater in the road, and knocked down a nearby granite wall. Police reported that two men carrying rifles were seen running across the field toward a third man pushing an automobile believed to be the getaway car. Two others riding in the car were injured and were identified as Frank Cubbon, the permanent under secretary of state to the Northern Ireland Office in Belfast, and Brian O'Driscoll, the chauffeur. The explosion occurred as the black Jaguar drove over the fifty to one hundred pounds of explosives, 150 yards from the official residence near Dublin, at 9:32 A.M. Ewart-Biggs was going to a meeting with the Irish foreign minister, Garret FitzGerald. The Irish government offered a reward of £20,000 for information leading to the arrest of the killers. The ambassador had been at his post for only twelve days. It was noted that he had been linked to British intelligence. He had supported the Algerian struggle for independence from France and said that he feared retaliation from rightist French militants. Ewart-Biggs had planned to engage in a high-profile diplomatic campaign, although he had taken several security precautions, including varying his route each day and having two security vehicles follow his car. On October 30, 1979, officials of the Immigration and Naturalization Service arrested Michael O'Rourke, twenty-seven, who was being questioned at FBI headquarters in Philadelphia. He was listed as Ireland's Public Enemy Number One after being linked to the Ewart-Biggs case. He was also wanted for questioning in the 1976 murder of a policeman. He blasted out of an Irish prison earlier in 1976. O'Rourke was living in Philadelphia under the name Patrick Mannion and apparently had violated U.S. immigration laws. 2798

July 23, 1976—Portugal—A bomb caused no injuries but extensive damage at the fourth-floor room of the Portuguese-German Democratic Republic Friendship Society in Lisbon. Windows of surrounding houses were shattered. The office is only a few yards from the U.S. embassy. The attack took place shortly before socialist leader Mario Soares was sworn in as prime minister of Portugal's first democratically elected government in half a century. Another bomb exploded at the Portugal-Poland Friendship Association. 2799, 3159

July 23, 1976—Chile—The MIR claimed credit for a parcel bomb mailed to the Argentinian Airlines manager. 3160

July 23, 1976—Italy—The International Ché Guevara Organization claimed credit for a bomb that knocked out several windows and the front door of the Argentine embassy in Rome. There were no injuries. 2800

July 23, 1976—Costa Rica—The Argentine embassy in San José was badly damaged by a bomb thrown by the Roberto Santucho Revolutionary Group. 2801

July 24, 1976—United States—An intrusion attempt was reported at the Prairie Island Units 1 and 2 licensed nuclear facility of the Northern States Power Company in Red Wing, Minnesota.

July 24, 1976—United States—Police on a stakeout in New York captured three Cuban exiles, members of Omega 7, who were attempting to light the fuse of a pipe bomb near the box office of a Manhattan theater where the pro-Castro July 26 Committee's Musical Festival was scheduled. The trio all lived in New Jersey and pleaded guilty to charges of planting the bomb at the Academy of Music. They were sentenced by the New York state supreme court to three years in prison. 2802

July 24, 1976—Mexico—Two Cuban exiles, members of the FLNC, were unsuccessful in an attempt to kidnap the Cuban Consul in Mérida, Daniel Ferrer Fernandez. They mistook Dartagnan Diaz, an official of the Cuban Fisheries Institute who was accompanying him, for the consul and fatally shot him. The killers were imprisoned in Mexico City on August 9, 1976, on charges of plotting to kidnap and murder Ferrer. Bombs had been found in the luggage of Orestes Ruiz Fernandez and Gaspar Eugenio Jimenez Escobedo, both Miami residents. 2803

July 24, 1976—Canada—A caller who used the FLQ slogan ''Nous vaincrons'' warned that a bomb had been planted in a washroom at the Olympic sports stadium in Montreal. A two-man bomb disposal unit found a shoebox containing an alarm clock and some wires but no explosives minutes before the end of a handball game between Japan and Yugoslavia that was attended by 2,242. 2804

July 24, 1976—Colombia—The Pedro Leon Arboleda commando of the EPL (Popular Liberation Army) claimed credit for two bombs that went off in the Chilean and FRG pavilions at the Eleventh Bogotá International Fair. Eight persons were injured and damage was estimated at $700,000 in Operation Tigre de Papel (''Paper Tiger''). A third bomb was found at the police station at the exhibit compound but was deactivated around midnight. 2805-2806

July 25, 1976—Israel—An Arab Druze serving in the Israeli border patrol was killed and three others were wounded when a bomb planted by Arab terrorists exploded in a restaurant in Nablus's Balata refugee camp on the West Bank. 2807

July 25, 1976—France—A bomb exploded at a Paris commercial firm that represents one Swiss and nine West German companies, causing considerable damage but no injuries. The next day a bomb exploded at dawn on the sidewalk outside a Greek travel agency in Paris, shattering windows but injuring no one. It was believed the explosions were to protest the Greek arrest of Rolf Pohle, a German terrorist. 2808-2809

July 26, 1976—Bahrain—The U.S. State Department warned shippers in the Persian Gulf against the possible hijacking of an oil ship in the region.

July 26, 1976—United States—The Farley Nuclear Power Plant of the Alabama Power Company in Houston County received a bomb threat.

July 26, 1976—United States—Stavros Sykopetrides, a New York City hotel cashier, was wrestled to the ground by security guards after lunging at former Turkish Prime Minister Bulent Ecevit with a loaded revolver during a protest demonstration. Ecevit was walking through the lobby of the Waldorf Astoria Hotel when the attack occurred. The Cypriot was indicted for assault and held on $100,000 bail. 2810

July 27, 1976—Colombia—A small device exploded at pavilion 216 of the International Fair-Exposition in Bogotá, occupied by the United States, causing $6,000 damage but no injuries. The blast occurred at 5:45 P.M. inside an air-conditioning unit. 2811

July 28, 1976—United States—The FALN was suspected of placing an incendiary device that was discovered in a pair of pants in the men's clothing department at Korvettes Department Store on Thirty-fourth Street in New York City at 9:30 A.M. 2812

July 29, 1976—Italy—A bomb exploded outside the Rome office of a subsidiary of Hoffman-La Roche, a Swiss chemical firm, causing considerable damage but no injuries. Hoffman owns the chemical factory at Seveso from which a highly toxic chemical had escaped after an explosion in early July, injuring a number of people. 2813

July 30, 1976—Israel—Two French tourists, Naftali Shlichter, and his sister Brouria, were taken to a hospital with leg injuries after one of them kicked a booby-trapped package lying on a Jerusalem sidewalk. Police detained more than one hundred suspects following the evening explosion in the city's Rommema quarter. 2814

August 1976—Ethiopia—Tom Davis, a British agricultural expert, was kidnapped but freed eight weeks later, according to the U.N. Development Bureau in Addis Ababa, on October 25, 1976. 2815

August 1976—United States—A Cuban exile group claimed in a Miami newspaper, "Very soon we will attack airplanes in flight."

August 1976—Belgium—The bodies of Uros Milicevic and Mijobrac Boskovic, two Serbian royalists known as Chetniks, were found in a Brussels house. Milicevic had been a friend of Stefan Markovitch, the bodyguard of Alain Delon, the French actor. Milicevic was the last person to see Markovitch before the latter was mysteriously slain in 1968. 2816

August 1, 1976—South Korea—After he was threatened with death, Larry Rozadilla, a World Boxing Council referee, reversed his decision in a fifteen-round boxing match, declaring the challenger, Yum Dong-Kyun, the winner of the super-bantam weight championship bout. He had initially declared champion Rigoberto Riasco of Panama the winner. However, he claimed he was beaten and dragged back into the ring by thugs associated with the promoters of the fight and forced to issue a statement saying, "I made a mistake in putting down my scores. It was raining and the judges' papers were all wet and I placed the scores in the wrong places. The Korean is the winner." Upon returning safely to Los Angeles, he said, "Because of attempts to inflict bodily harm on me, which included breaking the windows of my car, blocking our exit from the stadium, and a bomb threat in my hotel, I refrained from any statement until my safe return to the United States."

August 3, 1976—United States—The Dresden Units 1, 2, and 3 licensed nuclear facility of the Commonwealth Edison Company in Morris, Illinois, received a bomb threat.

August 4, 1976—El Salvador—Unidentified gunmen attacked the residences of the ambassadors from Spain and Nicaragua in San Salvador in the early morning. Nicaraguan Ambassador Edgar Escobar Fornos had arrived at his San Benito residence from a reception moments before a guard, Luis Alonso Cano Lima, was shot to death by the attackers, who stole his weapon and proceeded to the nearby Spanish residence. The gunmen fled by car after other police opened fire. 2817-2818

August 4, 1976—Philippines—Moslem rebels kidnapped the wife of a wealthy Chinese businessman, holding her in a cage while demanding $28,000 ransom. She was released unharmed on November 17, 1976, without the payment of the ransom. 2819

August 4, 1976—Colombia—A bomb exploded at the Summer Linguistics Institute in Bogotá, injuring five U.S. citizens who had just arrived from Peru. Several other bombs, including one at the Bank of America, exploded in northern Bogotá. 2820-2821

August 5, 1976—Ethiopia—Heavily armed members of the Somali Liberation Front stormed a tourist hotel at Moyale near the Ethiopian-Kenyan border, killing five persons, including a French tourist, Elizabeth Burst, and injuring twenty persons, including two French schoolteachers touring the area. The group ransacked the hotel, fired machine guns, and threw grenades. They kidnapped Alain Galaup, a French teacher, but released him on August 17. 2822

August 6, 1976—Egypt—Mohammed Ali Haitham, a former premier of South Yemen, was slightly wounded and his driver was killed in an assassination attempt in Cairo. 2823

August 6, 1976—Lebanon—The Body of Antoine Saab, a Christian cook who worked in the U.S. embassy's snack bar, was found floating in the Mediterranean. He had been abducted from his Beirut apartment near the embassy the previous week. Previously he had been a cook for rightist leader Camille Chamoun. 2824

August 8, 1976—Egypt—Two time bombs exploded in the afternoon on the fifth floor of a crowded government office complex in Cairo, wounding fourteen persons. The first explosion took place about noon, and the second went off ninety minutes later, injuring several policemen investigating the first blast. General Hassan Abu Basha, the deputy interior minister, announced that police arrested an Egyptian, Omad Abu Abkaiek, who was injured during the first explosion. The twenty-four-year-old Egyptian student confessed that he had received $750 from Libyan authorities as an advance payment and was promised $2,500 more after planting the bombs in Tahrir Square. On October 11, a military court sentenced one man to death and another to twenty-five years at hard labor for the attacks.

August 9, 1976—Lebanon—An explosion in Tyre sank the *Athena*, a Greek Cypriot cargo ship. None of the ship's ten crewmen or thirty passengers was on board. 2825

August 9, 1976—Argentina—An anti-Castro group in Miami claimed to have kidnapped Jesus Cejas and Crecencio Galanena Hernandez after they left the Cuban embassy in the evening to board a bus for the residence of Emilio Aragones, the Cuban ambassador. On August 16, the Associated Press received a letter containing a seven-line message and the red leather Argentine identification cards of the two. The letter claimed that the two had defected. 2826

August 11, 1976—Turkey—Four persons were killed and twenty-six injured when two PFLP terrorists threw grenades and fired submachine guns at a crowd waiting to board El Al flight 582, a B707 bound for Tel Aviv from Istanbul. The attackers were identified as Mahdi Muhammed, twenty-two, and Hussein Muhammed al Rashid, twenty-seven. Both carried forged Kuwaiti passports and claimed that Libya had financed their operation, which was to kill as many Israelis as possible in retaliation for the Entebbe raid. They had flown from Tripoli to Rome in the morning and then boarded an Alitalia flight to Istanbul. Rome airport authorities claimed that the terrorists may have been able to smuggle their weapons through because transit passengers are not searched. It was initially reported that they had carried on a fifteen-minute gun battle with police, who prevented them from hijacking the plane, which was parked one hundred feet away and was undamaged. Other reports claimed that the terrorists took a Turkish policewoman hostage and bargained with authorities, including Istanbul Governor Namik Kemal Senturk, for an hour before surrendering. The Turkish government denied that hostages had been taken. The terrorists were booked on a Pakistani Airlines flight to Baghdad and had joined the El Al passengers in the transit lounge. One of the passengers said that one of the terrorists' suitcases exploded, leading them to begin their attack. They ran up a flight of stairs and threw a grenade into the crowded corridor below. They then pulled guns from their baggage. The dead were identified as Harold W. Rosenthal, twenty-nine, of Philadelphia, a staff aide to U.S. Senator Jacob Javits; Yutako Hirano, a Japanese tour guide, and Solomon Weisbeck and Ernest Elias, both Israelis. Earlier reports that a Spaniard had died were inaccurate. Among the thirty injured were two U.S. citizens: Nona Shearer, forty, who had a bullet wound in the ankle, and Lucille Washburn, fifty-two, who suffered bruises. Rosenthal was en route to a seminar on Middle Eastern problems at the Van Leer Institute in Jerusalem as part of his liaison work for Javits with the Senate Foreign Relations Committee. The El Al later arrived safely in Tel Aviv with eighty-two passengers on board, six of them with shrapnel wounds. The attack set off a wave of indignation in the U.S. Congress, and Javits and Senator Hubert Humphrey scheduled hearings on state support to terrorists for September 1977. On November 16, 1976, a Turkish court sentenced the terrorists to death but commuted the sentences to life imprisonment. 2827

August 12, 1976—United States—The Turkey Point licensed nuclear facility of the Florida Power and Light Company in Florida City received a bomb threat.

August 13, 1976—Israel—Thirteen thousand dollars worth of equipment being used by a U.S. company conducting seismic tests for oil near the town of Jenin was damaged during the night by unknown individuals. The Israeli government was underwriting most of the cost of the research. 2828

August 14, 1976—United States—A car with diplomatic plates belonging to an official of the Indian embassy was destroyed by fire in Washington, D.C. 2829

August 14, 1976—Egypt—A bomb exploded in an Alexandria train, killing eight passengers and wounding sixty-six. On September 6, three Egyptians and a Libyan were arrested. Egyptian officials claimed that they were working for Libyan intelligence, who trained them and ordered the attack. On October 21, an Alexandria military court sentenced two of the Egyptians to death, while acquitting the two others. The train was loaded with workers and peasants bound for Aswan when the bomb exploded at 10:45 A.M. on a luggage shelf. Egyptian President Anwar Sadat claimed that this was part of a Libyan campaign of terror. He accused Libyan President Muammar Qaddafi of planning the Entebbe hijacking: ''Qaddafi paid the money, and the weapons were smuggled to Athens in a Libyan diplomatic pouch and were given to the terrorists by the Libyan embassy.''

August 14, 1976—El Salvador—The police guard at the Nicaraguan ambassador's residence was shot dead. 3156

August 14, 1976—Italy—Seventeen cars with Allied Forces in Italy license plates were firebombed in Sardinia. The autos belonged to U.S. Navy personnel. An incendiary device was thrown at the Naval Support Activity headquarters building on La Maddalena base, causing minor damage on August 15. No injuries were reported in any of the incidents, which were believed to be the work of Sardinian separatists. Police believed the attacks were related to the International Anti-Militarist March. 2831-2848

August 16, 1976—Italy—An aluminum tube filled with gunpowder exploded at the South African embassy in Rome, causing considerable damage but no injuries. A leaflet left in a phone booth was signed by the Proletarian Internationalism. 2849

August 16, 1976—United States—A fire was extinguished in the home of an Indian embassy employee in Montgomery County, Maryland, who had been victimized three days earlier. Although four people were in the home, no injuries were reported. 2850

August 18, 1976—Panama—A bomb placed in a hallway adjacent to Cubana's check-in desk at Belisario Porras International Airport exploded at 11:15 P.M., injuring no one but causing considerable damage. At 11:30 P.M., a second bomb exploded at the downtown office of Cubana, destroying plate glass windows but injuring no one. A local newspaper received an anonymous call from the Anti-Castro Command, saying it was fighting communism in Cuba and its penetration in Latin America. 2851-2852

August 19, 1976—Argentina—Leftist guerrillas assassinated Carlos Bergometti, thirty-eight, the deputy manager of Fiat's Materfer subsidiary, which manufactures railroad equipment. He was shot to death by several armed men as he left his Córdoba home. 2853

August 22, 1976—United States—The North Anna Units 1 and 2 licensed nuclear facility of the Virginia Electric and Power Company in Mineral received a bomb threat.

August 23, 1976—Austria—A homemade firebomb was removed from a staff car parked in front of the U.S. embassy in Vienna. 2854

August 23, 1976—Egypt—An Egyptair B737 flying ninety-six passengers and six crew members from Cairo to Luxor was hijacked by three armed men who demanded to be flown to Benghazi, Libya. The pilot told them he did not have enough fuel and was allowed to land at Luxor. The plane had left Cairo at 7:30 A.M. The hijackers threatened to blow up the plane and its passengers, most of whom were Egyptians, Japanese, and French tourists, unless five persons in jail in Cairo in connection with two assassination attempts were released. In the afternoon, women, children, and elderly passengers were allowed to leave the plane. The attackers continued to demand the release of three Libyans arrested in Cairo in March and charged with plotting to assassinate or kidnap Omar Abdullah Mahayshi, a former member of Libya's Revolutionary Command Council, who was granted asylum in Egypt, along with Salah Issa, director of the local office of the South Yemen airline company, and a Palestinian. Both had been arrested in Cairo in August in connection with an assassination attempt against a former prime minister of South Yemen, Mohammed Aly Haitham (see entry 2823). The prime minister and war minister, Mohammed el-Gamassy, flew to Luxor to take charge of the negotiations. It was reported that troops let the air out of the plane's tires. At 1 P.M., two officers disguised as mechanics were allowed to board the plane to see how the hijackers were armed, where they were, and what they were wearing. This information was used in the planning of a commando attack against the hijackers. Four commandos boarded the plane at 5:05 P.M., armed with screwdrivers and wrenches, and defeated the trio in hand-to-hand combat. The group was led by Ahmed Haim Badrawi, who said that he injured one of the hijackers. A second group of commandos armed with Soviet machine guns rushed aboard, firing eleven shots into the arms and legs of the two hijackers in the front of the plane. The operation lasted ten minutes. Brigadier General Nabil Shukri, recalling Israel's Entebbe raid, said, "If the Israelis can do it, we can do it." The Cairo newspaper *Al Ahram* said that Egypt's negotiating policy should be "never to yield to terrorists' demands at any price. We may lose an innocent person, even a hundred persons, but we will never release a criminal by yielding to his demand." All three hijackers were wounded, and some reports claimed that a steward was shot in the leg. Official sources denied that anyone except the hijackers was wounded. It was later determined that the plane was carrying sixteen Arab and seventy-nine non-Arab passengers, including twenty Frenchmen and four West Germans traveling under the auspices of the Club Méditerranée, and forty-one persons from the Tokyo Rotary Club. The terrorists claimed to be members of the Abdel Nasser Movement, but Reuters' Kuwait office received an anonymous phone call from the Palestine Revolution Movement claiming credit. The PLO denied all responsibility for the attack, as did Libya. The terrorists carried passports from Kuwait and Jordan, as well as a Palestinian travel document. They confessed to having received their directions in Libya, and one of them said they had been promised the equivalent of $250,000 to divert the plane to Libya. On September 18, they were fined and sentenced to hard labor for life but were acquitted on charges of collusion with Libya. The hijackers were identified as two Palestinians and an Egyptian: Ali Hahmed Usman, thirty-five, from Palestine; Mohammed Naguid, twenty-one, a Palestinian working in Kuwait; and Hahmed Suleiman, twenty-one, an Egyptian student. Three alleged accomplices were acquitted. 2855

August 24, 1976—Costa Rica—CORU bombs exploded at the San José offices of Iberia Airlines and Nanaco Shipping, injuring six. Both firms do business with Cuba. 2856-2857

August 25, 1976—United States—The Limerick Units 1 and 2 of the Philadelphia Electric Company in Pottstown, a licensed nuclear facility, received a bomb threat.

August 27, 1976—Argentina—Three people were injured when bombs hidden in flowers and other gift packages exploded. One of the victims was associated with Renault, another with IBM, and a third with Ford. The Montoneros later claimed credit. 2858-2860

August 28, 1976—France—Yvan Tuksor, forty-two, a Yugoslav political refugee, was killed and seven persons were injured in Nice when a bomb planted in Tuksor's car exploded while the car was stopped at a traffic light. Tuksor was the leader of a local Croatian nationalist movement. 2861

August 28, 1976—Vietnam—A former South Vietnamese soldier tried to hijack an Air France Caravelle as it was about to depart Ho Chi Minh City (Saigon) for Bangkok. The hijacker threatened to blow up the plane with his hand grenades but released the twenty passengers and crew unharmed. When police rushed the plane, he set off the grenades, killing himself and damaging the plane. No other injuries were reported. 5495

August 28, 1976—Iran—Three U.S. employees of Rockwell International were assassinated at 7 A.M. as they were being driven to work at an Iranian air force installation, Doshen Tappeh, in southeastern Tehran. The Iranian People's Strugglers (Mujahiddin e Khalq) used a Volkswagen to cut off the trio's Dodge from the front, while a second car cut them off from behind. Four gunmen jumped out, ordered the chauffeur to lie down, and blasted the car with Polish M-63 machine pistols and a Browning 9-mm pistol. The group then fled on foot and in the rear car. Reports claimed that the briefcase of one of the dead men was also stolen. The three had been working on project IBEX, a $1 billion electronic surveillance project for the Iranian military. It was reported that they used a car that never varied its routes or times. Authorities speculated that the killings were in retaliation for the deaths of Iranian guerrilla leader Hamid Ashraf and nineteen other terrorists during the previous week. While the recent crackdown was against the People's Sacrifice Guerrillas (Cheriks), it was believed that the two groups have some contact among their leaders. It was also reported that the IPS received Libyan backing and had been trained by the PFLP. The dead were identified as William C. Cottrell, forty-three, of Los Gatos, California; Robert R. Krongard, forty-four, of Sunnyvale, California; and Donald G. Smith, forty-three, of California. On September 5, 1976, security agents killed the driver of the Volkswagen, Hassan Alad-Push (also known as Hassan Ellaj-Pour), after tracing him through the car's dealer. A pistol used in the assassination was found with him. It was believed that he had used it to administer the coup de grace after his colleagues fired their machine guns. In another police shootout on November 17, 1976, Bahran Aram, the planner of the attack, was killed on a downtown Tehran street. 2862

August 30, 1976—Ireland—Firebombs exploded in two movie theaters and three bars in Dublin, twenty-four hours before the Parliament was scheduled to debate antiterrorist legislation. No one was injured. Police believed that a dozen bombs might have been planted. Damage was put at £1 million. 2863-2867

August 31, 1976—United States—The North Anna Power Station, a VEPCO licensed nuclear facility in Mineral, Virginia, received a bomb threat. Similar threats were received on September 1, 2, and 19.

September 1, 1976—Guatemala—A CORU bomb exploded at the Mexican consulate in Guatemala City, slightly injuring a receptionist and causing some property damage. The attack was reportedly in retaliation for Mexico's failure to release two CORU members who attempted to kidnap the Cuban consul in Mérida. 2868

September 1, 1976—Trinidad and Tobago—A CORU bomb exploded in front of the Guyana consulate general in Port of Spain, injuring three and causing extensive damage. The group said it was retaliating against Guyana's allowing Cuban troops and aircraft to stop in Guyana en route to Angola. The same day, a Guyanese boat anchored off Port of Spain was hit by saboteurs, who smashed the vessel's lifeboat, telecommunications, and other equipment. 2869-2870

September 1, 1976—Argentina—David Kraiselburd, the two-year-old U.S. citizen son of Raul Kraiselburd, an Argentinian newspaper publisher, was kidnapped near Buenos Aires. Five arrested suspects admitted on September 5,

1977, that although they had planned to demand a ransom, they had killed the child because they had no place to hide him. On September 27, 1977, four of the individuals were killed while trying to escape a La Plata prison. 3245

September 2, 1976—France—A bomb exploded in the commercial section of Bayonne near a Basque cultural association bookstore, causing property damage to area stores. The bomb went off a few hours before the opening of the trial of a Spanish Basque nationalist.

September 4, 1976—France—KLM flight 366, a DC9 flying from Malaga, Spain, to Amsterdam, was hijacked out of Nice by three armed hijackers. The plane was carrying seventy-eight passengers, including two Americans, and a crew of five. Most of the passengers were Dutch tourists. The hijackers had passed through a routine weapons search before boarding. The plane landed in Tunis and Cyprus for refueling. It circled off Israel's shore while the trio threatened to blow up the plane if the Israelis did not release eight prisoners, including Archbishop Hilarion Capucci and Kozo Okamoto (see incident 1056). Israel closed off Ben Gurion Airport and ignored the hijackers' demands. A deadline passed without incident. The Netherlands ambassador to Israel, Christian Arriens, talked the Israelis out of shooting down the DC9, which returned to Larnaca Airport in Cyprus. A PLO official and George Tombazos, a Cypriot minister, talked the trio into surrendering. The hijackers claimed they were members of a Libyan-based PFLP unit. The PLO and PFLP-GC said they had nothing to do with the incident. It was later determined that the passengers included five French, two Moroccans, two Indonesians, a West German, a Belgian, two Finns, and three Arabs. Passengers claimed that the attackers were armed with guns and hand grenades but did not ill treat them. Airline officials refused to fly the trio out of Athens, on their way to Baghdad, unless they were heavily guarded. Two of the group were identified as Hamdane Benhelel, thirty-one, an Algerian, and Mohamed Rustin, twenty-six, from Syria. It is believed they were given asylum in an undisclosed country. 2871

September 7, 1976—Corsica—Seven masked gunmen, members of the Corsican Nationalist Liberation Front, forced the pilot of an Air France B707 to taxi to the edge of Ajaccio airport. After ordering 181 people in the area to move back, they set off dynamite charges. Fifty people detained immediately after the attack were released, but another thirty were held for questioning.

September 7, 1976—Yugoslavia—Venezuelan-born PFLP terrorist Carlos (also known as Ilyich Ramirez Sanchez), twenty-nine, flew to Belgrade from Algiers for a few days' stay before flying on to Iraq. It was reported that he was traveling with five accomplices, two of them West Germans, including Hans-

Joachim Klein. Carlos is sought in twelve countries, and Western intelligence and diplomatic sources complained that the Yugoslavs did not arrest him.

September 8, 1976—Colombia—Argentine leftists were believed to have thrown Molotov cocktails at the Argentine consulate in Medellín, causing significant damage but no injuries. The attack may have been related to Chilean Solidarity Week. 2872

September 9, 1976—Argentina—The Montoneros assassinated an Argentine executive of the Chrysler factory in Buenos Aires in front of his home. One hundred twenty-one workers accused by Chrysler and Ford of promoting work stoppages and slowdowns had recently been fired. 2873

September 9, 1976—Austria—Fire in a Vienna office building caused minor damage to the entrance of the Chilean embassy. Police believed the arsonists were radical youths marking the anniversary of the overthrow of Allende. 2874

September 10, 1976—Italy—The six-year-old daughter of the Panamanian ambassador was kidnapped in Rome but found by police five hours later. Police held for questioning three women: a Panamanian, an Ecuadorian, and a Guatemalan. 2875

September 10, 1976—India—An Indian Airlines B737 flying from New Delhi to Bombay with eighty-four passengers and seven crew members was hijacked by six armed men who claimed to be Libyans wanting to fly to the Moslem holy city of Mecca, Saudi Arabia, to take part in the Haj pilgrimage. The passengers included thirty foreigners, among them thirteen West Germans, one Briton, and Gregory Spinner, twenty-five, a U.S. student who had recently graduated from Georgetown Law Center. The plane landed in Lahore, Pakistan. The hijackers allowed seven passengers, (three Indians, a Dutchman, and a West German couple with their child) to leave for health reasons. Later in the day, the leader, a bearded man apparently from the Indian subcontinent who spoke English, Urdu, Punjabi, and Bengali, left the plane with the rest of the seventy-seven passengers. He was arrested by Pakistan authorities. After more than nine hours on the ground, one of the hijackers told authorities that they would keep the plane and the passengers until the following morning, when they would issue further demands. However, police managed to drug the water that was brought on board the plane, and they entered the B737 and freed the seven crew while the remaining five hijackers slept. Initial reports claiming that the Pakistanis had conducted an armed commando raid on the plane proved to be exaggerated. On January 6, 1977, Pakistan released the six hijackers, citing lack of evidence to bring them to trial. 5496

September 10, 1976—United States—TWA flight 355, a B727 flying from New York to Chicago with eighty-six passengers and seven crew members, was hijacked by six Croatian nationalists at 8:19 P.M. Their leader handed a note to the flight steward, Thomas Van Dorn, shortly after the jet left La Guardia Airport. He in turn relayed the message to the pilot, Captain Richard Carey. The note read: "1. This airplane is hijacked. 2. We are in possession of 5 gelignite bombs, 4 of which are set in cast iron pens, giving them the same kind of force as a giant grenade. 3. In addition, we have left the same type of bomb in a locker across from the Commodore Hotel on 42nd Street. To find the locker, take the subway entrance by the Bowery Savings Bank. After passing through the token booth, there are 3 windows belonging to the bank. To the left of these windows are the lockers. The number of the locker is 5713. 4. Further instructions are contained in a letter inside this locker. The bomb can only be activated by pressing the switch to which it is attached; but caution is suggested. 5. The appropriate authorities should be notified from the plane immediately. 6. This plane will ultimately be heading in the direction of London, England." The hijackers were identified as Zvonko Busic, thirty, a Yugoslavian-born New Yorker; his U.S.-born wife, Julienne Eden Busic, twenty-seven; and three other Yugoslavian-born U.S. citizens, Petar Matavick, thirty-one, Frane Pesut, twenty-five, and Mark Vlasic, twenty-nine. They claimed to be members of the Croatian National Liberation Forces and the Fighters for a Free Croatia.

The New York City police bomb squad found a bomb and the hijackers' list of demands at Grand Central Station in Manhattan later that night. Two communiqúes from the group were to be published in five newspapers, or a second bomb would go off. The bomb squad took the bomb to a fifteen-foot-deep detonation pit in a police firing range in the Bronx. Although they waited two minutes for the bomb to go off, it exploded only when the group approached the pit. Officer Brian J. Murray, twenty-seven, was killed by the blast, which may have been caused by a time-delay booby trap. The officers had used a remote-control device to detonate a small explosive charge attached to the bomb, designed to break the external wires of the device. The officers had just begun to lift a protective wire mesh blanket from the bomb when there was a "bright flash and metallic bang, and the blanket went flying up in the air." Three officers were injured, including Henry Dworkin, Sergeant Terence McTigue, forty-one, and Deputy Inspector Fritz Behr, forty-three, commander of the New York Police Department scientific research division. The explosion gave immediate credibility to the hijackers' claim of having explosives on board the plane and elsewhere.

The *Los Angeles Times, Washington Post, New York Times*, and *Chicago Tribune* agreed to publish the hijackers' manifestos on their front pages. The hijackers had also demanded that the English-language *International Herald Tribune* in Paris print their communiqúes, but the incident ended before the *Tribune* needed to comply. The FAA aided TWA in arranging to drop the terrorists' leaflets over London, Paris, and Chicago, and the FBI was reported to have played a role in meeting the terrorists' demands for publicity. The U.S. State Department claimed that it had not gone against its publicly stated policy of not capitulating to terrorist demands.

The hijacked plane flew to Gander, Newfoundland, where it landed at 1 A.M. The group allowed thirty-five passengers to deplane while the plane refueled and was joined by a TWA B707, which was used to guide the 727 pilot to Europe. At 6:57 A.M., the 727 landed at Keflavik Air Base in Iceland, where the plane was refueled. Suitcases containing the leaflets were transferred from the 727 to the 707, which also landed. At 9:15 A.M., both planes took off for London, where the 707 dropped propaganda leaflets over the city. At 10 A.M., more propaganda leaflets, given by the hijackers to the freed thirty-five passengers, were dropped from a helicopter over Montreal. At 12:30, the 707 dropped leaflets over Paris, before landing with the 727 at Charles de Gaulle Airport at 1 P.M. (6 P.M. Paris time). There were reports that the hijackers had planned to fly to Belgrade, Yugoslavia. Upon landing in France, the group demanded to speak to President Ford, Secretary of State Kissinger, or U.S. Ambassador Kenneth Rush. Rush agreed to speak to the hijackers. He was met by the woman hijacker, a Norwegian passenger, and copilot Lou Senatore in the airport's control tower. During the negotiations, the passengers were twice forced to huddle in the plane's aisles while the hijackers informed them that they were going to die. A bishop aboard gave them last rites. French Interior Minister Michel Poniatowski was firm with the hijackers, saying that they could choose to surrender and be flown to Yugoslavia, be flown to the United States, or be killed if the passengers were injured or killed. The plane was blocked by vehicles so it could not take off, and one of its tires was punctured by police riflemen. The United States later protested the initial approach of the French. After tense negotiations, the group agreed to surrender peacefully. The remaining hijackers showed the passengers that the bombs were false. Three sticks of what looked liked dynamite were in a suitcase, and two cooking pots heavily taped with wires protruding and extending to a battery and electrical switch did not contain explosives. The devices contained what appeared to be putty tubes. One of the hijackers had placed some of the material around his chest and had threatened to set it off. The hijackers broke off sticks of the material and gave it to the passengers as souvenirs. Because the hijackers had entered France illegally, formal extradition procedures were waived and they were immediately returned to the United States.

After several jurisdictional battles between U.S. courts, the federal appeals court ruled on January 27, 1977, that the trial would take place in Brooklyn rather than Buffalo, New York. The U.S. court of appeals reversed a lower court ruling and restored two air piracy counts that had been dismissed by a U.S. district court on a motion by the hijackers, who were accused of kidnapping, air piracy, and second-degree murder. On May 12, 1977, a New York supreme court justice sentenced Mark Vlasic to a minimum of six, maximum thirty, years' imprisonment after he had pleaded guilty to a reduced charge of attempted kidnapping. On May 5, the other four hijackers had been convicted of air piracy and conspiracy. Busic and his wife were sentenced to life imprisonment. U.S. district court judge John R. Bartels said Busic could be paroled after ten years and his wife after eight. The other two received terms of thirty years on July 21. 2876

September 11, 1976—Holy See—The Ché Guevara Internationalist Brigade claimed credit for a bomb that exploded outside the Chilean embassy to the Vatican, causing slight property damage and no injuries. 2877

September 11, 1976—Italy—The Ché Guevara Internationalist Brigade set off bombs during the night outside the Rome offices of the USIS and the Brazilian airline Varig, causing slight property damage and no injuries. 2878-2879

September 11. 1976—Italy—Three youths on motorcycles threw 3 firebombs against the Saudi embassy during the evening, causing slight damage to the building and two cars parked on the street. Molotov cocktails were also thrown at the Rome offices of Honeywell International, the door of a building housing an Israel-connected travel agency, and the car of a U.S. Navy enlisted man. Police suspected that the bombings were in commemoration of the third anniversary of the overthrow of Allende. 2880-2883

September 12, 1976—Mexico—One person was killed and fifty-three were injured when a time bomb went off at the grave of a student leader slain in 1975 in Guadalajara. Two hundred fifty people were attending the ceremony. The killing was attributed to Marxist guerrillas.

September 13, 1976—Argentina—Patricia Ann Erb, nineteen, the daughter of a U.S. Mennonite missionary, was kidnapped during the evening from her Buenos Aires suburban home by three armed men who tied up her parents at around midnight. Two other children were also blindfolded. Other reports claimed that six armed right-wingers were involved. Patricia, of Jackson, Minnesota, had reputedly been involved in leftist politics. She was released on September 28 and claimed to have been held by police agents in what appeared to be a military prison. She turned up unharmed in a police station and was given a police escort on October 5 to the international airport, where she boarded a plane for Miami.

September 14, 1976—United States—A National Airlines flight to Miami with fifty-four passengers and six crew members returned to JFK International Airport at 3:45 P.M., seven minutes after takeoff, after a bomb warning was received. No bomb was found aboard the B727.

September 14, 1976—Argentina—The neo-Nazi Argentine National Socialist Front sent a communiqúe to the Buenos Aires news media, in which it threatened to kill the Vatican's diplomatic envoy, a former Argentine military president, and five other persons. 2884

September 15, 1976—Japan—An aged couple on an aerial sightseeing trip stabbed the pilot and a cameraman in a four-seat plane while flying south of Tokyo and then jumped into the sea. The wounded pilot made an emergency landing at Tokyo International Airport with the wounded cameraman. Patrol boats searched for the bodies of the couple.

September 15, 1976—Argentina—Montoneros fired submachine guns and threw three hand grenades against the Buenos Aires home of an Argentine Ford executive. No one was injured. 2885

September 16, 1976—United States—The Roman Catholic Church of St. Cyril and Methodius and St. Raphael at 502 West Forty-first Street in New York City was bombed. No one was injured in the nighttime explosion. The church was attended by Zvonko Busic, the leader of the Croatian hijackers of a TWA plane on September 10 (see incident 2876). During the incident, while the plane was parked in Paris, Mrs. Busic telephoned the Reverend Martin Cuvalo, the church pastor, to determine if the hijackers' manifesto had been published by the newspapers.

September 16, 1976—United States—A bomb attached to the hull of the Soviet container ship *Ivan Shepyetkov* exploded, causing minor damage but no injuries. United Press International and CBS received a call from a man claiming to belong to Omega-7, who said that a frogman attached the bomb to the bottom of the 530-foot ship, which was docked in Port Newark in Elizabeth, New Jersey. 2886

September 17, 1976—Ireland—A drunken man with a gun boarded an Aer Lingus B707 by the rear entry while the plane was parked on the apron at Shannon International Airport. The crew, which was loading cargo, was evacuated. The individual appeared at the top of the plane's steps and was talked down. He surrendered. No injuries were reported. 5497

September 19, 1976—United States—CORU published in Miami a detailed description of the attempt to kidnap the Cuban consul in Mérida, as well as a plan to dynamite the Cuban embassy in Mexico City.

September 20, 1976—United States—The Lucio Cabanas Unit of the New World Liberation Front bombed the Pacific Heights residence of the South African consul general in San Francisco, Anthony Drake. Although he and his family were in the residence, there were no injuries. However, the bomb knocked down and twisted an iron gate and sent pieces of metal from it across the street. The windows of homes across the street were shattered, and a car parked by the door was badly damaged by the 12:45 A.M. blast. The group condemned the racist policies of South Africa. 2887

September 20, 1976—Argentina—A fire caused $10,000 damage to the central electrical system of the new U.S. chancery building in Buenos Aires. Inspecting officials believed the fire was intentionally set and found cardboard jammed into the utility shaft where the fire started. 2888

September 20, 1976—Argentina—John G. Little, the Argentine executive of Schering Pharmaceutical Company, a subsidiary of a German-owned business, was assassinated on a street corner. 2889

September 20, 1976—Argentina—Several Montoneros in a truck fired on the Chrysler Febre-Argentina administrative office outside Buenos Aires. 2890

September 21, 1976—United States—The FALN set off a bomb equal to seven sticks of dynamite in a passageway between the twenty-third and twenty-fourth floors of the New York Hilton Hotel at 8 P.M. The blast injured no one but damaged the cement landing of the stairwell, burst a three-inch water pipe, cracked plaster, and shattered a window. Puerto Rican Govenor Rafael Hernandez-Colon was being honored twenty-one stories below. Two hundred demonstrators surrounded the hotel when the bomb went off. A female phoned the *New York Post* to claim credit, and a note was found taped to the base of a public telephone at the corner of Fifty-third Street and Third Avenue. The woman claimed that there was a bomb in another hotel, but a search was negative at the Statler Hilton. Earlier, Mayor Abraham Beame had attended the banquet, as had the Democratic candidate for the U.S. Senate, Daniel Patrick Moynihan. Police searched for two men who were seen in the vicinity before the explosion. Hernandez-Colon, who was scheduled to stay in a room on the hotel's forty-fifth floor, moved to an undisclosed location. 2891

September 21, 1976—United States—A bomb exploded in a Chevrolet sedan being driven on Washington's Embassy Row, killing two persons and wounding two others. The blast occurred at 9:35 A.M. as the car was driving past the Rumanian embassy, tearing a two-foot hole in the area around the driver. The car crashed into a Volkswagen parked in front of the Irish embassy. Among the dead was Orlando Letelier, forty-five, who was the Chilean ambassador to the United States between 1971 and 1973 during Salvador Allende's administration. Killed with him was Ronni Karpen Moffitt, twenty-three, an administrative assistant at the Trans National Institute, a division of the Institute for

Policy Studies. A passenger, Michael Moffitt, Ronni's husband and an institute research associate, was injured. Vassilios Vassiakostas, a Greek embassy employee, was cut on the cheek by a blast fragment. Investigators believed that the bomb, which could have been placed under the car while it was parked in front of Letelier's home that morning, used either an unsophisticated time-delay device or a remote-controlled radio detonator. Letelier had been a critic of the Pinochet regime in Chile, which earlier in the week had revoked his citizenship "for interfering with normal financial support to Chile." It was believed this referred to Letelier's attempts to halt U.S. aid to Chile because of widespread human rights violations. Suspicion for the attack centered on DINA, the Chilean intelligence service, as well as Chilean exiles, or CORU, the Cuban exile group, which accused Letelier of solidifying ties between Cuba and Chile. The leader of CORU, Orlando Bosch, claimed that the brothers Guillermo and Ignacio Novo Sampol had planted the bomb as a favor to the Chilean junta.

On May 11, 1979, a U.S. district court judge sentenced Michael V. Townley, a U.S.-born DINA agent, to serve a minimum of forty months, a reduced sentence, due to plea-bargaining for his testimony against other suspects. Two of three Cubans arrested received two life terms each, of which thirty years must be served. Two other Cuban exiles charged in the murder are still at large.

On October 1, 1979, Chile's supreme court reaffirmed its refusal to extradite or prosecute three former secret police officers named by Townley, claiming that the United States had not presented enough evidence to warrant any other order before a military court. The court declared the case closed, and the trio, held in custody in Santiago since the filing of the U.S. request a year ago, were freed. Townley had testified that he was working for General Juan Manuel Contreras Sepulveda, the former head of Chile's secret police, and Colonel Pedro Espinoza, and that he was aided in the assassination by Captain Armando Fernandez Larios. 2892

September 22, 1976—Italy—A bomb damaged the Rome regional office of Westinghouse at 4 A.M. but caused no injuries. 2893

September 22, 1976—Norway—A Norwegian air force lieutenant attempted to set fire to two U.S. war planes taking part in a NATO exercise and then critically wounded himself in a suicide attempt.

September 23, 1976—Ethiopia—In an unsuccessful assassination attempt, unidentified individuals threw hand grenades and fired machine guns at Major Mengistu Haile Mariam, the first vice-chairman of the ruling Ethiopian military council, and several of his colleagues. Mengistu was slightly wounded in the leg.

September 25, 1976—Italy—During protest marches by fifty thousand people demonstrating against Syria's intervention in Lebanon, the Ghassan Kanafani Commandos set bombs and firebombs at the warehouse of an Israeli-Italian company, three branches of the Bank of America and Italy, inside a suburban office of the Avis car rental company, in the Rome office of the United Hebrew Immigrant Aid Society, and outside a synagogue. The Avis office was extensively damaged. The group's communiqúe said, "Death to Zionism. Death to imperialism." The group later threw three firebombs during the night at a Lebanese Maronite monastery, but the devices failed to explode. 2894-2901

September 26, 1976—Israel—Ludvinna Janssen twenty-three, a blonde Dutch woman, was arrested at Ben Gurion International Airport while carrying a tin can designed to test the efficiency of metal-detecting devices. She was convicted of collaborating with Palestinian guerrillas and sentenced to six years. Her boyfriend, Marius Niewborg, flew on to India, where he was arrested for traveling on a forged passport and sent back to the Netherlands. 2902

September 26, 1976—Syria—Four members of Abu Nidal's Fatah dissident group Black June took over the Semiramis Hotel in Damascus and held ninety hostages. During a seven-hour gun battle with Syrian forces, four of the hostages, including three women, and the terrorists' leader were killed, and thirty-four hostages and an undisclosed number of Syrian troops were wounded. According to reports by the *New York Times*, "The guerrillas arrived at the hotel, a 7-story tan structure overlooking the Baraka River, in a blue Renault with Lebanese license plates at about 5 A.M. and were said to have asked for a room. On being informed by a reception clerk that the hotel was full, one of the intruders shot him in the hand and wounded an unidentified woman bystander. The guerrillas then reportedly ran to the fifth floor, taking hostages with them and in a few minutes the building was surrounded by at least 200 Syrian soldiers, including military policemen and special forces troops. At least 50 members of the special forces entered the hotel." At 9 A.M., the Syrian premier, General Abdul Rahman Khaleifawi, and Defense Minister Mustafa Tlas gave orders to storm the hotel. "Early in the battle the guerrillas shot into the street and the Syrians responded with several fusillades that left the hotel facade pocked with bullet marks. Inside the hotel, the Syrians used machine guns and tear gas as they climbed to the fifth floor. They were met by machinegun fire and rocket-propelled grenades. Fire trucks with telescope ladders were used by other soldiers to climb to the roof of the hotel and to carry down the wounded. By noon the battle was over. During the fighting, there were no reports that the guerrillas made any specific demands in return for the release of the hostages, who included many women and children. But there was an unconfirmed report that they asked to see the Ambassadors of Southern Yemen and Algeria. Whether these officials were notified or were present was not disclosed.'' An American couple, the Flints, was in the hotel but was not taken hostage. Although the U.S. embassy said that none of the hostages were U.S. citizens, the press claimed that Robert Castenbaum, an assistant NBC producer, was among them. The terrorists claimed to have been trained in Iraq. The PLO and Fatah denied responsibility for the attack and said that Nidal had been expelled from the group in 1970. The group said that it had aimed to obtain the release of thirty-three prisoners held by Syria for protesting against Syrian intervention in the Lebanese conflict. The dead terrorist was identified as Zuheir Abou Hashisha, a Palestinian. The superior security court of Syria quickly tried the surviving terrorists, who were hung the next day. They were identified as Jabbar Darnish, an Iraqi, and two Palestinians from Jordan, Mohammed Barqani and Mustasem Jayyoushi. President Hafaz Assad said, ''We shall hit back very hard. We denounced this criminal action committed by a gang that acted as if it were in Israel.'' 2903

September 26, 1976—Corsica—Corsican separatists shot and wounded a French Foreign Legionnaire, claiming that deserters had killed two shepherd brothers. They also bombed the legion commander's villa and an electric utility pylon in Corte.

September 27, 1976—Spain—A Molotov cocktail was thrown through the window of a Serrano store of a U.S. firm, damaging merchandise on display. The sprinkler heads were activated, and the fire was quickly contained. 2904

September 28, 1976—Colombia—U.S. industrialist Gustavo Curtis, fifty-five, the manager of Grancolombia Industries and Jacks Snacks food manu-facturers, a subsidiary of Beatrice Foods, was kidnapped in Bogotá during the evening when his car was rammed. The kidnappers included four men and a woman, who forced him to get out of the car and then fled toward the western part of Bogotá, along the road to the El Dorado Airport. Curtis's chauffeur, Simon Chacon, was tied up and abandoned near the university, with a message demanding 3 million pesos ($170,000) ransom. It was later reported that Curtis was being tried by a guerrilla group solely because he was an American. He was freed unharmed on May 18, 1977. Press reports differed as to whether a ransom of $140,000 was paid. 2905

September 28, 1976—Ecuador—A bomb exploded during the night at the Quito residence of an Argentine embassy counselor, Eugenio Fernando Bracht, who was slightly wounded. The blast also caused some property damage. 2906

September 29, 1976—France—Bombs exploded at the Banque Pastor (a Spanish facility) in central Paris and the Spanish consular office in suburban Saint-Denis, causing extensive property damage but no injuries. The explosions marked the first anniversary of the execution of five Basque terrorists in Spain. 2907-2908

September 30, 1976—Pakistan—Firebombs were thrown at Syrian Arab Airline offices in Rawalpindi and Karachi. The Rawalpindi office was not seriously damaged, but serious damage was reported at the Karachi office, where a police officer was badly burned. Rumors indicated that PLO supporters were responsible; others suggested that unknown individuals were protesting Syrian actions against Palestinians in Lebanon. 2909-2910

October 1, 1976—West Germany—A Molotov cocktail thrown through the window of the Syrian Arab Airlines office in Munich caused minor damage. 2911

October 1, 1976—Greece—Rolf Pohl, a Baader-Meinhof Group member, was extradited to Munich to complete his six-and-a-half-year sentence, which was interrupted when he was freed during the Lorenz kidnapping of February 27, 1975 (see incident 2246).

October 2, 1976—Barbados—A Venezuelan journalist reported that a bomb had been fastened under the wing of a Cuban plane but did not explode because it had fallen down as the plane taxied down the runway. The security official who found the bomb apparently did not report the case. 2912

October 2, 1976—Argentina—Five minutes after Argentine chief of state General Jorge R. Videla, fifty-one, left a reviewing stand at Campo do Mayo, a bomb exploded, injuring three military personnel. The bomb was packed in metal tubing supporting the reviewing stand. The last speaker, General Eduardo Catan, had described the victories of the army over the country's terrorists and summed up by saying, ''It could be that the guerrillas might still produce some notorious acts.''

October 3, 1976—United States—The Zion Unit 1 licensed nuclear facility of the Commonwealth Edison Company in Illinois reported an intrusion.

October 6, 1976—United States—The North Anna Power Station, a licensed nuclear facility of VEPCO in Mineral, Virginia, received a bomb threat. This was followed by two more threats that day, one on the seventh, one each on the thirteenth and fourteenth, three on the fifteenth, and one on November 3.

October 6, 1976—Barbados—At 2:30 P.M., a bomb exploded on board Cubana Airlines flight 455, a DC8 flying to Jamaica and Cuba with stops at Georgetown, Guyana, and Port of Spain, Trinidad. The plane had just left Bridgetown when the pilot reported an explosion on board and said that he would try to return. The plane crashed into the ocean, killing all seventy-three on board. Among them were fifty-eight Cubans, twenty-five of them Cubana employees, including the crew and sixteen members of Cuba's championship fencing team, eleven Guyanese, five North Koreans, two Trinidadians, and one person each from Colombia and Venezuela. An anti-Castro Cuban exile group, El Condor, claimed credit, as did CORU. On October 8, police in Port of Spain reported detaining for questioning two Venezuelans who left the plane in Barbados and returned to Trinidad the same night. On October 18, Hernan Ricardo Losano, who was carrying Venezuelan identity papers, claimed to have placed the bomb on board the plane. He was accompanied by Freddy Lugo. On October 14, Venezuelan authorities arrested Losano's employer, Luis Posada Carriles, CORU leader Orlando Bosch, forty-nine, and three other Venezuelans, identified as Oleg Gueton Rodriguez, Celsa Toledo, and Francisco Nunez. Bosch had entered the country on a false Costa Rican passport with a tourist visa and also carried a false Nicaraguan set of documents. The U.S. government had tried to extradite him. Bosch had been sentenced to four years in prison for carrying out illegal activities, including firing a bazooka at a Polish ship in 1968, but had violated his parole and fled to Venezuela on a false passport. It was later learned that Posada was a Cuban who was formerly head of the Venezuelan secret police, DISIP. Losano was an employee of the Caracas detective agency run by Posado. On October 22, Losano attempted suicide by slashing his wrist. He and Lugo had told police that they were photographers and had traveled to Trinidad to purchase cameras and equipment. There was evidence that they had contacts with Eric Searly, a Barbados political activist and boxing promoter. On October 25, it was learned that an FBI legal attaché in Caracas, Joe Leo, had had contact with Posada and Ricardo during his tour. It was also claimed that some of those arrested had received training by the CIA. Trinidad said it would expel the duo. On November 2, a Venezuelan judge indicted Bosch, Posada, Ricardo, and Lugo on qualified murder charges, which carry a maximum penalty of thirty years. Five others were released without charges. The evidence as to culpability was sketchy. It was reported that a British search team that found the sunken plane determined that the explosive used was C-4. Ricardo's girl friend took a call from him in Trinidad and relayed the message, "Tell Posada the truck has left with a full load," to Posada's secretary. Venezuelan security police said that they had uncovered CORU plans for terrorist attacks by Cuban exiles in the United States, Venezuela, Trinidad, Barbados, Guyana, Panama, and Colombia. It was also claimed that shortly after the explosion, a caller from Barbados telephoned the office of a private investigating company in Caracas, "The bus is full of dogs." 2913

October 7, 1976—India—An Air India 747 bound for Kuwait returned to New Delhi after receiving a bomb threat. 2914

October 7, 1976—Argentina—Bombs exploded during the night in Buenos Aires at the showrooms of foreign auto firms, including Ford, as well as a branch of the Bank of Boston, causing moderate property damage and no injuries. 2915-2917

October 7, 1976—Venezuela—Unidentified persons in a dark station wagon fired eight bullets at the Cuban embassy in Caracas at 11:15 P.M. No one was injured. 2918

October 8, 1976—Lebanon—Ali Hassan Salamah, believed to be the Black September planner of the Munich Olympics attack (see incident 1116), was critically wounded when he was shot in the stomach as he walked along a Beirut street. The Israeli secret service was believed responsible. 2919

October 9, 1976—Colombia—Anonymous telephone calls stated that the Pedro Leon Arboleda Urban Commando of the Maoist Popular Liberation Army (EPL) had tried and sentenced to death Spain's King Juan Carlos and Queen Sofia, who were due to visit the country. A state of siege had been decreed earlier by the government. 2920

October 10, 1976—Taiwan—The governor of Taiwan, Hsich Tung Min, sixty-nine, was injured in his Taipei home when a letter bomb exploded as he was opening it at 2 P.M. Reports indicated that his left hand had to be amputated. There were no indications of who was responsible.

October 10, 1976—Argentina—Domingo Lozano, forty-one, the Argentine manager of the French-owned Renault auto company, was shot and killed by gunmen who approached him while he was leaving a Córdoba church. Before fleeing, the attackers fired more shots into his body as his wife and six children looked on. 2921

October 11, 1976—Pakistan—Three Palestinians threw a hand grenade at the residence of the Syrian ambassador, Mohammad Bahir Dreii, in Islamabad. The bomb did not cause any damage to the building, but it bounced back and exploded, killing one of the attackers. The surviving pair, armed with pistols, attempted to attack the nearby Syrian embassy but were wounded and captured in the ensuing gun battle with police, three of whom were injured. On December 14, 1976, the Pakistani government released the two, allowing them to continue their studies in Lahore. The PLO denied any connection with the attack, and the PFLP was silent. 2922

October 11, 1976—Italy—Three members of Black June attacked the Syrian embassy in Rome, taking hostage three men and two women. They released one hostage who was seriously wounded in the leg during the initial assault, Hunen Hatem, an embassy counselor, who underwent surgery. The group then freed another hostage with the demand that they meet with the ambassadors of Algeria, Libya, and Yemen. However, two hours after the attack, they surrendered. Police said that the attackers, all in their twenties, were armed with three submachine guns, six grenades, and a pistol. Their leader, Nabil Hasnen, a twenty-five-year-old Palestinian, claimed that they had come directly from Lebanon and decided to surrender when they realized that they had not taken hostage the ambassador, Farouk al-Sharae, who was attending a ceremony elsewhere. According to Youssef Miro, one of the embassy employees who was taken hostage, the terrorists "came in, leveled their guns at us and said they wanted to revenge the massacre in Lebanon . . .to draw the attention of the world to the betrayal of the Syrian Government . . .We did not want to harm anyone. This action marks a new stage in the struggle of the Palestinian people." Miro said that five people escaped through the windows in the attack, which was quickly followed by police sharpshooters surrounding the building. The attackers were immediately jailed and charged with attempted murder. On November 6, 1976, a Rome court sentenced them to fifteen years in jail, to be followed by three years of supervised freedom. At their trial, the defendants identified themselves as Nabil Hasnen, twenty-five, of Lebanon; Jaad Mohammed, twenty, of Syria; and Ahmed Hossein, twenty-two, a Palestinian. The Syrians requested extradition. 2923

October 11, 1976—Argentina—Reverend Patrick Rice, an Irish priest who was a member of the Little Brothers of Charles de Foucauld, a French Roman Catholic association dedicated to working with the poor, was kidnapped by unidentified gunmen as he was saying mass in the Villa Soldati slum district of Buenos Aires. He was later found to be under arrest at the federal police security department.

October 13, 1976—Portugal—Bombs exploded at two luxury Lisbon hotels shortly before midnight, causing slight damage and no injuries. One bomb exploded near an office block close to the Sheraton's entrance; the other was on a Ritz porch. 2924-2925

October 14, 1976—Greece—In what it claimed was retaliation for the extradition of West German terrorist Rolf Pohle, the ELA firebombed the Athens office of the West German Siemens Corporation during the night, causing some damage. 2926

October 15, 1976—Cuba—In the aftermath of the bombing of the Cubana plane in Barbados that resulted in the death of seventy-three people, Cuban Premier Fidel Castro announced cancellation of the February 1973 antihijacking memorandum of agreement with the United States. The note had a six-month clause in it, effectively negating the treaty as of April 15, 1977. Castro accused the CIA of being behind the anti-Castro Cuban exile attempts and suggested that the agency was contemplating another assassination attempt against him. He claimed that he had intercepted a CIA message to one of its agents that said, ''Please report as soon as possible any information dealing with Fidel's attendance at the ceremony on the first anniversary of the independence of Angola on Nov. 11. If affirmative, try to find out complete itinerary of Fidel's visits to other countries during the same trip. . . . What is the official and private reaction to bomb attacks against Cuban offices abroad? What are they going to do to avoid and prevent them? Who is suspected as responsible? Will there be retaliations?''

October 16, 1976—Turkey—A cleaning woman found a bomb on top of an air conditioner of the Pan Am office in Izmir. 2927

October 17, 1976—Argentina—The Montoneros claimed credit for a bomb that exploded in a Buenos Aires military social club and injured fifty persons. Another bomb exploded at a naval arsenal, killing a seaman and injuring three others.

October 18, 1976—Argentina—Five gunmen riding in a car assassinated Enrique Aroza Garay, the Argentine executive of the German-owned Borgward automobile factory, as he was leaving his home in Ciudadela, a Buenos Aires suburb. 2928

October 19, 1976—Argentina—An American who threw a hand grenade at police who were surrounding a house where suspicious activity had been reported was shot to death by security forces. She was identified as a suspected leftist, Chris Ana Olson de Oliva, thirty, of Berkeley, California, daughter of a vice-president of Kaiser Industries. Her father, Carl Olson, had lived and worked in Córdoba in the 1950s. 2929

October 20, 1976—Argentina—The Montoneros kidnapped Bruno Quijano in Buenos Aires and demanded a ransom of $16 million. The victim was justice minister in President Alejandro Lanusse's administration from 1971 to 1973 and labor minister for President Arturo Frondizi from 1958 to 1962.

October 21, 1976—Venezuela—Thirty persons, most of them Dominicans, were arrested in a plot to kidnap the Dominican ambassador to Venezuela, Pedro Padilla Tonos. Reports indicated that he was to be held for the release of several prisoners whom the government described as common criminals, including Dr. Plinio Matos Moquete, who was jailed in Vias Vina on charges of robberies and other criminal actions. The kidnappers were to also have demanded a large sum of money and facilities from the Venezuelan government to leave the country. 2930

October 21, 1976—Trinidad and Tobago—El Condor threatened to bomb a West Indies Airways plane if Lugo and Ricardo, two suspects in the bombing of a Cubana plane in Barbados earlier in the month (see incident 2913), were not released. 2931

October 22, 1976—Ireland—President Cearbhall O'Dalaigh, sixty-five, resigned after a cabinet minister called him a "thundering disgrace" for what was termed procrastination regarding bills designed to curb the IRA. O'Dalaigh had asked the supreme court to rule on the constitutionality of the government's new antiterrorist measures before signing them into law.

October 24, 1976—United States—Save Our Israel Land firebombed the Tunisian U.N. mission, causing minor damage and no injuries. 2932

October 25, 1976—Puerto Rico—Aldo Vera Serafin, a Cuban exile who was involved with the Fourth Republic, which had ties to Orlando Bosch, the leader of CORU, was assassinated when two shots were fired at him during the night as he walked along a suburban San Juan street. Another prominent exile, José Rodriguez Gomez, was wounded. Vera, fifty-three, was named head of the technical investigations department, the main intelligence organ of the Cuban police, when Fidel Castro came to power in 1959. Vera fled Cuba in the early 1960s, however, after a split with Castro. 2933

October 27, 1976—Colombia—Two youths firebombed a car belonging to the U.S. military group commander while it was parked unattended on a Bogotá street. There were no injuries but minor damage. A British embassy car was also firebombed, presumably by students. 2934-2935

October 27, 1976—Spain—A man and a woman threw two bombs at the Moroccan embassy in Madrid and then fired submachine guns as they fled in a car. Two embassy employees were injured, one severely, and a passerby and a Spanish policeman were slightly wounded. The ground floor was wrecked, and diplomats' cars parked in front of the building were damaged. Speculation focused on the Polisario Front, although a spokesman in Algiers denied involvement. 2936

October 28, 1976—Iran—Iran returned to the Soviet Union Valentin Zasimov, a Soviet pilot who flew a small plane to Iran on September 23, where he requested political asylum in the United States. He was returned by the Persians under a Soviet-Iranian antihijacking agreement.

October 28, 1976—France—A bomb exploded in the garden behind the Interpol headquarters in a suburb of Saint Cloud near Paris, shattering every window in the building but causing no injuries. A caller to *France-Soir* said he was from a group of "Spanish ex-prisoners" (other reports said "Spain deportees") who were protesting because "of the support it [Interpol] gives the Spanish government in the repression of opponents of the regime." The Paris office of a West German firm was also bombed. Three days earlier, prior to the visit of Spanish King Juan Carlos, three factories, two of which import materials from Spain, were bombed, with five people slightly injured. Two banks, one of them Spanish, were also bombed. 2937-2939

October 28, 1976—Czechoslovakia—Flight OK 313, an Ilyushin 18 on a local flight from Prague to Bratislava with 105 passengers and 6 crew members, was hijacked on the ground by Rudolf Becvar, twenty-six, who was armed with a submachine gun, a pistol, a knife, and one hundred rounds of ammunition. He forced the pilot to fly him to Munich, where he surrendered to Bavarian authorities. The plane was returned with the passengers the following morning. Becvar was taken to Stadelheim Prison and was formally charged with "an attack against air traffic" on October 30. Becvar, who was born on November 19, 1950, had apparently sneaked onto the tarmac at the airport through a door reserved for airport personnel. The only casualty of the flight was an elderly male passenger who suffered a mild heart attack. Unconfirmed reports indicated that the passengers included several members of the Czech Communist party's Central Committee. The Czechs requested the return of the hijacker, claiming that he was sought for the murder of his brother, Stefan, and of an accomplice after the recent armed robbery of a taxi driver. The West Germans have no extradition treaty with the Czechs. However, it was pointed out that the West Germans were pressing for the passage of a U.N. convention on the taking of hostages and their response would have some effect upon its chances of passage. 5498

October 28, 1976—Northern Ireland—The Ulster Freedom Fighters claimed credit for the assassination of Maire Drumm, fifty-six, who had resigned a few weeks earlier as the vice-president of Sinn Fein, the political arm of the Provisional IRA. Gunmen disguised as doctors burst into her Mater Hospital room in Belfast during the night as she was recovering from treatment for a cataract and nervous exhaustion. Twenty thousand people marched at her funeral, including members of Cumman na Mban, the woman's IRA, and a children's brigade of the IRA, at Milltown Cemetery.

November 1, 1976—United States—Three people were arrested for threatening to pour a thousand gallons of home heating oil into Philadelphia's water supply unless $1 million was paid. The city complied with their instructions but received no signal to hand over the money. Those arrested included Louis Scott, twenty-five, an apprentice pipefitter at the Philadelphia naval base; David R. Nugent, thirty-five, a pipefitter from Pennsauken, New Jersey; and Kevin Grosso of Glenolden, New Jersey.

November 2, 1976—France—Homayour Keykavoussi, a counselor with the Iranian embassy, was shot four times in the chest and stomach at 7 P.M while on his way home in the residential seventeenth district of northern Paris. An off-duty policeman who tried to stop the attack was wounded in the thigh by a second gunman. The attackers escaped in the evening rush hour traffic on a bright orange motorcycle. The Reza Rezai International Brigades claimed credit for attacking Keykavoussi as he returned home from work, saying that he was a SAVAK agent. Ten Iranian students were detained for questioning. On January 12, 1977, a French court ordered the release of a student accused of the assassination attempt. Although Keykavoussi had identified the student as one of his attackers, the court ruled that newspaper photographs may have influenced the diplomat's recognition. 2940

November 3, 1976—Argentina—Two leftist gunmen shot to death Carlos Souto, an Argentine executive of Chrysler, as he left his Buenos Aires home for work. 2941

November 3, 1976—United States—Two bomb threats were received at the Waterford Steam Electric Station Units No. 3, a licensed nuclear facility of the Louisiana Power and Light Company in Taft.

November 4, 1976—Denmark—A Polish TU134 flying from Copenhagen to Warsaw with twenty-nine passengers and seven crew members was hijacked over Polish territory by Andrzej Jaroslaw Karasinski, twenty, who forced the pilot at 1:55 P.M.to fly to Vienna's Schwechat Airport. Austrian police armed with machine guns surrounded the plane, but the hijacker immediately surrendered. It was discovered that his weapons, initially believed to be a hand grenade and pistol, were actually partly chewed rye bread colored with shoe polish. He handed a note to the stewardess threatening to blow up the plane if his demand was not met. He was being deported to Poland after serving a four-month term in Denmark for burglary, theft, and forgery. Poland requested his extradition. Although the two countries have no extradition treaty, officials checked pre-World War II agreements to see if any of them applied in the case. On February 15, 1977, Karasinski was sentenced to four years by Judge Kurt Wachsmann, who said that the hijacker would not be expelled from Austria provided that no other criminal acts committed by him were brought to the court's attention. 5499

November 6, 1976—Turkey—Followers of the late Mahir Cayan, a Turkish terrorist killed in 1972, claimed credit for the bombings at the Istanbul offices of El Al, Dutch, and Iranian business firms and the Egyptian consulate. One person was injured in the night explosions. 2942-2945

November 7, 1976—Spain—The Madrid Cubana offices were bombed, causing heavy damage but no injuries. The Puerto Rican offices of the Associated Press received a phone call from the International, Secret and Revolutionary United Cells, an anti-Castro exile group, claiming responsibility. 2946

November 9, 1976—Costa Rica—The FSLN claimed credit for the bombing in San José of the Nicaraguan and Guatemalan consulates, which caused some damage and no injuries. Bombs were also found at the El Salvadorean consulate, as well as the residence of the Honduran ambassador. 2947-2950

November 13, 1976—Greece—Bombs destroyed vehicles in Athens belonging to a U.S. Air Force sergeant and the Syrian and Portuguese embassies. Two other bombs were found in the air force's exchange annex and in a vehicle. 2951-2955

November 14, 1976—Argentina—Unidentified attackers in a passing car bombed and machine-gunned the Buenos Aires residence of the Chilean embassy's press attaché, badly damaging the front of the building but injuring no one. 2956

November 17, 1976—Jordan—Four members of Black June armed with guns and hand grenades attacked the Intercontinental Hotel in Jordan and conducted a four-hour gun battle with King Hussein's helicopter-borne troops, leaving seven dead and five wounded. Three of the guerrillas, who had been trained for the raid in Iraq, were killed, and the fourth was seriously wounded. He was hanged in Amman on December 18. The group was protesting the Arab cease-fire in Lebanon, and at one point, one of the terrorists asked a hotel guest to transmit a demand that Jordan denounce the formation of an Arab peacekeeping force for Lebanon. Two hotel employees and two soldiers were reported killed, and a Dutch tourist was grazed in the temple by a bullet.

According to news dispatches reported in the *Washington Post*, "Witnesses said the four terrorists entered the Intercontinental, directly across the street from the U.S. embassy, about 9:50 A.M. They took Soviet-made submachine guns out of suitcases and started spraying bullets around the busy lobby, killing a hotel receptionist. All 300 rooms of the Intercontinental, a main meeting place of Jordanian as well as foreign political and business figures, were occupied when the attackers struck. Guests and visitors in the lobby screamed with fright when the attackers opened fire. Some threw themselves on the floor and others smashed windows with chairs and leaped onto a terrace one floor below. Police from a nearby substation arrived almost immediately and Jordanian army commandos arrived minutes later, encircling the hotel. Army helicopters dropped commandos...on the roof of the seven-story building. One guerrilla rushed to the roof and opened fire, killing a Jordanian officer, and then was shot dead himself. Three autos parked near the hotel were destroyed in the fierce gunfire, which continued for nearly four hours before troops moving from above and below trapped the Palestinians in the hotel's fourth floor. Then, a government spokesman said, Hussein personally ordered a final attack on the terrorists. . . .Guests at the hotel included a West German parliamentary delegation, several foreign diplomats and a number of journalists. The wounded guests included an American of Jordanian extraction, Fouad Kandalaft." 2957

November 17, 1976—Soviet Union—A bomb threat was made against the USA—200 Years Bicentennial exhibit in Moscow, delaying the showing for half a day. 2958

November 18, 1976—United States—A handwritten note was found in the rear galley of flight 150 of Eastern Airlines, a B727 flying seventy-four passengers and seven crew members from La Guardia Airport in New York to Montreal. The note claimed that a bomb was on board and demanded that the plane be diverted to Cuba. The plane landed at Montreal's Mirabel Airport, and the passengers disembarked. The threat was a hoax. 5500

November 19, 1976—Botswana—Bombs concealed in suitcases exploded in the Francistown headquarters of the Joshua Nkomo faction of the Zimbabwe African National Council, killing a child, injuring four other people, and causing serious damage. Police followed two vehicles to the Rhodesian border from the scene of the incident. 2959

November 26, 1976—United Kingdom—Three IRA men were convicted in Southampton of conspiracy to violate the Explosive Substance Act. The prosecution contended that the group intended to bomb the liner *Queen Elizabeth II*.

November 27, 1976—Sweden—Fifty pounds of explosives were found near the Ringhals nuclear plant during the evening. A newspaper received an anonymous phone call warning, "We have planted explosives near the Ringhals nuclear plant. This is our last warning. Next time the plant will be leveled to the ground."

November 29, 1976—Australia—A Melbourne radio station received a letter from the Group of Six warning that nuclear bombs would be detonated in Sydney and Melbourne unless the government announced an end to uranium mining and export by December 10.

November 30, 1976—West Germany—After a ten-month search, police arrested lawyer Siegfried Haag, who was accused of bombing three U.S. military installations in the previous four years.

November 30, 1976—Mexico—The Twenty-third of September Communist League was believed responsible for four bombs that exploded in Mexico City on the eve of the inauguration of President-elect José Lopez Portillo. A number of commercial buildings were damaged, including the Johnson and Johnson laboratory. The Poor People's Army claimed credit. 2960

December 1, 1976—Syria—Members of Black June shot and seriously wounded Syrian Foreign Minister and Deputy Premier Abdul Halim Khaddam while he was driving with his wife in a Damascus suburb. One shot struck him in the right shoulder, and another hit his left hand. He said he was saved from death when a headrest stopped one of the bullets. In a statement issued in Madrid, Black June said that they would "liquidate Syrian leaders" because of Syrian intervention in the Lebanese war. Khaddam claimed that there were two attackers armed with submachine guns who were riding on motorcycles. Syrian security officers claimed that the attackers were three Syrians and arrested one, whom they said was an army deserter. The PLO said that they had sentenced Abu Nidal, the Black June leader, to death. 2961

December 1, 1976—West Germany—The Revolutionary Cells claimed credit for the noontime firebombing of the U.S. Air Force officers' club at the Rhein-Main air base that injured eighteen, including nine Americans. The blast, which caused a fire requiring four hours to bring under control, caused $1 million damage. The most serious injury was a broken leg suffered by a visiting IBM employee. In a letter to the Associated Press, the terrorist group said that the base was a junction for U.S. military bases in Europe, Africa, and Asia and maintained a complete CIA telecommunications facility. The group also accused the U.S. Army of filling subway tunnels with lethal gas and water pipes with poison in experiments. It said the army had constructed a ghost town in West Berlin to train against civilian unrest and claimed that it pumped West Germany full of atomic and hydrogen bombs. It called the United States and West Germany imperialistic. 2962

December 4, 1976—Israel—Three Arab terrorists between ages nineteen and twenty-five were killed when a bomb they were assembling in a room above a Hebron barber shop exploded. 2963

December 5, 1976—Rhodesia—Albert Sumbe Ncube, twenty-six, a black Zimbabwe guerrilla, said during his court hearing in December that he had killed a Roman Catholic bishop and two missionaries, all of whom were West Germans. 2964

December 6, 1976—United States—An explosive device was found in a package in the mailroom of the transition headquarters of President-elect Carter at the Department of Health, Education and Welfare's north building at 3:35 P.M. The building was evacuated while the bomb was dismantled.

December 8, 1976—Soviet Union—An assistant of Soviet official Grigory Kuzmenko informed the director of the USA—200 Years Bicentennial exhibit across from Moscow's Sokolniki Park that they had received a telephoned bomb threat. The building was cleared at 4:30 P.M., forty-five minutes before the showing was scheduled to close for the day. No bomb was found. 2965

December 8, 1976—Mexico—The Mexican plant manager of the U.S.-owned Sylvania Electronics plant in Ciudad Juarez was killed by five members of the Twenty-third of September Communist League as the terrorists were leaving the plant after distributing communist propaganda to arriving workers. Two or three suspects were identified, but press reports conflicted on whether any of them had been arrested. 2966

December 8, 1976—Canary Islands—The Group for Self-Determination and Independence of the Canary Archipelago set fire to a Spanish-owned hotel on Grand Canary Island because the management had replaced sixty-five native employees with Spaniards. No injuries were reported.

December 9, 1976—United States—Antonio G. Polytarides, a Greek citizen who came to the United States two years previously as a tourist, was arrested and charged with illegally attempting to divert a shipment of one hundred machine guns to the Iraqi U.N. mission. The guns were received there on November 12 by Shams Uddin, a U.S. citizen who claimed to be the chauffeur for Al-Shaikhly, the Iraqi U.N. ambassador.

December 10, 1976—Egypt—Thomas Homan, the U.S. cultural attaché in Cairo, received an anonymous letter threatening him with death if he refused to distribute $100,000 to Egypt's poor. 2967

December 10, 1976—United States—The Calvert Cliffs Units 1 and 2 licensed nuclear facility of the Baltimore Gas and Electric Company in Lusby, Maryland, received a bomb threat.

December 10, 1976—United States—An envelope addressed to the Immigration and Naturalization Service exploded on a conveyor belt at the general post office in New York City but caused no injuries. A second unexploded bomb was discovered.

December 11, 1976—Philippines—Gunfire was directed at a bus taking three U.S. servicemen to work sixty miles north of Manila. One seaman was reported wounded. 2968

December 11, 1976—Northern Ireland—Fifty-two persons attending a wedding reception in a Portadown hotel were injured when a bomb exploded in the attic. The town, predominantly Protestant, is located thirty miles southwest of Belfast.

December 11, 1976—Spain—Five members of GRAPO (Antifascist Resistance Group October 1) kidnapped Antonio Maria de Oriol y Urquijo, sixty-three, president of the Council of State, member of the Council of the Realm, and one of Spain's richest men. Oriol was described as the fourth highest-ranking official in Spain. Basque sources initially claimed that the underground would demand a ransom of $15 million and the release of 150 ETA prisoners not covered by the summer amnesty decree of King Juan Carlos. The group had excellent information about Oriol's habits and entered his private office near Madrid's Retiro Park, claiming they were sent by a priest friend of his. The group then pulled out submachine guns and struck an Oriol employee who tried to stop them. Oriol's bodyguards were in a nearby apartment. Oriol's son claimed that some of the kidnappers were ETA members. The group threatened to kill Oriol if 15 prisoners were not released and flown to Algeria. The Spanish government met with the Algerian ambassador to discuss the situation but did not meet the group's demands. The group later changed its demands to the grant of amnesty for nearly 200 political prisoners. The government refused to deal with the group but promised to expand the amnesty after Oriol's release. On January 24, 1977, the group kidnapped Lieutenant General Emilio Villaescusa, sixty-four, president of the Supreme Military Tribunal. On February 11, 1977, the police put into effect Operation Achilles and rescued the two hostages with units supported by helicopters. Police arrested six persons in the two apartments where the hostages were being kept. Among the terrorists was Abelardo Collazo, who was believed to be GRAPO's leader. Another sixteen GRAPO members were arrested elsewhere. The police reported that the group had moved Oriol to a new hideout and that they had followed the car used to transport him. On February 12, it was announced that Spain had rounded up more than thirty suspects in the case. A host of press rumors had built up during the incident, including Oriol's being held in Portugal. 2969

December 13, 1976—Italy—Emanuela Trapani, seventeen, the daughter of the Milan representative of the U.S. firm Helene Curtis, was kidnapped as she was being driven to school. The Italian girl was released unharmed on January 27, 1977, and found in a telephone booth. Kidnapping is a common crime in Italy, and this may be a criminal case rather than one with political overtones.

December 13, 1976—Rhodesia—A lone guerrilla attacked a pilot and his wife as they were boarding their light plane at a bush airstrip in Wankie. She was slightly injured. The terrorist was killed by government troops.

December 13, 1976—Mexico—A Mexican employee at the Mexico City Chrysler plant was shot by members of the Twenty-third of September Communist League when he attempted to prevent them from distributing pamphlets to plant workers. 2970

December 15, 1976—Argentina—A bomb placed by the Norma Arrostito Commando of the Montoneros exploded at a Defense Ministry building in downtown Buenos Aires, killing fifteen and injuring thirty. The bomb was placed on the third floor of the eight-story building, inside a movie theater where an army officer was lecturing to an audience. Arrostito was shot dead on December 3 when thirty security agents raided a guerrilla hideout in Buenos Aires. The government announced that "as the result of a cowardly act," an army colonel, an air force major, two navy lieutenant commanders, and five civilians, including one woman, were killed in the blast.

December 15, 1976—Portugal—A Portuguese airliner chartered to fly Prime Minister Mario Soares to Brazil stopped in the Canary Islands after Lisbon officials received a bomb threat by an anonymous telephone caller. No bomb was found. 2971

December 15, 1976—Iraq—Free Iraq claimed credit for a bomb that exploded inside a suitcase on an Egyptian Airlines jet at Damascus. The plane had just landed at Baghdad international airport when the bomb went off. Some press reports claimed that 40 were killed and 300 injured. Iraqi authorities identified the dead as one Saudi Arabian and 2 Iraqis and claimed that more than 230 were injured. A British businessman, John Heath, was told that 7 persons had died in the blast, which blew glass more than a hundred yards. In Tehran, an Iranian pilgrim said he had counted 14 dead and 26 others being treated for injuries. He believed most of the injured were Egyptian pilgrims. The entire terminal building was gutted by the resulting fire, and the terminal's front end was torn away. Because the plane had arrived half an hour early and the bomb exploded fifteen minutes later, security officials believed that the explosive was meant to harm the passengers. The injured included citizens of Egypt, Iraq, Saudi Arabia, Syria, Lebanon, Japan, West Germany, and Greece. 2972

December 16, 1976—Colombia—A bomb went off in the pocket of a boy walking through the Chapinero store of a U.S. firm at 8:40 P.M. Seventeen additional bombs were found after the store was searched. The boy was held for questioning and charged with the bombing. 2973

December 17, 1976—Austria—After Waltraud Boock, twenty-six, a West German woman believed connected with terrorists, was arrested on December 13 in Vienna on suspicion of bank robbery, an anonymous caller warned of a bomb that exploded in the toilet of the license plate office of the Vienna Rossauer Barracks, a police headquarters. No one was injured, but two people were treated for shock. The caller claimed this was the Waltraud Boock Operation. Another bomb was found and defused in a street close to Vienna police headquarters. Another caller warned of a bomb to be placed at the Leanderbank Main Office in Vienna Am Hof First District.

December 18, 1976—Iraq—Kurdish rebels kidnapped four Polish agricultural experts in the northeast and demanded the release of Kurds imprisoned in Iraq. The group kidnapped two Frenchmen and an Algerian in February 1977. The Kurdistan Democratic party announced in London on March 29, 1977, that all seven hostages had been freed. The group called for world public opinion to stop what it termed the massacre of Kurds by the Iraqi army. 2974

December 19, 1976—West Germany—A fire in the noncommissioned officers' club of a U.S. Army barracks in Bad Hersfeld during the night caused $1,040,000 damage but no injuries. The building was completely burned out.

December 20, 1976—Rhodesia—A South African white tourist was killed when guerrillas fired machine guns at a ferry on Lake Kariba. 2975

December 21, 1976—United States—Palmtree J. Hinnant, Jr., who was born on July 13, 1939, took two hostages at gunpoint and commandeered a United Airlines DC8 at San Francisco international airport. He demanded a flight crew to fly him to the East Coast, fuel, food, brandy, his girl friend, and his luggage. He was granted the fuel, food, and brandy. The hostages were Jerry Dusenbury, a mechanic who took another mechanic's place because he could operate the radio and maintain communications with authorities, and Richard Funk, a shop manager. Hinnant, who was armed with a Luger-type automatic, was reported to have been a United mechanic who had been on sick leave since April 1975 and had been in and out of mental hospitals for thirteen years. Hinnant fired one shot throught the plane's window and slashed Funk, thirty-eight, several times with a knife. He surrendered his guns to two friends early the next day, ending a fourteen and a half hour siege by nearly one hundred FBI agents and sheriff's deputies. The assistant U.S. attorney in San Francisco deferred prosecution to local authorites. Hinnant was arraigned on charges of kidnapping, attempted extortion, and assault. Funk, his supervisor, said, ''I don't think he wanted to go any place. I think maybe he just wanted to get the plane up in the air and have us all crash and be killed.'' 5501

December 23, 1976—Iran—Security forces claimed to have killed eight Marxist guerrillas and captured eleven others in 2 gun battles in Tehran. Among the dead was Parvix Vzez-Zadeh, a Cuban-born communist.

December 24, 1976—Spain—A Madrid synagogue bombing caused no injuries. The Armed Groups for European Liberty phoned CIFRA News Agency to claim credit, saying AGEL members ''do not threaten, but execute. . . .Our enemies are Zionism and capitalism, and it is against them that our activities are directed.''

December 24, 1976—France—The Charles Martel Group, an extreme right-wing organization, claimed credit for the assassination of Prince Jean de Broglie, fifty-five, a member of Parliament and formerly a leading negotiator for Algerian independence. A twenty-year-old man talked to him on the Rue de Dardanelles for several minutes before firing several pistol shots point-blank into de Broglie. The group said that de Broglie helped to flood France with Arab workers from north Africa. Martel had founded the first French Christian kingdom in the eighth century and was the grandfather of Charlemagne. He stopped an Arab invasion of France in 732 at the Battle of Poitiers.

December 24, 1976—India—An Egyptian B707 crashed in flames north of Bangkok, killing all forty-two on board as well as thirty night shift workers at a factory at 3:41 A.M. Reports indicated fire on board the plane before it hit the ground.

December 24, 1976—France—An explosion at the Albanian embassy at 131 Rue de la Pompe in Paris during the night destroyed part of the building but caused no injuries. A rocket launcher was found in the gutter under a car parked a few yards away. A group indentifying itself as a military council fighting for the liberation of Albania from communism claimed credit. 2976

December 24, 1976—Lebanon—Unknown gunmen fired twelve rounds of gunfire at a central committee member of the PFLP and his wife in their western Beirut home. They were indentified as Abdel Wahhab al-Sayyed, a member of the PFLP's political bureau, and his wife, Khaldiyeh, a sister of Leila Khaled, a famed PFLP hijacker, who found the thirty-seven-year-old Sayyed when she went to call on the couple. A PFLP spokesman said, "Initial investigation has shown that the assailants were local reactionary forces operating on behalf of international imperialism, in collaboration with reactionary Arab regimes seeking capitulationist settlements in the Middle East." Mrs. Sayyed joined the PFLP in 1969 and held military assignments. Mr. Sayyed, born in Gaza, was expelled in the 1960s from Egypt and Syria because of his radical activites. He had been the PFLP representative to South Yemen. 2977

December 25, 1976—Mexico—Two tourists from Illinois were shot to death at point-blank range in their car on a main road eighty miles east of Mazatlán.

December 28, 1976—Costa Rica—Huber Matos, Jr., thirty-three, was wounded by two bullets fired at 11 P.M. as he walked toward his car in a parking lot near his San José restaurant. Matos is the son of a former commander of Fidel Castro's forces, who had been jailed in Cuba for seventeen years. Matos's mother, a New Jersey resident, requested State Department aid in arranging a prisoner exchange suggested by Chile in which her husband would be released for Jorge Montes, a prominent Chilean communist who was jailed after the 1973 coup. 2978

December 29, 1976—Ireland—A lone male tried to hijack a plane to Berlin from Dublin airport. He informed security officers at the public arrivals area that he had a bomb in his case and would set it off if he was not given a plane within thirty minutes. Security officers overpowered him and discovered that the suitcase contained wires and metal film canisters but no explosives. He was arrested and jailed in Mount Joy Prison. It appeared that he would only be fined for disturbing the peace. 5502

December 29, 1976—Lebanon—The Communist Action Group, a Lebanese leftist organization, was suspected of planting a bomb in a car that exploded outside a Christian Phalangist militia barracks in Beirut's Al Ashrafiyeh quarter, killing forty and wounding more than fifty.

January 1, 1977—Spain—The Adolf Hitler Command was suspected by police of setting a fire that destroyed the offices of *Berriak*, a Basque autonomist magazine, in San Sebastián during the night.

January 1, 1977—Italy—The Armed Proletarian Power (Potere Proletario Armanto) firebombed five cars belonging to U.S. Navy personnel in Santa Teresa di Gallura and Palau, two areas along Sardinia's northern coast. No injuries were reported. Another incendiary device was disarmed. 2980-2985

January 3, 1977—Colombia—A bomb was removed from an Avianca jet in Bogotá shortly before it was due to fly with 125 passengers to Caracas, Venezuela. A note near the device claimed the attack was a protest against ''Yankee imperialism'' and the Colombian government. 2986

January 3, 1977—France—Mahmoud Saleh, former temporary PLO Paris representative after the assassination of Mahmoud el Amchari in 1972, Fatah member, and Rejectionist, was assassinated by two men aged twenty-five who fired eight shots (including two into Saleh's forehead) with a large-caliber pistol during the night before escaping on foot. Saleh owned the Arabic bookshop on the Rue Saint Victor in Paris's Latin Quarter. The PLO blamed ''Zionist intelligence organs,'' specifically accusing ''Harley Libermann, former military attaché of the Zionist embassy in Paris, of perpetrating the assassination.'' The group claimed that Saleh was born in Sabastiyah in Nablus district. Israel refused to allow Saleh to be buried in his homeland. His Paris funeral was to be attended by a high-level PLO delegation, which sparked a major diplomatic incident (see January 7, 1977). 2987

January 3, 1977—Canary Islands—The South African Airways office in Las Palmas was bombed during the night, causing some damage but no injuries. Police believed the Algiers-based Canary Islands Independence Movement was responsible. 2988

January 4, 1977—United States—Police discovered bomb-making material in the Brooklyn apartment of Ramadan Abdullah, twenty-four, a murder suspect. Police theorized that the cache could be connected with the December 1975 La Guardia bombing (see incident 2532).

January 4, 1977—West Germany—A bomb caused a small fire at a fuel storage tank in the U.S. Army depot at Giessen. The Revolutionary Cells said the attack was against the ''pernicious influence of the United States.'' 2989

January 6, 1977—Syria—Two Syrians and a Palestinian were hung after their conviction of a series of bomb attacks carried out with the complicity of Iraq.

Nine other Syrians convicted of similar charges were given prison sentences ranging from one year to life.

January 6, 1977—Bangladesh—A hand grenade was thrown from a passing car at the USIS building in Chittangong, causing minor damage and slight injuries to a Bangladesh citizen during the evening. 2990

January 7, 1977—Spain—The Anitcommunist Armed Alliance sent death threats to three individuals in Córdoba, identified as Matias Camacho, president of the PSOE Provincial Committee; Joaquin Martinez, a lawyer; and Dr. Castilla del Pino. The group said it would carry out the threats if GRAPO executed Antonio Maria de Oriol y Urquijo (see incident 2969).

January 7, 1977—United States—Juan José Peruyero, an anti-Castro Cuban exile in his mid-forties, was gunned down by two Latin men who were waiting for him as he left his Miami home. Police questioned Roberto Carballo, the president of the 2506 Brigade Association, who had ousted Peruyero from leadership of the group the previous March. The organization is composed of Bay of Pigs veterans. 2991

January 7, 1977—United States—The INS reported that twenty-four Mexican terrorists were believed to have entered the United States to raid weapons and ammunition dumps at Fort Huachuca, a U.S. military base in Arizona, fifteen miles from the Mexican border. The base took precautionary measures.

January 7, 1977—Colombia—The Pedro Leon Arboleda Marxist-Leninist group claimed credit for the November 24, 1974, assassination of leftist lawyer Romero Buj and Amparo Silva, a woman, on one of Bogotá's main streets. Buj was married to Nidia Tobom, an associate of the famed Venezuelan-born terrorist Carlos (also known as Illich Ramirez Sanchez).

January 7, 1977—France—DST officials, apparently acting without higher official sanction, arrested Abu Daoud, thirty-nine, at a Paris hotel where he was staying with a Palestinian delegation attending the funeral of an assassinated Palestinian (see incident 2987). Daoud was believed to have planned the Munich Olympics massacre of September 5, 1972, and the West Germans claimed that he was in the hotel used by the terrorists just before the attack. Daoud had met with a French official before the arrest and claimed that he had been promised immunity while in Beirut before traveling to Europe. Daoud was arrested on an international warrant issued shortly after the Olympics attack. The French immediately came under strong pressure from Arab states, including Libya, Iraq, and Algeria, to release Daoud, whose true name is

Uchmed Daoud Mechamed Auda and who was traveling on an Iraqi passport under the name of Youssef Raji Hanna. The Israelis requested the French to hold Daoud for sixty days under provisional arrest, and the West Germans requested his extradition. It appeared that the French administration did not want to continue to hold Daoud, and on January 11 released him on legal technicalities and gave him a first-class seat on an Air Algeria flight to Algiers, where he was welcomed. The French claimed that the West Germans had not forwarded other documents or evidence supporting their warrant. The United States and Israel strongly protested the release, and Israel recalled its ambassador to France for consultation. The Germans also protested, although many observers believed they were relieved not to have to guard a terrorist whose release had been demanded during previous terrorist actions in 1973. The Soviets praised the French decision. The press reported that a U.S. counterterrorist group had tipped off the French regarding Daoud's true identity. It was later claimed that the Germans had also not followed up with an official demarche to accompany their request for extradition through Interpol.

January 9, 1977—Soviet Union—A bomb exploded in a Moscow subway, injuring twenty and killing seven. Three men were reported seen placing a parcel on the subway.

January 11, 1977—United States—William Saupe, described as being mentally ill, demanded that TWA flight 700, a B747 flying from New York to London, be flown to Uganda. He was subdued by other passengers after a brief skirmish and jailed in London. 5503

January 13, 1977—United States—Reports circulated that a radical splinter faction within Israel's Likud opposition bloc had paid $150,000 to professional assassins to kill U.S. Secretary of State Henry A. Kissinger for "selling out Israel during his Mideast shuttle diplomacy."

January 15, 1977—Zaire—Members of the Front for the Liberation of the Enclave of Cabinda (FLEC) raided a Fougerolle Company railway rebuilding site near the Cabinda border, killing several Congolese, damaging a tunnel under construction, and blowing up a number of bridges. They also kidnapped three French technicians and three Congolese workers but freed the Frenchmen on January 30, apparently without payment of a ransom. 2992

January 20, 1977—United Kingdom—Stewardesses Paii Dewoody and Jane Otto testified on February 9 in a Miami court that Audrey Bumgard, forty-five, of Galveston, Texas, an independent drilling supervisor on the North Sea oil project, swatted them sharply on their behinds during a National Airlines flight from London to Miami. Bumgard was charged with air piracy under the federal statute that makes it a felony, punishable by twenty years' imprisonment and $10,000 fine, for anyone who "while on an aircraft in U.S. jurisdiction, assaults, intimidates or threatens a crew member or flight attendant so as to interfere with his duties."

January 20, 1977—Mexico—Mitchell Andreski, the U.S. president of Duraflex Corporation, and his Mexican associate, Guillermo Flores Franco, thirty, were shot and killed by members of the Twenty-third of September Armed Communist League when they tried to prevent the group from passing out propaganda leaflets. Two other persons were wounded. The two were inspecting a construction site in the northeastern section of Mexico City. 2993

January 20, 1977—United States—The Independent Revolutionary Armed Commandos of Puerto Rico claimed credit for mailing four incendiary devices that were found in Manhattan. Reports conflicted as to their intended recipients, with addressees including former President Ford, President-elect Carter, the governor of Puerto Rico, the Justice Department, and the CIA. Some reports claimed that the devices exploded in a mail box and a midtown post office, slightly injuring a postman. 2994-2997

January 22, 1977—Zambia—Jason Moyo, fifty-three, the director of military operations for Joshua Nkomo's Zimbabwe African People's Union, was killed when a mail bomb exploded in his Lusaka office. The bomb, mailed in Botswana, injured four other people. It was believed that Moyo was expecting a package from a friend in Botswana and opened the bomb, believing the package had arrived. ZAPU claimed that the parcel was mailed "by agents of the Rhodesian racists and fascists." 2998

January 25, 1977—Argentina—Montoneros fired machine guns and threw a pipe bomb at the vacant suburban Buenos Aires home of a Goodyear executive. Leaflets supporting laborers in recent strife were left at the home, the tire plant, and the surrounding area. 2999

January 26, 1977—United States—A bomb threat was received at the VC Summers Nuclear Station Unit No. 1 of the South Carolina Electric and Gas Company.

January 27, 1977—Europe—Seventeen of the nineteen members of the Council of Europe signed the European Convention on the Suppression of Terrorism. Ireland and Malta refused to sign the convention at the Strasbourg meeting. The convention must be ratified by three states before coming into force.

January 27, 1977—Colombia—Three FARC gunmen fired machine guns from a moving car at the Paraguayan embassy in Bogotá, injuring no one. 3000

January 28, 1977—El Salvador—The Reverend Mario Bernal Londono, thirty-three, a Colombian Roman Catholic priest, and a local parishioner were kidnapped by guerrillas in front of the Apopa church, seven miles outside San Salvador, in an area that had experienced peasant unrest. The parishioner was later released in San Salvador. 3001

January 28, 1977—Ethiopia—A group of Ethiopian students, which fluctuated between thirty and ninety members, threw stones and attempted to set fire to U.S. and U.K. cultural centers in Addis Ababa. One student died, and six others were injured in the twenty-minute assault. Almost all of the U.S. center's ground-floor windows were broken. 3002

January 29, 1977—Lebanon—Two booby-trapped cars filled with explosives were found behind the Saidu city hall, eighteen miles south of Beirut. Several persons were arrested by the Arab peacekeeping force.

January 29, 1977—United Kingdom—Thirteen IRA bombs exploded in London one and a half miles west of Central Criminal Court, where four Irishmen accused of seven terrorist killings were on trial. No injuries were reported, but several fires were started by the explosions. Fifteen bombs were discovered in five Northern Ireland cities. It was believed that the attacks were to commemorate the fifth anniversary of Bloody Sunday, in which British troops fired on Irish protesters. 3003-3015.

January 31, 1977—Colombia—Six low-powered bombs exploded in the Bogotá office of Iberia Airlines, causing some damage but no injuries. Pamphlets left by the Revolutionary Workers Party called for support from revolutionary groups in Spain, Chile, Uruguay, Argentina, Portugal, and Bolivia. 3016

February 2, 1977—United Kingdom—An incendiary bomb exploded in a government office in Liverpool. The IRA announced a new guerrilla campaign against British cities. 3017

Feburary 2, 1977—Northern Ireland—Jeffrey S. Adgate, fifty-eight, British-born managing director of the DuPont International plant in Londonderry, was gunned down as he stepped from his car outside his home on the outskirts of the city. The IRA was believed responsible. On February 7, a twenty-two-year-old man was arrested and charged with the murder. 3018

February 3, 1977—United Kingdom—Two IRA incendiary bombs exploded in a central London bookshop, injuring no one. 3019

February 3, 1977—France—The Phalangist Security Group bombed a Palestinian library in Paris, causing considerable damage but no injuries. 3020

February 6, 1977—Rhodesia—Twelve armed black men shot to death seven foreign missionaries at the Masumi Catholic mission, fifty-seven miles east of Salisbury. Those killed included three Jesuits—two British priests and an Irish brother—and four Dominican nuns—three from West Germany and one from England. The attack came at 10 P.M., according to a survivor of the attack, Reverend Dunstan Myerscough, sixty-five. An elderly German nun, Sister Anna, was spared because her arthritis kept her from moving fast enough to line up for the guerrillas. Rhodesian police found 111 spent cartridges from Soviet-made machine guns. The mission housed four hundred boarding students and one hundred fifty African staff members. It appeared that the guerrillas were seeking to recruit the youths and took more than three hundred of them across the border into Botswana. A priest, Reverend Edgar Sommerreisser, accompanied one hundred forty parents across the border in an attempt to persuade them to return home. Only fifty-two returned, most of them girls aged between thirteen and sixteen. 3021

February 9, 1977—Egypt—The Kuwaiti newspaper *Al Qatab* reported that several Palestinian members of Black June were arrested by the PLO in Cairo, breaking up a plot to destroy U.S. Secretary of State Vance's airliner, which was scheduled to arrive a few days later. 3022

February 10, 1977—United Kingdom—A London court sentenced four IRA members to life imprisonment for seven killings, kidnappings, bombings, and shootings.

February 10, 1977—France—Alain Escoffier, twenty-seven, an extreme rightist, shouted anti-Soviet slogans while dousing himself with gasoline and setting himself on fire in the Paris office of Aeroflot. He was reportedly alive in a hospital several hours later.

February 10, 1977—Iraq—A Syrian agent was arrested after placing a booby-trapped suitcase in a Karbala mosque. The device was dismantled minutes before it was set to explode.

February 10, 1977—United States—An unspecific threat was made against the licensed nuclear facility of the Westinghouse Electric Corporation in Columbia, South Carolina.

February 12, 1977—Argentina—Seventeen bombs exploded at banks, electric power stations, and automobile showrooms throughout Buenos Aires but caused no injuries.

February 13, 1977—Turkey—A Turkish Airlines DC9 flying fifty-one passengers from Istanbul to Izmir was the scene of an attempted hijacking by Aslan Mintas, seventeen, a Turkish police cadet, who fired his pistol wildly to back up his demand to be flown to Yugoslavia. The pilot and a stewardess were slightly wounded. A passenger sneaked up and disarmed the hijacker as the plane was approaching its Izmir landing. Police arrested Mintas. 5504

February 14, 1977—Colombia—Fifty FARC members attacked the village of Macarena, ninety-five miles from Bogotá, at dawn, looting shops, killing one of four policemen in the town who conducted a two-hour gun battle with the terrorists, and kidnapping Richard C. Starr, a U.S. Peace Corps volunteer. The group fled into the mountains. Two hundred paratroopers were dropped into the mountains to pursue them, but it was believed that local residents, fearing guerrilla retaliation, helped the terrorists escape. On February 24, police reported that they had discovered the bodies of two heavily-armed guerrillas believed to have participated in the kidnapping in the vicinity of Guayabero Rivero in the La Macarena Mountains. On April 25, Agence France Presse reported that a ransom had been paid for Starr, who was released. The U.S. embassy neither confirmed nor denied the reports. Starr was released on February 11, 1980, after Jack Mitchell, of columnist Jack Anderson's staff, paid a $250,000 ransom on February 7 in Neiva, Colombia. 3023

February 15, 1977—United States—A bomb threat was received at the Arizona Public Service Corporation's Palo Verde licensed nuclear facility.

February 18, 1977—Argentina—An ERP bomb exploded at 8:40 A.M. fifteen meters from the side of the airfield in Buenos Aires from which President Jorge Videla's plane had taken off. The explosion blasted a fifteen-foot hole in the runway and caved in the canal in the Maldonado stream but caused no injuries. The plane was diverted to the First Air Brigade in Palomar, where it was confirmed that there was no damage, before it flew on to Bahia Blanca. Three other bombs were detonated by police.

February 18, 1977—United States—At 1:01 A.M., a bomb exploded in Chicago's Merchandise Mart, the world's largest commercial office building, causing $100,000 damage but no injuries. The bomb was placed in a coin-operated locker on the second floor near the boarding area for elevated trains and shattered some windows, ruptured a fire sprinkler pipe, and damaged four offices. A second bomb exploded at 1:04 A.M. eight blocks away at the U.S. Gypsum Company building, knocking out fifteen windows on the first two floors and causing $25,000 damage to the personnel office. The bombings were not similar to previous FALN bombings in Chicago, but an FBI spokesman said, "You'd have to assume it's some kind of terrorist group." No group took credit for the blasts.

February 18, 1977—United States—Two FALN bombs exploded during the night in New York City, shattering windows in the Gulf and Western and Chrysler buildings and injuring two. 3024-3025

February 18, 1977—Turkey—An early-morning bomb explosion caused moderate damage to the USIS library in Izmir. No injuries were reported. Several Ancilciler-TPLP members were charged in May. 3026

February 20, 1977—United States—A bomb exploded in the IBM building in New York City. No one claimed credit.

February 20, 1977—Mexico—Tijuana police rescued Roy Perguson, sixty-one, of Potrivilrie, California, from kidnappers after being held for more than forty-eight hours. The group demanded a $120,000 ransom, and were believed to be the Mexican Mafia, one of two gangs trying to gain control of the central California narcotics trafficking.

February 20, 1977—West Germany—Police arrested eighty-seven people and seized explosives, Molotov cocktails, wire-cutting tools, knives, and other equipment from leftist militants in connection with a mass demonstration against nuclear power at a site in Brokdorf. Most of the demonstrators apparently did not consider how far away the power plant was and discovered that they were exhausted by the time that they had hiked there, only to be confronted with 150 police. The group gave up and camped out, sang songs for a while and then left.

February 20, 1977—Italy—Franco Bartoli, twenty-nine, a convicted armed robber, took a Saluzzo family with three children hostage. He said he would free them in exchange for Pope Paul VI or Italian Interior Minister Francesco Cossiga. He said that the Pope would be available because all he does is "pray for his shares in the real estate business."

February 22, 1977—Syria—Dr. Muhammed el Fadel, fifty-eight, president of Damascus University, was shot to death outside his office. He had defended Palestinian guerrillas in Swiss and Greek trials.

February 22, 1977—Spain—Ten people were arrested by Spanish police in an arms factory for the Guerrillas of Christ the King. Among those arrested were Mariano Sanchez Covisa, the group's leader, and two Italians who were leading members of neofascist organizations in Italy wanted for several terrorist attacks. 3027

February 22, 1977—United States—Robert A. Dufala, thirty-nine, who claimed to be a Williamstown, New Jersey, member of a John Birch Society "hit team," went on trial in Camden for planning to kill Vice-President Rockefeller with a cyanide bullet on July 4, 1976. He said he was trying to prevent Henry Kissinger and the communists from taking over the world. The jury failed to reach a verdict, and a mistrial was declared on March 10, 1977.

February 22, 1977—Peru—Two bombs exploded in front of the Lima home of Colonel Manuel Bravo Yanes, the Cuban military, naval, and air attaché in Peru, causing considerable damage but no injuries. The home is adjacent to the official residence of Dr. Antonio Nunez Jimenez, the Cuban ambassador, in the San Isidro district. 3028

February 23, 1977—United States—Incendiary devices in envelopes addressed to the Banco Popular de Puerto Rico exploded in three Manhattan locations but caused no injuries or damage. The devices were similar to those sent recently in New York City to U.S. and Puerto Rican officials. 3029-3031

February 24, 1977—United States—Reuters reported from Denver that "skindivers recovered 2 stolen lead canisters holding deadly radioactive material today, ending a frantic 10-hour search, after police found 3 youths trying to smash open another canister, police said. The 3 youths, aged 16 to 18, led authorities to the spot in the South Platte River where they had tossed the canisters, police said. The canisters remained safely sealed, they added. The youths, whose names were withheld, stole a pickup truck yesterday outside a fast-food restaurant in suburban Sheridan, police said. The truck contained drilling equipment and 3 small canisters of the radioactive material, identified as Cesium 137, which is used in testing moisture density of soil.''

February 27, 1977—Egypt—An Egyptian working for Libyan intelligence planted a time bomb that exploded in a small Alexandria hotel, injuring nine.

February 28, 1977—Iraq—Kurdish rebels kidnapped an Algerian and two Frenchmen in the north and held them with four Poles whom they had kidnapped on December 18 (see incident 2974). The group demanded a stop to what they called the massacre of Kurds by the Iraqi army. The hostages were released on March 29 "on humanitarian grounds, as the state of their health had been deteriorating." 3032

March 1, 1977—United States—The Three Mile Island 1 and 2 licensed nuclear facility of the Metropolitan Edison Company received a bomb threat.

March 1, 1977—Rhodesia—The body of Reverend Manuel Rubio Diaz, fifty-eight, a Spanish-born Roman Catholic missionary who had lived in the country for twenty-eight years, was found bludgeoned to death in a remote area 170 miles south of the Salisbury and 80 miles from the Mozambique border. The area has been the scene of attacks by Zimbabwe guerrillas. 3033

March 2, 1977—Uganda—The Nairobi newspaper *Daily Nation* quoted West German intelligence sources in alleging that the PFLP had planned to hijack a plane that was to have taken remaining Americans out of Uganda. The group planned to fly the plane from Entebbe, possibly landing in Kenya. The story came on the heels of a week-long international crisis in which Idi Amin declared that no Americans could leave Uganda and called upon all Americans in the country to attend a meeting with him in Kampala. He later changed the site to Entebbe airport, leading observers to believe that the Americans would be deported. Amin changed the date of the meeting and later cancelled the meeting.

March 3, 1977—United States—The Millstone 1, 2, and 3 units of the licensed nuclear facility of the Northeast Nuclear Energy Company received a bomb threat.

March 4, 1977—West Germany—The chief prosecutor of Bavaria's supreme court announced the arrest of two Palestinians near Nuremburg on suspicion of being members of a group planning terrorist attacks in West Germany. 3034

March 5, 1977—Kenya—Kampala sources reported that a group of Ugandan exiles based in Nairobi planned to assassinate Ugandan President Idi Amin on January 24 as he opened an agricultural exhibition. A Ugandan female intelligence agent had penetrated the underground Christian network and foiled the plot.

March 5, 1977—Venezuela—Unidentified individuals fired a machine gun at the Colombian chauffeur of Wilfred Naimool, ambassador of Trinidad and Tobago, during the evening at the entrance to his home in Caracas. Alfredo Solis Aguirre, thirty, was wounded several times and taken to a hospital, where he was pronounced to be in critical condition. Police claimed that the attackers may have intended to steal the diplomat's automobile. 3035

March 6, 1977—Turkey—A bomb exploded in Ankara outside the Iraqi embassy, causing minor damage. A leaflet said the attack was "in memory of Arab patriots and Kurds." 3036

March 7, 1977—United States—Cory Moore, a black ex-marine armed with two pistols, took two white hostages at 2 P.M. and demanded to talk to President Carter about "why he did not speak out on poverty and why he did not apologize to black Americans for the injustices we have faced all these years." He released his first hostage, Shelly Kiggans, eighteen, a part-time clerk, eleven hours later in exchange for a television so he could watch the heavy media coverage of his demands. The president spoke to him for a few minutes at 4:13 P.M. on March 9, after which Moore released his second hostage, police captain Leo Keglovic, forty-eight, and surrendered. Moore was arraigned in Bedford, Ohio, municipal court on two charges of kidnapping. Observers questioned the wisdom of the presidential decision, suggesting that others would imitate Moore's actions. The president said, "The request was made to me to talk to Mr. Moore. I replied that I would be glad to talk to Mr. Moore after the officer is released. Perhaps it is a dangerous precedent but I have weighed the decision."

March 9, 1977—Egypt—Police arrested five for planting bombs on railway tracks west of Al-Alamein. The group confessed to working for Libyan intelligence, which had given them military training.

March 9, 1977—United States—In the first of three coordinated barricade and hostage operations, seven Hanafi Muslims took over the B'nai B'rith national headquarters at 1640 Rhode Island Avenue in northwest Washington, D.C. The group was led by the sect's spiritual leader, Khalifa Hamaas Abdul Khaalis, fifty-four, who was born Ernest Timothy McGhee. At around 11 A.M., the group drove a rented truck to the building and brought in rifles, handguns, machetes, long knives, and a crossbow. The amount of ammunition later found in the building made police believe that they had stored some of the material there ahead of time. Rifles and long knives were also found left in the van. They forced Andrew S. Hoffman, twenty, a George Washington University student who was walking past the building, to aid them in bringing the ammunition from the first to the third floor. After beating him to ensure compliance, they asked him his nationality. "I told them I was Italian and they let me go," he said. Hoffman is, however, one-half Jewish, which he did not mention to the anti-Semitic Hanafis. One hundred forty people were initially trapped inside the building, but 35 of them escaped, were freed during a police sweep of the building, or were released during negotiations because of illness. A total of 105 hostages were released thirty-nine hours later at the end of the siege. While it appeared that the group was hoping to seize the organization's high-ranking officials, most of the B'nai B'rith leaders were attending a luncheon at the Shoreham Americana Hotel in honor of Israeli Prime Minister Yitzhak Rabin.

The hostages initially were treated roughly by the Hanafis. Khaalis struck a hostage in the head and back with a weapon, causing him to bleed profusely. Dr. Sidney Clearfield, assistant national director of B'nai B'rith youth organizations, was one of many men who were pistol-whipped, punched, or hit with rifle butts. Shortly after the takeover, five of the seriously wounded hostages were allowed to leave the building. Steven Widdes, twenty-six, had lacerations in the head from a pistol-whipping. Wesley Hymes, thirty-one, a print-shop employee of B'nai B'rith, was stabbed and shot in the arm. He faced a year of surgery to repair the nerves and tendons of his left hand from machete wounds. Alton Kirkland, twenty-two, had knife wounds in his thigh, chest, diaphragm, spleen, stomach, and liver, which required three operations. Michael Smith received head injuries. Brian Golliday, twelve, received head and back injuries when struck with a gun. Sixteen other hostages were released about two hours after the siege began. Four men working on a new wing of the building escaped through an air-conditioning duct and were not injured. In all, forty hostages suffered from major or minor bruises, principally rope burns from being bound. Two hostages required stitches for cuts around their eyes.

After the attackers bound most of the hostages hand and foot, eight of the male hostages were unbound to allow them to paint over the windows. The treatment of the hostages varied from hour to hour, from concern for the sanitary conditions to threats of death. During an interview, Abdul Aziz, Khaalis's relative who remained at the Hanafi center, warned what would happen if the group's demands were not met: "Heads will be chopped off, a killing room will be set up. . .and heads will be thrown out of windows." As if to back this up, when one man complained about a heart condition, one of the captors said to Betty Neal, a secretary at the headquarters, "He's going to die anyway. I might as well chop his head off." One terrorist called out, "Any heroes here? Is anyone here ready to die?" When one of the hostages informed Khaalis that he could not be badgered, Khaalis singled him out as the first one to die if demands were not met. According to hostage Charles Fenyvesi, the leader "spoke of the killings in South Africa. He berated the American police for killing people and for failing to live up to a promise of immunity they had made to a kidnapper in Indiana." Despite these constant threats, four hostages who complained of chest pains were released during the day.

Khaalis's manipulation of the media was well orchestrated. He granted an interview over the telephone to WTOP newsman Max Robinson during the siege and informed Sergeant Robert Sharkey, Jr., of the Washington police homicide squad, "I told you I would get my revenge. This is only the third of four phases. The fourth phase you can't believe. You can't envision it."

Reporters from newspapers and radio stations throughout the United States, as well as from Mexico, France, and Australia, called, but Khaalis would not always speak with them. Despite the heavy press coverage, the phone appeared to be Khaalis's only source of information. When one of his men turned on a radio the first evening of the siege, Khaalis told him to turn it off because it got on his nerves. (However, it appeared that the radios were monitored in another siege location and that operational information was relayed to the B'nai B'rith headquarters, which appeared to be the command center for the three operations.)

At the end of the negotiations, police discovered sixteen firearms, numerous knives, and more than ten thousand rounds of ammunition (more than is found in some well-stocked sporting goods shops). Damage was estimated at $250,000.

Because of an agreement made during bargaining sessions, Khaalis was released. Those held on $50,000 bond included Abdul Adam, thirty-two (also known as George W. Smith); Abdul Shaheed, twenty-three (also known as Marvin Sadler); Abdul Hamid, twenty-two (also known as Hilvan Jude Finch); and Abdul Razzaq, twenty-three (also known as Nelson McQueen, Jr.). Those held on $75,000 bond were Abdul Latif, thirty-three (also known as Carl E. Roper), and Abdul Salaam, thirty-one (also known as Clarence White). Sadler, who had a twelfth-grade education, had no previous convictions. Finch had attended a West Point preparatory school. White had prior convictions for grand larceny, burglary, and possession of a deadly weapon. Latif was convicted in 1966 on charges of possession of a dangerous weapon and grand larceny, for which he was given probation. He was found not guilty by reason of insanity in a bank robbery in 1966. 3037

March 9, 1977—United States—At around noon, the Islamic Center at 2551 Massachusetts Avenue NW, in Washington D.C., was taken over by three Hanafi Muslims. According to Doron Shwaic, a student from Israel who was inside at the time of the attack, his tour group's bus driver ''came in excited and said, 'someone with a gun catch our leader [Tesdell]! We're all in danger.' '' Nester Pereira, a Nicaraguan foreign exchange student, also barely escaped being taken hostage at the center. Another student, Miriam Possenti of Venezuela, said she was taking photos outside the center when she noticed two black men entering an office. The terrorists were armed with two rifles, a shotgun, a pistol, knives, and machetes and went to the office of the director of the center, Dr. Mohammad Abdul Rauf, who was taken hostage along with ten others. Among the hostages were five Egyptian Center employees, three Americans, including Reverend Robert Tesdell of New York City, the tour guide, a Bangladeshi and a Colombian. The Turkish embassy reported that the caretaker, Davaz Mustapha, fifty-nine, and his son were also held. The seven male hostages were bound hand and foot using neckties and rope.

The attackers were masters of dramatic effects. They threatened to kill José Luis Mora, eighteen, the Colombian student, and held guns to his head; however, they were willing to negotiate for the release of ill hostages. Karl von Goetz, thirty, of Maryland, talked them into releasing Cecile, his half-sister. He initially tried to exchange himself for her but was turned down. Von Goetz, who claimed to have been a mercenary in Rhodesia, eventually obtained her release. She was rushed to George Washington Hospital and readmitted a few hours later with chest pains. Mushk Ara, eighteen, a student from Bangladesh who worked at the center, was released Wednesday night after her father, a Bangladesh embassy employee, phoned the center to talk with the terrorists. The group claimed they had no quarrel with his country and released her unharmed. Several of the hostages were allowed to telephone or receive calls from family members. A volatile situation occurred when a crank caller informed the gunmen that police were about to "take action." This tense atmosphere was relaxed by deputy police chief Maurice T. Turner, who talked with the terrorists over the phone. Several hostages pointed out that an all-news radio station was constantly playing.

The terrorists made use of the center's foreign ties. The three Moslem ambassadors who aided in the negotiations with the terrorists were all affiliated with the center. Khaalis ordered Rauf to phone New York to order a halt to the showing of the movie *Muhammad, Messenger of God*. Rauf said that "he gave me about twenty-five minutes to call some ambassadors of Muslim nations and tell them to do what they could to get the movie stopped. I called ambassadors in New York and Washington. I checked with Secretary of State Cyrus Vance. I finally got the consul general of Egypt in New York. I said he would call other ambassadors of Islamic nations and ask them to help get the film stopped. He also called New York Mayor Abe Beame."

One of the gunmen mused, "we're going to want Kissinger because we think he gave the signals for the 1973 murders" of members of Khaalis's family. Tesdell, a minister in the Christian Church Disciples of Christ, talked him out of his idea.

At the end of the siege, the attackers were released. They were identified as Abdul Rahman (also known as Clyde Cleman Young), who had a twelfth-grade education and no prior convictions; Abdul Rahim (also known as Phillip Alvin Young), who had attended Federal City College and received a journalism degree from Goddard College; and Abdul Qawee (also known as Samuel L. Young). They were brothers. Center assistant director Abdul Rahman Osman noted that one was a student who had attended two of his classes.

On March 21, the three were ordered jailed in lieu of $50,000 bond because the judge had received testimony that they would follow Khaalis's orders and that two hostages in the Center had been injured. A secretary at the center had cut her leg while being dragged from one room to another, and a caretaker had been beaten on the head and body. 3038

March 9, 1977—United States—The final Hanafi siege began at 2:30 P.M. at the Washington, D.C. City Council offices in the District Building at Fourteenth and E streets, Northwest, in Washington, D.C. Two men parked a Diamond taxi outside the Fourteenth Street entrance, left the emergency lights flickering, and went past the unguarded entrance and up to the stairs. One man carried a shotgun, the other a machete. At the top of the five flights of stairs, the gunmen mistakenly turned left, away from the mayor's office they had come to seize. On their way, they passed two young black news reporters, Stephen Colter and Maurice Williams. Besides the mayor, it appeared that the attackers were seeking city council member Arlington Dixon, who had sponsored a council-passed resolution favorable to the Nation of Islam (Black Muslims), the Hanafi rival. After firing a shotgun that hit several people, they moved down the corridor to the offices of council chairman Sterling Tucker and herded their hostages inside. Mayor Washington and other staff members locked themselves in their offices. Washington managed to leave the building under heavy escort at around 6 P.M. during the first night of the siege.

A shotgun blast killed Maurice Williams, twenty-four, of WHUR radio, who was pronounced dead on arrival at the hospital. It also wounded Mack Cantrell, fifty-one, a building guard. One pellet hit city council member Marion S. Barry, Jr., forty-one, and may have ricocheted. Cantrell, a guard, did not have time to fire his drawn weapon at the terrorists.

The thirteen hostages were bound with rope, masking tape, venetian blind cords, and phone cords. Twenty-eight others were trapped in nearby offices. For the first few hours, the terrorists refused to identify themselves, and there was some question of whether they were connected with the other attacks (such sieges had become more frequent in the United States during the past few months). Khaalis later affirmed that the two were indeed affiliated with him.

Police initially attempted to storm the building, firing shots. According to Alan F. Grip, a hostage, one of the terrorists pointed his gun at the floor and fired it, wounding Robert Pierce, fifty-two, a council aide and law student who was working as a legal intern. The gunmen directed the wounded Pierce to leave, but he responded that he was paralyzed and unable to. A woman volunteered to help him leave. It was later determined that part of his lower arm and wrist were blown away, and both of the long bones of his lower arm were completely severed, as were its principal nerves and arteries. Doctors stated that he would probably be paralyzed from the waist down for the rest of his life and would probably lose the use of his right hand.

During the negotiations, California Congressman Robert Dornan offered himself in exchange for a hostage. He was refused.

On Thursday night, Elsie Young, a receptionist, took advantage of the terrorists' growing fatigue and jumped through a broken glass partition to safety. Two hours after her escape, the terrorists released a hostage who complained of chest pains. He was identified as John Cockrell, executive director of the Restaurant Association of Metropolitan Washington. Four hours later, the group surrendered after a phone call from Khaalis. Damage from the attack was estimated at $10,000.

Abdul Muzikir, twenty-two, and Abdul Nuh were held on a $50,000 bond. Nuh held a B.S. degree and had no previous record of convictions. He was employed as a substitute teacher in the public-school system. Muzikir and Nuh were convicted of murder in the second degree, as was Khaalis. They were also convicted of assault with intent to kill Cantrell and Pierce. 3039

Addendum to incidents 3037-3039—Two years before the attack, Washington, D.C., police files on the Hanafi religious group had been destroyed as part of a drive to end controversy over surveillance projects. A police informant who had infiltrated the group's headquarters was also removed from the case. Police were able to piece together the following information about the group.

The Hanafis are one of the four schools of Islamic law within the Sunni sect, believing that the successor to the Prophet, Muhammad, should be elected. The Shi'a sect claims that the successor should follow blood lines. The U.S. Hanafis split from the Nation of Islam in 1967, attacking the Black Muslim antiwhite doctrine (which was later changed) and arguing that Elijah Muhammad was not a prophet of Allah. The group referred to the "Cassius X Clay gang." Recently the new Black Muslim leader, Wallace D. Muhammad, had returned from a trip to the Mideast with $16 million in Arab money and a proclamation from five Arab nations declaring him "the sole consultant and trustee for all American Muslim organizations." Observers theorized that this may have been the final indignity suffered at the hands of the Nation of Islam by Khaalis, who claimed to have been a Catholic once. During the sieges, Khaalis was furious that Wallace Muhammad came to Washington. Police refused to meet with Muhammad, who offered to act as an intermediary with Khaalis, fearing that the result would be bloodshed. (In another security-related decision by police, the customary nineteen-gun salute for British Prime Minister James Callaghan was cancelled for his White House visit at 10:30 A.M. for fear of startling the Hanafis.)

Khaalis's demands were for retribution and the correction of perceived indignities rather than for publicity for political causes. His primary demand was that seven Black Muslims who had been tried for the murder of Khaalis's family on January 18, 1973, be brought to him for his own application of vengeance. Many observers suggested that Islamic law allows state vengeance, but not individual vengeance. Five of the Muslims were serving jail terms, one had been released when a prosecution witness refused to testify, and the final one was subject to a retrial. The victims ranged in age from a nine-day-old baby to a twenty-five-year-old. They had been drowned, shot, and beaten to death. In a phone interview, Khaalis said, "The judge has to die like all of us have to die and he has to answer to the creator. So we leave this in the hands of

Allah . . .Nothing's going to exonerate the murderers, no matter what you say or anyone else says. The murderers have to die. If they don't die then there are others who can die in their place."

Khaalis also demanded $750 in court costs that had resulted from his outburst at the trial of the Black Muslims. The fee for his defense was sent to him at B'nai B'rith.

Khaalis demanded that the showing of the $18 million, three-hour film, *Muhammad, Messenger of God*, be halted. The nine theaters showing the movie in New York and Los Angeles complied. Moustapha Akkad, forty-four, the Syrian-born director of the film, said that he changed the film's title to *The Message* for its London premiere after the theater received threats. Orthodox Muslims, such as the Hanafis, interpret the Koran as forbidding any pictorial representation of Muhammad or even of his shadow. There was some dispute about the movie's treatment of the Prophet, whose uncle was played by Anthony Quinn. Akkad said that he had received approval from several Moslem countries but not from conservative Saudi Arabia. After the siege ended, Akkad said that he would reopen the showings to demonstrate that he would not give in to terrorism and that the film would be shown in Detroit, Kansas City, and Philadelphia starting March 23 and in Chicago on March 25. The film was financed largely with private capital from investors and banks in Kuwait, Libya, and Morocco. One press account said that Libya's President Muammar Qaddafi had invested in the film.

The Khalifa at one time requested that Mayor Walter Washington be traded for some hostages. This demand, as well as the one for the turning over of the seven Black Muslims, was refused. Khaalis set no deadlines or ultimatums during the negotiations, which were primarily conducted over the phone by deputy police chief Robert Rabe. The police allowed food, medicine, newspapers, and oral contraceptives to be sent in to the hostages. The Hanafis agreed that they would not harm the hostages if the police did not storm the buildings. Although the press speculated that the police may have been able to attack one of the locations successfully, most official spokesmen reported that attacks on the three locations would have to be well coordinated and that errors would cost the lives of hostages.

Although many news agencies cooperated with police, the degree of responsibility shown by many varied greatly. WMAL-TV news director Sam Zelman said he felt no need to honor a police request not to broadcast that some city employees had barricaded themselves in the District Building unknown to the raiders because the fact had already been published. WTOP radio broadcast unconfirmed reports that a group of motorcyclists ''who might be Hanafi Muslims'' were heading for the Grammercy Hotel. It was later learned that the motorcyclists were official escorts for the diplomats engaged in the negotiations. WTTG aired a forty-second segment of the proscribed *Messenger* film shortly after 7 P.M. during the first day of the siege. WTOP radio interviewed

Alan Grip, a hostage at the District Building, during the siege. Police complained that interviewers were tying up needed phone lines to the hostage sites and Hanafi headquarters. Press treatment of the incidents led U.S. U.N. Ambassador Andrew Young to suggest press curbs for such episodes. Whenever station WMAL broadcast that food had been brought to the B'nai B'rith building, one of the gunmen would appear a short time later to pick it up. This led police to deduce that the raiders were monitoring radio reports. WDCA-TV decided to cancel two future scheduled movies because a title and subject matter seemed potentially aggravating. *The Heroes of Telemark*, which includes scenes of Nazis murdering Norwegian hostages, and *Sinai Commandos*, about the 1967 Arab-Israeli war, were not shown. After a phoned demand from Khaalis, WTOP radio reporter Jim Bohannon apologized on television for referring to the group as Black Muslims, quoting an FBI press release.

Ambassador Georges Salomon of Haiti expressed a desire to assist in negotiations with the terrorists but was apparently refused. The Israelis pointed out that they were not involved in this incident. Aviezer Pazner, a spokesman for the embassy, said, ''Our security remains as it has always been—quite tight. We have not received any threats. We have not received any demands. Our security has always been tight because of terrorist threats.''

Three Muslim ambassadors aided in the final negotiations with the terrorists: Egyptian Ashraf Ghorbal, Ardeshir Zahedi of Iran, and Sahabzada Yaqub-Khan of Pakistan. They were brought into the case after clearance with Under Secretary of State Philip C. Habib and were brought to the police command center by Ambassador L. Douglas Heck, the chairman of the interagency Working Group of the Cabinet Committee to Combat Terrorism. Psychiatrists aiding in the negotiations included Dr. Steven Pieczenik of the State Department and the FBI's Patrick Mullaney.

Police initially insisted that Khaalis come out of the B'nai B'rith headquarters into the street to talk to the ambassadors, but Khaalis demanded that the group come to the eighth floor where the hostages were held. After telephoned bargaining, the meeting was held on the first floor as a compromise. Khaalis had wanted the two sides to come armed, but after another hour of arguing, no one carried guns. Present at the negotiating table were Washington chief of police Maurice Cullinane, deputy chief Robert Rabe, captain Joseph M. O'Brien, chief of the homicide division, the three ambassadors, Khaalis, and Aziz. The ambassadors quoted passages from the Koran stressing compassion, and Ambassador Ghorbal suggested the release of thirty hostages as a sign of good faith. The ambassadors also initially suggested that the gunmen might wish to seek asylum overseas. Zahedi indicated that there was ''a very sharp reaction that he was not interested.'' Khaalis responded, ''I am American. I live in this country, and I want to die in this country.'' The question of ransom was not raised, and the meeting ended amicably with Khaalis embracing the ambassadors at 11:10 P.M.

All of the hostages were released at 2 A.M. on March 11, with Khaalis and the three terrorists at the Islamic Center being released on their own recognizance. The deal apparently was agreed on in phone conversations between Cullinane, Rabe, and Khaalis around 1 A.M. After obtaining authorization by district and U.S. law enforcement officials, the police agreed to release Khaalis without bail and to allow the case to proceed at a normal pace through the courts. Four restrictions were placed upon Khaalis: he was not to travel outside the district; he must give up his passport by March 14; he must not possess any firearms; and he must not talk to reporters. The bail reform act under which the agreement was legal requires only personal bond (requiring no money) when a defendant has community ties and a minor prior criminal record (or none at all) and is considered by the judge as unlikely to flee before trial. Only two of the gunmen had prior criminal convictions. Six of the other terrorists were held on $50,000 bonds, and two others were held for $75,000 bonds. (The group seemed particularly close knit; five of them had worked at the same cab company, and one had worked at Abdul Aziz's Georgetown jewelry shop.) The decision to free Khaalis was widely debated by the press, the public, and law enforcement officials. One federal official remarked, "It makes a mockery of everything we've been doing in the last year to cut down crime. These are animals; you might have to make promises to save lives, but you sure as hell don't have to keep them once everybody's safe."

Khaalis's freedom was short-lived, ending in his arrest on March 31. A police wiretap of his telephone recorded him saying to an unidentified female, "They are going to pay in blood for it. I'm going to kill somebody. And they're gonna die for what they did. It don't matter to me. I keep telling people. Now they're gonna pay." His son-in-law, Abdul Aziz, was also arrested. Guns were seized at two Hanafi locations, in violation of Khaalis's liberty agreement. Aziz had just returned from Saudi Arabia and had been searched upon his return. Khaalis had replied, "I'll kill all two hundred. Up their asses now. They're playing rough, we'll play rough." (The two hundred were not further identified.)

The government charged each defendant with twenty-four counts of armed kidnapping. Press coverage of the trial in Washington was extensive, with Harry T. Alexander, the lawyer for Khaalis, receiving special attention. His constant outbursts led the judge to cite him for contempt of court, but at the end of the trial the judge congratulated all of the lawyers for the jobs they had done and withdrew the contempt citations. With the exception of Khaalis, the jury convicted each of eight counts of kidnapping that arose from the episodes in which they participated, acquitting them of the attacks in which they were not present. They were also acquitted of conspiracy. The judge set an early September 1977 date for final sentencing, with Khaalis facing a possible jail term of 325 years. On September 6, the sentences were: Abdul Adam, 44-132 years; Abdul Latif, 36-108 years; Abdul Shaheed, 36-108 years; Abdul

Salaam, 40-120 years; Abdul Hamid, 36-108 years; Abdul Razzaq, 40-120 years; Hamaas Kaalis, 41-123 years for the B'nai B'rith attack; Abdul Rahman and Abdul Rahim, 28-84 years, and Abdul Qawee, 24-72 years, for the Islamic Center attack; and Abdul Nuh, fifty-eight years to life, and Abdul Muzikir, seventy-eight years to life, for the District Building attack. In October 1979, the D.C. Court of Appeals upheld the convictions of the twelve, saying the government's evidence was overwhelming. Three defendants did not appeal further. Khaalis asked the full Court of Appeals to review the case. On February 19, 1980, the U.S. Supreme Court refused to review the convictions of eight Hanafis for conspiracy, armed kidnapping, and other charges. The group had challenged the government's use of wiretaps and questioned the competence of a juror.

March 10, 1977—Australia—A man with a gutteral foreign accent threatened to kill Queen Elizabeth in a bomb attack at a sports complex in Brisbane hours before she dedicated it. He was credited with several other threats received against her. 3040

March 11, 1977—Colombia—Giuseppe Mondini, the manager of the French and Italian Bank in Bogotá, was kidnapped by the Domingo Lain cell of the ELN, which demanded a ransom of $5 million and respect for the lives of certain political prisoners. He was released on June 5 after his family paid $85,000. Seven have been arrested. 3041

March 14, 1977—Spain—An Iberia Airlines B727 carrying twenty-nine passengers and seven crew members from Barcelona to Palma de Mallorca was hijacked by Luciano Porcari, thirty-six, a self-professed communist Italian automobile mechanic armed with a rifle and a pistol. He demanded to be flown to Abidjan, Ivory Coast, where he was given $140,000 by the government and his three-year-old daughter, Margarita, from his former African mistress. The plane, having refueled in Algeria before flying to the Ivory Coast, flew on to Seville, Spain, for refueling and continued to Turin, Italy, where several passengers were released. His estranged wife, Isabella Zavoli, refused to give him their daughter, Consuelo, five. Distributing $50,000 of the ransom money to the passengers and passing out some of the case of champagne he ordered brought on board, Porcari took pills to keep awake. His mother tried to negotiate with him by radio, but he said, "Listen, stop insisting. You make me nervous, like you always have." He also turned down negotiation attempts by his brother, Giancarlo. He flew on to Zurich, where he negotiated for ninety minutes with an Italian consular official. The plane flew in the direction of France but turned back after half an hour and returned to Zurich, where more hostages were released. The plane next circled Turin, where he was rebuffed by Zavoli, and finally flew on to Warsaw, Poland, where the plane was refueled. Porcari received permission to land in Moscow, but the pilot, claiming exhaustion, refused to fly on. Porcari flew back to Zurich, where a Spanish policeman and two unarmed Swiss police overpowered him. One of the policemen sustained a flesh wound in the leg. Ugo Moretti, a reporter for the Turin newspaper *La Stampa*, published excerpts of an eighty-page manuscript Porcari had given him a year before, describing his adventures in Somalia, Tanzania, Zambia, Malawi, Mozambique, Portugal, Spain, Canada, the Ivory Coast, Liberia, Guinea, Algeria, and Italy. Moretti had told him. ''It is all here, but it lacks the final chapter.'' ''You'll read the final chapter in the newspapers tomorrow morning. If we don't see each other again, take care of the book,'' was the reply. Porcari's three-year-old daughter was returned to her mother in the Ivory Coast on March 19, three days after the end of the hijacking. 5505

March 17, 1977—Japan—A Japanese ex-convict attempted to hijack a domestic All-Nippon airliner to the northern Japanese city of Sendai from Tokyo. The pilot refused, landing in Tokyo. The hijacker committed suicide with cyanide in the lavatory. He was armed with only a toy gun. 5506

March 17, 1977—Japan—A twenty-seven-year-old man wielding a knife took over an All-Nippon B727 with forty-three persons on board after takeoff at Sapporo. Passengers overpowered him. 5507

March 17, 1977—Ireland—Kieran McMorrow, an IRA leader, was captured after a gun battle near the border. 3042

March 19, 1977—Turkey—A Turkish Airlines B727 with 174 passengers, flying from Dharbakir to Ankara, was hijacked by two pistol-wielding eighteen-year-old Turks who forced the pilot to fly to Beirut. The hijackers, identified as Mohammed Hassan Guzel and Issmail Jama Ashan, demanded $300,000 in Turkish currency and a visit to the nearest Palestinian refugee camp. They released the 174 passengers, including two Americans, one and a half hours after the plane landed and surrendered to Lebanese authorities one hour later. 5508

March 19, 1977—West Germany—Approximately ten thousand demonstrators protesting the building of a nuclear power plant at Grohnde battled with police. Two hundred thirty police were injured. The protestors claimed eighty of them suffered injuries.

March 20, 1977—Ethiopia—Three Molotov cocktails were thrown from a moving car at the USIS building in Addis Ababa. Two of the bombs fell short of the building; the third struck an upper window but did not ignite. 3043

March 21, 1977—Canada—Robert McLagan, thirty-seven, a Vancouver resident, took over a Toronto bank and held sixteen hostages. Armed with a sawed-off shotgun, he demanded to be flown to Uganda so that he could kill Idi Amin. After twelve hours, the former mercenary soldier in Africa surrendered.

March 21, 1977—United States—FALN bombs exploded in New York City at the American Bank Note Company, which prints foreign currency, and at the FBI's Manhattan headquarters, damaging a ground-floor drugstore and cutting a passerby with flying glass. The group demanded an end to a federal probe of possible links between the FALN and the National Commission on Hispanic Affairs, which is funded by the Episcopal church. Earlier in the month, two lay ministers were jailed rather than testify before the grand jury. They were identified as Maria Cueto, thirty-three, and her secretary, Raisa Nemikan, twenty-seven, both Episcopals. 3044-3045

March 26, 1977—Uganda—The *Nairobi Standard* reported that the Uganda People's Passive Resistance Front, which it claimed was working inside Uganda, intended to poison the Ugandan coffee and tea crop in an attempt to cut off foreign exchange, which financed Amin's military supplies. The group claimed, "We shall naturally be saddened by any loss of life resulting from contact with contaminated Ugandan goods, but you must hold Amin and yourself responsible." Observers suggested that the group was a fiction created by exiles and doubted the credibility of the threat.

March 27, 1977—Ethiopia—Don McClure, seventy-one, a missionary from Blairsville, Pennsylvania, was shot and killed on the lawn of his Gode home by an armed guerrilla band. His son, Don McClure, Jr., and Graeme Smith, a representative of the U.S. aid group World Vision, escaped after being shot at by the attackers. The elderly McClure was packing to leave Ethiopia after living there for twenty-five years. 3046

March 27, 1977—Argentina—Six bombs exploded during the night in Buenos Aires, including one at the Sheraton Hilton, which injured nine people, 3047

March 28, 1977—Argentina—A bomb exploded outside a Buenos Aires building housing the offices of the Soviet commercial attaché and the residences of embassy members, injuring no one. Other bombs during the evening hit the headquarters of four cattle breeders' associations. 3048

March 29, 1977—Turkey—Unknown individuals fired a machine gun from a passing car at the Izmir home of James E. Moffett, the U.S. consul general, causing considerable damage but no injuries, although he and his family were in the residence. An unexploded bomb was found later in his garden. A bomb damaged the car of a teacher in the American school during the same evening. The next day, fifty youths threw several dozen rocks at the USIS building in Ankara, breaking several windows but causing no injuries. Several Acilciler-TPLP youths were arrested and charged in May. 3049

March 30, 1977—Greece—Eighteen vehicles with foreign service license plates were firebombed in Athens and in the area adjacent to the Hellenikon Air Base. Eleven of the cars belonged to Americans. The bombings may have been related to the opening the next day of the trial of several youths accused of attacks on U.S. cars. 3050-3067

March 30, 1977—United States—A six-by-nine inch manila envelope containing either an explosive or incendiary device mailed to President Carter was found in the White House mailroom inside the Executive Office Building at 2:45 P.M. Police who dismantled the bomb said that it may have partly detonated while in the mails.

March 30, 1977—Philippines—Captain Ernesto Agbulo, the pilot of a DC3 chartered to fly Filipino military passengers to their southern base, went berserk and sprayed the passenger cabin with machine-gun fire, killing seven and wounding sixteen near Zamboanga.

March 31, 1977—Colombia—The ELN exploded three bombs at the Bogotá Sears store, causing minor damage, to commemorate the death of Alexis Umana, a university student, during a confrontation with police in 1976. 3068

April 1977—Zaire—Glen J. R. Eschtruth, the head of the United Methodist Mission Hospital in Kapanga, was killed by rebels. The Michigan missionary was initially reported kidnapped. 3069

April 1977—Cyprus—The British High Commission received EOKA-B letters threatening that diplomats and servicemen would be kidnapped and killed if Kiriakos Kakis, a Greek Cypriot in the United Kingdom whose extradition was sought by Cyprus, was surrendered. Andreas Ppouris and Klavdhios Neokleous were arrested in November 1977 for the threats. 3298

April 1, 1977—Sweden—In raids on a villa and radio stop in Stockholm, police arrested fourteen West Germans, Austrians, and Latin Americans, who were plotting to kidnap former Immigration Minister Anna-Grete Leijon and hold her for the release of imprisoned Baader-Meinhof members in West Germany. Weapons and other military equipment were found at the locations. On April 3, the Swedes turned over two of the West Germans to Bonn. Norbert Erich Krocher, twenty-six, was wanted in a 1972 warrant for terrorist activities for a BMG splinter group, while Manfred Richard Adoneit, twenty-seven, was prominent in West Berlin extreme left groups. Swedish police claimed that the group had intended to bomb several public facilities, as well as to kill prosecutor K. G. Svensson. Three Latin Americans were sent to Cuba, from which they had come. They were identified as Armando Gonzales-Carillo and Thomas Okusane-Martinez of Mexico and Maria Christina Fuentes Corea of Chile. Alan Hunter was sent to England, where he was released. Martinez was reported to have participated in a 1972 hijacking. On April 4, Krocher's headquarters was raided. Police found fifteen pounds of explosives, medical equipment, and several books on bombing techniques. A police uniform was found, along with thirty false Swedish, German, and French passports. On April 18, Carl Persson, the chief of Sweden's police, announced that detailed plans had been found along with a map of the Spanish Sahara, which may have been the terrorists' destination. The attack was to have taken place on April 24, beginning with a staged car mishap. Leijon would have been placed in a specially prepared coffin, and a message would be sent from the address of Katarina Bangata 55 in Stockholm. The next day, two more messages would be delivered, demanding money and the release of eight BMG prisoners. A million dollars would be delivered within five days, and a U.S. Hercules transport plane with two crews and twenty-five tons of fuel would be made available, as would medicine, blankets, tents and gas masks. Swedish newspapers would publish a photo of Leijon in the "people's prison" with a "Prisoner of B 26" placard around her neck. The papers would also publish a terrorist message. On April 26, two terrorist songs would be sung on television in Swedish and German, and the film *Lost Honour of Katharina Blum* would be televised on both stations at specified times. The next day, the French film *L'Etat de Siege* would be shown. The terrorists planned to release Leijon on April 30, after all of their demands had been met. On July 28, Stockholm police announced that they had found more than two tons of stolen dynamite, which they believed was to be used to create a diversion during the kidnapping. 3070

April 5, 1977—France—The U. S. embassy in Paris was firebombed. 3071

April 7, 1977—Libya—The Libyans announced that five persons, including one Egyptian, were publicly executed in Benghazi for "terrorist sabotage."

April 7, 1977—Ethiopia—Insurgents kidnapped Canadian helicopter pilot William Waugh, forty-two, and an unidentified Ethiopian health worker but released them unharmed two days later. 3072

April 7, 1977—West Germany—A group of motorcycle-riding terrorists pulled alongside the official car of Siegfried Buback, fifty-seven, the nation's chief public prosecutor, and fired machine gun bursts. Buback was killed along with his driver. His seriously wounded bodyguard died in a Karlsruhe hospital on April 12. The Ulrike Meinhof Special Action Group claimed credit for attacking the chief prosecutor in the Baader-Meinhof trial as he was being driven to work. Police offered an $85,000 reward for the killers. On April 9, three men sought in the attack were reportedly spotted in Sweden. On May 3, 1977, police shot and seriously wounded Guenther Sonnenberg, along with an accomplice, Verena Becker, twenty-four, in a shootout in the town of Singen on the Swiss border. Ballistic tests showed Sonnenberg's machine gun had been the Buback murder weapon. Becker had been freed from prison after the February 1975 kidnapping of Peter Lorenz (see incident 2246).

April 9, 1977—Ireland—Frederick Parkinson, thirty-five, a Belfast truck driver and member of the Ulster Defense Association, was held on charges of conducting firebombings in the center of Dublin. According to police superintendent John O'Driscoll, "the accused was caught red-handed. He had been carrying devices which had not exploded and was caught when one exploded in his pocket." 3073

April 9, 1977—United States—The FALN claimed credit for planting eight incendiary devices that caused small fires in three Manhattan department stores. The group demanded the release of five Puerto Rican nationalists and denounced a federal grand jury investigating the FALN. 3074-3076

April 10, 1977—United Kingdom—Zuhair Akache fired into a car near Hyde Park in London and killed Qadi Abdullah Ali Hajri, sixty-five, deputy chief of the North Yemen Supreme Court, who had served as his nation's prime minister from 1972 to 1974; his wife, Fatimah, forty; and Abdullah Ali Hammami, a minister at the North Yemeni embassy. The killer escaped into a subway station. It was reported that he took an Iraqi Airways jet to Baghdad within five hours. He later appeared as Captain Mamoud, who led the October 13, 1977, Lufthansa hijacking (see incident 3207), where he died in a shootout with a rescue squad. 3077

April 10, 1977—Libya—Two hundred demonstrators sacked the Egyptian embassy in Benghazi. The next day, the Libyan consulate in Alexandria was set on fire.

April 11, 1977—Costa Rica—The Revolutionary Commandos of Solidarity claimed credit for bombs that exploded at the offices of Pan Am and Henderson and Company, as well as at a San José government building housing the U.S. military mission. Heavy damage but no injuries were reported. It was believed that the attack was in reprisal for the recent death in Nicaragua of FSLN leader Carlos Aguerero Echeverria, a Costa Rican. 3078-3080

April 11, 1977—Argentina—Leftist terrorists shot and killed an Argentine executive of a local firm operating under license from General Motors. The attack occurred in the early morning in Buenos Aires. The Montoneros claimed credit. 3081

April 12, 1977—France—The Action Front for the Liberation of the Baltic Countries claimed credit for firebombing two Paris offices of Franco-Soviet organizations. The front door of the France-Soviet Association offices near the Palais Royal gardens was slightly damaged. Extensive damage was reported at the Editions de Moscou publishing house. 3082-3083

April 13, 1977—Israel—Jerusalem police defused a small bomb connected to a battery-powered timer near a convention center. It was believed the bomb was to protest the tenth anniversary of Israel's capture of Jerusalem's Arab section. 3084

April 13, 1977—France—Luchino Revelli-Beaumont, fifty-eight, president of the French Fiat subsidiary, was kidnapped by the Committee for Socialist Revolutionary Unity, which demanded a $30 million ransom and set a deadline of June 11 for payment. On June 16, Hector Aristy, a former Dominican ambassador to the U.N. Educational, Scientific, and Cultural Organization, was charged in Paris with the kidnapping. He had been serving as an intermediary between the family and the kidnappers. The group lowered the demand to $8 million and then to $3 million. The victim was released unharmed near Versailles on July 11. The next day, Swiss police in Bern revealed that a ransom of $2 million had been paid by the family because the company had refused to negotiate. On July 21, Albert Chambon, a retired ambassador, was charged in Paris with protecting criminals by failing to tell police of the negotiations he had successfully participated in. Chambon, sixty-eight, a friend of the victim, said, "I feel I carried out not only my duty as a friend, but also that of a citizen, which consists in saving a human life." On July 26, Spain arrested seven persons believed involved. France requested extradition. 3085

April 14, 1977—Israel—Two Israelis armed with a pistol took over a section of the West German embassy in Tel Aviv, holding it for five hours before surrendering. The pair, identified as André Kilchinski, forty, and Henri Toronchik, thirty-four, held two empty rooms on the second floor and said they were angered over the slow progress of and world apathy toward trials of Nazi war criminals. They cited the Düsseldorf trial of fourteen defendants who were Nazi guards at the Maidenek concentration camp in Nazi-occupied Poland, a trial that had lasted one year and was expected to continue for two more. They promised to surrender if they were interviewed on Israeli television and if the embassy was closed for the day. The first demand was granted. 3086

April 15, 1977—Colombia—Victor Bigio, British manager of the textile firm Vanytex, was seriously wounded in Bogotá when he was shot several times by EPL assailants. 3163

April 19, 1977—El Salvador—Mauricio Borgonovo Pohl, thirty-seven, El Salvador's foreign minister, was kidnapped by gunmen from the Farabundo Marti Popular Liberation Front who invaded his home while he was eating breakfast. The group demanded that thirty-seven political prisoners be allowed to leave the country, threatening to kill their hostage. The government refused to negotiate and claimed to be holding only three terrorists (this figure was later increased to nine). The group sent several communiqués reiterating the demand. Borgonov's family asked Panamanian President Torrijos to intervene with President Molina. Pressure was also applied from a number of other Latin American nations, but the government refused to negotiate. French and Honduran diplomats offered to mediate. On May 10, Borgonovo's body, with three .22 caliber bullet holes in the head, was discovered beside a road ten miles southwest of San Salvador. The kidnappers said that Borgonovo, who had extensive business holdings, had been executed in a "revolutionary war to establish socialism." The next day, the White Warriors Union retaliated by attacking a meeting of a Catholic youth group headed by the Reverend Alfonso Navarro Oviedo, thirty-five. A teenager wounded in the assault later died. 3087

April 20, 1977—Namibia—SWAPO gunmen abducted eighty boys and forty girls, all blacks between the ages of twelve and twenty, from a Roman Catholic mission school in the north. Eleven students and six staff members later escaped, while the thirty guerrillas escorted the rest of the group across the Angolan border nine miles away. This appears to be a method of recruitment for the organization.

April 24, 1977—Libya—The Middle East News Agency reported that Muammar Qaddafi was wounded in the hand by a Libyan citizen who immediately committed suicide.

April 24, 1977—Israel—A bomb exploded on board a bus on its way to Beersheba, injuring twenty-eight, ripping out seats, and smashing windows. Arab passengers going to their jobs had left the bus ten minutes earlier and were suspected in the bombing. 3088

April 24, 1977—Poland—Polish police were reported to have stopped a hijacking attempt at Krakow airport by a Polish soldier who had seized a hostage and had attempted to take over a TU134 being prepared to fly to Nuremberg, West Germany. He fired several shots before being overpowered by soldiers dressed as mechanics. 5509

April 26, 1977—Ethiopia—Two members of the ELF attempted to hijack an Ethiopian Airlines flight between Makale and Gonder and divert it to Saudi Arabia or Sudan. Security guards shot and killed the attackers in a gun battle in which several passengers were wounded. 3089

April 27, 1977—France—Two Molotov cocktails were thrown at the West German consulate in Lille during the night. One hit the first floor but did not ignite. 3164

April 28, 1977—Cuba—Garland Grant, who had participated in the Black Panther hijacking of a Northwest Airlines jet to Havana on January 22, 1971, said that he desperately wished to leave Cuba, having spent five and a half years in Cuban prisons, in which he lost an eye in a beating by prison guards. Grant, who changed his name to Jesus Grant Gelbard, claimed to be living in a Havana hotel with fifteen other hijackers, who were also unhappy. "I just want to get back to the United States. I'm living like a dog in Cuba. There are more racism problems here than in the worst parts of Mississippi." He said that an American hijacker at Guanahay prison was killed when "his head was bashed against a wall."

April 28, 1977—West Germany—A Stuttgart court handed down life sentences to three surviving members of the Baader-Meinhof Gang—Andreas Baader, thirty-three; Gudrun Ensslin, thirty-six; and Jan-Karl Raspe, thirty-two—for the murders of four U.S. soldiers in bombings of U.S. installations in Frankfurt and Heidelberg in May 1972. They were also found guilty of thirty-four attempted murders and were given fifteen-year sentences for bombings of two police stations, a publishing house, and a judge's car, and for the attempted murder of policemen during the shootout in which they were arrested. The defendants had boycotted the trial for six weeks and were in poor physical condition as a result of their hunger strike. Their chief lawyer, Otto Schily, claimed that they should be tried as prisoners of war.

April 28, 1977—Guatemala—The GALGAS (Guatemalan Anti-Salvadorean Liberating Action Guerrillas) claimed that it would kill Salvadoreans who refused to leave the country. The group's press communiqué said, "For the sovereign freedom of Guatemalans, in face of the avalanche of Salvadoreans who daily invade Guatemala . . . We Guatemalans are not willing to endure this Salvadorean invasion any longer. In November we warned them that we did not want violence. They did not listen to us. Unfortunately, we have had to act. The unidentified bodies that have appeared on the southern coast, in the capital and in other places are those of Salvadorans who laughed at our warning. . . . We warn all Guatemalans and Guatemalan companies: You should not hire Salvadoreans nor cooperate with them in any way. On the southern coast our workers have been displaced by Salvadoreans and in the cities there are many unemployed Guatemalans because their jobs have been given to Salvadoreans.'' 3090

May 1, 1977—Mauritania—The Polisario Front kidnapped six French citizens —five men and a woman—in the mining town of Zouerate. Foreign Minister Louis de Guiringaud asked the Algerian ambassador to exert influence on the group to free the hostages. He was later told that Algeria has no power over the Polisario. Two French citizens died and the facility was extensively damaged during the mortar attack on the mining town of Zouerate. After intervention by the U.N. secretary general (see incident 3258), the hostages were released on December 23, 1977. 3091

May 2, 1977—Italy—Minutes after an Iberian airliner landed at Rome's Fiumicino Airport, Abuaisha Ali Fargani, a Libyan, used a knife to threaten the pilot and demanded that he be flown to Madrid to see his fiancée in Bilbao. He claimed to have explosives on the plane, which would be blown up if his demand was ignored. He allowed the other passengers to get off but kept the pilot, copilot, and navigator on board. Police negotiators diverted his attention, giving the pilot a chance to squirt him with a fire extinguisher. Fargani was overpowered. It was learned that he had been denied entry into Spain because he had no money. 5510

May 3, 1977—Rhodesia—A train on the Rhodesia-South African railway line was blown up near the Botswana border by black nationalists. A black rail worker was killed and another injured when the explosion threw two locomotives and several freight cars off the track.

May 6, 1977—Lebanon—Lars Gule, a Norwegian claiming to be a journalist, was arrested at Beirut airport before boarding a Lebanese flight to Frankfurt when twenty-five ounces of plastic explosives were found hidden in a book in his baggage. Detonators were also discovered. Gule said he obtained the explosives from a man named Ahmed in the Sabra district of Beirut. 3092

May 6, 1977—Mexico—A bomb exploded at a military checkpoint near the meeting site for Mexican President Lopez Portillo and Panama's President Torrijos several hours before the scheduled meeting. 3093

May 6, 1977—Soviet Union—Sixty Ethiopian students occupied the Ethiopian embassy for four hours in protest of the visit to Moscow of Lieutenant Colonel Mengistu Haile Mariam, the Ethiopian government's leader.

May 8, 1977—Japan—A Northwest Orient B747 flying from Tokyo to Honolulu was the scene of an attempted hijacking one hour after takeoff when Bruce Kohl Trayer, twenty-five, of Prairie du Chien, Wisconsin, held a razor at the throat of a stewardess and demanded to be flown to Moscow. The pilot, Captain Homer Sutter, later radioed that the purser had overpowered the hijacker by injuring him with a fire ax. Trayer's father had told him that Russia does not use food additives. The hijacker claimed to be ''fed up with the United States.'' He was arrested and hospitalized with a two-inch cut on his head. 5511

May 8, 1977—Argentina—A Montonero couple bound two doctors and two nurses at a private Buenos Aires clinic and then ambushed Admiral Cesar Guzzetti, fifty-eight, the foreign minister, bludgeoning him and shooting him twice in the head. The attackers held a pillow over the gun to muffle the sound of the shots. Guzzetti was partly paralyzed as a result.

May 11, 1977—Saudi Arabia—Saboteurs set fire to the Aramco-operated Abqaiq production center, causing $100 million in damage to a network of pipelines. The Beirut newspaper *Al Anwar* quoted sources as saying that the ''explosion was the result of an intentional act of sabotage'' by an unnamed foreign nation. 3094

May 12, 1977—Iran—Two terrorists were killed by Iranian security police while attempting to enter a ''Jewish Agency'' in Tehran. Two security men were also wounded in the machine-gun battle, which occurred twelve hours before the scheduled arrival of U.S. Secretary of State Cyrus Vance. SAVAK claimed that the two were members of an Islamic-Marxist organization. 3095

May 14, 1977—France—The Youth Action Group and the New Armenian Resistance Group claimed credit for bombing the Turkish tourism office in Paris, slightly injuring the building's caretaker. 3165

May 16, 1977—Portugal—FLEC said in Lisbon that it would blow up Gulf Oil's offshore drilling complex in Cabinda. The group criticized Gulf for paying the Angolan government $2 million per day in oil royalties. Gulf said it was making contingency plans. 3096

May 17, 1977—Spain—A GRAPO bomb exploded at 4 A.M. in a classroom of the U.S. cultural center in Madrid, stunning a watchman and badly damaging the center. Vice-President Mondale arrived in Madrid six hours later. 3097

May 19, 1977—Turkey—A small bomb caused slight property damage in the U.S. consulate compound in Istanbul. 3166

May 20, 1977—Spain—ETA gunmen disguised as hospital attendants raided the home of industrialist Javier de Ybarra, sixty-three, on the outskirts of

Bilbao. Ybarra is chairman of the Spanish subsidiary of Babcock and Wilcox, a U.S. engineering corporation. The group, which drove him away in an ambulance, demanded $15 million ransom for his release. On May 21, the government announced that it would permit twenty-three Basque prisoners to leave the country if they petitioned to be exiled. The next day, the government agreed to send five prisoners to Belgium. The group killed Ybarra after the expiration of the ransom deadline. After police failed to find the body, the ETA sent another communiqué explaining where the body was. He was found along an isolated mountain trail near Bilbao, shot in the head, on June 22. The Ybarra family apparently believed that he would be set free after the Spanish elections. 3098

May 23, 1977—Netherlands—In the first of two raids by South Moluccan terrorists, nine gunmen led by Max Papilaya, twenty-four, took over a 9 A.M. commuter train. Two members of the group pulled an emergency cord to halt the express between Assen and Groningen, allowing five others in masks to board and herd the hostages into first-class compartments. Minutes later, a second group took over a schoolhouse (see next incident). Thirty-four passengers, most of them elderly, were released, leaving fifty-six others as hostages. Both groups made the demands but set no deadlines. They requested cleaning equipment, food, and medical supplies, giving the impression that they were prepared for a long siege. It was determined later that the group had studied the operations of their comrades who had made similar attacks in December 1975 (and whose freedom they were now seeking) (see incidents 2505 and 2513) and were prepared to counter government tactics.

The attackers effectively created a climate of fear, firing their guns at a police helicopter that was circling the train. On May 25, they shoved three hostages with nooses around their necks out of the train and then hauled them back in after an hour. The next day, they displayed one of the hostages, bound and gagged, outside the train for fifteen minutes. On May 27, they fired warning shots later in the afternoon and refused to grant a request that a pregnant passenger be freed to prevent a miscarriage.

Dutch authorities turned down numerous requests from volunteers around the nation who wished to serve as substitute hostages, hoping that the terrorists would tend to develop a friendship with their hostages. The terrorists did relent somewhat in their demands. On May 30, they withdrew their demand to take their hostages with them to an unspecified location. KLM insisted on knowing the destination before it would recruit a volunteer crew.

The terrorists continued in their determination to achieve their goals, however. On June 2, they fired on a police command post and charged that officials were using two giant antennas to spy on them. They demanded that the dish-shaped antennas be removed. The devices had been erected at a nearby farmhouse for a video unit that was observing the train. Earlier in the day, the terrorists walked around outside the train and took snapshots of each other.

Press coverage was heavy, and at times the media exercised questionable judgment. On June 4, the press alleged that Dutch commandos had placed tiny listening devices under the train cars during the night (this later proved true). Power was also cut to the train's motors.

That same day, two mediators boarded the train and talked with the terrorists for six hours. The next day, the group released two women: A. H. Brouwer-korf, thirty-one, and Nelleke Ellenbroek-Prinsen, twenty-five, who was five months pregnant and suffered from thyroid problems and high blood pressure. On June 8, the terrorists released Theo van Hattem, forty-six, who may have suffered a slight heart attack.

Despite these minor gestures, the Dutch authorities became convinced that the terrorists would not back down, and at 5 A.M. on June 11, special commandos launched a simultaneous attack on the train and schoolhouse. Six F-104 Starfighter jets were flown over the train to scare and surprise the terrorists, while thirty marines raced across one hundred yards of open fields on the west side and blasted their way into the train. The group used special explosives to open the train's doors. Six of the South Moluccan terrorists were shot dead, as were a twenty-year-old woman and forty-year-old man who were shot in the head when they jumped to their feet, despite the soldiers' orders to lie flat (the same problem had occurred in the Entebbe raid). Seven other hostages, all of them women, were injured, as were two Dutch marines and another terrorist during the twenty-minute attack. The terrorists had segregated male and female passengers, and the gunmen were sleeping in the same first-class car as the women when the raid began. The two surviving terrorists were arrested.

The police later announced that within hours of the seizures, a group of royal marines and civilian and military police began practicing for the assault. Two special radars used to detect differences in heat were secretly used. These devices noted the movement of the terrorists, whose guns showed up on the radar. The commandos also used television cameras, binoculars, and other night-viewing devices.

On June 14, the Moluccan community, treating the dead terrorists as local heroes, buried the group. The first one buried was the only woman among the six slain, a twenty-two-year-old dental assistant. A Moluccan man said that she had been hit by 106 bullets and that a male terrorist had sustained 300 hits. Tensions between the Moluccan and Dutch community continued, with many threats made against the Moluccans by angry Dutch citizens. 3099

May 23, 1977—Netherlands—A few minutes after the attack on the train, four South Moluccans seized a primary school in the village of Bovensmilde, forcing 105 children and 6 teachers into the main classroom. Fifteen South Moluccan students were immediately freed. The terrorists had food and folding cots brought in for the children. They demanded a B747 to fly them, the group in the train, and twenty-one imprisoned comrades out of the country. The group never specified its ultimate destination, and observers suggested that it could be Vietnam, South Yemen, or Libya. Benin said that it would welcome the gunmen. The group set a deadline of 2 P.M. on Election Day for the release of the prisoners, which included the two groups who had participated in similar barricade operations in December 1975 (see incidents 2505 and 2513) as well as a group that had conspired to kidnap Queen Juliana in July 1975 (see incident 2327). Four of the prisoners were brought to a crisis center two days later, where they were interrogated about the hostage takers. It appeared that this group was well prepared for a long siege and in fact broke the other groups' records for patience.

   The Dutch and the Moluccans played a tense waiting game. The government said that the safety of the hostages had to be ensured before bargaining could begin. Justice Minister Andreas van Agt said, "We will not talk about any demands until all the children are liberated," while Prime Minister Jup Den Uyl vowed that "no hostages will leave the country." The negotiating team was run by two psychiatrists, Dick Mulder and Henk Havinga, who were in telephone contact with both groups of terrorists. The group in the school papered over the building's windows and fired warning shots at parents who tried to speak to them through megaphones. On May 25, they forced the children to scream from the windows, "We want to stay alive." Later the terrorists fired two short bursts of gunfire, one occurring when an elderly woman wearing a white smock wandered past the police guards and strayed close to the school. Police learned that she was not a nurse, as had been assumed, but a patient from a nearby mental asylum. The terrorists allowed two police to bring her back to safety.

   Telephone lines were set up between the train and school, and on May 25, the terrorists dropped their deadline. They released four children on May 26, and at 3 A.M. the next day, they released four more. Minutes afterward, the group released all of the children and one teacher after an infectious disease broke out. (Many observers claimed that the authorities had placed a mild drug in the food being brought to the site, but this was not confirmed.) Fifty children were rushed by ambulance to a Groningen hospital, but none of them was reported seriously ill with the stomach ailment. The terrorists agreed to free the children and one teacher after the remaining four teachers agreed to remain hostages and shield the terrorists from a police attack. The agreement was made without consultation with those on the train. It was later learned that the children who had been released previously had displayed some of the symptoms of the outbreak. Police learned in questioning the children that there were four terrorists rather than five as initially reported. A photographer claimed that he had snapped a picture showing a South Moluccan fleeing the school while the children were being released. He also claimed that the authorities had seized his film.

On June 1, the gunmen allowed mediators to intercede, having previously warned that people would be killed if mediators were introduced; however, both sides rejected each other's initial candidates. The gunmen proposed two persons perceived by the Dutch as too radical. The Dutch counterproposal of two persons was rejected in turn. A South Moluccan youth group, Pattimura, published a letter supporting the gunmen. On June 3, the standoff was broken when the groups agreed to two mediators from the Moluccan community. One was Ventje Soumokil, the widow of the short-lived Republic of South Moluccas leader in the 1950s, who was executed by Indonesia in 1966. The other was Dr. Hassan Dan, fifty-six, a retired general practitioner. The mediators talked to the terrorists on the train and managed to coax them into releasing a few hostages. On June 3, lawyers for some of the prisoners said that a few of them did not wish to accompany the gunmen out of the country.

The Dutch grew to believe that the stalemated positions could not be reconciled, and at 5 A.M. on June 11, troops attacked the two barricaded positions. The attack on the school took only ten minutes. Armored personnel carriers rushed the school on all four sides, and one of them broke through a wall. Marine commandos rushed in and met no resistance. There were no injuries, although the teachers were bruised and cut by falling brick and glass. The four terrorists were placed under arrest. There were reports that members of the Moluccan community had fired on the advancing commandos. On July 6, police arrested two unidentified Moluccans in Bovensmilde in connection with the siege.

On September 22, the seven surviving terrorists, aged between eighteen and twenty-eight, were sentenced to terms ranging from six to nine years. An eighth youth received a one-year term for helping plan the attacks. During the trial, Willem Soplanit, the school attack leader, said the ''guns were used only as a threat'' and that the group had agreed in advance not to kill any hostages. However, one of the train gunmen said that during the marine rescue, he ran into the women's compartment, hoping ''to shoot everybody'' but lost his nerve. 3100

May 25, 1977—United States—The Pedro Ruiz Botero Commandos bombed the Fort Lauderdale regional marketing office of Mackey International Airlines. The president of the firm immediately cancelled plans for flights to Havana. 3101

May 25, 1977—Mexico—Spanish businessman Jesus Bencerro Portillo was kidnapped in Mexico City by three individuals believed to be members of the Twenty-third of September Communist League. The group demanded a ransom of $438,000. 3167

May 26, 1977—Soviet Union—A Soviet Antonov 24 twin-engined turboprop flying eighteen passengers and five crew members from Riga, Latvia, to

Daugavpils was hijacked by Vasily Sosnovsky, thirty-seven, a Latvian mechanic, who forced the pilot to fly to Stockholm. He had pretended to be hiding a bomb under his coat. The plane was escorted in by Swedish jet fighters. The Swedes denied the Soviet request for extradition and granted Sosnovsky's plea for political asylum. Sosnovsky claimed that he had been punished in the Soviet Union for a previous escape attempt and would be happier in a Swedish prison than free in the Soviet Union. On July 27, he was sentenced to four years. 5512

May 28, 1977—Israel—A bomb went off near the entrance to the Joppa Gate in the Old City of Jerusalem, injuring a Canadian tourist and four others. Authorities closed the entrance and held several Arabs for questioning. 3102

May 29, 1977—Turkey—A bomb exploded at Istanbul's international airport, injuring forty-two persons, including an American woman. The bomb was planted in a luggage storage room, as was a bomb that exploded in a railway station and killed three. The 28 May Armenian Organization claimed credit for the attacks. The same day, one man was injured by gunfire in an assassination attempt against opposition leader Bulent Ecevit in new political violence that occurred during the final week of Turkey's national election campaign. 3103

May 29, 1977—Guatemala—El Salvador's ambassador to Guatemala, Colonel Eduardo Casanova Sandoval, was kidnapped in Guatemala City at 2:30 P.M. on the Avenue of the Americas, a residential district, by the Guerrilla Army of the Poor, using two vehicles. The location was the same as that of the 1970 kidnapping of German Ambassador von Spreti (see incident 0360). The group demanded that Inter-American Development Bank Secretary Jorge Hazeka read a five-page communiqué to the twelve hundred delegates attending the organization's eighteenth plenary session of the bank's governors. The communiqué was also to be distributed to all delegates, observers, press, and invited guests. The bank agreed, and Hazeka took twenty minutes to read the statement, which condemned Guatemala and El Salvador as "being at the service of the US and the great international monopolies." The communiqué went on to say, "The Salvadoran Government seemed to have given ample guarantees to enable you to meet at your ease. But the events which took place in conjunction with the elections in the neighboring country totally abolished the conditions which the great world capitalists require for the approval of their projects for penetration in our countries. . . .Because they did not have such a guarantee, the capitalists did not meet in El Salvador, which had been chosen as the site for their assembly. The capitalists feared, and with reason, that the Salvadoran people, angry at the repression and the fraud which the Molina regime has unleashed in the last 2 months, could with its demonstrations spoil the 'peaceful' and developist meeting of the imperialist bankers, their officials and their employees. In truth, the IDB governors' meeting in San Salvador would have been an additional affront to that nation, subjected now to one of the most violent, bloodthirsty and repressive campaigns since 1932. The Salvadoran brothers would not have let it take place without expressions of rejection and protest. . . .The governors, bankers, officials and employees of the imperialist enterprises of the various countries participating in this meeting are quite mistaken if they believe that they can still fool the Guatemalan people as the imperialists believe they deceive the people of our continent with their financial policy which is at the service of the dominant classes of the US, the great monopolies and the oligarchies of Latin America.'' Although President Kjell Laugerud refused to negotiate with the kidnappers, Sandoval was released unharmed on May 31 in Guatemala City. 3104

June 2, 1977—Costa Rica—A minor opposition presidential candidate, G. W. Villalobos, thirty-six, wrapped himself in a Costa Rican Flag and fired a .38 pistol at the San José home of fugitive U.S. financier Robert L. Vesco. No one was injured when three shots entered a window of the home, one blew out a tire on Vesco's 1975 Mercedes limousine, and two more hit the car's trunk. Villalobos was immediately arrested and charged with illegal possession of a firearm. He told reporters that it was time Vesco was thrown out of the country. Vesco is wanted on stock fraud charges in the United States and became eligible for Costa Rican citizenship later in 1977 after spending five years in the country. 3105

June 4, 1977—United States—An FALN bomb exploded after noon in the Cook County Building in Chicago, down the hall from the office of Acting Mayor Michael A. Bilandic. One person was injured. Later that day, riots broke out in the Puerto Rican district. A policeman shot and killed a rioter. Eighty others were reported injured. 3106

June 5, 1977—Lebanon—A Middle East Airlines B707, flight 322 from Beirut to Baghdad, was hijacked an hour into its flight by a man in a wheelchair who brandished a gun and a bomb. He was identified as a Lebanese, Nasser Mohammed Ali Abu Khaled, twenty-seven, who forced the pilot to land in Kuwait, despite the Kuwaitis' closing the airport and switching off the lights. Upon landing, he demanded $1 million from Kuwait, Iraq, and Saudi Arabia. He held the passengers on board the plane for six hours in 114 degree heat while negotiations were conducted by Kuwait Interior and Defense Minister Saad Abdullah Sabah, nephew of the ruling Sheik Sabah Salem Sabah. The hijacker fired one shot at commandos who boarded the plane disguised as technicians sent to fix the plane's air-conditioning system. Kuwaiti officials had agreed to the ransom demand but told Khaled that he would have to leave the plane to collect the money. When Khaled refused, the commandos were sent in to overpower him. No one was injured. Among the passengers were 56 Lebanese, 24 Iraqis, 8 Palestinians, 2 Kuwaitis, 3 Jordanians, 2 Syrians, 2

Britons, 2 South Yemenis, and a Saudi, as well as 3 infants. The crewmen were Lebanese. The plane was carrying 105 passengers and 7 crewmen. Kuwait released Khaled on August 28, 1977, for humanitarian reasons, claiming his motive was to obtain treatment for his paralysis. 5513

June 6, 1977—Italy—The Genoa office of Lufthansa was firebombed, causing minor damage. A leftist student charged with the attack said it was to protest West German policies concerning extremists. 3168

June 8, 1977—Colombia—The U.S. Consulate in Cali was bombed, causing some property damage. 3169

June 8, 1977—United States—The Carras Cruise Lines, a Greek-owned company based in New York, cancelled plans to sail the MTS *Daphne* from New Orleans to Havana four times per month after receiving several threats. 3107

June 9, 1977—Italy—A tall, thin, black-haired gunman shot and fatally wounded Taha Carim, sixty-two, Turkey's ambassador to the Vatican, as Carim was entering his Rome residence. The assailant fled on foot. Carim underwent surgery on his neck and shoulder wounds but died six hours later. In Beirut, the Justice Commandos for Armenian Genocide claimed credit for the "revenge." 3108

June 11, 1977—Soviet Union—A bomb went off in a taxi outside the Soviet-skaya Hotel in Moscow, which is often used by foreign dignitaries. An employee of the Moscow taxi administration told reporters that the bombing occurred when a taxi driver opened his trunk. The driver was injured, and damage was "insignificant." The hotel administrator said she had not heard the blast, "and even if I did I could not tell you because we do not release such information." In a rare public mention of urban terrorism in the Soviet Union, Tass reported on July 7 that the KGB had arrested a man in connection with the incident.

June 13, 1977—Syria—Two Syrians were hanged in Damascus's main square after being convicted of belonging to an assassination squad with the "instigation and financial support of the Iraqi regime." The court claimed that the group had killed four people, including an adviser of President Hafez Assad. Notices fixed to the bodies read, "In the name of the people of Syria, hanged for perpetrating killings and assassinations and sabotage acts against the Republic of Syria."

June 14, 1977—United States—Three Croatian terrorists forced their way into the Yugoslavian U.N. Mission at 2:30 P.M., wounding Radomir Medich, fifty-eight, a guard, in the abdomen. The group held the building for two hours and fooled police into believing they held a female hostage by using a falsetto voice. The group threw hundreds of leaflets into the street, demanding Croatian independence. They hauled down a Yugoslav flag and demanded that some of the leaflets be given to Kurt Waldheim, U.N. secretary-general. Waldheim received the leaflets. Some Yugoslav employees shouted, "Kill them. They'll never get justice." There was also a report that a Yugoslav had pulled out a machine gun and intended to storm the building. The terrorists eventually surrendered. Yugoslavia protested the United States's alleged tolerance of the gunmen. On June 16, the United States charged the group with conspiracy to kidnap the Yugoslav ambassador, Jaska Petric, and hold him for publicity. They were also charged by New York State for attempted murder. Marijam Buconjic, twenty-eight, of New Windsor, New York, Vladimir Dizdar, twenty-three, of Chicago, and Joco Brekalo, thirty, of St. Louis were found guilty of plotting to kidnap the ambassador on October 12 and were scheduled for sentencing on November 17. Dizdar was also convicted of shooting the chauffeur. Marijan Buconjic received seven years; Joza Brekalo, five years, and Vladimir Dizdar, four years. 3109

June 17, 1977—Turkey—A group protesting Dutch treatment of South Moluccans threw explosives at the Dutch consulate in Izmir, shattering several windows. 3110

June 17, 1977—France—Bombs wrecked the Paris offices of the France-USSR Magazine and slightly damaged the Soviet-owned Commercial Bank of Europe. Bombs were defused outside Tass and in a restaurant above the Aeroflot offices. The Solidarity Resistance Front claimed credit, saying that it was protesting the scheduled visit of Soviet leader Leonid Brezhnev, who arrived three days later amid tight security precautions. No one was injured in the bombings. 3111-3114

June 17, 1977—Cyprus—Four Arabs driving a car with diplomatic plates attempted to kidnap George Atallah, a Palestinian who was living in Lebanon, and force him aboard a Middle East Airlines flight to Beirut. Atallah, using crutches, had been admitted to a private Nicosia clinic with a leg injury and was released on June 16. The local press claimed that he was a member of Fatah who had expressed interest in returning to his birthplace, Israel, where he had been arrested for anti-governmental activities. The PLO was accused by the press of being behind the kidnapping attempt and of intending to place Atallah on trial and execute him. 3115

June 18, 1977—Syria—Suspected Syrian terrorists shot to death Brigadier General Abdul Hamid Razzouk, commander of the army missile regiment, on the steps of his Damascus home.

June 18, 1977—Bulgaria—A domestic Bulgarian flight from Vidin to Sofia with forty-nine persons on board was hijacked by Rumen Cankov Dimitrov, twenty-two, an auto mechanic, who ordered the pilot "to fly me to the West." It was later ascertained that he specified London or Munich. The pilot claimed to have enough fuel to fly to Belgrade, Yugoslavia, where the plane landed. Dimitrov was disarmed by a Yugoslav security policeman disguised as a Bulgarian pilot who had entered the plane. Dimitrov claimed that the hijacking had no connection with the Belgrade conference on the Helinski agreement. On June 19, the Bulgarian embassy said that it would not seek extradition and would leave the decision whether to try or expel him to the Yugoslavs. On June 23, Reuters reported that Bulgaria requested extradition, mentioning their anti-hijacking pact. 5514

June 19, 1977—United States—Dragisa Kasikovich, forty-four, the editor of a Serbian-American anticommunist newspaper, *Liberty,* and Ivanka Milosevich, nine, the daughter of his girl friend, were found dead in Chicago, each shot once in the head and once in the chest. The Serbian National Defense Council blamed Yugoslav secret service (UDB) agents for the attack. Jack Anderson, a syndicated American columnist, noted that Kasikovich had reprinted one of his columns that dealt with UDB harassment of exiles.

June 19, 1977—Yugoslavia—Croatian terrorists were blamed for a bomb that exploded in northern Yugoslavia aboard the Dortmund to Athens express train, killing one person and wounding two Finnish students and six Yugoslavs. 3116

June 19, 1977—Guatemala—Roberto Rischer Sandhoff, seventeen, died on June 21 from a bullet wound he received when four men attempted to kidnap him in Guatemala City. He was the son of Roberto Fischer Saravia, a Ford dealer and director of the El Dorado-Americana Hotel. One of his kidnappers also died. He was identified as Arturo Berganza Bocaletti, who police claimed had been in North Korea, Cuba, and the Soviet Union and had aided in the murder of U.S. Ambassador John Gordon Mein in 1968 (See incident 0088). 3117

June 20, 1977—France—Paris's international airport received two false bomb threats, and an unconfirmed report claimed that Soviet security men had requested the French police to be on the lookout for a sniper during the visit of Leonid Brezhnev. 3118-3119

June 20, 1977—El Salvador—The White Warriors' Union threatened to kill forty-seven Jesuits if they did not leave the country within thirty days. The deadline date coincided with the start of U.S. congressional hearings in the House Subcommittee on International Organizations on human rights in El Salvador. The group claimed that the Jesuits were involved in subversion. The

Jesuits remained at their posts. Many observers suggested that the terrorists had ties with the government. 3120

June 21, 1977—Chile—An LAN B727 flying from Antofagasta to Santiago with seventy-one passengers and seven crew members was hijacked by Carlos Tamayo, an employee of the Chilean Public Works Ministry, who diverted the plane to Mendoza, Argentina, where it was surrounded by police. Tamayo initially demanded that the plane be flown to Algeria but released all except the crew when the plane landed. He was talked into surrendering before he could carry out his threat to set off explosives. 5515

June 22, 1977—Cyprus—*I Simerini*, a local Nicosia newspaper, reported that a meeting of international terrorists had taken place in Cyprus and was addressed by Carlos, the Venezuelan-born terrorist, and George Habash, the PFLP leader.

June 24, 1977—United States—Bombs exploded at the suburban Pittsburgh home of John Badovinac, president of the Croatian Fraternal Union of America, causing $30,000 damage but no injuries. Badovinac said that he had twice before been threatened with death by Croatian separatists who disagree with the nonpolitical, non-separatist aims of his organization. 3121

June 26, 1977—Sri Lanka—Officials of the state-owned Ceylon Electricity Board believed that sabotage was responsible for a nationwide blackout during the night. An installation near Sri Lanka's main hydropower generating plant was damaged.

June 26, 1977—Brazil—A bearded gunman fired a single shot from a small-caliber gun at the car of Marvin Hoffenberg, fifty-one, the U.S. consul general in Recife, as he and his wife, Lucia, were leaving the Grande Hotel restaurant after a morning anniversary celebration. No one was injured. Observers speculated that the attack may have been related to Hoffenberg's arrangement to have Rosalynn Carter meet two American missionaries who reportedly were held naked and incommunicado for three days in a small cell. A few days later, a Brazilian law student said that he had fired the shot intending to frighten the consul's friend for flirting with his wife.

June 28, 1977—Costa Rica—A powerful bomb exploded at 6 P.M. at the San José entrance to the consulates of El Salvador and Nicaragua, causing extensive damage but no injuries. Police speculated that the attack was aimed at the El Salvador consulate. 3122

June 29, 1977—Dubai—A Gulf Air VC10 was hijacked after takeoff with its sixty passengers and four crew members by Samir Mohamed Hassan Sharara, twenty-six, from Bint Jubayl village in southern Lebanon. He was armed with a pistol with a silencer and two grenades and forced the pilot to land at Doha International Airport in Qatar, where he demanded a $125,000 ransom and safe passage to an undisclosed nation. He said he took over the plane to publicize the situation in "south Lebanon, which is subjected every day to thousands of shells and savage, repeated aggressions." Negotiations were conducted from 8:30 A.M. for two hours by Major General Hamad ibn Khalifah Al Thani, the crown prince and defense minister. The hijacker allowed the passengers to disembark. During this process, a force of Qatari troops boarded the plane and arrested Sharara. 5516

June 29, 1977—Israel—Several Arab terrorists broke into a Druze home in Al-Mari at 10 P.M. and shot and wounded three family members. The terrorists had been brought to the Lebanese border in a taxi. 3123

July 1977—Algeria—In interviews with Madrid's Cambio held in Algiers and an unspecified European capital, PFLP Executive Committee member Taysir al-Qubba'ah and Salah Yasir and Abu Yuhud, two Fatah dissidents, vowed to kill several Arab personalities, including Yasir Arafat, for "grave compromises with Zionism." The spokesman, who referred to the "real leaders, such as Abu Dawud," told the reporter, "It has not been possible to neutralize the Arab regimes. Hence it will be necessary to eliminate them. . . . Men like Arafat, Abu Mazin or Abu Iyad are nothing but traitors to the real interests of the Palestinian people. . . . Arafat and the present leadership of the organization robbed us of a good comrade in Paris not long ago. Mahmud Salih, secretary of the Arab bookshop, discovered the contacts the leadership was making with the Zionists. When he released tape recordings and written documents to the public which proved the existence of these contacts, they killed him." 3124

July 2, 1977—United States—Twenty-nine people, including six reporters, were sent to a local hospital after Buddy Cochran, thirty, of Americus, Georgia, drove his Jaguar into a crowded Ku Klux Klan rally in Plains, Georgia. Cochran claimed that he had a black friend in the marines in Europe and disagreed with the speech being made by Klan Imperial Wizard Bill Wilkinson.

July 2, 1977—Turkey—Five young men attempted to see the French ambassador at his Istanbul summer residence. They forced their way through the gate and cut phone lines. The guard, Musa Boran, was struck and shot at but managed to disperse the group by firing two shots at them, one of whom he claimed was French. 3125

July 3, 1977—Brazil—Delorme Mehu, Haiti's ambassador to Brazil, was shot and killed by two men in the northeastern town of Salvador. The assassins, identified as Geraldo Pereira dos Anjos and Israel Motta da Silva, claimed that they were hired by the Haitian embassy's first secretary, Louis Robert Mackenzie, who denied their charges. 3126

July 3, 1977—Egypt—Members of the At-Takfir wa Al-Hijrah (variously translated as Repent and Migrate, Society for Atonement and Flight From Evil, and Atonement and Migration Society), a rightist religious cult, kidnapped Shaykh Muhammad Husayn adh-Dahahabi, Egypt's former minister of religious affairs, from his home. Reports indicated that between four and nine men disguised as police armed with submachine guns entered his home. They placed him in one of his two cars and drove off. The second car was surrounded by neighbors, who were informed by the driver, "I have not been instructed to speak by my emir." The group phoned demands to news agencies, calling for $500,000, the release of sixty imprisoned members of the group, publication of a statement, and apology for past criticism of the group, which considers President Anwar Sadat a heretic, and campaigns for the liquidation of banks, destruction of night clubs and liquor stores, and a return to a puritan form of Islam. They set two deadlines for the demands to be met. Negotiations were reportedly carried out by lawyer Shawkat at-Tuni, who served as defense counsel for the organization. On July 4, police debunked reports that Dahahabi had been killed, noting that a phone call pinpointing the location of his body turned out to be false. However, his body was found on July 7 in a shabby house in the nightclub district of suburban Giza. Dahahabi, sixty-four, wearing a white robe and a scarf around his head and neck, had been shot through the left eye. Coroners said that he had been killed on July 4. Police arrested a bricklayer identified as Moustafa Abdel Maasood Ghazy, who claimed to have fired the shot. Hundreds of members of the group were arrested in the following week, including the leader of the Moslem fanatics, Shukri Ahmed Mustafa, thirty, who admitted to planning the kidnapping.

July 4, 1977—Syria—A bomb exploded in a car parked between the Syrian Air Defense Command Headquarters and the American School in Damascus, killing six persons and injuring eleven others, including Michel Duger, head of the French Commercial Mission, who was passing in his car and suffered head injuries. Police reported considerable damage to houses in the area, as well as to the front wall of the school. Documents found in the car's wreckage indicated that it had entered Syria from Iraq at the Abu Shamat border post on June 28. 3127

July 4, 1977—United States—A Vermont Transit Lines bus traveling through the Bronx, New York, was hijacked by a twenty-six-year-old Navy seaman identified only as Robinson, a Panamanian resident alien, who shot John McGavern, fifty, a librarian at the University of Hartford, in the neck to intimidate the other passengers. He ordered the bus driver, Norman Bozick, forty-one, to drive to Kennedy Airport, where the bus was cornered at TWA hangar 12. The airport was closed for one and a half hours. Robinson demanded a DC8 to Cuba and a ransom of $6 million. Although he allowed nine of the twenty-two passengers to leave, he also ordered the separation of the black from the white passengers and spoke of racial mistreatment in the United States. He was described as a Spanish-speaking black wearing blue jeans. Frank Bolz of the New York Police Department took over negotiations as a plane was readied for possible use. Susan Bruso, twenty-two, of Florence, Massachusetts, a member of the armed forces, attempted to subdue Robinson with a karate chop. In the confusion, he fatally shot a passenger, Nettie Blassberg, sixty who had been directed to stand on the bottom step of the bus exit. The bus driver lunged at him and was himself killed by the hijacker's .45 caliber weapon. Jimmy Lo, thirty-six, of Hong Kong, was shot in the chest when Robinson's command to "shut up" was mistaken for "stand up," a movement that scared the hijacker. Robinson surrendered after nine hours and was held without bail to undergo mental tests. Bath, Maine, authorities said he was being investigated in connection with stolen money orders. 3128

July 5, 1977—Chile—Four Chilean Socialists hijacked a Ladeco B727 flying from Arica on a domestic flight and diverted it to Lima, Peru, where they released fourteen women, two children, and one man. The flight had begun with fifty-two passengers and eight crew members. The hijackers were identified as Patricia Mairiam Castro Flores, eighteen, and three brothers with the last name of Alarcon Herrerra; Carlos, Willibaldo, and Patricio, who had hijacked a Chilean plane to Cuba in December 1969 (see incident 0295). The group demanded the release of two Chilean socialists, Carlos Iazo and Erick Snacke, from Santiago military jail. After five hours of negotiations with the Peruvian foreign minister, José de la Puente, and Interior Minister General Luis Cineros Vizquerra, the hijackers released their remaining hostages in return for asylum in the Venezuelan embassy. The group had requested clearance to fly to Venezuela and on to Paris. On July 9, they were granted asylum to Cuba. 3129

July 6, 1977—Israel—A pipe bomb planted under a vegetable stand in Petah Tiqva, a Tel Aviv suburb, killed one and injured twenty-two, four of them seriously, in a crowded open-air market. In Beirut, the PLO and PDFLP claimed credit. Fifty Arabs were rounded up for questioning. The trial of Brigitte Schultz, twenty-three, and Thomas Reuter, twenty-four, two West Germans who had been arrested in Nairobi along with three Palestinians planning to shoot down an El Al B707 with Strella rockets in January 1976, was scheduled to begin (see incident 2565). 3130

July 7, 1977—Switzerland—The Frankendorf villa of Rudolph Rupp, the deputy director of F. Hoffman-La Roche, Ltd., was bombed, causing minor damage and no injuries. Extremists said that this was a "first warning" to the company, which they claimed was responsible for the dioxin poisoning of the Seveso area in northern Italy in 1976 by a La Roche subsidiary.

July 7, 1977—France—Two European-looking gunmen in their twenties fired six pistol shots through the limousine window of the Mauritanian ambassador to France, injuring him in the jaw, arm, shoulder, and thigh. Ahmed Ould Ghanahalla was driven to the American hospital in Neuilly after the attack on the Avenue Malakoff in the sixteenth arrondissement of Paris, and was reported in satisfactory condition. The attackers, armed with either a .44 magnum revolver or a P-38, fled on foot toward the Place Victor Hugo. A woman called Agence-France Presse to claim credit for the Mustafa el Wali Bayyid Sayed International Brigade. Sayed was a former secretary-general of the Polisario Front who was killed in a raid on Nouakchott, Mauritania in June 1976. The Polisario Front in Algiers denied responsibility and blamed Moroccan intelligence, which it claimed was attempting to discredit the Polisario. "It is well known that Paris has always been chosen by the Moroccan intelligence services and their accomplices for the execution of such tasks." Moroccan Foreign Minister Ahmed Laraki claimed that the gunmen had been provided arms by Algeria. 3131

July 8, 1977—Lebanon—A B707 leased to Kuwait Airways by British Midland Airway was hijacked out of Beirut by six Fatah dissidents who claimed to be members of the Friends of the Arabs. They were led by Abu Saed, thirty-six, (also known as Abdul Karim Abu Hamdi), a PFLP-GC member who had served as the PLO's post office communications chief during the 1975-1976 civil war in Lebanon. The PLO indicated that he had received foreign intelligence assistance in his jailbreak shortly before the hijacking. The group, armed with grenades, one submachine gun, and smaller weapons, threatened to blow up the plane if the demands for the release of three hundred prisoners in Arab jails were not met. The plane first flew to Kuwait, where officials indicated that there were forty-five passengers and a crew of ten, including seven Britons. Saed demanded that Menachem Begin release Archbishop Hilarion Capucci. Kuwaiti Planning Minister Mohammed Youssef Adasani negotiated with the hijackers on the runway in Kuwait and agreed to allow them to fly to Aden. The group released several of their hostages and then traded twenty-eight others for the Kuwaiti chief of security, Brigadier Muhamed al-Hamad, the deputy chief representative of the PLO, Awni Battash, and an Al Fatah member, Abou al Ruzz. However, the plane landed in Damascus after two of the hijackers and three hostages overpowered Saed, an accused thief, defrauder, and extortionist. After he called them traitors, one of the gunmen told Saed, "We're not traitors. The demands you're making have nothing to do with what the hijacking was originally about." The group surrendered to Syrian authorities on July 10. Two days later, four persons working at Beirut airport were held on suspicion of having given weapons to the hijackers. 3132

July 9, 1977—Argentina—Peugeot executive Andres Gasparous was wounded when five leftist gunmen in an automobile fired on his home near La Plata. A police guard was killed and another wounded. 3170

July 10, 1977—Soviet Union—Two young men armed with a hand grenade that contained no explosives hijacked an Aeroflot TU134 twin-engine jet flying from Petrozavodsk, Karelia, to Leningrad and forced the pilot to land in Helsinki, Finland. The hijackers had initially demanded that the pilot fly to Arlanda Airport in Stockholm, but he apparently did not have enough fuel. The hijackers released the plane's five crew members but held seventy-nine passengers, including seven children. They demanded a Finnish crew to fly them to Sweden, but Sweden refused them entry. The hijackers then demanded that they be flown to some other country. Negotiations were initially hampered by a lack of Russian speakers at the airport. The authorities refused to discuss the hijackers' demands until the children were released. Six hostages escaped by jumping out of the plane's rear door. One man suffered a twisted ankle in this maneuver. When the hijackers slept, five crew also escaped during the night after locking the cockpit. The group released forty-two women and children the next day. The hijackers turned down an offer of a Cessna plane to fly them out of Finland, and they surrendered on July 11. The Soviets requested extradition the next day and vowed harsh punishment for the two when they were returned under terms of a Soviet-Finnish antihijacking treaty on July 15. Gennady L. Seluzhko, twenty-two, and Alexander Zagirnyak, nineteen, were sentenced to fifteen and eight years respectively on November 10, 1977. 5517

July 10, 1977—Syria—A bomb exploded in a parked car across from the Interior Ministry in a Damascus square, killing two and injuring fifty-three.

July 10, 1977—India—A mob stoned the car of Joseph Patrick O'Neil, the U.S. consul, in Krishnagar as he was repairing it. He had gone there to investigate a shooting incident at the Hare Krishna movement complex. Eleven members of the International Society of Krishna Consciousness, including three Americans, were detained after fifteen villagers were injured in a shooting incident. The villagers had attacked the center after a farmer was allegedly beaten by Krishna members.

July 11, 1977—Switzerland—The Zurich office of Air Iran was destroyed by firebombs. 3133

July 12, 1977—Panama—The British embassy received an anonymous call from an individual claiming to be a member of a Guatemalan nationalist commando, threatening to kidnap U.K. ambassador to Panama Robert John in reprisal for British plans to grant independence to Belize. 3134

July 12, 1977—Spain—A leftist group claimed credit for a bomb that damaged the French embassy's cultural service in Madrid. The GRAPO bomb exploded twelve hours after it struck the library. 3135

July 12, 1977—El Salvador—Two men armed with . 45 caliber pistols shot and killed Osmin Aguirre Salinas, the former president of El Salvador, as the eighty-two-year-old took a walk outside his San Salvador home. The killers fled in a waiting car with two other men.

July 14, 1977—Greece—American Express in Athens was bombed, shattering windows and damaging the main door. The car of an American professor at a U.S.-sponsored school was set on fire. A bomb was found in the U.S. Armed Forces Post Exchange. No injuries were reported. Individuals protesting alleged U.S. support for the former junta and tolerance of the Turkish invasion of Cyprus were suspected. 3246-3248

July 14, 1977—Ethiopia—Count Carl Gustaf von Rosen, sixty-seven, a Swedish nobleman who once led the Ethiopian air force, was killed in a guerrilla attack at the house of a local administrator near the town of Wode, where he was staying. Several others were killed in the attack. 3136

July 16, 1977—United States—An Alitalia B747 carrying 365 persons from New York to Rome made an emergency landing in Halifax, Nova Scotia, after receiving a bomb threat. No bomb was found. 3171

July 18, 1977—United Kingdom—Firebombs were thrown through the window and against a door of the Vietnamese embassy in London, igniting small fires that caused minor damage but no injuries. 3137

July 18, 1977—Netherlands—A firebomb was thrown onto the thatched roof of the Blaricum villa of Pieter Menten, seventy-eight, a Dutchman who was a suspected Nazi war criminal. The device started a fire early in the morning. It badly damaged the thirty-room house, which held a large part of his art collection, valued at millions of dollars. Most of the paintings and antiques were saved, and there were no injuries. Menten had been arrested in December 1976 and accused of killing two hundred persons, mostly Jews in Poland, while serving with the Nazis.

July 20, 1977—Israel—A bomb exploded at noon in a Nahariya supermarket, injuring five persons. Sixteen Arabs were rounded up. Another bomb exploded in a Jerusalem zoo at about the same time. 3138-3139

July 20, 1977—Japan—Taketomo Takahashi, forty-two, a JRA member, was arrested by Japanese police in Tokyo after being deported by Sweden, where he was arrested while carrying an Indonesian passport in Stockholm. The former assistance professor at Rikkyo (St. Paul's) University was charged with using a forged passport. It was believed that he was in charge of JRA research and arms procurement.

July 22, 1977—Mexico—Daniel Ferrer Fernandez, the Cuban consul in Mérida, was given special police protection after receiving several death threats. He had been the subject of an attack in July 1976 in which one of his companions was killed (see incident 2803). 3140

July 22, 1977—Peru—A Cuban fishing boat docked at a port near Lima was destroyed by a bomb. The International Commandos of Zone 6 of CORU claimed credit for the incident. No injuries were reported. 3249

July 23, 1976—Tanzania—Several people, including members of the armed services, were arrested in connection with a bomb that exploded outside a northern Tanzanian tourist hotel. It caused some damage but no injuries.

July 23, 1977—United States—The Alyeska Pipeline Service Company announced that there had been an attempt to damage the Alaska pipeline with five charges of dynamite. The flow of oil was not hampered by the explosions, which tore off twenty to thirty yards of insulation and bent support posts. On July 27, Larry D. Wertz, twenty-six, a fur trapper who lived one and a half miles from the site of the blast, was arrested. He was found walking out of the woods carrying a rifle and pistol. Several others were later arrested in connection with the case, including William J. Freeman, twenty-one, a cook and baker, and Donald E. Drum, nineteen, a painter whose father was a pipeline security guard.

July 25, 1977—United States—A dynamite bomb exploded at 3:20 A.M. at the Rockville, Maryland, home of Morris J. Amitay, forty-one, the executive director of the American Israel Public Affairs Committee, the major pro-Israel lobby in Washington. Damage was estimated at £50,000; no injuries were reported. Palestinian groups denied responsibility. Police later determined that a car seen speeding away from the scene was not related to the attack.

July 27, 1977—United States—Richard Sachs, twenty-three, of Jersey City, and Thomas George, twenty-two, of New York City dropped a bag containing cockroaches on the floor of the House of Representatives during a debate on food stamps. They claimed to be members of a sixty-one-member group, Members of American Youth for Action, which had called for a $3 per hour minimum wage. They were held on $500 bond.

July 28, 1977—Israel—Palestinian guerrillas claimed credit for a bomb that exploded in a Beersheba market, wounding 28. 3141

July 29, 1977—Italy—Seven pounds of dynamite caused minor damage to the Milan Swissair office. The Combatants for Communism, a leftist group, said it was protesting the long detention of Petra Krause in Swiss jails. She had been arrested in 1975 and charged with the bombing of an American bank in Zurich, as well as supplying arms to West German and Italian terrorists. She was held in investigative custody and was scheduled to go on trial September 19. 3142

July 30, 1977—Greece—A bomb exploded in Athens, damaging five U.S. military vehicles. It was believed to be in protest of a U.S. Greek military agreement. 3143

July 30, 1977—Turkey—Leftists were blamed for a bomb that exploded in the backyard of the U.S. consulate in Adana, which shattered windows but caused no injuries. A second undetonated bomb was discovered on consulate grounds. 3144

July 30, 1977—Italy—The Milan offices of Aeroflot were bombed, causing severe damage to the offices and to three vehicles parked in front of the building. No injuries were reported. No group claimed responsibility for the attack, but the press speculated that a right-wing group may have been retaliating for the Swissair bombing (see incident 3142). 3250

July 30, 1977—West Germany—Terrorists killed Juergen Ponto, head of the Dresden Bank, the second largest in Germany, during an attempted kidnapping during the night. The Red Morning claimed credit and called for the immediate release of all urban terrorists, threatening that ''more members of the exploiting class will be executed.'' Police on August 1 arrested Eleonore Maria Poensgen, twenty-three, in Frankfurt, who was identified by the widow as one of the attackers. Poensgen's lawyers presented fifteen witnesses at a press conference who backed her alibi that she was on her way to a party at the time of the attack. Police were also searching for Susan Albrecht, twenty-six, of Hamburg, a daughter of a friend of the Pontos, and six other accomplices, including several women.

July 31, 1977—France—Twenty-five thousand demonstrators marched on the Super Phoenix nuclear breeder reactor in Malville. One hundred extremists charged police barricades, touching off a riot in which 105 persons were injured and a French demonstrator, Vital Michalon, thirty-one, died, apparently from a heart attack. Police blamed extremists from ecological groups from Belgium, Italy, Switzerland, France, and West Germany for the attack. Police found guns, iron bars, helmets, gas masks, and wire cutters in the cars of some of the protesters at the plant, which is being funded by France, Italy, and West Germany.

August 1, 1977—Zambia—Bombs wrecked the Lusaka offices of the Zimbabwe African People's Union but caused no injuries. 3145

August 2, 1977—Turkey—The Izmir residence of the U.S. consul general was sprayed with automatic weapon fire in the early morning, but no injuries were reported. 3251

August 3, 1977—United States—FALN bombs exploded on the twenty-first floor of 342 Madison Avenue in New York City, which houses Defense Department security personnel, as well as at the Mobil Building at 150 East Forty-second Street. The first attack came at 11:30, when an employee noticed a handbag left on a window sill. He found a clocklike device and alerted fifty coworkers to flee the office. The bomb went off twelve seconds later, blasting the office doors off their hinges but causing no injuries. An hour later, the Mobil bomb killed Charles Steinberg, twenty-six, a partner in an employment agency in the building, and injured eight others. The FALN warned that bombs were located in thirteen other buildings, including the Empire State Building and the World Trade Center. One hundred thousand office workers were evacuated in the rain during the afternoon. Eighty more crank calls were received in Brooklyn. On August 4, New York Police announced the arrest for illegal possession of a shotgun, a revolver, and one hundred rounds of ammunition of David Perez, twenty-seven. His roommate, Vincent Alba, twenty-six, was also questioned. Marie Haydee Beltran Torres, twenty-two, was charged by federal authorities with the Mobil bombing. A federal grand jury in Chicago on September 7 indicted her husband, Carlos Alberto Torres, twenty-five, and Oscar Lopez Riviera, thirty-four, on conspiracy and a "variety of explosive-related charges." 3146-3147

August 4, 1977—Israel—Israeli forces reported killing two Arab terrorists, injuring a third, and arresting two more who had crossed the border and planned an attack three miles south of the Sea of Galilee in hopes of disrupting U.S. Secretary of State Cyrus Vance's visit to the Middle East. 3148

August 5, 1977—Italy—Two young men planting a dynamite bomb were killed when it exploded early in Turin. Police said they were connected with leftist terrorists and identified them as Aldo Orlando Marin Pinones, twenty-four, of Chile and Attilio di Napoli, nineteen, of Italy. 3149

August 6, 1977—Turkey—Automatic weapon fire was directed at the Istanbul Intercontinental Hotel, which is owned by Pan Am. Several windows were broken, but no one was injured in the attack. Later in the month, twenty-three members of the Acilciler faction of the Turkish Peoples Liberation Party/Front were arrested for this incident, as well as numerous bombings and bank robberies. 3252

August 6, 1977—Rhodesia—A bomb expoded in Woolworth's in Salisbury, killing eleven and injuring seventy-six, mostly blacks. The dead—eight blacks and three whites—included a black child. The second floor of the store was wrecked by the blast, which knocked out a large section of the eight-inch thick outer wall. Police said the bomb was composed of seventy-five pounds of TNT and had been placed at a parcel check-in-site. Authorities blamed Rhodesian guerrillas for the blast, although no group claimed credit. A suspect was arrested on October 28, 1977. 3150

August 8, 1977—United States—A bomb attributed to the FALN was found in the AMAX building in New York City. 3151

August 9, 1977—Rhodesia—In an attack on St. Paul's Roman Catholic mission 220 miles southwest of Salisbury, black nationalist guerrillas shot in the back and killed two white women missionaries, identified as Johanna Decker, fifty-nine, a German-born physician, and Sister Ferdinanda, an Austrian nun. The guerrillas assaulted and kicked black nurses, threatened them with rape, and forced patients from their beds. 3152

August 9, 1977—Mexico—American business executive William A. Weinkamper was dragged at gunpoint from his car while he was on his way home from his Mexico City office. He was released three days later after the payment of what some sources reported as a $2 million ransom. Weinkamper is manager of Clevite de Mexico, an automobile parts manufacturing subsidiary of Gould, Inc., of Cleveland. On August 19, police arrested two youths and recovered $100,000 of the ransom. 3172

August 11, 1977—Peru—The *Rio Jababo*, a Cuban ship, was damaged by an explosion in El Callao as fish were being unloaded. The Cuban government claimed that it was a case of sabotage, but Peruvian authorities attributed the explosion to a blowout of a boiler. Havana press reported that CORU claimed credit. 3173

August 12, 1977—France—The Paris-Cairo flight of an Air France jumbo jet was diverted out of Nice by Tarek Sajed Khater, nineteen, of Cairo, who held a biscuit tin aloft and informed the 242 people on board, "I have one thousand pounds of dynamite in here, and I can blow up all the passengers and the plane. . .fighting for the rights of the Islamic people." He forced the pilot to fly to Benghazi, but Libyan authorities prevented the plane from landing. The plane then overflew Corfu and landed in Brindisi, Italy, to refuel. During the flight, he recited Hamlet's soliloquy in English, French, and Arabic and dabbed his neck with perfume. Upon landing, he left the plane to talk to ground personnel and was locked out of the plane by the crew. He was immediately arrested by police, who grabbed an ax and small boxes containing a nonexplosive material. During five hours of questioning, he informed authorities that his father had been killed in the recent Egypt-Libya border clashes and that he was attempting to reconcile the two nations. He was charged with air piracy. 5518

August 14, 1977—United States—A bomb exploded near a Venezuelan air force plane parked at Miami international airport, causing no damage or injuries. The Luis Boitel Commando claimed it was retaliating for the jailing of CORU leader Orlando Bosch. 3153

August 15, 1977—United States—The *Washington Post* reported that federal agents in Miami "arrested a Bay of Pigs veteran, seized a cache of automatic weapons and confiscated 3 boats in thwarting plans by about a dozen Cuban exiles to raid their former homeland. Assistant U.S. Attorney R. J. Sanford said the boats and weapons were apparently to be used soon in a 'hit-and-run harassment raid somewhere on the Cuban coast.' The federal raiding party, made up of U.S. Customs agents, arrested only one person, Pedro Gil, 41, a member of the group that invaded Cuba in 1961. He was charged with violating federal arms export control laws. Authorities said other arrests may be made as the investigation progresses." 3174

August 15, 1977—United States—The Yugoslav consulate was damaged by a fire set in front of the building in the early morning in San Francisco. 3253

August 15, 1977—West Germany—A pipe bomb exploded in the Stuttgart office of leftist lawyer Klaus Croissant, causing damage to the office but no injuries to the two lawyers present. Croissant, who had fled to France two months previously, was suspected of relaying information to jailed members of the Baader-Meinhof Gang while acting as their defense attorney.

August 16, 1977—Israel—The PLO claimed responsibility for a bomb that exploded in a bus on its way from Kiryat Shmona to Tel Aviv. The bomb went off in Afula, injuring eight. Eleven Arabs on board or in the vicinity of the bus were detained for questioning. 3175

August 20, 1977—United States—Jerry Richard Mills, thirty-six, of Escondido, California, claimed he had a bomb and forced the pilot of a Western Airlines B707 flying from Honolulu to Denver to land at Salt Lake City. Mills demanded to be met by police and was held pending an appearance before a magistrate. The FBI claimed that it considered this incident a hijacking. Mills had boarded the plane in San Diego. No bomb was found, and none of the seven crew or twenty-four other persons on board was injured. 5519

August 21, 1977—Mexico—Two men, members of the People's Revolutionary Armed Forces (FRAP) took over a bus in Michoacán State and held forty hostages. They threatened to set off a hand grenade and kill the passengers if the government did not release Ramon Campana Lopez (also known as the Butcher), who was held for his involvement in the 1974 kidnapping of José Guadelupe Zuno, the father-in-law of former President Luis Echeverria. A shootout with police ensued at midnight after the guerrillas forced all men to the front of the bus. One of the grenades went off, killing ten and wounding fifteen. Reports differed as to whether one of the guerrillas was killed or had escaped. His colleague was wounded. Police reported that the FRAP consisted of former members of the Armed Revolutionary Movement (MAR), a group that had received aid from North Korea and the Soviet Union in late 1970. It was later reported that the hijackers had also demanded safe passage to the U.S. border.

August 21, 1977—France—A bomb exploded outside the Italian consulate in Paris, breaking most of its windows but causing no injuries. Police found two pamphlets titled "Solidarity with Kappler," a reference to a German S.S. colonel who had escaped from life imprisonment in Rome for war crimes. 3254

August 25, 1977—West Germany—A young couple, members of the Red Army Faction, entered the Karlsruhe apartment of an elderly couple, tied them up, and constructed a "Stalin organ," consisting of forty-two rockets constructed of lengths of water piping arrayed in a wide rifling arc. The missiles were fitted with contact fuses and were set to be fired sequentially by an electric clock. The group aimed the contraption at the offices of the new federal prosecutor, Kurt Rebmann, fifty yards away. The sixty-nine-year-old painter and his wife, age seventy-four, were able to reach a cupboard where they found a knife to cut their bonds. Police were alerted, and the attack was prevented.

August 26, 1977—Italy—A bomb exploded outside the Milan offices of the Italy-German Chamber of Commerce, injuring no one, in an apparent reprisal for the escape of Nazi war criminal Herbert Kappler. 3177

August 28, 1977—West Germany—Molotov cocktails were thrown into an IBM office building in Hamburg, causing slight damage and no injuries. 3255

August 29, 1977—Australia—Fire destroyed the chancery of the Indian High Commission in Canberra. The fire's cause was being investigated.

August 31, 1977—Portugal—Chile's newspaper *El Mercurio* reported that the Revolutionary Coordinating Junta (JCR), which includes members of the Chilean MIR, Argentinian ERP, Bolivian ELN, and Uruguayan Tupamaros, had held several meetings in its Lisbon headquarters.

September 1, 1977—Canada—A bomb exploded in a Toronto garage, killing three Serbians. The *Toronto Sun* reported that the three had planned to bomb the homes of sympathizers of Yugoslav President Tito and Yugoslav missions in six or seven cities in Canada and the United States in retaliation for the murder in Chicago in June of Dragisa Kasikovich (see June 19, 1977 incident). 3178

September 4, 1977—Lebanon—Wilhelm Schoettler, the court-appointed counsel for the three surviving members of the 1972 Munich Olympics terrorist team, said that they were living in Beirut on monthly life pensions of $1,000 each paid by the Libyan government.

September 5, 1977—West Germany—Foreign Ministry spokesmen denied reports that Palestinian guerrillas were being routinely issued work and residence permits. The statement refuted remarks by Fatah deputy Abu Iyad, who told a reporter of the Beirut weekly *Al-Usbu' Al-'Arabi* that "nowadays West Germany issues residence and work permits to commandos as long as they possess Fatah membership cards of those of the Palestinian Liberation Front."

September 5, 1977—West Germany—Hanns-Martin Schleyer, sixty-two, president of the West German employers' association, the Confederation of Industry, a member of the board of directors of Mercedes-Benz, and West Germany's most famous industrialist, was kidnapped by members of the Red Army Faction, successors to the Baader-Meinhof Gang. Between ten and fifteen terrorists firing submachine guns ambushed his two-car convoy at an intersection in Cologne during rush hour as he was being driven to his apartment. The group pushed a baby carriage across a one-way street, halting his Mercedes sedan. The terrorists then fired over two hundred rounds, killing two police escorts, a security agent, and a driver. They dragged Schleyer from his limousine into a minibus, which was later found abandoned in a garage under a Cologne high-rise building. The minibus contained a letter with a demand for the release of several West German terrorists.

The terrorists' demands were initially unclear. An individual phoned *Bild Zeitung* and said, ''This is the Action Society. . . .We demand the release of Baader and everyone imprisoned in Stammheim. Otherwise Herr Schleyer will be executed at 5:15 P.M. tomorrow.'' The Red Army Faction phoned two other news agencies with similar demands. Early in the morning of September 6, the central office of the German Press Association (DPA) in Hamburg reported that it received an anonymous call demanding the release of Ralf Reinders, Fritz Teufel, Gerald Klepper, Ronald Fritsch, Andreas-Thomas Vogel, Till Meyer, Waltraud Sieber, Ilse Jank, and Thomas Weslau. The Siegfried Hausner Commando Group of the RAF later cleared up matters, demanding freedom for eleven terrorists, who were to be accompanied on a flight out of the country by Martin Niemoeller, eighty-five, an evangelical theologian. (The pastor had been a German submarine commander during World War I but became a pacifist and a leader of church resistance against the Nazis.) Each of the prisoners was to be given the equivalent of $43,000 and be allowed to fly to the country of his or her choice. The government was further instructed to promise not to attempt to obtain extradition. Five of the eleven Baader-Meinhof Gang terrorists were women. The eleven were identified as Andreas Baader, Gudrun Ensslin, and Jan-Carl Raspe, the most well-known surviving members of the original Baader-Meinhof Gang, who were being held for a series of bank robberies and bombings (see incident 1027) in the early 1970s; Karl-Heinz Dellwo, Hanna Krabbe, and Bernd Roesner, who took part in the 1975 attack on the West German embassy in Stockholm (see incident 2282); Guenter Sonnenberg and Verena Becker, two suspects in the assassination of prosecutor Siegfried Buback; and Ingrid Schubert, Irmgard Moeller, and Werner Hopper, who were in custody for robbery, suspicion of murder, and attempted murder, respectively. It was reported that the jailed guerrillas said they would like to fly to South Yemen or North Korea, although rumors persisted that three of the prisoners preferred to stay in prison.

The West German government on September 9 named Denis Payot, president of the Swiss League for Human Rights, as its intermediary after a noon deadline for freeing the prisoners had passed without incident. Payot transmitted messages between the negotiators during Schleyer's incarceration, relying mainly upon media offices, which the terrorists used for messages.

The terrorists also passed several items proving that Schleyer was alive, usually tape recordings of his voice reading from the latest newspapers. Due to background noises on one of the tapes, the Dutch newspaper *De Telegraaf* reported that authorities believed Schleyer was being held on a boat in the Netherlands. Background noises were amplified and indicated the presence of water beating against something. Horns heard in the background were traced to signals used by Dutch vessels. An international search by Dutch and German officials was negative.

The Schleyer kidnapping, following closely the assassinations of Buback and Ponto and the aborted rocket attack in Karlsruhe, caused increased concern by the public regarding terrorism. Business executives sought increased protection through the legal system, and the sales of security services boomed. The government, deciding to remain firm in the face of the kidnappers' threats, refused to release the prisoners and was supported by the public, according to various polls. However, sources reported that a government official flew to Vietnam in what appeared to be an effort to find a nation willing to accept the prisoners if they were freed. Hans-Jurgen Wischnewski, a high government official, made a visit to Algeria to seek asylum for the prisoners in early September. Buoyed by the news, the terrorists allowed at least six deadlines to pass without harming Schleyer. However, many believed that the government was stalling for time, allowing it to conduct a nationwide hunt for the kidnappers' hideout. Schleyer's family claimed they had tried to pay a $15 million ransom. His son claimed that the government intentionally leaked word of the plan to a news agency so that the terrorists would cancel the arrangement.

The hijacking of a Lufthansa jetliner (see incident 3207) by terrorists apparently acting in concert with the kidnappers greatly increased the pressure on the government to effect the release of the prisoners. However, the successful rescue operation at Mogadishu, Somalia, turned the advantage back to the government but put Schleyer's fate in doubt. Schleyer's well-being was further put in jeopardy by the suicides in prison of Baader, Raspe, and Ensslin, as well as the self-inflicted wounds of Moeller. Leftists throughout Europe (see below) claimed foul play on the part of the German government and engaged in a rampage of bombing of German facilities.

On October 19, the Siegfried Hausner Command sent the following message to the French left-wing newspaper *Liberation* and to the Stuttgart office of DPA: "After forty-three days we have ended Hanns-Martin Schleyer's miserable and corrupt existence. Herr Schmidt, who from the start allowed in his power calculations for the possibility of Schleyer's death, can find him in the Rue Charles Peguy at Muelhouse in a green Audi 100 with a Bad Homburg registration. Owing to our grief and anger over the massacres of Mogadishu and Stammheim, his death is of no significance. Andreas, Gudrun, Jan, Irmgard and we ourselves are not surprised by the fascist stage-setting of the imperialists for the destruction of the liberation movement. We will never forget that Schmidt and the imperialists supporting him shed this blood. The struggle has only started. Freedom through armed anti-imperialist struggle." That night, police found the sedan in the French border town but initially did not find Schleyer's body. Fearing that a booby-trap had been rigged to the trunk, explosives experts were called in. However, only Schleyer's body was found. Although police originally claimed that his throat had been slashed, it was later noted that Schleyer was shot below the right ear. A bullet wound and two wounds were found on the top of his head, apparently caused by blows from a heavy instrument. The next day, Mulhouse police said he had been killed by three shots fired into his head at close range thirty-six hours before his body was found. The timing would place his death shortly after the Mogadishu raid. The group hoped that press reports of Schleyer's having been a Nazi party member prior to World War II (he also served in the S.S. during the war and spent three years in a French prison camp) would lessen public revulsion with their actions. However, Chancellor Schmidt defended his actions in not giving in to the terrorists, noting that the "prisoners whose release was demanded by the terrorists had been charged with thirteen murders and forty-three attempted murders between them."

Ninety minutes after the news of Schleyer's death, the Federal Criminal Office released the names of sixteen persons suspected of being involved in the crime. Among them were Susanne Albrecht, Silke Maier-Witt, Adelheid Schulz, Angelika Speitel, Siegrid Sternbeck, and Willy Peter Stoll, who were also on the wanted list in connection with the Ponto murder. Christian Klar was wanted for the Buback murder. Brigitte Mohnhaupt is believed to have accompanied Knut Folkerts, who was arrested in Holland in a shootout with police. Also named were Rolf Heissler, who had been released in exchange for Peter Lorenz in March 1975, and Friederike Krabbe, believed to be related to one of the Stockholm terrorists, Hanna Elise Krabbe. Also named were Christoph Wackernagel and Rolf Clemens Wagner, who were wanted for bombing attacks. The Federal Criminal Office noted that Joerg Lang, the former partner of radical lawyer Klaus Croissant, Inge Viett, who escaped from the Berlin women's jail, Elisabeth van Dyck, wanted in connection with arms thefts, and Julianne Plambeck, a noted terrorist, were also suspected of involvement in the kidnapping.

A state funeral held for Schleyer on October 25 was attended by twelve hundred mourners, including President Walter Scheel and Chancellor Helmut Schmidt, under tight security precautions. Both vowed to wipe out terrorism in Germany and bring Schleyer's killers to justice.

Stefan Wisniewski was arrested in France in May 1978 and extradited to West Germany a year later. On November 5, 1979, he was charged in Karlsruhe with murdering Schleyer and his bodyguards, kidnapping, attempted extortion, coercion and forging documents.

Rolf Wagner was arrested on November 19, 1979, after a gun battle with Swiss police. He was suspected of being the driver of the van used in the getaway. He was one of four terrorists arrested in Yugoslavia in May 1978 who were later released in a dispute over extradition of Croatian terrorists. 3179

September 6, 1977—El Salvador—Elena Lima de Chiorato, wife of American construction industrialist Louis Chiorato, was kidnapped in El Salvador in front of her husband's company offices as she was about to get into her family's car by individuals armed with machine guns who engaged in a shootout with her bodyguards.

September 6, 1977—Austria—A fire was reported in the German Democratic Republic pavilion after the conclusion of the Vienna Volkstimme Press Festival. The blaze, believed to be a case of arson, caused considerable damage, destroying a movie projector. The Austrian Communist party claimed a direct connection ''between this attack and the most recent neo-Nazi excesses.'' 3180

September 6, 1977—Colombia—A bomb exploded in a Sears store in Cali, injuring three persons. 3181

September 7, 1977—Ireland—The IRA murdered John Lawler, a Dublin hauler, apparently after he told police about his involvement in a plan to smuggle arms and explosives across the Irish Sea.

September 7, 1977—Iraq—Iraqi news media reported the arrest of Muhammad 'Isam Mahmud, a Syrian citizen who claimed to have been hired by the Syrian consul in Baghdad, Nasuh Juwayjati, to engage in acts of terrorism. Mahmud confessed to planting a bomb in a car in Ar-Rashid Street in Baghdad. The press reported that Juwayjati was given forty-eight hours to leave Baghdad. The Syrian press condemned the Iraqi allegations.

September 7, 1977—Mexico—Danish millionaire Andrea Kongsted Ellirisem was kidnapped in Otumba, Mexico State. Her captors demanded a ransom of around $40,000. She was rescued by police on September 17 after a shootout with five persons. The press claimed the incident was conducted by criminals.

September 7, 1977—United States—El Condor and the Luis Boitel Commandos claimed credit for bombs that went off in Washington, D.C. The Boitel Commandos had warned on September 2 that a series of bombs would go off along Route 1 between Homestead and Key West, Florida. The blasts occurred as leaders of eighteen Latin American nations traveled to Washington to witness the signing of the Panama Canal treaties. Six days earlier, the Cubans had also opened their first diplomatic office in Washington in seventeen years. The first bomb exploded at 2:40 A.M. in a driveway behind the ground-floor offices of Aeroflot and the Soviet embassy's maritime attachés. Windows were knocked out in the building, as well as in surrounding structures. Five minutes later, the Boitel Commandos phoned United Press to criticize Soviet support of the Castro regime, Cuban human-rights violations, and the use of Cuban military forces in Africa. Condor phoned United Press International in Miami to say, ''Listen carefully. The bomb that went off in Washington today was put by the Cuban anti-Communist commando El Condor in retaliation for giving away to the Communist the Panama Canal. Goodbye.'' A bomb then exploded in a flower pot in the Ellipse, a few yards away from the White House. The only damage was to the three-hundred-pound pot. Spokesmen estimated the damage at $145. Reports differed as to whether the bombs were made of C4 or were pipe bombs filled with gunpowder. Some reports indicated that Condor and the Boitel groups had merged. 3182-3183

September 7, 1977—Northern Ireland—A masked gunman who had entered the home of Jurgen Gradel, honorary West German vice consul in Ballymena, fired a shot in a ceiling before escaping into the night. No one was hurt. 3184

September 10, 1977—Turkey—A bomb exploded in front of the Turkish American Association in Adana, shattering all the glass on the ground floor but causing no injuries. 3256

September 10, 1977—United States—A Pan Am jetliner carrying 298 passengers and sixteen crew members made an emergency landing in Shannon, Ireland, after an anonymous caller told the airline's control center at New York's Kennedy Airport that a bomb was on board the New York to London flight and demanded $1 million to reveal its location. No bomb was found during the eight and a half hour delay.

September 10, 1977—Netherlands—Police arrested one man upon finding a blueprint by South Moluccans in Assen and Bovensmilde for taking hostages. One policeman was shot in the leg by a sniper during the house-to-house search. 3185

September 11, 1977—Israel—A bomb exploded in a Beersheba bus station's baggage room, wounding ten persons, two of them seriously, while Israelis were making last-minute preparations for Rosh Hashanah. 3186

September 11, 1977—Azores—A bomb damaged the new official residence of General Galvao de Figueiredo, the resident Portuguese minister.

September 12, 1977—France—Two gunmen fired ten shots from semiautomatic pistols in a predawn attempt to kill Princess Ashraf Pahlavi, fifty-seven, the twin sister of the shah of Iran. The duo, driven by a third terrorist in a white Peugeot sedan stolen from a local car dealer, forced the driver of her Rolls Royce to stop along a seaside road two miles from Antibes. She was riding home after an evening of gambling at the Palm Beach Casino in Cannes. Although the princess was unhurt, her lady-in-waiting, Kahainouri Forough, who was sitting in the princess's seat and may have been mistaken for her, was killed by a single bullet in the head. Arus Ettemadian, twenty-nine, an Iranian businessman driving the car, attempted to get away by crashing into the attack car and was wounded in the arm. A fourth passenger, Dijarchi Modergar, sitting in the back seat, was also unharmed. The Peugeot was found abandoned in Antibes. There was no attempt at robbery, and the gunmen remained silent during the attack. They were presumed to be anti-shah terrorists. 3187

September 13, 1977—Mexico—Dozens of bombs planted by the Popular Armed Revolutionary Front exploded in three towns, causing considerable damage. One report put the figure at $905 million, although estimates of $20 million are more credible. One of the five casualties was to a bomber who was seriously injured by an explosion at the Woolworth store in Guadalajara. Some reports indicated that the group responsible was the Union del Pueblo. 3188

September 14, 1977—Mexico—Bombs went off in a Sears Roebuck store and the Mexican-American Cultural Institute. Unexploded bombs were found outside a General Motors assembly plant and the headquarters of the Colgate Palmolive subsidiary. 3189-3192.

September 15, 1977—Australia—The Indian High Commission's military attaché, Colonel Iqbal Singh, was stabbed in the early morning in Canberra. The Indian press characterized the incident as a kidnapping attempt against him and his wife. Iqbal reportedly disarmed his assailant, who fled. The attacker, a twenty-six-year-old Australian, was apprehended later and claimed that he was seeking the release of P. R. Sarkar, the Ananda Marg leader. The Delhi Domestic Service quoted official sources as saying, ''The incident comes in the wake of a series of vandalism against Indian missions and Air India offices in Canberra and Sydney [sic]. These include the demonstrations over the last several months and stone throwing. The latest was the devastating fire at the Indian Chancery in Canberra about a fortnight ago. The demonstrations have been made by Anand Margis, mostly Australians. They claim responsibility for some of these acts.'' 3193

September 19, 1977—United States—An individual claiming to be a member of the Luis Boitel Commandos phoned the Associated Press at 1:50 A.M. and said, ''Listen carefully. We have planted bombs at several Miami Beach hotels. Unless our demands are met, we will take further action. Freedom for all Cuban political prisoners.'' Minutes later, bombs went off at the pool area of the DuPont Plaza in Miami and outside the Fontainebleau Spa, a health club attached to the hotel in Miami Beach. Explosions also went off at the Sheraton Four Ambassadors pool in Miami and in front of the Eden Roc in Miami Beach. Police estimated damage at $4,000, saying the bombs sounded ''more than anything else like an attention-getter at this point." Boitel was a Cuban political prisoner who died during a hunger strike at a Havana prison. 3194-3197

September 19, 1977—Switzerland—Peter Egloff, twenty-four, and Daniel van Arb, twenty-three, went on trial in Winterthur on charges of stealing weapons from army depots and passing them to urban terrorists in West Germany, France, Italy, and Spain. The Swiss pair were also accused of carrying out bomb attacks on diplomatic and business premises in Zurich between 1971 and 1974. 3198

September 22, 1977—Puerto Rico—Allan Randall, forty-three, a New York-born attorney, was shot to death in the garage of his Condado condominium in San Juan by two gunmen as he was getting into his car at 7 A.M. Randall was hit in the chin and neck with two bullets fired from a .32 caliber pistol. A message found in a phone booth a few blocks from the scene claimed that he was "condemned to death and was executed today by labor commandos" who alleged that he collaborated with the CIA and was part of a plan to "destroy gains won by the island labor movement." Randall had been the director of the annual convention of the Federal Bar Association, which was to discuss the problem of terrorism. The meeting was cancelled, but a small convention was held at the Mayflower Hotel. It was later reported that a short list of future victims was found pinned to Randall's body and in a nearby phone booth. One name was reportedly that of an individual who keeps computerized records on terrorism for an American intelligence agency.

September 22, 1977—Netherlands—Knut Folkerts, twenty-five, a Baader-Meinhof Group member wanted in the assassination of Bonn's chief prosecutor Siegfried Buback, was captured in a shootout with police that left one Utrecht officer dead and another seriously wounded. A female accomplice, identified as Brigitte Mohnhaupt, twenty-eight, escaped. It was believed that the duo had been involved in a shooting incident in the Hague earlier in the week, but they had escaped with the aid of two Dutch accomplices. Police believed that they may also have been involved in the death of banker Juergen Ponto and the kidnapping of Hanns-Martin Schleyer (see incident 3179). Folkerts received twenty years from a Dutch court on December 20. He claimed to be at war with the FRG. 3199

September 25, 1977—Netherlands—The German newspaper *Bild am Sonntag* reported that West German terrorists, including Knut Folkerts, planned to kidnap Prince Claus, husband of crown Princess Beatrix of the Netherlands. The Dutch Justice Department coordination center in the Hague called the report "pure and utter nonsense." 3200

September 25, 1977—Israel—Brigitte Schultz, twenty-four, on trial for complicity in the abortive missile attack on an El Al plane at Nairobi airport in January 1976, requested extradition to West Germany (see incident 2565). Two Israeli attorneys traveled to Bonn to file the appeal.

September 27, 1977—Iraq—The Lebanese magazine *Al-Usbu' Al-'Arabi* claimed that Wadi Haddad, chief of PFLP external operations, had been assassinated by his opponents in Iraq. The magazine noted that Haddad and George Habash, PFLP secretary-general, frequently disagreed. It also claimed that Venezuelan-born terrorist Carlos had replaced Haddad as chief of external operations.

September 28, 1977—West Germany—The federal prosecutor's office indicted Ralf Reinders, thirty-one; Ronald Fritzsch, twenty-six; Gerald Kloepper, twenty-three; Till Meyer, thirty-three; Fritz Teufel,thirty-four; and Andreas Vogel, twenty-one, of having been members of the 2 June Movement who murdered Guenter von Drenkmann, president of the Berlin Higher Court, in November 1974 and of kidnapping Peter Lorenz in February 1975 (see incident 2246). They were also accused of several bank robberies in which 861,340 marks were stolen and of stealing hunting weapons and other equipment from a gunsmith store. Their trial was expected to begin in March 1978.

September 28, 1977—West Germany—The federal government joined Austria and Sweden in ratifying the convention of the Council of Europe for joint action to combat terrorism. Ireland and Malta did not subscribe to the January 1977 convention, which was signed by seventeen foreign ministers. The convention directs that fugitive terrorists must be extradited or tried in the country in which they seek refuge. It enters into force three months after the third instrument of ratification is deposited.

September 28, 1977—India—A Japanese Airlines DC8 was hijacked out of Bombay airport, which has no metal detectors, by five members of the Hidaka Commando Unit of the Japanese Red Army, who forced the pilot to fly to Dacca, Bangladesh. The flight had originated in Paris and had made stops in Athens, Cairo, and Karachi en route to Bangkok with 142 passengers and 14 crew members. On board were 12 Americans and an Indonesian, along with numerous Japanese. The hijackers, armed with guns, grenades, and plastic explosives, ordered the passengers not to move and not to look at their faces.

A statement released in Beirut, Lebanon, by the JRA demanded the release of "revolutionary commandos" jailed in Japan. The statement denounced Japanese Emperor Hirohito as a war criminal and accused the Japanese government of concealing scandals, such as the Lockheed bribery case. The group's name was believed to refer to Toshihiko Hidaka, who committed suicide after being arrested in Jordan in 1975 for using a false passport. They demanded the release of nine radicals in Japanese prisons, along with a $6 million ransom, the largest for any hijacking. Included in the list of prisoners was a woman, Ayako Daidoji, twenty-eight, a leftist convicted of involvement in several bombings of business firms in 1974 and 1975 in Japan. Two of those whose release was demanded had no previous association with radical activities, being viewed as common criminals convicted of murder and robbery. However, they had been cell mates of other Japanese radicals now at large.

Negotiations were conducted by Bangladesh Vice-Marshal A. G. Mahmoud, who was able to talk the hijackers into ignoring several deadlines they had set. The group threatened to kill the passengers one by one and blow up the plane if their demands were not met. Their first victim was to be John Gabriel, who they believed was an American Jewish friend of President Jimmy Carter. The group also demanded sixty thousand $100 bills.

On September 29, the Japanese government agreed to pay the ransom. They later agreed to release the prisoners as well. The hijackers released Carole Wells Karabian, wife of a former California State assemblyman, and K. Krueger and G,. Verghese, his wife, and their one-year-old son, who carried Indian passports but reside in California. One of the passengers released at Dacca identified a photo of one of the hijackers as Norio Sasaki, twenty-nine, who was jailed for taking part in a bombing in Tokyo three years ago. He had been released in August 1975 during the JRA takeover of the U.S. consulate in Kuala Lumpur, Malaysia. As was the case in that incident, some of the prisoners whose release was demanded refused to go. Isao Chinen, who was accused of throwing a bomb at Crown Prince Akihito in 1975, balked, as did Toshio Omura, who was jailed for setting a bomb in a government office in 1969, who claimed to disagree with the hijacker's ideology. Curiously, the hijackers did not demand the release of Takahashi Taketomo, who had been deported to Japan from Sweden and was suspected of being a JRA leader in Europe.

The Japanese government's decision to release the prisoners was heavily criticized, particularly because they were flown to Dacca on October 1, Japanese Law Day. The money was also on the plane (some of it had to be obtained in New York). Early on October 2, the hijackers released fifty-nine of the hostages in exchange for the money and prisoners. It was determined that passengers from sixteen nations had been on board.

Soon after, an armed uprising began in Dacca at 5:50 A.M. A radio broadcast said the rebellion was backed by armed forces, students, peasants, and workers. At least four army officers were shot by soldiers taking part in the coup attempt. However, it appears that they did not enter the terminal building, and the coup was defeated by government forces. The hijackers were edgy during the disturbance, but none of the hostages was harmed. More than one hundred passengers were released in stages before the plane took off later that day. Bangladesh officials cleared the plane for takeoff despite a last-minute telephone appeal from Japanese Prime Minister Takeo Fukuda, who wanted all of the hostages released. The hijackers refused, saying ''We must get where we are going. It is very dangerous. We have imperialist and Zionist enemies. They could shoot down our plane and crew. They can't shoot us down if our passengers are on board.'' The plane flew to Damascus, Syria, and Kuwait, stopping to refuel and release seven hostages. Upon leaving Kuwait, twenty-two passengers and seven crew members were still on board. The plane finally landed in Algiers, where the hijackers surrendered to the authorities on October 3, 135 hours after the incident began. They were taken away from the airport in three black limousines. Most of the hostages immediately left Algiers. Thomas Phalen, twenty-nine, from San Francisco, chose to stay in the country.

A storm of controversy arose over the Algerian decision to grant the hijackers asylum, as well as the Japanese agreement to capitulate. Japanese officials noted that they had contacted ten nations for landing permission and had been turned down by all ten. Japan agreed to Algerian demands not to press for the return of the hijackers or ransom. This led to the resignation in protest of Justice Minister Hajime Fukuda, who took full responsibility for the Japanese decision. Responding to public protest, the Japanese government asked Algeria to bar the terrorists from leaving the country and to make sure that the money was not used for new terrorist actions. Algeria refused Japan's request, saying it ''will not tolerate that its good faith and good will be exploited.'' Japan later expressed the hope that the prisoners, terrorists, and money would be returned. The fate of the hijackers is unknown. On October 25, attempting to deflect growing international criticism of its becoming a haven for terrorists, Algeria defended its policy by saying that negotiating with terrorists saves lives and that it was honor bound to abide by agreements made with the hijackers. An Algerian official said that the conditions agreed to during the incident included that the terrorists could keep the ransom, would not be extradited, and would not be photographed by the press. He indicated that the terrorists may already have left Algeria, and ''the case is closed. . . .Experience shows that only by responding to skyjackers' demands has loss of life been avoided.'' While expressing relief that the Lufthansa case (see below) was ended without injury to the hostages, he noted that Algeria would not allow such a rescue operation on its soil.

Algeria claimed on October 18 that the ransom was hidden in Dacca, Kuwait, and Damascus before the hijackers arrived in Algiers. It claimed the terrorists each carried only $1,000. On October 27, Chief Japanese Cabinet Secretary Sunao Sonoda charged that the hijackers and prisoners had left Algeria, which had confiscated two-thirds of the ransom. Police said the hijack leader was Osamu Maruoka, twenty-six. The others were Kunio Bando, thirty; Norio Sasaki, twenty-nine; Kazuo Tohira, twenty-four; and possibly Jun

Nishikawa, twenty-seven. Maruoka was wanted in connection with the 1972 Lod Airport massacre, as well as the July 1973 JAL hijacking in Amsterdam (see incidents 1056 and 1595).

On October 12, police raided twenty sites in Tokyo and Osaka in search of evidence related to the hijacking. They confiscated eighty newspapers and memorandums and more than one hundred pieces of material evidence but made no arrests. The government and JAL also announced that they would be implementing new antihijacking security measures.

Shortly after the hijacking, an unknown individual claiming to be a member of the JRA granted interviews to the press, purporting to explain the actions of the hijackers. 3201

September 29, 1977—France—Guinean Consul Abulaye N'daw was hospitalized after being beaten by thirty demonstrators outside his Paris embassy. Six individuals were detained for questioning. 3202

September 29, 1977—Ethiopia—Armed men broke into the Italian embassy in Addis Ababa during the night and held Ambassador Marcello Guidi and several embassy staff for an hour. The group fled when local police arrived. 3203

September 30, 1977—France—An Air Inter Caravelle carrying ninety-one persons was hijacked over Paris by Jacques Robert, forty-three, who shot a stewardess in the arm and demanded radio air time to broadcast a taped message. Robert was identified as a mentally disturbed individual who had held up a Paris radio station at gunpoint in 1974. He demanded that the plane be refueled and flown to an unnamed destination. After the plane landed, police stormed it. Before he was overpowered, Robert set off his hand grenade, killing a passenger and injuring four others, including former Information Minister Philippe Malaud. The French pilots' union said the injuries "showed the absurdity of hasty, ill-timed and unsuitable operations" and said Orly security was inadequate. Robert was charged on October 3 with hijacking, murder, attempted murder of police officers, and taking hostages. 5520

September 30, 1977—France—Klaus Croissant, forty-eight, the attorney for Baader-Meinhof figures who was suspected of setting up a communications net between the jailed terrorists and their at-large comrades, was arrested by Paris police. Croissant had fled illegally to France in July, seeking asylum from West German charges of supporting terrorist groups. West German prosecutors, announced that they had also charged one of his colleagues, lawyer Siegfried Haag, thirty-two, with aiding in the planning and provision of weapons for the 1975 attack on the West German embassy in Stockholm. Haag had been in a West German jail since his November 1976 arrest. The West German Parliament passed a law permitting the isolation of jailed terrorists from each other and from their lawyers for temporary periods during times of emergency.

October 1977—Netherlands—On December 16, 1977, Dutch police reported that five men had admitted to staging armed attacks on the West German consulate and the residence of the American consul general in Rotterdam in October. 3305-3306

October 1977—Switzerland—Graziella Ortiz, heiress to Jorge Ortiz, an antique dealer belonging to the Patino family, a wealthy Bolivian tin-mining group, was kidnapped in Geneva. The police agreed not to interfere with the family's attempts to free her and allowed them to keep their promise to the kidnappers of remaining silent on the incident.

October 3, 1977—Lebanon—*Sana* in Damascus reported that "the Iraqi nationalist grouping has announced the death of struggler Ahmad al-Juburi, a member of the central command of the national socialist congress in Iraq and Khalid al-Harbaji, member of the fighters congress, who were assassinated at the criminal hands of the gangs of the fascist regime in Iraq in a street in Beirut on the night of Monday, 3 October 1977. The grouping has issued a statement on the occasion promising the masses of the Iraqi people to continue the struggle until the country is liberated from the rule of killers, and to remain faithful to the principles for which the two departed were martyred."

October 4, 1977—United States—A Pan Am jet carrying 288 passengers from San Francisco to Tokyo made an emergency landing in Vancouver when a note was found in a washroom claiming that eight bombs were on board. No bombs were found.

October 4, 1977—Panama—Students from Panama City University set fire to the car of the U.S. Ambassador while the chargé d'affaires, Raymond Gonzalez, was attending an exhibition in the architecture building. William Jorden, the ambassador, was out of the country. 3204

October 5, 1977—Ireland—Seamus Costello, thirty-eight, founder of the Irish Republican Socialist party, was assassinated on a crowded Dublin street by a gunman who fired two shotgun blasts into his face, reloaded, and fired again. The killer escaped in a waiting car. Costello was at odds with the IRA, although his supporters blamed "agents of British imperialism" for the murder.

October 11, 1977—Yemen—President Ibrahim al Hamdi and his brother, Colonel Abdullah Mohammed al Hamdi, were assassinated. A three-man presidential council, headed by Major Ahmed Hussein al Ghashmi, was formed to lead the country.

October 11, 1977—Czechoslovakia—A Czech YAK40 flying twenty-four passengers and three crew members to Prague was hijacked out of Karlovy Vary (formerly Carlsbad) by a man and a woman wielding pistols who forced the pilot to fly to Frankfurt. They were identified as Vlastimil Toupalik, thirty, and Ruzena Vickova, twenty-two, who were members of the airline's ground staff and who were dressed in Czech Airlines uniforms. The Germans allowed the plane to land when the pilot radioed ''in unmistakable terms that he had to fly to Frankfurt.'' After two and a half hours in which the hijackers demanded that the plane be refueled for a flight to Munich, they surrendered, requesting political asylum. The Czech news agency said Toupalik faced charges at home of failure to pay alimony. The hijackers were held on charges of ''endangering airline transportation.'' The passengers and the crew returned to Czechoslovakia. 5521

October 11, 1977—United States—Puerto Rican terrorists bombed facilities of General Motors and another firm in New York City. 3205-3206

October 13, 1977—Spain—Lufthansa flight 181, a B737 scheduled to fly from the Spanish resort island of Mallorca to Frankfurt, was hijacked fifty-five minutes after takeoff. Two women hijackers reached into their boots, withdrew guns and hand grenades, and along with two male accomplices diverted the plane to Rome. On board were eighty-two passengers and five crew members. Nationalities represented included Germans, a Spanish flight crew, a Swedish passenger, an Austrian flight attendant with four West German crew members, six West German beauty queens, and two Americans (Christine Santiago and her son, Leo, five, of Sandee, California). It was later learned that the terrorists had boarded the flight at the last moment, foregoing the usual search procedures. The German government immediately imposed a news blackout, which had been initiated during the Schleyer case (see incident 3179).

The hijackers set down in Rome for a refueling stop. Two identified themselves as Harda Mamoud and Walter Mohammed, who appeared to be their leader. Female voices heard in the background led authorities to believe that two female hijackers were on board. A statement in grammatical and concise Arabic delivered to Reuters in Beirut identified them as the Organization of Struggle Against World Imperialism, which confirms the ''objectives and demands'' of the Red Army Faction kidnappers of Schleyer. The group demanded the release of the same eleven terrorists (see incidents 2282 and 1027) in West German jails as had been mentioned in the Schleyer case, as well as the release of two Palestinian terrorists, identified as Mahde and Hussein, held in Turkish jails (see incident 2827). They demanded a ransom of $15 million and added that 100,000 marks be given to each prisoner. The terrorists demanded that the prisoners be flown to Vietnam, Somalia, or the People's Democratic Republic of Yemen (PDRY).

Upon establishing their demands, the hijackers took off for Cyprus, landing in Larnaca, although the Cypriot government at first barred their arrival. In what came to be known as Operation Oscar X-Ray, Hans-Juergen Wischnew-ski, Chancellor Schmidt's troubleshooter, carrying satchels with millions of marks, set off in a German jet, trailing the hijacked plane in the hopes of beginning negotiations. Simultaneously a West German commando unit began practicing assaults on a similar B737 in the Cologne airport hangar. Two squads of thirty-two men each boarded a third jet and headed for Cyprus that night. At 10:47 P.M. on October 13, the PLO representative in Cyprus, Saharia Abdul Rachim, appealed to the hijackers to release the women and children. The hijackers refused to talk to him. Soon afterward, the German jet carrying the commandos arrived in Akrotiri, fifty miles from Larnaca. Perhaps fearing an Entebbe-type raid, the hijackers took off for Bahrain.

On its way, the plane was refused permission on October 14 to land in Beirut, Damascus, Kuwait, and Iraq. Bahrain and Dubai, which were next on their itinerary, tried to prevent the plane's landing. Vietnam, Somalia, and PDRY, named by the hijackers as candidates to receive the released prisoners, indicated an unwillingness to receive them. (However, on October 15, it was reported that a Somali diplomat indicated that his country would accept the prisoners if it could help save lives.)

In Dubai that Sunday, Wischnewski was on the ground and managed to begin talking to the terrorists by radio. The German and Arabic-speaking hijackers let a first deadline slip by and set a new one. Perhaps to mask its intentions, Bonn announced on October 15 that a special jet carrying the squad of antiterrorist commandos which had been standing by for two days in Turkey had been called back to West Germany.

The West Germans rejected the demands of the hijackers the next day and pleaded successfully in the federal constitutional court against an injunction that would have forced it to release the urban guerrillas. The action had been brought by Schleyer's son, who argued that each citizen had the right to life and "physical inviolability" under the constitution. He therefore concluded that the government had an obligation to save his father's life by fulfilling the kidnappers' demands. The court, however, ruled that the government's obligation to an individual was overshadowed by its larger responsibility to the collective protection of all citizens, which was enhanced by taking deterrent steps, including the refusal of political blackmail attempts. Many commentators were surprised that West Germany took such a hard stance against the terrorists in the face of much greater pressure than they had faced in the kidnapping of an individual.

The hijackers hoped to increase that pressure by their treatment of the hostages, establishing an image of being quite willing to kill. They consistently refused requests to release sick, young, or female passengers. The leader of the hijackers called out the names of those he believed were Jewish and said they would be killed in the morning. However, he later changed his mind, saying he would not execute these "pigs," referring to three West German girls. The female hijacker took delight in brushing grenades against the heads of the passengers while the terrorist leader ranted against imperialism and Zionism. This pressure was added to when the hijackers fired three shots at Dubai engineers who had approached the aircraft to attach a mobile generator because the plane's lighting system had failed. Despite these hostile actions, the terrorist leader allowed the UAE defense minister to send in a cake to celebrate the birthday of flight attendant Ann-Marie Staringer.

At this point, the West Germans asked the government of Dubai (and later PDRY) to permit a commando raid. South Yemen refused; Dubai permitted the squad to land but demanded that Dubai armed forces take part in the operation. Before Dubai soldiers could be properly instructed by the West Germans, the hijackers ordered the plane into the air, forty minutes before the expiration of the second deadline in Dubai, and headed for PDRY. Dubai's chief negotiator, Defense Minister Sheik Mohammed bin Rashid al-Maktum, when asked about the aborted rescue, said, "Everything was considered. But I didn't want violence or anything that would have exposed lives to danger." Meanwhile Pope Paul offered himself as a substitute hostage.

The plane now headed for Oman, but the sultan refused permission to land. They went on to Aden, but PDRY attempted to prevent the landing as well. Pilot Juergen Schumann, thirty-seven, made a rough landing in a dirt strip alongside the main runway on October 16. He left the aircraft to inspect damage to the landing gear and wandered into an area cordoned off by security forces. Reports differ as to what next transpired, but it appears that he attempted to convince the authorities not to allow the damaged plane to take off again. When he got back to the cabin (some reports indicate that PDRY officials, fearing that the terrorists would kill the remaining hostages, forced the pilot to return), he was forced to kneel in the aisle while a one-question trial ("Are you guilty?") was held on whether he tried to escape. The leader of the hijackers fired a bullet through his head in front of the passengers, including seven young children. (It was later learned that the pilot had managed to alert the outside as to the number of hijackers by special signals.) On October 17, in revulsion at the actions of the hijackers, Foreign Minister Kurt Fischer telephoned from East Berlin to the office of West German Foreign Minister Hans-Dietrich Genscher and offered whatever diplomatic support he could provide in ending the incident.

Ten hours after landing in Aden, the terrorists forced the copilot to head the plane for Somalia. Passengers were forced to step over the pilot's body if they wanted to get water or have access to oxygen. Eventually the pilot's body was pushed into a closet. When the plane landed at Mogadishu, the wrapped body was dumped onto the runway. The pressure on the passengers intensified as the hijackers tied them up, poured alcohol from passengers' gift-shop liquor over them and in the cabin for eventual burning, and collected passports to throw out so that passengers could be identified after the planned explosion. Setting what they termed a final ultimatum, the hijackers rejected three Somali offers for safe passage in return for the release of the hostages.

International recoil at this action grew to a recognition of the need for immediate, forceful response. President Carter sent a private message to Somali leader Mohammed Siad Barre requesting him to aid the Germans in whatever way was necessary. Wischnewski, who had been refused permission to land in Aden and had been waiting in Saudi Arabia, landed in Somalia and contacted his commando team, which was on the Greek island of Crete. The team members of Grenzschutzgruppe Neun (GSG-9) set off before the Somali government gave permission for the rescue. Wischnewski meanwhile set up contact with the hijackers, and noting the necessity for more time, lied to the hijackers and led them to believe that the Baader-Meinhof prisoners had been released and were en route to Somalia. The ruse worked, and a new deadline, ten hours away, was set.

A slight hitch almost tipped off the operation to the hijackers. Michael Gurdus, an Israeli in Tel Aviv who monitors airwaves for radio and television, ran the story of the planned attack at 9 P.M. on his news show, several hours before the raid. He overheard the plane's pilot radio, "They are asking too many questions and want to know exactly what we are carrying and I cannot tell them." Later he intercepted a message indicating that the pilot was to land after dark with a minimum of landing lights. Saying "action might be imminent," he played some of the tapes during his news show. Israeli radio decided not to broadcast the news item, and international wire services quickly agreed to West German requests for a news blackout until after the rescue mission was completed. Gurdus defended his actions by saying that he had decided that the hijackers were not listening to messages from the outside and that the item was carried as one of many conflicting reports.

The plane soon after landed in Mogadishu with thirty assault commandos and thirty backup medical and communications personnel. Although they left the plane dressed in sports outfits, by midnight they were dressed in black, their faces blacked out. They moved on the plane at 2 A.M. on Tuesday,

October 18. Five minutes later, approaching from the rear of the plane, the commandos set up four stepladders. They then ignited an oil drum and rolled it toward the nose of the plane and away from the craft. The hijackers were drawn to the cockpit for a better look, allowing the commandos to open the plane's doors simultaneously. The raiders threw in specially designed British grenades that do not emit shrapnel but stun people with blinding light and deafening sound for several seconds. (Two special British advisers had accompanied the team to instruct them in the devices' use.) Rushing in, the commandos yelled "Hinlegen!" ("Get down!") Two of the terrorists were immediately killed in the cockpit. A third in the first-class compartment opened fire. Although hit by two bullets, he hurled a grenade toward the rear of the plane. Hit by more bullets, he detonated another grenade while falling, injuring several hostages in the feet. The fourth terrorist, a woman, opened fire through the door of the lavatory in the rear of the plane. She was quickly subdued. Six minutes after the beginning of the operation and 106 hours after the start of the hijacking, the passengers were safely out of the plane. One commando and four passengers were slightly injured. Stewardess Gabi Dillman, twenty-three, received minor injuries in the right leg due to grenade fragments.

Messages of congratulations to the Germans and the rescue team poured in from around the world. It was learned that the group was led by Lieutenant Colonel Ulrich Wegener, who was quickly promoted to full colonel. Wegener had participated as an observer in the Israeli Entebbe raid, and his group had profited from training by the Israeli group. The commando squad was part of a 170-man unit formed after the abortive rescue attempt in the 1972 Olympics tragedy. The unit's action was the first time German military troops had fired shots in anger overseas since World War II.

The euphoria of the Germans was tempered by the embarrassment to the government over the suicides of Andreas Baader, thirty-four, Jan-Carl Raspe, thirty-three, and Gudrun Ensslin, thirty-seven, and the attempted suicide of Irmgard Moeller, thirty. The group, part of the list of terrorists whose release was demanded, had been held in solitary confinement under special security precautions in a West German jail. Most leftists believed that prison authorities had engineered their murders, despite autopsies attested to by an international team of observers, which found the deaths to be suicides. On October 20, the Kuwaiti newspaper *Al-Hadaf* came up with an imaginative interpretation of their deaths. It argued that the German special forces took the foursome with them to Mogadishu as a preventive cover for their advance on the plane. Doha reported that the group was killed during the raid. "Andreas Baader . . . was permitted to speak to the hijackers from the Mogadiscio Airport control tower and . . .had assured the plane's hijackers that the exchange of hostages would take place shortly."

The identity of the hijackers remained a mystery, with reports conflicting as to their documentation. It was learned that they had used a cosmetic case with a

false bottom and a portable radio to smuggle pistols of East European manufacture and hand grenades on board the plane. The surviving female wore a Ché
Guevara tee-shirt and was shouting "Palestine will live" in Arabic when she
was captured. Some reports claimed that she carried an Iranian passport issued
to Maroona Mouna; her three dead comrades had Iranian passports in the
names of Soraya Avrary, Reza Abrasy, and Shanug Golan. Others identified
the woman, who suffered slight gunshot wounds in her shoulder and leg, as
Shahnaz Gholam, twenty-two. Other reports identified the dead terrorists as
Johannes Gerdus, a Dutch citizen, and Reza Abassy and Soraya Ansary of
Iran. Gerdus was believed to have been the group's leader, who identified
himself as Captain Mahmoud and Walter Mahmoud. On October 25, Arab
diplomats in Somalia claimed that the woman was born in Haifa, Israel. Iran
claimed that the passports had been forged. On October 27, the PFLP-Special
Operations claimed credit, saying that the hijack leader was Zuhair Akkasha, a
Palestinian refugee born in 1954 in a Lebanese camp. He had received aviation
engineering training in London. The fingerprints of Zuhair Yousof Akasha
matched those of the killer of North Yemen's former prime minister, Al Jehri
(see incident 3077). It was reported that Akasha's false Iranian passport was
made out to Ali Hyderi. The two other dead hijackers were identified as Nadia
Shehade Doebis, twenty-one, and Nabi Ibrahim Harb, twenty. Doebis was a
Palestinian from Lebanon who had studied economics. Harb was from a
Christian area of Lebanon. The message included what were alleged to be
photos of the trio. Al Manar, an Arabic weekly published in London, identified the surviving hijacker as Suheila Saleh, a Palestinian from Kuwait. The
message said the group had belonged to the PFLP. Many suggested that the
hijackers were members of an Iraqi-based group headed by Wadi Haddad.
Whatever the identity of the woman as of October 27, West Germany had made
no formal demand for her extradition from Somalia.

On October 19, White House spokesman Jody Powell refused to discuss the
degree of U.S. involvement in the rescue, saying, "There was a message and
there were several other steps taken in support of the decision" to overpower
the hijackers. Other reports indicated that Saudi Arabia had persuaded Siad to
allow the attack. On October 21, Somali President Mohammed Siad Barre
said, "Somalia's range of friends all over the world has grown considerably."
Following the cutoff of Soviet military assistance, Somalia's urgent needs for
arms became obvious in its Ogaden conflict. While Siad said there were "no
conditions" when he agreed to allow the raid, the West German government
announced the next day that it would continue furnishing equipment and other
aid to Somalia.

In the wake of Japan's embarrassment over caving in to hijackers (see
incident 3201) and Germany's jubilation over its success, many other nations
felt pressed to establish similar commando rescue squads. Zbigniew Brzezin-
ski, President Carter's special assistant for national security affairs, declared,

''The United States would be prepared to take whatever action it had to, or was capable of'' in the event of a future hijacking. The Pentagon announced that it had assembled and trained a special force drawn from all three branches of the armed services. The FBI noted that it has trained nine hundred to one thousand agents to deal with domestic terrorist incidents. On October 21, the Associated Press reported that thirteen countries maintain highly skilled commando units trained to rescue hijacking hostages. The countries were identified as the United States, West Germany, Israel, Britain, France, Switzerland, Belgium, Denmark, Italy, the Netherlands, Norway, Austria, and Indonesia. The British colony of Hong Kong also has such a group, and Egypt has also mounted rescue operations.

Concern with airport security was brought to the fore. On October 24, West Germany sent border guards to thirteen foreign airports to take over security checks for German-bound planes. The International Federation of Airline Pilots Associations called for a forty-eight-hour strike in the absence of U.N. action and to protest the killing of Schumann. Pilots from Sweden, the United Kingdom, Norway, Denmark, Greece, and Belgium quickly voted to join the strike.

On November 2, the West German goverment released a 224-page report on its response to terrorism, furnishing details on the attack. It claimed that Vietnam and four Arab countries had refused asylum to the eleven imprisoned terrorists. Minister of State Hans Juergen Wischnewski had made trips to Algeria, Libya, Iraq, Southern Yemen, and Vietnam to discuss the terrorists' demands. When the terrorists were informed of the refusals, they accused Bonn of pressuring those governments for such a response and suggested contacting Angola, Ethiopia, Guinea-Bissau, and Mozambique. The report revealed that all written communications received on behalf of the hijackers originated from the same typewriter that Schleyer's kidnappers had used. 3207

October 13, 1977—Argentina—A bomb exploded at the home of an Argentine executive of the Chrysler subsidiary. The explosion, which went off inside a car parked in front of the residence, killed a man and a woman and injured two other women. It was believed to have been placed by two people who were seen near the car that morning shortly before the blast. 3208

October 14, 1977—Argentina—Security officers discovered a terrorist arms factory, which they claimed was connected with one European and two Asian embassies. The facility supplied 9-caliber machine guns, 60-caliber mortars, and munitions for several extremist groups. It was also reported to be preparing to manufacture grenades and a grenade launcher for the Montoneros. The hideout was used by the Argentine Communist Marxist Leninist Maoist Oriented Party to funnel funds abroad for leftist propaganda campaigns and to hold several kidnap victims.

October 15, 1977—Israel—The Arab Revolutionary Movement claimed responsibility for a bomb that went off during the morning in the old city of Jerusalem, slightly injuring two tourists. 3209

October 16, 1977—Japan—Two men wearing white masks and claiming to be members of the Aso Red Army Commandos hijacked a bus in Nagasaki carrying twenty-four passengers during the afternoon. During the fifteen-hour siege, the hijackers, armed with a shotgun, dynamite, and a gasoline bomb, released four children and an elderly man. The group said, "We have no objective" but demanded to talk to Justice Minister Mitsuo Setyama. Police stormed the bus, killing Hisayuki Kawasaki, thirty-one, and arresting his colleague. Kawasaki had been arrested previously on theft and kidnapping charges. It was learned that the men were criminals who had used the terrorist ploy to give credibility to their demand.

October 17, 1977—Argentina—San Justo police killed two leftists passing out leaflets in front of a Chrysler plant after they were discovered awaiting workers who were to enter the factory. Setting down their pamphlets, the two opened fire on the police before being killed. 3210

October 18, 1977—West Germany—Hours after the news of the rescue at Mogadishu reached West Germany, authorities found the bodies of Andreas Baader, thirty-four, Jan-Carl Raspe, thirty-three, and Gudrun Ensslin, thirty-seven, who had committed suicide inside the maximum security prison built for them at Stammheim in Stuttgart. Irmgard Moeller, a fourth prisoner whose release had been demanded, had tried to stab herself in the chest with a bread knife. Despite allegations by their lawyers and European leftists that the trio had been killed, an autopsy attended by international representatives determined the deaths were suicides made to look like murders. Baader had fired two bullets into his cell walls and shot himself in the back of the head. Raspe died from a bullet wound shortly after being found in his cell at 8 A.M. Ensslin was found hanging from a wire from a window bar in her cell. Left unanswered were questions regarding how the prisoners had learned of the rescue attempt and how they had acquired the weapons. They were each held in a separate cell and had been barred from seeing each other or other prisoners since early September. They had been placed under a temporary ban on all outside contacts for convicted terrorists. On October 21, police discovered that a room to which the terrorists had access had nine ounces of explosives hidden under a floor molding. The cell had been occupied by terrorist Helmut Pohl. Authorities also discovered a small radio in Raspe's cell, along with secret cavities large enough to hold a gun. Additionally the terrorists had devised a crude communications system based upon their electric razors and the prison electrical system. Authorities speculated that the group's lawyers had smuggled in the material before the contact ban had gone into effect. The chief of the prison's security system, as well as the justice minister of Baden-Württemberg, were forced to resign.

October 18, 1977—Italy—The Walter Alasia Column of the Red Brigades phoned an Italian news service's Milan office, threatening to execute "various German fascists living in Italy masked under any label whatsoever . . .in honor of the comrades fallen in Germany."3211

October 18, 1977—Yemen—George Clift, a British embassy counselor in Sana, was found dead from poison in his apartment. His cook had vanished earlier.

October 18, 1977—Poland—The official Polish press agency reported that a hijacking had been foiled by the crew and police aboard a Polish LOT AN24 flying from Katowice to Warsaw. No passengers were injured. 5522

October 19, 1977—Australia—Meneghini, an Australian employee of the Air India office in Melbourne, was stabbed in the lung by an unidentified assailant. The sales representative's attacker escaped, leaving behind a note from the political wing of the Anand Marg, which threatened further violence. 3212

October 19, 1977—United States—In a letter to Montgomery County, Maryland, officials, an unidentified individual claimed he would dump four hundred cubic centimeters of germs into the water supply of the eastern seaboard at 6 A.M. the next day.

October 19, 1977—Italy—Hundreds of demonstrators rioted in Genoa, smashing a glass door at the West German consulate. Leftists in Turin bombed two West German auto showrooms. German businesses were bombed in Leghorn, Bologna, Milan, and Siena. In Venice, attackers set fire to the door of the German consulate. 3213-3219

October 19, 1977—France—Firebombs were thrown at three West German tourist buses in Paris and two in Nice. Police said damage was slight, but the Nice buses were destroyed. 3220-3221

October 20, 1977—Greece—Armenian extremists claimed credit for planting a bomb that destroyed the car of Metin Yalma, the assistant press attaché of the Turkish embassy in Athens. 3222

October 20, 1977—Australia—The Indian high commissioner in Melbourne, J. C. Ajmani, received a letter from the Universal Proutist Revolutionary

Front, which threatened "programmed assassination" of Indian trade officers, consuls, and other officials unless the Indian government freed Ananda Marg leader P. R. Sarkar. Ajmani said the group was a front for the Ananda Marg, but leaders of the sect denied the charge. The letter, dated October 14, was posted in Melbourne at 5 P.M. on October 19, claiming credit for the knife attack that day. 3223

October 20, 1977—Japan—An eighteen-year-old member of a Japanese rightist group was arrested after sneaking into the premises of the Soviet embassy and breaking a window pane with a steel pipe. He carried a petition demanding the return of four Soviet-held islands, which had been Japanese territory east of Hokkaido. The intrusion occurred at 2:22 A.M.

October 20, 1977—Greece—Economist Christos Kassimis, thirty-four, died after a gun battle with police after he was discovered attempting to bomb a West German factory in Athens. The leftist and two accomplices opened fire on police after they were asked to produce identification. 3224

October 20, 1977—France—The Red Army Faction of Southern France pledged that "100,000 attacks are going to be committed against German firms in Europe." 3225

October 20, 1977—United States—Frontier Airlines flight 101, a B737 scheduled to fly from Grand Island to Denver with stops in Lincoln and Omaha, was hijacked by Thomas Hannan, twenty-nine, of Grand Island. The hijacker had casually walked through a metal-detecting device, opened his carry-on suitcase for inspection, and pulled out a sawed-off shotgun. He pushed past a security guard at 6 A.M. and forced the pilot to fly to Kansas City, where the plane refueled and he allowed eighteen passengers, including eight women and eight children, to deplane. The B737 flew on to Atlanta, where, after the passage of a 5 P.M. deadline, he released two women flight attendants. He demanded $3 million, two machine guns, two pistols, two parachutes, and a reunion with George David Stewart, twenty-nine, who had been arrested with him in September after a $7,000 robbery at an Atlanta branch of a bank formerly headed by former budget director Bert Lance. Several reports alleged a homosexual relationship between the two friends. After releasing the remaining eleven passengers at the suggestion of FBI negotiators, Hannan committed suicide in the presence of the remaining two crewmen at 10 P.M. 5223

October 20, 1977—United States—Tomas Aristedes Baez Perez, thirty, lunged twice at the pilot of the Lear jet that was taking him from New York City to Santo Domingo. The pilot determined that the Dominican citizen's actions were too dangerous to continue the flight, and he landed at Richmond's Byrd

International Airport, where FBI agents met the plane at 10:20 P.M. On October 28, U.S. magistrate David C. Lowe dismissed charges of violating the federal Crime Aboard Aircraft statute regarding interference with a flight crew. Baez had been suffering from psychological problems, and his doctor was scheduled to meet him in the Dominican Republic. 5524

October 20, 1977—United States—A brick was thrown through the Air India ticket office on New York's Park Avenue. An explosive device thrown along with the brick did not explode. 3257

October 21, 1977—United States—A National Airlines DC10 with sixty people on board was diverted to Hamilton, Bermuda, during the night when a bomb threat was received while the plane was en route from Miami to Paris. No bomb was found. The plane arrived in Paris four hours later. 3226

October 21, 1977—United Nations—The International Federation of Air Line Pilots Associations called off plans for a two-day civil aviation strike after receiving assurances that the United Nations would take action against hijacking. However, Captain Derry Pearce, president of the group, warned that the pilots would still strike in protest of the death of the pilot of the Lufthansa plane (see incident 3207) if firm action was not taken by the United Nations.

October 22, 1977—The press reported that South Yemen, Uganda, Libya, and Algeria condemned Somalia for cooperating with the West Germans in the raid on Mogadishu.

October 22, 1977—France—Arsonists set fire to eight tourist buses in Paris and attempted to burn the West German tourism offices. A violent explosion severely damaged a Paris apartment where police found explosives and pamphlets favorable to the Baader-Meinhof Group. In Toulouse, butane gas bottles were set on fire at the West German consulate, a private German telephone company, and a computer manufacturing firm. The Andreas Baader Commando claimed credit for the Toulouse attacks. 3227-3231

October 22, 1977—Italy—Police reported that bombs caused minor damage to a German bus parked in Bolzano and to a BMW auto showroom in Sassari. 3232-3233

October 24, 1977—West Germany—West German Chancellor Helmut Schmidt was threatened with assassination by the Red Army Faction.

October 25, 1977—Mauritania—Polisario guerrillas attacked a railway maintenance inspection group, kidnapping three Senegalese women, two

Frenchmen, and fifteen Mauritanians. Algeria came under pressure from the families of the hostages and various governments to lessen support to the Polisario. In turn, Algeria warned France against attempting a rescue mission. The French denied such rumors, stating that a general alert had been ordered for specific units only. On December 14, the United Nations announced that Hakim Ibrahim Abel, Polisario representative for foreign affairs, had pledged to Secretary-General Waldheim that the hostages would be released. William Powell, Waldheim's spokesman, said, "The time, place and circumstances of their release will be the subject of a further announcement." After the intervention of French Communist party chief George Marchais, the Polisario handed over the French hostages to Waldheim on December 23. Released with them were five men and a woman, all French citizens, taken hostage at Zouerate on May 1. The group, released in Algiers, claimed that they had been whipped by their captors after an escape attempt by two of them failed. The men had gotten twenty-five miles away from where they were being held but were captured and returned to the Polisario by Algerian troops in October. Daniel Ballaude, one of the escapees, said, "We were stopped by two of our guards who were joined by two soldiers we had never seen before. In our opinion, by the way they spoke French, they were Algerians. They gave orders in French. We were kicked and punched." (See incident 3091.) 3258

October 25, 1977—Guatemala—The Guatemalan Anti-Salvadoran Liberating Action Guerrillas (GALGAS) claimed that the bodies of thirty Salvadorans were at the bottom of Amatitlán Lake. The group said it had killed 150 Salvadorans and added that the group's 17 founding members had been joined by 700 others who were concerned about uncontrolled emigration. Despite dragging operations by police, no bodies were found in the lake. Government Minister Donaldo Alvarez Ruiz remarked, "This organization and its alleged activities are nothing more than the product of the imagination of some insane persons."

October 25, 1977—Italy—An anonymous caller to Ansa in Milan warned that his group would assassinate West German Ambassador Hans Arnold in revenge for the deaths of the Baader-Meinhof prisoners: "We confirm that within the next 200 hours he will be executed by a suicide commando." 3234

October 25, 1977—Turkey—Turkish extremists bombed an Istanbul building housing a primary school and the West German cultural center, injuring three Turkish civilians. 3235

October 25, 1977—Italy—A West German business in Rome was bombed. 3236

October 25, 1977—Abu Dhabi—A gunman armed with a pistol and grenade fired a machine pistol in the terminal of Abu Dhabi international airport, killing Saif ibn Said al-Ghubash, forty-seven, minister of state of the United Arab Emirates and the second-ranking official in the Foreign Ministry. Most reports assume that the killer, who was wearing flowing robes, was aiming at Syrian Foreign Minister Abdel Halim Khaddam, forty-four, who ducked behind a flight of stairs and was unhurt. Reports conflict as to the assassin's identity, whether he was part of a conspiracy, and regarding his actions immediately after the killing. Some claim he was a Palestinian who resided in Syria. He was reported to have seized seven airport workers and forced them into a Czech cargo plane. Surrounded by UAE police, he surrendered at 1 P.M. Three other gunmen reported to have accompanied him escaped in the attack. He was identified as Salah Mohammed Khaled, nineteen, code named Abd an-Nasir Jamal Muhammad. A member of the Palestinian community said, "I just pray the man they got is not a Palestinian." Khaddam alleged, "The aggressor, who was arrested, came from Baghdad and was sent by the Iraqi regime to carry out a crime which above all benefits the Israeli enemy." Kuwait press claimed the murderer admitted to being the leader of the assassination attempt against Khaddam earlier that year in the suburbs of Damascus. PLO leader Yasir Arafat denounced the murder, as did his deputy, Salah Khalaf (also known as Abu Iyad). Fatah claimed the killer had left for Abu Dhabi by sea four months previously, accompanied by an Iraqi national, and that he was a member of the dissident Abu Nidal Mahmud Al-Banna group. On October 28, Black September-June claimed credit for the attack in a communiqué mailed in Paris to Agence-France Presse. It referred to the "attempted capital execution of the traitor . . .will not escape death the next time." It said Ghubash's death was the result of the links existing between the "state of the United Arab Emirates and the mercenary Syrian regime." The group said Black September-June was the result of the "total and integral fusion at all levels" of Black September and Black June. After a trial by a Moslem religious court, Khaled, a Palestinian born in exile in Iran, was executed at dawn on November 16, 1977. 3237

October 26, 1977—Italy—Bombs damaged several cars and three West German showrooms in Rome. 3238-3240

October 27, 1977—Japan—Osamu Mitsui, director of the National Police Agency's security bureau, claimed that hand grenades used by the Japanese Red Army in their attack on the French embassy in the Hague in 1974 (see incident 2050) were part of the arms that Baader-Meinhof Group members had stolen from a U.S. military base in West Germany.

October 28, 1977—Netherlands—Maurits Caransa, sixty-one, a Dutch real estate multimillionaire, was kidnapped by four men at 1 A.M. from an Amsterdam nightclub after playing bridge. He was forced into the back seat of a waiting car. An anonymous German-speaking caller told a newspaper, "We are the Red Army Faction. We have Caransa. You will hear from us." A second caller demanded the release of imprisoned West German terrorist Knut Folkerts, held for a shootout with police in the previous month (see incident 3199). The caller also demanded the abdication of Queen Juliana. Other callers claimed that South Moluccans were responsible. Police treated the case as the work of nonpolitical criminals. Ransom demands ranged from $20,000 to $16 million. After bargaining his captors down to $4 million, Caransa directed his bank to pay the ransom and was released at 1:30 A.M. on November 2. He said the kidnappers were not part of a political group. They had held him for five days handcuffed to a bed but did not mistreat or threaten him.

October 28, 1977—Italy—Bombs damaged two Volkswagen showrooms in Turin and an Opel showroom in Rome. They caused no injuries. 3241-3243

October 28, 1977—Portugal—A bomb damaged the Lisbon offices of Siemens, a West German electrical engineering company. No injuries were reported. 3244

October 28, 1977—Thailand—Police arrested eighteen persons, including student leaders and a labor unionist, on charges of conspiring to hijack a Thai Airways Company B737 and hold its passengers hostage for the release of all suspects in the October 6, 1976, riots at Thammasat University. It was alleged that students from Bangkok planned to meet their colleagues from the provinces at either Chiang Mai or Hat Yai airport. The plane was to be diverted to either an ASEAN (Association of South East Asian Nations) nation or a Thai neighbor. Thai authorities reported that those boarding any domestic flights in the future would undergo a thorough search. 5525

October 29, 1977—Vietnam—Air Vietnam flight 509, a DC3 flying from Ho Chi Minh City (formerly Saigon) to Phuquoc Island with thirty-four passengers and six crew members was hijacked by four individuals armed with a pistol and three knives fifteen minutes after takeoff. The group shot and killed flight engineer Tran Dinh Nguyen and radio operator Nguyen Duc Hoa and seriously injured steward Nguyen Huy Thom. The plane landed at Thailand's Utapao airfield, where the hijackers were denied asylum. Naval authorities also turned down their request to dispose of the dead bodies, but they did provide food, water, and fuel. The hijackers claimed they were heading for Kota Bharu, Malaysia, but were allowed to land at Seletar, Singapore, when the pilot radioed that he was running out of fuel at 5:33 P.M. The hijackers appealed for political asylum, and Singapore authorities considered the request. Hanoi claimed that "Singapore authorities also decided to hand the criminals over to the Vietnamese authorities," although Singapore denied the allegation. A twenty-six-year-old bachelor decided that he wished to leave Vietnam and refused to return with the other passengers. It was reported that he intended to settle in the United States or Australia. The hijackers—identified as Lam Van Tu, twenty-eight, Tran Van Tu, twenty-three, Nguyen Minh Van, twenty, and Tran Van Hai, thirty-three—apparently wanted to go to the United States or France. Shortly after landing, the pilot, Nguyen Van La, thirty-four, copilot Mai Ban Bay, and the rest of the passengers and crew returned in the DC3 to Vietnam. The injured steward returned on November 28.

Relations with Vietnam were impaired when Singapore announced in November that it had decided to try the hijackers and would deny the Vietnamese request for extradition. Singapore claimed that Vietnam was not a party to any of the three international conventions on hijacking and that the two countries lacked an extradition treaty. A Vietnamese trade delegation cancelled its scheduled visit to Singapore as a result. The senior state counsel for Singapore, Tan Teow Yeow, said the prosecution had seventeen witnesses, although it was speculated that some of them would be the hijacked passengers and crew. The hijackers faced charges of armed robbery, abduction, wrongful confinement, dishonestly retaining a stolen aircraft, and crimes under the arms offenses act. Tran Huu Loc (also known as Lam Nguyen Thoy), a shopkeeper who had decided not to return to Ho Chi Minh City, was expected to be a key witness.

On December 15, the four hijackers were sentenced to fourteen years for possession of arms. Lam Van Tu (also known as Lam Van Chat) was ordered to be given twelve strokes of the cane for possession of a .38 Smith and Wesson revolver and twenty-two bullets. The other three were sentenced to six strokes of the cane for being in Lam's company during the offense. 5526

October 31, 1977—Colombia—Armed members of the ELN kidnapped West German industrialist Dieter Montuar Heinscher, forty-one, during the night near Chigorodo. The hostage was an executive in Laumayer of Medellín, a coffee exporter. The group telephoned his family, demanding 20 million pesos (approximately $550,000) in bills of different denominations and of current circulation. 3259

October 31, 1977—United Kingdom—A. S. Ahluwalia, assistant in the supply wing of the Indian High Commission in London, was knifed at 6:40 P.M. while he was returning home. 3260

November 1, 1977—Italy—Molotov cocktails were thrown at the Mercedes showrooms in Milan. 3261

November 2, 1977—Lebanon—The PFLP announced that Dr. Wadi Haddad, head of its foreign operation bureau, had been expelled from the organization in 1976 as a result of a difference of opinion with PFLP leader George Habash over the use of hijacking. The PFLP statement noted that Haddad was responsible for the October 13 hijacking of a Lufthansa jet. It was believed that the former pediatrician was still masterminding the operations of some groups, including the Japanese Red Army.

November 3, 1977—United Nations—The General Assembly endorsed without a vote a resolution that had been approved by acclamation by the Special Political Committee, which condemned hijacking by states and individuals. The resolution, sponsored by forty-six nations, appealed to countries to ratify three conventions on hijackings, to improve security arrangements at airports, and to act to eliminate the threat of extortion by air pirates. It noted that an action taken against hijacking should be "without prejudice to the sovereignty or territorial integrity of any states."

November 4, 1977—Turkey—The trial at the Fourth High Criminal Court in Istanbul of two Palestinians who killed four persons and injured twenty others in August 1976 began (see incident 2827). They had been sentenced to life imprisonment for murder and causing injuries, but the supreme court of appeals reversed the sentences. The prosecutor asked for a sentence of five to ten years for infiltrating arms into Turkey. Mahdi Mohammad Zubeyde and Mohammad Rashid Husayn, who claimed innocence, said that they were fighting for the liberation of Palestine.

November 5, 1977—Worldwide—Several news agencies reported that the Red Army Faction had sent letters warning, "For each comrade assassinated [a reference to the Baader-Meinhof suicides], we shall blow up a Lufthansa plane in flight. There will be no way to prevent that. Therefore, everyone should know that if he boards a German plane on Nov. 15 or afterward, death will be on board." Lufthansa stock plummeted, and Lufthansa pilots were instructed to employ evasive landing and takeoff tactics. The press speculated that the terrorists had acquired SA-7 missiles. 3262

November 5, 1977—Taiwan—The Government Information Office announced that it had arrested three men, members of the People's Liberation Front, for sending letters to foreign-owned factories and businesses. The letters threatened to take violent measures against them unless they withdrew from Taiwan by June. They had apparently been sent in January. The three were identified as Tai Hua-kuang from Tsanghsien, Hopei Province; Lai Ming-lieh, from Chiayi, Taiwan; and Liu Kuo-chi, from Taichung, Taiwan. Police claimed that the group was aided by the People's Republic of China. 3263

November 5, 1977—Cyprus—The local press quoted the *Economist* as saying that a luxury villa in Larnaca was the scene of a meeting between Wadi Haddad's Revolutionary Popular Front for the Liberation of Palestine, the

Japanese Red Army, the Baader-Meinhof Gang, the National Front for the Liberation of Turkey, and terrorist groups based in Libya, Algeria, and South Yemen. It claimed that the groups were evaluating previous actions and were also diverting the attention of Western intelligence organizations from another, more important meeting of the organizations' leaders. The *Nicosia News Bulletin* reported, "The local representatives of the groups that attended had coolly informed the local authorities about the visitors and requested that they should be given special treatment and the freedom to move around the island at will. It seems that the Cypriot Government was a willing host. Cyprus appears to have become a primary base for international terrorist organisations involved in the Middle East. This is largely a result of the civil war in Lebanon, which has denied them safe bases there. Two years ago, Palestinian groups began to transfer some of their intelligence units to Larnaca and Limassol. Later, they moved operational units to Cyprus as well. Finally, a year or so ago, the Palestinian movements moved their financial operations from Lebanon to Cyprus, as well as important files and their gun-running network. Inevitably, Cyprus has become a centre for the black market in arms."

November 6, 1977—Israel—Greek Catholic Archbishop Hilarion Capucci, fifty-five, Syrian born, was released from Ramleh Prison and flown to Rome on board an Alitalia plane. The pope had requested his release. He had been sentenced to twelve years in 1974 after being convicted of smuggling guns and explosives from Lebanon to Israel in his official car. At least one Israeli is thought to have died from PLO use of these arms. His release had been demanded by several hijackers, including the Entebbe group. In a dramatic gesture, he kissed the ground, which he believed he would never see again, before he boarded the plane. The understanding reached between Israel and the Vatican specified that Capucci not be allowed to make anti-Israeli propaganda, that he be posted far from the Middle East, and that the pope's letter not deny his guilt. The papal letter said, "We are deeply concerned at the present serious health conditions of Archbishop Capucci, Melchite patriarchal vicar of Jerusalem, detained in an Israeli prison. We have also received requests from many quarters that a solution be sought through our efforts. We therefore ask your excellency to be so good as to make use of your prerogatives of clemency as president of the state of Israel in favor of Archbishop Hilarion Capucci and to have him released from prison. And we are confident that his release will not be detrimental to the state of Israel. Such an act cannot fail to be considered as one of friendly kindness towards us and will be truly appreciated. With confidence in your benevolent attention to our request we assure your excellency of our sentiments of highest consideration."

November 7, 1977—United States—Ambassador Heyward Isham, director of the State Department's Office for Combatting Terrorism, was shot in the leg at 8:45 P.M. as he was going home from work. He was just emerging from his car when two men, one armed with a pistol, attempted to rob him. Isham pulled out a curtain rod from the car and struck one of the men on the head with it. He gave chase to the duo, but one of them whirled and fired. The two escaped. Isham believed that the two were robbers and that the case was not politically motivated.

November 9, 1977—Nepal—Two explosive devices were thrown against the gate of the Indian embassy in Katmandu, causing no damage or injuries. A letter demanding the release of Ananda Marg leader Sarkar was found nearby. 3264

November 9, 1977—Hong Kong—The Indian high commissioner received a letter from the Proutist bloc demanding the release of Ananda Marg leader Sarkar. 3265

November 9, 1977—Austria—Walter Michael Palmers, seventy-four, the owner of a lingerie retailing company with stores in West Germany and Austria, was taken from his car and forced into another one as he was driving home during the evening in the Dornbach section on the western outskirts of Vienna. A note found in his car demanded a ransom of $3 million and claimed that political motives were not involved. Police treated the case as a non-terrorist incident. However, on November 25, 1977, the press reported that two Austrian students arrested by Swiss police at the Italian border checkpoint of Chiasso were found in possession of weapons and two million shillings worth of foreign currency, which had been paid as ransom two weeks previously. Othmar Keplinger, one of the pair, was a sympathizer of the Baader-Meinhof Gang and had visited terrorist Waltraud Boock, who was serving a prison term for bank robbery in Austria. Vienna police arrested three others in connection with the case. Palmers's family apparently paid the ransom. 3266

November 10, 1977—Austria—Austrian officials in West Berlin received calls from the Red Army Faction, which claimed that it would assassinate Austrian Chancellor Bruno Kreisky. 3267

November 10, 1977—Netherlands—Police followed two suspected Baader-Meinhof terrorists from their Amsterdam suburban apartment during the evening to a nearby telephone booth. Ten flak-jacketed policemen closed in. When an officer opened the booth's door and asked if he could make a call, one of the terrorists drew a gun while his colleague threw a hand grenade. Three policeman were slightly injured, as was Christoph Wackernagel, twenty-six, one of the sixteen terrorists on the wanted list from the Schleyer kidnapping (see incident 3179). Wackernagel had been employed as an actor earlier. The other person was initially identified as another of the sixteen, but West German officials claimed he was Gert Richard Schneider, twenty-nine, who was wanted for the October 31 bombing of a West German court in Zweibrücken, which did extensive damage but caused no injuries. The West Germans said they believed that all of the sixteen terrorists were now outside of West Germany. The extradition trial was set for January 12, 1978. 3268

November 10, 1977—France—A gasoline bomb was thrown at the Algerian consulate in Strasbourg, causing no injuries and slight damage. A caller to a local newspaper said the attack was in retaliation for Algerian support of the Polisario group, which was holding eight French citizens hostage. 3269

November 10, 1977—El Salvador—Fifteen hundred members of the People's Revolutionary Front, some armed with sawed-off guns, .45 caliber pistols, and machetes, held 225 employees of the Labor Ministry hostage. The group also held OAS official Luis Jesus de la Garza, a Mexican citizen, along with two cabinet officials. They demanded that a minimum wage for farm workers be raised to 11 colons ($40) per day and at times threatened the lives of the hostages. Other reports claimed that the group intended the occupation to be peaceful. Two days later, with the mediation of church officials and after the group had already released a pregnant woman, the group allowed the employees to leave unharmed.

November 11, 1977—South Korea—Arson was suspected as the cause of the explosion of thirty tons of dynamite being carried by a freight train through Seoul. Fifty-six persons were killed, 1,348 injured, 9,500 homes and buildings were destroyed, and 14,000 persons were left homeless. Damage was estimated at $10 million.

November 11, 1977—West Germany—The Bonn press reported that German intelligence sources believed some of the sixteen Red Army Faction terrorists wanted for the Schleyer killing (see incident 3179) were hiding in Iraq or had joined Palestinians in Lebanon.

November 12, 1977—West Germany—Ingrid Schubert, a Baader-Meinhof Gang member, was found dead in her cell at the Munich-Stadelheim prison at 1:10 GMT, hanging from her window by a rope made of bedsheets. She had last been seen alive an hour earlier. An autopsy indicated that she had committed suicide. She had been sentenced by a Berlin regional court to a thirteen-year term for attempted murder, participating in freeing Andreas Baader from prison, several robberies, and membership in a criminal association. She had been moved from Stammheim prison to Stadelheim on August 18, 1977.

November 12, 1977—Denmark—A bomb was thrown against a wall of the Indian ambassador's residence in Copenhagen. Police also found an unexploded device in the garden. 3270

November 13, 1977—Israel—A PDFLP bomb exploded near an Arab school in the Old City of Jerusalem's Christian section, killing a student and wounding four other persons. A second bomb exploded three hours later in the Jewish suburb of Talpiot, across the street from a nursery school. An Arab teenager was killed, and a man was injured. The PDFLP in Beirut said the bombings were in retaliation for Israeli shelling in southern Lebanon. Part of the Associated Press story was censored by the Israeli military. 3271-3272

November 13, 1977—Morocco—Members of the Polisario in a heavily armed launch fired sixty-five machine-gun and artillery rounds at a Spanish ship owned by the Pescanova fishing company eighteen miles off the Saharan coast. The attackers kidnapped three Spanish fishermen, putting them ashore near Cape Leven, from where a Saharan column was believed to have taken them to Tindouf. The Polisario initially denied charges of complicity, but on November 21, the Algiers Domestic Service reported that "the Defense Ministry of the Saharan Democratic Arab Republic has issued a communiqué which says that on the night of 14 November the fighters of the Saharan Popular Liberation Army attacked a Spanish fishing boat which violated the territorial waters of the SDAR with the intention of plundering Saharan maritime wealth." 3273

November 14, 1977—United States—An Air India B747 with 203 on board was diverted to Ireland's Shannon Airport on a flight from New York to London after receiving a bomb threat. None of the 184 passengers and 19 crew was injured, and no bomb was found.

November 15, 1977—Worldwide—The Indian minister of external affairs, Atal Bihari Vajpayee, revealed that the Universal Proutist Revolutionary Federation had threatened Indian diplomatic missions in Katmandu, New York, Washington, Paris, and Stockholm, demanding the release of P. R. Sarkar, founder of the Ananda Marg. 3274-3278

November 15, 1977—Cuba—Six young Cuban dissidents from Havana University crashed their car into the gate of the Venezuelan embassy and rushed in under a hail of police bullets. One of the group was captured by Cuban police, and another was wounded. A press blackout was ordered, but it was learned four days later that the Venezuelan government had pressed Cuba to give the group safe passage. They were flown to Caracas on a Venezuelan air force jet, accompanied by the ambassador, Adolfo Taylhardat. Guillermo Amallo, who had been wounded, was subsequently flown to a Caracas hospital, where he died.

November 15, 1977—United States—New York City police found a bomb in the Iran Air offices and defused it. The shah of Iran was visiting Washington, D.C., on an official state visit. 3279

November 16, 1977—France—The French government extradited radical leftist lawyer Klaus Croissant by air to West Germany during the evening. The extradition request accused him of improperly aiding Andreas Baader while he was in prison.

November 16, 1977—Chile—Valparaiso police reported that Enrique Lopez Olmedo, a Spanish citizen believed to be carrying out subversive activities, was killed in a police shootout after he had refused to identify himself. 3280

November 16, 1977—Afghanistan—Ali Khorram, the minister of planning, was assassinated outside his office by a lone gunman at 2:50 P.M. The individual was arrested.

November 16, 1977—Venezuela—A DC8 carrying Venezuelan President Carlos Andres Perez from Caracas to Brasilia was diverted to Manaus for two hours and fifteen minutes when a bomb threat was received. No bomb was found. 3281

November 16, 1977—Malaysia—A time bomb exploded in the Air India office's rest room on the fourteenth floor of a building in Kuala Lumpur, causing minimal damage but injuring two police constables. Seventy-four people were detained for questioning. Police believed the attack may have been the work of the Ananda Marg, although the clandestine Communist party of Malaya was also suspected because it had celebrated its anniversary the day before. 3282

November 17, 1977—Syria—Two bombs exploded in the Egyptian embassy in Damascus, causing no injuries and slight damage to the building, as well as to a store near the embassy. Fatah denied responsibility for the evening explosion, which came after President Sadat had departed Syria after meeting with President Asad regarding his decision to go to Israel to discuss his peace proposals. 3283

November 17, 1977—Lebanon—A bomb was thrown at the Egyptair offices in Beirut at midnight, causing some damage. 3284

November 18, 1977—Mexico—Mexican authorities claimed that two of the West German terrorists connected with the Lufthansa hijacking to Mogadishu had entered Mexico two weeks previously and were planning to contact Central American terrorist groups. A reward of $5,000 was offered. The West German government, through Interpol, requested Mexico to conduct a search.

November 18, 1977—Lebanon—During a demonstration in Beirut against President Sadat's proposed trip to Israel, a demonstrator fired three rockets at the embassy, killing a guard and wounding four others, as well as damaging the building. 3285

November 18, 1977—Greece—Thirty Arab demonstrators shot their way into the Egyptian embassy in Athens. A Greek security guard and seven of the demonstrators were wounded. The group remained in the embassy for ninety minutes before surrendering to police. 3286

November 19, 1977—France—A gasoline container was set on fire outside the Egyptian embassy's Cultural Center in Paris, causing slight damage. 3287

November 19, 1977—Malaysia—The Indian high commissioner in Kuala Lumpur received a letter from the Universal Proutist Revolutionary Federation, which threatened to kill Prime Minister Morarji Desai if Ananda Marg founder Sarkar were not released. 3288

November 19, 1977—Pakistan—Six students, believed to be Palestinians, drove up to the Egyptian consulate in Karachi at 5 P.M. and tried to set it on fire. They succeeded only in setting afire some carpets, which were extinguished before the blaze could do serious damage. The group escaped. 3289

November 19, 1977—Libya—A major fire was reported in the Egyptian embassy in Tripoli. The Libyan news agency reported that a hundred thousand people demonstrated against the Sadat trip. 3290

November 20, 1977—Iran—During rioting, about twenty youths attempted to break into the Lufthansa offices in Tehran. They stoned the windows and seriously injured a policeman. Lufthansa spokesmen said the attack was not directed solely against them, noting that other businesses had been attacked.

November 20, 1977—Pakistan—Four men, presumably Palestinian students, threw burning bundles of cloth soaked in gasoline from a car at the Egyptian consulate in Karachi. Firemen extinguished the blaze before it could do serious damage. Security forces were increased around the consulate and Egyptian Airlines offices. 3291

November 21, 1977—Jordan—A bomb exploded at the Egyptian embassy, causing some damage. 3292

November 23, 1977—United States—A plane was diverted after a deranged passenger took off his clothes and tried to pummel down the cockpit door.

November 23, 1977—France—Paul Lucas, thirty-nine, a former lieutenant in France's naval veterinary corps, drove a yellow pickup truck to the Elysée palace, where a chain prevented his continuing. He jumped out of the truck and fatally wounded Ahmed Abu Hammachè, forty-three, with a .22 caliber rifle. Lucas was soon overpowered. He had made death threats against French presidents since 1968. He told the clerk at the truck rental agency, "I'm going to get Giscard. I will get in at all costs." Lucas was described as a former mental patient.

November 26, 1977—Ireland—Eight IRA gunmen took supermarket shoppers hostage in Dublin when police surprised them in the middle of a holdup. The group took nine hostages to an upstairs storage room. They released one of the hostages during the negotiations and ended the siege at midnight after thirteen hours, harming no one. Police believed them to be members of a gang that had engaged in a series of holdups netting $3 million over the past year. 3293

November 27, 1977—France—The Tal az-Za'tar group claimed credit for a predawn bombing of the Bank Leumi le Israel in Paris, which caused extensive damage but no injuries. An anonymous caller told Agence-France Presse that the bombing was a warning to the "Zionist killers who recently bombarded Lebanon and those who support them." The group's name is taken from a Palestinian refugee camp in Lebanon, which was overrun by Christian militia in August 1976 after a fifty-four-day siege. 3294

November 28, 1977—United States—Silla Koteswar, thirty-five, assistant director for purchase for the Indian embassy supply mission, was stabbed with two hunting knives as he walked to his car in the parking lot at 6:40 P.M. in Washington, D.C. His assailant plunged one eight-inch blade into his right side and another four-inch blade into his neck before fleeing. Koteswar crawled back into the building before collapsing. The Indian embassy's spokesman said, "We suspect [the assailant] belonged to the Universal Proutist Revolutionary Movement." In Denver, the spokesman for the U.S. chapter of Ananda Marg, Ivo Nelson, denied responsibility and said that the group's founder, Sarkar, had disavowed any acts of violence aimed at securing his release and would refuse to accept a release obtained by such acts. Kay Nelson, speaking for the Washington Ananda Marg, also denied credit for the attack. 3295

November 29, 1977—Djibouti—A French school director and a soldier of the national army were killed and the director's wife was wounded by a group that fled to Ethiopia. 3296

November 29, 1977—Indonesia—Gunmen claiming membership in the Front for the Liberation of Aceh, Sumatra, attacked the Arun airstrip in the town of

Lhok Sukon, where employees of Bechtel, a U.S. firm, were laying pipeline for a liquefied natural gas plant. According to the Indonesian Defense Ministry, the robbers were armed with old rifles and machetes and fired random shots at the workers. One American, George Pernicone, fifty-three, assistant superintendent of Bechtel, was killed, and Donald Stayer, twenty-two, was wounded and flown to Singapore for emergency surgery. The group seized a company van and ordered its driver to take them to the jungle. The group was reportedly headed by an Indonesian who had lived for twenty years in the United States. 3303

December 1977—Australia—Yugoslavia complained of violent attacks against its consulate in Sydney and the bombing of the Yugoslav Airlines office in Melbourne. Foreign Secretariat spokesman Mirko Kalezic said, ''These attacks are not the first or only attacks by fascist terrorists against Yugoslav missions and representatives in Australia, which proves that anti-Yugoslav subversive and terrorist activity continues uninterrupted and organized on Australian territory.'' 3297

December 1, 1977—Kuwait—Dissident Palestinians occupied the offices of the Palestine Liberation Organization in Kuwait in protest of what they termed ''PLO compromising stands—stands represented in the PLO alliance with As-Sadat and other Arab reactionaries.''

December 1, 1977—Cyprus—Three British military bases were bombed by individuals believed to be connected with EOKA-B. The first two explosions went off around 1 A.M. at the Akrotiri air base in southern Cyprus. The base's water reservoirs were destroyed, and the Dhekelia base transformer station was damaged. The second bombing was at the radio antenna system of the Zyyi station, damaging a generator of the Dhekelia naval base. The final bomb went off at the Kissounsa village in a building housing a Dhekelia club as well as water pumps for the Episkopi base in Limmasol. On December 4, Cypriot police arrested eight former members of the EOKA-B. On December 13, the police obtained an eight-day extension for the detention of three persons identified as Onisiforos Kharalambous Kolossiatis (also known as Foris), Menelaos Athimis, and Erotokritos Mattheou (also known as Kritonis). The case was believed related to the extradition hearing in the United Kingdom of Kiriakos Kakis, a Greek Cypriot. Threats had been made against British installations in April 1977 (see incident 3298) regarding his extradition. 3299-3301

December 1, 1977—Czechoslovakia—Czech security forces broke up a plot by three armed men to hijack a domestic airliner to West Germany. 5527

December 2, 1977—Argentina—Gunmen in two vehicles machine-gunned a car of a Chrysler executive's bodyguards in a southern suburb of Buenos Aires, killing two and seriously wounding a third. 3302

December 3, 1977—Ireland—Dublin police captured IRA commander Seamus Twomey after a car chase. Twomey, fifty-six, a member of the IRA's Army Council, was arrested with another man after their car was rammed by the police, who had been seeking him since his escape in a hijacked helicopter from a Dublin prison on October 31, 1973. He had been serving a one-year sentence for IRA membership. (See incident 5420.)

December 3, 1977—Israel—A bomb exploded in a crowded market street in Jerusalem's walled Old City, hospitalizing two West German tourists, three Israeli Jews, and one Arab. The bombing occurred thirteen days after President Sadat of Egypt stopped to pray at the Al Aqsa mosque during his trip to Israel. 3304

December 4, 1977—Malaysia—A Malaysian Airlines System B737 scheduled to fly from Penang to Singapore with a stopover in Kuala Lumpur (KL) was hijacked ten minutes after it left the resort island. Reports differ as to the identity and number of hijackers and the movements of the plane. Some sources claim that the pilot, Captain G. K. Ganjoor, radioed KL airport that he was being hijacked, ending with "hijacker aboard"; other sources stated that he identified the Japanese Red Army as responsible. Some sources claim that the plane touched down briefly at KL, while others say that the pilot attempted to disobey hijacker orders against landing at KL but pulled up after gunfire broke out on board. It appears that the plane, which was due to land at KL at 7:55 P.M., forty minutes after leaving Penang, overflew the airport at 7:54. An eighteen-year-old youth in the village of Kampong Tajung Kutang, thirteen miles west of Johore Baharu, told police that at 8:15, the jet shot upward, then went into a dive, and exploded into flames. Other witnesses said there was a second explosion as the wreckage hit the ground. The ruins were spread over a square mile of swamps. No survivors among the seven crew members and ninety-three passengers were reported.

Seventy-three of the passengers were described as Malaysians; Singaporeans were among the other twenty. Malaysian Agriculture Minister Ali Haji Amad was reported on board, as were the Cuban ambassador to Japan and Malaysia, Mario Garcia Inchaustegui, and his wife, Gladys Delgado. Two of the passengers were World Bank officials: O. D. Hoerr, forty-one, an American, and S. S. Naime, forty-seven, of Afghanistan. Five Britons died, including Thomas Parr of Lyminster, Sussex, who worked for a Worthing medical company.

The minister of home affairs, Tan Sri Ghazali bin Shafie, said the pilot referred to only one hijacker. An airline spokesman said the pilot did not identify the hijackers. It was noted that it was unlikely that the attack was by the JRA because the B737 did not have the range to reach the Middle East, where the JRA is based. Japanese authorities noted that the JRA did not claim credit for this attack, and that according to the passenger list, there was only one Japanese on board. The JRA report may have arisen because four Japanese tourists mistakenly boarded the plane at Penang but deplaned before it left. The identity and number of hijackers probably will never be known for certain. 3307

December 5, 1977—West Germany—Richard Scott, three, the son of a U.S. Army sergeant, was kidnapped by a masked couple from the Dielheim home of his German grandparents. The boy's father, Sergeant Richard A. Neumann, was attached to C Troop, Fourth Armored Cavalry Regiment, First Infantry Division in Böblingen, West Germany. Police said they had been unable to locate the boy as of December 7.

December 6, 1977—Egypt—David Holden, fifty-three, chief foreign correspondent of the *London Sunday Times*, was found dead, shot in the back, at 8:30 A.M. in Nasser City, a Cairo suburb. He had apparently been killed three hours earlier, disappearing after taking a taxi from the Cairo airport. His body was without identification papers, luggage, or money, save a few Jordanian coins, and lay in a morgue until he was identified by the British embassy on December 10. On December 16, Cairo police arrested two Arab men and a woman in connection with the case. It was noted that Holden's suitcase and typewriter had been discovered in an abandoned, blood-spattered car. On December 18, the *London Sunday Mirror* reported that Holden had spotted the leader of a Palestinian guerrilla group on its way to Cairo to disrupt Israeli-Egyptian peace talks. The two were aboard the same plane from Amman, recognized each other, and from then on, his life was in danger. It was believed that Holden was carrying a message from King Hussein to President Sadat promising him support in the peace talks. 3308

December 7, 1977—United States—Amar Inam Rahman, nineteen, son of India's minister of education and science, was stabbed at 10:30 P.M. in the stacks of Georgetown University's library by an assailant who gave no explanation for his attack. He was reported in fair condition at Georgetown University Hospital. The press speculated that the attack was related to a stabbing on November 29 of the Indian embassy's attaché by a member of the Universal Proutist Revolutionary Movement, which had been threatening the embassy. 3309

December 7, 1977—Japan—*Unity*, the publication of the Japanese Red Army distributed by the Osaka newspaper *Jin Min Shimbun*, warned that the group would attempt to recover Kozo Okamoto, the surviving member of the May

1972 Lod Airport massacre (see incident 1056). The group also criticized Japanese revolutionary movements and called for the establishment of a provisional revolutionary government.

December 8, 1977—Hong Kong—An Air India B707 flying from Bombay to Calcutta, Bangkok, and Hong Kong was diverted to Tokyo after the airline's office in New Delhi was informed that a bomb had been planted on board. The plane landed at 12:28 P.M. and was searched for an hour. No bomb was found. 3310

December 8, 1977—Venezuela—Caracas's Radio Continente Network reported that Illich Ramirez Sanchez (Carlos) and Wadi Haddad, the leader of a breakaway faction of the PFLP, were in Caracas. It was speculated that their arrival was timed to coincide with the beginning of the OPEC conference.

December 8-10, 1977—Argentina—Sister Alicia Domon, forty, a French nun, was kidnapped with fifteen Argentine citizens identified as either mothers or relatives of persons who have disappeared, after leaving a church at the end of a mass organized by the Ecumenical Movement for Human Rights. It was reported that armed individuals driving a Renault 12 captured her. Two days later, Renée Duquet, sixty-one, known as Sister Léonie, was kidnapped at 11 A.M. by four persons driving an American car with license plates who came to her home in San Pablo parish in Buenos Aires. The press reported that the kidnappers had identified themselves as plainclothes policemen and that the French government, in its note requesting information on the cases from the Argentine government, had accused the police of responsibility. It was noted that the French nuns had been residing in Argentina as members of the Notre Dame de la Mothe congregation since the 1950s.

On December 17, Agence-France Presse in Buenos Aires received a communiqué purportedly by the Montoneros. Attached was a photo of the nuns posing before the group's flag and a photocopy of a letter sent by Sister Alicia. The group demanded that the Catholic church and the French government reject the "dictatorial regime of General Videla." It called for French asylum for those persecuted by the government and demanded that a report be made to the United Nations on the status of detainees and missing and kidnapped people. The group demanded the release by December 24 of twenty political prisoners, including former President Hector Campora, writer Rodolfo Walsh, union leader Lorenzo Miguel, Sergio Tomasella, Curima Fortunato, Alfredo Teofilo Olivo, Juan Carlos Parolini, Eduardo de Ayala, Gloria Ayala, and Nancy Ayala. Representatives of the Montoneros in Mexico and France denied responsibility for the attacks, claiming that they were engineered by the government to discredit the organization.

December 12, 1977—Austria—Lieselotte Boehm, forty-two, wife of Vienna textile millionaire Leopold Boehm, was kidnapped by two armed men during the evening in front of her Grinzing, Vienna, villa. They escaped with her in a white car. Police reported that no ransom demand had been made as of the next day.

December 13, 1977—Japan—Japan announced that it had distributed photographs of JRA members to all Japanese embassies and consulates in Europe and Southeast Asia, as well as to Japanese Airlines offices. The eleven terrorists were identified as Kunio Bando, Jun Nishikawa, Hisashi Matsuda, Kazuo Tohira, Norio Sasaki, Okudaira Junzo, Nihei Akira, Shirosaki Tsutomu, and Sensui Hiroshi, and two women, Daidoji Ayako, and Ekita Yukiko. The last five were prisoners who were released by the Japanese government during the JAL hijacking of September 28, 1977 (see incident 3201).

December 13, 1977—Lebanon—Cairo radio reports indicated that Syrian authorities were plotting to assassinate members of the Egyptian embassy in Beirut in hopes of interfering with the Egyptian-Israeli peace conference.

December 14, 1977—United Arab Emirates—A bomb exploded in the morning in the Egyptian Airlines office in Ash Shariqah, causing no injuries but destroying the office's front window, as well as the furniture and front of the Ash Shariqah Bank. 3311

December 14, 1977—Angola—UNITA claimed credit for burning down three hotels in Luso housing Bulgarian and East German technicians, killing at least ten. 3312

December 14, 1977—Yugoslavia—Two men threw two Molotov cocktails at the West German embassy at 9:30 P.M. The first fell on the edge of the pavement and failed to explode. The second exploded in front of the embassy entrance and started a fire, which was quickly extinguished. The men escaped. 3313

December 14, 1977—Venezuela—Caracas Radio Continente Network reported that members of the Directorate of Intelligence and Prevention Services arrested the reputed girl friend of Carlos, the PFLP Venezuelan terrorist. It was believed that she was part of a group planning to attack the OPEC meeting in Caracas. It was reported that she had been present in Paris when Carlos shot policemen attempting to question him (see incident 2324) in June 1975.

December 14, 1977—Cyprus—Second Lieutenant Achilles Kyprianou, nineteen, the son of President Spiro Kyprianou, was kidnapped during the night near a military base in the Troodus Mountains by two men. The group threatened to send his father the youth's head if twenty-five political prisoners were not released by 10 P.M. on December 15. President Carter and Senator Edward Kennedy sent messages of concern, and the deadline was reset. The group whose release was demanded included those convicted of assassinating American Ambassador Rodger Davies on August 19, 1974 (see incident 2022), as well as others being held in connection with the recent bombings of British military facilities (see incidents 3299-3301). Nicos Sampson, one of the EOKA-B prisoners, repudiated any prisoner release obtained by violence.

Kyprianou brought in Peter Walter, a Scotland Yard official, to advise him of how to conduct the government's response to the crisis. After a cabinet meeting, the kidnappers' demands were rejected, with the president affirming that the commonweal was of higher importance than his son's life. Three EOKA-B sympathizers offered to act as mediators but threatened to distort the negotiations by injecting their own demands. The Greek ambassador intervened and held a meeting between the president and two of the kidnappers, which resulted in the release of the son on December 18. He reported after the predawn meeting that he held been held in a six-foot square pit in the mountains and was given only bread and water.

It was reported that the kidnappers would be allowed to leave Cyprus for asylum in Greece. However, on December 19, Athens radio reported that Greece had agreed to allow the kidnappers' plane to land at Ellinikon airport but that they would have to fly to another country. Police claimed that five EOKA-B members were responsible, led by Vassos Pavlides, also known as the Doctor, who was chief of the Limassol cell of the group. The press reported that the Greek Cypriot Council of Ministers agreed to declare a general amnesty after the February 1978 presidential elections. Most analysts suggested that Kyprianou's stand against the kidnappers would aid him in his reelection campaign. 3314

December 15, 1977—Djibouti—Members of the People's Liberation Movement (MPL), an Afar group, were reported to have been responsible for tossing two grenades into a bar restaurant, Le Palmier en Zinc, which was frequented by French troops. The explosions killed the owner, Jean-Jacques Aufray, a French national, a Frenchwoman, a Djiboutian waiter and two others and wounded thirty-two. Aufray died while being flown to France for medical treatment with ten others injured in the attack. Afar leaders, as well as the Ethiopian government, denied involvement. Fifteen were arrested for the attack. 3315

December 16, 1977—Argentina—Five men and two women driving a van and white Peugeot 504 shot to death Andres Gasparoux, the French fifty-five-year-old technical director of Peugeot in Buenos Aires, as he was driving two blocks from his home. Alberto Lopez, a local police official, was wounded in the morning attack. 3316

December 17, 1977—Syria—Vienna's *Die Presse* and *Kurier* newspapers reported that after the visit of Austrian Foreign Minister Willibald Pahr, PLO minister Faruq Qaddumi warned that the PLO might resort to terrorism in the wake of the Sadat-Begin initiatives: "We will fight with every means for our cause...the use of any kind of force is not terrorism." Acts of force against civil aviation were not ruled out: "We must use force against all enemies and enemy targets." Qaddumi argued that an organization that is not recognized as an international political reality is not subject to international responsibilities.

December 18, 1977—France—In a clandestine press conference near Ajaccio, the Corsican National Liberation Front warned that it would engage in a new wave of operations in Corsica and mainland France.

December 18, 1977—Lebanon—An explosive-laden suitcase was removed from the Beirut residence of a senior Egyptian diplomat. 3317

December 19, 1977—Lebanon—A suitcase containing thirteen pounds of explosives was found inside the Egyptian embassy and defused. 3318

December 20, 1977—Lebanon—During the night, an Egyptian bank and the adjacent office of Egyptair were slightly damaged by a bomb in Beirut. 3319

December 20, 1977—Lebanon—Two 3.5-inch Katyusha rockets and dynamite were found hidden in a vegetable cart on a building near the Egyptian embassy in Beirut. The devices were defused one hour before they were scheduled to fire. 3320

December 20, 1977—Switzerland—After two people drove a French-registered auto from France into Switzerland, they were requested by two Fahy customs guards to leave their car for an identity check. The woman fired a pistol at the officers, wounding one in the chest and the other in the leg. The latter returned the fire, wounding her male companion in the foot. The couple escaped in their car, which they abandoned ten miles away in Porrentruy. They took a taxi, which was stopped at a roadblock outside Delemont. They surrendered without further resistance. They were initially identified as Willy Peter Stoll, twenty-seven, and Juliane Plambeck, both on the list of sixteen Baader-Meinhof Gang members wanted for the killing of Hanns-Martin Schleyer (see incident 3179). It was soon learned, however, that they had arrested Gabriele Kroecher-Tiedemann, twenty-six, who was wanted for shooting an Austrian policeman at point-blank range in the December 1975 attack on OPEC (see incident 2527). With her was Christian Moller, who was suspected of taking part in West German bank raids after he joined the group in July. Some of the money paid in the ransom of Walter Palmers (see incident 3266) (the family had paid a multimillion dollar ransom in American, Italian, Austrian, and Swiss currency) was found in the terrorists' car. 3321

December 20, 1977—Colombia—Several Guajira Region Indians fired shots at the Venezuelan consulate in Maicao, killing José Hernando Tapias, a building watchman. 3322

December 21, 1977—Argentina—Alberto Corchs, a Uruguayan employee of a Buenos Aires import company, was kidnapped during the afternoon by a group of men. His wife was kidnapped a few hours later from their Lucila home by men driving a Ford Falcon and a Renault 12. The eighteen-month-old son of Elena Lerena de Corchs was left with some neighbors.

December 21, 1977—Colombia—*El Tiempo* reported that an American woman with the surname of Speyton was kidnapped. She was identified as the daughter of a principal Coca-Cola stockholder. A rash of kidnappings had recently plagued the country, with twenty-three persons being officially reported to be held by criminals or guerrilla groups.

December 22, 1977—Lebanon—The Egyptian embassy ordered most of its staff back to Cairo after a bomb damaged a building housing three Egyptian organizations: Misr-Lebanon Bank, Egyptair, and the En Nasr Export-Import Company.

December 23, 1977—United States—A bomb exploded at 12:10 A.M. in the Miami Beach offices of Venezuela's Viasa Airlines, knocking a large hole in a wall, shattering heavy glass windows and door frames, but causing no injuries. The explosion occurred hours after the first scheduled flight from the United States to Cuba since the early 1960s took off from Chicago. No one claimed credit for the bombing, although an anti-Castro Cuban group had warned that it would sabotage Venezuelan planes if Orlando Bosch, a Cuban exile terrorist leader, was not released from a Venezuelan jail. 3323

December 25, 1977—Kuwait—A bomb was found and dismantled outside the office of Egyptair in Kuwait City. 3324

December 25, 1977—United States—Eastern Airlines flight 688, a DC9 flying the Miami-Jacksonville-Atlanta-Indianapolis route, was hijacked fifty-two miles south of Atlanta's Hartsfield International Airport by an individual who boarded the plane at 7 A.M. in Jacksonville after purchasing a ticket under the name of Nick Roland. The man gave a stewardess a note stating that he was wired with explosives, had a gun, and wished to go to Miami and then to Cuba. FAA spokesman Jack Barker said he "mentioned something about wanting to go to Cuba to free the children." However, he allowed the DC9 to land in Atlanta at 8:20 A.M. and released fourteen of the passengers fifteen minutes later. Negotiations conducted by Atlanta police lieutenant William Collier and FBI special agent William D. Cochran lasted for three hours. The hijacker was overpowered by the officer and two FBI men, who discovered that the bomb was a radio taped to the man's leg and the gun was a toy. None of the five crew or thirty-one passengers was injured.

The hijacker was identified as Austrian-born Nikolai Wischnewsky, thirty-two, a landscaper from Pearl River, New York. In November 1975, he had been arrested in Sloatsburg, New York, in a similar phony-bomb caper. He threatened a bait and tackle store manager, demanding ammunition and guns with what turned out to be a cigar box. He served twenty-one months of a three-year sentence for attempted robbery. He had been free on parole from New York's Dannemora State Prison for only a month before the hijacking. He was arraigned on federal charges of air piracy and held in Fulton County jail.

During the hijacking, Cochran asked a woman who was allowed to leave if she would like her husband to accompany her off the plane. She whispered that she was unmarried. "Well, pick one." "I'll take that one with the moustache," and walked off the plane with the man. 5528

December 26, 1977—United States—A bomb exploded at 1:20 A.M. in the Venezuelan consulate in New York, blowing out windows and showering the street crowded with shoppers with glass. No injuries were reported. Ten minutes later, a man called the Associated Press to claim credit for Omega Seven, and said that the group was protesting Venezuela's jailing of Orlando Bosch, an anti-Castro Cuban terrorist leader. 3325

December 27, 1977—Colombia—Bogotá Radio reported that a German industrialist had escaped a kidnapping attempt but that José Ignacio Barraquer, a Spanish ophthalmologist, Natan Lanisky, a German industrialist, and the wife of a Polish industrialist were being held by unknown individuals.

December 28, 1977—Iran—A few days before the scheduled visit of President Carter to Iran, a bomb damaged the Iran-America Society's coaching center in Tehran, injuring three persons, including a policeman. A letter signed by the National Front Forces of Iran, which was found on the doorstep of United Press International, said that the visit "is not welcomed by forces of democracy. . . .The peace-loving people of Iran cannot welcome a man who is pushing the world toward war and misery. . . .[Carter is promoting] a dirty plot for the surrender of Arab and Moslem rights to the Zionist state through the treachery of the old traitor Anwar Sadat. . . .[Carter is] the father of the human killer neutron bomb." Diplomatic sources noted that the language was far harsher than normally employed by the Front and speculated that the bombing was staged to discredit opposition to the shah, who had experienced demonstrations during his tour of the United States. 3326

December 28, 1977—West Germany—Baader-Meinhof Group member Verena Becker, twenty-five, a former telephone operator, was sentenced to life imprisonment for armed robbery and attempted murder. She struggled with her four guards and had to be subdued while the Stuttgart judge read the sentence. Her release had been demanded by the hijackers of a Lufthansa plane in October and by the kidnappers of Hanns-Martin Schleyer in September (see incidents 3179 and 3207). She was arrested in the summer after a shootout in southern Germany in which police seriously wounded a male companion.

December 28, 1977—Greece—A parcel bomb the size of a cigarette package was found in the U.S. embassy's mail and defused. 3329

December 29, 1977—Malta—Letter bombs arrived at the homes of two doctors in Valletta. One exploded in the hands of Karen Grech, sixteen, daughter of obstetrician Edwin Grech, killing her and wounding her twelve-year-old brother and South African-born mother. A labor party member of Parliament received a second bomb, which did not explode. The doctors were working at a government hospital despite a six-month industrial dispute between doctors and the government. The post office subsequently suspended delivery of parcels and bulky letters.

December 29, 1977—Puerto Rico—FBI agents disarmed a bomb thrown from a passing car at 1:45 A.M. at the Venezuelan consulate in San Juan. 3327

December 30, 1977—Guatemala—Deutschlandfunk, a Cologne, West Germany, radio station, reported that fifteen West German terrorists were believed to have entered Guatemala from Mexico disguised as tourists.

December 31, 1977—Guatemala—Roberto Herrera Ibarguen, a former foreign minister, was kidnapped near a bridge six miles from Guatemala City when his car was intercepted by unidentified individuals at noon. Police found the car and the bodies of two off-duty policemen who were serving as his guards.

December 31, 1977—United Kingdom—A bomb hidden in a car belonging to the Syrian embassy exploded during the night, killing Jawat Awad, a medical attaché, and Sayez Shibly, a chauffeur. The bomb went off blocks from Piccadilly Circus, where thousands of people were celebrating the New Year. The one-pound bomb damaged store fronts and blew out windows. 3328

1978—Czechoslovakia—A planned hijacking of a Karlovy Vary to Prague flight was foiled in mid-1978. On August 23, the Czech supreme court upheld a Prague city court sentence for preparing to jeopardize the security of a means of air transport and leave Czechoslovakia via force of arms. E. Dvorak and K. Kejmar received fourteen and four years, respectively, while the sentences of J. Cerny and A. Eisenhamerova were raised to nine and six years.

January or February, 1978—Nicaragua—A bomb went off at the Nabisco Cristal cookie and cracker factory in Managua during a two-week general work stoppage. The firm is 60 percent owned by the U.S. firm Nabisco, Inc.

January 2, 1978—West Germany—An Egyptian security official defused a four-pound bomb two minutes before it was set to explode in his embassy. The bomb was hidden in a plastic shopping bag in the embassy garden, propped up against a wall. The two packages of explosives were set to explode at noon.

January 3, 1978—United Kingdom—A pound of explosives shattered windows and caused a small fire in the north London branch of the Turkish bank in Green Lanes, Haringey, but caused no injuries. The New Armenian Resistance claimed credit for the predawn explosion.

January 3, 1978—Belgium—The New Armenian Resistance pushed a bomb into a letter box of the financial counselor of the Turkish embassy. The bomb went off before dawn, severely damaging his apartment building in Brussels.

January 4, 1978—United Kingdom—Said Hammami, thirty-five, PLO and Fatah spokesman in London, died when a twenty-four-year-old Middle Eastern man fired three shots into him in the basement of the Arab League headquarters. Although police initially were looking for four men seen leaving the scene, they later concluded that one terrorist had acted alone and that he had escaped into a crowd of Oxford Street shoppers. At the Beirut funeral, Abu Iyad, Yasir Arafat's chief assistant, accused Abu Nidal's Black June Organization of responsibility. Other observers suggested that Hammami had been killed for having contact with some Israelis and advocating some form of coexistence between Israelis and Palestinians. An anonymous individual called United Press International in London to claim credit for the Voice of the Palestinian Revolution.

January 6, 1978—France—A letter bomb addressed to the Syrian embassy and postmarked in Strasbourg, Austria, was intercepted by Paris police. French police warned the Syrian and other embassies of letter bombs addressed to them.

January 6, 1978—Libya—In an apparent attempt to assassinate Libya's Colonel Muammar Qaddafi, a bomb in a helicopter in which he was to have ridden exploded, killing two East German Communist party leaders who had been visiting an agricultural project outside Tripoli.

January 8, 1978—United States—The Montrealer, an Amtrak Washington to Montreal train, made an emergency stop in Windsor Locks, Connecticut, where 250 passengers were evacuated after an anonymous caller said a bomb was on board. No bomb was found.

January 11, 1978—Colombia—Three unknown individuals fired machine guns at the Venezuelan consulate, damaging windows and doors but causing no injuries.

January 12, 1978—United States—A bomb attributed to the Puerto Rican FALN exploded on the ninth floor of Macy's New York City department store, causing no injuries and little damage.

January 12, 1978—Ethiopia—A bomb was thrown at the car of Ethiopian President Mengistu Haile Mariam and visiting Cuban Defense Minister Raul Castro, who were visiting Harar, Ogaden. Although the two leaders were not injured, six Cubans and a Russian were killed in the attack, which was believed to have been engineered by army dissidents.

January 12, 1978—Venezuela—In a message to the Panama office of the ACAN news agency, the Pedro Luis Boitel Command threatened Venezuelan officials, including President Carlos Andres Perez, for the imprisonment of Orlando Bosch (see incident 2913).

January 14, 1978—Philippines—Moslem rebels ambushed a truck and exploded a land mine, killing four Filipino security guards at a B. F. Goodrich Tire Company plantation, and wounded eight other civilians on the island of Basilan.

January 14, 1978—Corsica—Corsican separatists blew up two radar units on a French air force base.

January 18, 1978—Ecuador—A male and female armed with pistols and explosives hijacked a SAETA plane on a domestic flight shortly after it took off from Quito at 4:30 P.M. and demanded to be flown to Cuba. The male asked to be taken to a Colombian town whose name the crew forgot, but the pilot told him he had only enough fuel to reach Guayaquil. During a refueling step there, the hijackers let some passengers deplane. A second refueling stop was made in Panama City, Panama. The hijackers surrendered to Havana authorities. The plane, remaining passengers, and six crew members returned to Ecuador the next day. The hijackers claimed that a fictitious third person was on board, ready to detonate explosives.

January 19, 1978—Indonesia—"T.Z., alias S.," commander of the Darul Islam Holy War Command, was tried for planning to hijack an airplane outside Indonesia to release detained Moslems and obtain a ransom. During the trial of the group, it was alleged that the group had requested three hundred thousand modern weapons from Libyan President Qaddafi in 1975. Money was also requested for the revival of the Darul Islam/Tentara Islam Indonesia, a rebel movement.

January 19, 1978—France—The U.S.-owned Discount Bank in Paris was bombed, causing minor damage and no injuries. At a fire in a Paris school, police found pamphlets vowing revenge for the death of Andreas Baader. A Discount Bank branch in a Paris suburb was also bombed, wrecking a van and shattering windows.

January 19, 1978—Argentina—Unknown individuals attacked the Chilean consulate in Córdoba, causing some damage but no injuries to personnel. One of the attackers, a twenty-four-year-old bank employee, was killed. The attackers painted slogans referring to the Beagle Channel dispute.

January 20, 1978—Israel—Sami Ben-'Ali Isma'il, twenty-three, a U.S. citizen of Palestinian descent, was arrested for PFLP membership, committing a crime in Israel, maintaining contact with a foreign agent, and undergoing weapons training in August 1976 in Libya under the guidance of Taysir Quba. He had originally been detained on December 21, 1977, upon arrival at Ben Gurion Airport when he intended to visit his dying father in Ramallah. Felicia Langer, Isma'il's attorney, represented American Terre Fleener in a similar case.

January 21, 1978—Greece—A time bomb exploded before dawn at the U.S. Information Agency office in Thessaloniki, causing extensive damage but no injuries. Another bomb went off at the local American Express bank and travel agency, causing no injuries. No one claimed credit for the bombings, which came hours before the arrival in Athens of U.S. Secretary of State Cyrus Vance.

January 24, 1978—Swaziland—The right arm of Ablom Duma, forty-five, a leading member of the outlawed African National Congress of South Africa, was severed when his booby-trapped mailbox exploded in Manzini.

January 26, 1978—Argentina—The Argentine Youth for Sovereignty claimed credit for firing several shots from a passing car at the LAN-Chile Airlines office in Buenos Aires, causing minor damage and no injuries. The group warned that the Argentine people would "not cede one inch of national territory" to Chile.

January 27, 1978—Netherlands—Five Dutch children living in Maastricht were hospitalized after eating Israeli-imported oranges that had been injected with mercury. On February 1, the Dutch government received a letter from the Arab Revolutionary Army Palestinian Commando saying that it intended "to sabotage the Israeli economy." Reuters received a letter addressed to eighteen European and Arab governments that said that "oppressed Palestinian workers" in the occupied territories were responsible. The PLO in Beirut denied any involvement and said the attack was intended to "shake the support and confidence won by the PLO among world public opinion." Some observers suggested that the oranges had been tainted in a European port where they had been shipped for repackaging and distribution.

January 29, 1978—Lebanon—One kilogram of TNT exploded at the Tunisian embassy, causing some damage but no injuries. The Tunisian Revolutionary National Organization claimed credit.

January 29, 1978—Chad—FROLINAT claimed to have killed all those on board a DC3 that it shot down by antiaircraft fire. At least three soldiers from France were killed, according to some press reports, although they were listed as missing by the Chad Ministry of Cooperation.

January 30, 1978—Chad—FROLINAT attacked another plane with antiaircraft fire. The DC4 was able to make a safe landing, and the French crew survived.

January 31, 1978—United States—FALN claimed credit for a bomb that exploded in a trash can outside the Consolidated Edison headquarters in Manhattan. The group said it was in support of a thirty-five-day electrical workers' strike in Puerto Rico. Another FALN bomb exploded under an unoccupied police car in Manhattan.

January 31, 1978—West Germany—An off-duty policeman became ill in Dortmund after eating a mercury-poisoned Israeli orange. The same day, poisoned oranges were discovered in Aachen and Frankfurt.

February 1978—West Germany—Five members of a right-wing extremist group were arrested for the theft of four automatic pistols from a Dutch soldiers' bivouac at the NATO training ground in Bergen, Lower Saxony. The group, a sports defense association, was believed to be planning more attacks on Bundeswehr soldiers to obtain their weapons and had been active in Schleswig-Holstein, Cologne, and Hamburg. They were classified as criminals by police in 1977. Some sources claimed that the group hoped to free Rudolf Hess from his Spandau jail in Berlin and worked "like the Red Army group in its initial stage."

February 1978—Colombia—In mid-February, the September 14 Workers Self-Defense Command bombed the Nicaraguan embassy "in solidarity with the exploited people of Nicaragua and with the fighters of the Sandinist National Liberation Front."

February 1, 1978—Costa Rica—Four Nicaraguans and a Costa Rican took over the U.N. office at 10 A.M. Mario Palma Flores, Efrain Medina Torres, Leonardo Aleman, Daniel Avea Castillo, and Felipe Chaves Alvarado left the office forty-eight hours later carrying the Nicaraguan flag and stating that they were satisfied with the support they had received.

February 1, 1978—West Germany—Pea-sized amounts of mercury were found in Israeli fruit in Darmstadt. Elsewhere, two children and two women suffered stomach ailments and skin eruptions after eating poisoned oranges.

February 2, 1978—West Germany—A twelve-year-old girl was hospitalized in Bremen after eating a tainted Israeli orange.

February 2, 1978—Sweden—Mercury injected into Israeli oranges was discovered to have caused skin discoloration.

February 2, 1978—Netherlands—Spanish oranges injected with mercury were discovered in the same southern Holland area where tainted Israeli produce had been found, lending credence to the Israeli claim that the poisoning had not necessarily taken place in Israel.

February 3, 1978—Pakistan—A male Pakistani armed with a grenade attempted to hijack a domestic Pakistani B747 flight from Islamabad carrying 357 persons. His grenade exploded, injuring three persons. The plane landed safely and the man was turned over to police. He was sentenced to death by a military court, and President Mohammed Zia ul-Haq rejected a clemency petition from the hijacker's mother. On November 5, 1979, Said Hussain was hanged at the Central Jail in Rawalpindi.

February 3, 1978—El Salvador—Twenty-four leftists took over the U.N. information office in San Salvador, later identifying themselves as members of the Popular Revolutionary Bloc after saying they were workers affiliated with the Workers' National Union and Union of Izalco Sugar Mill Workers. The group wished to "denounce the Salvadoran Government's Abuse of Human Rights" and demanded U.N. intervention toward the release of 120 workers and union leaders arrested on January 31 for calling a strike at Izalco Sugar Mill. After the police surrounded the office, the BPR vacated the offices in the evening after they were promised that the U.N. commission would be requested to investigate human rights cases. The guerrillas had also demanded the release of several prisoners another group had demanded in the 1977 kidnapping of Foreign Minister Mauricio Borgonovo, who was killed in April after the government claimed it did not hold the prisoners (see incident 3087). None of the U.N. employees held hostage was harmed.

February 5, 1978—United States—The Anti-Communist Latin American Army claimed responsibility for the 10:32 P.M. bombing of the Manhattan Mexican consulate, which slightly damaged a metal front door. The group demanded the freedom for the "anticommunist Cuban Oreste Ruiz and Gaspar Jimenez and Gustavo Castillo." Right-wing Cubans were believed responsible because the Mexicans were seeking to extradite two Cubans accused of murdering a Cuban official in Mérida, Mexico.

February 5, 1978—Belgium—Poisoned Israeli oranges were discovered. A lemon injected with mercury was found in Héverlé the next day.

February 6, 1978—United Kingdom—A woman found a mercury-poisoned Israeli orange in a bag of fruit she had bought in a London store.

February 7, 1978—Netherlands—Groningen authorities discovered ten contaminated Spanish oranges.

February 7, 1978—Philippines—Three Ananda Margis stabbed Jyoti Sarup Vaid, an Indian embassy official, in the embassy. Steven Michael Dwyer, twenty-eight, of Wichita, Kansas, and Victoria Sheppard, thirty-one, of Maryland, were sentenced to ten to seventeen years in prison for attempted murder on May 25 and ordered to pay the victim $13,333 plus the cost of the three-month trial. Vaid, the personal secretary to the chargé d'affaires, was stabbed in the chest and throat. Dwyer and Sheppard claimed to have been at the scene but said they were not involved; they had appeared to obtain visas. A Filipino judge ordered an investigation of the organization as possible security risks; it had fifty thousand members in the Philippines and was known for previous violent actions.

February 9, 1978—Puerto Rico—The People's Revolutionary Army claimed credit for bombing a branch of the Chase Manhattan Bank in support of a strike against the Water Resources Authority, a state-owned electric utility.

February 11-12, 1978—Corsica—Corsican separatists set off bombs at offices of companies from the French mainland, causing considerable damage but no injuries.

February 13, 1978—Italy—Italian health officials banned the sale of grapefruit in Milan and Bergamo after an Israeli-imported grapefruit in Bergamo was found to be poisoned with mercury. Later, tainted grapefruit was found in Milan.

February 14, 1978—Israel—A PLO bomb exploded on a bus during the evening in Jerusalem, killing two people, including a local resident of the Ge'ula neighborhood, and injuring forty-three.

February 14, 1978—El Salvador—The People's Revolutionary Army bombed and machine-gunned the Nicaraguan embassy destroying its doors and shattering its windows at 6:15 A.M., fifteen minutes after Ambassador Edgar Escobar Fornos arrived. He sustained scratches. The group's leaflets said it was attacking the Somoza regime.

February 14, 1978—Bolivia—A "Nationalist Commando" warned that a bomb had been placed at the Chilean chancery. No bomb was found on the ninety-ninth anniversary of the Chilean invasion of Bolivia's Antofagasta port.

February 16, 1978—Puerto Rico—Early in the morning, a bomb exploded at the Chase Manhattan branch office in Santurce, causing major damages but no injuries. Another bomb exploded within ninety minutes at the bank's branch in Rio Piedras, with the same results. A bomb exploded across the street at a Citibank branch. A bomb exploded at Woolworth's and at the U.S.-owned Barker store in San Juan. Later, the San Juan branch of Chase Manhattan was bombed.

February 17, 1978—Colombia—A medium-strength bomb exploded in the hotel offices of Lufthansa in Bogotá, causing no injuries but some damage. The Andreas Baader Brigade of the German Liberation Popular Front claimed credit and warned that this was the beginning of a number of attacks against U.S. and German enterprises designed to manifest solidarity with oppressed people. The press reported that German authorities had warned local police that German terrorists might be hiding in Colombia.

February 17, 1978—Colombia—Four men in a European-made car kidnapped José Bartolini Berlini, fifty, an Italian toy-factory owner, early in the morning in a downtown Medellín street. His car was later found near a soccer stadium by police who took fingerprints. On February 20, the family received a

letter demanding a 40 million peso ($1.4 million) ransom, along with proof
that they were holding him. He was rescued by the Administrative Department
of Security's antikidnapping squad on February 22 at 5 P.M. at a fashionable
home outside of Medellín. Three members of the ring were arrested without
shots being fired: Hernando Lopez Quintero, Guillermo Zapata Velez, and
Rodrigo Alberto Yepes. Berlini had lived in Colombia for fifteen years.

February 17, 1978—Northern Ireland—The IRA claimed it shot down a
British army helicopter, which crashed near the Eire border, killing a colonel
and seriously wounding the pilot and an army captain. A military spokesman
said there had been a gunfire exchange in the area before the crash.

February 17, 1978—Israel—A PLO time bomb hidden in a trash can near a
bench in the main square of Hebrew University in Jerusalem exploded, killing
an Arab and seriously wounding another. The victims were from the West
Bank and were not local students. Another explosive device found nearby was
defused.

February 18, 1978—Cyprus—Yusuf el Sebai, editor of *Al Ahram*, an
Egyptian newspaper, was assassinated by two gunmen at the Nicosia Hilton
Hotel. Sebai, former minister of culture and a close friend of President Sadat,
was secretary general of the Afro-Asian Peoples' Solidarity Organization,
which was meeting in Nicosia. One of his attackers forced him to the floor of
the hotel lobby and pinned him with his knee. The attackers shot him three
times in the head, killing him instantly, and then took thirty hostages with them
into a restaurant. They threatened to use their grenades to kill the hostages
unless Cyprus flew them out of the country. Among the hostages were delegates to the conference, including Moroccan Othman Benan; Sudanese As-
Sayid Mughrabi; Sulayman Haddad, Syria's military attaché; Abd al Muhsin
Abu Mayzar, the PLO's official spokesman; George Batal, a Lebanese Communist party member; Syrians Mustafa Amin and Dr. Mustafa Murad; and Mr.
Colombo, chief of Somalia's delegation. At 2 P.M., twelve hostages were freed
for safe conduct to Larnaca airport. One of them said that the terrorists claimed
to be Palestinians, although the PLO denied responsibility, condemning the
attack. The terrorists killed Sebai "because he published good things about
Israel" and because he had accompanied President Sadat on his November
1977 trip to Israel. The gunmen were later identified as Samir Mohammed
Hadar, twenty-eight, of Jordan, and Zayid Alali, twenty-six, who carried a
Kuwaiti passport.

At 3 P.M., the gunmen took their bound hostages to the airport on a minibus.
Seven of the eighteen hostages were traded for a Cyprus Airways DC8. Among
the released hostages was the South Yemeni delegation, whose freedom was
obtained by a Cypriot negotiating team headed by President Spyros Kyprianou.
Later in the evening, a Cypriot plane flew PLO leaders from Beirut to talk to

the terrorists for six hours. Vlassos Lyssarıdes, the Cypriot Socialist leader, served as an intermediary and joined Interior Minister Christodoulos Veniamin as substitute hostages. The Cypriot cabinet, which had erroneously identified the terrorists as Eritreans until the ELF denied involvement, met to direct negotiations. At 8:30 P.M., the plane took off with four volunteer crewmen and the original eleven hostages: four Egyptians, three PLO officials, two Syrians, a Somali, and a Moroccan (a Sudanese may have been among the hostages, according to one press account). At 8:55 P.M., the Libyan government denied landing permission to the overhead DC8. Kuwait, Somalia, and Ethiopia also closed their airports to the plane. PDRY later denied landing rights, and the plane landed at 3:45 A.M. on February 19 in Djibouti, which refused refueling until landing elsewhere was obtained. Algeria first granted but later retracted this permission. At 2:15 P.M., the plane left for Cyprus, arriving three and a half hours later at Larnaca airport. President Kyprianou suggested that the plane fly to Damascus, provided that the Palestinians surrender to the Syrians, who would turn them over to the PLO. Yasir Arafat agreed to this arrangement.

At 6:15 P.M., one hundred Egyptian commandos landed in a C130 plane and attacked the hijackers. Cypriot forces fired at the commandos, killing fifteen and wounding sixteen. The terrorists immediately surrendered. Cyprus claimed that Egypt had informed them that the plane was carrying a team of negotiators, not commandos. Egypt initially said that Cyprus had been correctly informed but the next day conceded that they had not mentioned the commandos, fearing a leak. Cyprus said that the terrorists were planning to surrender in any case. In the battle, seven Cypriot soldiers and a West German television cameraman were wounded. Cyprus rejected Egypt's extradition request, and Egypt suspended diplomatic relations on February 21. Several Western sources reported that a sixteen-man PLO squad fought alongside the Cypriots, using AK-47s.

On April 5, the gunmen were sentenced to death. A July 31 appeal was rejected, but on October 23, the president commuted their sentences. Authorities claimed that Riyad Samir al-Ahad, an Iraqi, had planned the attack.

February 19, 1978—Australia—Malaysian Prime Minister Hussein Bin Onn received a kidnap threat while he was attending the Afro-Asian Peoples' Solidarity Organization conference in Melbourne. Security services reported that a few people from Kuala Lumpur had gone to Melbourne to kidnap him. He replied that they were not Malaysian students, but he returned to Kuala Lumpur rather than meet with Malaysian students.

February 21, 1978—El Salvador—Two armed men kidnapped Manuel Luna Uzkuiame, a Bolivian economist and adviser to the United Nations in San Salvador, while he was driving to a meeting with a San Salvador private company. He escaped by disarming one man and forcing the driver of his car to crash in front of a patrol car in front of a police station. Police arrested one of the two, identified as Salvadoran citizen Inocente Oaxaca Fernandez. Luna and Oaxaca were both slightly injured. The other managed to escape.

February 21, 1978—United States—A firebomb was thrown against the garage door of an Egyptian official of the World Bank in Arlington, Virginia. The Jewish Committee of Concern claimed it ignited the gasoline can that had been filled with a flammable liquid to protest President Carter's approval of the sale of military planes to Egypt. The wife and sons of Saad S. Fishway were sleeping in the house at the time of the 3:57 A.M. fire but were uninjured. Damage was estimated at $200.

February 21, 1978—Nicaragua—The car of Eduilio Ferry, a Uruguayan financing specialist with the Inter-American Development Bank, was partially destroyed when it was firebombed at 5:30 P.M. in the bank parking lot in Managua. Three bullet holes were also found in the car. The bomb also damaged the car of architect Camilo Rosales. The explosion occurred on the forty-fourth anniversary of the death of guerrilla leader Augusto Cesar Sandino.

February 22, 1978—Spain—Eight Italians, a French woman, and two Spaniards were arrested in a raid on a light-arms factory in a Madrid apartment. One of those arrested was Mariano Sanchez Covisa, leader of the Warriors of Christ the King. All of the Italians had arrest records for fascist militancy, and some were wanted by Italian police. Giancarlo Rognoni, a terrorist who had been convicted in Italy, was known as the King of Black Plots.

February 28, 1978—Pakistan—Karachi officials detained an armed man they believed intended to hijack an aircraft on which the Sri Lankan finance Minister was traveling.

March 3, 1978—United States—During the night, a gasoline fire at the Yugoslav consulate in San Francisco caused $15,000 damage but no injuries.

March 4, 1978—France—A bomb exploded during the night in a car parked near the Iraqi embassy, destroying the car but causing no injuries.

March 4, 1978—Belgium—A bomb exploded during the night near the Iraqi embassy, damaging the entrance hall and shattering windows in nearby apartments. No casualties were reported.

March 4, 1978—United Kingdom—A woman peeling an Israeli orange in Haddington, Scotland, spotted mercury globules.

March 6, 1978—United Kingdom—A woman and two men, all British citizens, were charged with conspiracy to murder the Indian ambassador, an embassy employee, and employees of the Indian Tourist Office.

March 7, 1978—Zaire—Troops in Kinshasa arrested ninety-one persons alleged to have conspired to kill President Mobutu's children in hopes of provoking his resignation. Mobutu claimed that the plan also called for blowing up the Matadai-Kinshasa oil pipeline, the Inga hydroelectric dam across the Congo River, shops, movie theaters, newspaper buildings, and the French and Moroccan embassies.

March 8, 1978—Belgium—Baron Charles Bracht, sixty-three, Austria's honorary consul general and a businessman with worldwide holdings, was kidnapped during the night in Antwerp. His car was found at a nearby parking lot, where police believed he was abducted. His body was found on April 10 in a garbage dump on the outskirts of Antwerp. A medical examiner claimed he died on March 7 or 8 from a shot in the head, which may have been accidental. The Belgian police believed he was kidnapped for a monetary ransom, because he was president of a holding company with agricultural and real estate interests in Belgian hotels and apartments and in Zaire, Indonesia, Malaysia, Australia, and Brazil.

March 9, 1978—Taiwan—Shih Ming-Cheng, a crewman armed with an ax and scissors, attempted to hijack a China Airlines jet en route from Kaoshiung, Taiwan, to Hong Kong with 101 passengers and divert it to mainland China. A security guard on the plane shot and killed the flight engineer, who managed to injure the pilot and copilot during a scuffle. Shih reportedly had instructions for landing in China, acquired from mainland radio broadcasts that offered rewards to defectors.

March 10-11, 1978—Greece—During the night, three small bombs exploded under cars owned by Turkish diplomats in the Paleon Faliron-Kalamaki area of Athens, slightly injuring a Turkish diplomat, two policemen, and a passerby.

March 11, 1978—Israel—Fatah terrorists used a raft to land on a beach on the northern coast, seized a tour bus, and left forty-six dead and eighty-five wounded before being stopped. Fatah said the operation was named after "Martyr Kaml Adman," who was killed in an Israeli commando raid in Beirut on April 10, 1973.

Thirteen gunmen were launched from a larger ship in two rubber boats to the shore north of Maagen Hikhael, a kibbutz twenty miles south of Haifa. Two of the guerrillas drowned during the voyage. The surviving eleven asked an American woman walking on the beach their whereabouts, then shot her to death. Gail Rubin, thirty-nine, a photographer, was a relative of U.S. Senator Abraham Ribicoff (D-Conn.). The group then halted a taxi on the Haifa-Tel Aviv coastal highway. They killed several passengers. They then took over a Haifa-bound bus full of Sabbath tourists, killing and wounding some of the passengers in a crossfire. The terrorists forced the driver to turn around and drive toward Tel Aviv. While in transit, the terrorists fired at highway traffic, incurring further Israeli casualties. The terrorists fired on a second bus, killing more passengers, and herded the survivors, including thirty children, onto the first bus. Further down the road, six passengers of a taxi were taken as hostages on board the bus.

The bus crashed through one of a series of police roadblocks as the terrorists tossed hand grenades and fired at three policemen, killing one man. The bus then stopped near a larger barrier outside the Tel Aviv Country Club, seven miles north of town. Police marksmen shot out the bus tires and a gunbattle involving the terrorists, police, and troops who had been flown in by helicopter broke out. Some of the guerrillas exited the bus with seventy-one hostages. The bus burst into flames, due, according to some reports, to terrorist-set bombs. At least twenty-five people died in the explosion on the bus. There were no reports of Israeli military casualties. Nine terrorists were killed, and two taken into custody. One of those captured was Hussein Ibrahim Mahmoud Siyad, eighteen, who joined Fatah the year before, trained in al-'Izziyah in southern Lebanon, then received training in handling explosives and weapons in Ad-Damur and Al-Qasimiyah.

The terrorists claimed that the operation was planned by Abu Jihad, who supervised their training. The PLO claimed that the operation was headed by Dalal Mughrabi, twenty-five, a Palestinian woman, who was killed in the fighting. Fayad said the terrorists were to seize a building, preferably a Tel Aviv hotel, and demand the release of Kozo Okamoto, the JRA terrorist, Musa Jum'ah, who was caught in the Savoy Hotel attack, a female terrorist, and two other male terrorists. If these demands were rejected, the terrorists were to blow up themselves and the hostages. They also were to demand that the British and Romanian ambassadors, along with the U.N. representative in Israel, come to the hotel as hostages. They would then demand a U.N. plane to fly them, their hostages, and their freed colleagues to Damascus.

The terrorists were armed with Kalashnikov rifles, Czech-made mortar rounds, Soviet-made hand grenades, RPG launchers, a large quantity of explosives, pistols, M-16 rifles, and 52mm mortars. U.S.-made LAW anti-tank missiles were left in the taxi the terrorists initially attacked then abandoned.

Press sources indicated that the operation was timed to coincide with Israeli Prime Minister Menachem Begin's visit to the United States, which was to begin on March 11. Saudi Arabia, Libya, Kuwait, Jordan, and other Arab states praised the attack. Begin said the attack strengthened his government's resolve not to permit establishment of a Palestinian homeland. Three days later, Israeli land, air, and sea forces conducted retaliatory raids against PLO targets in Lebanon.

On October 23, 1979, an Israeli military court in Lod convicted Halen Hussein and Hussein Fayad of murder during the raid. The prosecutor, Lieutenant Colonel Amnon Starshov, recommended consecutive life sentences for Fayad, who was a minor at the time of the attack. Fayad quoted from the Koran, and said, "The victims died for the revolution. . . .I came here to show you who is a Palestinian and who speaks for the Palestinians." It was not certain whether his colleague was also a minor. The duo were sentenced to life imprisonment on October 25, 1979.

March 10-11, 1978—Greece—Three bombs went off during the night under the cars of Americans in the Terpsithea and Glifadha section of Athens, causing some damage.

March 12, 1978—Greece—A bomb exploded in an Athens theater showing a Soviet movie that evening, injuring eighteen persons. Greek police blamed ultrarightists.

March 13, 1978—Netherlands—Three South Moluccan gunmen seized an Assen government building at 10 A.M. and held seventy-one employees hostage. In the initial assault, at first believed conducted by four to six terrorists, one man was killed and five were injured. Two hundred other office workers escaped by leaping from windows and crawling down fire hoses, while the others were herded into a ground-floor corridor. In a letter delivered to the Justice Ministry in the Hague, the group demanded the release of twenty-one South Moluccan terrorists who had participated in previous attacks, $13 million, a bus to take them and the hostages to the airport, a plane to shuttle them to Amsterdam's airport, and a DC10 to take them to an undisclosed destination. A deadline was set for 2 P.M. the next day. The terrorists threatened to shoot two hostages each half-hour, if their demands were not met. Among the twenty-one whose release was demanded (all of whom were from Ceram or smaller islands in the southern end of the Moluccas) were seven who had taken over locations in 1977 to press the Dutch to recognize an independent South Molucca (see incident 3099 and 3100).

The attack began when a gunman seized a taxi and marched the driver at gunpoint into the provincial government's complex. He then pulled out a submachine gun and began firing and was soon joined by his colleagues. The group killed Karel de Groot, forty, chief of the Provincial Planning Office, who was shot and thrown out of a window. Among the wounded was a boy shot through the lung as he rode his bicycle past the building. The terrorists fired on an ambulance that had arrived to pick up the wounded.

According to the terrorists' request, two South Moluccan community leaders served as mediators and met with the gunmen for two hours the next day. The terrorists agreed to release one hostage and allowed seven hostages to call their families. The terrorists had threatened to kill their fifty-five male and sixteen female hostages if they saw any of the six truckloads of marines who had surrounded the building that evening. Dutch authorities used sophisticated eavesdropping devices to monitor the terrorists' movements.

When the terrorists gave the government thirty minutes to comply with their demands, Attorney General Harry Addens ordered a marine attack. The terrorists' claim that they had killed someone had been bolstered by a shot heard outside. (The hostage was later found to have been wounded.) After using an explosive to distract the gunmen, one hundred marines rushed in at 2:30 P.M. Seven hostages but no marines nor terrorists were injured during the twenty-minute shootout. The marines found Jan Tripp and Daan Huisinga, two provincial councillors, tied to chairs; they were to have been the first execution victims of the twenty-eight-hour-long siege. The terrorists were nineteen, twenty, and twenty-two years old and came from Assen. On April 17, Tripp, fifty-nine, died of a gunshot wound sustained during the incident.

March 13, 1978—United States—Clay Thomas, thirty, claiming to have a bomb, hijacked a United Airlines San Francisco to Seattle flight and diverted it to Oakland, where sixty-eight passengers and four flight attendants were freed. He then flew to Denver for refueling. FBI agents talked to the hijacker, who claimed to have terminal cancer, for one hour, and persuaded him to release his last three hostages, all crewmen. The three leaped thirty feet to the ground; one broke a leg. Thomas hoped to go to Memphis, and later perhaps Cuba, but surrendered at 7:55 P.M. Thomas, who was slightly injured during his arrest, was charged with air piracy. His bond was set at $250,000.

March 16, 1978—Italy—Twelve members of the Red Brigades killed five bodyguards during their kidnapping of former Premier Aldo Moro. The Rome abduction took place at 8:15 A.M. when Moro's sedan, accompanied by a police car, was ambushed as he was on his way to meet with Christian Democratic Premier Guilio Andreotti, who was going to request a vote of confidence for the first communist-supported government in thirty-one years. Moro, sixty-one, president of the ruling Christian Democrats, was cut off by two stolen cars from which three to five terrorists jumped out and fired machine guns. The two policemen in Moro's car died immediately, and two of the three in the follow car died later. The fifth bodyguard died after undergoing surgery. At the scene were found 710 bullets, some of which came from a rarely seen Soviet-made weapon and a Czech pistol. One of the stolen cars, which was used as the escape vehicle, was later found with stolen diplomatic plates.

The kidnappers demanded the release of jailed comrades and a suspension of the Turin trial of fifteen Red Brigades leaders, including founder Renato Curcio. They also called for the release of Armed Proletarian Nuclei members. On March 18, the group issued a communiqué announcing a "people's trial" of Moro, who was photographed in front of a Red Brigades flag. Because the government refused to negotiate, the Moro family requested Caritas International, a Roman Catholic relief organization, to act as an intermediary. In one of their nine communiqués, the Red Brigades said they would deal only with the government. On April 15, the group announced that Moro had been sentenced to death. Three days later, a message claimed that Moro's body could be found in a mountain lake, Duchess Lake, one hundred miles northeast of Rome. Police, soldiers, firemen, and skin divers found nothing after a three-day search. On March 20, a newspaper received a photo of Moro in apparently good health, holding the previous day's newspaper. On April 22, the government allowed a 9 A.M. deadline to pass without granting the terrorists' demands. Two days later, a new terrorist ultimatum called for the release of thirteen terrorists. On April 24, Luis Carlos Zarak, Panama's ambassador, said that his president had offered asylum to the prisoners in return for Moro's safe release.

On May 9, Moro's bullet-riddled body was found in the trunk of a car parked in downtown Rome. The burgundy Renault R-4 was parked on a small street around the corner from the headquarters of both the Christian Democrats and Communists. Moro's hands and feet were chained, and at least ten bullets were found in his chest and head. The car was found after police intercepted an anonymous call to one of Moro's secretaries at 1 P.M.

On May 18 and 19, three Red Brigades hideouts were discovered. One of them was believed to be the printing headquarters of the kidnappers. On September 14, Corrado Alunni, reputedly the new Red Brigades leader, was arrested in Milan in connection with the case. By then, seventeen persons had been charged, although eleven suspects were still at large. The next day, Marina Zoni, thirty-one, was arrested. On October 3, Lauro Azzolini, thirty-five, and Antonio Savino, twenty-seven, were arrested in a gun battle with police in which Savino and two police were injured. On April 16, 1979, Italian judiciary officials released new evidence implicating twelve people in the case. Several of them had been imprisoned for the previous nine days. Among them were educators, journalists, professors sympathetic to leftists, and Antonio Negri, professor of political science at Padua University. Ultraleftist Professor Franco Piperno, thirty-six, was arrested in Paris on August 18, 1979, and charged with murder. On September 14, 1979, after giving a press conference denying involvement in the case, Lanfranco Pace, thirty-two, was arrested by Paris police in a hotel. On September 24, 1979, after a gun battle with Rome police, Prospero Gallinari, twenty-eight, believed to have driven the car with diplomatic plates that blocked Moro's car, was arrested, along with Mara Nanni. Gallinari was hit twice in the legs, twice in the lower abdomen and in the left temple.

On January 3, 1980, Rome's public prosecutor asked that several individuals be tried in the Moro case. Corrado Alunni, Prospero Gallinari, Franco Bonisoli, Lauro Azzolini, Teodoro Spadaccini, and Giovanni Lugnini were charged with the kidnap and killing of Moro and the slaying of his five-man escort. Adriana Faranda, Valerio Morucci, Mario Moretti, Enrico Triaca, Gabriella Mariani, Antonio Marini, and Barbara Balzerani were accused of crimes connected to the ambush. Toni Negri was believed to have phoned Moro's wife on April 30, 1978 to announce that Moro would be killed. An eyewitness claimed that Negri was at the scene of the ambush, and that a woman congratulated him on the attack.

March 17, 1978—Spain—The ETA bombed the Lemoniz nuclear power station, killing two workers and injuring a dozen. Two U.S. nine hundred megawatt Westinghouse reactors were at the plant. It was not disclosed how much damage was caused to the power station's vital working parts. The group claimed that it had issued three warnings. Officials said there was no danger of contamination because uranium fuel was not yet in use at the plant, scheduled for completion in 1979.

March 17, 1978—Nicaragua—Three members of the FSLN stole 120,000 cordobas from a Bank of America branch in Managua. They used a stolen car for their getaway. Later they stole 150,000 cordobas from branches of Immobiliaria de Ahorro y Prestamo in the Linda Vista residential area and in Altamira.

March 18, 1978—France—A car bomb killed François Duprat, a member of the French ultrarightist National Front, in Rouen. Paris police arrested Antonio Bellavita, forty, a suspected Red Brigades member, from Milan, and five other extremists. Bellavita fled to France when three Italian arrest warrants were issued on charges of subversion, creation of an armed band, and public advocacy of an instigation to lawlessness. An Italian working for Interpol was instrumental in locating Bellavita, whose extradition was requested. The terrorist was believed to have helped organize the Red Brigades in 1973 and 1974.

March 18, 1978—United States—A small-caliber pistol was fired during the night at the windows of the Brazilian embassy chancery, shattering several glass panels but causing no injuries.

March 25, 1978—Australia—Canberra police found a sophisticated gelignite bomb that had been thrown onto the grounds of the residence of Jagdish

Ajmani, the acting Indian ambassador. Ajmani accused the Ananda Marg, whose spokesman, Mark Dimellow, denied the charge.

March 26, 1978—West Germany—The Brussels-based People's Army of the Oppressed in Zaire claimed credit for leaving an incendiary device in front of the door of the Zairian embassy.

April 1978—United Kingdom—Cyprus's High Commission received a telephone call warning that the building would be blown up if the killers of Yusuf as-Siba'i, Egyptian secretary general of the Afro-Asian People's Solidarity Organization, were executed. Scotland Yard placed a guard around the building after learning that Black June would try to free Samir Rhadir of Jordan and Zayid al-Ali of Kuwait, who were sentenced to death in Nicosia for the February 18 incident.

April 1978—Czechoslovakia—The Bratislava Regional Court on July 28 sentenced three people identified only by initials, for planning to hijack a plane on the Bratislava-Prague route. F. K. received nine and a half years' unsuspended sentence and K. J. received eight years' unsuspended sentence. Both were assigned to the Third Correctional-Educational Group. S. U. was sentenced to six years' unsuspended sentence and assigned to the Second Correctional-Educational Group on charges of planning to threaten the security of an aircraft and leaving the republic.

April 1, 1978—United States—A rifle-wielding fifteen-year-old boy boarded a Piedmont plane in Richmond, Virginia, and demanded to fly to New Jersey. He allowed the passengers to leave and surrendered after the pilot and copilot escaped through a cockpit window.

April 2, 1978—Pakistan—During the night, a grenade was thrown into the U.S. consulate general grounds in Lahore, causing little damage and no injuries. Observers believed the attack may have been by individuals seeking to avenge the death sentence of former Premier Zulfiqar Ali Bhutto (who had accused the United States of causing his overthrow to prevent the building of a Pakistani nuclear reprocessing plant).

April 7, 1978—Philippines—Four people being driven in a B. F. Goodrich truck were killed in an ambush by unidentified men while on their way to voting in parliamentary elections in Zamboanga Del Sur Province. Ten other occupants were wounded in the elections for the two hundred man interim national assembly. Goodrich has a rubber plantation in Kabasalan, a town 480 miles south of Manila in Mindanao, where Moslems had pressed for self-rule for five and a half years.

April 7, 1978—Algeria—The Canary Islands Intelligence Service, a previously unknown group, claimed credit for attacking Antonio Cubillo, the leader of the Movement for Self-Determination and Independence of the Canary Islands (MPAIAC). Cubillo was stabbed at the entrance to his Algiers home at 8:30 A.M. He lapsed into a coma from his multiple stab wounds in the back and stomach but recovered. The group claimed that it was established three months before to fight against "Marxism and those who try to attack the unity of Spain."

On April 9, Spaniards Juan Antonio Alfonso Gonzalez, thirty-one, and José Luis Cortes y Rodriguez, twenty, were arrested seven days after arriving in Algiers. A Madrid newspaper received a call from Algiers claiming that on the evening of April 8 the MPAIAC had executed two of the attackers. On April 10, Cubillo accused the Spanish security services (later joined by the Socialist party) of instigating the attack, which brought quick denials. On April 11, the governor of Santa Cruz said twenty persons had been detained in a crackdown on MPAIAC. On May 7, Gonzalez was sentenced by an Algiers court to death; Rodriguez received twenty years. Alfredo Gonzalez Garcia, described as the plot's organizer, was sentenced to death in absentia.

April 20, 1978—Egypt—The Egyptian State Security Prosecution Department in Cairo announced the arrest of twenty-four people belonging to an international terrorist consortium planning to carry out a series of attacks against peace negotiators from Egypt and Israel. They were described as eleven Palestinians, seven Jordanians, three Swiss, one Omani, one Egyptian, and a West German. The group called themselves Correct Course of Fatah (Al-Khat as-Sahih Lifatah), which had been headed by Wadi Haddad, according to the Egyptians. The group was now part of the Black June Organization, which Egypt held responsible for the January 1978 assassination of PLO London representative Said Hammami and the February 1978 killing of Yusuf as-Siba'i, a prominent journalist and friend of President Sadat. The chief of the group was George Bilinni, a Palestinian attached to a terrorist organization in Zurich. He was the link between Sergio Mantovani of Switzerland and Vera Marta Guenter (alias Elvira Gunter) of West Germany, both of whom had arrived in Cairo for terrorist attacks. Guenter studied Arabic at a German-run cultural center in Cairo, although some sources reported she also worked in television. Among those arrested were three Palestinians studying in Cairo, who were aided by two Jordanians. The group had received advanced weapons training. On May 20, Egyptian Attorney General Ibrahim al-Qalyubi ordered the release of Swiss journalist Jean Bakta and his wife, Doris. Egypt claimed that the group was linked to the Red Brigades of Italy.

April 21, 1978—Thailand—Bangkok police arrested two Australian and one American member of the Ananda Marg on charges of plotting to blow up the embassy of Australia, which had recently banned the sect.

April 25, 1978—Thailand—A bomb was reported on board a Thai Airways International jetliner flying seventy-eight passengers from Bangkok. A two-hour search was negative. Meanwhile Philippine authorities called an alert for the elite Metropolitan Command troops because of threats by the New People's Army to bomb power stations. No attacks took place.

April 26, 1978—Israel—A grenade was thrown into a parked tourist bus in Nablus's main square, killing two West German youth volunteers. The dead—an eighteen-year-old woman and a nineteen-year-old man—and injured were part of the Action Reconciliation Group, which sends West German youths abroad to do humanitarian work in countries whose people suffered under the Nazis, providing alternative service for conscientious objectors. Authorities called a curfew and arrested dozens of suspects.

May 4, 1978—France—Henri Curiel, cofounder of Egypt's Communist party and leader of a Paris-based organization that supported left-wing terrorists from around the world, was shot to death by two pistol-wielding youths at his Latin Quarter home. Organization Delta, a rightist group, claimed credit. The group was believed to be composed of opponents of France's decision to grant independence to Algeria. The organization was apparently responsible for a recent spate of anti-Algerian bombings in France directed primarily against immigrant workers.

May 6, 1978—Corsica—Autonomist groups were believed responsible for a bomb that destroyed two buildings owned by the Belgian army in Solaro.

May 7, 1978—Soviet Union—Tass reported that police killed a man who attempted to hijack a local Aeroflot flight abroad. Skubenko was killed while resisting arrest during the flight from Ashkabad, near the Iranian border, to Mineralniye Vodi.

May 8, 1978—Djibouti—Young Afar members of the National Independence Union, the Djibouti political party, kidnapped René Boucault, a French technician in northern Djibouti, and took him to Ethiopia. He was released unharmed to the French embassy in Addis Ababa on May 16. The group had called for democractic rights in Djibouti, the release of political prisoners, equality among the nationalities and workers of Djibouti, and the immediate establishment of an all-party group to draft a new constitution.

May 9, 1978—Rhodesia—Two black guerrillas armed with grenades and automatic rifles attacked a Juliasdale luxury hotel at night, killing two white Rhodesian women and wounding three persons, including a visitor from the United States. One guest was killed at her table, and a hotel employee died near the doorway. Minne Bolin, seventy-seven, of Apache Junction, Arizona, was struck in the head by flying glass when a grenade exploded outside the terrace windows. In the attack on the Montclair Hotel (located in a mountain resort town eighty miles east of Salisbury and twenty miles from Mozambique), the attackers fired three RPGs and AK-47 assault rifles at the dining room.

May 10, 1978—Colombia—Six members of the M-19 kidnapped William Barquero Montiel, fifty-one, Nicaragua's ambassador, during the morning from his north Bogotá home. Four men and two women—all heavily armed and dressed in religious habits—dragged him out of the embassy into his car. Due to a police dragnet, the group released him two hours later near Puente Aranda in southwestern Bogotá. The group claimed that they were protesting the Somoza dictatorship; Barquero believed that they were attempting to publicize the FSLN's activities.

May 10, 1978—Czechoslovakia—A Czech male claiming to have a bomb hijacked a Czech airliner with forty-six people on board to West Germany, where three adults and two children requested asylum from Frankfurt authorities. The hijackers were identified as Josef Katrincak, twenty-seven, Anna Katrincakova, and Radomir Sebesth, twenty-six, along with their children. The four-engine Ilyushin-18 had been flying from Prague to Brno and landed at 7:30 P.M. at Rhine-Mein Airport. Police believed that the explosives were carried on by the children of taxi driver Katrincak. Two of the hijackers were sentenced to three years by a Frankfurt court.

May 11, 1978—Colombia—An Avianca flight carrying 109 persons from Santa Marta to Bogotá was hijacked by two gunmen and diverted to Cali, Colombia; Aruba; and Willemstad, Curaçao. Two women and two children were released during the Cali refueling stop, where the hijackers demanded flight charts for Aruba, Curaçao, and Cuba. At the next stop, between twenty-four and forty passengers were freed or escaped. Aruba airport personnel refused to refuel the plane. The hijackers requested only food and did not indicate the purpose of the hijacking. The hijackers shot the flight engineer when he refused to take food on board a plane the hijackers had demanded. Bogotá Avianca officials said the hijackers demanded $53,000 for the plane's return. The plane landed at 6:27 P.M. at Willemstad, where a hijacker armed with a pistol and grenade was jumped by the pilots after ordering most of the passengers to disembark. Police overpowered him. The second hijacker was captured when his pistol discharged as he tried to blend in with the passengers. Two policemen and a hijacker were wounded.

May 11, 1978—Italy—Marzio Astarita, thirty-seven, an Italian manager of the Chemical Bank of New York, was shot in the legs four times by a masked man and woman in a Milan street ambush. The attackers escaped in a stolen car. An anonymous caller claimed credit for the Front Line and Fighting Communist Formations.

May 12, 1978—Italy—Five armed Red Brigades gunmen attacked a Honeywell warehouse, immobilizing the custodian and two cleaning women and setting the building on fire with gasoline, causing a billion lire damage.

May 13, 1978—United States—A firebomb was discovered at the Iranian embassy just before midnight.

May 14, 1978—United States—The Jewish Armed Resistance planted a bomb in the Manhattan offices of *Novoye Russkoye Slovo*, a Russian-language daily newspaper. The 3:30 A.M. explosion heavily damaged the first two floors and the printing facilities.

May 15, 1978—Oman—The People's Liberation Army ambushed and killed a British officer who was driving near the Red Line, north of Salalah, in southern Oman.

May 16, 1978—Laos—Rightist Laotian rebels ambushed and killed fourteen Soviet military advisers and their Vietnamese driver near Vientiane, at Kilometre 19 of the highway that parallels the Mekong River. The three-jeep convoy, which had left the city at 4 P.M., was attacked an hour later when the middle jeep triggered a land mine. The rebels opened up with heavy machine-gun fire, killing the Russians in the jeep.

May 16, 1978—Mexico—An Aeromexico DC-9 flying ninety-nine persons was hijacked to Mexico City, where the two hijackers, who falsely claimed to have explosives, surrendered. Raul Armendariz Guadarama, thirty-four, and Auerlio Lucero Dominguez, twenty-five, both of whom had been fired in a labor dispute on the Chihuahua Pacific Railroad in the north, had sought publicity and justice. Aeromexico ordered the screening of all luggage and the installation of x-ray machines at all Mexican international airports.

May 17, 1978—El Salvador—Fugio Matsumoto, fifty-four, Japanese president of Insinca (Central American Synthetic Industries), a textile firm, was kidnapped in the evening by seven armed men as he left his office. A shootout at his factory led to the wounding of Jorge Adalberto Campos, an Insinca guard. The next day, the Maoist Armed Forces of National Liberation (FARN) said that Matsumoto was a member of the Japanese, German, and U.S. business communities, which exploit El Salvador's economy and workers. FARN demanded the release of thirty-three political prisoners. On May 23, a government spokesman denied that there were any political prisoners in the country and refused to negotiate. The next day, Matsumoto's family ran full-page FARN advertisements in the newspapers *La Prensa Grafica* and *El Diaro de Hoy*, as the group demanded.

FARN also called for a general amnesty for those being tried under the Law for the Defense and Guarantee of Public Order, the abolition of that law, and a $4 million ransom. Their demands for prisoner release escalated: twenty-three on May 22, thirty-three on May 24, thirty-eight on June 22. A separate communiqué identified the kidnappers as National Resistance rather than FARN. On May 25, they threatened to kill Matsumoto the next day if their demands were unmet. On June 29, police announced that they believed he was killed between May 21 and 23. On July 5, an anonymous caller said that he would be put on trial and that the government and his family would be responsible for the outcome.

On August 11, Augusto Antonio Carranza Parada of FARN; Eduardo Sancho Castaneda, alias Nelson; Berta Ramirez Galan, alias Elvira; Jose Armando Lovos, alias Neto; José Alberto Ramos Martinez, alias Felipe; and several others were arrested. Carranza claimed that Matsumoto was killed on May 17 when he was being taken from the getaway car into a house at 14 El Cocal Avenue, Manzano District, when a .45 caliber pistol belonging to Neto, a FARN leader, accidentally fired. Matsumoto was buried the next morning on the Cliffs of Cerro (Sancasito), but the group decided to demand 10 million colones from Insinca anyway. The next day, the firm offered a reward for information leading to the discovery of Matsumoto. On October 4, his body was found buried on San Jacinto Hill, three kilometers south of San Salvador.

In March 1979, FARN accused General Romero's government of staging the ambush in which it claimed Matsumoto was wounded in the back by a bullet. FARN said the group was escaping with him from their hideout when the National Guard stopped their vehicle. The group also said the family offered only $40,000 ransom.

May 18, 1978—Rhodesia—Black nationalist guerrillas ambushed a jeep in Nyamapora, close to the Mozambique border, killing two Swiss Red Cross workers and their African assistant.

May 19, 1978—United States—Specialist 4 John G. McCarthy, twenty-one, took as hostage Felix Daniel, a ticket agent at McGhee Tyson Airport in Knoxville, Tennessee. McCarthy had crashed his car through the airport gate and fired at pursuing police officers. An unidentified FBI agent was slightly injured by metal fragments before McCarthy, whose hostage had escaped, surrendered. McCarthy was absent without leave from Fort A. P. Hill near Fredericksburg, Virginia. He had told his roommate he intended to hijack an airplane and was found armed with an M-16 rifle, a .45 caliber pistol, a large supply of ammunition, a bayonet, a parachute, and a gas mask.

May 20, 1978—France—An Air France Airbus scheduled to fly to Tel Aviv was delayed for two hours at Charles de Gaulle Airport after an anonymous bomb threat was received. A search was negative.

May 20, 1978—France—Israeli security officers at Paris's Orly Airport noticed a group of five men loitering among passengers awaiting an Iberia flight for Malaga, Spain, across from the El Al counter, where a charter group was to board flight 324 at 4:20 P.M. At 3:40 P.M., one of the men tried to go through the door to the El Al waiting room. An Israeli employee blocked his passage and was told by the individual that he was looking for the Zagreb flight. The individual joined his unticketed companions, who opened their luggage and pulled out Beretta machine pistols, which they fired at French police guarding the gate. The other two men vanished in the confusion. The three terrorists were killed in the gun battle, as was the chief brigadier of the French riot police. Three French policemen and three passengers were wounded. Police found plastique and hand grenades on the bodies of the terrorists. The trio had arrived earlier in the day from Tunis. One was identified as Mahmoud Awada, twenty-five, from Lebanon. The others carried Kuwaiti and Tunisian passports.

In Beirut, Lebanon, the Organization of the Sons of Southern Lebanon claimed credit, naming the action Operation al-'Abasiyah, after a village several kilometers northeast of Tyre where it claimed two hundred of its members had been killed in Israeli air raids. The group said that they were also reminding France of its colonialist past and that they had intended to attack several "Zionist enemy officers" who were scheduled to fly on flight 324. Israeli sources suggested that Abu Nidal's Black June Organization, possibly in concert with the Popular Front for the Liberation of Palestine, was responsible.

May 22, 1978—United States—A FALN incendiary device went off at 9:50 A.M., setting off a small fire in a second-floor tobacco shop of the Eastern Airlines Terminal of New York's JFK Airport, causing no injuries and slight damage.

May 22, 1978—United States—A FALN incendiary device went off at 9:57 A.M. in the Century Shop on the main concourse of Newark Airport's terminal A, near the TWA desks, causing no injuries and slight damage.

May 22, 1978—United States—A FALN incendiary device went off at 10 A.M. in a trash can in a men's room on the second level between the Eastern and Delta Airlines desks at New York's La Guardia Airport, causing no injuries and slight damage.

May 22, 1978—United States—A FALN six-inch pipe bomb went off at 9:40 A.M. on the sidewalk outside the Justice Department Building in Washington, D.C., slightly chipping marble on the building's facade. The time bomb, hidden amid shubbery east of the entrance, caused no injuries.

May 22, 1978—United States—FALN warned that bombs would explode at 10 A.M. in the O'Hare Hilton at O'Hare Airport in Chicago. No explosions were reported.

May 24, 1978—Soviet Union—Mikhail Timoshukov, claiming to represent the Russian Liberation Army, seized two Soviet hostages in the Moscow office of Finnair and demanded to be flown out of the country. Police exchanged shots with the hooded man armed with a double-barreled shotgun, drove him out with tear gas, and arrested him. Tass claimed he was an escaped convict from Kazakhstan, while other reports identified him as being from Semipolatinsk in western Siberia. He claimed to have a bomb and had told Finnair that he would name his destination later. The two hostages escaped at 2 P.M. while Timoshukov reloaded his shotgun. Lyudmila Semyonov, a secretary, was injured in the leg from flying glass from the eighteen to twenty shots fired in the gun battle. The other hostage was Sergei Supkov, a driver. Timoshukov was also reported injured.

May 24, 1978—United States—Barbara Ann Oswald attempted to divert a helicopter from St. Louis to a Marion, Illinois, federal penitentiary to help three inmates escape. She was shot to death after pilot Allan Parklage wrestled the pistol from her and fired when she reached for a second gun. Oswald had chartered the Fostaire Helicopter Company Bell 206B Jet Ranger with a $500 deposit and stated that she wished to fly to Cape Giradeau, Missouri, to inspect flooded property. She hoped to free Martin J. McNally and Garrett B. Trapnell, convicted hijackers, and James K. Johnson, a bank robber. The hijackers were serving time for 1972 hijackings. On December 22, Trapnell was convicted in Benton, Illinois, for conspiracy in Oswald's attempt.

May 26, 1978—Uganda—Kenya's Ministry of Foreign Affairs claimed that a bomb exploded on a Kenyan aircraft while it was parked at Entebbe airport. The plane crashed after the bomb exploded during the flight, killing former cabinet minister Bruce MacKenzie; pilot Paul Lennon; Gavin Whitelaw, a visiting British businessman; and Keith Savage, manager-director of Wilken Air Telecommunication.

May 26, 1978—France—Marion-Brigitte Folkerts, twenty-seven, was arrested upon arriving at Paris's Orly Airport from Beirut. She was suspected of having links to the Baader-Meinhof Gang and Japanese Red Army and was carrying West German and Lebanese passports. She was deported to West Germany and was to be charged with forging documents and belonging to a terrorist organization. Her husband, Uwe, and brother-in-law, Knut, had been previously arrested for terrorist activity.

May 29, 1978—Colombia—Juan Nicolas Escobar Soto, fifty-one, manager of the Texas Petroleum Company, was kidnapped in Bogotá by six men and two women. On January 3, 1979, his body was found when Colombian troops raided a guerrilla hideout during a search for fifty-seven hundred firearms—including rifles, bazookas, and mortars—that had been stolen from the Military Institutes Brigade by the M-19 on New Year's Day. Soto, for whom a large ransom had been demanded, was shot inside a tunnel in the Lucerna suburb, southwest of Bogotá, when the army and police closed in. He was shot twice in the heart and once in the abdomen. Colombian troops shot to death four others, although some sources claim that two guerrillas committed suicide in the shootout and a third kidnapper may have been shot by his comrades while taking refuge in the tunnel leading from their safe house. One of the dead terrorists was Eleodoro Argueyo Fonseca. A noncommissioned officer was reported wounded. A people's jail was discovered, consisting of a room under the floor made of cement with electrical installations independent of the house's main wiring. On January 5, three M-19 members were reported to have committed suicide after the raid. That day, the van used in the kidnapping was found in northern Bogotá. A woman was arrested in an apartment complex on Jimenez Avenue in Bogotá and was described as a key suspect in the Soto and arms cases. Two automatic weapons and a notebook containing the names of European-residing lawyers were found in the apartment.

May 31, 1978—West Germany—West German police claimed that the Red Cells had plotted to blow up a U.S. army hotel. An army spokesman reported that a bomb had exploded on March 24, 1978, but no one was injured.

June 2, 1978—Spain—Three members of the Justice of Armenian Genocide fired at the windshield of the Turkish ambassador's limousine when it stopped for a traffic light in Madrid, killing Ambassador Zeki Kuneralp's wife, brother-in-law, and chauffeur. Kuneralp's beige Mercedes was held up in a traffic jam at the Calle de Fortuny, and he was in the embassy nearby when the three young men attacked with pistols. One of the gunmen opened one of the Mercedes' car doors and fired a 9mm. The group escaped in a Ford Fiesta, which was found abandoned nearby. The next day, the Armenian Secret Army for the Liberation of Armenia also claimed responsibility and warned that the Spanish government would be attacked if police found the killers.

June 3, 1978—Rhodesia—Two white Roman Catholic missionaries, Pieter Geyerman, thirty-six, a German, and Andrew von Arx, forty-five, a Swiss, were shot and killed by black guerrillas on the veranda of the Embakwe Mission in the Plumtree District, near Rhodesia's southwestern border with Botswana.

June 3, 1978—Israel—A bomb went off in a bus in Jerusalem, killing six and wounding twenty, tearing off the back of the bus, and severing power lines in the Beit Vagan section of West Jerusalem near Mount Herzel. Among the dead were an Israeli youth, seventeen, and Richard Fishman, thirty, a student at the University of Maryland Medical School who was on vacation. The PLO claimed Fatah was responsible for bombing the bus, which had left the Arab section of East Jerusalem at 1 P.M. and picked up Jews going home for the Sabbath. The bomb was timed for the eleventh anniversary of the capture of East Jerusalem. It was placed on an overhead rack in the rear of the bus and consisted of an 81-mm mortar shell with a watch as a timer.

June 5, 1978—Czechoslovakia—Police foiled a hijack plan during a check of security installations at Prague's Ruzyne Airport. The Prague City Court sentenced K. S. and J. K. to nine years and Z. M. to eight years for planning a hijacking.

June 8, 1978—Rhodesia—Black nationalist guerrillas attacked a Salvation Army school for black girls outside Plumtree, fifteen miles from Rhodesia's southwestern border with Botswana. Killed in the attack on the Usher Institute were two teachers, Sharon Faith Swindells, twenty-five, of Northern Ireland and Diana Barbara Thompson, twenty-eight, of London. Injured were David Cotton, thirty-eight, of the United Kingdom and Guvnor Berit Pallson, thirty-seven, of Sweden.

June 9, 1978—Cyprus—Limassol authorities charged seven persons with conspiring between January 1, 1977, and April 8, 1978, to use explosives to damage the premises of political parties and foreign embassies and to use firearms against individuals. A preliminary hearing was scheduled for June 17 for Vasos Khristodhoulou Pavlidhis (alias Yiatros), Dinos Khristodhoulou Poyiatzis, Andreas Rodhotheou Khristofi, Anastasias Andreou Koyiotis, Kharalambous Yeoryiou Papakleovoulou (a captain in the National Guard), Andreas Kosta Khatzikharalambous Kostouris, and Andreas Evthimiou.

June 9, 1978—Portugal—The Action Group for Communism bombed the Argentine embassy in Lisbon, claiming its protest was timed to coincide with the World Cup Soccer Series in Argentina and to denounce the alleged killings of eight thousand persons and imprisonment of twelve thousand others by the military government.

June 12, 1978—West Germany—The People's Army of the Oppressed in Zaire left two incendiary devices that were found in the morning at a window of the Zairian embassy in Bonn. One of the devices had slightly singed a blind; the other had not ignited.

June 12, 1978—Czechoslovakia—A Brno court sentenced Ladislav Sevec to eight years and Tomas Stejskal and Zdenek Vardan to one year for conspiracy to hijack a Czech plane.

June 15, 1978—Kuwait—The Organization of the Sons of Palestine claimed credit for killing Ali Nasir Yasin, forty-four, a member of the PLO National Council and PLO representative in Kuwait. Yasin was found in front of the door of his home around 11 A.M., dead from gunshot wounds. Abu Iyad, a member of the Fatah Central Committee, denied that the OSP existed and accused Abu Nidal, a Black June Organization leader, of the assassination. Fatah, of which Yasin was a member, accused Iraqi agents of the murder.

June 15, 1978—Canary Islands—A bomb set by the Movement for the Autonomy and Independence of the Canary Island Archipelago wrecked the Las Palmas office of South African Airways.

June 17, 1978—Rhodesia—Archie Dunaway, fifty-eight, a white American Baptist evangelist, was stabbed to death by black nationalist guerrillas at the Sanyati Mission Hospital, where the McComb, Mississippi, native was director of the nursing school. The facility is 120 miles west of Salisbury.

June 18, 1978—El Salvador—The El Salvador ERP planted a bomb that went off during the night at the Argentine embassy, causing damage but no casualties. The ERP said it wished to "call attention to what was really happening" in Argentina, which the World Cup soccer championship obscured, and to demonstrate its solidarity with the struggles of Argentina's people and revolutionary organizations.

June 19, 1978—France—A bomb destroyed the offices of Ecuador's ambassador.

June 21, 1978—Guatemala—The government announced it had uncovered a terrorist plan to kidnap three or four ambassadors. The National Liberation

Movement was believed to be planning to assassinate government officials and high-ranking military officers.

June 21, 1978—Lebanon—During the night, unidentified persons fired from a Peugeot at an Iraqi embassy car in Beirut.

June 21, 1978—Thailand—A bomb was found after a telephoned warning on the U.S. Operations Mission's third floor in Bangkok.

June 23, 1978—Rhodesia—Black nationalist guerrillas bayonetted, axed, and clubbed to death eight British missionaries and four of their children at an Elim Mission School in the Vumba Mountains. Twenty guerrillas told two hundred students at the Emmanuel Secondary School, ten miles southeast of Umtali, to leave that day and return to their homes. Mary Fischer, a white teacher, was reported in critical condition after being dragged into the bush where she was assaulted. The only white resident of the school who escaped unharmed was teacher Ian McGarrick, who had been warned of the guerrillas' approach. The dead were identified as Catherine Picken, fifty; Elizabeth Wendy Hamilton, thirty-seven; Philip George Evans, twenty-nine; Susan Evans, thirty-three; Rebecca Evans, four; Peter McCann, thirty; Sandra McCann, thirty; Philip McCann, six; Joy McCann, five; Robert John Lynn, thirty-seven; Joyce Lynn, thirty-six; and Pamela Grace Lynn, three weeks.

On August 11, Rhodesian security forces killed two of the attackers, who were armed with two AK rifles. Captured notebooks led police to conclude that the guerrillas were under the command of Robert Mugabe, leader of the Zimbabwe African National Union, who had denied responsibility. Others believed that Joshua Nkomo's Zimbabwe African Peoples Union was involved.

June 24, 1978—Yemen—A bomb exploded in a South Yemeni diplomat's briefcase, killing President Ahmed Hussein al-Ghashmi and the envoy. The envoy was about to hand Ghashmi a message from his government's President Salim Rubayyi' 'Ali. Lieutenant Colonel Abdul Al'Aalem was believed responsible for the assassination. He was an army officer who had escaped to Aden four weeks earlier after his insurrection in the Ta'izz area in the south of Yemen was defeated by Ghashmi's forces. Yemen immediately blamed South Yemen's Marxist government and broke diplomatic relations.

June 24, 1978—United States—A militant Puerto Rican group claimed credit for six incendiary devices that exploded in three crowded suburban department stores shortly after noon during Chicago's annual Puerto Rican Day parade.

June 25, 1978—France—Bombs badly damaged the Paris offices of two East European firms.

June 28, 1978—Rhodesia—Three black gunmen killed Gregor Richert, forty-two, and Bernard Lisson, sixty-nine, at St. Rupert's Mission, ninety miles west of Salisbury. They arrived at 5 P.M. and shot the West German Jesuits as they stood in front of their house. They then addressed a dozen black staff members, including nuns, admitting to the murders. The killers took money from, but did not harm, the staff members. The guerrillas spoke Sindebele, the language of the Matabele, who live hundreds of miles away in the south. Matabele tribesmen are prominent among the Zambian-based guerrillas of Joshua Nkomo.

July 1978—United States—James R. Rose, Jr., thirty-one, a former navy diver and demolitions expert, was arrested in Miami, Florida, for plotting to bomb Soviet and Japanese whale boats moored in the harbor of Talcahuano, Chile. As of September, two brothers who had joined the plot—Bernard and Robert Reed—were still at large. The trio had acquired a two-man yellow submarine, explosives, and sophisticated diving equipment. The money for the attack was to come from an unnamed international environmental organization.

July 3, 1978—France—Juan José Etchave Orogengoa, forty, a former ETA leader, was critically injured when hit in the stomach by two machine-gun bullets in Saint-Jean-de-Luz. His wife, Rosario Etchave, forty-one, died instantly in her car as two gunmen fired from opposite sides of the street. The Etchaves had just closed their restaurant in the border town.

July 3, 1978—France—Talion Law bombed a Paris hall rented by the PLO, causing heavy damage but no serious injuries. The group was retaliating for a PLO bombing of a Jerusalem street market the previous week in which two Israelis died and twelve were injured.

July 3, 1978—Puerto Rico—A man and a woman armed with a gun took over Chile's consulate in San Juan, took hostage Consul Ramon Gonzalez Ruiz and Sergio Alejandro Nunez, who was on business there, and demanded the release of five Puerto Ricans held in federal jails for attempting to assassinate President Truman and firing pistols in the U.S. House of Representatives. The attackers initially claimed to be four people and to be holding four hostages. Pablo Marcano Garcia, twenty-six, and Nydia Guevas Rivera, twenty-four, did not belong to any known group. They phoned the State Department, television stations, newspapers, and wire services to condemn Chile's "murderous actions" against its people. On July 4, seventeen hours later, the terrorists surrendered and released their hostages unharmed. Marcano was held on $500,000 bail and Guevas on $250,000 bail.

July 9, 1978—United Kingdom—An Arab gunman shot and killed former Iraqi Prime Minister Abdul Razzak al-Naif, forty-four, as he walked from London's Intercontinental Hotel in the Mayfair District near Hyde Park toward a taxi. Naif died around midnight of two bullet wounds in the head. The twenty-five-year-old gunman hid behind a potted plant and fired a .38 caliber revolver from behind Naif. The doorman at a nearby hotel, a chauffeur, and a taxi driver captured the gunman. A second man was later arrested at Heathrow Airport. On July 26, Saadovn Chaker, reputed Iraqi intelligence chief, was detained in London and charged with instigating Naif's murder. That day, the United Kingdom expelled eight Iraqi intelligence officers because of terrorist threats. Two diplomats were barred from entering the country. Those expelled included five diplomats, who were given seven days to leave, two Iraq National Airlines employees, and an Iraq Bank employee. Officials claimed that the decision to shift the Middle East talks from central London to the moated Leeds Castle in Kent was unconnected with the explusions. Iraq retaliated by expelling ten Britishers, including eight diplomats.

July 10, 1978—United States—A small incendiary device planted by the Jewish Armed Resistance exploded at 9:30 A.M. near a Soviet tourist office in Rockefeller Center. The JAR was protesting the opening of the trials of Anatoly Scharanskiy and Aleksander Ginzberg, two prominent Soviet dissidents. The bomb was planted in a stairwell on the eighth floor, which is occupied by Intourist. Police found diesel fuel, pieces of a timer, and a dry-cell battery.

July 12, 1978—United States—During the night, a bomb exploded in a Queens, New York, apartment being used as an FALN bomb factory. Police found sixty-six sticks of dynamite, more than two hundred pounds of chemicals for making incendiary devices, blasting caps, smokeless and black powders, and dummy FALN letters in East Elmhurst. Three pipe bombs, which had been set to explode, were detonated at a police range. Police theorized, "The fact that the three bombs went off and then one hour later two incendiary devices went off in department stores leads us to believe they planned simultaneous explosions." The 5:20 P.M. explosion blew off both hands and part of the face of the bomb maker, William Morales, twenty-eight, whose last known address was 1734 Madison Avenue. Police were attempting to determine whether he was the same William Morales who in 1975 had been a member of the National Commission on Hispanic Affairs of the Protestant Episcopal Church, an organization that may have had links to the FALN.

July 15, 1978—United Kingdom—The Middle East peace talks, scheduled to begin in London, were moved after George Habash, PFLP leader, threatened to disrupt them. U.S. Secretary of State Cyrus Vance, Israeli Foreign Minister Moshe Dayan, and Egypt's Mohammed Ibrahim Akmel were to attempt to break the deadlocked negotiations.

July 16, 1978—United States—Kristina Katherina Berster, twenty-eight, a suspected terrorist from West Germany, was arrested as she attempted to enter Vermont from Canada using a fake Iranian passport bearing the name Shahrzad S. Nobari. The passport was one of a group stolen when radical Iranian students took over the Iranian consulate in Geneva, Switzerland, in June 1976. The FBI noted that Nobari, an Iranian who lived in Hamburg, FRG, had visited Los Angeles in December 1977 using a reissued passport. Berster was sought by the FRG for membership in the Socialist Patients' Collective, a group which included members of the Baader-Meinhof Group. She was imprisoned in the FRG for several months in 1973 for criminal conspiracy, illegal use of explosives and forging identity documents. She was released before her trial, and fled. Fingerprints and the "Green Book"–a compendium of wanted terrorists distributed by the West Germans to friendly governments—established her identity.

Authorities searched for two men and a woman who had accompanied Berster in an automobile to the border. Berster got out of the car, which proceeded into the U.S. The trio awaited her hidden behind a closed service station. Customs patrol officers arrested her as she attempted to cross at an unauthorized location near Alburg, Vermont. The trio asked why she had been detained and were themselves questioned by the border patrol. The trio were carrying valid U.S. passports and were released. They then drove back to Montreal. On July 17, two of them, including the woman, flew from Montreal to the United States.

Berster was held under $500,000 bond in Albany, New York. On July 24, a West German Supreme Court judge issued an arrest warrant for her. On July 27, a seven count federal indictment was handed down against Berster, including charges of the use of falsified documents and violation of immigration laws. On July 30, the FRG requested her extradition. Berster argued that she had come to the United States to escape harm in West Germany. Her attorney said that she would request political asylum. West Germany withdrew its extradition request when Berster wrote to the Interior Ministry saying she had revoked terrorism and would return freely to the FRG. After serving sixteen months in U.S. jails, she was deported to Hamburg, FRG, on November 1, 1979.

Her three companions were later identified as Ray Kajmir, thirty-three, an Iranian-born naturalized U.S. citizen, who owned a New York City boutique; Michael Vincent Diterlizzi, twenty-two, a Montreal resident; and Maria

Amendola, thirty, of New York. On August 12, 1978, a court in Burlington, Vermont, issued a ten-count indictment against Kajmir and Diterlizzi. Amendola was charged with the misdemeanor of joining the men in aiding Berster to elude examination by the Immigration and Naturalization Service. After pleading innocent, Diterlizzi was released on $10,000 personal recognizance bond and Amendola on $5000 bond. On October 28, Kajmir was found innocent on charges of aiding and abetting Berster. On November 3, Diterlizzi, who pleaded guilty to aiding Berster enter the United States, received an 18-month suspended sentence.

July 18, 1978—Colombia—The M-19 seized a bus carrying Venezuelan and Nicaraguan baseball players and lectured them for two hours with revolutionary rhetoric. The group spray-painted the bus with Sandinista and M-19 initials and anti-Somoza slogans. The bus had been on its way from the athletes' village to the sports complex in Medellín where the Central American and Caribbean games were being held.

July 19, 1978—Libya—Five members of Yasir Arafat's Fatah at 9 P.M. attacked the Tripoli offices of the Fatah Revolutionary Council, killing two and wounding one. Killed were advanced cadre geophysical engineer Yusuf 'Ali Darwaish (alias Ahmad Hassan) and signal corps Lieutenant 'Imad ad-Din Mustafa Shakir 'Ayyad (alias 'Imad Ash-Shaykh). After the guerrillas were arrested, the attack was denounced in a joint statement of the Palestinian Popular Struggle Front, the Palestinian Liberation Front, the Palestinian National Liberation Movement (Fatah) Revolutionary Council, the Popular Front for the Liberation of Palestine, and the Democractic Popular Front for the Liberation of Palestine. On July 27, the bodies were flown to Baghdad, Iraq, where they were received by members of the Palestine Armed Struggle Bureau of the Ba'ath Party National Command, members of the Political Committee of the Palestinian Revolution, and representatives of Arab liberation movements.

July 23, 1978—Colombia—The Popular Liberation Army was blamed for bombing the U.S. embassy in Bogotá during the night. A security wall was knocked down.

July 24, 1978—El Salvador—The Revolutionary People's Army (ERP) bombed the Guatemalan embassy at 5:20 A.M., destroying walls and glass windows but causing no injuries. The ERP was protesting the "climate of oppression in Guatemala" and referred to "the Panzos massacre in which over one hundred Indians were killed." It also hailed increasing activities to secure "Central America's liberation" and pledged solidarity with groups in

Nicaragua, Guatemala, and El Salvador. Several other groups claimed credit for the bombing.

July 28, 1978—Colombia—During the night, a bomb exploded at the Colombian-Soviet House in Medellín, seriously injuring the group's secretary-general, Guillermo Parra Ramirez.

July 28, 1978—India—A bomb exploded near the Calcutta home of the Soviet consul. Unidentified individuals hurled two bombs near his home while shouting slogans.

July 28, 1978—United Kingdom—A hand grenade was thrown under the car of Iraqi Ambassador Taha Ahmad ad-Dawud, wounding two passersby, at 2:15 P.M. outside the embassy in Kensington, West London. The ambassador was about to enter his car when he was killed. A terrorist lobbed a grenade under the car, whose wheels were blown into the area. Police searched for four "Arab-looking" men in Hyde Park. As of July 31, they were still searching for three Arab youths and a Lebanese girl believed involved. On August 2, a young man and woman were apprehended. Khouloud Moghrabi, nineteen, a Lebanese, and Abou-Naama Mohmoud, thirty, an Algerian, were held for a week without bail at Marylebone Magistrate's Court on charges of conspiracy to murder ad-Dawud.

July 31, 1978—France—Two PLO-affiliated terrorists seized eight hostages in the Iraqi embassy shortly before 10 A.M. after asking to see an Iraqi diplomat. When guards requested identification papers, they pulled submachine guns out of their overcoats, fired into the lobby, and tossed a grenade. One of the terrorists fled and threw his gun down on the sidewalk. His colleague took over the first floor and seized the hostages, injuring two embassy employees. That afternoon, he allowed an ambulance to evacuate a guard who had been shot in the head, abdomen, and leg. Sixteen Iraqi embassy officials remained barricaded in upper-floor offices. The PLO denied responsibility, but the Iraqi press agency claimed that the PLO had attacked the embassy "in coordination with Syrian intelligence." The terrorist was later identified as Ahmed Hammami, twenty-five, the brother of Sa'id Hammami, the London PLO representative who had been murdered in January. He demanded the release of a woman held in London for a failed assassination attempt against the Iraqi ambassador three days previously. He demanded a plane to take him to London to pick her up and then fly elsewhere.

Mundhir Tawfik el-Wandawi, Iraqi's ambassador, contacted the ambassadors of Kuwait, Qatar, and Algeria to mediate. He also waived extraterritorial rights and allowed a French police assault "if it proves necessary" to free the hostages, including chargé d'affaires Aref Abdel Karim. At 6:30 P.M.

the terrorist surrendered after negotiations with the Algerian and Iraqi ambassadors and an Arab League member. As the terrorist was being escorted out of the embassy by French police plainclothesmen, Iraqi guards opened fire, killing a French police inspector and wounding two other police officers and the captured terrorist. The police returned the fire, killing an Iraqi guard and wounding another. Ahmed Abdun, the director of the Arab League Bureau who had offered to serve as a mediator, was wounded in the leg. The Iraqi ambassador later said that his bodyguards were not shooting at the terrorist—rather it was unknown persons in the street outside who were coming to join Hammami. He claimed that this led the French police and his guards to respond. The French found this explanation fanciful and detained the three Iraqi gunmen, identified as two secretaries and an attaché, all of whom had diplomatic immunity. France decided to expel them.

August 1, 1978—Rhodesia—Thomas A. Wigglesworth, sixty-one, a retired British army officer, was kidnapped in the morning from his farm near Penhalonga and taken across the border into Mozambique by black nationalist guerrillas.

August 2, 1978—Pakistan—Two Arab terrorists opened fire on Iraqi officials entering their Karachi consulate general, injuring an Iraqi official and a police guard. Police bayonetted Taha Mahmoud, twenty, and captured Abdullah Ahmad, twenty-one, who was seriously injured. The two South Yemenis, who had come three days earlier from Jidda, Saudi Arabia, arrived at the main gate at 9:30 A.M. and fired at Consul General Amer Naji Zain Din as he entered the building. The terrorists seriously wounded Mohammad Ghaib, another consular official, as he drove up soon afterwards. Ahmad died of his wounds on August 5.

August 2, 1978—Lebanon—Iraq accused Palestinian rightists of having fired at the car of Iraqi Ambassador Qassem al-Samawi during the night, causing no damage to the car and no injuries to the driver or the ambassador's bodyguard. The ambassador was not in the car at the time of the attack.

August 3, 1978—Kuwait—Palestinian sources claimed that an assassination attempt had been made on PLO chief Yasir Arafat. Other sources claimed that the attack had been made in Lebanon, when Arafat's car, carrying Qatari diplomatic license number 2, was fired on near Al-Masna' while Arafat was traveling from Beirut to Syria.

August 3, 1978—France—Izz Ad-Din Al-Qalaq, forty, Paris PLO chief, and his aide, Hammad Adnan, were assassinated by two terrorists who had arrived by motorcycle along the Boulevard Haussman. As the gunmen shot their way into the building, one of them was captured by Arab League employees. The second reached Qalaq's third-floor offices and shot him twelve times. The terrorist then set off a grenade, killing Adnan. Two Jordanian PLO employees and a Tunisian Arab League employee were wounded by grenade fragments and bullets. The killer was caught attempting to escape from the roof. The terrorists were Hatem Abdul Kadir, a Palestinian with Jordanian nationality, and Ishem Mustapha, who had an Algerian passport. The Rejection Front of Stateless Palestinian Arabs, as well as Black September and June, claimed credit. The terrorists said they had killed Qalaq on the orders of Abu Nidal, Iraq-based leader of Black June. A later communiqué said the killing was a "reply to the chain of assassinations and murders prepetrated by the Palestinian right" and to the "reactionary policy led by PLO chief Yasir Arafat."

August 5, 1978—Pakistan—Four terrorists, hoping to assassinate PLO representative Yusuf Abu Hantash, burst into the PLO offices in Islamabad and machine-gunned to death a Pakistani policeman and three Palestinians: Saad Abu Nasar, the mission's Telex operator, Omar Khnafer, a medical student, and Mohammad al-Hussain, a guerrilla studying with the Pakistani army. That morning, the attackers arrived by automobile at the mission, a two-story villa. Two people with a box walked to the office gate, where they were stopped by a guard who asked to search the box, which was loaded with machine guns and hand grenades. As they argued, Nasar came out of the building. The terrorists took out their guns, killed the policeman and Nasar, and ran into the building shouting for Hantash, who hid in his office. The terrorists killed Khanfer in the visitors' room and Hussain in the backyard and escaped by throwing hand grenades to discourage pursuit. Witnesses said the terrorists spoke an Iraqi dialect of Arabic. Hantash accused the Iraqi government of directing the attack, but it denied the charge. On August 16, two more persons, in addition to two others previously arrested, were held for suspected involvement in the attack. Among the arrested, who were believed to be members of a group opposed to Yasir Arafat were Jamal Muhammad Abu Ahmad and Muhammad Hasan Abu Shahda, who were taken from a Lahore house 180 miles southeast of Islamabad. A Rawalpindi magistrate remanded them to police custody for thirteen days.

August 6, 1978—Netherlands—A KLM DC9 flying from Amsterdam to Madrid was hijacked by a Dutchman armed with a toy pistol, a spray can he claimed was a bomb, and a bottle he said contained a dangerous chemical. He forced his way into the cockpit and diverted the plane to Algiers, which initially denied permission for the plane to land. The Algerians relented after the Dutch ambassador's intercession. However, while the plane was over the Mediterranean, a crewman and three male passengers stormed the cockpit and overpowered hijacker Paul Gokkel, a Dutch student. No injuries were reported. The plane landed in Barcelona, Spain, where the hijacker was arrested. The Dutch government requested extradition.

August 8, 1978—Guatemala—A national police agent foiled an attempt by two men to kidnap Viviana Soriano, fifteen, the daughter of the Uruguayan ambassador. She was en route to the embassy when the well-dressed men used a jeep to block her car and tried to force her out of the vehicle in south Guatemala City. Her bodyguard prevented the kidnapping.

August 8, 1978—Puerto Rico—During the night, a bomb went off outside the San Juan auditorium where the Cuban Ballet was performing, causing no injuries or damage. Threatening phone calls had been received.

August 11, 1978—West Germany—The Justice Ministry in Hanover refused to parole Ronald Augustin, a Dutchman, who had threatened to murder U.S. Ambassador Walter J. Stoessel. Augustin had been convicted of aiding West German terrorists.

August 13, 1978—Lebanon—Shortly after midnight, a tremendous explosion demolished a Beirut nine-story apartment building, killing 161 (and possibly 200) and wounding 70 to 80. It appeared to have been triggered by a blast in a parked car, which set off munitions inside the structure. Rival Palestinian factions denied that the explosion was part of an interguerrilla feud. The building was the headquarters of the military command and central operations of the Palestine Liberation Front of Abul Abbas, and it also housed a Fatah office. Some Palestinians blamed the blast on the PFLP-General Command, headed by Ahmed Jebril, a former Syrian army captain. The PLF's Central Committee had adjourned at 11 P.M., an hour before the blast, after a three-day meeting. The PLF claimed 80 of its members were killed; Fatah lost 11 members. Abbas was not in the building, which was located in the al-Fakihani section of Beirut. The PLF denied that it and other groups stored arms in the building.

August 14, 1978—El Salvador—Six armed men kidnapped Kjell Bjork, thirty-five, a Swedish technical director of Telefonica LM Ericsson, when he left the offices of Dada and Company, located on the southern side of the Salvadoran Social Security Hospital in San Salvador. The gunmen forced him into his own car and drove off. On August 24, his firm received a note from the FARN demanding publication of its declarations in newspapers in Venezuela, Panama, Costa Rica, Nicaragua, Honduras, El Salvador, Guatemala, Mexico, Sweden, and Japan. Most newspapers, save those in El Salvador, agreed. The government forbade the publication, but Ericsson paid for censored blank spaces that appeared in the local newspapers. The FARN communiqués accused those governments of repression and human rights violations. After the printing of the advertisements FARN released Bjork unharmed on August 26.

On September 9, small farmer Miguel Angel Torres, twenty-three, and student Jesus Antonio Quintanilla Lara, twenty-two, were arrested for involvement. They said an undisclosed ransom paid by Bjork's family would finance local clandestine group campaigns. The kidnappers said they received training in Costa Rica by instructors from other Central American countries. Among the trainers was Eden Pastora, the FSLN's Commander Cero who led the seizure of the national palace in Managua, Nicaragua, on August 22, 1978.

August 14, 1978—United States—Croatian terrorists planted dynamite bombs on a U.N. window ledge and in a Grand Central Station locker in New York City. Neither exploded. The bomb on the window ledge of the Dag Hammarskjold Library was powerful enough to destroy the building. The group that claimed responsibility demanded the release of a Croatian accused of attempting to assassinate the Yugoslavian ambassador to Bonn.

August 15, 1978—Iran—During the night, a bomb exploded in Tehran's crowded Khansalaar Restaurant, killing an Iranian man suspected of carrying the bomb into the basement and wounding forty-five, including ten Americans.

August 16, 1978—Spanish Sahara—The Polisario Front was believed responsible for machine-gunning a Spanish fishing boat off the coast of Spanish Sahara, sixty miles north of Villa Ganeros. The captain was seriously wounded, and the boat's hull was badly damaged.

August 17, 1978—Libya—A Fatah member fired three shots at Husayn Muhammad 'Ali, an Iraqi embassy employee, as he was entering the embassy in the morning. Ali died soon after. Mahmud Ayat Ahmad al-Katib, alias Darrar Yusuf, twenty-five, was captured and found to be carrying a Jordanian passport, which he had used in traveling from Damascus on August 12. It was charged that he was told to assassinate the Iraqi ambassador by Khalid Abdullah, who provided his revolver.

August 17, 1978—United States—Two armed Croatians seized the West German consulate in Chicago and demanded that the government prevent the extradition of a colleague to Yugoslavia. The two men—Bozo Kelava, thirty-five, of San Francisco and Mike Kodzoman, thirty-one, of Chicago—entered the consulate on the tenth floor of a South Michigan Avenue building shortly after its 10 A.M. opening and asked to see the consul general. Upon learning he was vacationing, they pulled out hand guns and took eight hostages. Two hostages—Eva Raster, sixteen, daughter of Consul General Ego Raster, who was at home a few blocks away, and an elderly Austrian man—were released unharmed a few hours later. A secretary escaped and called the police, who alerted the FBI. The terrorists carried boxes that they claimed contained explosives. Those held hostage included Werner Ickstadt and Peter Brandt, administrative officers, Martin Murmann of the passport and visa section, and Marlies Stulgies and Henrietta Back, secretaries.

The Croatians demanded that West Germany release Stjepan Bilandzic, thirty-nine, who was imprisoned in Cologne for the attempted murder of Vladimir Topic, Yugoslavia's vice-consul, in Düsseldorf, in 1976. Bilandzic reputedly founded the Croatian National Resistance. Yugoslav authorities had requested his extradition for sending two individuals to Yugoslavia to begin a terrorist campaign. A Cologne court had ruled that he could be extradited, but his lawyers petitioned Germany's highest court for an injunction, arguing that extradition would be a death warrant, a belief echoed by the Chicago gunmen. They demanded to speak to Bilandzic in Cologne, and a telephone hookup was arranged at noon. Negotiators included West German diplomats, a priest, and Evon Bilandzic, Stjepan's brother. During the night, Stjepan urged Kelava and Kodzoman to surrender. They agreed and were held in a federal prison in lieu of $1 million cash bond each. Bilandzic was freed by a Cologne court in September and visited Chicago to raise money for a defense fund for the two. It was later revealed that Kodzoman was his distant relative. On December 1, the two were acquitted of kidnapping and conspiracy charges but convicted of imprisoning a West German diplomat with a deadly weapon. They faced a maximum sentence of ten years.

August 18, 1978—West Germany—Eight IRA bombs exploded at 11:06 P.M. at British army bases within a twenty-mile radius of British army headquarters at Moenchengladbach. The blasts caused structural damage at the bases in seven cities and towns, including Minden and Düsseldorf. The IRA was believed responsible after analysis of a bomb that did not explode in Bielefeld. The device weighed sixty pounds and was placed outside a barracks. Most of the bombs were set against buildings or fences outside guarded areas. Two bombs had been thrown over perimeter fences. West German security officials suggested that the IRA and West German terrorists had cooperated with Palestinians because IRA explosives usually consisted of commercial gelignite supplied from the Middle East. A young British female military officer was slightly injured by flying glass in one of the explosions. In October, the *Irish Times* received a phone call from the IRA saying, "We bombed the bases in West Germany to establish our ability to strike at British imperialism anywhere at any time."

August 19, 1978—Greece—The PFLP accused the Greek government of assassinating Bashir Ibrahim Jibril, one of its members, in Athens.

August 20, 1978—East Berlin—No one was injured in a gas explosion that blew part of the roof off the Czech ambassador's home. The incident may have been related to the tenth anniversary of the Soviet invasion of Czechoslovakia.

August 20, 1978—United Kingdom—A PFLP-Special Operations trio hurled hand grenades and fired submachine guns at a bus carrying an El Al crew to the Europa Hotel, where they were to stay, near Grosvenor Square, a few hundred yards east of the U.S. embassy. The terrorists killed an Israeli stewardess and wounded two others, along with seven British bystanders. One terrorist died from ricocheting fragments from his grenade. Another was captured, and a third escaped. A fourth man may have been involved. The next day, Israeli air force planes bombed terrorist bases in Ad-Damur and Burj al-Barajinah in Lebanon.

August 20, 1978—Belgium—During the night, demonstrators threw smoke bombs into a Paris to Moscow train to protest the 1968 Soviet invasion of Czechoslovakia. Two firemen were hospitalized.

August 22, 1978—Nicaragua—The national palace in Managua was taken over at 1 P.M. by twenty-five heavily armed FSLN members. They took more than fifteen hundred hostages who had been meeting in both houses of Congress. The hostages included five hundred legislators and government officials, including President Somoza's nephew, José Somoza Abrego, thirty-two, and his cousin, Luis Paillas Debayle, president of the Chamber of Deputies. A pickup truck drove to the side door on the east side of the palace while another drove to the other side. The guerrillas, wearing uniforms of the army's training battalion, entered the building. After being challenged by a guard, the terrorists pulled machine guns from their briefcases and killed him. Five more guards died elsewhere inside the building. The group was led by Eden Pastora (alias Commander Zero), forty-two; Hugo Torres (alias Uno), thirty-one, a law student; and Dora Maria Tellez Argueyo (alias Dos), a medical student. The group gave the government six hours to comply with their demands or they would kill all their hostages. They demanded a general amnesty for all political prisoners and publication of their communiqués in the newspapers, as well as on radio and television at 6 A.M., noon, and 6 P.M. until the operation was completed. They also called for the granting of the requests of the health sector, guaranteeing by decree the Hospital Labor Union's requests. The Somoza government and family were to pay $10 million through intermediaries in Venezuela, Panama, Mexico, Cuba, Costa Rica, and Nicaragua. One million in cash was to be turned over to the palace guerrillas, the Rigoberto Lopez Perez Command, named after a man killed in 1956 by Somoza's father. The operation itself was called Death to Somozaism—Carlos Fonseca Amador, named after the founders of the FSLN killed in a 1976 clash with the army. The terrorists demanded a guarantee of safe passage by air to

Panama and called for three airplanes to take the prisoners to Mexico, Venezuela, and Panama. Costa Rica offered to accept the political prisoners.

Managua's archbishop and two other Catholic prelates agreed to mediate, as did the Panamanian and Costa Rican ambassadors. The Red Cross was permitted to evacuate the twelve dead and fifteen wounded. Those casualties not from the initial attack came during a subsequent clash with government troops. One terrorist was wounded. Pastora warned against intervention by the troops and said he had grenades, automatic rifles, gas masks, and ammunition. The terrorists extended their original six-hour deadline after the government asked for twenty-four hours because the demands involved foreign governments. That night, three hundred women, children, and minor employees were freed, and a new deadline was set for 3 A.M. After the government allowed the media to broadcast FSLN statements, more women were freed. The terrorists then set a 3:30 P.M. deadline for their other demands to be met; otherwise they would begin killing the hostages, starting with three government officials. The government conceded shortly after, although the ransom was reduced during negotiations to $5 million and ultimately to $500,000.

Reports differed regarding the number and disposition of prisoners mentioned by the hostage takers. One source said the group demanded that Panama, Venezuela, and Mexico each send a plane for their group and fifty-nine released FSLN prisoners and that they were to be accompanied out of Nicaragua by the ambassadors of Venezuela, Mexico, Costa Rica, Panama, and Peru. Others said the group demanded release of eighty-four prisoners, who were to go to Panama. A Venezuelan Air Force C130 and a Panamanian COPA plane flew the group to Panama on August 24. The Panamanian government arranged to relocate them elsewhere. A pro-FSLN local group, Friends of Nicaragua, said the twenty-five who could not be located had probably been killed. On August 25, Mexico announced it would grant asylum on request. On September 2, twenty-two FSLN members arrived in Havana, where they were welcomed by the government.

Reportedly Pastora became a naturalized Costa Rican in September 1977. Other sources said that a Mexican, Victor Manuel Tirado Lopez, had led the assault. Others suggested that lawyer and university professor, Dr. Nora Astorga de Jenkins, could have been the third leader, but this was denied by Pastora, who said his FSLN faction supports a short-range armed insurrection.

August 25, 1978—United States—A passenger on a TWA B707 flying from New York to Geneva, Switzerland, threatened to blow up the plane if several prisoners were not released. While passengers were watching a movie as the plane flew over Ireland, a person in a black wig, moustache, and cape gave a stewardess two letters and instructed her to take them to the captain. The individual claimed to belong to the United Revolutionary Soldiers of the Council of Reciprocal Relief Alliance for Peace, Justice, and Freedom Everywhere and demanded the release of Rudolph Hess, Sirhan Sirhan, and five Croatians. He demanded that the seven be at Geneva Airport by 5 P.M. and that President Carter publicly announce Hess's release. Flight 830 was kept on the ground for eleven hours as authorities attempted to determine the hijacker's identity. He had threatened to detonate explosives he claimed were in two suitcases at 5:30 P.M. All passengers were taken off the plane, frisked, and questioned five times. Geneva police found hidden in the plane's toilet an orange-yellow cape, balloons, the black wig, a man's shirt, and a pair of glasses. Police later arrested Rudi Siegfried Kuno Kreitlow, sixty-three, alias Charles Frank Metel, of New York, an unemployed chauffeur. On February 24, 1979, he was convicted of threatening to blow up the plane with nine crew and seventy-eight passengers. He faced a maximum fine of $10,000 and twenty years in jail.

August 25, 1978—United Kingdom—Shots were fired at the London home of an unidentified Arab diplomat.

August 29, 1978—Mexico—Hugo Margain Charles, thirty-five, son of the Mexican ambassador to the United States, was kidnapped from his car by four men and women in another car. His bodyguards were pinned down by heavy gunfire, which wounded several people. Margain died shortly after from a bullet that had severed a leg artery. A note found at the scene was signed by the Twenty-third of September Communist League, and the family later received a telephoned ransom demand. However, police rejected the possibility that the group was responsible and believed that the attack was designed to undermine a planned government amnesty for political prisoners.

August 30, 1978—Poland—Alexander Detlev Tiede, thirty-two, hijacked a LOT Airlines Tupolev 134 carrying sixty-three passengers and eight crew members on a flight from Warsaw to East Berlin via Gdansk and diverted it to a U.S. military base in West Berlin. The East German hijacker was armed with an empty starter's pistol and was accompanied by a woman and an eleven-year-old child. U.S. military authorities held the trio after they landed at Tempelhof Airport. Seven other East Germans asked to remain in West Berlin for political reasons. Five hours later, the plane left for East Berlin's Schoenfeld Airport. Tiede was tried and convicted by a specially constituted U.S. court in Berlin.

September 2, 1978—Australia—Police arrested a group of nineteen Croatians at an isolated bush camp 150 miles south of Sydney, where they confiscated weapons, maps of Yugoslavia, and instructions on planting land mines.

September 3, 1978—Italy—A powerful bomb exploded during the night at the gate of the pope's vicar's residence in Rome, three miles from the Vatican.

Observers suggested the bombing was to protest the presence of Argentina President Jorge Videla at the papal installation.

September 5, 1978—Israel—Stephen Michael Hilmes, a U.S. bomb expert, died five days later from injuries suffered when a bomb went off in Jerusalem.

September 9, 1978—Peru—The Peruvian Anti-Communist Alliance kidnapped Roberto Fanjul, a Colombian newsman, in Lima. He was released the next day, physically abused, with a note accusing him of belonging to the Montoneros, an Argentine terrorist group, and entering Peru to contribute to Trotskyite plans.

September 9, 1978—United States—Omega-7 planted a powerful time bomb at Cuba's U.N. mission's doorway, blowing out scores of windows, wrecking several parked cars, digging a crater in the sidewalk, and injuring a mission guard and two other persons.

September 13, 1978—United Kingdom—Shahnawaz Bhutto, twenty-one, a student and son of former Pakistani Prime Minister Zulfigar Ali Bhutto, told a London telephone operator that there was a bomb at 10 Downing Street. On December 15, 1979, he was put on two years probation and ordered to pay up to $2,200 in court costs. His father was hanged by the Pakistani government in April 1979.

September 14, 1978—West Germany—In Weisbaden, the federal criminal police arrested Leila Bocook, twenty-five, an American teacher with Baader-Meinhof connections, and charged her with illegal possession of firearms.

September 16, 1978—Japan—A man hurled two Molotov cocktails, which failed to explode, in front of the U.S. Marine Corps headquarters in Nakaku-sugi, Okinawa. Guards arrested the man, who was demanding the abrogation of the U.S.-Japan security treaty.

September 16, 1978—Guatemala—The People's Guerrilla Army machine-gunned and wounded General Edmundo Meneses Cantanero, Nicaragua's ambassador, as he was walking through the center of Guatemala City. The group alleged that he had coordinated police repression plans and manuevers against Central American guerrillas. Meneses died of his wounds on September 29.

September 16, 1978—El Salvador—The Popular Liberation Forces fired machine guns at dawn at the U.S. embassy. The group's communiqué criticized "Yankee imperialism," demanded the release of political prisoners, and called for a reduction in the price of housing, fertilizer, rents, agricultural land, water, and electric power. It claimed the United States was active in Central American counterinsurgency campaigns.

September 17, 1978—France—At 7 A.M. two grenades were thrown over the fence of the Vietnamese embassy, causing no injuries or damage.

September 21, 1978—Austria—Police arrested a Yugoslav man at Schwechat Airport who had hidden a 7.65-mm pistol and ammunition in a loaf of bread and was attempting to board a Belgrade-bound Austrian Airlines plane. He may have been a member of a Croatian separatist group.

September 27, 1978—Guatemala—During the evening, a powerful time bomb destroyed the Guatemala City offices of Lanica, the Nicaraguan Airlines Company, but caused no injuries.

September 27, 1978—Honduras—Men and women phoned several threats to the Venezuelan embassy in Tegucigalpa, warning that the embassy and homes of the ambassador and other officials would be bombed. The threats began when it was learned that a Nicaraguan student who had been residing in Honduras had sought refuge in the embassy. The student alleged that a paramilitary group in sympathy with Nicaragua's Somoza regime existed in Honduras. The student also claimed that Honduran authorities cooperated with Nicaraguan agents operating in the capital city.

September 27, 1978—Honduras—Several men and women telephoned bomb threats to the Costa Rican embassy.

September 27, 1978—United States—Havana radio reported that a tiny anti-Castro exile group operating out of Miami claimed credit for blowing up a North American airliner while it was flying to Cuba.

September 28, 1978—United States—Anthony Cikoja, forty-eight, was killed by three .32 caliber bullets fired from a car as he left his Greenburgh, New York, home for work. Three months previously, he had received a letter from the "Croatian Intelligence Service" demanding that he send $5,000 to a Paraguayan address or be killed. The letter, written in a Croatian dialect, was signed by Tripimir Budrovic, "Commander of the Operations." Cikoja was of Croatian descent but had lived in the United States for twenty-seven years and was not involved in émigré politics. The next day, a Westchester man was charged with the murder.

September 29, 1978—Guatemala—Seventy-five unarmed employees of Duralita occupied the Swiss embassy and held Ives Berthoud, the ambassador, hostage. The group said their Swiss employers were mistreating them and had stopped operations to destroy their union. The workers requested the ambassador to intervene with Duralita's managers to rehire them and stop the harassing of their union. The workers also asked Berthoud to tell Eternite, Duralita's owner, to order local company representatives to respect their workers.

September 30, 1978—Turkey—A bomb was thrown at Egypt's Istanbul consulate, causing slight damage. The attackers had approached by boat.

September 30, 1978—Finland—Aarno Laminparras, thirty-seven, an Oulu building contractor, hijacked a Finnair plane carrying fifty persons and shuttled for sixteen hours between Oulu and Helsinki before releasing all of his hostages. He then ordered the three-man crew to fly to Amsterdam and then back to Finland. Before releasing the passengers, Laminparras collected a $170,750 ransom from Finnair and $37,500 from *Helsingin Sanomat*, a newspaper. At Oulu, the hijacker's wife picked up $125,000 from the plane. He also demanded and was given route maps for central and southern Europe, fuel, food, lemonade, cigarettes, and two bottles of whiskey. He finally surrendered when authorities agreed to allow him to return home with his wife provided that he turn himself in on the morning of October 2. He brought his pistol and some of the ransom home with him. Police arrested him at his home seven hours after he was released.

October 1978—Italy—Bjorn Borg, the Swedish tennis star, was threatened in Milan by a telephone call from Stockholm. He withdrew from his scheduled match.

October 1, 1978—Turkey—A bomb was thrown at the Israeli consulate in Istanbul, causing no injuries. Another bomb was thrown at the Egyptian consulate, with the same result.

October 2, 1978—United States—A TWA plane flying from Chicago to Rome, Italy, was diverted to Montreal after a bomb threat. A search at Deauville airport was negative, and the plane flew on to Paris and Rome. Among the passengers was Chicago's Cardinal John Cody.

October 3, 1978—El Salvador—During the morning, several members of the Faribundo Marti Popular Liberation Forces broke windows and threw incendiary devices into the Lanica (Nicaraguan Airlines) offices in San Salvador.

October 4, 1978—United States—A firebomb damaged the Danmarie Cabinet Company in Chicago, which is owned by Daniel Nicolic, an American of

Croatian descent. He reportedly received a letter from the "Croatian Intelligence Service" similar to that received by Anthony Cikoja, who was killed on September 28 for refusing to comply with their extortion demands.

October 4, 1978—Mexico—Two to four persons attempted to kidnap the sixteen-year-old son of Eden Pastora, the FSLN's Commander Zero, in Guadalajara. Pastora's wife said they wanted to make him fight against the Somoza regime.

October 10, 1978—Iran—Six armed men attempted to firebomb the Iraqi consulate in Khorramshahr. The group arrived at 5:30 A.M. in a van carrying five gallons of gasoline and explosives. After shooting and killing an Iranian guard, the group escaped without damaging the consulate.

October 10, 1978—Colombia—During the night, bodyguards fired on several armed men who stopped the car of Nicaraguan Ambassador Barquero Montiel in an apparent kidnap attempt. There were no injuries in the Bogotá incident. Barquero denied that he had been the object of a kidnap attempt.

October 11, 1978—Iran—Two persons driving a motorcycle threw two pipe bombs into a bus carrying ten Americans working for Bell Helicopter International in Isfahan. One of the bombs exploded, slightly injuring three Americans.

October 12, 1978—Northern Ireland—The Irish Freedom Fighters claimed responsibility for bombing a Dublin to Belfast train, killing one woman and injuring two other women. The name may have been an IRA cover for its Newry and South Armagh units. Three bombs exploded in the toilets of three of the train's coaches, causing serious damage. More than one hundred passengers were on the CIE train at the time. A warning telephone call was received that morning twenty-two minutes before the blast, but authorities were unable to warn the train because CIE staff had opposed placing radios in train cabs, believing that they would be attacked for cooperating too closely with security forces. The first bomb went off when the train was approaching Belfast's Botanic Halt, less than a mile from its central station destination. The Northern Ireland Railways chief executive said he was not aware of any bomb searches having been conducted in the republic. At 10:05 A.M., a woman reportedly phoned the Samaritans' Organization in Portadown warning that ten bombs were on board. CIE learned of the bombs at 10:13 A.M., and claimed, "At that time rail control at Connolly station was alerted by NIR in Belfast, and told that there were ten bombs on board the train from Dublin." CIE then informed Dublin Castle, and security forces arranged to search the train upon its arrival in Belfast.

October 16, 1978—United States—British Airways BA-282, a DC10 flying 231 passengers from Los Angeles to London, landed at Frobisher Bay on Canada's Baffin Island after U.S. authorities received a bomb threat. The plane flew on after a negative search, which took four hours.

October 17, 1978—France—Bruno Busic, chief of an anti-Yugoslav émigré organization, was assassinated in the Paris flat of another Yugoslav émigré.

October 17, 1978—Greece—A bomb exploded at an Athens firm in Kaningos Square selling Soviet goods, causing great damage. The 10 P.M. explosion on Khalkokondhilis Street broke windows of adjoining shops and of a private car. Half an hour later, a bomb exploded at Solomos Street 57, in the offices of a firm selling Soviet tractors, causing serious damage.

October 18, 1978—Nicaragua—The FSLN was believed responsible for an attack on Managua's Ciudad Jardin branch of the Bank of America and stealing 700,000 cordobas ($100,000). The four armed men had arrived in a taxi at 9:30 A.M.

October 21, 1978—Ethiopia—The Tigre People's Liberation Front kidnapped George W. Krois, thirty-six, an American pilot who had landed a helicopter in guerrilla-held territory to repair a U.N. locust plane, which had crashed. He was flying for the Canadian Viking Helicopters Company of Ottawa from Abi Adi. The group announced his capture, as well as that of three Ethiopians riding with him, on November 6 in Khartoum, Sudan. He was taken in Abergalle District near Gondar Province. Krois was freed on January 3, 1979. The group said, "We are forgotten both in the countries of the east and in the western countries. We want to make our struggle known and that is why we kidnapped this American citizen." No mention was made of the Ethiopians.

October 25, 1978—El Salvador—The Faribundo Marti Popular Liberation Forces (FPL) claimed responsibility for a bomb that exploded in the morning at the Guatemalan consulate in Chalchuapa, killing a watchman and causing considerable damage.

October 25, 1978—Turkey—Fifteen to twenty persons threw a bomb into a U.S. minibus that carried diplomatic plates in Istanbul. The group forced the U.S. cultural attaché, his secretary, and his driver out of the car. The attackers bombed the minibus and fired shots when a traffic policeman drew his pistol. Windows were shattered in nearby buildings, and a seventeen-year-old boy was slightly wounded by gunfire as he was passing by. The group escaped.

October 27, 1978—Nicaragua—Several revolver-wielding guerrillas stole 1.5 million cordobas ($214,285)—348,697 cordobas in cash and the rest in checks—from a car picking up deposits from the Bank of America's Montoya branch in western Managua. The driver was wounded.

October 27, 1978—Chile—A bomb of the type used by the Movement of the Revolutionary Left exploded inside a trash can in front of the Argentine consulate in Santiago, breaking several windows but causing no injuries.

October 30, 1978—Nicaragua—Four youths armed with revolvers held up a Banco de America branch in Santo Tomas. The branch manager was taken hostage but later released after the reported FSLN youths escaped that morning.

November 1978—Iran—A firebomb was thrown at the chauffeur-driven car of George Link, the American manager of the Oil Service Company of Iran in Ahwaz. The car caught fire but Link was unhurt. Ahwaz is an oil-producing area 340 miles southwest of Tehran. Link took a vacation in December and was replaced by his deputy, Paul Grimm, who was assassinated on December 23.

November 1, 1978—Netherlands—A man in his thirties and a woman in her twenties fired machine pistols at guards at a border checkpost, killing one Dutch border guard and injuring two others. They crossed the border near Kerkrade, in southern Limburg Province. They opened fire when challenged at a checkpoint. They stole a baker's van and fled into the Netherlands.

November 7, 1978—Mexico—Authorities arrested Washington Laino Amaral, a Tupamaro leader, in Mexico City. Although picked up for robbery, Laino admitted recruiting persons at the University of Mexico for the Tupamaros. He claimed that he had come from Nicaragua, where he participated in attempts to overthrow the Somoza government.

November 7, 1978—Guatemala—Ten Salvadorans were found dead in Guatemala City. Circumstances of the case led observers to believe that a terrorist group that kidnaps, tortures, and murders its victims was responsible. In 1977, the news media received anonymous announcements of the creation of the Guatemalan Anti-Salvadoran Liberation Action Group, which pledged to kill Salvadorans who took the jobs of Guatemalans.

November 7, 1978—Mexico—Brianda Domecq, thirty-six, the American-born daughter of a millionaire Spanish distiller, was kidnapped in Mexico City by individuals claiming membership in the Twenty-third of September Communist League. A $4.3 million ransom (one report claimed the ransom demand was $5 million) demand was later reduced to $1 million. She was taken while alone in her car on Mexico City's outskirts. Police learned of the group's hideout after seizing one of the men in a Mexico City department store as he left a note for her husband. Police raided the place, freed her, and captured five suspects. No one was injured in the raid, during which a sixth man escaped. Police claimed the group were common criminals.

November 7, 1978—Iran—A firebomb was thrown at a Tehran apartment in the Niavaran area, where a U.S. embassy employee, other foreign nationals, and an Iranian family lived.

November 9, 1978—Colombia—The M-19 overpowered a watchman and stole radiocommunications equipment and weapons from the Chrysler Colmotores Company in Bogotá.

November 9, 1978—Switzerland—During the early morning, a bomb exploded at the outer entrance of the United Bank of Switzerland facing Geneva's Cornavin train station, blowing in the adjoining door to the apartment block housing the Mexican and Sudanese consulates.

November 11, 1978—United States—A man claiming PLO membership phoned a bomb threat to the concert hall of Washington, D.C.'s Kennedy Center, where the Rinat Choir of Israel was performing.

November 11, 1978—West Germany—Three terrorists, apparently Yugoslav émigrés, attacked several Yugoslav citizens in Konstanz during the night, killing Radomir Gazija and wounding two others. Gazija's brother Nenad was among those attacked. Stejpan Vidovic, one of the attackers, was detained, while Ivan Andabak and Mladen Perisic escaped.

November 15, 1978—Soviet Union—Guards killed E. M. Maknayev, an armed man who attempted to hijack a Soviet airliner flying between Krasnodar and Baku, Azerbaidjan. The flight passes within 85 miles of the Iranian border and 140 miles of the Turkish border.

November 19, 1978—Guyana—U.S. Congressman Leo J. Ryan (D-California), fifty-three, and four others were killed in an attack while on a fact-finding mission of lawyers and journalists near Port Kaituma. The group was looking into reports of inhumane treatment of Americans who were residing at the Peoples Temple settlement in Jonestown, which had been erected in 1977 by its leader, Jim Jones, after it was attacked by San Francisco newspapers. Ryan and his party of twenty-five had been joined by nine defecting sect members and were boarding one of the group's two planes when an individual started shooting at them. Following the murders, Jones led a mass suicide of the more than nine hundred group members.

November 19, 1978—Israel—A bomb exploded on a bus carrying tourists through the West Bank, killing four, including a Belgian tourist, and injuring forty. A Swedish passenger was unharmed. The bus was between Jericho and Jerusalem, en route to Tel Aviv, near Maale Adumim, one of Israel's settlements in Arab lands. Police were uncertain whether the bomb was inside or strapped to the rear of the vehicle, which was destroyed. One report indicated that the bomb was thrown by a person who escaped in a waiting truck in the direction of the Jordan Valley. Fatah claimed credit, apparently to mark the first anniversary of President Sadat's visit to Israel.

November 19, 1978—Israel—The Voice of Palestine claimed that Palestinian revolutionaries set off a bomb in Jerusalem's commercial center, injuring a number of people, destroying the entrance of three shops, and shattering glass. Police claimed that they cleared the area and safely detonated the bomb after a shopkeeper noted a suspicious object wrapped in a carpet.

November 22, 1978—Peru—A bomb exploded in a Sears Roebuck department store in Lima, injuring several persons.

November 23, 1978—United States—Chicago police arrested Nikola Sivovic of Chicago and Rados Stevlic of Wayne, Illinois, suspected Serbian terrorists, for planning to bomb a Yugoslav reception. The FBI seized several bombs when they arrested three other Serbians—leader Stojilko Kajevic of Washington, D.C., Bosko Radonjic of Manhattan, and Nikola Kavaja of Paterson, New Jersey—in New York City on the same charges. The five were also indicted for conspiring to assassinate Yugoslav President Tito during his March 7-9 visit to Washington. A sixth Serbian was being sought. In February 1979, federal authorities dropped one of the charges. The group were reportedly members of SOPO, an anti-Communist Serbian émigré group.

November 24, 1978—El Salvador—Five members of the FARN kidnapped Frits Schuitema, thirty-four, a Dutch manager of the Phillips Electrical Company, from his car in San Salvador. The group raised a $1 million ransom demand to $4 million from his company and called for the publication of FARN statements in the *New York Times*, Dutch newspapers, and those of thirty other countries in Europe, America, and Asia. On December 26, FARN announced it had received $1 million from Phillips and that its publication demand had been made. However, it refused to release the hostage until El Salvador newspapers ran their advertisement, a demand the government rejected. Schuitema was freed unharmed on the night of December 30 after Dutch Overseas Radio broadcast the FARN manifesto. On November 26, the Marxist-Leninist Proletarian Guerrilla Army had claimed credit for the kidnapping.

November 25, 1978—El Salvador—In the early morning, a bomb exploded in the German-owned Bayer Company's warehouses, 138 kilometers east of San Salvador, causing a fire that destroyed the installation.

November 30, 1978—El Salvador—Ian Massie, forty-six, and Michael Chatterton, forty-five, manager and assistant manager of the Bank of London and Montreal, were kidnapped by the FARN as they were leaving their San Salvador offices. On December 10, the group demanded the release of the country's political prisoners. On December 26, the group set a December 30 deadline for beginning negotiations, threatening to kill the hostages. The group also demanded money and the publication of their manifesto in Salvadoran and foreign newspapers. San Salvador's archbishop formed a mediation commission with a diplomat and another individual, along with the Red Cross. On March 14, 1979, an anonymous caller said the hostages had been executed on January 29 and were buried near Matsumoto's body, a Japanese business executive who had been kidnapped. On March 23, FARN denied this and proposed direct negotiations with the company. On March 31, FARN said the firm had abandoned its employees. "The case of Massie and Chatterton is closed." The two were released in mid-1979.

November 30, 1978—Mozambique—A parcel bomb was sent to the Maputo offices of Robert Mugabe's Zimbabwe African National Union. Mugabe, co-leader of the Patriotic Front, blamed the Salisbury regime.

November 30, 1978—Italy—The Proletarian Squad detonated a bomb outside IBM's warehouses in Bologna, smashing windows and a wall but causing no injuries.

December 5, 1978—Iran—During the night, the homes of three Americans in Tehran's northern and eastern sectors were firebombed.

December 6, 1978—United States—The New Jewish Defense League destroyed an Egyptian diplomat's car in New York City with a firebomb.

December 6, 1978—Switzerland—At 8 P.M., a bomb exploded in front of the Turkish consulate in Geneva, shattering windows and damaging an elevator but causing no casualities.

December 7, 1978—El Salvador—Takakazu Suzuki, fifty-six, financial executive for Insinca (Industrias Sinteticas de Centro America—Central American Synthetics Industries, a Japan-El Salvador joint venture), was kidnapped by five machine-gun-wielding FARN youths as he drove his car in western San Salvador. The group demanded the release of five political prisoners, a monetary ransom, publication of a manifesto in the world's newspapers, and a solution to an Insinca factory strike. On December 13, the firm accepted the workers' demands. The government refused to negotiate. On December 13, the group sent the family a letter about their demands. Suzuki wrote a letter in Spanish asking that no forcible investigation be undertaken. On January 2, 1979, *Listin Diario*, a Dominican newspaper, published two pages of a FARN declaration.

December 8, 1978—Iran—Firebombs thrown by demonstrators burned down the Isfahan headquarters of Grumman, a U.S.-based defense contractor. Six Americans escaped from the four-story structure, and no injuries were reported.

December 8, 1978—Iran—During the night, the Tehran homes of an American and a British diplomat were firebombed, causing no injuries.

December 11, 1978—Lebanon—The Norwegian ambassador escaped a nighttime kidnap attempt thirty-six hours before the Nobel Peace Prize was awarded to Egyptian President Sadat and Israeli Prime Minister Begin. A rejectionist group planned to kill the ambassador if the prize was awarded.

December 12, 1978—Venezuela—Unidentified individuals forced open the Swiss embassy's main door with iron bars when no one was in the building. The group escaped with thousands of bolivars in cash.

December 12, 1978—Israel—Three Israelis armed with starter's pistols took over the West German Cultural Center in Tel Aviv to protest the coming expiration of the West German statute of limitations for Nazi war crimes. They surrendered peacefully after two hours and freed a woman hostage.

December 12, 1978—United States—The New Jewish Defense League doused with gasoline and set on fire the Coney Island, Brooklyn, home of Farouk Mansour, vice-consul of Egypt's U.N. mission. The next-door home of an elderly Jewish couple was heavily damaged.

December 14, 1978—Argentina—During the morning, a bomb exploded in front of the Chilean consulate in Comodoro Rivadavia.

December 14, 1978—United States—Edmund Casey, fifty-three, an Albany janitor, hijacked National Airlines flight 97, a B727 flying in the morning from New York to Miami with six crew members and forty-eight passengers, diverting the flight to Charleston, South Carolina. He had told a flight attendant that he was carrying acid and wanted to go to Cuba. FBI agents took him off the plane. Casey had no weapons, and no injuries were reported. He later claimed that he was drunk and called the episode ''a joke.''

December 17, 1978—Switzerland—A bomb was thrown at the Turkish Airlines office in Geneva, shattering windows but causing no injuries. A man claimed credit for a secret Armenian organization.

December 17, 1978—United Kingdom—An IRA bomb exploded behind a showcase of Maggs Department Store in Bristol at 2 A.M., injuring seven people.

December 17, 1978—United Kingdom—IRA bombs exploded at 2 A.M. in two Liverpool businesses, injuring two people at one location.

December 17, 1978—United Kingdom—IRA bombs exploded at 2 A.M. in four businesses in Coventry, Manchester, and Southampton, causing no injuries.

December 18, 1978—United Kingdom—An IRA bomb exploded near the British Museum in London. A guard was hospitalized for shock. Another IRA bomb exploded nearby. Elsewhere in London, an IRA bomb exploded in a YMCA basement parking lot. Three persons were hospitalized for smoke inhalation.

December 18, 1978—United States—New York City police arrested two men for plotting to bomb the Egyptian Tourist Office in Rockefeller Center. Bruce Barry Berger, thirty, of Manhattan was arrested near the target while carrying the bomb. Victor G. Vancier, twenty-one, of Queens identified himself as the New Jewish Defense League's executive director. The bomb—two wired sticks of dynamite—would have caused much damage.

December 20, 1978—Nicaragua—A group of Americans were shot at near Chinandega, eighty miles northwest of Managua. One American was wounded, two were missing, and three were arrested. Their car was also missing. A spokesman said the group probably worked in Honduras and were on a highway twenty miles south of Chinandega when they were attacked.

December 20, 1978—France—José Maria Benaran Ordenana, thirty (alias Argala), a leader of the ETA's military wing, was killed when a bomb hidden in his car exploded in the French Basque locality of Anglet near the Spanish border. He had been involved in an industrialist's kidnapping and the 1973 murder of Premier Blanco (see incident 1751).

December 21, 1978—India—Two members of the youth wing of Indira Gandhi's Congress party hijacked an Indian Airlines B737 flying from Calcutta to New Delhi via Ranchi, Patna, and Lucknow. Reportedly the plane was seized at Benares airport, 375 miles southwest of New Delhi, although other reports indicated that it was hijacked before it was due to land in New Delhi with 124 passengers and 6 crew members. The hijackers ordered the pilot to fly to Benares and demanded the release from jail of former Prime Minister Indira Gandhi, withdrawal of criminal charges against her and Sanjay Gandhi, her son, and the resignation of the government of the Janata party. The hijackers, Bhola Nath Pandey and Virenda Pandey, said they carried pistols and a hand grenade. One passenger escaped or was allowed to leave the plane shortly after landing in Benares. Vitar Pradesh State's chief minister, Ram Naresh, negotiated all night with the hijackers at Varanasi Airport. The hijackers demanded to speak with Prime Minister Morarji Desai. When they determined that Naresh could not fulfill their demands, the Pandeys asked to be taken to Lucknow (where they had boarded) to address a press conference. The hostages were released unharmed, and the hijackers were arrested. The pistols turned out to be toys, and the grenade was a cricket ball.

December 22, 1978—Iran—No one was injured when a gasoline bomb was thrown through the window of an American's Tehran home.

December 23, 1978—Cambodia—Three terrorists assassinated Malcolm Cadwell, forty-seven, British Marxist and Asian scholar who was visiting Phnom Penh at the government's invitation. Richard Dudman and Elizabeth Becker, two American journalists accompanying him, were not injured in the attack on the Phnom Penh Government Guest House, where they were staying. The terrorists got past three armed guards and sentries from the nearby government palace. One of the terrorists, armed with a pistol and a submachine gun, killed Caldwell at 1 A.M. One of the assassins committed suicide or was killed, a second was captured, and a third escaped. A government guard died, and two house attendants were wounded. The government blamed Khmer commandos who wished to "show that we cannot protect our friends." Caldwell, an expert on the economic history of Asian countries, was skeptical of the atrocities allegedly committed by the Pol Pot regime, about which he wrote sympathetic articles.

December 23, 1978—Iran—Paul Grimm, fifty-six, a Texaco executive and acting manager of the Oil Service Company of Iran (OSCO), was shot and killed by three armed men as he drove to work in Ahwaz at 7 A.M. They fired automatic weapons as his car slowed at an intersection. The attackers, with gauze or fabric wrapped around their faces, ran from behind a wall at the intersection and fired hand guns. On January 14, 1979, the Peoples Strugglers (Mujaheddin e Khalq) claimed credit. Grimm had received a note the week before warning him to leave Iran. Elsewhere in Ahwaz, Malek Boroujerdi, an Iranian production superintendent for OSCO, was gunned down while driving to work.

December 23, 1978—Iran—During the night, a U.S. military official's car was set on fire in Tehran, causing no injuries. Elsewhere in the city, a bomb wrecked the Western Electric Company's offices but caused no injuries.

December 26, 1978—Rhodesia—Gerhard Pieper, thirty-eight, a German Jesuit who ran the Kangaire Mission northeast of Mount Darwin, was shot and killed by thirty ZANU guerrillas. The terrorists accused him in front of black sisters of not providing higher education for the local population. The sisters were also accused of believing in a Christian deity rather than in the tribal spirits. The terrorists ordered the sisters to return to their convent, drank beer, and then shot Pieper several times at 7:30 P.M.

December 26, 1978—Turkey—The cars of two Americans in Izmir were firebombed, causing no injuries.

December 27, 1978—Costa Rica—The Guatemalan ambassador, who was in charge of Nicaraguan interests, protested to Costa Rican authorities the kidnapping of Nicaraguan citizens Nestor Alonso Ordonez, Santiago Sequeria, Angel Carillo, and Faustino Trigueros, whom the FSLN had taken to Costa Rica by force after beating and binding them.

December 30, 1978—United States—Omega-7 bombed the Cuban mission to the United Nations, as well as the glass facade of a Lincoln Center theater.

1979—Iran—During the early part of the year, sporadic violence, in the forms of threats, car burnings, and bombings, took place against foreign—and particularly U.S.—targets throughout Iran.

January 1, 1979—Rhodesia—Martin Holenstein, forty-four, a Swiss Roman Catholic missionary at the Selukwe rural African reservation, was kidnapped, apparently by nationalist guerrillas, while on his way to conduct New Year's Mass. His bullet-riddled body was found near the reservation on January 3. He had disappeared five days after another Catholic missionary, Gerhard Pieper, thirty-eight, a German Jesuit, was shot dead at a remote outpost in northeastern Rhodesia. Most church leaders in Rhodesia considered guerrilla groups responsible for the killings, but suggested that these acts were not necessarily ordered by the top-level guerrilla leaders.

January 8, 1979—Austria—An unsuccessful assassination attempt was made in Vienna against Colonel Masoud Barzani, thirty-five, son of the Kurdish leader Mustapha Barzani. He claimed that the evening attack was not conducted by rival Kurdish groups but was the responsibility of "the Iraqi secret service of the embassy, on Baghdad's orders."

January 12, 1979—Tunisia—Three Tunisians hijacked a Tunis to Djerba flight of an Air Tunisia B727 and diverted it to Tripoli, Libya. They released the seventy-five passengers, took off, but returned to Tripoli, where they released the eight crew members and surrendered to authorities after a thirteen-hour takeover. The hijackers, armed with pistols and grenades, had demanded the release of Habib Achour, jailed in October 1978 for his part in organizing a national strike, and Mohammed Masmoudi, a former Tunisian foreign minister. Both were said to have links with the Libyan government. Tunisian authorities requested extradition of the hijackers, identified as Chedly Ayari, a businessman, Chihab Dakhli, a printer, and Abdesselam Ferchichi, an employee of the Ministry of Agriculture.

January 13, 1979—France—A leader of a Basque separatist group was seriously wounded in a submachine gun ambush in a French town on the Spanish border. The attack was believed to have been in retaliation by Spanish rightists for bomb blasts in Spain's northern Basque region that resulted in the deaths of two policemen.

January 14, 1979—Iran—Martin Berkowitz, fifty-three, an employee of a U.S. construction firm, was stabbed to death in his Kerman home in southern Iran. The words "Go back to your own country" were scrawled on the wall. Berkowitz was a former air force colonel who had served in Vietnam and Korea and who was employed as an engineer on a copper mining project at the Sarchashmeh Mines near Kerman, run by Parsons-Jurdon, Ltd., a division of the Ralph M. Parsons Company of Pasadena, California. He had sent his family out of the country the previous month in the wake of continued anti-American violence.

January 16, 1979—El Salvador—Forty teenage leftist members of FAPU took over the Mexican embassy, the Organization of American States office, and the central headquarters of the Red Cross in San Salvador. Occupants of the Red Cross building were peacefully removed by the national guard later in the day. However, the youths in the Mexican embassy held 6 Mexicans and 150 Salvadorans hostage, most of the latter of whom had been awaiting visas to Mexico. The youths demanded the release of "hundreds" of political prisoners and missing persons, a general amnesty, and an end to alleged government repression. The takeover came less than twenty-four hours after forty mothers of prisoners staged a sitdown demonstration at the United Nations Information Office. The government denied it held any of the prisoners.

The youths requested the intervention of San Salvador's archbishopric for providing food, water, blankets and other supplies, which they alleged were being held up by the government. The Mexican ambassador, Alberto Sales Hurtado, ultimately served as a mediator between the FAPU members and the government. Early the next day, the youths released all but thirty-five hostages, most of the former being women. Later that day, the government agreed to grant safe conduct to the youths to travel to Mexico as political refugees. The youths then surrendered their weapons, which included twelve pistols, revolvers, and a carbine snatched from an embassy guard. The final agreement was reached a few hours before Salvadoran President Carlos Humberto Romero was scheduled to go to Mexico on an official three-day visit. On January 22, the FAPU members left for Mexico City.

January 16, 1979—Lebanon—Six Lebanese Shiite Muslims hijacked a Middle East Airlines 727 flying seventy-three passengers and three crew members from Beirut to Amman and diverted it to Jordan and Cyprus. Although the hijackers claimed that the plane was running out of fuel and they would blow up the plane if their demands were rejected, Cypriot Communications Minister Iliadhis refused to allow the plane to land at Larnaca airport and ordered a blackout of the airfield. After the plane circled Larnaca for fifteen minutes, it returned to Beirut, where the hijackers were arrested after releasing their hostages. The group had hoped to publicize their demand for the release of Shiite leader Musa Sadr, who disappeared in August 1978.

January 17, 1979—El Salvador—Members of the FARN kidnapped Ernesto Liebes, seventy-two, Israel's consul general and local millionaire coffee exporter. According to witnesses, the attack took place five kilometers from downtown San Salvador on the Panamerican Highway when Liebes's Cherokee vehicle was hit by a similar vehicle carrying four men. He was forced at machine-gun point to enter their car, along with a woman who had accompanied him.

On January 22, the FARN claimed that Alberto Garcia Calderon led the noon kidnapping and demanded the release of several political prisoners. The group called its operation Heroes of the Salvadoran Revolution Anastasio Aquin, Farabundo Marti, Feliciano Ama, Saul Santiago Contreras, Roque Dalton Garcia, Felipe Pena and Lil Milagro Ramirez. The government replied that it held no political prisoners and that those who violate the Law for the Guarantee and Defense of Public Order are tried by civil courts.

The FARN claimed that it had seized an M-1 carbine and a .45 caliber automatic pistol from Liebes's bodyguard and that several uniformed policemen nearby fled without trying to stop them. The group set a deadline of March

21, 7 P.M., for the release of five prisoners, publication of certain documents, and other demands or they would kill Liebes, two British bankers, and a Japanese businessman they held hostage.

Liebes's body was found on March 22 in an abandoned car in a San Salvador neighborhood following an anonymous phone call. He had been shot.

January 17, 1979—Denmark—Copenhagen was threatened with continued bomb attacks on public buildings unless the prime minister paid $2 million to the writer of three anonymous letters. During the previous week, one bomb had been defused, a second had been detonated by authorities, and a third had killed an Italian waiter who was carrying it.

January 18, 1979—United Kingdom—Two fuel depots on the Thames River were blown up by what Scotland Yard suspected was a special IRA ''sleeper unit'' assigned to live and work in the United Kingdom until receipt of a coded signal. No injuries were reported, although one of the explosions started a firestorm that lit up the sky and scorched nearby east London homes. An anonymous caller using the IRA identification code called a British news agency after the first explosion at a natural gas storage tank, identified the targets, and said, ''For God's sake do something. People are living there.''

January 20, 1979—Spain—A powerful bomb exploded early in the morning outside the Barcelona offices of Air France, causing slight damage but no injuries.

January 22, 1979—Italy—Sari Gilbert, a *Washington Post* correspondent, was attacked by a gunman at her Rome apartment. The man, posing as a special delivery postman, drew a gun after asking her to sign for a letter. ''I threw the receipt book in the man's face, slammed the door and shouted, 'Help, terrorists' from my window,'' she reported. The gunman and an accomplice escaped on a motorcycle.

January 22, 1979—Lebanon—Ali Hassan Salameh, alias Abu Hassan, thirty-six, reputed Black September mastermind of the 1972 Olympics massacre, was killed when a bomb exploded in a parked car as his car passed it near his western Beirut home. The 3:35 P.M. explosion appears to have been accomplished by remote control detonation of one hundred pounds of explosives in a rented car. Salameh and his four Palestinian bodyguards riding in his station wagon were killed, as were five passersby, including a German nun and an English student. Eighteen others were injured. His bodyguards in a follow car were unhurt.

Salameh was a refugee from the Jaffa area of Israel. His father, also a Palestinian militant, was killed when his Ramleh headquarters was blown up by Haganah in 1948. He joined Al Fatah before the 1967 Middle East war and rose to become chief of security for Yasir Arafat. He is reputed to have become chief of Fatah's foreign terrorist operations in 1971. Despite his reputation as a philanderer, Georgina Rizk, the 1971 Miss Universe, became his second wife in 1978. He had successfully avoided injury in several previous assassination attempts believed to have been conducted by agents of Israeli intelligence services.

The case remains unsolved. The Palestine Liberation Organization immediately blamed Israel, although other observers suggested that rival Palestinian factions or Lebanese Christian militia may have been involved. According to one press report, however, two weeks previously Christian Maronites had warned Salameh that the Israelis had assigned a new assassination team to his case. They were apparently repaying a favor; a week before the warning, he had protected Dany Chamoun, a young Christian leader, from a Palestinian mob. He apparently did not take extra security precautions in spite of the threat.

According to *Time* magazine, fourteen Israeli agents, including several who had been involved in the Lillehammer, Norway, operation against Salameh in July 1973 that resulted in the death of a Moroccan waiter who resembled Salameh, were responsible. One of the suspects posed as an eccentric middle-aged spinster, Erika Mary Chambers, who carried a British passport issued in 1975. Three months before, she had rented an apartment overlooking the Rue Verdun, near Georgina Salameh's home. A second suspect was Peter Scriver, who arrived from Geneva with a British passport 260896 (or 260899). He contacted the Lena Car Rental Company in Beirut and rented a Volkswagen from them on January 18. He checked out of the Mediterranean Hotel on that date, having stayed one evening. British authorities claimed they had never issued the passport. A third suspect identified himself as Ronald Kolberg, holder of a Canadian passport, who claimed to be a sales representative for Regent Sheffield, Ltd., a New York cutlery and kitchenware firm. The company reported that no one of that name was employed by them. It was believed that the two men rented the explosives-laden car and getaway vehicle from Lenacar and that the woman detonated the device by radio. Other versions of this story suggest that the assassins hid a radio transmitter in Salameh's car, which emitted a short-range signal when it passed the Volkswagen.

On January 26, Palestinian security forces detained five journalists: one American, two British, and two Dutch, who were attending the Salameh funeral when it was discovered that they were holding Israeli press cards. The same day, Beirut military authorities arrested Donald Webster Stecher (Fisher), an American, and Phillipe Robert Rivault (Rivaux) of France. The two men, detained in the mountain town of Aley, fifteen miles from Beirut, reportedly carried six passports each. On January 30, the Associated Press reported that Ronald Kolberg, twenty-five, a University of Tel Aviv biology student from Vancouver, Canada, had gone into hiding when it was discovered that a copy of his passport had apparently been used by the assassins.

On January 28, a time bomb planted by members of Salameh's guerrilla unit exploded in a crowded Netanya, Israel, market square, killing two persons and wounding forty-three others.

January 23, 1979—Europe—Several European capitals, including London, received leters from the ARA (believed to be the Arab Revolutionary Army) threatening to poison Israeli agricultural products destined for all European Economic Community countries, Yugoslavia, and Rumania. Similar letters had been received in the United Kingdom a year previously, followed by the contamination of several Israeli oranges with mercury. The letter to the Dutch government, which was shown to journalists, claimed that the contamination would be on a greater scale and would use more lethal substances.

January 24, 1979—United States—Five men, one carrying a revolver, claiming membership in the Revolutionary Communist Party (U.S.A.) Committee to Give a Fitting Welcome, smashed windows and threw paint during an attack on the Chinese embassy to protest the visit of Chinese Vice-Premier Teng Hsiao-ping. The group claimed to be supportive of the deposed Gang of Four. Police identified the attackers as Curtis Mohn, thirty-one; Gregory Ford, twenty-seven, of Brooklyn; Mark W. Jackson, twenty-seven, of Baltimore; James Joseph Nelson, twenty-five, of Massachusetts; and James E. Loudermilk, forty-one, of Elizabeth, New Jersey. They were charged with destruction of foreign government property, and Loudermilk was separately charged with assaulting a federal officer. On August 3, 1979, Judge June Green sentenced Nelson, Mohn, and Jackson to two years' probation for the destruction. Loudermilk was given a three-month suspended sentence and three years' probation and was found guilty of possession of an unregistered gun. Green ordered the foursome to pay the chancery $815 in restitution. In June, Green accepted the defendants' guilty pleas to the charge of harassing the Chinese chancery but reversed her decision after hearing objections by U.S. Attorney Earl J. Silbert that they should be tried on a more serious charge. Ford escaped penalty because his name was inadvertently dropped from the indictment for the misdemeanor charge.

January 28, 1979—United States—United Airlines flight 8, a B747 carrying 119 passengers and a crew of 12 from Los Angeles to New York City, was hijacked shortly after takeoff when Irene McKinney, forty-nine, of Los Angeles handed a stewardess a note saying that she was "willing to die for the cause, but I don't know what the cause is." She claimed to have nitroglycerin in her handbag and demanded that a Hollywood entertainer—Charlton Heston, Jack Lemmon, or Lindsay Wagner—go to a TWA ticket counter in the Los

Angeles airport terminal and read a message hidden there on national television. Although Heston was brought to the terminal, it was later determined that the hijacker had the message with her.

Pilot Thomas Cook, who had been with United since 1943, reported that the hijacking occurred when the plane was about ten miles west of Prescott, Arizona. He requested landing instructions for an FAA field near Atlantic City, New Jersey, but later decided to fly on to the flight's original destination, JFK International Airport in New York. Eight hours after the flight began, the hijacker agreed to release 25 passengers—7 men, 12 women, and 6 children—when FBI negotiators convinced her that those people were ill. She ultimately was disarmed by an FBI negotiator at 4 A.M. the next day. Her purse contained no bomb but did include a rambling twenty-five-page document explaining her concept for a universal religion based on a technological heaven on earth after a massive solar explosion. It was later learned that she was recently divorced and was distraught over losing custody of her two children.

Passengers reported that they were treated well, being serenaded by actor Theodore Bikel, who was a passenger on the plane along with actor Sam Jaffe and singer Dino Martin.

January 29, 1979—Turkey—A high-powered explosive device was thrown into the Turkish-British Cultural Center in Ankara at 8:15 P.M., causing damage to the building but injuring no one. Half an hour later, a bomb was thrown at the Commerce Ministry.

January 30, 1979—Cyprus—A PLO official received a death threat. Zakhariya Abd al-Rahim receive a telephoned threat from a man speaking Arabic. Three men in a car were later seen with guns near his office.

January 31, 1979—Spain—The Commando of Solidarity with Euzkadi, apparently a Basque separatist group, claimed credit for throwing a petrol bomb into the French tourist office in Barcelona during the evening. A small fire was quickly extinguished by firemen.

February 1979—Sweden—Tennis star Bjorn Borg cancelled a match in Goteborg after receiving a threatening letter mailed in Stockholm saying "Red Brigade—death sentence—Bjorn Borg." Attached was a photo of Borg posing in an Israeli army uniform during a fall visit to the Middle East. Borg had previously received a telephone threat, apparently from Stockholm, while in Milan the previous October. Copies of the letter were sent to Borg, Stockholm police, the Royal Tennis Club, and Swedish news services.

February 1, 1979—Greece—Two Irishmen were arrested after crossing the Turkish border and charged with arms smuggling for the IRA. Border police discovered hidden compartments in their van, which concealed thirty-six hand grenades, several automatic rifles, and substantial quantities of explosives. The duo confessed to an Alexandroupolis magistrate that they bought the arms in Syria and Lebanon but refused to specify their suppliers. They were identified as Sheamus Ruddy, twenty-seven, of Belfast and Phelim Lally, twenty-four, of Newry, County Down, both Northern Ireland residents although they held Irish Republic passports. They were charged with ''smuggling, possession and transportation of arms and explosives with the intention of supplying terrorist groups,'' for which they could receive ten years. The U.K. consul stated that he could not demand their extradition because they were not wanted for any offense in the United Kingdom.

February 8, 1979— Australia—Nine men were arrested during the night while planning a bombing campaign against targets throughout Melbourne. Police alleged that they were members of a Croatian nationalist organization planning to protest the appearance at a Sydney theater of Soviet singers. Six men were brought before a Sydney court and charged with possessing gelignite, detonators, and connectors. The other three men appeared in court in Lithgow, where they were charged with stealing, possessing exposives, and intent to commit malicious injury. They were all remanded in custody pending late February court appearances.

February 12, 1979—Spain—GRAPO claimed credit for exploding a low-power bomb during the evening in the the basement of the French embassy, which caused slight damage and no injuries. The blast blew out windows in the house opposite and damaged a parked car. GRAPO's communiqué explained that ''the action is in response to the latest measures adopted by France against Basque refugees in France.

February 12, 1979—Rhodesia—An Air Rhodesia Viscount was shot down by Patriotic Front guerrillas at 4:45 P.M. on its flight between Kariba and Salisbury, killing all fifty-nine aboard. PF leader Joshua Nkomo said in an interview in Addis Ababa that the plane had been scheduled to carry Lieutenant General Walls, Rhodesian army commander, and that the plane was therefore a legitimate military target. The ZAPU guerrillas apparently used Soviet-made Strela heat-seeking missiles, which explode in the jet pipes of turboprop engines. Many of the dead were foreign tourists. Among the five dead crew members was Regina Chigwada, twenty-three, a black trainee hostess who was scheduled to become the civilian airline's fourth black hostess.

February 13, 1979—Egypt—A bomb exploded during the night at the Sheraton Hotel in Cairo, injuring Zizi Mustapha, an Egyptian belly dancer, and four other persons. No group claimed credit.

February 14, 1979—Rhodesia—Black nationalist guerrillas fired at a second Air Rhodesia Viscount en route from Kariba to Salisbury but caused little damage and no injuries. Five bullet holes were found in the plane when it landed. The plane carried twenty-four passengers, including Captain Peter Travers, the company's general manager, who was on an inspection visit to the wreckage of his company's plane that had been downed two days earlier. The airline company's pilots adopted various evasive tactics, including low flying, to make aiming missiles more difficult.

February 14, 1979—Iran—Approximately 200 armed urban guerrillas attacked the U.S. embassy and held U.S. Ambassador William H. Sullivan and 101 members of the embassy staff for more than two hours. The attack began at 10:15 A.M. when guerrillas opened fire with thirty-caliber heavy machine guns, automatic rifles, and submachine guns from the roof of a hotel and other buildings in the area. Other youths then pinned down 19 marine guards while others scaled the walls and embassy gates from three sides and fired at the chancery. The marines fired tear-gas shells and led the staff to the communications room, which is windowless and has reinforced walls. Top-secret communications gear worth $500,000 was blown up by staff members as the attackers closed in. Employees also set fire to classified files in priority order, but many documents were left unprotected in areas penetrated by the attackers. The siege ended two hours later when forces loyal to the government of Ayatollah Khomeini and personally led by Dr. Ibrahim Yazdi, deputy prime minister, engaged the attackers and eventually placed the embassy under protection of his militia.

During the attack, an Iranian waiter at the embassy's restaurant was killed when he was shot in the chest after coming out to surrender to the attackers. One American suffered a heart attack during the melee and was allowed to be evacuated to a local hospital. Two Iranians were initially reported killed in the fighting between the attackers and Khomeini forces. A nearby hospital said five wounded Iranians were treated there. A marine guard, identified as Sergeant Ken Kraus, twenty-two, of Lansdale, Pennsylvania, was grazed on the forehead and wounded in the arm. Kraus said an attacker asked ''where our weapons were. I took them into the restaurant where we had hidden two or three weapons. He insisted there were more and that he would shoot me if I didn't tell him where. I said it was all we had, and he hit me in the chest with the gun butt and I fell to the floor. Next I heard a blast and started to bleed. We never fired a shot. The ambassador told us not to fire so as not to jeopardize our own lives and those of Iranians working in the kitchen.'' The attackers claimed they had been fired on by members of SAVAK, the deposed shah's security forces, from the embassy grounds.

Khomeini forces blamed the Communist Tudeh party, while others suggested the People's Fedayeen, which denied responsibility, was involved. A few attackers admitted belonging to Fedaye, a Marxist guerrilla group that had refused Khomeini's orders to turn in their weapons to his forces.

February 14, 1979—Afghanistan—U.S. Ambassador Adolph "Spike" Dubs, fifty-eight, was taken hostage in Kabul by armed terrorists and died in a police attempt to free him.

The ambassador, a former deputy assistant secretary of state for Near Eastern and South Asian Affairs, was abducted when his chauffeur-driven ochre Oldsmobile flying the U.S. flag stopped for a traffic light at 8:45 A.M. A man in a police uniform pulled a gun on his driver. Reports differ as to whether Dubs was then driven off in his car by three terrorists who joined the first or whether he was taken in another car near the American Cultural Center. Dubs had no guard riding with him. He was taken to the Kabul Hotel, where the terrorists holed up in room 117 and demanded the release of three individuals whom the government claimed were unavailable. Observers disagreed as to the identity of those whose release was demanded. Some believed that they were colleagues of the terrorists who had been arrested in the Marxist-oriented government's recent crackdown on political opponents. Several sources said the kidnappers wanted the release of three mullahs (Moslem holy figures). The government claimed they demanded the release of Bahruddin Bahez, whom it described as a "vicious criminal" from Badakshan Province who had been captured by the deposed regime and who had escaped the previous July by feigning illness and overpowering four policemen who were taking him to a clinic. The government claimed that it attempted to stall the terrorists by not admitting that the prisoners were not available. During the negotiations, one of the terrorists came downstairs to look for a key and was captured in the lobby.

American embassy pleas not to take any precipitate action and prolong the negotiations were ignored by the government. The U.S. embassy was unable to get through to Foreign Minister Hafizullah Amin or police commander Syed Daoud Tarun during the negotiations, although Soviet advisers were seen openly conferring with Afghan authorities at the hotel. The Soviet advisers refused to confer with U.S. officials at the scene. Several American sources claimed that three Soviet advisers and a Soviet embassy security officer, Sergei Bakhtourin, conferred closely with the police and probably influenced the police decision to attack the terrorists.

American officials received indications that the Afghan police were planning an assault on the hotel room when they requested Bruce Flatin, a U.S. political counselor, to talk to Ambassador Dubs in some language other than English—which the terrorists apparently spoke—to obtain information from him. The two exchanged a few words regarding the ambassador's health and the fact that the captors held revolvers. Their conversation in German was abruptly halted by the terrorists who noted that they were "aware of your tricks." Flatin refused an Afghan directive to tell Dubs to lie down in ten minutes, the time the police scheduled for the assault. Flatin once again called for calm negotiations but was ignored. According to information that the *Washington Post* claimed was in a leaked State Department cable, "One Soviet adviser helped to arm an Afghan policeman. Two other Soviet police advisers and Bakhturin went out to the balcony. The tall, senior Soviet adviser then made hand signals from the balcony, presumably positioning the snipers across the street. . . .Firemen with picks and axes arrived and joined the police. A photograph of the Ambassador was displayed to all members of the security strike force. One of the commandos then asked, 'Is that the terrorist?' He was told that it was the Ambassador, whom he was to avoid shooting."

According to the Afghan government, its hand was forced when the terrorists set a ten-minute deadline at 12:30 for accession to their demands. At 12:50, the police began a forty-second onslaught on the hotel room, using single-shot and automatic weapons. The Afghans claimed that upon opening the door, Ambassador Dubs was found alive, then was quickly brought to a local hospital, where he died. The U.S. embassy said that Dubs was already dead, having sustained a single small-caliber wound above the right eye, a large-caliber bullet wound in the heart area, and a wound in the left wrist. The Afghans held that the terrorists shot the ambassador during the assault, although it was impossible to determine at the scene what bullets had struck the ambassador. The U.S. embassy protested "in the strongest possible terms" to the Afghan government for its action.

The fate of the terrorists is cloudy. Some reports from Kabul said all were killed in the shootout. However, a State Department spokesman said three individuals were removed from the room—one dead, one unconscious and probably dead, and one injured but alive. When and where the third terrorist died is unknown. His body was in the morgue with the other three terrorists (apparently including the individual captured during the negotiations) when the U.S. political counselor was called in by the government to view the bodies.

The identity of the terrorists also remains a mystery. Early reports that they were Shiite Moslems were contradicted by those who blamed the Izdah al-Islam sect, an antigovernment group. The government claimed that they were not part of any organized antigovernment forces. No political or religious group has claimed responsibility for the attack. Observers said it could have been inspired by religious opposition to the leftist government or to dissent within the ruling Khalq party. Most analysts agreed that the attack was not anti-American in nature but was rather calculated to gain maximum publicity. It is generally agreed that the terrorists were Afghans, and some witnesses reported that the police addressed one through the hotel room door keyhole as "Najib," which may have been a code name.

The Soviet role became a matter of controversy. Tarun later said to two reporters, "There were no Russians present. This was our operation and we made the decision." The Soviets passed a note to the State Department, which

Tass quoted as having ''pointed out that the Soviet representatives had arrived at the place of the incident with aim [sic] of protecting the life of Soviet citizens, whom the terrorists were also threatening.''

February 19, 1979—Spain—Luis Abaitua, the manager of Michelin factory in Vitória, was kidnapped by the ETA-PM as he left his office to return home in his car. He was released by his captors at 2 A.M. on March 1, 1979.

February 19, 1979—Turkey—A powerful bomb was thrown from a passing car at the Pan American Airlines office in Alsancak, Izmir, damaging the building and surrounding area but causing no injuries.

February 20, 1979—Turkey—The car of a U.S. serviceman attached to the southeast NATO headquarters in Izmir was firebombed, causing no casualties.

February 20, 1979—Turkey—Unidentified individuals fired from a passing car at the Izmir apartment of a U.S. serviceman attached to the southeast NATO headquarters.

February 20, 1979—Italy—Parma police arrested two Italians and two West Germans who were found carrying a time bomb and other weapons in their car. Rudolph Piroh, twenty-five, was carrying a false Argentine passport for Frederick von Haltazan, born in Neumarket and resident in Buenos Aires, Martino Rocco and Carmela Pane were identified as anarchists residing in a Pisa student dormitory. The four, all aged twenty-three to twenty-five, claimed to be ''professional revolutionaries.''

February 23, 1979—Turkey—Sadik Cemil, a Cypriot student, was shot to death in the afternoon in the Aksaray section of Istanbul. His colleague was kidnapped by the person who fired the shot, and another of his friends was beaten by another group. The secretariat-general of the National Unity Party blamed the incident on fighting between extremist groups.

February 24, 1979—United Kingdom—Irish Republican guerrillas planted bombs that exploded in a crowded Woolworth store and in a parked van in Yeovil, England, injuring four persons.

February 27, 1979—Chile—A bomb exploded at 4:29 A.M. in the U.S.-Chilean Cultural Institute in Santiago, causing some damage.

February 27, 1979—Finland—Four members of the Ananda Marga religious sect attempted to hijack an Oslo to Moscow Aeroflot jetliner by threatening to use their Molotov cocktails to set it on fire. The group said they intended to immolate themselves in Moscow to protest their ''suppression in state capitalistic countries.'' The group surrendered to police without a fight at a scheduled stop at Stockholm's Arlanda Airport. An Indian male was released after questioning. The other three were found guilty on April 12, 1979, of attempted hijacking. A twenty-seven-year-old Swedish man and a forty-two-year-old Brazilian woman received three years each in jail, while a twenty-two-year-old West German woman received eighteen months.

March 1, 1979—Lebanon—According to a Baghdad radio broadcast, right-wingers assassinated a Syrian Social National party member and wounded three others in an ambush in the Al-Kurah area of northern Lebanon.

March 1, 1979—Colombia—A large envelope containing explosives was found in front of an elevator on the third floor of the Japanese embassy in Bogotá. A report to the foreign minister speculated that the M-19, which had used the same modus operandi and had threatened in a newspaper statement to attack foreign missions, may have been responsible.

March 7, 1979—Israel—Time bombs were discovered on three Arab-owned tourist buses operating out of Jerusalem. One bomb exploded at the Allenby Bridge over the Jordan River, injuring twelve persons, including two drivers, several porters, and a guide. Many of the tourists were reportedly Jordanians. Another bomb exploded after the passengers left the bus to visit the Mount of Olives. No one was injured, but the vehicle was destroyed. A third bomb was found on a bus at Afula in the Plain of Jezreel and was defused by security forces.

March 8, 1979—Nicaragua—Costa Rican radio reported that three members of the FSLN armed with machine guns hijacked a Navajo plane in Managua owned by President Somoza and ordered the captain to fly to Venezeula. The plane landed in Costa Rica's Juan Santamaria Airport, where it was parked for thirty-five minutes. Colonel Guillermo Marti, chief of air and maritime defense, talked to the hijackers on board the plane and convinced them to surrender. The hijackers requested political asylum after being arrested and were identified as Santiago Carmona Palacios, Marvin Wilson Camano, and Pablo Robleto Miranda, members of the Pablo Fonseca Amado Patrol of the FSLN. The commander of the Nicaraguan air force, Colonel Orlando Zeledon, denied that a plane owned by the president had been hijacked. "President Somoza had no planes of that type; therefore, the report is false,'' said another source of a Panama radio station.

March 9, 1979—Philippines—Reverend Lloyd G. Van Vactor, fifty-five, an American serving as a missionary for the United Church of Christ, was kidnapped from his principal's office in Dansalan College by heavily armed

Moslem rebels posing as Philippine soldiers. It was believed that they were members of the Moro National Liberation Front, although the MNLF leadership in the south denied responsibility for the incident. On March 14, a note received from the kidnappers threatened to kill the twenty-seven-year Philippine resident within three days if a ransom of 500,000 pesos ($67,500) was not paid. According to Bishop Estanislao Abainza, the MNLF had mentioned a 100,000 peso ransom in a letter the previous year threatening to kill the Stanton, North Dakota, native. Press reports indicated that the church's New York office had authorized the payment of the ransom, but the decision was apparently reversed two days later. The kidnappers also demanded that the mayors of Ganasi and Madalum in Lanao del Sur Province be replaced by two men who were close relatives of one of the kidnap leaders, Jalandoni Morohombsar.

Negotiations for Van Vactor's release were handled by the Libyan ambassador, Moustapha Dreiza; Van Vactor's son, Norman, twenty-two; four college officials; a prominent assemblyman from the region; and a retired army general. The missionary was allowed to send letters to his wife through rebel couriers and requested medicines. The Libyan ambassador reported that fifteen rebels were involved. Van Vactor's release came a day after a third ten-day deadline had expired. The kidnappers freed him at 7:30 P.M. on March 28 after they received assurances that no military operations would be launched against them. Van Vactor walked into his Mindanao Island home half an hour later, physically healthy but suffering a substantial weight loss.

Despite Ambassador Dreiza's reports that no ransom was paid, it was reported that the faculty and alumni of the college raised $2,700 for his ransom. The rebels kept $1,300 but returned the rest of the money, which will likely go to the Maizie Van Vactor Scholarship Fund, named after his wife, who died following abdominal surgery on the eighth day of her husband's captivity. He did not learn of her death while he was held.

On April 2, the Philippine military filed criminal charges in the city court in Marawi, 490 miles, south of Manila, against seventeen Moslem rebels. The chart sheet identified only three individuals: Jalandoni Moohombsar (alias Commander Allan), Avelino Langilao (alias Billy Jack), and Mabay Benito (alias Commander Bobby).

March 14, 1979—Italy—A Rome court sentenced Fernado Vaca Narvaja, an Argentine Montoneros leader, and his wife, Maria Josefa Fleming, to prison terms of forty months in absentia for illegal possession of weapons and forged identity documents. Vaca Narvaja was reputedly the deputy chief of the Montoneros.

March 15, 1979—Pakistan—A bomb found in a washroom of the U.S. consulate in Karachi was defused.

834   March 16, 1979

March 16, 1979—Egypt—Security authorities arrested Ibrahim Ad-Dayah, a Syrian, on his arrival at Cairo airport and claimed that he was a member of Saiqa, sent by Syrian intelligence to participate in a terrorist campaign. He was to blow up the Foreign Ministry building opposite the Arab League building at noon, ensuring the largest number of casualties, including Foreign Affairs Minister Butrous Ghali. He was told to conduct two other operations of his choosing, detonating charges in crowded areas to cause panic and give the impression of domestic instability. Egypt's interior minister reported that two centers for financing his operations were found. The caches held 28,000 Egyptian pounds, $26,000, 10,000 lira, other foreign currencies, and 40,000 pounds worth of jewelry. He was given Cairo telephone numbers of local Saiqa support contacts, which Egypt claimed were members of Syrian intelligence. After his arrest, Ad-Dayah contacted the numbers under Egyptian supervision, and the occupants were later arrested. A second Saiqa operative was arrested on April 15. Their release was demanded by terrorists who took over the Egyptian embassy in Ankara, Turkey, on July 13, 1979.

Ad-Dayah was later found to be Akram az-Zughbi from the Hawran district of Syria. He was recruited by Wadi Ali Hawriyah (alias Abu Ahmad) of Saiqa, Bilal Hasan (alias Abu Mazin), commander of Saiqa's militia, and Abu Ali, commander of the Saiqa security forces and his deputy Abu Salim, according to Cairo radio. Ad-Dayah was trained in explosives at Ad-Damur camp in Beirut by a Syrian officer, Ahmad al-Hallaq, and a Palestinian, Husayn Mas'ud.

March 17, 1979—United States—Continental Airlines flight 62, a B727 carrying eighty-nine passengers and eight crew members on a flight from Los Angeles to Miami with stops at Phoenix, Tucson, and Houston, was hijacked at 9:15 A.M. after leaving Phoenix by John Carleton Kivlen, fifty-two, of San Rafael, California. Kivlen told a stewardess he had a "cutter" and demanded that $200,000 be placed in two bags under the plane's wings after landing in Tucson and that he be flown to Cuba. Kivlen worked for Tymshare Transactions Service, a San Francisco computer firm, and had been arrested in Tampa, Florida, in 1969 on hijacking charges that were subsequently dropped. Upon landing, the well-dressed hijacker allowed everyone but stewardess Mary Ellen Paul to deplane. FBI agents boarded the plane and negotiated with the hijacker, mostly by passing notes. At a signal from the agents, the stewardess dashed into a plane lavatory and Kivlen was overpowered. Kivlen carried only a nail file. He later appeared before U.S. District Court Judge Leo Brewster on a charge of seizing or exercising control of an aircraft by force of violence. Bail was set at $1 million.

March 22, 1979—Pakistan—Mazzan Raki Davesh, an administrative attaché at the Palestine Liberation Organization mission in Islamabad, was shot to death in a dispute at his home during the evening. He was with his two wives and a nephew at the time of the shooting.

March 22, 1979—The Netherlands—Sir Richard Sykes, fifty-eight, the U.K. ambassador to the Hague, was killed by two gunmen as he was entering his silver Rolls Royce at his home to go to the embassy at 9 A.M. Four shots, one of which hit Sykes in the head, were fired by two gunmen ten yards away who escaped on foot down a nearby alley behind his garage into rush-hour shoppers and commuters. His uninjured chauffeur, Jack Wilson, rushed Sykes to a hospital five hundred yards away, where Sykes died two hours later. Karel Strauss, nineteen, Dutch valet to Sykes, was shot as he held open the limousine door and died in the same hospital after being taken there by ambulance. Alyson Bailes, a visiting London Foreign Office official who was sitting next to Sykes, was unharmed in what police characterized as a very professional operation.

One of the two men fleeing had dark blond hair and wore a dark suit and white shirt. The other had brown curly hair and wore a brown suit. Both seemed to be in their late thirties. Witnesses said that only weapon they saw was a long-barreled pistol. Hague police suggested on April 2 that a third man was involved. A witness saw a man wearing a light-colored cap and a striped pullover sitting inside a car near the envoy's residence during the attack.

On March 23, *De Telegraaf*, an Amsterdam newspaper, received an anonymous call claiming credit for the IRA: "This is only the beginning. It's war. Tomorrow we will kill either the Ambassador in Belgium, France, or Germany." Two Belfast newspapers received calls from purported IRA Provos saying that the killing of Sykes and a Belgian banker (see next incident) "could be the work of one of our groups but if it is, we know nothing about it." Other IRA Provo sources denied having made such a statement. The same day, a male speaking Dutch wth a Hague accent told three news organizations that the Red Brigade, apparently a previously unknown Dutch group, had carried out the killing on behalf of the IRA. Sykes's embassy had been fighting gun-running to Irish guerrillas from left-wing sympathizers in the Netherlands, according to press reports.

Sykes was known as a leading security authority among British diplomats. As deputy under secretary of state at the Foreign Office, he had been sent to Dublin to investigate the 1976 IRA murder of British Ambassador Christopher Ewart-Biggs (see incident 2798). Sykes wrote a government report recommending increased security precautions for U.K. diplomats abroad, particularly at their residences. However, Dutch police said there were no policemen on duty outside his home at the time of the attack because the embassy had not requested any guards.

March 22, 1979—Belgium—A few hours after the Sykes murder, two gunmen shot and killed banker André Michaux, forty-seven, as he was parking his car outside his suburban Brussels home. Police and British investigators believed the attackers may have killed the wrong man and were rather hoping to kill a British neighbor, Paul Holmer, assistant to the United Kingdom's permanent representative to NATO, Sir John Killick. Although some police sources initially suggested that the same men could have been responsible for the Sykes and Michaux murders, ballistics tests established that different weapons had been used. Belgian police arrested a male member of a leftist organization who may have been involved in Michaux's murder. Although he may not have taken part in the killing, police found two machine guns in his home.

March 23, 1979—Israel—The PLO claimed credit for a bomb that went off at 3 P.M. next to Zion Square, Jerusalem, in a garbage can near a downtown taxi stand. A seventy-two-year-old Israeli man was killed and twelve Israelis, a Canadian woman, and a German man were injured. The bombing came hours after Prime Minister Begin left for the United States to sign the Egyptian-Israeli peace treaty. The statement issued by the PLO in Beirut warned that it would step up its campaign to protest the treaty.

March 24, 1979—United States—Omega-7, an anti-Castro Cuban exile group, claimed credit for bombs that went off in the New York and New Jersey:

The first bomb injured four TWA baggage handlers at New York's JFK International Airport who were placing a bag on a cart hauling luggage for TWA flight 17, scheduled to fly 180 passengers to Los Angeles. Police suggested that the 8:45 P.M. blast may have gone off prematurely, because a caller phoned later to warn of the bomb. The FBI said the four or five sticks of dynamite, set off by a timing device, would have blown a hole in the TWA jet.

Another bomb went off in the New Jersey Cuban Program in Weehawken, which handles immigration, job placement, and social work for Cubans. The final bomb damaged Almacen Pharmacia in Union City, which ships medicine to Cuba.

Omega-7 said this was the start of a campaign to attack firms dealing with the Castro regime. TWA was a target apparently because of its charter flights to Cuba.

On March 27, the FBI said that it was searching for two Cuban exile fugitives, José Dionisio Suarez and Virgilio Pablo Paz, to question about the blasts. They had been charged with the 1976 car bombing of former Chilean Ambassador Orlando Letelier (see incident 2892).

March 25, 1979—Syria—In an apparent protest against the signing of the Egyptian-Israeli peace treaty in Washington, D.C., two bomb blasts shattered windows of the U.S. embassy in Damascus during the evening. Someone in a car shouted "To hell with the traitorous agreement" before throwing a bomb into the embassy garden and driving off. The other bomb went off near the rear of the embassy, causing no serious damage and no injuries. No one claimed responsibility.

March 26, 1979—Turkey—A bomb went off during the evening at the Israeli embassy in Ankara, causing no casualties. A caller claimed credit for a group called Turkish Revolutionaries, who were protesting the signing of the Egyptian-Israeli peace treaty.

March 27, 1979—Turkey—A bomb was thrown from a car with an Izmir license plate into the entrance of the Turkish-American Association's movie theater, causing no injuries. The 9:40 P.M. blast damaged two cars parked at the hall's entrance and shattered windows of buildings nearby.

March 27, 1979—Bangladesh—The Egyptian ambassador was taken hostage in his home by several individuals for several hours before being released unharmed.

March 27, 1979—France—The Autonomous Intervention Collective Against the Zionist Presence in France and the Israeli-Egyptian Peace claimed credit when a bomb was thrown into a hostel for Jewish students in the Paris Latin Quarter. Thirty-two students, most of them French or Israeli, were injured, two of them seriously, Ibrahim Souss, the Paris PLO representative, condemned the bombing and suggested that it was the work of French anti-Semites: "We wage our battle in the occupied territories, not in France." Another bomb went off in a Jewish-owned perfume shop on the Avenue de l'Opera, wrecking the shop but injuring no one.

March 28, 1979—Spain—The ETA claimed credit for attacks on the offices of the Crédit Lyonnais in San Sebastián and on a French truck. It threatened to continue attacking French interests as a reprisal for any future actions taken by France against Basque refugees.

March 30, 1979—Turkey—A bomb was thrown into the garden of the U.S. embassy, shattering windows of the embassy and nearby buildings but causing no injuries.

March 30, 1979—United Kingdom—Airey Neave, sixty-three, war hero and Conservative party spokesman on Northern Ireland, died at 3 P.M. when a half-pound bomb hidden in his blue Vauxhall sedan exploded as he drove up the exit ramp to the House of Commons underground garage. Many observers believed he would have become home minister or Northern Ireland secretary under the government of his close friend, Margaret Thatcher. Neave's murder was the first assassination of a member of Parliament since the 1812 shooting of Prime Minister Spencer Perceval in the House of Commons lobby.

The IRA and Irish National Liberation Army (INLA) claimed credit for the blast. Police tended to believe INLA's statement, noting that the group had previously used this type of sophisticated device. In a phone call to Dublin newspapers, INLA said, "This is the first attack in a new campaign against British political and military establishment and will continue until there is a complete withdrawal of the British political and military presence from Ireland." The IRA claim noted, "We have this message for the British government: Before you decide to have a general election you had better state that you have decided not to stay in Ireland." Scotland Yard investigators said the bomb was a two-stage device probably attached magnetically to Neave's car. Some observers suggested that an agency or country in the Middle East with access to advanced technology was involved. The INLA calls itself the military wing of the Irish Republican Socialist party, which broke away from the IRA four years ago.

Police officers believed the bomb had been placed by a man who escaped on a motorscooter. All but one of the six men questioned in Dublin about possible links to the murder were released as of April 8. The London Press Association, quoting intelligence sources, said the assassins were unknown to the main IRA circles in Ulster. They may have been an active service unit of two or three people who could have returned to Ireland before the bomb exploded.

Neave was a member of the Royal Artillery in World War II. He was wounded and taken prisoner in the battle for Calais in 1940. Disguising himself as a German soldier, he became the first U.K. officer to escape from the Nazi's allegedly escape-proof Colditz prison. After the war, he served on the prosecution staff of the Nuremberg war trials. Although he staunchly opposed demands that British troops be withdrawn from Ulster, shortly before his murder, he had promised to look into allegations of mistreatment by Ulster police of IRA prisoners.

April 1979—Spain—According to Havana radio, Dr. Rosendo Canto Hernandez, president of the Spanish Committee for the Reunification of the Cuban Family, was attacked by two persons armed with pistols and knives as he was leaving the Casa de Cuba in Madrid. His left kneecap was fractured. Canto claimed his attackers were Spanish fascists with ties to Cuban rightist exiles in Miami.

April 2, 1979—Lebanon—Two men fired two rocket-propelled grenades from 150 yards away into the U.S. embassy, causing some damage but no injuries. The first grenade exploded in the air, and the second went through a second-floor window and exploded inside an empty office at 2:45 P.M. Later that day, the Arab People (Ash-Shab al-'Arabi) claimed responsibility and condemned the United States, Egypt, and Israel.

April 3, 1979—West Germany—A bomb hidden in a parcel to be taken by Lufthansa jet to Israel exploded in a mail-sorting shed at Rhein-Main, Frankfurt's international airport, injuring ten workers and doing substantial damage to the shed. One of the victims lost an arm in the 7:25 A.M. blast. Because Lufthansa handles mail for El Al Airlines, Palestinian terrorists were believed responsible.

April 4, 1979—Australia—Dimicias Speranzo, thirty-four, an Italian immigrant carrying bombs on his body and in his hands, grabbed a woman in the Sydney airport terminal and took over a Pan Am B747 scheduled to fly to Los Angeles. He demanded to be flown to Italy to meet with the Pope and Communist leader Enrico Berlinguer and then to be flown on to Moscow. Ninety-four minutes after he first held a knife to the woman's throat, an antihijack squad shot him. He died several hours later of multiple wounds.

April 5, 1979—Cyprus—A bomb exploded early in the morning at the entrance of the Israeli embassy, shattering windows.

April 5, 1979—Cyprus—A bomb exploded at dawn in the offices of a tourism agency representing Egyptair. According to a Nicosia radio station, police on April 18 arrested a Palestinian who was formerly employed by the Nicosia PLO office. Two other Palestinians were arrested and questioned in the case. Egypt later arrested a Saiqa member in Egypt for the bombing.

April 6, 1979—United States—A bomb exploded at the Cerritos, Los Angeles, residence of Frank Striskovich, a Croatian community activist. Another bomb went off at the Rossmor, Los Angeles, home of Mario Forgiarini. Kris Brkic, his predecessor as president of a coalition of nineteen Croatian community organizations, was shot to death on November 22, 1978, on the lawn of his Glendale home after he had refused to pay from $5,000 to $15,000 to extortionists in Paraguay who had mailed letters to fifty prominent Croatians demanding payment to the separatist group.

April 6, 1979—Spain—The ETA's military wing claimed credit for bombing the French consulate in San Sebastián, seriously injuring two police guards. The ETA accused the French government of collaborating with Spanish authorities in a crackdown on ETA members in France.

April 6, 1979—France—Unknown saboteurs set off five explosive charges at a factory of the Naval and Industrial Constructions of the Mediterranean firm, heavily damaging two nuclear research reactors that were to be shipped to Iraq later in the month. The firm was also manufacturing smaller reactor components for Belgium and West Germany. The Iraqi reactors' beehive-shaped pressure vessel for atomic fuel rods was destroyed and set back by at least eighteen months the delivery of the hardware. The unmarked four-thousand-foot square structure had little physical security—no fences or other obvious measures and only three night watchmen. Credit for the explosion at La Seyne sur Mer, on the Mediterrenean coast, was claimed by an anonymous French ecologist group, who said, "We have succeeded in neutralizing machines that are dangerous for the existence of human life. The Harrisburg catastrophe proves once again the dangers of the atomic industry. We have gone into action and we will do whatever is necessary to safeguard from nuclear horrors the life of the French population and the human race." A French government official, however, suggested that the Israeli government, which had stressed the danger of nuclear proliferation of the Iraqi reactors, may have been involved.

April 9, 1979—West Berlin—An explosive charge packed in a fire extinguisher was detonated on the Metropolitan Railroad (S-Bahn) tracks between the stations of Grossgoerschenstrasse and Schoeneberg in the evening. The S-Bahn is administered by the German Democratic Republic.

April 9, 1979—Italy—Juan Paillacar Soto, a twenty-five-year-old Chilean, was arrested by Italian police who suspected him of being a leader of the leftist Revolutionary Action Group.

April 9, 1979—United States—An anonymous individual claiming membership in Black September said a bomb was aboard a Delta Airlines flight carrying 137 passengers from Chicago to Atlanta. A two-hour search at Chicago's O'Hare Airport found no bomb.

April 12, 1979—Turkey—Three masked men firing pistols from a stolen Turkish-made Anadol automobile killed a U.S. Army officer and wounded another before speeding off down an Izmir side street. The attack came at 5 P.M. when the men, in uniform, were walking down the street of Izmir's Alsancak District near the 26 August Gate of Culture Park. Master Sergeant Edward A. Claypool, twenty-three, of Richards, Missouri, who was attached to the Turkish-U.S. Logistics wing of NATO, was killed at the scene. Sergeant Jeffrey P. Vail, twenty-two, of Myrtle Beach, South Carolina, was seriously wounded. The leftist Turkish People's Liberation Army, which had spent eight years underground, claimed credit for the attack. Police instituted a massive manhunt and later found the car in the Jewish cemetery on the old Kemal Pasa Road. Inside the car, police found two empty cartridges and two bullets.

April 15, 1979—Egypt—Police arrested Joseph Salim Abdallah, a Lebanese, upon his arrival at Cairo airport from Beirut and discovered that his suitcase contained explosives similar to those of a colleague who had been arrested on March 16. The Egyptians claimed that Salim was a first lieutenant in the Syrian intelligence service who was attached to the Saiqa office in Beirut. He was to conduct three operations in Egypt. The first was to place explosives in the

Sheraton Hotel, either in the restaurant or the nightclub to be sure of injuring as many guests as possible. He had been given a large sum of money to stay at the hotel and allow his explorations for the operation. He was told that an operative had been sent on this attack, but they had heard nothing further from him after he placed the explosives in an office in a hotel rest room. For his second attack, he was to place explosives in offices in At-Tahrir Square. In the third attack, he was to choose an operation involving the placing of explosives to create fear among the police and public. He was also to contact his colleague to find out why had he not attacked the Egyptian Foreign Ministry. The Egyptians claimed that Salim cooperated with them during his interrogation, providing information on Cuban supervision of Saiqa training and planning.

Egypt later said Salim's real name was 'Ali Samih Najm, who was deputy head of the Saiqa security office in Al-Hamra' in Beirut, under the command of Syrian Captain 'Isam al-Hamawi. Police said he was trained by Abu Salim and his explosives were prepared by Ahmad al-Hallaq. His release was later demanded by terrorists who took over the Egyptian embassy in Ankara on July 13, 1979.

April 15, 1979—Cyprus—Nicosia international airport, which is under U.N. control, was the scene of control tower sabotage, according to Nicosia radio.

April 16, 1979—Lebanon—A bomb went off in the morning in front of the JFK American Center in Beirut, causing structural damage but no casualties. A second bomb did not detonate. The bombing was believed to be a protest of the Egyptian-Israeli peace treaty.

April 16, 1979—Belgium—Palestinian terorists, hoping to take over El Al flight 334 from Tel Aviv via Vienna with 160 passengers at Zaventem Airport in Brussels, threw grenades and conducted a gun battle with police that left a dozen people injured. The El Al passengers were spared by the firm's practice of parking a distance from airline terminals. The terrorists, foiled in their hopes to reach the B707 at 2 P.M., went to a corner of a raised visitors' platform and lobbed a gasoline bomb and a light hand grenade into the arrival area below, injuring five Belgians. Armed with Soviet-made rifles and submachine guns, they then raced into a nearby self-service restaurant, where they shot seven more Belgians in a gun battle. El Al security men and Belgian police shot one of the terrorists in the shoulder and arrested the two terrorists in the restaurant. Police spokesmen said two more terrorists, possibly including a woman, may have escaped in the confusion. One of those arrested was carrying a list of demands showing that the group had planned to take over the plane. Belgian police would not release most of the demands to the press and would say only that the terrorists called for Prime Minister Wilfried Martens to come to the airport and for another plane to take them out of Belgium. Police later began a search of the homes of Palestinian sympathizers in the area.

The two arrested terrorists initially claimed PLO membership, but Naim Khader, the PLO representative in Brussels, denied any knowledge of the terrorists, as did Mahmoud Labadi, PLO spokesman in Beirut. Later a previously unknown Black March Organization claimed credit and demanded the release of the terrorists. Belgian state radio claimed the two captured were from the PFLP, and the press noted that in March, several PLO members spoke of reviving Black September to protest the Egypt-Israeli peace treaty.

The two had traveled to Brussels from Beirut via Paris and stayed in various hotels. They carried apparently forged Iranian, Iraqi, and Lebanese passports. They contacted a woman who aided them, although police were unable to determine if she participated in the attack at the airport. On August 16, Dhaled Dayekh Dokh and Husseini Rad Mahmoud, both from the Israeli-occupied Gaza strip, were sentenced to eight years for attempted murder and for carrying illegal weapons and false identity papers.

April 17, 1979—Rhodesia—An executive jet carrying Gabonese and Malian officials from Gabon to Nairobi, Kenya, made a forced landing at Victoria Falls airport after being shot at by black nationalist guerrillas.

April 19, 1979—Afghanistan—In an attack on an army base, Afghan insurgents killed three Russian advisers.

April 19, 1979—West Germany—The body of Jozo Molos, thirty, a Croatian émigré, was found in the Cologne woods with two bullet holes in the head and chest. He had been imprisoned in West Germany in the early 1970s on charges of planning to assassinate a Yugoslav consul. Stjepan Bilandzic, a Croatian émigré leader, denied that Molos was a member of his group but said that he believed the death was politically motivated and was probably perpetrated by the Yugoslav secret service.

April 19, 1979—Spain—The ETA sent a letter to the Japanese ambassador in Madrid that said, ''The Iberduero company is reported to have sought a credit to finance the nuclear centre of Lemoniz. We suppose that the Japanese financiers know the problems as a whole stemming from the construction of this centre, as well as the powerful opposition of the Basque people to this centre, which involves great uncertainty about its future. . . .The ETA organization will not allow the people's will to be ignored and, consequently, it will use all its military power against the atomic centre in order to stop it from functioning.''

April 19, 1979—Spain—GRAPO claimed credit for a night explosion in the Valencia showroom of a Ford agent. It damaged thirteen cars and blew out windows.

April 19, 1979—Egypt—A parcel from Syria exploded in Cairo's general post office, killing the woman who was handling it and wounding three women and a man. A few days later, the Eagles of the Palestine Revolution, believed to be a cover name for Saiqa, claimed credit for the blast at the Al-'Atabah postal customs office.

Five days later, Egyptian authorities revealed the arrests on March 16 and April 15 of two Saiqa members who were to conduct a bombing campaign in Egypt. Egpytian security officials also discovered that two other operatives, one a woman, had stayed at the Mena House Hotel, where they left a large suitcase filled with clothes and a small suitcase containing a large cigar box packed with explosives. They had fled the country.

April 21, 1979—Northern Ireland—Twenty armed men, members of the IRA and INLA, used five trucks to block a crossroad and take over a freight train that had just crossed the Irish border into County Armagh. An armed man forced the engineer to stop at Kileen Bridge, a few miles from the border. Six or seven men placed five milk containers filled with explosives in the locomotive, set time fuses, and escaped in the hijacked trucks. The explosion blocked the main road and rail links between Northern Ireland and Ireland.

April 24, 1979—Austria—The Eagles of the Palestine Revolution claimed credit for the bombing of a Jewish synagogue in Vienna. PLO representative Husayn in Vienna denied responsibility. Two suspects (see below) were arrested two days later on the German-Austrian border.

April 25, 1979—El Salvador—Panama radio reported that Alfredo Zapata, former chief of the Investigation Department of the National Police and security chief for the U.S. embassy, escaped from an evening attack when two people shot at him as he was entering his San Carlos residence. He jumped to the floor of his vehicle and repelled the attack.

April 25, 1979—Iran—Two women wearing black chadors and armed with Colt 45s were arrested after Iranian authorities received reports of a planned hijacking attempt at Tehran's Mehrabad Airport.

April 26, 1979—West Germany—Two suspected PLO members were arrested at the Passau-Achleiten crossing point on the Austrian-Bavarian border when police searching their rented car found fifty kilograms of explosives, time fuses, and eleven passports with photographs not of them. Bonn authorities believed that the two intended to pass the documents to Palestinians either already in Germany or intending to arrive soon. They initially identified themselves as Lebanese—Beorg Mechal and Salim Sejann—and were later identified as Mohammad Hamadi and Alim Seyaan, both thirty-three. They had planned to bomb an Israeli ship in Hamburg harbor. They were also suspected of having been involved in the April 24 bomb attack on a Jewish synagogue in Vienna. They were held in Munich for trial.

On April 29, two Arabs, both around twenty-five, were arrested on the German-Dutch freeway crossing point at Elten (Lower Rhine). They were driving a French car and had forged Iranian passports for the Passau pair. In July, the Lebanese and Iranian duo were charged with planning attacks on Jewish institutions, refineries, and oil storage depots in West Germany.

During the trial in Straubing, Mohammad Hamadi, thirty-five, of Lebanon, described himself as a Palestinian freedom fighter and said that refusal to carry out his organization's orders would have meant his death. His codefendants— Lebanese Salim, thirty-one, Iranian Mohammad Zahedi, twenty-five, and Rashim Musawi, twenty-five—denied membership in any Palestinian organization. Hamadi said he was to take the explosives from Vienna to Hamburg for transshipment to an Israeli port and that he had not intended to use the explosives in Germany. Salim, now a French citizen, denied any knowledge of the explosives and claimed to be on a business trip. Zahedi said he had been hired by Hamadi to bring a car from Europe to Beirut. Musawi, a geography student, claimed he had met his friend Zahedi in Rome by accident.

On July 20, 1979, the Passau regional court found Hamadi and Salim guilty of having prepared a bombing attack and sentenced them to two and a half years. Zahedi and Musawi were sentenced to four months for forging documents and unlawful entry into the country.

In a related case, the public prosecutor at Berlin's regional court on June 14 indicted five Lebanese, an Algerian, and a German on suspicion of "joint preparation of a crime involving explosives and the unauthorized possession of explosives." Investigations indicated the group had planned to bomb a fuel depot in the Lankwitz suburb. Apparently a three-man PLO commando from Beirut had entered from East Berlin and had been aided by the others.

April 28, 1979—Puerto Rico—Omega-7, an anti-Castro group, claimed credit for shooting Carlos Muniz Varela, twenty-six, a Cuban exile who was president of Varadero Tours, which organized visits to Cuba for San Juan's Cuban community.

April 30, 1979—Rhodesia—Michael Lewy, nineteen, of Alta Loma, California, was killed in a guerrilla ambush in the southwestern Bikita district. A ranch spokesman said he was working as a volunteer at the Devuli Ranch to gain experience in cotton growing and cattle ranching and was due to leave in July.

April 30, 1979—Spain—A homemade bomb exploded outside a Renault showroom in Bilbao, shattering the windows of surrounding buildings. Police blamed Basque separatists.

May 1, 1979—Colombia—The Maoist Popular Liberation Army (EPL) claimed credit for placing a bomb against a wall of the U.S. Marine guard residence in Bogotá, which destroyed a window, two doors, and several windows and injured a U.S. Marine and two Colombian women during the night. Windows of twenty neighboring buildings were shattered.

May 4, 1979—France—Domingo Iturbe Abasolo, an ETA leader, was seriously injured in a noon attack in Biarritz.

May 4, 1979—El Salvador—Members of the Popular Revolutionary Bloc (BPR), the most militant of three student-peasant groups banned by the military government, took over the Costa Rican embassy, where they held Ambassador Julio Esquivel Valverde, a secretary, two servants, and another employee hostage. Three of the attackers were reported injured in the initial assault, although they were armed with automatic weapons. Negotiations for their demands were conducted simultaneously with those for the release of the French embassy employees also held hostage by the BPR (see below). During the night of May 6, all of the Costa Rican embassy hostages escaped while their captors ate. The BPR claimed that the hostages had been evacuated in the face of government threats against their safety. The government did not rush the embassy after the diplomats had left, however, because the grounds were treated as extraterritorial. On May 9, the occupants surrendered after being granted political asylum in Costa Rica. The next day, Costa Rican President Rodrigo Carazo ordered his diplomats out of El Salvador after business attaché Jorge Pacheco and commercial attaché José Antonio Arollo received death threats in the wake of the hostages' escape. The BPR accused the Costa Rican government of deceit during the negotiations.

May 4, 1979—El Salvador—Fourteen men and two women wearing red and yellow masks of the Popular Revolutionary Bloc took over the French embassy. One of the guards at the embassy was injured in the hips, and a Salvadoran servant who was shot was taken to the hospital. The group took hostage Ambassador Michel Dondenne, sixty-two, counselor Jean Duffaud, three secretaries, and a Salvadoran. Meanwhile another BPR group took over the Costa Rican embassy. The two groups demanded the release of five recently arrested dissidents, including members of the BPR. The government denied that the five were in custody. However, the local radio reported that an unofficial government source said that Numa Escobar, BPR political training secretary, and Facundo Guardado, BPR secretary-general, could be released by paying a $15 fine. The president of El Salvador refused to negotiate with "subversives," but left open the possibility of dealing with "honorable" intermediaries. The BPR also asked the captive ambassadors to participate in the negotiations and asked them to publish a communiqué addressed to the world that demanded an end to "oppression" by the military government. It asked the diplomats to submit a report to the U.N. Human Rights Commission and the OAS regarding the situation of imprisoned BPR members, whom they claimed had been tortured.

On May 6, the French and Costa Rican governments offered the captors political asylum but were rebuffed by the BPR members, who said that they acted to obtain the release of their colleagues, not their own asylum. El Salvadoran Foreign Minister José Antonio Rodriguez Porth said his country had agreed to give the dissidents safe conduct out of the country.

On May 7, fifteen labor unions shut down factories for more than two hours in sympathy with the BPR cause. Another group took over the Metropolitan Cathedral in San Salvador. On May 9, El Salvador offered them and the French embassy group amnesty. Several demonstrations took place in support of the captors on May 8. Police opened fire on the crowd on the cathedral steps, killing at least twenty-three persons. A state of siege was declared May 23 following the assassination by left-wing guerrillas of Education Minister Carlos Antonio Herrera-Rebollo. On May 31, foreign diplomats requested a meeting with President Carlos Romero and demanded increased security protection following the murder of Hugo Wey, the Swiss chargé d'affaires.

At the end of the month, the occupations seemed almost ended. However, on May 31, the French embassy group reversed their decision to accept Panamanian asylum and demanded amnesty in their own country, which all along had been denied. That night, a piqued Panamanian Foreign Ministry withdrew its asylum offer and recalled the plane it had sent to fly the dissidents to Panama. Later that night, Mexico offered to break the deadlock by granting asylum to twenty-five occupiers of the French and Venezuelan embassies (the latter having been taken over on May 11). Shortly before the end of the occupations the next day, special French envoy Philippe Cuvillier and Peruvian Ambassador Adelmo Risi met with the leftists on the French embassy steps to work out final details. The French embassy group left at noon on June 1, and Ambassador Dondenne and five other embassy employees appeared ten minutes later. Later that day, a French military DC8 carried twenty-five BPR members, the Panamanian chargé d'affaires, and a French diplomat to Panama, where the dissidents were granted asylum. The next day, the leftists departed for Cuba. On June 2, members of the United Popular Action Front (FAPU) who had taken over the cathedral a second time on June 1 left the building because their colleagues no longer needed their aid.

May 6, 1979—Turkey—A bomb exploded in the rest rooms of the foreign airlines transit lounge at Istanbul's Yesilkoy Airport at 5:20 P.M., causing great damage but no injuries. A second bomb exploded five minutes later in a bus used to transport passengers from the terminal to planes. No injuries were reported.

May 7, 1979—Switzerland—A bomb exploded before dawn at the Spanish embassy in Bern, causing damage but no injuries.

May 11, 1979—El Salvador—According to Agence-France Presse, police shot and killed four members of the People's Revolutionary Bloc at noon who were trying to set fire to a Volkswagen dealership in San Salvador.

May 11, 1979—El Salvador—Nine members of the BPR took over the Venezuelan embassy, holding Ambassador Santiago Ochoa Antich and seven other employees hostage. The group had two semiautomatic pistols, although one of the militants claimed that this was to be a peaceful occupation. One shot was apparently fired by a guard during the takeover, but no injuries were reported. The takeover came two hours after the release by the government of two of the five BPR leaders who had been arrested in April and whose release was demanded by the BPR members who occupied the French and Costa Rican embassies. Ricardo Mena, a student leader, was freed during the night; Facundo Guardado, twenty-four, BPR secretary-general, was ordered released by a judge after two weeks' detention. The group demanded the release of the other three people mentioned by their colleagues in the other embassies, but the government denied holding them. They later demanded the return of three BPR members who had received asylum in Costa Rica after occupying that embassy. According to BPR member Julio Flores, "They did not receive asylum. They are continuously questioned and have no liberty." They next called for the release of four persons arrested on May 8 in front of the national cathedral, vowing, "We will stay here as long as necessary, fortified by the memory of those who died May 8." At least twenty-three students were killed and seventy wounded when police opened fire on the cathedral demonstrators.

Relations between the captors and hostages oscillated between friendly and tense. On May 12, the rebels unloaded their guns and gave the captives their ammunition, and the ambassador told a reporter who was allowed to enter the embassy: "They think Venezuela respects human rights and is a democractic country." However, relations chilled after a tennis ball was thrown into the embassy by BPR members who had left a note on the ball saying that a message previously transmitted in that manner carried instructions for the occupiers. The BPR members searched through the embassy but were unable to locate the first message. When they demanded that the ambassador allow them to look through locked embassy files, he replied that this was Venezuelan property. He later told reporters that this amounted to a humiliation of his country and that he had to escape. This was accomplished through one of several visits by his wife, who smuggled a pistol to Ochoa. The ambassador waved his gun and told his captors that his group had a nonexistent submachine gun. His group escaped through a nearby door and requested more arms from a Salvadoran policeman, who balked. He and four other hostages then climbed to freedom on May 20 through a back window while military attaché Colonel Witemundo Hernandez shouted to distract the captors. Although Hernandez and a few Salvadoran secretaries remained behind to maintain an official presence in the embassy, they too left the embassy that midnight.

A special Venezuelan envoy who was sent to San Salvador to negotiate his ambassador's release returned home on May 20 after Venezuela agreed to a police plan to cut off electricity, water, and food and starve the terrorists. Ambassador Ochoa returned to his embassy the next day and attempted to talk the occupiers into surrender. Venezuela guaranteed their safety as long as they stayed inside the embassy or agreed to asylum. Ochoa later asked for the Red Cross or the archbishop's offices to negotiate with those inside the embassy.

On May 22, students sympathizing with the occupiers attempted to break a government barricade and bring food to the embassy. Police fired on the group, killing fourteen youths and injuring twenty-two others, while themselves sustaining no casualties. Although police pointed out several small-caliber pistols lying near some of the bodies, witnesses said that neither the positions where the guns lay nor their clean condition corresponded to the bloody hands of the dead. In response to this violent turn of events, Venezuela sent three military aircraft to carry home fifty Venezuelan residents of El Salvador. On May 24, Venezuela requested papal mediation. Later that day, the Federation of University Centers of the Central University of Venezuela took over the El Salvadoran embassy in Caracas to protest events in El Salvador. On May 28, the government agreed to a Venezuelan request to bring food to the occupiers. On June 1, the siege ended by an agreement tied to the release of those held hostage in the French embassy. The Venezuelan embassy occupiers joined their colleagues in flying to asylum in Cuba.

May 11, 1979—Turkey—Four leftists in a speeding car fired machine guns at seven to nine American enlisted men awaiting a bus in Atakoy, an Istanbul suburb, to take them to Cakmakli's NATO ammunition depot. Corporal Thomas Mosley, twenty-one, was killed and Dwight Muir suffered light wounds. The Marxist Leninist Armed Propaganda Unit, a faction of the Turkish People's Liberation Front, claimed credit, saying that the base protected the "interests of American imperialism and its local collaborators."

May 13, 1979—Honduras—Yolanda Cosse Quiroz, Costa Rican consul in San Pedro Sula, was severely injured when one blond man and a swarthy man beat her unconscious and then robbed her in her office. The attackers, who had Nicaraguan accents, had requested documents to enter her country, claiming that they had fled Nicaragua because of its political violence. They painted slogans on her office walls, "Somoza yes, dirty Costa Ricans no." According to Panamanian radio, she believed the two men were Nicaraguan agents displeased with Costa Rica's views of the Somoza regime.

May 15, 1979—El Salvador—Four of five bombs planted against the doors of the Costa Rican consulate in Santa Ana by the Popular Liberation Forces exploded, causing considerable damage but no casualties.

May 15, 1979—El Salvador—Eight members of the FPL attacked revenue police guarding the South African embassy, seized the rifles of two slain policemen, and escaped in two cars.

May 18, 1979—Nicaragua—Twenty political opposition leaders, two priests, several labor leaders, and several newsmen received anonymous death threats by telephone and in a printed leaflet. The newsmen were identified as Agustin Fuentes, Latin-Reuter correspondent; Juan Maltez of Associated Press; Filadelfo Martinez of Acan-EFE; Danilo Aguirre, subdirector of *La Prensa*; Manuel Montalvan, Rodolfo Tampia Molina, José Esteban Quezada, Manuel Espinosa Henriquez, and Aaron Sanchez.

May 18, 1979—United States—An 11:57 P.M. explosion smashed a dozen windows and damaged a door in the rear of the building housing part of the Cuban Interests Section in Washington, D.C. Police issued a lookout for two men seen running from the area. An hour later, Omega-7 claimed responsibility. No injuries were reported.

May 23, 1979—United States—Zvonko Simac, twenty-five, and Mario Rudela, twenty-one, Croatian nationalists, were killed when a pipe bomb they were transporting accidentally exploded in their pickup truck in San Pedro, Los Angeles.

May 29, 1979—Colombia—Two men kidnapped Carolina Villegas Londono, nine, daughter of Diego Villegas, Bolivian consul in Medellín, while she was waiting for her morning school bus in front of her home. On July 15, it was reported that the kidnappers were demanding 20 million pesos ($500,000) ransom.

May 29, 1979—Turkey—A powerful explosion shattered windows of the Turkish-American Cultural Association in Ankara but caused no injuries.

May 30, 1979—El Salvador—Hugo Wey, forty-nine, commercial attaché and chargé d'affaires of the Swiss embassy, was killed by gunmen who hemmed in his car in the San Salvador suburb of Escalon as he drove to work. Police speculated that the attackers had intended to kidnap him but shot him in the temple when he attempted to flee. No group claimed responsibility, although two weeks previously the FPL had ''declared war'' on diplomats.

June 1, 1979—United States—A bomb was sent through the mail to a former Nazi SS officer living in Paterson, New Jersey. Similar bombs were sent to American Nazis in Arlington, Virginia, Cicero and Chicago, Illinois, and Lincoln, Nebraska. The International Committee Against Nazism and the Jewish Action Movement phoned wire services to assert that bombs had been sent. The Associated Press was told that "this is only a warning. . . .There'll be more tomorrow."

June 1, 1979—Greece—An Athens court convicted ten people, including a U.S. citizen, for forming a right-wing terrorist organization and participating in thirty-four bombings. Sentences ranged from ten months to life. A junior army officer was acquitted. The Greek-American, Dimitrios Koundanis, twenty-nine, who worked at a U.S. Navy communications base in Greece, received three and a half years for possessing arms and participating in a terrorist group.

June 2, 1979—Turkey—David Goodman, twenty-six, of Fort Lauderdale, who had been running a private English-language school in Adana, was shot to death by two gunmen when he answered his apartment doorbell. The killers fled on foot after the morning attack. No group claimed responsibility.

June 5, 1979—Nicaragua—The FSLN captured Guatemalan military attaché Colonel Ruben Castaneda, forty-six, near the city of León as he was driving to Managua from Guatemala. On June 13, he sent a letter to President Somoza asking him to relinquish power. He was released to the Costa Rican government at the Nicaraguan border on June 14.

June 8, 1979—United Kingdom—Six letter bombs exploded at Birmingham post offices, injuring five persons.

June 8, 1979—Australia—A Trans-Australia Airlines DC9 flying thirty-seven passengers (including two children) from Melbourne was hijacked by a mentally unbalanced, red-haired, bearded man with an Irish accent who held a semiautomatic shotgun to the head of the pilot. After ninety minutes on the ground at Brisbane's Eagle Farm Airport, the hijacker was overpowered when a stewardess knocked the shotgun from his hands, three stewardesses and two pilots rushed him, and some of the one hundred policemen surrounding the plane burst in. No injuries were reported.

June 11, 1979—United States—Delta Airlines flight 1061, an L1011 Tristar carrying 195 passengers and a crew of 12 from New York to Miami and Fort Lauderdale, was hijacked as it passed near Wilmington, North Carolina, at 7 P.M. The plane landed safely in Havana at 8:35 P.M. Cuban President Fidel

Castro arrived at 10:35 P.M. at José Martí International Airport to supervise the arrest of the hijacker, who was identified as Eduardo Guerra Jimenez, thirty-seven, the former Cuban air force pilot who flew a Cuban MIG17 on October 5, 1969, to Homestead Air Force Base and landed it near President Carter's plane. He was expected to be tried in Cuba.

June 12, 1979—Spain—A bomb set by the ETA killed a worker at the Lemoniz nuclear power plant.

June 13, 1979—Guyana—Two bomb explosions injured one person at the black-oriented House of Israel church in Guyana. Church officials blamed the attack on the opposition Peoples Progressive party, a charge denied by its leader, Cheddi Jagan. The church, which preaches that Jesus was black and that blacks "are the real Jews and God's chosen people," is run by Rabbi Edward Washington, who fled Cleveland, Ohio, after being convicted of extortion and sentenced to five years in jail in 1972 when he was known as David Hill.

June 14, 1979—United Kingdom—Three more letter bombs were found at the central sorting office at Birmingham. The letters were addressed to civil servants. The IRA was believed responsible.

June 15, 1979—El Salvador—William Rocha, the Nicaraguan manager of National Cash Register, was kidnapped when he left his office in downtown San Salvador. He was released at dawn on June 27.

June 16, 1979—Israel—Authorities arrested two U.N. officers after their car smashed into an Israeli car on the Jerusalem highway. Police found two suitcases stuffed with explosives, ammunition, and three submachine guns. On June 22, Lieutenant Colonal Alfred Gom, a Nigerian serving with the U.N. Interim Force in Lebanon, admitted to smuggling weapons from south Lebanon for the Palestine Liberation Organization.

June 16, 1979—West Germany—The Robert E. D. Straker Commando of the Territorial Resistance Army claimed credit for leaving a five-liter can of combustible liquid, which burst into flames in the Aeroflot office in Frankfurt. The fire set off a sprinkler system and caused water damage of 30,000 deutsche marks. The group's communiqué number one, bearing the code word Delta, said it would continue its "struggle against left-wing and right-wing extremist parties, communists, fascists, left-wing and right-wing terrorists."

June 20, 1979—Lebanon—Adil Wasfi (alias Khalid al-'Iraqi), an Iraqi national and deputy editor in chief of the *Filastin Ath-Thawrah* ("Palestine

Revolution,'' the PLO news magazine), was assassinated in Beirut in a morning attack. Iraq denied involvement. *Al-'Arab*, a Qatari newspaper, reported on July 1 that Palestinian security forces had arrested most of the eighty-one members of a group that had carried out the murder.

June 20, 1979—United States—Nikola Kavaja, forty-five, Serbian nationalist and mechanic from Paterson, New Jersey, hijacked American Airlines flight 293, a B727 that had taken off from New York's La Guardia Airport at 11:16 A.M. with 127 passengers and 8 crew members for Chicago. Kavaja took over the plane at 12:29 P.M. by claiming to have dynamite strapped to his body and also alleging to have an accomplice on board. He demanded the release of Reverend Stojilko Kavejic, forty-three, a Serbian Orthodox priest, who, together with the hijacker and four other Serbs, were arrested in November 1978 on charges of bombing and conspiracy to murder. The hijacker initally demanded the release of Kavejic and a safe flight to Peru, which he later changed to Johannesburg, South Africa. Kavaja had been freed on $350,000 bond and was on his way to Chicago to be sentenced for his part in the 1975 bombing of the Yugoslav consulate in Chicago, for which the group had been convicted on May 24. Facing sentence with the pair were Nikola Zivovic, fifty-two, of Chicago; Rados Stevlic, forty, of suburban Wayne; Zivotije Savic of suburban Downers Grove; and Bosko Radonjic of New York City. The last two pleaded guilty, while the others were convicted on bombing and conspiracy charges. They all belonged to SEPO, a Serbian acronym for Freedom for the Serbian Fatherland.

After landing in Chicago, Kavaja released the passengers and five of the crew members. Among the released passengers was Howard Morland, a journalist who had been in the news when the U.S. government filed suit to stop publication in *Progressive* magazine of his article on how to manufacture a nuclear bomb. Kavaja's lawyer, David Boeshich, then boarded the plane and accompanied him to New York, where they boarded a larger B707. They flew to Ireland's Shannon Airport, where Kavaja ended his twenty-two-hour odyssey by surrendering. He was deported from Ireland on June 22 and sent back on the same plane, with five Irish police guarding him. On June 22, he was sentenced to twenty years for the 1975 incident. On November 9, he was convicted of air piracy and bail-jumping.

June 21, 1979—Gabon—Robert Bossard, French managing director of Diesel-Gabon, and his wife were killed when a bomb exploded in their car after he turned on the ignition.

June 22, 1979—Israel—Vasco Mariz, the Brazilian ambassador, received an anonymous telegram threatening him with death after Brazil's rejection of an extradition request for Nazi war criminal Gustav Franz Wagner.

June 24, 1979—Afghanistan—A member of a Soviet advisory mission was reported killed in Kabul during weekend clashes between armed Hazara tribesmen and government forces.

June 25, 1979—Belgium—General Alexander M. Haig, Jr., fifty-four, supreme commander of allied forces in Europe, escaped anassassination attempt when a bomb went off a split second too late. The attack came as he was being chauffeured to work in his black Mercedes 600 sedan. His convoy was going over a fifty-foot bridge off a secondary road in the town of Obourg about halfway between his Casteau, Mons, headquarters and his home when a remote-controlled land mine exploded. The blast tore a hole ten feet wide and three feet deep in the bridge and showered concrete blocks onto the roof of a follow car, injuring two Belgian and one U.S. security men. Between one hundred and three hundred pounds of TNT or plastic explosive damaged the exhaust and trunk of Haig's car, which was nonetheless operable. The occupants of Haig's car, as well as those in the lead car, were uninjured. After checking on the fate of his security guards, Haig went on to work. When asked if his presidential aspirations were linked to the blast, he replied, "I don't think I have quite enough support in the United States at the moment to justify such drastic action. . . .They say when you get through Monday morning, the rest of the week is easy. So I am optimistic. . . .I thought I should go out with a bang, but this is too much."

Police investigators found a wire cable leading 150 to 200 yards away from the bridge that had been covered by an inch of earth. Grass had grown back to hide any trace of activity. The detonator consisted of four nine-volt batteries taped together and activated by a household switch. Police also found a construction worker's helmet, a thermos bottle, and a walkie-talkie. No fingerprints were found, and there was no indication where the materials were purchased. Belgian police questioned several Mons leftists, drivers in the area, and NATO personnel but developed no leads. They were aided in the investigation by NATO military security and French, West German, and British police. Several witnesses, including General Haig, said they saw two motorcyclists leaving the scene, and the Belgian news service Belga reported that a motorcyclist was arrested at Ath, about twelve miles away.

Several organizations claimed credit for the attack, including the Julien Lahaut Brigade, named after a Belgian Communist who was murdered after World War II; Revenge and Freedom; and the Andreas Baader Commando of the Red Army Faction. The Baader Commando's letter said, "We made a technical error; the general's car was traveling at a speed of two meters per tenth of second, and this was the amount of time it took to manually detonate the twenty kg of explosives. As a result, the explosion occurred right between the general's car and that of the escort vehicle which was following it." According to *Der Spiegel*, Hamburg security experts believed that the terrorists had intended to kill British NATO General Jack Harman and suggested that the Irish Republican Army was responsible. The IRA and ETA had used mines under cars in previous assassination attempts. General Haig stated that he had known for a year that he was a target of a group he declined to name. One military source said that the Italian Red Brigades had sent a threat against him. Despite these threats, Haig said that his limousine was not armor plated. However, he did take the precaution of using a variety of routes to work.

Haig had taken over as commander of the Supreme Headquarters of the Allied Presence in Europe (SHAPE) in December 1974 after serving as President Nixon's White House chief of staff. He was scheduled to retire five days later after thirty-one years of military service. He was replaced by outgoing army chief of staff General Bernard Rogers, fifty-seven, who had recently announced that the army planned to establish a 110,000-member strike force to respond to crises in the Middle East. This led several observers to suggest that a Palestinian group may have been responsible for the Haig attack.

June 25, 1979—Iran—An unidentified man phoned the Revolutionary Guards to warn that a bomb was in a suitcase aboard a Pan Am B747 scheduled to depart Tehran's Mehrabad International Airport. A two-hour search conducted by French and Iranian police located no bomb.

June 26, 1979—Mexico—Reports of an attack on the shah of Iran's residence in Cuernavaca were denied. A few weeks before, Iranian Ayatollah Khalkhali, believed to be chief of the Revolutionary Courts, had promised a reward for the future assassin of the deposed shah. A helicopter pilot reported that he had taken Reza Pahlevi, nineteen, son of the shah, for a ride and that the craft's motors may have been mistaken for gunfire.

June 26, 1979—Afghanistan—An Iranian newspaper reported that Afghan Moslem rebels captured two Soviet advisers in Herat.

June 26, 1979—Pakistan—Two French diplomats were pulled from their car and beaten near an area believed by observers to be the site of Pakistan's first uranium enrichment plant. Ambassador Pol le Gourrierce lost a tooth and First Secretary Jean Forlot was beaten unconscious and suffered a fractured skull.

June 29, 1979—West Germany—The Robert E. D. Straker Commando of the Territorial Resistance Army claimed credit for planting a bomb that failed to go off in the Soviet Intourist information office in Frankfurt-am-Main. The terrorists scattered leaflets at the scene.

June 30, 1979—Iran—Twelve armed individuals attacked the runway of Tehran's Mehrabad Airport and stopped a plane from leaving for London when the son of Ayatollah Montazeri, Mohammad Montazeri, and the son's friend, Asghar Jamal Fard, were prevented from leaving the country because their passports had not been renewed. The duo asked to leave or for their luggage to be returned. Their second request was granted. On July 1, the two students left on a Syrian plane for Damascus. The ayatollah, in a nationally broadcast statement, denounced his son for holding the 150 passengers on the first Syrian plane hostage.

June 30, 1979—Puerto Rico—Igoberto Gonzalez Sanches, forty-six, a Cuban key-punch operator living in Puerto Rico, brandished a bottle of rum and took over Eastern Airlines flight 932, a B747 flying 293 passengers and 13 crew members from San Juan to Miami, and demanded to go to Cuba. He was overpowered by two male flight attendants and two first-class passengers and was handed over to FBI agents when the jet landed on schedule in Miami. A federal judge set bond at $500,000.

July 1, 1979—Nicaragua—The FSLN kidnapped Colin Avery, an engineer from Brighton, England, while visiting a friend in Jinotepe, twenty-five miles north of Matagalpa.

July 2, 1979—France—Shortly after midnight, the engineer of the Paris to Madrid train *Puerta del Sol* slowed down when he noticed tires burning on the tracks. Members of the group Basque Justice, possibly a cover name for the ETA, fired 11.43 caliber bullets from machine pistols at the train for a minute and then fled. No injuries were reported. Fifteen bullet marks were found on the front coaches and seven empty 9-mm cartridges were recovered 2.5 miles south of Saint-Jean-de-Luz in the French Basque region. The previous week, the ETA had warned France that it would attack its representatives in the Basque country. Paris radio reported a 30 percent drop in French tourists crossing the border.

July 3, 1979—Spain—A bomb exploded in the Bilbao offices of the French Citroen auto firm, causing serious damage but no injuries.

July 5, 1979—Spain—ETA was blamed for bombing a Madrid branch of the National Bank of Paris, causing extensive damage but no injuries.

July 5, 1979—Belgium—A bomb exploded on the sixteenth floor of an Antwerp office building, damaging the British consulate and a Swissair office but causing no injuries. The blast shattered windows, spraying glass onto the Avenue de France below. The West German consulate is located two floors below.

July 6, 1979—Israel—The Palestine Liberation Organization claimed credit for planting a bomb in a grove near the U.N. mission in East Jerusalem. It wounded three French tourists who had gotten off a bus to take pictures.

July 6, 1979—France—A bomb exploded in a Paris underground parking lot, destroying the car of Beate and Serge Klarsfeld, the latter the chairman of the Jewish Association for the Condemnation of Nazi War Criminals, who two days before had applauded the West German Parliament's decision to continue prosecution of Nazis.

July 8, 1979—France—The Avengers of the Armenian Genocide bombed the Paris offices of Turkish Airlines, the Turkish Tourism Information Office, and the Turkish labor attaché's office, causing material damage but no injuries. A fourth bomb later exploded at the Paris OECD Turkish Bureau. The group said, ''With these explosions we are keeping the world aware of the existence of the Armenian people. We demand that the Turkish government—which is occupying our country and is an extension of the Ottoman Empire—stand by its responsibilities and return the Armenian lands to their true owners.''

July 9, 1979—Tunisia—A Global International Airways B707 hired by a Brussels firm, Young Cargo Airlines, to fly Red Cross supplies from Beirut to San José, Costa Rica, was diverted to Tunisia's Bizerta military airfield. A spokesman for the Kansas-based firm said the plane had been hijacked for a PLO gunrunning mission on behalf of the Nicaraguan FSLN. Three Palestinians were reported on board the plane. The pilot became suspicious and gave an excuse for landing at the civilian Tunis-Carthage airport, where the plane was placed under police guard. Three of the four crew members were taken to the U.S. embassy in Tunis. A representative of the chartering company was also reported on board the plane.

July 10, 1979—West Germany—Irish terrorists were blamed for setting off three bombs at the officers' mess of the Twenty-sixth Field Regiment and the sergeants' mess of the Second Field Regiment in Dortmund, which caused minor damage and no injuries.

July 10, 1979—Costa Rica—Several gunmen fired from a Chevrolet Nova in a morning attack on the Nicaraguan embassy, wounding two people, including the Nicaraguan consul, Santamaria. The person driving the car was arrested.

July 13, 1979—El Salvador—The United Popular Action Front threw stones and small homemade bombs at the U.S. embassy during the afternoon, breaking windows.

July 13, 1979—Turkey—Shortly after the morning rush hour, four Palestinian members of the Red Eagles of the Palestinian Revolution took over the Egyptian embassy in Ankara. The group was believed to be a Saiqa terrorist arm. The attack began when a yellow Mercedes drove up to the embassy. Four men armed with grenades and submachine guns jumped out and shot and killed the two Turkish policemen guarding the entrance, while a fifth attacker drove away. They then shot off the lock of the main gate and rushed onto the grounds. They threw two bombs and fired on Egyptian policemen, wounding at least two of them. They then entered the embassy and took Ambassador Ahmed Kamal Ulama, fifty-five, the military attaché, eleven Egyptians, and seven Turkish employees hostage. A Turkish policeman and the embassy's Turkish coffee boy managed to escape during the confusion of the attack. Approximately a thousand Turkish riot police, detectives with automatic weapons, elite troops, and sharpshooters surrounded the embassy, but the terrorists managed to hold off the authorities' armored cars by firing at them through the windows.

The group demanded the release from Egyptian jails of Ibrahim Dayi and Abdullah Joseph Salim, two Eagles who had been arrested separately at Cairo airport for transporting explosives and planning to conduct a wave of bombings in Egpyt. They demanded that Turkey recognize the PLO and sever relations with Egypt and Israel, condemn "American imperialism," and provide bus transportation to the airport where a plane would take them and their hostages to safety in an undisclosed Arab country. Iran said it would not allow such a plane to land at Tehran or any other Iranian airport. The group threatened to kill all of their hostages by blowing up the embassy but let several deadlines pass during negotiations handled by Hasan Fehmi Gunes, the Turkish interior minister.

The PLO disavowed the attack. Abdul Muhssen Abu Mayzar, PLO spokesman in Damascus, said, "We have nothing to do with this operation, nor do any of the organizations affiliated with the PLO or its national council." Mahmoud Lebadi, PLO spokesman in Beirut, claimed that Yasir Arafat's group was not involved. Egypt, however, held the PLO responsible and vowed to retaliate against those believed involved. It later said that it would not crack down on the Palestinian community in Egypt. Several Cairo newspapers claimed that Libyan President Qaddafi and Syrian President Assad had planned the operation.

Egypt gave Turkey permission to storm the embassy but requested that all peaceful means first be exhausted. Turkish military authorities were reported to be pressing for an attack, but Prime Minister Bulent Ecevit refused to give such an order.

Egypt refused to release the jailed terrorists and announced that they had been sentenced to life imprisonment at hard labor. Egyptian Prime Minister Mustafa Khalil said the gunmen wanted to "liquidate them physically because of the full confessions they made about the Eagles group.'' They reportedly told the Turkish ambassador they feared for their lives if released.

The terrorists released a Turkish secretary, apparently with a message for the authorities, a few hours after seizing the embassy. Just before midnight they accepted food and aspirins.

The following day saw a series of escape attempts, some successful. At 5:30 A.M., two Egyptians fled through the back and front doors to safety. They were identified as Ismail Mohammed Abel Khalil, the commercial attaché, and Halife Afifi Ced Ibrahim, an administrative assistant in the commercial office. Two Turkish policemen next tried to escape, but one was hit by gunfire. A policeman outside the embassy was wounded when he tried to help the two to safety. The gunmen were apparently also unaware of the presence of two Egyptian employees in a back room. When the guerrillas began searching the embassy, the employees crawled onto a third-floor window ledge. Hasan Cemal, a chauffeur, slipped and fell, landing on his head. He later died of brain injuries. Mohammed Ali Abdullah survived the sixty-foot jump with two broken legs and broken ribs. Police trained fire hoses on the windows to prevent terrorist gunfire while they rescued the escaping hostages.

Later in the day, Turkey accepted a PLO offer to mediate. However, Lebanon refused to allow a Turkish Airlines plane, scheduled to fly the mediators led by Abu Firas to Ankara, to land. The four PLO mediators and their two bodyguards drove from Beirut to Damascus, where they were picked up by the plane. Accompanied by a Libyan embassy official, three of the PLO members entered the embassy by a back door that afternoon and talked to the gunmen for twenty minutes. They returned in the evening and obtained the release of three women hostages—an Egyptian diplomat and two Turkish aides. The PLO mediators spent the night talking to the terrorists as tension around the building eased. At 8 A.M. on July 15, the terrorists freed unharmed the remaining nine of the original seventeen hostages and surrendered to police. They waved clenched fists and shouted, ''Long live the Palestinian revolution,'' and brought the ambassador and some of his staff to a balcony, where they had him wave a victory gesture. Turkey and Egypt claimed that no concessions had been made to the terrorists.

Prime Minister Ecevit sent a message of thanks to Yasir Arafat and announced that the PLO would be allowed to open an Ankara office in a few weeks. Permission to open the office had been provisionally granted three years previously but was stalled over reports of Palestinian training of Turkish leftists. Ecevit also thanked the ambassadors of Iraq, Libya, Kuwait, Syria, and Saudi Arabia for the ''excellent example of international cooperation.''

The terrorists were taken in two autos to a Marmara chalet that had once been Kemal Ataturk's residence and now served as a Foreign Ministry guesthouse. After being questioned there, they were taken to a security center. They were identified as Nirvan Kibanu, born in Damascus in 1955; Husayn Sulayman

Abdallah, born in Damascus in 1956; Muhammad Abu Zera, born in Darha, Syria, in 1960; and Mustafa Bitayti, born in Beirut in 1960. They were indicted on July 28 by the Ankara martial law comand military tribunal for carrying out hostile acts aimed at damaging relations between Turkey and Egypt; of premeditated murder; smuggling firearms into the country; smuggling, possessing, and using bombs; threatening the liberty of more than one person; and other armed acts. On October 25, a military court sentenced the four Palestinians to two death sentences each for killing the two Turkish guards. Defense lawyers said they would appeal the death sentences, which must also be approved by Parliament, and could be commuted to life imprisonment. Five Turks were convicted as accomplices, and were given sentences ranging from six months to twenty years. Two PLO members, one who served as mediator— Abu Selim and Abu Taleb—were said to have been involved in the preparation and planning of the attack. Some observers remained skeptical regarding the terrorists' fate, recalling that the two Palestinians who had attacked Yesilkoy Airport in August 1976 had recently escaped from jail and had been reported in Lebanon.

Police investigations disclosed that the terrorists had carried forged passports. Some of them had flown to Istanbul from Damascus, while the rest crossed the Turkey-Syrian border. On August 7, Ankara radio reported the arrest of Omer Faruk Erden, owner of an Istanbul farm, and Sukru Akbayrak, Hulusi Caglar, Nurettin Yildiz, Halit Adil Zayit, Isik Cetinli, and Ferit Yogurtcu for assisting the Palestinian raiders. In a police search of the home where the individuals were arrested, authorities found a Kalashnikov rifle, 20 knives, 150 rounds of ammunition, a bulletproof vest, and two hand radio receivers. One of those arrested was a woman.

July 15, 1979—Costa Rica—In a nighttime attack, unidentified gunmen fired four or five shots from a speeding auto at the San José residence of U.S. Ambassador Marvin Weissman, causing no injuries. Weissman's family was away on vacation. One of the bullets struck a window of the ambassador's daughter's room.

July 16, 1979—Lebanon—The Eagles of the Palestinian Revolution threatened Turkish embassy personnel if their imprisoned colleagues in Ankara were harmed. After the Turkish ambassador in Beirut contacted the PLO, Palestinian guards were sent to the embassy.

July 18, 1979—Nicaragua—Former members of Nicaragua's National Guard commandeered four planes at Managua airport and forced the pilots to fly them and their relatives to safety. A four-engine jet owned by the Miami-based Groth Air Services flew 147 refugees, including five Americans, to Miami after the Guard troops told the crew, ''You don't leave Nicaragua without taking these people or we'll shoot the plane down.'' The plane had carried ten thousand pounds of medical supplies to Managua that morning and was scheduled to return with a load of beef. A guardsman said, ''Your beef today is going to be on the hoof.'' A Red Cross DC8 flew 150 Nicaraguans, including National Guardsmen and their wives and children, to Guatemala City. An Electra and a DC9 belonging to the British-Nicaraguan Red Cross were diverted to San José, Costa Rica.

July 18, 1979—Guatemala—Vice-Foreign Minister Alfonso Lima, sixty-four, was kidnapped by the Rebel Armed Forces (FAR) while he was being driven by his chauffeur, Miguel Angel Escobar Ochoa, from his home to the national palace. The group submitted its demads to the government through the Costa Rican embassy. It called for the release of two FAR members—Oscar Ballesteros and Julio Cesar Verdugo Valenzuela—and a peasant who had been arrested a month ago. The government's spokesman, Donaldo Alverez Ruiz, claimed that the FAR members were not in jail and refused to negotiate with the terrorists. The group later demanded suspension of vehicle searches and called upon Lima's family and the government to arrange for the distribution of a FAR communiqué to the local news media. The government complied. The group next delivered what it claimed was a letter from Lima in which he resigned and blamed the government for prolonging his captivity. He was released in Guatemala City on August 3 and said that he had been pressured into signing the document and intended to stay in his job.

July 19, 1979—Finland—Following a three-hour gun battle, police at Kemi airport slightly wounded and overpowered a potential hijacker. Earlier the man had shot and wounded a woman in Haparanda, Sweden, fifteen miles away.

July 20, 1979—Chile—A plane carrying Uruguayan Foreign Minister Adolfo Folle home after a five-day official visit returned to Santiago's Pudahuel Airport after receipt of a bomb threat.

July 20, 1979—United States—Ronald Rimerman, thirty-six, a biochemist from Portland, Oregon, hijacked United Airlines flight 320 carrying 118 passengers, four flight attendants, and three crewmen from Denver to Omaha by claiming to have a bomb and demanding to go to Havana. Upon landing in Omaha, he allowed all but the three crewmen to leave. FBI agents boarded the plane and attempted to talk to him, but he refused to negotiate and would communicate only with the crewmen. Three FBI agents overpowered him in a brief scuffle and escorted him from the B727 two and a half hours after it landed. He had boarded a plane in Portland and transferred to the United flight in Denver. He was not armed.

July 24, 1979—Turkey—A bomb exploded in the Istanbul offices of the U.S. Wells Fargo Bank, causing damage but no injuries. The Revolutionary Left claimed credit. The bank had been involved in a controversial loan of $125 million to Turkey, secured against various Turkish agricultural exports. The government was forced to repeal the agreement following accusations that it was mortgaging the country's products.

July 25, 1979—France—Zuhair Muhsen, forty-three, chief of the Palestinian guerrilla organization Saiqa (Thunderbolt) and head of the PLO's military department, was assassinated at 1 A.M. as he was returning to his luxury fourth-floor apartment in Cannes' Gray d'Albion Hotel after an evening at the Palm Beach Casino. While his wife held the door open, a man rushed out from a service stairway and fired a shot into his head from six feet away. Police were searching for two men who fled the scene, described as looking European or Arabic. Muhsen underwent surgery an hour later at Saint Roch Hospital in Nice. He died the next day when life support systems were switched off at 4:30 P.M. by brain surgeon Jean Duplay, who pronounced the case hopeless.

Speculation quickly arose to the identity of the killers. The PLO blamed Israeli intelligence and its agents, a euphemism for Egypt after the signing of the Egypt-Israel peace treaty. Saiqa blamed the Camp David accords. The PLO sent a four-man team, composed of Muhsen's brother Majid, Abu az-Za'im, Muhammad Daghman, and Abu as-Sa'ud, to France to investigate. Muhammad Shihadah, a minor Palestinian guerrilla, died in al-Jinah, Lebanon, when fighting broke out after Fatah and Saiqa blamed each other for the assassination. Cairo newspapers said the killing could be due to "corruption by the Baathists and evil rulers among the Palestinian organizations so as to dominate them and use them in serving the Baathist purposes and objectives." Other observers claimed that there was Iraqi opposition to Muhsen, who had recently spoken against Syria's proposed union with Iraq. On July 29, *La Suisse*, a Geneva newspaper, received a typewritten letter in poor French from a group claiming to be disaffected PLO members who killed Muhsen because he "cold-bloodedly risked the life of all other Palestinians."

On August 20, Geneva police arrested Muhsin Jarudi, twenty-two, a Lebanese student, in connection with the murder. Shawqi Armali, the PLO's deputy observer at the U.N. facilities in Geneva, requested the Swiss to hand him over or allow the PLO to interrogate him. France and Syria made similar requests through Interpol.

Muhsen was born on the West Bank in 1936. He joined the Syrian Baath party in 1953 and the Syrian-backed Saiqa organization in 1968. He had been a math teacher and had graduated from Lebanese University with a political science degree. He rose to leadership positions within the PLO and was a member of the fifteen-man executive committee. He arrived in France secretly on a false passport on July 20 after leading a delegation to the African Summit

Conference in Monrovia, Liberia. His killing took place during a PLO diplomatic offensive in Western Europe, including secret meetings between Farouk Kaddoumi, the PLO foreign minister, and French Foreign Minister Jean François-Poncet in Paris.

July 25, 1979—Bangladesh—Nazrul Islam, an unemployed Bangladeshi in his early twenties, rushed from the rear of a Bangladesh Airlines Fokker Friendship F27 with a knife and pistol and forced the pilot to land at Calcutta's Dum Dum Airport. Speaking English and Bengali, he pretended to have two accomplices and threatened to blow up the plane, its thirty-nine passengers, and four crewmen if he was not given $1 million and another plane to fly to an undisclosed destination. He released three passengers, including Mrs. Mahfuza Khatoon, thirty, wife of a Bangladeshi atomic scientist, and her ten-week-old baby. Three more passengers escaped by jumping from the plane after a fire broke out during attempts to repair the air conditioning system. Passengers were asked to stack their valuables near the flight deck and to remain seated, with their seat belts on. All of the passengers were Bangladeshis, save one Japanese tourist. When food and drink were brought on board, paramilitary police surrounded the plane. The hijacker threatened to commit suicide but later gave up after holding the plane for ten hours. The plane had been on a domestic flight between Jessore, southwest Bangladesh, and Dacca. Police later discovered that Islam's gun was a toy and that no explosives were on board.

July 25, 1979—Spain—Spanish police raided a GRAPO safe house in Madrid and found plans to kidnap or kill a high-ranking U.S. Air Force officer in the Royal Oaks military housing community. Police arrested Alfonso Rodriguez Garcia, twenty, who confessed to twenty killings and Maria del Carmen Lopez-Anguita, twenty-one, who confessed to fourteen since joining GRAPO late last year. They were arrested in a taxi en route to a meeting with their chief to discuss who the target—preferably the highest-ranking officer—was to be. The group had surveilled the Americans at least six times in the last six months and had compiled a map of the area, which police also discovered. The couple were trying to make final indentification of the officers' rank badges before going into operation. Police also found an armaments cache, including several automatic weapons and a time bomb in a briefcase. The couple was accused of being responsible for bombing a Madrid cafeteria on May 29. They said they were lieutenants of José Maris Sanchez Casas, believed to be GRAPO's leader. Two of their group were still at large, according to police.

July 27, 1979—Netherlands—Two Moluccan suspects arrested during police searches for passports stolen from the Groningen town hall were found to be planning to kidnap Prime Minister Andreas van Agt and other public figures.

July 29, 1979—Spain— ETA bombs went off in Madrid's two rail stations and at the airport, killing 5 and wounding 113 at 1 P.M. , half an hour after a caller sent a warning. The bomb at Barajas International Airport killed one person and injured at least 9 others, including 2 U.S. tourists, Eugene de Matteo, sixty-three, of San Francisco, and his wife, Terese, sixty-one, who were waiting for a San Francisco-bound flight. At the Charmartin railway station, a Danish tourist was killed and several others were injured. The third bomb went off at Atocha rail station, killing 2 and injuring several. A communiqué sent to Agence-France Presse in Paris warned that other bombs had been planted in Spanish tourist regions and would be set off if Spain did not return Basque prisoners held in Soria to the Basque area.

August 1979—Mozambique—According to the Associated Press, anti-government guerrillas shot and killed five Soviet advisers to the Marxist government.

August 1979—Uganda—After the killings of an Italian businessman and a British professor, representatives of all diplomatic missions in Kampala called upon the government for greater military protection.

August 1, 1979—Lebanon—The Imam as-Sadr Brigades threw a bomb at the Libyan News Agency office in Beirut at 8 P.M. , injuring an employee.

August 2, 1979—France—Two ETA members were shot just across the French border. One of them died later in a hospital. A San Sebastián newspaper received a call from the Spanish National Action vowing, "These attacks were just the beginning of the armed offensive against ETA."

August 2, 1979—United States—Michele Sindona, fifty-nine, an Italian financier, was apparently kidnapped by Proletarian Justice after he left his lavish Pierre Hotel cooperative apartment on New York's Fifth Avenue at 7:15 P.M. In a call to the Italian news agency Ansa, the group claimed that it would execute the former Vatican financial adviser at dawn on August 11. Sindona had been free on $3 million bail and was due to go on trial September 10 on ninety-nine counts of bank fraud in the 1974 collapse of the Franklin National Bank, the biggest bank failure in U.S. history. Sindona was accused of siphoning $45 million in Franklin funds, most of which were lost in foreign exchange speculation.

On September 10, Sindona's Rome lawyers received a Brooklyn-postmarked letter with a photo of Sindona holding a placard reading, in Italian, "The fair trial will be done by us." Four Sindona lawyers were to be prepared to answer within ten minutes ten questions regarding Sindona's financial dealings to the Proletarian Committee of Subversion for Better Justice. Sindona appeared at a

New York hospital on October 16 with a bullet wound in his left thigh. He said that the Proletarian Committee of Subversion for Better Justice released him after he agreed to pay a ransom and furnish evidence of corruption by wealthy rightists in Italy. He claimed he was forced into a car by a sixty-year-old blond man holding a pistol, who spoke in broken Italian and appeared to be Greek. He was moved to four places during his captivity, and was shot when he attempted to escape. A psychiatrist believed that Sindona had been kidnapped, but police authorities remained unconvinced.

August 5, 1979—Canary Islands—Three deserters from the Juan de Austria regiment of the Spanish Foreign Legion drove onto the Puerto Rosario, Fuerteventura, airport runway in a stolen police jeep and commandeered an Iberian Airlines DC9 that was unloading passengers from Las Palmas, Gran Canaria Island. They took hostage eighteen passengers, two cleaning women, the pilot, the copilot, and a stewardess and demanded to be flown to a place of asylum. They first ordered the plane to fly to Casablanca, Morocco, but were denied landing permission. Algeria next turned them down. The plane then flew to Lisbon, Portugal, where it was allowed to land, apparently on Moroccan request. In Lisbon, they asked for fuel and food for two days and for information on the fastest route to Bordeaux, France. France, however, turned them down. After fourteen and a half hours in Lisbon airport, they released twelve passengers and four airport personnel. They then indicated that they wanted to fly to Zimbabwe-Rhodesia. One of the hijackers exclaimed, "We are not terrorists. We are deserters from the Spanish Foreign Legion. We are ready to hand over our weapons." They flew on to Geneva, Switzerland, where they surrendered fifteen minutes after landing. They were later identified as Frenchmen Noel Seijen, twenty-nine, Jean Lyschin, twenty-five, and French-born Chilean citizen Sergio Munoz Cadaval, twenty-two. No injuries were reported in the twenty-four-hour episode. Spanish officials said there would be no extradition request. The Swiss government intended to charge the hijackers with deprivation of liberty and blackmail, which carried maximum sentences of twenty years.

August 7, 1979—United States—Police found a bomb on the grounds of the Bethesda, Maryland, interests mission of Taiwan, which handles diplomatic functions.

August 8, 1979—Chile—A Lufthansa flight from Santiago to Lima, New York, and Frankfurt was delayed in La Paz, Bolivia, three and a quarter hours while German and Bolivian authorities searched the plane after receiving a bomb threat. No bomb was found.

August 8, 1979—Mexico—The Iranian Fedayeen group published a communiqué in the Mexican morning newspaper *Uno Mas Uno* that threatened the exiled shah by stating, "Neither in Mexico nor anywhere else in the world will you be able to escape the punishment that awaits you. The tribunal is comprised of the Iranian people, a people who destroyed the rotting columns of a centuries-old empire during a bloody struggle. The Iranian people are not incapable of executing this irrevocable decision, which has been accepted by world opinion. It is not just a threat; it is the will of a heroic people that will be carried out in the not too distant future." The message was written in Persian and Spanish.

August 12, 1979—Afghanistan—The Afghan National Liberation Front claimed to have killed thirty Soviet civilians and a number of Afghan soldiers at the shrine of Kherqua Mubarrakin Kandahar in south Afghanistan.

August 13, 1979—Lebanon—At 9 A.M., a rocket-propelled grenade and machine-gun fire was directed at the car of the Iraqi ambassador, 'Abd al-Husayn Hasan, who was wounded in the back and foot. His aide and driver were also wounded, and the car was destroyed. He had left his home for the embassy in the Ar-Ramlah al-Bayda section of Beirut and was one hundred meters from the embassy in the Al-Awaz'i area when the projectile was fired from the Ar-Rumul ad-Dakiliyah area.

August 16, 1979—Guatemala—A man who signed aboard as A. R. Kagan, twenty-four, of Massachusetts, hijacked Eastern Airlines flight 980 from Guatemala City to Miami carrying ninety-one people aboard. The knife-wielding hijacker was overpowered when the plane was in a landing pattern over Havana. The plan made it safely to Miami, ninety minutes behind schedule.

August 17, 1979—Lebanon—A bomb exploded at 9 P.M. at the West German embassy on Al-Hamra' Street in Beirut.

August 17, 1979—Iran—Two rocket-propelled grenades were fired early in the morning at the U.S. Embassy after a caller told the Revolutionary Guards to vacate the compound. One of the grenades failed to detonate; the other broke windows and damaged plaster in the embassy's former commissary restaurant, which was being converted into a new consular and visa department. No injuries were reported. The attack may have been carried out by militiamen who had been removed from their posts at the embassy the previous week.

August 21, 1979—Italy—The Red Guerrilla claimed credit for kidnapping British businessman Rolf Schild, fifty-five, his wife, Daphne, and their daughter, Annabelle, fifteen, in Sardinia. On September 6, Schild, joint chief executive of the Huntleigh Group Electronics Company, was released in very bad condition by the kidnappers, who demanded $24.5 milion ransom for his wife and daughter. The kidnappers had kept them under a brushwood shelter for all but a few days, when they were moved to a cave in the mountains. His firm said it would not help pay the money. According to a Huntleigh spokesman, ''That must be absolutely out of the question. This is a quoted [public] company with shareholders whose interests have to be protected.''

On November 1, the kidnappers threatened to cut off the ears of the women if negotiations were not quickly resumed with the company of the German-born engineer. All contact had been broken off on October 13 when go-betweens for Schild at an evening meeting were badly beaten when the kidnappers found they had brought no money.

On February 19, 1980, Sardinian police arrested eleven men in a series of predawn raids on mountain homes in the island's interior. The group was believed responsible for a series of kidnappings, including the Schild episode. Police recovered sixty thousand dollars believed to have been paid in ransoms. It was suggested that some had been paid by Schild. The group was believed to have links with the Red Brigades terrorist group.

Annabelle was freed on March 22, 1980, after the family paid $650,000 ransom.

August 21, 1979—Spain—The ETA was blamed for bombing a French bank in Bilbao.

August 22, 1979–Switzerland—The Armenian Liberation Army claimed credit for throwing a bomb at the Turkish consulate in Geneva shortly after the vice-consul had driven away. The driver of a passing car and two pedestrians were slightly injured, although there was little damage.

August 22, 1979—Guatemala—José Roberto Soundi, a Salvadoran banker, was killed as he and a companion were driving in Guatemala City. Two cars blocked his path. The occupants opened fire and threw a bomb at the car. Soundi's companion was reported to be in critical condition.

August 22, 1979—Colombia—A mentally unbalanced man hijacked a Colombian military plane with forty-nine passengers aboard at a local airport. The Avro craft was reported running low on fuel and crashed near Bogotá, killing the pilot and four other people.

August 23, 1979—Spain—The ETA was blamed for the early morning bombing of the Saragossa branch of the French bank Société Générale de Banque en Espagne. The blast wrecked the offices and damaged a pharmacy twenty yards away. Two hours later, a bomb damaged the French immigration office in the Basque border town of Irun. No injuries were reported.

August 23, 1979—Argentina—A bomb exploded in the Córdoba branch of the Israeli bank, causing some damage but no injuries.

August 23, 1979—United States—An explosive and an extortion note addressed to United Airlines were found in a piece of luggage in a men's room at Portland international airport. The note threatened United property, but the bomb was safely defused. Police did not believe that the threat was related to a hijacking that occurred later in the day.

August 23, 1979—United States—A United Airlines B727 flying 112 passengers and 7 crew members from Portland to Los Angeles was forced to return to Portland by James R. Allbee, twenty-six , of Portland, who claimed to have a bomb. He surrendered to the FBI at 2:25 A.M. and was found not to have a bomb in a package he was holding.

August 24, 1979—United Kingdom—Potentially dangerous radiation pulses were detected coming from the Israeli embassy. The embassy was unable to explain the source of the radiation.

August 24, 1979—Morocco—Fifty Central African Empire (CAE) students held Bernard Beloum, their ambassador, hostage and demanded immediate payment of scholarships that they claimed had been due since last October. Beloum said he had twice wired his capital for instructions but had not received a reply.

August 24, 1979—Libya—Mohammed Assomunah, twenty-eight, a Libyan student dissatisfied with his government, hijacked a Libyan Airlines B727 flying from Benghazi to Tripoli on its way to Frankfurt, West Germany. The plane, carrying fifty-nine passengers, mostly Libyans, and a crew of nine, was initially ordered to fly to Greece but was denied landing permission in Athens. The gunman then demanded to fly to Cyprus but was again denied landing permission. The plane headed toward Beirut and Damascus, but returned and landed in Larnaca airport, Cyprus, when it ran low on fuel. The hijacker surrendered to police and requested political asylum. The next day, Cyprus handed him over to a Libyan delegation.

August 25, 1979—Ireland—James McCann, one of the IRA's most wanted men, was arrested when police in Naas, thirty miles south of Dublin in County Kildare, came across a van hauling eight hundred pounds of cannabis. One of the four men near the vehicle, under whose load of bananas was hidden $2.3 million worth of marijuana, fired an automatic pistol at police. In the ensuing fight, one man was captured, but the other three escaped in a car, which crashed after an eight-mile chase. Police then captured two of the three.

McCann had escaped from jail after being arrested in a 1971 Belfast bombing. He had been sought by British, West German, and Dutch authorities but had successfully avoided extradition attempts when arrested in Canada two years earlier and in France in 1978.

August 25, 1979—Italy—David Tserkes, thirty-seven, a Russian emigrant resident in Israel, was arrested in Venice when his Opel was found to contain three kilograms of TNT, several detonators, several slow-burning fuses, and other bomb-making paraphernalia. He had arrived from Haifa on the *Apollonia*, a Greek ship, and was his way to Munich.

August 27, 1979—West Germany—A bomb exploded in the Frankfurt offices of Turkish Airlines, damaging the building and injuring a German woman going by in a streetcar. Police were looking for two middle-aged men seen driving from the scene just after the explosion. An anonymous caller, claiming to be from a revolutionary organization, telephoned the Associated Press twenty minutes before the explosion to warn that a bomb would be detonated at a "Turkish institution." Later the Armenian Secret Liberation Army claimed credit.

August 27, 1979—Ireland—Earl Louis Mountbatten of Burma, seventy-nine, second cousin of Queen Elizabeth, was killed shortly after noon when a bomb exploded on his twenty-nine-foot *Shadow V*, a green and white fishing boat that had just pulled out of Mullaghmore, a fishing village in County Sligo near the border. Lord Mountbatten died instantly when the fifty pounds of explosives went off. His grandson, Nicholas, fourteen, and his friend, Paul Maxwell, fifteen, also were killed. The dowager Lady Brabourne, eighty-two, mother-in-law of Lord Mountbatten's daughter, Lady Patricia Brabourne, died of her injuries the next day. Lady Patricia was seriously injured. Her husband, film and television director Lord Brabourne (John Ulick Knatchbull), and son Timothy, Nicholas's twin, were reported in satisfactory condition at a nearby hospital. The Irish National Liberation Army and the Irish Republican Army claimed credit, the latter saying that the execution was part of a "noble struggle to drive the British intruders out of our native land."

Two patrolmen in a separate car had accompanied the earl on the half-mile drive from his home to the mooring, a standard procedure for them. However, they did not regularly inspect his boat or accompany him on it. The local police superintendent said, "It was at his own request that he was not guarded constantly." Police officials speculated that the bomb may have been planted in his boat, which was left at an unguarded mooring a few yards from a stone jetty, and then set off either by remote control from the nearby hills or by a timing device. The bomb may have also been placed in one of the lobster traps the earl kept there, which exploded when pulled out of the water. Two skindivers had been reported in the area. Witnesses disagreed as to the speed of the boat and whether a trap was being pulled up at the time of the explosion. This was to have been the last weekend of a three-week trip to Classiebawn Castle where Lord Mountbatten spent part of the summer for the last three decades.

The Irish Republic offered a 100,000 pound reward for information leading to the arrest of the perpetrators, while the Ulster Defense Association threatened to "take the law into its own hands" if IRA violence was not stopped. An Irish police patrol had arrested two individuals at 9:30 A.M., a few hours before the bomb went off, who were suspected of being involved. Thomas McMahon, thirty-one, an upholsterer, and Francis McGirl, twenty-four, a farmer, were stopped in their car eighty miles away from Mullaghmore near the town of Granard, County Leitrim, in a routine police inspection. They seemed unusually nervous, and McGirl used a fictitious name and address. Police records indicated that McMahon was an IRA expert in bomb mechanisms and McGirl came from a family of IRA activists. Both had Eire addresses. They were held on charges of IRA membership but were later released on a technicality. They were immediately rearrested and taken to Dublin's special no-jury criminal court, where they were charged with the murder. Traces of nitroglycerin and sea water were found in their clothing. On November 23, a Dublin court found McMahon guilty and sentenced him to life imprisonment. The presiding judge refused to allow an appeal. McGirl was found innocent of the slaying but was charged to stand trial on January 21, 1980, on charges of belonging to the outlawed IRA. Irish police believe seven other men were involved in the murder.

Mountbatten, an uncle of Prince Phillip, was England's leading World War II hero. He had been chief of the British defense staff, last viceroy of India, admiral of the fleet, allied commander-in-chief in Southeast Asia, and first sea lord. Burma, where he had governed, declared a week of mourning.

August 27, 1979—Northern Ireland—Shortly after the Mountbatten murder, the IRA claimed credit for two bombs that killed eighteen British soldiers and wounded at least eight others in an ambush at Warrenpoint, on the border with Ireland. Troops traveling by truck between two army bases were injured when a bomb hidden in a civilian truck loaded with straw exploded as they passed. An army truck and jeep were demolished by the explosion of what the IRA claimed was twelve hundred pounds of dynamite. Gunmen then opened fire on the troops from inside Ireland on the other side of Carlingford Lake. This pinned down the troops for fifteen minutes and prevented ambulances from rescuing the wounded. When an army helicopter arrived to pick up the casualties, a second bomb hidden in a nearby stone house and consisting of five hundred pounds of explosives went off, damaging the helicopter and injuring two more soldiers. The pilot managed to take the wounded back to his base. There were reports that the gunmen used automatic rifles and that local residents, golfers from a nearby course, and passing tourists were injured.

Michael Hudson, twenty-nine, son of one of the queen's coachmen at Buckingham Palace, was killed in the crossfire. Shortly after the explosion, the IRA Provisionals in South Down claimed credit, although they denied that they had fired guns. Among the dead was Lieutenant Colonel David Blair, forty, commanding officer of the First Battalion of the Queen's Own Highlanders, a Scottish infantry regiment, the most senior army officer to be killed in direct guerrilla violence in Northern Ireland. A major also died.

August 28, 1979—Belgium—At 3 P.M., an IRA bomb blew up an outdoor stage in the Brussels Grand Palace minutes before a British military band was scheduled to give a concert marking Brussel's one-thousandth birthday. Seven members of the duke of Edinburgh's Royal Regiment Band, stationed in Ossendorf, West Germany, were injured, as well as eleven tourists, including two children. Damage from the blast was estimated at between $134,000 and $167,000. The plastic explosives were placed under the stage floor in the back, away from the square where there were hundreds of tourists. Casualties would have been much higher if traffic had not prevented the band from starting on time. Only six members of the band were on stage setting up instruments when the bomb went off. The other eighteen were changing into their red dress uniforms. A Brussels burgomeister later received a call from the IRA claiming credit.

August 28, 1979—Berlin—Four persons drove to the Oberbaumbruecke border crossing at Kreusberg, on the western side of the Berlin wall and threw a Molotov cocktail onto the eastern side at 8:40 P.M. East Berlin authorities said that several of their border troops were injured, and a sentry box was set on fire. The perpetrators escaped.

August 29, 1979—United Kingdom—A gasoline bomb thrown at an Irish social club in Nottingham caused no damage.

August 30, 1979—United States—A man claiming to represent the IRA warned that two bombs had been placed on one of three British frigates docked at Philadelphia's waterfront. The ship was evacuated, but no explosives were found.

August 30, 1979—Spain—Police defused two bomb set at the Bilbao showrooms of French auto firms.

September 1979—West Germany—The Yugoslav press reported that four Yugoslav émigrés fired on diners at the Balkan Grill in Frankfurt. Salih Mesinovic, thirty-eight, was killed. Police arrested one terrorist near the grill and another in his apartment. Warrants were issued for Anton Kujundzic and Ivan Livajica.

September 1, 1979—Afghanistan—Abdul Qayyum, spokesman for the Afghan Islamic Society, claimed that his group had captured and killed eight Soviet advisers in the guerrilla battle for the Jamb area.

September 1, 1979—Mexico—Spokesmen for the exiled shah of Iran denied that an attack had been made by three members of the Twenty-third of September Communist League against his residence in Cuernavaca.

September 3, 1979—Turkey—A bomb was thrown at the Libyan embassy, breaking windows of the embassy and surrounding buildings at around 7:40 P.M.

September 3, 1979—Lebanon—At midnight, a bomb exploded in the southern entrance of the Lufthansa offices in the Sabbagh building of Beirut's Al-Hamra Street, causing heavy damage but no injuries. The previously unknown Organization of Avenging Palestinian Youth claimed credit for this attack, as well as for three other bombings at that office and the Federal Republic of Germany's embassy. It demanded the release of jailed Palestinians in West Germany within a week.

September 5, 1979—Spain—Police detonated a bomb found in a Peugeot showroom in San Sebastián after receiving a telephoned warning.

September 7, 1979—Lebanon—Alitalia flight 713, a DC8 flying 172 passengers and 11 crew members from Tehran to Rome with a refueling stop in Beirut, was hijacked at 12:30 P.M. by three Lebanese Shi'ite students wearing Western clothing. The trio, originally identified as Kurds, took Colt revolvers out of their boxes of chocolates and told pilot Aldo Onorati that they wanted to refuel in Nice. France, citing a four-year policy, denied the plane landing rights. The plane set down at Rome's Fiumicino Airport at 3:25 P.M. Three helicopters flew 80 commandos of the army's antiterrorist squad to surround the plane. Italy's pilots' union demanded a boycott of Beirut and Tehran airports and claimed that their poor security was responsible for the incident. Most of the hostages were Iranians, although there were 10 Italians plus Stephen Fazio, nineteen, of New York, a student at the American University of Beirut. The hijackers requested food and drinks and wanted an electric generator to power the plane's air conditioning system.

The hijackers demanded to be flown to Cuba to address the summit meeting of the Non-Aligned Movement. They claimed that the Iranian-born leader of the Shi'ite sect of Islam, Imam Musa Sadr, fifty-four, and two aides vanished in Libya on August 31, 1978. Friends said Sadr had never left Tripoli, while Libyan officials said he left on an Alitalia flight to Rome. Italy said it had no record of his entry. Cuba said it would allow the hijackers to come for humanitarian reasons, but the hijackers were later informed that the flight would be impossible because of a tropical storm.

While the identity of the hijackers was in doubt (one report said the hijackers had claimed to be Palestinians), a Palestine Liberation Organization representative in Rome would say only, "We are currently checking with our headquarters in Beirut." Later Mohamed Sharnas, the Arab League's representative in Rome, spoke to the hijackers in Arabic and defused a tense moment in the negotiations. He persuaded the hijackers to release the 36 passengers whom they had not yet freed and to fly to Iran. The plane left Rome with the hijackers, the original crew of 9, 2 relief pilots, an engineer, and passenger Robert Saliba, who served as translator. Upon landing in Tehran, an Iranian religious leader, Hojjatoleslam Sajjadi, went to the plane to negotiate with the hijackers. They left with him and met Interior Minister Hashem Sabaghian and Vice-Premier Sadegh Tabatabai and surrendered, ending a twenty-hour incident. Sabaghian said that the three would be jailed pending consultations with Lebanese authorities: "We have sympathy for their motive, but not for their methods." The hijackers was identified as Haydar Asad Jamal Ad-Din, born in Al-Ghubayrah in 1952, Khudur Jafar Jamal Ad-Din, born in Al-Ghubayrah in 1956, and Fahmi Muhammad Jabaq, born in 1956. On September 11, Italian officials said they would request extradition.

The Iranians agreed to the hijackers' demand that their English-language communiqué be broadcast on Iranian television. Tehran Domestic Service ran the message, which read: "In the name of Allah, the compassionate, the merciful: to the heads of government meeting in Havana, Cuba: A year and a few days have passed since the disappearance of the Imam Musa As-Sadr together with Shaykh Muhammad Ya'qub and 'Abbas Badr Ad-Din. The entire world knows where the imam and his companions are, but nobody has taken the smallest step since Colonel Al-Qaddafi has bought the conscience of the world with a handful of dollars and a few barrels of oil. We demand that you clarify the mysteries surrounding the case of Imam Musa As-Sadr and his friends. We know the details. All the world leaders, without exception, know where the imam is and who has perpetrated this crime of his disappearance since the imam and his friends are not just a few suitcases which have disappeared en route from Libya to Italy. We, therefore, call for the release of the imam and his friends as soon as possible. Otherwise we proclaim to the world that we will be permitted to take any step and that no obstacle will bar our way. Act in accordance with the Koran which says: God, his apostle and the pious shall soon see your work. Signed: The Organization of the Standard Bearers of Imam Musa As-Sadr."

The hijacked plane had been previously used by the late Pope Paul VI during his 1970 trip to the Philippines and Australia.

September 7, 1979—United States—President Carter granted clemency to four Puerto Rican terrorists, who flew on to Puerto Rico to receive a heroes' welcome. Oscar Collazo, sixty-seven, was serving a life term for attempting to assassinate President Truman in 1950. Lolita Lebron, Irving Flores Rodriguez, and Rafael Concel Miranda fired on the U.S. House of Representatives in 1954, wounding five congressmen.

September 7, 1979—Afghanistan—Six West Germans were shot and killed by bandits or Moslem rebels who may have mistaken them for Soviet advisers to the government. Schoolteachers Johannes Koischus and Rolf Truxa, their wives, and Kioschus's two children were picnicking near Lataband Pass, eight miles west of their Kabul homes, when they were attacked.

September 8, 1979—Lebanon—Unidentified gunmen riding in a Mercedes Benz shot at the U.S. embassy shortly after a policeman arrested a man who tried to forcibly enter the building. No injuries were reported.

September 9, 1979—Afghanistan—Gaeton Dion, of Disraeli, Quebec, was shot and killed when suspected Moslem guerrillas attacked a tourist bus en route from Herat to Kandahar. The bus was one of several that travel between Europe and India. Later reports indicated that Kurt Marfurt, twenty-six, of Zurich, Switzerland, was killed as he crouched for cover on the bus floor. Russ Anthony Shanks of Sydney, Australia, suffered multiple bullet wounds in his stomach and legs.

   The forty European, U.S., and Canadian survivors of the attack said that the bus was chartered by the U.K. firm, Masic Bus Company, and was scheduled to drive from Istanbul to New Delhi through Pakistan. However, despite passengers' protests, the Turkish driver decided to save gas by going through Afghanistan. Shortly after dawn, the bus took on four Afghan soldiers to serve as guards and joined a convoy of other buses and trucks. The Turkish driver became impatient forty-five minutes out of Herat and drove ahead of the convoy. A shot was fired from the right of the bus, causing the driver to stop. The attackers opened up from the left side of the vehicle. The Afghan soldiers returned the fire. After the attack, the driver disappeared, and a Swiss tourist drove the bus back to Herat.

September 11, 1979—Northern Ireland—Men armed with submachine guns forced a train to stop at Cloughogue Bridge after it had crossed the border from Dundalk, Ireland. They forced the driver and a guard, the only persons on the train, to walk back to the Republic and then sent the sixteen-car train on. It crashed three miles down the track, blocking the main Belfast-Dublin line. Security sources believed the IRA was responsible.

September 12, 1979—West Germany—A Lufthansa B727 flight originating in Paris was hijacked out of Frankfurt at 9:55 A.M. and flew on to its original destination of Cologne. The hijacker, Rafael Kappel, thirty-one, a writer from

Rothenburg-on-Fulda, was armed with a toy pistol and demanded to talk with Chancellor Helmut Schmidt on television. Upon the plane's landing at 10:25 A.M. at Cologne, Hans-Juergen Wischnewski, minister of state, supervised the negotiations from the airport tower after Schmidt refused to talk to the hijacker. Kappel released the 121 passengers and four of the eight crew members after he was allowed to record a television message. The recording, which was not transmitted by the West German television network, included Kappel's demands for the development of nuclear power, improvement in maternity benefits (including a three-year paid leave for pregnant working women), better medical treatment for those with psychological problems, abolition of compulsory military service, and equitable distribution of the world's wealth. He also complained that ex-convicts are branded for life because of unfavorable entries in their identity documents. At 10 P.M., Kappel freed the remaining 4 crew members and surrendered.

September 13, 1979—France—Pedro Elizaran, a Spanish Basque separatist, was wounded when two men fired submachine guns at him from a car as he prepared to enter his home in Biarritz. The Spanish Armed Group told a Madrid newspaper that it had wounded Gusto Elizaran Sarasola, twenty-four.

September 13, 1979—France—The Spanish Armed Group claimed it bombed a restaurant in Saint-Jean-de-Luz belonging to Juan José Etchave, who had recently staged a hunger strike to press for political refugee status for Spanish Basque exiles.

September 15, 1979—Turkey—Peter Pulton, twenty-nine, a U.S. consular official, was slightly wounded when he was caught in the middle of a gunbattle between Istanbul police and terrorists.

September 17, 1979—France—The Spanish National Association said it bombed a country house belonging to relatives of Spanish exile José Maria Zaldua.

September 17, 1979—Puerto Rico—Three bombs went off at the National Guard's Tortuguero armory near Vega Baja, west of San Juan. A National Guard truck was burned in a separate attack attributed to nationalist terrorists inspired by the release of four Puerto Rican terrorists ten days previously. No injuries were reported.

September 18, 1979—Austria—A bomb went off in the regional museum on the fourth floor of the New Castle of Voelkermarkt in Carinthia at 5 P.M. Political motives were suspected because the museum was exhibiting a documentary about the 1918-1922 Carinthian defense struggle. Luka Widmar of

Ljubljana, Yugoslavia, was injured, as was Mira Blei-Lorger of Maribor, Yugoslavia, who ran to a doctor two hundred meters away. The leg of a man was later amputated, but his life was saved. Karl Petschnig, nineteen, of Jaunstein, first claimed responsibility but was sent to a psychiatric hospital for examination and later released. Widmar and Blei-Lorger later confessed to planting the bomb but said that they had not intended to cause injury and had set the timer to 10 P.M. At the time of Blei-Lorger's arrest, her passport did not agree with the name she gave, their claims to be Italians from Rome were shown to be false, and she refused to recognize a passport found at the bomb site as her own.

September 19, 1979—Israel—A plastique explosive hidden on a bicycle parked in front of the Atara Café on Jerusalem's Ben Yehuda Street went off, killing one person and injuring thirty-eight. The Arab Liberation Front claimed responsibility and said that a second bomb exploded, bringing the casualty rate to fifty. Policemen found a second device and defused it. Several arrests were reported. The bombing came while a group of U.S. black leaders were visiting Lebanon to meet with PLO leaders.

September 21, 1979—El Salvador—Dennis McDonald, thirty-seven, a U.S. engineer and general manager of Aplar, a subsidiary of Beckman Instruments of California, and Fausto Buchelli, a Puerto Rican, were kidnapped in San Salvador as they left their factory at 5 P.M. Two vehicles intercepted their car. José Luis Paz Viera, their Salvadoran driver and bodyguard, was machine-gunned to death by the attackers, who stopped the Aplar van in front of a women's prison. The Revolutionary Party of Central American Workers (PRTC) claimed responsibility. During the week of October 7, Beckman ran advertisements in a dozen foreign newspapers to satisfy the kidnappers' demands. An ad in the October 10 edition of *The New York Times* (a similar ad ran in the *Los Angeles Times*) cost $30,960. Beckman spokesmen would not say how much all of the ads in Latin American and European newspapers cost. On November 7, McDonald and Buchelli were released unharmed and returned to southern California. The firm refused to say whether it had paid a monetary ransom.

September 23, 1979—El Salvador—During an attack by two dozen gunmen on the Armed Forces Instruction Center on the grounds of the President's residence, three young U.S. citizens traveling in a rented car were shot to death. The San Francisco residents were identified as William Kong, Edwin Oswaldo Mendoza, and Moises Edgardo Magana. The last two were naturalized U.S. citizens from Santa Ana. Panama City radio ACAN reported that the three youths had participated in the attack. The U.S. consulate requested a thorough investigation.

September 23, 1979—Guatemala—Vernor Koller, the German owner of a ranch with several thousand head of cattle, and Pedro Valerio, the ranch's Austrian administrator, were kidnapped in El Naranjo, a village five hundred kilometers from Guatemala City. Their bullet-riddled bodies were found in the Cedro River on October 2.

September 29, 1979—Afghanistan—The Islamic Movement of Afghanistan claimed that it had invaded the Soviet embassy and killed six employees. Tass quickly denied the allegation, calling it American propaganda.

September 30, 1979—Guatemala—Richard Brink, manager of a furniture factory, and his son, Clarence, were kidnapped during the night in Guatemala City when they went to their store after a guard had phoned them to say that he was "facing problems."

October 2, 1979—United States—The FBI office in Newark, New Jersey, received a letter which read, "From FALN. Pope John Paul is to be shot in New York." The Puerto Rican terrorist group's letter directed the Bureau to an Elizabeth, New Jersey, apartment occupied by two El Salvadorans. The FBI found a submachine gun and four boxes of ammunition. Although the duo were not in the apartment at the time of the search, the woman was later found, questioned, and released. Alberto Roberto Gustave, thirty-six, a truck driver, appeared voluntarily at the U.S. embassy in El Salvador for questioning. The FBI and Secret Service concluded that the couple had nothing to do with the unsubstantiated threat, and suggested that the weapons were planted in their apartment.

October 7, 1979—Guatemala—Sixteen male members of the Guerrilla Army of the Poor (EGP), armed with submachine guns, jumped out of two vans at a softball field in Guatemala City and kidnapped Jorge Raul Garcia Granado, twenty-seven, son of Raul Garcia Granado, a wealthy cotton grower who is a distant relative of the president, General Romeo Lucas Garcia, as he stepped from his car. The attackers killed a chauffeur and bodyguard during the seizure. The group demanded that a 9000-word statement denouncing the government and praising Cuba be placed by the family in more than a dozen newspapers in Latin America, the United States, Canada, and Europe. *El Tiempo*, a Colombian daily, refused to run the thirty-two-page manifesto. The ad ran in the *Washington Post*, *San Francisco Chronicle*, and *New York Times*. The family had no estimate of the total cost, but the *Times* noted that it charged $24,187.50 for the space. The group also demanded that the father of the victim pay an $8 million ransom.

October 7, 1979—Nicaragua—During the evening, four machine-gun bullets were fired from a camper by several individuals alleged to be Sandinistas at a

Colombian embassy building housing Somozist refugees. No injuries were reported.

October 8, 1979—Nicaragua—A shot was fired through the front door of the Spanish embassy, causing no injuries.

October 11, 1979—El Salvador—The Farabundo Marti Popular Liberation Forces set on fire four cars belonging to the U.S. Peace Corps, which were parked in the Corps' parking lot.

October 12, 1979—Netherlands—A lone gunman drove up next to a Volkswagen with diplomatic plates and fired five shots while the victim waited for the light to change. Ahmet Benler, twenty-seven, son of the Turkish ambassador, died of his injuries. In a call to the Agence-France Presse offices in Paris, the Justice Commando of the Armenian Genocide claimed credit for the Hague attack. The group initially incorrectly identified the victim as a British diplomat.

October 14, 1979—Iran—Two men on a motorcycle fired a bullet into the head of Hans Joachim Leib, 32, killing him as he left his northern Tehran suburban home for work as the West German financial manager of the Iranian subsidiary of Merck Pharmaceutical Company. A note left on the body said that Forghan, a fundamentalist Moslem terrorist group (which is opposed to clerical rule), believed him to be a polytheist who supported capitalism. Leib had taken his post in June 1978, living in Tehran with his wife and son.

October 16, 1979—Libya—A Libyan Arab Airways Fokker Friendship on a domestic flight with forty passengers was hijacked by three men who told the pilot they wanted to go to Italy or Switzerland. The pilot set down in Valletta, Malta, to refuel. The young Arab trio was persuaded to surrender by Maltese Prime Minister Dom Mintoff, who left for Tripoli after the negotiations. The group was taken into custody.

October 16, 1979—Honduras—The body of Major Pablo Emilio Salazar, alias "Commander Bravo," one of the toughest military commanders in the ousted Somoza regime in Nicaragua, was found in Tegucigalpa. He had been tortured before being shot to death.

October 18, 1979—United States—Puerto Rican terrorists claimed credit for "more than one-dozen explosive charges placed Wednesday night" in Chicago and Puerto Rico. Police investigated the possibility that they were responsible for placing four sticks of dynamite attached to a timing device in a Chicago building housing the headquarters of several Republican groups as well as the Illinois Citizens for Kennedy, as well as phony bombs found at the Manhattan offices of the Democratic and Republican parties. In Chicago, dynamite bombs went off in the Cook County Building, while another was dismantled in a nearby building housing the Cook County Republican offices. Another three sticks of dynamite broke windows in an unoccupied building at the Great Lakes Naval Training Center in North Chicago. Bomb threats were made against the residence of Chicago Mayor Jane Byrne. The FBI was investigating a Puerto Rican threat to bomb the Indian Point nuclear power station near Peekskill, New York.

October 19, 1979—Lebanon—A hand grenade was thrown during the early morning into the residence of the Libyan ambassador in the Bi'r Hasan quarter of Beirut. The grenade exploded a few yards from the residence. The armed attackers fled pursuing embassy guards.

October 23, 1979—Philippines—Moro National Liberation Front pirates hijacked the Malaysian vessel Haleha Baru Adal forty kilometers from Samporna, Malaysia. Three of the forty-four passengers were killed and two were missing after the pirates stole property worth more than 8000 Malaysian dollars from the passengers. Seventeen of the Malaysian passengers were either released voluntarily or rescued by the Philippine Armed Forces. During the night of October 29, the final hostages, a Malaysian mother and her two children, were rescued from the terrorists' hideout in Siasi, Sulu, southern Philippines, after a gun battle in which the leader of the gang and four of his followers were killed.

October 24, 1979—El Salvador—Leftist members of the Popular Revolutionary Bloc took over the Ministries of Labor and Economy and San Salvador. They released 276 hostages on October 29, but still held three cabinet members, a Chilean official of the Organization of American States, and eight others. On November 6, the group released the remaining hostages after Juan Chacon, twenty-two, leader of the bloc, announced an agreement with the government which gave it a thirty-day truce in street battles that had taken more than eighty lives in two weeks. The group called for the government to double the $3-a-day minimum wage, freeze food prices, and report on the fates of 300 people who disappeared during the previous regime. The government agreed to fine bus owners who overcharged fares and asked companies to pay severence wages to workers dismissed when the firms closed during violent demonstrations.

October 27, 1979—United States—A bomb exploded at 10 P.M. at the Cuban Mission to the United Nations, blowing out windows but causing no injuries. A member of Omega Seven told the Associated Press that the explosives were to have been used to assassinate Fidel Castro during his visit to the United Nations two weeks ago, but that security was too thorough. He called for the immediate release of all political prisoners in Cuba. Police claimed they had been tipped that another device was set to explode in the area.

October 28, 1979—El Salvador—The Faribundo Marti Popular National Liberation Forces claimed credit for a bomb which exploded at the Bank of America branch office in San Salvador causing heavy damage but no injuries. According to an FPL communiqué left at the scene, the attack was to support the demands of Popular Revolutionary Bloc members who had taken over government ministries.

October 29, 1979—United States—The Prague domestic news service claimed that an unidentified individual fired two shots at the car of a Czech diplomat in the U.S.

October 30, 1979—Philippines—Five armed individuals, believed to be members of the Moro National Liberation Front in Baloi, Lanao Del Norte, southern Philippines, kidnapped Sin Pil-ho, Korean supervisor of the Hanil Development Corporation, a subcontractor of the Agus hydroelectric project, and his Filipino driver in Nangka, Baloi town. The duo was taken to the hinterlands of neighboring Pantao Ragat town. Military authorities negotiated the group's ransom demands.

October 30, 1979—El Salvador—About 300 leftists firing guns attempted to take over the U.S. embassy. Marine guards and Salvadoran troops who quickly arrived at the scene used tear gas to repel the attackers who were climbing the embassy fence. Two Marines were slightly wounded, including one whose ear was grazed by a bullet. A Molotov cocktail was hurled onto the western side of the building. Gunshot damage to the embassy was reported. There were no reports of injuries to the attackers during the 45-minute melee. Ambassador Frank Devine was not in the embassy when the members of the Popular League 28 reached the building. The previous day, at least twenty-six demonstrators were killed and 100 wounded in gun battles between leftist street demonstrators and security forces backing the new civilian-military junta.

October 30, 1979—United States—A Pacific Southwest Airlines flight carrying 101 passengers was hijacked over southern California by John Gray of Seattle, who claimed to have a bomb and demanded to be taken to Mexico City. He surrendered to Tijuana authorities when the plane landed to refuel.

October 31, 1979—El Salvador—Several hooded youngsters conducted a ten-minute gun battle with guards at the Guatemalan embassy. The building's facade was damaged, and some of the terrorists may have been wounded during their escape.

November 3, 1979—United States—A small pipe bomb exploded in the luxury apartment building housing members of the Albanian U.N. mission, causing minor damage. Police suggested that a disgruntled former employee or tenant was responsible, and that the bomb was not directed against the Albanians.

November 4, 1979—Iran—Five hundred radical Moslem students attacked the U.S. Embassy in Tehran, seizing 100 hostages after a two-hour battle in which fourteen Marine Guards lobbed tear-gas canisters. The terrorists later picked up Jerry Plotkin, a California electronics businessman, at a Tehran hotel and brought him to the embassy. The students called for the extradition of the exiled Shah of Iran, who thirteen days before had left Mexico for hospital treatment in New York for lymphatic cancer.

The students claimed thay they were armed with only ten pistols, although they later said that they had mined the embassy grounds and had placed explosive charges throughout the buildings. They threatened to kill the hostages and blow up the embassy compound if the U.S. attempted a military rescue.

There was some question as to who was in charge of the attack, and with whom the U.S. could negotiate. The Bazargan cabinet resigned on November 6, leaving all formal authority in the Khomeini-led Revolutionary Council. A series of Foreign Ministers—Ibrahim Yazdi, Abol Hassan Bani-Sadr, and Sadegh Ghotbzadeh—followed, and were frequently defied by those holding the embassy. It appeared that there may have been up to five different groups of students among those holding the embassy—fundamentalist Phalange, Qom theological students, Tehran university students, leftists, and Communists. ABC news reported that the CIA believed some of the students may have been trained by the Popular Front for the Liberation of Palestine. Although the students said that they were loyal only to Khomeini, many observers suggested that they were leading the handling of the negotiations.

On November 22, Mahmoud Labadi, the PLO spokesman, said that the PLO (which had offered to mediate in the dispute) had been told that the hostages would be released if the Shah left the U.S. for another country. One week later, Mexico said that it would not allow the Shah to return. Egypt offered him asylum. On December 15, the Shah was flown to Panama from San Antonio, Texas, after successful surgery. Iran requested extradition from Panama, and the students said that this would not affect the freedom of the hostages, whom they threatened to try as spies.

While the takeover initially appeared to be student-led, the government quickly moved to back the demands of the students. On November 12, Abol Hassan Bani-Sadr upped the ante, saying that Iran demanded U.S. recognition that the Shah is a criminal and must be extradited, the return to Iran of the Shah's fortune, and an end to "American meddling" in Iranian domestic affairs. He announced an oil embargo on the U.S. at the same time President Carter was announcing that the U.S. would no longer buy Iranian oil. It was also noted that L. Bruce Laingen, the U.S. chargé, and two other U.S. diplomats were being held at the foreign ministry.

The American response consisted of incrementally increasing pressures on Iran, as well as diplomatically isolating Tehran. Numerous anti-Iranian protests in the U.S. underscored widespread support for the president's actions. On November 13, Attorney General Benjamin Civiletti said the 50,000 Iranian students in the U.S. would have to prove that they are enrolled as full-time students and have committed no crimes, or face deportation. On December 11, a U.S. district judge ruled this crackdown unconstitutional, as it singled out a particular nationality for separate treatment. This ruling was overturned on December 27 by a U.S. Court of Appeals decision. On November 14, the U.S. froze Iranian government assets and blocked Iran's call for a UN Security Council debate. The U.S. had previously banned the sale of military spare parts to Iran. On November 23, Finance Minister Bani-Sadr said Iran would refuse to honor $15 billion worth of foreign debts involving loans from twenty-eight private banks. On November 23, the U.S. Department of Defense cancelled pilot training for Iranians. On December 12, the U.S. ordered all but 35 of the 218 Iranian diplomats in the U.S. to leave within five days.

Internationally, the U.S. focused on obtaining condemnations of Iran's actions by governments and international organizations. Scores of governments agreed that Iran had violated fundamental international legal norms. On November 9, UN Security Council President Sergio Palacios de Vizzio of Bolivia asked that the hostages be released, in accordance with a council consensus. On December 4, the council again called for the release of the hostages, and said that the UN could be used as a forum for the settlement of Iran's dispute with the U.S. Secretary-General Kurt Waldheim was authorized to use his ''good offices'' in settling the crisis. On November 25, Waldheim had called for a Security Council meeting on his own initiative, a move which has rarely been used in the UN. On December 31, the council approved by a vote of 11-0-4 a U.S.-sponsored resolution calling for economic sanctions if Waldheim's trip to Iran was not successful in obtaining the release of the hostages by January 7, 1980. Waldheim met with hostile demonstrations and was not allowed to meet with the hostages. The U.S. agreed to temporarily postpone consideration of a sanctions resolution when Iranian UN diplomats claimed to have a proposal to solve the crisis. On January 13, 1980, the U.S.S.R vetoed a U.S.-sponsored sanctions resolution which had passed the Security Council, 10-2.

In Geneva, on November 29, the U.S. announced that it would petition the International Court of Justice for interim measures, noting that Iran had violated three international agreements on protection of diplomats, the UN Charter, and the 1955 U.S.-Iran Treaty of Amity. Iran refused to participate in the deliberations. On December 15, the ICJ unanimously ruled in favor of the U.S. position, calling upon Iran to release the hostages and remove all unauthorized personnel from the embassy grounds.

For its part, Tehran claimed that the issue was not its holding of hostages, but rather the crimes of the Shah and alleged American intelligence collusion with the former regime. Numerous demonstrations involving tens of thousands of individuals underscored support for this position by Tehran residents. On November 13, the Revolutionary Council called for the interrogation of the Shah by a team of Iranian-picked investigators to prepare for his eventual trial in Iran. Ayatollah Khomeini repeatedly referred to the Embassy as a "nest of spies," and claimed that the hostages had lost their diplomatic immunity due to their actions. On December 1, the students announced that they had discovered a secret State Department cable regarding cover arrangements for two alleged CIA employees. On December 6, the students said they had found a forged Belgian passport, and a set of instructions for using this cover, for yet another alleged CIA employee who was being held. On December 8, the foreign minister said Iran would form an international tribunal to review "the crimes of the U.S. government in Iran," and that the "spies" would be displayed before this tribunal. This was a departure from previous Iranian statements that the hostages would be tried in Islamic courts, or possibly by the students.

The Iranians sequentially released several of the hostages being held, ultimately holding only those who they claimed were spies. Thirty Iranian employees were freed shortly after the students seized the embassy. Three other non-Americans were released the next week. On November 18, as part of their careful attempts to exploit the heavy media coverage of the embassy siege, the students brought forward three hostages before television cameras. The trio—Kathy Gross, twenty-two, a secretary, and two black Marine security guard sergeants, Ladell Maples, twenty-three, and William Quarles, twenty-three—were released the next day. On November 18, the director of Iranian media said women and blacks would be released. Khomeini so ordered on that day, saying "Islam reserves special rights for women," and that "blacks for a long time have lived under oppression and pressure in America and may have been sent [to Iran under duress]." Four white women and six black men flew to Paris on November 20. The female secretaries were identified as Lillian Johnson, thirty-two, Elizabeth Montagne, forty-one, Terry Tedford, twenty-four, and Joan Walsh, thirty-three. The blacks were Marines David Walker, twenty-five, and Westley Williams, twenty-two, contracting officer Lloyd Rollins, forty, and three Air Force administrators, James Hughes, thirty, Terry Robinson, twenty-seven, and Joseph Vincent, forty-one. On November 22, the students released a Bangladeshi, a Korean, a Pakistani, and two Filipinos. Those remaining, including blacks and a woman, were dubbed spies.

Visits by outsiders to the hostages were also carefully orchestrated as media events by the students. Visitors were not allowed to see all of the hostages, leading observers to suggest that some of the hostages had been removed from the embassy grounds. The Iranians refused to state how many hostages were being held. On November 10, envoys from Syria, France, Sweden, and Algeria were the first outsiders permitted to visit the hostages. After they left, the Iranians circulated a petition, in very poor English, which they claimed was signed by thirty-three hostages who requested the Shah's extradition. The four diplomats reported that the hostages were bound with ropes, even when they slept, and were spoon-fed. These reports were later confirmed by the released hostages. On November 11, Papal envoy Monsignor Ammibale Bugnini visited the hostages, but Khomeini rebuffed the Pope's plea to release them. On December 10, the students allowed NBC News to interview a hostage, Marine Corporal William Gallegos. On November 25, and again in December, Representative George V. Hansen (R-Idaho) visited the embassy to attempt to negotiate with the students, but was allowed to see fewer then twenty of the hostages. On December 25, following the sending by Americans of a million Christmas cards to the hostages, religious services were held for forty-three hostages by Cardinal Leon-Etienne Duval of Algeria, Reverend William Sloane Coffin of New York, Reverend William Howard, President of the National Council of Churches, and Auxiliary Bishop Thomas Gumbleton of Detroit. The priests reported that the hostages showed some strain from their ordeal, but that one of them had whispered that their televised denunciations of the Shah and American policy were given under duress.

On January 2, 1980, the students accused press attaché Barry Rosen of being "a famous spy and plotter."

Letters from several hostages, including some of those who had been accused of being spies, trickled out of the embassy to the hostages' families and the *Washington Post*. John Thomas, a member of an Amerindian group who attended a World Liberation Day conference in Tehran, brought back 151 letters written by forty of the hostages.

A delegation of forty-nine members of the Committee for American-Iranian Crisis Resolution met with the militants for three days in mid-February. Three clergymen in the group were allowed to visit hostages Paul Lewis and William Gallegos.

On February 9, Ayatollah Khomeini's son and Greek Catholic Archbishop Hilarion Capucci (who had been held in an Israeli prison for smuggling arms to Palestinian terrorists in the mid-1970s) visited the hostages.

In late January, the Canadian government helped smuggle out of Iran six Americans who had escaped from the embassy during the initial attack. The group first hid in the Tehran home of Robert G. Anders, a consular official, and then moved to the Iran-American Society to establish a telephone link with Washington. They hid at several locations before being given shelter at the Canadian embassy. Under cover of a general personnel drawdown at the embassy, the Americans used Canadian passports to slip out of the country with the rest of the Canadian embassy staff. New Zealand Prime Minister Robert Muldoon later revealed that his embassy had also aided the escape. The Canadian heroism triggered an outpouring of pro-Canadian sentiments in the United States.

In a flurry of behind-the-scenes negotiations, the U.S. agreed to the U.N. sending a panel to Tehran to investigate Iranian complaints against the Shah. The panel consisted of Louis Pettiti, sixty-four, French author, former president of the Paris Bar Association, and a judge on the European Court of Human Rights; Andres Aguilar, fifty-four, Venezuela's former ambassador to the United States, who had been a member of the Inter-American Human Rights Commision; Mohamed Bedjaoui, fifty, Algeria's U.N. Ambassador; Adib Daoudi, fifty-six, a Syrian diplomat; and Hector W. Jayewerdene, sixty-three, the Queen's Counsel in Sri Lanka, brother of Sri Lanka's president, and a member of the U.N.'s subcommittee for protection of minorities. In March, 1980, the group took evidence of torture in Iran but were held up in their hopes of visiting the hostages. On March 6, the embassy militants said that they would transfer responsibility for the hostages to the Revolutionary Council, but last-minute stalling by the students prevented the panel from immediately visiting the hostages.

On March 23, the Shah flew from Panama City to final asylum in Egypt.

On April 7, the U.S. broke diplomatic relations with Iran, imposed an economic embargo banning all exports to Iran except food and medicine, ordered a formal inventory of Iranian financial assets in the U.S., and cancelled all future visas for Iranian travel in the U.S. On April 22, the European Community agreed informally not to purchase Iranian oil priced above OPEC-set prices. On May 18, the European Community agreed to cancel contracts signed with Iran after November 4 except for food and medicine, although some problems with implementation of this E.C. agreement arose.

Visits to and interviews with the hostages continued during the second quarter of 1980. On April 14, International Red Cross officials claimed that they had been permitted to see all of the hostages. Three U.S. clerics were allowed to perform Easter services at the embassy. On April 21, Barbara Timm was permitted to visit her son, Marine Sgt. Kevin Hermening, twenty.

On April 24, an attempt by U.S. military forces to rescue the hostages failed when three of the eight helicopters assigned to the mission became unavailable due to various mishaps in the desert near Tabas, Iran. During the preparation for the flight from Tabas to Tehran, the rescue team was forced to detain a busload of fifty Iranians who came onto the scene. After a decision to call off the mission, a helicopter crashed into one of the transport planes, killing eight of the rescue squad. After being displayed by an Iranian cleric at the U.S. Embassy, the remains of the men were returned to the U.S. Secretary of State Cyrus Vance resigned in protest over the wisdom of the mission. The Iranian students claimed that they would prevent future rescue attempts by moving the hostages out of the embassy to other locations throughout Iran. As of early June, they claimed that hostages were in Mashad, Tabriz, Isfahan, Shiraz, Qom, Qazvin, Najafabad, Jahrom, Arak, Mahallat, Yazd, Gorgan, Zanjan, and Hamedan.

On May 24, the International Court of Justice unanimously ordered Iran to release the hostages, and said in a 12-3 decision that Iran must pay damages to the U.S.

In early June, ten Americans, including former U.S. Attorney General Ramsey Clark, ignored a Presidential ban on American travel to Iran and attended a three-day international conference in Tehran on U.S.-Iranian relations.

November 5, 1979—Iran—Moslem students took over the British embassy and held twenty-seven British citizens hostage after Ayatollah Khomeini accused the United Kingdom of sheltering former Iranian Prime Minister Shahpour Bakhtiar.

November 7, 1979—Italy—Police found two SA-7 Strela missiles inside a van driven by three leftists as they were driving between Rome and Ortona. The missiles were believed to have been smuggled to the Rome branch of the Autonomous Workers Movement by the Lebanese freighter *Sidon* on November 7. Police later arrested Salem Abu Anzek, a Jordanian, in connection with the incident.

November 9, 1979—Angola—A bomb went off at 8:05 P.M. near the Luanda embassy of the German Democratic Republic, killing Paulino Malaue and injuring at least five employees, as well as several Angolan passersby.

November 9, 1979—United States—One Sudanese and four Iranian students were arrested at the Minnesota governor's mansion and charged with conspiring to kidnap Governor Al Quie at 4:45 P.M. Two persons were arrested in a car which police sources had said was to be used in the kidnapping. The other three were arrested inside the mansion, where Gretchen Quie, the governor's wife, was hosting an international student reception. Two shotguns and a handgun were taken from the car. The students were later released, due to lack of evidence.

November 11, 1979—El Salvador—The Popular Liberation Army bombed a McDonald's restaurant in San Salvador, killing one person.

November 11, 1979—Lebanon—Forty Lebanese and Iranian students, led by two mullahs, jumped over an iron fence and occupied the garden of the U.S. embassy in Beirut for two and a half hours, demanding the return to Iran of the Shah. U.S. Marine guards made no attempt to intervene. Lebanese security guards prevented the youths from approaching the embassy entrance. Syrian peacekeeping troops finally fired submachine gun bursts into the air and swung their rifle butts, injuring at least twenty of the students and the two mullahs before the group left. The previous week, Palestinian officials claimed to have prevented Iranian youths from attacking the U.S. embassy.

November 13, 1979—Portugal—Two gunmen fired machine gun bursts and threw a grenade into the car of Israel's ambassador in Lisbon, Ephraim Eldar. His bodyguard died as he reached for his revolver. The ambassador survived by staying in the car, but a bullet broke a bone in his right forearm, another wounded him in the thigh, and he suffered shrapnel wounds. His driver, a policeman guarding the Israeli embassy, and a female passerby were also wounded in the attack. The Israeli Foreign Ministry said the duo escaped in a car which disappeared in traffic. Israel claimed that this was a result of Yasir Arafat's visit to Lisbon ten days previously at the Arab solidarity meeting. The Palestine Liberation Organization denied responsibility.

November 15, 1979—United States—An altimeter-controlled bomb exploded shortly after the takeoff from Chicago's O'Hare Airport of American Airlines flight 444, a B727 flying to Washington's National Airport. The pilot heard a thump shortly after the 11:20 A.M. takeoff. Smoke poured into the passengers' compartment, and the pilot made an emergency landing at Washington's Dulles Airport. No injuries were reported to the seventy-two passengers and eight crew members, and the plane landed safely at 12:50 P.M. The 10½ inch by 7½ inch by 9½ inch package carrying the explosives, three D dry cell batteries, and the altimeter was placed in a mail bag. Authorities said that the bomber would have had no idea of knowing onto which plane the mail bag would be placed. Two Chicago radio stations and a newspaper received calls claiming credit for the Iranian Student Association. "There will be more bombs, larger bombs, unless the deportation of Iranian students is stopped." The message referred to President Carter's decision to deport Iranian students illegally in the U.S., as a means of pressuring the Iranian government to release Americans held hostage in the embassy in Tehran. In Washington, the Iranian Students Association denied responsibility. American, United, and Trans-World Airlines temporarily suspended carrying mail on their flights. Damage to the plane was reported to be minor. The package reportedly carried $8.50 worth of postage.

November 15, 1979—United States—Federal officials arrested seven male and one female Iranian students for attempting to smuggle three disassembled Winchester 30.06 rifles, matching scopes, fifteen boxes of ammunition, and a street map of Washington, D.C. with "certain embassies marked," just as one of the men was about to board TWA flight No. 900 from Baltimore-Washington International Airport to New York's Kennedy International Airport. The Iranians spoke of taking the rifles to Iran. They claimed to all be attending Baltimore-area colleges, and were jailed on bonds ranging from $25,000 to

$250,000. Seyed Abrahim Mosavi purchased the rifles for more than $1,000 cash, and had spoken to a gun dealer about purchasing machine guns, pistols, a 12-gauge riot control shotgun and a Heckler and Koch assault rifle, according to the store owner. The group was charged with dealing in firearms without a license, placing firearms on an interstate commercial airliner without notifying the carrier, and conspiracy. On November 26, charges were dismissed against Abolghsaem Karaee, twenty-eight, Mohammad S. Tofighi, twenty-five, and his wife, Shahla Amenli, twenty-five. A federal grand jury in Baltimore indicted the other five on the aforementioned charges. They were identified as Bagher Moomeney, twenty-eight, who was to travel to Iran with the weapons; Seyed Abrahim Mosavi, twenty-six, who purchased the guns; Sirous Salahvarzi, twenty-nine; Mohammod Reza Bahadoritoolabi, twenty-four; and Friedoon Rostami, twenty-eight. The grand jury also indicted a seaman who was not at the airport at the time of the arrest: Alireza Yeganeh, twenty-six, for conspiracy and dealing in firearms without a license.

On February 22, 1980, Friedoon Rostami and Sirous Salahvarzi pleaded guilty to lesser crimes in exchange for agreeing to leave the United States at the end of the semester in civil engineering at the Community College of Baltimore. On February 25, 1980, Bagher Moomeney pleaded guilty to placing guns on a common carrier. U.S. District Judge Shirley Jones dismissed charges against Mohammod Toolabi, who agreed to leave the U.S. at his own expense after his semester in civil engineering at the Community College of Baltimore ended on May 31. On March 5, 1980, after deliberating for seven hours, jurors acquitted Seyed Abrahim Mosavi of attempting to smuggle rifles and ammunition aboard the plane. Moomeney was told on April 10, 1980 by a federal judge who gave him a suspended sentence to leave the country "with reasonable haste."

November 19, 1979—Switzerland—After a shootout in which a woman passerby was killed, another woman was injured, a policeman was wounded in the abdomen and a second one in the arm, Rolf Klemens Wagner, thirty-five, a member of the West German Red Army Faction, was arrested. His three male bank robber colleagues, who had just robbed a Zurich bank in an underground shopping center of $250,000, escaped. Wagner was arrested as he sat quietly awaiting a tram. Some of the money was found in the terrorists' getaway car. Wagner was suspected of being the driver of the van used in the kidnapping of German industrialist Hanns-Martin Schleyer on September 5, 1977 (see incident 3179). He was one of four West German terrorists arrested in Yugoslavia in May 1978 who were later released in an extradition controversy between Yugoslavia and West Germany.

November 20, 1979—Saudi Arabia—Between 200 and 500 heavily armed rebels raided the Grand Mosque at Mecca during dawn prayers, seizing hundreds and perhaps thousands of worshippers of thirty nationalities. The attackers said that they sought reversal of Saudi modernization and the abolition of television, professional soccer, and the employment of Saudi women outside the home, in favor of a fundamentalist society based upon conservative Shi'ite tenets.

The raiders closed the doors leading out of the courtyard, and presented Mohammed ibn-Abdullah Qahtani as the Mahdi, the enlightened one long awaited as the final prophet. An Islamic prophecy says that the Mahdi will be proclaimed at dawn prayers at the Grand Mosque and that fighting in the streets of Mecca will accompany his coming. The attack took place on the Moslem Year 1400's first day.

Saudi Arabia initially clamped down on all reports of the takeover, leading to the spread of numerous rumors. Several sources blamed the Iranian regime for the attack. Ayatollah Khomeini of Iran claimed that the U.S. was behind the sacrilege, leading to anti-U.S. riots in several Moslem countries. Responding to a request from Washington, Interior Minister Nayef declared that the U.S. was not involved.

Saudi National Guardsmen blew up the mosque gates and fought their way inside against the rebels, who were armed with submachine guns, rifles, and pistols. The commander leading the Saudi assault was killed. Most of the hostages escaped or were freed by the Saudis several hours after the takeover, but the rebels held out for two weeks. Saudi troops used tanks, heavy artillery, snipers, and tear and asphyxiating gases against the attackers, who had taken up sniper positions in the mosque's minarets. Frequent Saudi claims of victory were proven premature, and it was not until December 3 that Saudi troops routed the last of the rebels occupying the Mosque's basement.

Casualty figures vary. Some accounts indicated that 300 rebels, 65 soldiers, and 20 pilgrims were killed, and that at least 200 people were wounded. The Saudis announced that they had captured 170 rebels, most of whom were expected to be beheaded after questioning. Sheik Mohammed Bin Sebil, a mosque imam, said a guard was killed and two were seriously injured in the takeover. The Mahdi was killed in the final battle. He was identified as a twenty-seven-year-old dropout Islamic law student previously known to police as a religious agitator.

In questioning the surviving terrorists, the Saudis learned that the attack was to be part of a general uprising against the Saudi regime. A simultaneous attack on a shrine in Medina was aborted when the raiders discovered that troops were coincidentally praying there. A large demonstration of foreign workers in the oil fields was also to take place. The raiders had hoped to take hostage King Khalid, who cancelled a planned appearance at the mosque due to illness. The intruders fanned out at the mosque, searching the faces of the faithful in hope of finding the king. One of the captured rebels was a National Guard colonel. Most were Saudi nationals, with the rest coming from Pakistan, North and

South Yemen, Morocco, and Kuwait. Some prisoners admitted that they had been training in South Yemen.

The previously-unknown Union of the Peoples of the Arabian Peninsula later claimed credit, saying the attack was part of a "national progresive Islamic Arab revolution."

On January 9, 1980, 63 of the 170 militants arrested in the Mosque were beheaded in the early morning. The locations of the executions and nationalities of those executed were: Mecca: nine Saudis, two South Yemenis, one Egyptian, one Kuwaiti, one Sudanese, and one Iraqi; Riyadh: seven Saudis, two Egyptians, and one Kuwaiti; Medina: one South Yemeni, two Egyptians, and four Saudis; Damman: three Saudis, one Kuwaiti, one Egyptian, one South Yemeni, and one North Yemeni; Buraydah: five Saudis, one South Yemeni, and one Egyptian; Tabuk: three Saudis, one South Yemeni and one Egyptian. As the executions were held in the early morning, few Saudis saw the carrying out of the Koranic sentences, which were not televised. Juhaiman Bin Seif, the military commander of the group, was among those executed. The 107 other individuals, including 23 women and boys, were given various prison and "re-education center" terms. Another 38 persons were found not guilty and were released.

The Saudis reported that 12 officers and 115 noncommissioned officers were killed in the mosque battle. Another 49 officers and 402 noncommissioned officers and soldiers were injured. Officials reported 75 terrorists killed during the siege, while 27 later died from their injuries. Fifteen bodies were found when the mosque vaults were cleared. The final government tallies indicated that 270 people were killed and more than 550 wounded. At least 117 rebels and 26 pilgrims were among the dead.

November 21, 1979—Pakistan—Mobs believing that the U.S. was involved in the attack on Mecca attacked the U.S. consulate in Karachi, destroyed the American library in Lahore, and burned the American Center and British library in Rawalpindi. The Bank of America office in Islamabad was set on fire. American Express and Pan American Airways offices were also attacked.

November 21, 1979—Pakistan—Two Americans and two Pakistani employees of the U.S. embassy were killed when a mob attacked and burned down the U.S. embassy. The attack began when busloads of 300 to 400 students from nearby Quaid-i-Azam University drove to the embassy to protest the rumored U.S. involvement in the attack on Mecca. The attackers quickly overcame Pakistani guards and tore down protective grills. One of them seized a guard's rifle and shot in the head and killed Marine Corporal Steven Crowley, 19, who was defending the embassy from the roof. As word of the attack spread, the mob grew, with estimates ranging from 20,000 to 50,000 participants. Although an inflammatory statement by Iran's Ayatollah Khomeini was initially blamed for the attack, his broadcast over Tehran radio did not come until two hours after the siege began.

The government sent a few police to the embassy, but they were quickly overwhelmed by the mob. Three helicopters flying overhead apparently did nothing to thwart the mob. U.S. Ambassador Arthur W. Hummel, lunching at home when the noon attack began, spent hours trying to get the Pakistanis to send troops. U.S. Secretary of State Cyrus Vance also asked Pakistani President Mohammed Zia ul-Haq for aid, but it was five hours before troops cleared the embassy roof of armed demonstrators.

The students seized and beat Agency for International Development employee Thomas G. Putscher, thirty-two, took him from the compound, and held him hostage for five hours before releasing him.

The Americans and Pakistani employees fled to the steel-encased code room, while the attackers set the building on fire. Smoke poured into the room, while the raiders fired rifles down the ventilator shafts. The ninety Americans finally escaped through a steel hatch to the roof, which had been cleared of attackers by the Pakistani police.

The $21 million embassy chancery was destroyed, as was housing for fifty persons in the compound. The burned bodies of two Pakistani employees of the embassy were later found outside of the code room. The charred body of Army Warrant Officer Bryan Ellis, thirty, was found in his gutted apartment in the compound. At least two demonstrators later died of their injuries. Marine Sergeant Mike Sirois, twenty-seven, was treated at the British embassy for burns on his forearms, which may have been caused by the tear gas canisters he was tossing at the invaders.

The Pakistanis were criticized for their slow response, and over three hundred dependents and nonessential embassy personnel left the country soon after, leaving seventy people to man the embassy and other installations. President Carter later announced that there would be a personnel drawdown in ten Moslem countries where violence might break out.

Fourteen persons were arrested and faced trial by Pakistani military courts on charges of murder, assault, and arson.

November 21, 1979—Zambia—Tony Joyce, a correspondent for the Australian Broadcasting Corporation, was shot in the head somewhere east of Lusaka on the Great East Road, which leads to Malawi.

November 23, 1979—Malaysia—The U.S. embassy in Kuala Lumpur was evacuated after receiving a bomb threat. No bomb was found.

November 23, 1979—India—Mobs believing that the U.S. was responsible for the Mecca attack injured eight policemen when they tried to attack the U.S.

consulate in Calcutta. The crowd of 1000 set fire to cars, looted shops, and attacked the Soviet consulate. Two groups of demonstrators were organized by Indira Gandhi's Congress Party and a Moslem party.

November 23, 1979—Argentina—A bomb exploded at the home of Lopez Akimenco, the planning and industrial relations manager of the local Swift meat-packing plant at La Plata. The early morning attack caused damage but no injuries.

November 23, 1979—Japan—Kazumi Nomura, armed with a bottle opener and a small plastic knife, hijacked a Japan Air Lines DC10 flying from Osaka to Tokyo with 345 passengers and a crew of eleven and diverted it to Narita Airport in Tokyo for refuelling. He demanded to be flown to the Soviet Union, and threatened the life of a crew member. He was overpowered by the crew, but Toshiyuki Nishihiro, thirty-nine, the pilot, was injured on the wrist.

November 24, 1979—United States—A teenager armed with a knife demanded that an American Airlines B727 flying from San Antonio to Los Angeles fly him to Iran. The plane landed as scheduled at El Paso with seventy-one persons on board. After four hours of negotiations, the former paratrooper from Fort Benning, Georgia, was taken into custody, and held on $500,000 bail. He was released from the Army infantry during training because he was unable to adjust to the military. None of the 20 on board was injured. Hijacker Gerald James Hill was from Chester, Massachusetts.

November 24, 1979—United States—The FALN, a Puerto Rican independence group, claimed credit for three bombs which exploded during the night at two Chicago military recruiting offices and the Naval Armory. No injuries were reported.

November 25, 1979—Spain—The Secret Armenian Army for the Liberation of Armenia claimed credit for two bombs which went off in front of the Madrid offices of Alitalia, Sabena of Belgium, British Airways, and Trans World Airlines. The SALA said these were airlines of world imperialists, and that the attack was to serve as a warning to Pope John Paul II to cancel his trip to Turkey. Two people were slightly injured.

November 25, 1979—Turkey—Mehmet Ali Agca, a Turkish right-wing terrorist, escaped from prison and threatened to assassinate Pope John Paul II during his three-day visit to Turkey. Agca is accused of murdering journalist Abdi Ipekci. Agca said the attack would be "revenge" for the attack in Mecca.

Late November 1979—France—Armenian nationalists bombed the Turkish Airlines office in Paris, wounding three police guards.

November 25, 1979—United States—Eulalio Negrin, a member of the Committee of 75, which has negotiated the release of Cuban political prisoners, was shot to death as he opened his car door in the Cuban community of Union City, New Jersey. He was hit five times by fire from a semiautomatic weapon. Omega Seven claimed responsibility. During the spring, Negrin had opened the New Jersey Cuban Social Club to help reunite Cuban families. Omega Seven soon bombed that storefront.

November 27, 1979—France—A Ukrainian nationalist group claimed responsibility for firebombing and destroying three Soviet vehicles. Two Soviet embassy cars were parked near the homes of the embassy staff, and a minibus was parked in front of the Soviet trade mission in Paris.

November 28, 1979—United States—The Dallas clothing store of Mansor Morid, twenty-nine, an Iranian, was damaged by a fire apparently set by arsonists protesting the holding of the U.S. embassy in Tehran. Anti-Iranian slogans were painted on the store's walls, and two empty gasoline cans and two cans of spray paint were found at the scene. Damage was estimated at $4000.

November 28, 1979—El Salvador—Archibald Gardner Dunn, fifty-eight, the South African ambassador, was kidnapped as he was leaving his embassy for lunch by twelve to eighteen terrorists armed with submachine guns. The group threw him in the back of a blue pickup truck they had stolen minutes before the kidnapping, and fled without firing a shot.

Coincidentally, the El Salvadoran government had decided to break diplomatic relations with South Africa and announced this decision on November 29. The government nonetheless promised to do everything in its power to secure the ambassador's safe release.

Numerous hoax calls were received, but the government ultimately accepted as credible a claim of responsibility by the Farabundo Marti Popular Liberation Forces. The FPL demanded the payment of an undisclosed sum of money to be negotiated with the family; El Salvador's severance of relations with Israel, Chile, and Argentina; diplomatic recognition of Asian governments struggling for their sovereignty and of the Palestine Liberation Organization; release of political prisoners; and the trials of former Presidents Arturo Armando Molina and Carlos Humberto Romero, and the military chiefs who collaborated with them. The group set a December 27 deadline for the publication of its two declarations in the world's newspapers. It deemed the break in relations with South Africa as "demogogic" and an attempt to divert international attention, although it also had some positive aspects. The FPL expressed solidarity with Zimbabwe and other southern African countries dominated by the Republic of South Africa.

On the 29th, Dunn's relatives said the Republic was willing to negotiate his release. South Africa sent Johannes Volschenk to negotiate. Archbishop Oscar Romero offered to mediate. Robin Gardner Dunn, thirty-one, the ambassador's son, offered to join his father because of the ambassador's ill health.

Dunn had served in El Salvador for the past six years. He was the subject of an unsuccessful similar kidnapping attempt in which his driver was killed soon after his initial arrival in the country..

On December 23, 1979, the kidnappers said they would execute Dunn on January 15 if their manifesto was not published in 102 countries. Salvadoran papers allowed the kidnappers' December 27 deadline to pass without publishing the communiqués. On December 28, the South African government asked Panama to help obtain Dunn's release. The request was made through Panama's ambassador to the U.S. On December 31, the Salvadoran radio station YSU received two handwritten notes from Dunn addressed to his wife and a friend, Salvadoran industrialist Ernesto Rivas Gallont, who agreed to mediate. Dunn also requested for a woman identified as Delmi to intercede for his release. A Cuban reporter was permitted to interview Dunn and released an FPL manifesto on April 23, 1980. The group had previously threatened to set a deadline for Dunn's execution but decided to await reports on Dunn's activities from the South African Revolutionary Liberation Front.

November 30, 1979—Thailand—Two explosions went off in the American embassy compound at 6:40 A.M., nicking the concrete lip of a fountain and damaging some palm trees. Seventy M-79 grenade fragments were found. No injuries were reported. Two Thai men were reported cleaning the pool shortly before the explosion. When it was determined that such work had not been authorized, police began a search for the duo. Police later found an M-72 anti-tank rocket launcher, loaded with a rocket, at a construction site fifty meters from the embassy gates. Thai Prime Minister Kriangsak Chomanan suggested that Moslem separatists might have been responsible.

December 1979—Afghanistan—Two Soviets were killed as they toured Kabul's old bazaar unescorted.

December 1979—Bahrain—The Sons of the Occupied Territory Organization claimed credit for a bomb which shattered the glass front of a Manama complex housing the offices of Gulf Air and KLM Royal Dutch Airlines. No injuries were reported. The group, apparently Palestinians, said they were protesting against "airline companies allied with imperialism and Arab reactionaries."

December 1979—Iran—*The Washington Post* reported that foreign intelligence services alerted the Iranian government to two plans to assassinate Ayatollah Ruhollah Khomeini. The *Post*'s source speculated that Iranian political exiles in Paris were responsible.

December 2, 1979—Thailand—The U.S. embassy received a bomb threat at 12:45 P.M. from a man speaking Thai who said ''You'd better be careful today because something may be thrown over the wall.''

December 2, 1979—Libya—As estimated 2000 Libyans claiming to support Iran set fire to the U.S. embassy in Tripoli, destroying the first floor and damaging much of the second of the four-story building. The twelve American diplomats, two wives of staff employees, and six Libyan employees managed to escape unharmed through a side door after burning classified materials. The group eventually was dispersed by an automatic tear gas system. The Libyan authorities did not respond to requests by the embassy for protection, despite the fact that the U.S. had agreed not to post Marine guards at the facility. Some State Department officials noted that some of the attackers wore military uniforms, and that sound trucks were allowed at the scene. On December 4, the State Department announced a cutback of its diplomatic activities in Libya. Two days later, the Libyans expressed willingness to pay for the damages to the embassy.

December 3, 1979—West Germany—A bomb exploded in the early morning at the Frankfurt office of the American Morgan Guaranty Trust Company, causing some damage but no injuries. Police were informed by telephone that a suspicious person had placed a bag against the building. While police threw stones at the bag, the bomb exploded. Police suggested that the attack was connected with the Iranian crisis, as Morgan had obtained an attachment order from a German court against Iranian shares in the Krupp Company as a guarantee for outstanding credits. Police discounted letters saying that the target was the Metal Association, which promotes atomic energy, as the modus operandi did not fit the Revolutionary Cells.

December 3, 1979—Puerto Rico—Two sailors were killed and ten others injured when a U.S. Navy school bus carrying thirteen enlisted men and five enlisted women was ambushed by Puerto Rican terrorists at 6:42 A.M. The terrorists blocked the bus with a green truck on highway 867 bisecting the U.S. Naval Security Group Activity, a communications facility ten miles west of San Juan at Sabana Seca. They hit the bus with forty rounds from their M-16 rifles, then escaped in a van, which was found abandoned in Levittown, a San Juan suburb. John Robert Ball, of Madison, Wisconsin, the driver of the bus and a communications expert, was killed immediately. Also reported dead was Emil E. White, a radioman from Charlotte Amalie, St. Thomas, in the Virgin Islands. The five women were all wounded, as was Petty Officer Joseph R. Key, twenty-two, of El Paso, Texas. Three terrorist groups—the Organization of Volunteers for the Puerto Rican Revolution, the Puerto Rican Popular Army, and the Armed Forces of Popular Resistance—said that they were protesting the death three weeks previously of Angel Rodriguez Cristobal in a Tallahassee, Florida prison. He was arrested while protesting the Navy's use of Vieques Island, off Puerto Rico, for target practice. Prison authorities said he committed suicide by hanging, but the terrorists claimed he was murdered. Juan Mari Bras, fifty-one, the secretary-general of the Puerto Rican Socialist Party, defended the killing, labelling it an "act of war, still very isolated, of a sector of the independence movement."

December 3, 1979—United States—Cubana de Aviacion shifted the departure of its Soviet-built airliner from Newark to JFK Airport after receiving a threat from Omega 7 against the first regular charter service between Havana and New York.

December 4, 1979—United States—The United Americans phoned the State Department twice, threatening to kidnap fifty Iranian students in the United States and execute them if the hostages in Iran were harmed. The callers threatened students in Washington, D.C., California, Texas, Illinois, and New York.

December 4, 1979—United States—A bomb exploded in the New York offices of Union Travel Service, slightly injuring two employees and causing extensive damage. Croatian exiles threatened to detonate two other bombs if their political demands were not publicized.

December 4, 1979—Argentina—Robert Cox, the editor of the English-language *Buenos Aires Herald*, said that he would leave the country after his ten-year-old son received a letter from the Montoneros threatening to murder his family.

December 4, 1979—Ireland—The nine members of the European Community signed the European Convention on the Suppression of Terrorism, which deems that, for the purposes of extradition, the following crimes are not to be considered "political": air hijacking, hostage taking, attacks on diplomats, using a bomb, or attempting to do same or being an accomplice in such crimes. The convention allows any signatory to try a suspect even though the crime may have been committed on the territory of another signatory.

December 5, 1979—Thailand—A device thrown over the wall of the U.S. consulate in Chiang Mai at 4 P.M. was initially believed to be a bomb. It was later found to be only five dry cell batteries.

December 7, 1979—United States—At 11:40 P.M., a bomb exploded at the Cuban U.N. mission, causing damage and injuries to two policemen.

December 7, 1979—Guatemala—Three Nicaraguan businessmen and a Guatemalan companion were found shot to death in a faked auto accident. Felipe Gutierrez Garcia, Felipe Silva and Ramon Molina Gomez, as well as their Guatemalan friend, Alejandro de Jesus Medrano Mijangos, were shot with handguns, then placed into their car which was set on fire and pushed down a steep cliff. Local observers suggested that "the deaths have all the characteristics of a political vendetta which indicates that there is a Nicaraguan terrorist group in Guatemala looking for former officials or friends of deposed President General Anastasio Somoza Debayle."

December 7, 1979—France—Prince Shahriar Shafik, thirty-four, son of the deposed Iranian Shah's twin sister, Princess Ashraf, and a former captain in the Iranian Navy, was assassinated at 1 P.M. while he was walking down a street in Paris' 16th district near the home of his sister, Princess Azzadeh. A lone gunman wearing a motorcycle helmet walked up behind him and shot him in the neck with an automatic pistol. As Shafik lay bleeding, the gunman fired a second shot into his head, then escaped the scene. He was described as being 25 to 30 years old, athletically built, and of medium height.

Ayatollah Sadegh Khalkhali, the self-appointed leader of Iran's revolutionary tribunals, said that his Fedayen-e-Islam assassination squads were responsible. However, Shafik's name had not appeared on the hit lists of the Shah's relatives previously announced by the Tehran government. Iranian embassies in London and Vienna said that Khalkhali did not speak for the Iranian government.

The Moslem Liberation Front also claimed credit for the assassination, saying that Shafik was an enemy of Islam and of the Iranian people. They charged that the French had sided with "international Zionism," and proclaimed "Long Live Khomeini."

Iranian exiles suggested that Iran's secret police, Savama, was responsible. General Farouzian, the second-ranking member of Savama, had spent three weeks in Paris recently, allegedly because of differences with the chief of Savama. However, General Kaveh, the head of Savama, was also seen at Farouzian's Paris hotel. Many exiles alleged that five former Savak safehouses in Paris were now being used by Savama. Shafik's lawyer, Marc Valle, said General Hossein Fardust, a senior Savama official, had spent forty-eight hours in Paris the previous week. Princess Azzadeh claimed that she and Shafik had noticed motorcyclists driving near the house the previous week, but that French authorities had turned down their requests for protection. The princess backs *Free Iran*, an exile newspaper, and reportedly is attempting to form a military exile group, the Iran Liberation Army.

On December 10, the British Home Office announced that it was questioning a young Iranian in Dover who had travelled from London to Paris and back on the day of the assassination. The next day, he was expelled to Paris. An investigation by the French indicated he was apparently not the murderer.

December 9, 1979—Italy—Two bombs exploded at the Rome offices of Pan American Airways, World Airways, British Airways, and Philippine Airlines, injuring twelve persons. Armenian exiles claimed responsibility.

December 9, 1979—Puerto Rico—Two unidentified gunmen fired on a U.S. Navy sentry vehicle patrolling inside the perimeter of the Roosevelt Roads Naval Base during the night, causing no injuries. The duo escaped. No group claimed responsibility.

December 11, 1979—El Salvador—A bomb exploded at 10:30 P.M. at the Israeli embassy, damaging furniture and shattering windows but causing no injuries. The Revolutionary Peoples Army (ERP) said it was protesting fascist Zionism and racism. The ERP expressed solidarity with the Palestine Liberation Organization and the Farabundo Marti Popular Liberation Forces.

December 11, 1979—Guatemala—The National League for the Protection of Guatemala vowed to kill Mexican President Jose Lopez Portillo during his visit to Guatemala, saying that Guatemalans, particularly those arrested, were ill-treated in Mexico. The league said it was responsible for poisoning animals in the Mexican Gasca Brothers Circus.

December 11, 1979—Spain—A gasoline bomb damaged the Madrid office of Amnesty International. No one was injured.

December 11, 1979—United States—A powerful bomb exploded at 9:38 P.M. at the Soviet U.N. mission, injuring four Soviets and four New York policemen, none of them seriously, and damaging the building. The anti-Castro Cuban exile group Omega 7 said that it was protesting "Soviet colonialism which threatens our Hispanic-America and the free world." The bomb was planted in the driveway of the mission's garage. The Soviets loudly protested the bombing, saying that the United States called for protection of its diplomats in Iran, but was unable to protect diplomats at home.

December 12, 1979—Lebanon—Gunmen fired on the Volvo-244 auto of a Palestinian official near an Arab deterrent force roadblock in Beirut during the night. Gunmen inside the car returned the fire. One person was wounded.

December 12, 1979—El Salvador—Members of the February 28 Popular League (LP-28) seized an office building in San Salvador, taking hostage twelve Salvadorans and U.S. Peace Corps volunteer Deborah Loff, twenty-four, of Succasunna, New Jersey. The group demanded lower taxes and market stall rents, and installation of a Marxist national government. The group released four Salvadorans on December 14, but the mayor said that such economic reductions would wreck the market system. The group released Loff and Oscar Oreliana, manager of the San Jacinto Market, moments before ending their occupation on December 21. The group said that the government had agreed to a 25 percent reduction in stallholders' rents.

December 12, 1979—El Salvador—The U.S. embassy was evacuated after receiving a bomb threat at noon.

December 13, 1979—Iran—Shots were fired on the Japanese embassy at 1 A.M., causing no injuries. Two rifle bullet marks were found on the front outside wall.

December 14, 1979—Belgium—A parcel bomb exploded in Brussels' main mail-sorting center, seriously injuring two postal workers. The package had been mailed in Belgium for a foreign address, which was not immediately determined. No one claimed responsibility for the blast.

This may have been the first in a wave of IRA letter bombs mailed from Belgium to prominent Britishers listed in an old copy of *Who's Who*. The different-sized packets were wrapped like Christmas gifts in colorful paper, and hand-addressed, at times to old addresses of the individuals. Police said that the IRA was retaliating for the arrest of twenty-five IRA members in London the previous week. Operations in Belgium would be more difficult to police. The IRA claimed credit for the letter bomb attacks, saying that it was singling out "members of the establishment" to underscore the continuing protest in Northern Ireland's Maze Prison by convicted IRA terrorists who claim political prisoner status.

December 14, 1979—United Kingdom—An Iraqi man, arriving in London on a Middle Eastern Airlines flight from Beirut, was arrested after he was found to be carrying explosives and detonators concealed in tubes of instant shaving foam.

December 14, 1979—Turkey—Four Americans were shot to death in an ambush near their suburban Istanbul homes as they were arriving home for work at the Cakmakli military base at 5:40 P.M. The four were getting out of their car in the Florya district when five men and one woman pulled them from their car and shot them before fleeing in a stolen blue or white Turkish-made sedan. The Turkish chauffeur of their military car, Kamil Korkmaz, was wounded. Police found forty-six spent cartridges from the Kalashnikov rifles the terrorists had used. A retired Turkish army colonel fired a shotgun at the terrorists from the house where the Americans lived, possibly wounding some of the terrorists.

The dead were identified as U.S. Army Sergeant James Smith, forty, and three civilians of the Boeing Aircraft subsidiary on a contract at the NATO munitions depot: Jim Clark, sixty-three, Elmer Cooper, sixty-five, and Robert Frantz, forty-eight.

The Marxist-Leninist Armed Propaganda Unit of the Turkish Peoples' Liberation Front/Party claimed credit for the attack, saying, ''Guerrillas of the cell sought to punish the four American military officials. The goal of the attack is to expose American plots designed to suppress popular movements particularly in Iran and the Middle East in general.'' On February 13, 1980, Turkish authorities announced the arrest of Nazli Caglayan, alias The Scorpion, a woman believed to have masterminded the killings, along with three accomplices. Later, Suleyman Polat, leader of a squad of fifty-six terrorists arrested by government forces, submitted a thirty-two-page written confession to the killings.

December 15, 1979—France—The Voice of Lebanon reported that Paris police arrested an individual who had a loaded pistol and who intended to assassinate Faruq Qaddumi, the chief of the Palestine Liberation Organization's Political Bureau.

December 15, 1979—Cyprus—A tall and heavily built gunman fired a silenced weapon at two Palestine Liberation Organization officials who were entering their Renault with diplomatic plate JY 929, killing both shortly after 6 P.M. He ran to a small white rented car with ZJJ plates, and drove off with a second individual. The dead were Ibrahim Abdul Azis Raghif, alias Abu Safwat, thirty-five, a member of Fatah's office in Beirut, and Samir Toukan, alias Salim Ali, thirty, the second secretary of Fatah's office in Cyprus. Ali's wife, a Greek Cypriot, was not hurt in the attack.

The PLO accused Israel of the attack. Israel replied that Abu Safwat was in Cyprus to organize raids against Egyptian and Israeli targets. The Marj 'Uyun Lebanon Voice of Hope claimed that Libya was behind the assassination, in an attempt to protect its embassies from attacks by the PLO, with which it was feuding. A Nicosia newspaper received a phone call from the National Patriotic Front M.P. 14/31, which said, "Our intention was to do it on the 14th and not the 15th. Samir had collaborated with Greek Cypriots and mainland Greeks in crimes they had committed and were intending to commit in the future against the Greek nation....We warn those Greek Cypriots and mainland Greeks who collaborate with the Palestinian organization that they will suffer the same fate."

Police asked Interpol's aid in finding Jeffrey Sowden, who resides in Britain and holds a South African passport, and Ahmad Najib Burji, who resides in Beirut and holds a Lebanese passport.

December 17, 1979—United Kingdom—A half-pound bomb exploded at 9 P.M. at the Turkish Airlines office in Hanover Street in London's West End, causing considerable damage but no injuries. Police said the bomb was either thrown from a passing car or placed against a window. The Front for the Liberation of Armenia told Agence France-Presse, "This is a warning for Turkish fascism and British imperialism. We will continue our struggle against world imperialism and its pet, Turkish fascism, until the liberation of Armenia. As well, we back the IRA and all revolutionary movements in Ireland in their fight against British fascism."

December 17, 1979—Sweden—Zairean Ambassador Mobuto Dongo Yema, forty-three, brother of Zaire's President Mobutu Sese Seko, died in Stockholm's Danderyd Hospital during the night after apparently having been poisoned by "oppositional elements" from Zaire. He was conscious upon arriving at the hospital, but was vomiting blood, and died within the hour. Hours earlier, he had requested protection from Swedish authorities because of death threats, and had previously asked permission to carry a gun. On January 18, 1980, Swedish police said that the ambassador died from a drug overdose.

December 17, 1979—United Nations—The General Assembly adopted by consensus a convention against the taking of hostages. The convention calls for states to prosecute or extradite hostage-takers "without exception whatsoever." The convention was opened for signature on December 18, and will come into effect when twenty-two states have ratified it.

December 17, 1979—United Kingdom—Two IRA letter bombs exploded at post offices in Dover and Gerrards Cross, slightly injuring two postal workers. The intended addressees could not be determined, but it was believed that the packages were part of a batch mailed from Belgium to prominent Britishers.

December 18, 1979—United Kingdom—A package bomb was spotted before being opened at the suburban Cheshire home of Sir William Mather, director of the National Westminster Bank and a financial advisor to Queen Elizabeth II. His wife became suspicious of the Belgian postmark, and Sir William then noticed some strange-looking wires inside. He quickly put the package in the garden and called the police, who safely detonated the IRA bomb.

December 18, 1979—Philippines—Jeremy Ladd Cross, forty, of Lawrence, Massachusetts, a U.S. businessman, was shot in the neck by two men on motorcycles. He and his Filipino wife were leaving their offices in suburban Pasay City.

December 19, 1979—United Kingdom—An IRA letter bomb was delivered to the suburban London home of Lord Croham, former head of the Civil Service who is now an industrial advisor to the head of the Bank of England and a Deputy Chairman of the state-owned British National Oil Corporation. Lady Croham noticed that the package was addressed to "Sir Douglas Allen," her husband's title before he was made a life peer in 1978. He became suspicious after seeing the package's Belgian postmark. Police safely defused the bomb.

December 19, 1979—United Kingdom—A London postman found an IRA letter bomb in a Paddington sorting office addressed to Sir Arthur Knight, chairman of the Courtaulds Textile Company and the National Enterprise Board, a state body that aids industrial development. The bomb was defused. The device was addressed to a home he sold a year ago.

December 19, 1979—United Kingdom—An IRA letter bomb was delivered to the home of Sir Charles Villiers, chairman of the state-owned British Steel Corporation. Lady Villiers, a wartime refugee from Belgium with friends there, became suspicious when she did not recognize the handwriting on the package. She said, "I knew immediately that there was something odd. I thought there was a fair chance that it was a bomb because of all the publicity." Police were called in to defuse the bomb.

December 19, 1979—El Salvador—The Revolutionary People's Army set fire to the Alfa Romeo dealership in the western part of San Salvador in reprisal against police treatment of leftist demonstrators.

December 19, 1979—West Germany—A Ukrainian nationalist group claimed credit for setting fire during the night to the Munich office of Aeroflot, the Soviet airline. The ground floor of the Bernheim building in Lehnbach Square was damaged. The 15 October Commando said it was fighting for Ukrainian liberation and demanded "the immediate withdrawal of Soviet occupation troops." The group's name may come from the 15 October 1959 death of

Stephen Bandera, a Ukrainian nationalist, who died from potassium cyanide poisoning. Damage was estimated at DM300,000.

December 19, 1979—Venezuela—An Abu Dhabi newspaper reported that an attempt was made to poison the food of Dr. Mani' Sa'id al-'Utaybah, the UAE's Minister of Petroleum and Natural Resources, during the OPEC meeting in Caracas. The attempt was foiled.

December 20, 1979—Greece and Turkey—Following the deaths of two PLO representatives in Cyprus, Israeli representatives received telephoned threats.

December 21, 1979—Egypt—Cairo airport officials arrested Iranian Falah ad-Din Mohammad Gotchen as he arrived from Athens. He confessed that he was a member of the Iranian Fedayeen Islam organization, led by Shaykh Mohammad Sadegh Khalkhali, which was designed to export the Iranian revolution. He was to set six fires in Cairo, then move on to commit similar acts in other Egyptian cities, including Aswan and Alexandria. He had been given 215,000 Iranian rials for the operation by Grisha al-Ibrahimi, who had recruited Gotchen for the organization. On January 6, 1980, Egyptian authorities reported that they were investigating individuals Gotchen claimed were members of the organization. He was remanded to custody.

December 21, 1979—United States—Two security guards found a ticking bomb in some bushes near the Bethesda, Maryland, offices of the Taiwan Coordination Council for North American Affairs, which handles Taiwanese interests in the U.S. One of the guards threw the bomb from the building. The device, in a box the size of a paperback book, exploded at 7:20 A.M. in the air.

December 21, 1979—United Kingdom—A postal sorter spotted an IRA letter bomb addressed to a British Cabinet minister, Employment Secretary James Prior.

December 21, 1979—United Kingdom—An IRA letter bomb was defused.

December 22, 1979—United Kingdom—An IRA letter bomb was defused.

December 22, 1979—United Kingdom—Explosives experts defused an IRA letter bomb found in a London mail sorting office. It was addressed to the Mansfield home of Norman Siddall, deputy chairman of the National Coal Board.

December 22, 1979—United States and United Kingdom—FBI and New York City policemen raided the Nutley, New Jersey, offices of an electronics firm on a federal warrant and recovered bombs, booby traps and firearms. Scotland Yard agents raided a building in Crewe, seizing documents and taking several persons into custody. Two undercover detectives at the New York Hilton Hotel pursuaded two gunrunners that they were Caribbean revolutionaries, paid the men a $56,000 deposit for a $2 million sale of 10,000 machine guns, then arrested them. Police later uncovered briefcase bombs, letter bombs, grenades, poison darts, and scores of documents. One of those arrested, Frank Edward Terpil, claimed to be a former CIA employee who subsequently provided arms to Libya, had trained terrorists, advised Idi Amin, and had sold $3.2 million in weapons to the Ugandans. George Gregory Korkala drives an automobile with diplomatic plates registered to Uganda's United Nations mission. He was identified as the owner of the Amstech Corporation, the Nutley firm. John Dutcher, described by New York police as a "self-proclaimed assassin," was also held at the Hilton as a material witness. The trio were held without bail, and face a maximum of twenty-five years in prison if they are convicted of all the charges against them.

December 22, 1979—Zimbabwe-Rhodesia—After the signing of the peace accords between black nationalists and the interim Rhodesian government, three black gunmen sprayed the Salisbury family home of Robert Mugabe, Patriotic Front co-leader, with gunfire. Patrick Mugabe, twelve, was shot through the leg and Innocent Mugabe, twenty-seven, was grazed in the cheek. The duo were Mugabe's nephews. The Patriotic Front blamed agents of the former government of Bishop Abel Muzorewa for the attack.

December 22, 1979—France—Yilmaz Kolpan, thirty-one, press attaché of the Turkish embassy and manager of the Turkish Tourism and Information Bureau on the Champs-Elysées, was machine-gunned to death in front of Fouquet's, the Paris sidewalk café. Anonymous telephone callers to news agencies in Paris and Beirut said the Armenian Justice Commando Against Genocide intended to "shoot every Turkish political man in Europe and give the Armenians the rights they are not given by the Turkish Government."

December 23, 1979—Italy—The Armenian Secret Army for the Liberation of Armenia claimed credit for bombing the Rome offices of Air France and TWA. Some damage but no casualties were reported. A third bomb blew up in the staircase of a small hotel.

December 23, 1979—Iran—Unidentified gunmen knocked on the door of the Tehran home of Syrian Ambassador Ibrahim al-Yunis at 2 A.M. When a Revolutionary Guard guarding the residence opened the door, the gunmen fired Israeli-made Uzi machine guns. Reinforcements rushed to the scene, but the gunmen escaped in a waiting car.

December 24, 1979—United Kingdom—Two IRA bombs mailed from Belgium were defused by police.

December 26, 1979—Uruguay—A bomb destroyed the Montevideo monument to Franklin Roosevelt. The base of the statue was damaged by a bomb on April 22, when unidentified individuals claimed that they attacked the monument because FDR was "a Jew and a Mason."

December 28, 1979—El Salvador—The People's Liberation Forces attempted to bomb the San Salvador offices of the First National City Bank during the morning. A night watchman was killed while trying to prevent the attack. A terrorist and a bystander were killed in the explosion.

List of Organizations and Acronyms

This list includes names of organizations for which responsibility was claimed or attributed for specific terrorist actions described in the chronology. The inclusion of any group should not be interpreted as an evaluation of that organization's goals or motivations. Some attacks may have been carried out without the approval or even foreknowledge of the organization's leaders. Other claims of responsibility may have been falsely made by opponents of the organization who are attempting to discredit their enemies.

Many of the groups listed are cover names for organizations that wish to deny responsibility for a particular action that produced counterproductive results. Some names may have been used by common criminals to throw off police investigators or by psychotics seeking public recognition. No attempt has been made to pierce these covers, and the names provided by the claimants have been accepted.

Sources are often vague regarding the names of the group responsible or unclear about the amount of legally acceptable evidence available that leads to attribution of responsibility. The names of the major suspects in such vague cases have been used.

The list is organized according to the probable nationality of the terrorists or, when ambiguous, by the terrorists' area of operations. For some organizations, I have been unable to identify the full name so provide just the acronym.

GROUPS WITH INDETERMINATE NATIONALITY

Ché Guevara Brigade
International Ché Guevara Organization
International Revolutionary Front
Islamic Liberation Organization
Moslem International Guerrillas
VFVP   LBF

WESTERN HEMISPHERE

Argentina

Argentine Anti-Communist Alliance (AAA)
Argentine Liberation Front (FAL)

Argentine National Organization Movement (MANO)
Argentine National Social Front
Argentine Youth for Sovereignty
Comite Argentino de Lucha Anti-Imperialisto
Descamisados Peronistas Montoneros
ERP-August 22
Frente de Liberacion Nacionel del Vietnam del Sur
Maximo Mena Command
Montoneros
Movemento Peronista
Peronist Armed Forces (FAP)
People's Revolutionary Army (ERP; Ejercito Revolucionario del Pueblo)
Revolutionary Armed Force (FAR)

Bolivia

National Liberation Army (ELN)
Nationalist Commando

Brazil

Action for National Liberation (ALN)
Armed Revolutionary Vanguard-Palmares (VAR-Palmares)
Aurora Maria Nacimiento Furtado Command
Revolutionary Movement of the Eighth (MR-8)
Vanguarda Popular Revolucionaria (VPR)

Canada

Canadian Hungarian Freedom Fighters Federation
Quebec Liberation Front (FLQ)

Chile

Chilean Socialist Party
Proletarian Action Group
Revolutionary Movement of the Left (MIR)

Colombia

Group of Revolutionary Commandos-Operation Argimiro Gabaldon
Invisible Ones
Military Liberation Front of Colombia
Movement of April Nineteenth (M-19)
National Liberation Armed Forces
National Liberation Army (ELN)
People's Revolutionary Army-Zero Point
Popular Liberation Army (EPL)

Red Flag (Bandera Roja)
Revolutionary Armed Forces of Colombia (FARC)
Revolutionary Workers Party
September 14 Workers Self-Defense Command
United Front for Guerilla Action

Costa Rica

Revolutionary Commandos of Solidarity
Roberto Santucho Revolutionary Group

Cuba

Abdala
Alpha 66
Anti-Castro Commando
Anti-Communist Commandos
Brigade 2506
Condor
Coordination of United Revolutionary Organizations (CORU)
Cuba Action
Cuban Action Commandos
Cuban Anti-Communist League
Cuban C-4 Movement
Cuban Liberation Front
Cuban National Liberation Front (FLNC)
Cuban Power (el Poder Cubano)
Cuban Power 76
Cuban Representation in Exile
Cuban Revolutionary Directorate
Cuban Revolutionary Organization
Cuban Youth Group
International Secret Revolutionary United Cells
JCN
Latin American Anti-Communist Army
Movement for Cuban Justice
Movement of the Seventh (M-7)
National Integration Front (FIN; Cuban Nationalist Front)
Omega 7
Pedro Luis Boitel Command
Pedro Ruiz Botero Commandos
Pragmatistas
Scorpion (el Alacran)
Second Front of Escambray
Secret Anti-Castro Cuban Army

Secret Cuban Government
Secret Hand Organization
Secret Organization Zero
Young Cubans
Youths of the Star

Dominican Republic

Dominican Popular Movement (MDP)
Twelfth of January Liberation Movement
United Anti-Reelection Command

El Salvador

Armed Forces of National Liberation (FARN)
Faribundo Marti Liberation Labor Forces (FPL; Popular Liberation Front)
February 28 Popular League (LP-28)
People's Revolutionary Army (ERP)
Popular Revolutionary Bloc (BPR)
Revolutionary Party of Central American Workers (PRTC)
United Popular Action Front (FAPU)
White Warriors Union

Guatemala

Guatemalan Anti-Salvadoran Liberating Action Guerrillas (GALGAS)
Guatemalan Nationalist Commando
National League for the Protection of Guatemala
National Liberation Movement
Peoples Guerrilla Army of the Poor (EGP)
Revolutionary Armed Forces (FAR; PGT/FAR; Rebel Armed Forces)
Revolutionary Movement of November 13 (MR-13)

Guyana

People's Temple

Haiti

Coalition of National Liberation Brigades
Haitian Coalition

Mexico

Armed Communist League
Armed Vanguard of the Proletariat
Mexican People's Revolutionary Army
People's Armed Command
People's Liberation Army

People's Revolutionary Armed Forces (FRAP)
Twenty-third of September Communist League
United Popular Liberation Army of America

Nicaragua

Sandinist National Liberation Front (FSLN)

Paraguay

Political Military Organization
Popular Colorado Movement (MoPoCo, dissident faction of Colorado party)

Peru

Armed Nationalist Movement Organization (MANO)
Condor
Movement of the Revolutionary Left (MIR)
MTR
Peruvian Anti-Communist Alliance (AAP)
Revolutionary Vanguard

Puerto Rico

Armed Commandos of Liberation
Armed Forces of Popular Resistance
Armed Front for National Liberation (FALN)
Independence Revolutionary Armed Commandoes
MIRA
Organization of Volunteers for the Puerto Rican Revolution
People's Revolutionary Army
Puerto Rican Liberation Front
Puerto Rican Popular Army
Puerto Rican Resistance Movement

United States

Black Panther Party (BPP)
Black Revolutionary Assault Team
Hanafi Muslims
Hungarian Peace and Freedom Fighters
International Committee Against Nazism
Jewish Action Movement
Jewish Armed Resistance (JAR)
Jewish Armed Resistance Strike Force
Jewish Armed Resistance Strike Movement
Jewish Armed Resistance Strike Unit
Jewish Committee of Concern

Jewish Defense League (JDL)
Jewish Defense League-Wrath of God
Jewish Underground Army
New Jewish Defense League
New World Liberation Front (NWLF)
Pan Epirotic Federation of America and Canada
Red Guerilla Family
Republic of New Africa
Revolutionary Action Party
Revolutionary Affinity Group Six
Revolutionary Communist Party (USA) Committee to Give a Fitting Welcome
Revolutionary Force Seven
Save Our Israel Land (SOIL)
Student Struggle for Soviet Jewry
United Americans
United Revolutionary Soldiers of the Council of Reciprocal Relief Alliance for
    Peace, Justice, and Freedom Everywhere
Weatherman faction of Students for a Democratic Society
White Panthers

Uruguay

Armed Popular Front (FAP)
National Liberation Movement (MLN; Tupamaros)
Organization of the Popular Revolution-33 (OPR-33)
PCU
Raul Sendic International Brigade

EUROPE

Albania

Anti-Communist Military Council

Austria

Justice Guerrilla

Belgium

Julien Lahaut Brigade
Revenge and Freedom

Cyprus

Enosis Movement (EOKA-B)
National Patriotic Front M.P. 14/31

France

Action Front for the Liberation of the Baltic Countries
Andreas Baader Commando
Autonomous Intervention Collective Against the Zionist Presence in France
Avengers
Charles Martel Group
Committee for Socialist Revolutionary Unity
Committee of Coordination
Group for the Defense of Europe
International Solidarity
Jewish Self-Defense Front
Masada Action and Defense Movement
Movement for the Defense of Europe
Movement of Youthward Brothers in War of the Palestinian People
New Order
Organization Delta
Red Army Faction of Southern France
Sixth of March Group
Solidarity Resistance Front
Talion Law
We Must Do Something
Youth Action Group

Greece

Army Officers Representing the Free Greek Spirit
ELA
Free Greeks
Greek Anti-Dictatorial Youth (EAN)
Greek Militant Resistance
Greek People
Independence-Liberation-Resistance (AAA)
National Youth Resistance Organization
Organization of November 17
Patriotic Front
Peoples Resistance Organized Army
Popular Liberation Organized Army
Popular Resistance Sabotage Group-11 (LAOS 11)
Popular Resistance Sabotage Group Number 13 (LAOS Number 13)
Popular Resistance Sabotage Group People Number One (LAOS People Number 1)
Popular Revolutionary Resistance Group
Union of Officers Struggling for the National Idea

Italy

Armed Communist Formations
Armed Proletarian Nuclei (NAP)
Armed Proletarian Power
Autonomous Workers Movement
Black Order (Ordine Nero)
Combatants for Communism
Proletarian Committee of Subversion for Better Justice
Proletarian Internationalism
Proletarian Justice
Proletarian Squad
Red Brigades (BR)
Red Guerrilla
Revolutionary Action Group

Netherlands

Red Brigades
Revolutionary Peoples Resistance of the Netherlands

Spain

Anti-Fascist Resistance Group of October 1 (GRAPO)
Basque Nation and Freedom (ETA; Euzkadi Ta Azkatasuna)
Commando of Solidarity with Euzkadi
Hammer and Sickle Cooperative
Iberian Liberation Movement (MIL)
International Revolutionary Action Group (GARI)
Juan Paredes Manot International Brigade
Nationalist Intervention Group
Popular Revolutionary Armed Front (FRAP)
Spanish Armed Group
Spanish National Association
Warriors of Christ the King

Sweden

B-26

Switzerland

Les Beliers de Jura
Petra Kraus Group

Portugal

Action Group for Communism
ARA

Portuguese Anti-Communist Movement
Portuguese Liberation Army
Revolutionary Internationalist Solidarity

Union of Soviet Socialist Republics

October 15 Commando

United Kingdom

Black Liberation Army
Irish Freedom Fighters
Irish National Liberation Army (INLA)
Irish Republican Army-Provisional Wing (IRA-Provos)
Red Flag 74
Sinn Fein
Ulster Defense Association (UDA)
Ulster Volunteer Force (UVF)
Young Militants

West Germany

Andreas Baader Commando of the Red Army Faction
Baader Solidarity Group
German Liberation Popular Front, Andreas Baader Brigade
Holger Meins Brigade
Holger Meins Kommando, Revolutionary Cell
International Anti-Terror Organization
Puig Antich-Ulrike Meinhof Commando
Red Army Faction (RAF; Baader-Meinhof Gang; BMG)
Revolutionary Cell Brigade Ulrike Meinhof
Robert E. D. Straker Commando of the Territorial Resistance Army
Second of June Movement
Socialist Patients Collective
Ulrike Meinhof Commando

Yugoslavia

Croatian Intelligence Service
Croatian National Liberation Forces-Fighters for a Free Croatia
Croatian National Resistance
Freedom for the Serbian Fatherland (SOPO)
Trotskyist Organization
Young Croatian Army for Freedom
Young Croatian Republican Army

AFRICA

Angola

National Union for the Total Independence of Angola (UNITA)
Popular Movement for the Liberation of Angola (MPLA)

Cabinda

Front for the Liberation of the Enclave of Cabinda (FLEC)

Canary Islands

Canary Islands Independence Movement
Canary Islands Intelligence Service
Movement for Self-Determination and Independence for the Canary Islands
    (MPAIAC)

Chad

Chadian National Liberation Front (FROLINAT)

Djibouti

National Independence Union (UNI)

Ethiopia

Eritrean Liberation Front (ELF)
ELF-General Command
ELF-Revolutionary Council
Popular Liberation Forces (PLF)
Tigre Peoples Liberation Front (TPLF)

French Somaliland

Popular Liberation Movement
Somali Coast Liberation Front (FLCS)

Mozambique

Mozambique Liberation Front (FRELIMO)
Mozambique Revolutionary Council (COREMO)

Rhodesia-Zimbabwe

Patriotic Front (PF)
Zimbabwe African National Union (ZANU)
Zimbabwe African Peoples Union (ZAPU)

Somalia

Somali Liberation Front

Spanish Sahara

Mustafa el Wali Bayyid Sayed International Brigade
Popular Front for the Liberation of Saguia el Hamra and Rio do Oro
    (POLISARIO)

Zaire

Peoples Army of the Oppressed in Zaire
Peoples Revolutionary Party

ASIA

Afghanistan

Afghan Islamic Society
Afghan National Liberation Front
Afghan National Liberation Movement
Islamic Movement of Afghanistan

Bangladesh

National Socialist Party (JDS)

Burma

Kachin Independence Army

India

Ananda Marg
Kashmiri Liberation Front
Universal Proutist Revolutionary Front

Indonesia

Darul Islam Holy War Command
Free South Moluccan Youth Organization
Front for the Liberation of Aceh-Sumatra

Japan

Anti-Japan Armed Front of East Asia
Chosen Soren
Japanese Red Army (JRA; Arab Red Army; Army of the Red Star; breakaway
    of United Red Army; Red Army Faction; Rengo Sekigun)
Maruseido (Marxist Youth League)
Okinawa Liberation League
VZ 58 (name of Czech weapons used by Japanese Red Army)

Philippines

Kabataang Makabayan
Moro National Liberation Front (MNLF)
Peoples Revolutionary Front

Taiwan

People's Liberation Front
World United Formosans for Independence

Thailand

Pattani Liberation Front

MIDDLE EAST AND NORTHERN AFRICA

Algeria

Soldier of the Algerian Opposition
United Liberation Front of New Algeria

Iran

Fedayeen
Forghan
Iranian Peoples Strugglers (IPS; Mujahiddin e Khalq)
Iranian Students Assocation (ISA)
Moslem Liberation Front
National Front Forces of Iran
Reza Rezai International Brigades

Iraq

Free Iraq

Israel

Irgun Zevai Leumi
Wrath of God

Jordan

Jordanian Free Officers Movement
Jordanian National Liberation Movement

Lebanon

Imam As-Sadr Brigades
Lebanese Revolutionary Guard
Lebanese Revolutionary Socialist Movement

Lebanese Socialist Revolutionary Organization (Shibbu Gang)
Phalange
Phalangist Security Group
Revolutionary Arab Youth Organization
Socialist Labor Party
Standard Bearers of Imam Musa As-Sadr Organization

Oman

Peoples Liberation Army

Palestine

Abdel Nasser Movement
Action Organization for the Liberation of Palestine (AOLP)
Arab Communist Organization (CAO)
Arab Liberation Front (ALF)
Arab People (Ash-Shab al-'Arabi)
Arab Revolutionary Army-Palestinian Commando
Arab Revolutionary Movement
Arm of the Arab Revolution
Black June Organization (BJO)
Black March Organization
Black September-June
Black September Organization (BSO)
Commando Muhammed Boudia
Correct Course of Fatah (Al-Khat as-Sahih Lifatah)
Eagles of the Palestine Revolution (EPR; Red Eagles)
Fatah
Friends of the Arabs
Ghassan Kanafani Commandos
Group of the Fallen Abd al Kadir al Husayni
Mount Carmel Martyrs
National Organization of Arab Youth
National Youth Group for the Liberation of Palestine
Organization of Arab Nationalist Youth for the Liberation of Palestine
    (ANYOLP)
Organization for the Victims of Zionist Occupation
Organization of the Struggle Against World Imperialism (SAWIO)
Organization of Avenging Palestinian Youth
Organization of the Sons of Occupied Territories
Organization of the Sons of Palestine
Organization of Victims of Occupied Territories
Palestine Liberation Army (PLA)
Palestine Liberation Organization (PLO)

Palestine Popular Struggle Front (PSF)
Palestine Rejection Front
Palestine Revolutionary Forces
Palestine Revolutionary Movement
Popular Democratic Front for the Liberation of Palestine (PDFLP)
Popular Front for the Liberation of Palestine (PFLP)
PFLP-General Command
PFLP-Special Operations
Punishment Squad (al Icab)
Rejection Front of Stateless Palestinian Arabs
Saiqa (Thunderbolt)
Seventh Suicide Squad
Sons of the Occupied Land
Squad of the Martyr Patrick Arguello

Saudi Arabia

Union of the Peoples of the Arabian Peninsula (UPAP)

Turkey

Acilciler
Armenian Liberation Army
Avengers of the Armenian Genocide
Front for the Liberation of Armenia
Justice Commandos of the Armenian Genocide
Justice of Armenian Genocide
Marxist-Leninist Armed Propaganda Unit (MLAPU)
Mayir Cayan Suicide Group
New Armenian Resistance Group
Secret Armenian Army for the Liberation of Armenia (Secret Armenian
    Liberation Army; SALA)
Slave Kortin Yanikiyan Group
Turkish Peoples Liberation Army (TPLA)
Turkish Peoples Liberation Front (TPLF)
Turkish Revolutionaries
Turkish Revolutionary Youth Federation
28 May Armenian Organization
Yanikian Commandos

Yemen

Eagles of National Unity

Index
Terrorist Incident Location Dates, 1968-1979*

Abu Dhabi
September 09 75
October 25 77

Afghanistan
May 01 73
February 14 79
April 19 79
June 24 79
June 26 79
August 12 79
September 01 79
September 07 79
September 09 79
September 29 79
December xx 79

Algeria
October 06 72
January 03 76
January xx 76
July xx 77
April 05 78

Angola
June 08 69
April 08 75
September xx 75
October 09 75
October 23 75
November 21 75
April 07 76
December 14 77
November 09 79

Argentina
February 09 68
March 08 68
October 01 68

October 03 68
October 9 68
October 16 68
June 19 69
June 26 69
September 09 69
October 06 69
October 07 69
October 08 69
November 20 69
December 05 69
March 03 70
March 07 70
March 24 70
March 27 70
March 29 70
April 13 70
June 18 70
June 27 70
August 09 70
September 07 70
September 09 70
September 15 70
October 02 70
October 05 70
October 13 70
October 16 70
October 20 70
October 21 70
October 28 70
October 29 70
November 12 70
November 19 70
November 20 70
November 27 70
November 30 70
December 18 70
January 11 71
March 15 71

April 14 71
April 22 71
April 27 71
May 03 71
May 15 71
May 17 71
May 23 71
July 09 71
July 09 71
March 21 72
May 12 72
June 09 72
June 30 72
August 15 72
September 05 72
October 16 72
November 07 72
November 09 72
December 06 72
December 10 72
December 27 72
February 03 73
February 05 73
March 28 73
April 02 73
April 08 73
April 30 73
May 01 73
May 21 73
May 23 73
May 31 73
June 06 73
June 18 73
June 19 73
June 23 73
July 02 73
July 04 73
July 08 73
August 11 73

September 18 73
September 19 73
September 21 73
October 01 73
October 08 73
October 09 73
October 20 73
October 22 73
October 23 73
November 17 73
November 22 73
November 23 73
November 28 73
December 06 73
December 21 73
December 28 73
January 02 74
January 03 74
January 19 74
January 21 74
February 12 74
February 23 74
March 12 74
March 16 74
March 25 74
April 04 74
April 12 74
May 03 74
May 03 74
May 27 74
June 03 74
June 15 74
June 19 74
June 25 74
July 17 74
July 23 74
August 06 74
August 27 74
September 08 74

*Unknown dates are designated by xx.

Bolivia, cont.

September	22	70
September	22	70
October	07	70
December	07	70
May	12	71
June	07	71
August	21	71
August	21	71
September	24	71
May	13	73
May	10	76
February	14	78

Botswana

November	19	76
January	22	77

Brazil

March	19	68
April	15	68
April	29	68
October	12	68
October	14	68
October	18	76
October	27	68
June	11	69
September	04	69
September	06	69
September	20	69
September	29	69
October	13	69
November	12	69
January	23	70
January	24	70
March	11	70
April	05	70
April	21	70
April	26	70
June	11	70
July	01	70
July	16	70
July	24	70
August	22	70
September	30	70
December	07	70
February	05	71
August	25	71
October	30	71
November	03	71
November	09	71

January	11	72
February	05	72
February	07	73
February	21	73
May	18	73
August	12	73
October	01	73
February	19	74
July	03	76
July	xx	76
July	03	77

Bulgaria

December	02	70

Burma

May	04	73
March	04	75

Burundi

October	23	70

Cambodia

December	01	70
February	27	71
June	01	71
June	16	71
September	07	71
September	26	71
September	27	72
December	23	78

Canada

April	13	68
May	24	68
May	20	69
October	01	69
June	21	70
September	10	70
September	11	70
October	05	70
October	10	70
November	26	70
October	18	71
April	04	72
December	12	72
January	21	74
August	19	74
August	22	75
July	24	76
September	01	77

Canary Islands

January	03	77
June	15	78

Chad

April	21	74
January	29	78
January	30	78
February	02	78

Chile

February	20	68
March	12	68
March	16	68
October	10	69
December	19	69
July	30	70
August	04	70
August	30	70
October	08	70
October	10	72
October	13	72
July	25	73
July	27	73
August	12	73
August	15	73
August	27	73
September	04	73
December	08	73
May	01	76
July	23	76
July	05	77
November	16	77
October	27	78
February	27	79
July	20	79
August	08	79

Colombia

February	16	68
March	05	68
October	06	69
October	07	69
October	14	69
March	18	70
April	02	70
April	02	70
June	04	70
July	06	70
November	07	70
October	01	71

October	14	71
November	26	71
March	10	72
July	17	72
September	21	72
May	30	73
October	04	73
January	31	75
April	xx	75
August	05	75
September	27	75
December	16	75
January	14	76
January	30	76
February	16	76
February	27	76
March	30	76
April	03	76
July	17	76
July	24	76
July	27	76
August	04	76
September	08	76
September	28	76
October	09	76
October	27	76
December	16	76
January	03	77
January	27	77
January	31	77
February	14	77
March	11	77
March	31	77
April	15	77
June	08	77
September	07	77
October	31	77
December	20	77
January	11	78
February	15	78
February	17	78
May	10	78
May	29	78
July	18	78
July	23	78
July	28	78
October	11	78
November	09	78
March	01	79
May	01	79
May	29	79

Ethiopia, cont.

Month	Day	Year
March	xx	76
June	11	76
June	15	76
June	xx	76
August	05	76
August	xx	76
January	28	77
March	20	77
March	27	77
April	07	77
April	26	77
June	22	77
July	14	77
September	29	77
January	12	78

Finland

Month	Day	Year
February	27	79

France

Month	Day	Year
February	18	68
March	18	68
January	09	70
September	27	70
March	22	71
March	25	71
April	18	71
April	30	71
March	21	72
May	10	72
May	25	72
May	30	72
July	13	72
August	30	72
October	04	72
October	06	72
November	13	72
December	08	72
December	23	72
January	08	73
January	28	73
March	15	73
April	04	73
April	05	73
May	24	73
June	28	73
August	02	73
August	28	73
September	05	73
December	14	73
December	20	73
December	xx	73
January	06	74
February	01	74
March	01	74
May	03	74
July	03	74
July	16	74
July	25	74
July	26	74
July	28	74
August	03	74
August	23	74
August	xx	74
September	13	74
September	15	74
October	25	74
December	15	74
December	16	74
December	19	74
January	13	75
January	19	75
February	08	75
March	02	75
March	06	75
March	30	75
April	10	75
May	03	75
May	07	75
May	22	75
May	xx	75
June	05	75
June	12	75
June	27	75
June	28	75
July	26	75
August	28	75
August	29	75
September	16	75
September	26	75
October	07	75
October	08	75
October	14	75
October	18	75
October	24	75
December	10	75
unknown	xx	75
January	09	76
January	12	76
January	31	76
February	06	76
February	11	76
February	12	76
February	20	76
February	22	76
March	07	76
March	08	76
March	21	76
April	12	76
April	23	76
May	09	76
May	10	76
May	11	76
May	17	76
May	27	76
May	28	76
June	03	76
June	04	76
July	14	76
July	25	76
July	26	76
August	28	76
September	04	76
September	29	76
October	25	76
October	28	76
November	02	76
December	24	76
January	03	77
February	03	77
April	05	77
April	12	77
April	13	77
April	27	77
May	14	77
June	17	77
June	20	77
July	07	77
August	21	77
September	12	77
September	29	77
October	19	77
October	20	77
October	22	77
November	10	77
November	15	77
November	19	77
November	27	77
January	19	78
January	23	78
March	04	78
March	18	78
May	04	78
May	20	78
May	26	78
June	19	78
June	25	78
July	03	78
July	31	78
August	03	78
September	17	78
October	17	78
December	20	78
January	13	79
March	27	79
April	06	79
May	04	79
July	02	79
July	06	79
July	08	79
July	25	79
August	02	79
September	13	79
September	17	79
November	xx	79
November	27	79
December	07	79
December	15	79
December	22	79

Gabon

Month	Day	Year
June	21	79

Ghana

Month	Day	Year
September	21	73
April	01	76

Greece

Month	Day	Year
December	26	68
June	11	69
July	23	69
August	09	69
November	27	69
December	21	69
January	05	70
March	14	70
July	25	70
September	02	70
September	08	70
September	09	70
November	26	70
January	01	71
February	07	71
March	13	71
April	26	71
May	14	71
July	03	71
July	08	71

Iran, cont.

October	14	79
November	04	79
November	05	79
December	xx	79
December	13	79
December	23	79

Iraq

March	01	75
December	15	76
December	18	76
February	28	77

Ireland

May	30	70
February	28	71
September	04	71
December	13	71
February	02	72
March	20	72
June	08	72
June	10	72
October	05	72
December	01	72
January	01	73
January	xx	73
January	24	74
March	12	74
April	26	74
May	17	74
September	29	74
September	15	75
September	15	75
October	03	75
November	29	75
February	12	76
March	31	76
April	xx	76
July	03	76
July	21	76
August	30	76
March	17	77
April	09	77
November	26	77
October	12	78
August	25	79
August	27	79

Israel

January	13	68
February	20	68

February	21	68
February	24	68
March	18	68
April	18	68
August	06	68
August	18	68
August	19	68
August	21	68
September	04	68
November	22	68
December	29	68
December	31	68
February	21	69
February	25	69
March	06	69
May	15	69
May	30	69
June	19	69
June	20	69
June	24	69
August	07	69
August	15	69
August	26	69
September	02	69
October	22	69
October	23	69
November	19	69
January	01	70
January	24	70
February	23	70
May	22	70
August	13	70
November	06	70
February	25	71
March	02	71
March	04	71
March	22	71
April	11	71
June	04	71
June	11	71
June	23	71
July	07	71
September	16	71
January	05	72
January	16	72
May	01	72
May	30	72
June	20	72
July	11	72
September	16	72
September	29	72
October	25	72

November	03	72
April	21	73
July	19	73
July	23	73
December	04	73
December	05	73
February	11	74
April	11	74
May	15	74
May	27	74
June	04	74
June	13	74
June	25	74
August	07	74
August	10	74
September	02	74
September	04	74
November	19	74
November	30	74
December	06	74
December	11	74
December	20	74
March	05	75
June	15	75
June	23	75
July	04	75
July	09	75
July	18	75
October	05	75
October	24	75
October	27	75
November	09	75
November	13	75
November	20	75
November	23	75
January	02	76
January	09	76
January	13	76
March	20	76
May	03	76
May	10	76
May	25	76
June	27	76
July	18	76
July	25	76
July	30	76
August	13	76
September	26	76
December	04	76
April	13	77
April	14	77
April	24	77

May	28	77
June	29	77
July	06	77
July	20	77
July	28	77
August	04	77
August	16	77
September	11	77
October	15	77
October	25	77
November	13	77
December	03	77
January	20	78
February	14	78
February	19	78
March	11	78
April	26	78
June	02	78
September	05	78
September	30	78
November	19	78
November	20	78
December	12	78
March	07	79
March	23	79
June	16	79
June	22	79
July	06	79
September	19	79

Italy

February	19	68
July	22	68
June	18	69
August	29	69
September	13	69
January	04	70
March	01	70
May	03	70
May	30	70
September	25	70
October	06	70
October	24	70
October	30	70
July	22	71
July	28	71
April	21	72
May	28	72
June	03	72
August	05	72
August	16	72
October	16	72

Lebanon, cont.											
March	04	73	October	29	75	September	08	79	January	20	74
April	01	73	November	12	75	October	19	79	February	04	74
April	14	73	November	13	75	November	11	79	February	05	74
April	16	73	November	24	75				February	24	74
April	27	73	November	xx	75	**Lesotho**			March	14	74
April	28	73	December	06	75	April	13	70	March	21	74
April	29	73	December	08	75				March	22	74
April	30	73	December	18	75	**Libya**			May	14	74
May	01	73	December	25	75	September	11	70	August	28	74
May	02	73	January	01	76	November	19	77	**November**	**08**	**74**
July	23	73	January	10	76	March	06	78	November	14	74
September	24	73	January	xx	76	July	19	78	November	18	74
October	18	73	February	16	76	August	17	78	November	25	74
November	25	73	February	23	76	October	16	79	December	05	74
March	03	74	March	19	76	December	02	79	January	27	75
March	15	74	**April**	20	76				January	28	75
March	16	74	April	22	76	**Malaysia**			March	07	75
May	01	74	April	xx	76	December	06	70	April	02	75
May	08	74	May	16	76	October	04	72	May	17	75
May	28	74	June	16	76	October	10	72	July	19	75
July	03	74	June	27	76	October	14	72	September	02	75
July	21	74	July	09	76	October	31	72	November	28	75
August	02	74	August	06	76	October	xx	72	November	29	75
August	29	74	August	09	76	November	02	72	January	19	76
September	01	74	October	08	76	October	19	73	May	23	76
September	xx	74	December	24	76	August	04	75	May	25	76
October	11	74	May	06	77	February	10	76	June	05	76
November	01	74	July	08	77	November	16	77	July	16	76
December	10	74	November	17	77	November	19	77	July	24	76
December	12	74	November	18	77	December	04	77	November	30	76
December	15	74	December	18	77	November	23	79	December	08	76
December	21	74	December	19	77				December	13	76
December	xx	74	December	20	77	**Malta**			January	20	77
January	28	75	January	29	78	April	23	71	May	06	77
February	11	75	June	21	78				May	25	77
February	17	75	August	02	78	**Mauritania**			July	22	77
February	20	75	August	03	78	May	01	77	August	09	77
February	xx	75	August	13	78	October	25	77	September	13	77
April	16	75	December	11	78	**Mexico**			September	14	77
May	13	75	January	16	79	May	16	70	August	29	78
May	31	75	January	22	79	September	18	71	October	04	78
June	29	75	March	01	79	October	02	71	November	07	78
August	02	75	April	02	79	November	19	71	August	08	79
September	xx	75	April	16	79	July	17	72			
October	04	75	June	20	79	September	16	72	**Morocco**		
October	22	75	July	16	79	October	07	72	November	10	72
October	25	75	August	01	79	November	08	72	November	27	72
October	26	75	August	13	79	May	04	73	March	03	73
October	27	75	August	17	79	October	10	73	March	05	73
October	28	75	September	03	79	November	26	73	October	11	74
			September	07	79	December	03	73	November	13	77

Philippines, cont.

March	04	70
June	06	70
September	08	70
November	22	70
January	23	71
February	12	71
February	16	71
March	30	71
June	12	71
August	30	71
May	11	72
June	05	72
July	04	72
July	18	72
August	25	72
August	26	72
September	23	72
Unknown	xx	72
April	13	74
July	25	75
August	26	75
August	30	75
September	26	75
November	07	75
February	28	76
April	07	76
May	15	76
May	21	76
June	14	76
August	04	76
December	11	76
January	14	76
January	18	78
February	07	78
February	26	78
April	07	78
April	25	78
October	23	79
October	30	79
December	18	79

Poland

January	26	75

Portugal

October	23	70
November	20	70
October	27	71
November	08	71
September	11	75

September	27	75
January	16	76
February	12	76
April	22	76
July	21	76
July	23	76
October	13	76
December	15	76
May	16	77
October	28	77
June	09	78
November	13	79

Puerto Rico

November	23	70
March	xx	72
June	14	72
April	24	73
April	04	74
April	10	74
April	22	74
April	23	74
July	26	74
August	06	74
October	08	74
October	09	74
October	28	74
November	12	74
December	28	74
February	24	75
November	01	75
October	25	76
December	29	77
February	08	78
February	09	78
February	16	78
July	03	78
August	08	78
April	28	79
September	17	79
December	03	79
December	09	79

Rhodesia, Zimbabwe

May	24	72
October	10	72
April	18	76
May	xx	76
December	05	76
December	20	76

February	06	77
March	01	77
August	06	77
August	09	77
May	09	78
May	18	78
June	03	78
June	08	78
June	17	78
June	23	78
June	28	78
August	01	78
November	30	78
December	26	78
January	01	79
February	12	79
April	17	79
April	30	79

Saudi Arabia

April	14	73
May	11	77
November	20	79

Scotland

March	04	78

Sierra Leone

October	26	70

Singapore

February	19	70
April	xx	73
January	31	74

Somalia

March	23	75
April	12	76

South Africa

May	08	70
November	09	70
July	20	72
December	31	74
April	28	75

South Korea

August	15	74

South Yemen
(People's Democratic Republic of Yemen)

June	24	78

Spain

January	07	68
March	25	68
February	17	69
December	12	69
December	01	70
May	29	71
August	24	71
April	19	72
September	15	72
November	02	72
January	17	73
January	26	73
May	01	73
May	02	73
December	20	73
January	21	74
February	08	74
February	13	74
April	09	74
September	08	74
September	11	74
October	11	74
May	16	75
August	13	75
August	22	75
September	09	75
September	15	75
September	28	75
April	04	76
May	12	76
May	26	76
July	20	76
September	27	76
October	27	76
November	07	76
December	11	76
February	22	77
May	17	77
May	20	77
July	12	77
October	13	77
February	22	78
March	17	78
June	02	78
June	03	78
January	20	79
January	31	79
February	12	79
February	19	79
March	28	79

Turkey, cont.

July	02	77
July	30	77
August	02	77
August	06	77
September	10	77
October	25	77
January	22	78
September	30	78
October	01	78
October	25	78
December	26	78
January	29	79
February	19	79
February	20	79
February	23	79
March	26	79
March	27	79
March	30	79
April	12	79
May	06	79
May	11	79
May	13	79
May	29	79
June	02	79
July	13	79
July	24	79
September	03	79
September	15	79
November	25	79
December	14	79
December	20	79

Uganda

May	03	70
July	07	70
July	07	70
May	26	78
August	xx	79

United Arab Emirates

December	14	77

United Kingdom

July	18	69
August	17	69
August	25	69
December	05	69
December	17	69
May	06	70
May	09	70

May	10	70
July	23	70
September	07	70
September	12	70
September	27	70
October	06	70
September	20	71
December	15	71
February	22	72
May	09	72
December	24	72
February	20	73
March	08	73
March	10	73
May	20	73
August	18	73
August	21	73
August	22	73
August	23	73
August	24	73
August	25	73
August	29	73
August	30	73
September	08	73
September	12	73
September	17	73
September	18	73
December	17	73
December	18	73
December	21	73
December	22	73
December	26	73
December	29	73
December	31	73
January	05	74
January	06	74
January	20	74
January	21	74
January	24	74
January	31	74
February	03	74
February	04	74
February	12	74
March	26	74
April	06	74
May	04	74
May	19	74
June	15	74
June	17	74
July	04	74
July	16	74
July	17	74

October	05	74
October	10	74
October	22	74
November	06	74
November	07	74
November	18	74
November	21	74
November	25	74
November	27	74
November	xx	74
December	16	74
December	18	74
December	21	74
December	22	74
January	xx	75
August	18	75
August	25	75
August	26	75
August	27	75
August	28	75
August	29	75
September	05	75
September	28	75
September	xx	75
October	09	75
October	12	75
October	23	75
October	29	75
November	03	75
November	09	75
November	12	75
November	18	75
November	27	75
December	06	75
December	21	75
January	07	76
February	12	76
February	18	76
February	18	76
March	04	76
March	15	76
March	27	76
July	10	76
January	29	77
February	02	77
February	03	77
April	10	77
July	18	77
October	31	77
December	31	77
January	03	78
January	04	78

February	06	78
February	17	78
March	06	78
July	09	78
July	15	78
July	28	78
August	20	78
August	25	78
September	13	78
December	17	78
December	18	78
January	18	79
February	24	79
March	30	79
June	08	79
June	14	79
August	29	79
December	14	79
December	17	79
December	18	79
December	19	79
December	21	79
December	22	79
December	24	79

United States

January	02	68
January	09	68
January	25	68
February	08	68
February	21	68
March	19	68
April	25	68
May	26	68
May	30	68
June	05	68
June	21	68
July	04	68
July	07	68
July	09	68
July	14	68
July	15	68
July	16	68
July	19	68
July	30	68
August	03	68
August	08	68
August	17	68
September	03	68
September	16	68
October	23	68
November	15	68

Unites States, cont.			November	24	79	February	25	71	March	12	69
December	23	77	November	25	79	June	28	71	June	30	69
December	26	77	November	28	79	October	21	73	August	30	69
January	08	78	December	03	79	March	25	76	September	08	69
January	12	78	December	04	79	March	30	76	November	09	69
January	31	78	December	07	79	March	31	76	December	05	69
February	05	78	December	11	79	November	17	76	December	12	69
February	21	78	December	21	79	December	08	76	December	13	69
March	03	78	December	22	79				February	10	70
March	18	78				**Vatican City**			February	13	70
May	13	78	**Uruguay**			September	11	76	February	17	70
May	14	78	February	13	68				February	21	70
May	22	78	May	02	68	**Venezuela**			April	22	70
June	24	78	September	10	68	May	06	70	April	25	70
July	10	78	October	07	68	April	06	71	May	01	70
July	12	78	June	20	69	July	01	71	May	03	70
July	16	78	June	27	69	October	08	71	May	05	70
July	xx	78	September	10	69	May	17	72	May	06	70
August	14	78	December	26	69	May	18	72	May	08	70
August	17	78	January	01	70	May	21	72	May	10	70
September	09	78	June	12	70	May	23	72	May	14	70
September	10	78	June	23	70	May	24	72	July	28	70
September	27	78	June	30	70	May	25	72	August	12	70
September	28	78	July	31	70	June	08	72	September	06	70
October	02	78	August	07	70	October	10	72	September	09	70
October	04	78	August	19	70	December	05	72	October	08	70
October	16	78	September	04	70	May	18	73	November	25	70
November	11	78	September	11	70	November	20	73	January	16	71
November	23	78	October	08	70	March	14	74	February	12	71
December	06	78	December	01	70	October	25	74	March	01	71
December	12	78	December	11	70	October	30	74	March	07	71
December	18	78	January	08	71	November	03	75	April	01	71
December	30	78	April	06	71	February	13	76	February	02	72
January	24	79	April	07	71	February	17	76	February	06	72
March	24	79	June	23	71	February	19	76	February	08	72
April	09	79	June	xx	71	February	27	76	February	22	72
May	18	79	July	12	71	April	23	76	May	11	72
May	23	79	August	09	71	October	07	76	May	12	72
June	01	79	September	07	71	October	21	76	May	17	72
June	20	79	November	29	71	Unknown	xx	76	May	24	72
August	02	79	March	21	72	March	05	77	June	15	72
August	07	79	April	03	72	November	16	77	September	05	72
August	30	79	April	03	72	December	12	78	September	20	72
October	02	79	July	28	72	December	19	79	December	24	72
October	18	79	December	26	79				December	28	72
October	27	79				**West Germany**			January	10	73
October	29	79	**USSR**			February	16	68	January	11	73
October	30	79	March	01	68	October	26	68	March	21	73
November	03	79	March	02	68	January	08	69	April	23	73
November	09	79	January	02	71	March	09	69	June	09	73
November	15	79	February	19	71	March	11	69	July	26	73

Index
Types of International Terrorist Attacks, by Date of Incident, 1968-1979*

*Unknown dates are designated by xx.

Assassination, cont.

Month	Day	Year
July	25	79
August	01	79
August	12	79
September	07	79
October	12	79
October	14	79
October	17	79
October	26	79
November	25	79
December	01	79
December	07	79
December	14	79
December	15	79
December	17	79
December	18	79
December	22	79

Barricade-Hostage

Month	Day	Year
June	09	70
August	31	70
September	17	70
October	05	70
February	10	71
September	05	72
October	06	72
December	28	72
January	20	73
January	27	73
February	20	73
March	01	73
July	19	73
September	05	73
September	28	73
October	16	73
October	18	73
February	06	74
May	15	74
May	22	74
September	02	74
September	04	74
September	13	74
September	27	74
October	25	74
October	26	74
November	18	74
December	05	74
December	27	74
January	19	75
March	05	75
April	24	75
April	28	75
June	15	75
August	04	75
September	05	75
September	15	75
September	28	75
October	08	75
November	05	75
November	11	75
December	04	75
December	06	75
December	21	75
February	03	76
February	23	76
September	26	76
October	11	76
March	09	77
May	23	77
November	26	77
February	03	78
March	13	78
July	03	78
July	31	78
August	17	78
August	22	78
September	29	78
December	12	78
January	16	79
February	12	79
February	14	79
May	04	79
May	11	79
July	13	79
October	24	79
November	04	79
November	05	79
November	20	79
December	12	79

Conspiracy

Month	Day	Year
January	02	68
November	15	68
December	02	68
June	14	69
September	xx	69
December	05	69
December	17	69
September	08	70
December	29	70
September	23	72
January	09	73
February	15	73
March	15	73
April	xx	73
May	20	73
September	11	73
October	18	73
December	20	73
January	20	74
April	22	74
June	13	74
June	27	74
August	13	75
August	22	75
September	03	75
May	01	76
September	26	76
February	09	77
March	04	77
October	25	77
January	20	78
March	06	78
April	20	78
April	21	78
May	31	78
June	09	78
June	20	78
July	xx	78
November	23	78
March	16	79
April	15	79
April	25	79
June	29	79
July	25	79
July	27	79
December	15	79

Exotic Pollution

Month	Day	Year
November	22	73
January	27	78
Janaury	31	78
January	31	78
February	01	78
February	02	78
February	05	78
February	06	78
February	07	78
February	13	78
March	04	78
August	24	79
November	xx	79

Explosive Bombing

Month	Day	Year
February	08	68
February	16	68
February	18	68
February	20	68
February	21	68
February	22	68
March	12	68
March	15	68
March	16	68
March	18	68
March	19	68
March	24	68
March	25	68
April	13	68
April	25	68
April	29	68
May	24	68
May	26	68
May	30	68
June	21	68
July	04	68
July	07	68
July	09	68
July	12	68
July	14	68
July	15	68
July	16	68
July	18	68
July	19	68
July	20	68
July	30	68
August	03	68
August	08	68
August	17	68
August	18	68
August	19	68
August	21	68
September	03	68
September	04	68
October	03	68
October	07	68
October	09	68
October	14	68
October	16	68
October	27	68
October	31	68

Explosive Bombing cont.

Month	Day	Yr	Month	Day	Yr	Month	Day	Yr	Month	Day	Yr
October	14	71	July	18	72	April	16	73	December	21	73
October	16	71	July	xx	72	April	21	73	December	26	73
October	24	71	August	05	72	April	24	73	December	30	73
October	27	71	August	08	72	April	28	73	December	31	73
November	08	71	August	16	72	April	29	73	December	xx	73
November	09	71	August	25	72	April	30	73	January	06	74
November	10	71	August	29	72	May	01	73	January	09	74
November	23	71	September	10	72	May	07	73	January	11	74
December	05	71	September	14	72	May	13	73	January	18	74
December	11	71	September	16	72	May	23	73	January	20	74
December	13	71	September	17	72	May	24	73	January	24	74
January	05	72	September	27	72	June	09	73	February	03	74
January	17	72	September	29	72	June	17	73	February	12	74
January	22	72	October	04	72	June	28	73	February	16	74
January	26	72	October	16	72	July	04	73	February	23	74
January	27	72	November	03	72	July	10	73	February	24	74
January	xx	72	November	05	72	July	22	73	March	07	10
February	02	72	November	09	72	July	24	73	March	10	74
February	06	72	November	15	72	July	25	73	March	12	74
February	08	72	November	23	72	July	26	73	March	14	74
February	17	72	December	01	72	July	27	73	March	16	74
February	22	72	December	07	72	August	02	73	March	22	74
March	02	72	December	08	72	August	12	73	March	26	74
March	10	72	December	11	72	August	15	73	March	xx	74
March	29	72	December	12	72	August	18	73	April	04	74
March	xx	72	December	24	72	August	23	73	April	06	74
April	04	72	December	xx	72	August	27	73	April	08	74
April	15	72	January	07	73	August	29	73	April	09	74
April	20	72	January	08	73	September	04	73	April	10	74
April	21	72	January	17	73	September	05	73	April	14	74
May	03	72	January	24	73	September	07	73	April	18	74
May	09	72	January	24	73	September	08	73	April	19	74
May	10	72	January	25	73	September	10	73	April	21	74
May	11	72	January	28	73	September	12	73	April	22	74
May	12	72	February	21	73	September	17	73	April	24	74
May	18	72	March	03	73	September	19	73	April	30	74
May	23	72	March	04	73	September	24	73	May	01	74
May	24	72	March	05	73	October	01	73	May	03	74
May	25	72	March	07	73	October	02	73	May	04	74
May	31	72	March	08	73	October	05	73	May	08	74
June	03	72	March	10	73	October	09	73	May	14	74
June	08	72	March	28	73	October	19	73	May	17	74
June	09	72	March	29	73	November	17	73	May	19	74
June	10	72	March	xx	73	November	26	73	May	22	74
June	14	72	April	01	73	December	03	73	May	23	74
June	15	72	April	04	73	December	05	73	May	28	74
July	11	72	April	05	73	December	14	73	May	30	74
July	17	72	April	09	73	December	17	73	June	01	74
			April	12	73	December	18	73	June	02	74
			April	14	73	December	20	73	June	05	74

Explosive Bombing cont.											
			August	18	76	May	19	77	November	13	77
			August	24	76	May	25	77	November	15	77
March	27	76	August	28	76	May	28	77	November	16	77
March	29	76	September	01	76	May	29	77	November	17	77
March	31	76	September	11	76	June	04	77	November	21	77
April	02	76	September	16	76	June	08	77	November	27	77
April	03	76	September	20	76	June	17	77	December	01	77
April	22	76	September	21	76	June	19	77	December	03	77
April	23	76	September	22	76	June	22	77	December	04	77
April	24	76	September	25	76	June	24	77	December	14	77
April	29	76	September	28	76	June	28	77	December	15	77
April	30	76	September	29	76	July	04	77	December	18	77
May	02	76	October	02	76	July	06	77	December	19	77
May	03	76	October	06	76	July	10	77	December	20	77
May	06	76	October	07	76	July	12	77	December	23	77
May	09	76	October	13	76	July	14	77	December	25	77
May	10	76	October	16	76	July	20	77	December	26	77
May	12	76	October	25	76	July	22	77	December	28	77
May	14	76	October	27	76	July	28	77	December	29	77
May	17	76	October	28	01	July	29	77	December	31	77
May	25	76	November	06	76	July	30	77	December	xx	77
May	26	76	November	07	76	August	01	77	January	02	78
May	27	76	November	09	76	August	03	77	January	03	78
May	28	76	November	13	76	August	05	77	January	14	78
June	06	76	November	19	76	August	06	77	January	19	78
June	08	76	November	30	76	August	08	77	January	21	78
June	09	76	December	01	76	August	11	77	January	22	78
June	14	76	December	04	76	August	14	77	January	24	78
June	25	76	December	15	76	August	16	77	January	29	78
June	27	76	December	16	76	August	21	77	January	31	78
June	xx	76	January	03	77	August	23	77	January	xx	78
July	01	76	January	04	77	August	26	77	February	05	78
July	02	76	January	06	77	September	01	77	February	08	78
July	03	76	January	25	77	September	07	77	February	09	78
July	09	76	January	29	77	September	10	77	February	11	78
July	10	76	January	31	77	September	11	77	February	13	78
July	17	76	February	03	77	September	13	77	February	14	78
July	18	76	February	18	77	September	14	77	February	15	78
July	20	76	February	22	77	September	19	77	February	16	78
July	21	76	March	06	77	October	11	77	February	17	78
July	23	76	March	21	77	October	13	77	February	19	78
July	24	76	March	27	77	October	15	77	February	21	78
July	25	76	March	28	77	October	19	77	March	04	78
July	26	76	March	31	77	October	20	77	March	07	78
July	27	76	March	xx	77	October	21	77	March	10	78
July	29	76	April	11	77	October	22	77	March	12	78
July	30	76	April	13	77	October	25	77	March	17	78
July	xx	76	April	24	77	October	26	77	March	25	78
August	04	76	May	06	77	October	28	77	April	02	78
August	09	76	May	14	77	November	06	77	April	26	78
August	16	76	May	17	77	November	12	77	May	06	78

Incendiary Bombing, cont.

July	28	70
August	08	70
September	07	70
September	18	70
September	22	70
September	25	70
October	06	70
October	08	70
October	09	70
October	14	70
November	12	70
November	25	70
December	03	70
January	17	71
January	25	71
February	14	71
February	16	71
March	02	71
March	06	71
March	07	71
March	15	71
March	20	71
March	25	71
May	15	71
June	12	71
July	01	71
July	09	71
July	25	71
August	09	71
August	22	71
September	07	71
September	15	71
October	01	71
October	08	71
October	30	71
November	03	71
November	22	71
November	26	71
February	02	72
April	16	72
April	19	72
April	25	72
May	11	72
May	12	72
May	17	72
June	18	72
September	15	72
October	07	72
October	10	72
November	02	72
December	23	72
December	26	72
December	28	72
January	10	73
January	17	73
February	05	73
March	22	73
March	23	73
April	05	73
April	09	73
April	23	73
April	25	73
May	01	73
May	02	73
May	18	73
May	26	73
June	20	73
July	20	73
August	29	73
August	30	73
September	08	73
September	14	73
September	28	73
October	08	73
December	08	73
December	18	73
December	xx	73
January	06	74
February	08	74
February	11	74
February	16	74
March	01	74
March	03	74
March	07	74
March	14	74
March	23	74
April	xx	74
May	29	74
June	11	74
July	21	74
August	09	74
August	17	74
August	26	74
September	16	74
October	06	74
November	03	74
November	05	74
November	14	74
November	22	74
November	25	74
December	24	74
December	27	74
December	xx	74
January	xx	75
March	24	75
April	02	75
April	10	75
April	xx	75
May	16	75
July	23	75
August	28	75
September	23	75
September	26	75
September	27	75
September	28	75
September	xx	75
October	25	75
October	29	75
January	02	76
January	09	76
January	12	76
January	21	76
February	11	76
February	12	76
March	08	76
March	12	76
March	14	76
March	19	76
March	20	76
April	04	76
April	12	76
April	14	76
April	17	76
April	23	76
May	06	76
May	12	76
May	14	76
May	17	76
May	19	76
May	20	76
May	26	76
May	xx	76
June	01	76
June	02	76
June	03	76
June	04	76
June	19	76
June	24	76
July	12	76
July	14	76
July	28	76
August	13	76
August	14	76
August	15	76
August	16	76
August	23	76
August	30	76
September	08	76
September	09	76
September	11	76
September	20	76
September	27	76
September	30	76
October	01	76
October	14	76
October	24	76
October	27	76
January	01	77
January	28	77
February	02	77
March	20	77
March	30	77
April	05	77
April	09	77
April	12	77
April	27	77
May	11	77
June	06	77
July	11	77
July	14	77
July	18	77
August	15	77
August	28	77
September	01	77
September	06	77
October	04	77
October	19	77
October	21	77
October	22	77
November	01	77
November	10	77
November	19	77
November	20	77
December	02	77
December	14	77
January	12	78
February	21	78
March	03	78

Kidnapping, cont.

Month	Day	Year
October	22	75
October	23	75
October	24	75
October	25	75
October	26	75
October	27	75
October	29	75
November	07	75
November	21	75
November	xx	75
December	22	75
December	xx	75
January	14	76
January	xx	76
February	27	76
February	28	76
March	xx	76
April	20	76
April	29	76
May	15	76
May	21	76
May	23	76
May	25	76
May	xx	76
June	11	76
June	15	76
June	26	76
June	xx	76
July	09	76
July	13	76
July	24	76
August	04	76
August	05	76
August	09	76
August	xx	76
September	01	76
September	10	76
September	28	76
October	21	76
December	11	76
December	18	76
Unknown	xx	76
January	15	77
January	28	77
February	14	77
February	28	77
March	11	77
April	01	77
April	07	77
April	13	77
April	19	77
April	20	77
May	01	77
May	20	77
May	25	77
May	29	77
June	17	77
June	19	77
June	28	77
August	09	77
September	05	77
September	07	77
September	10	77
September	15	77
September	25	77
October	03	77
October	25	77
October	28	77
October	30	77
November	09	77
November	13	77
November	29	77
December	14	77
December	29	77
January	18	78
January	23	78
February	02	78
February	17	78
February	21	78
February	26	78
March	07	78
March	16	78
April	15	78
May	08	78
May	10	78
May	17	78
May	29	78
July	18	78
August	01	78
August	08	78
August	14	78
August	29	78
September	09	78
October	04	78
October	11	78
October	21	78
November	07	78
November	24	78
November	30	78
December	07	78
December	11	78
December	27	78
January	01	79
January	17	79
February	14	79
February	19	79
March	09	79
March	27	79
May	13	79
May	29	79
June	05	79
June	15	79
August	02	79
August	21	79
September	21	79
September	23	79
October	30	79
November	09	79
November	28	79

Letter Bombing

Month	Day	Year
January	09	68
January	25	68
February	03	69
February	xx	69
August	08	69
October	06	70
November	09	70
December	16	71
January	02	72
March	20	72
July	19	25
July	25	72
July	xx	72
September	16	72
September	19	72
September	20	72
September	21	72
September	23	72
October	04	72
October	10	72
October	14	72
October	25	72
October	26	72
October	27	72
October	31	72
October	xx	72
November	02	72
November	06	72
November	10	72
January	24	73
January	xx	73
April	xx	73
August	18	73
August	21	73
August	24	73
August	25	73
August	27	73
August	28	73
September	11	73
September	17	73
September	18	73
October	26	73
December	17	73
December	22	73
January	21	74
January	31	74
February	01	74
February	04	74
February	05	74
February	12	74
February	13	74
May	07	74
May	22	74
December	31	74
August	20	75
September	15	75
May	27	76
June	03	76
June	14	76
July	23	76
August	27	76
January	20	77
January	22	77
February	23	77
December	28	77
December	29	77
January	06	78
November	30	78
March	01	79
April	03	79
April	19	79
June	01	79
June	08	79
June	14	79
November	15	79
December	14	79
December	17	79
December	18	79
December	19	79
December	21	79
December	22	79

Other Armed Attack, cont.

Month	Day	Year
June	01	78
August	16	78
August	20	78
September	16	78
September	17	78
October	10	78
October	25	78
November	01	78
December	20	78
January	24	79
February	14	79
April	01	79
April	17	79
April	25	79
April	28	79
May	15	79
September	07	79

Sabotage

Month	Day	Year
February	21	68
December	29	69
April	02	71
April	07	71
July	xx	71
September	09	71
January	xx	72
February	22	72
January	01	73
December	xx	73
April	21	74
July	04	74
August	13	76
September	01	76
April	15	79
April	30	79

Shootout with Police

Month	Day	Year
May	16	70
May	13	73
June	27	75
April	03	76
July	16	76
October	19	76
March	17	77
September	22	77
October	17	77
November	10	77
November	16	77
December	20	77

Sniping

Month	Day	Year
February	09	68
March	08	68
September	16	68
January	09	69
October	14	69
August	18	70
September	04	70
September	10	70
September	18	70
September	22	70
September	xx	70
December	06	70
February	20	71
March	16	71
October	20	71
March	21	72
May	21	72
May	28	72
December	05	72
April	16	73
July	04	73
December	11	73
July	04	73
December	11	73
July	17	74
October	30	74
December	07	74
January	19	75
January	xx	75
April	08	75
June	16	75
August	13	75
September	14	75
October	28	75
December	25	75
January	08	76
January	10	76
February	12	76
February	17	76
February	27	76
March	07	76
April	02	76
May	01	76
May	23	76
August	04	76
September	20	76
October	07	76
November	14	76
January	27	77
March	29	77
June	02	77
August	02	77
August	06	77
December	20	77
January	11	78
January	26	78
March	18	78
June	21	78
August	25	78
February	05	79
February	20	79
May	05	79
May	20	79
July	02	79
July	15	79
August	13	79
August	17	79
September	01	79
September	13	79
September	16	79
September	23	79
October	07	79
October	08	79
October	30	79
October	31	79
November	21	79
November	23	79
December	09	79
December	12	79
December	13	79

Theft, Break-in

Month	Day	Year
April	15	68
September	10	68
October	07	68
June	27	69
August	29	69
September	10	69
September	29	69
October	10	69
October	20	69
December	26	69
June	12	70
June	23	70
June	30	70
September	02	70
September	03	70
September	11	70
September	xx	70
October	07	70
October	21	70
October	28	70
November	20	70
November	27	70
November	30	70
December	11	70
December	18	70
January	07	71
January	11	71
February	05	71
April	14	71
April	22	71
August	21	71
August	xx	71
October	xx	71
November	xx	71
March	21	72
February	01	74
February	03	74
March	17	74
April	26	74
May	27	74
August	28	74
September	xx	74
December	xx	74
February	xx	75
May	14	75
June	28	75
September	27	75
October	28	75
November	12	75
November	13	75
January	xx	76
March	31	76
April	20	76
April	xx	76
February	15	78
March	17	78
October	18	78
October	27	78
October	30	78
November	09	78
December	12	78

Threat

Month	Day	Year
February	16	68
February	19	68
March	01	68
March	02	68
April	18	68
August	08	68
October	18	68

Threat, cont.										
April	15	78	July	15	78	October	xx	78	June	05	79
April	25	78	August	11	78	November	11	78	June	22	79
May	20	78	August	xx	78	January	23	79	August	08	79
May	22	78	September	10	78	January	30	79	October	18	79
June	03	78	September	27	78	February	xx	79	November	25	79
June	21	78	October	02	78	April	19	79	December	02	79
			October	16	78	June	01	79	December	11	79
									December	12	79
									December	20	79

Index
Groups Claiming Responsibility or Believed Involved in International Terrorist Attacks, by Date of Incident, 1968-1979*

*Unknown dates are designated by xx.

Black September, cont.
March   07   73
March   12   73
March   15   73
April   09   73
April   16   73
April   27   73
April   28   73
April   30   73
June   09   73
August   05   73
September   07   73
October   18   73
October   21   73
December   10   73
January   07   74
February   02   74
December   11   74

Bolivian Dissidents
April   22   70
June   15   70
June   16   70
June   17   70
September   21   70
September   22   70
October   07   70
August   21   71
February   14   78

Bolivian Peasants
May   12   71

Brigade 2506
April   06   76

Burundi Rebels
October   23   70

Canadian Hungarian Freedom Fighters Federation
October   18   71

Canaries Intelligence Service
April   05   78

Canary Islands Independence Movement
January   03   77

Catalan Separatists
May   16   75

Charles Martel Group
December   14   73
December   18   73
March   02   75
April   10   75
November   13   77

Che Guevara Brigade
May   11   76
September   11   76

Chilean Socialist Party
July   05   77

Chilean Leftists
October   10   72

Chosen Soren
August   15   74

Coalition of National Liberation Brigades
January   23   73

Colombian Students
June   04   70
April   xx   75
October   27   76

Colombian Indians
December   20   77

Comite Argentino de Lucha Anti-Imperialisto
May   12   72

Combatants for Communism
July   29   77

Committee of Coordination
May   25   77

Commando Muhammed Boudia
August   03   74
August   25   74
September   15   74
November   18   74
January   13   75
January   19   75
June   27   75

Commando of Solidarity with Euskadi
January   31   79

Committee for Socialist Revolutionary Unity
April   13   77

Condor
September   19   74

Coremo
January   xx   71

Correct Course of Fatah
April   20   78

CORU (Committee of United Revolutionary Organizations)
July   10   76
August   24   76
September   01   76
October   06   76
July   22   77
August   11   77

Croatian Intelligence Service
September   28   78

Croatian Liberation
November   23   78
June   20   79

Croatian National Liberation Front
September   10   76
February   08   79

Cuban Action Commandos
February   06   75
February   26   75
March   27   75
April   03   75
April   13   75
May   02   75
May   07   75
July   15   75

Cuban Anti-Communist League
December   xx   73

Cuban Representation in Exile
June   14   69

Cuban Revolutionary Directorate
August   02   73

Cuban Action
December   30   73
January   21   74
August   13   75

Cuban C-4 Movement
November   09   74

Cuban Liberation Front
October   12   71
December   30   73

Cuban Power 76
November   27   75

Cuban Revolutionary Organization
July   09   76

ETA (Basque Nation and Freedom)

December	01	70
May	29	71
January	17	73
December	20	73
May	20	77
March	17	78
February	19	79
March	28	79
April	03	79
April	06	79
April	19	79
April	26	79
June	12	79
July	02	79
July	05	79
July	29	79
August	21	79
August	23	79
September	20	79

Ethiopian Army Dissidents

January	12	78

Ethiopian Students

February	02	70
January	28	77

Front for the Liberation of Aceh and Sumatra

November	29	77

FALN (National Liberation Armed Front)

June	14	74
August	31	74
October	26	74
December	11	74
January	24	75
April	03	75
June	14	75
June	xx	75
October	27	75
December	29	75
June	08	76
July	12	76

July	28	76
September	21	76
February	18	77
March	21	77
April	09	77
June	04	77
August	03	77
August	08	77
August	23	77
January	12	78
January	31	78
May	22	78
July	12	78
November	24	79
November	25	79

FALN Argentine Liberation Front

March	24	70
October	21	70
October	28	70
November	30	70
December	18	70
October	16	72
February	03	73
April	02	73
September	14	74

FAP (Peronist Armed Front)

November	20	69
November	27	70
November	22	73
April	04	73
August	27	74
June	21	76

FAP of Uruguay

March	21	72
April	03	72

FAPU-United Front for Popular Action

January	16	79
July	13	79

FAR-ARG (Revolutionary Armed Forces of Argentina)

December	10	72
September	19	73

December	28	73
February	12	74

FARC (Revolutionary Armed Forces of Colombia)

January	31	75
January	14	76
January	27	77
February	14	77
October	30	77

Faribundo Marti Liberation Front

March	12	76
April	19	77
October	03	78
October	25	78
May	20	79
October	11	79
October	28	79
November	28	79

FARN (Armed Forces of National Liberation)

May	17	78
August	14	78
November	24	78
November	30	78
December	07	78
January	17	79

Fatah

March	18	68
August	18	68
August	19	68
December	29	68
December	31	68
August	15	69
September	08	69
September	08	69
January	24	70
May	04	70
June	09	70
November	06	70
March	15	71
July	07	71
August	24	71
August	xx	71

September	08	71
September	16	71
October	04	71
May	08	72
September	11	72
November	23	72
January	01	73
March	01	73
March	15	73
April	21	73
September	11	73
June	25	74
November	30	74
March	05	75
July	04	75
November	13	75
July	xx	77
March	11	78
June	02	78
August	02	78
August	17	78
September	30	78
November	19	78

FIN

December	11	72
December	xx	72
March	29	73

FLCS (Front for the Liberation of the Somali Coast)

March	23	75
February	03	76

FLEC (Front for the Liberation of the Enclave of Cabinda)

January	15	77
May	16	77

FLNC (Cuban National Liberation Front)

June	14	72
December	xx	73
January	20	74
March	14	74
March	16	74
April	09	74

Indeterminate Amboonese and Moluccan Terrorists

August	31	70
December	27	74
December	xx	74
March	xx	75
July	xx	75
December	04	75
May	23	77
September	10	77
July	27	79

Indeterminate Angolan Guerrillas

June	08	69

Indeterminate Anti-Castro Cubans

March	19	68
July	30	68
November	15	68
December	11	68
May	20	69
June	08	69
May	10	70
October	16	73
November	12	74
December	28	74
August	09	75
October	17	75
October	xx	75
November	28	75
November	29	75
December	08	75
March	03	76
April	03	76
May	01	76
July	17	76
August	09	76
September	21	76
June	08	77
July	22	77
August	15	77

Indeterminate Arab Guerrillas

January	13	68
February	20	68

February	21	68
February	24	68
August	06	68
August	21	68
September	04	68
December	29	68
February	25	69
March	06	69
May	15	69
May	22	69
June	19	69
August	07	69
August	25	69
August	26	69
September	02	69
November	19	69
December	05	69
January	01	70
February	17	70
February	23	70
April	15	70
June	07	70
June	10	70
August	22	70
September	01	70
September	02	70
September	03	70
Septmber	08	70
September	10	70
September	17	70
September	18	70
October	05	70
December	29	70
February	25	71
April	02	71
June	11	71
June	23	71
June	xx	71
August	21	71
September	05	71
September	09	71
September	15	71
September	16	71
October	24	71
January	05	72
January	16	72
August	30	72
September	12	72
September	17	72
September	19	72

September	29	72
October	25	72
January	09	73
January	11	73
April	27	73
April	xx	73
May	01	73
May	20	73
July	23	73
September	05	73
November	22	73
December	05	73
January	05	74
January	20	74
April	22	74
June	04	74
June	09	74
June	13	74
July	03	74
August	02	74
September	02	74
October	11	74
December	15	74
April	16	75
May	13	75
July	09	75
July	18	75
August	02	75
October	02	75
October	04	75
October	05	75
October	24	75
October	27	75
October	29	75
November	23	75
November	24	75
January	02	76
January	xx	76
April	xx	76
May	03	76
June	xx	76
July	02	76
July	18	76
July	25	76
July	30	76
October	11	76
December	04	76
March	04	77
April	13	77
April	24	77

May	06	77
May	11	77
May	28	77
June	29	77
July	20	77
July	28	77
August	04	77
September	11	77
October	25	77
November	18	77
November	19	77
November	20	77
December	06	77
February	18	78
February	19	78
July	19	78
July	31	78
August	02	78
August	05	78
August	13	78
November	19	78
Novmeber	20	78
December	11	78

Indeterminate Argentine Guerrillas

October	03	68
June	19	69
Septmber	09	69
June	09	72
March	28	73
January	15	76
October	07	76

Indeterminate Argentine Leftists

June	15	74
November	25	74
April	07	76
April	13	76
May	04	76
August	19	76
Septmeber	01	76
September	08	76
October	19	76
November	03	76
July	09	77
October	17	77

Indeterminate		
Turkish Guerrillas,		
cont.		
February	20	79
February	23	79
April	14	79
May	05	79
May	06	79
May	28	79
May	29	79
June	01	79
November	01	79
November	25	79
December	09	79
Indeterminate West		
German Leftists		
March	12	69
Indeterminate		
Yugoslavs or		
Croatians		
March	15	68
March	24	68
April	13	68
July	18	68
September	03	68
November	10	68
April	xx	69
June	09	69
June	30	69
November	29	69
August	01	70
October	21	70
February	10	71
April	07	71
November	23	71
January	26	72
January	27	72
March	29	72
June	15	72
June	20	72
September	15	72
September	17	72
August	28	74
October	xx	74
March	30	75
June	07	76
June	28	76
June	14	77
June	19	77

June	24	77
June	xx	77
September	01	77
August	14	78
August	17	78
September	02	78
October	04	78
November	23	78
April	06	79
May	23	79
Indeterminate		
Zimbabwe		
Guerrillas		
April	18	76
May	18	78
June	03	78
June	08	78
June	17	78
June	28	78
August	01	78
April	30	79
Indeterminate Com-		
munist Insurgents		
April	25	78
Indeterminate		
Corsican Indepen-		
dence Rebels		
January	14	78
February	11	78
May	06	78
Indeterminate		
Eritrean Guerrillas		
October	21	78
Indeterminate		
Loatian Guerrilla		
May	16	78
Indeterminant		
Lebanese Terrorists		
September	07	79
November	11	79
Indeterminate		
Palestinians		
April	03	70
May	11	79

Indeterminate		
South Moluccans		
January	29	78
Indeterminate		
Turkish Terrorists		
March	26	69
Indian Students		
July	22	68
August	11	69
International		
Anti-Terror		
Organization		
September	20	72
International		
Che Guevara		
Organization		
July	23	76
International Revo-		
lutionary Front		
June	03	76
International Secret		
Revolutionary		
United Cells		
November	07	76
International		
Solidarity		
February	06	76
International		
Brigade Against		
Repression in		
Europe		
October	15	79
Invisible Ones		
October	06	69
IRA (Irish		
Republican Army)		
March	26	74
November	xx	77
December	17	78
December	18	78
January	18	79

March	22	79
March	30	79
April	21	79
June	14	79
June	25	79
August	27	79
August	28	79
September	11	79
October	17	79
December	14	79
December	17	79
December	18	79
December	19	79
December	21	79
December	22	79
IRA-Provos (Irish		
Republican Army		
Provisional Wing)		
September	04	71
February	02	72
February	22	72
June	08	72
January	xx	73
March	08	73
March	10	73
August	18	73
August	21	73
August	22	73
August	23	73
August	24	73
August	25	73
August	27	73
August	28	73
August	29	73
August	30	73
September	08	73
September	12	73
September	17	73
September	18	73
December	17	73
December	18	73
December	21	73
December	22	73
December	26	73
December	28	73
January	06	74
January	21	74
January	24	74
January	31	74
February	03	74

Justice Commandos of the Armenian Genocide, cont.

October	24	75
June	09	77
June	02	78
October	12	79

Justice Guerrilla

April	17	74

Kabataang Makabayan

March	30	71
August	30	71

Kachin Independence Army

March	04	75

Kashmiri Liberation Front

January	30	71

Kurdish Sympathizers

March	01	75
December	18	76
February	28	77

Latin American Anti-Communist Army

October	08	74
October	09	74
October	28	74
December	15	74
February	05	78

Laos People Number One

January	18	74

Laos-11

June	02	74
June	12	74

Laos Number-13

January	18	74

Lebanese Leftists

October	25	75
October	26	75
October	27	75
July	09	76

Lebanese Liberation

March	07	80

Lebanese Revolutionary Socialist Movement

March	16	74

Lebanese Revolutionary Guard

April	14	73

Lebanese Rightwing Guerrillas

March	01	79

Leftist Acapulco Guerrillas

November	19	71

Les Beliers

July	13	72

Luis Boitel Commando

August	14	77
January	12	78

Mount Carmel Martyrs

July	20	73

Mayir Cayan Suicide Group

March	10	75
November	06	76

Mustafa El Wali Bayyid Sayed International Brigade

July	07	77

M-19

May	10	78
May	29	78
July	18	78
November	09	78
March	01	79

M-7

July	26	74
August	06	74
October	08	74

Malay-Arab Group

October	31	72
October	xx	72
November	02	72

Mano Argentine National Organization Movement

March	27	70
March	29	70

Mano-Peru

February	04	74
February	05	74

Martyr Abou Mahmoud Squad of Anyolp

November	21	74

Maruseido

November	14	74
November	22	74

Marxist Group

May	22	75

Masada—Action and Defense Movement

October	04	72

Maximo Mena Command

October	16	72

Military Liberation Front of Colombia

September	27	75

MIR (Movement of the Revolutionary Left)

June	08	75
October	27	78

MIR-Chile

July	23	76

MIRA

December	14	70
August	22	71

MNLF (Moro National Liberation Front)

September	26	75
November	07	75
February	28	76
April	07	76
May	21	76
February	26	78
March	09	79
October	23	79
October	30	79

Montoneros

August	15	72
September	05	72
September	19	73
February	12	74
September	08	74
September	16	74
September	19	74
February	26	75
March	09	75
August	22	75
October	24	75
October	29	75
January	29	76
August	27	76
September	09	76
September	15	76
September	20	76
January	25	77
April	11	77
March	14	79

Mopoco

August	27	73

Patriotic Front
September 02   70
February   12   79

Patriotic Front (ZANU)
June   23   78
December   26   78

Pattani Liberation Front
April   23   74

PCU
September 07   71

PDFLP (Popular Democratic Front for the Liberation of Palestine)
March   06   69
May   15   74
May   22   74
September 04   74
November   19   75
November   30   74
December   20   74
November   13   75
November   20   75
July   06   77
November   13   77

PDFLP
November   13   77

Peoples Armed Commandos
September   18   71

Peoples Liberation Army
March   22   74

Peoples Resistance Organized Army
February   23   74

Peoples Revolutionary Armed Forces
May   04   73

September   13   77
September   14   77

Peoples Revolutionary Army
April   30   74
February   14   78
June   18   78
July   24   78

Peoples Revolutionary Front
January   22   71

Peoples revolutionary Party
May   19   75

Pedro Ruiz Botero Commando
May   25   77
September 07   77
September 19   77

Peoples Liberation Front
January   xx   77

People's Liberation Army (of Oman)
May   15   78
June   01   78

People's Temple
November   19   78

People's Army in Zaire (APOZA)
March   26   78
June   12   78

Peoples Guerrilla Army (EGP)
September   16   78

Peoples Revolutionary Army in Puerto Rico
February   09   78
March   12   80

Peoples Strugglers
May   21   75
July   03   75
August   28   76
December   23   78

Peruvian Anti-Communist Alliance
September 09   78

Peruvian Students
October   23   69
August   28   75

Petra Kraus Group
June   18   74
February   27   75

PFLP (Popular Front for the Liberation of Palestine)
July   22   68
November   22   68
December   26   68
February   18   69
February   21   69
February   25   69
March   06   69
May   30   69
June   20   69
June   24   69
July   18   69
July   18   69
August   17   69
August   25   60
August   29   69
September 08   69
October   22   69
October   23   69
December   21   69
January   24   70
February   10   70
February   21   70
March   28   70
March   29   70
June   07   70
June   09   70
June   10   70
July   22   70
July   25   70
September 06   70

September 09   70
April   11   71
April   18   71
June   04   71
July   28   71
September 20   71
February   22   72
May   30   72
July   11   72
August   05   72
November   03   72
April   04   73
April   16   73
December   20   73
December   31   73
January   24   74
January   31   74
February   06   74
March   15   74
August   03   74
August   07   74
August   10   74
December   11   74
October   22   75
December   21   75
January   09   76
January   25   76
May   25   76
June   27   76
August   11   76
September 04   76
July   xx   77
January   20   78
July   15   78
November 08   79

PFLP-GC (Popular Front for the Liberation of Palestine-General Command)
February   21   70
May   22   70
January   02   72
June   20   72
August   16   72
April   16   73
July   01   73
April   11   74
June   13   74
June   29   75
July   08   77

Red Brigade of the Netherlands
March   22   79

Red Cells
May   31   78

Red Flag 74
November   07   74
November   21   74

Red Guerrilla
August   21   79

Red Guerrilla Family
January   14   76

Red September
April   14   77

Rejection Front of Stateless Palestinian Arabs
August   03   78

Republic of New Africa
November   27   71

Revenge and Freedom
June   25   79

Revolutionary Action Party
August   29   70

Revolutionary Affinity Group 6
August   01   70

Revolutionary Commandos of Solidarity
April   11   77

Revolutionary Commandos of the People
February   08   78

Revolutionary Force 7
July   01   70
July   02   70

Revolutioanry International Solidarity
September   11   75

Revolutioanry Peoples Resistance of the Netherlands
June   18   72

Revolutionary Vanguard
November   21   74

Revolutionary Workers Party
January   31   77

Revolutionary Action Group
April   09   79

Revolutionary Movement of the Left
December   19   69
February   27   79

Reza Rezai Inter-national Brigades
November   02   76

Robert E. D. Straker Commando
June   16   79
June   29   79

Slave Kortin Yanikiyan Group
February   20   75

Sardinian Separatists
August   14   76
August   15   76

Save Our Israel Land
October   24   76

Secret Anti-Castro Cuban Army
May   17   76
October   24   75

Secret Armenian Army for the Liberation of Armenia
December   18   75
June   02   78
June   03   78
November   18   79
November   25   79

Second Front of Escambray
December   02   68
September   xx   69

Secret Cuban Government
March   30   71
July   xx   71
March   xx   72
December   12   72
March   xx   73
July   24   73
December   xx   73

Secret Hand Organization
February   04   74

Secret Organization Zero
April   13   74
November   01   75

Shan Tribesmen
May   04   73

Shibbu Gang
October   18   73
May   08   74
July   21   74

June   29   75
June   16   76

Shiite Muslims
January   16   79

Sinn Fein
May   30   70

Socialist Labor Party
October   22   75

Socialist Patients Collective
April   24   75
July   16   78

Solidarity Resistance Front
June   17   77

Soldier of the Algerian Opposition
August   xx   74
August   18   75

Somali Liberation Front
August   05   76

Sons of the Occupied Land
February   06   74
May   30   74
December   04   79

Sons of Palestine
June   15   78

South Moluccan Suicide Command
March   13   78

Spanish Armed Group
September   13   79
September   17   79

Spanish Deportees
October   28   76

Wrath of God, cont.

January	25	73
April	05	73
April	09	73
April	12	73
June	17	73
June	28	73
July	21	73
December	10	73
October	08	76
January	03	77

Yanikian Commandos

October	26	73

Young Croatian Army for Freedom

February	07	76

Young Croatian Republican Army

January	12	76

Young Cubans

April	04	72

Young Militants

December	21	75

Young Militants Association

May	17	74

Youth Action Group

December	15	74
December	16	74
May	14	77

Youth Wing of the Communist Party

December	20	78

Youths of the Star

October	06	75

Zaire Rebels

April	xx	77

Zero Point

May	18	73

12 January Liberation Movement

September	27	74

14 September Workers Self-Defense Command

February	15	78

2 June Movement

February	02	72

23 September Communist League

October	10	73
March	21	74
November	18	74

December	05	74
January	28	75
July	19	75
September	02	75
May	25	76
July	16	75
September	02	75
May	25	76
July	16	76
December	08	76
December	13	76
January	20	77
May	25	77

28 May Armenian Organization

May	29	77

6 March Group

March	06	75

7th Suicide Squad

August	05	73

About the Author

EDWARD F. MICKOLUS is an Intelligence Analyst with the Office of Political Analysis, U.S. Central Intelligence Agency. His articles have appeared in the *International Studies Quarterly, Journal of Irreproducible Results, Orbis,* and many other journals and books. He is the author of the bibliographic reference, *The Literature of Terrorism* (Greenwood Press, 1980).